KU-106-158

The Art of French Cooking

3750 RECIPES CREATED BY THE GREAT CHEFS OF FRANCE, INCLUDING

Ali-Bab · E. Darenne · E. Duval
A. Escoffier · Ph. Gilbert · P. Montagné
H.-P. Pellaprat · Urbain-Dubois

From hors d'oeuvre to pastries,
from the specialities of the great Paris restaurants
to the heritage of French provincial cookery,
historic and modern menus, traditional French gourmet lore,
and a sommelier's guide to the correct selection and service of wines
with detailed lists of vintage years

Translated by JOSEPH FAULKNER

Edited by BART WINER

PAUL HAMLYN · LONDON

PUBLISHER'S NOTE

We take great pride in presenting the first English edition of the world-famous L'ART CULINAIRE FRANÇAIS, originally published in France by Flammarion. This encyclopedic cookbook is the most prized collection of recipes ever presented to the French public. As soon as it was published in France, Flammarion became a household word, as familiar and important to food lovers as the name "Webster" is in the field of dictionaries.

Ernest Flammarion began this tremendous undertaking in 1945. He collected, in one huge volume, all the most precious cooking secrets that French chefs had discovered during 250 years of exacting experience—including famous recipes created by Carême, the master chef who prepared banquets for Napoleon and Prince Talleyrand and who founded the great tradition of *haute cuisine* . . . recipes by Urbain-Dubois, grand master of the kitchens to William I, Emperor of Germany . . . and, of course, superb recipes by Escoffier, the most respected name among gourmets of our century.

In short, THE ART OF FRENCH COOKING is the *ne plus ultra* of cookbooks, and we present it with every certainty that it will delight English-speaking readers as much as it has already delighted today's generation of gourmets in France.

KITCHEN MEASUREMENTS

The recipes in this book give solid measures in pounds and ounces, which are identical in Britain and America. Liquid measures, however, are sometimes given in American cups and tablespoons, which are slightly smaller in capacity than British Standard cups and spoons. The American Standard ½ pint measuring cup has a capacity of 8 fluid ounces; the British Standard Imperial ½ pint measuring cup has a capacity of 10 fluid ounces; i.e. American cup and spoon measures are exactly ⁴⁄₅ of the British measures.

It should also be noted that in U.S.A. and France the word chicorée or chicory refers to the curly-leaved salad vegetable, and endive to the straight white-leaved vegetable. In Great Britain the curly-leaved vegetable is known as endive and the straight white-leaved vegetable as chicory.

CREDITS

The illustrations for this book were taken in France, in cooperation with the firms listed below:

PUIFORCAT—silverware
COLOM—baskets of fruit
NOËL—linens
ROUARD—table service
DEHILLERIN—cooking utensils

Les Établissements Nicolas lent their invaluable experience for the chapter on wines, M. Colom for the chapter on fruits and M. Depoix-Linzeler for the chapter on the art of table setting.

We give our sincerest thanks to all the helpful friends who have assisted in the production of this book.

PUBLISHED BY PAUL HAMLYN LTD. WESTBOOK HOUSE, FULHAM BROADWAY, LONDON, BY ARRANGEMENT WITH GOLDEN PRESS, INC. AND LIBRAIRIE FLAMMARION.

PRINTED IN FRANCE

CONTENTS

STOCKS, SAUCES AND GARNISHES

THICK AND CLEAR SOUPS

HORS D'OEUVRES

EGGS

SALT-WATER FISH AND FRESH-WATER FISH

MEAT

POULTRY

GAME

VEGETABLES, ITALIAN PASTES AND FARINACEOUS FOODS, SALADS

MIXED ENTREES

PASTRY

CHEESE, FRUITS

PROVINCIAL COOKING

FOREIGN COOKING

HOME CANNING AND PRESERVING

LIST OF COLOR PLATES

GENERAL REFLECTIONS ON CULINARY ART AS EXPRESSED IN THIS WORK

Though eating is a natural necessity of all living beings, cookery—the agreeable and sensible preparation of food—was refined and perfected in the march of civilization, and, after passing through numerous stages, became an art. We do not have to inform anyone that French cooking has been long ranked among the finest.

A number of our cooks have become famous and have founded schools. From Marie-Antoine Carême to Escoffier, all, or almost all, have bequeathed us their professional testaments in the form of cookbooks. These cookbooks were appropriate to the period in which they were written, and some of them are truly bibles of gastronomy.

Like everything in life, cooking has had to adapt itself to the caprices of fashion and, above all, to yield to economic necessity. Prosperous times meant an unstinted cooking; times of want, cooking restrictions. But French cooking has always maintained its superiority by adapting itself without falling in quality, and thus has always remained at the top of world gastronomy.

In our time, the cookery of Carême, as it was served at the Tuileries or at Prince Talleyrand's, is out of the question; even the art of cooking of Dubois and Bernard and of the fine houses of the Second Empire remains only a model. But it is always in principles that one finds enlightenment. That is why we say that modifications of form and presentation imposed by circumstances never will alter the basis, the very essence, of French cooking.

Thus, with the hope of satisfying the most cultivated palates, we have gathered together in this volume an anthology of the best recipes by modern culinary authors. We have not selected only those recipes which qualify as great or fancy cookery, but have borrowed from works that present the art of cooking in its entirety. Home-cooking, as practiced daily by the housewife, is clearly explained and will certainly not be the least interesting or the least appreciated part of this work.

Placed side by side in this volume will be found the sumptuous recipes of Ali-Bab or Montagné, of Escoffier or Gilbert, and those for simple, everyday cooking; as well as recipes for pastries, desserts, ice cream, etc.; all of the *plats de douceur,* or sweet dishes, as they used to be called.

We have also given a good deal of space to regional cooking, those specialties of the French provinces which have made the reputation of their region of origin. It is not possible to speak of Toulouse without recalling *cassoulet,* of Marseille without thinking of *bouillabaisse,* of Caen without its tripe. This gourmand folklore has become a part of the annals of cooking in France.

We have also looked across the French borders to glean good foreign recipes, which have been so appreciated by French gourmets that they have appeared on French menus after being adapted to French taste.

Finally, at the end of the book, you will find some recipes for preserving and canning.

Postscript: Out of respect for our authors' texts, we have reproduced the recipes just as we have found them in the original works. Some of them are presented in the indicative mood, while others are in the imperative. For example, one author writes "Prepared in the following manner," while another one says "Take so much," "Cook," etc. We apologize for what must seem a contradiction to the rules of writing, which state that once the mood of a verb has been chosen it should remain the same from one end of the work to the other.

For the sake of objectivity and impartiality we sometimes repeat the same recipe as given by different authors.

A BACKWARD GLANCE AT COOKING

We thought that it would be interesting to begin this anthology of modern cooking with a backward glance at the culinary arts as they were practiced by the master chefs of 150 years ago.

First we present three "restorative prescriptions" very much in vogue, it seems, in their day—taken from *The Physiology of Taste* by Brillat-Savarin. It is evident that, for material and other reasons, the methods employed at the time have largely disappeared.

A. Take 6 large onions, 3 carrots, a handful of parsley; chop everything and put it into a casserole, which you heat, browning the mixture with a piece of good fresh butter.

When it is ready, put in 6 oz. sugar candy, 20 grains of powdered amber, a crust of grilled bread, and 3 bottles of water. Boil ¾ hr., adding new water to compensate for loss through boiling so that there will always be 3 bottles of liquid.

While these things are going on, kill, pluck, and clean an old rooster, which you then mash, flesh and bones, in a mortar with an iron pestle; also chop 2 lb. choice beef.

This done, mix the 2 kinds of meat, adding a sufficient quantity of salt and pepper.

Put it into a casserole on a hot fire, so that the heat penetrates, and from time to time throw in a little fresh butter to keep the mixture from sticking while being sautéed.

When you see that it is browned—that is, when the osmazome is roasted—pour in the broth, which is in the first casserole, bit by bit, and when it has all been poured in keep at a rolling boil ¾ hr., always taking care to add hot water to keep the same amount of liquid.

At the end of this time the operation is finished and you have a potion whose results are certain as long as the patient has still retained a properly functioning stomach.

To administer it, give a cup of it every 3 hr. until bedtime the first day; on the following days, a good cupful in the morning and the same amount in the evening until the 3 bottles have been finished. Keep the patient on a light but nourishing diet, such as chicken legs, fish, sweet fruits, jams. It is almost never necessary to make a new batch. Toward the fourth day he will be able to return to his regular occupations and should make up his mind to be wiser in the future, if possible.

By eliminating the amber and sugar candy it is possible to use this method to make a fine soup worthy of being served at a connoisseurs' dinner.

The old rooster may be replaced by 4 old partridges and the beef by a piece of leg of mutton without lessening the effectiveness and agreeable taste of the preparation.

The method of chopping the meat and browning it before adding the liquid may be considered a general rule if one is in a hurry; it is a rule based on the idea that meat has a higher caloric value if treated in this way before being put into water. This method may be used whenever you need a good fatty soup and do not care to wait 5 or 6 hr. for it to cook, which sometimes happens—especially in the country. Naturally, those who avail themselves of this idea will praise the professor.

B. It would be a good thing if everyone knew that though amber, considered as a perfume, may be unpleasant to the uninitiated whose nerves are delicate, it has a remarkably tonic and exhilarating effect when taken internally. Our ancestors used it a great deal in cooking and were none the worse off.

I know for a fact that Marshal Richelieu, of glorious memory, constantly chewed amber pastilles. As for myself, when I have one of those days when I feel my age or think with difficulty and feel oppressed by some unknown power, I mix some powdered amber, the size of a bean, with sugar in a good cup of chocolate and always feel simply marvelous. With the help of this tonic life becomes relaxed, thought is set free, and I do not have that insomnia which invariably follows the weak cup of coffee taken to produce the same effect.

C. Prescription A is intended for robust constitutions, decisive people, and those who wear themselves out through action.

I have been drawn by the occasion to compose another potion, one more agreeable to the taste and with a gentler effect, which I reserve for weak constitutions, for undecided characters, for those, in a word, who become exhausted without effort. Here it is:

Take a knuckle of veal weighing at least 2 lb.; divide it into 4 parts lengthwise, bone and flesh; brown with 4 sliced onions and a handful of water cress; when it is nearly cooked pour on 3 bottles of water and allow to boil 2 hr., taking care to replace whatever liquid evaporates. Now you already have a good veal broth. Salt and pepper moderately.

Mash separately 3 old pigeons and 25 live crayfish; combine both of these and brown as described in Prescription A, and, when you see that the mixture is thoroughly heated and is beginning to stick to the pan, pour on the veal broth and cook 1 hr. Strain the enriched broth. It may be taken morning and night, or perhaps morning only, 2 hr. before luncheon. This is also a delicious soup.

I was induced to prepare this last potion by a pair of writers who, finding me in a good frame of mind and having confidence in me, took advantage (as they expressed it) of my wisdom.

They made good use of it and have not had cause to regret it. The poet, who had been simply elegiac, became romantic; the lady, who had written only one pallid novel with an unhappy ending, turned out a second and better one that ended with a fine and happy marriage. In both cases there was an exaltation of powers, and I believe, in good conscience, that I may take a little of the credit.

MENU FOR 25 TO 30 PERSONS

FIRST SERVICE

4 SOUPS

Garbure - Printanier - À la Reine - Purée of Peas and Rice

4 DISHES AFTER THE SOUP

Salmon Génoise - Pike Hollandaise
Chicken Flamande
Sirloin on the Spit with Fried Potatoes

12 ENTREES

Aspic of Rabbit Fillets
Hot Quail Pie - Chicken Mayonnaise
Rice Casserole garnished with Veal Strips
Sliced Chicken Maréchale - Quenelles - Larded Young Hare
Pigeon Cutlets
Mutton Chops Soubise
Sweetbreads with Sorrel - Mackerel Fillets
Rouen Duckling with Crayfish Butter

SECOND SERVICE

4 LARGE SIDE DISHES

Chicken Galantine - Savoy Sponge Cake
Glazed Ham - Brioche

4 ROAST DISHES

Two Pheasants, one larded
Quails - Fried Sole and Fried Smelts

6 SIDE DISHES

Peas in Sugar - Spinach Pie
Asparagus - Broad Beans in Lemon Jelly - Cucumbers in Cream
Small Grilled Cabbages - Chartreuse of Fruit
Two Salad Bowls

THIRD SERVICE OR DESSERT

8 DECORATED PLATES

Garnished with preserved fruit - Candies and other bonbons

8 TAMBOURS

Garnished with cookies -
marzipan, macaroons, meringues, etc.

8 FRUIT COMPOTES

8 PLATES OF FRUIT IN SEASON

2 CHEESES 2 SUGAR BOWLS

Carême, Prince Talleyrand's head chef, who is still the uncontested master of cooking, gives us a few examples in his *Art de la cuisine française* of what princely meals used to be, meals that were always served with the same style regardless of the number of guests.

In his *Art de la cuisine française,* Carême plans the table setting, the seating arrangements, and the dishes for each service. It would be impossible to be more precise or to give a better understanding of the complexity of serving a dinner, which was made still more difficult because the utensils and the cooking methods were so rudimentary compared to those at the disposal of our present-day chefs.

Here are a few recipes taken from this rare and much-sought-after book:

CHICKEN FILLETS MARÉCHAL FILETS DE POULETS À LA MARÉCHALE

Slice off 14 chicken fillets according to the rule and remove the *filets mignons* (tenderest part of the breast cut from under the wings). Trim, then marinate in salt, pepper, a few sprigs of parsley, and the juice of 1 lemon. Prepare *fines herbes* with chopped parsley, chopped mushrooms and truffles, and a shallot chopped very fine and well blanched. Heat these *fines herbes* in butter, adding a piece of chicken glaze the size of a walnut and a little grated nutmeg. Pour this onto a plate and allow it to cool so that it may be used for stuffing the chicken fillets in the center. Make a small incision in the pieces where the *filets mignons* were attached. Dip them in beaten egg, then in bread crumbs, and moisten with clarified butter in order to bread them again. Grill them on a piece of oiled paper ¼ hr. before serving, and fill the incisions with truffles. Crown with the *filets mignons,* which you will have fried in a light batter, and pour a semiglaze Espagnole Sauce on top not thick enough to coat the pieces.

QUAILS WITH FINES HERBES IN A CASE CAILLES AUX FINES HERBES EN CAISSE

Place 8 quails prepared like those *à la jardinière* (cooked with vegetables) in a well-buttered casserole. Heat chopped parsley, chopped mushrooms and truffles, and 2 chopped and blanched shallots, in butter. Moisten these *fines herbes* with 1 glass Madeira and pour them over the quails. Cook 20 min. with fire above and below, then drain them after skimming off the fat. Finish the *fines herbes* with 1 tbsp. Espagnole Sauce. Have ready a large case made of oiled paper. Place the quails, covered with *fines herbes*, in the case with the breasts outside, leaving a well in the center of the case. Cover with strips of pork fat and a circle of buttered paper. Enclose the case in a double thickness of paper. Bake in the oven ½ hr. before serving. Take out of the oven when ready to serve, remove the paper and fat strips, skim off the fat, place sliced mushrooms in the center of the quail case, and dress with Italienne Sauce.

MACKEREL FILLETS MAÎTRE D'HÔTEL FILETS DE MAQUEREAUX À LA MAÎTRE D'HÔTEL

Choose 6 fine, soft-roed mackerel firm to the touch, with bright eyes, silvery skins, and light-blue backs; such are the desired conditions to ensure their freshness. Remove the gills and then through the hole made take out the intestines and the roe, making sure not to break the latter. Wipe them off well without washing them. Slice off the fillets in the same way you would whiting fillets—in other words, by holding the mackerel turned toward you with the left hand on the back and inserting the blade of the knife at the head and drawing it down to the tail at a slight slant and sliding on the backbone. When the fillets have been cut off, trim them without removing the skin; cut off all of the parts around the stomach that held the intestines. Place the fillets according to size, skin side down, in a sautéing pan with plenty of butter. When they have been thus arranged, throw a pinch of salt on top, sprinkle with the juice of 1 lemon, pour melted butter over them, and cover with a round piece of paper. Place the sautéing pan on a hot fire 10 min. before serving. As soon as the butter begins to boil, remove from the fire and slip the knife blade under the fish to loosen them. Turn them over and put back on the fire. As soon as they are firm to the touch, drain them on a white cloth. Remove the skin and arrange them in a crown; in the center place the soft roes, which have been sautéed in butter and covered with thickened Maître d'Hôtel Sauce.

Let us stop here with these examples and note that most of these recipes could be served today without eliciting any surprise—which proves that Carême was indeed an innovator for his time, one to whom we still refer today.

Pastrymaking in Carême's day was quite different from today's, especially in the decoration of the pieces of pastry. Pastrymaking was extremely complicated and required a great deal of talent on the part of the practitioner, who, according to Carême, had to have as great a knowledge of architecture as of his own profession. His *Pâtissier royal,* which was the counterpart of his *Art de la cuisine française,* shows us engravings in which the actual pastry has almost disappeared under its monumental decoration. There are temples, cascades, kiosks, helmets, balloons, etc., in which spun sugar played a major role.

To be complete, we believe we ought to give a few of these recipes:

WATERFALL URN CASSOLETTE À CASCADE

(*Note:* Modern *cassolettes* are small ramekins of porcelain or silver or are made of pastry and served with hors d'oeuvres. In Carême's day the word referred to a kind of incense burner.)

The urn is made of short paste covered with pink sugar; it is garnished with small white crusts made of almond paste into which you put rose whipped cream. The garlands are made of spun sugar, as are the 3 iced fountains in the bowls between the feet of the urn. This arrangement gives a great deal of elegance to the piece. The 3 bases are of short paste with colored almonds. The three ornaments are composed of puffs glazed with caramel, lemon cookies, and little nougats trimmed with Chantilly cream.

INDIAN PAVILION PAVILLON INDIEN

This large piece is octagonal in shape; it should be white with orange-colored roofs; the other details should be purplish red, yellow, or pink.

The base has 3 levels with 8 fluted sides; the one in the middle should be covered with sugar of the same color as the details of the pavilion. The 3 ornaments are made of almond-paste crusts filled with pistachio cream, puffs with rose icing sprinkled with rock sugar, and almond cookies covered with the icing called "royal" and sprinkled with pistachios.

These two examples suffice to give an idea of the work executed by Carême. But in addition to these artistic pieces there is a chapter in his *Pâtissier royal* devoted to regular pastrymaking: *génoise,* flaky paste, tortes, tarts, cookies, puffs, cream puffs, biscuits, etc. It is of singular interest that among the *pithiviers* (an almond cake typical to the town of Pithiviers) we find *pithiviers* with kidneys; in other words, chopped and cooked veal kidneys were added to the almond cream. In others we find beef marrow, which is a little more acceptable, since tortes and tarts with marrow were made thirty-five to forty years ago and are still enjoyed by some today.

Here are some small cakes made of flaky paste from quite an original recipe:

PEARLY OAK LEAVES FEUILLES DE CHÊNE PERLÉES

Have ready a pastry cutter 3 in. long and 1½ in. wide, fluted in the shape of an oak leaf. Cut the leaves from flaky paste and bake on a tin sheet. Next whip 2 egg whites and mix with 3½ oz. fine sugar; spread this lightly over the cakes and make a line lengthwise down the centers. With the tip of a pearling cone, form a small oval pearl of egg white and place it thus: put it near the line in the center of the leaf, slanting it a little, and finishing it at the end of the first indentation in the leaf; next place another one about ¼ in. away. Place 6 on one side and 6 on the other, slanting in opposite directions so as to form six pairs of chevrons. Powder with sugar and place in the oven at low heat. Allow the cakes to color slightly, then place in the center of each pearl a little ribbon of pistachio icing and between each a thin ribbon of red-currant or apple jelly and a larger ribbon down the middle to separate the pearls.

This explanation is a little confusing, so we shall end our journey into the past here and go on to the recipes of Urbain-Dubois and Bernard, who are a little closer to us, since they were the grand masters of the kitchens of the King of Prussia, who became William I, Emperor of Germany.

Between Carême and Urbain-Dubois there was Jules Gouffé, who wrote *Le Livre de la cuisine* and *Le Livre de la pâtisserie,* both beautifully illustrated. He was a cook of great merit and deserves the honor of being included.

Dubois and Bernard brought out the first edition of their splendid work, *La Cuisine classique,* in 1856 and the eighth edition in 1878. The work of this period was grandiose and bridges the gap between the cooking of Carême and that of the great modern chefs: Escoffier, Montagné, Gilbert, Moisson, Fétu, Cubat, Falcoz, Tony Girod, Caillat, Pellaprat, and other more modest artisans whose names are little known, or unknown, but whose ability has contributed to raising French cooking to the realm of art.

To all these pioneers, this book (drawn from their books) carries the gratitude of all gourmets and even gourmands.

Here are a few recipes taken from *La Cuisine classique,* which we give to document our readers on this mid-nineteenth-century work:

TURKEY HEN IMPÉRIALE DINDE À L'IMPÉRIALE

Dress a turkey hen; remove the breastbones in order to stuff the entire stomach with a firm dressing of forcemeat mixed with a few diced truffles. Truss the turkey for roasting, with the legs tied down; singe it, and stud the breast with pieces of fine pork fat. Place it in a long casserole larded with pork fat, ham, and chopped vegetables; half fill the casserole with good bouillon; bring to a quick boil to reduce the liquid by ½. At this point add 1 glass Madeira and the same amount of good stock and a few raw truffles. Cover the turkey with buttered paper, put the lid on the casserole, and bring it near the opening of the oven or reduce the heat, keeping a fire on the lid of the casserole. Finish cooking it slowly, basting from time to time. Drain off the juices, skimming the fat, reduce to a semiglaze, and glaze the turkey with it. Arrange the turkey on a platter on a bed of cold, molded rice.

At either end of the platter place white rice molded into a bowl shape. Fill the bowls with a *montglas* (diced ingredients bound with Madeira Sauce) composed of pickled tongue and mushrooms; encircle this mixture with a chain of small, round truffles. Finally, group around the turkey a garnish composed of whole truffles, cockscombs, and mushroom caps. Glaze the truffles with a brush and lightly dress the cockscombs and mushrooms with sauce; serve the rest of the sauce in a sauceboat.

PULLETS SCOTCH STYLE POULARDES À L'ÉCOSSAISE

Make a platform of bread in the shape of a pyramid; fry it and fix it to the center of a platter. When it is cold, cover it with ordinary forcemeat; dry this in the oven. Next fashion a pretty crust of rice; fry it and then place it on the platform, sticking it with 2 small skewers. Make 4 semicircles of rice, forming them into an irregular, hollowed-out border. Stick these all around the inside of the platter; this rice is intended to hold the pullets when they have been dressed.

Remove the breast and backbones from 4 medium-sized pullets. Stuff them with raw, firm forcemeat. Truss them in a round shape with the feet pulled back into the skins of the drumsticks. Place them in a casserole lined with pork fat and thin-sliced vegetables; fill the casserole ¾ full with cooking stock. Bring the liquid to a boil, and immediately lower the heat; cook slowly, basting often. Just before serving, drain and untruss the pullets; cut the breasts almost all the way off, leaving a small attachment, and put them back in place. Set the pullets almost upright, leaning them against the pyramid; between each one place a small pickled beef tongue, also sliced and reconstructed; fill the interstices with mushrooms and truffles; fill the cup with a small garnish or decoration. Glaze the tongues and truffles; lightly coat the pullets with Velouté reduced with mushroom cooking liquid. Serve the remaining sauce separately.

The menus reproduced on the following pages will show, better than any commentary, what was considered a good meal in the last century.

Menu of a dinner served at the Tuileries, January 6, 1820.

2 SOUPS

Spring-Vegetable Health Soup - Crayfish Bisque

4 LARGE DISHES

Fawn on the Spit

Turbot with Oyster Sauce - Carp Régence

Sweetbread Casserole Saint-Hubert

16 ENTREES

Glazed Fillets with Lettuce - Sautéed Partridge Fillets with Truffles

Grenadins of Young Rabbit Fillets Toulouse

Venison Chops Soubise

Cutlets Villeroi, Vénitienne Sauce

Chicken Quenelles in Thick Consommé

Small Skewers Belle-vue in Jelly

Cutlets of Young Hare in Blood

Pullets with Tarragon - Kromeskis with Velouté

Blanquette of Pullet Fillets Conti

Perch Waterfish

Chicken à la Reine Chivry

Small Meat Pies with Béchamel Sauce

Lamb Fillets with Asparagus Tips

Purée of Game Polonaise

4 LARGE DISHES

Crayfish Bush

Sultana with Chantilly Cream - Cheese Soufflé

Glazed Wild-Boar Ham

3 ROAST DISHES

Bohemian Pheasants - Red Partridges - Morvan Woodcocks

16 SIDE DISHES

Asparagus Stalks - Cauliflower with Parmesan Cheese

Mushrooms Provençale - Truffles in Champagne

Lettuce with Dressing - Spinach in Consommé

Salad Piémontaise - Cucumbers in Consommé

Orange Jelly

English Cream

Pancakes with Candied Lemons

Poached Eggs with Gravy - Souffléed Cakes - Macaroni Italian Style

Apples with Vanvres Butter - Waffles Flemish Style

2 Special Plombières

DESSERT

8 Large Baskets of Fruit

4 Small Baskets, etc.

Menu of a Paris restaurant during the siege in the Franco-Prussian War. (Reproduced verbatim.)

December 25, 1870
99th day of the siege

HORS D'OEUVRES

Butter - Radishes - Stuffed Donkey's Head - Sardines

SOUPS

Purée of Red Beans with Croutons
Elephant Consommé

ENTREES

Fried Gudgeons - Roast Camel English Style
Jugged Kangaroo
Roast Bear Chops with Poivrade Sauce

ROASTS

Haunch of Wolf, Venison Sauce
Cat flanked by Rats
Water-cress Salad
Antelope Terrine with Truffles
Mushrooms Bordelaise
Buttered Green Peas

SIDE DISH

Rice Cake with Jam

DESSERT

Gruyère Cheese

WINES

FIRST SERVICE

Sherry
Latour Blanche 1861
Ch. Palmer 1864

SECOND SERVICE

Mouton Rothschild 1846
Romanée Conti 1858
Bellenger frappé
Grand porto 1827

Coffee and Liqueurs

Café Voisin, G. Braquenas, 261, rue Saint-Honoré

Here is a really imposing menu for a Christmas dinner given at the Savoy Hotel in London and prepared by M. A. Escoffier, the eminent chef of that establishment (1899) :

SAVOY HOTEL

MENU

Fresh Caviar - Bouquet of Shrimps - Royal Natives
Clear Turtle Soup - Borscht Russian Style
Suprême of Sole Aurore
Red-Mullet Fillets with Soft Roe
Pullets Royale
Timbales of Truffles in Champagne
Saddle of Venison Master of the Royal Hunt
Crayfish Mousseline
Woodcock Delights
White Lady Sherbets
Ortolan Cocotte
Quails with Orange
Nasturtium Salad
New Asparagus
Foie Gras poached in Champagne
Soufflé Chantilly
Iced Pineapple
Tangerines Orientale
Filbert Cookies - Delicacies
Scotch Shortbread
Fruit

WINES

Johannisberger cabinet 1874
Pommery, extra dry, 1884
Château Rauzan Segla 1875
Château Coutet, Marquis de Lur-Saluces
Mise du Château Étampé 1861
Grande Champagne 1830
Grandes Liqueurs

Turkish Coffee

(Table setting, Paule Marrot.)

Fig. 1. — *Intimate luncheon.*

Fig. 2. — *Informal dinner.*

(Table setting, Renou and Genisset.)

(Table setting, Pa

Fig. 3. — *Dinner in the country.*

Fig. 4. — *Formal dinner.*

SEATING ARRANGEMENTS

It is not easy to assemble a group of guests and keep them happily seated together, side by side, for an hour—not to say two hours or more. This is not only a question of good food and good wines: the success of a dinner depends more on good humor, on an atmosphere of friendliness that is felt by the guests. Without doubt, a well-served table provides a smooth plane of understanding; it is no less true that guests get along better if they are seated with that in mind and grouped according to their tastes.

The real art of serving is, therefore, above all the art of inviting.

The circumstances motivating a dinner party give it a general tone; for example, intimate or formal, social or official. But regardless of the type of dinner, the mistress of the house must take care in making up a harmonious guest list of persons who have common interests and respect for each other. All combinations are possible, however; a variety of dispositions and characters (if not carried to excess) may animate the party agreeably, mix charm with wit, and add beauty to intelligence and warmth to seriousness. Respectful young people may be placed beside those of advanced years and budding talents beside those who have already arrived.

Once the choice has been made, placing the guests around the table comes next, and the order of their seating will determine the order in which they are served, with one reservation—ladies are served before gentlemen.

Indeed, the rules are simple: the hosts, facing each other at the middle of the table, divide the guests by placing the most important male guest to the right of the mistress of the house, the most important female guest to the right of the master; then to their left, respectively, those who are second in rank, and the remainder distributed to right and to left on both sides in descending order. The sexes are alternated, naturally, married women being "evaluated" according to the "worth" of their husbands. The two ends of the table thus become the poor corners, and care must be taken to place intimate friends and young people there, so that they will not take offense at their distance from the center of the table.

It is nevertheless difficult not to cause some secret discontent, but how can it be avoided? Everyone cannot be seated in the place of honor.

Many hosts today ease the difficulty by adding the two poles at the ends of the table to the two poles at the middle. This revives the old notion of the head of the table being the master's place and the foot the wife's. Today head and foot are equal; the hosts revaluate them when seated there. The guests near them are greatly honored and those seated at the center of the table are flattered by being given the places of the heads of the house and being the center of the group.

The individual importance of each guest must be understood in order to establish precedence in seating. This importance depends on age, profession, and social standing. But these elements are not always so easy to evaluate. Age? The exact age of a man is often unknown and, more often, the exact age of a woman. One should, therefore, beware of appearances, which may be misleading. Profession? Only one takes precedence over any other, not excluding sex and age: men of the Church. All of the others are evaluated relatively. In the legal world judges come first; in the military, the army; among writers, men of letters; in the teaching profession, university professors. The host should not be blamed for being faithful to his own social category and giving favored positions to outstanding members of his own set, provided that this preference does not appear obviously hidebound. It is not possible, in any case, to establish a hierarchy of officialdom or of the professions that will apply to every situation or to say that "the gown takes precedence over the military" or vice versa.

Social position is sometimes difficult to define: some, who put all their efforts into appearances and maneuver themselves into first place, are often inferior to those of real worth who, being modest, seek no honors. It is therefore a delicate matter, no matter how much attention you pay to the subject, to establish the precedence of each guest at the dinner table.

However, certain titles assure indisputable right of precedence to those who hold them and to the wives who share these honors. Custom has codified the hierarchies for which we give the following ready reckoner: men of the Church go before all, as we have said—at least in Catholic circles; next come the bearers of the highest titles of nobility: princes and dukes—provided they come from countries where such titles are not mass-produced; next, titularies of positions that authorize the appellation of Excellency: ambassadors and ministers (but important men of state, naturally, should go before anyone). Then the Academicians and Members of the Institute. The Académie Française, probably because it includes dignitaries of the Church, princes and dukes, ambassadors and ministers, admirals and generals, is considered by some to bestow all privileges upon its members, giving them the absolute right of pre-eminence. However, distinctions may be made among members of that august body; although many of them are illustrious, there are some who do not deserve to be placed, even in dining, before all others. Next come high officials: judges, prefects, admirals, generals, eminent university professors. Important ranks in the Legion of Honor may also be considered. Here ends the list of "fixed stars" in the firmament of honors. But other celebrities in society, the arts, literature, and science are the "variable stars" who may be made to shed a not less flattering light.

Is it difficult to know which one of two married men should precede the other? One has to make a choice, even if it comes to drawing straws. But the wives are the compensation: the wife of the loser is placed before the wife of the winner.

These rules may be used to satisfy the self-esteem of each guest. But there are other rules, more psychological than social, that are also important and will come naturally to you. For example: place people side by side whose similar tastes and education will suggest pleasant subjects of conversation; arrange the good talkers as you would the lights; place two brilliant minds opposite each other so that they may bat the ball back and forth in general conversation. If you find that you have placed someone less favorably than you may have wished, you may console him with a charming neighbor or by giving him a chance at some point in the conversation to show his worth.

Hospitality, when it is really understood, is not just a matter of custom and good sense. It is also—and above all—a matter of feeling.

THE ART OF TABLE DECORATION AND SERVICE

We do not presume to lay down fixed rules for setting and decorating a table; like any other demonstration of a refined civilization, this one is free from the severities of strict etiquette and reflects, rather, the personality of the host, his taste, his imagination, and his education. It is not necessary to emphasize the fact that the table should harmonize with the dining room and, without too much strictness, have a certain unity of style. It should have the same degree of elegance as the party one plans to give; and there lies a question of tact and discrimination outside the domain of this study.

Nevertheless, there are a few fundamental principles, rooted in French tradition as well as in the desire for quality and elegance, that govern the laying of the table and the sequence in serving. The photographs of four tables, each laid according to a different plan, illustrate the first part of this essay, which is devoted to decoration.

SETTING AND DECORATING THE TABLE

Special care must be taken in selecting the tablecloth, since it will serve as the basic foundation for the whole arrangement. White is preferred for evening, and it may be plain, damask, lace-trimmed, or embroidered with gold thread, with napkins to match. Individual place mats are reserved for small luncheons. In any case, avoid tablecloths that are too ornate.

An elementary rule for comfort is to leave plenty of space between each guest so that each one may be perfectly at ease. The distance may be measured in laying the plates. These should be of white china for evening, round or contoured, with a gold band or discreet decoration. If you have an antique service, it must be in keeping with the décor of the table and the style of the silver. One dinner plate per guest, whether soup or consommé is served (we shall discuss later how soup is to be served), and in no case two plates superposed.

Glasses should be of thin crystal, with stems. The reason we forbid stemless glassware is that the hand extinguishes the play of lights; we also advise against marbled, etched, faceted, or colored glasses. The material of the glass or crystal should be, as it were, absent: the most transparent is the best. The glass worthy of a great wine pardons its presence by letting itself be forgotten.

A good wineglass should be of the proper size, thin, light, balanced, yet stable. The cup should not flare out, but, on the contrary, tend to narrow in, like a tulip. The stem, like the leg of an elegant woman, should be free of vain ornaments that detract from the line. Neither square, nor hexagonal, nor octagonal, it is unostentatiously cylindrical. The total height of the base and stem should be a little less than the height of the cup itself. The base is round. The glass illustrated on page 35 (Figure 5) is perhaps the ideal glass. The material it is made of is light. While solid, it has the fineness of a hair; while slender, it maintains its equilibrium. The tulip-shaped cup, without any exaggerated inclosure of the lip, is borne on a stem of faultless proportions.

Nothing disturbs the gyration of the liquid within, the hand's caress, the sight for the eyes and the bliss for the nose. No ornament, no etching, no beveling . . . everything for the wine!

Never fill the wineglass more than half full. It is better to stay below the halfway mark, well below, even to a third of the glass. Our great French wines are endowed with various spirits and pleasing nuances that are shown to better advantage by not being confined to too small a glass or overwhelmed by too full a one. Let the little genie on leaving the wine bottle frisk and frolic; he will know how to reward you.

The glasses are placed in a line at the head of the plates, or slightly on the bias, with the largest glass for water on the left and, in descending scale, as many glasses as there will be wines served during the meal. For champagne use neither of the so-called champagne glasses, either bowl- or cone-shaped, both of which are unsuitable for its proper enjoyment, but a glass that is rather large, and set back from the others. For a formal dinner, champagne may be served in a silver-gilt goblet.

The silverware is always the most beautiful ornament on the table; its quality, polish, choice, and arrangement will give the decoration of the table its tone and class. The setting of each place should be as follows: to the left of the plate, the dinner fork, then the fish fork, if such a course is served; to the right, the knife, blade turned toward the plate, and the fish knife. If the meal begins with soup, the spoon should be placed to the right of the fish knife; if the occasion calls for it, it may be replaced by an oyster fork. Never put forks, knives, or spoons between the plate and the glasses; this would be a grave error in taste—in France, at least. Do not allow unaesthetic knife rests, which serve no purpose anyway, since forks and knives are changed for each course. These replacements should be left on the plate and not placed on the tablecloth. French tradition calls for the prongs of the forks placed pointing downward on the cloth, and not in the other direction, thus showing the engraved arms or initials. In the same way, the spoons should be laid bowl down. Allow us to point out, as one of the refinements of a fine home, the small, individual butter plates of silver or crystal with their knives, placed to the upper right of the dinner plates, and, for formal dinners, the bread plates placed on the opposite side.

A Nordic custom is being introduced into France, and we shall mention it for its genuine sumptuousness: we mean the plates called "service plates," made of silver, round and flat, and a little larger in diameter than the plates that are placed on them. They stay in front of the guests during each and every course and are seen during the changing of courses, with their large initials or coat of arms in the center. They are not removed until the cheese is served, so that the place before the guest is not bare, even for the shortest moment, until dessert.

The center of the table, intended to hold a permanent decoration throughout the meal, requires particular attention and scrupulous care in regard to size and color. Whether it is a mirror holding a silver or antique pottery tureen (to be used only as a decoration, of course), a basket of flowers or fruit, or a floral decoration enlivened with various objects, the centerpiece should reflect the mood of the mistress of the house or the importance of the occasion. Flowers should be arranged very carefully, since they add their freshness and vivacity of color to the table décor, and should not be so voluminous as to be annoying to the guests. They will do for the table what borders and hedges do for the harmonious geometry of a French garden.

An elegant dinner deserves to be lighted by candles in low candelabra at the ends of the table or around the center. Their flames, mingled with discreet electric lighting, will lend a lovely warmth to the atmosphere of the evening. They will make the silver and crystal sparkle, play upon the colors of the wines in the glasses, and enhance the complexions of the ladies and the glitter of their jewels. Carefully regulate the height of the candles so that they are neither too high nor too low, to avoid unflattering shadows on faces. Be sure, also, that they are not placed in the way of the guests. All that remains is to place, with symmetry and practicality, the saltcellars, spice and mustard containers, and the water and wine carafes if it is to be an intimate meal. There are no carafes on a sumptuously laid table unless they are used for decorative purposes. Just before the arrival of the guests, the glasses are filled with iced water and the butlers offer more if it is needed during the meal and between the various servings of wine.

Let us not forget the napkins. Carefully folded, they may be placed on the plates or, to the left of the plates, hiding the bread. They should not be folded into pretentious and complicated arrangements. A dinner table is not a showpiece.

All is ready now, and the guests' places are designated by cards, if there are enough of them to justify this practice. The rules of precedence have been tactfully observed in the arrangement of the seating, without omitting certain affinities. The hostess inspects her table for the last time; the time is drawing near for the arrival of the first guests.

TABLE SERVICE

A fine dinner party is not only a show of elegance and aesthetics. The success deserved by the smartness of the table and the artistry of the cooking depends on one thing more. One cannot conceive of a fine home without impeccable service, and this is the final instrument of success. Service will assure continuity to the rhythm of the meal, without hurrying, without dragging, and above all without any untimely interruptions. Nothing destroys the atmosphere of a dinner party more than slow or insufficient service. Exaggeration of the reverse turns a meal into a kind of marathon in which everyone finishes exhausted. Faultless servants know how to go unnoticed; they work in silence, not mechanically, but with constant attention to the needs of the guests. A butler can successfully serve from six to eight persons, no more. His dress should be sober; he wears white gloves. The waitress wears a white apron.

When the guests enter the dining room by the open double doors, the candles have just been lighted. The butlers, who draw back to allow the guests to enter, seat the ladies.

The ladies are always served first, starting with the one seated to the right of the host. Then comes the turn of the one to the left, and the other ladies by order of precedence, until the hostess has been served last, but before any of the gentlemen, for whom the same protocol is observed. The plates should be served from the left and removed from the right.

The soup plates are brought in one by one on dessert plates, and these are substituted for the service plates used in the original setting. After the soup, the soup plates and spoons are removed and are replaced by flat plates; the place before the guest is never left bare. If the following dish is a hot one, the plates must also be hot. This imperative rule applies to the whole meal; it is as important as changing the plates for each course. The forks and knives just used will be removed and others brought, laid flat on the new plate. The salad is served in special crystal dishes shaped like crescent moons. These are distributed at an opportune time and are placed to the left of the service plates, whose round shape fits into the crescent.

Silver serving dishes are always preferred, for both aesthetic and gastronomic reasons, since they hold the heat better and thus safeguard the quality of the food. They come in various appropriate shapes: dishes for fish, roasts, stews, and soufflés; deeper dishes for vegetables; cake plates, etc. They are accompanied by various sauceboats. They are brought direct from the kitchen and served immediately. Be sure not to adopt a practice that should be reserved for restaurants—"presenting" the prepared dishes before passing them to the guests. This would show a complete lack of taste and judgment, even though the trimmed dish is a masterpiece of culinary art. The guests may admire it when the butler serves the guest of honor, who will naturally call it to the attention of all the guests.

The dishes should be arranged in such a manner that one may serve oneself easily. Fish, in particular, should have the meat cut away from the bones and replaced in its original form. Meats, roasts, fowl, or game should not be carved at the table by the host—even if he is in the habit of doing so—except at intimate meals. Remember that cold dishes must be served very cold, even iced in certain cases.

This is not the time to extol the merits of wine, but to explain how its arrival at the table is honored. The choice of the wine is usually left up to the host, who should show a subtle science in his selection. It is not served with the soup. The first service of wine immediately follows the first course. The butler serves each guest from the right and fills the appropriate glass about two-thirds full while discreetly announcing the name of the wine and the vintage year. Before serving, he will have poured off the first few drops in the butler's pantry to remove any particles of cork and to make sure that the wine is free from fault. Another wine is served with the following course, in another glass, but without removing the first glass served. Meanwhile, the butlers watch attentively to serve more as the guests require it and to make sure that the water glasses are filled. Wines should be served at the proper temperature to bring out the flavor: room temperature for red wines; champagne and white wines chilled. At intimate meals, carafes of wine and water are placed on the table at the guests' disposal, and a fine wine is served with the main course.

But let us return to the progress of the dinner: cheeses immediately follow the seasoned course. The dinner plate is now replaced by a smaller plate with a fork and a dessert knife with a steel blade. It is not necessary to point out that the guests are constantly supplied with bread and that the individual butter plates are replenished if necessary. The cheeses are served on appropriate plates, with glass or wooden bottoms, and with as many serving knives as there are different kinds of cheeses. They are only served once. We have mentioned that a fork should be served with the knife and cheese plate; even though it is seldom used in eating cheese, it should be served anyway, as a sign of delicacy.

A sort of short intermission should now take place as a prelude to a veritable change of scenery. The table is now stripped of all that was used in the preceding courses, except for the central decoration and the wineglasses, which stay where they are. The saltcellars, spice and mustard containers, undergo the same fate as the plates, silverware, and bread and butter plates. The butlers proceed with this operation adroitly and speedily, at the same time brushing the crumbs from the cloth in front of the guests. Next they bring in the dessert plates, which they have prepared before dinner on a butler's tray. On these plates are a crystal or silver finger bowl, with warm water and a slice of lemon; on either side of the bowl are a dessert fork and spoon and two dessert knives, one with a steel blade for certain pastries and the other with a silver blade for fruit.

May we be permitted to suggest that the serving of the dessert be particularly subtle? The atmosphere of the meal, relaxed and jolly, thanks to the quality of the food and wine and the warmth of the conversation, should be enhanced by a greater sense of well-being because of the new décor. The dessert plates should be still more beautiful, unusual, and decorative than the plates that preceded them. Although gilded silverware is a great luxury, it is still a good idea to have the whole dessert service, including the plates, made of this precious material.

Individual ash trays are also distributed. Sugar shakers take the place of saltcellars on the table, and cake plates loaded with *petits fours* tempt the appetites of the guests. The meal ends with sweet dishes and fruit.

Confident as she may be in the ability of her servants, the good hostess is constantly attentive during the entire meal so that not a single mistake or act of negligence spoils the impeccable service. Meanwhile, she does not neglect her guests, paying special attention to each one, subtly directing the conversation, changing it if necessary, or picking it up if it seems to lag. She rises from the table only at the end of the meal, to go into the drawing room for coffee and liqueurs, after she has ascertained that all her guests are ready to leave the table.

We feel certain that such a hostess will not deserve the cutting rejoinder of an epicure asked one day to give his impression of a dinner: "Everything was cold," he said, "except the ice cream." But we would like to recall the charming expression of Mme du Deffand: "Dining is one of the four aims of man; I have forgotten what the other three are."

THE MENU

The custom of writing on a card what will be served the guests does not seem to date far back into antiquity; the oldest menus we possess, called *Escriteaux* (announcements), date back to the sixteenth century. They have been greatly modified since then.

There are various types of menus, the principal ones being: 1. Restaurant and large hotel menus, which are necessarily entirely different from bourgeois menus, since they cater to different needs and are made according to different rules. 2. Menus for large banquets, weddings, and other celebrations. 3. Family menus. 4. Menus for dinner parties or luncheon parties, when the family meal takes on a more ceremonial aspect.

But regardless of what type of menu it may be, there are certain basic rules, laid down by master chefs in agreement with famous gourmets, which are immutable and may not be disregarded. In this book, intended for large restaurants as well as for family kitchens, we shall examine in turn the most sumptuous and the simplest menus.

Rules governing table service and, consequently, menus: for contrast, white meat should follow red meat, or vice versa; the same for sauces: a white sauce should follow a brown sauce and have an entirely different flavor. The same vegetables used for a garnish should not be found twice on the same menu, whether they are garden vegetables or mushrooms; if the latter have been served with the fish, they should not be a part of the meat dish. Only truffles may reappear in several courses, in which they usually play only a decorative role. The same thing goes for cooking wines used in making sauces. Fish cooked in white wine should be followed by a brown sauce made with port or Madeira. If this observation is not heeded, you will find the same flavor in every course.

Order in which the courses should be served: soup (for dinner), which may be preceded by oysters in winter or melon in summer. When the number of guests is fairly large offer two soups: a clear consommé, garnished in various ways, and a cream soup. The soup is usually followed by hot fish, but sometimes by cold fish. Next comes the entree—poached or braised fowl, or small cuts of meat, or game or hot ham with a garnish; then follows the roast, which may be meat, fowl, or game, but always different from the preceding course. The salad accompanies the roast, but if a cold dish follows the roast, such as a *pâté*, *chaud-froid*, or aspic mousse, the salad should be served with this cold dish. An exception is made in the case of *foie gras*, which has too delicate a flavor to be eaten with a vinegary salad.

Fig. 5. — *Types of recommended glassware. Number 4 is a parfait glass.*

Fig. 6. — *1. Aperitif glass. 2. Liqueur glass. 3. Brandy glass. 4. Port glass. 5. Champagne glass.*

Next come the vegetables, formerly called *entremets,* or side dishes. Today the *entremets* include only sweet dishes, either hot or cold, or ice cream with wafers or sugared cookies. Cheeses should be served before the dessert course, and not after, as some pseudo-gastronomes would have it. Two cheeses are usually served, a rich one and a dry one: for example, Camembert and Gruyère, Pont-l'Évêque and Cheshire, Brie and Port-Salut. No dinner is good without cheese: with this course one really tastes a fine meal. *Petits fours,* almost obligatory, do not figure on the menu. They stay on the table.

We do not advise listing the wines for each course on the menu. This makes too much of a banquet menu. The guests will simply want the wines to be good, but if the host feels that his cellar deserves to be appreciated, he may have the wines discreetly announced to each guest by the servant pouring the wine.

For the same class of luncheon, replace the soup with hors d'oeuvres, varied according to season. Oysters, chilled melon, port, sherry, or any other wine of the same sort may be substituted for the hors d'oeuvres. In general, luncheons may be a little less filling because there is frequently not sufficient leisure time for lingering at the table—one of the reasons militating in favor of dinner parties instead of luncheon parties.

We have assembled a few menus of different kinds. Their value lies in giving ideas, in serving as a base. The hostess can modify and vary them in innumerable ways, without, however, changing the order of the courses. An exception is made in the case of *foie gras,* which should, in our opinion, come at the beginning of the meal, when served in homes, and not at the end as dictated by custom. Ordinarily, guests are no longer hungry when this dish is served and cannot give it the full appreciation it deserves, which is really a shame.[1]

Note: Dinner menus become luncheon menus simply by replacing the soup with hors d'oeuvres, and the other way around.

BUFFET LUNCHEONS SERVED AT TABLES

There is a difference between the buffet luncheon served at tables and the standing buffet luncheon. The former is usually served in the bride's home to close friends immediately after the wedding ceremony. This luncheon is served at small tables. For the most part the menu is made up of cooked dishes arranged on a buffet. Butlers and their helpers serve the food on small plates, the guests making their own choices. The menu ordinarily starts with both cold and hot consommé, followed by either hot Foie Gras Patties or Patties à la Reine. Frequently, for the sake of convenience, only cold patties are served. The main dishes may be Ham in Aspic, Chicken Galantine, Foie Gras Mousse, Chicken Chaud-Froid, Lobster in Mayonnaise, Mixed Salad, and pastries such as Mousseline Brioche, assorted cookies, Petits Fours, Millefeuilles, etc. The beverages are usually red and white Bordeaux wines, champagne, hot coffee, and Viennese Coffee, served with fruit sherbets and ice creams.

Luncheon is served at small tables for two, three, or four guests. At each place there should be a tea napkin, salad fork, rolls, and an ice-cream spoon.

[1] This is a personal opinion, approved many times by numerous gourmets, which never fails to raise an argument.

When the home is not equipped for this kind of service, caterers should be called upon who can provide the dining room, chairs, tables, and all of the service, including butlers and waiters.

STANDING BUFFET LUNCHEONS

The standing luncheon is more and more replacing the seated luncheon. It is given for the same kind of formal occasion, usually in the middle of the afternoon. The guests are received by the bride's parents and sometimes by the bride and groom, if they have not already left on their honeymoon. After passing through the receiving line, the guests move on to the buffet, which is spread with all sorts of sandwiches, brioche loaves filled with *foie gras,* thin slices of brown bread buttered or covered with jelly, and especially a great many pastries, Petits Fours, glazed oranges, stuffed dates, nuts, etc.

The minimum amount of pastries needed to serve 300 guests at a buffet luncheon should be: 600 assorted small cookies, 400 assorted sandwiches and stuffed rolls, and 20 large cakes to be sliced as needed: a Brioche Ring (easier to cut and serve than a large Mousseline Brioche), Mocha, Chocolatine, Paris-Brest, and Progress cakes, Sponge-Cake Roll, Génoise with jam, Genoa Loaf, Pithiviers, etc.

Although not obligatory, a platter of cold meat is sometimes served. If served, we advise ham or beef fillet—meat without bones—which is easier for standing guests to manage than a chicken leg or other meat that must be cut from the bone.

The butlers stand behind the buffet on which the foods are arranged. To one side they have the ices, Viennese Coffee or iced chocolate, and the other beverages to be served. The liquid refreshments always include white wine, orangeade, lemonade, cherry squash, and, above all, champagne. The plates and forks should also be near at hand, and the butlers should have a pair of cake servers so that they never have to touch the food with their fingers. At least two butlers are needed in addition to a maid or two to wash and dry glasses, plates, and forks as required. As a rule, the luncheon should be over by six o'clock.

TYPICAL BUFFET MENU FOR ONE HUNDRED GUESTS

Hot and Cold Consommé

COLD DISHES

Salmon decorated with Mayonnaise, Chantilly, or Green Sauce
Chicken Galantine
Glazed Ham
Beef Fillet with Foie Gras (Strasbourgeoise)
Pheasant Galantine (in season)
or
Woodcock Pie
Pâté de Foie Gras
One or two dishes of Chicken Chaud-Froid
Truffled Foie Gras Aspic
or
Foie Gras Loaf
or
A Mousse (of your choosing)
300 sandwiches and stuffed rolls:
ham, roast beef, foie gras, cheese,
hard-boiled eggs, etc.

PASTRY

Éclairs, Cream Puffs, Brioches, Millefeuilles, Madeleines,
Condés, champagne biscuits, cookies, fruit tartlets
If desired, an ornamental cake with several layers or some
large layer cakes
Assorted Petits Fours

VARIOUS BEVERAGES

Punch, sirups, Bavarian creams, hot and iced chocolate and coffee
2 qt. fruit ices, 2 qt. ice cream

EVERYDAY MENUS

SPRING AND SUMMER

LUNCHEONS

Cucumber Salad
Blanquette of Veal with Mushrooms
New Potatoes Fondantes
Fruit

•

Radishes and Butter
Grilled Tournedos
Potatoes Lyonnaise
Lettuce Salad
Fruit

•

Tomato Salad
Fresh Cod Fillets Boulangère
Cold Ham in Jelly
Cheese
Rhubarb Tartlets

•

Celery with Rémoulade Sauce
Grilled Mutton Chops
French-fried Potatoes
String Beans
Peaches and Apricots

•

Melon
Chicken Sauté Portuguese Style
Cauliflower with White Sauce
Fruit

•

Muzzle
Veal Cutlets Breaded English Style
Green Beans
Pastry

DINNERS

Leek Soup
Poached Eggs Portuguese Style
Peas with Bacon
Fruit Compote

•

Vegetable Soup
Cod with Caper Sauce
Boiled Potatoes
Spinach English Style
Strawberry Cream

•

Cabbage Soup
Whiting in White Wine
Boiled Potatoes
Peas French Style
Fruit

•

Health Soup
Veal Birds
Stuffed Eggplant
Salad
Fruit Compote

•

Onion Soup
Chicken Rissoles with Tomato Sauce
Squab with Turnips
Fruit

•

Julienne Vegetable Soup
Scrambled Eggs Normande
Risotto Milanaise
Molded Cream Custard

EVERYDAY MENUS

AUTUMN AND WINTER

LUNCHEONS

Shrimps and Butter
Toulouse Cassoulet
Chicory (Endive) Salad
Pear Compote

•

Lyon Sausage
Tournedos Benjamin
Fried Oyster Plant
Rice Cake

•

Marinated Herring Fillets
Veal Chasseur
Potato Croquettes
Cheese
Floating Island

•

Beet Salad
Garnished Sauerkraut
Potatoes English Style
Cheese
Fruits

•

Mans Rillettes
Pork Chops Grand'mère
Mashed Potatoes
Coffee Soufflé

•

Marinated Mushrooms
Saddle of Roast Hare with Chestnuts
Apple Charlotte

DINNERS

Saint-Germain Soup
Whiting-Pollock Fillets Dugléré
Jugged Hare
Pear Compote

•

Tapioca Soup
Beef au Gratin Marius
Potatoes Anna
Chestnut Pudding

•

Cream-of-Lettuce Soup
Coquilles Saint-Jacques Parisienne
Veal Casserole with Carrots
Crêpes Suzette

•

Navy-Bean Soup
Fried Whiting with Lemon
Roast Pheasant
Salad
Praline Ice Cream

•

Pot-au-feu
Salt Beef
Escarole Salad
Eggs in Snow

•

Country-style Soup
Hare Loaf Normande
Endive (Chicory) Salad
Fruit Crusts

MENUS FOR SIMPLE MEALS WITH GUESTS

SPRING AND SUMMER

LUNCHEONS

Assorted Hors d'Oeuvres
Eggs en Cocotte with Cream
Grilled Mutton Chops
Potatoes Fondantes
Salad
Cheese
Strawberries with Chantilly Cream

•

Artichokes Greek Style
Whiting or Trout Meunière
Grilled Deviled Chicken
Potato Straws
Cheese
Chocolate Soufflé

•

Tomatoes Antiboise
Red Mullet Niçoise
Grilled Rib Steak Maître d'Hôtel
New Potatoes in Butter
Cheese
Peaches Cardinal

•

Melon
Poached Eggs Florentine
Squabs with Peas
Salad
Cheese
Rhubarb Tartlets

•

Lobster Pastry Boats
Stuffed Eggs Chimay
Beef Fillet Bouquetière
Cheese
Coffee Parfait

DINNERS

Chicken Consommé
Grilled Salmon Steak with Anchovy Butter
Bresse Pullet on the Spit
Asparagus with Mousseline Sauce
Cheese
Meringues Germaine

•

Crayfish Bisque
Sole Fillets Marguery
Leg of Lamb English Style with Vegetables
Salad - Cheese
Pithiviers

•

Cream-of-Artichoke Soup
River Trout Hussarde
Chicken Galantine in Aspic
Muguette Salad
Cheese
Strawberry Ice Cream

•

Cream Soup Dubarry
Sole Fillets Normande
Chickens en Cocotte Bonne Femme
Green Salad
Cheese
Omelet Norwegian Style

•

Cream-of-Asparagus Soup
Pike Quenelles Lyonnaise
Chicken Sauté Demidov
Salad - Cheese
Apricots Mireille

MENUS FOR SIMPLE MEALS WITH GUESTS

AUTUMN AND WINTER

LUNCHEONS	DINNERS
Oysters Stuffed Eggs Aurore Chicken Sauté Marengo Lobster Aspic Russian Salad Cheese Crêpes Suzette Fruit	Cream-of-Barley Soup Sole Birds Favart Chicken Colette Saddle of Venison Purée of Celery Applesauce Salad - Cheese Pears Flambé
•	•
Assorted Hors d'Oeuvres Brill Fillets Dugléré Lamb Chops Capucine Ham in Aspic Salad Cheese Bananas Flambé	Saint-Germain Soup Turbot with Mousseline Sauce Veal Liégeoise Beef Fillet Godard Artichoke Bottoms with Duxelles Salad - Cheese Pears Bourdaloue
•	•
Oysters Fried Perch Sweetbreads Financière Woodcock Pie Salad Cheese Millefeuilles with Cream Fruit	Royal Springtime Consommé Boiled Trout with Melted Butter Roast Ham in Crust Spinach Loaf with Parmesan Cheese Foie Gras Mousse in Aspic Cheese Nesselrode Pudding with Sabayon Fruit
•	•
Patties à la Reine River Trout Muguette Venison Chops Bélisaire Salad Cheese Mont-Blanc with Chestnuts	Cream-of-Mushroom Soup Brill Fillets Portuguese Style Braised Veal Chartreuse Salad Cheese Chocolate Profiteroles

SUPPER MENUS

SPRING AND SUMMER

Consommé Madrilène
Lobster Américaine
Pullet en Cocotte Bonne Femme
Roast Saddle of Lamb
Green Beans
Salad - Cheese
Peach Melba

•

Consommé with Tapioca
Sole Fillets Newburg
Squabs with Peas
Ham Cones Tsarine
Cheese
Fruits Chilled
in Champagne

•

Melon with Port
Cream-of-Fresh-Pea Soup Clamart
Lobster Parisienne with Tartar Sauce
Beef Fillet Portuguese Style
(with Stuffed Tomatoes)
Roast Duck on the Spit
Glazed Turnips
Cream Cheese
Strawberries in Kirsch

•

Jellied Chicken Consommé
Salmon Galantines
Lamb Chops Châtelaine
Sliced Duckling Montmorency
Salad
Cheese
Bombe Alhambra
Pastry Straws
Fruit in Season

•

Cream-of-Asparagus Soup
Brill Amiral
Braised Veal Chartreuse
Chicken Chaud-Froid
in Aspic
Salad
Cheese
Ice Cream Countess Marie

•

Melon with Port
Bass Régence
Ham in Crust with Madeira Sauce
Truffles in Ashes
Bagration Salad
Cheese
Omelet Norwegian Style
Fruit

•

Faubonne Soup
Lobster Thermidor
Chicken Tarragon
Baron of Lamb Byzantine
Irma Salad
Cheese
Denise Cups

Assorted Hors d'Oeuvres
Turbot Cambacérès
Saddle of Veal Chartreuse
Pullet Néva
Muguette Salad
Cheese
Snowball Bombe

SUPPER MENUS

AUTUMN AND WINTER

Oysters
Consommé with Profiteroles
Cold Salmon Trout Norwegian Style
Pheasant Salmis Saint-Julien
Saddle of Veal Renaissance
Salad
Cheese
Fauvette Bombe

•

Consommé with Vermicelli
Pike with White Butter
Quails Turkish Style
Beef Fillet Richelieu
Foie Gras Aspic
Salad - Cheese
Pineapple Bourdaloue
Shortbread Cookies

•

Cream-of-Chicken Soup Princesse
Sole Fillets Caprice
Pullet Derby
Saddle of Venison Metternich
Rice Pilaf
Salad
Cheese
Frozen Orange Surprise

•

Cream-of-Lettuce Soup
Lobster Newburg
Rice Creole
Pullet Châtelaine
Foie Gras Croustade with Aspic
Salad
Cheese
Pears Sultane

•

Germiny Soup
Brill in Chambertin
Saddle of Venison Creole
Stuffed Artichokes Barigoule
Périgord Eggs
Parisian Salad
Cheese
Deviled Pineapple

•

Cream-of-Chestnut Soup
Sole Fillets Joinville
Quails in the Nest
Ham Fitz-James with Madeira Sauce
Truffles in Napkin
Green Salad
Cheese
Armenonville Cup

•

Chicken Consommé
Turbot Parisienne
Pullet Derby
Leg of Venison with Chestnuts
Strasbourg Pâté de Foie Gras
Mixed Salad
Cheese
Charlotte Parisienne

Oysters
Salmon Trout Chivry
Partridges Normande
Beef Fillet Régence
Foie Gras Suvarov
Windsor Salad
Cheese
Pears Hélène

QUANTITIES PER SERVING

(GROSS WEIGHT)

	Ounces
Fish	8
Rock lobster	10
Lobster	12
Beef, Veal, Pork — with bones	7
Beef, Veal, Pork — without bones	5
Beef fillet	6
Lamb, Mutton — with bones	8
Lamb, Mutton — without bones	6
Ham, whole	10
Ham, sliced	6
Tongue, beef or veal	8
Calf's liver	4
Boned calf's head	8
Chicken	12
Duck	14 to 16
Turkey	14
Goose	16
Foie gras	3 to 4
Rabbit	6 to 8
Hare	8

VEGETABLES

	Ounces
Potatoes	8
Asparagus	12
Carrots	6
Spinach	14
Green beans	10
Peas	10
Salad	8

DRIED VEGETABLES

Beans	2
Lentils	2¼
Peas	2¼
Rice	1½

Italian pastes	2

Pastes for soups (see p. 195)

Eggs for hors d'oeuvres	1 per person
Eggs, fried, poached	2 " "
Eggs, scrambled, omelet	3 " "

Soup, 1 qt. for 5 persons

Sauce, 1 qt. for 20 persons

PASTRY

Owing to the great variety of ingredients used in pastry recipes, it is impossible to give exact weights. Since very little weight is lost in cooking it is usually safe to allow 2 to 2½ oz. per serving.

Approximate number of PETITS FOURS to the pound:

Matches	60	Glazed Fours	35
Cheese patties	30	Dry Fours	65
Brioches	40	Masked fruits	30
Carolines, puffs	35	Brandied fruits	35
Croissants	55	Palm leaves	50
Various cookies	55	Milk or brioche rolls	45

Filled rolls 35

WINES

Preparation of the Wine

Let us suppose that you are going to serve a well-aged red wine, a full-bodied Burgundy, sensual and voluptuous in a masculine way, or a gentle Bordeaux, vibrant and voluptuous in a feminine way. I cite these two types of wines since it is impossible to list all of them. But the same truths hold good for other wines, whether we are concerned with the Côtes-du-Rhône wines, as vigorous as the sun that shines upon them, or those from other vineyards strong enough to allow long and slow aging without spoiling.

The "bottle" has been selected to go with the menu and the guests. The victim of this beautiful sacrifice has been chosen. But we still have to bring the fine old red wine from the wine cellar or storeroom to the place where it is to be drunk. Careful! This is a delicate operation.

Bringing Wine to Room Temperature

To bring a bottle of wine to room temperature means to let it stay in one room of the apartment—the dining room, usually—until it takes on the temperature of that room. Placing the bottle near heat or the fire or dipping it a few times in hot water is a barbarous custom: heating the wine is *not* bringing it to room temperature. Of course, heating the wine is faster and requires less care and respect, but it is not done without harm to the wine. A noble wine, like any other delicacy, is sensitive to sudden heat. A corner of the fireplace, a radiator, hot water, have a deadly effect. The bouquet of the wine flees, the color changes.

Twenty-four hours are sufficient for wine to reach room temperature. But bottles of Bordeaux and, possibly, Burgundy should be allowed to stand forty-eight hours so that the sediment collects on the bottom before the decanting procedure.

Decanting Wine

Through the years red wines usually leave a deposit in the bottom of the bottles. The purpose of decanting is to separate the clear liquid from the residue; otherwise, oxidation will take place on contact with the air. This oxidation, if prolonged, is detrimental to Burgundies but favorable to Bordeaux, whose bouquet will be brought out in full if the decanting is done at the right time. Therefore, Burgundy is decanted just before it is to be served and only if it contains a deposit. Red Bordeaux should always be decanted from one to two hours before it is to be drunk. This time limit is not absolute, but if it is observed you can be sure that you will not make a serious error. It goes without saying that the shortest time holds for light wines and the longest time for full-bodied wines; between these two extremes, the time can be set only according to the origin and the year of the wine.

Decanting Procedure

1. Let the bottle stand upright for forty-eight hours in the room where it will be drunk. This way, the sediment will fall to the bottom.

2. When the time has come, uncork the bottle very carefully, preferably with a corkscrew with handles, avoiding in so far as possible moving the bottle and therefore stirring up the sediment.

3. Light a candle. Using its light, examine the bottom of the bottle to discover where the sediment has collected most abundantly.

4. Place a glass funnel in the wine carafe to be used for serving. Set the lit candle to the right. Take the bottle in your right hand almost level with the bottom, taking care that the part where the sediment is heaviest stays down. Tilt the bottle very slowly, using the index finger of the left hand for leverage. Rest the neck of the bottle on the glass funnel.

5. Pour very slowly. The air should enter the bottle without causing any glug-glug sounds. Pour faster when the level of the wine is most horizontal the length of the bottle. The candle should now light up the main part of the bottle. Follow the progress of the sediment toward the mouth of the bottle and as it approaches it slow down the speed of pouring, then quickly set down the bottle as soon as it reaches the mouth. When the decanting is well done—which is easier to do than to explain—the waste is insignificant: no more than a liqueur glassful.

Note: The carafe should first be brought to the right temperature in hot water. Drain it well, then "wine" it by pouring in a liqueur glassful of wine, shaking the wine throughout the carafe, and throwing it away.

Temperature

Red Bordeaux is drunk at the temperature of the room where it has been "brought to room temperature," not lower than 64° F. All other red wines—Burgundy, Côtes-du-Rhône, Beaujolais, Touraine, etc.—are brought to a temperature a few degrees below that of the room where they are to be drunk. It is therefore necessary to bring them to room temperature in a room somewhat colder. Sometimes, through a trick of the thermometer, the wine seems too cold. The remedy is simple. Warm the wineglass a little by holding it in the hands. Certain connoisseurs like to hatch their pleasure this way. They are the true wine lovers, who close their eyes when drinking to "listen to" the wine. However, this cupping of the wineglass is only the final bit of perfecting. Be careful not to conclude that this is the way to bring a wine to room temperature.

Bringing a wine to room temperature means allowing the temperature of the wine to rise slowly and naturally. Any artificial method is a great mistake.

To Pluck the Bouquet

In every great bottle of wine there is a mysterious marvel that poets of the vine call the bouquet. This little genie, the perfume of the wine, is extraordinarily sensitive. He is afraid of humidity, cold, and heat. For no reason at all, he will shrivel up and hide. You must take infinite pains with this mollycoddle.

When you order a fine-vintage wine in a restaurant, the wine steward often brings you the bottle delicately cradled in a wicker basket. But when it is cold, does the basket make it any the better? Often you are told that the wine has been brought to room temperature. But what do the words mean? Most often, the bottle has been placed near the fire. The wine arrives tepid at the table, which is frightful. Heating is not the same as bringing to room temperature.

If you wish the little genie, bouquet, to materialize completely, you must woo him the following way. Just before dining, fill a carafe with rather hot water; after a few minutes, pour the water off. Then take the bottle of wine and pour a half liqueur glassful of the wine into the heated carafe; shake it thoroughly. This way, the whole inside will be impregnated with the wine's perfume. Then slowly decant the rest of the bottle.

If you follow this method, the bouquet, the little genie, will come out of hiding into a temperate and aromatic atmosphere, disport himself, let you know that he is satisfied; all that's left is to sing his praises.

This problem of bouquet is so important that I have taken the liberty of adding words of advice from a Burgundian connoisseur of great experience, M. Charles Brunot. "The bouquet," he writes, "is composed of several unstable ethers. Divine, born of celestial alcohols, they need oxygen to come into being and, to evaporate, only a slight accent of heat. Decanting is not only to leave the lees or sediment in the bottom of the bottle. It allows the ether molecules to oxidize on contact with the oxygen in the air. Although before swallowing the wine, you can keep it in your mouth a long time or warm it by hand, the evaporation will take place too late. It is therefore lost, unprofitably, in the stomach. You must therefore take care to start this evaporation by previously and gently raising the temperature."

Such are the general rules.

Cooling (White Wines)

The technique of cooling white wines has given rise to a good deal of controversy. Opinions about this lack no diversity—indeed, originality. One banishes the refrigerator, heaven knows why. Another scorns the ice bucket, while others prefer to chill the wineglass by jiggling a piece of ice in it. Others—and they are the most cautious—expose the bottles to the open air when the temperature is just right, but carefully avoid placing them in drafts. Of all these methods, only one should absolutely be discarded: the chilled glass. No matter how it is done, some drops of water are always left in the glass; they mix with the wine, without profit to the wine or to you, the drinker. Let us therefore hold on to the other methods of cooling: outdoor exposure, the ice bucket, the refrigerator.

Temperature

All white wines, including champagnes, which are customarily iced, must be drunk cool but not cold, let alone iced—with certain exceptions. With excessive cold, the wine—metaphorically speaking—withdraws into its shell and hides its beauties. The bouquet, for example, does not begin to be given off below a temperature of 50° F. However, you must take into account the fact that a wine served at about 40° F. in a room where the temperature is about 65° F. reaches about 54° F. in ten minutes. At this moment the wine will taste much better, but it will have lost certain of its qualities through being aerated too long. Since one generally drinks wine within the first five minutes following its serving, this delay must also be taken into account in determining the temperature to which the wine should previously have been brought. All white wines—Alsatian, Anjou, Bordeaux, Burgundy, champagne, etc.—should be chilled to a temperature between 46° and 50° F. so that in the five minutes following service they will be drunk at a temperature of between 50° and 54° F. This is without doubt the ideal temperature for truly appreciating all the qualities of a white wine.

Port, Madeira, Sherry, and Dessert Wines

White port is served a little colder than room temperature; red, a little warmer. If there is any sediment, it can be decanted. Port is indifferent to oxidation, but it is very sensitive to cold.

Madeira is served 5 to 6 degrees above room temperature.

Sweet sherry is served 5 degrees above room temperature; dry sherry, 5 degrees below.

Dessert wines—muscatel, Banyuls, Malaga, etc.—are drunk at room temperature.

Exceptions

The exceptions mentioned earlier are the very great vintage wines of Anjou and white Bordeaux and the great white Burgundies. It is a question of year. For the Anjou and Bordeaux wines: the wines of the great years that are particularly liqueurlike. For the Burgundies: the wines of the great years that are particularly full-bodied and saplike. They should be chilled to a temperature between 41° and 43° F.

For wine brought to the height of its glory, all that's left is to sing its praises.

CORRECT WINES TO BE SERVED WITH VARIOUS DISHES

RED WINES

(*a*) Dishes with which light wines are preferable:

Ham pie with cheese
Kidneys and bacon en brochette
Lamb chops
Leg of lamb
Saddle of lamb
Lamb Villeroi
Roast veal
Sweetbreads
Grilled mutton chops
Chicken giblets
Roast larks
Roast quail
Lentils
Peas
Potatoes Maître d'Hotêl
New potatoes in butter
Foie gras
Game pies made of game birds listed above and below
Roast thrush
Roast partridge
Roast squab
Roast guinea hen
Roast chicken

Roast young turkey
Lettuce

Chicken en cocotte
New kidney beans

(*b*) Dishes requiring full-bodied or stronger wines:

Leg of mutton
Mutton stew
Saddle of mutton with vegetables
Beef { steak / filet mignon / sirloin / rumpsteak / tournedos / roast }
Duck { roast / with olives / Rouen / with turnips }
Goose Cassoulet
Duck livers Périgueux
Chicken { Chasseur / Marengo }

Pigeon Crapaudine
Woodcock
Snipe
Venison
Pheasant
Hare
Partridge with cabbage
Boar
Teal
Cardoons with gravy
Braised celery
Mushrooms Bordelaise
Cauliflower au gratin
Artichoke bottoms
Beans with pork
Fried potatoes
Pies made of game listed above

WHITE WINE

(*a*) Dishes with which dry white wines are preferable:

Oysters, shellfish
Eggs
Lobster with mayonnaise
Cold fish with mayonnaise
Grilled fish
Fried fish
Roast fowl
Duck with olives
Duck with turnips
Wilted lettuce

Braised celery
Roast lamb
Braised endive (chicory)
Braised turnips
Cauliflower au gratin
Crayfish
Galantine
Ham
Frosted biscuits

(*b*) Dishes with which mellow or semidry wines are preferable:

Patties à la Reine
Sweetbreads
Timbales
Tripe à la Mode de Caen
Vol-au-vent
Bouillabaisse
Lobster Américaine
Sole Normande
Fish with white sauce
Fatty or rich fish
Chicken sautés
Chicken with rice

Asparagus with white sauce
Cardoons
Kidney beans (fresh haricot beans)
Artichoke bottoms
Navy beans (dried haricot beans)
Lentils
Noodles and macaroni
Peas
Potatoes
Foie gras
Desserts

COMPARISON OF VINTAGES

BORDEAUX

A. RED WINES

1872 - Mediocre year. Wines lack maturity and strength.
1873 - Mediocre year. Vintage spoiled by frost.
1874 - Good year. Light but fine and elegant wines.
1875 - Very good year. Light and elegant wines.
1876 - Mediocre year.
1877 - Moderate success. Elegant wines.
1878 - Great year. Wines distinguished by their perfect harmony.
1879 and 1880 - Mediocre years. Insufficient wines.
1881 - Moderate success. Wines a little harsh.
1882, 1883, 1884 - Mediocre years. Mildew.
1885 and 1886 - Bad years. Mildew.
1887 - Average year. Wines a little harsh.
1888 - Mediocre year. Wines too light.
1890 - Fairly good year. Wines full-bodied but harsh.
1891 - Fairly good year. Wines thin but fine and elegant.
1892 - Uneven quality; many wines turn bad.
1893 - Very good year. Mellow wines with plenty of body.
1894 - Mediocre year. Green wines from diseased vines.
1895 - Mediocre year. Most of the wines failed to develop properly.
1896 - Average year. Wines soft and smooth but lacking in warmth.
1897 - Bad year.
1898 - Good year. Full-bodied, rather firm wines. Some good bottles to be found, especially in the Graves region.
1899 - Very great year. Wines full-bodied and mature, but sometimes a little harsh.
1900 - Very great year. Mellow, elegant wines.
1901 - Mediocre year. Grapes spoiled during the harvest. Meager wines.
1902 - Mediocre year. Immature wines, thin and without distinction.
1903 - Bad year. Watery wines without body.
1904 - Great year. Wines moderately full-bodied, mellow.
1905 - Good year. Wines thin but elegant.
1906 - Very great year. Wines very full-bodied but a little harsh and slow in maturing; a few very fine bottles.

1907 - Good year. Wines light, fine, elegant.
1908 and 1909 - Mediocre years. Meager wines.
1910 - Bad year.
1911 - Average year. Saint-Emilion wines are smooth and finished.
1912 - Mediocre year. Uneven maturity, wines thin and meager.
1913 - Mediocre year. Wines arid and without charm.
1914 - Average year. Wines thin and meager.
1915 - Bad year. Wines mildewed and sick.
1916 - Very great year. Wines rich and mellow, a little harsh at the start, later becoming smooth and elegant. 1916 wines have more body than those of 1918.
1917 - Mediocre year. Wines that were fruity in the beginning later became watery, harsh, and without finesse.
1918 - Very great year. Mellow wines with great elegance. They are less finished but finer and smoother than those of 1916.
1919 - Mediocre year. Wines thin and without polish.
1920 - Great year. Wines moderately full-bodied but very well balanced and distinctive. More subtle than 1918 wines.
1921 - Great year. Wines mature, rich, and mellow.
1922 - Good year. Wines have too little body but are tender and elegant.
1923 - Mediocre year. Wines thin and meager. Because of the drought the grapes failed to mature and consequently the wines are sometimes tinged with a taste of the stem.
1924 - Great year. Fine bouquet, moderately full-bodied, mellow wines.
1925 - Mediocre year. Most wines thin, although some have charm.
1926 - Great year. Wines smooth and mellow with much subtlety. They mature rapidly.
1927 - Mediocre year. Weak wines. A few, though light, are pleasant.
1928 - Great year. Mellow wines of very distinguished character. They are fruitier and have more body than those of 1924.
1929 - Great year. Wines have a good deal of body and flavor, richer than the 1928 wines.
1930 - Bad year. Weak wines.
1931 - Mediocre year. Thin wines, sometimes a little green.
1932 - Bad year.
1933 - Good year. Wines have too little body but some are quite fruity.
1934 - Very good year, although unevenly successful. The successful wines are flavorful and fruity.
1935 - Mediocre year. Weak wines.
1936 - Mediocre year. Wines light.
1937 - Great year. Full-bodied wines with fine flavor.
1938 - Average year. Light wines with some bouquet.
1939 - Good year. Wines flavorful and richer than those of 1938.
1940 - Good year. Wines have a fine bouquet, are light, and mature rapidly.
1941 - Mediocre year. Wines very weak.
1942 - Good year. Smooth and flavorful wines.
1943 - Very good year. Wines strong and distinguished.
1944 - Average year. The smooth wines are rather neutral.

1945 - Very good year. Some fine bottles may develop, but the wines have a great deal of body and are sometimes a little harsh.
1946 - Very good year. Wines supple, with taste and body.
1947 - Great year. Wines have a fine bouquet and much character.
1948 - Very good year. Fresh wine, with aroma, charm, and character.
1949 - Great year. Full-bodied wines, solid, strong.
1950 - Fairly good year. Wines quick to mature.
1951 - Mediocre year.
1952 - Good year.
1953 - Very good year. Wines balanced, well rounded.
1954 - Average irregular year, a few successes.
1955 - Successful year. Supple, complete wines.
1956 - Average year. Wines with sufficient finesse.
1957 - Very good year. Full-bodied wines with a certain amount of finesse.
1958 - Quite a good year.
1959 - Very good year.
1960 - Light, very quick-maturing wines.

B. WHITE WINES

1879 - Mediocre year.
1880 - Average year.
1881 - Average year.
1882 - Mediocre year.
1883 - Mediocre year.
1884 - Fairly good year.
1885 - Mediocre year.
1886 - Mediocre year.
1887 - Good year.
1888 - Ordinary year.
1889 - Ordinary year. Thin wines.
1890 - Fairly good year.
1891 - Good year. The wines are elegant and strong, but lack sweetness.
1892 - Fairly good year. Wines liqueurlike at start, but lost this quality rapidly.
1893 - Very great year. Wines mellow and with very good tone.
1894 - Mediocre year. Wines dry out rapidly.
1895 - Mediocre year. Wines meager and harsh.
1896 - Average year. Wines not quite mature.
1897 - Bad year.
1898 - Good year. Wines a little dry but with tone.
1899 - Suduiraut was almost the only wine to achieve a fine quality, the rest being more or less dried out.
1900 - Great year. Very elegant wines.
1901 - Very great year. Much richer wines than in 1900, but with less finesse. The Yquem and Climens are most remarkable.
1902 - Very mediocre year.
1903 - Bad year.
1904 - Great year. Wines with tone.
1905 - Bad year.

1906 - Good year. Wines a little scanty and decidedly inferior to those of 1904.
1907 - Mediocre success. Wines too dry.
1908 - Very great year. Wines with liqueur quality and great tone. Certain ones are decidedly outstanding.
1909 - Average year. Wines are strong enough but lack finesse. A few good bottles.
1910 - Bad year.
1911 - Bad year. Wines too dry, not mellow.
1912 - Average year. Wines thin, lacking in sweetness.
1913 - Mediocre year.
1914 - Very good year. Wines sufficiently strong and with good bouquet. A few fine bottles.
1915 - Bad year (mildew). Immature, weak wines with a disagreeable acidity.
1916 - Good year. Elegant wines with good bouquet, but lacking the liqueur quality of those of 1914.
1917 - Good year, but not generous. Some wines are mediocre while others have bouquet, tone, and a very fine quality.
1918 - Good year. Light wines. Some are agreeably mellow.
1919 - Great year. Liqueur quality and tone. Richer than the 1917 wines, but heavier than those of 1921.
1920 - Mediocre year. Meager wines with no attraction.
1921 - Very great year. Wines of the highest quality, refined yet strong. They have more tone and finesse than those of 1919.
1922 - Mediocre year.
1923 - Uneven year. In general the wines are rather thin.
1924 - Good year. Mellow wines with tone, but less "complete" than those of 1921, 1926, and 1929.
1925 - Uneven year. Light wines. A few are green but others are mellow enough and very agreeable.
1926 - Great year. Fine wines, mellow, with much tone, but sometimes a little heavy.
1927 - Great year. Heady wines, liqueurlike, preserving their quality better than and often finer than those of 1926.
1928 - Good year. Full, mellow wines lacking the tone of the great years.
1929 - Very great year. Full-bodied, mellow wines with much tone.
1930 - Bad year.
1931 - Bad year. Weak, vinegary wines.
1932 - Bad year.
1933 - Mediocre year. Light wines, sometimes heady and preserving their quality.
1934 - Good year. Spirited, heady wines, somewhat mellow.
1935 - Bad year.
1936 - Average year. Wines fine but thin.
1937 - Very great year. Fine, very heady wines, mellow and distinguished. More tone than those of 1929.
1938 - Average year. Sufficient tone.
1939 - Average year. Wines have more tone than in 1938.
1940 - Good year. Spirited wines with tone.
1941 - Mediocre year.

1942 - Very good year. Heady, liqueurlike wines.
1943 - Very great year, probably exceptional. Wines complete, with tone and liqueurlike quality.
1944 - Mediocre year.
1945 - Good year. Wines have sufficient liqueur quality.
1946 - Mediocre year.
1947 - Great year. Wines full of tone, liqueur quality, and well balanced.
1948 - Good year. The wines are quite sweet, pleasant.
1949 - Great year. The wines are sweet, mellow, very aromatic.
1950 - Good year.
1951 - Mediocre year.
1952 - Good year.
1953 - Good year.
1954 - Average year.
1955 - Good year. Some pleasant, successful wines.
1956 - Mediocre year. Frost limited production.
1957 - Good year. Small harvest.
1958 - Average year.
1959 - Very good year.
1960 - Light, very quick-maturing wines.

BURGUNDY

A. RED WINES

1886 - Great year. Fine and distinguished wines.
1887 - Great year. Wines of very good quality, well balanced, full-bodied, and fruity.
1888 - Wines light, thin, and a little green.
1889 - Wines of good quality. Small harvest owing to vine diseases.
1890 - Wines weak and incomplete.
1891 - Wines delicate, lacking in body.
1892 - Wines tender, not very fruity.
1893 - Average year. Light wines, rather neutral.
1894 - Great year. Wines of good quality and constitution, robust and full-bodied. Very well matured.
1895 - Good year. Wines mellow, full-bodied, with nice bouquet.
1896 - Mediocre year. Light wines.
1897 - Mediocre year. Wines harsh and bitter.
1898 - Fruity wines, but a little thin.
1899 - Great year. Full-bodied wines that keep well, but a little harsh.
1900 - Great year. Wines light and tender; uneven quality; large harvest.
1901 - Bad year.
1902 - Bad year.
1903 - Mediocre year. Wines thin, dry, and acid.
1904 - Great year. Wines tender, supple. Have a good bouquet and keep well.
1905 - Bad year. Wines flat and without taste.
1906 - Very great year. Wines preserve their quality and are more complete than those of 1904.

1907 - Good year. Wines very light but very elegant.
1908 - Mediocre year. A few good wines.
1909 - Bad year. Wines green and thin.
1910 - Almost no harvest.
1911 - Very great year. Mellow, full-bodied wines.
1912 - Average year. Wines vigorous but rather lacking in character and finesse.
1913 - Bad year.
1914 - Good year. Wines light and flavorful; a few batches came out very well.
1915 - Very great year. Wines generous, rich, full-bodied, with fine constitution. Capable of being kept a very long time.
1916 - Good year. Wines light and distinguished.
1917 - Mediocre year. Wines bitter and thin.
1918 - Good year. Wines have bouquet but are a little thin.
1919 - Good year. Wines full-bodied and succulent but a little harsh.
1920 - Good year. Wines mellow and supple.
1921 - Great year. Very fine wines with bouquet and much distinction. They have less body than those of 1915 or 1923.
1922 - Average year. Wines light but pleasant.
1923 - Very great year. Wines complete, full-bodied, mellow, spirited, and easily preserved.
1924 - Good year. Wines sufficiently strong yet fine; not much body.
1925 - Mediocre year. Wines scarce. A few fine bottles may be found, however.
1926 - Great year. Wines very heady, full-bodied.
1927 - Mediocre year. Most wines rather thin; a few bottles with good enough bouquet to be found.
1928 - Great year. Wines mellow, flavorful, with great elegance.
1929 - Very great year. Wines complete, full-bodied, and mellow, with a more subtle distinction than those of 1928.
1930 - Bad year. Wines thin but with bouquet.
1931 - Bad year. Wines acid and thin.
1932 - Bad year. Wines harsh.
1933 - Bad year. Wines thin and acid.
1934 - Very good year. Wines mellow, tender, with fine bouquet.
1935 - Bad year. Wines thin and acid.
1936 - Bad year. Wines thin and flat.
1937 - Good year. Wines full-bodied and heady.
1938 - Average year. Wines preserve their quality and have bouquet.
1939 - Mediocre year. Thin wines.
1940 - Mediocre year. Wines harsh and without distinction.
1941 - Average year. Wines thin.
1942 - Good year. Wines have bouquet and are supple.
1943 - Good year. Wines have bouquet and are supple; more body than 1944.
1944 - Mediocre year. Wines very thin.
1945 - Very good year. Wines full-bodied with bouquet.
1946 - Very good year. Supple wines with distinctive bouquet.
1947 - Great year. Rich wines, supple, tender, and with fine bouquet.
1948 - Very good year. Aromatic wines, smooth, but fragile.
1949 - Great year. Sirupy wines. aromatic, heavy.

1950 - Good year.
1951 - Average year. Thin wines.
1952 - Very good year. Full-bodied wines.
1953 - Very good year. Full-bodied wines.
1954 - Mediocre year. Thin wines.
1955 - Very good year. Delicate and elegant wines.
1956 - Average year. Light wines without much color.
1957 - Good year. Production limited by frost.
1958 - Average year.
1959 - Very great year.
1960 - Bad year.

B. WHITE WINES

1925 - Average year. Light wines.
1926 - Great year. Complete, vigorous wines.
1927 - Good year. Elegant wines, sufficiently distinctive and vigorous.
1928 - Great year. Distinctive, vigorous wines.
1929 - Very great year. Complete and very vigorous wines.
1930 - Bad year. Weak wines.
1931 - Average year. Wines thin but with enough bouquet.
1932 - Mediocre year. Thin wines.
1933 - Bad year. Wines thin and acid.
1934 - Good year. Wines supple, tender, and with a bouquet.
1935 - Bad year. Wines thin and acid.
1936 - Bad year. Wines thin and flat.
1937 - Bad year. Wines without character.
1938 - Good year. Wines with flavor and sufficiently vigorous.
1939 - Average year. Wines without great character.
1940 - Harvest almost nonexistent.
1941 - Mediocre year. Wines thin and acid.
1942 - Good year. Wines supple and flavorful.
1943 - Very good year. Wines with bouquet and vigor.
1944 - Mediocre year. Weak wines.
1945 - Very good year. Wines with flavor and body.
1946 - Very good year. Fine wines with much bouquet.
1947 - Great year. Very fine wines with bouquet and vigor.
1948 - Very good year. Fine wines, aromatic, agreeable, and fresh.
1949 - Great year. Very smooth, perfumed, solid.
1950 - Fairly good year. Smooth wines.
1951 - Mediocre year.
1952 - Good year. Full-bodied wines.
1953 - Average year.
1954 - Mediocre year.
1955 - Very good year.
1956 - Average year. Vigorous wines, with character.
1957 - Average year. Production limited.
1958 - Average year, but with several successes.
1959 - Very great year.
1960 - Average year.

BEAUJOLAIS – MACONNAIS

A. RED WINES

1926 - Great year. Wines very full-bodied.
1927 - Mediocre year.
1928 - Very great year. Mellow wines with a fine bouquet.
1929 - Bad year. Harsh wines.
1930 - Mediocre year. Weak wines.
1931 - Mediocre year.
1932 - Mediocre year.
1933 - Great year. Fine wines with very good bouquet.
1934 - Good year. Wines full-bodied, supple, and fruity.
1935 - Mediocre year. Wines thin and neutral.
1936 - Bad year. Wines harsh and without charm.
1937 - Very good year. Wines full-bodied and heady.
1938 - Good year. Fine wines, supple, and with good constitution.
1939 - Mediocre year.
1940 - Good year. Wines light and fruity.
1941 - Mediocre year. Harsh wines.
1942 - Good year. Wines full-bodied and succulent.
1943 - Average year.
1944 - Bad year. Nervous wines.
1945 - Very good year. Supple wines with body and bouquet.
1946 - Very good year. Supple wines with bouquet.
1947 - Very great year. Very fine wines with fine bouquet and admirable constitution.
1948 - Average year. Little character.
1949 - Great year. Wines with substance, solid, very aromatic.
1950 - Good year.
1951 - Bad year.
1952 - Very good year. Supple and fruity wines.
1953 - Exceptional year. High quality.
1954 - Average year.
1955 - Very good year.
1956 - Average year. Vigorous wines.
1957 - Good year. Wines of character.
1958 - Average year.
1959 - Uneven year: some great successes and some failures.
1960 - Mediocre year.

B. WHITE WINES

1926 - Great year. Full-bodied distinctive wines with fine bouquet.
1927 - Average year.
1928 - Good year. Sufficient body.
1929 - Very great year. Wines with body, finesse, and much class.
1930 - Average year.
1931 - Average year.
1932 - Average year.

1933 - Average year.
1934 - Good year. Full-bodied, supple, and fine wines.
1935 - Bad year. Wines green and acid.
1936 - Bad year. Wines acid and tasteless.
1937 - Bad year. Wines dry and without charm.
1938 - Good year. Wines with flavor and bouquet.
1939 - Mediocre year.
1940 - Average year. Light wines.
1941 - Average year. Light wines with bouquet.
1942 - Good year. Full-bodied wines with bouquet.
1943 - Average year. Supple wines.
1944 - Bad year.
1945 - Mediocre year. Deficient wines.
1946 - Very good year. Fine, distinctive wines with bouquet.
1947 - Great year. Full-bodied wines with bouquet.
1948 - Average year. Light wines.
1949 - Great year. Very perfumed wines, very well balanced.
1950 - Fairly good year.
1951 - Mediocre year.
1952 - Good year.
1953 - Very good year. Supple wines hinting at fine qualities.
1954 - Average year.
1955 - Very good year.
1956 - Lean, but occasionally harmonious wines.
1957 - Average year. Quite supple wines.
1958 - Average year.
1959 - Great year.
1960 - Average year.

CHABLIS

1924 - Good year. Abundant harvest.
1925 - Average year. Light wines, sometimes a little green.
1926 - Good year. Full-bodied wines, quick to mature.
1927 - Great year. Wines have great finesse and bouquet, preserve their quality.
1928 - Mediocre year. Almost no harvest. Acid wines.
1929 - Very great year. Full-bodied, fine, distinctive wines.
1930 - Good year. Light wines with bouquet.
1931 - Mediocre year. Green wines.
1932 - Mediocre year. Thin wines.
1933 - Average year. Rather light wines with bouquet.
1934 - Very good year. Fruity wines with body.
1935 - Average year. Light wines.
1936 - Bad year.
1937 - Very good year. Full-bodied wines.
1938 - Average year. Wines with bouquet.
1939 - Bad year.
1940 - Average year.
1941 - Average year. Light wines.

1942 - Very good year. Wines with bouquet.
1943 - Very good year. Well-rounded wines with fine bouquet.
1944 - Average year. Pleasant wines.
1945 - Harvest spoiled by frost.
1946 - Very good year. Flavorful, full-bodied wines with bouquet.
1947 - Good year. Very strong wines with body.
1948 - Very good year. Aromatic wines, fresh, with character.
1949 - Great year. Smooth wines, strong, perfumed.
1950 - Fairly good year. Fruity wines.
1951 - Mediocre year. Acid wines.
1952 - Good year. Supple wines.
1953 - Very good year, harvest reduced by frosts.
1954 - Mediocre year, much reduced by frosts.
1955 - Very good year, wines of great refinement.
1956 - Very poor harvest, due to frost. Mediocre wines.
1957 - Good year. Wines of character.
1958 - Average year. Frost.
1959 - Very great year.
1960 - Average year.

ALSACE

1925 - Fairly good.
1926 - Very good.
1927 - Mediocre.
1928 - Very great.
1929 - Great.
1930 - Average.
1931 - Good.
1932 - Good.
1933 - Average.
1934 - Very good.
1935 - Average.
1936 - Good.
1937 - Very good.
1938 - Very good.
1939 - Fairly good.
1940 - Mediocre.
1941 - Good.
1942 - Very good.
1943 - Great.
1944 - Average.
1945 - Good.
1946 - Average.
1947 - Great year.
1948 - Good year.
1949 - Great year.
1950 - Fairly good year.
1951 - Average year.
1952 - Good year.
1953 - Very good year.
1954 - Good year.
1955 - Very good year.
1956 - Very good year.
1957 - Good year.
1958 - Average year.
1959 - Excellent year.
1960 - Large harvest, average quality.

ANJOU—TOURAINE

A. WHITE WINES

1924 - Good year. Well-made wines with some tone.
1925 - Average year. Supple wines; thinner and with less tone than those of 1924.
1926 - Great year. Very mellow wines. Almost no quantity.
1927 - Average year. Poor harvest.

1928 - Great year. Mellow wines with tone.
1929 - Great year. Full-bodied wines with good flavor.
1930 - Average year.
1931 - Very good year. Fine wines; rather light but with tone.
1932 - Mediocre year.
1933 - Good year. Full-bodied, mellow wines.
1934 - Mediocre year. Wines thin but fruity.
1935 - Bad year.
1936 - Bad year.
1937 - Good year. Wines not very mellow but with tone.
1938 - Mediocre year.
1939 - Bad year.
1940 - Average year.
1941 - Mediocre year.
1942 - Good year.
1943 - Great year. Liqueur-quality wines.
1944 - Good year.
1945 - Great year. Fine liqueur quality to the wines; very small harvest.
1946 - Mediocre year. Wines too dry.
1947 - Great year in Touraine, with fine, mellow wines. Average year in Anjou; wines too dry.
1948 - Good year. Dry wines, but aromatic.
1949 - Very good year. Mellow wines, perfumed, very strong.
1950 - Fairly good year.
1951 - Mediocre year. Wines immature.
1952 - Good year. Wines supple.
1953 - Very good year. Balanced wines.
1954 - Average year. Wines a little acid.
1955 - Very good year.
1956 - Mediocre year; the wines had much acidity.
1957 - Average year.
1958 - Good year.
1959 - Very great year.
1960 - Average year.

B. RED WINES

1925 - Mediocre year.
1926 - Great year. Wines complete, but almost no harvest.
1927 - Very ordinary quality; poor harvest.
1928 - Great year. Very fruity wines.
1929 - Great year. Subtle, elegant wines with fine bouquet.
1930 - Mediocre year.
1931 - Mediocre year.
1932 - Mediocre year.
1933 - Mediocre year. Harsh wines.
1934 - Average year. Wines supple and fruity.
1935 - Bad year.
1936 - Bad year. Light wines.

1937 - Very good year. Wines subtle, mellow, and fruity.
1938 - Mediocre year.
1939 - Average year.
1940 - Average year.
1941 - Mediocre year.
1942 - Good year.
1943 - Very good year.
1944 - Average year.
1945 - Great year. Very small harvest.
1946 - Good year.
1947 - Great year.
1948 - Good year.
1949 - Great year. Very perfumed wines.
1950 - Average year.
1951 - Bad year.
1952 - Fairly good year.
1953 - Very good year.
1954 - Fairly good year.
1955 - Very good year. Fruity and well-balanced wines.
1956 - Good year. Thin wines, but they have character.
1957 - Mediocre year.
1958 - Average year.
1959 - Very great year.
1960 - Large harvest; average year.

CÔTES-DU-RHÔNE

1911 - Very good.
1912 - Good.
1913 - Good.
1914 - Very good.
1915 - Fairly good.
1916 - Very good.
1917 - Fairly good.
1918 - Unusually good.
1919 - Good.
1920 - Good.
1921 - Very good but rather uneven.
1922 - Fairly good.
1923 - Good.
1924 - Very good.
1925 - Good.
1926 - Very good.
1927 - Fairly good.
1928 - Very good.
1929 - Very good.
1930 - Good.
1931 - Good.
1932 - Fairly good.
1933 - Very good.
1934 - Very good year.
1935 - Average year.
1936 - Great year.
1937 - Good year.
1938 - Very good.
1939 - Great year.
1940 - Average.
1941 - Average.
1942 - Good year.
1943 - Very good year. Complete, well-rounded wines.
1944 - Good year. Fine wines.
1945 - Very great year. Very fine wines with character.
1946 - Good year. Wines with body and subtlety.
1947 - Very good year. Wines very supple and full-bodied.
1948 - Average year.

1949 - Great year. Solid, robust, perfumed wines.
1950 - Good year.
1951 - Fairly good year. Light wines.
1952 - Very good year. Full-bodied wines.
1953 - Average year.
1954 - Mediocre year.
1955 - Very good year.
1956 - Very good year.
1957 - Average year.
1958 - Average year.
1959 - Mediocre year.
1960 - Good year.

ARBOIS

1937 - Great year.
1938 - Average year.
1939 - Average year.
1940 - Mediocre year.
1941 - Mediocre year.
1942 - Good year.
1943 - Great year.
1944 - Average year.
1945 - Great year.
1946 - Very good year.
1947 - Very good year.
1948 - Good year.
1949 - Very good year.
1950 - Good year.
1951 - Mediocre year.
1952 - Good year. Wines of character.
1953 - Very good year.
1954 - Average year.
1955 - Very good year.
1956 - Mediocre year.
1957 - Good year.
1958 - Quite a good year.
1959 - Good year.
1960 - Largest harvest, average year.

JURANÇON

1934 - Great year. Full-bodied, heady, very mellow wines.
1935 - Good year. Wines that preserve their quality and have bouquet.
1936 - Bad year. Meager wines.
1937 - Very good year. Very supple wines with bouquet.
1938 - Average year.
1939 - Average year.
1940 - Good year.
1941 - Very good year.
1942 - Very good year.
1943 - Very good year.
1944 - Good year.
1945 - Good year.
1946 - Very good year. Wines with tone.
1947 - Good year. Sufficiently vigorous wines with tone.
1948 - Good year.
1949 - Very good year.
1950 - Good year.
1951 - Average year.
1952 - Very good year.
1953 - Very good year.
1954 - Mediocre year.
1955 - Good year. Refined wines.
1956 - Very good year. Plenty of character.

1957 - Average year.
1958 - Quite a good year.
1959 - Very good year.
1960 - Good year.

MONBAZILLAC

1937 - Good year.
1941 - Mediocre year.
1942 - Great year.
1943 - Great year.
1944 - Mediocre year.
1945 - Great year.
1946 - Mediocre year.
1947 - Great year.
1948 - Average year.
1949 - Very good year.
1950 - Good year.
1951 - Mediocre year.
1952 - Very good year.
1953 - Average year; frosts.
1954 - Fairly good year.
1955 - Very good year.
1956 - Practically no harvest. Frost.
1957 - Small harvest. Good year.
1958 - Average year.
1959 - Very good year.
1960 - Average year.

POUILLY-SUR-LOIRE

1931 - Average year.
1932 - Average year.
1933 - Good year. Supple, fruity wines.
1934 - Very good year. Full-bodied wines.
1935 - Average year. Thin wines.
1936 - Good year. Supple wines with bouquet.
1937 - Very good year. Full-bodied wines.
1938 - Average year.
1939 - Average year.
1940 - Average year.
1941 - Mediocre year.
1942 - Good year.
1943 - Good year.
1944 - Mediocre year.
1945 - Very great year. Wines with fine bouquet. Small harvest.
1946 - Good year. Small harvest.
1947 - Great year.
1948 - Good year.
1949 - Great year. Wines with character, fruity.
1950 - Fairly good year.
1951 - Mediocre year.
1952 - Good year. Full-bodied, strong wines.
1953 - Very good year, wines very refined.
1954 - Average year.
1955 - Good year.
1956 - Good year. Vigorous wines.
1957 - Small harvest. Fairly good year.
1958 - Very small harvest. Average year.
1959 - Very great year. Complete wines.
1960 - Very big harvest. Fairly good year.

CHAMPAGNE

1932 - Good year. Very supple wines with a bouquet.
1933 - Very good year. Wines full-bodied and heady.
1934 - Great year. Fine wines; elegant, vigorous, and with fine bouquet.
1935 - Average year. Meager wines.
1936 - Mediocre year. Insignificant wines.
1937 - Very good year. Full-bodied wines; not so fine as 1934.
1938 - Fairly good year.
1939 - Mediocre year.
1940 - Very good year. Small harvest.
1941 - Good year.
1942 - Very good year. Very elegant wines.
1943 - Very good year. Wines with body.
1944 - Good year. Well-balanced wines.
1945 - Mediocre year.
1946 - Good year. Well-balanced wines.
1947 - Good year. Full-bodied wines.
1948 - Good year. Fine and elegant wines.
1949 - Great year. Very well-balanced wines, but solid, and with substance.
1950 - Average year.
1951 - Bad year.
1952 - Fairly good year.
1953 - Very good year. Very balanced.
1954 - Fairly good year.
1955 - Good year.
1956 - Small harvest. Average year.
1957 - Good year.
1958 - Average year.
1959 - Great year.
1960 - Large harvest. Average year.

SPIRITS AND LIQUEURS

DISTILLATION AND IMPROVEMENT

Everyone knows that alcohol, being very volatile, escapes easily in the form of steam from liquids when they are heated to a certain degree. The steam is passed through a still and by a cooling process is restored to its liquid form.

Wine is the liquid that produces the finest quality alcohol (spirits, brandies, cognac, champagne brandy). The best French spirits are those from the two Charentes, then, in diminishing scale, from Gers (armagnac), Montpellier, etc. The action of the wooden casks on spirits is as important as it is for wines. Therefore woods are chosen whose chemical composition contains the necessary substances to improve the liquor. The best woods are oak and chestnut. Staves from Danzig, Stettin, Angoulême, Bosnia, and the northern parts of North America are particularly well known for this purpose.

When the spirits have acquired the desired degree of alcohol through distillation, they are put into special casks where they turn amber through aging and take on part of the aromatic flavor of the wood, the other part being natural to the alcohol and to the wine from which it was extracted.

When the spirits, or brandies, have matured in the kegs, they are poured into bottles and are well corked with long, sound stoppers. The bottles are marked with all the necessary seals and labels to guarantee the origin and are shipped off.

Spirits acquire flavor and maturity only in the proper casks. After they have been put into bottles they no longer improve. So, if a champagne brandy is aged ten or fifteen years and then is put into bottles, it will never be any older, from the standpoint of maturity, even though it is not opened until a century later. There is no point, therefore, in marveling over a bottle of brandy that seems venerable because of its great age. The brandy can only have the same qualities it had when it was put into its glass house. A brandy of 1900, bottled in 1910, will still be only ten years old in 1950.

Aging indefinitely in the cask, say for a few decades, is not only costly but impossible without spoiling.

ORIGINS

WINE BRANDIES[1]

The most desirable brandies are cognac and armagnac.

Cognac comes from the Charente region and is made by distilling wines called Folle-Blanche, which are very acid and disagreeable in taste. On the other hand, the brandy is very mellow and has a finely developed bouquet that comes only after much aging. The taste is fine and "long"; that is to say, it lasts in the mouth and nose after the brandy is swallowed.

The Charente brandies are classified by four regions:

1. La Grande Champagne, including the towns of Cognac, Segonzac, and Jarnac. This is the region that produces the best brandies.

2. La Petite Champagne, which surrounds La Grande Champagne and extends from Châteauneuf to Barbezieux. The brandies of this region have less bouquet than those of La Grande Champagne, but have the advantage of aging more quickly.

3. Les Borderies, to the north of La Grande Champagne. These brandies have a highly developed bouquet but are rather lacking in mellowness and subtlety.

4. Les Bois, which surround the three preceding regions and include even the isles of Ré and Oléron. This region produces brandies that age rapidly but are of average or inferior quality.

Armagnac brandies are perfumed, fine, pleasant, and produce a warm glow in the stomach; but unlike Cognac brandies, the taste is fleeting. They have been classified by three regions:

1. Le Haut-Armagnac, comprising Cazaubon, Gabarret, Condom, Valence, Vic-Fézensac.

2. Le Tenarèze, to the west of the Haut-Armagnac and including Montréal, Castelnau, Aignan, Eauze.

3. Le Bas-Armagnac, which extends to the west from the Tenarèze to the junction of the departments of Landes, Gers, and Lot-et-Garonne. This section produces the finest of these brandies.

VARIOUS BRANDIES AND LIQUEURS

In addition to wine brandies in France are brandies made by the distillation of grapeskins. In certain regions, such as Burgundy, Touraine, and Champagne, these brandies are much admired. These grapeskin brandies (*eaux-de-vie de*

[1] Concentration and rectification of these brandies provide industrial alcohols.

marc) have a very peculiar and persistent woody taste and acquire real finesse only after long aging.

In Brittany, and especially in Normandy, cider is distilled to make a brandy called Calvados. Its subtlety and fine flavor recall the actual taste of the apple and even its aroma.

Cherries and mirabelle and quetsch plums are distilled into kirsch, *mirabelle,* and *quetsche,* all equally appreciated by connoisseurs. They may be distinguished from other types of brandies by a slight taste of prussic acid, which comes from the stones of the fruit. The best come from the Vosges and Alsace, where a highly perfumed raspberry brandy (*framboise*) is also made.

In other countries spirits are distilled from barley and wheat (whiskies), from juniper (gin), rice, etc.

We shall merely mention the innumerable liqueurs made in almost all parts of France, using wine brandy as a base with sugar and the juices of fruits or aromatic plants, such as chartreuse, kümmel, Grand Marnier, curaçao, Médoc cordial, cherry brandy, anisette, peppermint, etc.

LIQUEUR WINES

These sweet, heady wines have an important place in both private and formal parties. They are usually served at the beginning of the meal, but may be served also as a dessert wine. Most of them come from the South of France, Portugal, and Spain. The best and most well known of these wines are (in alpha betical order): Banyuls, Frontignan, Grenache, Madeira, Malaga, port, and sherry.

The liqueur wines of Corsica are similar to Malaga and Madeira.

PROPER WAY TO DRINK LIQUEURS

At the end of a good dinner it is customary to offer a brandy or a liqueur to the guests after the coffee has been served. Some people are opposed to this custom, and quite wrongly, for a small glass of good quality brandy or liqueur cannot injure the health, unless, naturally, the custom is abused.

Really to enjoy a liqueur, but especially a brandy such as cognac, champagne, armagnac, etc., an appeal should be made first to the eye; and for that, avoid fancy glasses, for the reasons already given under "Setting and Decorating the Table."

A brandy, which should never be served chilled, should be slightly warmed before touching the lips by being gently rotated in a glass held cupped in the hands. True lovers of fine brandies never fail to do this, for it liberates the aroma of the brandy. For this purpose a brandy glass (balloon shape) should be used (Figure 3, p. 34).

After enjoying the quality of the liqueur by inhaling its aroma (a test that an inferior liqueur can never pass), sip it slowly. M. Dagouret gives us his impressions on this subject:

"At the very moment a fine brandy enters the mouth, all of its finest qualities should burst forth like fireworks and as quickly become extinguished, leaving behind only the soothing and subtly penetrating sensation of its bouquet, without any of the harsh aftertaste common to ordinary spirits."

Fig. 7. COCKTAIL ACCESSORIES

1. Silver cup to hold hot-drink glass. 2. Mixing spoon. 3. Cocktail strainer. 4. Shaker. 5. and 6. The two tumblers of the shaker. 7. Nutmeg grater. 8. Lemon or orange squeezer. 9. Mixing glass. 10. Ice shovel.

COCKTAILS AND VARIOUS BEVERAGES

Nowadays no cookbook is considered complete unless it devotes a section to fashionable drinks. Cocktails, praised by some and condemned by others, have been in public favor for some time, and for this public we have included a broad summary of the bartender's science as interpreted by two masters in this field: Dagouret and Mayor Olivier.

GENERAL REMARKS ON THE PREPARATION OF HOT, COLD, AND CHILLED DRINKS

Long Drinks: Long drinks are served in tall glasses, either tumblers or stemware, in which they are usually prepared. They are cooling, thirst-quenching, and refreshing.

If you have no fresh fruit, use brandied, canned, or frozen fruit. However, the extra amount of sugar in preserved fruit must be taken into consideration.

Short Drinks: Short drinks are served in small tumblers or Madeira or Bordeaux glasses; chilled liqueurs, pousse-café, etc., in their special glasses. These drinks are appetizers or aids to digestion, tonic, stimulating, or soothing to the stomach.

Hot Drinks: Hot drinks, tall or short, should be served in glasses with stems to avoid burning the fingers. If a tumbler is used, it should be placed in a metal holder made to fit it. Straws or spoons are also used. To keep the glasses from breaking they should be rinsed in hot water before being filled. Dissolve the sugar in hot water before adding the liquor, otherwise use simple sirup. These drinks are warming (naturally), stimulating, helpful to the digestion, and fortifying.

COCKTAILS (Da.)

Quantities and proportions given in the following recipes are for one person. For several persons multiply the quantities given by the number of glasses to be served.

PREPARATION

Cocktails are made in shakers, glass tumblers, or the final serving glass.

Each recipe gives the size of the glass for the mixture. If several cocktails are to be served at the same time, a larger glass must be used for the preparation.

It is not necessary to give all the recipes for cocktails; when you know how to make a Brandy Cocktail, you also know how to make a Chartreuse Cocktail, Benedictine Cocktail, or x, y, z cocktail.

In countries where absinthe has been outlawed, anise, gentian, or a similar liqueur may be used.

Finally, be sure never to use a shaker in preparing drinks with an effervescent base such as champagne, lemon soda, cider, etc. They should be mixed with a spoon.

A dash of bitters or such from a bottle with a dropper cap equals 3 or 4 drops, depending on the force of the shake.

A jigger is a 1½ oz. measure used in the United States.

ABSINTHE COCKTAIL

Shaker ¼ full of chopped ice; ½ tsp. simple sirup; 1 drop angostura, 2 drops anisette; 1 liqueur glass absinthe; ¾ jigger water.

Put the top on the shaker. Shake well. Strain into a cocktail glass onto a twist of lemon peel. Serve with small straws.

AFTERNOON COCKTAIL

Highball glass ½ full of crushed ice; 1 liqueur glass maraschino; 1 liqueur glass Fernet-Branca; 1 liqueur glass cognac; split bottle of soda or seltzer.

Stir with a spoon. Serve with long straws and 2 half slices of orange.

BRANDY COCKTAIL

Mixing glass ¼ full of chopped ice; ½ tsp. sugar; 2 dashes angostura; 2 dashes curaçao; 1¼ jiggers cognac.

Stir and strain into a cocktail glass. Add a piece of lemon peel. Short straws.

BRONX COCKTAIL

Mixing glass ¼ full of chopped ice; ½ jigger gin; ½ jigger dry vermouth; ½ jigger sweet vermouth; juice of ¼ orange.

Stir and strain into a cocktail glass. Twist of orange peel; short straws.

BRUT COCKTAIL

Mixing glass ¼ full of chopped ice; 1 dash angostura; ½ jigger *amer picon ;* 1 jigger dry French vermouth.

Stir and strain into a cocktail glass. Short straws.

CALVADOS COCKTAIL

Mixing glass ¼ full of chopped ice; 2 dashes sirup of gum; 2 dashes angostura; 2 dashes curaçao; 1¼ jiggers Calvados.

Stir and strain into a cocktail glass. Twist of lemon peel; short straws. (Calvados is brandy made from cider.)

CHAMPAGNE COCKTAIL

Highball glass ¼ full of chopped ice, ½ tsp. simple sirup; 3 dashes angostura; 2 dashes curaçao.

Fill the glass with champagne. Stir with a spoon. Add a twist of lemon peel. Serve as it is with long straws.

DERBY COCKTAIL

Shaker ¼ full of chopped ice; 2 dashes angostura; 2 dashes curaçao; 3 dashes maraschino; 1¼ jiggers champagne brandy. Shake. Strain into a short highball glass. Add two fresh strawberries and a twist of lemon peel. Fill with champagne. Serve with straws.

DEVIL COCKTAIL

Shaker ¼ full of crushed ice; 1 liqueur glass green crème de menthe; 1 liqueur glass old brandy; 2 dashes angostura; 2 dashes curaçao; pinch of cayenne. Shake and strain into a cocktail glass. Add a zest of lemon peel and serve with straws.

FANCY COCKTAIL

(Fancy Brandy, Fancy Gin, etc.)

Fancy cocktails are prepared the same way as other cocktails, the only difference being that the rim of the cocktail glass is moistened with lemon juice and then frosted by being dipped into powdered sugar. A cherry or an olive may be placed in the bottom of the glass.

There is no need to list all of the recipes for fancy cocktails, since it would only be a tiresome repetition.

GIN COCKTAIL

Mixing glass ¼ full of chopped ice; 2 dashes angostura; 2 dashes curaçao; 1 tsp. simple sirup; 1¼ jiggers gin.

Stir. Strain into a cocktail glass with a twist of lemon peel.

JERSEY COCKTAIL

Mixing glass with a few pieces of ice; 1 tsp. angostura; ½ tsp. powdered sugar; 1½ jiggers cider.

Stir. Strain into a cocktail glass with a twist of lemon peel.

KÜMMEL COCKTAIL

Shaker ¼ full of chopped ice; 2 dashes curaçao; 2 dashes angostura; ½ tsp. simple sirup; 1¼ jiggers kümmel.

Shake well. Strain into a cocktail glass containing a few drops of lemon juice. Straws.

LONDON COCKTAIL

Mixing glass ¼ full of chopped ice; 2 dashes curaçao; 2 dashes orange bitters; ½ tsp. anisette; 1¼ jiggers gin.

Stir. Strain into a cocktail glass. Straws.

MADEIRA COCKTAIL

Mixing glass ¼ full of chopped ice; 2 dashes angostura; 2 dashes curaçao; 2 dashes sirup of gum; 1¼ jiggers Madeira.

Stir. Strain into a cocktail glass and add a twist of lemon peel.

MANHATTAN COCKTAIL

Mixing glass ¼ full of chopped ice; 3 dashes angostura; ½ tsp. simple sirup; 1 liqueur glass rye whisky; ¾ jigger Noilly vermouth.

Stir. Strain into a cocktail glass containing a twist of lemon peel. Short straws.

MARTINI or MARTINEZ COCKTAIL

Mixing glass ¼ full of chopped ice; 2 dashes angostura; ½ tsp. simple sirup; 1 liqueur glass gin; ¾ jigger Turin vermouth.

Stir. Strain into a cocktail glass with a twist of lemon peel. Short straws.

METROPOLITAN COCKTAIL

Mixing glass ¼ full of chopped ice; 2 dashes orange bitters; 1 tsp. simple sirup; 1 liqueur glass cognac; ¾ jigger Noilly vermouth.

Stir. Strain into a cocktail glass containing a twist of lemon peel. Short straws.

OLD MAN COCKTAIL

Mixing glass ¼ full of chopped ice; 2 dashes angostura; 2 dashes curaçao; ½ tsp. simple sirup; ¾ jigger rye whisky; ¾ jigger Turin vermouth.

Stir. Strain into a cocktail glass.

OYSTER COCKTAIL

In a cocktail glass: 2 dashes angostura; pinch of celery salt; a few drops of tarragon vinegar; ½ tsp. Worcestershire sauce; ½ liqueur glass cognac; 3 fresh oysters.

Stir. Serve with a spoon.

ROSE COCKTAIL

Mixing glass ¼ full of chopped ice; 1 jigger French vermouth; ⅓ jigger kirsch; ⅓ jigger red-currant sirup.

Stir. Strain into a cocktail glass with a cherry. Short straws.

The kirsch and currant sirup may be replaced by cherry brandy.

ROSE DRY COCKTAIL

Mixing glass ¼ full of chopped ice; 1 jigger gin; ¼ jigger lemon juice; ¼ jigger grenadine.

Stir. Strain into a cocktail glass. Short straws.

ST. JAMES COCKTAIL

Shaker ¼ full of chopped ice; 2 dashes angostura; 2 dashes curaçao; 1 tsp. simple sirup; 1¼ jiggers St. James rum.

Shake well and strain into a cocktail glass with a twist of lemon peel. Short straws.

SHERRY COCKTAIL

Mixing glass ¼ full of chopped ice; 2 dashes angostura; 2 dashes curaçao; ¼ tsp. powdered sugar; 1¼ jiggers sherry.

Stir. Strain into a cocktail glass containing a twist of lemon peel. Short straws.

SODA COCKTAIL

Highball glass; a few large pieces of ice; 4 dashes angostura; 4 dashes curaçao; ½ tsp. powdered sugar. Fill with soda.

Stir with a spoon. Serve in the same glass with slices of orange or lemon. Straws.

SWISS COCKTAIL

Mixing glass ¼ full of chopped ice; 2 dashes angostura; 2 dashes maraschino; ½ tsp. simple sirup; ½ liqueur glass absinthe; ½ liqueur glass gentian; ¾ jigger water.

Stir. Strain into a cocktail glass with frosted rim. Straws.

VERMOUTH COCKTAIL

Mixing glass ¼ full of chopped ice; 2 dashes angostura; 2 dashes curaçao; ½ tsp. simple sirup; 1¼ jiggers Noilly vermouth.

Stir. Strain into a cocktail glass with a twist of lemon peel. Short straws.

WHISKY COCKTAIL

Mixing glass ¼ full of chopped ice; 2 dashes angostura; 2 dashes curaçao; 1 tsp. simple sirup; 1¼ jiggers of the whisky desired.

Stir. Strain into a cocktail glass containing a twist of lemon peel. Short straws.

ZIZI COCKTAIL

Shaker ¼ full of crushed ice; 2 dashes angostura; pinch of cayenne; 1 liqueur glass green crème de menthe; 1 liqueur glass champagne brandy.

Strain into a double cocktail glass or small highball glass and fill with iced champagne. Straws.

CUPS (Da.)

This refreshing, tasty, and thirst-quenching drink may be served equally well at meals, in place of wine, and in the afternoon or evening, at parties, instead of punch.

When served at the table, it is prepared in a pitcher or special carafe and is poured like ordinary wine.

For buffets it is prepared in a bowl and ladled out into wineglasses or cups, which should always be stemware. Several pitchers of punch may also be laid out on the buffet, since this manner of serving is faster than with a ladle.

BADMINTON CUP

In a pitcher: half of a medium-sized cucumber, peeled and sliced; strips of the peeling; 5 oz. sugar; 1 bottle red Bordeaux; pinch of nutmeg. Allow the sugar to dissolve; chill on ice 1 hr. Before serving, add a bottle of soda or seltzer.

Serve in water glasses or place the pitcher on the table.

BALAKLAVA NECTAR

Place in a large bowl: juice of 1 lemon and the peeling sliced very thin and cut into small pieces; 2 tbsp. powdered sugar; 1½ jiggers maraschino; ½ cucumber sliced very thin; 2 bottles red wine; 2 bottles soda water; a few pieces of ice.

Add a bottle of champagne. Mix well with a spoon. Decorate with fruit. Serve, with a ladle, in glasses or cups.

BOLE IZ FRUKTOF (RUSSIAN CUP)

(1) Into a casserole put: 1 bottle red Bordeaux, 1 bottle champagne, 3 oz. sugar, 1 glass Madeira, a pinch of powdered cinnamon.

Bring to a boil. Chill on ice, then pour in a cupful of sliced fruit and a few pieces of ice. Serve with a ladle.

(2) I have also prepared this cup differently, by adding the champagne later, after the cup was chilled, and without boiling it. The sparkling drink is preferable.

CHABLIS CUP

In a special carafe: a few pieces of ice, 1¼ jiggers raspberry sirup, 1¼ jiggers curaçao, 1 jigger cognac, fruit in season, a sprig of mint, strip of cucumber peeling. Pour in a bottle of chablis and send, as is, to the table or buffet.

CHAMPAGNE CUP

(1) For 1 glass per person: in a glass or cup ½ filled with crushed ice: 1 tsp. powdered sugar, 3 dashes cognac, 3 dashes curaçao. Chill. Add fruit in season, sprig of mint or cucumber strip. Fill with champagne. Stir with a spoon. Serve with straws.

(2) For 6 persons: in a large bowl or special carafe: 1 tbsp. powdered sugar, 1 liqueur glass brandy, 1 liqueur glass curaçao, 1 sliced orange and ½ sliced lemon, pineapple, strawberries, cherries, grapes, etc., mint leaves or borage, cucumber peel, 1 bottle soda.

Let stand 1 hr. on ice, then add 1 bottle chilled champagne. Stir. Serve with a ladle into cups. For 12 persons, 18, 24: double, triple, or quadruple the quantities.

CLARET CUP

(1) Per person: in a glass or cup ½ filled with crushed ice: 1 tsp. powdered sugar, 3 dashes curaçao, 3 dashes maraschino, fruit in season, slice of orange, cucumber peel.

Fill with red wine. Stir. Serve with straws.

(2) For 6 persons: in a large bowl or special carafe: 1 tbsp. powdered sugar, 1 orange and ½ lemon sliced, cherries, strawberries, grapes, diced pineapple, 1 liqueur glass maraschino, 1 liqueur glass curaçao, 1 bottle red wine.

Let stand 1 hr. on ice. Before serving, add 1 bottle soda and a few pieces of ice. Stir. Serve with a ladle or send to the table in a carafe.

GINGER-ALE CUP

In the carafe: 1 tbsp. powdered sugar, 1 liqueur glass cognac, 1 liqueur glass curaçao, 1 liqueur glass maraschino, 1 sliced orange, ½ sliced lemon, fruit in season, diced pineapple, strip of cucumber peel or sprig of mint. Let stand

1 hr. on ice. Before serving, add 2 bottles ginger ale and a few pieces of ice. Stir. Send the carafe to the table or pour into glasses first.

MARQUISE AU CHAMPAGNE

This is only a kind of Champagne Cup.

In a large bowl: 1 wineglass sirup of gum, 1¼ jiggers maraschino, 1¼ jiggers kirsch, apricots, pineapple, pears, diced apples, 1 lemon and 1 orange sliced, raspberries, strawberries, grapes, cherries, 1 bottle mineral or soda water.

Chill 1 hr. Before serving, add 1 bottle chilled champagne. Stir. Serve, with a ladle, in glasses or cups.

SAUTERNE CUP

(1) Into a glass ½ filled with ice, pour ½ liqueur glass raspberry sirup, 3 dashes curaçao, 3 dashes cognac. Chill well. Decorate with fruit in season, peel, etc. Fill with sauterne. Serve with straws.

(2) To make with a full bottle in a carafe: a few pieces of ice; quadruple the quantities given above. Pour in the bottle of wine and serve.

EGGNOGS (Da.)

In Scotland eggnog is called "old man's milk."

The essential ingredient of this fine drink, hot or cold, is the whole egg or simply the yolk. Do not forget the nutmeg.

EGGNOG (Da.)

Fill the shaker ⅓ full of crushed ice; add 1 fresh egg, 1 tbsp. powdered sugar, 1¼ jiggers whisky; fill with cold milk. Shake well. Pour into a highball glass and sprinkle with nutmeg. Serve with straws. (Add a glass of liqueur, if desired.)

FRENCH EGGNOG

Into a large heated glass: 2 egg yolks, 2 tbsp. powdered sugar, 1¼ jiggers rum or cognac. Fill with very hot milk. Stir with a spoon and sprinkle with nutmeg.

SHERRY EGGNOG

Into a shaker ⅓ filled with ice, put 1 whole fresh egg, 1 tbsp. powdered sugar, 1 wineglass sherry. Fill with cold milk. Shake well. Pour into a tall glass and sprinkle with nutmeg. Serve with straws.

FIZZES (Da.)

The fizz is a short, cold drink, the distinguishing features being lemon juice, white of egg, and sparkling water or Vichy water.

A long drink may also be made by doubling the proportions.

BRANDY FIZZ

Shaker ¼ filled with crushed ice, 1 tbsp. powdered sugar, 1 tbsp. egg white, juice of ½ lemon, 1 jigger cognac. Shake well. Strain into a highball glass and fill with soda water.

GIN FIZZ

Shaker ¼ filled with crushed ice, 1 tbsp. powdered sugar, 1 tbsp. egg white, juice of ½ lemon, 1 jigger gin. Shake well. Strain into a highball glass and fill with soda.

FLIPS (Da.)

Originally a flip was a hot drink made with boiling beer mixed gradually with beaten eggs and rum and seasoned with nutmeg and ginger. Smoothness and froth were obtained by pouring the mixture from one pitcher held very high into another lower one and so on back and forth.

Today the flip is made hot or cold, as desired, and a hot liquid or ice is used, depending on the circumstances and the season. If a hot drink is prepared, do not forget to transfer the mixture several times to make it foam nor to heat the glasses before serving.

BRANDY FLIP

A shaker ½ full of ice, 1 tsp. powdered sugar, 1 fresh egg well beaten, 1¼ jiggers cognac. Shake well and strain into a 4-oz. glass. Season with nutmeg and serve with straws.

EGG FLIP (HOT)

Into a shaker put: 1 tbsp. powdered sugar, 1 beaten egg, a pinch of spices. Mix well.

Fill with very hot beer. Using a warmed highball glass, pour the mixture back and forth several times until foamy. Sprinkle with nutmeg and serve.

PORT FLIP

Shaker ½ full of crushed ice, 1 tbsp. powdered sugar, 1 fresh well-beaten egg, 1 wineglass red or white port. Shake well and strain into a 4-oz. glass. Nutmeg. Straws.

WHISKY FLIP

Shaker ½ full of crushed ice, 1 tbsp. powdered sugar, 1 fresh well-beaten egg, 1¼ jiggers whisky. Shake well and strain into a 4-oz. glass. Nutmeg. Straws.

GROGS (Da.)

Many people confuse grog with punch; the latter may be served hot or cold, but grog must always be very hot.

Grog is a stimulating and warming cold-weather drink. It is also a good preventive against a cold or a remedy at the beginning of one.

It is usually served in a special heatproof grog glass, but may be served in any preheated glass. Use a metal holder for glasses without stems.

AMERICAN GROG

(1) In a grog glass: 1 tbsp. powdered sugar or simple sirup, 1 jigger cognac, 1 jigger rum, ½ jigger curaçao. Fill ¾ full with weak tea. Stir and add a slice of lemon. Serve boiling hot with a spoon.

(2) To make 1 qt.: 3 oz. rum, 3 oz. cognac, 2½ oz. curaçao, 3 oz. simple sirup, ½ pt. very strong black tea. Mix well while still cold.

(3) To serve in a grog glass: 1¼ jiggers of the mixture given above. Fill ¾ full with boiling water. Serve with a slice of lemon and extra sugar if needed. Spoons.

BLACK GROG

In a grog glass: 1 tbsp. molasses; 1¼ jiggers rum. Fill ¾ full with very hot black tea. Slice of lemon. Spoon.

BRANDY GROG

In a grog glass: 1 tbsp. powdered sugar; 1¼ jiggers cognac. Fill ¾ full with boiling water. Slice of lemon. Spoon. (This is the ordinary, everyday grog.)

FRENCH GROG

In a grog glass: 1 tbsp. powdered sugar; ½ jigger cognac; ½ jigger rum. Fill ¾ full with boiling water. Slice of lemon. Spoon.

HONEY GROG

In a grog glass: 1 tbsp. honey; 1¼ jiggers cognac. Fill ¾ full with boiling water. Slice of lemon. Spoon.

RUM GROG

In a grog glass: 1 tbsp. powdered sugar; 1¼ jiggers rum. Fill ¾ full with boiling water. Slice of lemon. Spoon.

WHISKY GROG

In a grog glass: 1 tbsp. powdered sugar; 1¼ jiggers whisky. Fill ¾ full with boiling water. Slice of lemon. Spoon.

PUNCHES (Da.)

Punch may be made whatever way seems best, hot or cold, long or short. Sometimes it is prepared with milk instead of water.

Hot Punch: Serve in a short grog glass with slices of lemon or orange, extra sugar on the side, and a teaspoon. If it is served in a tumbler, use a metal glass holder. Heat the glass.

Cold Punch: Serve in a large glass with fruit in season: strawberries, cherries, grapes, etc., and slices of orange, lemon, or pineapple. Provide straws. Sometimes it is also served in cups.

Punch may be prepared hot or cold for several persons at one time or in large quantities for parties. In the latter case use a silver bowl (hot) or a porcelain bowl (cold) and serve with a punch ladle in special cups.

BRANDY PUNCH (COLD)

Shaker ¾ full of crushed ice; 1 tsp. orange juice, 1 tbsp. powdered sugar, 1 tbsp. cold water, 1 jigger rum, 1¼ jiggers cognac. Shake well. Add fresh fruit and a slice of orange. Straws.

BRANDY PUNCH (HOT)

In a heated grog glass or short highball glass: 1 tsp. lemon juice, 1 tsp. powdered sugar, 2 dashes curaçao, 1 jigger cognac. Fill with boiling water and mix well. Slice of lemon. Nutmeg. Spoon.

CANADIAN PUNCH

Tall highball glass ½ full of crushed ice; 1 tsp. lemon juice, 1 tbsp. powdered sugar, 1 jigger rum, 1¼ jiggers rye whisky, slices of orange and pineapple. Fill with cold water and stir. Straws.

CHAMPAGNE PUNCH

Tall highball glass ½ full of crushed ice; 1 tbsp. lemon juice, 1 tbsp. strawberry sirup, ½ slice pineapple, 1 slice orange. Fill with champagne. Stir with a spoon. Strawberries, cherries, currants, grapes. Straws.

CIDER PUNCH

Shaker ½ full of crushed ice; 1 tsp. lemon juice, 1 tbsp. powdered sugar, 1 jigger cognac, lemon peel cut in diamond shape, 1 strip cucumber peel. Shake well. Fill with cider. Stir. Orange slices. Serve with long straws.

CLARET PUNCH (COLD)

Shaker ½ full of crushed ice; 1 tbsp. powdered sugar, 1 slice lemon and 2 slices orange. Fill with red Bordeaux. Shake well. Garnish with berries in season. Straws.

CLARET PUNCH (HOT)

Heat in a pan: 1¼ jiggers red Bordeaux, 1 tsp. lemon juice, 1 tbsp. powdered sugar, 3 dashes curaçao, 1 jigger cognac. Pour into a heated highball glass. Add hot water. Nutmeg. Slice of lemon. Spoon.

MILK PUNCH (COLD)

Mixing glass ⅓ full of crushed ice; 1 tbsp. powdered sugar, 1 jigger cognac, 1 jigger rum. Fill with cold milk and stir. Strain into a highball glass. Nutmeg. Straws.

MILK PUNCH (HOT)

Large grog glass, heated; 1 tbsp. powdered sugar, 1 jigger cognac, 1 jigger rum. Fill with hot milk. Stir. Nutmeg. Spoon.

TEA PUNCH (HOT)

In a silver tumbler: 1 tsp. lemon juice, 1 tbsp. powdered sugar, 1 jigger rum, 1 jigger cognac. Mix. Set aflame. Fill with very hot, strong tea. Spoon.

VARIOUS COLD DRINKS

LEMONADE AND ORANGEADE LIMONADE and ORANGEADE (M. O.)

½ lb. granulated sugar, juice of 6 lemons, grated peelings of 2 lemons, 1 qt. water. Stir until the sugar is dissolved and pour through a fine mesh strainer or cloth.

Orangeade is made the same way by substituting 6 oranges for the lemons, grated peeling of 1 orange, and juice of 2 lemons.

FROZEN MARQUISE MARQUISE GLACÉE (M. O.)

Make a hot Marquise (see Marquise Paulette, p. 83), leaving out the cognac. Add about 3 cups strong tea, juice of 2 oranges and 1 lemon, and ½ cup rum.

When the punch has cooled, pour into a freezer and let freeze somewhat.

ROMAN PUNCH PUNCH À LA ROMAINE (M. O.)

7 oz. simple sirup; 1 bottle dry white wine; juice of 4 lemons and 3 oranges; grated peelings of 1 lemon and 1 orange.

Mix the sirup and wine; add juice and grated peels; steep 1 hr., then strain into a freezer. Freeze like ordinary sherbet; when the mixture begins to thicken, add ¼ its volume of Italian Meringue (p. 557) or whipped cream.

ZABAGLIONE WITH SHERRY SABAYON AU XÉRÈS À LA FRONTERA (M. O.)

For 10 persons: break the yolks of 10 eggs into a pan and mix with 1 tbsp. water; add 9 oz. powdered sugar and ½ bottle Villamil sherry. Whip the mixture over a slow fire until it is poached and frothy. This Zabaglione is served with hot puddings.

If you prefer to serve the Zabaglione chilled, continue to beat it, after it has been taken off the stove, until cooled and then mix in 1 pt. whipped cream. Pour it into an ice-cream mold and pack in ice or pour into champagne cups and chill in the refrigerator.

ORANGE SALAD SALADE D'ORANGES (Da.)

In a salad bowl: peeled oranges, sliced and then quartered. Sprinkle with powdered sugar and moisten with brandy and a very little water. Chill on ice. Serve in cups.

It may also be served in half an orange rind placed in a bed of crushed ice.

SHERBETS SORBETS

For Granités, Marquises, Punch, Spooms, see pp. 669–670.

CHAMPAGNE SILK SOYER AU CHAMPAGNE (Da.)

Highball glass ½ full of crushed ice; 1 tsp. orange juice; 2 dashes maraschino; ¼ jigger curaçao; 1 jigger grenadine.

Fill with champagne and stir with a spoon. Decorate with slices of orange. Serve with straws.

NORMAN HOLE TROU NORMAND (Da.)

In Normandy they have a custom of serving a glass of Calvados in the middle of a long dinner or after Tripe à la Mode de Caen to whet the appetite again. This is called "making a Norman hole"—that is, the Calvados supposedly burns a hole through the food already eaten.

Serve a liqueur glass of Calvados. Some may prefer a wineglass of old Calvados.

At formal dinners, instead of the *trou normand,* spoom, sherbet, snow (grated ice cream), or punch can be served before the roast.

VIE EN ROSE VIE EN ROSE (Da.)

Shaker ½ full of crushed ice; 1 jigger grenadine; juice of ¼ lemon; 1 jigger kirsch.

Shake well. Add soda or seltzer and stir. Serve with straws.

VARIOUS HOT DRINKS

TEMPERANCE DRINKS (Drinks without alcohol) (Da.)

To make this book as complete as possible and yet avoid making a new subdivision, we have included under this heading beverages that call for a slight addition of spirits or wines. If these are being prepared for total abstainers or children, the liquor may be omitted.

POSSETS BAVAROISES (Da.)

Posset always used to be a hot drink made with tea and hot milk sweetened with a capillaire (orange-flower simple sirup). Today it is served hot or cold, in any flavor desired.

ENGLISH POSSET BAVAROISE À L'ANGLAISE (Da.)

For 2 persons: put 1 egg yolk and 2 tbsp. powdered sugar into a saucepan. Mix well and heat over a low flame. Pour in, while constantly beating, ½ pt. boiling tea and 1 jigger rum. Continue to whip. When it becomes frothy, serve in heated glasses or cups.

COFFEE POSSET BAVAROISE AU CAFÉ (Da.)

For 2 persons: put 1¼ jiggers capillaire and 1 egg yolk into a saucepan over low heat. Bind by whipping. While beating, add ½ pt. hot coffee. When the foam coats the spatula, serve in heated glasses or cups.

CHOCOLATE MILK POSSET BAVAROISE AU CHOCOLAT (Da.)

For 2 persons: heat 3 oz. chocolate dissolved in a little water. Beat 1 egg yolk with 1¼ jiggers capillaire and pour into the chocolate while stirring. Add ½ pt. boiling milk and continue beating. When the foam coats the spatula, serve in heated glasses or cups.

WATER POSSET BAVAROISE À L'EAU (Da.)

Boiling-hot tea. Sweeten with capillaire. Serve in heated cup or glass.

MILK POSSET BAVAROISE AU LAIT (Da.)

Half hot tea; half boiling milk. Sweeten with capillaire. Serve in heated glass or cup.

ORGEAT POSSET BAVAROISE À L'ORGEAT (Da.)

1¼ jiggers orgeat (an almond-flavored sirup), boiling water or tea. Serve in heated glass or cup.

MILK POSSET WITH ORGEAT BAVAROISE D'ORGEAT AU LAIT (Da.)

1¼ jiggers orgeat; 1¼ jiggers hot tea. Fill with boiling milk. Serve in heated glass or cup.

BISCHOFF (M. O.)

Lightly grill the peel of 2 oranges. Pour 1 bottle Bordeaux into a mixing bowl and add a pinch of grated nutmeg, the orange peel cut into small pieces, and a stick of cinnamon. Let steep 12 hr.

Before serving, pour another bottle of Bordeaux into the infused wine, add 10 oz. sugar, and heat without boiling. Strain through a cloth and serve in punch cups.

ENGLISH BISCHOFF (M. O.)

Let steep 24 hrs. in 1 cup Villamil port: peel of 1 lemon grilled and cut into small strips, 5 oz. sugar, 4 cloves, and a pinch of grated nutmeg.

Just before serving, add 1 bottle Villamil port and heat in a *bain-marie.* Strain and serve in punch cups.

CHOCOLATE CUP FOR PARTIES CHOCOLAT EN TASSES POUR SOIRÉES (M. O.)

Melt ½ lb. good chocolate in a little water over a low flame. Dissolve 6 oz. sugar in 1 qt. milk, add a vanilla bean, and bring to a boil. Pour the boiling milk little by little over the chocolate. Beat with a whisk to make it foamy and to avoid lumps. The chocolate must not boil.

MARQUISE PAULETTE MARQUISE PAULETTE (M. O.)

Heat without boiling 1 bottle good white wine, 8 oz. sugar, a piece of lemon peel, 4 cloves. Strain through a fine linen cloth into a punch bowl and add ½ cup hot, flaming cognac. Serve in punch cups with a slice of lemon.

HOT ORANGEADE ORANGEADE CHAUDE (M. O.)

8 oz. sugar in 1 qt. water. Bring the liquid to a boil and pour over 6 oranges and 1 lemon, peeled so that none of the white skin adheres and thinly sliced. Add the peel of 1 lemon and 1 orange and let steep 10 min. in a *bain-marie.* Strain through a cloth and color with a little carmine.

HOT WINE FRENCH STYLE VIN CHAUD À LA FRANÇAISE (M. O.)

Dissolve 6 oz. sugar in 1 bottle good Bordeaux with a stick of cinnamon and lemon peel. Heat the wine without boiling until a white foam forms on the surface. Serve very hot in punch cups with peeled slices of lemon.

COFFEE (Da.)

The different types of coffees are classed below according to quality:

(1) *Mocha* (Arabia), small, yellow, uneven, and wrinkled beans. *Java* (Island), large, long, chestnut, yellow, or green beans.

(2) *Martinique* (Island), medium, long beans, green or yellow. *Mysore* (India), medium, closed beans. Same quality as Mocha.

(3) *Bourbon* (Island), small, round, green or yellow. Not quite so good as the preceding.

(4) *Brazil,* yellow or green. Similar but inferior to Bourbon.

(5) *Cuba, Jamaica, Puerto Rico,* all inferior to Martinique.

(6) *Guadeloupe, Cayenne,* same observation.

One type of bean does not make good coffee; it is necessary to blend 2 or 3 types to produce fine color and aroma. Excellent coffee is now being harvested in Madagascar and on the Ivory Coast.

Preparation:

It is useless to give all of the ways of making coffee. Everyone knows that aside from coffee made in a percolator or by drip method there is no really good coffee. The important thing is not to lose the aroma and flavor while making it and to use good coffee. Use only recently roasted coffee and do not grind it until ready to use. Like any other infusion, coffee should not be boiled.

COFFEE WITH CHICORY CAFÉ À LA CHICORÉE

Chicory is cheaper than coffee, to which it imparts some color but no flavor except that it makes it bitter. For many people, however, bitterness is synonymous with strength and quality.

To test whether there is any chicory in ground coffee, drop 1 tsp. into ½ glass water and shake. The coffee will float and the chicory will fall to the bottom.

COFFEE WITH CREAM CAFÉ CRÈME

Black coffee with a little pitcher of fresh cream. In certain households the cream is really only milk.

DOUBLE-STRENGTH COFFEE CAFÉ DOUBLE

Filtered coffee made by using very hot coffee instead of boiling water. Nothing better.

BLACK COFFEE CAFÉ NOIR

Ordinary coffee. Sugar as desired.

TURKISH COFFEE CAFÉ TURC

Prepare with coffee pulverized with a pestle in a mortar. No matter how fine the grinder is it never grinds the coffee fine enough.

The equipment is highly specialized and consists of small pots, like saucepans, with long handles, similar to those which bartenders use to warm beer, but even smaller. They are wide at the bottom and narrow at the top. The coffee is served in tiny cups held in containers with stems. Usually several cups are drunk.

Place 1 of the small pots, ⅔ full of water and containing a pinch of sugar, on a small alcohol stove. Orientals do not take sugar. When the water boils, add 1 small coffeespoonful of powdered coffee per person. When the coffee starts to rise, remove it from the heat, by means of the long handle, and swing it back and forth in the air. Some people tap the pot, but it is better to swing it to make the foam fall. Replace on the fire and make it rise again, repeating this 3 times. Pour into the small cups. Drink it at once and ask for more. Turkish Coffee should have the consistency of light cream. To keep the coffee from having time to settle it should be prepared at the table.

For those who are not accustomed to it, 2 or 3 drops of cold water added to the coffee in the pot when it is ready will make some of it settle and not be so thick. Of course, this destroys some of its character. Anyone who has drunk good *caoua* prepared by an expert *caouadgi* will not ask for anything better. We must still insist that ground coffee will not do so well as coffee that has been pulverized in a mortar.

Serve sugar candy and a glass of cold water on the side.

RUSSIAN COFFEE CAFÉ RUSSE

Prepared in a reversible coffee maker, which does not allow the aroma to escape while the coffee is being made.

VIENNESE COFFEE CAFÉ VIENNOIS

(1) Fill a water tumbler (without ice) almost full of iced, sugared coffee and 2 tbsp. cold milk. Stir. Top with a dome of sweet whipped cream. Serve with a spoon and straws.

(2) Other recipe: bring to a boil 1 cup cream with 3 oz. sugar. Mix with 1 qt. strong, hot coffee. Let cool. Serve very cold in cups or glasses. Top with Chantilly Cream (p. 552).

TEA (Da.)

Tea, a plant native to China and Japan, is now being raised in Brazil and has long been an important product of India and the East Indies. The beverage is made by steeping the dried leaves.

Teas shipped by sea always lose a little of their fragrance. The best are called "caravan teas" because they are brought by the overland route from China through Russia. After these the best are:

Green teas: Assam, chulan, hyson.

Black teas: souchong, Pakao, Ceylon.

As with coffee, the best teas are a blend.

Preparation:

In France tea is usually made badly. Here is the best way:

A glazed crockery teapot is preferable, but one of porcelain, metal, or enamel may be used.

Pour 1 cup boiling water into the pot. Put on the lid. Shake to wet and heat all the interior. After a minute, pour out the water. Put in 1 small tsp. tea for each person. Pour in just enough boiling water to cover the tea. Cover and let steep 3 min. Add the required amount of boiling water. Serve at once, otherwise bitterness will spoil the aroma.

Water that has been boiled several times or too long will not make as good tea as freshly boiled water.

VARIOUS INFUSIONS (Da.)

These should be prepared in a teapot. Quantities given are per cup or person:

Star anise (badian) : seeds of 1 star.

Camomile: 6 flowers.

Mint: a pinch.

Fennelflower: a good pinch.

Elderberry: a good pinch.

Linden blossom: a good pinch.

Verbena: a good pinch.

Add boiling water and let steep 5 min. Serve with sugar on the side and, if desired, orange-flower water.

KITCHEN UTENSILS
COOKING PROCEDURES

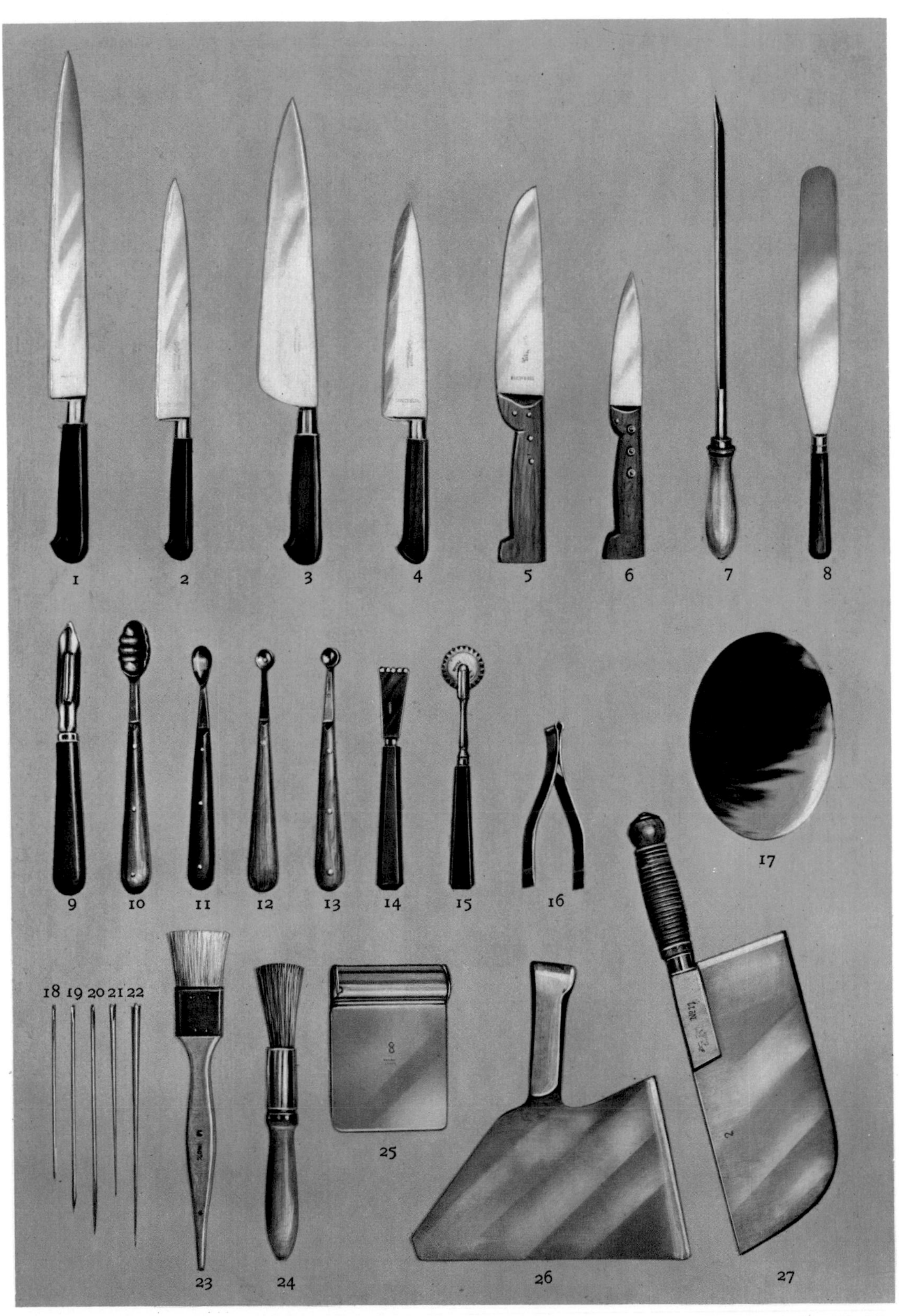

Fig. 8 - *1. Cook's knife. 2. Knife for fish fillets. 3 and 4. Kitchen knives. 5. Butcher's knife. 6. Boning knife. 7. Handled larding pin. 8. Spatula (Palette knife). 9. Paring knife. 10. Oval, ridged cutting spoon. 11. Plain oval cutter. 12 and 13. Ball cutters. 14. Orange or lemon peeler. 15. Pastry cutting wheel. 16. Pincers. 17. Pastry blender. 18, 19, 20. Trussing needles. 21 and 22. Skewers. 23. Flat brush. 24. Round brush. 25. Pastry cutter. 26. Butcher's chopper. 27. Meat cleaver.*

Fig. 9 - *1. Ridged caramel roller. 2. Pastry roller. 3. Pastry-bag for decorations. 4. Cone-shaped mold for creams. 5 and 6. Pastry-bag tubes with ridged openings. 7. Pastry-bag tube with plain opening. 8. Dariole mold. 9. Caramel cutter. 10 and 11. Wire beaters for sauces. 12. Wire beater for eggs. 13. Conical strainer. 14. Cooky cutter. 15. Cooky cutter with scalloped edges. 16. Rectangular tartlet mold. 17, 18, 19 and 20. Wooden spatulas. 21. Mold for fritters. 22 and 23. Plain and fluted molds for pastry boats. 24 and 25. Fluted and plain tartlet molds.*

Fig. 10 - *1. Tray for Génoise cake. 2. Square cake pan. 3. Round cake pan. 4. Mousseline mold. 5. Pound-cake pan. 6. Long, plain pâté mold. 7. Brioche mold. 8. Charlotte mold. 9. Pudding or crumb-cake mold. 10. Mold for genoa loaf. 11. Tart or flan circle. 12. Kugelhopf mold. 13. Savarin mold. 14. Oval pâté mold. 15. Round pâté or timbale mold.*

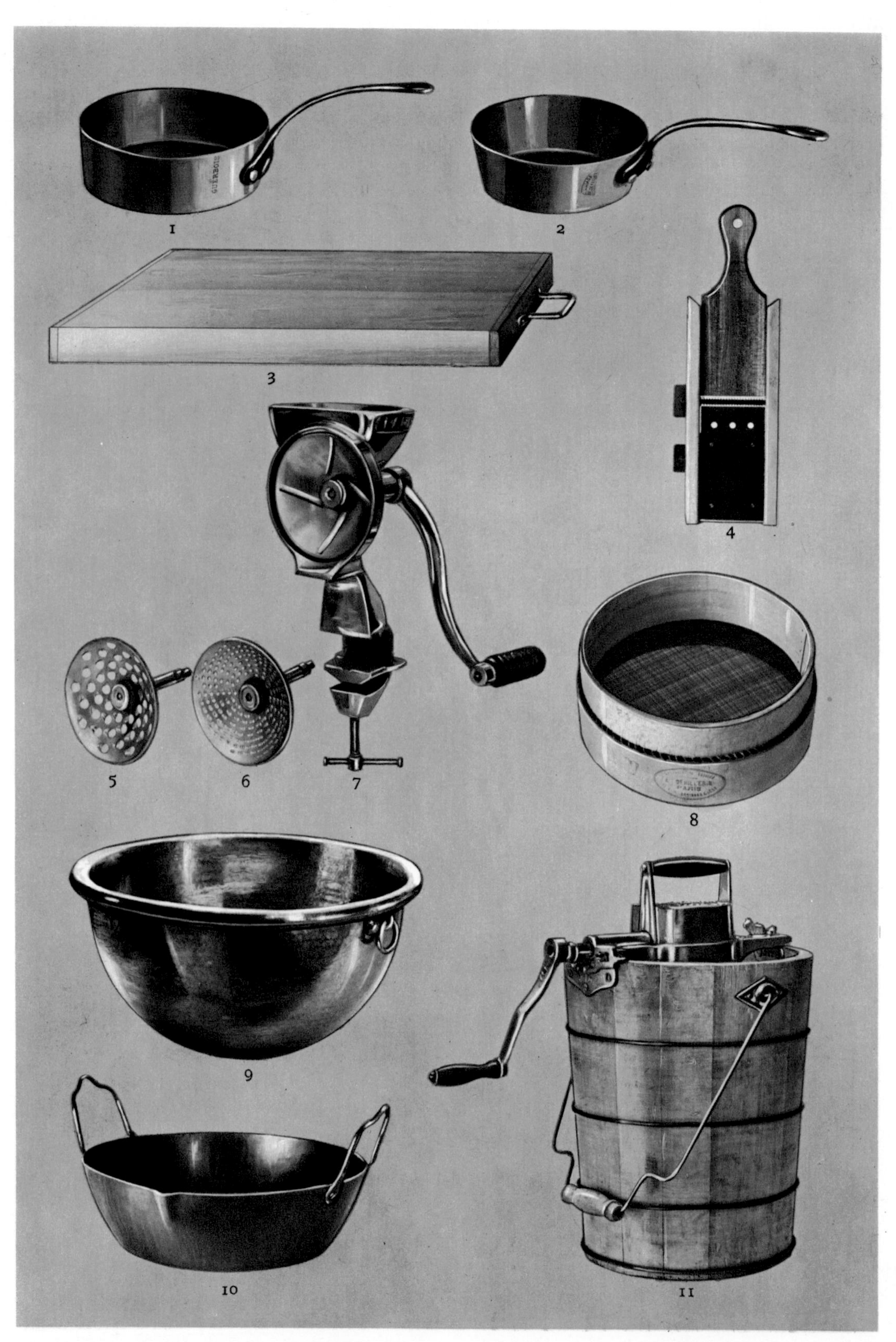

Fig. 11. - *1 and 2. Frying or sauteing pans. 3. Chopping board. 4. Vegetable grater. 5 and 6. Grinder cutting disks. 7. Grinder. 8. Sifter with cloth screen. 9. Copper bowl for beating egg whites. 10. Deep-fat frying pan. 11. Ice-cream freezer*

Fig. 12. Eggs in aspic *(1)*.
Pour a little aspic jelly into the molds. Leave in refrigerator until firm. Decorate with ham or tarragon leaves.

Fig. 13. Eggs in aspic *(2)*.
Poach the eggs, dry them on a cloth, trim them, and gently place them into the molds.

Fig. 14. Eggs in aspic *(3)*.
Finish filling the molds with jelly. Put back into refrigerator. Be sure the jelly has set before unmolding.

Fig. 15. Eggs in aspic *(4)*.
Dip the molds in warm water to make removal easy. (Recipe p. 261.) If eggs are served in ramekins, place the decoration on top of the egg instead of on the bottom.

Fig. 16
If you do not have a special fish scraper, use one of the shells in wich you ordinarily serve mixed sea food.

Fig. 17. Fish Fillets *(1)*.
Use a large, sharp knife. After scraping, gutting, and cleaning the fish, cut it into even slices.

Fig. 20. Sole Fillets *(1)*.
Cut a small incision at the fail of the sole. Pull off the skin with one tug.

Fig. 21. Sole Fillets *(2)*.
Run a sole fillet knife between the black-bone and the flesh to remove the fillet.

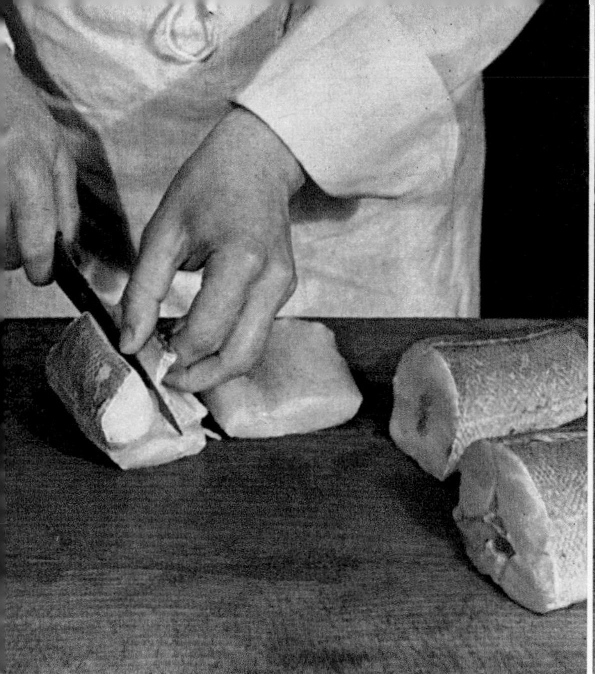

Fig. 18. Fish Fillets *(2).*
Remove the bones from each slice by following the spine with the point of a flexible knife called a sole fillet knife.

Fig. 19. Fish Fillets *(3).*
Remove the skin by pulling the knife back and forth in a sawing motion. *(Recipe p. 285.)*

Fig. 22. Stuffed Trout (or other fish) *(1).*
Cut the fish down the back and remove all bones from the raw fish. Use scissors to sever the blackbone at its two extremities.

Fig. 23. Stuffed Trout *(2).*
Stuff with Pike Forcemeat. It is easier and quicker if you use a pastry bag. Sew up the back of the fish with needle and thread. *(Recipe p. 313.)*

Fig. 24. Lobster Américaine *(1)*.
Cut the live lobster into even-sized pieces following the joints. Hold firmly in the left hand.

Fig. 25. Lobster Américaine *(2)*.
Cut off the claws and slice the back in two. With a sharp blow of the back of the knife, crack open the claws.

Fig. 28.
To split a cooked rock or spiny lobster, cut the tail open first, then the head and the body. Use a knife with a strong blade.

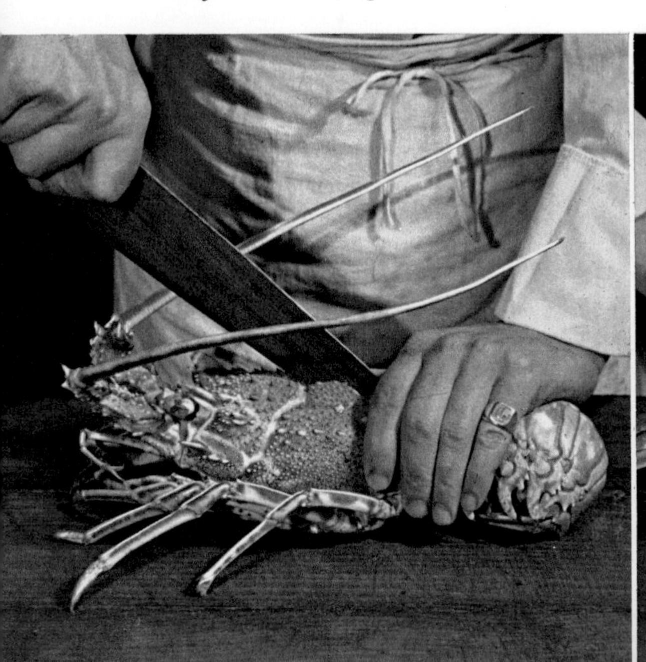

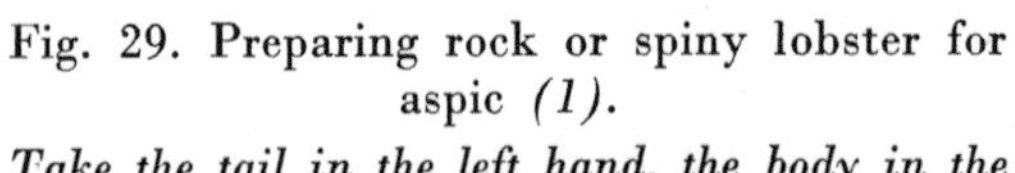

Fig. 29. Preparing rock or spiny lobster for aspic *(1)*.
Take the tail in the left hand, the body in the right hand, and pull to separate the two.

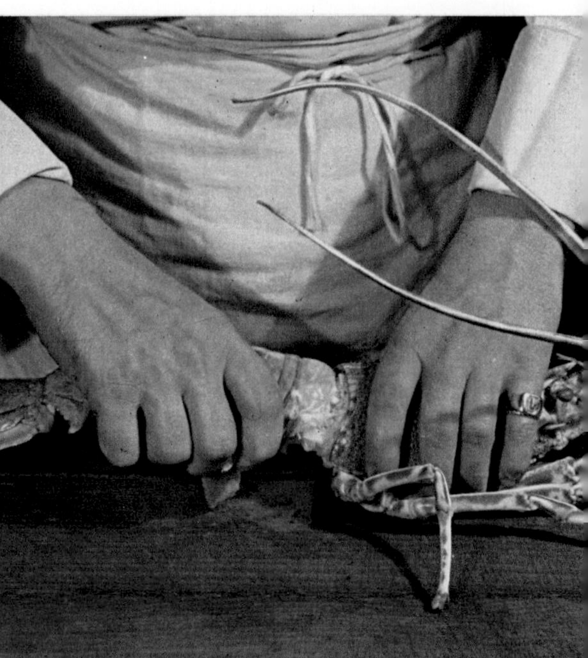

Fig. 26. Lobster Américaine *(3)*.
Throw away the little pocket containing gritty matter. This is the only part of the lobster not used.

Fig. 27. Lobster Américaine *(4)*.
Save the coral and intestines to be used in binding the sauce. (Recipe p. 316.)

Fig. 30. Preparing rock or spiny lobster for aspic *(2)*.
Cut the under part of the body with scissors taking care not to cut the flesh with the points.

Fig. 31. Preparing rock or spiny lobster for aspic *(3)*.
Gently separate the tail meat from the shell by passing the fingers between the shell and meat.

Fig. 32. Lobster or rock-lobster aspic *(1)*. *Place the mold in a bowl of ice and fill to the top with liquid jelly.*

Fig. 33. Lobster or rock-lobster aspic *(2)*. *When the jelly begins to harden around the inside of the mold, pour out the liquid part in the middle. Decorate the bottom and sides of the mold.*

Fig. 36. Coquilles Saint-Jacques *(2)*. *Using a knife or metal spatula, separate the meat and other parts from the shell in one stroke.*

Fig. 37. Coquilles Saint-Jacques *(3)*. *Cut away the coral with scissors, holding the rest of the meat in the left hand.*

Fig. 34. Lobster or rock-lobster aspic *(3)*. *Place the sliced lobster meat in the center and finish filling the mold with jelly. Put on ice to set.* *(Recipe p. 318.)*

Fig. 35. Coquilles Saint-Jacques (scallops) *(1)*. *Open the shell with a round, strong knife.* *(Another method is explained on p. 324.)*

Fig. 38. Coquilles Saint-Jacques *(4)*. *Separate the meat from the viscous parts by pressing with the thumb. The sticky, filmy parts are not to be eaten.*

Fig. 39. Coquilles Saint-Jacques *(5)*. *Fill the deep part of the scallop shell with a mixture bound with Normande or other sauce. Place the meat and strips of coral on top.*

Fig. 40. Coquilles Saint-Jacques *(6)*.
With a spoon spread over the filled shells. This should be done neatly and without smearing.

Fig. 41. Coquilles Saint-Jacques *(7)*.
Using a pastry bag with a fluted tube, trim the edge of the shells with a band of potatoes Duchesse. The shells are now ready for the oven. (Recipe p. 324.)

Fig. 44. Oysters *(3)*.
For long-shaped oysters, use the tip of the knife.

Fig. 45. Sea Urchins *(1)*.
Use scissor tips to make a hole in the middle of the top of the sea urchin.

Fig. 42. Oysters *(1)*.
ress the edge of an oyster knife against the hinge of the shell.

Fig. 43. Oysters *(2)*.
Press the tips of the fingers of the left hand hard against the knife. When the muscle has been cut, the oyster will open immediately.

Fig. 46. Sea Urchins *(2)*.
sing the hole as a starting point, cut the sea rchin from the inside out 3/4 the way around.

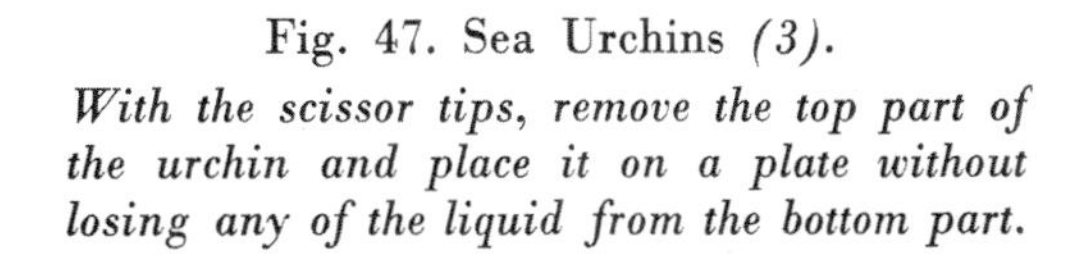

Fig. 47. Sea Urchins *(3)*.
With the scissor tips, remove the top part of the urchin and place it on a plate without losing any of the liquid from the bottom part.

Fig. 48. Clams *(1)*.
Open the shell from the side, working very quickly to slide the knife between the two halves of the shell.

Fig. 49. Clams *(2)*.
When the shell is open slide the knife betweer the clam and the upper half of the shell, ther remove this part of the shell by bending it back

Fig. 52.
Veal grenadins being studded with strips of fat, using a larding needle. Only the tops are studded.

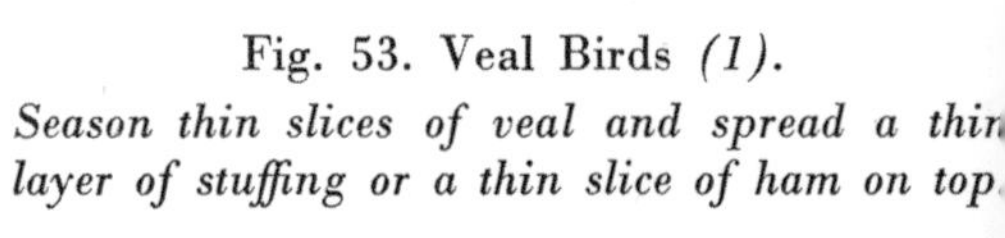

Fig. 53. Veal Birds *(1)*.
Season thin slices of veal and spread a thin layer of stuffing or a thin slice of ham on top.

Fig. 50.
Larding a piece of meat with a larding needle and strips of pork fat.

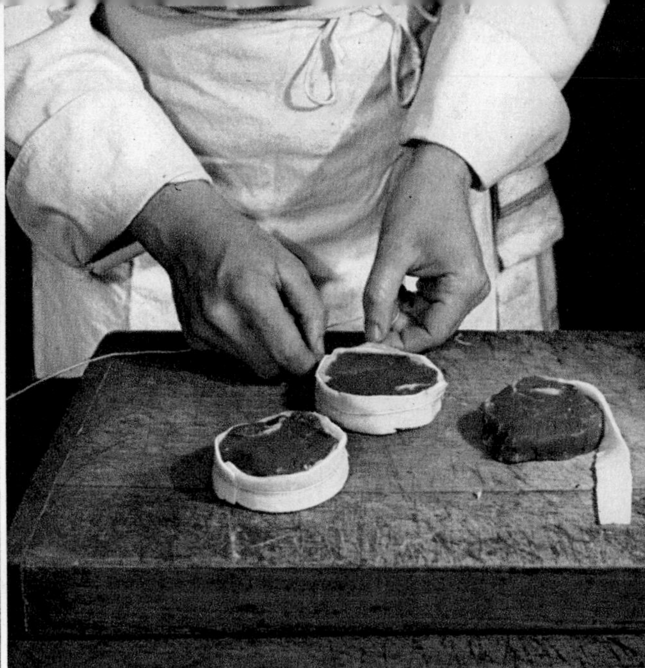

Fig. 51.
Tournedos larded with a band of pork fat tied on with a piece of string.

Fig. 54. Veal Birds *(2).*
After rolling the veal birds, tie them with string in at least two places. They are now ready to be cooked. (Recipe p. 343.)

Fig. 55. Cooked Ham.
Slip the fingers between the fat and the rind and pull off the rind. The rind may be used to line the bottom of the pans for braised dishes.

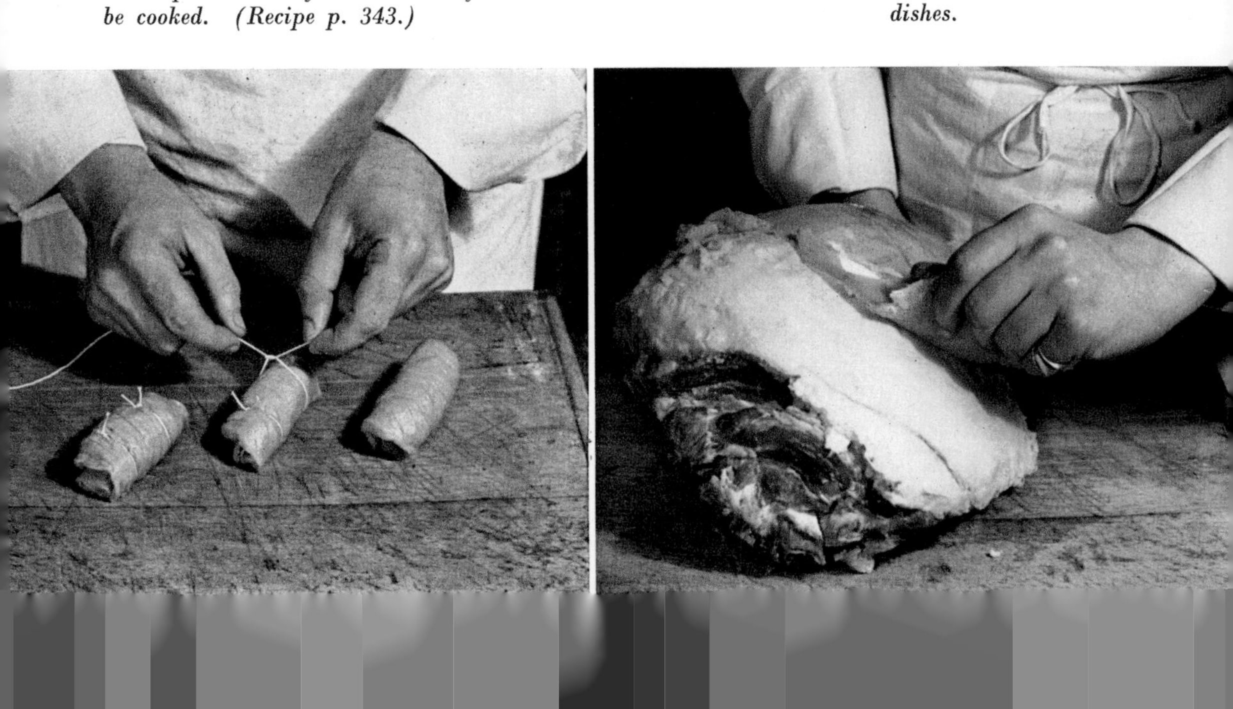

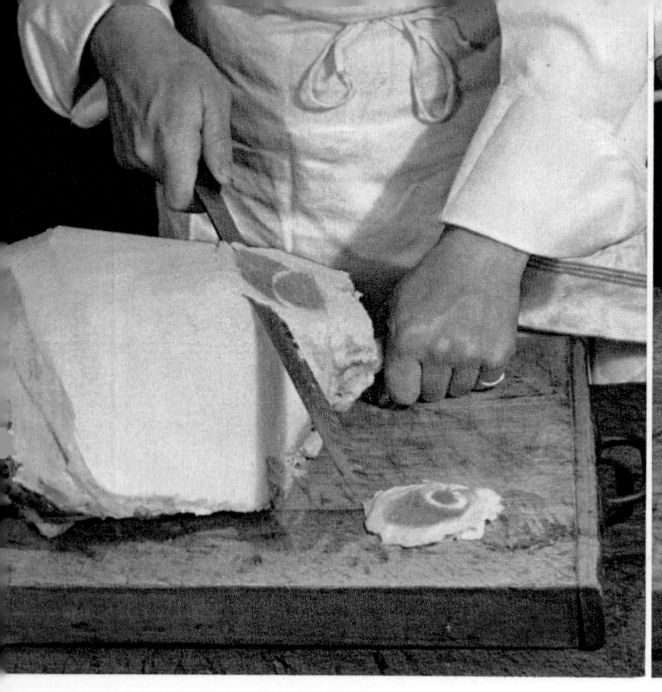

Fig. 56.
Use a long knife with a flexible blade to cut the ham. The slices should always be very thin.

Fig. 57. Ham cones *(1)*.
Cut the ham slices as shown in the photograph using a pattern made of cardboard or paper

Fig. 60. Dressing a chicken *(1)*.
Cut open the neck from the back with a sharp knife.

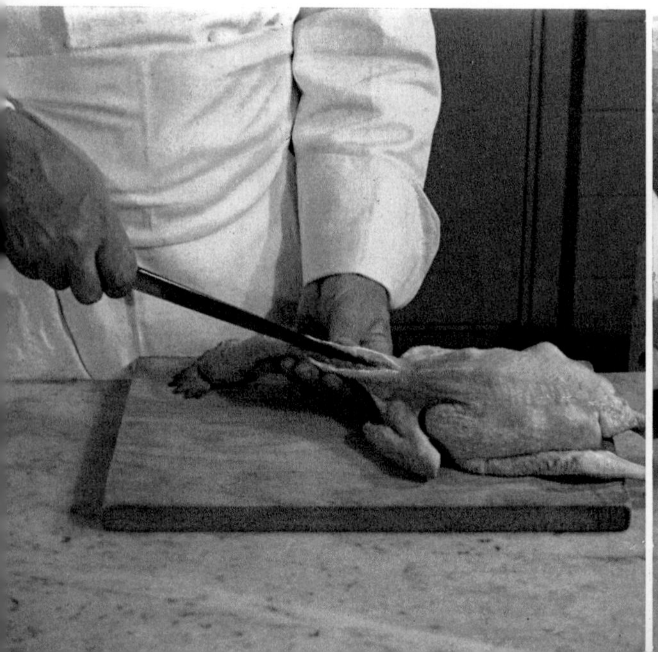

Fig. 61. Dressing a chicken *(2)*.
Raise the head of the chicken in the left hand while cutting the skin of the neck halfway around.

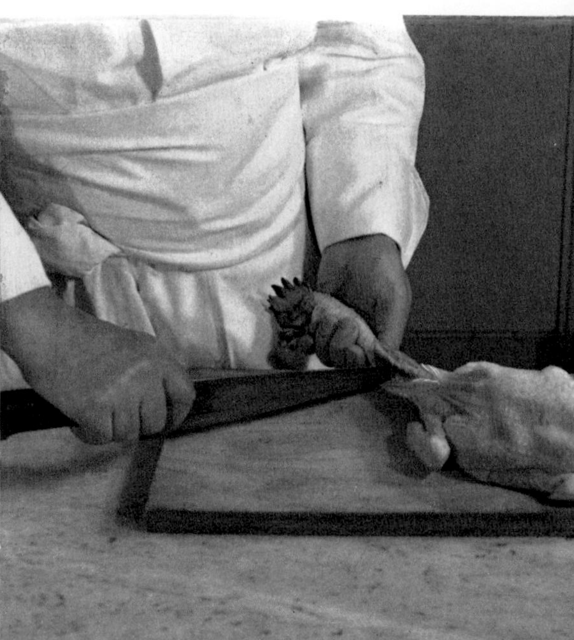

Fig. 58. Ham cones *(2)*.
Put the ham slices into the cone molds, pushing them into place with the thumb.

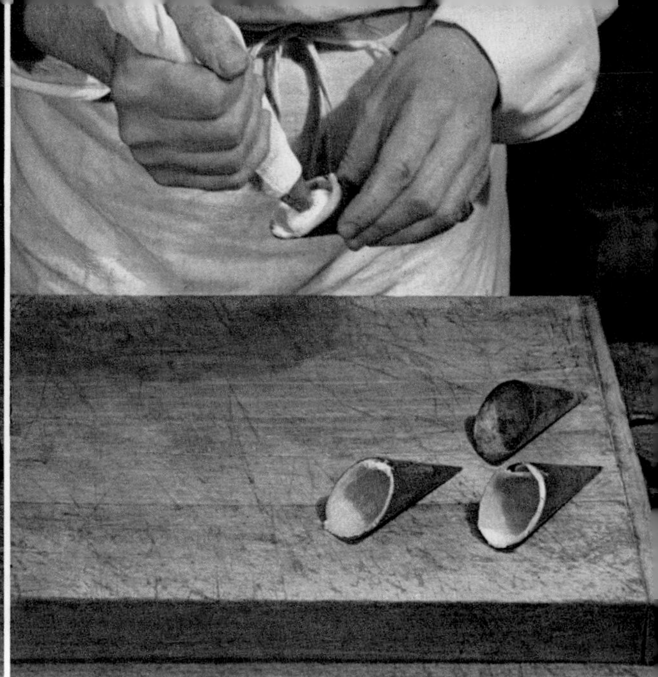

Fig. 59. Ham cones *(3)*.
Use a pastry bag to fill the cones with foie gras or other stuffing. A spatula may be used if there are only a few to fill. *(Recipe p. 371.)*

Fig. 62. Dressing a chicken *(3)*.
Cut off the neck where it joins the body by pressing sharply on the knife.

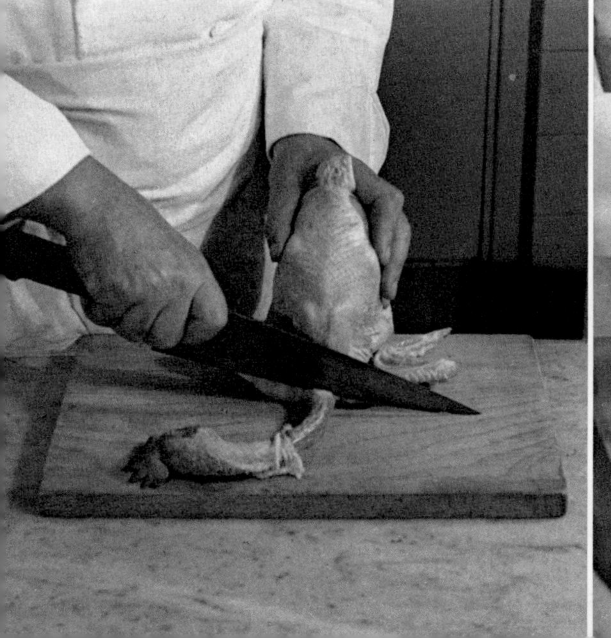

Fig. 63. Dressing a chicken *(4)*.
Remove the crop and lungs by inserting the index finger into the breast cavity.

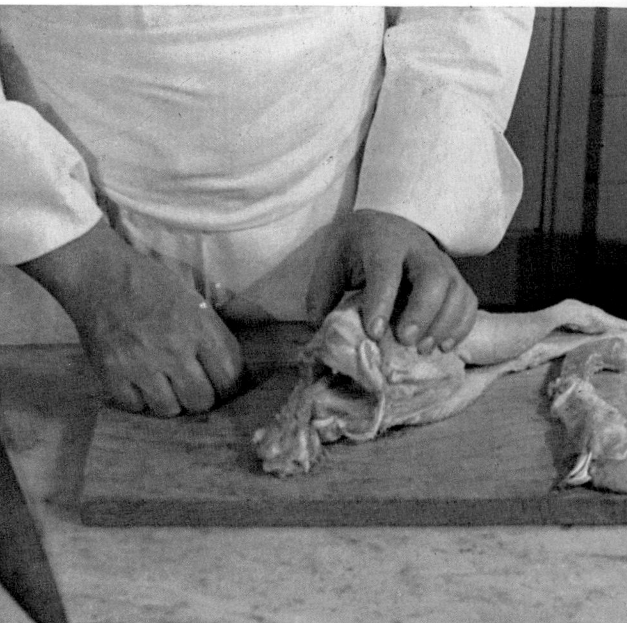

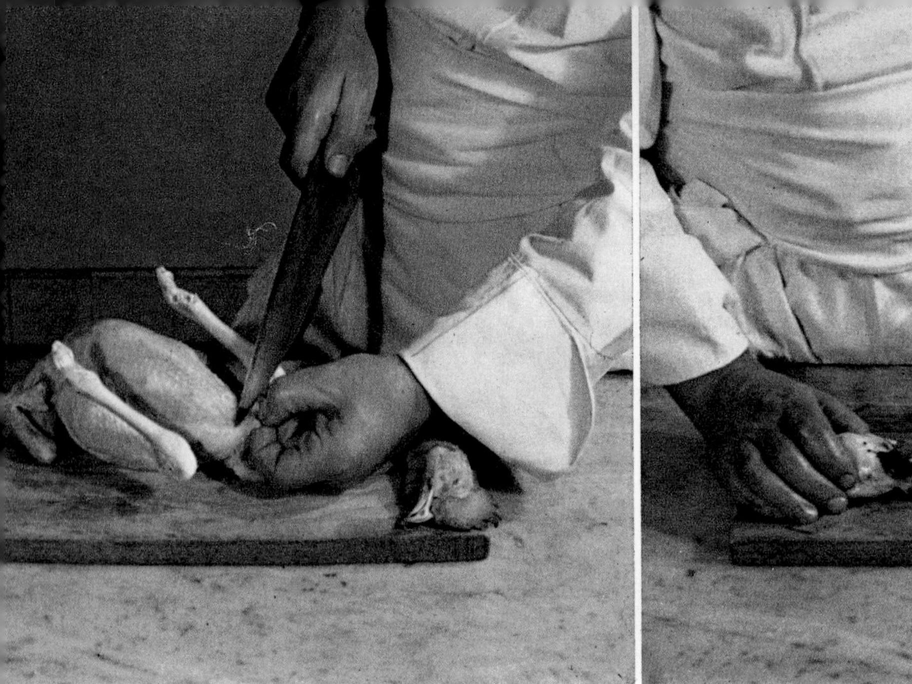

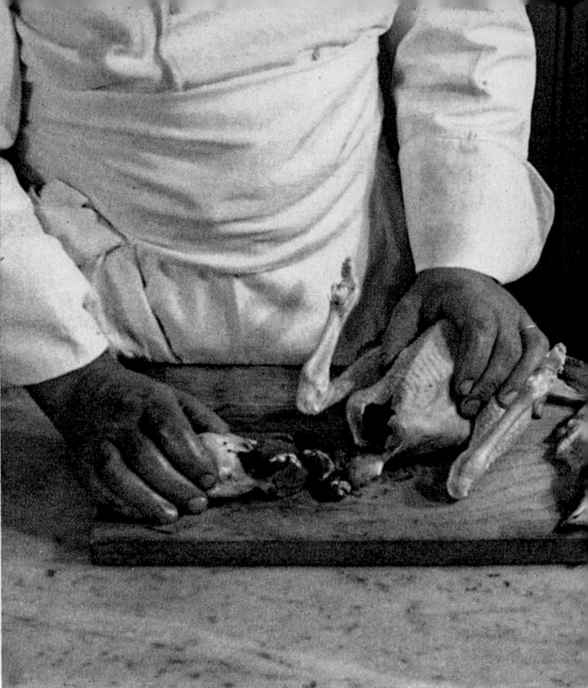

Fig. 64. Dressing a chicken *(5)*.
Cut open the tail end of the chicken by holding the tail between the thumb and the index finger.

Fig. 65. Dressing a chicken *(6)*.
Through this opening, take out the inner organs - gizzard, intestines, viscera, etc. - by simply pressing on the chicken.

Fig. 68. Trussing a chicken *(3)*.
Restring the trussing needle and sew through the back of the chicken.

Fig. 69. Trussing a chicken *(4)*.
Hold down the legs and pass the needle in the opposite direction through the stomach of the chicken to truss down the legs. Tie the string in a double knot.

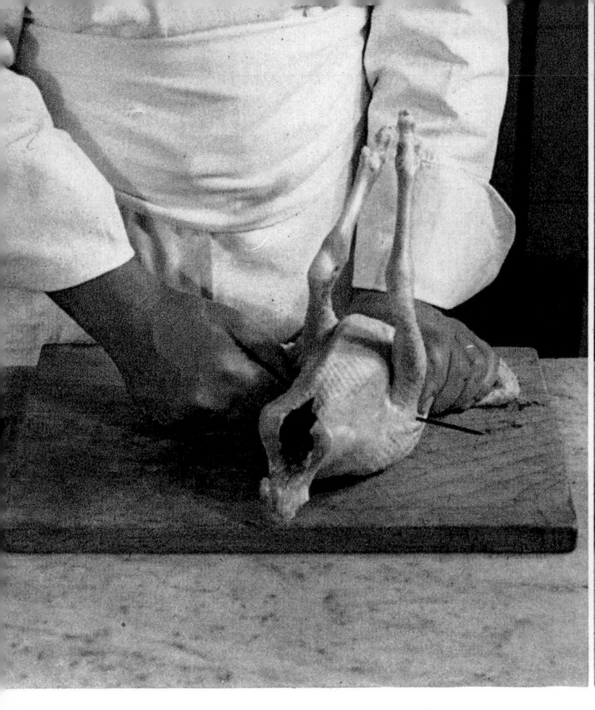

Fig. 66. Trussing a chicken *(1)*.
Lift up the legs and skewer them from one side to the other with a trussing needle and string.

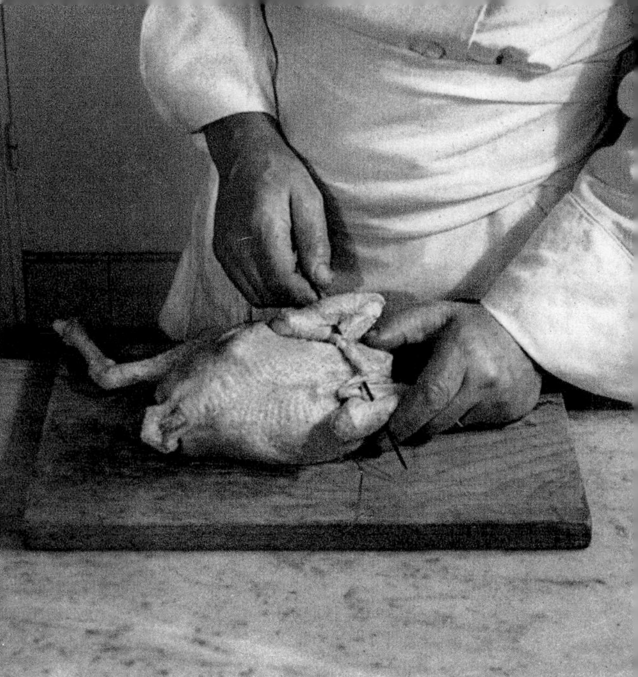

Fig. 67. Trussing a chicken *(2)*.
Turn the chicken over and sew the wings together with a piece of the skin of the back and neck. Pull tightly and make a double knot.

Fig. 70. Trussing a chicken *(5)*.
The cleaned and trussed chicken is now ready for roasting. The legs may be left sticking up, as shown, or cut off midway.

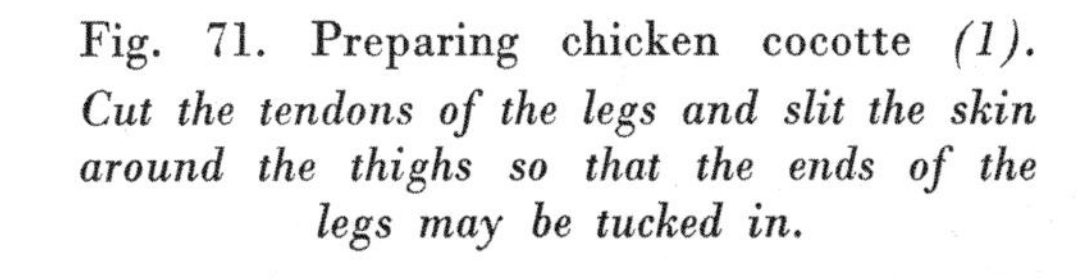

Fig. 71. Preparing chicken cocotte *(1)*.
Cut the tendons of the legs and slit the skin around the thighs so that the ends of the legs may be tucked in.

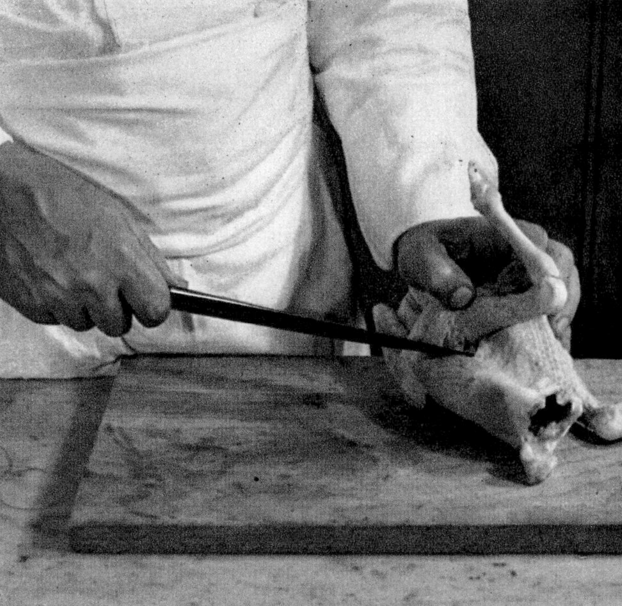

Fig. 72. Preparing chicken cocotte *(2)*. *Truss like a roasting chicken. The illustration shows the way it should look for chicken cocotte. (Recipe p. 394.)*

Fig. 73.
Cleaned neck and giblets ready to cook. These include comb, neck, heart, liver, and gizzard. (Recipe p. 410.)

Fig. 76. Preparing chicken galantine *(3)*. *Spread the skin out on a cloth or napkin. Fill with alternate layers of pork forcemeat, sliced chicken, pork fat or bacon, ham, and truffles.*

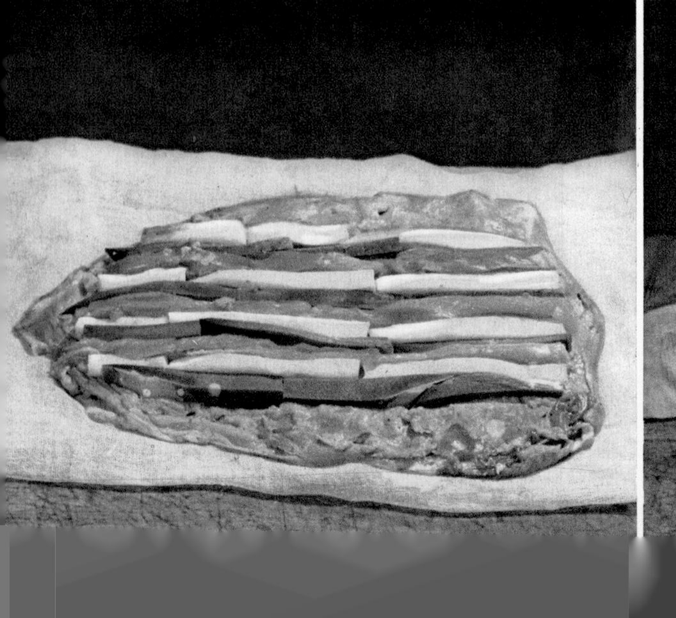

Fig. 77. Preparing chicken galantine *(4)*. *Roll it all in the cloth or napkin and tie solidly with string. Cook according to the directions. (Recipe p. 419.)*

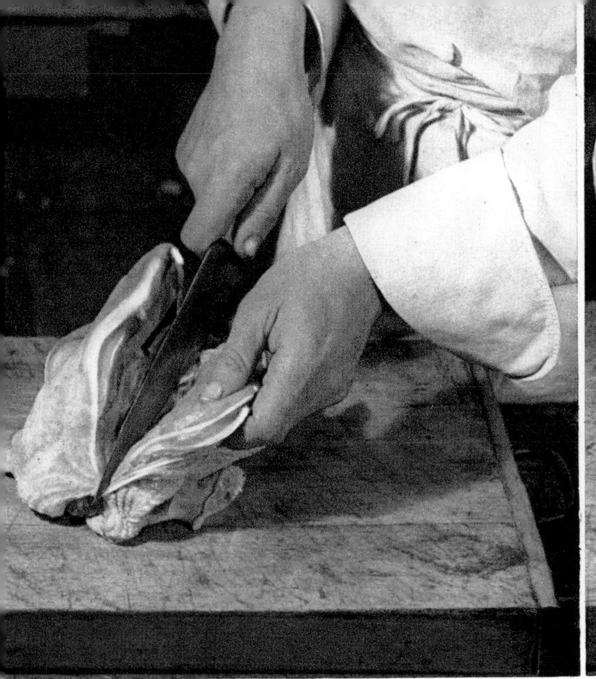

Fig. 74. Preparing chicken galantine *(1)*.
After the chicken has been cleaned, split it down the back without disturbing the skin on the sides. Separate the flesh from the carcass.

Fig. 75. Preparing chicken galantine *(2)*.
Remove the carcass and the rest of the bones without tearing the skin.

Fig. 78. Carving roast chicken *(1)*.
Remove the thigh by cutting toward you while holding it with a fork. Pressing down with the back of the knife will hold the chicken on the board.

Fig. 79. Carving roast chicken *(2)*.
Cut the wing and separate the bone at the joint. (The same carving procedure is followed on both right and left sides.)

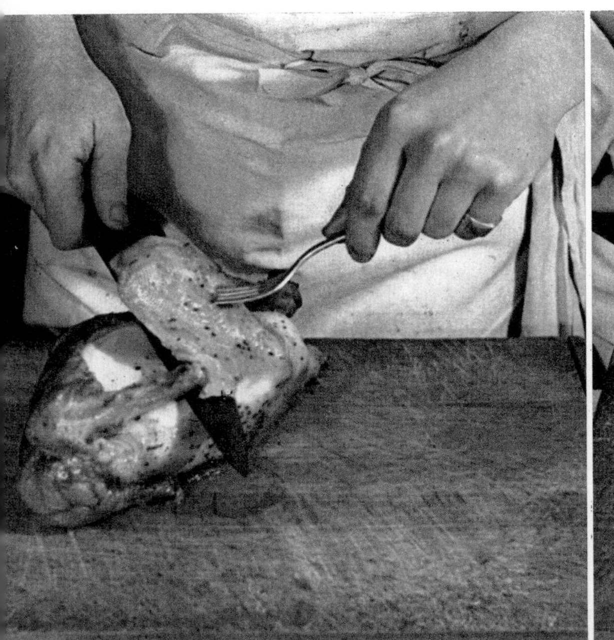

Fig. 80. Carving roast chicken *(3)*.
Separate the carcass from the breast and cut into pieces. (At the table this may be done with carving shears.)

Fig. 81. Potatoes Duchesse *(1)*.
Croquette shape. Roll by hand on a lightly floured board. Fish quenelles are made the same way.

Fig. 84. Potatoes Duchesse *(4)*.
Small-loaf or roll shape. Mold them by hand and finish with the point of a small knife.

Fig. 85. Potatoes Duchesse *(5)*.
Various shapes made by hand and with a pastry bag.

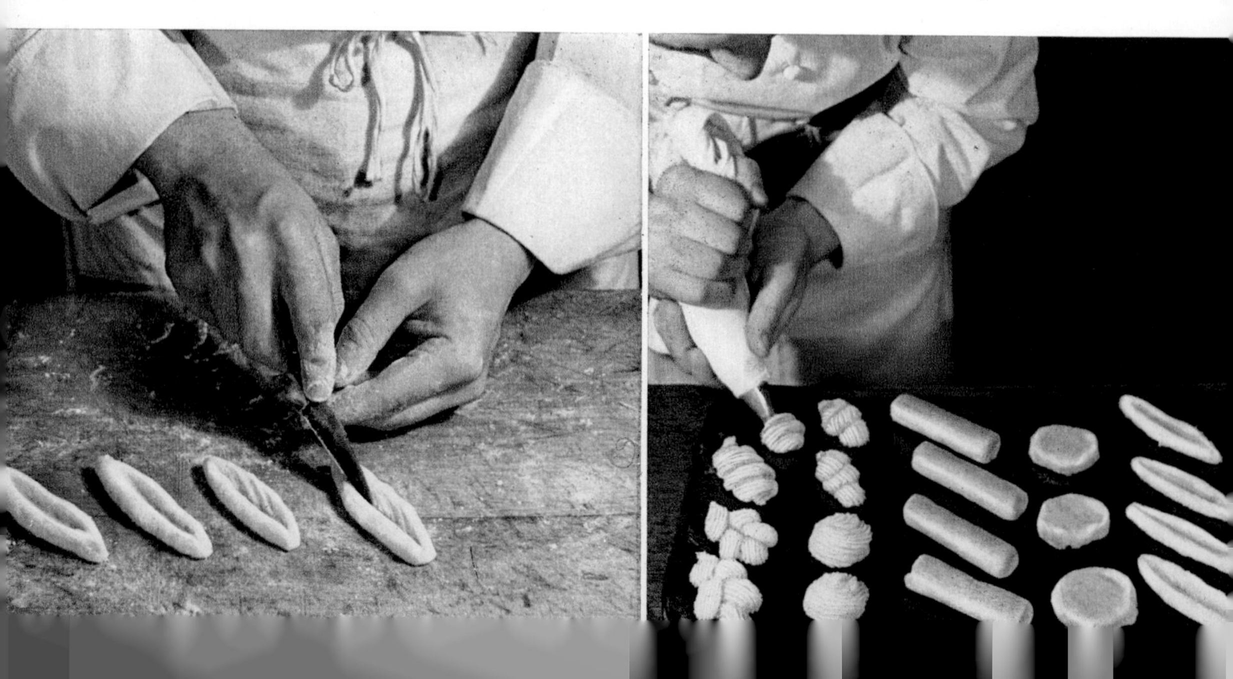

Fig. 82. Potatoes Duchesse *(2)*.
Flat-cake shape. Flatten and shape the potatoes with the side of a knife.

Fig. 83. Potatoes Duchesse *(3)*.
Brioche shape. Mold in two pieces like pastry brioches.

Fig. 86. Souffleed potatoes.
How to cut the potatoes to make them puff.

Fig. 87. Potatoes Parisienne.
The potatoes are cut with a bell cutter. *(Recipe p. 509.)*

Fig. 88. Fluting mushrooms.
Use an ordinary small knife; can be made with a special utensil, but that takes a certain amount of dexterity.

Fig. 89. Artichoke bottoms *(1)*.
Pull away all the leaves around the base of the artichoke. This facilitates the following operation with the knife.

Fig. 92. Puff paste *(1)*.
Flour arranged in a well. Placed this way, the flour prevents the liquid ingredients - water, milk, eggs, etc. - from running down the marble or baking board.

Fig. 93. Puff paste *(2)*.
Put the salt in the middle of the well, pour in the water, and mix gently with the finger tips.

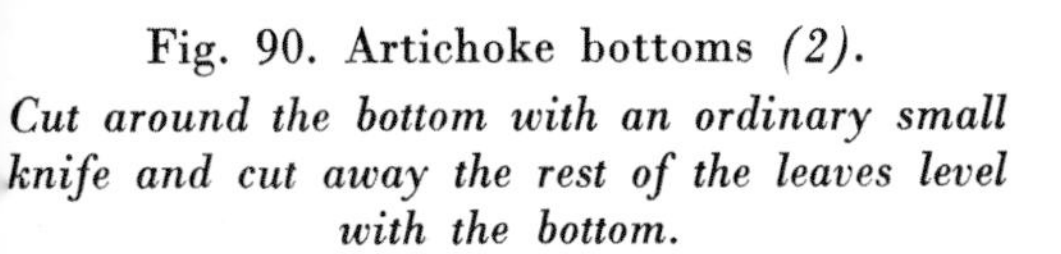

Fig. 90. Artichoke bottoms *(2)*.
Cut around the bottom with an ordinary small knife and cut away the rest of the leaves level with the bottom.

Fig. 91. Artichoke bottoms *(3)*.
Lemon juice will prevent the artichoke bottoms from turning brown. Before cooking, soak them in water containing lemon juice.
(Recipe p. 490.)

Fig. 94. Puff paste *(3)*.
Flatten out the paste, put the butter on top (lightly worked by hand), and cover it with the paste.

Fig. 95. Puff paste *(4)*.
Use a rolling pin to roll out the paste into a long even, rectangular shape.

Fig. 96. Puff paste *(5)*.
Fold this length of paste in 3. This step is called the first "turn". Every 2 turns, let the paste stand at least 1/4 hr.

Fig. 97. Puff paste *(6)*.
Stick the finger tips into the paste in order not to make a mistake about the number of turns. Here the paste has been turned 4 times.

Fig. 100. Patties *(3)*.
Brush the bottom crusts with beaten egg, then stick the hollowed-out circles on top. Let stand a moment, then bake.

Fig. 101. Vol-au-vent *(1)*.
On a layer of puff paste turned 6 times, use a pattern and a small knife to cut out 2 rounds crusts.

Fig. 98. Patties *(1)*.
On a layer of puff paste turned 6 times and rolled out thin, use a fluted cutter to cut out 2 circles for each patty crust.

Fig. 99. Patties *(2)*.
Using a plain cutter smaller than the first one, cut out the center of half of the circles. Place the others on a buttered baking tray.

Fig. 102. Vol-au-vent *(2)*.
Cut a circle out of the inside of one of the 2 round crusts. Put the solid crust on a buttered baking tin and brush the surface with beaten egg. Press the hollow circle of paste on top.

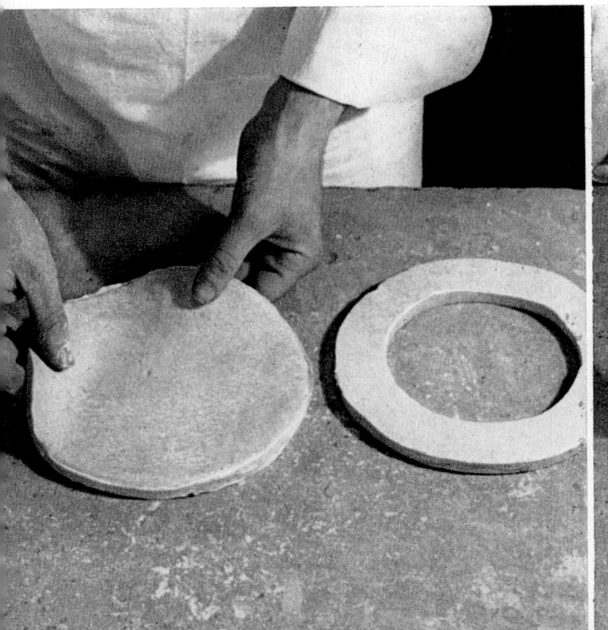

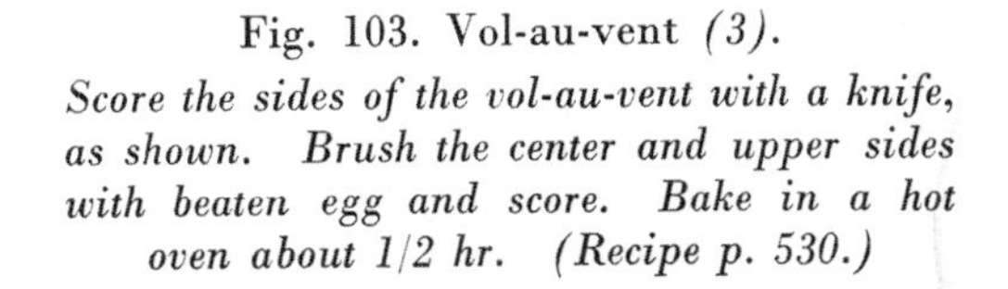

Fig. 103. Vol-au-vent *(3)*.
Score the sides of the vol-au-vent with a knife, as shown. Brush the center and upper sides with beaten egg and score. Bake in a hot oven about 1/2 hr. (Recipe p. 530.)

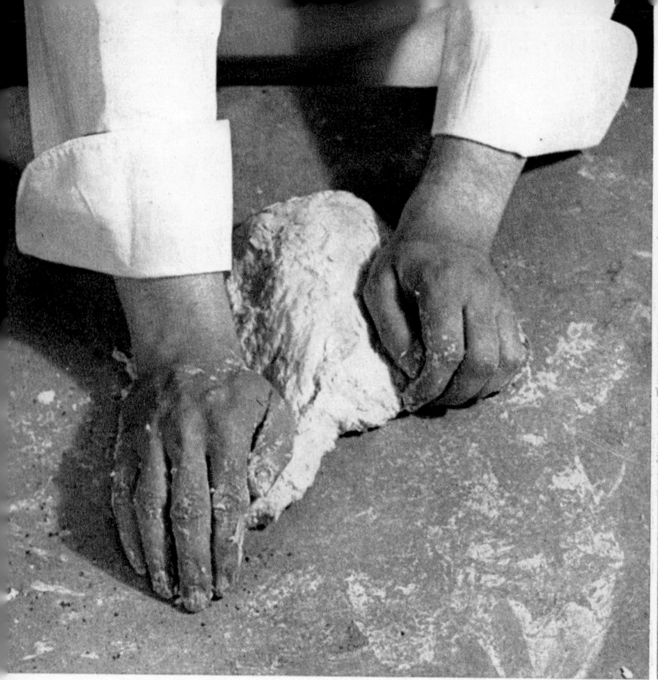

Fig. 104.
Knead the paste by hand to obtain perfect consistency. Puff paste is never kneaded. Follow the recipes given.

Fig. 105.
When the tart has been lined in the pan or circle flan, raise the rim a little to pinch it with special pincers. (See fig. 16, p. 89.)

Fig. 108.
Use a pastry tube with a large, plain tube to make éclairs and salambos (of choux paste). (Recipe p. 589.)

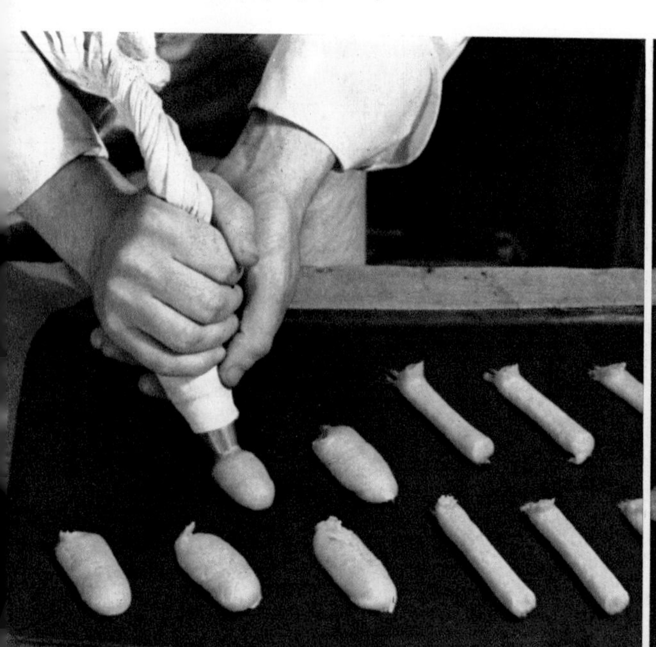

Fig. 109.
Make carolines and small puffs like éclairs, using a smaller plain tube with the pastry bag. Dry baking tray. (Recipe p. 603.)

Fig. 106. Polkas.

With a scalloped cutter, cut a bottom crust from pie paste, then use a pastry bag to make a border of choux paste. Bake on a greased tin. (See p. 597.)

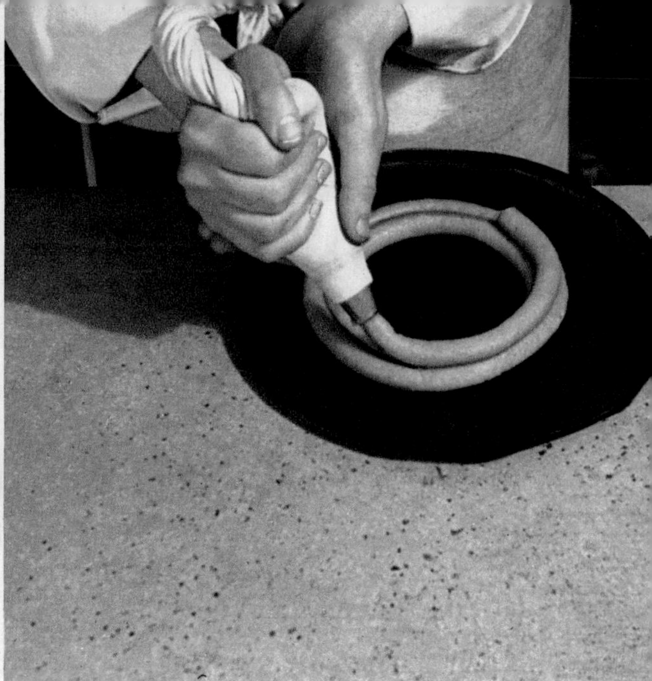

Fig. 107. Paris-Brest.

Using a pastry bag, with a large plain tube, make a crown of 3 circles of choux paste, 1 on top the other 2. Bake on a dry baking tray. (Recipe p. 578.)

Fig. 110.

Squeezing macaroons out of a pastry bag with a large, plain tube onto a baking tray covered with white paper. (Recipe p. 592.)

Fig. 111.

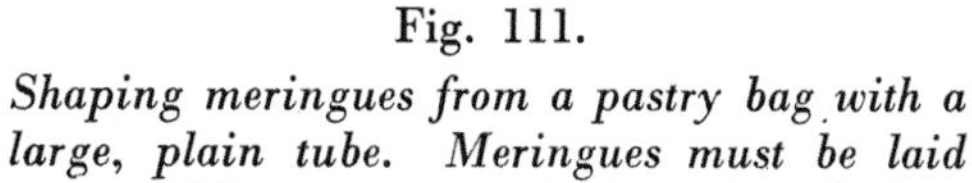

Shaping meringues from a pastry bag with a large, plain tube. Meringues must be laid out quickly to prevent falling. Bake on a buttered, floured tray. (Recipe p. 597.)

Fig. 112. Mocha cake *(1)*.
Cut a Génoise cake in 2 and spread with a layer of coffee butter cream. Lay the other half of the cake on top.

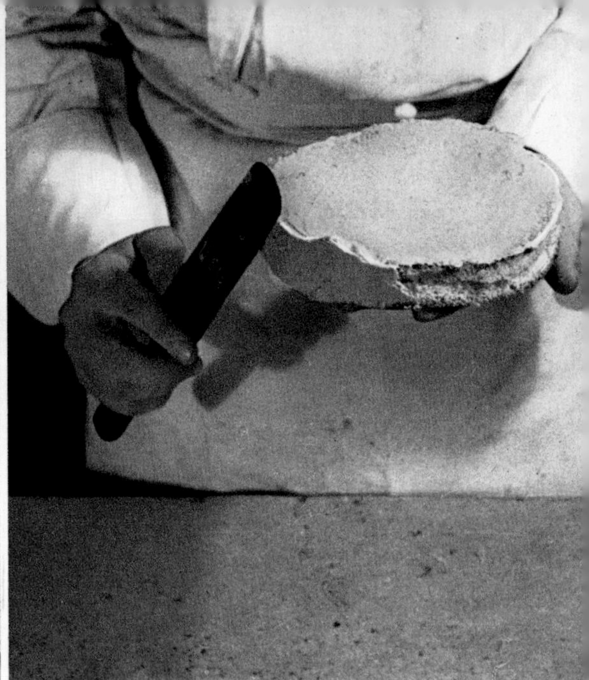

Fig. 113. Mocha cake *(2)*.
Spread a thin layer of the same butter cream over the top and sides. Do this neatly, without making swirls or holes.

Fig. 116. Weaving butter cream.
This decoration is not difficult, but takes a little patience. (Instructions are given in the recipe for Gift from Nice p. 569.)

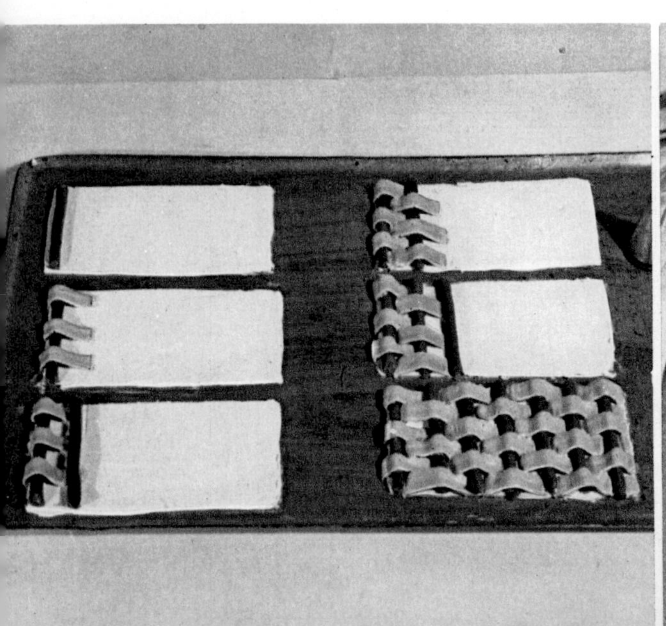

Fig. 117. Frosted Petits Fours *(1)*.
Use small, variously shaped cookies for bases and decorate with a pastry bag, using various flavors of butter creams.

Fig. 114. Mocha cake *(3)*.
Cover the side of the cake with chopped, toasted almonds by holding the chopped nuts in the hollow of the right palm and dipping the cake into it.

Fig. 115. Mocha cake *(4)*.
Decorate the top by using a pastry bag with a fluted tube. The designs are made according to individual taste. *(Recipe p. 575.)*

Fig. 118. Frosted Petits Fours *(2)*.
Cover with fondant flavored and colored to go with the butter cream. The petits fours are placed on a raised grill.

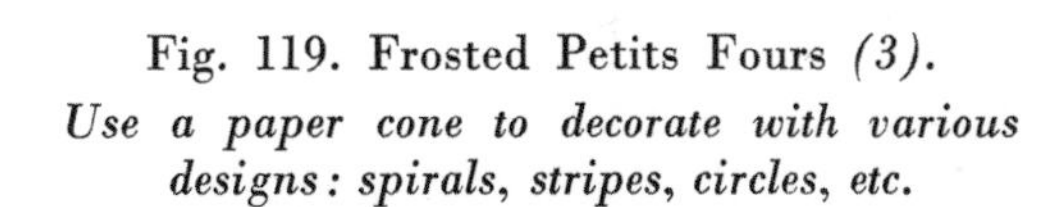

Fig. 119. Frosted Petits Fours *(3)*.
Use a paper cone to decorate with various designs: spirals, stripes, circles, etc.

Fig. 120.
Cooking sugar to the ball stage. The sugar forms a ball when pressed by the fingers. (Complete directions for cooking sugar are given on p. 561.)

Fig. 121. Sugar flowers *(1)*.
Form rose petals from sugar cooked to the "crack" stage by pressing between the thumb and the index finger. (Instructions on p. 608.)

Fig. 122. Sugar flowers *(2)*.
Weld the petals onto a central bud (also made of sugar) by heating over an alcohol lamp.

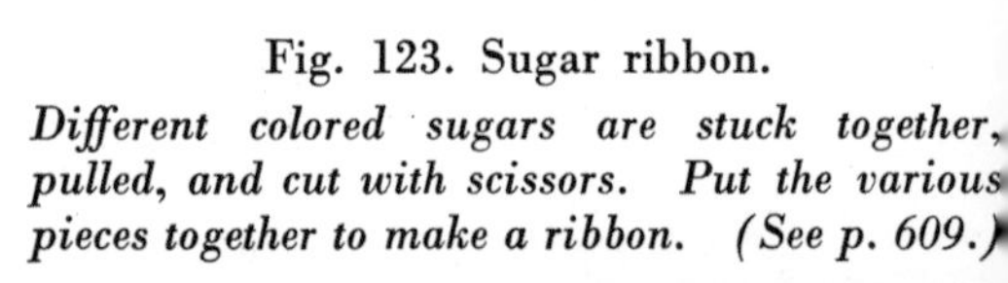

Fig. 123. Sugar ribbon.
Different colored sugars are stuck together, pulled, and cut with scissors. Put the various pieces together to make a ribbon. (See p. 609.)

BASIC COOKING METHODS

There are four principal ways to cook food, with variations and subdivisions of each of these basic methods: *boiling, roasting, grilling* or *broiling* (a type of roasting), and *frying*.

BOILING

Boiling is perhaps the most frequently used method of cooking food. Sometimes it is done with lots of water and a very hot fire, as in the case of green vegetables or certain meats that must be blanched before cooking (sweetbreads, tongue, heads, and most shellfish). Other foods must be boiled gently with a minimum of water or other moistening, especially when *braising* is called for. We braise stew, beef à la mode, and some vegetables after blanching them: celery, lettuce, sorrel, etc. A third manner of boiling is called *poaching*. This is a way of cooking food in water, broth, wine, or gravy so that the liquid does not come to a full boil, but gently simmers. Each one of these three methods of boiling is different from the others, and each has a specific purpose.

BRAISING

Of all the ways of cooking food, braising is perhaps the most difficult and expensive. It requires great care in preparation, quality meats, and excellent juices and stocks for moistening. The best meats for braising come from beef cut from animals from 3 to 6 years old and mutton from sheep from 1 to 2 years old.

If the piece of meat to be braised comes from leg of beef or lamb, it should first be larded, because these meats are not fatty and prolonged cooking runs the risk of drying them out. This is not necessary for sirloin or side of beef, which has veins of fat running through it.

Whether larded or not, meat is improved if it is marinated for a few hours in wine before being braised. The proper way to marinate is to season the meat with salt, pepper, and spices; roll it, and place it into a container, just large enough to hold it, between two layers of flavoring vegetables. Pour on 1 cup wine per 2 lb. meat. Let marinate a few hours, turning from time to time. As a garnish for braising, prepare for each lb. of meat 1 oz. onions and 1 oz. carrots cut in thick slices and browned in butter or fat, also a *bouquet garni* containing a clove of garlic and 1 oz. blanched fresh pork rind.

When the meat has been well marinated, let it drain in a strainer ½ hr. and then sponge it off with a dry cloth.

Heat some fat from clarified consommé in a thick-bottomed casserole or stewpan large enough to hold the meat and, when it is very hot, put in the meat. Brown it on all sides. The time it takes to brown it and the depth of the crust will depend on the size of the meat. When the meat has been browned, remove it and, if it is a lean piece, tie on some strips of bacon or pork fat with strings.

Put the vegetable garnish and *bouquet garni* into the bottom of a pot or Dutch oven and lay the meat in on top. Add the wine used in the marinade and reduce quickly on a hot fire until it becomes sirupy. Cover the meat with good brown stock and bring to a boil again. Cover the pot and boil slowly and steadily on a medium fire. Let the meat cook until no blood escapes when it is pierced with a fork. While cooking, the stock will be rapidly absorbed and the meat will become dry if it is not frequently basted with stock and turned. The meat must be kept covered with juicy stock constantly if it is to soak up the sauce and have the richness that makes braised meat different from that prepared in any other way.

Braised white meats, as prepared today, are not, properly speaking, really braised. Breast, loin, shoulder, and saddle of veal are braised, as are fricandeau and sweetbreads of veal, turkey hens, fat pullets, and sometimes, though less often, joints or saddles of lamb. All these meats are braised alike, except that the timing differs according to size. The garnish is the same as for red meat, except that the vegetables are merely turned in butter rather than browned. White stock is used instead for moistening.

Except for sweetbreads, which are always blanched before being braised, the meat or fowl to be braised can be lightly browned in butter on all sides to seal in the juices, so that the meat will dry out less. However, this procedure is not indispensable.

Next place the meat in a pot with the vegetable garnish. Half cover the meat with veal stock that has been reduced until it is sirupy. Baste frequently while cooking. A white meat is braised when, on being pierced deeply with a skewer, it exudes a colorless juice.

ROASTING

Everyone knows what a roast is, and the saying that the only good roast is the one cooked on a spit is still true. However, the spit has disappeared with the grill in the modern household, except in outdoor cookery. Only commercial establishments have them now. Roasts are made today in gas or electric ovens, which have been developed until they are almost perfect.

Fowl, tender cuts of meat, pork, game, and, sometimes, fish may be roasted.

Trim the meat to be roasted, pull tendons if necessary, and stud with small pieces of pork fat. Thin strips of fat may be tied on the outside; this is especially effective in keeping the breast of chicken moist and tender. Place the roasting meat in a very hot oven to sear the outside and seal in the juices. However, it must not be seared to such an extent that too heavy a crust is formed and the heat cannot enter the meat. Generally speaking, the smaller the roast, the hotter the oven should be to seal the outside quickly. Chickens should be greased with butter, but roasts of beef, unless they have been larded, must be well greased outside with good beef-fat drippings or lard, for butter will not do. Fatty meats such as mutton, pork, duck, and goose should not be greased, since they supply their own grease while roasting. Game fowl should always be banded with strips of bacon or pork fat, and large game roasts, such as venison, boar, and deer, for example, must be studded with thin strips of pork fat and marinated.

Cooking time is measured by the weight of the roast: ¼ hr. per lb. of red meat if it is to be rare. Salt the meat after basting it for the first time, but salt it only slightly, adding a little at a time. The salt penetrates slowly as the heat opens the pores of the meat. If all of the salt is put on in the beginning, the melting fat will wash it all down into the bottom of the pan.

It is hard to say what is the best way to tell when the roast has been properly cooked. Primarily, it is a matter of experience. A meat roast, if it is done, should seem elastic and rise again when it is pressed in the middle. An infallible test for any kind of fowl is to raise it without piercing it and let the juice run out from the inside. If it is clear, the roast is cooked; if it is pink, the roast needs more time in the oven. When the fowl has been pricked with a fork at the joint of the thigh, the juice should also be clear.

Important advice: Never put water in the roasting pan; juice for basting must come from the roast itself. A good gravy should preserve the flavor of meat, but you must not use beef broth to make a fowl or game-fowl gravy.

When the roast is cooked, place it on a platter and skim the fat off the juice from the roast. Save the fat for other roasts. On the bottom of the roasting pan you will find either gravy from the roast or burnt gravy sticking to it. The latter may be heated with a little water or broth until it melts and makes a good gravy, which may then be browned and thickened, if desired.

Sometimes meat, but especially fowl, is cooked on top of the stove in a casserole, Dutch oven, or cocotte, and this too may be considered roasting as long as only butter or good fat with no liquid is used. If an oven is not handy, you can cook a meat roast this way. Brown the meat in butter or fat, season it, cover the pot, and set it over a very moderate fire, turning it on all sides as it roasts. Since the cover keeps the heat in, pot-roasting does not require quite so much time as oven-roasting. For pot-roasting, Escoffier warns not to moisten the meat while cooking, or it will be braised. Like other roasts, the gravy is made from the juices after the meat has been cooked and removed.

In this same section we shall consider sautés.

Sautés are small pieces of meat such as tournedos, veal cutlets, liver, etc., or fowl and game cut in pieces, seasoned, floured or not, and seared in hot fat. White meats must be seasoned, floured, and well browned in a pan. After they have been well browned to seal in the juices, they are put uncovered into the oven to finish cooking, or in a covered pan on top of the stove, over a slow fire, and basted once or twice.

We shall now discuss grilling, which really belongs in the same category as roasts, because it is really roasting over a live fire in the open air. Let us see what Escoffier has to say on the subject.

USE OF THE GRILL

Grilling dark meats: The main problem in grilling is the proper temperature to be maintained for each type of meat. The larger the piece of meat and the more blood it contains, the hotter and faster it must be seared to seal in the juices. If we are using large pieces of meat, such as beef or mutton, the brown coating must be all the thicker for the meat to have excellent quality and especially to be juicy. The pressure of these juices against the brown coating will be all the stronger as they are more abundant, and this pressure will increase proportionately as the juices are heated. If the grill temperature is well regulated so that the heat penetrates progressively, the following results will be obtained:

The heat, striking directly against the side of the meat in contact with the grill, first makes the fibers contract, then penetrates the meat in successive layers, pushing the juices toward the raw side until they form beads on it. The meat should then be turned over, and the flow of juices will start the other way. The cooked crust of the first side heated will stop the flow, and a few drops will push through to the surface, indicating the degree to which the grilled meat has been cooked.

It stands to reason that if a very large piece of meat is being grilled the heat must be turned down as soon as the outside crust is formed, so that the inside is evenly heated. Otherwise the outside will be like a black cinder and will keep the heat from penetrating the inside. The end result will be a roast with a charred exterior and a raw interior. Small pieces of meat should be seared on the outside and cooked for only a few minutes to be properly done. In this case, there is no need to lower the heat.

Example: A rump steak or a Chateaubriand (a thick fillet of beef) should be seared over a very hot fire to seal in the juices, and then the fire should be lowered to allow the interior to cook through. Thin steaks and chops must also be seared, but the heat does not have to be turned down, for it takes only a short time for the heat to penetrate and cook the inside.

Preparations and care while grilling: The meat should be liberally covered with butter before being put on the grill, and then more butter should be added during the grilling to prevent the drying out of the parts in contact with the fire. Turn the meat over with a flat turner or, better still, special tongs. You must never pierce the meat, or you will make an easy opening for the juices to flow away, ruining all the precautions taken to seal in the juices.

How to tell when the meat is cooked: Press the crust with your finger. If it is firm, the meat is cooked through. If there is no resistance and the surface contracts, the meat is not done. If a few drops of pink blood squeeze out onto the crusty surface, you may be sure that the meat has cooked long enough.

Grilling white meats: The quick searing and sealing of the outside necessary for dark meats is not needed for white meats since there is no concentration of red blood. This type of grilling requires a moderate heat and frequent basting with butter to keep the meat from drying out. The meat may be considered cooked when the juice that runs out is completely colorless.

FRYING

Almost anything may be fried: eggs, fish, meat, vegetables, and desserts.

Cooking foods by frying is sufficiently difficult to make a little instruction and advice necessary, for just as there is nothing more digestible and appetizing than a dish properly fried, there is also nothing more indigestible than one improperly fried. The base for frying is fat or oil, but just any fat will not do. The ideal fat, almost the only kind used in professional cookery, is fat from beef kidneys. Veal fat is not good unless mixed with beef fat; it is too fine, besides, and is better saved for other cooking uses. Mutton fat is not to be considered because it has too strong a taste. Peanut oil is especially good for fish because a high degree of heat can be obtained without burning. Pork fat is also excellent for frying.

As a general rule, the smaller the piece to be fried, the hotter the oil or fat should be.

Oil is preferable for fish. If the piece of fish weighs more than 4 oz., small incisions should be cut on both sides to let the heat penetrate: this is for fish that are spindle-shaped, such as whiting, herring, and mullet; flat fish such as sole or plaice do not need to be cut. Fish should always be "sealed" or seared by having the oil very hot. You can tell if it is being seared by a light smoke escaping that has a fishy odor. Be sure that the quantity of frying oil is at least as much in volume or weight as the quantity of fish being put in, so that the fish will not cool it and turn out boiled instead of fried. Keep the fire hot, so that the oil will be just as hot after the fish have been put in as before. Fried fish should usually be dipped first in cold, slightly salted milk, rolled in flour, and shaken to get rid of the excess flour.

All fried foods, especially fish, must be served immediately after cooking, nice and crisp, salted, and arranged on a doily or napkin to absorb the grease.

Breaded dishes like meat or vegetable croquettes, *rissoles,* fritters, and so on are also fried; they are described in their respective chapters.

Souffléed potatoes need beef-kidney fat, for oil is too difficult to use for this recipe unless one is experienced.

Some meats and vegetables are first cooked one way and then fried, like tripe and salsify, to cite two examples.

A last word of caution: after using fat for deep frying, let it stand about 20 min. before straining it into a container for storage, to avoid burning yourself. It is absolutely necessary to strain it, to remove particles of flour, bread crumbs, etc , which have settled in it and would burn next time the fat was used.

PREPARING FAT FOR FRYING

Take, for example, 4 lb. beef-kidney fat, for you must always use a large amount of fat: it is economical, since you will run less risk of burning it than with a small amount; besides, every dish that is fried must swim in fat. Cut this fat in very small pieces, or have the butcher do it; place the pieces in the deep-frying pan, and cover completely with water. Cook slowly until all of the water has evaporated. When all the fat has been rendered, little bits of well-browned cracklings will float on top. When a bluish, strong-smelling smoke begins to rise, the fat is clear and ready.

Strain the liquid fat through a fine sieve and press through all of the fat possible. To purify the fat, fry a couple of quartered onions or clean potato peelings in it, to absorb any strong flavor remaining. It is better to sacrifice 2 onions than to spoil the first thing cooked in the fat. These directions, while not needed by a professional chef, are included to help the housewife or home cook.

COOKING TIME AND CARVING INSTRUCTIONS FOR ROASTS

RIB ROAST OF BEEF

15 min. per lb. Be sure to leave the roast in the warmer for at least 20 min. before carving. Cut all the way across in thin slices, using a carving knife with a long, thin blade or a ham knife.

FILLET OF BEEF

12 min. per lb. Leave in the warmer 15 min. after cooking, to let the meat settle and make carving easier. This principle holds good for all cooked meats. Slice with a thin knife, without pressing on the roast, to avoid losing the blood.

ROAST BEEF

12–15 min. per lb., depending on shape. Two roasts, each weighing 3 lb., may require different timing. A round, thick roast will require 15 min. per lb., whereas a long roast will need only 12.

VEAL ROAST

30 min. per lb. Slice a little thicker than beef. Always serve well done.

LEG OF MUTTON

15 min. per lb. If the meat is of good quality, it has enough fat and therefore need not be greased before cooking. Slice it not too thick and not too thin, slanting the knife to make the slices thicker and in the opposite direction to cutting ham.

SADDLE OF MUTTON

15 min. per lb. The carving is difficult to explain. First, detach the two sides of the top saddle completely and then cut the lean meat lengthwise in strips, putting them back into place. The rolled-up flaps of the saddle are left as they are, to support the bones of the saddle on the platter.

ROAST LAMB, LEG OR SADDLE

25 min. per lb. This meat should be well cooked. Carve the same as mutton.

PORK

Should also be well cooked, 30 min. per lb. Always slice thin according to the shape of the piece.

HAM

Hot or cold, the skin and part of the fat must be removed. Slice very thin, bringing the knife from the top down toward the narrow, bone end, in the opposite direction to cutting leg of mutton.

ROAST CHICKEN (HEN OR LARGE CHICKEN)

50 min. for an unstuffed chicken and 1¼ hr. for a stuffed chicken. Slice the breast lengthwise in thin slices. Cut the legs from the breasts with a few strokes of the knife, separating the bone. Try to reconstruct the chicken after carving, or arrange the slices of meat around the carcass, which has been cut in pieces and placed in the center of the platter.

ROAST SPRING CHICKEN

13–15 min. per lb. Cut in pieces, separating the bones, with a knife or poultry shears. The breast may be cut in long slices and then put back into place along with the legs and thighs, reconstructing the chicken as much as possible.

ROAST CHICKEN (BROILING SIZE)

Cook for 20 min. and cut in quarters.

DUCK

15 min. per lb. Carve the same as a goose; the breast in long slices, legs in pieces. Rouen duck, which is always served rare, should be roasted in a very hot oven for 25–30 min.; the breast is cut in long, narrow strips.

TURKEY

A small, young turkey takes 1 hr. and a large turkey 1¾-2 hr. Carve the breast in slices like chicken and the legs in medium-sized pieces. Legs and carcass in the center of the platter, with the white meat placed around them.

GOOSE

Should be very well done. Roast in a moderate oven to make the fat ooze out. Toward the end of the cooking turn the heat up to brown the skin. If the goose is not stuffed, allow 20 min. per lb.; 25 min. per lb. if stuffed with dressing or chestnuts. Cut the breast in long, narrow strips, the legs in pieces.

PIGEONS

Pigeons weighing 12 oz. (dressed), 20–25 min. Cut in half or, if very large, in 3 pieces—a small half of each side with leg and wing, with the breast as the third piece.

GUINEA HEN

The meat is very dry and must be covered with strips of bacon or larded with strips of fat. Roast ¾ hr. and carve as you would spring chicken.

PHEASANT

Roast in a hot oven 25–30 min., according to weight. Carve the breast in long slices.

PARTRIDGE

Roast 15–20 min. in a very hot oven. Cut in 2 or 4 parts, according to size.

LEG OF VENISON

12 min. per lb. Should always be served rare. Slice the same as ham.

SADDLE OF VENISON

12 min. per lb. Carve the 2 fillets off the top. Cut them in slices across rather than lengthwise as in the case of saddle of mutton, otherwise the slices will be too long and too big. Arrange the slices in their original shape.

BOAR

Same treatment as venison.

SAUCES FOR HOME COOKING

The recipes for sauces requiring kitchen stocks as a base, given by Montagné and Escoffier, are suitable only for professional cooks and restaurant kitchens. Does that mean you have to give up the idea of having good French cooking at home? Certainly not. The wide-awake homemaker with Continental taste who wishes to prepare a meal in the best French tradition does not have to upset her budget or spend hours in the kitchen. After studying the recipes of the great master chefs, she can produce most of the sauces by simplifying the directions. Here is how it is done: white sauces are for the most part made by using the cooking juices of the meats that call for these sauces. Thus, for a *blanquette* of veal or creamed chicken, the veal or chicken is cooked in a kind of court bouillon (a little water, salted and seasoned with aromatic herbs and sometimes a few vegetables), and the sauce is made from the resultant broth.

However, brown sauces, such as Madeira Sauce, to name only one, call for much greater care if you want to succeed. These sauces can be made without using expensive stocks by making a brown roux from 2 tbsp. flour, 1½ oz. good fat or lard (not butter; it turns black and makes the gravy bitter), and some bouillon. If you have no bouillon made from *pot-au-feu* or soup bones available, use a ready-made commercial concentrate. Add 2 tbsp. tomato purée or 3 or 4 fresh tomatoes. Stir the sauce constantly until it boils and then cook slowly for at least ½ hr. Skim off the froth and grease and correct the seasoning. Now you have a basic brown sauce that may be used for Madeira Sauce or any other merely by adding either a *mirepoix* of vegetables (see p. 136), or mushrooms, or browned onions, or truffles. With this basic sauce the most modest cook can imitate almost all of the sauces made by the great chefs.

Whenever possible, the brown sauces should be enriched by the juices or stock of the meat they are to accompany. For example, if you are making a sauce to go with game, finish it with some of the strained cooking juices from the game; the same goes for fowl. Remember always to cook the sauce slowly and to skim off the froth and grease to make it smooth and not too thick. White sauces can sometimes be rather thick, or at least creamy, but brown sauces never.

The superiority of French cooking is founded on sauces. They bring out the best qualities of the food. In a fine restaurant the sauce cook ranks next to the head chef.

Other authors of cookbooks evidently feel the same. You have only to look at the space reserved for the chapter on stocks and sauces. However, the stock from which the sauces are made can only be achieved really in great restaurants and first-class hotels; home cooking does not allow this kind of luxury. Nevertheless, we shall give all the necessary directions so that even the simplest everyday cooking will take inspiration from great cooking and resemble it as much as possible, if only sufficient pains are taken.

We must add also that we agree with health experts that a diet of rich sauces and gravies will have unpleasant repercussions on the digestive system, especially if accompanied by generous quantities of wine worthy of enhancing fine food. And so from time to time family cooking should "take the cure" with a more restful, though just as carefully prepared, menu, making the next feast all the more appreciated.

Stocks are divided into two principal classes: white stock for making white sauces and brown stock for brown sauces.

We shall now pass the pen to our masters, Escoffier and Montagné, who in their books *Le Guide culinaire* and *Le Grand Livre de la cuisine* (in collaboration with Prosper Salles) gave us the finest culinary documentation of our epoch, especially concerning cooking for large hotels and restaurants.

STOCKS SAUCES AND GARNISHES

STOCKS, SAUCES AND GARNISHES

BASIC ELEMENTS IN SAUCEMAKING

STOCK FOR QUANTITY COOKING

ORDINARY WHITE STOCK FONDS BLANC ORDINAIRE (M.)[1] (*For 10 qt.*)

This stock is obtained from the cooking of white meats, chicken bones, knuckle of veal, etc. The stock must be cooked slowly and evenly to keep it clear. That is one of the essential conditions that determine the purity and smoothness of the veloutés made from it.

Basic ingredients: 24 lb. veal (neck, knuckles, or fresh trimmings), 2 lb. carrots, 1 lb. leeks, ½ lb. onions, 6 oz. celery, a large *bouquet garni* (parsley, thyme, and bay leaf), 2 cloves. *Liquid:* 11 qt. water (or thin white consommé). *Seasoning:* If water is used, 2 oz. salt; if consommé is used, put in less salt, since consommé is salted.

Preparation: Put the boned meat tied with string and the bones cut in small pieces into the pot. Add the water or white consommé. Bring to a boil. Skim off

[1] A list of the names of authors whose initials appear at the beginning of each recipe will be found on p. 819.

the foam. Add the vegetables. Cook 3 hr. at a slow but steady boil. Strain through cheesecloth.

Note: Chicken giblets or carcasses may be added to the basic ingredients. To make the stock very savory a trussed hen may also be added. The chicken, as well as the other meats, may be used later for various stuffings, pastes, hashes, etc. When the white stock is finished, the same bones may be boiled again. This second broth, after boiling 3 hr., may be strained through cheesecloth and used as the liquid for a new preparation of white stock.

CHICKEN WHITE STOCK FONDS BLANC DE VOLAILLE (M.)

Make exactly like Ordinary White Stock, adding 2 hens and some giblets.

BROWN STOCK FONDS BRUN OR ESTOUFFADE (M.) (*For 10 qt.*)

This concentrated broth, used as the liquid ingredient of Espagnole and Semiglaze Sauces, must be prepared most carefully. It should be perfectly clear and have an undisguised flavor. By undisguised flavor we mean that only beef and veal should be used and that it is wrong to add leftovers or other meat trimmings. It is advisable that the basic ingredients have a standard quality and that therefore only absolutely fresh meats be used.

Basic ingredients: 10 lb. lean beef, 4 lb. beef knuckle, 10 lb. veal knuckle, 4 lb. meaty veal bones chopped in small pieces, 8 oz. fresh, blanched pork rind, 2 lb. carrots, 1 lb. leeks, ½ lb. onions, 6 oz. celery, a large *bouquet garni*, 2 cloves, 1 clove garlic. *Liquid:* 14 qt. water (or white consommé). *Seasoning:* Same as for white stock.

Preparation: Put the vegetables, pork rind, and herbs in the bottom of a 15-qt. kettle. Place the meat and bones on this bed of flavorings. Brown over a low flame, stirring occasionally. Remove the grease formed while browning. Pour in the water or consommé. Salt. Bring to a quick boil, skim off foam and grease, and cook 8-10 hr. at moderate heat. Strain the stock through a fine sieve. Boil it down, carefully skimming off impurities. Use as required in recipes.

BROWN VEAL STOCK or VEAL GRAVY FONDS DE VEAU BRUN OR JUS DE VEAU (M.) (*For 5 qt.*)

Into a large kettle put 6 oz. fresh, blanched pork rind, 12 oz. carrots, and ½ lb. onions sliced thick. On top of this layer place 6 lb. meaty veal bones, finely chopped and browned in the oven, and 6 lb. boned shoulder and knuckle of veal tied with string and also browned in the oven. The kettle covered, simmer on the fire 25 min. Add 5 qt. White Stock (p. 133). Reduce the liquid by boiling until it becomes sirupy. Add 6 qt. more White Stock. Bring to a boil, skim, and cook 5 hr. at a gentle, constant boil. Remove the pieces of veal before the stock is completely cooked, so that they may be used as chopped meat or in other ways. Strain the stock through cheesecloth and boil again until reduced by ⅓. Use the stock as directed.

Note: This stock, which is not too thick, since it was reduced only once, is used for making gravies for sautés (tournedos, veal cutlets, chicken, etc.). It is also used for enriching the flavor of Semiglaze Sauce and special meat jellies.

GAME STOCK FONDS DE GIBIER (M.) (*For 2½ qt.*)

Put 6 lb. mixed ground-game trimmings and 2 trussed partridges (all previously browned in the oven) into a kettle on top of a layer of 4 oz. fresh, blanched pork rind, 4 oz. carrots, 4 oz. onions sliced in rings. Pour in ½ bottle dry white wine. Cook until it turns to a glaze, or becomes sirupy. Add 3 qt. white veal stock. Add a *bouquet garni* made of stalks of parsley, thyme, bay leaf, 2 sage leaves, and 6 juniper berries. Bring to a boil, skim, and simmer 3 hr. Strain and use as directed.

Note: The partridges used to make the stock can be used later as a purée, chopped, etc., in other recipes.

VEGETABLE STOCK (MEATLESS) FONDS (MAIGRE) DE RACINES (M.) (*For 2½ qt.*)

Brown in butter 8 oz. carrots, 8 oz. onions, 4 oz. leeks, 6 oz. celery, 2 oz. parsnips, and 4 parsley roots, all sliced thin. Season with salt and a little sugar. When the vegetables have been well browned, pour 3½ qt. water over them. Add 8 oz. mushroom stems and peelings chopped in large pieces and a *bouquet garni* consisting of a branch of fennel, a sprig of thyme, and ¼ bay leaf. Cook 1½ hr. at a full boil. Strain the stock, pressing the vegetables to extract all the juice. Boil the stock to reduce it by ⅓.

Note: This meatless stock is good for making sauces for certain diets. Dry vegetables such as beans, lentils, chick-peas, etc., cooked without meat, also make an excellent stock for diet recipes.

ORDINARY MEAT GLAZE GLACE DE VIANDE ORDINAIRE (M.)

Thoroughly reduce clear and greaseless brown stock by boiling several times, straining the stock through cheesecloth after each boiling. When the glaze is sufficiently reduced—when it coats a spoon dipped into it—pour into small jars and keep in the refrigerator.

Note: Meat glaze can also be made from white veal stock.

CHICKEN or GAME GLAZE GLACE DE VOLAILLE OU DE GIBIER (M.)

Make exactly like Ordinary Meat Glaze, above, using either chicken or game stock.

Note: Except for a few special recipes requiring meat glaze as an additional ingredient, it is better to use this glaze very sparingly. Stocks and sauces should have their own special flavor and quality, if they are properly made, and it is useless—even harmful—to strengthen the flavor by adding a rather large amount of meat glaze. Meat glazes are only practical in large restaurants, where there is a ready supply of bones and meat trimmings still containing sufficient natural juices to be reduced into the concentrated gravy we call meat glaze.

MATIGNON (M.)

A *matignon* is a sort of vegetable mash used to cover meats that are braised or stewed for a long time. The usual proportions are 4 carrots, 2 onions, ½ stalk celery, and parsley roots, all sliced thin; powdered thyme and bay leaf, pepper and salt. Cook slowly in butter or fat until the vegetables form a pulp. If the *matignon* is to be used with meat dishes, cook a little chopped ham with it.

MIREPOIX

RICH MIREPOIX FOR ESPAGNOLE SAUCE MIREPOIX GRASSE POUR ESPAGNOLE (M.)

Dice in large pieces 4 carrots, 2 onions, ½ stalk celery, and 8 oz. lean bacon. Brown everything in a stewpan, adding a sprig of thyme, a bay leaf, and a few branches of parsley. When the vegetables are well browned, add to sauces or stocks.

MEDIUM MIREPOIX FOR BRAISED DISHES MIREPOIX MOYENNE POUR PIÈCE BRAISÉE (M.)

Dice very fine the same quantity of vegetables listed in the preceding recipe. This is called a *salpicon*. Brown in butter until it forms a mash, seasoning with salt and pepper; add powdered thyme and bay leaf. Pour in ½ cup white wine and reduce. Add some chopped ham if a rich mirepoix is desired.

Note: In French cooking the word *salpicon* refers to any ingredient diced into about ⅛-in. cubes. We speak of a salpicon of fish, chicken, game, sweetbreads, ham, truffles, or vegetables. These are *simple* salpicons. A *compound* salpicon consists of several harmonious ingredients blended with a sauce. Example: *salpicon chasseur, salpicon financier, à la reine,* etc.

MIREPOIX BORDELAISE FOR CRAYFISH MIREPOIX BORDELAISE POUR ÉCREVISSES (M.)

Dice fine 4 oz. carrots, 4 oz. onion, and ½ oz. parsley (or chop fine and squeeze in a cloth to extract the water). Add a pinch of powdered thyme and bay leaf. Cover and cook slowly and thoroughly in butter. Place in a jar covered with waxed paper and save until needed.

ROUX

This is the thickening medium that is combined with stock to make sauces.

WHITE ROUX ROUX BLANC (M.)

Melt 1 lb. butter without browning it. Add 1½ lb. sifted flour to the butter. Mix well with a spatula. Cook at low heat for a few minutes, stirring constantly. This roux is used in making Béchamel Sauce and Velouté.

GOLDEN ROUX ROUX BLOND (M.)

Make the same as White Roux, using the same amounts of butter and flour. Cook the roux a little longer until it becomes slightly golden in color. Use in making sauces for poultry, sweetbreads, etc.

BROWN ROUX ROUX BRUN (M.)

Like White or Golden Roux, Brown Roux should, in principle, be made with butter. However, in current usage the butter is often replaced with fat from the soup pot after the fat has been carefully purified and clarified. This makes an excellent roux, and one much less expensive than that made with butter. Brown Roux is made with the same proportions of butter (or fat) and flour as the other roux, but it must cook very slowly, at a moderate heat, and much longer than the others to give it its brown color. It is used to bind brown sauces, especially Espagnole Sauce.

Note: Brown Roux made with butter must be watched very carefully or the butter, which quickly turns black, will give the flour a bitter taste. We advise using some of the good fat left over from roasting, which should always be on hand in a well-organized household.

BROWN SAUCES

BASIC SAUCES

ESPAGNOLE or **SPANISH SAUCE** SAUCE ESPAGNOLE (E.) (*For 5 qt.*)

Brown Roux (p. 137) for binding: 1½ lb.; Brown Stock (p. 134) : 12 qt.; Mirepoix (below) for flavoring: 6 oz. diced pork fat, 10 oz. diced carrots and 6 oz. diced onions, 2 sprigs of thyme, 2 small bay leaves.

Preparation: (1) Bring 8 qt. stock to a boil; add the roux, mixing it well with a spatula or wire whisk, and bring to a boil again, constantly stirring. Reduce the heat and cook at a slow, even boil.

(2) Add the Mirepoix, prepared as follows: melt the pork fat in a frying pan and add the diced carrots and onions, thyme and bay leaves; heat until the vegetables are lightly browned. Carefully drain off all the fat and put the vegetables into the sauce. Pour 1 glass white wine into the frying pan and reduce by ½. Add this also to the sauce and cook the sauce slowly 1 hr., skimming frequently.

(3) Strain the sauce through a cone-shaped sieve into another stewpan, pressing the Mirepoix lightly. Add another 2 qt. stock and simmer slowly and steadily 2 hr. Strain the sauce into an earthenware dish and spoon it until it is completely cool.

(4) The next day put the sauce into a thick-bottomed casserole or pot with 2 more qt. stock, 1 qt. tomato purée or the equivalent in fresh tomatoes, about 4 lb. If tomato purée is used, we advise putting it into the oven first until it is almost brown, to destroy the acidity. The tomato will help to clarify the sauce and, at the same time, give it a more appetizing color. Bring the sauce to a quick boil over a hot fire while stirring briskly with a spatula or wire whisk. Lower the flame and cook at a slow boil 1 hr., skimming carefully from time to time. Strain through a sieve and spoon it until it is completely cool.

Note: There is no way of knowing how many times this sauce will have to be skimmed and boiled to remove the impurities and excess fat. It all depends on the quality of the stock used in its preparation. If the very finest stock is used, it should be possible to prepare Espagnole Sauce in 6 hr.

SEMIGLAZE SAUCE SAUCE DEMI-GLACE (E.)

The sauce commonly called Semiglaze is really Espagnole Sauce (p. 137) at the height of its perfection, after the final boiling and skimming. It is finished by adding meat glaze or other glaze and is seasoned with some wine, which naturally changes its character and determines how it is to be used.

Note: We advise always adding the wine off the stove. Boiling will make the wine evaporate before it can give any flavor to the sauce.

For these basic sauces, we should like to remark, one may borrow indiscriminately from the recipes of Escoffier or Montagné, both stars of equal magnitude in the culinary firmament. All authors of cookbooks have drawn upon these same modern masters for their information and references. Even simple recipes for home cooking are based upon their works. The same is true of easier recipes by Heyraud, Pellaprat, and other authors to be found further on in this work, recipes that will not frighten the home cook.

BROWN SAUCES (COMBINATIONS)

BIGARADE SAUCE SAUCE BIGARADE (E.)

For braised duckling: strain, skim off the fat, and reduce the stock made from braising the duckling. After reducing the stock, strain it again through cheesecloth and thin it with the juice of 4 oranges and 1 lemon per qt. sauce.

For pot-roasted duckling: skim the fat off the stock, bind it with a little arrowroot mixed with 1 oz. caramelized sugar dissolved in 1½ tbsp. vinegar; add orange and lemon juice as above.

Both of the preceding recipes should be finished with 2 tbsp. orange peel and 1 tbsp. lemon peel, cut julienne style—in very thin, long strips—and well blanched.

BORDELAISE SAUCE SAUCE BORDELAISE (E.)

Reduce 1½ cups red wine, with 2 tbsp. chopped shallots, mignonette pepper, thyme, and ½ bay leaf, to ½ cup. Add 3 oz. Espagnole Sauce (p. 137); simmer 15 min., skimming from time to time, and strain through a cloth or a sieve.

Season to taste with 1 tbsp. melted meat glaze, juice of ¼ lemon, 2 oz. beef marrow diced or cut in rings and poached.

Especially good with grilled red meats.

Note: It should be noted that nowadays Bordelaise Sauce is wrongly prepared with red wine instead of with white wine, as it was made originally.

BOURGUIGNONNE SAUCE SAUCE BOURGUIGNONNE (E.)

Take 3 pt. good red wine seasoned with 5 sliced shallots, parsley sprigs, thyme, ½ bay leaf, 1 oz. mushroom peelings, and reduce by ½. Strain through cheesecloth; bind with butter kneaded with flour (1½ oz. butter and 1 oz. flour); when finished, add 3 oz. butter and season with a little cayenne pepper.

To be used with egg dishes and other household specialties.

CHARCUTIÈRE SAUCE SAUCE CHARCUTIÈRE (E.)

Add to 1 qt. Robert Sauce (p. 144), just before serving, 4 oz. gherkins cut in short, thick julienne strips.

Used with grilled pork and other meats requiring a highly seasoned sauce.

CHASSEUR SAUCE I SAUCE CHASSEUR (E.)

Sauté in butter 6 oz. sliced raw mushrooms with 2½ tbsp. chopped shallots. Sauté for a few min., add 1½ cups white wine, and reduce by ½. Add 1½ cups Tomato Sauce (p. 146) and 1 cup Semiglaze Sauce (p. 138); boil a few minutes, and finish with 6 oz. butter and 1½ tbsp. chopped chervil and tarragon.

CHASSEUR SAUCE II SAUCE CHASSEUR (E.)

Lightly brown 6 oz. sliced raw mushrooms in butter and oil. Add 1 tbsp. chopped shallots and almost immediately pour off ½ the fat. Moisten with 1 cup white wine and 1 small wineglass cognac and reduce by ½. Finish with 1½ cups Semiglaze Sauce (p. 138), ½ cup Tomato Sauce, (p. 146), and ½ tbsp. meat glaze. Boil 5 min., then sprinkle on 1 tsp. chopped parsley.

BROWN CHAUD-FROID (HOT-COLD) SAUCE SAUCE CHAUD-FROID BRUNE (E.) (*For 1 qt.*)

1½ pt. Semiglaze Sauce (p. 138), 3 oz. truffle essence, 1 pt. aspic jelly.

Add the truffle essence to the Semiglaze Sauce; reduce over a hot fire while adding the aspic jelly bit by bit. It should be reduced by about ⅓.

Correct the seasoning and see if the sauce has the proper consistency.

Finish with 1½ oz. Madeira or port; strain through cheesecloth, and cool by spooning until it will coat whatever ingredient it is to be used with.

BROWN CHAUD-FROID SAUCE FOR DUCK SAUCE CHAUD-FROID BRUNE POUR CANARDS (E.)

Prepare the sauce as directed above, substituting 4 oz. duck stock made from duck scraps for the truffle essence. Reduce until a little thicker than in the preceding recipe.

When it has been strained, finish with the juice of 3 oranges and 2 tbsp. orange peel cut in very thin julienne strips. The orange peel must be well blanched and drained until dry.

BROWN CHAUD-FROID SAUCE FOR GAME SAUCE CHAUD-FROID BRUNE POUR GIBIER (E.)

Make the same as ordinary Brown Chaud-Froid Sauce, above, replacing the truffle essence by 6 oz. Game Stock (p. 135) made from the carcasses of whatever game meat is to be covered.

TOMATO CHAUD-FROID SAUCE SAUCE CHAUD-FROID TOMATÉE (E.)

Take 1 qt. already reduced, very smooth tomato purée. Reduce it again, adding 1 pt. aspic jelly to the purée bit by bit; continue to cook until only 1 qt. sauce remains.

Strain through cheesecloth and spoon until the sauce is cool enough to use.

VENISON SAUCE SAUCE CHEVREUIL (E.)

Prepare 1 qt. Ordinary Poivrade Sauce (p. 143): (1) with a Mirepoix (p. 136) made with ham, if the sauce is to go with marinated meat; (2) with game trimmings, if it is to go with a piece of game. Strain through a sieve, pressing hard, skim, and add, a spoonful at a time, 3 oz. good red wine. Season with a little cayenne pepper and a pinch of sugar, and strain.

COLBERT SAUCE SAUCE COLBERT (E.)

This name has been wrongly given to Colbert Butter (p. 163), which is a Maître d'Hôtel Butter to which meat glaze has been added. To differentiate this butter from Chateaubriand Sauce (p. 266) some cooks add tarragon to it, but this is not an absolute rule. In fact, the two preparations are entirely different. Chateaubriand Sauce is a thin meat glaze with melted butter and chopped parsley added, whereas Colbert Sauce or Butter has butter as its principal ingredient, with the meat glaze only for extra flavoring.

DIABLE SAUCE SAUCE DIABLE (E.)

Since this sauce is generally used only in small quantities, we shall give proportions to make 6 oz. sauce. Take 1½ cups white wine with 3 chopped shallots and reduce by ⅔. Add 6 oz. Semiglaze Sauce (p. 138) and boil for a few minutes. Season generously with cayenne pepper. Especially good with grilled chicken or pigeon.

Note: This sauce is made just as frequently with vinegar instead of white wine, with a final addition of *fines herbes* (finely chopped parsley, tarragon, chives, and, sometimes, chervil). However, we prefer the recipe given above.

ESCOFFIER DIABLE SAUCE SAUCE DIABLE ESCOFFIER (E.)

This sauce may now be bought, already prepared, in stores. All that is necessary is to add freshly softened butter to it. It goes especially well with grilled or poached fish, but may be used with any kind of grilled meat.

DIANE SAUCE SAUCE DIANE (E.)

Prepare 15 oz. very smooth, thick, highly seasoned Poivrade Sauce (p. 143). Add 12 oz. whipped cream (or 6 oz. whipping cream that doubles in quantity when whipped) and 2 tbsp. chopped truffles and chopped hard-boiled egg whites. To be used with venison chops, noisettes, and steaks.

DUXELLES SAUCE SAUCE DUXELLES (E.)

Take 6 oz. white wine and 6 oz. mushroom cooking juices containing 2 tbsp. chopped shallots and reduce by ⅔. Add 1 pt. Semiglaze Sauce (p. 138),

4 oz. tomato purée, and 4 tbsp. Dry Duxelles (p. 176). Boil 5 min. and finish with ½ tbsp. chopped parsley. Used especially with gratinated dishes.

Note: Duxelles Sauce, which is frequently confused with Italienne Sauce (p. 142), should never be made with ham or pickled tongue added.

TARRAGON SAUCE SAUCE ESTRAGON (E.) (*For 1 pt.*)

Drop 1 oz. branches of tarragon into 6 oz. boiling white wine. Cover and let steep 10 min. Add 1 pt. Semiglaze Sauce (p. 138) or thickened Veal Gravy (p. 134); reduce by ⅓, strain, and finish with 1 tsp. chopped tarragon. Good with noisettes of white meats, fowl, etc.

FINANCIÈRE SAUCE SAUCE FINANCIÈRE (J.)

Madeira Sauce (p. 142) flavored with truffle essence.

FINES HERBES SAUCE SAUCE AUX FINES HERBES (E.)

Drop into 6 oz. boiling white wine a good pinch each of parsley leaves, chervil leaves, tarragon, and chives. Let steep 20 min.; strain through a cloth and add 1 qt. Semiglaze Sauce (p. 138) or thickened Veal Gravy (p. 134). Boil a few minutes and finish with 2½ tbsp. chopped herbs (the same as those used in the beginning) in equal proportions and a dash of lemon juice.

GENEVOISE SAUCE SAUCE GENEVOISE (E.)

Brown in butter a finely chopped Mirepoix made of: 4 oz. carrots, 3 oz. onions, a pinch of thyme and bay leaf, 1 oz. parsley. Add 2 lb. salmon heads and a pinch of mignonette pepper and cook slowly ¼ hr. Drain off the butter and pour in 1 qt. red wine. Boil until reduced by ½, add 1 pt. meatless Espagnole Sauce (p. 137); cook slowly 1 hr. Press through a strainer, let stand a few minutes, and skim off the fat. Add 1 pt. red wine and 1 pt. fish stock; boil down until the sauce has the desired consistency, skimming off impurities. Strain and season with 1 tbsp. anchovy essence and 6 oz. butter added while stirring slowly. Use with salmon or trout.

Note: This sauce was originally called Génoise by Carême. However, first Reculet and then Gouffé called it Genevoise, which doesn't make much sense, since no red wine is made in Geneva. Although wrong, this name has prevailed and is the one we use—noting, however, that whether under the name of Génoise or Genevoise, Carême, Reculet, Dubois, and Gouffé all call for the use of red wine.

GODARD SAUCE SAUCE GODARD (E.)

Add a Mirepoix made with ham (p. 136) to 12 oz. champagne or dry white wine and reduce by ½. Add 1 qt. Semiglaze Sauce (p. 138) and 6 oz. mushroom essence, cook slowly 10 min., and strain through a cone-shaped sieve. Reduce by about ⅓ and strain again. Used especially with Godard Garnish (p. 181).

GRAND-VENEUR SAUCE I SAUCE GRAND-VENEUR (E.)

Make a clear Poivrade Sauce with venison stock (p. 143), then add, per qt. sauce, 3 oz. hare's blood diluted with 3 oz. Marinade (see p. 167). Heat a few minutes, taking care not to let the sauce boil, and strain through a sieve.

GRAND-VENEUR SAUCE II SAUCE GRAND-VENEUR (E.)

Thin Poivrade Sauce (p. 143), with 2 tbsp. red-currant jelly and 7 oz. cream added per qt. sauce. To be used with venison.

GRATIN SAUCE SAUCE GRATIN (E.)

Take 9 oz. white wine and 9 oz. fish stock (made from the fish with which the sauce is to be used) containing 1½ tbsp. chopped shallots, and reduce by ½. Add 3 tbsp. Dry Duxelles (p. 176) and 15 oz. meatless Espagnole (p. 137) or Semiglaze Sauce (p. 138) and simmer 5-6 min. Finish with ½ tbsp. chopped parsley. Use with fish prepared au gratin.

HUSSARDE SAUCE SAUCE HUSSARDE (E.)

Cook 2 onions and 2 shallots, chopped fine, in butter until golden brown. Pour in 12 oz. white wine, reduce by ½, and add: 12 oz. Semiglaze Sauce (p. 138), 2 tbsp. tomato purée, 6 oz. white stock, 3 oz. lean, raw ham, 1 crushed clove garlic, and a *bouquet garni.* Cook slowly 25–30 min. Remove the ham and strain the sauce through a sieve, pressing it with a spoon. Heat and finish with the ham diced fine, a little grated horseradish, and a good pinch of chopped parsley. Used for grilled or spitted red meats.

ITALIENNE or **ITALIAN SAUCE I** SAUCE ITALIENNE (E.)

Add to 1 qt. Semiglaze Sauce containing tomatoes (p. 138): 4 tbsp. Dry Duxelles (p. 176) and 5 oz. lean, cooked ham, diced fine. Cook 5–6 min. Finish with 1 tbsp. chopped parsley, chervil, and tarragon.

Note: When this sauce is to be served with fish, reduce the fish stock and add it to the sauce, but leave out the ham.

LYONNAISE SAUCE SAUCE LYONNAISE (E.)

Lightly brown in butter 3 medium-sized, chopped onions so that they are almost completely cooked. Pour in 6 oz. white wine and 6 oz. vinegar, reduce by ⅔, and add 1 pt. Semiglaze Sauce (p. 138). Cook slowly 5–6 min., skimming, and strain through a sieve.

Note: Depending upon the type of dish with which this sauce is to be served, the onion may be left in the sauce or strained off.

MADEIRA SAUCE SAUCE MADÈRE (E.)

This is a Semiglaze Sauce (p. 138) that has been reduced and then restored to its normal consistency by adding, off the stove, 3 oz. Madeira per qt. sauce.

MATELOTE SAUCE SAUCE MATELOTE (E.)

Take 9 oz. fish Court Bouillon (water with herbs, in which fish is cooked: see p. 293) made with red wine and 1 oz. mushroom peelings; boil until reduced by ⅔. Add 1 qt. meatless Espagnole Sauce (p. 137), bring to a boil, strain, and finish with 6 oz. butter and a pinch of cayenne pepper.

MARROW SAUCE SAUCE MOELLE (E.)

This sauce is made exactly like Bordelaise Sauce (p. 138). No butter is used except when the sauce is to accompany a vegetable. In any case, the sauce has added to it, before serving, 6–7 oz. finely diced and poached beef marrow and 1 tbsp. chopped and blanched parsley per qt. sauce.

MOSCOVITE SAUCE SAUCE MOSCOVITE (E.)

Have ready 1 pt. Poivrade Sauce (p. 143) made with venison stock. Add to this sauce 3 oz. Malaga, 1 tbsp. juniper-berry juice, 1½ oz. grilled pine nuts or grilled, shredded almonds, 1½ oz. dried currants soaked in warm water. Serve with venison.

PÉRIGUEUX SAUCE SAUCE PÉRIGUEUX (E.)

To 1 pt. full-bodied and rather thick Semiglaze Sauce (p. 138), add 4 oz. truffle essence and 4 oz. chopped truffles. Serve with small entrées such as timbales, hot meat pies, etc.

PIQUANT SAUCE SAUCE PIQUANTE (E.)

Add 2½ tbsp. chopped shallots to 9 oz. white wine and 9 oz. good vinegar; boil until reduced by ½. Add 1 qt. Espagnole Sauce (p. 137) and cook 10 min., skimming. Finish off the stove with 2 tbsp. chopped gherkins, parsley, chervil, and tarragon. This sauce is usually served with grilled, boiled, or roast pork. It is also good with boiled beef and sliced meats.

ORDINARY POIVRADE SAUCE SAUCE POIVRADE ORDINAIRE (E.)

Cook in oil, until the vegetables are brown, a Mirepoix (p. 136) made of 4 oz. carrots, 3 oz. onions, sprigs of parsley, bits of thyme and bay leaf. Pour in 3 oz. vinegar, 6 oz. Marinade (p. 166), and reduce by ⅔. Add 1 qt. Espagnole Sauce (p. 137) and cook slowly ¾ hr. Ten min. before straining the sauce, add 8 crushed peppercorns. If the pepper is put in earlier, it will hurt the sauce somewhat, since the taste of pepper will be too pronounced. Strain through a sieve, using a little pressure, and thin the sauce with 6 oz. Marinade; simmer 35 min., skimming, until reduced to the desired consistency. Strain again and add 2 oz. butter. Serve with marinated or nonmarinated meats.

POIVRADE SAUCE FOR GAME SAUCE POIVRADE POUR GIBIER (E.)

Brown in oil a Mirepoix (p. 136) made of 5 oz. carrots, 5 oz. onions, 2 lb. leftover ground-game meat, bits of thyme and bay leaf, and sprigs of parsley. When brown, drain off the oil, add 9 oz. vinegar and 6 oz. white wine, and reduce completely. Add 1 qt. Espagnole Sauce (p. 137), 2 qt. brown game stock, and 1 qt. Marinade (p. 166). Cover and cook slowly—in the oven, if possible—for 3½ hr. About 8 min. before straining the sauce, add 12 large crushed peppercorns. Press through a strainer. Thin the sauce with 1 cup Game Stock (p. 135) and 1 cup Marinade; simmer ¾ hr., skimming, or until reduced to 1 qt. Strain for the last time and add 3 oz. butter.

Note: Although game sauces are not usually buttered, we advise adding a little butter. Sauce prepared this way is slightly less hot, but gains in smoothness and finesse.

PORTUGAISE or **PORTUGUESE SAUCE** SAUCE PORTUGAISE (E.) (*For 1 qt.*)

Chop a large onion very fine and heat it in hot oil until it begins to turn golden, then add 1½ lb. peeled, crushed, and drained tomatoes, a clove of crushed garlic, salt, pepper, and a little sugar if the tomato is acid. Cover the pan and cook slowly. To finish the sauce, add a little tomato essence, the necessary amount of clear Tomato Sauce (p. 146), 3 oz. melted meat glaze, and 1 tbsp. fresh crushed parsley.

PROVENÇAL SAUCE SAUCE PROVENÇALE (E.)

Peel, crush, and drain 12 good tomatoes. Put them into a flat stewpan containing 7 oz. hot smoking oil; season with salt, pepper, and a pinch of powdered sugar; add a small clove of crushed garlic and 1 tsp. chopped parsley. Cover and cook slowly ½ hr.

Note: This sauce is made in many different ways, but we have decided to give the true bourgeois recipe, which is really a tomato fondue.

RÉGENCE SAUCE SAUCE RÉGENCE (E.)

Take 9 oz. Rhine wine containing 3 oz. precooked Mirepoix (p. 136) and 1 oz. raw truffle peelings, and reduce by ½. If truffles are out of season, they may be replaced by 3 oz. truffle essence. Add 1½ pt. Semiglaze Sauce (p. 138), cook a few minutes more, skimming, and strain. Used for meat dishes following the soup course.

ROBERT SAUCE SAUCE ROBERT (E.) (*For 1 pt.*)

Cook a large, rather finely chopped onion in butter without browning it. Add 4 oz. white wine, reduce by ⅔, add 6 oz. Semiglaze Sauce (p. 138), and cook 10 min. on a slow fire. Strain through a cone-shaped sieve (or not—this is optional) and add, off the fire, a pinch of powdered sugar and 1 tbsp. mustard. Usually served with grilled pork.

Note: Robert Sauce must not be allowed to boil after the mustard has been added.

ROMAINE or **ROMAN SAUCE** SAUCE ROMAINE (E.)

Cook 2 oz. sugar until it becomes a light caramel and dissolve it in 3 oz. vinegar. After the sugar has been dissolved, add 12 oz. Espagnole Sauce (p. 137) and 6 oz. Game Stock (p. 135). Reduce by ¼, strain through a sieve, and add 1 oz. grilled pine nuts and 1 oz. sultanas and 1 oz. dried currants picked and soaked in warm water.

Note: This sauce is usually served with venison, but it is also very good with marinated meat if the Game Stock is replaced by ordinary Brown Stock (p. 134).

ROUENNAISE SAUCE SAUCE ROUENNAISE (E.) (*For 1 pt.*)

Prepare 8 oz. Bordelaise Sauce (p. 138), taking care to use a fine red wine. Press 3 medium-sized duck livers through a sieve and poach this purée in the Bordelaise Sauce without letting it boil. Boiling would cause the purée to become granulated. Strain the sauce and season to taste. This is the special sauce for roast Rouen duck.

SALMI SAUCE SAUCE SALMIS (E.)

The basis of this sauce, which is similar to a thick soup, is always the same. Only the liquid ingredients vary, depending on the type of bird or game used and whether the game is fat or lean.

Brown 6 oz. finely chopped Mirepoix (p. 136) lightly in butter. Add the skin and chopped carcasses of the birds or game with which the sauce is to be served. Pour in 6 oz. white wine, reduce by ⅔, and add 1 qt. Semiglaze Sauce (p. 138). Cook slowly ¾ hr. and press hard through a strainer to extract the quintessence of the flavorings and the carcasses. Thin this thick gravy with 8 oz. stock made from the kind of bird or game it will accompany. If the game is lean and the recipe recommends a meatless base, mushroom cooking juice should be substituted for the stock. Cook ¾–1 hr., skimming frequently, or until the sauce has been reduced by ⅓. Bring to the proper consistency and quality by adding mushroom cooking juice and truffle essence. Strain, and add a little butter.

Note: The addition of about 2 oz. butter is optional.

TURTLE SAUCE SAUCE TORTUE (E.)

To 3 oz. boiling Veal Stock (p. 134) add the following: a good pinch of sage, a small pinch of marjoram, a pinch of rosemary, a basil leaf, a pinch of thyme and bay leaf, a bit of parsley, and 1 oz. mushroom peelings. Cover, let steep 25 min., and add 4 peppercorns 2 min. before straining. Strain through cheesecloth, then add 14 oz. Semiglaze Sauce (p. 138) mixed with 6 oz. Tomato Sauce (p. 146). Reduce by ¼ and strain through a sieve. Flavor with 2 oz. Madeira, a little truffle essence, and cayenne pepper.

Note: Though this sauce should have a certain tang, the cayenne should be measured with the greatest care.

VENISON SAUCE SAUCE VENAISON (E.)

To 1½ pt. prepared Poivrade Sauce for Game (p. 143), add 3 tbsp. melted red-currant jelly mixed with 3 oz. cream. The jelly and cream should be added off the stove and just before serving. This sauce is used with big game animals.

ZINGARA SAUCE SAUCE ZINGARA (E.)

Reduce 6 oz. white wine by ⅔ and some mushroom cooking juice by ½. Add 8 oz. Semiglaze Sauce (p. 138), 5 oz. Tomato Sauce (p. 146), 2 oz. white stock, and cook 5–6 min., skimming. Season with a pinch of cayenne pepper and finish with a julienne made of 3 oz. lean ham and pickled tongue, 2 oz. mushrooms, and 1 oz. truffles. Special sauce for veal or fowl.

WHITE SAUCES

BASIC SAUCES

ALLEMANDE or **PARISIENNE SAUCE** SAUCE ALLEMANDE OT PARISIENNE[1] (M.)
(*For 1 qt.*)

Mix 5 egg yolks with 8 oz. cold white stock and 2 oz. mushroom essence (or mushroom cooking juice boiled down). Add 1 qt. very smooth Velouté (p. 147). Season with a little freshly ground pepper and a dash of grated nutmeg. Mix well. Cook in a flat, heavy-bottomed sautéing pan until the sauce is thick enough to cling to the spatula. Strain. Keep the sauce hot in a *bain-marie* or double boiler, the surface of the sauce dabbed with butter. Just before serving, add 4–5 oz. butter.

Note: This sauce may be slightly acidulated by adding a little lemon juice.

BÉCHAMEL SAUCE SAUCE BÉCHAMEL OT BÉCHAMELLE AU GRAS (M.)
(*For 2½ qt.*)

Moisten ¾ lb. White Roux (p. 136) with 2½ qt. milk previously boiled. Mix well. Add to the sauce 6 oz. diced lean veal cooked in butter till white with 2 oz. sliced onion. Season with salt, pepper, and a little nutmeg, and add a small *bouquet garni.* Simmer 1 hr. and strain. Keep hot in a *bain-marie* or double boiler, dabbing the surface of the sauce with butter to prevent a skin from forming.

Note: This sauce may be made meatless by leaving out the veal.

SUPRÊME SAUCE SAUCE SUPRÊME (M.) (*For 1 qt.*)

This sauce marks the highest degree of succulence a Velouté can reach. Here is how it is made:

Preparation: To 1 qt. very smooth Velouté (p. 147), add 1 qt. Chicken White Stock (p. 134) and 4 oz. mushroom essence. Cook over a hot fire, constantly stirring with a spatula, until the sauce has been reduced by ⅔. Add 6 oz. fresh heavy cream and reduce until the sauce clings to the spatula. Strain through a sieve and, just before serving, add 4 oz. butter.

TOMATO SAUCE SAUCE TOMATE (E.) (*For 1 qt.*)

Take 6 lb. fresh tomatoes and cut them in ½; remove the seeds without pressing the tomatoes; chop them and put them into a stewpan with 3 oz. butter or, preferably, 5 tbsp. olive oil; add ½ tbsp. salt, a pinch of pepper, and a bouquet of parsley containing ½ clove of garlic. Cover the pan and cook 30–35 min. over a low fire. Strain through a fine sieve and pour the sauce into an earthenware dish; spread a little butter over the surface, and keep in reserve. If no fresh tomatoes are available, canned tomatoes will do.

---

[1] Note by Escoffier: "We know of no reason that justifies calling this sauce German rather than Parisian. The name Parisian has been adopted by some chefs, but not so generally as one might wish." Therefore, in this book, you will find recipes using either name, depending upon the author.

VELOUTÉ or **RICH WHITE SAUCE** VELOUTÉ OR SAUCE BLANCHE GRASSE (M.)

(*For 3 qt.*)

Velouté is not a sauce in itself but only the first step in the preparation of Allemande Sauce and Suprême Sauce. The usual proportions are: 12 oz. flour, 9 oz. sweet butter, 3½ qt. white stock.

Preparation: Make the usual White Roux (p. 136) by mixing the flour in melted butter and cooking it without browning. Let the mixture cool slightly before adding the white stock, which should also be merely warm and not hot. If the mixture is too hot, the Velouté will not be smooth. Once the stock and roux have been mixed, heat over a hot fire, stirring constantly. Skim the sauce and let it simmer about 1½ hr. Strain into an earthenware bowl and spoon frequently while cooling. Dab the surface with butter.

FISH VELOUTÉ VELOUTÉ DE POISSON (M.)

Prepare the same as above, substituting fish stock for the white stock.

WHITE SAUCES (COMBINATIONS)

AURORE SAUCE SAUCE AURORE (E.)

Purée of very red tomatoes added to the Velouté (above), the proportions being 3 parts Velouté to 1 part tomato purée. Finish the sauce with 4 oz. butter per qt. sauce. Serve with eggs, white meats, and fowl.

AURORE SAUCE FOR FISH SAUCE AURORE (MAIGRE) (E.)

Follow the recipe given above, using Fish Velouté (above) with the tomato purée. Finish with 5 oz. butter per qt. sauce.

BANQUIÈRE SAUCE SAUCE BANQUIÈRE (M.)

Put 8 oz. chicken Velouté and 6 oz. brown veal stock into a stewpan. Reduce by ⅓ over a hot fire, meanwhile adding gradually 3 oz. fresh heavy cream and 2 oz. Madeira. Remove from the stove and add 4 oz. butter. Strain. For chicken, sweetbreads, and ragouts of cockscombs and cock's kidneys.

Note: This sauce is also called Pâtissière Sauce.

BÉARNAISE SAUCE SAUCE BÉARNAISE (M.)

In a small stewpan reduce almost completely 6 oz. vinegar (or, if this is too strong, a mixture of 3 oz. vinegar and 3 oz. white wine) containing 1 oz. finely chopped shallots, 2 oz. crushed tarragon and 1 oz. crushed chervil, a pinch of salt, a good pinch of mignonette pepper, and a dash of powdered thyme and bay leaf. Allow the vinegar and herbs to cool, then add 5 or 6 egg yolks (depending on size) mixed with 1 tbsp. water. Heat over a very low flame or in a double boiler, beating with a wire whisk. As soon as the yolks begin to thicken a little, add 1 lb. melted butter bit by bit, continuously whipping. When the mixture is very smooth and has the consistency of mayonnaise, strain through a sieve. Just before serving, add 1 tbsp. chopped tarragon and ½ tbsp. chopped chervil and season with a dash of cayenne pepper or paprika and, if needed, a dash of lemon juice. Serve with grilled meats or fish.

Note: In spite of its name, this sauce does not come from Béarn (ancient province in the Pyrenees). In the anecdotal history of cookery we learn that it was first made at the Pavillon Henri IV at Saint-Germain-en-Laye.

TOMATO-BÉARNAISE or CHORON SAUCE SAUCE BÉARNAISE TOMATÉE OR SAUCE CHORON (M.)

Prepare the Béarnaise Sauce as described above (p. 147) and add ⅓ its volume of very thick Tomato Sauce (p. 146).

Note: Usually, chopped tarragon and chervil are not added to Choron Sauce. This sauce is sometimes incorrectly called French Sauce.

BEAUHARNAIS SAUCE SAUCE BEAUHARNAIS (M.)

Add to the Béarnaise Sauce (p. 147) ⅓ its volume of very thick tarragon purée. Strain. Used for tournedos and noisettes.

Note: This sauce should be pale green.

BUTTER or BÂTARDE SAUCE SAUCE AU BEURRE OR SAUCE BÂTARDE (E.)

Combine 2 oz. flour with 2 oz. melted butter. Pour over it 14 oz. boiling water containing a pinch of salt; beat briskly with a wire whisk; add the yolks of 5 eggs mixed with 2 tbsp. cream and a dash of lemon juice; strain. Remove from the stove and finish with 12 oz. fresh butter. Serve with asparagus or boiled fish.

Note: We advise keeping this sauce warm in a *bain-marie* or double boiler after it has been bound, and not adding the butter until just before serving.

BRETONNE SAUCE SAUCE BRETONNE (M.)

Prepare the same as Bretonne Sauce for Fish (below), substituting chicken Velouté (p. 147) for the fish stock.

BRETONNE SAUCE FOR FISH SAUCE BRETONNE (MAIGRE) (M.)

Lightly braise in butter a thin julienne of equal proportions of celery, leeks, and onions. Add ¼ its volume of raw mushrooms also cut in thin julienne strips. Pour in 3 oz. fish stock. Reduce almost completely. Remove from the stove and, just before serving, add 6 oz. White-Wine Sauce (p. 155) or Normande Sauce (p. 153). Mix well.

Note: Sometimes this sauce is completed with 2 tbsp. julienne of truffles.

CARDINAL SAUCE SAUCE CARDINAL (E.)

Add to 3 cups Béchamel Sauce (p. 146): 1½ oz. fish stock and 1½ oz. truffle essence, reduced by ¼; 3 oz. cream. Finish off the stove with 4 oz. very red Lobster Butter (p. 164) and season with a pinch of cayenne pepper. Serve with fish.

CHANTILLY SAUCE SAUCE CHANTILLY (M.)

Take some Suprême Sauce (p. 146) that has been reduced until very thick and add, at the last moment, ⅓ its volume of stiff whipped cream. (This mixture must be made off the stove.)

Note: A Hollandaise Sauce (p. 151) with whipped cream is sometimes served under this same name. Serve with fowl, sweetbreads, asparagus.

ORDINARY WHITE CHAUD-FROID SAUCE SAUCE CHAUD-FROID BLANCHE ORDINAIRE (M.)

Mix 15 oz. Allemande Sauce (p. 146) with 12 oz. white chicken jelly and reduce by ⅓. While cooking, add 6 oz. fresh cream. Strain through cheesecloth. Spoon until cool. Serve with fowl, poached and soft-boiled eggs, sweetbreads.

WHITE CHAUD-FROID SAUCE WITH SUPRÊME SAUCE SAUCE CHAUD-FROID BLANCHE AU SUPRÊME (M.)

Take 15 oz. chicken Velouté (p. 147), 15 oz. Chicken Aspic (p. 169), and 7 oz. fresh heavy cream; cook until reduced by ⅓. Serve with the same dishes as above.

WHITE CHAUD-FROID SAUCE WITH VARIOUS ESSENCES SAUCE CHAUD-FROID BLANCHE AUX ESSENCES DIVERSES (M.)

Prepare the sauce as described above, adding while cooking about 6 oz. of one or another of the following essences: celery, mushroom, tarragon, truffle, etc. Serve with the same dishes as Ordinary White Chaud-Froid Sauce.

CHAUD-FROID SAUCE À LA MADRILÈNE or PINK CHAUD-FROID SAUCE SAUCE CHAUD-FROID À LA MADRILÈNE OR SAUCE CHAUD-FROID ROSE (M.)

Prepare Ordinary White Chaud-Froid Sauce, above, and add, before straining, 4 oz. concentrated tomato juice; season with paprika and finish, after straining, with 2 tbsp. peeled pimentos cut in julienne strips, cooked in consommé and drained. Serve with the same dishes as other *chaud-froid* sauces.

PAPRIKA CHAUD-FROID SAUCE SAUCE CHAUD-FROID AU PAPRIKA (M.)

When reducing Ordinary White Chaud-Froid Sauce, above, add 2 tbsp. chopped onion melted in butter, seasoned with paprika, and cooked in white wine. The color of this sauce should be slightly pink. Use like Ordinary White Chaud-Froid Sauce.

GREEN CHAUD-FROID SAUCE SAUCE CHAUD-FROID VERTE OR VERT-PRÉ (M.)

While reducing the Ordinary White Chaud-Froid Sauce, add 4 oz. green herbs steeped in white wine (chervil, tarragon, parsley, chives). Before straining the sauce, add 2 tbsp. tarragon and chervil purée in equal amounts. Serve with Chicken Chaud-Froid (p. 413) called *à la printanière* or *au vert-pré.*

CHIVRY SAUCE SAUCE CHIVRY (M.)

Steep some chervil, tarragon, parsley, chives, and fresh burnet in a little white wine. Add it to an ordinary Velouté (p. 147) and cook until it thickens. Finish with Green Butter (p. 163). Strain. Serve with eggs, poached chicken. braised sweetbreads, etc.

CHORON SAUCE SAUCE CHORON (M.)

Same as Tomato-Béarnaise Sauce (p. 148).

CURRY or **INDIENNE SAUCE** SAUCE AU CURRY or À L'INDIENNE (M.)

Prepare the same as the Curry Sauce that follows, replacing the Béchamel Sauce with chicken Velouté (p. 147). Serve with eggs, fowl, or braised sweetbreads.

Note: Other curry sauces will be found in the section dealing with Chicken Curry (p. 404).

CURRY or **INDIENNE SAUCE FOR FISH** SAUCE AU CURRY or À L'INDIENNE (MAIGRE) (M.)

Heat 2 oz. sliced onions in butter without letting them brown too much. Add ½ small peeled, diced apple; 1 small peeled, drained, crushed tomato; ½ clove crushed garlic; and a *bouquet garni* made of parsley root, celery root, thyme, and bay leaf. Sprinkle with 2 tbsp. curry powder. When this has been well blended, pour in 4 oz. coconut milk.[1] Reduce this mixture by ⅓; add 3 tbsp. Béchamel Sauce (p. 146) or Fish Velouté (p. 147). Mix well; strain through a sieve, pressing the sauce through. Bring the sauce to a boil. Finish, before serving, with 6 oz. heavy cream and juice of ½ lemon.

CURRY SAUCE SAUCE AU CURRY (M.)

Cook 2 oz. sliced onions in butter without letting them brown too much. Sprinkle with 2 tbsp. curry powder. Add a *bouquet garni* made of parsley and celery roots, thyme, and bay leaf. Pour in 12 oz. rather thin Béchamel Sauce (p. 146), 3 oz. fish stock, and 3 oz. coconut milk. Reduce by ⅓ and strain. Finish with heavy cream and lemon juice, as indicated in preceding recipe.

TARRAGON SAUCE SAUCE À L'ESTRAGON (M.)

Reduce almost completely 6 oz. white wine containing 1 oz. crushed tarragon. Add 12 oz. chicken Velouté (p. 147) and reduce again. Remove from the stove and add 4 tbsp. fresh cream and 2 tbsp. butter. Strain. Add 1 tbsp. chopped tarragon before serving. For eggs, fowl, and sweetbreads.

FINES HERBES SAUCE SAUCE AUX FINES HERBES (M.)

Take 6 oz. white wine containing 1 sliced shallot, 2 crushed parsley roots, and 1 dessertspoon crushed chervil; reduce by ⅔. Pour in 12 oz. chicken Velouté (p. 147) or, if the dish is meatless, Béchamel Sauce (p. 146). Boil 5 min. and strain. Before serving, add 4 tbsp. cream and 1 tsp. chopped tarragon. For poached eggs, fowl, and sweetbreads.

FRENCH SAUCE SAUCE À LA FRANÇAISE (M.)

Prepare as in recipe following, replacing the Béchamel Sauce with chicken Velouté (p. 147) made with mushroom essence. Finish the sauce with Crayfish Butter (p. 164). For poached eggs, fowl, sweetbreads.

---

[1]Coconut milk is extracted by grating the pulp of the nut, diluting it with warm water (or milk), and pressing it through a cloth.

FRENCH SAUCE FOR FISH SAUCE À LA FRANÇAISE (MAIGRE) (M.)

Reduce 12 oz. Béchamel Sauce (p. 146) diluted with 4 oz. fish stock. Add a clove of crushed garlic, a dash of nutmeg, and 2 tbsp. mushroom essence. Boil 5 min. and strain. Finish with 3 oz. crayfish tails.

Note: Carême, from whom Montagné adapted this recipe, states that this sauce goes very well with carp, pike, or salmon loaves and that it may be decorated with crayfish tails and fluted mushrooms. It was first served by Prince Paul of Württemberg.

HENRY IV SAUCE SAUCE HENRI IV (M.)

Take some very thick Béarnaise Sauce (p. 147) and add ⅔ its volume of thick Veal Stock (p. 134) reduced to a glaze. Serve with steaks and chops or with grilled or breaded and pan-fried fish fillets.

HOLLANDAISE or **ISIGNY SAUCE** SAUCE HOLLANDAISE OT ISIGNY (M.)

Reduce almost completely 1½ oz. water seasoned with a pinch of salt. Let the stewpan in which the salt water was boiled cool. When it is cold, put in 4 egg yolks diluted with 1 tbsp. cold water. Cook the yolks over a very low flame, constantly beating them with a wire whisk, until they have the consistency of rather thin mayonnaise. Add 1 lb. melted butter while still beating over the fire. If it becomes too thick, 1 or 2 tbsp. water may be added bit by bit to thin it. Season to taste and add a finger of lemon juice. Strain and keep hot in a *bain-marie* or double boiler.

Note: This is a typical French sauce with the delicious flavor of Normandy butter, which is its principal ingredient. It seems right to us, therefore, to call it Isigny Sauce. For meat or meatless dishes, this sauce has innumerable uses. It may be used to cover poached or soft-boiled eggs, with various vegetables boiled or cooked in butter, or with fowl and sweetbreads.

HONGROISE or **HUNGARIAN SAUCE** SAUCE HONGROISE (M.)

Make exactly like Hongroise Sauce for Fish (below), substituting chicken Velouté (p. 147) for Fish Velouté. Serve with eggs, fowl, sweetbreads, noisettes of lamb, veal cutlets.

HONGROISE or **HUNGARIAN SAUCE FOR FISH** SAUCE HONGROISE (MAIGRE) (M.)

Cook 1 medium-sized chopped onion in butter without letting it brown. Season with 1 tbsp. paprika. Add 3 oz. dry white wine and a *bouquet garni* made of parsley roots, thyme, and bay leaf. Reduce by ⅔. Add 9 oz. Fish Velouté (p. 147) and simmer 20 min. Add 3 oz. fresh heavy cream while simmering. Remove the *bouquet garni,* strain, and finish with 3 oz. butter.

IRISH SAUCE SAUCE À L'IRLANDAISE (M.)

To 12 oz. ordinary Hollandaise Sauce (above), add 1 tbsp. chopped, blanched mint leaves. Serve with boiled vegetables, soft-boiled or poached eggs, and giblets.

IVORY SAUCE SAUCE IVOIRE (M.)

Add 3 tbsp. white veal stock reduced to a glaze to 12 oz. Suprême Sauce (p. 146). Serve with poached chicken, soft-boiled or poached eggs, and giblets.

JOINVILLE SAUCE SAUCE JOINVILLE (M.)

To 9 oz. Normande Sauce (p. 153), add 3 oz. Crayfish Butter (p. 164) and 1 tbsp. champagne brandy set aflame.

MALTAISE or **MALTESE SAUCE** SAUCE MALTAISE (M.)

Add the grated peel of 1 orange (blood orange, preferably) and its juice to ordinary Hollandaise Sauce (p. 151) and strain.

MIKADO SAUCE SAUCE MIKADO (M.)

Make exactly like Maltaise Sauce (above), substituting the grated peel and juice of 2 tangerines for the orange. Special sauce for asparagus.

MORNAY SAUCE SAUCE MORNAY (E.)

Add 6 oz. stock of the fish with which the sauce is to be served to 1 qt. Béchamel Sauce (p. 146), reduce by ⅓, and add 2 oz. grated Gruyère and 2 oz. grated Parmesan cheese; heat until melted. Finish with 4 oz. butter. If used for other than fish dishes, leave out the fish stock.

MOUSSELINE SAUCE SAUCE MOUSSELINE (M.)

Mix 2 parts rather thick Hollandaise Sauce (p. 151) with 1 part whipped cream. The whipped cream should not be added until just before serving. For boiled or braised vegetables, especially asparagus.

MOUSSEUSE SAUCE or **VIRGIN BUTTER** SAUCE MOUSSEUSE OR BEURRE À LA VIERGE (M.)

Put 10 oz. soft butter into an earthenware dish heated with boiling water, but well dried. Season with a pinch of salt. Beat the butter with a wire whisk until it is very creamy, gradually adding a finger of lemon juice and 2 or 3 tbsp. cold water. A few tbsp. whipped cream may be added, if desired, just before serving. Serve with boiled fish or asparagus.

Note: This preparation is not a sauce in the exact sense of the word, but since it is served as one we include it among these recipes.

NANTUA SAUCE SAUCE NANTUA (E.)

Add 6 oz. cream to 1 qt. Béchamel Sauce (p. 146) and reduce by ⅓. Strain, then bring the sauce back to its normal consistency by adding 4–5 oz. cream. Finish with 5 oz. very smooth Crayfish Butter (p. 164) and garnish with 20 small crayfish tails.

NEWBURG SAUCE WITH RAW LOBSTER SAUCE NEW-BURG AVEC LE HOMARD CRU (E.)

Cut a lobster weighing 1½–2 lb. into small pieces. Remove the soft parts and crush them with 1 oz. butter and set to one side. Cook the pieces of lobster meat in 2 oz. butter and 4 tbsp. oil; season with salt and cayenne pepper. When the shell has turned red, drain off all of the fat and add 2 tbsp. cognac set aflame and 6 oz. Marsala or old Madeira. Reduce the wine by ⅔; pour 6 oz. cream and 6 oz. fish stock over the lobster, and cook slowly 25 min. Drain the pieces of lobster in a sieve, remove the meat from the shell, and dice. Finish the sauce by mixing in the soft parts of lobster previously set aside; bring to a quick boil a few times to make sure it is cooked, then mix in the diced lobster meat; test the seasoning and correct if necessary.

Note: The addition of the diced lobster meat is optional. The meat may also be cut into thin slices and used for decorating the fish with which the sauce is to be served.

NEWBURG SAUCE WITH COOKED LOBSTER SAUCE NEW-BURG AVEC LE HOMARD CUIT (E.)

Cook the lobster in an ordinary Court Bouillon (p. 277). Remove the tail meat and cut in slices. Arrange these slices in the bottom of a well-buttered sautéing pan; season well with salt and cayenne pepper and heat on both sides to turn the outside red. Cover the slices of lobster with good Madeira and cook until the wine is almost entirely reduced. Beat the yolks of 3 eggs with 6 oz. cream and, just before serving, pour over the lobster; spoon gently, off the stove, until perfectly combined.

Note: Originally these two Newburg Sauces, as well as Américaine Sauce (p. 316), were made for and served exclusively with lobster. The combination of sauce and lobster made a unique dish. However, it could only be served at luncheon, for people with delicate stomachs could not eat it at night. To remedy this situation we have adopted the custom of serving lobster sauce with fillets and *mousselines* of sole, using the lobster meat only as a garnish. This innovation has been well received. By using curry or paprika for flavoring, some excellent variations of this sauce may be made, which go particularly well with sole and other lean white fish. It is a good idea to serve a little Rice Indian Style (p. 512) with fish prepared this way.

NINON SAUCE SAUCE NINON (M.)

Add 6 oz. cream to 12 oz. chicken Velouté (p. 147) flavored with truffle essence. Season with a pinch of curry powder and cook for a few minutes on a hot fire. Strain. Add 2 tbsp. finely diced vegetables and 1 tbsp. Dry Duxelles (p. 176). For soft-boiled and poached eggs, artichoke bottoms, and braised celery.

NORMANDE SAUCE SAUCE NORMANDE (E.)

To 3 qt. Fish Velouté (p. 147) add: 3 oz. mushroom cooking juice, 3 oz. mussel cooking juice, 6 oz. stock from sole, a few drops of lemon juice, and 5 egg yolks mixed with 6 oz. cream. Cook over a hot fire until reduced by ⅓. Strain, and finish with 3 oz. rich cream and 5 oz. butter. This sauce is usually served with Sole Normande (p. 301), but may be used to advantage with any number of dishes.

Note: In general, we do not approve of adding to any recipe the water oysters have been cooked in. This water, which is simply salty, has no flavor. It is always preferable to use a few spoonfuls of mussel cooking juice instead.

PALOISE SAUCE SAUCE PALOISE (M.)

Make an ordinary Béarnaise Sauce (p. 147), substituting an equal quantity of fresh mint for the tarragon used in the boiling. After straining the sauce, add 1 tsp. chopped mint. For small steaks and chops.

POULETTE SAUCE SAUCE À LA POULETTE (M.)

This sauce is especially served with Sheep's Trotters Poulette (p. 359). It is merely a kind of Allemande Sauce (p. 146) made with mushroom essence, a finger of lemon juice, and chopped parsley.

PRINTANIA SAUCE SAUCE PRINTANIA (M.)

Add green asparagus butter (see Printanier Butter, p. 165) to ordinary Suprême Sauce (p. 146). Used with soft-boiled or poached eggs and giblets.

Note: Dishes with which this sauce is served should always be garnished with mushrooms sautéed in butter.

RAVIGOTE SAUCE SAUCE RAVIGOTE (M.)

Make the same as Ravigote Sauce for Fish (below), using chicken Velouté (p. 147) instead of Béchamel Sauce or Fish Velouté. For soft-boiled and poached eggs, fowl, and sweetbreads.

RAVIGOTE SAUCE FOR FISH SAUCE RAVIGOTE (MAIGRE) (M.)

Take 3 oz. vinegar containing 1 chopped shallot, ½ tbsp. chopped chervil and tarragon, a sprig of thyme, and a bit of bay leaf, and reduce by ⅔. Add 3 oz. fish stock, swirling it around the saucepan, then add 6 oz. Béchamel Sauce (p. 146) or Fish Velouté (p. 147). Bind with 3 egg yolks. Cook for a few moments, beating with a wire whisk; remove from the stove and add 3 oz. butter; strain. Just before serving, add 1 tbsp. chopped chervil and tarragon.

SMITANE SAUCE SAUCE SMITANE (M.)

Cook 4 oz. chopped onions in butter until soft. Add 3 oz. white wine, 3 tbsp. reduced veal stock, and 12 oz. sour cream. Boil for a few moments and add a dash of lemon juice. Strain.

SOUBISE SAUCE or **ONION CULLIS** SAUCE SOUBISE or COULIS D'OIGNONS (M.)

A Soubise is a garnish rather than a sauce. The preparation of Soubise Purée, or Onion Purée, will be found in the chapter on vegetables (p. 504). When this purée is used to cover poached or soft-boiled eggs, fowl, white meats, giblets, etc., it should be diluted with a few tbsp. fresh cream and finished with a little butter.

VALOIS or **FOYON SAUCE** SAUCE VALOIS or FOYON (M.)

This sauce is only a variety of Béarnaise Sauce (p. 147). Prepare it by adding melted meat glaze to ordinary Béarnaise Sauce. For small steaks and other small grilled or sautéed pieces of meat.

VÉNITIENNE or **VENETIAN SAUCE** SAUCE VÉNITIENNE (M.)

Prepare the same as Vénitienne Sauce for Fish (p. 155), substituting chicken Velouté (p. 147) for Fish Velouté. Serve with soft-boiled or poached eggs, fowl, and sliced sweetbreads.

VÉNITIENNE or VENETIAN SAUCE FOR FISH SAUCE VÉNITIENNE (MAIGRE) (M.)

Boil 3 oz. vinegar with 1 chopped shallot and a sprig of tarragon until reduced by ½. Add 7½ oz. fish stock and reduce by ½. Add 6 oz. Fish Velouté (p. 147) and reduce by ½, while adding 6 oz. fresh heavy cream bit by bit. Remove from the stove and finish with 4 oz. Green Butter (p. 163) and 1 tbsp. heavy cream. Strain.

Note: This sauce should be pale green. It may also be prepared by adding Green Butter to a White-Wine Sauce (below) containing vinegar reduced with shallot and tarragon.

VÉRON SAUCE SAUCE VÉRON (M.)

Make the same as Véron Sauce for Fish (below), substituting Allemande Sauce (p. 146) for Normande Sauce. Finish the sauce (as below) with concentrated tomato juice and anchovy essence. Serve with noisettes of lamb, sliced sweetbreads, sliced chicken.

VÉRON SAUCE FOR FISH SAUCE VÉRON (MAIGRE) (M.)

Mix equal parts of Normande Sauce (p. 153) and Béarnaise Sauce (p. 147). Finish with Espagnole Sauce (p. 137) made with fish stock, 1 tbsp. concentrated tomato juice, and ½ tbsp. anchovy essence.

VILLEROI SAUCE SAUCE VILLEROI (M.)

Add 6 oz. mushroom essence (or reduced mushroom cooking juice) to 15 oz. Allemande Sauce (p. 146) and reduce over a hot fire. Cook until the sauce is thick enough to cling to the spatula. Strain through a sieve.

Note: Villeroi Sauce is used with dishes that have been dipped in egg, breaded, and fried in deep fat. Most of these dishes are termed *à la Villeroi,* breading being their distinctive characteristic. Foods prepared this style should be small in size. Lamb sweetbreads or sliced veal sweetbreads, cockscombs and cock's kidneys, sliced lamb or veal brains, and many other things are cooked this way.

WHITE-WINE SAUCE SAUCE VIN BLANC (E.)

This sauce can be prepared 3 different ways:

First method: To 1 qt. Fish Velouté (p. 147) add 6 oz. fish stock (of the fish it is to go with) and 4 egg yolks; reduce by ⅓, remove from the stove, and add 6 oz. butter. White-Wine Sauce prepared in this manner is especially suitable for glazing.

Second method: Boil 3 oz. good fish stock until reduced by ½. Add 5 egg yolks and 1 lb. butter, following the same procedure as for Hollandaise Sauce (p. 151).

Third method: Break 5 egg yolks into a saucepan and heat slightly; add 1 lb. butter, stirring in gradually, and, bit by bit along with the butter, 3 oz. very good fish stock.

COLD SAUCES

AÏOLI SAUCE or **PROVENÇAL BUTTER** SAUCE AÏOLI OR BEURRE DE PROVENCE (M.)

Pound 4 small cloves of garlic (about 1 oz.) very fine in a mortar. Add 1 raw egg yolk, a pinch of salt, and 7 oz. oil, pouring the oil at first drop by drop and then in a thin trickle when the sauce begins to thicken. The mixture should be made in the mortar by stirring vigorously with a pestle. While mixing, thin the sauce by gradually adding the juice of 1 lemon and ½ tbsp. cold water.

Note: If the sauce begins to separate, it can be bound together again with the yolk of a raw egg, as when making Mayonnaise (p. 157).

ANDALOUSE or **ANDALUSIAN SAUCE** SAUCE ANDALOUSE (E.)

Add 7 oz. very smooth, very red tomato purée to 2½ cups rather thick Mayonnaise (p. 157); add, finally, 3 oz. finely diced pimento.

CHANTILLY SAUCE SAUCE CHANTILLY (E.)

Prepare 2½ cups very thick Mayonnaise (p. 157), using lemon juice instead of vinegar. Before serving, add 4 tbsp. very stiffly whipped cream, then correct the seasoning. Served especially with warm or cold asparagus.

Note: Add the whipped cream just before serving, or the sauce may curdle.

GÉNOISE or **GENOESE SAUCE** SAUCE GÉNOISE (E.)

In a mortar pound 1½ oz. freshly blanched pistachios and 1 oz. pine nuts (or, if unavailable, sweet almonds) into a fine, smooth paste, adding 1 tsp. cold Béchamel Sauce (p. 146). Strain this paste through a fine sieve into a mixing bowl and add 6 egg yolks, a pinch of salt, and a pinch of pepper; mix well with a wire whisk; blend in 1 qt. oil and the juice of 2 medium-sized lemons. Finish the sauce with 3 tbsp. herb purée made with parsley and chervil leaves, tarragon, chives, and fresh burnet in season. The herbs should be in equal quantities, blanched 2 min. in boiling water, strained, cooled, crushed, and pressed through a fine sieve. This sauce is usually served with cold fish.

GRIBICHE SAUCE SAUCE GRIBICHE (E.)

In a mixing bowl press the yolks of 6 freshly cooked hard-boiled eggs into a smooth paste, adding 1 tsp. mustard, a large pinch of salt, and a good pinch of pepper. Mix in 1 pt. oil and 1½ tbsp. vinegar. Finish with 4 oz. chopped gherkins and capers, 1 tbsp. chopped, mixed parsley, chervil, and tarragon, and the whites of 3 hard-boiled eggs cut in short julienne strips. This sauce is usually served with cold fish.

ITALIENNE or **ITALIAN SAUCE II** SAUCE ITALIENNE (E.)

Cook half a calf's brain in a strongly spiced Court Bouillon (p. 277); let cool and press the brain through a fine sieve. Mutton or beef brains may be substituted. Put the purée of brains into a mixing bowl, beat it till smooth, and add a Mayonnaise Sauce made of 5 egg yolks, 1 dessertspoon salt, a generous pinch of pepper, 1 qt. oil, and juice of 1 lemon (see below). Finish the sauce with 1 tbsp. chopped parsley. This sauce may be served with any cold meat.

MAYONNAISE SAUCE MAYONNAISE (E.)

Mayonnaise is used in most cold sauces and for this reason may be considered a basic sauce just as Espagnole Sauce and Velouté are basic. It is very simple to prepare, but certain factors must be borne in mind:

Proportions: 6 egg yolks (the tread or chalaza of the egg must be removed), 1 qt. oil, 1 dessertspoon salt, a good pinch of white pepper, 1½ tbsp. vinegar or the equivalent in lemon juice if you want a very pale sauce.

(1) Beat the egg yolks, adding salt, pepper, and a few drops of vinegar or lemon juice. (2) Add the oil drop by drop in the beginning and then in a trickle when the sauce begins to thicken. (3) From time to time break the body of the sauce by adding a little vinegar or lemon juice. (4) Finally, add 3 tbsp. boiling water to bind the sauce and prevent it from separating when it is stored.

Note: (1) The idea that seasoning the egg yolks causes Mayonnaise to separate is not shared by experts. On the contrary, it has been demonstrated scientifically that the liquefied salt helps the eggs to bind the sauce. (2) It is an absolute mistake to believe that Mayonnaise should be made on ice, and the contrary of the truth, since coldness is the most frequent cause of Mayonnaise separating. In cold weather the oil should be warmed a little or at least brought to room temperature. (3) Mayonnaise separates because of 3 mistakes: (*a*) adding too much oil at the start; (*b*) using oil that is too cold; (*c*) using too much oil in relation to the number of eggs.

STIFF MAYONNAISE SAUCE MAYONNAISE COLLÉE (M.)

Add 6 oz. melted Aspic Jelly (p. 168) made from meat or fish to 12 oz. Mayonnaise. Mix briskly with a wire whisk.

Note: This sauce, which is used for covering cold fish or sliced shellfish (as well as eggs or fowl), should be used as soon as the jelly has been added to the Mayonnaise.

MOUSQUETAIRE SAUCE SAUCE MOUSQUETAIRE (E.)

To 1 qt. Mayonnaise (above) add 4 oz. finely chopped shallots cooked in 4 oz. white wine until completely reduced, 3 tbsp. melted meat glaze, 1 tbsp. chopped chives. Season with a pinch of cayenne or freshly ground pepper. Serve with cold meats.

Note: The shallots may be pressed through a strainer or even preferably added to the sauce in the form of a purée.

MUSTARD SAUCE WITH CREAM SAUCE MOUTARDE À LA CRÈME (E.)

Put into a mixing bowl 3 tbsp. mustard, a pinch of salt, a pinch of pepper, and a finger of lemon juice. Mix, and add slowly, as when making Mayonnaise (above), 6 oz. very fresh heavy cream. Serve with hors d'oeuvres.

RÉMOULADE SAUCE SAUCE RÉMOULADE (E.)

To 1 qt. Mayonnaise (above), add: 1½ tbsp. mustard; 4 oz. gherkins and 2 oz. capers, chopped and mashed; 1 tbsp. chopped parsley, chervil, and tarragon, and ½ tbsp. anchovy essence.

RUSSIAN SAUCE SAUCE RUSSE (E.)

Pound in a mortar 4 oz. soft parts of lobster and 4 oz. caviar, adding 2 or 3 tbsp. Mayonnaise (p. 157). Strain through a fine sieve and mix in 3 cups Mayonnaise. Season the sauce with 1 tbsp. mustard and 1 tbsp. Derby Sauce (bottled).[1] Serve with cold fish and shellfish.

TARTAR SAUCE SAUCE TARTARE (E.)

In a mixing bowl work the yolks of 8 hard-boiled eggs into a smooth paste; season with a big pinch of salt and freshly ground pepper; mix in 1 qt. oil and 2 tbsp. vinegar. Finish with 2 tbsp. green-onion or chive purée, pounded in a mortar, thinned with 2 tbsp. Mayonnaise (p. 157), and strained through a fine sieve. This sauce may be served with cold fowl, meat, fish, and shellfish; it is also served with meat and fish prepared *à la diable,* or deviled.

GREEN SAUCE SAUCE VERTE (E.)

Drop into boiling water and blanch for 5 min.: 2 oz. spinach leaves, 2 oz. water cress, 2 oz. parsley, chervil, and tarragon leaves in equal amounts. Strain, cool quickly, press out the water, and crush the herbs in a cloth so as to squeeze out 3 oz. thick juice. Add this juice to 1 qt. very thick, highly seasoned Mayonnaise (p. 157). Serve with cold fish and shellfish.

VINAIGRETTE SAUCE or COLD RAVIGOTE SAUCE VINAIGRETTE or RAVIGOTE FROIDE (M.)

Mix in a bowl 1 tbsp. onion chopped fine, washed, and squeezed in a cloth, 1 tbsp. chopped parsley, 1 tbsp. chopped chervil and tarragon, 1 tbsp. capers, salt, and pepper. Add 3 oz. vinegar and 9 oz. oil. Mix.

Note: This sauce is usually served with calf's or sheep's head and feet, but may also accompany cold fish and shellfish. When it is used with calf's head, add part of the brains, well drained and diced fine or crushed with a fork. Sometimes chopped hard-boiled eggs are added, which makes the sauce a little like the Rémoulade Sauce that used to be made in certain regions of France.

VINCENT SAUCE SAUCE VINCENT (E.)

First method: Blanch in boiling water for 2–3 min.: 4 oz. sorrel leaves, parsley, chervil, tarragon, chives, and very tender shoots of burnet, all in equal quantities; 2½ oz. water-cress leaves, and 2½ oz. spinach leaves. Drain, cool, press out the water, and mash these herbs very fine with the yolks of 6 freshly cooked hard-boiled eggs. Press through a strainer, catching this purée of herbs in a mixing bowl. Add a pinch of salt and pepper and yolks of 5 raw eggs; blend in 1½ pt. oil and as much vinegar as is needed. Finish the seasoning with 1 tbsp. Derby Sauce (bought prepared).

Second method: Prepare the herb purée as described in the first method. Add Mayonnaise (p. 157) to this purée, and finish the same way. Serve with cold fish and shellfish.

Note: This sauce was created by Vincent Lachapelle, one of the master chefs of the eighteenth century.

---

[1] See note under Deviled Sauce, p. 160.

HOT ENGLISH SAUCES

CRANBERRY SAUCE SAUCE AUX AIRELLES (E.)

Cook 1 lb. red cranberries in 1 qt. water in a covered pot. When the berries are cooked, drain them and press through a fine sieve. Add to the purée thus obtained enough of the cooking water to make a rather thick sauce, and add sugar according to taste. This sauce may be bought ready prepared. All you need do is heat it, adding a little water. It is especially served with roast turkey.

ALBERT SAUCE SAUCE ALBERT (E.)

Mix 6 oz. grated horseradish with 6 oz. white consommé and simmer 20 min. Add 6 oz. English Butter Sauce (see below), 4 oz. cream, 1½ oz. bread crumbs. Cook over a hot fire until thickened; press through a strainer with a wooden spoon; bind with 2 egg yolks, and season with a pinch of salt and pepper. Finish with 1 tsp. mustard mixed with 1 tbsp. vinegar. Serve with braised beef.

AROMATIC SAUCE SAUCE AUX AROMATES (E.)

Steep 10 min. in 1 pt. consommé: 1 sprig of thyme, a large pinch of basil, a pinch each of savory, marjoram, sage, and chives, 2 chopped shallots, a little nutmeg, and 4 peppercorns. Strain the infusion through a cone-shaped sieve and bind it with 2 oz. Golden Roux (p. 136); boil for a few minutes, and finish with juice of ½ lemon and 1 tbsp. chopped, blanched chervil and tarragon. Serve with large pieces of boiled meat or fish.

ENGLISH BUTTER SAUCE SAUCE AU BEURRE À L'ANGLAISE (E.)

This sauce is made like French Butter Sauce (p. 148), except that it should be thicker, the proportions being: 3½ tbsp. butter, 3½ tbsp. flour, 3 cups boiling water seasoned with a pinch of salt, 5–6 drops of lemon juice, 7 oz. butter. It is not necessary to bind with egg yolks.

ROEBUCK SAUCE SAUCE CHEVREUIL (E.)

Mince 1 medium-sized onion and 3 oz. raw ham. Brown lightly in butter; add a *bouquet garni* and 4 oz. vinegar, and reduce almost completely. Add 9 oz. Espagnole Sauce (p. 137) and simmer 15 min., skimming. Remove the *bouquet garni* and finish with 1 wineglass port and 1 tbsp. red-currant jelly. Serve with venison.

SHRIMP SAUCE SAUCE CREVETTE À L'ANGLAISE (E.)

To 1 qt. English Butter Sauce (above) seasoned with cayenne pepper, add 1 tsp. anchovy essence and 5 oz. shelled shrimp. Serve with fish.

DEVILED SAUCE SAUCE DIABLE (E.)

Take 4 oz. vinegar containing 1 tbsp. chopped shallots and reduce by ½. Add 7 oz. Espagnole Sauce (p. 137) and 2 tbsp. tomato purée; cook 5 min. Finish with 1 tbsp. Derby Sauce and a good pinch of cayenne pepper, and strain through a sieve. This sauce is usually served with grilled fowl.

Note: Derby Sauce is highly recommended for seasoning certain hot or cold sauces. It is much better than Worcestershire Sauce and may be bought in most stores.

SCOTCH EGG SAUCE SAUCE ÉCOSSAISE (E.)

Prepare a Béchamel Sauce with 2½ oz. butter, 1¼ oz. flour, 12 oz. boiling milk, and the usual seasoning (see p. 146). As soon as the sauce begins to boil, add the finely chopped whites of 4 hard-boiled eggs. Just before serving, mix in the yolks of 4 hard-boiled eggs pressed through a strainer. Serve with codfish.

GOOSEBERRY SAUCE SAUCE AUX GROSEILLES (E.)

Cook in a copper saucepan 1 qt. young green gooseberries (topped and tailed and washed) with 5 oz. sugar and 3 oz. water. Press through a fine sieve. This purée is served with grilled mackerel.

OYSTER SAUCE SAUCE AUX HUÎTRES (E.)

Prepare a Golden Roux with 2 dessertspoons butter and 1½ dessertspoons flour (see p. 136). Blend in 3 oz. milk and 3 oz. cream. Season with a pinch of salt, bring to a boil, and simmer 10 min. Strain, season with cayenne pepper, and add 12 poached, sliced oysters. Serve with boiled fish.

ENGLISH EGG SAUCE SAUCE AUX OEUFS À L'ANGLAISE (E.)

Make a White Roux with 2 oz. butter and 1 oz. flour (see p. 136). Blend in 1 pt. boiling milk; season with salt, white pepper, and a little nutmeg; bring to a boil and simmer slowly 5–6 min. Add 2 hot, diced hard-boiled eggs, whites and yolks. Usually served with haddock and cod.

BUTTER-AND-EGG SAUCE SAUCE AUX OEUFS ET AU BEURRE FONDU (E.)

Melt ½ lb. butter and add: juice of ½ lemon, salt and pepper, 3 hot, diced hard-boiled eggs, and 1 tsp. chopped, blanched parsley. Serve with boiled fish.

ONION SAUCE SAUCE AUX OIGNONS (E.)

Cook 8 oz. thin-sliced onions in 3 cups milk with salt, pepper, and nutmeg. As soon as the onions are cooked, drain, saving onions and liquid. Chop the onions. Make a White Roux with 1½ oz. butter and 1½ oz. flour (see p. 136), blend in the milk used for cooking the onions, bring to a boil, add the chopped onions, and simmer 7–8 min. The sauce must be very thick. It may be served with rabbit, fowl, tripe, boiled mutton, braised game, etc., and is always poured over the meat.

BREAD SAUCE SAUCE AU PAIN (E.)

To 1 pt. boiling milk add 3 oz. fresh white bread crumbs, a large pinch of salt, 1 small onion stuck with a clove, 1 oz. butter. Cook slowly 15 min.; remove the onion; stir the sauce with a wire whisk till smooth, and finish with 3 oz. cream. Serve with roast chicken or game birds.

Note: When Bread Sauce is served with roast chicken, a sauceboat with the roasting juices of the chicken should be served at the same time. For game birds, add a dish of bread crumbs fried in butter and a plate of potato chips.

FRIED BREAD SAUCE SAUCE AU PAIN FRIT (E.)

To 6 oz. consommé add 2 tbsp. very lean, finely diced ham and 2 chopped shallots. Let simmer gently 10 min. Separately, fry 2 oz. bread crumbs in butter and, just before serving, add to the consommé. Finish with a pinch of chopped parsley and a dash of lemon juice. This preparation is served with small roast birds.

APPLESAUCE SAUCE AUX POMMES (E.)

Prepare some ordinary Apple Marmalade (p. 814), very lightly sugared and seasoned with a pinch of powdered cinnamon. Beat until smooth with a wire whisk before serving. This sauce is served warm with duck, goose, pork, roasts, etc.

Note: The practice of serving Applesauce with roasts is not by any means peculiar to England; the same custom is followed in Germany, Belgium, and Holland. In these countries roast game is always accompanied by Applesauce or Cranberry Sauce (p. 159) or a hot or cold fruit compote.

PORT-WINE SAUCE SAUCE AU PORTO (E.)

Boil 4 oz. port with 1 tbsp. chopped shallots and a sprig of thyme until reduced by ½. Add the juice of 2 oranges and ½ lemon, 1 tsp. grated orange peel, a pinch of salt, and a few grains of cayenne. Cook, then strain through cheesecloth, and add 15 oz. thickened Veal Gravy (p. 134). Serve with wild duck and game birds in general.

Note: This English sauce is served in many French restaurants.

HOT HORSERADISH SAUCE SAUCE RAIFORT CHAUDE (E.)

Same recipe as Albert Sauce (p. 159).

REFORM SAUCE SAUCE RÉFORME (E.)

This sauce is a combination of Poivrade Sauce (p. 143) and Semiglaze Sauce (p. 138), with the addition, per pt. sauce, of a garnish made of: 2 medium-sized gherkins, white of 1 hard-boiled egg, 2 medium-sized mushrooms, 2 dessertspoons truffles, 1 oz. pickled tongue, all cut into short julienne strips. This sauce is often served with mutton chops.

SAGE-AND-ONION SAUCE SAUCE SAUGE ET OIGNONS (E.)

Bake 2 large onions. When they are cold, peel and chop them, then mix them with 6 oz. bread crumbs soaked in milk and pressed to squeeze out the excess liquid. Add 2 tbsp. chopped sage and season with salt and pepper. Used for stuffing ducks.

Note: This sauce is sometimes served separately in a sauceboat after 5 or 6 tbsp. good juice from the roast have been added. Often, also, chopped, cooked beef suet is added, in the same proportion as the bread crumbs.

YORKSHIRE SAUCE SAUCE YORKSHIRE (E.)

Cook thoroughly in 6 oz. port 1 tbsp. orange peel cut in tiny strips. Strain off the orange peel and add to the wine: 1 tbsp. Espagnole Sauce (p. 137), 1 tbsp. red-currant jelly, a pinch of powdered cinnamon, a pinch of cayenne. Cook for a moment, strain through a cloth, and finish the sauce with the juice of 1 orange and the tiny strips of orange peel. Serve with roast or braised duckling and braised ham.

COLD ENGLISH SAUCES

CAMBRIDGE SAUCE SAUCE CAMBRIDGE (E.)

Mash and blend the yolks of 6 hard-boiled eggs, 4 well-washed anchovy fillets, 1 tbsp. tiny capers, 1 tbsp. chervil, tarragon, and chives in equal proportions. Add 1 tsp. mustard, 4 oz. oil, and 1 tbsp. vinegar; prepare the same way as Mayonnaise (p. 157). Season with a dash of cayenne pepper and press through a strainer with a spoon. Beat with a wire whisk and finish with 1 tsp. chopped parsley. Serve with any cold meat.

CUMBERLAND SAUCE SAUCE CUMBERLAND (E.)

To 4 tbsp. melted red-currant jelly add 3 oz. port; 1 dessertspoon finely chopped, blanched, and crushed shallots; 1 tbsp. each of well-blanched orange and lemon peel, cut in tiny julienne strips and well drained and cooled; juice of 1 orange and ½ lemon; 1 tsp. mustard; a dash of cayenne pepper and a dash of powdered ginger. Mix well. Serve with cold venison.

GLOUCESTER SAUCE SAUCE GLOUCESTER (E.)

To 1 qt. very thick Mayonnaise (p. 157) add 6 oz. sour cream mixed with juice of ½ lemon, a pinch of chopped fennel, and 2 tbsp. Derby Sauce (ready prepared). This sauce is mainly served with cold meat.

MINT SAUCE SAUCE MENTHE (E.)

Cut into fine julienne strips or chop 2 oz. mint leaves. Put into a bowl and add 1 oz. powdered sugar, 4 oz. vinegar, a pinch of salt, pepper, and 4 tbsp. water. Mix well. Serve with hot or cold lamb.

OXFORD SAUCE SAUCE OXFORD (E.)

Make Cumberland Sauce, as described above, with the following changes: (1) grate the orange and lemon peel instead of cutting in julienne strips; (2) use only ½ tbsp. each of orange and lemon peel. Use with the same dishes as Cumberland Sauce.

COLD HORSERADISH SAUCE SAUCE RAIFORT (E.)

Mix in a bowl 1 tbsp. mustard with 2 oz. grated horseradish, 2 oz. powdered sugar, a pinch of salt, 15 oz. cream, 9 oz. bread crumbs soaked in milk and pressed to remove excess liquid, and 2 tbsp. vinegar. Serve very cold with boiled or roast beef.

Note: Be sure to add the vinegar at the very end.

BUTTERS

GARLIC BUTTER BEURRE D'AIL (E.)

Blanch well 8 oz. peeled garlic. Drain thoroughly and pound in a mortar, add 11 oz. butter, and press through a sieve.

ALMOND BUTTER BEURRE D'AMANDES (M.)

Pound 4 oz. blanched almonds in a mortar, adding ½ tbsp. cold water. Add 4 oz. butter and press through a sieve.

Note: Filbert, Hazelnut, and Pistachio Butters are made the same way.

ANCHOVY BUTTER BEURRE D'ANCHOIS (E.)

Pound 4 oz. washed and dried anchovy fillets into a paste. Add 11 oz. butter and press through a sieve.

BERCY BUTTER BEURRE BERCY (E.)

Boil 6 oz. white wine containing 1 tbsp. finely chopped shallots until reduced by ½. Let stand until cool, then add 4 oz. softened butter, 9 oz. diced beef marrow that has been poached and well drained, 1 tbsp. chopped parsley, a good pinch of salt and ground pepper, and juice of ½ lemon.

CAVIAR BUTTER BEURRE DE CAVIAR (E.)

Pound 3 oz. pressed caviar until it becomes a fine paste, add 9 oz. butter, and press through a sieve.

COLBERT BUTTER BEURRE COLBERT (E.)

Add 2 tbsp. melted meat glaze and 2 tsp. chopped tarragon to 8 oz. Maître d'Hôtel Butter (p. 164).

RED BUTTER FOR COLORING BEURRE COLORANT ROUGE (E.)

Take leftover lobster, shrimp, and crayfish shells; scrape off any substance adhering to the interior or exterior of the shells. Dry them well and pound in a mortar, adding the same weight in butter as in shells. Heat in a double boiler to melt the butter, stirring frequently; strain through cheesecloth into a bowl chilled with ice; when the butter has become solid again, squeeze in a cloth to extract the water.

Note: If no lobster, shrimp, or crayfish shells are available, paprika may be used for coloring the butter. In any case, we advise against the use of red vegetable coloring for sauces.

GREEN BUTTER FOR COLORING BEURRE COLORANT VERT (E.)

Wash and drain 2 lb. spinach. Shake the leaves to dry thoroughly. Extract the juice by tightly squeezing the spinach leaves in a cloth; put this juice into a saucepan and heat in a double boiler until it coagulates. Pour the thickened juice onto a stiff napkin and let it drain. Scrape off the coloring substance from the napkin with a knife and, in a mortar, mash it into a paste with twice its weight in butter. Strain through a sieve and keep in a cool place.

Note: This natural green coloring is much more effective than artificial coloring.

SHRIMP BUTTER BEURRE DE CREVETTES (E.)

Pound 6 oz. shrimp in a mortar, mix with 6 oz. butter, and press through a sieve.

CURRIED or **INDIAN BUTTER** BEURRE AU CURRY OR À L'INDIENNE (M.)

To 9 oz. butter add 1 tbsp. chopped onion cooked in white wine and cooled and 1 tbsp. curry powder. Mix well. Press through a sieve.

SHALLOT BUTTER BEURRE D'ÉCHALOTES (M.)

Slice 4 oz. shallots, blanch them, and drain well. Mash them into a paste in a mortar and add 8 oz. butter. Mix well. Press through a sieve.

CRAYFISH BUTTER BEURRE D'ÉCREVISSES (E.)

Mash into a paste some leftover crayfish (cooked with a Mirepoix as for Crayfish Bisque, p. 198). Mix with the same weight in butter, and press through a sieve.

BUTTER FOR SNAILS BEURRE POUR LES ESCARGOTS (E.) *(For 50 snails)*

To 12 oz. butter add 1¼ oz. finely chopped shallots, 1 clove garlic crushed to a paste, 1 tbsp. chopped parsley, 1 tsp. salt, and a generous pinch of pepper. Mix well by kneading and keep in a cool place.

TARRAGON BUTTER BEURRE D'ESTRAGON (E.)

Blanch 5 oz. fresh tarragon leaves 10 min., drain, cool, press out the water, and pound into a pulp in a mortar. Add 9 oz. butter and press through a sieve.

LOBSTER BUTTER BEURRE DE HOMARD (E.)

Pound into a paste the soft parts, eggs, and coral of lobster. Mix with the same weight in butter and press through a sieve.

YELLOW BUTTER BEURRE JAUNE (M.)

Mix equal parts of hard-boiled egg yolks and butter until perfectly smooth.

MILT or **SOFT-ROE BUTTER** BEURRE DE LAITANCES (M.)

This butter is made either with milt, or soft roe, from smoked and salted herring, soaked in water and drained, then well crushed in a mortar, with double its weight in butter added, or with milt, or soft roe, from fresh fish (herring or otherwise) poached in white wine for a short time and then mixed with the butter.

MAÎTRE D'HÔTEL BUTTER BEURRE MAÎTRE D'HÔTEL (E.)

Knead 9 oz. butter until soft and mix with 1 tbsp. chopped parsley, 1 tsp. salt, a good pinch of pepper, and juice of ¼ lemon.

Note: The addition of 1 tbsp. mustard is recommended as a variant of Maître d'Hôtel Butter, which goes particularly well with grilled meat or fish.

FLOUR BUTTER BEURRE MANIÉ (E.)

This butter is used when it is necessary to thicken sauces quickly, as for matelote sauces. Make it by mixing 3 oz. flour with 4 oz. butter. When used for thickening a sauce, the sauce must not be allowed to boil, or it may take on the disagreeable flavor of raw flour.

MARCHAND DE VINS BUTTER BEURRE MARCHAND DE VINS (E.)

Reduce by half 6 oz. red wine containing 1 oz. chopped shallots. Add a pinch of salt, a pinch of ground pepper, 1 tbsp. melted meat glaze, 6 oz. soft butter, juice of 1/4 lemon, 1 tbsp. chopped parsley. Mix well. Serve with grilled steak.

MONTPELLIER BUTTER BEURRE DE MONTPELLIER (E.)

Drop into a copper pan of boiling water: 4 oz. water-cress leaves, parsley, chervil, chives, and tarragon leaves in equal proportions, and 1 oz. spinach leaves. At the same time blanch separately 1 1/2 oz. finely chopped shallots. Drain and cool the herbs and shallots. Press all the water out of the shallots and herbs and mash together into a paste. Add 3 medium-sized gherkins, 1 tbsp. pressed capers, 1 small clove of garlic, and 4 anchovy fillets. Pound all of this into a fine paste and finish with 1 1/2 lb. butter, 3 hard-boiled egg yolks, and the yolks of 2 raw eggs. Continue mixing and add 6 oz. oil little by little. Strain through a fine sieve. Beat the preparation with a wire whisk until smooth; add salt if necessary and a pinch of cayenne pepper. Serve with cold fish or spread over the fish to decorate it when served buffet style.

MONTPELLIER BUTTER FOR DECORATIVE DETAILS BEURRE DE MONTPELLIER POUR CROÛTONNAGE DE PLATS (E.)

When this butter is specially prepared to use for decoration and fancy-shaped ornaments, leave out the oil and egg yolks, both cooked and raw. Spread the butter with an even thickness on a tray to facilitate cutting it. Chill in a cool place, but not over ice.

MUSTARD BUTTER BUERRE DE MOUTARDE (E.)

Add 1 1/2 tbsp. French mustard to 9 oz. soft butter and keep in a cool place.

PISTACHIO BUTTER BEURRE DE PISTACHES (E.)

Pound 6 oz. freshly blanched pistachios into a paste, while moistening with a few drops of water; add 9 oz. butter and press through a sieve.

PRINTANIER BUTTER BEURRE PRINTANIER (M.)

This butter, which is especially used for canapés (and other cold hors d'oeuvres), is made with a base of different green vegetables, such as fresh peas, fresh green beans, green asparagus tips, etc. The vegetables are first blanched in boiling salted water, then, after being completely cooked, are drained, cooled, and wiped dry. Pound them into a pulp in a mortar and mix with 8 oz. butter per 4 oz. vegetable.

HORSERADISH BUTTER BEURRE DE RAIFORT (E.)

Pound 2 oz. grated horseradish into a paste, mix with 9 oz. butter, and press through a sieve.

SMOKED-SALMON BUTTER BEURRE DE SAUMON FUMÉ (M.)

Make the same way as Anchovy Butter (p. 163), replacing the anchovies with an equivalent amount of smoked salmon.

TRUFFLE BUTTER BEURRE DE TRUFFES (M.)

Pound 4 oz. raw truffles in a mortar, add 8 oz. butter, season with a dash of spices, and mix. Strain through a fine sieve.

VARIOUS CULLISES COULIS DIVERS (E.)

Pound crayfish shells, or the remains of prawns, or the soft parts, eggs, and coral of lobsters and rock lobsters. Add 4 tbsp. fresh cream per 4 oz. mashed shellfish and strain. These cullises should be made at the last minute.

MARINADES AND BRINES

There are many types of marinades and brines, but the purpose of all of them is: (1) to penetrate the meat soaked in them with the spices used in their preparation; (2) to make certain meats tenderer; (3) sometimes to preserve the meats, especially when atmospheric disturbances might make them spoil. Finally, the ingredients depend upon what is being marinated or pickled.

QUICK MARINADE MARINADE INSTANTANÉE (E.)

This is a good marinade to use when you want to marinate a small steak or chop to be grilled and haven't much time. Better yet, it may be used with those meats which are among the ingredients that make up such cold preparations as galantines, terrines, pâtés, etc. (1) If the meat is to be grilled, sprinkle it with finely sliced shallots, chopped parsley, thyme, and bay leaf, salt and pepper. Proportions depend upon the size of the meat. Pour a mixture of oil and lemon juice over the meat, the proportions being ½ lemon per tbsp. oil. (2) If you are preparing strips of veal, sliced game, ham, pork, etc., season the meat with salt and pepper and marinate in 3 parts white wine, 3 parts cognac, and 1 part oil. This seasoned liquor is later used in making the forcemeat for the marinated meat. In any case, turn the meat frequently in the marinade to make sure it permeates the meat.

UNCOOKED MARINADE FOR MEAT OR VENISON MARINADE CRUE POUR VIANDES DE BOUCHERIE OU VENAISON (E.) (*For 2 qt.*)

Flavoring: 4 oz. carrots, 4 oz. onions, 1½ oz. shallots, 1 oz. celery, 2 cloves garlic, 3 sprigs of parsley, 1 sprig of thyme, ½ bay leaf, 6 peppercorns, 2 cloves.

Liquid Ingredients: 5 cups white wine, 12 oz. vinegar, 5 oz. oil.

Preparation: Season the meat with salt and pepper. Slice the carrots, onions, and shallots thin and put half of them into the bottom of a pan just large enough to hold the piece of meat and the marinade. Cover the meat with the rest of the vegetables and spices and add the white wine, vinegar, and oil. Keep in a cool place and turn the meat frequently in the marinade.

COOKED MARINADE FOR MEAT OR VENISON MARINADE CUITE POUR VIANDES DE BOUCHERIE OU VENAISON (E.) (*For 2 qt.*)

Flavoring: Same as for Uncooked Marinade, above.

Liquid Ingredients: 5 cups white wine, 9 oz. vinegar, 5 oz. oil.

Preparation: Lightly brown in oil the finely sliced carrots, onions, and shallots with the herbs and spices already mentioned. Add the white wine and vinegar and cook slowly ½ hr. Do not pour the marinade over the meat until it is completely cold.

UNCOOKED OR COOKED MARINADE FOR VENISON ROASTS

MARINADE CRUE OU CUITE POUR GROSSE VENAISON (E.) (*For 2 qt.*)

Flavoring: Use the same ingredients as given in the previous marinade recipes, adding ½ oz. rosemary.

Liquid Ingredients: 1½ qt. vinegar, 10 oz. oil.

Preparation: Whether preparing it hot or cold, follow the directions given in previous recipes.

COOKED MARINADE FOR MUTTON, VENISON STYLE

MARINADE CUITE POUR LE MOUTON EN CHEVREUIL (E.) (*For 2 qt.*)

Flavoring: Use the same ingredients as indicated in previous recipes and in the same proportions, adding 10 juniper berries, a pinch of basil, and a pinch of rosemary.

Liquid Ingredients: The same as those used for cooked marinade for meat or venison.

Preparation: Lightly brown in oil the sliced onions, carrots, and shallots and the herbs; add the white wine and vinegar and cook over a low fire ½ hr.

COOKED MARINADE FOR MUTTON, CHAMOIS STYLE

MARINADE CUITE POUR LE MOUTON EN CHAMOIS (E.) (*For 2 qt.*)

Flavoring: Same as for Uncooked Marinade, with the addition of 15 juniper berries, ½ oz. basil, and ½ oz. rosemary.

Liquid Ingredients: 1½ qt. good red wine, 9 oz. vinegar, 5 oz. oil.

Preparation: Same as above. When possible, the marinade may be made with good wine vinegar, using the following proportions: 24 oz. red wine, 18 oz. wine vinegar, 5 oz. oil. The same amount of wine vinegar as wine may be used, provided the wine vinegar is not too acid.

GENERAL REMARKS ON MARINADES (E.)

(1) Meats are more quickly marinated when soaked in a cooked marinade. In allowing time for meats to marinate, take into consideration the type and size of the meat, the temperature of the meat and the room, and the humidity. (2) We absolutely forbid the use of pure vinegar in any marinade for meat and tender venison; its corrosive action destroys the flavor of the meat. Pure vinegar may be used only in marinating tough game, such as wild boar, stag, reindeer, etc.

STORING MARINADES (E.)

If a marinade is to be kept for a long time, especially in summer, it is a good idea to add ½ tsp. boric acid per 2 qt. marinade. Moreover, in summer the marinade should be boiled every 2 days and in winter every 4 or 5 days, and freshened after each boiling with 6 oz. of the same wine it is made of and 3 oz. vinegar.

SALT BRINE SAUMURE AU SEL (E.)

In making this brine use 1½ oz. saltpeter per 2 lb. bay salt. The total quantity of salt and saltpeter will be determined by the size and quantity of the pieces to be salted. The meat should be kept covered and weighted down.

Preparation: First pierce the meat to be salted rather deeply with a large skewer, then rub with pulverized saltpeter. Next place it in a container with the salt and a sprig of thyme and ½ bay leaf per 2 lb. salt.

LIQUID BRINE FOR TONGUE SAUMURE LIQUIDE POUR LANGUES (E.)

Proportions: 5 qt. water, 4½ lb. bay salt, 6 oz. saltpeter, 12 oz. brown sugar, 12 peppercorns, 12 juniper berries, a sprig of thyme, and a bay leaf.

Preparation: Boil all of the ingredients in a large pot; pierce the tongue with a skewer and rub with salt and saltpeter; when the brine has completely cooled, pour it over the tongue. A medium-sized tongue should be soaked in brine for 8 days in winter or 6 days in summer.

ASPIC JELLIES

All jellies or aspics are made from a stock whose basic ingredient determines the special flavor of the jelly and, therefore, its use. To make the jelly solidify without resorting to artificial stiffening substances, use the gelatinous parts of meat such as calf's feet, pork rind, etc., which also assure its smoothness. However, and principally in summer, it is always absolutely necessary to test the degree of consistency of the stock being used by putting it on ice, before clarifying the jelly, in order to add a few leaves of gelatin, if needed. In any case, never more than ⅓ oz. gelatin (6 leaves) per qt. should be used, and the gelatin should be very transparent, brittle, and without any gluey taste. It should never be used without first being softened in cold water or at least well washed. We do not recommend the use of artificial coloring in the preparation of ordinary aspics, since these should have their own natural coloring. Furthermore, adding a little Madeira at the end will be sufficient to give the clear amber tone characteristic of aspics.

STOCK FOR ORDINARY ASPIC FONDS POUR GELÉE ORDINAIRE (E.)

(*For 5 qt.*)

Nutritive Ingredients: 4 lb. veal knuckle, 3 lb. chopped veal bones, 3 lb. leg of beef. These meats and bones must be lightly browned in the oven. *Gelatinous Ingredients:* 3 calf's feet, boned and blanched; 10 oz. blanched fresh pork rind. *Flavoring Ingredients:* 8 oz. carrots, 8 oz. onions, 2 oz. leeks, 2 oz. celery, a strong *bouquet garni*. *Liquid:* 8 qt. water. *Cooking Time:* 6 hr.

Preparation: Make the same way as Brown Stock for sauces (p. 134), but the color should be lighter.

STOCK FOR WHITE ASPIC FONDS POUR GELÉE BLANCHE (E.)

Use the same ingredients and the same proportions as in making Ordinary

Aspic (p. 168), with very white stock in place of water. Prepare in the same way and cook 6 hr.

STOCK FOR CHICKEN ASPIC FONDS POUR GELÉE DE VOLAILLE (E.) (*For 5 qt.*)

Nutritive Ingredients: 3 lb. veal knuckle, 3 lb. leg of beef, 2 lb. chopped veal bones, 3 lb. chicken bones, giblets, and especially the scalded feet. *Gelatinous Ingredients:* 3 calf's feet, boned and blanched. *Flavoring Ingredients:* The same as for Ordinary Aspic (p. 168), but in smaller amounts. *Liquid:* 8 qt. clear white stock. *Cooking Time:* 4½ hr.

Preparation: Make the same way as stock for sauces.

STOCK FOR GAME ASPIC FONDS POUR GELÉE DE GIBIER (E.) (*For 5 qt.*)

Nutritive Ingredients: 2 lb. veal knuckle, 4 lb. leg of beef, 1½ lb. chopped veal bones, 3½ lb. bones and remains of game. Brown all of these in the oven. *Gelatinous Ingredients:* 3 calf's feet, boned and blanched. *Flavoring Ingredients:* The same vegetables and herbs as for Ordinary Aspic (p. 168), but increase the proportion of celery and thyme by ⅓ and add 8 juniper berries. *Liquid:* 8 qt. water. *Cooking Time:* 4 hr.

Preparation: Make the same as Game Stock for sauces (p. 134).

FISH STOCK FOR ORDINARY ASPIC FONDS DE POISSON POUR GELÉE ORDINAIRE (E.) (*For 5 qt.*)

Basic Ingredients: 1½ lb. inexpensive fish such as gurnet, weever, and whiting, 1½ lb. bones and trimmings of sole. *Flavoring Ingredients:* 8 oz. chopped onions, 2 parsley roots, 4 oz. peelings and fresh mushrooms. *Liquid:* 6 qt. clear, strong fish stock. *Cooking Time:* 45 min.

Preparation: Make the same way as fish stock.

STOCK FOR FISH ASPIC WITH RED WINE FONDS POUR GELÉE DE POISSON AU VIN ROUGE (E.)

This stock is ordinarily the Court Bouillon used in cooking the fish, such as carp, trout, etc. (see p. 277). Equal quantities of good red burgundy and the fish stock are used for this fish aspic, along with gelatinous ingredients to make the aspic solidify. The vegetable and herb flavoring is furnished by the ingredients used in cooking the fish.

GENERAL REMARKS ON THE USE OF STOCKS IN MAKING ASPIC (E.)

Stock used in making aspic should, as often as possible, be prepared the day before. When ready, the stock should be skimmed of fat, strained, and left to cool in an earthenware dish. As the stock cools it will coagulate and the remaining fat will gather on the surface and solidify, making it easy to remove. At the same time, particles of sediment that managed to pass through the cloth or strainer will settle in the bottom of the dish because of their weight, making it possible to pour off the clear stock.

HOW TO CLARIFY ASPIC

ORDINARY MEAT ASPIC GELÉE GRASSE ORDINAIRE (E.) (*For 5 qt.*)

(1) First of all determine the consistency of the stock, so that, if necessary, more gelatin may be added. (2) Have the stock for the aspic ready, the fat and sediment removed. (3) Put into a thick-bottomed pot of suitable size: 1 lb. very lean, finely chopped beef, 2 tsp. chervil and tarragon, and 3 egg whites. (4) Pour the cold, or barely tepid, aspic stock on the chopped meat and mix well with a wire whisk or a spatula. Bring to a boil over a not-too-hot fire, while stirring gently, to combine the egg whites with the gelatin, thereby clarifying the aspic. Simmer ¼ hr. and strain through a cloth.

Note: Do not add wine to the aspic until it is almost cold. It is a mistake to add any kind of wine while clarifying the aspic, for boiling will spoil or at least change the taste of the wine. On the contrary, added to the aspic almost cold, the wine keeps its flavor intact. The aspic must have sufficient body when the wine is added so that this extra liquid will not weaken its consistency and keep it from solidifying. Wines like Madeira, Marsala, or sherry may be used, in the proportion of 3 oz. wine per qt. aspic. Rhine wines, champagne, and fine white wines may be added at the rate of 6 oz. wine per qt. aspic. It is better not to use any wine at all than one of inferior quality, which may impair the flavor of the aspic.

GAME ASPIC GELÉE DE GIBIER (E.)

Clarify Game Aspic in the same way as Ordinary Meat Aspic, above. However, ordinary Game Aspic, without any special flavor, should be reinforced with ½ lb. lean chopped beef and ½ lb. dark game meat. If the aspic is to have a special game flavor, it will be necessary to use the meat of the particular game the aspic is to be served with, such as partridge, pheasant, grouse, etc., when clarifying it. All game aspics are improved by adding 2 tbsp. champagne brandy per qt. aspic, provided the brandy is of superior quality. Better leave out the brandy if it is mediocre. Without the flavor of the brandy, the aspic, however imperfect, can be passable, but flavored with common brandy it will be bad.

WHITE FISH ASPIC GELÉE DE POISSON BLANCHE (E.)

Fish aspic may be clarified 2 ways: (1) by using 3 egg whites per 5 qt. aspic and by adding ½ lb. chopped whiting to compensate for diluting the aspic with the egg; (2) with fresh caviar, or pressed caviar, if fresh is not available, in the proportion of 2 oz. per qt. aspic, and clarifying as explained in the recipe for Fish Consommé (p. 192). Fish aspics may be flavored with dry champagne or a very fine white burgundy (see remarks on use of wine in aspic under Ordinary Meat Aspic, above).

Note: Certain types of fish aspics may be given a special flavor by using 4 small crayfish per qt. aspic. The crayfish should be sautéed and cooked as for a bisque (see p. 198), then mashed finely and added to the fish stock 10 min. before straining it.

FISH ASPIC WITH RED WINE GELÉE DE POISSON AU VIN ROUGE (E.)

Clarify with 4 egg whites per 5 qt. aspic. The red wine almost always decomposes during the cooking of the fish or the clarification of the aspic, resulting in the precipitation of the tannic-acid coloring matter. This decomposition seems to be caused by contact with the gelatin suspended in the fish stock, and no way is known, at present, to prevent it. To compensate for the absence of color, artificial coloring (carmine liquid or red vegetal) must be added, but this must be done with the greatest care, for the aspic should not become any darker than a somewhat heightened pink.

CHICKEN ASPIC GELÉE DE VOLAILLE (E.)

Chicken aspic is clarified exactly like Ordinary Meat Aspic (p. 170), using the same aromatic ingredients (chervil and tarragon), except that the amount of lean beef is halved, the other half being replaced by the same amount of chicken neck—in other words, ½ lb. chopped lean beef and ½ lb. chopped chicken neck.

Note: Excellent results in clarifying the aspic are obtained by adding crushed roast-chicken bones, which have been well dried in the oven to get rid of fat.

GARNISHES

VARIOUS FORCEMEATS FARCES DIVERSES (E.)

Forcemeats are used very often for garnishes or, made in any one of a variety of ways, may form the basic element of a garnish. There are 5 principal types of forcemeats: (1) forcemeat with veal and fat, called *godiveau* in ancient cookery; (2) forcemeat whose basic ingredients may vary but which is always combined with panada to give it body; (3) forcemeat made with cream, according to the modern method, used for mousses and mousselines; (4) a special forcemeat called gratin, with chopped liver as the principal ingredient, which includes several varieties but is always made the same way; (5) simple forcemeats ordinarily served with cold dishes such as galantines, *pâtés,* and terrines.

PANADAS FOR FORCEMEATS PANADES POUR FARCES (E.)

There are several sorts of panadas, each depending on the kind of forcemeat and the dish the forcemeat goes with. Generally, the amount of panada used should not be more than half the weight of the basic ingredient of the forcemeat, whatever it is made of. If eggs and butter are mixed into the panada, they must be taken into consideration in calculating the general proportions used in the forcemeat. Panadas should always be used cold, except Panada E. When the panada is ready, it should be spread out on a buttered platter or tray to cool more quickly and be covered with a buttered paper or have butter spread over its surface to avoid the crust made by contact with the air. The panada recipes given below make 1 lb. net. If more or less panada is desired, it will be easy to change the proportions accordingly.

PANADAS

A. BREAD PANADA PANADE AU PAIN (E.)

(*For forcemeats made of fish.*)

Ingredients: 9 oz. boiling milk, ¼ lb. stale white bread crumbs, 1 tsp. salt.

Preparation: Soak the bread crumbs thoroughly in the milk; heat over a hot fire until the paste has sufficient consistency to stick to a spoon; remove from the stove and spread on a buttered platter or tray to cool.

B. FLOUR PANADA PANADE À LA FARINE (E.)

(*Suitable for any forcemeat.*)

Ingredients: 9 oz. water, pinch of salt, 2 oz. butter, 6 oz. sifted flour.

Preparation: Bring the water, salt, and butter to a boil in a stewpan; remove from the stove and mix in the flour; heat again over a hot fire, constantly stirring, until a smooth paste is formed; spread the paste out onto a tray, as described above, and let cool.

C. FRANGIPANE PANADA PANADE À LA FRANGIPANE (E.)

(*For chicken and fish forcemeats.*)

Ingredients: 5 oz. flour, 4 egg yolks, 3½ oz. melted butter, generous pinch of salt, pinch of pepper, a dash of grated nutmeg, 6 oz. milk.

Preparation: Blend the flour and egg yolks in a stewpan; add the melted butter, salt, pepper, nutmeg; dilute very gradually with the boiling milk; cook 5–6 min., constantly stirring with a wire whisk. When the panada has thickened to the desired degree, pour out and cool.

D. RICE PANADA PANADE AU RIZ (E.)

(*For various forcemeats.*)

Ingredients: 8 oz. rice, 15 oz. white consommé, ¾ oz. butter.

Preparation: Pour the consommé over the rice, add the butter, bring to a boil, and cook in the oven 40–45 min. without touching the rice. After removing it from the oven, beat vigorously with a spoon to crush the rice, and let stand till cool.

E. POTATO PANADA PANADE À LA POMME DE TERRE (E.)

(*Suitable for large quenelles stuffed with veal and other white meats.*)

Ingredients: 2 medium-sized freshly boiled, peeled potatoes, 9 oz. milk, salt, white pepper, a little nutmeg, ¾ oz. butter.

Preparation: Boil the milk until reduced by 1/6 and add the butter, seasoning, and the potatoes cut in thin slices; cook 15 min. This preparation should be used while it is still warm because the purée will become sticky if it is mixed cold.

FORCEMEATS

Regardless of the basic ingredient used, whether veal, chicken, game, fish, or shellfish, forcemeats are all made the same way. A recipe typical of each kind of forcemeat is given below. Other recipes may be prepared simply by changing the ingredients.

FORCEMEAT WITH PANADA AND BUTTER FARCE À LA PANADE ET AU BEURRE (E.)

(*For ordinary quenelles, decorated borders for entrees, etc.*)

Ingredients: 2 lb. carefully trimmed meat, 1 lb. Flour Panada (p. 172), 2 tsp. salt, 1/4 tsp. pepper, pinch of nutmeg, 1 lb. butter, 4 whole eggs and 8 yolks.

Preparation: Dice the meat and pound in a mortar with the seasoning. Remove the meat and pound the panada. Then add the butter, put the seasoned meat back in, and, using a pestle, pound vigorously to assure an even mixture. Next add the eggs and yolks, 1 or 2 at a time; strain through a sieve into a bowl, and stir with a spatula until very smooth.

Note: In making any kind of forcemeat, a small portion of it should be poached as a test before continuing to make forcemeat balls or quenelles.

FORCEMEAT WITH PANADA AND CREAM FARCE À LA PANADE ET À LA CRÈME (E.)

(*For light quenelles.*)

Ingredients: 2 lb. trimmed meat, 3/4 lb. Frangipane Panada (p. 172), 5 egg whites, 1 tsp. salt, 1/4 tsp. white pepper, dash of nutmeg, 5 1/2 cups heavy cream.

Preparation: Whatever meat is used, pound it, adding the egg whites a little at a time. Add the panada, and pound thoroughly with a pestle until the ingredients are well mixed. Press through a fine sieve into a bowl, beat with a spatula until smooth, and chill on ice 1 hr. Then dilute little by little with 1/3 of the cream, finally adding the other 2/3 half whipped. The forcemeat should now be very white, smooth, and creamy.

Note: Unless you have the finest quality heavy cream, it would be better to make Forcemeat with Butter (recipe above), using Frangipane Panada.

LIGHT FORCEMEAT WITH CREAM or MOUSSELINE FORCEMEAT FARCE FINE À LA CRÈME or MOUSSELINE (E.)

(*For mousses, mousselines, soup quenelles, etc.*)

Ingredients: 2 lb. trimmed meat, 4 egg whites, 5 1/2 cups fresh, heavy cream, 2 tsp. salt, and 1/3 tsp. white pepper.

Preparation: Pound the finely minced meat and seasoning in a mortar; add the egg whites little by little, and press through a fine sieve. Put the forcemeat into a sautéing pan; beat with a spatula until smooth, and chill on ice 2 hr. Next dilute it gradually with cream, blending it carefully, without removing the pan from the ice.

Note: (1) The quantity of cream given in this recipe is the average amount used, since different meats and fish can absorb more or less cream, depending on their albuminous characteristics. (2) This forcemeat (the finest and most delicate of forcemeats) can be used with any meat, game, fowl, fish, or shellfish as the base. (3) Fresh meats rich in albumin, such as fowl and veal, need less egg white than older and well-hung meats. In fact, when this forcemeat is made with sliced spring chicken, while the flesh is still warm, the egg whites can be left out. (4) When good cream is available, this forcemeat should be prepared in preference to any other, especially if shellfish is used for a base.

CHICKEN QUENELLES QUENELLES FINES DE VOLAILLE (M.)

(*For soup.*)

The forcemeat: Make a mash of 5½ oz. (net weight) lean meat of chicken (white preferably), adding 1 egg white. Season with salt, white pepper, and a little grated nutmeg. Press through a fine sieve. Put into a bowl over ice; beat it with a spatula, while adding, bit by bit, 3 oz. fresh heavy cream. *The quenelles:* The forcemeat may be made into balls either by squeezing it from a pastry bag with a plain round tube or by shaping it with a teaspoon. Make the balls very small and lay them in a buttered pan. Pour boiling white consommé over them and poach by simmering gently.

Note: Quenelles for soup may be varied by adding different ingredients, such as chopped truffles or mushrooms, *fines herbes*, chives, etc. They may also be made with very white veal for economy's sake.

VEAL FORCEMEAT WITH BEEF SUET OR GODIVEAU

A. GODIVEAU WITH ICE GODIVEAU MOUILLÉ À LA GLACE (E.)

Ingredients: 2 lb. loin of veal with sinews removed, 3 lb. very dry beef suet, 8 whole eggs, 1 oz. salt, 1 tsp. white pepper, generous pinch of nutmeg, 1½ lb. chopped ice or 3 pt. ice water.

Preparation: Dice the veal and chop into mincemeat, adding the seasoning. Then chop the beef suet, which has been cut in pieces, with the skin and fibers well removed. Pound the chopped veal and the chopped suet separately, then combine them and pound together until thoroughly mixed; add the eggs 1 by 1 while continuing to pound. Press through a sieve and spread the stuffing in a thin layer on a tray and keep on ice until the next day. The following day pound again and add the ice (or ice water), broken into small pieces to facilitate mixing, bit by bit. Always test the forcemeat after the ice has been added—if it is too firm, add a little ice water, and if it is too light, bind with a little egg white.

Note: Quenelles made from Godiveau are principally used for garnishing Vol-au-vent (p. 530) and for the Financière Garnish (p. 181) that accompanies roasts. Like the others, these quenelles can be squeezed from a pastry bag, but they are usually rolled by hand and poached in salted water. However, they are even better if they are cooked in a slow oven rather than poached in liquid. Make the Godiveau rather moist; squeeze them from a pastry bag with a plain tube onto buttered papers, which in turn are put on buttered trays, and heat in a slow oven 7–8 min., until a few drops of grease form on the outside of the balls. Remove from the oven, place a tray or a marble slab on top, turn them upside down, and as soon as they are merely warm, pull the papers off. Then let them cool completely and arrange them on dishes or, better yet, wicker racks.

B. GODIVEAU WITH CREAM   GODIVEAU À LA CRÈME (E.)

Ingredients: 2 lb. loin of very white veal with sinews removed, 2 lb. very dry beef suet, 4 whole eggs and 3 yolks, 20 oz. cream, 1 oz. salt, 1 tsp. pepper, and a pinch of nutmeg.

Preparation: Chop the veal and suet separately into a fine mincemeat; mix them together in a mortar, season, and pound until perfectly combined; add the whole eggs and the yolks 1 by 1, continuing to pound vigorously. Press through a sieve, spread out on a tray, and chill on ice until the next day. The following day chill a mortar or mixing bowl in advance by packing ice inside; pound the mixture again, this time mixing the cream in gradually. Test the forcemeat before shaping all the quenelles and correct the composition if necessary.

C. LYONNAIS GODIVEAU or PIKE FORCEMEAT WITH SUET

GODIVEAU LYONNAIS or FARCE DE BROCHET À LA GRAISSE (E.)

Ingredients: 1 lb. boned and skinned pike (net weight), 1 lb. very dry beef suet trimmed and crumbled (or ½ beef fat and ½ very white beef marrow), 1 lb. Frangipane Panada (p. 172), 4 egg whites, ½ oz. salt, ½ tsp. pepper, and a dash of nutmeg.

Preparation: Pound the pike into a mash; pound the suet separately, adding the panada (very cold) and the egg whites little by little. Mix the pike with the suet, add the seasoning, pound vigorously, and press through a sieve. Put the mixture into a mixing bowl, blend thoroughly with a spatula, and keep on ice until needed. Another method is to add the panada to the mashed and seasoned pike, press it through a sieve, put it back into the mortar, and pound it vigorously. Then add the suet in small bits (or the melted fat and marrow), constantly pounding. Put into a bowl and chill on ice.

GRATIN FORCEMEAT   FARCE GRATIN (E.)

(*For meat pies, canapés, small game, and duckling.*)

Quantities for 2 lb. forcemeat: 12 oz. fresh fat bacon ground, 24 oz. chicken livers, 4 or 5 sliced shallots, 1 oz. mushroom peelings, ½ bay leaf, a sprig of thyme, 1½ tsp. salt, ⅓ tsp. pepper, a dash of allspice.

Preparation: Melt the bacon and heat it in a sautéing pan; add the chicken livers with the shallots, mushrooms, and seasoning, and sear them quickly. Do not brown—the livers must be very rare to make a pinkish forcemeat. Let become almost cool, pound into a paste, press through a sieve, beat smooth in a bowl. Cover with buttered paper and keep in a cool place.

FORCEMEAT FOR POULTRY AND GAME FARCE POUR VOLAILLE ET GIBIER (E.)

The net weight of the poultry or game fowl used in making this forcemeat will determine the proportions of the other ingredients. Thus, a chicken weighing 3 lb. cleaned will usually furnish 1 lb. breast meat for the forcemeat. The other ingredients will therefore be in the following proportions: 8 oz. well-trimmed veal, 8 oz. lean pork, 2 lb. fresh bacon fat, 4 whole eggs, 2 oz. spiced salt, 3 oz. brandy.

Preparation: Chop the meats and baconfat separately; mix them together in a mortar with the seasoning; pound them into a fine paste, adding the eggs 1 by 1 and the brandy at the very last; press through a sieve.

DUXELLES

DRY DUXELLES DUXELLES SÈCHE (E.)

The basic ingredient is invariably chopped mushrooms, and it can be made with any edible mushroom. Heat 1 tbsp. chopped onion and 1 tbsp. chopped shallot in 1 oz. butter and 1 oz. oil. Add ½ lb. finely chopped mushroom peelings and stems pressed in a towel to extract the moisture. Brown until almost all the liquid has evaporated; season with salt and pepper and finish with a pinch of chopped parsley; put into a bowl and cover with buttered paper.

DUXELLES FOR STUFFED VEGETABLES DUXELLES POUR LÉGUMES FARCIS (E.)

Use for stuffing tomatoes, mushrooms, etc. Take 4 tbsp. Dry Duxelles (above) ; add to it 1½ oz. white wine and reduce almost completely. Add 3 oz. Semiglaze Sauce (p. 138) with a strong tomato base, a small clove of crushed garlic, 1 oz. bread crumbs. Let simmer until it has thickened to the proper consistency for use.

BASIC MIXTURES AND PREPARATIONS FOR COLD GARNISHES

MOUSSES, MOUSSELINES, and **COLD SOUFFLÉS** MOUSSES, MOUSSELINES, and SOUFFLÉS FROIDES (E.)

Hot or cold, Mousses and Mousselines are the same except for their size, shape, and the way in which they are used. A Mousse, whether cold or hot, is usually made in a large mold, its capacity depending upon the number of people to be served. Mousselines, on the other hand, are molded with a spoon, pastry bag, or in special molds in the shape of large quenelles, 1 for each guest. Soufflés are molded in small cassolettes, or small individual casseroles.

COMPOSITION OF THE BASIC MIXTURE FOR COLD MOUSSES AND MOUSSELINES (E.)

Ingredients: 1 qt. purée of poultry, game, *foie gras,* fish, shellfish, or whatever the principal ingredient is to be; 7 oz. melted Aspic Jelly (p. 168) ; 12 oz. Velouté (p. 147) ; 12 oz. cream, which when whipped will make 18 oz. The proportions may be slightly modified, depending upon the basic ingredient used; also, some Mousses are made with either Aspic Jelly or Velouté.

Preparation: Add the Aspic Jelly and the Velouté (or only 1 of the 2, if desired) to the basic purée, mixing thoroughly in a bowl over ice; next add the whipped cream. Please note that the seasoning must be carefully tested and corrected in making any cold preparation.

Note: The cream should be only half whipped; if it is completely whipped, the Mousse will not be so smooth and will have a rather dry taste.

MOLDING COLD MOUSSES (E.)

Formerly—and this method is still used by many—Mousses were molded in plain or fancy molds lined with a layer of very clear jelly and decorated with ingredients in keeping with the Mousse. Today, we prefer this method: set a layer of very clear Aspic Jelly (p. 168) in the bottom of a silver timbale; using fresh butter, stick a band of white paper on the outside of the timbale so that it is about ¾ in. higher than the rim of the timbale and when it is removed will make the Mousse resemble a soufflé. The band of paper can also be placed inside the timbale; it is removed just before serving, by detaching it from the Mousse with a knife blade dipped in warm water and pulling it gently off. As soon as the timbale is garnished, the Mousse is put in a cool place to set. Mousses can also be made in little silver cassolettes, but this method is better reserved for cold soufflés, in order to show a difference between them, even though they may be made of the same ingredients. Mousses can also be prepared in modern silver or crystal utensils, especially game and *foie gras* Mousses. The preparation is simply poured into the center of the utensil (at the bottom of which a layer of Aspic Jelly has set) and carefully smoothed; it is put in a cool place to set, and the decorations are applied directly on the Mousse, which is finally glazed with Aspic Jelly. When a game Mousse is made, it is surrounded with *suprême* of game glazed with Aspic Jelly.

MOLDING COLD MOUSSELINES (E.)

Cold Mousselines may be molded either with a layer of Aspic Jelly (p. 168) or with a Chaud-Froid Sauce (p. 139). In either case, they should be made in an egg-shaped mold.

First Method: Line the molds with very clear Aspic Jelly; then put in a layer of the Mousse mixture containing the principal ingredient, such as chicken, game, fish, shellfish, or truffles. Garnish with a salpicon (see Medium Mirepoix, note, p. 136) made of the same basic ingredient. Cover with another layer of the Mousse mixture, smooth the top into a dome shape, and put into the refrigerator to harden.

Second Method: Cover the bottoms of the molds with the Mousse mixture; garnish with a salpicon made of the same ingredient; cover with another layer of Mousse mixture, and put into the refrigerator. When the Mousselines have solidified, remove from the molds and cover with a Chaud-Froid Sauce (p. 139) in keeping with the basic ingredient; decorate with small pieces of truffles, chicken, or whatever the Mousseline is made of. Glaze with Aspic Jelly to protect the decoration. Cover the bottom of a crystal or silver platter with a layer of clear Aspic Jelly and let it set; arrange the Mousselines on this bed; pour some more jelly over them, and keep in the refrigerator until ready to serve.

COLD SOUFFLÉS SOUFFLÉS FROIDS (E.)

Cold Soufflés are the same as Mousses so far as their composition is concerned, but instead of being made in large molds they are made in small cas solettes, 1 for each person. They are molded like Mousses—in other words, the Mousse mixture is placed on a layer of Aspic Jelly that has set in the bottom of the cassolettes; these have a paper band around them so that the mixture can be filled above the rim, giving the effect of a hot soufflé when the paper band is removed after the mixture has hardened.

Note: The principle of these 3 preparations, all of which have the same base, may be stated quite simply: (1) a Mousse, even though it could be served under the name of soufflé, should still be called a Mousse to avoid confusion, and is made in a mold large enough to serve all the guests; (2) Mousselines are like large quenelles, whether or not stuffed with a salpicon, and are served 1 to a person; (3) Cold Soufflés are small Mousses molded in cassolettes or similar dishes and are also served 1 to a person.

ASPICS ASPICS (E.)

The main point to remember in preparing any aspic is that the jelly must be tasty, absolutely limpid, and with just the right stiffness. When aspics are molded as they were in the ancient cuisine, the molds used are always those with a hollow in the center, whether plain or decorated. Ring molds can also be used, but generally only when the center of the aspic is filled with a garnish. The first step in making a molded aspic is to decorate the bottom and sides of the mold. To do that, after the mold has been well chilled with crushed ice, pour in some half-set jelly and roll the mold over ice so that the jelly will stick to the bottom and sides; lay the decorative pieces in this cold jelly, which immediately holds them. The question of decoration depends on the taste and imagination of the cook and can scarcely be prescribed; all one can say is that the decoration must be placed perfectly and be plainly seen when the aspic is removed from the mold. The ingredients used in the decoration must also be in keeping with the principal ingredient of the aspic. These are usually truffles, poached and shaped egg white, gherkins, capers, various leaves, thin radish rings, lobster coral, pickled tongue, etc. If the aspic filling is made of various sliced meats, rectangles of *foie gras,* etc., and the mold is so large that this must be made in several layers, a bed of jelly must be placed between each layer of filling, which is not added until the jelly it is laid upon has sufficiently solidified. The aspic is always finished with a rather thick layer of jelly. As soon as possible surround the mold with ice to set the aspic, but without using salt, because that would disturb the smoothness of the jelly.

To unmold: Dip the mold in hot water, dry it quickly, turn the mold upside down on a folded napkin, bed of molded rice, or block of carved ice. Surround the aspic with jelly cut in small squares, diamond shapes, etc., or with chopped jelly.

Note: A molded aspic necessarily requires a fairly stiff jelly, which is always a serious drawback, for this sort of jelly hasn't the quality of ordinary jelly. However, modern culinary practice has adopted this method: first, a bowl or mold of silver, crystal, or porcelain is embedded in ice and then the bottom is covered with a layer of jelly, which is allowed to harden. The ingredients of the aspic are then added, and a layer of half-congealed jelly is placed on top. In this method, the decoration, if any, is made directly on the aspic ingredients before they are set in place.

CHAUDS-FROIDS (E.)

The cooked meats, poultry, or game to be covered with Chaud-Froid Sauce (p. 139) are usually small pieces, although whole roasts or joints may be treated the same way. However, the larger pieces have special names. If the Chaud-Froid is made up of small separate pieces, these are usually dipped in the sauce and placed on a grill. When the sauce is cold, the pieces are decorated, glazed with jelly, and the excess sauce is trimmed off. If a large piece is used, it should be completely covered at one time with very cold but very runny Chaud-Froid Sauce; then it is decorated and glazed with jelly. Small Chauds-Froids are served either on a base or around the border of a mound of bread, rice, or semolina; or they may be served in a timbale or a deep silver, porcelain, or crystal dish. Large pieces of meat served as Chauds-Froids may be placed on a platter or in a bowl laid in a bed of ice. Poultry and game fowl made into Chauds-Froids should be cut into uniform pieces, with the skin removed. Wings and drumsticks are not used, but set aside for some other purpose. Chauds-Froids made of sliced meats are usually combined with mushrooms, cockscombs and cock's kidneys, which should be covered with sauce, and with truffles, which are simply glazed with jelly.

COLD LOAVES PAINS FROIDS (E.)

In old-style cooking these were merely a kind of forcemeat that had been molded, chilled, then decorated and glazed with jelly. Modern cooking no longer includes this recipe, and Cold Loaves have been replaced by Mousses.

GARNISHES FOR COLD DISHES (E.)

There are various garnishes for cold dishes, depending upon the nature of the preparation: halves or quarters of stuffed eggs, decorated and glazed; small tomatoes stuffed or otherwise garnished, or large stuffed tomatoes cut into quarters; small timbales or pastry boats with vegetable salad; French rolls or tartlets with tomato purée bound with jelly; very white hearts of lettuce; anchovy fillets, olives, etc.

GARNISHES

Proportions are for 10 servings

ALGÉRIENNE or ALGERIAN GARNISH GARNITURE À L'ALGÉRIENNE (E.)

(For cuts of meat)

10 sweet-potato croquettes shaped into small loaves; 10 small tomatoes, drained, seasoned, and cooked slowly in a finger of oil. Serve with thin Tomato Sauce (p. 146) mixed with grilled, peeled pimentos cut in tiny julienne strips.

AMÉRICAINE or **AMERICAN GARNISH** GARNITURE À L'AMÉRICAINE (E.) (*For fish*)

This garnish invariably calls for slices of lobster meat prepared *à l'américaine* (see p. 316). Serve with a lobster sauce.

AMIRAL GARNISH GARNITURE AMIRAL (M.) (*For fish*)

Poached oysters, breaded and fried; Mussels Villeroi (p. 323); very small shells of Crayfish au Gratin (p. 315); large, thick slices of truffles. Serve with Normande Sauce (p. 153) finished with Crayfish Butter (p. 164).

ARMENONVILLE GARNISH GARNITURE ARMENONVILLE (M.) (*For fish*)

Slices of truffles alternated with slices of boiled potatoes, arranged in a border. Serve with White-Wine Sauce (p. 155) containing mushrooms cut in fine julienne strips and sautéed in butter.

BASQUAISE or **BASQUE GARNISH** GARNITURE BASQUAISE (M.) (*For fish pan-fried in oil*)

Julienne of pimentos cooked in oil; mushrooms sautéed in oil. Serve with Tomato Sauce (p. 146) flavored with a little chopped garlic.

BOULANGÈRE GARNISH GARNITURE À LA BOULANGÈRE (E.) (*For mutton, lamb, and poultry*)

½ lb. sliced onions browned in butter, 1½ lb. potatoes cut in quarters or sliced, 1 tsp. salt, and ½ tsp. pepper. These ingredients should be mixed together and placed around the meat after it has been browned. Cook with the meat. When this garnish is used with chicken, make the following change: potatoes cut in the shape of olives; small onions previously browned in butter. Serve with a little good gravy.

BOUQUETIÈRE GARNISH GARNITURE À LA BOUQUETIÈRE (E.) (*For roast meats*)

½ lb. carrots and ½ lb. turnips cut into balls and glazed; ½ lb. small Potatoes Château (p. 506); ¼ lb. green peas and ¼ lb. diced green beans, mixed in butter just before serving; ½ lb. cauliflower in flowerets. Arrange these vegetables around the roast in small separate mounds, alternating the colors; cover the cauliflower lightly with Hollandaise Sauce (p. 151). Serve with gravy from the roast, skimmed of fat and made very clear.

BOURGUIGNONNE GARNISH GARNITURE À LA BOURGUIGNONNE (E.) (*For braised beef*)

1 lb. small glazed onions, ½ lb. quartered mushrooms sautéed in butter, 5 oz. diced browned bacon. These ingredients should be arranged around the piece of meat at the proper time. The base of the liquid used for cooking the beef must always be an excellent red wine—that's the hallmark of a dish labeled *à la bourguignonne*. Serve with the braising sauce.

CARDINAL GARNISH GARNITURE À LA CARDINAL (E.) (*For fish*)

10 fine slices of lobster tail, 10 slices of very black truffle, 2½ oz. lobster meat, and 2 oz. diced truffles. Serve with Cardinal Sauce (p. 148).

CHAMBORD GARNISH GARNITURE CHAMBORD (E.) (*For large braised fish*)

10 quenelles of fish forcemeat made with truffles and molded with a spoon; 4 large decorated oval-shaped quenelles; 8 oz. fluted mushrooms; 10 slices of soft roe, seasoned, floured, and sautéed in butter; 8 oz. truffles cut in olive shape; 6 crayfish, shelled or not, cooked in Court Bouillon (p. 277), 6 croutons fried in butter. Make the sauce from the stock used in braising the fish.

CHÂTELAINE GARNISH GARNITURE CHÂTELAINE (E.) (*For meats and poultry*)

10 artichoke bottoms filled with thick Soubise Sauce (p. 154), 30 shelled chestnuts cooked in the braising liquid of the meat, 12 oz. Potatoes Noisette (p. 509). Sauce: the stock used in cooking the meat, added to Madeira Sauce (p. 142).

CHOISY GARNISH GARNITURE CHOISY (E.) (*For tournedos and noisettes*)

10 halves of braised lettuce, 20 small Potatoes Château (p. 506). Sauce: Buttered Meat Glaze (p. 135).

DIEPPOISE GARNISH GARNITURE DIEPPOISE (M.) (*For fish*)

Mussels cooked in white wine and drained, shelled shrimps, White-Wine Sauce (p. 155).

FINANCIÈRE GARNISH GARNITURE À LA FINANCIÈRE (E.) (*For meats and poultry*)

20 ordinary quenelles of veal or chicken forcemeat, depending on whether the garnish is used with meat or poultry; 6 oz. small fluted mushroom caps; 4 oz. cockscombs and cock's kidneys; 2 oz. sliced truffles; 12 blanched olives. Financière Sauce (p. 141).

FLORENTINE GARNISH GARNITURE FLORENTINE (M.) (*For fish and eggs*)

Blanch spinach leaves, chop them coarsely, cook in butter, and place as a bed under fish fillets cooked in white wine. Mornay Sauce (p. 152).

GODARD GARNISH GARNITURE GODARD (E.) (*For roasts and poultry*)

10 quenelles of Forcemeat with Panada and Butter (p. 173), with chopped mushrooms and truffles added, and shaped with a spoon; 4 large oval quenelles decorated with truffle and very red tongue; 10 small fluted mushroom caps; 5 oz. cockscombs and cock's kidneys; 8 oz. fine glazed lamb sweetbreads or glazed and sliced veal sweetbreads; 10 truffles cut in the shape of olives. Godard Sauce (p. 141).

HENRY IV GARNISH GARNITURE HENRI IV (E.) (*For noisettes and tournedos*)

Medium- or small-sized artichoke bottoms filled with tiny Potatoes Noisette (p. 509) rolled in melted meat glaze. Béarnaise Sauce (p. 147).

HONGROISE or **HUNGARIAN GARNISH** GARNITURE HONGROISE (E.) (*For various dishes*)

Mold cauliflower flowerets in small cups or ramekins and empty onto an ovenproof platter that has been buttered; sprinkle the cauliflower with grated cheese; and cover with Mornay Sauce (p. 152) containing paprika and chopped, glazed ham. Serve with a thin sauce seasoned with paprika.

INDIENNE or **INDIAN GARNISH** GARNITURE À L'INDIENNE (E.) (*For fish, meats, and poultry*)

5 oz. Patna rice prepared Indian style (see Rice Indian Style, p. 512). Curry or Indienne Sauce (p. 150).

ITALIENNE or **ITALIAN GARNISH** GARNITURE À L'ITALIENNE (E.) (*For meats and poultry*)

20 small Artichoke Quarters Italian Style (p. 490), 10 Macaroni Croquettes (p. 240) bound with grated cheese and shaped like disks. Italienne Sauce (p. 142).

JARDINIÈRE GARNISH GARNITURE À LA JARDINIÈRE (E.) (*For meats*)

5 oz. carrots and 5 oz. turnips scooped into balls with a plain or grooved vegetable spoon, or column-shaped, and cooked in consommé and glazed; 5 oz. green peas, 4 oz. small kidney beans (young haricot beans), and 5 oz. French beans cut in diamond shapes, all 3 vegetables with melted butter added just before serving and kept separate; 10 flowerets of freshly cooked cauliflower. Arrange these vegetables around the meat in separate mounds, alternating the colors; cover each floweret of cauliflower with 1 tsp. Hollandaise sauce (p.151). Serve with clear gravy.

JOINVILLE GARNISH GARNITURE JOINVILLE (M.) (*For fish*)

Fish fillets prepared Joinville style are especially characterized by their garnish, a border of quenelles of Pike Forcemeat (p. 175). As a variation, the fish fillets cooked in white wine may be garnished with a salpicon (see note, p. 136) of shrimps, truffles, and mushrooms bound with Joinville Sauce (p. 152).

MAILLOT GARNISH GARNITURE À LA MAILLOT (E.) (*Serve with meats, especially ham*)

10 carrots and 10 turnips cut in the shape of large olives and cooked in consommé, 20 small glazed onions, 10 braised halves of lettuce, 4 oz. green peas, and 4 oz. French beans mixed with butter. Sauce: thickened gravy.

MARÉCHAL GARNISH GARNITURE MARÉCHAL (E.)

(*A*) For calves' sweetbreads, cuts of meat, and poultry: 10 spoon-shaped quenelles of truffled chicken forcemeat, 2–2½ oz. sliced truffles mixed with

Italienne Sauce (p. 142), 20 cockscombs. Serve with Semiglaze Sauce (p. 138) made with Madeira.

(*B*) For sliced poultry, sliced calves' sweetbreads, lamb noisettes and chops: a slice of glazed truffle on each portion of meat; asparagus tips with butter (or, if asparagus is not in season, very tiny green peas). Meats with which this garnish is served are always breaded with a mixture of ⅔ bread crumbs and ⅓ finely chopped truffles.

MILANAISE or **MILANESE GARNISH** GARNITURE À LA MILANAISE (E.) (*For cuts of meat*)

1 lb. blanched macaroni cut in short pieces; 2 oz. each pickled tongue, ham, mushrooms, and truffles, all sliced in thin julienne strips; 2 oz. Gruyère and 2 oz. Parmesan cheese, grated; 3 oz. tomato purée; 4 oz. butter. Serve with clear Tomato Sauce (p. 146).

MIRABEAU GARNISH GARNITURE MIRABEAU (E.) (*For grilled red meats*)

20 strips of anchovy fillets arranged crisscross on the piece of grilled meat, 10 large pitted olives, a border of blanched tarragon leaves, 5 oz. Anchovy Butter (p. 163).

NANTUA GARNISH GARNITURE NANTUA (M.) (*For fish*)

Crayfish tails with Nantua Sauce (p. 152) arranged in a border around fish cooked in white wine or placed in small pastry boats or patty shells. Sometimes sliced truffles are added to this garnish. Reduced fish stock is added to the Nantua Sauce.

NIÇOISE GARNISH GARNITURE NIÇOISE (M.) (*For grilled or pan-fried fish*)

Tomato Fondue (p. 194) with a little Anchovy Butter (p. 163) and chopped tarragon added; anchovy fillets placed crisscross on the fish; capers and black olives (or pitted green olives, if preferred). Slices of lemon, peeled to the flesh, on the fish.

NORMANDE GARNISH GARNITURE À LA NORMANDE (E.) (*For fish*)

10 oysters and 10 mussels, poached and trimmed, 10 small mushroom caps, 4 oz. shelled shrimps, 10 slices of truffles, 10 medium-sized crayfish cooked in Court Bouillon (p. 277), 10 gudgeons or small smelts breaded and fried, 10 small diamond-shaped bread croutons fried in butter just before serving or some baked puff-paste rosettes. Normande Sauce (p. 153).

Note: The use of truffles in this garnish is optional.

ORIENTALE GARNISH GARNITURE À L'ORIENTALE (M.) (*For fish*)

Small tomatoes stuffed with Risotto (p. 513), zucchini sautéed in oil, cooked pimentos, black olives. Tomato Fondue (p. 194), somewhat thin, seasoned with curry. Serve Rice Pilaf (p. 512) separately.

PARISIENNE or **PARISIAN GARNISH** GARNITURE À LA PARISIENNE (E.) (*For cuts of meat and poultry*)

1¼ lb. Potatoes Parisienne (p. 509), 10 artichoke bottoms cooked in butter and garnished in dome shape with a salpicon (tiny cubes) of equal parts of tongue, mushrooms, and truffles bound with thick Velouté (p. 147); glaze under a hot flame or with a salamander. Serve with Semiglaze Sauce (p. 138).

PORTUGAISE or **PORTUGUESE GARNISH** GARNITURE PORTUGAISE (E.) (*For cuts of meat and poultry*)

10 small whole tomatoes stuffed with Duxelles (p. 176), 30 Potatoes Château (p. 506). Serve with Portugaise Sauce (p. 144).

PRINCESSE GARNISH GARNITURE PRINCESSE (M.) (*For fish*)

Green asparagus tips covered with butter, sliced truffles. Normande Sauce (p. 153).

Note: Usually served with quenelles, mousses, and fish loaves, but may also be used to garnish fish fillets cooked in white wine.

PRINTANIÈRE GARNISH GARNITURE À LA PRINTANIÈRE (E.) (*For poultry and meat sautés*)

5 oz. each of small early-spring carrots and turnips cut in balls, cooked in consommé, and glazed; 20 small new onions glazed in butter; 5 oz. green peas; and 5 oz. blanched asparagus tips. Cook the vegetables 8–10 min. together with the meat or poultry they are to accompany, before serving.

PROVENÇAL GARNISH GARNITURE À LA PROVENÇALE (E.) (*For roast meats*)

10 small whole tomatoes, 10 large mushrooms stuffed with Duxelles (p. 176) with a pinch of garlic added. Provençal Sauce (p. 144).

RÉGENCE GARNISH GARNITURE RÉGENCE (M.) (*For fish*)

Large quenelles of Pike Forcemeat (p. 175) finished with Crayfish Butter (p. 164), poached oysters, carp or pike soft roe poached in white wine (usually stuffed into little pastry boats; see p. 233), mushrooms cooked in white wine, sliced truffles. Normande Sauce (p. 153).

RICHELIEU GARNISH GARNITURE RICHELIEU (E.) (*For roast meats*)

10 small tomatoes and 10 medium-sized mushrooms stuffed in the usual way; 10 small lettuces or halves of lettuce, braised; 20 potatoes cut in the size and shape of pigeons' eggs and cooked in butter just before serving. Serve with the cooking juices of the meat skimmed of fat, strained, and slightly thickened.

ROSSINI GARNISH GARNITURE ROSSINI (E.) (*For noisettes and tournedos*)

10 good slices of *foie gras* sautéed in butter and seasoned, 4 oz. sliced truffles. Serve with Semiglaze Sauce (p. 138) with truffle essence.

STRASBOURGEOISE GARNISH GARNITURE À LA STRASBOURGEOISE (E.) (*For geese and turkeys*)

1¼ lb. braised sauerkraut, 10 rectangles of salt pork cooked with the sauerkraut, 10 slices of sautéed *foie gras*. Serve with the gravy from the bird.

TOULOUSAINE GARNISH GARNITURE À LA TOULOUSAINE (E.) (*For poultry and Vol-au-vent*)

20 quenelles of chicken forcemeat, 10 slices of braised lambs' or calves' sweetbreads, 4 oz. cockscombs and cock's kidneys, 8 oz. very white mushroom caps, 2 oz. sliced truffles. Parisienne Sauce (p. 146) with mushroom essence.

VERT-PRÉ GARNISH GARNITURE VERT-PRÉ (E.)

(*A*) For grilled meats: bunches of water cress or garden cress, mounds of Potato Straws (p. 509). Serve with Maître d'Hôtel Butter (p. 164).

(*B*) For white meats and duckling: 12 oz. green peas, 12 oz. French beans, 8 oz. asparagus tips, mixed in melted butter. Serve with clear gravy.

ZINGARA GARNISH GARNITURE À LA ZINGARA (E.) (*For veal and poultry*)

4 oz. lean ham and pickled tongue sliced in thin julienne strips, 4 oz. mushrooms and 2 oz. truffles also cut in julienne. Serve with Semiglaze Sauce (p. 138) fortified with tomato and tarragon.

THICK AND CLEAR SOUPS

THICK AND CLEAR SOUPS

This chapter on cooking will interest all gourmets, for while soup may not be the most important part of a dinner it is none the less the first act, the curtain raiser, if we may call it that, and its composition and excellent quality will augur what is to follow. We recommend that for a fine dinner great care be taken with the soup. France is the classical land of soup, and, as Montagné says, quoting the good-natured Chrysale in Molière: "One lives on good soup, not fine talk." This assertion makes fine talk a little too cheap, since it also has its value, especially at the table, but the body will mellow with the good soup as the mind with the fine talk.

This chapter is divided into consommés, which include thin soups; bouillons, which are still plainer; soups thickened with puréed vegetables or with cream and egg yolks; and soups with bread, noodles, etc. Thin soups, consommés, cream soups with flour or vegetables, all have bouillon as their base, a broth made from Pot-au-Feu (p. 190) or stock rich in aromatic and nutritive juices. The starting point is always the national Pot-au-Feu, the bouillon which can be transformed into a full-bodied consommé or used to thin creams, purées, or thick soups, as you will learn from the recipes that follow. Clear consommés must be perfect in taste and smoothness; they are usually garnished with vegetables cooked separately, with noodles, tapioca, seminola, or sago, with a *royale* (see pp. 195–196), with fried croutons or with quenelles, with tomatoes, ham, Threaded Eggs (p. 194), or truffles (as will be explained in the following pages).

One recommendation is essential: always serve soup piping hot.

Throughout the centuries soups have been prepared in various ways according to the taste of the period. For example, in the Middle Ages they were seasoned with verjuice, ruby wine, saffron, and even mustard, as noted by Taillevent, head chef for Charles VI, in his memorable book, *Le Viandier*. Spoons already existed at that time, although forks were not to appear until much later.

At banquets it is customary to serve the guests a choice of 2 soups: a clear, garnished consommé and some sort of cream soup or bisque.

We repeat for soups what we said earlier about sauces. When cooking for the family, one cannot have at hand the famous bouillons and consommés used in fancy cooking. Therefore, the housekeeper must use meat broth when she has it and most of the time make her soups from boiled vegetables, enriching the more delicate soups with a commercial concentrate.

BASIC SOUPS AND CONSOMMÉS

ORDINARY PETITE MARMITE PARISIENNE PETITE MARMITE ORDINAIRE À LA PARISIENNE (M.) (*For 8–10 persons*)

Nutritive Ingredients: 1¼ lb. rump (or chuck) of beef, 1 lb. top ribs of beef, ½ lb. oxtail (cut up in slices), 1 marrowbone (tied in a muslin bag), 1 small chicken (1½–2 lb.) browned in the oven, chicken giblets. *Flavoring Ingredients:* ¾ lb. carrots and ½ lb. turnips (both net weight, cut in the shape of large olives), 4 oz. white of leeks cut in pieces, 4 oz. celery cut in pieces, 6 oz. heart of cabbage (blanched), 1 medium-sized onion stuck with a clove. *Liquid:* 4 qt. white consommé. *Garnishes:* In addition to the vegetables indicated above, which are the principal garnish, serve at the same time fine slices of bread (the long, thin French loaf) dried out in the oven, along with bread crusts with grated cheese and the soup poured over them. *Cooking Time:* 3½ hr.

Preparation: (1) Put the nutritive ingredients listed above into a large marmite (an earthenware soup pot). Add the consommé, covering the meat completely. Slowly bring to a boil. Skim carefully. (2) Add the vegetables listed above, except the cabbage (previously blanched), which is best cooked separately in white consommé with a little fat. Correct the seasoning. Simmer about 3 hr.

Serving: Petite Marmite should be served in the same pot in which it was made. The broth should be absolutely clear. Serve at the same time: (1) the heart of cabbage cooked in the rich consommé; (2) fine slices of French bread dried out in the oven, or toasted bread crusts. With Petite Marmite Parisienne it is also customary to serve rectangular slices of the soft part of the bread, toasted, and covered at the last moment with the marrow cooked in the pot. Put into each plate 2 small slices of beef (preferably from the top ribs), a slice of breast of chicken, and a piece of oxtail.

Note: The recipe given above is the one used in most fine eating places. In certain restaurants Petites Marmites are made in advance in pots varying in size from 2 to 6 servings. In other restaurants the soup is made in a large pot and served by the plate. The proportions of meat and vegetables given above may be adapted for preparing similar dishes.

Remarks: The Petite Marmite served in fine restaurants is often called (quite wrongly, we think) a bad imitation of the simple and savory Family Pot-au-Feu (below). This accusation is without foundation most of the time. Our long experience allows us to state that this succulent soup was generally made properly, with neither care nor necessary ingredients lacking. Petite Marmite is also occasionally called Pot-au-Feu. While the method of making the latter is similar, it differs from Petite Marmite, as the following recipes will show.

FAMILY POT-AU-FEU POT-AU-FEU FAMILIAL (P.) (*1 qt. for 4 persons*)

To make 4 qt. bouillon, take 5 qt. cold water, 2 lb. beef (chuck or shank), 1 soupbone (knucklebone), 6 oz. carrots, 2 oz. turnips, 3 or 4 leeks, 1 large onion, 1½ oz. bay salt, a small *bouquet garni* of chervil, parsley, bay leaf, and thyme, and 1 clove to be stuck into the onion. Put the meat and soupbone into the cold water, place on the stove, and slowly bring to a boil. Skim thoroughly, then salt and add the vegetables. When it begins to boil again, skim once more, then cover and cook slowly 3 hr. The bouillon should be clear and amber-colored. The color may be darkened by adding a little coloring such as caramel.

OXTAIL POT-AU-FEU or **FRENCH OXTAIL SOUP** POT-AU-FEU À LA QUEUE DE BOEUF OF POTAGE QUEUE DE BOEUF À LA FRANÇAISE (M.)

Nutritive Ingredients: 1 oxtail cut in even pieces, 3 lb. knuckle of veal. *Flavoring Ingredients:* 2 large onions and 2 large carrots cut in thick slices, 2 leeks cut in pieces, 2 stalks of celery sliced thin, 1 clove of garlic not peeled, 2 cloves, and a *bouquet garni* made of parsley stems, thyme, and bay leaf. *Liquid:* 3 qt. white consommé.

Preparation: Put the vegetables into a marmite heated with 1 tbsp. fat from clarified soup stock. Lay the knuckle of veal (cut crosswise in 2 or 3 pieces) on top of the vegetables and add the pieces of oxtail blanched and tied in a muslin bag. Cover the pot and cook gently until the vegetables and meat are slightly browned, then add the consommé, the garlic, and the *bouquet garni.* Bring to a boil, skim, season (if necessary). Simmer 5 hr. with the pot ¾ covered.

Clarifying: Strain the bouillon from the pot. Skim off the fat. Clarify it the following way (which is considerably different from that ordinarily used for consommés) : put ½ lb. lean beef and ½ lb. lean veal, diced, into a flat-bottomed stewpan and brown. Sprinkle with 2 oz. arrowroot. Cover with the consommé strained through a cloth. Simmer 45 min. Strain again through a cloth.

Garnish: Pieces of the oxtail, 12 oz. carrots and 6 oz. turnips scooped out in little balls and cooked in consommé. Serve in the same pot the soup was made in.

Note: This soup may also be garnished with the same vegetables cooked in the pot and cut into pieces the shape of a clove of garlic. Complete by adding a little Madeira at the last moment.

CLARIFIED CONSOMMÉ or **DOUBLE** or **RICH CONSOMMÉ** CONSOMMÉ CLARIFIÉ OF CONSOMMÉ DOUBLE OF RICHE (M.) (*For 4 qt. clarified consommé*)

Rich Consommé, to use the name it is generally given (a rather ostentatious term that we never use), to justify its name ought to be absolutely succulent. It should also have a fine amber color and be quite clear. Furthermore, we must say, basing our words on the authority of physiologists, that, rich though it is in extractive juices, Double Consommé is not a food in the precise sense of the word; to be truly nutritive it should be completed with some sort of Italian paste or bread. Here is how it is prepared:

Nutritive and Flavoring Ingredients: 4 lb. chopped lean beef, 6 oz. carrots diced fine, 6 oz. leeks diced fine. *Clarifying Ingredients:* 2 very fresh egg whites. *Liquid:* 5 qt. white consommé. *Cooking Time:* 1½ hr.

Preparation: Put the chopped meat and diced vegetables into a deep pot with a heavy bottom (or a tin-lined copper marmite). Add the egg whites. Mix these ingredients. Pour the cold white consommé into the pot. Bring to a boil, stirring frequently. As soon as the boiling is well pronounced, lower the flame and let simmer 1½ hr. Strain through a napkin.

ORDINARY FISH CONSOMMÉ CONSOMMÉ (SIMPLE) DE POISSON (E.) (*For 10 qt.*)

Nutritive Ingredients: 6 lb. pike, 2 lb. carp, 2 lb. tench, 2 lb. backbone of soles, 4 lb. heads of turbot or large whiting. *Flavoring Ingredients:* 1½ lb. onions cut in rings, 8 oz. parsley stems or roots, 1 lb. leeks, 1 stalk of celery (2 oz.), 1 bay leaf. *Liquid:* 9½ qt. water and 1 qt. white wine. *Seasoning:* 3 oz. salt. *Cooking Time:* 40–50 min. of simmering.

DOUBLE FISH CONSOMMÉ CONSOMMÉ (DOUBLE) DE POISSON (E.) (*For 4 qt.*)

Ordinary Fish Consommé (above) : 4 qt. *Other Ingredients:* 3 lb. boned fish (equal proportions of pike and whiting) pounded in a mortar, while adding 3 egg whites and 4 oz. leeks and 4 oz. parsley stems chopped fine.

Cooking Time: 25–30 min.

Clarifying: Put the fish pounded with the egg whites and chopped vegetables into a pot with a bottle of dry white wine. Mix, add the Ordinary Fish Consommé, bring to a boil, and let simmer.

Notes on Clarifying Fish Consommés: In clarifying fish consommé, you can reduce the amount of fish by ½, provided you replace it with 1¼ oz. caviar per qt. consommé. You can also use only caviar, 2½ oz. per qt. Ordinary Fish Consommé, following this procedure:

Pound the caviar (fresh or pressed) in a mortar; mix this purée with cold Ordinary Fish Consommé. Bring to a boil, stirring constantly. Lower the flame and let simmer 20 min. Then strain the consommé through cheesecloth. If it is not going to be used immediately, keep it in a covered double boiler or *bain-marie* to prevent a gelatinous skin from forming on the surface.

CLARIFIED CHICKEN CONSOMMÉ CONSOMMÉ DE VOLAILLE CLARIFIÉ (M.) (*For 4 qt.*)

Basic Ingredients: 1 medium-sized hen, trussed and browned in the oven; 6 chicken giblets chopped raw; 2 lb. lean ground beef. *Clarifying:* 2 egg whites. *Liquid:* 5 qt. white consommé. *Cooking Time:* 1 hr., 40 min. (depending on the tenderness of the hen; add to the cooking time, if needed).

Preparation: Proceed the same as for Clarified Consommé (p. 191). Strain through a cloth.

Remarks: The hen called for above may be replaced by a corresponding quantity of chicken giblets. Carcasses of roast chickens may also be added to this preparation. When a hen is used, it must not be too tough. The hen can be used later to make croquettes, chicken hash, or other dishes.

COLD CONSOMMÉS CONSOMMÉS FROIDS (A.)

Cold Consommés may be served as refreshment at social functions, as a dinner soup in summer, and with suppers. They are always clarified and must never be served with any solid ingredients added. They should be very rich and have a consistency similar to hot consommé with tapioca; if clearer, they will seem to lack body, and if thicker, they will be less appealing. They can be flavored with ingredients that will give them a special tone—game stock, mushrooms, truffles, tomatoes, pimento, celery, tarragon, brandy, liqueurs, or wines (Cyprian, Madeira, malmsey, Marsala, port, etc.). But the flavor chosen must be used with discretion; for 1 qt. consommé the following proportions are sufficient: 6 oz. mushrooms or truffles, 8 oz. tomatoes, 4 oz. celery, ½ oz. pimento, 3 oz. tarragon, 2¾–3¼ oz. wine, 1¼–1½ oz. brandy. When adding liqueurs or game stock, use only a little bit at a time and sample after adding each time, for it is impossible to give the proportions: they depend on the bouquet and alcoholic content of the liqueurs and, for game stock, on the kind of game used and how fresh it is.

Here is a concrete example of how to prepare cold consommé with tomatoes and port. For 6 persons take: 2½ lb. top round of beef without fat or bones, 2 lb. top ribs of beef, 2 lb. carrots, 1 lb. ground beef, 1 lb. tomatoes, 1 lb. knucklebone, 4 oz. port, 4 oz. turnips, 3 oz. white of leek, 1 oz. bay salt, ⅛ tsp. pepper, 4 qt. water, 3 chicken giblets, 2 egg whites, and parsnips, celery, bay leaf, thyme, clove, and garlic, more or less, according to taste. With all these ingredients, except the ground beef, egg whites, and port, make a bouillon that should be allowed to cook until only 2 qt. remain. During this process, remove the tomatoes before they disintegrate. Let the bouillon cool and skim off the fat. Put the skimmed bouillon into a stewpan, add the ground beef and the egg whites (lightly beaten), bring to a boil, then cook long enough to reduce the liquid to about 1½ qt. Strain the consommé through a cloth, add the port, and chill in the refrigerator.

VARIOUS INGREDIENTS FOR GARNISHING SOUPS

CHIFFONADE and CHERVIL TOPS CHIFFONADE and PLUCHES (E.)

Chiffonade is made of finely shredded lettuce and sorrel leaves, braised to a pulp in butter. In certain cases it is made of only strips of sorrel and lettuce blanched in salted water a few minutes before being put into the soup. Chervil Tops consist of only the leaves without stems and are a savory complement added to the soup only at the last moment.

CRUSTS and CROUTONS CROÛTES and CROÛTONS (E.)

Crusts are generally made from French bread (the long, thin, crusty loaves) split lengthwise and then cut into inch-thick strips. After the doughy bread on the inside of the crusts has been removed and the corners of the crusts trimmed, they should be lightly buttered or moistened with fat from unclarified soup stock and put into the oven to dry. Allow 1 crust per person. Soups sometimes are served with ordinary household bread cut in thin slices. In certain cases, these slices are dried in the oven; in others, they are sprinkled with grated cheese and then browned in the oven. Croutons are made from the soft part of the bread cut into ¼-in. cubes. They are fried in clarified butter—if possible, just before serving. Allow 2 tbsp. croutons to 1 qt. soup, or about 1½–2 oz.

GAME FORCEMEAT FOR QUENELLES FOR SOUP FARCE FINE DE GIBIER POUR QUENELLES À POTAGES (E.)

Proceed according to the method of preparation and the proportions given under Chicken Forcemeat for Quenelles (below), substituting slices of game for chicken.

FISH FORCEMEAT FOR QUENELLES FOR SOUP FARCE FINE DE POISSONS POUR QUENELLES À POTAGES (E.)

The preparation is the same as for Chicken Forcemeat for Quenelles (below), using fish fillets in keeping with the soup and increasing the number of egg whites by ¼.

CHICKEN FORCEMEAT FOR QUENELLES FOR SOUP FARCE FINE DE VOLAILLE POUR QUENELLES À POTAGES (E.)

Finely pound 4 oz. sliced, uncooked chicken in a mortar, adding 1 egg white a little at a time. Season with a pinch of salt, a dash of nutmeg, and press through a sieve. Work the mixture over ice, then blend in 1 oz. heavy cream.

TOMATO FONDUE and **DICED TOMATOES** FONDUE DE TOMATES and DÉS DE TOMATES (E.)

Tomato Fondue is used in various ways as a garnish, but it is always prepared the same way. The tomatoes used ought to be perfectly ripe, pressed, free of seeds, and well peeled. Scald them in boiling water for a few seconds to facilitate the removal of the skins. The flesh of the tomatoes is then finely sliced and cooked with 1 oz. butter to every 4 oz. tomatoes, a pinch of salt, and a good pinch of powdered sugar. Be careful to cook the tomatoes only till they "melt," not till they turn into a purée.

For Diced Tomatoes to be used as a garnish, choose very red but rather firm tomatoes and remove skins and seeds. The raw, peeled tomatoes are cut into cubes as even as possible, dropped into boiling white consommé, or lightly salted boiling water, and poached 7–8 min. They are then taken out with a perforated ladle and put directly into the soup they are to garnish.

JULIENNES and **BRUNOISES** JULIENNES and BRUNOISES (E.)

These are sometimes juliennes (thin matchlike strips) and brunoises (tiny dices) of ordinary vegetables, used as a simple or a supplementary garnish, in the proportions of 1 or 2 tbsp. per qt. soup. Other times they are juliennes and brunoises of poultry, game, or fish fillets, or pickled tongue, or artichoke bottoms, the usual proportions being 1 or ½ tbsp. per qt. soup, depending on whether the garnish contains few or many ingredients.

THREADED EGGS FOR GARNISHING CLEAR CONSOMMÉ OEUFS FILÉS POUR GARNITURE DE CONSOMMÉ CLAIR (E.)

For 2 qt. consommé: beat 1 egg as for an omelet and strain through cheesecloth. Pour into a cone-shaped sieve with fine holes, holding it over a pan of boiling consommé; wave it back and forth over the consommé until all of the egg has drained away. The egg will solidify instantly and should be lifted out with a perforated skimming ladle and dropped immediately into the consommé with which it is to be served.

VARIOUS PASTES FOR CLEAR SOUPS PÂTES DIVERSES POUR POTAGES CLAIRS (E.)

Florence Snow (*Neige de Florence*) : This special product is served separately, at the same time as the consommé, in medium proportions of 1–1½ oz. for 10 persons. Each guest takes as much as he wants and mixes it directly into his consommé.

Italian Pastes (*Pâtes d'Italie*) : Use 2–2½ oz. per qt. consommé. Poaching time is 8–12 min., depending on thickness and quality.

Pearl Barley (*Perles du Japon*) : Use 2½–2¾ oz. per qt. consommé. Poaching time: 20–25 min.

Rice (*Riz*) : When used as the only garnish, allow 1¾ oz. raw rice per qt. consommé. Should be poached in consommé separately, the grains not sticking together. Poaching time: 20–25 min.

Salep: Same amount as pearl barley per qt. consommé. Poaching time: 18–20 min.

Sago (*Sagou*) : Same proportions and poaching time as for salep.

Tapioca: Exactly the same as for the 2 products above.

Vermicelli (*Vermicelle*) : Allow 2–2½ oz. per qt. consommé. Poaching time: 5–12 min., depending on thickness and quality.

Note: (1) It is always helpful to pour salted boiling water over Italian pastes and vermicelli before poaching them in the consommé. (2) Most pastes for soup can easily be measured by the spoonful; an ordinary tbsp. or soupspoon holds about 1 oz.

PROFITEROLES FOR SOUPS PROFITEROLES POUR POTAGES (E.)

In the cooking of olden days, Profiteroles were nothing more than little balls of homemade bread. With good reason, the modern cook has substituted those made of Choux Paste, which are infinitely more delicate. These Profiteroles are made about the size of a hazelnut and are baked the way other things fashioned of Choux Paste are. They are usually stuffed with some sort of purée and should be baked quite dry. There are usually about 30 to a serving.

Proportions of Choux Paste for 100 Profiteroles: 3 oz. water, 6 oz. butter, ⅓ oz. salt, 8½ oz. sifted flour, 5 medium-sized eggs. The paste should be kept rather firm. (For preparation, see Ordinary Choux Paste, p. 548.)

VARIOUS ROYALES

Proportions for the following *royales* will make a garnish for 2 qt. consommé. Thus, it is easy to increase or decrease them according to need and consequently to regulate the poaching time. We only give the principal recipes here, deeming it useless to prolong the list, since their preparation is always the same, whatever principal ingredient is used. We must call attention here to the strict rule that a *royale* must not, indeed cannot, be cut until it is completely cold; in other words, until the inside has definitely hardened by cooling. Also, the shape of a *royale,* whatever it may be, must be perfectly regular and even. Finally, to assure these preparations the extreme delicacy they require, the quantity of whole eggs or yolks called for must not be exceeded if they are to solidify properly.

ORDINARY ROYALE ROYALE ORDINAIRE (E.)

Steep 2 pinches of chervil in 1½ oz. boiling consommé. Beat together, as for an omelet, 1 whole, medium-sized egg with 3 yolks; add the consommé bit by bit. Strain through a cloth, remove the resulting mousse, and pour into buttered molds. Poach in a *bain-marie* or double boiler, taking great care that the water does not boil. Poaching time for dariole molds (medium cupcake molds): 12–15 min. Poaching time for a loaf: 25–30 min. for an 8-oz. mold.

CARROT or CRÉCY ROYALE ROYALE DE CAROTTE OR ROYALE CRÉCY (E.)

Cook 3 oz. sliced carrots thoroughly in butter, add 1 tsp. cold Béchamel Sauce (p. 146) and 2 tbsp. cream, and strain. Season with a pinch of sugar; bind with 1 small whole egg and 2 yolks; poach in a *bain-marie* or double boiler as described above.

CREAM or DESLIGNAC ROYALE ROYALE À LA CRÈME OR ROYALE DESLIGNAC (E.)

Beat together, as for an omelet, 1 medium-sized egg and 3 yolks, blend in 6 oz. cream, season with a pinch of salt and a dash of grated nutmeg, and strain through cheesecloth. Poach in a *bain-marie* or double boiler as explained above.

GAME ROYALE ROYALE DE GIBIER (E.)

Finely pound 2 oz. cooked game meat of whatever sort in a mortar. Add 1½ tbsp. cold Espagnole Sauce (p. 137), 1½ oz. heavy cream, 1 small whole egg and 2 yolks beaten together as for an omelet. Strain and poach as usual.

ASPARAGUS ROYALE ROYALE DE POINTES D'ASPERGES (E.)

To 4 oz. half-boiled asparagus tips, add 1½ tbsp. Béchamel Sauce (p. 146), 2 tbsp. cream, a pinch of chopped spinach, and 3 egg yolks. Strain and poach as explained.

FISH or SHELLFISH ROYALE ROYALE DE POISSON OR DE CRUSTACÉS (E.)

Pound in a mortar 2½ oz. sole fillets poached in butter, or the same amount of cooked fish or meat of shellfish, depending on the type of soup for which the *royale* is being made. Add 1 tbsp. Béchamel Sauce (p. 146), 2 oz. cream, and a dash of nutmeg, and strain. Bind with 3 egg yolks and poach.

TOMATO ROYALE ROYALE DE TOMATE (E.)

Mix 3 oz. very red tomato purée, which has been strained through cloth, with 2 tbsp. white consommé. Season with a little salt and powdered sugar; bind with 1 small whole egg and 2 yolks, and poach.

TRUFFLE ROYALE ROYALE DE TRUFFE (E.)

Finely pound 4 oz. very black truffles in a mortar, while adding 1½ tbsp. very reduced cold Semiglaze Sauce (p. 138), and 3 egg yolks. Strain and poach.

POULTRY ROYALE ROYALE DE VOLAILLE (E.)

Finely pound 2 oz. cooked white meat of poultry in a mortar; add 1½ tbsp. Béchamel Sauce (p. 146), 1½ oz. cream, and a dash of nutmeg. After the mixture has been strained, bind with ½ egg and 2 yolks. Poach as usual.

BOUILLONS

VEGETABLE BOUILLON BOUILLON DE LÉGUMES (P.)

Vegetable Bouillons are prescribed for many diets. Here is how they are made. Cut into rather small pieces: 3 carrots, 1 turnip, 2 leeks, 1 potato, 1 small head of lettuce, 1 stalk of celery, a branch of chervil (never use cabbage). Cover with plenty of water, salt lightly, and cook over a low fire 1 full hr. without covering the pot. If, for example, 1½ qt. water is used, it will be reduced during cooking to ¾ qt., or by ½. Strain the bouillon and add tapioca or Italian pastes, depending upon the prescription. In certain cases, as indicated by the doctor, dried vegetables, beans, lentils, or rice may be added.

CRUSTS IN THE POT CROÛTES AU POT (P.)

After making Pot-au-Feu (p. 190), prepare small crusts by removing the white part from several slices of bread and toast lightly in the oven. Cut the carrots, turnips, and leeks cooked in the bouillon into small, regular pieces. Add a small amount of green cabbage cooked separately in bouillon and then also cut into pieces. Put the vegetables into a tureen and pour the bouillon over them through a strainer. Add the crusts and a pinch of chopped chervil. The crusts may be moistened with a little fat from the Pot-au-Feu before toasting.

BELLE FERMIÈRE SOUP POTAGE BELLE FERMIÈRE (C.)

Use the bouillon from a soup pot largely made of beef, including round of beef and a chicken or the equivalent in giblets, thoroughly skimming off the fat.

Garnish: For 1 qt. bouillon, 5 oz. white-heart cabbage cut in julienne strips and cooked in bouillon, 2 oz. fine macaroni boiled, 2½ oz. fresh French beans cooked quickly in boiling salted water and still rather firm. Cut the beans into small sections without letting them cool.

JULIENNE SOUP POTAGE JULIENNE (P.)

Cut the white of a few leeks lengthwise into small strips. Do the same with carrots, turnips, 1 cabbage, and 1 onion. Season with salt and a dash of sugar; mix everything and then put into a casserole and pour over it a few tbsp. fat skimmed from bouillon. Cover as tightly as possible and cook slowly, preferably in the oven, until the vegetables become slightly brown. Next pour in the desired amount of bouillon for the soup, simmer ¼ hr., skim off the fat before serving, and sprinkle with chopped chervil.

MIMOSA SOUP POTAGE MIMOSA (A.)

Cut in thin slices French beans cooked beforehand in salted water. Press some yolks of hard-boiled eggs through a colander with large holes. Heat some very good bouillon and then, just before serving, put in the sliced beans and the little balls of egg yolk; they should resemble the leaves and flowers of mimosa. This is a very pretty and tasty soup.

MACARONI SOUP POTAGE AUX PÂTES D'ITALIE (P.)

Same process as for Vermicelli Soup (p. 198), pouring the macaroni slowly into the boiling soup, 2 oz. per qt.

PEASANT SOUP POTAGE À LA PAYSANNE (P.)

Cut carrots, leeks, turnips, cabbage, and potatoes into small thin slices. Put these vegetables into a casserole containing 2 oz. butter and season with salt and a pinch of sugar. Cover tightly and allow the vegetables to cook down slowly over low heat, then add plenty of water and ⅓ oz. salt per qt., and cook ½ hr. Serve over a few slices of bread, with chopped chervil on top.

TAPIOCA SOUP POTAGE AU TAPIOCA (P.)

Drop into boiling bouillon, while stirring constantly, 2 tbsp. tapioca per qt. soup. Stir frequently while cooking to avoid a skin forming on the surface, but, if one does form, carefully remove it before serving. It takes 10 min. to cook tapioca. Semolina is cooked exactly the same way.

VERMICELLI SOUP POTAGE AU VERMICELLE (P.)

Drop the vermicelli into the boiling bouillon, allowing 2 oz. per qt. soup, and cook about 15 min., depending on the thickness of the vermicelli. Always serve the bouillon well skimmed of fat.

THICK SOUPS CREAMS OR CULLISES (M.)

These soups, which are also called cullises, are made of some ingredient reduced to a purée and clear Béchamel Sauce (prepared with 4 oz. White Roux to 1 qt. milk; see p. 146). Cream soups do not require binding with egg yolks, which differentiates them from Veloutés. They are finished with fresh cream (6 oz. per qt. soup) and butter (3–4 oz. per qt. soup).

Note: Binding the cream soups at the end with butter is optional. We advise it because it makes these soups smoother. The proportions of the various ingredients used in cream soups are given in the following recipes. We also give, in this chapter, certain soups that, while not bound with Béchamel Sauce, have certain similarities to cream soups.

CRAYFISH BISQUE or CULLIS BISQUE OR COULIS D'ÉCREVISSES (E.)

Proportions: 30 crayfish of medium weight, about 1½ oz. apiece. *For the Mirepoix:* 2 oz. carrots, 2 oz. onions, a pinch of thyme and bay leaf, 3 parsley sprigs, 1 tsp. flaming brandy, 6 oz. white wine. *For Binding and Liquid:* 4½–6 oz. cooked rice and 1½ qt. white consommé.

Preparation: (1) Finely chop the Mirepoix and brown in butter; add the crayfish, well washed and gutted; sauté them in the Mirepoix until the shells are quite red. Season with 1 oz. salt and a little ground pepper; pour on the brandy and white wine, and cook until reduced. Next cover with 6½ oz. consommé and cook 10 min. (2) Cook the rice in ¾ qt. consommé. (3) Remove the shells from the crayfish, keeping the tails and 10 shells. (4) Pound the remainder very fine in a mortar; add the rice and the stock from cooking the crayfish; and put through a sieve. Dilute this purée with 1 pt. consommé; bring to a boil; strain through a cone-shaped sieve, and keep hot in a *bain-marie* or double boiler.

Finish, just before serving, with 6 oz. butter and 3 oz. cream. Season lightly with cayenne pepper.

Garnish: The remaining tails diced; the trimmed shells stuffed with creamed fish forcemeat poached at the last moment.

CREAM-OF-ARTICHOKE SOUP I CRÈME D'ARTICHAUTS (M.)

Blanch and slice 8 large artichoke bottoms and cook in butter in a casserole. Pour over 1¾ qt. Béchamel Sauce (p. 146). Simmer gently 25 min. Strain the soup, pressing it through with a spatula. Pour the soup into a casserole and add 1 pt. white consommé (or milk, if the soup is to be prepared meatless). Finish the soup, off the stove, with 6 oz. fresh heavy cream and 6 oz. butter.

Note: Cream soups can be garnished with a salpicon (tiny cubes) of the basic ingredient, or, if you wish, various quenelles, or other preparations in harmony with the soup. For Cream-of-Artichoke Soup, 1 or 2 whole artichoke bottoms may be set aside to be diced and added to the finished soup.

CREAM-OF-ARTICHOKE SOUP II CRÈME D'ARTICHAUTS (M.)

Prepare the cream soup as explained in the preceding recipe, but put into the Béchamel Sauce only ½ the quantity of artichoke bottoms. Pound the rest of the artichoke bottoms (cooked in butter) in a mortar with 6 oz. butter. Press this artichoke butter through a fine sieve and add to the soup at the last moment.

Note: Cream soups ought to be very smooth, and it is best to strain them through cheesecloth after creaming and buttering.

CREAM-OF-WHITE-ASPARAGUS SOUP or **ARGENTEUIL CREAM SOUP** CRÈME D'ASPERGES BLANCHES OR ARGENTEUIL (M.)

Proceed according to the recipe for Cream-of-Artichoke Soup (above), substituting 2 lb. (net weight) scraped white asparagus for the artichokes. Cook the asparagus (only the tender parts) in butter and continue as above.

Note: This cream soup may be garnished with diced white asparagus tips cooked in salted water.

For this soup, and for all of the following cream recipes, milk should be used in place of white consommé when a meatless soup is desired.

CREAM-OF-GREEN-ASPARAGUS SOUP or **LAURIS CREAM SOUP** CRÈME D'ASPERGES VERTES OR LAURIS (M.)

Same as above, using green instead of white asparagus.

CREAM-OF-CELERY SOUP CRÈME DE CÉLERI (M.)

Proceed as for Cream-of-Artichoke Soup (above), using 4 stalks of celery, blanched and cooked in butter, instead of artichokes.

Note: This cream soup may also be prepared with celery root or celeriac.

CREAM-OF-MUSHROOM SOUP CRÈME DE CHAMPIGNONS (M.)

Add 1 pt. very smooth mushroom purée to the Béchamel Sauce. Boil a few moments. Finish with fresh cream and butter. Strain.

CREAM-OF-CAULIFLOWER SOUP or **DUBARRY CREAM SOUP** CRÈME DE CHOU-FLEUR OR DUBARRY (M.)

Same as Cream-of-Artichoke Soup, with cauliflower cooked in butter instead of artichokes (see Dubarry Cream Soup, p. 200).

CREAM-OF-SHRIMP SOUP CRÈME DE CREVETTES (M.)

Cook briskly in butter, with 3 tbsp. fine Mirepoix (p. 136), 1½ lb. large shrimps (or prawns). Add 3 oz. dry white wine. Drain the shrimps; mix their cooking juices with the Béchamel Sauce. Pound the shrimps into a paste (saving 20 shelled shrimps for the garnish). Add this shrimp purée to the soup. Press through a strainer with a spatula. Heat well. Finish with fresh cream and butter. Garnish with shrimps, diced.

CURRIED CREAM-OF-SHRIMP SOUP CRÈME DE CREVETTES À L'INDIENNE (M.)

Proceed as above, using small shrimps and seasoning with curry.

DUBARRY CREAM SOUP CRÈME DUBARRY (P.)

Blanch a small cauliflower 8–10 min. Prepare a little roux made of a bit of butter and 2 tbsp. flour; add 1½ qt. bouillon, and when it boils put in the cauliflower and let cook slowly. After cooking 40 min., skim the soup and strain everything through a fine sieve. Bring to a boil again with a little milk, bind with egg yolks and cream, and garnish with small croutons or cauliflower flowerets. The soup should be very creamy. This soup can also be made from leftover cooked cauliflower, when there is not enough to serve as a vegetable.

CREAM-OF-CRAYFISH SOUP CRÈME D'ÉCREVISSES (M.)

Cook 30 crayfish as in the recipe for Crayfish Bisque (p. 198). Pound into a fine paste and add the Béchamel Sauce. Finish as in the recipe for Cream-of-Shrimp Soup (above).

CREAM-OF-SPINACH SOUP CRÈME D'ÉPINARDS (M.)

Add to the Béchamel Sauce 2 lb. blanched spinach cooked in butter. Strain, and finish with fresh cream and butter as usual.

CREAM-OF-SEAFOOD SOUP CRÈME DE FRUITS DE MER À LA MARINIÈRE (M.)

Cook mussels, cockles, and clams in white wine. Drain them, saving the liquid, and remove the shells. Add the cooking liquid to the Béchamel Sauce. Strain this cullis. Finish with fresh cream and butter as usual, and at the last moment add the shellfish listed above.

CREAM-OF-NAVY-BEAN SOUP CRÈME DE HARICOTS BLANCS (M.)

Add to 1 qt. Béchamel Sauce (p. 146), 1 qt. navy-bean purée. Dilute with white consommé (or milk). Finish with cream and butter according to the usual procedure.

CREAM-OF-NAVY-BEAN-AND-ONION SOUP CRÈME DE HARICOTS BLANCS SOUBISÉE (M.)

Same method as above; put into the Béchamel Sauce 4 large, sliced onions cooked in butter without browning. Finish in the usual way.

CREAM-OF-FRENCH-BEAN SOUP CRÈME DE HARICOTS VERTS (M.)

Blanch 1½ lb. French beans 10 min. in salted water, then cook in butter. Put the beans into the Béchamel Sauce. Cook 15–18 min. Strain. Finish with fresh cream and butter in the usual way.

CREAM-OF-OYSTER SOUP or **CANCALAISE CREAM SOUP** CRÈME AUX HUÎTRES or CANCALAISE (M.)

Poach in their own juice 24 oysters removed from the shells. Drain, trim, and cut each into 2 or 3 pieces. Add the oyster cooking juice to the Béchamel Sauce prepared the usual way but to which 1 medium-sized onion, sliced and cooked in butter without browning, has been added. Dilute to the desired consistency. Finish with cream and butter; strain. Add the poached oysters and some chervil tops.

Note: Cream-of-Cockle Soup and Cream-of-Mussel Soup are prepared the same way.

CREAM-OF-LETTUCE SOUP CRÈME DE LAITUES (M.)

Blanch 10 small heads of lettuce, drain, squeeze out excess liquid, and cook in butter. Put the lettuce into the Béchamel Sauce. Cook 45 min. Strain; finish with cream and butter.

Note: Cream-of-Chicory, Cream-of-Endive, and Cream-of-Escarole Soups are prepared the same way.

CREAM-OF-CHESTNUT SOUP CRÈME DE MARRONS (M.)

Braise 1 lb. (net weight) peeled chestnuts, seasoning them with a little celery salt and a pinch of sugar. Press the chestnuts through a fine sieve. Add this purée to the Béchamel Sauce. Mix well. Strain. Finish the soup with cream and butter.

CREAM-OF-TURNIP SOUP or **FRENEUSE CREAM SOUP** CRÈME DE NAVETS or FRENEUSE (M.)

Cook 1 lb. thinly sliced, blanched turnips in butter. While cooking, add the white of 1 large leek thinly sliced. Add the turnips to the Béchamel Sauce. Cook 45 min. Strain. Finish with cream and butter as usual.

NISSARDE CREAM SOUP CRÈME À LA NISSARDE (M.)

Peel 2 lb. squash or vegetable marrow, cut in thick slices; cook with 3 oz. butter, a pinch of salt, and a pinch of sugar. When the squash has become quite soft, strain through a sieve to make a purée. Dilute this purée with 1½ qt. Béchamel Sauce (p. 146). Mix well. Boil for a few moments. Strain. Add 6 oz. tapioca cooked in consommé. Finish with cream and butter.

CREAM-OF-BARLEY SOUP I CRÈME D'ORGE (M.)

Wash pearl barley several times, changing the water each time, and cook gently in white consommé for 3 hr. (⅘ lb. barley to 1½ qt. consommé) along with a garnish composed of the finely sliced white of 1 leek and 1 stalk of celery sliced the same way. Strain through a sieve, pressing with a spatula. Finish the soup with cream and butter.

Note: This cream soup may be garnished with pearl barley cooked in consommé.

CREAM-OF-BARLEY SOUP II CRÈME D'ORGE (M.)

Make a White Roux (p. 136) of 5 oz. butter and 6 oz. barley flour. Add 2 qt. ordinary consommé. Put into this mixture a veal knuckle, 6 oz. pearl barley washed in water, the white of 1 leek and 1 stalk of celery, both sliced fine, also 2 sliced carrots. Season. Cook 3 hr. at a very slow boil. Take out the veal knuckle. Strain the soup through a sieve, pressing with a spatula. Finish the soup with cream and butter.

CREAM-OF-SORREL SOUP CRÈME D'OSEILLE (M.)

Add 1 lb. sorrel, well cooked in butter, to the Béchamel Sauce. Boil 5 min. Strain the soup through a sieve and finish with cream and butter as usual.

PARABÈRE CREAM SOUP CRÈME PARABÈRE (M.)

Add 6 oz. julienne of carrots, white of leek, and celery, and chervil tops to a Béchamel Sauce flavored with onion and diluted to the desired consistency with consommé (or milk), strain, and finish with cream and butter.

CREAM-OF-LEEK SOUP CRÈME DE POIREAUX (M.)

Proceed as with Cream-of-Artichoke Soup (p. 199), substituting for the artichokes 1 lb. (net weight) white of leeks finely sliced and cooked in butter. Finish in the usual manner.

Note: This cream soup is usually served with small diced croutons fried in butter.

CREAM-OF-FRESH-PEA SOUP I CRÈME DE POIS FRAIS (M.)

Same as Cream-of-Artichoke Soup (p. 199), using instead 1½ qt. fresh green peas cooked French style (see p. 505). Strain and finish according to the usual method.

CREAM-OF-FRESH-PEA SOUP II CRÈME DE POIS FRAIS (M.)

Pound in a mortar with 8 oz. butter 1½ qt. fresh green peas that have been cooked in salted water and drained. Strain the pea butter through a fine sieve and add to the Béchamel Sauce. Finish the usual way.

CREAM-OF-RICE SOUP CRÈME DE RIZ (M.)

Cook ½ lb. well-washed and drained rice 45 min. in 1½ qt. white consommé. Add 3 tbsp. butter. Strain through a sieve. Finish with cream and butter. Garnish with rice cooked in consommé.

Note: This soup can also be made with rice flour. Cream-of-Oatmeal Soup is made the same way.

CREAM-OF-JERUSALEM-ARTICHOKE SOUP CRÈME DE TOPINAMBOURS (M.)

Proceed as in making Cream-of-Artichoke Soup (p. 199), substituting for the artichokes 2 lb. Jerusalem artichokes cooked in butter. Finish in the usual manner.

Note: Cream-of-Chinese-Artichoke Soup and Cream-of-Sweet-Potato Soup are prepared the same way.

CREAM-OF-CHICKEN SOUP or CREAM SOUP À LA REINE CRÈME DE VOLAILLE OR À LA REINE (M.)

Cook a meaty chicken (weighing about 2 lb. after dressing) in a somewhat thin Béchamel Sauce (p. 146). Drain the chicken and bone it. Save some of the sliced breast, which will be diced and used for the garnish. Pound the rest of the meat as fine as possible in a mortar. Put this purée into the Béchamel Sauce and bring to a boil. Strain through a sieve and finish with 6 oz. cream and 6 oz. butter. Garnish with the diced white meat.

CREAM-OF-CHICKEN SOUP MARY STUART CRÈME DE VOLAILLE MARIE STUART (M.)

Prepare the cream soup as described above. At the last moment add a garnish composed of 3 tbsp. carrots cut into balls (with a vegetable ball cutter) and cooked in white consommé, the same amount of fresh green peas cooked in salted water and well drained, and chervil tops.

CREAM-OF-CHICKEN SOUP PRINCESSE CRÈME DE VOLAILLE PRINCESSE (M.)

Proceed as for ordinary Cream-of-Chicken Soup (p. 202). Garnish with 3 tbsp. green asparagus tips cooked in salted water and drained, diced chicken, and chervil tops.

Note: Cream-of-Chicken Soup may also be garnished with pearl barley, rice, etc.

SPECIAL THICK SOUPS (M.)

These soups are most often made by mixing various purées with one or more complementary ingredients. A certain number of them, belonging for the most part to the Parisian school of cooking, are finished by binding with egg yolks and cream. (Quantities given in the following recipes are calculated to serve about 10 persons.)

AMBASSADOR SOUP POTAGE AMBASSADEUR (M.)

To 2 qt. fresh pea purée add 3 oz. sorrel and lettuce Chiffonade (p. 193) cooked in butter, 5 tbsp. rice cooked in consommé, chervil tops.

Note: Although the recipe for this soup calls for a purée of fresh peas, it is often made with a purée of split peas.

AMPHITRYON SOUP POTAGE AMPHITRYON (M.)

Add 6 oz. Tomato Fondue (p. 194), 5 tbsp. vermicelli cooked in consommé, and chervil tops to 2 qt. Parmentier Purée (see Parmentier Soup, p. 207).

ANDALUSIAN SOUP POTAGE ANDALOU (M.)

Add 4 tbsp. julienne of pimento or sweet pepper cooked in consommé, 6 oz. tapioca also cooked in consommé, and chervil tops to 2 qt. tomato purée.

ARTOIS SOUP POTAGE ARTOIS (M.)

Add 6 oz. finely diced vegetables braised in butter and then dropped into consommé, and some chervil tops, to 2 qt. navy-bean purée.

BALVET or JUBILEE SOUP POTAGE BALVET OR JUBILÉE (M.)

Purée of fresh peas thinned with white consommé; vegetables from the stock pot.

BANVILLE SOUP POTAGE BANVILLE (M.)

Purée of leeks together with ⅓ that amount of tomato purée, completed with celeriac or celery root and onion cut in julienne strips, braised in butter, and dropped into consommé; chervil tops.

CERES SOUP POTAGE CÉRÈS (R.)

Beat 2 egg yolks and mix with a small quantity of carrot purée. Pour into small cream pots (earthenware custard molds or ramekins will do) and let set in a *bain-marie* or double boiler. Cool and cut into small squares. Do the same with purée of green peas or asparagus tips, adding a little chopped spinach. Prepare a cauliflower purée and mix with 2 well-beaten egg whites. Let set, as above, in a *bain-marie* or double boiler, cool, and cut into small squares. Put all of this into the soup tureen, and pour in bouillon slightly thickened with tapioca or cornstarch or potato starch.

CHAMPENOIS SOUP POTAGE CHAMPENOIS (M.)

Mix ⅔ Parmentier Purée (p. 207) with ⅓ celery purée. When the soup is done, finish with 6 oz. celeriac or celery root and carrots diced fine, braised in butter, and dropped into consommé; chervil tops.

CONDÉ SOUP POTAGE CONDÉ (P.)

Same procedure as for Navy-Bean Soup (p. 205), using kidney beans. Neither requires binding with egg yolk, but it may be done just the same.

CONTI SOUP POTAGE CONTI (P.)

Same process as above, using lentils.

WATER-CRESS SOUP POTAGE AU CRESSON (P.)

Put 1 lb. potatoes and a handful of water cress into water and cook together. As soon as it is well done, press through a fine sieve; dilute this purée with milk, water, or bouillon so as to make a creamy soup. Butter and season, then garnish with croutons or with water-cress leaves blanched for a few minutes in boiling water.

DARBLAY SOUP or **JULIENNE DARBLAY** POTAGE DARBLAY or JULIENNE DARBLAY (M.)

Add 6 oz. julienne of vegetables (cut into thin strips) to 2 qt. Parmentier Purée (p. 207). The julienne should first be braised in butter. Bind the soup in the usual manner with egg yolks and fresh cream; finish with 4½ oz. butter and chervil tops.

LIGHTNING SOUP POTAGE ÉCLAIR (P.)

This soup justifies its name by the rapidity with which it can be made. Bring 1 full qt. lightly salted water to a boil and cook 6 oz. vermicelli in it. When this is cooked, beat 2 whole eggs with 1 pt. warm milk in the soup tureen itself, pouring in the vermicelli while mixing. Season and serve.

FAUBONNE SOUP POTAGE FAUBONNE (M.)

Mix equal parts of navy-bean purée and julienne purée (see Darblay Soup, above) in consommé; add chervil tops.

Note: In some restaurants this soup is made with purée of fresh green peas (or split peas) and julienne purée in consommé.

FONTANGES SOUP POTAGE FONTANGES (M.)

Purée of green peas finished with sorrel Chiffonade (p. 193) and chervil tops.

FONTENELLE SOUP POTAGE FONTENELLE (M.)

Purée of white asparagus finished with lettuce Chiffonade (see p. 193) and chervil tops.

GENTILHOMME SOUP POTAGE GENTILHOMME (M.)

Lentil purée with game stock. (Cook the lentils with a partridge browned in the oven and a Mirepoix [p. 136] of vegetables cooked in butter.) Garnish with very small game quenelles (with, sometimes, truffles cut in julienne strips or in tiny balls with a vegetable spoon).

GERMAINE SOUP POTAGE GERMAINE (M.)

Cook gently in butter 1 pt. julienne (thin strips) of carrots, white of leek, and celeriac or celery root. Add to this julienne, when it is quite soft, 1¾ qt. thin purée of lettuce. Cook it all together. Finish with 4½ oz. tapioca cooked in consommé and 3 oz. fresh cream; chervil tops.

GERMINY SOUP POTAGE GERMINY (M.)

Pour 1½ qt. ordinary consommé over ½ lb. sorrel Chiffonade (p. 193). Bring to a boil; at the last minute bind with 10 egg yolks mixed with 1 pt. fresh heavy cream. Let thicken on the fire as in making English Cream (p. 550), stirring with a spatula, until it almost comes to a boil. Finish, off the stove, with 6 oz. butter and chervil tops. Serve with thin-sliced French bread.

NAVY-BEAN SOUP (SOISSONS STYLE) POTAGE AUX HARICOTS BLANCS (SOISSONNAIS) (P.)

Cook 1 pt. navy beans in water, as explained in the chapter on vegetables (p. 491), then press through a fine sieve. Add to this purée the liquid in which the beans were cooked and some milk to give the soup the consistency of Velouté. Butter, season properly, and garnish with bread croutons fried in butter. The soup can be bound with 1 egg yolk, but off the stove. For variety, this soup may also be garnished with rice, vermicelli, tapioca, sorrel, etc. The rice or vermicelli should be cooked separately, the sorrel melted in butter beforehand, and the tapioca cooked in the soup before binding (thus keeping the soup thinner, tapioca thickening it too much).

LAMBALLE SOUP POTAGE LAMBALLE (M.)

Mix equal parts of purée of fresh peas and consommé with tapioca.

Note: This soup is also prepared with purée of split peas.

LONGCHAMP SOUP POTAGE LONGCHAMP (M.)

Add to 1½ qt. purée of fresh peas, 3 oz. sorrel Chiffonade (p. 193) and 1 pt. consommé with vermicelli; chervil tops.

MACARONI SOUP POTAGE AU MACARONI (R.)

Cook the macaroni in long pieces. Cook in boiling salted water and, when tender, immerse in boiling bouillon for 5 min. Drain and put in layers in the bottom of a soup tureen, sprinkling each layer with grated Gruyère cheese. Fill with piping-hot bouillon.

MALGACHE SOUP POTAGE MALGACHE (M.)

Cook 4 oz. finely sliced onion in butter without browning. Season with salt and 1 tsp. curry. Dredge with 2 tbsp. flour. Pour in 1½ qt. white consommé. Mix well. Add 4 tbsp. peeled, diced tomatoes and 2 tbsp. rice. Finish by cooking it all together.

MARIA SOUP POTAGE MARIA (M.)

Purée of small navy beans garnished with small green peas cooked English style (p. 505) and chervil tops. Diced croutons fried in butter.

MONSELET SOUP POTAGE MONSELET (M.)

Purée of split peas accented with a Mirepoix (p. 136) containing a good amount of celery, white of leek cut in julienne strips and cooked in butter, lettuce Chiffonade (p. 193), and chervil tops.

MONT-BRY SOUP POTAGE MONT-BRY (M.)

To 1½ qt. Cream-of-Chicken Soup (p. 202), add 1 pt. consommé with tapioca. Complete at the last moment with 3 oz. julienne (thin strips) of mushrooms cooked in butter, and 3 oz. fresh cream.

SNOW SOUP POTAGE NEIGE (M.)

Cook a handful of sorrel in butter. Cover with boiling water, salt, and put in some slices of bread with the crust removed. Cook over a slow fire ½ hr. Heat some milk, bind with egg yolks, and fold in the whites of the eggs whipped to a froth. Add to the soup and serve.

CHRISTMAS SOUP POTAGE DE NOËL (R.)

Take some almonds, shell them, and soak them in warm water a few minutes to remove the skins. Pound them in a mortar, wetting them with milk, and press forcefully through a sieve. Bring some milk to a boil and sugar or salt it. Flavor with vanilla. Bind with 1 tbsp. tapioca and pour into a soup tureen. Mix in the almond milk. Fry some small circles of bread without crusts in butter, sprinkle with sugar, and glaze in the oven; add to the soup. Exquisite, and with a very delicate flavor.

ONION SOUP POTAGE À L'OIGNON (A.)

To prepare Onion Soup one may use sliced onion more or less browned, or left colorless, covered with water or with some sort of meat or meatless bouillon or even with milk. Remove the onion or leave it in the soup. If a clear soup is desired, it may be served as it is, or it may be bound with egg or otherwise; other ingredients also may be added, such as tomatoes, cheese, etc.

Soups may be prepared similarly from onion purée, or cream of onions, or cream of onions with Velouté (p. 147). Garnish these soups with fried croutons or croutons with grated Parmesan cheese. It is easy to devise many onion soups, each different from the others.

PARMENTIER SOUP POTAGE PARMENTIER (P.)

Take the white of 2 or 3 leeks, depending on size, slice thin, brown in butter till golden; add 1 lb. potatoes cut in quarters and enough water to cover; salt, and let cook. When cooked, press through a fine sieve and thin with a little water and boiled milk. Bring to a boil, skim, and bind with 1 egg yolk. Pour into a soup tureen and add butter. Garnish with small croutons fried in butter.

SPLIT-PEA or SAINT-GERMAIN SOUP POTAGE AUX POIS CASSÉS or SAINT-GERMAIN (P.)

First soak and then cook ½ lb. split peas in just enough water to cover them, not more. Do not salt. When they have been brought to a boil, skim, then add 1 onion and 1 carrot cut in pieces. Cover and cook slowly. When they are well cooked, or almost dry, press through a fine sieve and thin the purée with 1 qt. water or bouillon to make the soup creamy but not too thick. Then salt and add a pinch of sugar to counteract the tartness of the pea purée. Bring this to a boil, skim, then add butter off the stove. Garnish, according to taste, with small bread croutons fried in butter, or with rice or tapioca, vermicelli, sorrel, etc.

PURÉE-OF-SEA-EEL SOUP POTAGE PURÉE DE CONGRE (A.)

For 6 persons, take 5½ lb. sea eel, ½ lb. small shrimps cooked in the proper Court Bouillon (p. 277), ½ lb. tomatoes, ¼ lb. butter, 3 oz. grated Gruyère cheese and 2 oz. grated Parmesan cheese, 1 oz. fish stock, a pinch of saffron, 3 qt. water, 3 potatoes, 3 onions, 1 small carrot, 1 bay leaf, a sprig of thyme, parsley, curry, and salt.

Cut the sea eel in slices about 2 in. long, split the head in 4 parts, and cook everything in a kettle with the water, carrot, 1 onion, thyme, bay leaf, saffron, parsley, and salt. Boil 1¼ hr., then take out the fish. Remove the bones, pound the meat to a pulp in a mortar, and press through a sieve.

Shell the shrimps, keeping the tails, and boil the scraps for a few minutes in the fish broth, which will then be strained off. In this same broth cook the potatoes, then mash them and press them through a sieve.

Meanwhile, cook the tomatoes separately in their own juice with 1 onion and some parsley; press them through a sieve. Finally, brown 1 sliced onion in 2 oz. butter; add the fish stock and the cooked tomatoes. Set this mixture aside for a moment. Thoroughly mix the fish broth, the mashed eels, the mashed potatoes, then the onion-and-tomato mixture just set aside, and, last, the grated cheeses. Season with curry, add 1½ oz. butter cut into small pieces, trim with the shrimp tails, and serve hot with croutons fried in the rest of the butter. This soup is absolutely wonderful.

PURÉE-OF-PARTRIDGE SOUP POTAGE PURÉE DE PERDRIX (A.)

For 6 persons, take 3 qt. game consommé (made by cooking the carcasses, necks, etc., of game fowl and vegetables in salted water), 1 cup mushrooms, $3/4$ cup Cream-of-Rice Soup (p. 202), 1 partridge, butter. Roast the partridge, bone it, and put the bones and trimmings through a press, saving the juice. Cook the peeled mushrooms in butter. Make a mash of the partridge meat and the mushrooms, pressing them through a fine sieve. Put the game consommé into a pot, bring to a boil, add the Cream-of-Rice Soup, let cook, then add the mashed mushrooms and partridge and the juice obtained from the press. Pour into a soup tureen and serve immediately. This is a fine soup for a hunt dinner. Soup from game animals may be made the same way.

ROSSINI SOUP POTAGE ROSSINI (R.)

Cut some large onions in rings and cook in butter without browning until they can be crushed and reduced to a purée. Dredge with flour. Salt, pepper, and add boiling water. Cook separately until soft 2 or 3 large tomatoes with thyme, parsley, salt, and pepper. Reduce this to a purée and put through a sieve. Pour this purée into the cream of onions, mix the 2 over a low fire, add grated Gruyère or Parmesan cheese, and pour over fried croutons.

SAINT-CLOUD SOUP POTAGE SAINT-CLOUD (M.)

This soup (one of Carême's recipes) is nothing more than a purée of fresh peas enriched with purée of lettuce and served with diced croutons fried in butter.

HEALTH SOUP POTAGE DE SANTÉ (M.)

Add 4 oz. sorrel Chiffonade (p. 193) cooked in butter to $1\frac{1}{2}$ qt. somewhat thin Parmentier Purée (p. 207). Bind in the usual manner with egg yolks and fresh cream; complete with butter and chervil tops. On a separate plate, serve thin slices of French bread with the crust removed.

SOLFERINO SOUP POTAGE SOLFÉRINO (M.)

Cook 3 thin-sliced leeks in butter. Add $1\frac{1}{4}$ lb. seeded, quartered tomatoes and a *bouquet garni* containing a clove of garlic. Cover with 2 qt. consommé and add 4 medium-sized potatoes cut into round slices. Cook $1\frac{1}{2}$ hr., remove the *bouquet,* and press through a sieve. Thin with 1 pt. consommé, add butter, and strain through cheesecloth. Garnish with small potato balls (scooped out with a vegetable spoon and cooked in white consommé) and chervil tops.

Note: French beans cut in diamond shape and cooked in salted water sometimes complete the garnish for this soup.

VELVET SOUP POTAGE VELOURS (M.)

Add 1 pt. consommé with tapioca to $1\frac{1}{2}$ qt. carrot purée.

SOUPS

Translator's Note: The difference between the soups (*potages*) given in the preceding recipes and the soups (*soupes*) that follow is largely a matter of consistency and the occasion for which the soup is prepared. Consommés, cream soups, and soups thickened into a purée and enriched with eggs and cream, as presented in the preceding chapter, may be served at a stylish dinner. The soups that follow are the more ordinary (though none the less delicious) types served at family meals.

PANADA or BREAD SOUP PANADE (P.)

This soup is made with crusts of bread left over from a meal. Made the following way, it will be judged excellent, contrary to an old prejudice against cooking bread in soup, and is quickly done. Put the bread crusts into a pan and cover well with cold water, add salt and pepper, and place on the stove. When it has been brought to a full boil, remove from the fire and beat vigorously with a wire whisk, add 1 pt. boiling milk, correct the seasoning, then beat 1 whole egg (or 2) with 1 cup milk and pour into the soup, which should be boiling hot but off the fire. Add 1 tbsp. butter and serve. Panada or Bread Soup should be rather thick and form a mush.

GARLIC SOUP SOUPE À L'AIL (R.)

Peel a handful of garlic and put into boiling water. Salt and cook ¼ hr. Cut some very thin slices of bread and moisten them with fine olive oil. Place them in the bottom of a soup tureen. Pour in the soup, adding 2 egg yolks for binding, if desired. This soup, which is highly relished in the South of France, is given to children as a medicine for worms.

CABBAGE SOUP SOUPE AUX CHOUX (P.)

Cook some pickled pork or a piece of well-soaked salt pork in a soup pot. When it starts to boil, skim and garnish like Pot-au-Feu (p. 190). Add 1 or 2 green cabbages cut into quarters and let cook 1½ hr. Add a few potatoes cut into quarters and a small sausage and cook until done. Cut some slices of bread and soak them in the soup while cooking, adding a few vegetables as well. No need to butter this soup. It is also a good idea to add carrots and leeks, as in Pot-au-Feu. The cabbage, pork, and sausage make this dish a main course.

COUNTRY-STYLE VEGETABLE SOUP SOUPE AUX LÉGUMES À LA PAYSANNE (A.)

Take all the varieties of vegetables that you like and some breast of pork. Clean or peel the vegetables and cut them into pieces or leave them whole, depending on size. If you use cabbage, first blanch it to remove the bitterness. Put some pork fat and goose fat into a frying pan and brown first the breast of pork and then the larger vegetables. Put the pork, with the necessary amount of water, into a stewpan; bring to a boil; skim; add the blanched cabbage, a little salt and pepper, and then the other vegetables, those that take longest to cook first, so that they cook without falling to pieces. Finally, taste it, correct the seasoning with salt and pepper, then add some fresh butter cut into little pieces and let it melt. Pour the contents of the stewpan into a soup tureen containing slices of bread, mostly crusts. Serve. The younger and fresher the vegetables, the better this soup will be. With new, freshly picked vegetables, it is delicious.

ONION SOUP WITH CHEESE SOUPE À L'OIGNON AU FROMAGE (P.)

Brown slowly in butter about 4 oz. finely sliced onions. When they are rather brown, sprinkle on 1 tbsp. flour; slowly cook to a darker brown and then cover with 1½ qt. water; salt, pepper, and cook 10 min. After putting some slices of household bread sprinkled with fresh Gruyère cheese in the bottom of a soup tureen, pour in the soup, cover, and let stand about 10 min. before serving. If you do not wish to serve the onion with this soup, you can strain it when pouring it over the bread. This soup may also be served gratinated, with or without onion. To do this, make the soup a little thicker, put it into a tureen that can go into the oven, cover the surface with grated cheese, and heat in a very hot oven until the top turns a golden brown.

ONION SOUP WITH MILK soupe à l'oignon au lait (P.)

In the country, where there is plenty of good milk, this soup can be made by cooking 2 large onions, sliced very fine, in butter until yellow but not brown. Cover with 1½ qt. milk, preferably already brought to a boil. Cook slowly, so that the milk will not boil over, for a good ¼ hr., season well, and pour over bread. No need to use butter.

SORREL SOUP soupe à l'oseille (P.)

Clean 6 oz. sorrel, removing the stems; wash it and press out the water between the hands, then cut into small strips. Drop it into a stewpan containing 2 oz. very hot butter. Stir it until it is reduced to a pulp, then cover with 1½ qt. water. Add 3 large mealy potatoes, peeled and cut into quarters, salt, and let cook ½ hr. Press the potatoes through a sieve or simply mash them with a fork. If the soup is too thick, add a little water. Break 1 whole egg into a soup tureen, add 1 cup cold milk, and beat. Pour in the soup, adding slices of bread and a little chopped chervil. Do not let it boil with the egg. Vermicelli or other pastes may be cooked in the soup instead of using bread.

LEEK-AND-POTATO SOUP soupe aux poireaux et pommes de terre (P.)

Lightly brown in butter 2 or 3 leeks cut into small pieces; add about ⅔ lb. potatoes cut into quarters; cover with 1½ qt. water; salt, and cook slowly. When everything is cooked, mash the potatoes into a purée and pour everything into a soup tureen over slices of household bread toasted in the oven; then add a piece of fresh butter.

PUMPKIN SOUP soupe au potiron (P.)

Take about 1 lb. pumpkin, cut it into pieces, and cook in salted water. Put it through a fine sieve and then thin the purée with milk to give it a creamy consistency; next season and sugar lightly. Cut a few thick slices of household bread, put them into the soup, and let them cook until pulpy about 10 min. Take off the fire, butter, and pour into a soup tureen.

TOMATO SOUP soupe à la tomate (P.)

Lightly brown in butter 1 sliced carrot and 1 sliced onion, then add 1 heaping tbsp. flour and 1–1¼ lb. ripe tomatoes, crushed by hand, including seeds and juice. Dilute with 1 qt. water and add salt, pepper, 2 lumps of sugar, a sprig of parsley. Cook slowly ¾ hr. and then put through a strainer with holes small enough to retain the tomato seeds. Put back into the stewpan and thin with any preferred bouillon or, if that is lacking, with water. It should be a little creamy. Add a little fresh butter and 3 tbsp. rice cooked separately for 20 min. in bouillon. This soup is delicious. Tapioca—3 tbsp.—may be used instead of rice.

HORS D'OEUVRES

HORS D'OEUVRES

These little tidbits, which may be prepared in a multitude of delightful ways, are becoming ever more successful and are to be seen in restaurants as well as in private homes. Many of these hors d'oeuvres are made from leftovers of the day before, such as fish, meat, or vegetables, and with a little taste and ingenuity one can make new kinds every day. Hors d'oeuvres have a pleasing freshness, especially in summer; the mayonnaise and vinaigrette dressings customarily used as seasoning whet the appetite. But their appearance must be pleasant and simple—never lose sight of the fact that these little delicacies are intended to stimulate the appetite, not to satisfy it. Thus, the first course of a luncheon should not be loaded with real dishes but with what gastronomes call palate-ticklers.

Hors d'oeuvres may be divided into several categories: there are the relish dishes, garnished with items presented as they are, such as radishes, sausages, olives, shrimps, etc.; hors d'oeuvres prepared as salads, and those requiring a little more work, such as canapés, little pastry boats, and shells. The whole gamut will be run in the following pages, with recipes signed by some of the greatest chefs of modern times, whose names should guarantee their quality.

In this chapter the homemaker will find the art and method of using up those little leftovers she does not know what to do with. Whether it be fish, meat, egg, or vegetable, nothing should be wasted; especially in these times and in this book, which is written for all classes of society and has for its primary goal to create style and quality without neglecting the question of economy, which is basic in cooking.

VARIOUS CANAPÉS (M.)

Canapés were formerly called Russian and were one of the principal ingredients of the *zakuska,* a sort of before-dinner meal served in a room adjoining the real dining room. These canapés are now generally called French, legitimately enough, since the greater number are a part of French custom. Canapés are trimmed in various shapes, squares, rectangles, rounds, diamonds, etc., from thin undercrusts of light bread. Canapés are fried in clarified butter or toasted, depending upon the nature of the garnish used. Canapés are also made with black bread. Canapés may also be made (and this makes a more delicate preparation) from the undercrusts of slightly salted brioches or from rye brioches. The variety of canapés is infinite, and the garnishes used are innumerable. The way these canapés are decorated should always be secondary to their flavor. The main point to observe is always to make them small and, as far as possible, to vary their shape as well as the ingredients that garnish them.

ANCHOVY CANAPÉS CANAPÉS AUX ANCHOIS (M.)

Spread Anchovy Butter (p. 163) on toasted canapés cut in rectangles. Decorate by placing thin strips of anchovy fillets on top in an *x*. Fill the interstices of the *x* with the chopped yolk of a hard-boiled egg, chopped egg white, and chopped parsley. (Figure 124, Page 216.)

HARLEQUIN CANAPÉS CANAPÉS À L'ARLEQUINE (M.)

Any desired shape. Spread the toasted canapés with any of the butters on pp. 163–166. Garnish, making different combinations of colors, with pickled tongue, smoked ham, smoked salmon, truffles, hard-boiled egg yolks and whites chopped separately, chopped parsley. All of these ingredients should be chopped or diced into tiny cubes. Make a border of butter, using a paper cone.

ARMORICAN CANAPÉS CANAPÉS À L'ARMORICAINE (M.)

Round shape. Spread Lobster Butter (p. 164) on canapés fried in butter. Border of Red Butter (p. 163). Fill the middle of the canapé with diced lobster. On each canapé put a little slice of lobster topped with Stiff Mayonnaise (p. 157).

AVEYRONNAIS CANAPÉS CANAPÉS AVEYRONNAIS (E.P.)

Oval shape; fresh white bread. Spread with butter, then, with a fluted tube, garnish with a mixture of equal parts of Roquefort cheese and butter. Place half a nut on the center. (Figure 125, Page 216.)

BEAUHARNAIS CANAPÉS CANAPÉS À LA BEAUHARNAIS (M.)

Oval shape. Spread Printanier Butter (p. 165) on toasted canapés. Border of Yellow Butter (p. 164). Fill the middle with a salpicon (tiny cubes) of breast of chicken alternated with a salpicon of truffles.

CAVIAR CANAPÉS CANAPÉS AU CAVIAR (M.)

Round shape. Cover toasted canapés with natural butter or Caviar Butter (p. 163). Make a border of butter, garnish with fresh caviar, and put a round slice of peeled lemon on top. (Figure 124, Page 216.)

SHRIMP CANAPÉS CANAPÉS AUX CREVETTES (M.)

Round shape. Spread with Shrimp Butter (p. 164). Garnish with shrimps arranged as a rosette. In the middle place a little rose of fresh butter, squeezed from a pastry bag with a fluted tube, or simply a small caper.

DANISH CANAPÉS CANAPÉS À LA DANOISE (M.)

Any desired shape; black bread. Spread the toasted canapés with Horseradish Butter (p. 165). Garnish with alternate strips of smoked salmon, herring fillets, and caviar. Border of Horseradish Butter.

HADDOCK CANAPÉS CANAPÉS AU HADDOCK (E.P.)

Oval shape; fresh white bread. Spread with butter and cover with a slice of haddock. Glaze with gelatin (p. 555). Place at the center a small mound of red caviar and decorate each end with Shrimp Butter (p. 164), using a paper cone. (Figure 125, Page 216.)

MIKADO CANAPÉS CANAPÉS MIKADO (E.P.)

Round shape; fresh white bread. Spread with butter. Place a slice of hard boiled egg on the bread. Remove the yolk. Garnish the center in a dome shape with red caviar, then on top place a pinch of finely chopped truffles. Border of Shrimp Butter (p. 164) around the egg white. (Figure 125, Page 216.)

ASPARAGUS TIP CANAPÉS CANAPÉS AUX POINTES D'ASPERGES (E.P.)

Oval shape; fresh white bread. Spread with butter. Cover with a slice of red pickled tongue. Place lengthwise 3 small asparagus tips. Glaze with gelatin (p. 555), then make a border of Montpellier Butter (p. 165) on the asparagus. (Figure 125, Page 216.)

SOFT-ROE or **MILT CANAPÉS** CANAPÉS DE LAITANCES (W.)

Spread with Mustard Butter (p. 165) and garnish with soft roe or milt previously poached in white wine. Border of *fines herbes.*

MONTMORENCY CANAPÉS CANAPÉS MONTMORENCY (W.)

Spread small, square canapés with Anchovy Butter (p. 163). Place on top, using a pastry bag filled with Tuna Cheese (see *Note*, below), 4 small balls surmounted by a fifth; top with mayonnaise mixed with anchovy purée; around the base of the canapé put a sprinkling of mixed lobster coral and truffles.

Note: Tuna Cheese is a kind of tuna butter in which ½ the butter is replaced by very soft Gruyère cheese. Roquefort may be used for these "cheeses," but always with some flavoring or coloring agent and the butter.

LOBSTER-CORAL CANAPÉS CANAPÉS AUX OEUFS DE HOMARD (W.)

Spread with Lobster Cheese (see *Note,* above); on top, arrange lobster coral previously marinated in salt and lemon juice; border with a ribbon of Lobster Butter (p. 164).

SPRINGTIME CANAPÉS CANAPÉS À LA PRINTANIÈRE (M.)

Cut in diamond shapes. Spread the canapés with Montpellier Butter or Printanier Butter (p. 165). Garnish with chopped hard-boiled eggs. Decorate with a cross of fresh butter and very green water-cress leaves or chopped parsley and chervil. (Figure 124, Page 216.)

RÉJANE CANAPÉS CANAPÉS RÉJANE (W.)

Spread round canapés with Lobster Cheese (see *Note,* above, under Montmorency Canapés); on top make a mound of chopped eggs mixed with mayonnaise. Completely cover with thin mayonnaise and around the base make a border of lobster coral.

Note: If lobster coral is not available, cook egg yolks in a double boiler, delicately color them, and then chop.

RUSSIAN CANAPÉS CANAPÉS À LA RUSSE (W.)

Spread round canapés with cayenne butter. With a very small pastry cutter stamp out round, rather thin slices of pickled tongue, ham, smoked salmon, Gruyère cheese, and truffles, all exactly the same size. Cut these circles in 2, making half-moons. Cover the canapés with circles made from 2 different half-moons. These varicolored canapés make an attractive effect.

ROSETTE CANAPÉS CANAPÉS ROSETTE (E.P.)

Round shape; fresh white bread. Spread with butter. Cover with a slice of hard salami. Place on each slice a small gherkin cut in fan shape. Glaze with gelatin (p. 555), decorate with butter, using a paper cone. (Figure 124, P. 216.)

CANAPÉS WITH SMOKED SALMON OR OTHER SMOKED FISH CANAPÉS AU SAUMON FUMÉ OU AUTRES POISSONS FUMÉS (M.)

Any desired shape. Spread toasted canapés with Smoked-Salmon Butter (p. 165). Garnish with very thin slices of smoked salmon. Border of chopped parsley.

COLD HORS D'OEUVRES

MARINATED FRESH ANCHOVIES or ANCHOVY ESCABECHE ANCHOIS FRAIS MARINÉS OR ESCABÈCHE D'ANCHOIS (M.)

This method of preparation, much used in Spanish cooking, may be applied to various small fish, smelts, sardines, red mullet, etc. Here is the way to make Escabeche: (1) Brown the fish rapidly in very hot oil after first cleaning, trimming, drying, and dusting with flour. As soon as the fish (anchovies, sardines, or whatever) are well browned on both sides, lay them out in a rectangular earthenware pan or deep dish. (2) Add 5 unpeeled cloves of garlic, 1 medium-sized onion and 1 medium-sized carrot, both sliced thin (per 2 lb. fish, net weight), to the oil used in cooking. Brown these ingredients. Add 9 oz. vinegar and 3 oz. water. Season with salt, a branch of thyme, a piece of bay leaf, 2 sliced pimentos, and 4 or 5 stalks of parsley. Boil this Court Bouillon 10 min. Pour it boiling over the fish. Let the fish marinate 24 hr. in this in a cool place. Serve as is, in the same dish in which the fish were marinated.

ANCHOVY FILLETS CHAVETTE ANCHOIS (FILETS D') CHAVETTE (M.)

Arrange anchovy fillets (soaked to remove the salt, trimmed, and wiped dry) in a relish dish on a bed of lettuce Chiffonade (see p. 193) seasoned with oil and vinegar. Garnish around the dish with little mounds of diced beet alternated with mounds of diced potato salad. Pour olive oil and a dash of vinegar over the anchovy fillets. Sprinkle with chopped hard-boiled eggs and chopped parsley.

ANCHOVY FILLETS CÔTE D'AZUR ANCHOIS (FILETS D') CÔTE D'AZUR (Fa.)

Roll the fillets into rings on the tip of the finger; place them on potato salad; fill the rings with chopped hard-boiled eggs and make a border around the relish dish of tomatoes or beets sliced thin and cut in half-moons or of the 2 alternated. (Figure 127, Page 217.)

Fig. 124 - 1. Anchovy canapés (p. 214). 2. Caviar canapés (p. 214). 3. Springtime canapés (p. 215.) 4. Rosette canapés (p. 216).
Fig. 125 - 1. Aveyronnais canapés (p. 214). 2. Haddock canapés (p. 215). 3. Mikado canapés (p. 215). 4. Asparagus-tip canapés (p. 215).

Fig. 124

Fig. 125

Fig. 126

Fig. 127

Fig. 128

Fig. 129

ANCHOVY FILLETS NÎMOISE ANCHOIS (FILETS D') À LA NÎMOISE (Fa.)

Anchovy fillets in oil, cut in long strips and placed on potato salad in a relish dish; place chopped whites of hard-boiled eggs along one side of the dish and the chopped yolks along the other. Decorate both ends of the dish with parsley. (Figure 129, Page 217.)

ANCHOÏADE ANCHOÏADE (Fa.)

Very highly esteemed in the South of France, where this anchovy cream is prepared as follows: pound the anchovies (soaked in water to remove the salt and then wiped) in a mortar with a little oil and a dash of vinegar. Spread on a slice of homemade bread and place slices of hard-boiled egg and thin slices of onion on top. Put it in the oven for a few minutes and serve immediately.

ARTICHOKES GREEK STYLE ARTICHAUTS À LA GRECQUE (M.)

Strip and carefully trim some very small artichokes. Blanch 4 min. in boiling salted water acidulated with a dash of lemon juice. Drain the artichokes and let them cool. Cook them 25 min. in the following, previously prepared Court Bouillon: boil 6 oz. water, 1½ oz. olive oil, juice of 2 lemons (strained through a cloth), and a *bouquet garni* made of a stalk of celery, a stalk of fennel, thyme, and bay leaf. Add 1 tsp. coriander seeds, a few grains of white pepper, and ½ tsp. salt. Place the artichokes in an earthenware dish and cover with the Court Bouillon in which they were cooked. Chill thoroughly before serving.

Note: These artichokes should be served as they are, cold, in an earthenware or glass dish; they may also be arranged on a relish dish.

ARTICHOKES WITH POIVRADE or VINAIGRETTE SAUCE ARTICHAUTS À LA POIVRADE OR À LA VINAIGRETTE (M.)

Small, very tender, raw artichokes arranged in a cluster in a glass bowl half filled with ice. Serve with oil, vinegar, salt, and pepper.

Note: The artichokes may also be trimmed and quartered and arranged in a relish dish. Pour highly seasoned Vinaigrette Sauce (p. 158) over them.

ARTICHOKE BOTTOMS ARTICHAUTS (FONDS D') (M.)

These bottoms (chosen as small as possible) are first blanched, cooled, and drained, then marinated 1 hr. in oil, vinegar (or lemon juice), salt, and pepper. They are garnished in various ways. When garnished, and, as the case may be, decorated with truffles, beets, or otherwise, the bottoms are arranged on a relish dish or hors d'oeuvre plate. They may be surrounded by Aspic Jelly (p. 168) or, depending on the other preparations, decorated with curly parsley, etc.

ARTICHOKE BOTTOMS ANDALOUSE ARTICHAUTS (FONDS D') À L'ANDALOUSE (M.)

Garnish with a salpicon (tiny cubes) of pimento, tomatoes, and potatoes bound with mayonnaise seasoned with paprika and stiffened with gelatin. Sprinkle with chopped chives.

ARTICHOKE BOTTOMS BRY-MONT ARTICHAUTS (FONDS D') À LA BRY-MONT (M.)

Garnish with tuna purée bound with mayonnaise; sprinkle with chopped hard-boiled egg yolks mixed with chopped parsley.

Fig. 126 - Cones of smoked salmon (p. 228).
Fig. 127 - Anchovy fillets Côte d'Azur (p. 216).
Fig. 128 - Tartlets Stanley (p. 221).
Fig. 129 - Anchovy fillets nîmoise (p. 217).

ARTICHOKE BOTTOMS WITH VEGETABLE SALAD ARTICHAUTS (FONDS D') À LA MACÉDOINE DE LÉGUMES (M.)

Garnish with a salad made from various vegetables seasoned with oil and vinegar; on each bottom, a small ball of cauliflower.

ARTICHOKE BOTTOMS MAZARIN ARTICHAUTS (FONDS D') MAZARIN (W.)

Small bottoms of fresh artichokes cooked in white wine, drained, cooled, and filled with leftover, diced lobster bound with thick mayonnaise. Garnish in mounds and decorate with chopped egg whites and chopped parsley in equal parts; arrange on a bed of parsley in a relish dish and stick a pink shrimp or prawn into each one. (Figure 131, Page 224.)

PASTRY BOATS WITH LOBSTER[1] AND OTHER SHELLFISH BARQUETTES À LA LANGOUSTE ET AUTRES CRUSTACÉS (M.)

Fill pastry boats (made of Short Paste, p. 545) with a salpicon (tiny cubes) of lobster mixed with mayonnaise. On this filling, stick very small slices of lobster coated with Aspic Jelly (p. 168), decorated with chervil leaves. Border of chopped, hard-boiled egg yolks.

PASTRY BOATS MOSCOVITE BARQUETTES À LA MOSCOVITE (M.)

Pastry boats (made of Short Paste, p. 545), baked dry, and garnished with a salpicon (tiny cubes) of breast of chicken and truffles mixed with thick mayonnaise well seasoned with paprika. In the center place a few small asparagus tips and a piece of lemon peel arranged like a basket handle. (Figure 133, P. 225.)

PASTRY BOATS NEPTUNE or NIÇOISE BARQUETTES À LA NEPTUNE OR À LA NIÇOISE (M.)

Little boats made of Short Paste (p. 545) without sugar and baked until crisp, filled with reduced Tomato Fondue (p. 194), a little garlic and parsley, very cold. Place on top a thin slice of tuna and a small piece of hard-boiled egg (an egg cut into 8 pieces). Chopped parsley around the edges of the crust. (Figure 130, Page 224.)

PASTRY BOATS NORMANDE BARQUETTES À LA NORMANDE (M.)

Garnish the pastry boats (made of Puff Paste, p. 544) with a salpicon (tiny cubes) of shrimp tails, mushrooms, and truffles bound with Stiff Mayonnaise (p. 157). Place 1 oyster (poached and drained) on each pastry boat. At each end place a large mussel (poached in white wine and well drained). Top the pastry boats with White Fish Aspic (p. 170). (Figure 133, Page 225.)

PASTRY BOATS WITH TUNA OR OTHER MARINATED FISH BARQUETTES AU THON OU AUTRES POISSONS MARINÉS (M.)

Garnish the pastry boats (made of Short Paste, p. 545) with a salpicon (tiny cubes) of tuna and hard-boiled eggs bound with mayonnaise. On each boat place 3 or 4 small slices of marinated tuna. Decorate with chervil leaves.

---

[1] *Translator's Note:* Since the spiny, European lobster known as *langouste* is not available in this country, we have substituted lobster, but rock-lobster tail meat may also be used.

CELERY GREEK STYLE CÉLERIS À LA GRECQUE (M.)

Trim heads of celery, divide into quarters, blanch, cool, and prepare them in same manner as Artichokes Greek Style (p. 217).

CELERY TARTARE CÉLERIS À LA TARTARE (M.)

Cook well-cleaned celery in salted water. Drain, cool, and dry. Cut the stalks into 4 sections. Arrange on a relish dish and cover with Tartar Sauce (p. 158); sprinkle capers on top and surround with half slices of scalloped lemon.

Note: Celery with Mayonnaise is prepared the same way.

CELERIAC or CELERY ROOT WITH MUSTARD CÉLERI-RAVE À LA MOUTARDE (M.)

Cut the celeriac (celery root) into a fine julienne (thin strips). Season with mustard, oil, vinegar, salt, and pepper.

Note: In Parisian restaurants celeriac or celery root is usually served raw with thick mayonnaise seasoned with mustard. It is also prepared with mayonnaise seasoned with curry, paprika, ketchup, or other condiment. Celery stalks, with threads removed and cut in thick julienne strips, may be prepared the same way. Stalk celery and celeriac can also be seasoned with Vinaigrette (p. 158) or Rémoulade Sauce (p. 157).

In addition to the recipes given above, celeriac may also be prepared in pastry boats or round pastry shells; once cooked in water, it should be marinated and then the pastry shells should be garnished with different items.

MARINATED CÈPES[1] CÈPES MARINÉS (M.)

Trim and thoroughly wash 2 lb. small cèpes, firm and of the same size. Blanch 10 min. in salted, acidulated water. Drain and cool. Put them into an earthenware dish and cover with the following boiling, strained marinade: boil 12 oz. vinegar and 6 oz. olive oil with 4 crushed garlic cloves, a branch of thyme, ½ bay leaf, 6 peppercorns and 6 coriander seeds, 2 parsley roots and a large stalk of fennel; season with salt. Cook this marinade for several minutes. Keep in a cool place 24 hr. before serving.

Note: This recipe is applicable to all types of mushrooms.

MARINATED MUSHROOMS CHAMPIGNONS MARINÉS (M.)

Pick out some fine, rather large white mushrooms. Use only the caps. Wash and peel, then cut in slices and arrange in a relish dish. Soak 2 hr. in advance with a sauce made of lemon juice, salt, ground pepper, and oil. Serve as they are, without being cooked.

MUSHROOMS IN WHITE WINE CHAMPIGNONS DE COUCHE AU VIN BLANC (W.)

Clean and peel small mushrooms; turn them in oil in a frying pan, cover with white wine, lemon juice, a little sugar, 1 tbsp. vinegar, salt, cayenne pepper, a stalk of celery, and a few coriander seeds. Cook for a moment; then, when cool, serve in the cooking juices.

---

[1] Cèpes are a giant kind of mushroom with brown top and white underside found in a wild state in America, but not developed for commercial use.

MARINATED RED CABBAGE CHOUX ROUGES MARINÉS (M.)

Trim and wash the cabbage, then cut it up into very fine julienne strips. Sprinkle it with salt, put it into an earthenware dish, and let it macerate 48 hr., turning it from time to time. Drain, press, and put into a stone jar, sprinkling well with black pepper and crushed bay leaves (and, if desired, several cloves of garlic). Cover with vinegar (boiled or raw). Let marinate 24 hr.

MARINATED GREEN CABBAGE CHOUX VERTS MARINÉS (M.)

Same method of preparation as for red cabbage, above.

COCKLES (OR MUSSELS) WITH MAYONNAISE COQUES (OU MOULES) À LA MAYONNAISE (M.)

Cooked cockles (or mussels), carefully washed and sponged; mix them in mayonnaise with paprika, then surround them with a thin ribbon of thick, cold tomato purée squeezed from a paper cone.

ZUCCHINI BENOÎTON COURGETTES À LA BENOÎTON (M.)

Fry thick slices of unpeeled zucchini in oil, not letting them brown too much. Drain and let cool. Place on these slices a salpicon (tiny cubes) of hard-boiled eggs and marinated tuna mixed with thick mayonnaise. Arrange the zucchini in a relish dish; surround them with sweet peppers cut in julienne strips and diced tomatoes, arranged in alternate clusters. On each slice of zucchini place a slice of lemon peeled to the flesh, moisten with oil and vinegar, and sprinkle with chopped chives.

ZUCCHINI MOSAIC COURGETTES À LA CAILLOU (M.)

Cook thick slices of unpeeled zucchini 5 min. in salted water. Drain, wipe dry, and marinate in oil, vinegar, salt, and pepper. Arrange the slices of zucchini in a relish dish, alternating them with thin slices of drained, salted tomatoes. Make a border of julienne of pimento and lettuce Chiffonade (p. 193), arranged in alternate mounds, around these vegetables. Garnish with hard-boiled eggs cut into quarters. Dress with oil and vinegar; sprinkle with chopped basil.

ZUCCHINI GREEK STYLE COURGETTES À LA GRECQUE (M.)

Cut the zucchini into quarters and trim these quarters into large pod shapes. Cook them in a Court Bouillon prepared the same way as for Artichokes Greek Style (p. 217). Serve very cold with the Court Bouillon.

ZUCCHINI TURKISH STYLE COURGETTES À LA TURQUE (M.)

Prepare and cook the zucchini as described in Zucchini Greek Style (above), but season the Court Bouillon or marinade with 1 tsp. saffron (while reducing the Court Bouillon). Let cool. Arrange on an oval platter. At each end of the platter place some cooked white rice and along the sides a border of pimentos cut into julienne strips. Moisten with a few tbsp. Court Bouillon. Sprinkle with chopped parsley.

SHRIMPS or **PRAWNS** CREVETTES GRISES OU ROSES (M.)

Arrange cooked shrimps or prawns in a relish dish with tufts of curly parsley Or hang them by the tail around the rim of a goblet filled with fresh parsley—to. give the effect of a bouquet. (Figure 134, Page 225.)

SHRIMP (SALAD or MAYONNAISE) CREVETTES (SALADE OR MAYONNAISE DE) (M.)

Salad: Shell the shrimps or prawns and season them in a salad dressing, either of oil and vinegar with chopped parsley, or with mayonnaise, or with Tartar Sauce (p. 158). Arrange in a relish dish and surround with half slices of lemon, the rim of which has been scalloped. Sprinkle with chopped parsley.

Mayonnaise: Season the shelled shrimps with very thick mayonnaise. Arrange in a relish dish or in small crystal glasses. Garnish with hard-boiled egg quarters, hearts of lettuce, capers.

SHRIMPS STANLEY or TARTLETS STANLEY CREVETTES À LA STANLEY OR TARTELETTES STANLEY (M.)

Season the shrimps with mayonnaise seasoned with curry. Arrange them in little tartlet shells (made of Short Paste, p. 545) ; garnish each with ½ tbsp. highly seasoned tomato-and-pepper salad. On each tartlet place a slice of hard-boiled egg cut crosswise. Moisten with a little oil. (Figure 128, Page 217.)

VARIOUS STUFFED ÉCLAIRS and KAROLY ÉCLAIRS FOURRÉS DIVERS and KAROLY (M.)

These hors d'oeuvres are also called Carolines. They are stuffed with various foods: purées of meat and fish; mousses of ham, *foie gras,* and game; salpicons of chicken, etc. They may be served as they are or coated with a White or Brown Chaud-Froid Sauce (pp. 149, 139) made with or without meat, depending on the main ingredient used as a stuffing.

SPINACH JACQUELINE ÉPINARDS JACQUELINE (M.)

Cook picked and washed spinach rapidly in plenty of salted, boiling water. Drain, cool, and press out the excess water. Chop roughly. Season with oil, vinegar, salt, and pepper. Arrange in a dome on a crystal salad plate. Surround with a garnish of small alternate mounds of beets, hard-boiled eggs (yolks and whites), and celeriac or celery root, all diced small. Garnish the top of the spinach with slices of lemon peeled to the flesh; sprinkle with chopped parsley. (Figure 321, Page 525.)

HEARTS OF CHICORY FLAMANDE GOURILOS À LA FLAMANDE (W.)

Hearts of chicory (or escarole) cooked in a Court Bouillon as for Artichokes Greek Style (p. 217) ; arrange on a relish dish, placing on 1 group a small bouquet or mound of crushed tomatoes, on another a salad of sliced carrots, on a third a mound of sliced mushrooms; a bit of chopped, mixed herbs on all of them.

HEARTS OF CHICORY ORANAISE GOURILOS À L'ORANAISE (W.)

Hearts of chicory (or escarole) well blanched, then prepared Greek style (see Artichokes Greek Style, p. 217) with a little saffron added.

FRESH HERRING DIEPPOISE HARENGS FRAIS À LA DIEPPOISE (M.)

Poach the herring in a marinade made of white wine and vinegar, with round, scalloped slices of carrots, sliced celery, and sliced onions added (these vegetables previously cooked in the marinade), seasoned with salt, peppercorns, thyme, bay leaf, and parsley. Let the herring cool in the marinade.

FRESH HERRING SPANISH STYLE HARENGS FRAIS À L'ESPAGNOLE (M.)

Cook the herring, seasoned with salt and paprika, in very hot oil until stiff. Arrange them in an ovenware dish on a bed of sliced onions and crushed tomatoes that have first been cooked in oil and seasoned with salt and pepper. Place sweet pimentos, cut into julienne strips, and 2 chopped garlic cloves on the herring. Moisten with oil and lemon juice. Cover and bake in the oven. Let cool in the cooking juice. Before serving, sprinkle with chopped parsley and on each herring place a slice of lemon peeled to the flesh.

MARINATED HERRING HARENGS MARINÉS (M.)

Preparation: Cut fillets from herring that has previously been skinned. Trim these fillets, removing all bones. Soak the fillets in cold water for 2 hr. (herrings may also be desalted in milk or in a mixture of milk and water). Soak the milt or soft roe and the roe at the same time. Drain the herring, milt, and roe. Dry everything well and cut the fillets lengthwise into 2 or 3 pieces, according to size. Place the herring fillets in a rectangular earthenware dish, alternating them with the milt and roe (these can also be marinated in separate dishes). Sprinkle each layer of herring with thin slices of onion cut in rings and tiny pieces of bay leaf. Fill the dish full and pour olive oil over everything, enough to cover the fish. Let macerate 48 hr. in a cool place.

To serve: Serve the herring fillets as they are, in the same dish, or, if desired, arrange them in hors d'oeuvre dishes, alternating the fillets with the milt and the roe. Surround with half slices of lemon, the rim scalloped. Place a row of onion rings on the herring fillets. Moisten with oil from the marinade.

Note: Sometimes thin slices of scored raw carrots are added to the marinade. This addition only makes the dish more attractive. The herring can be soaked 1 hr. in dry white wine before being put into the marinade.

GREEN BEANS INDIAN STYLE HARICOTS VERTS À L'INDIENNE (M.)

Cook the green beans in salted water with a finely sliced onion. Drain; season with mayonnaise flavored with curry. Arrange in a relish dish. Surround with a border of tomatoes that have been peeled, seeded, diced, salted, and drained; season with oil and vinegar. Place a row of peeled, thinly sliced lemon on the beans.

GREEN BEANS NIÇOISE HARICOTS VERTS À LA NIÇOISE (M.)

Dice the green beans. Blanch 5 min. in boiling salted water. Drain, and cook with somewhat thin Tomato Fondue (p. 194) seasoned with crushed garlic. When the beans are cooked, add 1 tbsp. chopped tarragon and 1 tbsp. capers. Arrange in a relish dish; garnish with slices of lemon peeled to the flesh.

GREEN-BEAN SALAD HARICOTS VERTS EN SALADE (M.)

Cook the beans in salted water, keeping them somewhat firm. Drain and season while hot with oil, vinegar, salt, and pepper. Arrange in a relish dish or bowl; sprinkle with chopped parsley and chervil, or with chopped chives.

JALANGUI DOLMA (EGGPLANT TURKISH STYLE) JALANGUI DOLMA (AUBERGINE À LA TURQUE) (W.)

Take your eggplant, cut around the inside starting from the stem end, then roll it as you would a hard-boiled egg you want to shell. The inside of your eggplant will come out like a long stopper. Save some of it to use as a plug when your eggplant is stuffed with a Risotto made as follows: take 12 oz. finely sliced onion cooked in oil and 5 oz. Rice Pilaf (p. 512), moisten with 1 pt. White Stock (p. 133), add 5 oz. crushed tomatoes, 2 oz. sliced pimentos, 4 finely cut mint leaves, and the inside of your eggplant cut into cubes; season highly. When this is done, braise your eggplants in White Stock with a little crushed tomato and ¼ cup olive oil. When cooked, set them up and place on top the little that is left from the cooking liquid. Serve very cold.

LETTUCE HELDER LAITUES HELDER (W.)

Same cooking procedure as for Mushrooms in White Wine (p. 219). Use crushed tomatoes instead of coriander seeds. First blanch the lettuce.

LETTUCE PORTUGUESE STYLE LAITUES À LA PORTUGAISE (W.)

Blanch the heads of lettuce and then cook in white wine, lemon juice, salt, pepper, and a *bouquet garni*. When cooked and cooled, arrange the heads of lettuce on a platter and between each head place a mound of Rice Portuguese Style (made with tomato and onion) and a mound of grated horseradish.

WATERMELON MELON D'EAU or PASTÈQUE (M.)

Served in slices, like any fresh melon. It may also be prepared with Frontignan, port, or other dessert wine, following the recipe for Portuguese Melon.

PORTUGUESE MELON or **GOLDEN MELON** MELON DU PORTUGAL or MELONE DE ORO (M.)

This melon, whose white flesh tastes rather like a peach, was introduced into France some years ago. Its success comes from the fact that it arrives in the middle of winter, when French melons, such as cantaloupes, are no longer available. It is prepared in the following manner: cut a circular piece out of one side of the melon, to drain out the water and seeds. Lightly sugar the inside of the melon and pour in 7 or 8 oz. dessert wine—Frontignan, malmsey, port, sherry, etc. Replace the lid on the melon. Place the melon in a terrine and surround with crushed ice. Let it cool 2 hr. before serving. Serve by the spoonful, covering each portion with wine from inside the melon.

BOLOGNA SAUSAGE MORTADELLE (M.)

Cut in slices. Arrange on a plate. Garnish with curly parsley.

Note: Bologna sausage may also be served cut in very thin slices and rolled into cones like Bayonne or Milan ham. Nevertheless, we advise not cutting Bologna sausage too thin.

MUSSELS WITH CURRY or **INDIAN STYLE** MOULES AU CURRY or À L'INDIENNE (M.)

Cook the mussels in white wine, remove the shells, and season with mayonnaise flavored with curry. First reduce the liquid in which the mussels have cooked. Strain it when cool, and add to the mayonnaise.

Note: Dry the mussels well before seasoning.

MUSSELS INDIAN STYLE MOULES À L'INDIENNE (W.)

Add curry to the liquid the mussels are cooked in, and serve them in the center of a rice ring. (Figure 135, Page 232.)

MUSSELS WITH MAYONNAISE MOULES À LA MAYONNAISE (M.)

Cook the mussels. Season with very thick mayonnaise.

MUSSELS NIÇOISE MOULES À LA NIÇOISE (M.)

Cook the mussels. Remove the shells. Put them into a Tomato Fondue (p. 194) to which you have added: desalted (by soaking in water) and diced anchovy fillets, capers, chopped tarragon, 1 or 2 tbsp. oil, and the reduced and strained liquid in which the mussels were cooked.

OX MUZZLE MUSEAU DE BOEUF (M.)

After being pickled, the ox muzzle is desalted and cooked in water for 6 hr. Drain, let cool. Slice finely; season with oil, vinegar, salt, pepper, chopped onions and parsley. Arrange in relish dishes.

EGGS GERMAN STYLE OEUFS À L'ALLEMANDE (W.)

Arrange in an hors d'oeuvre dish a relish of hard-boiled eggs and capers in Horseradish Sauce (p. 162). On top place a few shavings of horseradish.

EGGS CLÉMENCE OEUFS À LA CLÉMENCE (W.)

Cut hard-boiled eggs in half, crosswise. Mash the yolks with an equal amount of tuna in oil; season; stuff the whites, and keep them cool. Then cut each half egg in two. Arrange them in a bed of green mayonnaise on a relish dish and stick pink shrimps along both sides. (Figure 136, Page 232.)

EGGS CRESSONNIÈRE OEUFS À LA CRESSONNIÈRE (W.)

Cover your eggs with mayonnaise mixed with a purée of water cress; garnish with a few leaves and bunches of water cress.

EGGS HUNGARIAN STYLE OEUFS À LA HONGROISE (W.)

Cut hard-boiled eggs in half; coat with mayonnaise seasoned with paprika and a little grated onion.

EGGS INDIAN STYLE OEUFS À L'INDIENNE (W.)

Relish of hard-boiled eggs and apples, mixed with mayonnaise seasoned with lemon and curry powder; garnish with Rice Indian Style (p. 512).

EGGS JOINVILLE OEUFS À LA JOINVILLE (W.)

Cut thin slices of hard-boiled eggs, arrange them on a little Cream of Shrimp (p. 200) bound with mayonnaise. Stick pink shrimps in the eggs.

EGGS MADRILÈNE OEUFS À LA MADRILÈNE (W.)

Place alternate thin slices of hard-boiled eggs, tomatoes, and onions on a relish dish; dress with Vinaigrette Sauce (p. 158) seasoned with mustard and sprinkle *fines herbes* on top.

HARD-BOILED-EGG SALAD WITH MAYONNAISE OR TARTAR SAUCE

OEUFS DURS À LA MAYONNAISE, EN SALADE, À LA TARTARE (W.)

Cut the eggs in quarters (or halves); arrange on relish dishes; season with oil, vinegar, salt, pepper, and *fines herbes,* or cover with mayonnaise or Tartar Sauce (p. 158). Surround with half slices of scored lemon, half slices of beets or tomatoes. (Figures 137-138, Page 232.)

Fig. 130 - Pastry boats Neptune (p. 218).
Fig. 131 - Artichoke bottoms Mazarin (p. 218).
Fig. 132 - Stuffed eggs senora (p. 226).

Fig. 130

Fig. 132

Fig. 131

Fig. 133

Fig. 134

EGGS MOSCOVITE OEUFS À LA MOSCOVITE (W.)

Arrange soft-boiled (*mollet*) eggs (see p. 253) on a vegetable salad, coat with thin mayonnaise, make a border of sliced tomatoes around the plate or relish dish, and, at the last moment, sprinkle the eggs with pink paprika.

EGGS NIÇOISE OEUFS À LA NIÇOISE (W.)

Arrange on an hors d'oeuvre plate a salad of crushed tomatoes and chopped hard-boiled eggs, seasoned with a purée of fish; decorate with some small black olives and anchovy fillets on top.

EGGS PORTUGUESE STYLE OEUFS À LA PORTUGAISE (W.)

Arrange quarters of hard-boiled eggs on a relish dish; garnish them with a ragout made of shrimps, crushed tomatoes, and sliced pimentos, seasoned with mayonnaise, lemon juice, and a crushed garlic clove. Cover the eggs with Tomato Jelly (p. 813).

EGGS PROVENÇAL OEUFS À LA PROVENÇALE (W.)

Cut hard-boiled eggs in half, arrange them on a relish dish, coat them with mayonnaise with anchovy purée added; place a few anchovy fillets on top.

EGGS RAVIGOTE OEUFS À LA RAVIGOTE (M.)

Arrange soft-boiled (*mollet*) eggs (see p. 253), coat them with Cold Ravigote Sauce (p. 158), place a few blanched tarragon leaves on top.

EGGS RÉJANE OEUFS À LA RÉJANE (W.)

Mix sliced hard-boiled eggs and sliced celeriac or celery root in mayonnaise strongly seasoned with mustard; arrange in a relish dish with a little chopped fennel on top.

EGGS RIGOLETTO OEUFS À LA RIGOLETTO (W.)

Cut hard-boiled eggs in the same way as lemons, so as to have two halves with a saw-tooth design. Garnish each half with a small vegetable salad mixed with mayonnaise.

EGGS RUSSIAN STYLE OEUFS À LA RUSSE (M.)

Arrange your hard-boiled eggs on Russian Salad (p. 525), cover with mayonnaise, and on top sprinkle chopped tongue, ham, and truffles.

EGGS VIVANDIÈRE OEUFS À LA VIVANDIÈRE (W.)

Cut hard-boiled eggs in half, scoop out the yolks, and stuff with a ragout of shrimps bound with mayonnaise.

VARIOUS STUFFED HARD-BOILED EGGS OEUFS DURS FARCIS DIVERS (M.)

Cut the eggs in half lengthwise. Remove the yolks; put these yolks through a fine sieve and add some complementary ingredient to them. Stuff the egg halves with this composition, smoothing it into a dome. Arrange the eggs on an hors d'oeuvre plate. Season with oil, vinegar, salt, and pepper, or, depending on the nature of the ingredients, coat with mayonnaise, Tartar or Green Sauce, or others of the same type (pp. 157–158). Garnish around the sides with beets, slices of lemon, curly parsley, etc.

Note: Instead of cutting the eggs lengthwise, they may be shaped like little

Fig. 133 - 1. Pastry boats moscovite (p. 218).
2. Pastry boats normande (p. 218).
Fig. 134 - Arrangement of pink shrimps or prawns (p. 220).

barrels. The yolks are removed, reduced to a purée, and mixed with another ingredient such as purée of anchovy, salmon, or tuna, very thick Tomato Fondue (p. 194), chopped cooked ham or tongue, shrimp, caviar, botargo (salted or smoked mullet roe), various salpicons, etc. The whites are then filled with the mixture. Stuffed eggs prepared this way may be arranged directly on a plate; placed on small round slices of bread (the crusts removed) spread with a butter made from some harmonizing ingredient (see Butters, pp. 163–166); or placed on very small artichoke bottoms cooked until tender and marinated, or even in little boats made of Short Paste (p. 545) or of various vegetables scooped out: beets, cucumbers, zucchini, etc.

STUFFED EGGS MIREILLE OEUFS FARCIS À LA MIREILLE (P.)

Hard-boiled eggs cut in half; remove the yolks and stuff the whites with tuna-and-tomato purée; place on each a small anchovy fillet rolled into a ring around a pitted olive stuffed, if desired, with capers. Arrange the eggs in an hors d'oeuvre dish on a bed of Potato or Tomato Salad (p. 523).

STUFFED EGGS MONTIJO OEUFS FARCIS À LA MONTIJO (W.)

Take hard-boiled eggs, cut them in half, remove the yolks and put them through a sieve with a few anchovy fillets and a piece of butter; season highly; stuff your eggs with this purée, then cover with mayonnaise mixed with anchovy purée; decorate with a few thin strips of Spanish pimento.

STUFFED EGGS SEÑORA OEUFS FARCIS À LA SEÑORA (P.)

Cut hard-boiled eggs in half, lengthwise or crosswise, remove the yolks and mash them with a little tuna and 3 anchovy fillets in oil; fill the whites, but not to excess, then place them on sprigs of parsley in a relish dish. Put a thin, firm slice of tomato on each halved egg, a small round piece of tuna on the tomato, and on top a pitted black olive. Serve chilled. (Figure 132, Page 224.)

SMOKED GOOSE (BREAST OF) OIE FUMÉE (POITRINE D') (M.)

Cut the breast in thin slices, arrange on a plate, garnish with curly parsley. Serve with grated horseradish.

VARIOUS OLIVES OLIVES DIVERSES (M.)

Arrange in a relish dish with pieces of chopped ice on top.

Note: Excellent stuffed olives may also be found already prepared. Below, we give the way to prepare stuffed olives.

STUFFED OLIVES (LARGE) OLIVES FARCIES (GROSSES) (M.)

Remove the pits with an olive pitter. Stuff them with any of the following: anchovy purée, tomato purée, red-pimento butter, or any other garnish. Arrange them on a relish dish and moisten them with oil.

ORANGE BASKETS PANIERS D'ORANGES (P.)

Cut the oranges in a basket shape, scoop them out, and fill with a salad made of heart of lettuce, beets, potatoes, and pippins, all mixed with mayonnaise; season well. Place on top a thin slice of orange and, in a ring, bits of nuts. Do not fill the baskets too far in advance because the white, inner skin of the orange will give the contents a bitter taste.

VARIOUS RILLETTES[1] RILLETTES DIVERSES (M.)

Rillettes from Tours are the best known, but excellent ones are prepared in other parts of France. Serve in the jars in which they come.

VARIOUS CRACKLINGS RILLONS DIVERSES (M.)

The best known are those from Blois. Arrange on small plates or in relish dishes.

RED MULLET ORIENTALE ROUGETS À L'ORIENTALE (M.)

Brown some very small red mullets, seasoned with salt and paprika, in oil. Place them in an ovenware dish. Cover with Tomato Fondue (p. 194) with crushed garlic, chopped parsley, and lemon juice added. Cook the red mullets in this fondue. Place a slice of lemon peeled to the flesh on the fish. Sprinkle with chopped parsley. Chill well. (Figure 139, Page 233.)

RED MULLET WITH SAFFRON ROUGETS AU SAFRAN (M.)

Like Red Mullet Orientale (above), with 1 tsp. saffron added to the Tomato Fondue.

ROYANS ROYANS (M.)

This is the name given in Bordeaux to a variety of sardine with extremely delicate flesh. Use the same recipes for *royans* as given for fresh sardines prepared as hors d'oeuvres.

VARIOUS SALADS SALADES DIVERSES (M.)

Apart from green salads, called seasonal salads, and certain prepared salads served at the same time as the roast, or after, depending upon their nature, a certain number of salads are served as hors d'oeuvres. Below is a list of these salads, together with the way they are seasoned.

ARTICHOKE (BOTTOM) SALAD SALADE (DE FONDS) D'ARTICHAUTS (M.)

The bottoms sliced; seasoned with oil, vinegar, salt, pepper, and chopped parsley and chervil.

Note: The bottoms may also be cut into large cubes.

SAVELOY SALAD SALADE DE CERVELAS (M.)

Cooked saveloy (a kind of sausage), sliced. Arrange on Potato Salad (p. 523). Cover with Vinaigrette Sauce (p. 158) seasoned with mustard. Sprinkle with chopped parsley. Garnish with thin onion rings (or sprinkle with chopped chives).

CRAB SALAD SALADE DE CRABE (M.)

See Hard-Shell Crab Russian Style, p. 321.

SHRIMP SALAD SALADE DE CREVETTES (M.)

Season the shelled shrimps with oil, vinegar, salt, pepper, and *fines herbes,* or with mayonnaise. Serve well chilled.

CRAYFISH SALAD SALADE D'ÉCREVISSES (M.)

Season the crayfish tails as described, above, for Shrimp Salad.

[1] Rillettes are potted mincemeats made of pork, etc.

SPINACH SALAD SALADE D'ÉPINARDS (M.)

Spinach cooked in whole leaves, drained, cooled, dried, and arranged in a mound on a salad plate, seasoned with oil, vinegar, salt, and pepper; sprinkled with chopped hard-boiled egg yolks and chopped parsley.

HERRING-FILLET SALAD SALADE DE FILETS DE HARENGS (W.)

Take whole herring fillets; skin, soak in water to remove salt, and trim; then arrange on an hors d'oeuvre plate with onion rings; pour a little olive oil on top. They can also be arranged on Potato Salad (p. 523) in a bowl.

FISH or CHICKEN SALAD SALADE DE POISSON OT DE VOLAILLE (P.)

Leftover fish or chicken, skinned, arranged on a salad plate, covered with mayonnaise, and decorated with hard-boiled eggs and heart of lettuce.

CHICKEN SALAD SALADE DE VOLAILLE (M.)

This salad is prepared with leftover poached or braised chicken. Skin the pieces of chicken; cut them in thin slices. Arrange them on lettuce Chiffonade (p. 193) in a salad bowl or relish dish. Season with oil, vinegar, salt, pepper, and chopped parsley, chervil, and tarragon.

Note: This salad can be garnished with quartered hard-boiled eggs, lettuce hearts, and capers. The chicken can also be covered with mayonnaise. But prepared this way and garnished with hard-boiled eggs, lettuce, capers, anchovy fillets, the dish is no longer considered a salad but a cold entree.

SARDINES SARDINES (M.)

Fresh sardines can be prepared as hors d'oeuvres, using all the recipes given for anchovies, smelts, herring, and red mullet. Sardines thus prepared are served in the same dishes in which they are cooked, sprinkled with chopped parsley and garnished with slices of lemon peeled to the flesh.

SARDINES IN OIL (CANNED) SARDINES CONSERVÉES À L'HUILE (M.)

Sardines in oil prepared in French canneries are most highly regarded. These sardines are prepared *au naturel*—in other words, simply marinated in oil or seasoned in different ways: with tomatoes, pimentos, truffles, etc. Serve these sardines as they are, in their own can, or, if you wish, in an hors d'oeuvre dish garnished with hard-boiled eggs, capers, slices of scored lemon, curly parsley, etc. (Figure 140, Page 233.)

Note: A great number of hors d'oeuvres may be made with canned, marinated sardines. They are used for this purpose in the form of fillets, purées, and salpicons. They are used in all of these various forms to garnish pastry boats, canapés, tartlets, and other preparations for which the recipes are given in this chapter.

SMOKED SALMON (CONES OF) SAUMON FUMÉ (CORNETS DE) (P.)

The smoked salmon is bought ready-made, cut in very thin slices. Cut the slices in triangles, roll them into cones, and in each one, to hold the shape, place a bunch of curly parsley. Arrange them on an hors d'oeuvre plate and place a small butter rose, or quarter of a hard-boiled egg, in the opening of each one. (Figure 126, Page 217.)

TUNA MARINATED IN OIL THON MARINÉ À L'HUILE (M.)

Serve arranged on a plate. Garnish with capers in vinegar, tomatoes, olives, hard-boiled eggs, etc.

TUNA MIRABEAU THON À LA MIRABEAU (P.)

Make a purée of tuna in oil, well mashed with a little butter. Arrange it in a mound on an hors d'oeuvre dish and stud the top with pitted green olives filled with thick tomato purée (this last can be omitted).

TUNA MIREILLE THON À LA MIREILLE (P.)

The same purée (as above) on an hors d'oeuvre dish. Cover with thin slices of small tomatoes, with a good pinch of chervil tops on each.

TOMATOES ANTIBOISE TOMATES À L'ANTIBOISE (M.)

Delicately hollow out some very small tomatoes, chosen for uniformity ot size and shape. Hollow them out without breaking them. Macerate them 2 hr. in oil, vinegar, salt, and pepper. Stuff them with the following preparation: 2 oz. chopped tuna in oil, mixed with 2 hard-boiled eggs and 2 tbsp. capers and *fines herbes,* also chopped. Bind it all together with 1 tbsp. mayonnaise mixed with anchovy essence. Shape this stuffing into a dome on the top. Arrange the tomatoes on an hors d'oeuvre plate. Moisten them with the liquid in which they were macerated. Surround with half slices of scored lemon. (Figure 141, P. 240).

TOMATOES SCOTCH STYLE TOMATES À L'ÉCOSSAISE (M.)

Choose 6 round, firm tomatoes. Cut into quarters. Remove the seeds and pulp from these quarters without breaking them and macerate as described in Tomatoes Antiboise (above). Stuff with the following preparation: purée of cooked salmon bound with 1 tbsp. Stiff Mayonnaise (p. 157) with a little Worcestershire sauce added.

Note: These tomatoes can also be stuffed with a purée of anchovies, herring, turbot, etc.

TOMATOES MENTONNAISE TOMATES À LA MENTONNAISE (M.)

Small tomatoes, drained and marinated, stuffed with a purée of hard-boiled egg yolks mixed with desalted anchovy fillets (diced fine) and chopped parsley. Arrange on a relish plate; on each tomato place a slice of lemon peeled to the flesh. The tomatoes may also be stuffed with celery and Rémoulade Sauce.

TOMATO SALAD or **TOMATOES VINAIGRETTE** TOMATES EN SALADE or À LA VINAIGRETTE (M.)

Peel the tomatoes (after scalding them). Cut in slices of equal thickness. Arrange in a line. Sprinkle with salt. Let them drain 30 min. Remove the seeds. Arrange the tomatoes on relish plates; season with oil, vinegar, and pepper; sprinkle with chopped parsley.

Note: Tomatoes Vinaigrette may also be cut into quarters. A seasoning that goes very well with this preparation is chopped basil. To present this simple salad most attractively, it may be encircled with Cucumber Salad (p. 523), just as Cucumber Salad may be encircled with Tomato Salad.

HOT HORS D'OEUVRES

OR SMALL ENTREES

For family cooking, this chapter presents very appetizing ways of serving all sorts of leftovers: as rissoles, croquettes, fried mixtures, tartlets, or pastry boats, etc., making it possible to prepare dishes that are both economical and tasty.

ANCHOVY STICKS ALLUMETTES AUX ANCHOIS (M.)

Spread fish forcemeat (see p. 173) mixed with Anchovy Butter (p. 163) on a strip of Puff Paste (p. 544) about 3 in. wide and 1/8 in. thick. Cut the strip into very narrow rectangles. On each rectangle place an anchovy fillet. Bake in the oven 12–14 min. A thin covering of Puff Paste may be placed on top. Fashion in the shape of a fish. (Figure 142, Page 240.)

OLD-FASHIONED or **CAPRICE STICKS** ALLUMETTES À L'ANCIENNE OF CAPRICE (M.)

As above, with purée of breast of chicken bound with reduced Velouté (p. 147), and very small slices of lean ham alternated with thin slices of truffles.

SHRIMP STICKS ALLUMETTES AUX CREVETTES (M.)

As above, with fish forcemeat (see p. 173) mixed with Shrimp Butter (p. 164) and shelled shrimps.

CHEESE STICKS ALLUMETTES AU FROMAGE (P.)

Roll out the Puff Paste (p. 544) the last 2 times, sprinkling generously with grated Gruyère cheese and a little paprika, and cut into strips about 1 in. wide; place them on a pastry sheet, brush the tops with beaten egg, and sprinkle with cheese. Bake in a hot oven and serve hot. They may also be twisted into corkscrew shapes. (Figure 143, Page 241.)

STICKS WITH VARIOUS FILLINGS ALLUMETTES AUX SALPICONS DIVERS (M.)

Spread the Puff-Paste strips (p. 544) with various salpicons (tiny cubes), meat or meatless, 1 ingredient or a mixture of several, mixed with white or brown sauces. Cut and bake the sticks as described above.

ATTEREAUX ATTEREAUX (E.)

An hors d'oeuvre of bygone cooking that modern cooking is bringing back into favor. In fact, the Attereau is any brochette whose ingredients, cut in small slices of the same size, are spitted. The ingredients are alternately spitted on a small wooden skewer and covered with a reduced (that is, thick) sauce, which is characteristic of the preparation. When the sauce has hardened, the Attereaux are trimmed, breaded English style—that is, (1) floured, (2) dipped in beaten egg with a little olive oil, (3) dipped in bread crumbs—and fried just before serving. When they are served, the wooden cooking skewer is replaced by an ornamental silver skewer. They are then placed on a napkin with a border of fried parsley or else they are stuck upright in a circle on a mound of rice or fried bread, with a bouquet of fried parsley in the middle.

ATTEREAUX GENEVOISE ATTEREAUX À LA GENEVOISE (E.)

Chicken livers sautéed in butter (browned on the outside, but rare inside), braised lamb's sweetbreads, poached brains, mushrooms, truffles, and artichoke bottoms, all cut in squares of about 1 in., spitted on skewers, and covered with very thick Duxelles Sauce (p. 140). Chill, cover with a layer of forcemeat softened with beaten egg, and bread English style (see recipe for Attereaux, p. 230), giving the Attereaux a cylindrical shape. Fry quickly; replace the wooden skewers with silver serving skewers, and arrange as described on p. 230.

OYSTER ATTEREAUX VILLEROI ATTEREAUX D'HUÎTRES VILLEROI (E.)

Poach some large oysters; trim them and spit them in sixes on wooden skewers, alternating them with slices of cooked mushrooms. Cover with Villeroi Sauce (p. 155) to which the reduced oyster liquid has been added. Bread English style (see under Attereaux, p. 230); roll the Attereaux into cylinders. Fry quickly and arrange as usual.

ATTEREAUX WITH PARMESAN CHEESE or **PARMA BROCHETTES**
ATTEREAUX AU PARMESAN or BROCHETTES DE PARME (E.)

Preparation: 8 oz. semolina cooked in 1 qt. white consommé, allowing about ½ hr. for cooking. Add to the semolina, off the stove, 6 oz. grated Parmesan cheese and 4 oz. butter. Spread out on a buttered tray to about ¼-in. thickness and let cool well. Cut into small circles about the size of a quarter with a ring cutter. Spit these circles on wooden brochettes, alternating with slices of fresh Gruyère cheese of the same size and thickness. Bread English style (see under Attereaux, p. 230), fry quickly, and replace the wooden brochettes with silver serving skewers.

PASTRY BOATS (STUFFED) BARQUETTES (GARNIES) (M.)

Pastry boats differ from tartlets only in the shape of the patty shell, which is oval instead of round. The pastry-boat molds are usually lined with Short Paste (p. 545) or trimmings of Puff Paste (p. 544). For certain boats the molds may also be lined with semolina, polenta, the mixture for Potatoes Duchesse (p. 507), etc. By definition, pastry boats ought to be filled with meatless ingredients, fish, shellfish, mollusks. In current practice, however, these hors d'oeuvres are frequently prepared with meat.

PASTRY BOATS ANDALOUSE BARQUETTES À L'ANDALOUSE (M.)

Fill the pastry boats with a little very thick Tomato Fondue (p. 194) seasoned with paprika. On each boat place a small slice of marinated tuna. Cover with 1 tbsp. pimento cut in julienne strips and cooked in oil. Sprinkle with fried bread crumbs that have been well drained. Put into a very hot oven for just a moment. Arrange on a napkin; garnish with parsley.

PASTRY BOATS BORDELAISE BARQUETTES À LA BORDELAISE (M.)

Fill the boats with large mushrooms sliced fine and sautéed in oil with a few chopped shallots. On each boat place a very small sole fillet sautéed in butter. Cover with 1 tbsp. highly seasoned Mirepoix Bordelaise (p. 136). Sprinkle with chopped parsley.

PASTRY BOATS CARÊME BARQUETTES CARÊME (M.)

Fill the boats with a salpicon (tiny cubes) of soft roe or milt, mushrooms, and truffles bound with reduced Fish Velouté (p. 147). On each boat place 2 poached oysters alternated with slices of truffles. Cover with Normande Sauce (p. 153). Glaze in the oven.

PASTRY BOATS CREOLE BARQUETTES À LA CRÉOLE (M.)

Fill the boats with a mixture of cooked rice and Tomato Fondue (p. 194). On each boat place cooked okra and a salpicon (tiny cubes) of sweet peppers cooked in butter. Sprinkle with bread crumbs fried in butter and then drained. Place in the oven for a moment.

SHRIMP PASTRY BOATS or **PASTRY BOATS JOINVILLE** BARQUETTES DE CREVETTES OF JOINVILLE (E.)

Fill the bottoms of the boats with a fine salpicon (tiny cubes) of shrimps bound with Velouté (p. 147) mixed with Shrimp Butter (p. 164). Cover with sauce and decorate with shrimps. (Figure 144, Page 241.)

DEVILED PASTRY BOATS or **DEVILED-CRAYFISH PASTRY BOATS** BARQUETTES À LA DIABLE OT BARQUETTES D'ÉCREVISSES À LA DIABLE (M.)

Fill the boats with Crayfish Bordelaise (p. 315) highly seasoned with cayenne pepper. Cover with Bordelaise Sauce (p. 138). Sprinkle with fried, drained bread crumbs. Place in the oven for a moment.

PASTRY BOATS DUCHESSE BARQUETTES DUCHESSE (M.)

Line the boat molds, well buttered, with the mixture for Potatoes Duchesse (p. 507). Fill the boats with a salpicon (tiny cubes) of chicken, truffles, and mushrooms bound with reduced Velouté (p. 147). Cover the boats with a layer of the mixture for Potatoes Duchesse. Brush the tops of the boats with beaten egg and place in the oven to brown.

SOLE-FILLET PASTRY BOATS BARQUETTES DE FILETS DE SOLE (M.)

Fill the boats with a salpicon (tiny cubes) of sole fillet and mushrooms bound with reduced Fish Velouté (p. 147). On top of this mixture place some small slices of sole fillet. Cover with Normande Sauce (p. 153). Sprinkle with fried, drained bread crumbs. Place in the oven for a moment.

Note: Pastry boats with other fish may be prepared the same way.

LOBSTER PASTRY BOATS HONGROISE BARQUETTES DE HOMARD À LA HONGROISE (M.)

Fill the boats with a salpicon (tiny cubes) of leftover lobster and mushrooms bound with paprika sauce, also called Hongroise or Hungarian Sauce (p. 151). On each boat put 2 small slices of lobster. Cover with paprika sauce. Glaze in the oven. Sprinkle with chopped lobster coral mixed with chopped parsley.

OYSTER PASTRY BOATS BARQUETTES D'HUÎTRES (M.)

Fill the boats with poached, drained, trimmed oysters. Cover with Normande Sauce (p. 153). Sprinkle with fried bread crumbs. Place in the oven for a moment.

Fig. 135 - Mussels indian style (p. 223).
Fig. 136 - Eggs Clémence (p. 224).
Fig. 137 & 138 - Eggs with mayonnaise (p. 224).

Fig. 136

Fig. 135

. 137

Fig. 138

Fig. 139

Fig. 140

OYSTER PASTRY BOATS MONSELET BARQUETTES D'HUÎTRES MONSELET (M.)

Fill the pastry boats with a salpicon (tiny cubes) of artichoke bottoms and truffles mixed with cream. Sprinkle with Parmesan cheese; moisten with melted butter; heat quickly in the oven until a crust forms. On each boat place 3 fried oysters (dipped in flour, beaten egg, and bread crumbs).

OYSTER PASTRY BOATS MORNAY BARQUETTES D'HUÎTRES MORNAY (M.)

As above. Cover with Mornay Sauce (p. 152). Sprinkle with Parmesan cheese. Heat in the oven until a crust forms.

OYSTER PASTRY BOATS NORMANDE BARQUETTES D'HUÎTRES À LA NORMANDE (M.)

Fill the boats with a salpicon (tiny cubes) of mussels, shrimps, and mushrooms bound with Normande Sauce (p. 153). On each boat place 2 poached oysters, alternated with slices of truffles. Cover with Normande Sauce. Glaze in the oven.

OYSTER PASTRY BOATS OSTENDAISE BARQUETTES D'HUÎTRES À L'OSTENDAISE (E.)

Fill the boats with poached, trimmed oysters bound with a creamy Béchamel Sauce (p. 146) mixed with fish stock. Sprinkle the tops with chopped truffles.

SOFT-ROE OR MILT PASTRY BOATS BARQUETTES DE LAITANCES (M.)

Fill the boats with a salpicon (tiny cubes) of mushrooms bound with Béchamel Sauce (p. 146). On each boat place 2 pieces of milt or soft roe (from herring or other fish) cooked in butter *à la meunière* (see p. 279). Sprinkle with chopped parsley. Cover the boats at the last moment with brown butter in which a small quantity of freshly sifted bread crumbs has been fried.

SOFT-ROE OR MILT PASTRY BOATS WITH PARMESAN CHEESE BARQUETTES DE LAITANCES AU PARMESAN (E.)

Fill the bottoms of the boats with 1 tbsp. Mornay Sauce (p. 152); on the sauce put a piece of soft roe or milt poached in white wine. Cover this, using a pastry bag, with a Parmesan-cheese-soufflé mixture (see Cheese Soufflé, p. 249) and bake 7–8 min. in a moderately hot oven.

PASTRY BOATS LOMBARDE BARQUETTES À LA LOMBARDE (M.)

Line the buttered pastry-boat molds with a mixture of semolina and Parmesan cheese. Fill the insides of the boats with chicken ravioli filling (see Ravioli, Filling *c*, p. 521). Cover with a thin layer of semolina. Unmold. Dip in flour, beaten egg, and bread crumbs. Fry at the last moment. Arrange on a doily. Garnish with fried parsley. (Figure 143, Page 241.)

PASTRY BOATS NEPTUNE BARQUETTES À LA NEPTUNE (M.)

Fill with shrimps, small mushrooms, mussels, and oysters bound with Normande Sauce (p. 153) with some thin Shrimp Butter (p. 164) added.

Note: Also made in tartlets. (Figure 144, Page 241.)

Fig. 139 - Red mullet orientale (p. 227).
Fig. 140 - Arrangement of sardines in oil (p. 228).

PASTRY BOATS PARMESANE BARQUETTES À LA PARMESANE (M.)

Line the boat molds as described in Pastry Boats Lombarde (p. 233), using a mixture of polenta and Parmesan cheese. Fill the boats with a salpicon (tiny cubes) of anchovies and hard-boiled eggs bound with Béchamel Sauce (p. 146). Finish the same way as Pastry Boats Lombarde.

FRITTERS BENEDICTINE BEIGNETS À LA BÉNÉDICTINE (E.)

Mixture composed of ⅔ Brandade of Salt Cod (p. 290) and ⅓ potato purée. Divide into pieces about the thickness of a walnut and shape into oval disks. Just before serving, dip in thin Frying Paste (p. 558) and fry in hot deep fat.

FRITTERS MATHURINE BEIGNETS À LA MATHURINE (E.)

Mixture of Choux Paste (p. 548) without sugar and diced herring fillets and sardines in oil. Proportions: 1 oz. of each per 4 oz. Choux Paste. For preparation and method of frying, proceed exactly as for ordinary Souffléed Fritters (see Pastry, p. 612).

FRITTERS PALERMITAINE BEIGNETS À LA PALERMITAINE (M.)

Prepare fritters of Choux Paste with Parmesan cheese as described above. Stuff the fritters, after frying them, with unsugared Pastry Cream (p. 552) with cheese added.

Note: Fritters stuffed with a cream base are prepared the same way with various cheeses: Cheshire, Dutch, Brie, etc.

FRITTERS WITH PARMESAN CHEESE BEIGNETS AU PARMESAN (M.)

Prepare ordinary Choux Paste (without sugar). When it is finished, add grated Parmesan cheese in the proportion of ⅓ cheese to ⅔ Choux Paste. Divide this mixture into pieces the size of a hazelnut and fry in very hot deep fat.

FRITTERS PIGNATELLI BEIGNETS PIGNATELLI (E.)

Add to 5 oz. ordinary Choux Paste (without sugar) : 2 tbsp. very lean, cooked, diced ham; 1 oz. almonds, finely shredded and lightly toasted. Prepare the same way as ordinary Souffléed Fritters (p. 612).

BEURRECKS TURKISH STYLE BEURRECKS À LA TURQUE (E.)

Cut 8 oz. fresh Gruyère cheese into tiny diced bits and blend with 3 tbsp. very thick, almost cold Béchamel Sauce (p. 146). Chill the mixture well. Shape into the form and size of an ordinary cigar. Roll each piece in an oval of paper-thin noodle paste (see Fresh Noodles, p. 520) and join the edges of the paste with beaten egg. Bread English style (dip in flour, beaten egg, then bread crumbs); fry at the last minute before serving. (Figure 145, Page 248.)

Note: Beurrecks may be made in rissoles of various shapes, but should always be breaded English style. Beurrecks are made in Constantinople on street corners with a dexterity and ingredients that in no way resemble ours.

BLINI BLINIS (A.)

Blini are a kind of small pancake, made in various ways, that are very popular in Russia, especially during Lent. Here is the recipe. For 6–8 persons take: 2 lb. wheat flour, 1 lb. buckwheat flour, 11 oz. clarified butter, 1 oz. brewer's yeast, 1 qt. unskimmed milk, 5 fresh eggs, powdered sugar, salt. Mix the 2 types of flour well. Break the eggs; separate the yolks from the whites. Dissolve the yeast in the milk, which has been slightly warmed. With the milk and the flour mixture prepare a batter a little thicker than that used for ordinary (French) pancakes. Stir in 6 oz. warm, clarified butter, the yolks of the eggs, sugar and salt to taste; mix well. Beat the egg whites till stiff; fold them into the batter. Let the batter rise overnight. Take some small, round frying pans without handles, about 3 in. in diameter and ½ in. deep. Pour 1 tbsp. batter into each and, with the aid of a baker's paddle, place in a wood-burning oven, under the flame; moisten during the baking with the remainder of the melted butter. The blini should be thin, evenly browned on both sides, light, and crisp. Arrange the blini on a silver platter and serve them with sauceboats of clarified butter and sour cream and with fresh caviar.

For variety, the blini may be made with oatmeal flour, grits, semolina, rice flour, etc. (Figure 143, Page 241.)

PATTIES (PREPARATION OF SHELLS FOR) BOUCHÉES (PRÉPARATION DES CROÛTES DE)

See Mixed Entrees, p. 529.

OLD-FASHIONED PATTIES BOUCHÉES À L'ANCIENNE (M.)

Fill the patty shells with a purée of breast of chicken with cream and a salpicon (tiny cubes) of truffles. For each patty make a covering of a round, thin slice of ham heated in Madeira and, on the ham, place a slice of truffle.

Note: In certain cases the cover for the patty shell is replaced by a slice of truffle or some other ingredient suitable to the filling.

PATTIES BANQUIÈRE BOUCHÉES À LA BANQUIÈRE (M.)

Fill with a salpicon (tiny cubes) of cockscombs and cock's kidney, truffles, and mushrooms bound with chicken Velouté (p. 147) reduced with fresh cream and flavored with sherry. Slices of truffles as covers.

PATTIES BOUQUETIÈRE BOUCHÉES À LA BOUQUETIÈRE (M.)

Fill with diced vegetables bound with chicken purée (or sole purée, if a meatless dish is wanted) slightly thinned with cream.

Note: The diced vegetables may also be bound with Velouté (p. 147).

PATTIES CAMBACÉRÈS BOUCHÉES CAMBACÉRÈS (M.)

Fill with a salpicon (tiny cubes) of mussels, mushrooms, and truffles bound with Fish Velouté (p. 147), to which diced vegetables have been added. On each patty place a slice of truffle and, on top of that, a frog's leg Villeroi (that is, dipped in egg and bread crumbs and fried in deep fat).

PATTIES CARDINAL BOUCHÉES CARDINAL (M.)

Fill with a salpicon (tiny cubes) of spiny lobster (or lobster), truffles, and mushrooms bound with Nantua Sauce (p. 152) or Fish Velouté (p. 147) finished with Lobster Butter (p. 164).

PATTIES CARÊME BOUCHÉES CARÊME (M.)

Fill with chicken purée with cream. On each patty place a small slice of *foie gras* and, on that, a slice of truffle.

SHRIMP, CRAYFISH, LOBSTER, SPINY LOBSTER, OYSTER, MUSSEL, AND OTHER SHELLFISH PATTIES BOUCHÉES AUX CREVETTES, AUX ÉCREVISSES, AU HOMARD, À LA LANGOUSTE, AUX HUÎTRES, AUX MOULES, ET AUTRES COQUILLAGES (M.)

Fill with one or another of these salpicons (tiny cubes) bound with Fish Velouté (p. 147) finished with a butter made from the shellfish chosen (see Butters, pp. 163–166).

PATTIES MONTGLAS BOUCHÉES MONTGLAS (M.)

Fill with a salpicon of *foie gras*, pickled tongue, breast of chicken, truffles, and mushrooms bound with Semiglaze Sauce (p. 138) containing Madeira.

PATTIES NANTUA BOUCHÉES À LA NANTUA (M.)

Fill with crayfish tails bound with crayfish purée Nantua (see Nantua Sauce, p. 152).

PATTIES PÉRIGOURDINE BOUCHÉES À LA PÉRIGOURDINE (M.)

Fill with a salpicon of *foie gras* and truffles bound with very thick Madeira Sauce (p. 142). Slices of truffles for covers.

PATTIES PRINCESSE BOUCHÉES PRINCESSE (M.)

Fill with a salpicon of breast of chicken, truffles, and asparagus tips bound with chicken Velouté (p. 147) reduced with sherry. Place a bunch of asparagus tips on each patty.

PATTIES À LA REINE I BOUCHÉES À LA REINE (J.)

Fill with a salpicon of veal sweetbreads, brains, forcemeats, and mushrooms bound with Velouté (p. 147).

PATTIES À LA REINE II BOUCHÉES À LA REINE (M.)

Fill with chicken purée bound with chicken Velouté (p. 147). Slices of truffles as covers.

Note: The patties may also be filled with a salpicon of chicken, truffles, and mushrooms bound with Velouté.

PATTIES SAINT-HUBERT BOUCHÉES SAINT-HUBERT (M.)

Fill with game purée, or, if desired, a salpicon of game, bound with reduced Game Stock (p. 135) finished with game essence.

PATTIES SURCOUF BOUCHÉES SURCOUF (M.)

Fill with sole purée bound with Fish Velouté (p. 147) and truffles diced fine. Slices of truffles as covers.

PATTIES TITAŸNA BOUCHÉES TITAŸNA (M.)

Fill with a salpicon of fresh mushrooms and lean ham bound with paprika sauce (see Hongroise or Hungarian Sauce, p. 151). Place on each patty 1 tsp. shredded sweet peppers (green and red) cooked in butter.

PATTIES TOURANGELLE BOUCHÉES À LA TOURANGELLE (M.)

Fill with a salpicon of truffles and mushrooms bound with a red-wine sauce made with fish stock (see White-Wine Sauce, p. 155). Place on each patty a quenelle of truffled Pike Forcemeat (p. 175).

PATTIES LA VARENNE BOUCHÉES LA VARENNE (M.)

Fill with a salpicon (tiny cubes) of sweetbreads bound with Velouté (p. 147). On each patty place a slice of truffle and, on the truffle, a small bunch of buttered asparagus tips.

PATTIES, VOL-AU-VENT and CROUSTADES WITH HARD-BOILED EGGS BOUCHÉES, VOL-AU-VENT and CROUSTADES D'OEUFS DURS (P.)

Puff-Paste (p. 544) patty shells and vol-au-vent or timbales and croustades of Short Paste (p. 545) may also be filled with creamed hard-boiled eggs or hard-boiled eggs with Béchamel Sauce (p. 146). They make excellent entrees for Lent.

PATTIES (SMALL) USED AS GARNISHES BOUCHÉES (PETITES) COMME ÉLÉMENT DE GARNITURES (E.)

Apart from their special role as hot hors d'oeuvres, patties are also often used as garnishes, or as part of a garnish, for fish and game courses served after the soup. In this case, they are made smaller and are filled with ingredients in harmony with the dish they go with. They are also served with certain vegetables, especially celery and cardoons.[1] In this special case, they are filled with diced, poached marrow mixed with meat glaze. A round slice of poached marrow forms the cover, and they are arranged around the vegetable.

TINY STUFFED BRIOCHES BRIOCHES MIGNONNES FARCIES (A.)

Prepare some Brioche Paste without sugar (p. 546); make into very small brioches. When they are baked, cut the tops off and scoop out the insides. Put them into the oven to dry. Fill the empty brioches with a cheese mixture made of very thick Suprême Sauce (p. 146) to which grated Cheshire, Gruyère, or Parmesan cheese, and a sprinkling of black truffles, chopped fine, have been added. Put the tops of the brioches back on and heat for a moment in an open oven. Arrange them on a plate covered with a doily and serve.

VARIOUS CASSOLETTES CASSOLETTES DIVERSES (M.)

Also served as a small entree, this hors d'oeuvre is only a substitute for patties. Cassolettes are made of various materials: porcelain, earthenware, or silver. They are now making more practical and elegant glass cassolettes that may be put into the oven. The fillings, salpicons, and other mixtures given for pastry boats, patties, crusts, and tartlets may also be used for cassolettes.

CASSOLETTES BOULONNAISE CASSOLETTES À LA BOULONNAISE (P.)

Using a pastry bag with a large round tube, on a pastry sheet make some small round forms, with a thin bottom, of Potatoes Duchesse (p. 507). Brush with egg and bake to a golden brown in a very hot oven. Arrange on a round platter and fill the centers with a mixture of mussels and cooked leftover fish bound with a fish sauce. Place a round slice of truffle on each cassolette. In place of a truffle, a shrimp may be stuck in the center or the cassolettes may be sprinkled with chopped parsley. (Figure 146, Page 248.)

Note: The filling for this same kind of cassolette may be varied and the cassolette named according to the filling used. They may be filled with a mixture of shrimps, or *foie gras*, or leftover chicken or ham, etc.

[1] Thistlelike plant related to the artichoke.

CASSOLETTES DUCHESSE CASSOLETTES DUCHESSE (M.)

The cassolettes are made with Potatoes Duchesse (p. 507), as on p. 237. After spreading the preparation on a floured marble slab or a baking board, roll it out like piecrust and cut with a plain circular pastry cutter. Cut smaller circles to be used as tops. Dip in flour, beaten egg, and bread crumbs and fry in deep hot fat. Hollow them out and fill with various salpicons, then cover with the small tops set aside. These cassolettes may be filled with all the preparations given for patties and similar pastry crusts. (Figure 147, Page 248.)

CANNELLONI CANNELLONI (H.)

Same paste and same fillings as for Ravioli (p. 521). Roll out the paste thicker than for Ravioli and cut with a knife into squares about 2½–3 in. per side. Poach in boiling salted water, cool, and drain on a cloth. With a knife spread the filling on the surface of each square and roll it up. Arrange them side by side on a buttered baking dish sprinkled with cheese. Sprinkle more cheese over them and moisten with Veal Stock (p. 134). Simmer over low heat.

CHESHIRE CAKE CHESTER CAKE (P.)

Make a paste with 6 oz. flour, 3 oz. butter, 3 oz. grated Cheshire cheese, a pinch of salt, a little cayenne, 2 egg yolks; knead well. Spread out the paste with a rolling pin and cut into thin, round pieces about 2 in. in diameter. Brush with beaten egg and bake in a hot oven. Put them together, 2 by 2, placing in the center a Cheshire-cheese cream made by mixing in ½ cup thick, boiling Béchamel Sauce (p. 146), 1 egg yolk, 2 oz. Cheshire cheese, a small piece of butter, salt, and cayenne. Serve very hot.

COLUMBINES COLOMBINES (Gi.)

Preparation is the same as for Pastry Boats or Rissoles Chevreuse (p. 248), the sole difference being that they are made in tartlet molds. The envelope or crust is made of semolina mixed with Parmesan cheese and egg yolks. Any type of filling given for patties may be used (salpicons or purées), provided it has the same consistency as a croquette mixture. The name is always determined by the principal ingredient used in the filling.

CHICKEN AU GRATIN IN SHELLS COQUILLE DE VOLAILLE AU GRATIN (P.)

Slice up leftover cooked chicken and make some highly seasoned Mornay Sauce (p. 152) with cheese. This makes a delicious light entree. Put some of the sauce in the bottom of scallop shells and the cut-up chicken on top. Cover copiously with sauce and sprinkle with cheese and bread crumbs. Brown in the oven. The edges of the shells may be bordered with Potatoes Duchesse (p. 507), using a pastry bag with a serrated tube, if there is not enough chicken to fill the shells.

CRÊPES COLETTE or **PANCAKES** CRÊPES COLETTE OR PANNEQUETS (P.)

To use up a small amount of leftover cooked chicken: make 6 or 8 crêpes without sugar (see p. 614 for batter); make a hash of the chicken and mushrooms well bound with a cream sauce and seasoned. Fill each crêpe with 1 tbsp. hash and roll into a cigar shape. Put them into a buttered ovenware dish, top with 1 tbsp. Mornay Sauce (p. 152), sprinkle with cheese, gratinate in a hot oven (that is, until a brown crust forms), and serve.

STUFFED CRÊPES MORNAY CRÊPES FARCIES À LA MORNAY (P.)

Make some very small crêpes without sugar (see p. 614). Fill the centers with a hash made of chicken, or sweetbreads, or brains, etc., and some mushrooms. Bind with 1 or 2 tbsp. White Sauce (p. 147). Fold up the 4 sides of the crêpes to enclose the stuffing and place, with the folds underneath, in a buttered baking dish. Cover with 1 tbsp. Mornay Sauce (p. 152), sprinkle with grated Gruyère cheese, and gratinate in a hot oven.

VARIOUS SPREAD CRÊPES CRÊPES FOURRÉES DIVERSES (M.)

Preparation: Make the crêpes very thin, using no sugar. Spread them with any mixture bound with Béchamel (p. 146) or Semiglaze Sauce (p. 138). Stack the crêpes 1–1½ in. high. Cut the stacks into small rectangles. Place these rectangles on a buttered baking dish. Sprinkle with Parmesan cheese. Gratinate in the oven.

Note: These crêpes are also called pancakes. They may be sprinkled with bread crumbs instead of cheese.

SPREAD CRÊPES ANTIBOISE CRÊPES FOURRÉES À L'ANTIBOISE (M.)

Spread the crêpes with a mixture of marinated tuna and diced hard-boiled eggs bound with Béchamel Sauce (p. 146) finished with Anchovy Butter (p. 163).

SPREAD CRÊPES INDIAN STYLE CRÊPES FOURRÉES À L'INDIENNE (M.)

Spread the crêpes with a mixture of diced onions and mushrooms (cooked in butter) seasoned with curry and bound with Béchamel Sauce (p. 146).

SPREAD CRÊPES PARMESANE CRÊPES FOURRÉES À LA PARMESANE (M.)

Spread the crêpes with Parmesan cheese mixed with cream.

SPREAD CRÊPES PÉRIGOURDINE CRÊPES FOURRÉES À LA PÉRIGOURDINE (M.)

Spread the crêpes with *foie gras* purée mixed with chopped truffles.

SPREAD CRÊPES RAMPONNEAU CRÊPES FOURRÉES RAMPONNEAU (M.)

Spread the crêpes with a salpicon (tiny cubes) of chicken liver, ham, and mushrooms bound with very thick Semiglaze Sauce (p. 138).

KROMESKIS CROMESKIS (H.)

These are small, spherical croquettes made with a chicken-croquette mixture (see p. 240) wrapped in salted crêpes, dipped in Frying Paste (p. 558), and fried. Serve on a doily. Tomato Sauce (p. 146) or Périgueux Sauce (p. 143) served separately.

TOASTED HAM AND CHEESE SLICES I CROQUE-MONSIEUR (P.)

Cut stale bread into small rectangles and cover each slice with a small slice of broiled ham; cover the ham with 1 tbsp. very thick Béchamel Sauce (p. 146) bound with 1 or 2 egg yolks and a rather large amount of grated Parmesan cheese. Place the crusts on a plate with broiling-hot butter and heat in the oven 5 min.

TOASTED HAM AND CHEESE SLICES II CROQUE-MONSIEUR (P.)

Prepare the slices of bread as on p. 239, but place a slice of fried ham on top of a good slice of Gruyère cheese and cover with a second slice of bread. Moisten with plenty of melted butter. Place in a very hot oven to toast the bread and melt the cheese. Powder with paprika before serving.

CROQUETTES CROQUETTES (M.)

Croquette mixtures are made from various salpicons (tiny cubes) of meat, poultry, fish, shellfish, etc., bound with a white or a brown sauce. In addition to the basic ingredient of these mixtures, chicken or otherwise, add diced mushrooms and truffles and, depending on the recipe, lean ham and pickled tongue. The proportions used in combining these ingredients are: 12 oz. sauce (which should always be very thick) to 1 lb. salpicon.

Preparation: Dice very fine the materials used in the salpicon. Put into a frying pan, moisten with a little Madeira, cover, and heat in the oven. Bind this mixture with Allemande Sauce (p. 146), Béchamel Sauce (p. 146), or, depending on the ingredients used, a brown sauce such as Semiglaze Sauce (p. 138) with Madeira, Game Stock, etc. Spread the mixture out evenly on a buttered platter and butter the top to prevent a crust from forming. Let cool. Cut in pieces weighing 2–3 oz. Shape them (while rolling them in flour) into forms such as corks, eggs, etc. Dip in flour, beaten egg, and then bread crumbs. At the last moment before serving, fry the croquettes in boiling deep fat. Drain them. Arrange them on a doily or napkin; garnish with fried parsley. Serve with a sauce that goes with the basic ingredients.

Note: The various croquettes can be made in the shape of cutlets or chops, with a piece of macaroni with a paper frill around it stuck in the end of the croquette. (Figure 148, Page 249.)

CROQUETTES BIGNON CROQUETTES BIGNON (M.)

Salpicon (tiny cubes) of crayfish and truffles bound with crayfish purée. Round shape. Nantua Sauce (p. 152).

Note: These croquettes are especially used as a garnish for fish.

CROQUETTES BRANTÔME CROQUETTES BRANTÔME (M.)

Salpicon of *foie gras,* breast of chicken, and truffles bound with Allemande Sauce (p. 146) finished with Madeira. Shape into corks or stoppers. Semiglaze Sauce (p. 138) with truffle essence.

CROQUETTES DIVETTE CROQUETTES DIVETTE (M.)

Potatoes Duchesse mixture (p. 507) combined with a salpicon of ham and mushrooms, seasoned with paprika. Cork shape. Tomato Sauce (p. 146).

CROQUETTES L'ÉCHELLE CROQUETTES L'ÉCHELLE (M.)

Very thick mushroom purée with a salpicon of ham and truffles. Round shape. Velouté (p. 147) with *fines herbes.*

MACARONI CROQUETTES CROQUETTES DE MACARONI (M.)

Salpicon of (blanched) macaroni with diced truffles and mushrooms. Bind with thick Béchamel Sauce (p. 146) mixed with grated cheese. Cork shape. Tomato Sauce (p. 146).

Fig. 141 - Tomatoes antiboise (p. 229).
Fig. 142 - 1. Anchovy sticks (p. 230). 2. Friands (p. 243).
3. Pasties parisienne (p. 246).

Fig. 141

Fig. 142

Fig. 143

Fig. 144

CROQUETTES NÎMOISE CROQUETTES À LA NÎMOISE (M.)

Salpicon of codfish mixed with diced truffles. Round shape. White-Wine Sauce (p. 155).

CROQUETTES À LA REINE CROQUETTES À LA REINE (M.)

Purée of breast of chicken, with diced truffles and mushrooms added. Cork shape. Velouté (p. 147) with cream.

CROQUETTES SAGAN CROQUETTES SAGAN (M.)

Salpicon of calf's brains, artichoke bottoms, and onions (the last cooked in butter) mixed with thick Béchamel Sauce (p. 146) seasoned with curry. Oval shape. Curry Sauce (p. 150).

CROQUETTES SÉVIGNÉ CROQUETTES SÉVIGNÉ (M.)

Salpicon of breast of chicken, mushrooms, and truffles bound with Soubise Purée (p. 504). Cork shape. Buttered Semiglaze Sauce (p. 138).

CHICKEN CROQUETTES CROQUETTES DE VOLAILLE (M.)

Salpicon of chicken, mushrooms, and truffles bound with Allemande Sauce (p. 146). Semiglaze (p. 138) or Tomato Sauce (p. 146).

CHEESE CRUSTS CROÛTES AU FROMAGE (A.)

There are a great number of possible combinations for cheese crusts. Here are a few examples:

CHESHIRE-CHEESE CRUSTS CROÛTES AU CHESTER (A.)

Take: 5 oz. flour, 4 oz. grated Cheshire cheese, 3½ oz. butter, 1½ oz. heavy cream, a pinch of salt, cayenne. Make a paste of these ingredients without kneading it; let it stand 3 hr., then roll out to make not too thick a crust. Cut it with a round cutter 2 in. in diameter, brush the circles with beaten egg, and bake in a hot oven. Make sandwiches of these circles with a layer of grated Cheshire and Gruyère cheeses softened with butter in between. Serve very hot on a doily.

Cheshire-Cheese Crusts may also be served cold. After baking the crusts, let them cool and fill them with a cream cheese prepared as follows: beat 3 egg yolks in 6 oz. heavy cream; season with a pinch of salt, a tiny pinch of cayenne, and a little rum or whisky to taste; thicken over a low fire; let the mixture cool almost completely, then add 1 oz. butter and 3 oz. Cheshire cheese or 3 oz. grated Cheshire and Gruyère cheeses mixed. Spread the surfaces of 2 crusts and fit together as sandwiches. Arrange on a doily.

PARMESAN-CHEESE CRUSTS CROÛTES AU PARMESAN (A.)

Take: 5 oz. flour, 5 oz. grated Parmesan cheese, 4 oz. butter, 2 oz. water, salt, and cayenne pepper. Prepare a flaky paste (see p. 544), folded 8 times, with the flour, butter, water, salt, and cayenne, sprinkling each fold or layer of paste with grated Parmesan cheese. Let stand 15 min. Roll the paste out until ⅜ in. thick; cut in diamond shapes, brush with beaten egg, and bake in a very hot oven. Serve on a doily.

Gruyère-Cheese Crusts are prepared the same way.

ROQUEFORT-CHEESE CRUSTS CROÛTES AU ROQUEFORT (A.)

Take: 5 oz. flour, 4 oz. Roquefort cheese, 4 oz. butter, 1 oz. cream, a pinch

Fig. 143 - 1. Cheese sticks (p. 230). 2. Pastry boats lombarde (p. 233). 3. Blini (p. 234).
Fig. 144 - 1. Pastry boats Joinville (p. 232). 2. Tartlets Neptune (p. 233).

of salt, 1 egg yolk, paprika or cayenne to taste. Mix into a paste without kneading; let stand 20 min.; roll out until rather thin; cut into ovals; bake in a hot oven; let cool. Spread the surface of the crusts with a mixture of Roquefort and butter to taste. Put together in twos to make sandwiches. Serve on a doily.

These crusts may also be served with the following cream: beat 3 fresh egg yolks in 6 oz. heavy cream; season with a pinch of salt and a tiny pinch of paprika or cayenne. Thicken over a low fire. Off the fire, add 3 oz. Roquefort and 2 oz. butter; blend thoroughly; put back on the fire and stir until sufficiently thick. Watch this carefully. Remove from the fire and flavor with a dash of kirsch. Let cool completely. Make sandwiches of the crusts with the cream in the middle. Serve on a doily.

Hot cheese crusts may be used as hors d'oeuvres; cold cheese crusts are sometimes served at the end of the meal, in place of cheese.

FONDUE FONDUE (B.-S.)

Allow 1 egg per serving for each guest. Take a piece of good Gruyère cheese weighing ⅓ the weight of the eggs, and a piece of butter weighing ⅙ the weight of the eggs. Beat the eggs well in a stewpan and then add the butter and the cheese, grated or sliced. Place on a hot stove and stir with a spatula until the mixture is thick and smooth; add a pinch more or less of salt, depending on whether the cheese is more or less aged, and a strong amount of pepper, which is one of the outstanding characteristics of this ancient dish. Serve on a warm plate; bring out the best wine; drink heartily, and it will be marvelous.

(Recipe for fondue quoted from the papers of M. Trolliet, Bailiff of Moudon, canton of Berne.)

FONDUE BRUXELLOISE FONDUE À LA BRUXELLOISE (H.)

Cook a very thick Béchamel Sauce (p. 146), bind it, mix in plenty of cheese, spread it out on a tray, and butter the top. Chill and cut in various shapes. Bread the pieces, fry them, and arrange them on a doily.

CHEESE FONDUE FONDUE AU FROMAGE (H.)

Reduce some white wine and add to it some very creamy Gruyère cheese chopped coarsely; melt it without stirring too much with a wooden spoon, and finish with a good dash of kirsch and freshly ground pepper. Fondue is served in the pan in which it was made, over a chafing dish, accompanied by toast or plain bread.

FONDUE PIÉMONTAISE FONDUE À LA PIÉMONTAISE (H.)

The only cheese used for this recipe is Piedmont cheese (Fontina) soaked in cold milk. Melt fresh butter in an earthenware casserole; add the cheese, after draining, and stir with a wooden spoon until melted. Bind with 3 egg yolks per 8 oz. cheese, and, at the last moment, add some thinly sliced white truffles. Should be served in the cooking dish.

CHICKEN FRIANDISES FRIANDISES DE VOLAILLE (H.)

Chilled, thickly bound chicken purée cut into small balls, breaded, and fried. Suprême Sauce (p. 146) served separately. Small spherical croquettes are also served under this name.

FRIANDS FRIANDS (M.)

Small patties of flaky paste usually filled with a forcemeat of veal (or chicken), beef marrow, and mushrooms (see Forcemeats, p. 171). Formerly the filling had added to it ⅓ its weight in seeded, soaked Malaga raisins. Fresh cream was added while the forcemeat was mashed. Friands are prepared like small *pâtés* or pasties, but in an elongated shape. (Figure 142, Page 240.)

VARIOUS FRITOS FRITOTS DIVERS (M.)

This hors d'oeuvre is made of various ingredients: slices of brains, sweetbreads, chicken; pieces of sheep's trotters, calf's head, tongue, fish, etc., marinated for 1 hr. in oil, lemon juice, salt, pepper, and chopped parsley. These are dipped in Frying Paste (p. 558) and fried at the last moment in very hot deep fat. Arrange on a doily. Garnish with fried parsley. Serve with Tomato Sauce (p. 146).

MIXED FRITOS FRITOTS MISTOS (H.)

The *frittura mistos* is an assortment of breast of chicken, chicken croquettes, small quartered artichokes, brains, broccoli, sweetbreads, leaf spinach, etc., dipped in a thin Frying Paste made of flour, whole beaten eggs, salt, pepper, and an almost imperceptible dash of garlic (see p. 558). Fry separately, at the last moment, in smoking hot oil in a frying pan. Do not cover after cooking, or the fried paste will become soggy. They should be served crisp.

CHEESE GALETTES or **FLAT CAKES I** GALETTE AU FROMAGE (A.)

For 6 persons take: 1 lb. flour, 14 oz. butter, 1 pt. water, 6 oz. Gruyère or Parmesan cheese, ½ oz. salt, 1 egg yolk. Make a Flaky Paste (p. 544) with the butter, flour, water, and salt. Sprinkle with finely grated cheese after each of the last 2 folds. Roll out the paste until it is about ⅜ in. thick. Cut into circles or squares, as desired; make small gashes in the top surfaces; brush with egg yolk beaten with a little water; place in a hot oven. A half-hour's cooking generally suffices to turn out fine glazed flat cakes. It is important not to open the oven before the pastry is through baking; otherwise, the dough will fall.

As a variant, the paste may be cut into sticks after being rolled out a little thinner. These sticks, often called Cheese Straws (*pailles au fromage*), are placed on a tin baking tray, each separated from the others, and are baked in the oven like the flat cakes. Cheese Straws are served with clear consommés.

CHEESE GALETTES or **FLAT CAKES II** GALETTE AU FROMAGE (M.)

Cut Flaky Paste (see above) in circles about 2 in. in diameter. Prick them with the point of a knife to prevent their puffing up while baking. Bake in the oven. Spread the flat cakes with a cream of Parmesan cheese seasoned with a little cayenne. Press the flat cakes together in twos and keep them hot in the warmer until time to serve.

These flat cakes are often served as savories (at the end of the meal, in place of a sweet).

GALETTES or **FLAT CAKES PÉRIGOURDINE** GALETTES PÉRIGOURDINE (M.)

Prepare the flat cakes as described above. Instead of cheese, fill with *foie gras* purée with chopped truffles added.

GNOCCHI FLORENTINE GNOCCHI À LA FLORENTINE (H.)

Take some Choux Paste (p. 548) and add twice its volume in purée of boiled potatoes—that is, simply pressed through a sieve—and season with cheese, *fines herbes,* and chopped cooked ham. Shape the *gnocchi* with a wet spoon, place them on a buttered plate, sprinkle with Parmesan cheese, dot with butter, and gratinate in the oven—that is, till a brown crust forms.

GNOCCHI PARISIENNE GNOCCHI À LA PARISIENNE (H.)

To some salted Choux Paste (p. 548) add ⅕ its volume in purée of boiled potatoes and grated Parmesan cheese. Squeeze the *gnocchi* from a pastry bag (with a large plain tube) into water and bring to a boil. Cool and drain on a cloth. Next cover them with a cream sauce, place in a baking dish, sprinkle with grated Parmesan cheese and dot with butter, and put into the oven to rise.

GNOCCHI PARISIENNE TIMBALE GNOCCHI (TIMBALE DE) À LA PARISIENNE (H.)

Prepare the *gnocchi* and cover with cream sauce as described above. Place them in a timbale lined with Puff Paste (p. 544), cover with the same paste, prick with a fork, brush with beaten egg, and bake in the oven.

POTATO GNOCCHI NIÇARDE GNOCCHI DE POMMES À LA NIÇARDE (H.)

Mash the pulp of baked potatoes and, on a baking board, knead into a paste with a little more than the same amount of flour. The paste should be smooth. Form into balls the size of a hazelnut and press them lightly against the tines of a fork so as to make a fold in the middle. Poach them in salted water. Season with a layer of grated Parmesan cheese and melted butter and simmer with

GNOCCHI ROMAINE GNOCCHI À LA ROMAINE (H.)

Bring to a boil 1 qt. milk with 3½ oz. butter, salt, and nutmeg. When boiling, drop in gradually 8 oz. medium semolina and stir vigorously. When the semolina is cooked and firm, mix in 1 beaten egg and grated Parmesan cheese. Mix briskly and spread on a buttered tray until ¾ in. thick. Let cool and cut into circles with a plain, round cutter. Roll them in grated Parmesan cheese, arrange in an ovenware dish, butter, and gratinate in the oven. (Figure 149, Page 249.)

GOUGÈRE BOURGUIGNONNE GOUGÈRE BOURGUIGNONNE (A.)

For 8 persons take: 6 oz. water, 6 oz. flour, 2 oz. butter, 3 oz. Gruyère cheese, 3 fresh eggs, salt. Cut the cheese into cubes about ½ in. square; do not grate it. Put the water, butter, and salt into a stewpan and bring to a boil; sprinkle in the flour while stirring. Cook on a moderate fire, constantly stirring, until the taste of flour has disappeared. This should take about ½ hr. Remove from the fire, let cool a little, then break in the eggs 1 by 1, constantly stirring. The paste should be very smooth and not too thick. Then, and then only, add the cheese and mix again. Make a crown or ring of the paste on a pastry sheet and place in a hot oven. Bake 20–30 min. Do not open the oven door while baking or the paste, which will puff up quite high, will fall. Gougère is served hot or cold. (Figure 150, Page 256.)

CHICKEN MAZAGRAN MAZAGRAN DE VOLAILLE (E.)

Make a border of the mixture for Potatoes Duchesse (p. 507) on an oval buttered plate, as for Sole Suchet. (Figure 180, Page 300.) Fill the center with sliced chicken, truffles, and mushrooms bound with Suprême Sauce (p. 146). Brush the potato border with egg yolk and brown in the oven. When the plate is removed from the oven, cover the chicken mixture with fresh bread crumbs browned in butter. Surround the base of the *mazagran* with a ring of small chipolata sausages grilled or fried in butter.

SMALL CHICKEN MAZAGRANS MAZAGRANS (PETITS) DE VOLAILLE (P.)

To use up a little leftover cooked chicken: line buttered tartlet molds with Potatoes Duchesse (p. 507). Make a hollow in the center to be filled with leftover chicken (cut into tiny pieces) mixed with a few slices of cooked mushrooms and bound with a little sauce, either Madeira (p. 142) or Tomato Sauce (p. 146). Using a pastry bag with a rather large serrated nozzle, cover with Potatoes Duchesse; place in a very hot oven 6–8 min. Unmold and serve with the same sauce as that used inside, only a little thinner.

CHICKEN MOUSSE MOUSSE DE VOLAILLE (P.)

Take an old hen used for making bouillon and prepare a very creamy, highly seasoned purée; after straining it, mix with Béchamel Sauce (p. 146) and 3 whole eggs. Prepare a mold decorated as for Chartreuse of Partridge (p. 468) and fill with the purée. Poach in a *bain-marie* (or large double boiler) ½ hr. Let settle 10 min. and then unmold. Serve with Suprême Sauce (p. 146).

PARMESAN-CHEESE STRAWS PAILLETTES AU PARMESAN (H.)

Roll out Puff Paste (p. 544), sprinkle with Parmesan cheese and cayenne pepper, cut in long thin strips, and bake in the oven. Serve with soups. When sprinkled with sugar instead of cheese and pepper, they may also be served with ice cream. (See also the recipe for Cheese Galettes, p. 243.)

SMALL PÂTÉS or PASTIES PETITS PÂTÉS (M.)

Patties (pp. 235–237), as we have remarked, are filled after the shells are baked; small *pâtés* or pasties are filled or stuffed before being baked, which of course means that they must be made in 2 pieces, 1 to cover the other. The bottom crust ought to be very thin and made from the trimmings of Puff Paste (p. 544) to prevent its rising. The top crust, ⅛ in. thick, should be joined to the bottom crust in the usual manner—that is, by moistening the edges with water. Small pasties, like patties, are made in all sizes. It is better, however, not to make them too big, for their ingredients make them heavy enough.

SMALL PÂTÉS or PASTIES HONGROISE PETITS PÂTÉS À LA HONGROISE (M.)

Fill the pasties, before covering them, with a salpicon (tiny cubes) of ham bound with thick Velouté (p. 147), to which chopped onion, cooked in butter and strongly seasoned with paprika, has been added. Brush the pasties with beaten egg. Bake in the oven 18–20 min.

SMALL PÂTÉS or PASTIES WITH GRAVY PETITS PÂTÉS AU JUS (M.)

Fill with pork forcemeat (see Forcemeats, pp. 171–176) to which chopped mushrooms and chopped parsley have been added. Finish as described on p. 245. At the last moment, pour 1 tbsp. thick, brown Veal Gravy (p. 134) through a hole (made specially for this) in the top of each pasty.

SMALL PÂTÉS or PASTIES WITH GRAVY (OLD METHOD) PETITS PÂTÉS AU JUS (P.)

Line small brioche molds with Short Paste (p. 545) and bake dry (that is, lined with tissue paper filled with fruit stones to keep the pastry from losing its shape). Bake separately as many small disks cut from the same paste, to be used as covers. After baking, empty the crusts and fill with quenelles, mushrooms, brains, chopped olives, bound with a good, full-bodied gravy seasoned with Madeira. Place the covers on top. Serve hot on a napkin. These pasties take the place of patties when it is too hot for the cook to make Puff Paste.

SMALL PÂTÉS or PASTIES PARISIENNE PETITS PÂTÉS À LA PARISIENNE (M.)

Prepare the pasties in the usual way. Fill them, before covering with the top crust, with pork forcemeat mixed with veal (or chicken) forcemeat (see Forcemeats, pp. 171–176). To this filling add Veal Stock (p. 134) reduced with Madeira.

Note: Chopped truffles may be added to the forcemeat. (Figure 142, Page 240.)

SMALL PÂTÉS or PASTIES PÉRIGOURDINE PETITS PÂTÉS À LA PÉRIGOURDINE (M.)

Fill the pasties, before covering them, with a forcemeat made of diced *foie gras* and truffles.

Note: Infinite varieties of small *pâtés* or pasties may be prepared by filling them with the mixtures, stuffings, and salpicons given for patties and similar dishes.

PIROJKY MOSCOVITE PIROGUIS À LA MOSCOVITE (E.)

Mixture: 10 oz. cooked white fish, without skin or bones; 5 hard-boiled eggs; 5 oz. cooked *vesiga* (sturgeon spinal marrow; see *Note,* p. 310). Chop and mix the fish, eggs, and *vesiga.*

Preparation: Make some Kulibiak Paste (p. 778) or ordinary Brioche Paste (p. 546) without sugar. Cut the desired number of bottom crusts with a plain oval cooky cutter. Fill the centers with ½ tbsp. of the mixture given above. Lightly moisten the edges of the ovals and bring them together, pinching them tightly, so as to enclose the filling. Keep the pirojky ½ hr. in a rather warm place and then bake 20 min. in a hot oven. Just before serving, pour 1 tsp. Colbert Sauce (p. 140) into each.

FOIE GRAS POMPONNETTES LUCETTE POMPONNETTES DE FOIE GRAS À LA LUCETTE (Gi.)

Paste: For 20 pomponnettes sift ½ lb. flour on the baking table and shape into a well. In the center place ⅓ oz. fine salt, 2 oz. chopped almonds (sifted and lightly toasted), 6 oz. butter, 4 egg yolks, and about 3 oz. water. Combine the ingredients, knead the dough twice, wrap in a cloth, and leave 1 hr. in a cool place.

Filling and shaping the pomponnettes: Press 8 oz. cooked *foie gras* through a sieve, collecting the purée on a plate. Take 1/3 of it and add 2 tbsp. chopped truffles, then divide this truffled purée into 20 parts. In the center of each one place a freshly shelled pistachio and roll into a ball the size of a hazelnut. Now envelop these balls in more purée of *foie gras,* making a slightly larger ball, and place on a floured plate. Roll out the paste until between 1/8 and 1/4 in. thick; cut into 20 circles with a round, fluted cooky cutter about 2 1/2 in. in diameter. Lightly moisten the edges, place a *foie gras* ball in the center of each one, and close the pastry around the balls by gathering the edges of the pastry together so as to form a small pouch. Place them together, 2 by 2, with the gathered ends of the pastry together. Moisten the connecting parts and stick the balls together in pairs. Drop these little pomponnettes into very hot deep fat. Arrange on a napkin with fried parsley.

QUICHE LORRAINE I QUICHE DE LORRAINE (H.)

The Quiche Lorraine is very popular with bathers at summer resorts in the Vosges. Here is an easy recipe, kindly contributed by M. P. Sauvan of Nice: (1) Line a flan circle or pie tin with ordinary Short Paste (p. 545). (2) Mix 4 oz. flour with milk, 8 egg yolks, a pinch of salt, 1 pt. heavy cream slightly sour, and grated nutmeg. Strain through a cone-shaped sieve. (3) Fill the flan with this mixture and bake 15 min. in a rather hot oven. Serve hot as soon as it is taken out of the oven.

Note: If desired, the pie crust may be lined with slices of broiled smoked bacon before the filling is added.

QUICHE LORRAINE II QUICHE À LA LORRAINE (E.)

Line a well-buttered deep griddle or pie pan about 7 in. in diameter with ordinary Short Paste (p. 545). This should serve 10 persons. Line the bottom of the crust with thin slices of bacon, blanched and lightly browned in butter. The bacon slices may be alternated with thin slices of Gruyère cheese, but this is optional and contrary to local custom. Fill the pan, which has been lined with Short Paste and bacon slices, with a mixture composed of 12 oz. cream, 3 small eggs, a pinch of salt. Complete with 1 oz. butter, cut in small pieces and scattered over the mixture. Bake 30–35 min. in a medium oven. When the *quiche* has cooled until merely warm, cut into triangles.

SMALL QUICHES WITH HAM QUICHES AU JAMBON (PETITES) (E.)

Line deep tartlet molds with Short Paste (p. 545) or trimmings from Puff Paste (p. 544). In the bottom place a thin, round slice of lean ham and fill with the mixture given above. The proportions should be sufficient for 15 tartlets. Bake 15–18 min. in a medium oven.

RAMEKINS RAMEQUINS (M.)

To 1/2 lb. ordinary Choux Paste (made without sugar) add 2 oz. grated Gruyère cheese and 2 oz. of the same cheese diced. Using a pastry bag with a large plain nozzle, squeeze out balls of the above mixture, about the size of Brussels sprouts, onto a baking sheet. Brush with beaten egg, and on each ball place a thin slice of Gruyère cheese. Bake in a moderately hot oven 12–15 min. (Figure 151, Page 256.)

Note: This hors d'oeuvre belongs in the repertory of old French cooking. It bears some resemblance to a *gougère* (see p. 244), which used to be made quite often and is made with the same mixture except that it is shaped into a ring instead of into small cabbages. These ancient recipes were prepared somewhat differently from the way they are made today. The following old recipes will show how ramekins were prepared in the seventeenth century.

CHEESE RAMEKINS RAMEQUINS DE FROMAGE (M.)

Take some cheese; melt it in butter with a whole or mashed onion, salt, and plenty of pepper; spread this on a piece of bread and hold a shovel full of hot coals over it. Serve hot.

RAMEKINS WITH CHIMNEY SOOT RAMEQUINS DE SUIE DE CHEMINÉE (M.)

"Your bread having been placed in a frying pan a little more than half filled with butter or oil, powder the top with soot, salt, and strong pepper, and serve hot."

We do not think we are going too far if we state that this recipe holds first place for originality.

RISSOLES RISSOLES (A.)

Rissoles are fried preparations made from fillings bound with sauce, cooled, and wrapped in paste. The paste used for Rissoles is usually Puff Paste (p. 544), but Short Paste (p. 545) or ordinary Brioche Paste (p. 546), all without sugar, can also be used. The traditional shapes are the following: gathered pouch, turnovers with plain or saw-tooth edges, and small square, round, oval, or rectangular pasties. Roll out whatever paste is used to a thickness of 1/8–3/16 in.; from this paste cut fairly large circles. On the circles place small forcemeat balls, balls of salpicon (meat or other elements cut in small cubes) bound with a very thick sauce, or small garnishes. Moisten the edges of the circles and close either by folding the circles over themselves, forming half-moons, or by using other unfilled circles as tops. Give them any shape mentioned above. Rissoles are sometimes breaded. They are always fried in deep hot fat. When they are nicely browned, they are drained and served as a hot hors d'oeuvre or an entree on a plate covered with a napkin and decorated with fried parsley. Rissoles are never served with sauces.

Here are some examples of fillings:

(*a*) Oysters covered with lobster purée bound with Allemande Sauce (p. 146) made with fish stock and seasoned with curry. (*b*) Shrimps with Béchamel Sauce (p. 146) mixed with very firm Shrimp Butter (p. 164). (*c*) Salpicon of lobster and truffles with very thick lobster sauce (see Newburg Sauce, pp. 152–153). (*d*) Fish quenelles made of pike, whiting, or salmon, for example, with butter, Panada (p. 171) made of bread crumbs and fish bouillon, and very reduced Allemande Sauce made with fish; and, in general, any mixture for patties can be used. (Figure 152, Page 256.)

CHICKEN RISSOLES or PASTRY BOATS CHEVREUSE RISSOLES OU BARQUETTES DE VOLAILLE À LA CHEVREUSE (Gi.)

Mixture: Bring 1 qt. white bouillon to a boil and sprinkle in 5 oz. semolina. Cook slowly until the semolina has absorbed all the bouillon and formed a thick

Fig. 145 - Beurrecks turkish style (p. 234).
Fig. 146 - Cassolettes boulonnaises (p. 237).
Fig. 147 - Cassolettes duchesse (p. 238).

Fig. 145

Fig. 146

Fig. 147

Fig. 148

Fig. 149

paste. Then add, while stirring with a wooden spoon, 2 oz. grated cheese, 4 egg yolks, and 2 oz. butter. Pour the semolina out on a plate, level it with a knife, and butter the surface to prevent a crust from forming while it cools.

Salpicon: Dice some leftover breast of chicken, cooked mushrooms and truffles, allowing ⅔ chicken to ⅓ mushrooms and truffles. Put all of this into very reduced Allemande Sauce (p. 146). Pour this mixture out on a plate and butter the top, as above.

Forming the rissoles: When the 2 preparations (semolina and the salpicon) are cold, butter as many small boat-shaped tin molds as are needed. The proportions given for semolina will make 20–24 rissoles. Line the bottom and sides of the molds with a layer of semolina ⅛ in. thick. Put in 1 tbsp. salpicon and cover with a thin layer of semolina; smooth with a knife blade. Dip the molds in hot water and empty the contents upside down on a tray, side by side. Dip each rissole in flour, beaten egg, and bread crumbs. Smooth each one with a knife blade to give them the right shape and arrange again on the tray. Five minutes before serving, drop them into hot deep-frying fat; drain them after 2 or 3 min., or when they are sufficiently browned; salt lightly and arrange on a folded napkin with a bunch of fried parsley in the center.

Remarks: All mixtures with sauces covered with semolina or paste and fried are called rissoles. The preparations we have given above may be made in any number of shapes or molds, but the boat-shaped tin molds are the most usual and the easiest to use. They may be used for a multitude of things, which is why we advise their being included among the small kitchen utensils.

History: These rissoles are called Chevreuse, not for their shape or filling, but for the semolina covering. We do not know whether this method of preparation was inspired by the beautiful Mme de Rohan Montbazon (the Duchesse de Chevreuse), but considering the interest this confidante of Anne of Austria had in cooking, we may assume it.

RISSOLES À LA REINE RISSOLES À LA REINE (H.)

Using a round cooky cutter with scalloped edges, about 2 in. in diameter, cut some circles out of Puff Paste (p. 544). In the center of each place 1 tbsp. filling for Patties à la Reine II (p. 236). Moisten the edges and fold over to make a half-moon, pressing the edges together. They may be fried or baked in the oven; in the latter case, they should first be brushed with beaten egg.

Note: Rissoles are filled with the same garnishes as patties. Serve with Périgueux (p. 143), Madeira (p. 142), or Tomato Sauce (p. 146).

CHEESE SOUFFLÉ SOUFFLÉ AU FROMAGE (P.) (*For 8 persons*)

Melt 2 oz. butter in a stewpan; mix in 1½ oz. flour, and moisten immediately with 1 cup milk; salt, pepper, and bring to a boil while stirring with a wire whisk. When it begins to boil, it becomes like a thick Béchamel Sauce. Remove it from the fire, add a piece of butter, a pinch of grated nutmeg, and 4 egg yolks. Add 3 egg whites beaten to a froth and, at the same time, 4 oz. grated Gruyère cheese. Mix briskly with a spoon. Pour the mixture into a buttered soufflé dish sprinkled with cheese. Bake 20–22 min. in a moderately hot oven and serve immediately in the dish in which it was baked. Porcelain timbales are generally used.

Fig. 148 - Chicken cutlets (p. 240).
Fig. 149 - Gnocchi romaine (p. 244).

CHICKEN SOUFFLÉ SOUFFLÉ DE VOLAILLE (P.)

Make a purée by mashing leftover chicken with a little Béchamel Sauce (p. 146) ; season, press through a sieve, and heat. Remove from the stove and add 2 or 3 egg yolks and 2 beaten egg whites per ½ lb. Treat as other soufflés.

ONION TART TARTE AUX OIGNONS (P.)

Make a tart of Short Paste (p. 545) without sugar and, for the filling, slice 3 or 4 medium-sized onions and cook slowly in butter without browning too much; next mix in 6 oz. rather thick milk sauce (Béchamel, p. 146), season with salt, pepper, and nutmeg, then remove from the stove. Beat 2 eggs with a little cream and add to the mixture. Grill a few very thin slices of smoked bacon and place them on the bottom crust after pricking it with a fork. Fill the tart with the cream of onions and bake 40 min. in an oven rather hot at the start, then turned down till moderately hot.

TARTLETS WITH PARMESAN CHEESE TARTELETTES AU PARMESAN (H.)

Line the molds with Puff Paste (p. 544) and fill with Parmesan-cheese soufflé mixture (see Cheese Soufflé, p. 249). Allow 2 beaten egg whites for 1 qt. mixture. Decorate with diamond-shaped pieces of Gruyère cheese and bake in the oven.

Note: It is also possible to use a cold cream made of the following: 4 whole eggs, salt, nutmeg, 2 oz. flour. Place grated cheese in the bottom and on top of the cream filling; 1 qt. makes 40 tartlets.

SMALL CHICKEN TIMBALES TIMBALES DE VOLAILLE (PETITES) (P.)

Mash cooked chicken and mix with 3 oz. Béchamel Sauce (p. 146) per 5 oz. chicken, 2 tbsp. rich cream, salt, pepper, grated nutmeg, and 1 whole egg. Press this purée through a metal sieve and poach 10 min. in a *bain-marie* or double boiler, in small buttered molds, either baba or brioche molds. Unmold and cover the timbales with Suprême Sauce (p. 146) or some other sauce.

CHEESE CORKSCREWS TIRE-BOUCHONS AU FROMAGE (P.)

Make 2 folds of Puff Paste (p. 544) trimmings, sprinkling with grated cheese and a tiny pinch of cayenne pepper. Roll out the paste in thin strips about 2 in. wide and cut into pieces about the length of a finger. Take both ends and twist into a corkscrew. Place on a tray and bake in a hot oven.

SCOTCH TOAST TOAST À L'ÉCOSSAISE (P.)

Grill the toast and garnish with a very thick Butter Sauce (p. 148) to which chopped capers and anchovy purée have been added; sprinkle with Parmesan cheese and brown in the oven. The toast may also be garnished with eggs scrambled with cheese; capers and anchovy fillets on top.

EGGS

EGGS

"A treatise on the egg—that Proteus of cooking—has yet to be written," Monselet once said in one of the *Lettres gourmandes* published by *L'Événement.*

Since then, many books especially devoted to the element the ancients considered the symbol of the world have been written, but none have been able to sum up the multitude of egg recipes created on the spur of the moment or from imagination.

We are not, therefore, undertaking to succeed in a single chapter where others have not been able to in whole books devoted to the subject. We shall limit ourselves to recipes in current usage, adhering, as far as possible, to the uniformity of preparation and name that has been our rule.

The chapter on eggs is divided into three sections:

The first section includes eggs baked, poached, soft-boiled, molded, fried, in cocottes and cases, hard-boiled, scrambled, and cold.

The second section includes omelets.

The third, plovers' eggs.

BAKED EGGS OEUFS SUR LE PLAT (E.)

Eggs treated this way are really a kind of poached egg whose merit depends on just the right degree of cooking. Their preparation hinges upon these 3 points: (1) cooking the white until it becomes milky; (2) shining, mirrorlike quality of the yolk; (3) extra care to keep the eggs from sticking to the bottom of the plate.

Principle of preparation: The proportions in the recipes for this kind of egg are uniformly for 2 eggs. The normal quantity of butter used is ⅔ oz.: half in the utensil, and the other half poured melted over the 2 yolks. Actually, *oeufs sur le plat* (literally, "eggs on the plate") are either baked in the oven or cooked directly over a slow fire, in ovenware dishes, of course.

POACHED AND SOFT-BOILED EGGS OEUFS POCHÉS ET MOLLETS (E.)

The recipes for poached eggs being applicable to soft-boiled eggs, we shall consider the two together, calling attention to the fact that in both cases the eggs must be strictly fresh.

Preparation of poached eggs: Boil water in a frying pan with ⅓ oz. salt and 1 tbsp. vinegar per qt. water. Break the eggs into the water at the spot where the water is boiling. Allow 3 min. for poaching in water held at 203° F., or until the white solidifies sufficiently to enclose the yolk and permit handling of the egg: a poached egg being, in short, merely a soft-boiled egg without the shell. Cool the eggs; trim them, and keep them in hot water with ⅙ oz. salt per qt. water.

Preparation of soft-boiled (mollet) eggs: Drop the eggs into boiling water and cook 6 min. from the time the water starts to boil again. Cool, remove the shells immediately, and keep hot in the same way as poached eggs.

Dressing for poached and soft-boiled (mollet) eggs: These methods are most often used: (1) on bread croutons (made without the crust) slightly hollowed, trimmed plain or with fancy edges. Oval croutons for poached eggs, round for soft-boiled eggs, both kinds of croutons fried in clarified butter. (2) On oval pieces of flaky pastry for poached eggs, on rings with scalloped edges for soft-boiled eggs. (3) In borders of various fillings, depending on the recipe. These borders are designed with a pastry bag or by hand on a buttered plate. They are made round or oval and may be plain or decorated. Depending on the ingredient used, they are either poached or browned in the oven. (4) In tartlet pastry shells and garnished according to the recipe. When dressed on fried croutons, flaky pastry, or tartlets, the eggs should be covered with sauce first.

MOLDED EGGS OEUFS MOULÉS (E.)

Among the various recipes for eggs, those calling for molding are certainly the most decorative. However, since they take a relatively long time to prepare, poached or soft-boiled (*mollet*) eggs are usually preferred, since they can be cooked quickly. These eggs are made in variously shaped molds and are decorated according to the nature of the preparation. The eggs are broken directly into the molds or are combined with another preparation and poached in a *bain-marie.* Poaching time is 10–12 min., and the whole process requires a minimum of 15 min. The eggs are almost always unmolded onto small pieces of toast, after being allowed to set for a few minutes after coming out of the *bain-marie* to make the unmolding easier. Regardless of the recipe, the molds should always be heavily buttered.

EGGS IN COCOTTES AND CASES OEUFS EN COCOTTES ET EN CAISSES (E.)

(The eggs are poached in ramekins or other small porcelain or earthenware dishes. Cases used to be made of pleated paper; now they are made of china.) These eggs belong to still another category of poaching. They are normally cooked 10 min. in a *bain-marie.* However, the timing may vary by a few minutes, depending on the type of utensil used and the thickness of its sides and bottom, which the heat must penetrate before having any effect on the eggs. Eggs in cocottes or cases are served on a napkin or paper doily. To speed up the operation, always heat the dishes before breaking the eggs into them.

FRIED EGGS OEUFS FRITS (E.)

Of all the recipes for preparing eggs, those for fried eggs are relatively the least significant. The fried eggs served so regularly in England and America for breakfast are only eggs cooked in a frying pan. In those countries, a real fried egg is unknown. In general, the garnish for this kind of egg is served separately; the eggs are arranged on napkins or toast, with fried parsley in the center.

Principles of Preparation: Any well-purified fat may be used in cooking these eggs, but oil is most often used and produces the best results. To prepare fried eggs well, they should be cooked only 1 at a time. Heat some oil in a small frying pan until it begins to smoke slightly; slide in an egg broken onto a plate and seasoned; then, using a wooden spoon, completely cover the yolk with the white part, which has solidified through sudden contact with the hot oil. Drain on a cloth and continue the operation until the desired number of eggs have been cooked.

HARD-BOILED EGGS OEUFS DUR (E.)

Although seemingly unimportant, the cooking time for hard-boiled eggs should be definite. It is useless to continue boiling them for too long a time, since the eggs become tough, especially the white part on account of its albuminous content. For uniformity of cooking, the eggs should be put into a strainer with large holes so that they all may be plunged into the boiling water at the same time. From the moment the water begins to boil again, allow 8 min. for cooking medium-sized eggs weighing about 2 oz.; 10 min. for large ones weighing 2½ oz. As soon as they are cooked, pour off the hot water and plunge them into cold water so that the shells may be removed without damaging the eggs.

SCRAMBLED EGGS OEUFS BROUILLÉS (E.)

This way of preparing eggs is incontestably the finest of all—provided, of course, that the eggs are not overcooked and that they remain soft and creamy. Scrambled eggs are usually served in silver timbales, but they may also be served in special pastry crusts, in hollowed-out brioches, or in patty shells or tartlets.

Scrambled eggs used to be served in timbales surrounded with variously shaped croutons or with small bits of flaky paste baked in such shapes as crescents, diamonds, rings, palmettes, etc. This method has some good points and still may be followed. In olden days, scrambled eggs were cooked only in a *bain-marie* or double boiler: it guaranteed perfect cooking, but made the operation rather long. It can be done more quickly right over the fire, but at low heat, and not violently, thereby assuring that perfect homogeneity of molecules which makes the eggs smooth.

Principles of Preparation: Gently heat 2 oz. butter in a thick-bottomed, flat saucepan; add 6 eggs well beaten with salt and pepper; heat over a slow fire and stir with a wooden spoon, avoiding any increase in temperature, which will cause the egg molecules to solidify instantly and form lumps—something scrambled eggs should never have. When the eggs have reached the proper consistency, remove the pan from the fire and finish them with 2 oz. butter cut into tiny pieces and, if desired, 3 tbsp. cream. Scrambled eggs should be beaten with a wire whisk only when absolutely necessary.

Note: In the recipes for scrambled eggs given further on, the proportions call for 6 eggs.

COLD EGGS OEUFS FROIDS (E.)

Cold eggs, like all cold preparations, should be treated with taste and arranged and decorated with the greatest care.

EGGS ALEXANDRA OEUFS ALEXANDRA (E.)

Cold: Cover some trimmed and dried cold poached eggs with White Chaud-Froid Sauce (p. 149). Place a fine, scalloped slice of truffle on each egg; cover with cold, melted white Aspic Jelly (p. 168); trim off any excess sauce and place the eggs in oval tartlet shells made from trimmings of Puff Paste (p. 544) and garnished with lobster mousse (see Basic Mixture for Cold Mousses, p. 176) that has already set. Border the eggs with a ribbon of caviar. Arrange the tartlets in a ring on a platter with chopped Aspic Jelly in the center.

EGGS ALGÉRIENNE OEUFS À L'ALGÉRIENNE (P.)

Scrambled: Make scrambled eggs with cream and mix in some grilled, peeled, diced green peppers and quartered small tomatoes.

EGGS AMERICAN STYLE OEUFS À L'AMÉRICAINE (E.)

Fried: Here "fried eggs" means merely eggs cooked in butter in a frying pan. Cook 2 eggs, slide them onto a hot plate, and garnish with 2 slices of grilled bacon on one side and 1 grilled tomato on the other.

Note: There is no real reason for calling these eggs "American Style," except that Americans and the English are very fond of them. However, since this name has prevailed, we shall stick to it.

EGGS ANDALOUSE OEUFS À L'ANDALOUSE (E.)

Cold: Poach the eggs and cover them with some very fine tomato purée to which ⅓ as much Soubise Purée (p. 504) and 1 pt. Aspic Jelly (p. 168) per qt. Soubise Purée have been added. Fill as many oval tartlet molds as there are eggs with tomato purée thickened with jelly. Unmold when they have set, and on each place an egg. Arrange them in a circle on a plate and surround with a chain of very thin onion rings, cooked but not browned, interlaced. Garnish the center with chopped white Aspic Jelly.

EGGS ENGLISH STYLE OEUFS À L'ANGLAISE (P.)

Poached: Drain the poached eggs on a cloth and arrange them on thin slices of well-broiled smoked bacon. Pour bacon fat over them, if the bacon was pan-broiled, or melted butter, if the bacon was cooked on a grill.

EGGS ARCHIDUC OEUFS ARCHIDUC (E.)

Poached or soft-boiled (mollet): Sauté in butter some thinly sliced chicken livers and ¼ their weight of truffles; melt the glaze in the sautéing pan with a little cognac. Fill some tartlet shells with the chicken livers and place the eggs, previously covered with Hongroise or Hungarian Sauce (p. 151), on top.

Fig. 150 - Gougère bourguignonne (p. 244).
Fig. 151 - Ramekins (p. 247).
Fig. 152 - Rissoles (p. 248).

Fig. 151

Fig. 150

Fig. 152

Fig. 153

Fig. 154

EGGS ARGENTEUIL OEUFS ARGENTEUIL (E.)

Poached or soft-boiled (*mollet*): Fill some tartlet shells with asparagus tips blanched and then cooked in butter; on this garnish place 6 white asparagus stalks arranged like the spokes of a wheel with the tips extending beyond the edge of the shell. In the center of each wheel place an egg covered with cream sauce mixed with ½ its volume of green asparagus purée.

Scrambled: Add 2 tbsp. white asparagus tips, heated in butter, to the scrambled eggs. Arrange in a timbale with a pretty bouquet of the same asparagus tips planted in the middle.

Cold: Cover very cold soft-boiled (*mollet*) eggs with White Chaud-Froid Sauce (p. 149) mixed with ⅓ its volume of green asparagus purée. Place a green asparagus salad in the center of a round plate. Around the salad make a circle of boiled potatoes sliced thin with a fancy cutter to about the size of a quarter. Arrange the eggs in a rosette around the salad.

EGGS AURORE OEUFS À L'AURORE (P.)

Poached: Arrange the eggs on croutons and cover with well-buttered Aurore Sauce (p. 147). Sprinkle the tops with hard-boiled egg yolks pressed through a sieve.

Hard-boiled: Prepare the eggs with Béchamel Sauce (p. 146), place in a baking dish, and sprinkle with the chopped yolks of 1 or 2 hard-boiled eggs. Brown in the oven and make a ring of Tomato Sauce (p. 146) around the plate.

Stuffed: Cut hard-boiled eggs in half lengthwise; remove the yolks and put them through a sieve, then mash with a little butter, salt, pepper, 1 tbsp. tomato purée, and 2 tbsp. Béchamel Sauce (p. 146). Using a pastry bag, fill the whites with this mixture, moisten with butter, and place in a very hot oven 5–8 min. Arrange them on a bed of well-buttered Aurore Sauce. (Fig. 153, Page 257.)

BACON AND EGGS OEUFS AU BACON (E.)

Baked: These eggs may be prepared 2 ways: (1) Brown some bacon slices in butter in a frying pan. Place them in the bottom of the egg dish with some of the fat, break the eggs on top, and cook as usual (on a slow fire or in the oven). (2) (English method) Broil slices of bacon and arrange them on either side of the eggs. The eggs are cooked in a frying pan and may or may not be trimmed with a round cutter before being slid onto a plate.

EGGS BALZAC OEUFS BALZAC (E.)

Scrambled: Mix the scrambled eggs with 2 oz. diced truffles and 2 oz. diced pickled tongue. Arrange the eggs in a timbale and surround with small round croutons fried in butter and then covered (using a pastry bag) with a rosette of very thick Soubise Sauce (p. 154). On the eggs make a band of Semiglaze Sauce enriched with tomatoes (p. 138).

EGGS BEAUGENCY OEUFS À LA BEAUGENCY (P.)

Poached: Place the eggs on rather large artichoke bottoms; coat with Béarnaise Sauce (p. 147), and on top place a thin slice of poached beef marrow.

Fig. 153 - Stuffed eggs aurore (p. 257).
Fig. 154 - Poached eggs cardinal (p. 259).

EGGS BÉCHAMEL OEUFS À LA BÉCHAMEL (P.)

Hard-Boiled: Cut the eggs in very thin, round slices and heat them, without boiling, in a good, well-buttered Béchamel Sauce (p. 146) rather strongly seasoned.

EGGS BENEDICTINE OEUFS BÉNÉDICTINE (E.)

Poached or soft-boiled (mollet): Fill some tartlet shells with Brandade of Salt Cod (p. 290) lightly mixed with truffles. Place the eggs, coated with a cream sauce, on top.

EGGS BERCY OEUFS BERCY (E.)

Baked: Cook the eggs as usual. Serve them with a grilled sausage or 4 small chipolata sausages laid between the yolks, and surround with a band of Tomato Sauce (p. 146).

EGGS BERGÈRE OEUFS À LA BERGÈRE (P.)

En cocotte: Mix together a small piece of soft butter and 2 oz. chopped, cooked mushrooms, a little chopped parsley, salt, and pepper. Line the bottom and sides of the cocottes or ramekins with this mixture. Break an egg into each and cook as explained on p. 254.

EGGS IN BLACK BUTTER OEUFS AU BEURRE NOIR (P.)

Baked: Heat some butter in a baking dish until it begins to darken, then break the eggs into it. Baste with butter browned in a separate pan. Pour 1 tbsp. vinegar into the latter pan while still very hot, then pour this over the eggs. Salt and pepper before serving in the cooking dish.

EGGS BOIELDIEU OEUFS BOIELDIEU (E.)

Poached or soft-boiled (mollet): Fill some tartlet shells with a salpicon (tiny cubes) of breast of chicken, *foie gras,* and truffles bound with chicken Velouté (p. 147). Place the eggs on top and coat them with reduced, thickened chicken gravy.

EGGS BONVALET OEUFS BONVALET (E.)

Poached or soft-boiled (mollet): Place the eggs, coated with chicken Velouté (p. 147), on round or oval croutons slightly hollowed in the center, encircled with a small groove, and fried in butter. Using a paper cone, fill the grooves in the croutons with a ribbon of Béarnaise Sauce (p. 147) thickened with tomato, thus encircling the eggs; decorate each egg with a fine slice of scalloped and glazed truffle.

EGGS BORDELAISE OEUFS À LA BORDELAISE (E.)

Fried: Prepare as many halves of Tomatoes Provençale (p. 515) as there are fried eggs, adding a pinch of chopped shallot to each tomato half. When they are cooked, fill them with finely sliced mushrooms sautéed Bordeaux style (see Cepes Bordelaise, p. 502). Place a fried egg on each garnished tomato half. Arrange in a circle on a round plate and serve with fried parsley in the middle.

EGGS BOURGUIGNONNE OEUFS À LA BOURGUIGNONNE (E.)

Poached or soft-boiled (*mollet*) *:* In a small copper saucepan bring to a boil 1 qt. red wine containing herbs (shallots, parsley, thyme, and bay leaf) and seasoning. Strain through a cloth; boil down by ½; and bind with 2 oz. Flour Butter (p. 164). Remove from the fire and add some butter. Arrange the eggs on buttered toast and coat with the sauce.

Note: According to local custom, the eggs are poached directly in the herb-filled wine, seasoned, and drained. The wine is strained through a cloth, reduced, bound into a sauce, and buttered. The eggs are placed on toast rubbed with garlic.

EGGS CARDINAL OEUFS À LA CARDINAL (P.)

Poached: Place the eggs on croutons and coat with Cardinal Sauce (p. 148). Top each egg with a slice of truffle. (Figure 154, Page 257.)

EGGS CAVOUR OEUFS CAVOUR (E.)

Fried: Cut tomatoes in half, drain and scoop them out, and cook them in oil in a frying pan. Arrange the tomatoes on a serving dish; fill each half with Risotto Piémontaise (p. 513), and on top place a fried egg. Serve with an accompanying sauceboat of reduced Veal Gravy (p. 134).

EGGS WITH MUSHROOMS OEUFS AUX CHAMPIGNONS (P.)

Scrambled: Cut 3½ oz. raw mushrooms, carefully peeled and washed, in thin slices. Sauté them in butter until they are browned and add them to the scrambled eggs.

EGGS CHANTILLY OEUFS CHANTILLY (E.)

Poached or soft-boiled (*mollet*) *:* Fill patty shells (made of Puff Paste, p. 544) with a mixture of 3 parts of purée of fresh peas to 1 part very stiff whipped cream. On top of each filled patty shell place an egg thinly coated with Mousseline Sauce (p. 152).

EGGS CHARTRES OEUFS À LA CHARTRES (E.)

Poached or soft-boiled (*mollet*) : Place each egg, covered with thickened Veal Gravy (p. 134) flavored with tarragon, on a piece of toast fried in butter. Decorate each egg with a star made of blanched tarragon leaves.

Cold: Line egg-shaped molds with a coating of clear Aspic Jelly (p. 168); decorate with blanched tarragon leaves; place a poached egg in each mold, and finish filling with the jelly. Unmold just before serving; arrange in a ring; garnish the center with chopped jelly and border the plate with very firm Tarragon Butter (p. 164) cut into squares.

EGGS CHASSEUR OEUFS CHASSEUR (E.)

Baked: Cook the eggs as explained previously and arrange on either side a mound of sliced chicken livers sautéed *à la chasseur* (seasoned, floured, and sautéed in butter, then covered with Chasseur Sauce, p. 139).

Poached or soft-boiled (*mollet*) : Fill tartlet shells with sliced chicken livers sautéed *à la chasseur* (see p. 259). Coat the eggs with Chasseur Sauce and top with a pinch of chopped parsley. Place an egg on each filled tartlet.

Scrambled: Place the scrambled eggs in a timbale and in the center put a garnish of sliced chicken livers sautéed *à la chasseur.* Sprinkle with chopped tarragon and chervil and surround with a band of Chasseur Sauce.

EGGS CHÂTILLON OEUFS CHÂTILLON (E.)

Scrambled: Put the scrambled eggs into a timbale. In the center place a nice bunch of sliced mushrooms sautéed in butter. Place a pinch of chopped parsley on the mushrooms; surround them with a ribbon of Meat Glaze (p. 135), and finish with a border of crescents made of Puff Paste (p. 544).

EGGS CHIMAY OEUFS À LA CHIMAY (P.)

Stuffed: Prepare the same way as stuffed Eggs Aurore (p. 257), adding some finely chopped mushrooms cooked in butter to the purée of egg yolks, then a little chopped parsley. Stuff the eggs, place them in a baking dish, and cover with a thick Mornay Sauce (p. 152). Sprinkle with a handful of grated cheese and bread crumbs, moisten with melted butter, and brown in the oven. Serve immediately.

EGGS COLBERT OEUFS À LA COLBERT (P.)

En cocotte: Prepare Eggs with Cream, as described below, adding a pinch of chopped *fines herbes* to the cream. Then, when the eggs are cooked, surround the yolks with a ribbon of Colbert Butter (p. 163).

EGGS IN CONES OEUFS EN CORNETS (P.)

Scrambled: Make pastry cones like those sold in pastry shops and fill them with either plain or garnished scrambled eggs. Close the open end of the cone with a round slice of ham, truffle, etc.

EGGS WITH CREAM OEUFS À LA CRÈME (P.)

En cocotte: Heat the cocottes or ramekins a little and pour in a finger of boiling cream; break very fresh eggs into them. Place the cocottes in a *bain-marie,* season the eggs, and simmer 2 min. over a low flame, then, covering them with a baking sheet, put them into the oven 3 min. Arrange the cocottes on a napkin or paper doily.

EGGS WITH SHRIMPS OEUFS AUX CREVETTES (P.)

Scrambled: Sauté shrimps in butter and add them to the scrambled eggs.

EGGS WITH CROUTONS OEUFS AUX CROÛTONS (P.)

Scrambled: Fry in butter about 20 croutons cut in small cubes from stale bread with the crust removed. Do not dry them out or brown them too much. Mix them with the scrambled eggs at the last moment.

EGG KROMESKIS OEUFS (CROMESQUIS D') (P.)

Finely dice hard-boiled eggs and bind with a little very thick Béchamel Sauce (p. 146). Season well and reduce on the fire with 1 whole raw egg yolk for every 6 hard-boiled eggs. Chill and then divide the mixture into pieces about the size of a small egg. Roll them into the shape of a stopper or cork with a little flour, dip them in Frying Paste (p. 558), and fry in very hot deep fat; arrange on a napkin with parsley. Serve Tomato Sauce (p. 146) separately.

EGG CROQUETTES OEUFS (CROQUETTES D') (P.)

Same procedure as described on p. 260, rolling the croquettes a little larger and dipping them in bread crumbs instead of Frying Paste. Serve with a separate dish of Tomato Sauce (p. 146), or Périgueux Sauce (p. 143), etc.

EGGS DAUMONT OEUFS DAUMONT (E.)

Poached or soft-boiled (mollet): Cook some large fresh mushrooms in butter, mix them with a salpicon (tiny cubes) of shrimps bound with Nantua Sauce (p. 152), and place the eggs on top, coated with Nantua Sauce. Decorate each egg with a slice of scalloped, glazed truffle.

DEVILED EGGS OEUFS À LA DIABLE (E.)

Break the eggs into a frying pan containing very hot butter. Turn them without breaking the yolks and slide them onto a plate. Pour browned butter over them and a dash of vinegar reduced in the frying pan.

EGGS ELIZABETH OEUFS ÉLISABETH (P.)

Stuffed: Remove the yolks from hard-boiled eggs by making a hole on the side, but keeping the whites whole. (Save the piece of white removed to use as a plug later on.) Make a purée of the yolks by mixing them with a little Béchamel Sauce (p. 146), butter, and 2 mashed artichoke bottoms put through a sieve. Stuff the eggs with this filling and replace the pieces of white removed to extract the yolks. Place each egg on a fried crouton cut the same size as the egg. Coat them with Mornay Sauce (p. 152) mixed with paprika and sprinkle a pinch of grated cheese on top; brown in the oven. Arrange them in a ring on a round plate and fill the center with sliced artichoke bottoms and mushrooms bound with a little Madeira Sauce (p. 142). These eggs are very good and may be served at a formal luncheon. Using this recipe as a basis, you can vary the fillings.

EGGS WITH TARRAGON OEUFS À L'ESTRAGON (P.)

Poached, cold: Line the molds with Aspic Jelly (p. 168) and decorate with blanched tarragon leaves. Place an egg in each mold and finish filling with the jelly, which has been strongly seasoned with tarragon. Let set, then unmold onto a bed of chopped jelly. (Figure 155, Page 264.)

EGGS FLORA OEUFS FLORA (E.)

Poached or soft-boiled (mollet) : Cover one half of each egg with chicken Velouté (p. 147) and the other half with Tomato Sauce (p. 146). Sprinkle a pinch of chopped parsley on the half covered by Tomato Sauce and a pinch of chopped truffle on the Velouté. Place each egg on a piece of Puff Paste (p. 544) made in any desired shape.

EGGS FLORÉAL OEUFS FLORÉAL (E.)

Poached or soft-boiled (mollet) : Cover the eggs with Velouté (p. 147) mixed with chopped chervil and place chervil tops on each egg. Arrange the eggs on pieces of Puff Paste (p. 544) cut a little larger than the eggs. Using a pastry bag with a tube with a small serrated opening, make a wavy ribbon of purée of very green peas around the edge of each piece of pastry.

EGGS FLORENTINE OEUFS À LA FLORENTINE (P.)

Poached: Prepare Spinach English Style (p. 514) and cover the bottom of a baking dish with it. Drain the poached eggs well and place them on top of the spinach. Cover with Mornay Sauce (p. 152). Sprinkle with grated cheese and bread crumbs, moisten with melted butter, and brown in a hot oven.

EGGS FORESTIÈRE OEUFS FORESTIÈRE (P.)

Scrambled: Add 4 oz. small wild mushrooms (morels) sautéed in butter and 2 oz. lean bacon, also fried in butter, to the scrambled eggs. Sprinkle with chopped parsley. Cepes may be used instead of the morels.

EGGS FROU-FROU OEUFS FROU-FROU (E.)

Cold: Neatly trim some very small poached eggs; coat them with a Chaud-Froid Sauce (p. 149) made with cream and mixed with ⅓ as much purée of hard-boiled egg yolks. Decorate the top of each egg with a scalloped ring of black truffle and around the base of the egg make a thin circle of chopped truffles. Glaze with cool, melted Aspic Jelly (p. 168) and keep on ice. Prepare a salad of small peas, asparagus tips, and diced or diamond-cut green beans; bind the salad with Stiff Mayonnaise (p. 157). Mold this salad in an oiled dome-shaped mold or form it into a pyramid in the center of a round plate. Surround it with a circle of chopped Aspic Jelly; arrange the eggs in a ring around the salad, sticking them onto the circle of jelly, and border the plate with slices of very clear jelly. (Figure 156, Page 264.)

EGGS GRAND-DUC OEUFS GRAND-DUC (E.)

Poached or soft-boiled (*mollet*) : They may be made 2 ways: (*a*) Place the eggs on fried croutons and arrange them in a circle on a plate. Place a crayfish tail between each egg and a slice of truffle on top of each egg. Cover with Mornay Sauce (p. 152) and glaze quickly in the oven. On removing from the oven, place a nice bunch of buttered asparagus tips in the center.

(*b*) Arrange the eggs in a pastry shell baked in a pie tin large enough to accommodate the desired number of eggs. Place a slice of truffle on each egg and a crayfish tail between each egg. Cover with Mornay Sauce and glaze quickly in the oven.

EGGS GRAND'MÈRE OEUFS GRAND'MÈRE (E.)

Scrambled: Prepare ordinary scrambled eggs, adding, while they are still very hot, 1 oz. small diced croutons fried in butter. Place in a timbale with a pinch of chopped parsley in the center.

EGGS HALÉVY OEUFS HALÉVY (E.)

Poached or soft-boiled (*mollet*): Fill tartlet shells with half Tomato Fondue (p. 194) and half salpicon (tiny cubes) of breast of chicken bound with Velouté (p. 147). Cover half of each egg with Tomato Sauce (p. 146) and the other half with Parisienne Sauce (p. 146). Draw a ribbon of Meat Glaze (p. 135) between the 2 sauces. Arrange the eggs on the filled shells.

EGGS HUSSARDE OEUFS À LA HUSSARDE (P.)

Stuffed: Mix a generous portion of chopped onions slowly cooked in butter with hard-boiled egg yolks put through a sieve, and season highly with paprika. Stuff the whites of halved hard-boiled eggs with this filling. Put them into a baking dish, moisten with melted butter, and place 5 min. in a very hot oven. Arrange the eggs on tomato slices sautéed in butter with onions and paprika. Moisten with cream flavored with lemon and paprika.

HAM AND EGGS OEUFS AU JAMBON (P.)

Fried: Place fried eggs on slices of fried or grilled ham and separate each portion with Tomato Fondue (p. 194).

EGGS JOINVILLE OEUFS JOINVILLE (P.)

Poached: Place the eggs on croutons or small pastry crusts and cover with Shrimp Sauce (p. 159). Stand a shrimp up on top of each egg or decorate with three small shelled shrimps. (Figure 158, Page 265.)

BACON AND EGGS OEUFS AU LARD (P.)

Fried: Prepare the same way as for Ham and Eggs (above), using lean salted or smoked bacon instead of the ham.

EGGS MARIETTE OEUFS MARIETTE (P.)

Molded: Partially cook scrambled eggs, allowing 6 eggs for 4 persons; add 2 beaten raw eggs, and pour this composition into small, well-buttered porcelain ramekins. Cook in a *bain-marie* and then, when firm, unmold onto a Risotto with cheese (p. 513). Have the rice in a baking dish and shaped like a flat cake. Cover the whole with Béchamel Sauce (p. 146) with cheese. Sprinkle a little grated cheese on top and brown very quickly in a hot oven so as not to harden the eggs.

EGGS MARINIÈRE OEUFS À LA MARINIÈRE (P.)

Scrambled: Like Eggs Normande (p. 266), replacing the oysters with mussels; decorate the tops of the eggs with grilled small mushroom caps; sprinkle parsley on top.

EGGS MARSEILLAISE OEUFS À LA MARSEILLAISE (P.)

Scrambled: Cut 2 small eggplants in half. Macerate them in salt and fry in oil; scoop out the flesh, chop it, and mix it with an equal amount of scrambled eggs. Refill the eggplant shells with this mixture and surround with a ring of garlic-flavored tomato cullis (see p. 198).

EGGS MASSÉNA OEUFS À LA MASSÉNA (P.)

Poached: Place the eggs on artichoke bottoms and coat with Périgueux Sauce (p. 143); place a slice of truffle on each egg.

MIRROR EGGS OEUFS AU MIROIR (P.)

These are very fresh eggs cooked on a fireproof plate, put into a very hot oven or under the broiler for 1 min. to give the yolks that white film which forms on very fresh eggs, a sort of milky veil in which, as in a mirror, images seem to be reflected. They should be prepared at the last minute and served immediately.

EGGS MISTRAL OEUFS À LA MISTRAL (P.)

Baked: Between each egg place half a small tomato cooked in oil; in each tomato half place a pitted olive.

EGGS MONSEIGNEUR OEUFS MONSEIGNEUR (P.)

Poached: Make a fine purée of some leftover fish, such as cod, halibut, flounder, etc., and mix the purée with butter and Béchamel Sauce (p. 146). Fill tartlet shells made of Short Paste (p. 545) with the purée and place poached eggs on top. Cover with well-buttered Béchamel Sauce or a fish sauce left over from the evening before.

EGGS MORENO OEUFS MORENO (P.)

Scrambled: Fill emptied tomato halves cooked in oil with scrambled eggs and put some fried onions in the middle.

Fried: Grill as many tomato halves as there are eggs to be served. Fry 2 or 3 onions, cut in thick rings, in oil. Place a fried egg on each tomato half and arrange the fried onion rings in the center of the plate.

EGGS WITH MORELS OEUFS AUX MORILLES (P.)

Scrambled: Mix a handful of mushrooms (morels) sautéed in butter, and 12 very small slices of bacon browned in butter, with the scrambled eggs. Or, if you wish, add only the bacon to the eggs and arrange the mushrooms in a bouquet in the middle.

EGGS MORNAY OEUFS MORNAY (P.)

Poached: Drain the eggs, place them on bread croutons broiled in butter, and coat with very thick, highly seasoned Béchamel Sauce (p. 146) with cheese. Powder with grated cheese and bread crumbs, moisten with butter, and brown in a very hot oven.

MOSAIC EGGS OEUFS MOSAÏQUE (E.)

Cold: Line molds shaped like egg halves with clear Aspic Jelly (p. 168). Decorate in a mosaic pattern with pickled tongue, poached egg white, truffles, and green beans, all cut in small diamond shapes. Place a poached egg in each mold; finish filling with the jelly, and let congeal. Prepare Russian Salad (p. 525) separately and put it into a dome-shaped mold previously lined with jelly and decorated mosaic fashion, as described above. Just before serving, unmold the salad onto a round plate, surround it with the eggs, and cover the rest of the plate with diced jelly.

EGGS MOSCOVITE OEUFS À LA MOSCOVITE (E.)

Cold: Slice off both ends of some hard-boiled eggs. Encircle the eggs on top and bottom with 3 strips of anchovy fillets, like hoops of a barrel, which the egg is supposed to represent, and in the middle place a tiny piece of truffle to represent the bung. Carefully empty the eggs with a small corer and fill with caviar.

Fig. 155 - Poached eggs with tarragon (p. 261).
Fig. 156 - Poached eggs frou-frou (p. 262).

Fig. 155

Fig. 156

Fig. 158

Fig. 157

Fig. 159

making the caviar come out to a point on the top of each egg. Place each egg on a very white artichoke bottom and encircle with a band of chopped jelly. (Figure 159, Page 265.)

EGGS NIÇOISE OEUFS À LA NIÇOISE (E.)

Poached or soft-boiled (*mollet*): Cut some potatoes in the shape of artichoke bottoms; cook them in butter like Potatoes Château (p. 506) and garnish with buttered, diced string beans. Place the eggs on top, and on each egg put a small mound of Tomato Fondue (p. 194). Encircle each egg with a ribbon of thick Veal Gravy (p. 134).

Cold: Cover cold poached eggs with thick mayonnaise lightly seasoned with tomato. Decorate each egg with a chervil leaf and arrange the eggs around a salad of green beans, tomatoes, and potatoes seasoned with oil and vinegar.

EGGS NINON OEUFS À LA NINON (Gi.)

Poached: Take 3 small bunches of asparagus, of which the tips will be set aside and assembled in small bunches tied with a loop of string. Cut all that is left of the tender part of the stalks in sections about 1 in. long and drop, together with the tied tips, into a small copper saucepan containing lightly salted boiling water. Cook rapidly over a hot fire to keep the asparagus green.

Meanwhile, poach 12 small eggs, which must, as we constantly repeat, be absolutely fresh. Break the eggs into a large saucepan of boiling water, slightly salted and containing a few drops of vinegar. If, as we have already said, the eggs are very fresh, the whites will immediately envelop the yolks while solidifying, but if the contrary is true, the whites will spread in the water, with deplorable results. As soon as all the eggs are in the water, lower the flame and let the eggs poach—that is, let the whites solidify without boiling. Drain them in a bowl of warm water when they are ready. Empty the asparagus into a strainer. Save the bunches of bound tips and put the rest through a fine sieve. Put this asparagus purée into a small stewpan, bind with 2 tbsp. Béchamel Sauce (p. 146), and heat it to the boiling point, then finish, off the stove, with 3½ oz. butter. Note that this purée should be thick and have a pale-green color. If the shade of green is not just right, it may be corrected with a drop of vegetable coloring.

Take the poached eggs 1 by 1 to trim them correctly and arrange in a ring on a plate. Between each egg and its neighbor place some asparagus tips so that the clear green contrasts with the white of the eggs. In the center of the ring pour the emerald-colored purée.

Variant: Cover the eggs with Parisienne Sauce (p. 146) and decorate with a slice of truffle. (Figure 157, Page 265.)

EGGS NORMANDE I OEUFS À LA NORMANDE (E.)

Baked: Fill the bottom of the baking dish with 2 tsp. cream seasoned with salt and pepper, 1 tsp. fish essence, 6 shucked raw oysters with their own juice. Break the eggs on top and cook until the yolks show a milky film. Surround with a border of Normande Sauce (p. 153).

Poached or soft-boiled (*mollet*) : Coat the eggs with Normande Sauce and place them on tartlet shells filled with 3 poached oysters bound with Normande Sauce.

Fig. 157 - Poached eggs Ninon (p. 265).
Fig. 158 - Poached eggs Joinville (p. 263).
Fig. 159 - Poached eggs moscovite (p. 264).

EGGS NORMANDE II OEUFS À LA NORMANDE (P.)

Scrambled: Add 12 poached oysters to the scrambled eggs and serve in boat-shaped patty shells.

EGGS WITH SORREL or SPINACH OEUFS À L'OSEILLE OR AUX ÉPINARDS (P.)

Hard-boiled: Cut hard-boiled eggs in half while still hot and place on sorrel braised in cream. The sorrel can be replaced by spinach, or, sometimes, by a combination of the two. Hard-boiled eggs can also be prepared Florentine or Mornay style, like the poached eggs of the same name.

EGGS PALACE OEUFS À LA PALACE (P.)

Poached: Fill the bottoms of small cocottes or ramekins with 1 tbsp. mushroom purée. Lay the eggs on top and cover with a Cheese Soufflé mixture (p. 249). Sprinkle with grated cheese, place in a warm *bain-marie*, and send to the oven for 3 or 4 min.

EGGS PARISIENNE OEUFS À LA PARISIENNE (E.)

En cocotte: Line the bottoms and sides of cocottes or ramekins with a layer of chicken forcemeat (see Forcemeats, p. 176) mixed with an equal amount of chopped tongue, mushrooms, and truffles. Break the eggs into the lined cocottes. Poach as usual; and, when ready, encircle with a band of Semiglaze Sauce (p. 138).

EGGS PARMENTIER OEUFS PARMENTIER (E.)

Baked: Bake some medium-sized potatoes. Open them with an oval pastry cutter (saving the lid thus formed) and scoop out the insides. Make mashed potatoes of this while still very hot and half fill the potato skins with it. Break an egg into each potato, moisten with cream, and bake in the oven. Just before serving, replace the potato lids and serve on a napkin.

EGGS PÉRIGUEUX or PÉRIGOURDINE OEUFS À LA PÉRIGUEUX OR PÉRIGOURDINE (P.)

Poached: Place the eggs on croutons, cover with a well-buttered Périgueux Sauce (p. 143), and decorate each egg with a slice of truffle.

EGGS PETIT-DUC OEUFS PETIT-DUC (E.)

Poached or soft-boiled (mollet): Place each egg in a large, slightly hollowed-out, grilled mushroom. Cover with Chateaubriand Sauce (below).

Chateaubriand Sauce: Thin Meat Glaze (p. 135) with butter and chopped parsley.

EGGS POLIGNAC OEUFS POLIGNAC (E.)

Molded: Heavily butter some baba molds; decorate the bottoms with a large slice of truffle; break the eggs inside; season and poach as usual. Unmold each egg onto a small slice of toast; arrange in a circle; and cover with melted Maître d'Hôtel Butter (p. 164) mixed with a little melted Meat Glaze (p. 135).

EGGS PORTUGUESE STYLE OEUFS À LA PORTUGAISE (P.)

Poached: Fill buttered tartlet molds with a Risotto (p. 513) made with tomatoes and cheese, and unmold them in a ring onto a round baking dish. Place a poached egg on each, cover with Mornay Sauce (p. 152), and glaze in a hot oven. Surround the eggs with a circle of gravy flavored with tomato.

Baked: Place a small mound of tomatoes, peeled, crushed, and sautéed in butter, between each egg. Sprinkle the tomatoes with chopped parsley.

Scrambled: Add 5 oz. diced tomatoes, sautéed in butter, to the scrambled eggs. Arrange in a timbale and, in the center, place a mound of sautéed tomatoes sprinkled with parsley.

Hard-boiled: Cook some chopped onions in butter without browning, and mix with Béchamel Sauce (p. 146). Sauté some thick slices of tomato in butter and place them in the bottom of a timbale; cover the tomatoes with sliced hard-boiled eggs. Season the Béchamel Sauce with red pepper and pour over the eggs, let simmer, and serve with chopped parsley on top.

EGGS POULETTE OEUFS À LA POULETTE (P.)

Hard-boiled: Mix slices of hard-boiled eggs and mushrooms with Poulette Sauce (p. 154). Add the juice of ½ lemon and chopped parsley.

EGGS PRINCESS MARIE OEUFS PRINCESSE MARIE (E.)

Scrambled: Make some small timbales of Puff-Paste (p. 544) trimmings in dariole molds; cut out some covers with a scalloped ring cutter and brush lightly with beaten egg; in the center of each cover place a smaller, saw-toothed piece of paste, but do not brush this one with egg. Bake the timbales and covers in a low oven. Fill the timbales with scrambled eggs mixed with Parmesan cheese and finished with 2 tbsp. Velouté (p. 147) reduced with truffle essence and 2 tbsp. diced truffles. Place a cover on each timbale and serve on a napkin.

EGGS RAVIGOTE OEUFS À LA RAVIGOTE (E.)

Cold: Line small oval molds with jelly and decorate with slices of gherkins, tarragon leaves, and capers. Pour into each mold 1 tbsp. Rémoulade Sauce (p. 157) mixed with jelly but still liquid. Lay in the poached or soft-boiled (*mollet*) egg so as to cover the egg with sauce. Let congeal and unmold at the last moment onto oval, scalloped slices of clear jelly.

EGGS À LA REINE OEUFS À LA REINE (E.)

Poached or soft-boiled (*mollet*): Fill tartlet shells with a thick chicken purée; place the eggs, coated with Suprême Sauce (p. 146), on top.

En cocotte: Fill the bottoms of the cocottes with very finely minced breast of chicken bound with a thick Velouté (p. 147). Break an egg into each, poach them, and surround the yolks with a ribbon of Suprême Sauce.

Cold: Level with the grooves, cut the heads off small brioches baked in molds and hollow out the crusts. Line the inside with minced breast of chicken bound with mayonnaise lightly seasoned with cayenne; place a soft-boiled (*mollet*) egg coated with mayonnaise in each crust; decorate the top with a piece of truffle and glaze with jelly. (Figure 160, Page 272.)

EGG RISSOLES OEUFS (RISSOLES D') (P.)

Prepare a hard-boiled-egg mixture as for Egg Kromeskis (p. 260) ; when it is cold, wrap each piece, cut in the shape of a small egg, in Short Paste (p. 545) ; moisten the edges all around and pleat like a turnover. Fry in deep hot fat; serve on a napkin with fried parsley. This is served without sauce.

EGGS WITH KIDNEYS OEUFS AUX ROGNONS (P.)

Baked: Between each egg place half a mutton kidney, grilled or sautéed, and moisten with Périgueux Sauce (p. 143).

EGGS ROSITA OEUFS ROSITA (E.)

Cold: Cover poached eggs with White Chaud-Froid Sauce (p. 149) with lobster coral mixed in it. Decorate them in fish-scale style, using truffles cut in crescents of graduated size, and glaze with jelly. Place them in a circle on a bed of chopped clear jelly; surround with a chain of very small tomatoes, pressed, marinated, and stuffed with chopped tuna in oil.

EGGS ROSSINI I OEUFS ROSSINI (E.)

Baked: Cook the eggs in a frying pan. Cut them with a plain ring cutter and place each one on a round slice of *foie gras* sautéed in butter. Cover the yolk of the egg with a slice of truffle. Encircle each egg with a ribbon of Semiglaze Sauce (p. 138) made with truffle essence.

Poached or soft-boiled (*mollet*) : Arrange the eggs on tartlet shells filled with a slice of *foie gras* sautéed in butter. Cover the eggs with thickened Veal Gravy (p. 134) with Madeira and place a large slice of truffle on each egg.

EGGS ROSSINI II OEUFS À LA ROSSINI (Gi.)

Poached: Place poached eggs on oval-shaped croutons of the same size fried in clarified butter and lightly spread with *foie gras* purée. Cut as many circles of raw *foie gras* the size of a quarter as there are eggs. Lightly salt and pepper the *foie gras* circles, dip in flour, and cook slowly in butter, turning them. If cooked *foie gras* is used, merely heat the circles in the oven. Place a piece of this *foie gras* on each egg and, on top of the *foie gras,* a slice of truffle. Serve Périgueux Sauce (p. 143) separately.

Note on the name Rossini: Foie gras and truffles are the characteristics of all dishes served under this name, dedicated to the celebrated composer, who was particularly fond of this way of preparing food.

EGGS SÉVIGNÉ OEUFS À LA SÉVIGNÉ (Gi.)

Poached: Pound 4 oz. leftover breast of chicken in a mortar with a few tbsp. Velouté (p. 147) , heat slowly, and strain through a sieve. Place in a saucepan, season well, and mix in a few very black, diced, cooked truffles. Fry in butter some oval croutons about the size of the eggs and slightly scoop out the centers to hold the chicken purée. Arrange these ovals in a ring on a round plate, place a poached egg on each, and cover the eggs with 1 tbsp. good Velouté (p. 147) reduced with the cooking juices of mushrooms and lightly buttered. On each egg place a round slice of truffle about the size of a quarter.

EGG SURPRISE OEUFS EN SURPRISE (P.)

Stuffed: Remove the yolks from hard-boiled eggs as for Eggs Elizabeth (p. 261) and stuff with a fine mince of any meat, or mushrooms, or tomatoes, or *foie gras;* save the yolks for some other use. Dip the eggs in rather thin Frying Paste (p. 558), after rolling them in flour, and fry in very hot deep fat 5 or 6 min. before serving. Arrange on a napkin with fried parsley and accompany with a sauce that will go well with the stuffing used in the eggs.

EGGS SUZETTE OEUFS SUZETTE (P.)

Poached: Bake some medium-sized potatoes in the oven without removing the skins. Cut a piece off the top and scoop out the pulp, leaving only enough around the skins so that the potato holds its shape. Mash a small amount of the pulp with butter and cream and season. Use this to fill the bottoms of the potato shells and place a small poached egg in each shell. Coat lightly with Mornay Sauce (p. 152) and brown quickly in the oven.

EGGS TARTARE OEUFS À LA TARTARE (P.)

Cold: Cover poached or soft-boiled (*mollet*) eggs with thick Tartar Sauce (p. 158) and arrange them around a purée of tuna in oil mixed with a little mayonnaise and well seasoned. Decorate the eggs with capers and anchovy fillets.

EGGS WITH TOMATO SAUCE OEUFS (SAUCE) TOMATE (P.)

Fried: Arrange the fried eggs on a napkin with a bouquet of fried parsley in the middle. Serve Tomato Sauce (p. 146) separately.

EGGS À LA TRIPE OEUFS À LA TRIPE (P.)

Cold: Same procedure as for hard-boiled Eggs Béchamel (p. 258), adding a good amount of sliced onions cooked in salted water and buttered.

Note: This bizarre name has neither rhyme nor reason, but since it has been accepted by usage we shall conform. Besides, the dish is excellent.

EGGS WITH TRUFFLES OEUFS AUX TRUFFES (P.)

Scrambled: Dice some cooked truffles and mix them with the scrambled eggs. On top place some slices of truffle moistened with butter.

EGGS VIROFLAY OEUFS VIROFLAY (P.)

Poached or soft-boiled (*mollet*) : Fry some brioche crusts (made without sugar) in butter. Scoop out the insides and fill with spinach leaves blanched and cooked in butter. Coat the eggs with Parisienne Sauce (p. 146) and place them on the filled crusts.

Molded: Line buttered baba molds with spinach leaves blanched and cooked in butter. Break the eggs into the molds, poach, and unmold onto toast; coat with Parisienne Sauce.

EGGS XAVIER OEUFS À LA XAVIER (P.)

Poached: Fill pastry crusts with minced leftover lobster bound with Cardinal Sauce (p. 148). Place a poached egg on each and cover with the same sauce. Sprinkle with hard-boiled egg yolks pressed through a sieve and a little chopped chervil.

EGGS YVETTE OEUFS YVETTE (P.)

Scrambled: Mix ordinary scrambled eggs with 2 tbsp. Nantua Sauce (p. 152), 1 tbsp. asparagus tips, and 1 tbsp. diced crayfish tails. Place the eggs in tartlet shells made of Puff-Paste (p. 544) trimmings, with a slice of glazed truffle on each.

EGGS ZINGARA OEUFS À LA ZINGARA (P.)

Poached: Place the eggs on fried croutons and coat with tomato-flavored Semiglaze Sauce (p. 138) to which a fine julienne (thin strips) of ham, tongue, truffles, and mushrooms has been added. Sprinkle with chopped parsley.

OMELETS

The theory of preparing an omelet is at once simple and complicated, for tastes vary greatly about it. Some like their omelets well done, others like them just done, and still others think they should be runny. The main thing is to know the preferences of your guests. We shall not dwell on the method of making an omelet, which is, above all, a question of practice and dexterity. We shall simply say that the desired result is homogeneity of the egg molecules and general smoothness. After all, what is an omelet? Scrambled eggs enclosed in a covering of coagulated egg; nothing else. The following recipes all call for a 3-egg omelet with a tiny pinch of salt and pepper for seasoning and 1 tbsp. butter for cooking it. When the omelet has been rolled and turned out onto a plate, it should be spread with a little butter to make it shine; this is optional but recommended.

CÈPE (MUSHROOM) OMELET OMELETTE AUX CÈPES (P.)

Same procedure as for Morel Omelet (p. 271).

MUSHROOM OMELET OMELETTE AUX CHAMPIGNONS (P.)

Finely slice 5 oz. well-cleaned raw mushrooms; sauté them in butter; when they are slightly browned, add them to the beaten eggs.

OMELET CHASSEUR OMELETTE CHASSEUR (P.)

Slice thin and sauté in butter 2 or 3 chicken livers and 2 mushrooms; salt, pepper, and bind with 1 or 2 tbsp. Semiglaze Sauce (p. 138). Keep this hot without letting it boil. Make the omelet as usual and, before rolling it, spread with the chicken-liver-and-mushroom mixture. When it has been placed on a plate, slit the top and put in 1 tbsp. chicken livers that have been set aside. Sprinkle with a pinch of chopped parsley.

SHRIMP OMELET OMELETTE AUX CREVETTES (P.)

Spread the omelet, before rolling it, with a few tbsp. shrimp bound with Shrimp Sauce (p. 159). Slit the top and put in a small bunch of shrimps sautéed in butter. Run a band of Shrimp Sauce around the omelet. (Figure 161, P. 272.)

CROUTON OMELET OMELETTE AUX CROÛTONS (P.)

Add bread croutons fried in butter to the beaten eggs.

SPANISH OMELET OMELETTE À L'ESPAGNOLE (E.)

Add to the beaten eggs: 1 part finely sliced onion cooked in butter, 2 parts Tomato Fondue (p. 194) with chopped parsley. Make the omelet in the shape of a pancake.

OMELET FERMIÈRE OMELETTE À LA FERMIÈRE (P.)

Make a Ham Omelet (below), but do not roll it. When it has been cooked, slide it onto a round plate and sprinkle with chopped parsley.

FINES HERBES OMELET OMELETTE AUX FINES HERBES (P.)

While beating the eggs, add a suitable quantity of finely chopped parsley, chervil, tarragon, and chives.

FLORENTINE OMELET OMELETTE À LA FLORENTINE (E.)

Spread the omelet, before rolling it, with 2 tbsp. leaf spinach, blanched and cooked in butter. Surround the omelet with a border of Béchamel Sauce (p. 146).

OMELET GRAND'MÈRE OMELETTE GRAND'MÈRE (E.)

To the beaten eggs add a pinch of chopped parsley and, while still hot, 1 oz. diced bread croutons sautéed in butter. Make the omelet immediately.

HAM OMELET OMELETTE AUX JAMBON (P.)

Dice cooked ham and sauté in butter before adding it to the beaten eggs.

BACON OMELET OMELETTE AU LARD (P.)

Cut thin slices of bacon and blanch 2 min. in water to remove the salt; brown them in a pan and add to the eggs.

OMELET LORRAINE OMELETTE LORRAINE (E.)

Add 1 oz. grilled, lean bacon cut in small pieces, 1 oz. fresh Gruyère cheese in thin slivers, a pinch of chopped chives, and 1 tbsp. heavy cream to the eggs. Make the omelet as usual.

OMELET MASSÉNA OMELETTE MASSÉNA (E.)

Spread the omelet, before rolling it, with 1 oz. finely sliced artichoke bottoms sautéed in butter and bound with 1 tbsp. Tomato Sauce (p. 146). Place 2 fine slices of poached beef marrow covered with Meat Glaze (p. 135) on the omelet. Surround the omelet with a border of Béarnaise Sauce (p. 147).

MOREL (MUSHROOM) OMELET OMELETTE AUX MORILLES (P.)

Slice the morels (mushrooms) and sauté them in butter; bind them with 2 tbsp. Semiglaze Sauce (p. 138), and spread over the omelet before rolling it. Slit the top of the omelet and insert 1 tbsp. morels.

MOUSSELINE OMELET OMELETTE MOUSSELINE (E.)

Beat 3 egg yolks in a bowl with a small pinch of salt and 1 tbsp. heavy cream. Beat the whites very stiff and add to the yolks. Pour this mixture into a large frying pan containing 1 oz. very hot butter. Cook the omelet quickly, giving the pan a few shakes to bring the edges of the omelet in toward the center. When the mixture is equally firm all over, roll the omelet and turn it out onto a plate. Serve immediately.

SORREL OMELET OMELETTE À L'OSEILLE (P.)

Finely shred a handful of sorrel and heat it in butter in a stewpan until soft and pulpy. Add it to the beaten eggs and make an omelet.

OMELET PARMENTIER OMELETTE PARMENTIER (P.)

Dice potatoes and cook them in butter; add to the eggs.

OMELET COUNTRY STYLE OMELETTE À LA PAYSANNE (P.)

To the beaten eggs add a few slices of browned lean bacon, some sliced potatoes sautéed in butter, and a little sorrel cooked in butter until soft. When the omelet is well cooked on one side, turn it over like a pancake and slide it onto a round plate.

ASPARAGUS-TIP OMELET OMELETTE AUX POINTES D'ASPERGES (P.)

Add to the beaten eggs some green asparagus tips, cut about 1 in. long, cooked in salted water, and sautéed in butter. When the omelet is finished, make an opening in the top and insert a small bunch of asparagus tips. (Figure 162, Page 273.)

KIDNEY OMELET OMELETTE AUX ROGNONS (E.)

Spread the omelet, before rolling it, with 1½ tbsp. veal or mutton kidneys, diced, seasoned with salt and pepper, sautéed quickly in butter, and bound with Semiglaze Sauce (p. 138). After the omelet has been placed on a plate, make an opening in the center and insert 1 tbsp. of the same filling. Surround with a band of Semiglaze Sauce.

OMELET ROSSINI OMELETTE ROSSINI (E.)

Add 1 tbsp. cooked *foie gras* and 1 tbsp. diced truffles to the beaten eggs. On top of the omelet place a small rectangle of heated *foie gras* and a slice of truffle at either end. Surround with a band of Semiglaze Sauce (p. 138) made with truffle essence.

OMELET SAVOYARDE OMELETTE À LA SAVOYARDE (E.)

Add 2 tbsp. heavy cream, 1 oz. raw potatoes sliced in thin rings and sautéed in butter, and ¾ oz. fresh Gruyère cheese cut in thin slivers to the beaten eggs. Make the omelet in the shape of a pancake.

TUNA OMELET OMELETTE AU THON (B.-S.)

Preparation: For 6 persons, take the soft roe, or milt, of 2 carps, wash well, and blanch 5 min. in boiling, salted water. Take a piece of fresh tuna about the

Fig. 160 - Cold eggs à la Reine (p. 267).
Fig. 161 - Shrimp omelet (p. 270).

Fig. 160

Fig. 161

Fig. 162

Fig. 163

size of an egg and a small shallot chopped very fine. Chop the soft roe and tuna together, mix well with the shallot, and place all in a stewpan with a large enough piece of butter; sauté until all the butter has melted. This is the distinguishing feature of the omelet. Take another piece of butter, mix with parsley and chives, moisten with lemon juice, and place on an oval fish platter and heat. Beat 12 very fresh eggs and carefully mix in the sautéed tuna and soft roe. Make the omelet in the usual manner, but longer, thick, and moderately soft. Transfer it adroitly to the platter prepared to receive it and serve to be eaten immediately.

This dish should be reserved for a really fine luncheon or a get-together of enthusiasts for fine food, when the guests appreciate what they are eating and take their time. Serve with a fine old wine, and the results will be marvelous.

Notes on Preparation: (1) The soft roe and tuna should be sautéed without boiling, which causes it to harden and prevents mixing well with the eggs. (2) The platter should be deep enough so that the butter sauce can be concentrated in one corner and served with a spoon. (3) The platter should be warm, otherwise the porcelain will absorb all the heat from the omelet and there will not be enough left to melt the Maître d'Hôtel Butter on which the omelet is placed.

OMELET VOSGIENNE OMELETTE VOSGIENNE (P.)

Mix the beaten eggs with thin strips of grilled, smoked bacon, thin slices of Gruyère cheese, and a little heavy cream. Make the omelet as usual.

EGG SYMPHONY SYMPHONIE D'OEUFS (A.) (*For 6 persons*)

Take 12 eggs. Hard-boil 2, let cool, and chop. Poach 6 eggs and keep warm. With the 4 remaining eggs make a thin, simple omelet in a large pan; it may be flavored or not or contain some hot ingredients, depending on taste. When the omelet is cooked, sprinkle it with the chopped hard-boiled eggs and place the poached eggs on top; fold the omelet, slide it onto a plate, and serve. The omelet should be served so that each guest receives a poached egg in his portion. A sauceboat of Tomato Sauce (p. 146), or Béchamel Sauce (p. 146), or cream acidulated with lemon juice to taste may be served at the same time. A more elegant way to serve this dish is to prepare as many small omelets as there are guests, with a poached egg in each omelet. (Figure 163, Page 273.)

PLOVERS' EGGS OEUFS DE VANNEAU ET DE PLUVIER (E.)

Though differing in plumage, the lapwing and the plover have the same habits and habitat and their eggs are similar. These eggs, almost the size of pigeons' eggs, have pale-green shells with black specks. When cooked, the albuminous part of the egg turns milky white but does not become so firm as the whites of other eggs. All of the ordinary egg recipes may be applied to these eggs, but they are usually served hard-boiled and cold. To hard-boil them, allow 8 min. from the time they have been put into boiling water and the water re-

Fig. 162 - Asparagus-tip omelet (p. 272).
Fig. 163 - Egg symphony (p. 273).

sumes boiling. To assure freshness before cooking, plunge the eggs into a panful of cold water; the eggs that float on the surface are of doubtful freshness and should therefore be discarded.

PLOVERS' EGGS IN ASPIC OEUFS DE VANNEAU EN ASPIC (E.)

Cold: Line a mold with a decorative border with Aspic Jelly (p. 168) and decorate as desired; set the pieces forming the decoration in place with a few more drops of jelly, then cover with a few tbsp. jelly, and let congeal. On this jelly arrange the shelled, hard-boiled plovers' eggs with the point of the egg down, so that when removed from the molds the eggs will be standing up. Finish filling the mold with jelly, pouring it in in successive layers. Unmold onto a napkin when ready.

PLOVERS' EGGS IN A NEST OEUFS DE VANNEAU DANS UN NID (E.)

Cold: Mold a nest of Montpellier Butter (p. 165) on a round plate, fashioning the outside with a paper cone. Cook the eggs soft-boiled (*mollet*) ; cool, shell, and place in the nest around the sides. Fill the center with clear Aspic Jelly (p. 168) and surround the nest with golden cress.

PLOVERS' EGGS GABRIELLE OEUFS DE VANNEAU GABRIELLE (E.)

Cold: Line dariole molds with Aspic Jelly (p. 168) and sprinkle the interior with beads of lobster coral. In each mold place a cold, soft-boiled (*mollet*) plover egg with the point down; finish filling with jelly, and let congeal. Unmold each egg onto a tartlet shell. Using a pastry bag with a tube with a grooved opening, surround the base with a ribbon of purée of creamed sole fillets.

PLOVERS' EGGS ROYALE OEUFS DE VANNEAU À LA ROYALE (E.)

Hot: Line as many tartlet molds as there are eggs with chicken purée bound with eggs, and poach. Unmold, arrange them in a circle, and remove a small portion of the center of each tartlet to hold a hot, shelled, soft-boiled (*mollet*) egg upright. Coat the egg with thin mushroom purée and sprinkle with chopped truffles.

FISH

SALT-WATER FISH AND FRESH-WATER FISH

CHOICE AND PREPARATION OF FISH FOR COOKING (P.)

Everyone knows that freshness is the first thing to look for in buying fish. It is also necessary to be able to distinguish between good fish and the merely mediocre. A really fresh fish has a shiny appearance, quite red gills, flesh firm to the touch, and skin almost always sticky. (There are, however, exceptions.)

Fish with scales must be scaled before being cleaned (the firmer the belly, the easier the scaling) . To do this, scrape the fish strongly with a rather sharp knife, working from the tail toward the head, or against the scales. There are, moreover, special scaling knives to do this job easily and properly.

Next clip off the fins with strong scissors and cut off the tail about midwya. Clean the fish by removing the gills and inserting a finger through these holes to pull out the intestines; cut open the belly of the fish with a knife to remove the rest of the entrails; wash it quickly in running fresh water and wrap it in a clot.h

Once the fish has been cleaned, any of the following cooking methods may be used: cooking in a Court Bouillon, braising, poaching, roasting, grilling, frying, and *à la meunière.*

COURT BOUILLON COURT-BOUILLON (P.)

Anyone familiar with French cooking knows what a Court Bouillon is. It consists of enough water to cover the fish, 2 oz. vinegar per qt. water, onions, shallots, parsley, thyme, bay leaf, ½ oz. salt, 5 or 6 peppercorns. This ordinary Court Bouillon may be modified, depending on the fish being prepared, by replacing the vinegar with 8 oz. of white wine.

When large fish such as sea bass, pike, cod, salmon trout, and salmon are cooked whole, they should be started in a cold Court Bouillon and enough cooking time should be allowed for the vegetables to cook and impart their flavor to the fish. If small fish or slices of fish are to be cooked, boil the Court Bouillon alone first, let it cool, then drop in the fish and replace on the stove.

Fish must never be boiled in Court Bouillon. An exception to this rule is made for Bouillabaïsse (p. 735) , various fish stews, and shellfish. When the Court Bouillon containing the fish comes to a boil, the heat should be lowered to let it simmer for ¼ hr. per lb.: this is why the cooking time of a large fish is the same as that of its Court Bouillon and why small fish which cook rapidly would not take on any of the flavor of the herbs and vegetables if the Court Bouillon were put on the fire at the same time as the fish.

If the fish is to be served cold, it should be allowed to cool in the Court Bouillon and then be drained.

BRAISING BRAISAGE (P.)

This method of cooking is especially used for large fish served whole or in thick slices: Carp Chambord (p. 308) or a thick slice of tuna or conger eel. Place a few slices of onions, carrots, and shallots lightly browned in butter in the bottom of the braising pan. Place the fish on top, put a very thin slice of pork fat on top of the fish, and pour in white or red wine to fill the pan halfway, without covering the fish. The type of wine used will depend on the sauce that is to go with the fish. Season and bring to a boil on the stove, then place in the oven and cook slowly, basting frequently. Cooking time will depend upon the size of the fish. The strip of pork fat may be replaced by a piece of oiled paper. The cooking juices of fish prepared this way are always added to the sauce that accompanies them; often, moreover, the juices themselves, bound with flour and butter, make up the sauce.

POACHING POCHAGE (P.)

A poached fish is a fish cooked with very little liquid, without boiling. Poaching is used chiefly for cooking sole, river trout, chicken turbot, or for fillets or slices of fish. Cold water should be run through white-fleshed fish to drain out all of the blood: sole, turbot, brill, etc.

Butter the bottom of a frying or roasting pan, sprinkle it with sliced onions or shallots, place in the fish, and season with salt and pepper. Fill the pan halfway only with white or red wine, Madeira or champagne, cooking juices of mushrooms, or fish stock made from bones and scraps of fish. Cover the fish with buttered paper and place it in the oven. Cook without boiling (cooking time depends on weight, size, and type of fish), basting from time to time. Make a sauce from the cooking juices to accompany the fish.

ROASTING RÔTISSAGE (P.)

Fish may be roasted just as well as meat, but we must add that this method of cooking is not suitable to all fish; they must be rather large and firm of flesh—for example, conger eel, gilthead, pike, carp. Cover them well with butter and put in a very hot oven, basting frequently. Though little used, roasting rather fatty fleshed fish makes very interesting dishes.

GRILLING GRILLADE (P.)

If you wish to serve fish grilled or "on the grill"—for often they are cooked in the oven, though called grilled—first flour the fish and brush the surface with oil before placing them on a preheated grill. If the fish weighs more than 6 oz., it should be slit in several places along both sides so that the heat will penetrate and cook the insides without burning the skin. Cut these slits about ¼ in. deep. When the fish is cooked on one side, turn it over on the other, and baste often with oil or melted butter during the cooking. Whole fish or slices of large fish can be grilled.

FRYING FRITURE (P.)

Generally, fish are fried in oil because oil can be heated until very hot without burning and the fish are thus easily seared. The smaller the fish, the more they must be seared, and not too many at one time, so the oil won't cool. When frying a large fish, slit it as for grilling. Serve the fish as soon as it is fried, so that it will be golden and crisp.

It is a good idea, before frying, to dip the fish in salted cold milk and roll them in flour to give them a crisp crust and a golden color. Salt the fish when draining off the oil and serve on a napkin with slices of lemon and, if you wish, a bunch of fried parsley.

MEUNIÈRE (P.)

Fish cooked *à la meunière* should be dipped in milk and flour and pan-fried in very hot butter; large fish should be slit, as described above. This method is especially suitable for small fish such as trout, sole, whiting, and mackerel. Slices of large fish may also be prepared *à la meunière.* Directions for serving will be given in the recipes.

SALT-WATER FISH

HADDOCK and FRESH COD AIGLEFIN and CABILLAUD (P.)

Both these fish become salt cod after curing. When fresh, they are cooked in a Court Bouillon (p. 277) either whole or in slices and are served with any fish sauce. They can also be fried in slices or cooked in the frying pan, but the meat is apt to fall apart. See the recipes for fresh cod (pp. 283–284).

SEA BASS KRONSTADT BAR À LA CRONSTADT (P.)

Cold: Cook the fish in a Court Bouillon (p. 277) and let it cool partially in this liquid before draining. Place it on a fish platter with a garnish of 6 or 8 stuffed hard-boiled eggs prepared the following way. Cut the eggs in half, press the yolks through a sieve, mix with butter and 1 tbsp. mayonnaise, and divide this cream into 2 parts. Mix ½ with spinach-and-water-cress purée and the other ½ with thick tomato purée and a dash of red coloring. Using a pastry bag with a tube with a serrated opening, fill ½ the whites with the green mixture and the other ½ with the red, arranging the stuffed eggs around the fish in alternating colors.

Carve the fish without moving the pieces, to make it easy for the guests to serve themselves. If any of the egg filling is left over, it may be used for decorating the fish. Cover the whole arrangement of fish and eggs with a thin layer of Aspic Jelly (p. 168) and border the plate with thin slices of lemon. Serve with Green Sauce (p. 158). (Figure 164, Page 280.)

SEA BASS RÉGENCE BAR RÉGENCE (J.) (*For 10 persons*)

Bone a bass weighing 4 lb. (see directions, p. 95). Season the flesh and spread the interior with a good thickness of Pike Forcemeat (p. 175). Close the fish and sew it carefully so that it will have its original appearance, and poach 40–45 min. in a Court Bouillon made with white wine (p. 277). When cooked, let cool until tepid and drain; remove the skin and the thread; let cool. Arrange on a platter. Cover the fish, except the head and tail, with a thin layer of Choux Paste (p. 548) made without sugar. Brush with beaten egg, then, using a teaspoon, make a pattern of fish scales. Place in the oven and leave long enough to bake the paste. Surround the fish with fried parsley and on either side place 4 or 5 unshelled crayfish, cooked in Court Bouillon, with the heads turned toward the ends of the platter. Serve, separately, Joinville Sauce (p. 152) with tiny cubes of truffles and shrimps added.

Note: Lacking fresh-water crayfish, we had to trim this dish with sea crayfish, which makes a less attractive effect. (Figure 165, Page 280.)

BRILL AMIRAL BARBUE À L'AMIRAL (M.) (*For 12 persons*)

(1) Take a brill weighing 5 lb. and make a cut lengthwise on the dark side to separate the fillets from the backbone. Break the backbone in 2 or 3 places so that the fish may be cooked without breaking the flesh. Place 2 tbsp. butter seasoned with salt and pepper inside the brill. (2) Place the fish on the buttered grill of a flat roasting pan. Season with salt and pepper. Pour over it 1 pt. fish essence (prepared with Chablis). Bring to a boil on top of the stove and finish cooking in the oven at a low heat, basting frequently. (3) Remove the fish from the cooking pan, trim it, remove the black skin and the backbone. Place the fish on a large serving platter.

Sauce: Strain the cooking liquid through a fine strainer and cook until reduced by ½; add 6 oz. Fish Velouté (p. 147) and reduce over a hot fire, while adding gradually 10 or 12 oz. fresh heavy cream, until the proper consistency has been reached. Finish the sauce with 4 oz. Crayfish Butter (p. 164), 2 tbsp. champagne brandy (set aflame), and a dash of cayenne pepper. Strain through a sieve. Sponge off the excess moisture from the fish, cover it with this sauce while it is piping hot, and surround it with a Garnish Amiral (p. 180)—that is, Mussels and Oysters Villeroi (p. 323), very small shells filled with crayfish tails, mushroom caps, and slices of truffle.

BRILL ASTURIENNE BARBUE À L'ASTURIENNE (M.)

(1) Stuff the brill with whiting forcemeat made without cream (see Forcemeats, p. 173, and under Sole Fillets Cardinal, p. 294), with a chopped onion, cooked in butter until soft, added, and seasoned with paprika. Place the brill on a buttered baking dish covered with a layer of pimentos and mushrooms cut in julienne strips and cooked in butter. Pour in 6 oz. white wine and season with salt and paprika. Sprinkle the top of the fish with tiny pieces of butter and cook in the oven, basting frequently. (2) When the fish is cooked, drain off the cooking juice. Reduce this stock and add it to some Mornay Sauce (p. 152) prepared separately. Cover the fish with this sauce and surround it with small tomatoes cooked in oil. Sprinkle with grated Parmesan cheese and moisten with melted butter. Brown quickly in the oven.

BRAISED BRILL BARBUE BRAISÉE (A.) (*For 6 persons*)

Take 1 cup white wine (Graves or sauterne), 1 cup fish stock (seasoned and flavored with herbs and vegetables), 3 oz. peeled mushrooms, 1 oz. butter,

Fig. 164 - Sea bass Kronstadt (p. 279).
Fig. 165 - Sea bass Régence (p. 279).

Fig. 164

Fig. 165

Fig. 166

Fig. 167

1 brill weighing about 3 lb., 1 small shallot, parsley. Gut, clean, and trim the fish. Slice the mushrooms and chop the shallot and parsley, and place them in the bottom of a fish roasting pan. Place the brill on the buttered grill of the roasting pan and pour the wine and cold fish stock over it. Bring to a boil on top of the stove and then place in the oven to cook, basting frequently. When cooked, slide the brill onto a platter and keep warm. Strain the cooking juice and save it to mix with a Régence Sauce made of these ingredients: 8 oz. Alsatian wine (Riesling or Riquewihr) or Rhine wine, 8 oz. fish stock, 1 oz. mushrooms, 1 oz. truffle trimmings, Normande Sauce (p. 153). Mix the wine and fish stock, add the mushrooms and truffle trimmings, and boil down by ½; reduce the cooking juice from the brill and add; reduce this combined liquid even further, then add an equal amount of Normande Sauce. Strain.

Garnish the platter with truffles cut in the shape of olives, soft roe poached in fish stock, forcemeat balls of pike and crayfish (see Forcemeats, p. 173) shaped with a spoon, and small croquettes of souffléed potatoes. Cover the fish smoothly with some of the sauce and serve the rest of the sauce in a sauceboat.

As a variation the brill may also be served with poached oysters, small croquettes, very white mushrooms, and small Potatoes Duchesse (p. 507). Serve with Shrimp Sauce, prepared as follows:

For 6 persons, take: 2 cups fish stock, 5 oz. shrimps, 3 oz. butter, 2½ oz. fresh heavy cream, 2 oz. flour, 1 tbsp. raw lobster coral, paprika, and cayenne pepper. Peel the shrimps, saving the shells. Make a White Roux (p. 136) with 1½ oz. butter and 1½ oz. flour. Mix this with the fish stock and cook slowly 20 min., skimming frequently; next pour in the cream, the mashed lobster coral, and heat slowly until reduced by ¼. Remove from the stove and add Shrimp Butter made with the rest of the butter, the shrimp shells, and a few shrimps (see p. 164); season with paprika or a dash of cayenne. Strain the sauce and add the remainder of the shrimps. This Shrimp Sauce should be pale pink.

BRILL IN CHAMBERTIN BARBUE AU CHAMBERTIN (M.)

Prepare the brill as directed in the recipe for Brill Amiral (p. 280), but pour over it 1 qt. fish stock made with Chambertin (a red burgundy). Add a large amount of mushroom peelings to the garnish (see *Note,* below). Cook in the usual manner, drain the fish, trim, and serve on a platter.

Sauce: Strain the cooking juice and reduce it by ⅔, then add 12 oz. well-skimmed Espagnole Sauce (p. 137) made with fish stock, reduce for a few minutes on a hot fire, while spooning with a wooden ladle; strain through cheesecloth and pour over the fish.

Note: The garnish for fish braised in white or red wine is optional and depends upon the other dishes included in the menu. With brill braised with Chambertin, we have often served a garnish of mushrooms and small pieces of sole fillets rolled in flour and sautéed in butter.

BRILL DEAUVILLE BARBUE À LA DEAUVILLE (P.) (*For 10 persons*)

To serve the fish more easily, it is best to slice it into fillets; remove these fillets the same as you would those of sole. Take a thick, very white brill weighing 4 lb. Wash the fillets, the backbone, and the head (with the gills removed). Make a fish stock with Madeira and cook it for 15 min. Cut 2 oz. very red carrots, 1 oz. onions, white of 2 leeks, 1 oz. mushrooms, and 1 truffle into thin julienne

Fig. 166 - Brill french style (p. 282).
Fig. 167 - Sauteed cod Bombay (p. 283).

strips. Mix this julienne in a stewpan with a little hot butter, season with salt, cover the pan, and cook 10 min. at low heat in the oven. Strain the fish stock through a fine sieve into this julienne, let simmer for a minute, and pour over the brill fillets set in a baking dish. Poach 15 min. without boiling. Remove the fillets and place them on a serving platter. Reduce the cooking juice of the fish on a hot fire, while adding 2 oz. heavy cream and 2½ oz. Béchamel Sauce (p. 146). Season this sauce, which should be creamy, and pour it over the fish without straining it, leaving the vegetables in this exquisite sauce. Surround the fish with 12 large grilled mushroom caps stuffed with shrimps bound with Shrimp Sauce (p. 159).

BRILL FILLETS DROUOT BARBUE (FILETS DE) À LA DROUOT (P.) (*For 5 persons*)

Remove the fillets from a brill weighing 2 lb. Make the usual Court Bouillon with the bones, head, etc. (p. 277). Strain the Court Bouillon over the fillets, cover them with a buttered paper, and poach 15–20 min. in the oven. Reduce the cooking juice of the fish and use it to make a Béchamel Sauce (p. 146) bound with egg yolks; remove from the stove and add some butter and correct the seasoning. Arrange the brill fillets on a long fish platter and surround them with a ring of sliced potatoes boiled in their jackets. Cover the fish and potatoes with grated cheese and coat with the sauce. Sprinkle the top with more grated cheese and white bread crumbs. Pour melted butter over it and brown in the oven. Serve very hot as soon as it is removed from the oven.

BRILL FANCHON BARBUE FANCHON (M.)

Line the bottom of a buttered baking dish with thin julienne strips of celery root or celeriac and mushrooms cooked in butter. Place the brill on top and moisten with Chablis and a little lemon juice. Cook in the oven. Drain off the cooking juice, reduce it, add butter, and strain. Pour this sauce over the fish. Glaze quickly. Surround with diced potatoes browned in butter.

BRILL FRENCH STYLE BARBUE À LA FRANÇAISE (M.)

Prepare and cook the brill in white wine in the usual way.

Sauce: Reduce the cooking juice, bind with 12 oz. Fish Velouté (p. 147), and finish with fresh cream and butter. Divide the sauce into 2 parts, adding very green Tarragon Butter (p. 164) to 1 part and leaving the other white. Strain the 2 sauces separately.

Garnish: Small Cassolettes Duchesse (p. 238) filled with a ragout of Mussels Poulette (p. 323); crayfish cooked in Court Bouillon (p. 277); large slices of truffles.

Dressing: Cover half the fish with the green sauce and the other half with the white and arrange the garnish around the fish. Separate the two sauces with a band of truffle slices. (Figure 166, Page 281.)

BRILL MIROMESNIL BARBUE À LA MIROMESNIL (P.)

Carefully remove the fillets from the side with the black skin; salt and pepper; place in a fish pan with white wine and shallots, and poach. Next make White-Wine Sauce (p. 155), adding to it, just before serving, a little fresh tomato purée, to give it a delicate pink tint, and a little cayenne. Cover the brill with this sauce and scatter a few strips of truffles on top. As a garnish, use grilled mushroom caps stuffed with fresh tomato purée thickened with bread crumbs. Around the edge of the dish make a ring of bread croutons fried in butter, alternated with the mushroom caps.

STUFFED BRILL NANTUA BARBUE FOURRÉE À LA NANTUA (M.)

Prepare and cook the brill in white wine in the usual way. When it is cooked, drain it and place it on a buttered platter. Turn it over onto a second buttered platter so that the bottom side will now be up. Slice off the 2 fillets, remove the backbone, and fill the inside of the fish with a layer of very thick crayfish purée. Replace the 2 fillets carefully so that the fish will have its original form. Remove all of the black skin covering these fillets. Replace the fish onto the first platter, turning it over again so that it will be right side up. Trim the side bones and heat well in the oven.

Sauce: Reduce the cooking juice of the brill, adding 12 oz. crayfish purée mixed with 5 tbsp. fresh cream. Remove from the stove and add 6 oz. butter.

Garnish: Small patties filled with a ragout of crayfish Nantua (p. 236).

BRILL PARISIENNE BARBUE À LA PARISIENNE (M.)

See Turbot Parisienne, p. 304.

BRILL FILLETS PORTUGUESE STYLE BARBUE (FILETS DE) À LA PORTUGAISE (A.) (*For 4 persons*)

Take 1 lb. tomatoes, 1 cup water, 8 oz. white wine, 6 oz. butter, 5 oz. mushrooms, 1 brill weighing about 2 lb., carrots, onions, parsley, thyme, bay leaf, salt, and pepper. Remove the fillets from the brill, saving the head, bones, and skin. Place the head, bones, and skin in a stewpan with the water, wine, carrots, onions, parsley, thyme, bay leaf, salt, and pepper; cook slowly for about 1 hr. Strain the fish stock thus obtained through a cone-shaped sieve. Cook the brill fillets in the oven with some of this fish stock and 2 oz. butter. When cooked, remove the fillets from the oven and keep hot. Cook the rest of the fish stock with the cooking juice from the fillets until reduced to a good consistency. Prepare a Portuguese Garnish (p. 184): peel, seed, and cut the tomatoes into pieces; peel and slice the mushrooms. Put the tomatoes, mushrooms, and a medium-sized onion, chopped parsley, and 2 oz. butter into a stewpan; cook until the liquid has completely evaporated, which takes about 15 min. Arrange the fillets on a platter and surround them with the garnish of tomatoes and mushrooms; cover smoothly with the reduced fish stock and add the rest of the butter cut in small pieces. Heat in the oven for a few minutes and serve. Fillets of sole, chicken turbot, or turbot can be prepared the same way.

BRILL SAINT-LAURENT BARBUE SAINT-LAURENT (M.)

Cut 4 not-too-deep slits in a medium-sized brill. Season with salt and pepper, sprinkle with flour, moisten with oil, and grill over a low flame. Arrange it on a serving dish on a bed of Tomato Fondue (p. 194). Surround with a ring of sliced mushrooms sautéed in butter and seasoned with paprika. Serve with Bordelaise Sauce (p. 138).

SAUTÉED COD BOMBAY CABILLAUD (SAUTÉ) À LA BOMBAY (M.)

Cut the flesh of the cod into 1½-in. squares, season with salt and curry, and dredge with flour. Sauté the fish quickly in a frying pan with clarified butter.

Arrange it in a border of Rice Indian Style (p. 512). Around this border place alternate mounds of Tomato Fondue (p. 194) and diced eggplant sautéed in oil. Sprinkle with chopped parsley. Cover the fish with Curry Sauce (p. 150) just before serving or serve the sauce separately. (Figure 167, Page 281.)

COD BOULANGÈRE CABILLAUD À LA BOULANGÈRE (M.) (*For 5 persons*)

Heat 2 tbsp. butter in an earthenware baking dish and place a 2-lb. slice of cod in it. Season with salt, pepper, and a little powdered thyme and bay leaf. Moisten with melted butter and place in a hot oven. Cook 12 min. Surround the fish with 24 small buttered potato balls half cooked in a frying pan and 10 small glazed onions. Replace in the oven to finish cooking; baste frequently. Sprinkle with chopped parsley.

FRIED COD CABILLAUD FRIT (P.)

Dip some thin slices of cod in milk and then in flour. Fry 8–10 min. in very hot deep fat and serve with lemon quarters.

COD WITH PARSLEY SAUCE CABILLAUD (SAUCE) PERSIL (P.)

Cook slices of cod weighing about 6 oz. each in a Court Bouillon (p. 277) and serve with a white sauce to which a pinch of chopped parsley has been added.

COD PORTUGUESE STYLE CABILLAUD À LA PORTUGAISE (E.) (*For 5 persons*)

Cut the cod into slices weighing about ½ lb. each. Season with salt and pepper and place them in a sautéing pan containing (for 5 slices): 4 oz. butter, 3 oz. oil, 4 oz. chopped onion browned in butter, 1 small crushed clove of garlic, 2 pinches of crushed parsley, 1½ lb. pressed and crushed tomatoes, 4 oz. rice ¾ cooked in salted water, and 6 oz. white wine. Cover the pan and bring to a boil over a hot fire, then lower the heat and cook 10 min. Remove the cover to reduce the liquid, and finish cooking, which takes 8 min. more. Place the slices on a long fish platter and cover with the cooking juice and vegetable garnish.

BAKED MINUTE PLAICE or **FLOUNDER** CARRELETS SUR LE PLAT À LA MINUTE (P.)

Clean the fish and cut 4 shallow slits on each side with the point of a knife, forming a kind of square pattern. Place the fish in a baking dish and sprinkle with salt and pepper, 3 or 4 chopped shallots, and some chopped parsley; pour in enough white wine till it is level with the fish, sprinkle the top of the fish with bread crumbs, dab with butter, and cook in a very hot oven so that the fish are cooked and the top is browned. All fish or slices of fish can be prepared this way: sole as well as whiting, or pieces of large fish.

SLICED POLLACK or **WHITING ENGLISH STYLE** COLIN (TRONÇON DE) À L'ANGLAISE (P.)

All large fish or slices of fish can be prepared "English style." Cook the fish in a well-seasoned Court Bouillon (p. 277) without boiling, 9–10 min. per lb. fish. Drain the fish and serve it on a napkin, surrounded by Potatoes English Style (p. 506), sprigs of parsley, slices of lemon, and, if you wish, cooked mushrooms. Serve melted butter separately.

POLLACK FILLETS BERCY COLIN (FILETS DE) À LA BERCY (P.)

Remove the fillets from the pollack, and make a Court Bouillon with the bones, head, tail, etc. (p. 277). Cook 1 tbsp. chopped shallots in butter, add a little white wine, and reduce by ½; add the fish bouillon, salt, pepper, lemon juice, chopped parsley, and 2 tbsp. butter mixed with 1 tbsp. flour. Bring to a boil once or twice and pour over the raw fish fillets placed in a baking dish; sprinkle with bread crumbs and brown in a hot oven. Sprinkle with chopped parsley before serving.

POLLACK or TURBOT DUGLÉRÉ COLIN or LOTTE À LA DUGLÉRÉ (P.)

These 2 fish can be prepared the same way, cooked in slices or in fillets without bones and skin. For this recipe, however, fillets are preferable. (To remove the bones and skin and slice the fillets, see figures on p. 94.) Cook them with salt and pepper and 1 glass white wine. Separately, lightly brown 4 oz. finely sliced onions, then add 1 lb. tomatoes, peeled, pressed, and chopped, and cook with the onions until reduced to a purée. When the fish has been cooked, drain off the white wine from the cooking and pour it into the tomato purée, binding with 2 oz. butter mixed with 1 tbsp. flour. This sauce should be creamy, not too thick, and well seasoned. Pour it over the cooked fish fillets and sprinkle with chopped parsley.

POLLACK FILLETS FLORENTINE COLIN (FILETS DE) À LA FLORENTINE (P.)

Cook the fillets as described above. Cook separately 3 lb. well-stripped spinach in salted water; drain, cool, press by hand to remove excess water, and sauté in butter. Place the spinach in the bottom of a baking dish and the fish fillets on top; cover with Mornay Sauce (p. 152) and brown in the oven. Any fish can be prepared this way.

POLLACK FILLETS MORNAY COLIN (FILETS DE) À LA MORNAY (P.)

Cook the fish fillets in white wine as described above. When the fillets have been cooked, remove them and reduce the white-wine cooking liquid over a hot fire. Make a very thick Béchamel Sauce (p. 146) and thin it a little with the reduced white-wine cooking liquid. Add 2½ oz. grated Gruyère cheese to this sauce. Place the fish in a baking dish, cover with the sauce, sprinkle with bread crumbs, moisten with melted butter, and brown in a hot oven.

POLLACK FILLETS BREADED ENGLISH STYLE COLIN (FILETS DE) PANÉS À L'ANGLAISE (P.)

Season the pollack fillets with salt and pepper, dip them in milk, roll them in flour, then carefully dip them in egg white beaten with the same amount of oil. Next, cover them with golden bread crumbs. Place the fillets in a baking pan (iron or tin-plated copper), moisten them with oil, and cook 8–10 min. in a very hot oven. Serve with Maître d'Hôtel Butter (p. 164). They can also be served with Tomato Sauce (p. 146) or potatoes cooked any fashion.

SLICED POLLACK RUSSIAN STYLE COLIN (TRONÇON DE) À LA RUSSE (J.)

Cold: Poach the fish as directed in the recipe for Sliced Pollack English Style (p. 284), let cool partially, drain, and remove the skin. Cover the pollack with Aspic Jelly (p. 168) after decorating it with some small truffle designs. Finish trimming with chopped jelly. Place the slice of pollack toward one end of the platter; at the other end make a dome of Russian Salad (p. 525). Cover with hard-boiled egg whites, yolks, and truffles (all chopped separately). Alternate the colors. Finish with jelly triangles and parsley. (Figure 168, Page 288.)

CONGER EEL IN THE POT CONGRE À LA COCOTTE (P.) (*For 5 persons*)

A common fish like the conger eel is excellent prepared the following way. Take a slice of eel weighing about 2 lb., cut off the fins, and brown it in butter in a Dutch oven or iron cocotte with 20 small onions around it. When everything is nicely browned, pour in 1 glass white wine, season with salt, pepper, and a *bouquet garni;* cover and cook slowly, in the oven or over a low flame, for 40 min. Serve the fish with the small onions and Potatoes English Style (p. 506) around it. Bind the cooking juice with a nut of butter mixed with flour and cover the eel with this sauce.

ROAST GILTHEAD[1] DAURADE RÔTIE (P.)

A gilthead, if large enough, is very good roasted. Cut a few shallow slits in the fish and cover it with a thin strip of bacon. Roast in a very hot oven, basting frequently with butter; when the fish is cooked, the bacon fat will have melted and browned it nicely. Place it in a platter, then add shallots and white wine to the cooking pan; reduce by ½, and add a piece of butter and 2 or 3 oz. cream. Sprinkle the fish with freshly ground pepper before serving. The same recipes given for pollack may be used for gilthead.

FRIED SMELTS ÉPERLANS FRITS EN BUISSON (P.)

Gut and clean the smelts, but do not let them soak in the water, which will soften the flesh. When they have been washed and drained, soak them 5 min. in cold, salted milk, remove, and roll in plenty of flour. Drop them, a few at a time, into plenty of very hot fat (preferably oil). Cook until crisp. Serve in a pile on a napkin with lemon quarters and parsley.

HADDOCK HADDOCK (M.)

This excellent dish comes to us from England and Scotland. The haddock should be cut into fillets and moderately smoked. There are many ways of preparing smoked haddock, of which the following are the most used.

HADDOCK IN MELTED BUTTER HADDOCK AU BEURRE FONDU (M.)

Plunge the fish into lightly salted boiling water (or in salted, boiling milk). When the liquid comes to a boil again, lower the heat and let the fish poach, covered and without boiling, 15 or 20 min., depending on the size of the fish. Arrange it on a fish platter and pour a few tbsp. cooking juice over it. Serve with a separate dish of melted butter and Potatoes English Style (p. 506).

Note: Boiled haddock may also be served with fresh butter or with Egg Sauce (p. 160).

GRILLED HADDOCK HADDOCK GRILLÉ (M.)

Salt the fish lightly and spread the surface with melted butter. Grill it over a low flame. Serve with melted butter and Potatoes English Style (p. 506).

[1] A delicate-fleshed European, but especially Mediterranean, fish, silvery-blue, with a golden crescent between the eyes.

MARINATED HERRING HARENGS MARINÉS (M.) (*For 5 persons*)

Cold: Take ½ cup white wine, ¼ cup vinegar, 2 medium-sized onions, 1 medium-sized carrot, 2 shallots, parsley, thyme, bay leaf, salt, and peppercorns. Cook 20 min., then pour, while still boiling, over 10 small herrings which have been well cleaned and wiped dry. Place the fish in an earthenware baking dish (avoid metal) and cover with a piece of oiled or buttered parchment paper. Cook 20 min. in the oven, remove, then pour a finger of oil over them and let cool; serve as they are in their marinade. (For cold hors d'oeuvres.)

HERRING IN MUSTARD SAUCE HARENGS SAUCE MOUTARDE (P.) (*For 6 persons*)

Clean 6 herrings, dip them in flour, and pan-fry in butter or in oil as for fish *à la meunière* (see p. 279). Serve with a white sauce (not bound with egg yolks) with 1 tsp. mustard added to it. The herring may be grilled instead of pan-fried, if preferred.

FRENCH SOLE or **DAB** LIMANDE (P.)

This fish, sometimes called lemon sole, though prepared like Dover sole, does not approach its delicacy, and the flesh is less firm. However, it is superior to plaice or flounder. Small French soles should be fried whole; the large ones can be cut into fillets and prepared like sole or cut into slices and prepared like burbot. Recipes given further on for sole may be used in preparing French sole.

BURBOT LOTTE (P.)

This is also a common, inexpensive fish, sold without head, entrails, or bones. It can be prepared with any of the recipes for pollack; served with good sauces, it makes a fine dish. Since the flesh renders a good deal of water while cooking, it does not require very much liquid for cooking. For the same reason it is not easily fried.

BURBOT IN RED WINE LOTTE AU VIN ROUGE (P.)

Cut a piece of burbot into fillets and poach them in ½ cup red wine, salt, pepper, shallots, and a *bouquet garni.* Meanwhile, cook 20 small onions and as many mushrooms in butter over a low fire. When the burbot is cooked, drain off the juice and reduce by ½. Then thicken it with 2 oz. butter mixed with 1 oz. flour. Bring to a boil a few times and darken the sauce with caramel coloring (because the cooked wine has an unattractive color). Let the fish, onions, and mushrooms simmer in this sauce a few minutes.

MACKEREL ALGÉRIENNE MAQUEREAU À L'ALGÉRIENNE (M.)

Bone the mackerels and season the insides with salt and pepper; fill them with 1 heaping tbsp. shredded pimentos stewed in oil. Line the bottom of a baking dish with Tomato Fondue (p. 194) seasoned with paprika and place the fish on top, one pressed tightly against another. Sprinkle with bread crumbs and moisten with oil. Bake in the oven. Decorate the mackerels with slices of lemon peeled to the flesh, and sprinkle with chopped parsley.

Note: Mackerel Algérienne can also be prepared the same way as Red Mullet Algéroise (p. 292). Though similarly named, these recipes differ considerably.

GRILLED MACKEREL MAÎTRE D'HÔTEL MAQUEREAUX GRILLÉS MAÎTRE D'HÔTEL (P.)

Take some very small mackerels, clean them carefully, wash and dry them, and roll them in flour. Sprinkle them with oil, place them on the grill, and salt several times, a little at a time; grill them on both sides. Mackerels weighing 4–6 oz. take 12–15 min. to cook; heavier ones must be slit in several places to let the heat penetrate. Serve them on a hot platter with lemon quarters and Maître d'Hôtel Butter (p. 164). If the mackerels are too large, the fillets may be sliced off and pan-fried or grilled.

Note: All fish may be garnished or served with steamed potatoes.

MACKEREL FILLETS MIREILLE MAQUEREAUX (FILETS DE) MIREILLE (P.)

Season the fillets, flour them, and pan-fry them in very hot oil. When they are cooked, arrange them on a platter. Change the oil in the pan and, when it is very hot, drop in a handful of chopped raw mushrooms and 1 onion, 1 shallot, and 1 clove garlic, all chopped. Brown everything well and pour over the fillets and then sprinkle them with a little boiling vinegar. Surround the fish with sliced tomatoes sautéed in oil, and sprinkle everything with chopped parsley.

MACKEREL WITH PARSLEY SAUCE MAQUEREAUX SAUCE PERSIL (P.)

Cut some large mackerels into thick slices, leaving out the heads, and cook with water, salt, vinegar, and a handful of parsley sprigs. Make a white sauce, using 3 parts milk and 1 part cooking juice of the fish, with a large pinch of chopped parsley and juice of ½ lemon added. The sauce should be highly seasoned. This recipe is for fish too large to grill.

MACKEREL WITH TOMATOES AND BREAD CRUMBS MAQUEREAUX AUX TOMATES, GRATINÉS (A.) (*For 4 persons*)

Take 1½ lb. tomatoes, 5 oz. butter, 4 small soft-roed mackerels weighing together a little more than 1 lb., 1 clove garlic, sifted bread crumbs, chopped parsley, salt, and pepper. Pour boiling water over the tomatoes and remove the skins. Heat the clove of garlic in 3 oz. butter without browning it, then remove. Brown the tomatoes in this garlic-flavored butter, sprinkle with parsley, salt, pepper, and continue to cook until the liquid is reduced. Clean the mackerels, split them along the back, and remove the heads and bones. Season the open fish, wrap them in oiled paper, and grill them. Butter the bottom of a baking dish with 1 oz. butter, put in half the tomatoes, place the grilled mackerels (with the paper removed) on top, cover with the rest of the tomatoes, and sprinkle with bread crumbs with small bits of the remaining butter on top. Brown 10 min. in the oven. This recipe can be used for other fish: fried weever and whiting, roast pollack, grilled gurnard, gilthead cooked in Court Bouillon (p. 277), etc.

WHITING COLBERT MERLAN À LA COLBERT (M.)

Cut open the back of the fish to remove the backbone. Dip the fish in milk, flour, beaten egg with a little oil, and bread crumbs. Fry it in deep fat. Arrange it on a long fish platter and fill the opening in the fish with Colbert Butter (p. 163). Garnish with fried parsley and lemon quarters. (Figure 169, Page 288.)

Fig. 168 - Sliced pollack russian style (p. 285).
Fig. 169 - Whiting Colbert (p. 288).

Fig. 168

Fig. 169

Fig. 170

Fig. 171

FRIED WHITING MERLANS FRITS (P.)

Dip the fish in salted milk and then roll in flour. Drop them into very hot deep fat, a few at a time, depending on the amount of hot fat, which you should not let cool; cook 8–10 min.; drain, salt, and serve immediately on a napkin with fried parsley and a lemon quarter per person. Fried fish must always be crisp, dry, and served immediately. Whiting can be prepared like sole and other fish, but the meat is delicate and cannot stand too much handling. The best method apart from frying is *à la meunière* (see p. 279).

WHITING AU GRATIN MERLANS AU GRATIN (P.)

Finely chop 6 oz. cleaned raw mushrooms; brown them in butter with 2 chopped shallots and some chopped parsley; add 1 tsp. flour, let brown slightly, and pour in ½ cup white wine, 1 tbsp. tomato purée, salt, and pepper. Cook 10 min. and pour over the whiting in a baking dish; sprinkle with bread crumbs and bits of butter and brown in the oven.

WHITING IN WHITE WINE MERLANS AU VIN BLANC (P.) (*For 4 persons*)

Poach 4 whitings in ½ bottle white wine, salt and pepper. Whiting weighing 5 or 6 oz. takes 10 min. to cook. Meanwhile, prepare a white sauce; when the whitings are poached, drain off the cooking juice and boil until reduced to about 5 or 6 tbsp. Add this juice to the white sauce and pour over the whitings. Any fish can be prepared this way.

SALT COD ARMENIAN STYLE MORUE À L'ARMÉNIENNE (M.)

Soak the cod well to remove the salt and slice the fillets into long thin strips. Season with paprika, and dip in beaten eggs and bread crumbs. Pan-fry in oil, browning the fish on both sides. Place the fish on a long platter on a layer of rather thick Tomato Fondue (p. 194). Garnish the top of the fillets with shredded pimento cooked in butter, mixed with finely shredded lemon peel blanched in hot oil and drained. Serve with a side dish of Rice Pilaf (p. 512).

SALT COD BACCALAO or BISCAÏENNE MORUE BACCALAO OR À LA BISCAÏENNE (M.) (*For 4 persons*)

Soak the cod to remove salt, cut into pieces, and poach. Put 4 oz. oil per lb. cooked cod into a casserole, and add 2 large sliced onions, 4 sliced, seeded pimentos, and 1 crushed clove of garlic. Brown lightly. Add 1½ lb. peeled, sliced tomatoes. Cook over a hot fire, adding a few tbsp. liquid from poaching the cod (or good fish stock), and thicken with some highly seasoned Flour Butter (p. 164). Now add the cod. Let simmer at low heat. Serve with bread croutons fried in oil and quarters of hard-boiled eggs, and on each piece of fish place shredded pimento. Moisten with a dash of oil, sprinkle with parsley, and serve with Rice Cuban Style (p. 512).

Note: If desired, potatoes can be cooked with the cod.

SALT COD BENEDICTINE MORUE À LA BÉNÉDICTINE (M.)

Prepare the cod as for Brandade (p. 290), adding ⅓ its weight in mashed potatoes before mixing in the oil. Place the cod in a buttered baking dish. Shape into a mound or dome and moisten with melted butter. Brown in the oven.

Fig. 170 - Brandade of salt cod (p. 290).
Fig. 171 - Red mullet Monte-Carlo (p. 293).

BRANDADE OF SALT COD MORUE (BRANDADE DE) (P.) (*For 3 persons*)

Poach 1 lb. very white cod without cooking it too well. Pick and flake it well; put it into a stewpan containing 3 oz. very hot oil, and mash it well with a spatula. Add a crushed clove of garlic and, little by little, while stirring vigorously, 6 oz. very hot olive oil. When the mixture has absorbed 6 or 8 tbsp. oil, mix in 3 tbsp. boiling milk. Continue adding oil and boiling milk until it contains 9 oz. oil (including the first 3 oz. put in before the garlic) and 4½–6 oz. milk and has the consistency of mashed potatoes. Taste and correct the seasoning, which should be a little peppery. Mold the Brandade into a pyramid or dome and garnish with small triangular bread croutons fried in oil. (Figure 170, Page 289.)

CREAMED CODFISH MORUE À LA CRÈME (P.)

The pieces of salt cod should be thoroughly soaked to remove as much salt as possible, then dipped in flour and cooked slowly in butter in a frying pan so that the heat penetrates the center of the cod. Cut open one of the pieces to see if the center is white; if it is pink, the codfish should be cooked a little longer. When it is cooked and just beginning to brown, turn onto a platter. Pour 6 oz. heavy cream per lb. cod into the frying pan, add a dash of vinegar, and boil 2 min. Pepper lightly, salt if necessary, and pour over the fish.

SALT COD WITH SPINACH or **SALT COD ROMAINE** MORUE AUX ÉPINARDS OR À LA ROMAINE (M.)

Poach the codfish and flake it. Cook some chopped spinach leaves in a pan with very hot oil and add diced anchovy fillets, a little crushed garlic (this is optional), and chopped parsley. Spread a layer of this spinach on the bottom of a baking dish and place the codfish flakes on top, cover with another layer of spinach, sprinkle with bread crumbs, moisten with oil, and brown in the oven.

SALT COD SPANISH STYLE MORUE À L'ESPAGNOLE (A.) (*For 6 persons*)

Take 1¼ lb. soaked cod, 1¼ lb. potatoes, 1 lb. tomatoes, ¾ lb. fresh red Spanish pimentos or 4 oz. powdered red Spanish pimento, 4 oz. olive oil, 1½ oz. onions, 1 clove garlic, 1 tbsp. flour, 1 tsp. freshly ground pepper, *bouquet garni* (parsley, thyme, bay leaf), sifted bread crumbs, salt.

Poach the codfish, drain it, and remove the bones; cut it into pieces; save 8 oz. cooking liquid. Peel the pimentos, slice into thin strips, and sprinkle with half the pepper. Chop the onions and brown them in oil; add the tomatoes (cut in pieces), garlic, *bouquet garni,* the rest of the pepper, and the cooking juice set aside. Cook 10 min., thicken with the flour, and cook for a few more minutes. Taste and finish seasoning with a little salt if necessary; strain the sauce. Meanwhile, steam the potatoes, peel and slice them. Line the bottom of a baking dish with a layer of potatoes, place a layer of cod on top, then a layer of pimento strips, and moisten with a little of the sauce. Continue making alternate layers until all the ingredients have been used, sprinkle with bread crumbs, and cook in the oven for about ½ hr., or until the liquid has almost completely evaporated.

This is an excellent preparation.

SALT COD WITH BEANS MORUE AUX HARICOTS (A.) (*For 6-8 persons*)

Take 1½ lb. well-soaked cod fillets, 1 lb. dried beans, 8 oz. butter, 6 oz. cream, 3 onions, 2 carrots, 2 medium-sized leeks, 1 clove garlic, 1 *bouquet garni* (parsley, thyme, bay leaf), blanched chopped parsley, salt, and pepper. Soak the beans for a day in cold water to make them swell and soften.

Cook the beans in salted water with the leeks, carrots, 1 onion, and the *bouquet garni.* Strain the beans and save the broth; keep both hot. At the same time, cook the codfish in water; remove the skin and bones; slice the fillets and keep hot. Cook the garlic and the remaining 2 onions in 4 oz. butter, without browning them, and add the broth from cooking the beans; salt, pepper, and cook until the liquid has been flavored with the garlic and onions. Strain it through a fine sieve and thicken it with the purée made by pressing a few tbsp. cooked beans through a sieve. Beat this sauce with a wire whisk, adding the rest of the butter and the cream; heat the sauce and test the seasoning, which should be somewhat hot. Place the sliced codfish and the beans in a dish, sprinkle with chopped parsley, and pour the sauce over it before serving.

Another way of serving this dish is to add 9 oz. concentrated tomato purée to the sauce at the same time as the bean purée. Cook until you have a tomato sauce of the desired consistency and finish with butter and cream.

SALT COD LANGUEDOCIENNE MORUE À LA LANGUEDOCIENNE (M.)

Poach square pieces of well-soaked salt cod in water. At the same time, brown some quartered potatoes in a pan with ½ butter and ½ oil. Season the potatoes with salt and pepper and, when they start to brown, sprinkle with flour. Mix them well while still on the fire, and add a little crushed garlic, a *bouquet garni,* and some chopped parsley. Add a little water and a few tbsp. cooking juice from the codfish. Cover the potatoes and finish cooking. A few minutes before serving, put the squares of codfish, well drained, into the pan with the potatoes and simmer together a few moments. Serve in a timbale or in a deep platter.

Note: This dish can be prepared entirely with oil. It is also called Salt Cod Carcassonnaise (*Morue à la carcassonnaise*).

SALT COD HOME STYLE MORUE À LA MÉNAGÈRE (P.)

Soak the cod in water 24 hr. to remove the salt, changing the water several times. Cut the codfish into small pieces and poach it in fresh water without boiling. Just as it is ready to boil, lower the flame and let it cook 10 min. Before cooking the fish, boil some potatoes with the jackets on and make a Béchamel Sauce (p. 146) with 1 large chopped onion, cooked in butter without browning, added to it. Thin the sauce with a little of the cooking water from the codfish. Peel and slice the potatoes; flake the codfish on top, throwing away skin and bones, and pour the sauce over all, after seasoning it with a little pepper.

SAUTÉED SALT COD WITH TOMATOES MORUE SAUTÉE AUX TOMATES (P.) (*For 5 persons*)

After soaking the salt cod and cutting it into squares, dip it in flour and pan-fry in very hot butter. But do not cook too quickly; it should take 12–15 min. Remove the fish to a plate and put 1 lb. (per 2 lb. cod) tomatoes, peeled, drained, and chopped into big pieces, into the pan with the butter used in cooking the codfish. When the tomatoes are cooked, season, but not too strongly, with salt, pepper, chopped parsley, and, if desired, a little finely chopped garlic. Cook another minute and pour over the codfish.

GRAY MULLET VINTIMILLE MULET À LA VINTIMILLE (P.) (*For 4 persons*)

Take a gray mullet weighing about 1½ lb.; cut incisions on both sides and place it in a long buttered baking dish; surround the fish with rather thick slices of peeled zucchini, sprinkle both fish and vegetable with chopped herbs, and season everything highly. Pour melted butter over it and cook in the oven ¾ hr.; serve as is in the baking dish. If zucchini is not available, use eggplant.

SKATE WITH BLACK BUTTER RAIE AU BEURRE NOIR (P.)

Cut the skate into pieces and cook it in a Court Bouillon well flavored with vegetables (p. 277) ; drain, skin and trim, and place the fish on a long platter. Heat a large piece of butter in a pan until it turns black. Season the skate with salt, pepper, chopped parsley, and capers. Pour the black butter over the fish, then drop a few tbsp. vinegar into the same pan and pour over the fish.

There are only a few ways to serve skate, which is a very good fish.

RED MULLET ALGÉROISE ROUGET À L'ALGÉROISE (M.)

Cover the bottom of a baking dish with Tomato Fondue (p. 194) seasoned with a little powdered saffron and mixed with chopped fennel. Arrange small red mullets on this layer of tomato. Season with salt and pepper, add a little white wine, and sprinkle oil on top of the fish. Cook in the oven. When the red mullets are cooked, sprinkle with bread crumbs and oil and brown lightly in the oven. Serve with chopped parsley and a slice of lemon on each fish.

RED MULLET EGYPTIAN STYLE ROUGET À L'ÉGYPTIENNE (P.) (*For 6 persons*)

Professional chefs prepare paper cases cut the same size as the fish for this dish. We recommend the following method. Sauté in oil 1 lb. peeled, quartered tomatoes; season with salt, pepper, chopped parsley, and a pinch of crushed garlic. Also sauté in oil 6 or 8 small red mullets, cleaned and dipped in flour. Use half the tomatoes to make a layer in the bottom of a long baking dish and place the mullets on top; cover the fish with the rest of the tomatoes, sprinkle with bread crumbs, and brown in a very hot oven.

GRILLED RED MULLET WITH FENNEL ROUGET GRILLÉ, AU FENOUIL (A.)

Place 12 sprigs of fresh fennel on the grill of a dripping pan, and on top place the mullets, which have been cleaned, slit in several places, seasoned, and turned in a pan with clarified butter; grill them on both sides at low heat, taking care not to burn the fennel and turning the fish delicately so as not to break them. Arrange them on a hot plate and cover them with Maître d'Hôtel Butter (p. 164) strongly flavored with lemon juice. Red mullets prepared this way will have a much better flavor than if cooked in the traditional manner, which is to marinate them in oil, lemon juice, and fennel and then grill them.

RED MULLET MONT-BRY ROUGET MONT-BRY (M.)

Half cook the red mullets in a pan with oil. Place them in a long baking dish on top of a layer of Dry Duxelles (p. 176) mixed with chopped parsley and

Fig. 172 - Sole fillets caprice (p. 294).
Fig. 173 - Timbale of sole fillets Escoffier (p. 296).

Fig. 172

Fig. 173

Fig. 174

Fig. 175

seasoned with paprika. On each red mullet place 2 slices of tomato and 2 slices of zucchini, both cooked in oil. Surround with a ribbon of Tomato Sauce (p. 146). Sprinkle with bread crumbs and oil and brown lightly in the oven.

RED MULLET MONTE CARLO ROUGET À LA MONTE-CARLO (P.)

Place grilled mullets on slices of buttered toast cut to the same size and shape as the fish and spread with Anchovy Butter (p. 163). Serve with Potato Straws (p. 509) and lemon slices. (Figure 171, Page 289.)

RED MULLET NIÇOISE ROUGET À LA NIÇOISE (M.)

Cold: Brown some small red mullets, seasoned with salt and pepper, in olive oil. Place them in a baking dish. Cover them with a not-too-thick Tomato Fondue (p. 194) seasoned with crushed garlic and chopped tarragon. Finish cooking slowly in the oven. Decorate the mullets with anchovy fillets arranged in a grillwork pattern and lemon slices. Moisten with a few drops of lemon juice, and chill well before serving.

JOHN DORY SAINT-PIERRE (J.)

This very delicate fish is not much sought after because of its hideous appearance. All the recipes given for brill, turbot, and sole can be used in preparing John Dory. However, it is preferable to use only the fillets.

SOLE BERCY SOLE À LA BERCY (M.) (*For 2 persons*)

Proportions for a sole weighing about 1 lb.: Season the fish with salt and pepper and place it in a buttered baking dish lined with chopped shallots and parsley. Pour some reduced fish stock (or, simply, dry white wine) over it. Dot with 1 tbsp. butter divided into bits and cook in the oven, basting frequently. When the sole is cooked, pour off the cooking juice and reduce it in a small pan, add 1 tbsp. butter and a few drops of lemon juice, and pour over the fish. Glaze in a very hot oven.

SOLE BOISTELLE SOLE BOISTELLE (M.)

This is a variation of Sole Bonne Femme, below. Place the sole in a buttered baking dish and surround it with thick slices of raw mushrooms. Season with salt and pepper and moisten with very reduced fish stock. Cook in the oven, basting frequently. Sprinkle with chopped parsley before serving.

SOLE BONNE FEMME SOLE BONNE FEMME (P.)

Sprinkle the bottom of a buttered baking dish with 2 oz. sliced raw mushrooms, 1 chopped shallot, and some chopped parsley. Place on top the prepared sole—that is, the black skin removed, the head cut off, trimmed, and well washed. Pour ½ glass white wine over the fish, salt and pepper, cover with a buttered paper, and poach in the oven. Drain off the liquid and reduce well, then add ½ cup Hollandaise Sauce (p. 151). Cover the fish with this sauce and glaze it very quickly under the broiler or in a very hot oven, so the top will be golden but the sauce won't have time to boil and separate.

SOLE FILLETS BOURGUIGNONNE SOLES (FILETS DE) À LA BOURGUIGNONNE (E.)

Cook some thin onion rings in butter and use them to line the bottom of a buttered baking dish. Place the fillets lengthwise on top; surround them with

Fig. 174 - Grilled sole (p. 297).
Fig. 175 - Sole fillets La Vallière (p. 298).

sliced mushrooms sautéed in butter; season with freshly ground pepper; pour in 3 oz. Mâcon wine (a red Burgundy), and poach in the oven. Pour off the cooking liquid, reduce by ⅔, bind with a little butter mixed with flour, and finish with 1 oz. butter. Cover the fish with this sauce and glaze in the oven.

SOLE FILLETS CAPRICE SOLES (FILETS DE) CAPRICE (P.)

Dice finely 1 tbsp. carrots and 1 tbsp. truffles and cook 5 min. in butter in a covered saucepan; add 1 small glass Madeira and let simmer 2 min.; pour this over the fillets, which should be folded in half and seasoned with salt and cayenne pepper. Poach in the oven. Reduce the cooking juice, then add a few tbsp. Joinville Sauce (p. 152) and heavy cream. Cover the fillets with this sauce without straining it, and decorate each fillet with ½ tomato sautéed in butter; in each tomato place a cooked mushroom cap and a little chopped parsley. (Figure 172, Page 292.)

SOLE FILLETS CARDINAL I SOLES (FILETS DE) CARDINAL (A.) *(For 4 persons)*

Take 1 pt. water, 1 cup white wine, 5 oz. butter, 1 oz. champagne brandy, 1 oz. stale bread crumbs, ½ oz. salt, ⅓ oz. flour, a few peppercorns, 12 crayfish, 2 soles weighing together about 1½ lb., 1 whiting weighing about ½ lb., 1 egg, 1 egg yolk, 1 medium-sized carrot, 1 medium-sized onion, a *bouquet garni,* milk, lemon juice, nutmeg, cayenne, red coloring.

Soak the crayfish in milk 2 hr. Prepare a Court Bouillon with the water, wine, brandy, carrot and onion sliced, *bouquet garni*, salt and pepper and cook ½ hr. (see p. 277). Clean the crayfish and drop them into the boiling Court Bouillon; remove them after cooking 15 min. Save the Court Bouillon. After removing the tails, scrape the meat from 8 crayfish, keeping the shells intact; remove the shells from the tails and keep them hot. Pound the crayfish meat and waste shells in a mortar with 2 oz. butter and strain through a sieve. Save this Crayfish Butter for later use with the sauce.

Take 4 oz. whiting and pound it in a mortar with bread crumbs soaked in milk; add 1 oz. butter, 1 whole egg, salt, and a little nutmeg; pound it again, then strain this forcement through a sieve. Slice the fillets from the sole and cover them with the Whiting Forcemeat; sprinkle with a little lemon juice, and fold the fillets in half. Put the unused parts of the sole and whiting into the Court Bouillon used for cooking the crayfish, and cook until the liquid is reduced by ½; strain. Place the small end of the sole fillets in the empty crayfish shells that you have saved, and place these in a flat-bottomed pan. Pour the reduced Court Bouillon over the fish, cover the pan, and cook 10 min.; keep hot.

Make the Cardinal Sauce: mix the flour with the rest of the butter, moisten with the reduced Court Bouillon in which the fillets were cooked; boil a few minutes. Remove from the stove and bind the sauce with the egg yolk, then mix in the Crayfish Butter and season to taste with cayenne pepper and lemon juice; add the red coloring. Heat. (See also p. 148.)

Arrange the crayfish shells filled with the sole fillets in a ring on a platter, place the crayfish tails in the center, and cover the tails and the part of the sole outside the shells with the Cardinal Sauce. Serve the remainder of the sauce in a sauceboat.

As a variation, the fillets may be served on a ring of the Whiting Forcemeat. Put the forcemeat into a ring mold and cook in a *bain-marie.* Unmold onto a platter and garnish the top with the sole fillets. In the center of the ring, place a salpicon (tiny cubes) of mushrooms, pike quenelles, and crayfish tails bound with Cardinal Sauce.

SOLE FILLETS CARDINAL II soles (filets de) cardinal (P.)

Poach sole fillets, folded in half, with a glass of good sauterne. Cook some crayfish in a Court Bouillon (p. 277), and cook ½ lb. mushrooms the usual way. Reduce the cooking liquid from the sole and the crayfish and add it to a fine cream sauce made somewhat thick because of this addition. To this sauce add some Crayfish Butter (p. 164), season with red pepper or cayenne pepper, and add red coloring. Arrange the sole fillets on a long fish platter. Surround with crayfish meat and the mushrooms; coat with the sauce. The platter may also be decorated with 4 whole crayfish, if they are readily available.

SOLE FILLETS CHAUCHAT soles (filets de) chauchat (E.)

Fold the fillets and poach them with butter and lemon juice. Cover the bottom of a platter with Mornay Sauce (p. 152), arrange the fillets in the center, and surround them with thick slices of small boiled potatoes; cover the fillets with Mornay Sauce and glaze in the oven.

SOLE FILLETS CHEVALIÈRE soles (filets de) à la chevalière (E.)

Fold the fillets and stuff them, pointed end first, into large crayfish shells. Poach in white wine and butter. In the center of a large service plate, shape into a pyramid a julienne of lobster tail, mushrooms, and truffles bound with a little Lobster Sauce (see p. 152). Arrange the sole fillets around this pyramid so that the crayfish tails stand upright, and encircle with a ribbon of White-Wine Sauce (p. 155). Border the plate with baked palmettes made of Puff Paste (p. 544).

SOLE FILLETS CHOISY soles (filets de) choisy (M.)

Fold the fillets and cook them in dry Marsala with mushroom peelings. Place each fillet into half a heart of braised lettuce (using fish stock, not bouillon). Arrange them on a molded ring of fish forcemeat. Fill the center of the ring with Pike Forcemeat balls made with truffles (p. 175).

Sauce: Add reduced Espagnole Sauce (p. 137) made with fish stock, buttered and strained, to the cooking juice from the fillets.

SOLE FILLETS CUBAT soles (filets de) cubat (E.)

Poach the fillets with the cooking juice from mushrooms and butter. Spread the bottom of a platter with mushroom purée and arrange the fillets on top, with 2 slices of truffle on each fillet; cover with Mornay Sauce (p. 152) and glaze.

SOLE DUGLÉRÉ sole à la dugléré (M.)

Slice the sole crosswise into even portions and place in a buttered pan lined with 2 peeled, pressed, diced tomatoes and 1 tsp. chopped parsley. Season with salt and pepper. Add ½ medium-sized sliced onion, a sprig of thyme, and a small piece of bay leaf. Sprinkle 1 tbsp. melted butter over the fish and add 1½ oz. dry white wine. Cook with the pan covered. Drain the sole and arrange on a platter. Reduce the cooking sauce and bind with 2 tbsp. Fish Velouté (p. 147); remove from the stove and add 2 tbsp. butter. Cover the fish with this sauce.

Note: It is an established principle that all fish prepared *à la Duglêré* should be cut crosswise in thick slices. However, in the case of sole, the fish may be left whole. Instead of binding the cooking sauce with Velouté, it may be thickened with a mixture of butter and flour, or even, according to certain chefs, with a mixture of flour and water (called *à la meunière*). Also, this preparation may be seasoned with a tiny pinch of crushed garlic.

SOLE FILLETS DUSE SOLES (FILETS DE) À LA DUSE (E.)

Spread the fillets with fish forcemeat (p. 173); fold them and poach in fish stock. Place them in the bottom of a buttered Savarin mold (round mold with a hollow center) large enough to hold the necessary number of fillets. Finish filling the mold with Rice Pilaf (p. 512) cooked in fish stock, pressing it down lightly. Unmold immediately onto a round plate, cover with Mornay Sauce (p. 152), and glaze. After removing the plate from the oven, fill the center of the molded fish and rice with shrimps well bound with White-Wine Sauce (p. 155), and sprinkle this garnish with chopped truffles.

TIMBALE OF SOLE FILLETS ESCOFFIER SOLES (TIMBALE DE FILETS DE) ESCOFFIER (E.)

Cold Dish: For an ordinary-sized mold, prepare 12 medium-sized fillets to be made into *paupiettes*—that is, spread with a mixture and rolled up. Spread 6 of these fillets with a fine fish forcemeat (see p. 173) finished with Lobster Butter (p. 164) and Red Butter (p. 163); spread the other 6 with the same fish forcemeat with very black truffle purée added. Roll them up into "birds." Poach them in a good fish stock and let cool in the cooking liquid. When they are cold, drain them, wipe them dry, trim the ends, and cut each roll crosswise into 4 round slices. Line a round mold lightly (a mold with 2 levels, an outer ring and a higher dome center) with Aspic Jelly (p. 168) and place on ice to set. Lay in the circles of sole, dipped in half-set jelly to assure their sticking almost immediately to the other jelly in the ring part. Arrange them according to the same color, or in alternating colors, so that the mold will have a neat design. Finish filling the mold (the dome) with cold crayfish mousse (see p. 177). Keep the mold on ice 2 hr. and unmold, just before serving, onto a cut-glass platter or silver timbale. (Figure 173, Page 292.)

SOLE BIRDS FAVART SOLES (PAUPIETTES DE) FAVART (M.)

Spread the fillets with Pike Forcemeat seasoned with chopped tarragon (p. 175), and roll into birds. Poach in sauterne. Place each sole bird in a small pastry boat half filled with chopped creamed mushrooms. Cover the birds with Nantua Sauce (p. 152) made with the reduced cooking liquid from the sole birds. Sprinkle with Parmesan cheese and brown in the oven.

SOLE FERMIÈRE or **SOLE RUSSIAN STYLE** SOLE À LA FERMIÈRE OF À LA RUSSE (M.)

Season the sole with salt and pepper and place in a buttered pan on a layer of carrots, celery, leeks, onions, and parsley roots sliced thin and cooked in butter. Pour in some reduced fish stock. Bring to a boil on top of the stove, then finish cooking in the oven, basting often. Before serving, add 1 tbsp. fresh butter and a dash of lemon juice.

Fig. 176 - Sole fillets marquise (p. 299).
Fig. 177 - Golden sole meunière (p. 300).

Fig. 176

Fig. 177

Fig. 178

Fig. 179

SOLE FILLETS FLORENTINE SOLES (FILETS DE) À LA FLORENTINE (E.)

Poach the fillets in fish stock and butter. Place them on a bed of leaf spinach first lightly blanched, then cooked in butter; cover with Mornay Sauce (p. 152), and glaze.

SOLE GANDILLON SOLE GANDILLON (C.)

Lightly brown the sole in butter; surround with peeled, drained, crushed tomatoes cooked in butter with a little crushed garlic and some shallots. On the center of the sole place some shredded sorrel leaves cooked in butter till soft and some slices of lemon peeled to the flesh and seeded. Brown plenty of butter, then throw in a small amount of fresh white bread crumbs, and as soon as they are nicely browned, pour butter and crumbs over the fish. Serve immediately so that the dish will arrive at the table with the butter still bubbling hot.

JELLIED SOLE FILLETS WITH TOMATOES SOLES (FILETS DE) À LA GELÉE AUX TOMATES (P.) (*For 6 persons*)

Cold Dish: Fold 12 sole fillets in half and poach 10 min. in white wine with a little chopped shallot and parsley; let cool. Then season some tomato halves, let them macerate in oil and vinegar, and then roll into balls by squeezing in a cloth. Place the fillets on a silver platter with the tomatoes on top and cover with Aspic Jelly lightly tinted pink with red coloring (p. 168); let set, and surround the platter with a ring of scalloped lemon slices.

SOLE FILLETS GRANDGOUSIER SOLES (FILETS DE) GRANDGOUSIER (Gi.) (*For 4 persons*)

Slice the fillets from 2 soles, flatten them, and soak in cold water, then dry them, fold in half, and poach in a fine dry white wine with 2 tbsp. champagne brandy and 8 oz. sliced raw mushrooms. When the fillets are poached, drain them and reduce the cooking liquid by ¾. To this liquid add 1 tbsp. tomato purée and 6 oz. fresh tomatoes skinned, drained, and cut into small pieces. Cook until creamy, remove from the stove, add butter, and season with a little paprika. Place the fillets on a long hot platter, cover copiously with this sauce, then around them place 8 small artichoke quarters, first blanched 15 min., then cooked, covered, in butter. Stick a shrimp into each artichoke quarter and surround the platter with crescents made of Puff Paste (p. 544).

GRILLED SOLE SOLE GRILLÉE (M.)

Cut a few shallow slits in the sole; season with salt and pepper, roll in flour, sprinkle oil or melted butter on the surface, and cook on a grill at low heat. Place the fish on a very hot platter and garnish with fresh parsley. Serve with Maître d'Hôtel Butter (p. 164), Shallot Butter (p. 164), or any sauce usually served with grilled fish. Border with parsley and lemon slices. (Figure 174, Page 293.)

SOLE FILLETS INDIAN STYLE I SOLE (FILETS DE) À L'INDIENNE (M.)

Cut each fillet into 2 or 3 pieces and fry in clarified butter. Place the pieces on Rice Indian Style (p. 512). Serve with a separate boat of Curry Sauce (p. 150).

Note: Dishes called *à l'indienne*, or "Indian Style," may be made in different ways. Following is another method of preparing curried sole fillets.

Fig. 178 - Sole fillets normande (p. 301).
Fig. 179 - Sole fillets Saint-Germain (p. 302).

SOLE FILLETS INDIAN STYLE II SOLE (FILETS DE) À L'INDIENNE (M.)

(*For 2 persons*)

Take a sole weighing about 1 lb. and slice the fillets into narrow strips. Roll up these strips to form small "birds" and secure them with string or thread. Prepare the following sauce separately. Cook 1 medium-sized chopped onion in butter without browning. When the onion is almost cooked, add ½ small diced potato, 1 skinned tomato chopped in large pieces, a little crushed garlic, a little cardamom, and ½ tbsp. chopped parsley. Sprinkle with 1 tbsp. powdered curry, mix, moisten with 9 oz. coconut milk (or almond milk), season, and cook 20 min. Finish with 3 oz. fresh cream and a dash of lemon juice. Fifteen min. before serving, place the sole birds in this sauce and simmer till cooked. Place in a timbale and serve with a platter or vegetable dish of Rice Indian Style (p. 512).

SOLE FILLETS JOINVILLE I SOLES (FILETS DE) JOINVILLE (P.)

Spread the fillets with Whiting Forcemeat (see under Sole Fillets Cardinal I, p. 294), fold in half, and poach in fish stock. Arrange them in a circle, each overlapping the next, and in the center place a garnish of shrimps, mushrooms, and truffles. Cover everything with Shrimp Sauce (p. 159) with the reduced fish stock added to it. Stick a pink shrimp into each fillet and place a few slices of truffle in the center.

SOLE FILLETS JOINVILLE II SOLES (FILETS DE) JOINVILLE (E.)

Fold the fillets and poach them in the cooking liquid from mushrooms and butter. Stick a small crayfish claw into each fillet and arrange the fillets in a circle, with the pointed ends overlapping on top. In the center place a Joinville Garnish (p. 182) and cover both garnish and sole fillets with Joinville Sauce (p. 152); on each fillet place a slice of truffle brushed with Meat Glaze (p. 135).

SOLE FILLETS JOINVILLE III SOLES (FILETS DE) JOINVILLE (E.)

This is the old method. Poach the fillets, keeping them very white, and stick a crayfish claw into each. In the center of a platter shape a salpicon Joinville (tiny cubes of shrimp, truffle, and mushroom bound with somewhat thick Joinville Sauce, p. 152) into a dome and cover with more Joinville Sauce. Arrange the fillets around the dome, with the pointed ends overlapping on top; place a slice of very black truffle on each fillet and border the platter with thin, scalloped slices of lemon. In this method of dressing, only the garnish is covered with sauce, while the sole fillets form a white ring around it.

SOLE FILLETS LA VALLIÈRE SOLES (FILETS DE) LA VALLIÈRE (E.)

Spread the fillets with fish forcemeat (see p. 173), fold them, stud with truffles (make small incisions in the fillets to hold thin slices of truffles), and poach in fish stock. Arrange them in a circle, each overlapping the next, on a shallow border of Mousseline Forcemeat (p. 173) poached in advance; cover lightly with Normande Sauce (p. 153) and place a slice of truffle on each fillet. Into the center of the ring pour a garnish composed of poached, sliced soft roe, poached oysters, crayfish tails, and very white small mushrooms, bound with Normande Sauce finished with Crayfish Butter (p. 164). (Figure 175, Page 293.)

SOLE FILLETS MÂCONNAISE SOLE (FILETS DE) À LA MÂCONNAISE (M.)

Fold the fillets. Poach 2 of them in fish stock with white wine and 2 in fish stock with red Mâcon (a Burgundy). Arrange them on a platter, alternating them. Cover the fillets cooked in white wine with White-Wine Sauce (p. 155) and those in red wine with a red-wine sauce finished with Espagnole Sauce (p. 137) (made with fish stock) and Anchovy Butter (p. 163). Garnish with small mushrooms sautéed in butter and fried mussels. Made with Bordeaux, this dish is called Sole Fillets Bordelaise.

SOLE FILLETS MAGISSON SOLES (FILETS DE) MAGISSON (M.)

Dip the fillets in egg and bread crumbs mixed with chopped parsley. Cook them in butter. Place them on a long platter on a bed of chopped onion cooked in butter until soft. For the sauce, brown in butter mushrooms cut in julienne strips, at the last minute adding gherkins cut the same way. Pour this piping hot over the fish. Squeeze lemon juice over the fillets and sprinkle with chopped parsley.

SOLE FILLETS MANON SOLES (FILETS DE) MANON (E.)

Spread the fillets smoothly with fish forcemeat (see p. 173), roll them into "birds," and poach in the cooking liquid from mushrooms. Arrange them in a circle on a platter bordered with a band of Potatoes Duchesse (p. 507) (pressed from a pastry bag with a tube with a large fluted opening), brushed with beaten egg, and browned in the oven in advance. In the center of the platter make a garnish of asparagus tips, truffles and mushrooms cut in julienne strips, all mixed with butter; lightly cover the sole birds with Fines Herbes Sauce (p. 150) without spilling any on the garnish.

SOLE FILLETS MARGUERY SOLES (FILETS DE) MARGUERY (M.)

Poach the fillets in fish stock with reduced white wine. Drain them, wipe them dry, and place them in a baking dish. Surround the fish with a garnish of mussels poached in white wine (then well drained) and shelled shrimps. Cover with White-Wine Sauce (p. 155) with the fish stock, reduced to a glaze, added. Glaze quickly in a very hot oven or under a broiler.

SOLE FILLETS MARQUISE or **CROUSTADE OF SOLE MARQUISE**

SOLE (FILETS DE) MARQUISE OR CROUSTADE DE SOLE MARQUISE (M.)

Fold the fillets, season with salt and pepper, dip in flour, and fry in hot butter (*à la meunière*). Lay them in a ring in a deep pie crust with the edges slightly raised. In the center place a ragout of crayfish tails and sliced mushrooms and truffles bound with Royale Sauce (below). On this ragout shape a mound of very small Pike Forcemeat balls (p. 175) made with Crayfish Butter (p. 164). Cover the sole fillets with golden fish glaze to which a little Madeira and butter have been added. Serve with a separate dish of Royale Sauce. (Fig. 176, P. 296.)

Royale Sauce: Add to some well-strained Normande Sauce (p. 153) 3 tbsp. mushrooms and truffles, cut in julienne strips, cooked in sherry.

SOLE FILLETS MAZARIN SOLES (FILETS DE) MAZARIN (M.)

Dip the sole fillets in flour, beaten egg with a little olive oil, and bread crumbs and fry in clarified butter. Place them on a long fish platter, and on top of the fillets lay a row of sliced zucchini sautéed in butter, tomato halves also sautéed in butter, and slices of truffle. Moisten with several tbsp. Maître d'Hôtel Butter (p. 164) seasoned with paprika.

SOLE MEUNIÈRE or **SOLE IN BUTTER** SOLE À LA MEUNIÈRE (M.)

Season the sole with salt and pepper and dredge with flour. Cook in a frying pan of very hot butter. Brown well on both sides. Place the sole on a very hot fish platter. Sprinkle with chopped parsley, a dash of lemon juice, and, just before serving, pour over it the cooking butter heated until almost black (having added a little fresh butter before heating it). Serve immediately, while the butter is still bubbling.

GOLDEN SOLE MEUNIÈRE SOLE À LA MEUNIÈRE DORÉE (M.)

Same preparation as above. Serve the sole garnished simply with lemon quarters and no brown butter. (Figure 177, Page 296.)

Note: All fish prepared *à la meunière*, or pan-fried in butter, should be served as simply as possible. It is a waste to decorate them with affected garnishes such as slices of lemon decorated with radish roses, beets, parsley, and other flowery trimmings hardly compatible with this recipe. However, when feasible, before the brown butter is poured over it, the fish may be moistened with a little golden fish glaze or Espagnole Sauce (p. 137) made with fish stock (well skimmed and reduced). This addition will bring out the flavor of the dish.

SOLE MEUNIÈRE WITH VARIOUS GARNISHES SOLE À LA MEUNIÈRE AVEC GARNITURES DIVERSES (M.)

Sole, either whole or filleted, prepared as above, may be garnished in various ways. Here are a few of the garnishes most often used:

Sole Meunière with Eggplant: Slices of eggplant sautéed in butter.

Sole Meunière Catalane: Mounds of shredded pimento alternated with Tomato Fondue (p. 194) and diced potatoes sautéed in butter.

Sole Meunière with Mushrooms: Sliced mushrooms sautéed in butter. (Figure 236, Plate 44.)

Sole Meunière with Cucumbers: Cucumbers cut in the shape of small balls, cooked in butter.

Sole Meunière with Zucchini: Zucchini slices sautéed in butter.

Sole Meunière with Tomatoes: Seeded tomato halves sautéed in butter.

SOLE FILLETS MURAT SOLE (FILETS DE) MURAT (M.) (*For 2 persons*)

Slice the fillets from a sole weighing 1 lb. and cut the fillets into strips. Season them, dip them in flour, and sauté in butter *à la meunière.* In another pan sauté in butter 1 medium-sized diced potato and 1 diced artichoke bottom (previously blanched). Mix the sole fillets and the vegetables in one frying pan. Pile them up on a round platter and on top place 4 tomato slices sautéed in oil. Sprinkle with chopped parsley, add a dash of lemon juice, and pour a little brown butter over everything.

SOLE FILLETS NEWBURG SOLE (FILETS DE) NEW-BURG (E.)

Take a cooked lobster and prepare Lobster Newburg (p. 318), taking care to cut the tail into as many slices as there are sole fillets; keep these slices hot. Dice the remainder of the lobster meat and add to the sauce. Fold the fillets in half and poach in fish stock. Arrange the fillets overlapping in a circle with a slice of lobster on each fillet; cover with the lobster sauce with the diced lobster meat added to it.

Fig. 180 - Sole Suchet (p. 302).
Fig. 181 - Sole fillets Urbain-Dubois (p. 302).
Fig. 182 - Salmon trout Chivry (p. 313).

Fig. 180

Fig. 181

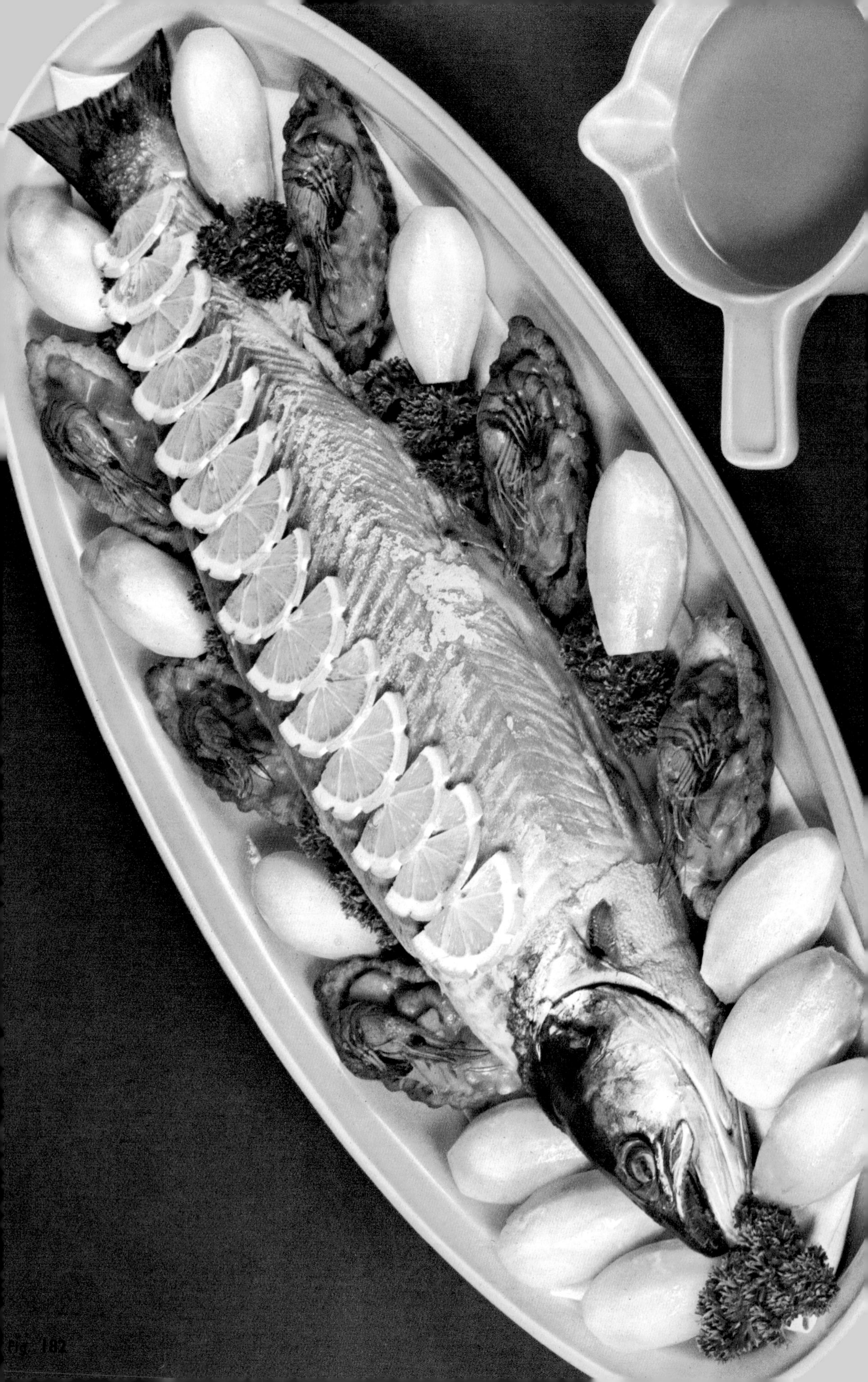

Fig. 182

Fig. 183

Fig. **184**

Fig. **185**

SOLE FILLETS NORMANDE SOLE (FILETS DE) NORMANDE (E.) (*For 2 persons*)

Proportions for a sole weighing about 1 lb.: Poach the fillets in fish stock and mushroom juice. Drain well and surround the fillets with poached, trimmed mussels and shrimps. Make a line down the middle of the platter with 4 poached oysters and 4 fine mushroom caps. Place in the oven for a few moments, tilt the platter upon removing to pour off any liquid, and cover garnish and fish smoothly with Normande Sauce (p. 153). Complete the garnish with a few truffle slices placed in a line across the top, and, around the platter, small pastry crescents, fried gudgeons, and 4 medium-sized crayfish. (The truffle slices are optional.) (Figure 178, Page 297.)

Note: We regret that we could not find crayfish to illustrate this dish. See Boiled Crayfish, p. 315.

BREADED, SAUTÉED JULIENNE OF SOLE FILLETS SOLES (JULIENNE DE FILETS DE) PANÉE, SAUTÉE (A.) (*For 4 persons*)

Take 1 cup white wine, ½ lb. butter, ⅘ cup fine, fresh bread crumbs, ⅘ cup water, 4 oz. mushrooms, ¼ cup heavy cream, 1 tbsp. flour, 2 medium-sized soles providing approximately 1 lb. fillets, 2 fresh egg yolks, 1 medium-sized carrot, 1 medium-sized onion, 1 *bouquet garni,* four spices (see *Note,* below), salt, and pepper. Slice the fillets from the sole and save the bones and trimmings. Put into a casserole: wine, water, sole bones and trimmings, mushrooms, carrot, onion, *bouquet garni,* salt, pepper, and a little of the spices; let cook until a sufficiently concentrated fish stock is obtained. Cook the sole fillets in this. Slice the fillets into julienne strips. Brown the bread crumbs in 5 oz. butter and then add the julienne of fish, sautéeing the fish and bread crumbs until all the slices of sole are covered with crumbs. Mix the flour with a little butter, moisten this mixture with the cooking liquid from the fillets, reduce further if necessary, bind this sauce with the egg yolks, and finish with the remainder of the butter and the cream. Heat. Serve with the sauce in a separate sauceboat and small dishes of grated Parmesan and Gruyère cheese.

Note: Four spices: mixture of 5 oz. white pepper, 1 dessertspoon powdered clove, 1 oz. ginger, 1⅛ oz. grated nutmeg.

SOLE PORTUGUESE STYLE SOLE À LA PORTUGAISE (M.)

Season the sole with salt and pepper and cook it in oil. Place it in a baking dish. Surround with Tomato Fondue (p. 194) cooked in oil, strongly seasoned with chopped onion and a little crushed garlic. Sprinkle with bread crumbs, moisten with oil, and glaze quickly in a hot oven. Sprinkle with chopped parsley.

FAN OF SOLE FILLETS RENAISSANCE SOLES (ÉVENTAIL DE FILETS DE) RENAISSANCE (P.) (*For 6 persons*)

Cold Dish: Take 12 sole fillets, 6 oz. Chaud-Froid Sauce (p. 149), 1 lb. vegetables. Poach the sole fillets in a Court Bouillon made with the bones, white wine, and jelly (p. 277). After cooking, press the fillets until they are very flat; cover with the sauce thickened with cream; arrange the fillets on a bed of semolina shaped like a fan. Decorate the fillets with bits of truffles and glaze with Aspic Jelly (p. 168). Garnish each space with a band of truffled jelly, and, to finish, alongside the fillets arrange a vegetable salad mixed with mayonnaise. Trim this dish artistically, making a border of jelly or lemon slices.

Fig. 183 - Salmon trout norwegian style (p. 314).
Fig. 184 - Turbot Cambacérès (p. 304).
Fig. 185 - Turbot parisienne (p. 304).

SOLE DELIGHTS SAINTE-ALLIANCE SOLES (DÉLICES DE) SAINTE-ALLIANCE (C.)

Place a fine crayfish tail inside each folded fillet and cover each with a thin slice of salmon cooked in Chablis. Nantua Sauce (p. 152).

Garnish: Fluffy Pike Forcemeat balls (p. 175) crammed into crayfish shells to simulate the tail; small pastry triangles.

SOLE FILLETS SAINT-GERMAIN SOLES (FILETS DE) SAINT-GERMAIN (M.)

Spread the fillets with melted butter; season them and cover them with fresh bread crumbs; moisten with butter, and grill over a low flame. Place on a long platter and garnish with small new potatoes (or Potatoes Noisette, p. 509) browned in butter. On each fillet place 1 tbsp. Béarnaise Sauce (p. 147). Between each fillet run an even line of golden fish glaze. Sprinkle with chopped parsley. (Figure 179, Page 297.)

SOLE SUCHET SOLE À LA SUCHET (P.)

Cut a small quantity of very red carrots into fine julienne strips; cook slowly in butter in a tightly sealed pan. Meanwhile, use a pastry bag to border a long platter with Potatoes Duchesse (p. 507), then prepare Sole in White Wine (p. 303). Arrange the sole in the middle of the potato ring, after first browning the potatoes in the oven. Cover the fish with White-Wine Sauce (p. 155) and sprinkle the carrots and shredded truffles on top. (Figure 180, Page 300.)

SOLE FILLETS SYLVESTRE SOLE (FILETS DE) SYLVESTRE (M.)

Take a sole weighing about 1 lb. Cook the fillets, folded, with 1 tbsp. Mirepoix (p. 136) cooked in butter and 2 tbsp. sherry. When ⅔ cooked, add 1 tbsp. salpicon (tiny cubes) of mushrooms and ½ tbsp. salpicon of truffles. Arrange the sole fillets on a platter and garnish with very small tomatoes stuffed with sole purée, sprinkled with bread crumbs and oil, and browned in the oven. Cover the sole with a sauce made by reducing the cooking liquid, adding 3 oz. cream, reducing again, and finishing with 1 tbsp. butter.

SOLE FILLETS URBAIN-DUBOIS SOLES (FILETS DE) URBAIN-DUBOIS (M.)

(*For 6 persons*)

(1) Line a buttered ring mold with 12 pieces of sole fillets well flattened and seasoned. Place the fillets in the mold diagonally, lightly overlapping each other, so that they stick out of the mold at their 2 ends. Spread the fillets with a thin layer of Pike Forcemeat (p. 175). Fill the empty space remaining in the mold with crayfish tails mixed with Nantua Sauce (p. 152). On top of this mixture, which should be spread out in an even layer, place a thin layer of Pike Forcemeat. Fold over the ends of the fillets sticking out of the mold and press everything well down.

(2) Poach in a *bain-marie*, covered and at moderate heat. Let stand a few minutes before unmolding. Unmold onto a round service plate.

Garnishes: 12 poached scallops cut in half, dipped in flour, beaten egg with a little olive oil, and bread crumbs, and fried in clarified butter. Make a pile of the scallops in the center of the platter.

Sauce: Cover the ring with Normande Sauce (p. 153). Place 12 thick slices of truffles on top. Serve the rest of the sauce separately. (Figure 181, Page 300.)

SOLE IN WHITE WINE SOLE AU VIN BLANC (M.) (*For 2 persons*)

Take a sole weighing approximately 1 lb. Make a vertical incision down the side from which the skin is removed. Gently raise the fillets so that they are partially detached from the backbone. Into this opening place ½ tbsp. butter and a little salt. Put the sole into a buttered pan with the open side underneath. Season with salt and pepper. Moisten with 3 tbsp. fish stock made with white wine. Cover the pan and poach gently. Drain the fish, place on a platter, cover, and keep warm. Reduce the poaching liquid and finish it with White-Wine Sauce (below). Strain this sauce and cover the sole, which has been wiped dry, with it.

White-Wine Sauce: Cook 9 oz. fish stock made with dry white wine and mushroom pieces until reduced by ⅔. Add 6 oz. Fish Velouté (p. 147). Reduce by ½. Bind with the yolks of 4 eggs. Cook for a few moments while beating with a wire whisk. Remove from the stove and finish with 4 oz. butter. Correct the seasoning and add a dash of lemon juice (the lemon juice may be omitted if the white wine is acid). Strain through a fine sieve.

Note: When covered with sauce, the sole can be served as is, or, if preferred, glazed in the oven. The glazing must be done as quickly as possible, in a very hot oven, to prevent the sauce fom separating.

SOLE FILLETS IN RED WINE SOLES (FILETS DE) AU VIN ROUGE (A.) (*For 4 persons*)

Take 1 cup water, ⅘ cup red wine, 5 oz. butter, 2½ oz. mushrooms, 1 oz. Anchovy Butter (p. 163), ⅔ oz. flour, 2 soles weighing about 1½ lb. together, 2 cloves, 1 medium-sized carrot, 1 small turnip, 1 onion, 1 shallot, 1 clove of garlic, 1 *bouquet garni* (parsley, thyme, bay leaf, chervil, and celery), fish heads and bones, lemon juice, salt, pepper, and cayenne.

Remove the fillets, saving the trimmings. Peel the vegetables; slice the carrot and the turnip; chop the mushrooms; stick the cloves into the onion. Put the water, wine, mushrooms, fish heads and bones, sole trimmings, carrot, turnip, onion, shallot, garlic, *bouquet garni*, salt, pepper, and cayenne into a pot; cook until a flavorful and concentrated fish stock is obtained, and then strain. Place the sole fillets in a well-buttered porcelain baking dish; season with salt and pepper; moisten with a few tbsp. fish stock, and bake in the oven at low heat without browning. Keep hot.

Prepare the following sauce: make a roux with 2 oz. butter and flour; pour in the remainder of the fish stock, and you will have a Fish Velouté. Add the cooking liquid from the soles, using a wire whisk to bind the sauce; add the remainder of the butter, the Anchovy Butter, and a little lemon juice; heat; taste for seasoning and, if necessary, add salt, pepper, and cayenne. Arrange the fillets on a platter, cover with the sauce, and serve.

BRAISED TUNA WITH MUSHROOMS THON BRAISÉ AUX CHAMPIGNONS (P.)

Brown a thick slice of tuna in a pan with ½ butter and ½ oil; add a large sliced onion, 2 shallots in rings, and 4 or 5 tomatoes peeled and quartered; moisten with ½ glass white wine and 3 oz. brown sauce. Season, cover, and braise ½ hr. Remove the fish, reduce the cooking sauce, and press it through a sieve to make a purée; place it on the fire again with a few mushrooms sautéed in butter. Cook 10 min. and pour over the fish.

GRILLED TUNA MAÎTRE D'HÔTEL THON GRILLÉ MAÎTRE D'HÔTEL (P.)

Season a thick slice of fresh tuna and roll in flour, dip in oil, and place on a grill heated in advance to keep the fish from sticking to the bars. Grill the fish well on both sides, basting with oil from time to time. When the fish is cooked, the backbone should be removed easily. Serve with Maître d'Hôtel Butter (p. 164) and lemon quarters.

TURBOT CAMBACÉRÈS TURBOT CAMBACÉRÈS (M.)

Make a long cut down the black side of the turbot and carefully detach the fillets from the spine. Season the inside of the fish. Place it on the buttered grill of a fish poaching pan. Cover it with celery and leeks cut in thin julienne strips (previously cooked in butter). Pour in 2 cups champagne and 2 cups fish essence. When ¾ cooked, add a julienne of truffles and mushrooms. Baste the turbot frequently to glaze it lightly. Drain it and place on a long platter.

Sauce: Reduce the cooking liquid by ⅔, bind with 6 oz. Fish Velouté (p. 147), and finish with cream and butter. This sauce should not be strained.

Garnishes: Fried Mussels Villeroi (p. 323), frogs' legs Villeroi, small crayfish croquettes, fluted mushrooms. (Figure 184, Page 301.)

TURBOT IMPÉRIALE TURBOT À L'IMPÉRIALE (M.)

Boiled turbot, placed on a fish platter with grill, garnished with small shells of crayfish with Nantua Sauce (p. 152) with bread crumbs on top and browned in the oven, fried *nonats* (young gobies), oysters and Mussels Villeroi (p. 323), all arranged in alternate mounds around the fish. Serve separate sauceboats of lobster sauce (see p. 152) and Hollandaise Sauce (p. 151), and boiled potatoes.

TURBOT or BRILL PARISIENNE TURBOT OR BARBUE À LA PARISIENNE (M.)

Make a long cut down the black side of the turbot and gently detach the fillets from the backbone. Place it on the buttered grill of a fish poaching pan. Pour in 2 cups champagne and 2 cups fish essence. Baste frequently and glaze lightly while cooking. Meanwhile, prepare Lobster Américaine (p. 316) and keep the tail meat hot; make Lobster Butter (p. 164) with the rest of the lobster meat, the coral, and the creamy parts. Drain the turbot and place it on a long fish platter; cover it with White-Wine Sauce (p. 155) with Lobster Butter added. On top of the turbot lay the slices of lobster tail meat alternated with slices of truffle. Garnish the rim of the platter with truffled pike quenelles (see Pike Forcemeat, p. 175) and stuffed mushrooms. (Figure 185, Page 301.)

BREADED SLICED TURBOT TURBOT (ESCALOPES DE) PANÉES (A.)

Remove the skin and bones from a turbot; slice the fillets; season with salt, pepper, and lemon juice; dip in flour, then in a beaten egg, and finally in dry, sifted bread crumbs. Place the breaded slices in a buttered porcelain baking dish and bake in the oven 10 min., basting with the cooking juices. Serve in the baking dish. Serve separately a sauceboat of Italienne Sauce prepared the following way. Melt some butter in a stewpan and brown 2 chopped shallots and some chopped mushrooms in it; cook until the water from the mushrooms has evaporated, and then add chopped parsley, crushed tomatoes or tomato purée, salt, pepper, fish stock; cook until the sauce is sufficiently concentrated. Strain it and then add some *fines herbes*.

Sliced brill, sole fillets, whiting, etc., can be prepared the same way.

Fig. 186 - Matelote of eel bourguignonne (p. 306).
Fig. 187 - Pike Brymont (p. 307).

Fig. 186

Fig. 187

Fig. **188**

Fig. **189**

STUFFED CHICKEN TURBOT TURBOTIN FARCI (A.)

Take a chicken turbot weighing 3 or 4 lb. and a medium-sized live lobster. Clean the turbot, wipe it dry, split it down the back on either side of the backbone, which you remove by slipping a knife under it, without spoiling the shape of the fish. This operation requires great care.

Prepare a stuffing made of fresh salmon, mushrooms, *fines herbes*, sifted bread crumbs; moisten with port or sherry; season with salt, pepper, and curry; bind with 1 whole egg and 1 yolk. Stuff this filling into the hollow in the turbot left by the removal of the backbone. Cook some truffles in champagne brandy and save until later. Place the chicken turbot on the buttered grill of the fish poaching pan; pour some white wine and fish stock over it; baste frequently while cooking; reduce the cooking stock and thicken it with a little potato starch.

Meanwhile, cut the lobster into thick slices and cook it *à l'américaine* (p. 316). When it is cooked, remove the meat from the shell and cut it into thin slices. Keep hot. Reduce the cooking stock. Place the waste lobster meat into a mortar and pound it, adding a little cream, the brandy used in cooking the truffles, the lobster coral and creamy parts. Pound again, moisten with the reduced cooking stock, and press through a strainer and then a sieve. Put this sauce back onto the stove and add the cooking stock from the chicken turbot; heat, while stirring, without letting it come to a boil, and add butter after removing from the stove.

Place the chicken turbot on a platter; on top, the length of the fish, arrange a line of lobster slices so that they overlap but are separated from each other by slices of truffle. Garnish the sides of the platter with small truffled salmon quenelles and stuffed mushrooms. At either end of the platter, make a mound of pink shrimps. Serve the sauce separately. This is a very beautiful dish.

FISH SOUFFLÉ SOUFFLÉ DE POISSON (P.) (*For 4 persons*)

Remove the flesh from any leftover fish and, using a fork if the fish is tender (or a chopper, if it is not), mash into a fine purée. Thin the purée with an almost equal amount of very thick Béchamel Sauce (p. 146), season well, heat, and when it begins to boil, remove from the stove. Mix in 4 egg yolks for each ½ lb. fish, and 3 whites beaten stiff. Pour the mixture into a buttered soufflé dish and bake about 20 min. at low heat. Serve immediately, as you would any soufflé.

FRESH-WATER FISH

GRILLED SHAD MAÎTRE D'HÔTEL ALOSE GRILLÉE MAÎTRE D'HÔTEL (P.)

Shad, which is found at the mouths of rivers in the springtime, is an exceptionally delicious fish, but contains a great many bones. After scaling, cleaning, washing, and drying the shad, dip it in flour and make shallow cuts along both sides; then spread the surfaces with oil and grill it. If a grill is not available, it can be baked in a very hot oven and basted with butter several times. It takes 15 min. per lb. to cook shad. Serve with Maître d'Hôtel Butter (p. 164).

SHAD PROVENÇALE ALOSE À LA PROVENÇALE (P.) (*For 6 persons*)

Cook in oil until soft 2 lb. sorrel cut into strips; add 1 large chopped onion and ½ lb. fresh peeled, drained, and chopped tomatoes. When all this has

Fig. 188 - Pike chops princesse (p. 307).
Fig. 189 - Pike loaf dieppoise (p. 308).

cooked down, add a little chopped garlic and 1 or 2 tbsp. pulverized bread crumbs. Meanwhile, either grill or bake the shad. Place ½ the sorrel fondue in a baking dish or braising pan, place the shad on top, and cover with the rest of the sorrel; place in a slow oven and braise 3 hr. Serve in the baking dish.

SHAD TOURANGELLE ALOSE À LA TOURANGELLE (P.) (*For 6 persons*)

Clean the shad well and stuff it with the following filling: soak 4 oz. stale bread crumbs (for a 3-lb. shad) in milk; press the bread crumbs and crumble them; then mix in 2 chopped onions cooked in butter and plenty of chopped herbs as well as 1½ oz. butter and the soft roe or roe of the shad well crushed together. Boil and drain a few handfuls of finely chopped sorrel, beet greens, green cabbage leaves, and the white of 4 or 5 leeks. You will need a good quantity of these vegetables, for they cook down considerably. Place them in the bottom of a baking dish, put the fish on top, and cover with ½ bottle of Saumur white wine; season, cover with oiled paper, and cook in the oven 1 full hr. Finally, reduce the cooking juice and mix in 1 cup cream. Serve the shad in the dish it was cooked in.

MATELOTE OF EEL BOURGUIGNONNE ANGUILLE (MATELOTE D') BOURGUIGNONNE (P.)

A matelote can be made with any fish having firm flesh, but it is preferable to make it with a mixture of fish rather than with 1 type. Here is a recipe for eel.

Wash, clean, and skin the eel and cut it into sections about 3½ in. long; put these pieces into a pot on a bed of thinly sliced onions, shallots, and 1 clove garlic, a few peppercorns, and a small *bouquet garni.* Pour good red wine over the fish, salt lightly, then simmer 20 min. When the fish is cooked, remove the pieces 1 at a time to another casserole, then reduce the cooking liquid by ⅓ so that there will not be too much sauce. Bind this sauce by mixing in 2 oz. fresh butter kneaded with ½ tbsp. flour. The sauce should become creamy the first time it is brought to a boil, but since cooked wine produces an unappetizing color, it is necessary to darken the sauce with a little caramel coloring. Add to the pieces of eel 15 small onions cooked separately and slowly in butter and 5 oz. mushrooms also cooked in butter. Strain the sauce through a fine sieve onto the eel. Taste the sauce to correct the seasoning and serve the matelote with a garnish around it of bread croutons fried in oil and crayfish cooked in Court Bouillon (p. 277). (Figure 186, Page 304.)

EEL POULETTE ANGUILLE À LA POULETTE (Fa.)

Those who do not like Matelote of Eel with red wine may prepare it the same way, but cook it in white wine instead of red. Make a white sauce with butter, flour, the cooking stock from the eel, and add very white mushrooms and poached mussels and oysters. Bind the sauce with 2 egg yolks and a little cream. Serve with a border of bread croutons fried in butter.

GRILLED EEL TARTARE ANGUILLE (GRILLÉE) À LA TARTARE (M.)

Cook 3-in. sections of eel in a Court Bouillon made with white wine (p. 277). Let the eel cool in the Court Bouillon. Drain and dry the pieces of eel; spread with oil or melted butter; cover completely with fresh bread crumbs, and moisten with oil or melted butter. Cook on a grill over a low flame, browning both sides. Serve with Tartar Sauce (p. 158).

PIKE WITH WHITE BUTTER BROCHET AU BEURRE BLANC (P.)

Cook the pike in an ordinary Court Bouillon (p. 277), drain it, remove all the skin, and place it on a hot platter, then pour White Butter Sauce (p. 687) over it, or serve the sauce separately for important occasions.

BLANQUETTE OF PIKE BROCHET EN BLANQUETTE (P.)

Cut the pike into rather thick slices and brown in butter. Dredge with flour, moisten with ½ white Anjou wine and ½ water, add small onions and mushrooms, season well, and cook slowly. Remove the pike and bind the cooking liquid with 2 egg yolks and a little heavy cream.

Pike may be cooked like Trout au Bleu (p. 312) or served with any of a variety of sauces made from the cooked Court Bouillon. The skin must always be removed before serving.

PIKE BRYMONT BROCHET BRYMONT (M.) (*For 10 persons*)

(1) Stuff a 4¼-lb. pike with fish forcemeat mixed with diced truffles. Season with salt and pepper, cover with thin strips of bacon, and braise in white wine (mixed with very reduced fish stock made with white wine). (2) Drain the pike, remove the strips of bacon, and place the fish on a long platter. Baste with a few tbsp. reduced and buttered cooking stock from the pike and glaze lightly in the oven.

Sauce: Strain the cooking stock and reduce it. Bind with egg yolk as in making White-Wine Sauce (p. 155).

Garnishes: 10 crayfish croquettes; 10 strips of breaded fried eel; 10 breaded fried gudgeons; Potatoes Noisette (p. 509). Arrange these garnishes in alternate mounds. Serve with White-Wine Sauce (p. 155). (Figure 187, Page 304.)

PIKE CHOPS PRINCESSE BROCHET (CÔTELETTES DE) PRINCESSE (M.)

Fill buttered chop-shaped molds with fine Pike Forcemeat (p. 175). Poach. Unmold the chops and place each on a small pastry-boat crust half filled with a salpicon (tiny cubes) of mushrooms and truffles bound with reduced Fish Velouté (p. 147). Arrange the chops in a circle on a round platter. Garnish the center of the platter with asparagus tips in butter. Cover the chops with Normande Sauce (p. 153), and on each place a large slice of truffle cut round. (Figure 188, Page 305.)

PIKE QUENELLES LYONNAISE BROCHET (QUENELLES DE) À LA LYONNAISE (M.)

Forcemeat: 2 lb. boned pike, 4 lb. beef-kidney fat, 4 lb. very thick Pastry Cream made without sugar (p. 552), 8 egg whites, 1 pt. fresh heavy cream, salt, pepper, grated nutmeg. (1) Chop the boned pike and the beef fat and pound separately in a mortar; mix the pike and fat and pound in a mortar while adding the Pastry Cream. Blend in the egg whites, season, and strain through a fine sieve. Place in a bowl and work over ice, mixing in the fresh cream drop by drop. (2) Make the quenelles in the shape of big stoppers or corks and poach a few moments in salted water. Drain them and place them to swell in the following ragout.

Ragout and Sauce: This ragout is usually made of such garnishes as cubed olives, mushrooms, truffles, lambs' brains, and, sometimes, sweetbreads. The sauce used to bind this ragout is an Espagnole Sauce made with fish stock and reduced while adding a few oz. Madeira (p. 137). The quenelles should boil for some time in this ragout so that they puff up, which is the distinguishing feature of this dish. Arrange in a timbale, a Vol-au-Vent crust (p. 530), or merely on a platter.

Note: Another recipe is given in the section on Forcemeats, p. 175.

PIKE LOAF DIEPPOISE BROCHET (PAIN DE) À LA DIEPPOISE (P.) (*For 8 persons*)

The Pike Forcemeat for this loaf is not made like that given in the recipe above; you need the fillets of a small pike or pickerel weighing about 1½ lb. in order to have 1 lb. net meat for 8 persons. Pound this meat with salt and pepper and mix in 1 cup rather thick, very cold Béchamel Sauce (p. 146), then 3 oz. rich cream, 1 whole egg, and 2 yolks. After straining this purée through a sieve, put it into a buttered mold, and cook in the oven in a *bain-marie* 25–30 min. Using the bones and trimmings of the pike, make a fish stock with white wine. Next blend in a saucepan 2 oz. butter and 1½ oz. flour, adding 6 oz. water and the fish stock reduced to 3 oz. Add the 2 egg yolks and stir briskly on the fire before adding butter and chopped herbs. Unmold the pike loaf onto a round platter and pour the sauce over it. Shrimps or mussels should be used as a garnish on top. (Figure 189, Page 305.)

PIKE LOAF NEMOURS BROCHET (PAIN DE) À LA NEMOURS (P.)

Same recipe as the preceding. For the garnish, make small round potato croquettes, the size of small plums, and Shrimp Sauce (p. 159). Unmold the loaf, cover with Shrimp Sauce, and garnish with the potato croquettes (in which a little shrimp has been mixed).

PICKEREL FILLETS HOME STYLE BROCHETON (FILETS DE) À LA MÉNAGÈRE (P.) (*For 4 persons*)

Chop 6 oz. raw mushrooms into large pieces; spread them out on the bottom of a buttered baking dish, and on top lay the fillets of 2 small pikes or pickerels weighing about 1 lb. each; pour on white wine, season, cover with buttered paper, and place in the oven. Bake 10–15 min.; drain off the cooking liquid, reduce by ½, bind with butter mixed with a little flour, and add more butter before serving. Pour this sauce over the fish.

CARP CHAMBORD CARPE CHAMBORD (M.) (*For 6 persons*)

(1) Stuff a carp weighing 2½ lb. with fine Pike Forcemeat (p. 175). Sew up the opening of the fish. Remove the skin over the fillets and stud the fillets with truffles cut in the shape of pegs. (2) Cover the carp with strips of bacon or pork fat held in place by tying with string. Place it on the buttered grill of a fish pan and place the grill into the pan over a layer of sliced carrots, onions, and celery cooked in butter until soft. Fill the pan to ⅔ the height of the fish with 1 part fish stock and 2 parts red wine. Bring to a boil on top of the stove; cover; finish cooking in a moderately hot oven. (3) Drain the carp and remove the strips of fat. Reduce the cooking liquid, add butter, strain, and then baste the fish with it and glaze in the oven. Place the carp on a serving platter without anything underneath or on top of a large slice of bread, with the crust removed,

Fig. 190 - Salmon Kulibiak (p. 310).
Fig. 191 - River trout Lily-of-the-valley (p. 313).

Fig. 190

Fig. 191

Fig. 192

Fig. 193

fried in butter, stuck to the platter with paste so as to separate the fish from the garnishes. (The carp may also be placed on a bed of rice.)

Sauce: The cooking stock strained, reduced, and finished as for Genevoise Sauce (p. 141).

Garnishes: Along the sides of the carp place, in alternate mounds, 12 pike quenelles (shaped with a spoon), 12 fluted mushroom caps cooked in butter and a little lemon juice, 24 glazed truffles cut in the shape of olives, 12 breaded fried gudgeons, 12 pieces of carp soft roe prepared Villeroi style. At each end of the platter place 3 crayfish in their shells, cooked in Court Bouillon (p. 277). Cover with a few tbsp. sauce (given above), and serve the rest of the sauce in a sauceboat.

Note: The decoration of this dish may be enhanced by sticking skewered truffles and crayfish into the fish. The garnish may also include some large pike quenelles decorated with pieces of truffle fixed with egg white.

Remarks: Formerly, the garnish for Carp Chambord included a great number of ingredients that, to say the least, scarcely went with the fish they accompanied.

STURGEON WITH TURTLE SAUCE ESTURGEON (TRONÇON D') SAUCE TORTUE (U.-D.)

Cut a slice of sturgeon from the middle. Split it and clean it underneath and remove skin and scales; stud it with pieces of pork fat, roll it, and tie with string as you would a veal roast. Salt it and wrap it in buttered paper. Bake slowly about 1 hr., basting with butter, then unwrap it and place it on a hot platter. Garnish one side with molded fish quenelles, the other with fluted mushroom caps. Cover the garnishes with a little Turtle Sauce (p. 145) or Matelote Sauce (p. 142), and serve the remainder of the sauce separately. Glaze the fish a little with melted butter.

LAMPREY STEW LAMPROIE (CIVET DE) (A.)

Take a live lamprey, cut off the head and tail, drain the blood, clean it, and plunge into boiling water for 3 min., then remove the skin and cut into pieces. Brown the lamprey slices in olive oil for a few moments with white of leek. Cook separately chopped bacon fat, shallots, parsley, and bay leaf. Sprinkle this with flour, moisten with good red wine, season with salt and pepper, and add the browned lamprey and leeks. Cook together 2 hr. Just before serving, bind the sauce with the lamprey blood and some chicken blood so that it becomes very dark; taste it and correct the seasoning, if necessary, with salt, pepper, nutmeg, and powdered sugar. Serve with fried croutons.

This stew can be canned very successfully. To prepare it for canning, after browning the ingredients mentioned above, put them into tin cans, seal tightly, and finish cooking 3 hr. in a *bain-marie.* When serving canned lamprey, open the can, heat in a *bain-marie,* empty the contents into a hot dish, and garnish with fried croutons prepared at the last moment.

This recipe may be used for eels. It is also very good for salmon.

GRILLED SALMON SAUMON GRILLÉ (M.)

Cut the slices to be grilled from the thick center part of the fish. These pieces should be about 1 in. thick. Season, spread the surfaces with oil or melted

Fig. 192 - Crayfish bush (p. 315).
Fig. 193 - Crayfish au gratin (p. 315).

butter, place the slices on a grill well heated in advance, and brown on both sides over a very hot flame. Finish cooking at moderate heat. Grilled Salmon is usually served on a butter sauce such as Maître d'Hôtel Butter (p. 164), Anchovy Butter (p. 163), Ravigote Sauce (p. 154), etc. It may also be served with Béarnaise Sauce (p. 147) or any other special sauce for grilled fish. Like all grilled fish, Grilled Salmon is usually served with boiled potatoes.

GRILLED SALMON WITH ANCHOVY BUTTER SAUMON GRILLÉ AU BEURRE D'ANCHOIS (A.) (*For 6 persons*)

Take 2 lb. fresh salmon, 6 oz. butter, 3 oz. salted anchovies. Make Anchovy Butter the following way: wash the anchovies, soak them a little in water to remove the salt, dry them, remove the bones, pound the flesh in a mortar with butter; press through a fine sieve. Cut the salmon into ½-in. steaks, then grill over a hot fire, without any seasoning, 3 or 4 min. on each side. (The grill should be heated and greased in advance.) Serve on a hot platter with a sauceboat of the melted anchovy butter.

SALMON KULIBIAK SAUMON (COULIBIAC DE) (M.) (*For 15 to 18 persons*)

The paste: Prepare in an earthenware bowl a leaven of 9 oz. flour, 6 oz. warm milk, and ⅓ oz. yeast. Mix this leaven with a spatula until smooth and put in a warm place to rise. When it has risen nicely, add 9 oz. flour, 9 oz. melted butter, 7 whole eggs, and a pinch of salt. Knead this paste until very smooth; turn it over on a floured baking board or marble slab and work it gently. Place it back in the bowl and let it stand in a warm place about 1 hr.

Garnishes: (*a*) Cut 1½ lb. skinned, boned salmon into long thin fillets. Season these fillets with salt and paprika and cook them in a buttered baking dish with 3 oz. white wine and the juice of 1 lemon. (*b*) Chop 10 oz. spinal marrow of sturgeon (see *Note,* below) and cook at low heat with a little butter and 1 heaping tbsp. chopped shallots and chives cooked in butter till soft. Add 2 tbsp. chopped fennel and parsley. Empty onto a plate, and when cold add 4 hard-boiled eggs either diced or sliced and 4 oz. chopped mushrooms cooked in butter. (*c*) Cook 8 oz. semolina in consommé. When it is cooked, spread it out on a platter and dry it in the warmer, then strain it through a wide-meshed sieve.

Preparation and baking of the kulibiak: Roll the paste into a ball on a floured baking board and roll it out into an oblong about ¼ in. thick, 1½ ft. long, and 1 ft. wide. Place this layer of paste on a floured cloth and spread it with alternate layers of the ingredients given above, taking care to spread these layers in the center of the paste, leaving a border of paste around the mixture about 3 in. wide. Fold the paste over the filling and join the edges with beaten egg. Put the kulibiak on a buttered baking sheet with the joined edges down and let it set 30 min. in a warm place. Brush with beaten egg, sprinkle with bread crumbs, cut a small gash on top, and put into a hot oven. Arrange on a long platter and serve with a sauceboat of melted butter. (Figure 190, Page 308.)

Note: The spinal marrow of sturgeon is used only for certain dishes in Russian cooking. Tests made by Escoffier have revealed that: (1) normal soaking time in cold water to cause the marrow to swell is 5 hr.; (2) at this point, the marrow has increased in volume a little more than 5 times; (3) 3 qt. liquid are needed to cook 2 oz. marrow, which after soaking weighs about 10 oz.; it should be cooked slowly, with a cover; (4) cook small pieces 3½ hr. and larger pieces 4½ hr.

SALMON GALANTINE SAUMON (GALANTINE DE) (A.) (*For 12 persons*)

Cold Dish: Take a center cut of salmon weighing about 4 lb., 1½ lb. pollack, whiting, or gurnard and scraps of sole, 9 oz. Frangipane Panada (p. 172), 9 oz. dry white wine, 1 oz. blanched pistachios, 12 crayfish, 1 pike weighing a little more than 1½ lb., butter, *bouquet garni,* egg whites, lemon juice, four spices (see *Note,* p. 301), nutmeg, salt, pepper, cayenne. Scale the salmon and remove the skin and bones without spoiling the fillets. Save all the scraps. Scrape, clean, and dry the pike. Remove all the meat without leaving any bones. Save all the scraps. Cut the salmon into fillets lengthwise, the 2 large fillets cut into 4 strips, and the 2 smaller ones each into 3 strips; season with salt and pepper.

Preparation of the fish stock: Put into a pot 2 qt. water, the pollack, whiting, or gurnard cut into pieces, the trimmings of sole, salmon, and pike, *bouquet garni,* white wine, salt, pepper, a little of the four spices; bring to a boil, skim, and cook ½ hr. over a very low fire. Press through a strainer. Cook the gutted crayfish in the fish stock; remove the shells and save the tails. Using the shells and 2 oz. butter, make a Crayfish Butter (see p. 164).

Preparation of the forcemeat: Cut the pike into small pieces and pound in a mortar, then add the crayfish tails and pound again. Finally, mix in the Frangipane Panada and the Crayfish Butter; season with salt, pepper, and nutmeg to taste.

Preparation of the galantine: To make a galantine measuring 5 in. on each side, place a piece of parchment paper 18 in. long and 8 in. wide on the table; butter it; spread out on top a layer of forcemeat ⅓ in. thick, leaving a margin of about 3 in. around the paper. Lay out 2 rows of pistachios laid end to end the length of the filling; on top place 3 long strips of salmon alternated with 2 shorter strips; cover with forcemeat. Repeat this operation, making alternate layers of pistachios, salmon, and forcemeat until all the ingredients have been used; finish with a layer of forcemeat. Roll the galantine crosswise into a cylinder, and fold the edges of the paper to seal in the ingredients. Cover the roll with cloth without making any wrinkles; tie the ends tight against the paper; wrap a band of cloth lengthwise around the galantine without squeezing it. Place the galantine on a grill in a pot and pour hot fish stock over it until completely covered; bring to a boil; reduce the heat, and let simmer ¾ hr. You can tell whether the galantine is cooked if it feels firm. Remove the galantine, let it cool a bit, remove the cloth band, and open the cloth cover. Place small boards against the sides of the galantine, holding them in place with some heavy object so as to press tightly against the galantine, and on top place another board, weighted down with about 2 lb.; let cool 12 hr. under this pressure.

Preparation of the jelly: Strain the cooking juice through a fine sieve; give it body, if necessary, with a little calf's jelly; clarify it with egg whites; season with a dash of cayenne and lemon juice; strain through a napkin.

Decoration: Remove the galantine from the cloth and paper. Place it on a platter and cover it with part of the jelly somewhat softened; let it set. Decorate with the remainder of the jelly cut into patterns according to taste.

For variety, sole fillets may be used instead of pike and soft roe of carp instead of crayfish.

SALMON GALANTINE TAILLEVENT SAUMON (GALANTINE DE) TAILLEVENT (M.) (*For 12 persons*)

Cold Dish: Remove all the bones from the center part of a salmon weighing about 4½ lb. without tearing the skin. Be sure that it is well scaled. Take ⅔ of the meat and cut it into long slivers of the same size; marinate these slivers 2 hr. in oil, lemon juice, salt, pepper, and chopped parsley. Sear them in butter and chill again.

Forcemeat: Using the rest of the salmon meat, prepare a forcemeat. Add to this an equal quantity of Pike Forcemeat mixed with cream (p. 175). Add diced truffles to this forcemeat and mix well.

Garnishes: Make 12 small sole birds stuffed with Pike Forcemeat containing anchovy purée. Cook these birds in butter. Let them cool. Use the same forcemeat to stuff 48 large pitted, blanched olives. Peel 12 round truffles and macerate them in cognac, salt, pepper, spices.

Preparation of the galantine: Spread a moistened cloth out flat on a table. In the center of the cloth make a square of very thin strips of pork fat the same size as the salmon skin. Place the salmon skin on the fat with the outside of the skin down. Season with spiced salt. Cover the center of the skin with a thin layer of forcemeat extending about 4 in., leaving about a ¾-in. margin of skin around the edges. On top of this layer of forcemeat place the slivers of salmon meat and the sole birds, separating one from the other with a little forcemeat. Cover this with another layer of forcemeat. In the center of this layer place the truffles packed tightly together. On each side of the truffles lay a row of stuffed olives. Cover all of this with a layer of forcemeat. Place the remainder of the salmon slivers on top and cover again with a layer of forcemeat. Bring the skin as well as the strips of fat over this last layer. Roll the galantine in the cloth and tie securely with string at each end and in the middle.

Cooking the galantine: Place the galantine on the grill of a fish poaching pan. Cover with fish Aspic Jelly (p. 168) previously prepared, strained, and chilled. Bring to a rolling boil, then reduce the heat, and let simmer 1½ hr. Leave the galantine in the liquid until almost cool, then drain it, remove the cloth and the strips of fat, and roll it again in another cloth. Tie it well and press it into shape as you would a Chicken Galantine (see p. 419).

Serving the galantine: This galantine can be served as it is, on a silver plate, surrounded with chopped jelly. It can also be covered with White Chaud-Froid Sauce (p. 149) made from fish stock and decorated with truffles, egg whites, lobster coral, chervil leaves, etc., fixed into place with half-congealed jelly. When covered with sauce and decorated, the galantine should be glazed with jelly. Place it on a bed of molded rice or bread. Decorate the border with decorative pieces of jelly. Serve with mayonnaise or Green Sauce (p. 158).

BOILED TROUT or **TROUT AU BLEU** TRUITES AU BLEU (E.)

For this recipe, it is absolutely essential to use live trout. Have ready a shallow pan of boiling Court Bouillon strongly flavored with vinegar (p. 277). About 10 min. before time to serve the trout, stun them with a blow on the head, eviscerate and clean them quickly, then plunge them into the boiling liquid,

Fig. 194 - Dressing for lobster Américaine (p. 316).
Fig. 195 - Lobster Américaine (p. 316).

Fig. **194**

Fig. **195**

Fig. **196**

Fig. **197**

where they shrivel up immediately, with the skin breaking in several places. It takes only a few minutes to cook a trout weighing about 6 oz. Drain the trout and serve immediately on a napkin with curly parsley around them. Serve with Hollandaise Sauce (p. 151) or melted butter.

Note: If the trout are served cold, they should be accompanied by a Ravigote Sauce (p. 158) made with oil.

TROUT HUSSARDE TRUITES À LA HUSSARDE (E.)

Stuff medium-sized trout with fish forcemeat (see p. 173) mixed with 4 oz. chopped onion, cooked in butter, per lb. forcemeat (see p. 95 for directions). Arrange them in a buttered pan, on a bed of finely sliced onions cooked in butter but not browned; add a *bouquet garni* and, per 8 or 10 trout, 4 oz. butter and 6 oz. Chablis. Poach uncovered, basting frequently. Arrange the trout on a platter; strain the cooking stock, including the onion, through a sieve, bind with a little Fish Velouté (p. 147) or Flour Butter (p. 164). Add more butter after removing the sauce from the stove, pour it over the trout, and glaze quickly in a very hot oven.

TROUT MANTOUE TRUITES À LA MANTOUE (G.)

Take 12 small mountain trout or, if not available, river trout. Clean and wash them, then detach the fillets from either side of the backbone, removing the latter. Spread a thin layer of fish forcemeat (see p. 173) mixed with finely chopped truffles over each fillet. Put the fillets back together again, giving the trout their normal shape, and sew them with a thread. Place them side by side in a buttered pan lined with sliced carrots, onions, and shallots, a *bouquet garni,* a few peppercorns, and mushroom peelings. Pour in fish stock and white wine until the trout are half covered. Bring to a boil, then cover with buttered paper, and cook slowly in an open oven 20–25 min., basting frequently. Be sure that the liquid merely simmers. Remove the trout from the liquid, place on a platter, cover with Italienne Sauce (p. 142) made with fish stock, and sprinkle lightly with chopped parsley.

RIVER TROUT LILY-OF-THE-VALLEY TRUITES DE RIVIÈRE À LA MUGUETTE (P.)

Cold Dish: Poach the trout in the usual manner and let cool. Remove the skin carefully, leaving only the head and part of the tail covered. Decorate with green of leek, blanched tarragon leaves, yolk and white of hard-boiled eggs. Glaze with Aspic Jelly (p. 168). Place the trout upon a bed of chopped jelly. (Figure 191, Page 308.)

SALMON TROUT CHIVRY TRUITE SAUMONÉE À LA CHIVRY (P.)

The trout is poached in a good Court Bouillon made with white wine (p. 277). Season the Court Bouillon well and cook it in advance. When cold, pour it over the trout placed in a fish poaching pan. Bring to a boil and then reduce the heat to prevent the meat from breaking. The trout must not be cooked at more than a simmer if it is to be served attractively. While it is cooking, make some small patty shells in boat-shaped molds. Fill these shells with a salpicon (tiny cubes) of shrimps and mushrooms bound with Cardinal Sauce (p. 148), and also make a hot green sauce called Chivry Sauce (p. 149). Place the trout on its side on a long platter and remove the skin; set a row of thin lemon slices the

Fig. 196 & 197 - Arrangements of lobster aspic russian style (p. 318).

length of the trout; surround with curly parsley and the filled patty shells, with 3 boiled potatoes between each patty shell. Serve very hot, with the sauce in a separate dish. (Figure 182, Page 300.)

Note: Salmon trout, a fish of the first order, makes a superb dish for elegant dinners. Serve it hot, cooked in Court Bouillon or (more rarely) braised, and accompanied with one of the finer sauces.

SALMON TROUT NORWEGIAN STYLE TRUITE SAUMONÉE À LA NORVÉGIENNE (E.)

Cold Dish: When the trout has been poached and cooled, remove the skin, decorate it, and glaze thickly with Aspic Jelly (p. 168). Set a very clear layer of jelly in the bottom of a serving platter, on top of this jelly make a bed of molded rice and place the trout on top. Stick a row of pink shrimps (the tails shelled) into the trout, and surround with small timbales of cucumbers blanched, marinated, and filled with a purée of smoked salmon; small whole tomatoes or peeled tomato halves pressed in a cloth to round them, decorated with a bit of parsley and leaves of Green Butter (p. 163) squeezed from a paper cone; small boats shaped from beets, cooked and marinated, and filled with shrimp salad; hard-boiled egg halves glazed with jelly. Serve Russian Sauce (p. 158) separately.

Note: The garnish may be varied according to taste and circumstance: pastry-shell boats filled with a purée of smoked salmon; small artichoke bottoms garnished with shrimp salad; hard-boiled egg halves, and lettuce salad. (Figure 183, Page 301.)

GLAZED SALMON TROUT IN CHAMPAGNE TRUITE SAUMONÉE (GLACÉE) AU VIN DE CHAMPAGNE (M.)

Cold Dish: Prepare a fish Aspic Jelly (p. 168), using ½ dry champagne and ½ rich fish stock. Pour this cold jelly over a salmon trout placed on the grill of a fish poaching pan. Simmer slowly. Let stand in the liquid until almost cool. Drain the trout and remove the skin, leaving only a narrow band of skin at either end of the fish. Decorate the skinned part with truffles, hard-boiled egg white, chervil leaves (fixed with half-congealed jelly). Cover the trout (which must be well chilled) with half-congealed jelly (made from the cooking liquid and clarified the usual way). Chill well in the refrigerator. Place the trout in a deep oval platter, and pour a layer of jelly around the fish, then chill again in the refrigerator.

FROGS

FROGS' LEGS FRIED IN BATTER GRENOUILLES EN BEIGNETS (P.)

Buy some nice fat frogs' legs and cut off the toes with scissors. Before cooking, macerate them for a while in salt, pepper, chopped parsley, and a little vinegar. Dry them off just before cooking, and dip them in Frying Paste (p. 558). Fry 5 min. in deep hot fat. Serve with fried parsley.

Note: If you wish to pan-fry them, you may add some bread crumbs fried in butter or chopped garlic or shallots. Mushrooms browned in butter or diced potatoes may also be added. They may be mixed in with a Risotto (p. 513) or prepared Indian style (curried) in a border of creole rice (made with tomatoes, onions, and peppers).

FROGS' LEGS POULETTE GRENOUILLES À LA POULETTE (P.)

Cook the frogs' legs slowly in butter in order not to brown them and let them simmer in Poulette Sauce (p. 154). Decorate with chopped parsley.

SAUTÉED FROGS' LEGS GRENOUILLES SAUTÉES (P.)

Dip the frogs' legs in flour and sauté them in very hot butter; salt and pepper generously and serve moistened with piping-hot butter, lemon juice, and chopped parsley.

CRUSTACEANS

CRAYFISH BORDELAISE ÉCREVISSES À LA BORDELAISE (A.) (*For 10 persons*)

Take 1½ pt. milk, 1 pt. dry white Bordeaux, 1⅛ lb. butter, ¾ cup champagne brandy, ¾ cup fish stock, ¾ cup Fish Velouté (p. 147), ¾ cup concentrated tomato sauce, 8 oz. carrots, 8 oz. onions, 1 oz. shallot, 1 oz. parsley, ½ oz. tarragon, 60 live crayfish, thyme, bay leaf, salt, pepper, cayenne.

Soak the crayfish in the milk 10 hr. Chop together carrots, onions, shallots, tarragon, and ½ oz. parsley. Put the chopped vegetables into a pot with 4 oz. butter, thyme, bay leaf, salt, and pepper; cook well. Remove the intestines from the crayfish; drop them into the pot, sprinkle with cayenne, and sauté them until they become very red; pour in the brandy and light it. Remove the crayfish and keep them warm. Add the wine to the cooking stock and reduce it by about ⅓. Then add the crayfish, fish stock, Fish Velouté, and tomato sauce; cook 10 min. Place the crayfish in a timbale; keep warm. Strain the sauce, cook it until concentrated, then add the rest of the butter and the rest of the parsley blanched and chopped; pour it over the crayfish.

BOILED CRAYFISH ÉCREVISSES À LA NAGE (P.)

Cook the cleaned crayfish in a good Court Bouillon well seasoned with vegetables and a little white wine (p. 277). Cook 10 min. at a rolling boil, then let cool and serve as is, in the cooking liquid. Always use live crayfish.

Note: During the last few years we have not been able to get any of the fine German and Czechoslovakian crayfish. For this reason we show very few in the illustrations. Crayfish from the rivers of France are very small and are eaten only in the regions in which they are found.

CRAYFISH BUSH ÉCREVISSES (BUISSON D') (P.)

Cook the crayfish as directed above and arrange them in a pyramid with curly parsley on a special rack called a crayfish bush. (Figure 192, Page 309.)

CRAYFISH AU GRATIN ÉCREVISSES (GRATIN D') (P.) (*For 4 persons*)

Cook 24 crayfish in a well-seasoned Court Bouillon with white wine (p. 277). Remove the shells, saving 6 or 8 of the best-looking shells, and make a Crayfish Butter (p. 164) with all the rest. Prepare a rather thick cream sauce and add the Crayfish Butter to it. Simmer the crayfish meat in this sauce. Make a pastry shell in a mold, or a ring of Potatoes Duchesse (p. 507) squeezed from a pastry bag with a tube with a fluted opening, and brown in the oven. Season the crayfish well and pour them with the sauce into this crust. Sprinkle a pinch of grated cheese on top and glaze under a broiler or in a very hot oven. Decorate the top with the reserved crayfish shells and serve immediately. (Figure 193, Page 309.)

LOBSTER AMÉRICAINE I HOMARD À L'AMÉRICAINE (E.) (*For 3 persons*)

The lobster must be alive. Cut the tail into slices; remove all the legs; break the claws to facilitate removal of the meat after cooking; cut the body of the lobster in two lengthwise; remove the sac found at the top of the head, which usually contains gravel. Save the intestines and the coral; season the pieces of tail meat with salt and pepper. (See pictures, p. 96.)

To prepare a lobster weighing about 1 lb.: Heat 4 tbsp. oil and 1 oz. butter until very hot in a deep frying pan; drop in the pieces of lobster; sauté them until the flesh becomes firm and the shell turns bright red. Holding the lid tightly on the pan, pour off the fat; sprinkle 2 chopped shallots and a crushed clove of garlic onto the lobster pieces; add 1 small glass of flaming cognac, 6 oz. white wine, 4 oz. fish stock, 1 tbsp. melted meat glaze, 3 pressed, peeled, chopped tomatoes or 1½ tbsp. tomato purée, 1 pinch crushed parsley, and a dash of cayenne. Cover the pan and cook in the oven 15–20 min. Remove the lobster pieces and place them on a platter; remove the shell from the slices of lobster meat and the meat from the claws and place them in a timbale; arrange the half shells of the lobster on top so that they lean on each other and stand up. Keep hot. Reduce the cooking sauce to 6 oz.; add the chopped intestines with ½ tbsp. butter; cook for a few moments, and strain. Heat again without boiling, remove from the fire, and finish with 4 oz. butter divided into small pieces; pour over the lobster pieces and sprinkle with a pinch of crushed parsley. (Figures 194-195, Page 312.)

LOBSTER AMÉRICAINE II HOMARD À L'AMÉRICAINE (E.)

Prepare the lobster as described above. Take only the meat from the tail and the claws, place it in a timbale, and cover with the sauce.

Note: This second recipe, which is the one used in modern English and American cooking, does not use the top halves of the lobster. They are generally used in preparing Red Butter (p. 163).

LOBSTER BORDELAISE HOMARD À LA BORDELAISE (E.) (*For 3 persons*)

Cut the live lobster into pieces as when making Lobster Américaine (above); season the pieces. Sear the meat and color the shell in 2 oz. clarified butter, then pour off ½ the butter and add 2 tbsp. chopped shallots and 1 crushed clove of garlic, 3 tbsp. flaming cognac, and 3 oz. white wine; cook until reduced by ½. Add 7 oz. fish stock, 6 oz. Espagnole Sauce (p. 137) made with fish stock, 4 oz. Tomato Sauce (p. 146), a *bouquet garni*, a pinch of salt, and a dash of cayenne. Cover and cook 15 min. Remove the tail and claw meat as in the recipe for Lobster Américaine; place them in a small pan and keep hot. Add the chopped intestines to the sauce, cook for a moment, reduce the sauce to 6 oz., strain, and pour over the lobster meat. Heat the lobster and sauce without boiling. Finish with a few drops of lemon juice, 3 oz. butter divided into small pieces, ½ tbsp. chopped chervil and tarragon. Shake the pan over the fire to mix everything together. Arrange in a timbale and sprinkle with a little chopped parsley.

LOBSTER CARDINAL HOMARD CARDINAL (E.)

Plunge the live lobster into a boiling Court Bouillon (p. 277). As soon as it is cooked, split it in two lengthwise; remove the meat from the tail; cut the tail meat into slices and keep hot in several tbsp. Cardinal Sauce (p. 148). Remove the claws, and take out the meat by working it with a knife through a large hole or by cutting the under edges of the claws with strong scissors. Do this without breaking or spoiling the appearance of the claws. Dice the claw meat and the meat from the body of the lobster; mix this with an equal amount of cooked diced mushrooms and ½ that amount of diced truffles; bind this mixture with a few tbsp. lobster sauce. Using a part of the mixture, fill the empty claws and spread the rest in an even layer in each ½ of the lobster shell. On top of this layer of filling lay the slices of lobster tail meat alternated with slices of truffles. When both halves of the lobster have been prepared this way, place them on a platter and, to steady them, place the claws on either side. Cover slices and claws with Cardinal Sauce, sprinkle with grated cheese, moisten with melted butter, and glaze quickly in a very hot oven or under a broiler.

GRILLED LOBSTER HOMARD GRILLÉ (E.) (*For 3 persons*)

Generally, the live lobster is split lengthwise down the middle, seasoned, and grilled over a slow fire, allowing ½ hr. for a lobster weighing about 2 lb. Nevertheless, it is preferable to cook the lobster in a Court Bouillon (p. 277) until ¾ done. Treated this way, the lobster meat will be tenderer than when grilled raw. If you cook it first in a Court Bouillon, split the lobster after removing it from the liquid, pour melted butter over it, and grill until the cooking is completed. Break the claws to make it easy to remove the claw meat, place the lobster on a napkin or a grill, surround with curly parsley, and serve with a dish of Deviled Sauce (p. 140) or any other highly seasoned sauce for grilled fish.

LOBSTER MOUSSE BERCHOUX HOMARD (MOUSSE DE) BERCHOUX (M.) (*For 6 persons*)

Forcemeat: In a mortar, pound 1 lb. lobster meat into a fine mash. While pounding, season with salt and a pinch of paprika. Add 2 egg whites drop by drop. Press this forcemeat through a fine sieve into a pan. Chill on ice 2 hr. Keeping it still on ice, work 21 oz. fresh heavy cream into it. Pour this mousse into a buttered charlotte mold decorated with large round slices of truffle. Fill the mold only ¾ full. Place the mold in a *bain-marie* and poach 30 min. at moderate heat.

Garnishes: Breaded fried oysters; small pastry boats filled with crayfish tails bound with Nantua Sauce (p. 152); fluted cooked mushrooms; Laguipière Sauce (below) containing chopped truffles.

Sauce: To 12 oz. Butter Sauce (p. 148), add 2 tbsp. golden fish glaze and a dash of lemon juice. Strain. This sauce may also be prepared with White-Wine Sauce (p. 155) as a base.

LOBSTER MOUSSELINES HOMARD (MOUSSELINES DE) (M.)

Mousselines are made with the lobster forcemeat given above. They may be molded with a spoon or squeezed from a pastry bag and poached in salted water. They are garnished in various ways and topped with a sauce to harmonize with the garnish, or are covered with Mornay Sauce (p. 152) and glazed.

LOBSTER NEWBURG I HOMARD À LA NEW-BURG (E.)

Lobster Newburg is made in 2 ways: (1) with raw lobster, a method particularly suitable for large affairs; (2) with cooked lobster, which is the correct method. (Take a lobster weighing about 2 lb.)

LOBSTER NEWBURG II (WITH RAW LOBSTER) HOMARD À LA NEW-BURG (E.) (*For 3 persons*)

Cut up the live lobster and sauté it in oil and butter as for Lobster Américaine (p. 316). When the meat has become firm and the shell has turned red, pour off all the fat; pour 3 tbsp. flaming cognac and 6 oz. Marsala over the lobster. Cook until the liquid is reduced by ⅔; season, and add 12 oz. cream and 3 oz. fish stock. Cover and cook 15 min. Remove the lobster pieces, extract the meat from the shells, and keep hot in a covered dish. Bind the sauce with the chopped intestines and 1 oz. butter and boil for a few instants. Strain the sauce and pour it over the lobster meat.

LOBSTER NEWBURG III (WITH COOKED LOBSTER) HOMARD À LA NEW-BURG (E.) (*For 3 persons*)

Cook the lobster in a Court Bouillon (p. 277), remove the meat from the tail by removing the bottom membrane, and cut it into regular slices. Place these slices in a well-buttered sautéing pan, season them well, and heat on both sides until the outer skin turns pink. Next pour in enough Madeira until the slices are almost covered, and cook until nearly all the wine has evaporated. Just before serving, pour a mixture of 4 oz. cream and 2 egg yolks over the lobster meat. Roll the pan gently back and forth over the fire until the sauce is well bound by the cooking of the egg yolks; pour immediately into a warm timbale.

Note: (1) It is not possible to prepare this lobster in advance, since the sauce cooks very rapidly. (2) It may also be served in a ring of Potatoes Duchesse (p. 507) browned in the oven in advance. Usually, however, it is served with creole rice (rice with tomatoes, onions, and peppers).

LOBSTER ASPIC RUSSIAN STYLE HOMARD (ASPIC DE) À LA RUSSE (E.)

Cold Dish: Cover the lobster slices with Stiff Mayonnaise (p. 157); decorate them with truffles, lobster coral, etc., and place them, standing, in a ring mold well lined with clear Aspic Jelly (p. 168); place the slices in such a way that the decorated sides will show after the aspic is unmolded. Finish filling the mold with jelly; let it set; unmold just before serving, and fill the center of the ring with Russian Salad (p. 525).

Second Recipe: Line a plain mold with Aspic Jelly. Place the lobster slices decorated with truffles around the sides of the mold, with the slices overlapping each other. Fill the empty space in the center with Russian Salad. Finish filling the mold with jelly and let set. Serve with 6 small artichoke bottoms garnished with Russian Salad, half of them tinted light pink; glaze all of them with jelly after decorating with truffles. (Figures 196-197, P. 313 and directions, P. 98.)

LOBSTER THERMIDOR HOMARD THERMIDOR (M.)

Split a live lobster in half lengthwise. Crack open the claws and remove the gills from the shell. Salt, baste with olive oil, and roast in the oven about 20 min. Remove the meat from the tail and dice into large pieces; remove part of the shell from the claws. In a separate pan reduce fish stock, white wine, meat gravy, chervil, tarragon, and chopped shallots to a glaze. Add some thick Béchamel Sauce (p. 146) and English mustard to this reduced sauce. Boil for a few moments and add 1 part fresh butter to 2 parts sauce. Spread a little of this sauce in the bottom of the empty lobster shells, lay in the tail meat, and cover these as well as the claw meat with the rest of the sauce, sprinkle with grated Parmesan cheese, and glaze under a hot flame.

Note: This recipe may also be used for lobster cooked in a Court Bouillon. In this case, the diced lobster meat should be browned a little in butter.

Remarks: Lobster Thermidor was created at the Café de Paris. We owe this recipe to M. Tony Girod, head chef of this celebrated Paris restaurant.

LOBSTER PILAF HOMARD (PILAF DE) (A.) (*For 4 persons*)

Take 2 cups concentrated white bouillon or consommé, 1½ cups white wine, 1½ cups rice, 5 oz. mushrooms, 5 oz. shrimps, 5 oz. butter, 4 oz. carrots cut into tiny cubes, 2½ oz. heavy cream, 1½ oz. chopped onion, 1 jigger cognac, a small sprig of parsley, a few peppercorns, 1 pt. mussels, 12 oysters, 2 whitings weighing about 1 lb. together, 2 small soles weighing about 1 lb. together or scraps of soles, 2 egg yolks, 1 hard-roed live lobster weighing about 3 lb., a *bouquet garni,* a bay leaf, a few sprigs of thyme, flour, lemon juice, four spices (see *Note,* p. 301), salt, and pepper.

Shell the shrimps and save the shells. Peel the mushrooms and cook them in ½ oz. butter and a little lemon juice; save the peelings. Cook the mussels in their own juices; blanch the oysters in their juices. Mix mussels, oysters, mushrooms, and shelled shrimps together; keep hot. Save the cooking juices of the oysters, mussels, and mushrooms. Place in a saucepan ¾ oz. butter, cut carrot, parsley, thyme, bay leaf; brown slowly; cover and let cook until almost dry. Next pour in the wine, cognac, cooking juices of oysters, mussels, and mushrooms; add peppercorns, washed mushroom peelings, whitings and soles or scraps of soles previously turned in a pan with ½ oz. butter, a little of the four spices to taste; and continue cooking. Cook the fish stock until concentrated and press it lightly through a strainer.

While preparing the fish stock, cook the lobster 20 min. in water salted with bay salt. Remove the shell, cut the meat into slices, and save the insides, the scraps, and the coral; keep hot. Make a Lobster-Shrimp Butter, using 1 oz. butter, the scraps and roe of the lobster, and the shrimp shells (see p. 164). Wash and drain the rice. Cook the chopped onions without browning in 2 oz. butter; next add the rice and the *bouquet garni;* turn in the pan for a few moments, then add the white bouillon or consommé; season with salt and pepper and cook in the oven 20–25 min., until the liquid has been completely absorbed and the rice grains are fluffy and whole. Finish the sauce: mix the flour with the rest of the butter without browning it, moisten with reduced fish stock, and cook. Bind this Velouté with the cream and egg yolks; add a little lemon juice if necessary; blend the sauce with the Lobster-Shrimp Butter; strengthen the seasoning.

Mold the rice into a ring on a platter; glaze it lightly with the sauce; in the center place the mixture of oysters, shrimps, mussels, and mushrooms bound with a little sauce; decorate each slice of lobster meat with a piece of lobster coral and place them on the rice ring. Serve rest of sauce separately.

This dish may be garnished with truffles if desired, but with or without truffles Lobster Pilaf is an attractive dish. Spiny lobster, or sea crayfish, may be prepared the same way.

SPINY LOBSTER or SEA CRAYFISH[1] EN BELLEVUE PARISIENNE

LANGOUSTE EN BELLEVUE À LA PARISIENNE (M.)

Cold Dish: Remove all of the meat from the shell of the lobster and fill it with lettuce Chiffonade (p. 193) or a vegetable salad mixed with Stiff Mayonnaise (p. 157). Decorate the slices of lobster meat with truffles, chervil leaves, and lobster coral and glaze with Aspic Jelly (p. 168).

Garnishes: Small artichoke bottoms filled with a salad of various vegetables (with a salpicon of lobster bound with thick mayonnaise added to the salad), decorated with truffles, and glazed with jelly; halves of hard-boiled eggs decorated with truffles and glazed with jelly; hearts of lettuce. Mayonnaise. (Figure 198, Page 320.)

Note: Small tomatoes, all the same size, may be used instead of the artichoke bottoms.

SPINY LOBSTER CABOURG LANGOUSTE À LA CABOURG (P.)

Cook the lobster in a Court Bouillon (p. 277). Split it in half lengthwise and cut the tail meat into slices. Cut the meat of the legs into small pieces and mix with mussels, mushrooms, and sliced truffles. When everything is cooked it is mixed with a Normande Sauce (p. 153) made from the cooking juices of the mussels and mushrooms and bound with egg yolks. Pour this composition into the bottom of the lobster shell and place the sliced tail meat on top. Cover with sauce and glaze in a rather hot oven. To serve, place the lobster on a long platter and decorate with truffle slices and fried, breaded gudgeons.

SPINY LOBSTER CARDINAL LANGOUSTE CARDINAL (E.)

Same recipe as for Lobster Cardinal (p. 317).

SPINY LOBSTER THERMIDOR LANGOUSTE THERMIDOR (M.)

Same recipe as for Lobster Thermidor (p. 318). (Figure 199, Page 321.)

SPINY-LOBSTER CHOPS VICTORIA LANGOUSTE (CÔTELETTES DE) À LA VICTORIA (Gi.)

Cooking the lobsters and preparing the mixture: Cook 2 or 3 medium-sized spiny lobsters in boiling water with salt, vinegar, carrots, onions, sprigs of parsley, peppercorns, thyme, and bay leaf, allowing 15–20 min. per lb. lobster. Let cool, then remove the tails (see directions, p. 97), remove the shell, and cut the meat into 7 or 8 even slices. Remove the meat from the legs and the body and dice, together with any scraps left in the tail and a sufficient amount of cooked mushrooms and truffles. Put this diced mixture into a very thick Normande Sauce (p. 153), lightly seasoned with cayenne, to which a piece of Spiny-Lobster Butter has been added (see Lobster Butter, p. 164). Mix everything well, pour onto a buttered platter, and let cool.

Making the chops and sauce: With this mixture, divided into even-sized pieces weighing 2 or 3 oz. each, form small chop-shaped croquettes, using either

[1]All recipes calling for spiny lobster (French *langouste*) may be applied to lobster or rock-lobster tails.

Fig. 198 - Spiny lobster en bellevue parisienne (p. 320).

Fig. 198

Fig. 199

Fig. 200

a mold or a knife. Dip them in milk, flour, beaten egg, and bread crumbs; correct their shape while sticking bread crumbs on top, and place them on a tray. Separately, prepare Normande Sauce, add butter to it, and finish with 1 oz. Spiny-Lobster Butter. Add the sliced lobster tail meat, small cooked mushrooms, and sliced truffles to this sauce; keep hot in a *bain-marie.*

Cooking and serving: Fry the chops in deep hot fat 5 min. before serving; as soon as they have browned, drain them on a cloth, salt lightly, and arrange them in a ring, overlapping, on a platter. Using a pointed piece of fried bread, fix a paper frill onto the end of each chop. In the center of the ring of chops, pour the ragout of lobster, mushrooms, and truffles (kept hot), and serve immediately.

HARD-SHELL CRAB RUSSIAN STYLE TOURTEAU À LA RUSSE (P.)

Cold Dish: Cook the crab in a Court Bouillon (p. 277). Let it cool and then remove the legs and claws as well as the flat part of the shell (plastron). Remove all the contents of the shell; trim the meat found in the interior, removing all the hard parts, and dice it. Take the meat out of the legs and claws and dice that, too. Season the meat with mayonnaise mixed with the yellowish creamy substance found inside the crab. Wash and dry the crab shell and fill with this mixture. Mold the filling into a dome. Decorate with slices of tomatoes, hard-boiled eggs, gherkins, a thin ribbon of mayonnaise made with a paper cone or a pastry bag, curly parsley. (Figure 200, Page 321.)

MOLLUSKS

SNAILS (PREPARATION OF) ESCARGOTS (PRÉPARATION DES) (M.)

(1) Wash in several waters to remove all dirt from the shells and the diaphragm. Using the point of a small knife, remove the diaphragm closing the shells; place the snails in a bowl with rock salt, vinegar, and a little flour (the quantity determined by the number of snails); let them soak 2 hr. to make them disgorge their viscous slime, turning them from time to time. Next, wash them again in running water to remove all mucous substances from the shells.

(2) Place them in a saucepan with cold water, bring to a boil very slowly, carefully removing the scum produced by the remainder of the mucous substances; let boil 8 min.; drain and cool.

(3) Cover completely with equal parts of white wine and water; add ⅓ oz. salt per qt. liquid, thick rings of carrots and onions, sliced shallots, garlic cloves, a *bouquet garni,* and a few peppercorns. Cook at a slow, even boil 3–3½ hr., depending on the size of the snails. When cooked, drain them in a strainer, remove snails from shells, and immediately cut off the cloaca (the black end of the helix). Wash shells in warm water, drain, and set on a rack to dry.

Notes: (*a*) We do not think it necessary to mention here the traditional bag of ashes without which, according to old wives' recipes, the snails would not cook. This item is mentioned religiously in certain cookbooks. (*b*) In Burgundy, it is customary, when preparing snails in shells or fried in batter, to sauté them in butter for a few moments with finely chopped shallots and crushed garlic without letting them brown—this, in the following proportions: 2 oz. butter, 1

Fig. 199 - Spiny lobster thermidor (p. 320).
Fig. 200 - Hard-shell crab russian style (p. 321).

oz. shallots, 2 cloves of garlic, a pinch of salt and pepper, and a dash of spices or nutmeg, according to taste. This final seasoning is important because the snails absorb very little of their seasoning while cooking.

SNAILS BOURGUIGNONNE ESCARGOTS À LA BOURGUIGNONNE (M.)

Place a bit of Butter Bourguignonne (below), about the size of a bean, in the bottom of each shell; place the snail in the shell and close the opening with more of the same butter, pressing it down tightly. Place them in a snail pan (or baking dish); baste with a little white wine. Sprinkle the butter with fine bread crumbs and bake 8 min. in a very hot oven.

Butter Bourguignonne: For 100 snails: 1 lb. butter, 3 oz. finely chopped shallots, ⅔ oz. grated garlic, 2 oz. chopped parsley, 1 tbsp. salt, a few ground peppercorns, ½ tsp. spices. Mix all these ingredients well.

OYSTERS HUÎTRES (M.)

True oyster lovers never eat these delicious mollusks any way except raw. We admit that oysters, served raw, are the most delectable hors d'oeuvres one can eat. We must take into account, however, that there are a great many recipes for serving oysters hot and that most of these dishes are excellent. The best French oysters are the Armoricans and those from Cancale, Belon, Marennes, Courseulle, and Arcachon. The most valued foreign oysters are: Zeeland (Holland), Ostend and Victoria (Belgium), Natives and Colchester (Great Britain), Red Bank (Ireland), Blue Point and East River (United States), Malpeque (Canada).

OYSTER PATTIES NORMANDE HUÎTRES (BOUCHÉES AUX) À LA NORMANDE (M.)

Poach and trim the oysters; place them in patty shells half filled with a salpicon (tiny cubes) of mushrooms, shrimps, and truffles bound with Normande Sauce (p. 153). Cover smoothly with Normande Sauce. On top of each patty place a slice of truffle.

OYSTER BROCHETTES HUÎTRES (BROCHETTES D') (M.)

Place poached and trimmed oysters on skewers, alternating them with sliced mushrooms cooked in butter. Dip the brochettes in milk, beaten egg, and bread crumbs. Grill over a slow fire. Serve with Maître d'Hôtel Butter (p. 164).

MUSSELS CHARENTES MOULES DES CHARENTES (P.)

Open the mussels and remove 1 shell. Prepare a mixture of chopped parsley, garlic, and bread crumbs. Put plenty of butter into a saucepan and, when the butter is very hot but not brown, drop in the mussels. Turn the mussels in the butter, sprinkle on the bread-crumb mixture, and remove from the saucepan when the juice has been absorbed and the bread crumbs begin to brown. Salt and pepper.

CREAMED MUSSELS MOULES À LA CRÈME (P.) (*For 3 persons*)

Take ½ lb. mushrooms, 1 cup cream, 4 oz. butter, 4 oz. carrots, 1 oz. flour, 3 qt. mussels, vinegar (optional), a *bouquet garni,* pepper. Clean the mussels carefully; peel and chop the mushrooms. Cook the carrots sliced thin and the *bouquet garni* slowly in 1½ oz. butter for about ½ hr.; pepper, then add the mussels, and sauté them a sufficient length of time for them to pop open and be cooked; keep them hot. Put 1 oz. butter into a saucepan with the chopped mushrooms, then add the flour; stir in the pan without letting the mixture brown; moisten with the strained cooking juice from the mussels; cook for a few minutes; blend into the sauce the remainder of the butter and the cream; add some vinegar. Remove a valve from each shell and arrange the mussels on a platter or on as many plates as there are guests.

MUSSELS MARINIÈRE MOULES À LA MARINIÈRE (P.) (*For 4 persons*)

Take 4 qt. mussels. Wash, scrape the shells, and wash again in several waters. Clean them well in cold water, but do not let them soak, or they will open and lose their sea water. Cook them in a rather large kettle with pepper (no salt), parsley, thyme, and 2 chopped shallots; pour in ½ glass white wine, cover, and boil until all the mussels have opened. To make sure that all of the mussels have opened, stir several times, bringing those on the bottom to the top. Remove from the pot as soon as cooked. Pour the cooking liquid into a large stewpan and place on a hot fire to boil; add a large piece of fresh butter and a pinch of chopped parsley. When the liquid has been reduced to ½ its original volume, pour it over the mussels, from which, meanwhile, you have removed 1 shell. Serve immediately.

MUSSELS POULETTE MOULES À LA POULETTE (P.) (*For 2 persons*)

Cook as directed in the preceding recipe. Strain the cooking liquid, let any sediment fall to the bottom, and use the clear liquid to make a white sauce. To make the sauce, melt 1 oz. butter (per 2 qt. mussels), mix with 1½ tbsp. flour, and immediately pour in the cooking liquid from the mussels and a little cream (or milk). Add 1 egg yolk and bring to a quick boil while beating briskly with a wire whisk. Remove from the heat when it first begins to boil, butter the sauce, taste it and correct the seasoning if necessary, add a little parsley, and serve at the same time as the mussels.

MUSSELS VILLEROI MOULES À LA VILLEROI (P.)

Cook some large mussels, shell them, dry them, and dip them in thick Béchamel Sauce (p. 146) bound with egg yolk. Let the mussels cool, then dip them twice in flour, beaten egg, and bread crumbs, and fry in hot deep fat. This method of preparing mussels is used when a garnish is needed for large fish, but Mussels Villeroi are delicious served as a small entree.

MUSSEL PILAF ORIENTALE MOULES (PILAF DE) À L'ORIENTALE (P.)

Prepare Mussels Marinière (above) and make the Rice Pilaf (p. 512). Make a Velouté (p. 147) from the mussel cooking liquid and mix in a strong pinch of curry or saffron according to taste. Mix the shelled mussels into this sauce and pour into the center of the rice arranged in a ring.

Note: Mussels flavored with curry are called Indian style or creole style. In general practice, mussels are used as garnishes. These garnishes may be prepared Villeroi style, or fried in batter, or mixed with shrimps, mushrooms, crayfish tails, etc.

SEA URCHINS OURSINS (E.)

Sea urchins are principally served as hors d'oeuvres. Trim off the spikes first, then open the flat side of the shells with scissors; pour out the water and remove the digestive tract. The edible portion is made up of the ovaries, usually purplish red in color, which are scooped out with bits of bread, as one might eat a soft-boiled egg served in the shell, which gives the sea urchin its other name, "sea egg." (See directions, p. 101.)

DEVILED SCALLOPS SAINT-JACQUES (COQUILLES) À LA DIABLE (P.)

Cook the scallops as for Scallops Parisienne (below), then chop them fine; brown 1 chopped onion in butter, sprinkle it with 1 tsp. flour, moisten with the strained cooking liquid from the scallops, and add the chopped scallops, a piece of stale bread the size of an egg (soaked in cold milk, squeezed in the hand, then crumbled). Add chopped parsley, salt and ground pepper, 1 tsp. mustard, and cook everything together for a few minutes. Fill the scallop shells with this mixture, sprinkle with bread crumbs, moisten with butter, and brown in the oven or under the broiler.

SCALLOPS WITH MAYONNAISE SAINT-JACQUES (COQUILLES) À LA MAYONNAISE (M.)

Cold Dish: Cook the scallops in white wine, slice them, and season with oil, vinegar, salt, and pepper. Make a bed of lettuce Chiffonade (p. 193) in each shell and lay the scallop slices on top. Cover with mayonnaise. Decorate the top with strips of lobster coral, anchovy fillets, and capers. Garnish around the shells with quarters of hard-boiled eggs and hearts of lettuce.

SCALLOPS PARISIENNE I SAINT-JACQUES (COQUILLES) À LA PARISIENNE (P.)
(*For 6 persons*)

Place 6 scallop shells on the stove or in the oven 5 min. to open them. Remove the scallops from the shells and save the deep half of the shell. Wash the scallops in several waters to remove all of the sand and cut out the black part, which is the intestine. Cook the scallops in a small Court Bouillon made of enough white wine to cover the scallops, 1 sliced onion and 1 sliced shallot, a small *bouquet garni,* salt, and pepper (p. 277). Cook 10 min. Cook separately 5 oz. mushrooms. Next make a rather thick sauce with 2 oz. butter, 1 tbsp. flour, and the strained cooking juice from the scallops; add milk, cook the sauce for a few minutes, then cut the scallops and mushrooms into small pieces and add; mix well in the sauce and season highly. Stir on the fire 5 min., then remove, and add 2 oz. grated Gruyère cheese. Pour this mixture into the well-cleaned shells, sprinkle grated cheese and bread crumbs on top, and brown in the oven or under the broiler. Serve piping hot.

Note: Another method for opening the shells is shown on p. 99.

SCALLOPS PARISIENNE II SAINT-JACQUES (COQUILLES) À LA PARISIENNE (M.)

Braise the scallops and slice them. Sauté some thin-sliced or diced mushrooms in butter. Mix them together with Béchamel Sauce (p. 146) or Fish Velouté (p. 147). Pour this mixture into the shells bordered with a band of Potatoes Duchesse (p. 507) brushed with beaten egg. Sprinkle the mixture with bread crumbs and moisten with melted butter. Brown in the oven or under the broiler. (See directions, p. 100.)

MEAT

MEAT

This chapter on butcher's meat includes recipes for preparing beef, veal, mutton, and lamb, as well as the brains, tongues, liver, kidneys, feet, and so on from these animals. Furthermore, it is customary to include pork—and such pork products as puddings and sausages—in this chapter.

Advice on the quality of meats and their various modes of cooking: Meat to be grilled or roasted should be tender and aged, the texture so smooth that it feels velvety to the touch.

Beef should be very red and grained, streaked with fat, but not excessively so. Whitish meats come from young animals and do not contain much blood; dark meats come from bulls and old animals. Cooking time for cuts of red meat weighing 3–4 lb. is based on 15 min. per lb., but cuts under 1 lb. take more than 15 min. because they must first be completely seared on all sides.

Veal should be very white and served well done. Mutton, to be good, should be somewhat fatty—dry mutton will not make a good roast. Lamb should be white and, like veal, served well done.

During the summer heat, don't overindulge in meat; besides, it isn't at its best then, especially beef and mutton. Veal, however, if it is of good quality, can be eaten at any time of the year. This doesn't mean that you should completely give up meat in summer—only, serve the meat with a good deal of vegetables.

Portions: 5 oz. raw meat per person, or 4 oz. net weight.

Meats may be roasted, grilled, braised, sautéed, or, sometimes, boiled, as in the case of blanquettes and as found in most recipes for heart, head, feet, etc.

BEEF

BRAISED BEEF AIGUILLETTE DE BOEUF BRAISÉE (P.)

(*Tr. Note:* French butchers do not cut meat into the same roasts, chops, and steaks that we find in American or English butchershops. The *aiguillette* is a small, lean piece of meat cut between the rump and the round. This recipe may be applied, however, to any piece of beef suitable for a pot roast.)

Lard the beef with strips of pork fat rolled in spiced salt mixed with chopped parsley and a little crushed garlic. Brown it on all sides in a cocotte or Dutch oven with some fat and a few slices of onions and carrots. Then drain off the fat and pour in ½ bottle white wine. Cook until the liquid is reduced by ½, then pour in enough thin brown sauce to bring the liquid to the top of the beef; season and add a *bouquet garni ;* cover tightly and simmer for about 3 hr., or until the meat is well done. Skim the fat off the gravy, strain it, and cook some more if it needs thickening. The braised beef may be served with Macaroni Napolitaine (p. 520), cabbage braised with bacon, rice, etc., the macaroni being especially suitable.

SIRLOIN OF BEEF ALOYAU (E.)

The sirloin is cut from that part of the steer's back extending from the haunch to the floating ribs, including the whole fillet. This cut may not properly be called sirloin unless it includes the fillet, or undercut, and the upper fillet, which the French call *contrefilet.* If the whole joint is to be cooked, it should be shortened by removing the flank and by cutting the ligament, lying along the backbone against the upper fillet, in several places. A little fat should be left on the undercut and all the fat must be left on the upper fillet. In modern cookery, if the sirloin is to be braised, it is cut crosswise into pieces weighing between 6 and 7 lb. For roasting, it is better kept whole. Served as a large joint, the sirloin is braised or roasted and usually served rare. Braised sirloin, unless it is of top quality, usually turns out to be dry. All the garnishes given for beef fillet may be served with the sirloin, but generally the heavier garnishes are preferred, such as: Bourgeoise, Celery, Flemish, Richelieu, Provençal, etc. The accompanying sauce should be the one indicated for the garnishes.

COLD SIRLOIN ALOYAU FROID (E.)

Sirloin served cold should first be trimmed and then covered with a rather thick layer of Aspic Jelly (p. 168). It is served on a platter surrounded with jelly, the border decorated with jelly slices cut into fancy shapes.

BEEFSTEAK BEEFSTEAK (E.)

In principle, the beefsteak is cut from the head end of the fillet, but it can also be taken from the upper fillet or the sirloin. Beefsteak may be prepared according to any of the recipes for rib steak (*entrecôte*).

BEEF BOURGUIGNONNE BOEUF À LA BOURGUIGNONNE (P.) (*For 4 persons*)

When the butcher trims cuts of beef to order or for his display, he saves all the lean scraps and those streaked with fat for beef to be prepared Burgundy style, or *à la bourguignonne.* No special cuts are needed for this dish, but you may, if you so desire, ask for a piece of the haunch, rump, or neck cut into cubes a little smaller than those used for stew.

Brown 1 lb. beef in lard or oil (not butter, which is a useless expense) over a very hot fire. Add a few small onions or quartered large onions. When meat and onions are well browned, sprinkle with 1 tbsp. flour and let this also turn brown; add a crushed clove of garlic, then enough red wine to cover the meat, or ½ wine and ½ water. Darken the sauce with caramel coloring (which makes it not better, but better-looking); add 1 tbsp. tomato purée, salt, pepper, *bouquet garni,* and 4 oz. bacon fat cut in thick strips and browned in the frying pan; cover and cook slowly for about 2½ hr.; skim the fat off the sauce, add 4 oz. raw mushrooms, and finish cooking 15 min. Serve with chopped parsley on top.

BEEF DAUBE BOEUF EN DAUBE (P.) (*For 4 persons*)

Take 1 lb. beef (same type as in the preceding recipe, but cut in larger pieces); lard each piece of beef through the center with a piece of fat bacon rolled in some chopped parsley and garlic. Place the pieces of beef in a pot containing a few pieces of pork rind; add 2 onions and 2 carrots cut in quarters, a *bouquet garni,* salt, pepper, and pour in enough red wine almost to cover the meat. Cook slowly 4 hr. Bind the sauce with a few tbsp. thick tomato purée. Skim the fat off the sauce and serve, after thickening the sauce, if necessary, with a little Brown Roux (p. 137) or a little potato starch thinned with cold water. A larding needle is needed to lard the pieces of meat.

Fig. 201 - Rib steak bordelaise (p. 330).
Fig. 202 - Rib steak Mirabeau (p. 330).

Fig. 201

Fig. 202

Fig. 203

Fig. 204

BEEF WITH EGGPLANT MARIUS BOEUF GRATINÉ MARIUS (P.)

Peel and slice 2 eggplants; salt the slices and let drain 10 min.; flour them and fry in oil; place them in a baking dish. Put 1 lb. drained, quartered tomatoes into the oil remaining in the frying pan; add garlic, seasoning, and chopped parsley. Cook the tomatoes down completely. Cover the eggplant slices with very thin strips of beef; pour and spread the tomatoes on top. Sprinkle with bread crumbs, moisten with oil, and brown in the oven.

BEEF À LA MODE BOEUF À LA MODE (P.) (*For 6 persons*)

It is a good idea to prepare a large amount of Beef à la Mode, since it is excellent reheated and may also be served cold in aspic, which is the way some people prefer it. Take 2 lb. beef, from the haunch, rump, sirloin, or round. Roundsteak may be bought ready prepared at the butcher's, well larded with pieces of fat needed to keep it from being too dry. Also take ½ calf's foot and 5 oz. pork rind. Brown the beef on all sides in a cocotte with a little lard, then pour in enough water (and, if desired, 1 glass white wine) to cover the meat. Around the meat, put in the boned calf's foot and the pork rind blanched 5 min. in boiling water; add salt, pepper, *bouquet garni;* cover and cook slowly 1½–2 hr.; then add 30 small onions and enough thick carrot slices to make up the garnish. If the gravy is too pale, darken it with caramel coloring, and if you have no small onions, use large onions quartered. Finish cooking slowly another 1½ hr., then skim the fat off the sauce, and serve the beef with its garnish, with the calf's foot, cut into pieces, mixed in. Serve the leftovers cold the next day.

SAUTÉED BEEF LYONNAISE BOEUF SAUTÉ LYONNAISE (P.)

This recipe is very good for using up leftover boiled beef. Slice 2 or 3 onions and brown them slowly in a frying pan. In another pan, grill the beef in butter or in fat. After browning these ingredients separately, sauté them together for a few minutes with salt and pepper and serve, without sauce, with a dash of vinegar on top and a little chopped parsley.

BEEF BALLS BOULETTES DE BOEUF (P.)

Mix some chopped beef with a small amount of sausage meat, a little white bread soaked in bouillon, squeezed dry, and crumbled, salt, pepper, parsley, and chopped onions cooked in butter. Divide this mixture into small balls, roll them in flour and fry in lard. Serve Tomato Sauce (p. 146) separately.

BEEF CARBONNADES FLAMANDE CARBONNADES DE BOEUF À LA FLAMANDE (P.)

Sauté some rather thick beefsteaks in a frying pan, then place them in a pot on a thick layer of sliced onions lightly sautéed in lard (butter is not necessary). Cover with another layer of onions, then season and pour in ½ bottle beer. Add a *bouquet garni* and 1 cup brown sauce. Cover and cook slowly in the oven at least 2 hr. Skim the fat off the sauce and serve as is. It can be served with any starchy vegetable.

UPPER FILLET CONTREFILET (E.)

The upper fillet—the cut of beef, along the backbone, extending from the haunch to the floating ribs—is treated the same as the fillet, and therefore all the recipes for beef fillet may be used for it. It is usually boned for braising, but if it is

Fig. 203 - Pan-roasted beef fillet bouquetière (p. 331).
Fig. 204 - Beef fillet Godard (p. 332).

to be roasted, it is preferable to keep the bone, as is done in England. In this case, the long ligament must be cut in different sections to keep the roast from losing its shape, and the bones of the back must be broken near the heel so that they may be removed easily in carving. If the upper fillet is of top quality, it is best roasted.

COLD UPPER FILLET CONTREFILET FROID (E.)

When served as a cold cut, the upper fillet must first be trimmed carefully, then covered with Aspic Jelly (p. 168) and served on a platter trimmed with chopped jelly and a border of jelly slices.

RIB STEAK BORDELAISE ENTRECÔTE À LA BORDELAISE (P.) (*For 3 persons*)

Pan-fry the rib steak rare, then remove it from the pan and drop in a chopped shallot; brown it for a minute, add a pinch of flour, pour in 1/4 cup red wine and 1/4 cup bouillon, darken the sauce with caramel coloring, season, and add 1 1/2–2 oz. diced raw beef marrow; let the beef marrow cook in the sauce until half melted. Pour this sauce over the steak. If possible, place a row of marrow slices on top of the steak. (Figure 201, Page 328.)

RIB STEAK FORESTIÈRE ENTRECÔTE À LA FORESTIÈRE (E.) (*For 6 persons*)

Sauté the steaks in butter. Place them on a platter and surround them with 10 oz. morels (mushrooms) and 10 oz. diced potatoes sautéed in butter and arranged in alternate mounds with rectangles of lean bacon, blanched and browned. Sprinkle a little chopped parsley on the mushrooms and potatoes. Melt the glaze in the sautéing pan with a few tbsp. white wine; add 5 oz. good veal gravy; strain this sauce and serve it separately.

GRILLED RIB STEAK MAÎTRE D'HÔTEL ENTRECÔTE GRILLÉE À LA MAÎTRE D'HÔTEL (P.)

The rib steak, as its name implies, is a slice of meat cut from between 2 ribs, but for those who like lean meat it may also be cut from the upper fillet. The grill should be preheated over a white-hot fire. When the bars of the grill are very hot, the lightly oiled and salted steak is placed on it. The thicker the steak, the higher the grill should be raised from the fire, so that the meat will not be too charred. Serve with Maître d'Hôtel Butter (p. 164).

If a grill is not available, rib steak can also be fried in butter, but this method is not so good. Avoid too hot a fire, or the butter will blacken before the meat is cooked and give it a disagreeable taste.

RIB STEAK MIRABEAU ENTRECÔTE MIRABEAU (P.)

Grill the steak and spread the top with butter blended with a little anchovy essence. Place a few strips of anchovy fillets in oil on top the steak and a border of pitted olives around it. (Figure 202, Page 328.)

RIB STEAK VERT-PRÉ ENTRECÔTE VERT-PRÉ (M.)

Grill. Garnish with Potato Straws (p. 509) and water cress. Serve with Anchovy Butter (p. 163) or Maître d'Hôtel Butter (p. 164).

ESTOUFFADE ESTOUFFADE (P.) (*For 6 persons*)

(1) Cut up 1¼ lb. chuck and 1¼ lb. fat-covered beef from the lower ribs; the meat should be cut into cubes weighing about 3½ oz. Brown ½ lb. diced, blanched lean bacon in butter; drain it. Brown the pieces of beef in the bacon fat with 3 medium-sized onions cut in quarters. Add a crushed clove of garlic, 1 tsp. salt, pinch of pepper, and sprinkle with 2 tbsp. flour. Stir while browning. Next pour in 1 bottle red wine and 1 qt. brown stock, bring to a boil, add a *bouquet garni*, cover, and cook in the oven 2½–3 hr.

(2) Pour all of this into a strainer placed over a bowl. Place the pieces of beef and bacon in a sautéing pan; add ½ lb. mushrooms quartered and sautéed in butter. Let the sauce stand for ¼ hr. to let the fat rise to the surface. Skim off the fat and bring the sauce to the proper consistency either by cooking it until it is reduced if it is too thin or diluting it with a little stock if it is too thick. Strain it over the meat and let simmer for a good ¼ hr. before serving.

PAN-ROASTED BEEF FILLET BOUQUETIÈRE FILET DE BOEUF POÊLÉ À LA BOUQUETIÈRE (P.)

A garnished beef fillet is usually served roasted. However, I recommend pan-roasting it, and here is the way it is done. Sear it first in an iron pot with a little good fat. When it is browned on all sides, add 1 sliced onion and 1 sliced carrot. Then, when the vegetables have begun to color, pour a little Madeira or white wine and 1 cup Semiglaze Sauce (p. 138) over the fillet. Season, cover, and cook in the oven, allowing 15 min. per lb. meat. The fillet turns out rare; it has absorbed the flavor of the sauce just as the sauce has been improved by cooking with the meat. Also, not having a crust like a roast, the fillet is easily cut. Since all garnished fillets are cooked the same way, you need only decide on the kind of garnish, and these are numerous. Bouquetière Garnish (p. 180) is made of early-spring vegetables: carrots, turnips, green beans, small peas, cauliflower, and potatoes correctly cut, cooked separately, and sautéed in butter, then, as the name indicates, arranged in small bouquets around the fillet, which is basted with the skimmed sauce from the cooking. (Figure 203, Page 329.)

BEEF FILLET DAUPHINE FILET DE BOEUF À LA DAUPHINE (Gi.)

Remove the tendons from the fillet, lard it, and tie it a few times with string to keep its shape. Place it in a braising pan on a bed of pork rind, sliced carrots and onions, *bouquet garni,* and peppercorns, and begin braising it as directed on p. 121. Pour in enough salted or unsalted Veal Gravy (p. 134), white wine, and Madeira (1 part white wine and Madeira to 2 parts Veal Gravy) to cover the fillet halfway. Bring to a boil on top of the stove and finish cooking in the oven at low heat, basting frequently. Allow 12 min. per lb. if the fillet is to be rare, and 15 min. for medium. Remove the fillet from the braising pan 10 min. before serving, and place it in a flat pan. Baste it with a few tbsp. of its own cooking juice, and place it in the oven for a few minutes to glaze the surface and brown the pork fat.

Sauce: Strain the cooking juice and skim off the fat. Reduce it if it is too thin, and add enough Espagnole Sauce (p. 137) so that the sauce will be thin rather than thick. Bring to a boil a few times and finish at the last moment with a glass of fine Madeira. Be sure not to let the sauce boil after adding the Madeira.

Serving: Place the fillet on a long platter and surround it with a garnish of Potatoes Dauphine (p. 507).

BEEF FILLET GODARD FILET DE BOEUF GODARD (E.)

Lard the fillet with strips of pork fat and tongue, alternating them, and pan-roast it (see directions, p. 331). Place it on a platter and surround it with a Godard Garnish (p. 181) arranged in bouquets covered lightly with sauce. Place decorated quenelles at the middle and both ends of the platter. Serve with a dish of Godard Sauce (p. 141), with some of the stock from the pan-roasting, skimmed, strained, and reduced, added. (Figure 204, Page 329.)

BEEF FILLET MODERNE FILET DE BOEUF À LA MODERNE (E.)

Lard the fillet with pork fat and tongue; pan-roast it and glaze it just before serving. Place it on a platter and on either side arrange small vegetable molds, with decorated quenelles at either end of the platter and braised heads of lettuce in the spaces between the vegetable molds. Serve separately a gravy made by skimming and straining the cooking stock and lightly binding it with arrowroot. (Figure 219, Page 348.)

BEEF FILLET RÉGENCE FILET DE BOEUF À LA RÉGENCE (M.)

Stud with truffles and marinate in Madeira; spread Matignon (p. 135) over it, cover with strips of bacon, and braise with Madeira. Place the fillet on a base of fried bread (without the crust). Surround the fillet with a garnish composed of large decorated quenelles, slices of *foie gras* sautéed in butter, fluted mushrooms, medium-sized truffles cooked in Madeira, cockscombs.

Sauce: The cooking stock enriched with Semiglaze Sauce (p. 138) with truffle essence.

FILETS MIGNONS FILETS MIGNONS (E.)

Filets mignons are usually cut from the tail of the beef fillet. They should be trimmed into flat triangles. This is an excellent way to use up those parts of the tenderloin too thin to make *tournedos.*

Preparation of filets mignons: After seasoning, dip the *filets mignons* in melted butter and bread them. Lightly press the bread-crumbed surface, cross-rule it with the back of a knife, baste with melted butter, and grill slowly.

Serve with any vegetable garnishes, and any of the following sauces: Béarnaise (p. 147), Choron (p. 148), Valois (p. 154), etc.

Note: Sauces should be served separately.

BEEF FRICADELLES WITH TOMATO SAUCE FRICADELLES DE BOEUF SAUCE TOMATE (P.)

Grind up some leftover beef into a hash; mix in ½ its volume of very dry puréed potatoes. Season with salt, pepper, *fines herbes,* and chopped onions cooked in butter. Then add 1 whole egg per lb. mixture. Divide into balls and roll them into shape with a little flour. Fry the balls in a pan with a little fat, and serve with a separate dish of Tomato Sauce (p. 146), or Piquante Sauce (p. 143.)

BEEF HASH AU GRATIN HACHIS DE BOEUF AU GRATIN (M.)

Mix the minced beef with Semiglaze Sauce (p. 138) and chopped onion cooked in butter until soft. Line a baking dish with Potatoes Duchesse (p. 507) squeezed from a pastry bag or with overlapping slices of boiled potatoes. Brush the border of potatoes with beaten egg. Place the beef hash in the center. Sprinkle with bread crumbs. Baste with melted butter. Brown in the oven.

BEEF HASH PARMENTIER HACHIS DE BOEUF À LA PARMENTIER (P.)

Grind up some leftover boiled beef as finely as possible. Brown 1 large chopped onion in lard, add a pinch of flour, then 1/4 cup white wine and 1 or 2 cups water. Put in the ground meat and a little tomato, season highly, and let simmer 3/4 hr., stirring from time to time. While this is cooking, make some puréed potatoes, strain them through a sieve, and mix with beef bouillon instead of milk. Place the hash in a baking dish, cover it entirely with the puréed potatoes, and brown in a very hot oven. When, after 8 or 10 min., the potatoes form a crust, brush the surface with a little melted butter or a beaten egg to glaze it well. This hash is a very nutritious dish for a large family.

BEEF MEDALLIONS DUBARRY MÉDAILLONS DE BOEUF DUBARRY (E.)

Sauté the medallions, place them on fried croutons, and cover them with golden Meat Glaze (p. 135). Surround them with little loaves or balls of cauliflower topped with Mornay Sauce (p. 152) and browned in the oven. Serve with buttered Veal Gravy (p. 134). (Figure 205, Page 336.)

Note: Medallions, merely another form of *tournedos,* are either sautéed or grilled. See the recipes for *tournedos* (pp. 334–335).

BEEF MIROTON MIROTON DE BOEUF (P.)

This is a good recipe to use for boiled beef left over from a *pot-au-feu.* Slice fine 2 or 3 large onions and brown them slowly in good fat from a roast or some lard. When browned, sprinkle them with 1 tbsp. flour; pour in some beef bouillon if there is any, or water; add a little tomato purée, salt, pepper, and a dash of vinegar. Cook gently 20 min., then heat the slices of boiled beef in this sauce. Serve as is, after skimming the fat off the sauce.

Note: When the sauce is made with water, it is a good idea to add a little meat extract or ready-prepared beef-bouillon cubes. This keeps the sauce from being too flat.

BEEF LOAF PAIN DE BOEUF (P.) (*For 3 persons*)

Grind up 1/2 lb. cooked beef; mix in 2 oz. stale bread crumbs soaked in bouillon; salt, pepper, chopped herbs, 1/2 cup Béchamel Sauce (p. 146), and 1/2 cup thick tomato purée. Heat well, remove from the stove, and bind with 2 whole eggs; pour into a buttered charlotte mold and cook 25–30 min., in a *bain-marie,* in the oven. Unmold and serve moistened with whatever sauce you prefer, such as Tomato (p. 146), Chasseur (p. 139), Piquante (p. 143), etc.

RUMP OF BEEF ENGLISH STYLE POINTE DE CULOTTE DE BOEUF À L'ANGLAISE (P.)

This is an excellent luncheon dish and a good way to serve a piece of boiled beef rare. Take a piece of tip of rump or rump steak weighing about 4 lb.; place it in a large pot with cold water as for making a *pot-au-feu ;* bring it to a boil, skim carefully, and add a garnish of carrots, turnips, leeks, and *bouquet garni,* then add 2 or 3 cabbages cut in quarters and previously blanched in boiling water.

Season well and cook together, allowing ¼ hr. per lb. meat. Serve on a platter, meat and vegetables together, and save the cooking stock to make soup for dinner. (Figure 206, Page 336.)

RUMP STEAK RUMSTEAK (E.)

The rump steak is cut from the head of the sirloin. It may be grilled or sautéed. Any of the recipes for rib steak (*entrecôte*) may be used in preparing it.

STEWED STEAK STEWED STEAK (P.)

When a slice of rump steak or rib steak is too tough to be grilled, it can still make a delicious dish if prepared the following way. Brown it on both sides in a cocotte or Dutch oven in fat from a roast, then remove it and drop a few diced onions and carrots into the fat. Brown these vegetables, then pour in ½ cup white wine, ½ cup beef bouillon, 3 or 4 tbsp. tomato pureé, salt, pepper, and *bouquet garni ;* put the meat back into the pot. Cover tightly and cook very slowly for about 3 hr. Skim the fat off the gravy and serve as is, with chopped parsley sprinkled on top.

TOURNEDOS BEAUGENCY TOURNEDOS À LA BEAUGENCY (P.)

Sauté the steaks in butter and place them on croutons, cover with thickened gravy, and on each *tournedos* place an artichoke bottom filled with Béarnaise Sauce (p. 147), with a large slice of poached beef marrow in the middle. In the center of the platter place some Potatoes Noisette (p. 509). (Figure 207, P. 337.)

Note: Tournedos are choice steaks cut from the fillet and average in weight about 3½ oz.

TOURNEDOS BENJAMIN TOURNEDOS BENJAMIN (E.)

Sauté the steaks and place them on thin fried croutons. Surround them with small potato croquettes made of Potato Dauphine mixture (p. 507) with truffles, allowing 3 croquettes per steak. Place a small stuffed mushroom on each steak. Serve a separate dish of Semiglaze Sauce (p. 138) with the glaze in the sautéing pan melted with Madeira and added to it.

TOURNEDOS CLAMART TOURNEDOS À LA CLAMART (M.)

Sauté in butter. Garnish with small artichoke bottoms filled with buttered peas or Peas French Style (p. 505).

Sauce: The juices in the sautéing pan with Madeira and veal stock added.

TOURNEDOS HENRY IV TOURNEDOS HENRI IV (P.)

Grill the steaks and place them on croutons; using a spoon, make a narrow ribbon of thick Béarnaise Sauce (p. 147) around the edge of each steak. Fill the center of the platter with Potatoes Pont-Neuf (p. 509). (Figure 208, Page 337.)

TOURNEDOS MARIE LOUISE TOURNEDOS MARIE-LOUISE (P.)

Sauté the steaks in butter, place them on croutons, and cover with thin Semiglaze Sauce (p. 138). On each steak place an artichoke bottom filled with Soubise Purée (p. 504) and decorated with a cooked mushroom cap. Surround with Potatoes Duchesse (p. 507). (Figure 209, Page 340.)

TOURNEDOS MONÉGASQUE TOURNEDOS À LA MONÉGASQUE (M.)

Sauté the steaks in butter. Place a rather thick slice of eggplant sautéed in oil on each. Garnish with Tomato Fondue (p. 194) and black olives.

Sauce: The cooking juice in the pan melted with white wine, with tarragon added, and finished with tomatoed Veal Stock (p. 134). (Figure 210, Page 340.)

TOURNEDOS ROSSINI TOURNEDOS ROSSINI (E.)

Sauté the *tournedos;* place them on fried croutons covered with melted Meat Glaze (p. 135). On each *tournedos* place a slice of *foie gras* sautéed in butter and, on that, a few fine slices of truffle. Melt the cooking juice in the pan with Madeira and blend with Semiglaze Sauce (p. 138) made with truffle essence.

BEEF BRAINS, TONGUE, KIDNEY, ETC.

BEEF MARROW AMOURETTES (M.)

The spinal marrow of beef is a prolongation of the brain and has the same substance.

After washing in cold water, remove the covering film. Soak again in cold water to make the marrow very white and poach in a Court Bouillon made with vinegar as for Brains (below). After being cooked and drained, beef marrow can be prepared in a variety of ways. It is especially used as an ingredient of certain garnishes. It is also used to garnish vol-au-vents, meat pies, and timbales. Beef marrow is also used in the mixture for croquettes, or on hot canapés, in fritters, with mayonnaise or Vinaigrette Sauce, etc. All the recipes for beef brains may be used in preparing marrow.

BRAINS CERVELLE (M.)

Preparation: Soak in cold water, remove the thin membrane covering the brain, and soak again in cold water until very white. Cook in a vinegared Court Bouillon flavored with sliced carrots and onions, *bouquet garni,* salt, and pepper (p. 277). The Court Bouillon may be made in advance or at the last minute, the important thing being to have it at a full boil when the brains are dropped in. This is the only way to keep the brains firm.

Cooking Time: About 25 min. After the brains have been cooked, they may be prepared according to particular recipes. For some recipes, however, raw brains are used.

BRAINS IN BLACK BUTTER CERVELLE AU BEURRE NOIR (M.)

Cut the brains into rather thick slices. Arrange them on a round platter with diced beef marrow in the middle. Season them with salt and freshly ground pepper. Heat well. Just before serving, pour 3½ oz. piping-hot black butter over the brains. (Add 2 tbsp. parsley leaves to the butter before pouring it over the brains.) Heat a finger of vinegar in the same pan and pour over the brains.

BEEF BELLY LYONNAISE GRAS-DOUBLE À LA LYONNAISE (P.)

The belly, sold in butchershops already prepared but not cooked, takes a long time to cook. Cut it into long strips and brown it in good fat over a very hot fire. When it begins to brown, add 1 tbsp. flour per lb. belly; brown it a little longer, then add enough water almost to cover it, salt, pepper, flavor with a little tomato purée and a good quantity of sliced large onions previously browned separately in a frying pan. Cover and cook slowly for at least 1½ hr. and serve with a dash of vinegar and chopped parsley on top.

BEEF TONGUE LANGUE DE BOEUF (H.)

Trim the waste part off the back of the tongue, and plunge the tongue for a minute into boiling water to make it easier to remove the outer skin; then braise it as you would Braised Beef (p. 327). Tongue may be garnished with any buttered, diced, or puréed vegetable. If you use salted or marinated beef tongue, let it soak in running water overnight.

GRILLED OXTAIL QUEUE DE BOEUF GRILLÉE (M.)

Cut the tail into pieces 3–3½ in. long. Cook about 3½ hr. in consommé. Let it cool in the consommé. Drain the pieces, dip them in melted butter and bread crumbs, and grill them over a slow fire. Serve with mashed potatoes or with any other garnish usually served with grilled meats. For the sauce, use any of the special sauces for grilled meats such as Bordelaise (p. 138), Diable (p. 140), Piquante (p. 143), Robert (p. 144), etc.

BEEF KIDNEY ROGNON DE BOEUF (E.)

Beef kidney is only sautéed. However, in England, it is used in beef-and-kidney pies and in puddings.

Preparation: Strip the skin off the kidney, remove the fat, and cut it into medium-thick slices. If the kidney is from an old steer, it is a good idea to plunge it into boiling water for a moment and then drain and dry immediately. Sauté the kidney in butter over a hot fire for just a moment without cooking it, then put it into a strainer to drain out the blood, which has an alkaline odor and must be thrown away. Into the pan used in sautéing the kidney, pour white or red wine, Madeira, mushroom juice, or any other liquid that goes with the kidney recipe. Reduce this liquid, then add 4 oz. whatever sauce is to be used; boil for a few moments and strain. Sauté the kidney in this sauce, along with whatever garnishes are to accompany it. Remove from the stove and finish with 2 oz. butter.

Note: Once the kidney has been placed in the sauce, it must not be allowed to boil again, otherwise the kidney will become leathery.

BEEF KIDNEY IN MADEIRA ROGNON DE BOEUF AU MADÈRE (E.)

Sauté the kidney, drain, and place in Madeira Sauce (p. 142) enriched with butter.

BEEF TRIPE TRIPES DE BOEUF (M.)

Beef tripe has 4 distinct parts, all of which are used in preparing Tripe à la Mode de Caen (p. 337).

The 4 parts are: the fat part of the belly, which may be bought already cooked and rolled into cylinders under the name of *gras-double ;* the extremity of the belly, which begins the honeycombed part; the white honeycombed part; the brown honeycombed part.

In preparing Tripe à la Mode de Caen, not only are the above parts of the intestine used, but also the hoofs of the animal, previously scalded, the dewclaw removed, and boned. The hoofs provide the gelatin necessary in this dish.

Fig. 205 - Beef medallions Dubarry (p. 333).
Fig. 206 - Rump of beef english style (p. 333).

Fig. 205

Fig. 206

Fig. 207

Fig. 208

TRIPE À LA MODE DE CAEN TRIPES À LA MODE DE CAEN (M.)

Tripe à la Mode de Caen belongs to the earliest days of French cooking and is associated with the gallimaufries and other rich ragouts that delighted fourteenth-century gourmands.

This dish, the glory of Norman cooking, is famous throughout the whole world. In Paris, restaurants specialize in making it and deliver it to the home. In spite of the fact that this dish has been commercialized and may be bought ready-made, we feel it worth while to present a detailed recipe.

Preparation: Proportions for a whole tripe (that is, the 4 parts of the stomach lining mentioned on p. 336) : 2 ox hoofs, 12 large onions (4 of them with a clove stuck in), 8 medium-sized carrots, a large *bouquet garni*, 12 leeks, 1 tsp. salt per lb. tripe, 1/4 tsp. pepper per lb., 1 3/4 qt. dry plain cider, 9 oz. Calvados or cognac. There should be enough liquid, whether cider or water (water can be used in place of cider), to cover the tripe fully.

(1) *Cleaning and cutting the tripe:* Soak the tripe for a long time in running water, blanch it in a lot of boiling salted water for 15 min., and cool. Examine it carefully to make sure it is clean, wash it again, and drain. Cut up the tripe into pieces about 1 1/2 in. square. Season with salt and pepper. Remove the bones from the feet, split each half into 2 pieces, break the bones.

(2) *Cooking:* In the bottom of a deep kettle (in Normandy they use a very deep earthenware pot with a small opening) put the carrots, onions, *bouquet garni,* leeks, bones of the feet. Place the seasoned tripe on top of these ingredients; in the center place the feet. Pour in the cider (or water) and the Calvados or cognac (the liquid should cover the tripe well). Bring to a boil on top of the stove. Seal the cover of the pot tightly. Place in the oven and cook 10 hr. at a low, steady heat.

Serving the tripe: Tripe is usually served in special small pots, one for each guest. It may also be served in deep bowls set into larger bowls containing hot water to keep it piping hot, which is very important. Before serving tripe, remove the bones of the feet, the vegetables, and the *bouquet garni,* and the gravy must be skimmed of all the fat.

Remarks: (*a*) Sometimes beef fat is added to the tripe in preparing it for cooking. This is to make the tripe whiter. (*b*) We call attention to the practice, without necessarily recommending it, of using calves' feet instead of ox hoofs. The calves' feet may, however, be cooked separately and added to the tripe just before serving. But, let it be understood, do not leave out the ox hoofs.

VEAL

The quality of veal may be judged by its whiteness. Veal from calves which have not yet been turned out to graze is called milk-fed veal; this has the whitest meat. However, young calves just beginning to eat grass also provide very good veal, and this is the type most commonly found in the butchershops. Veal, like lamb or pork, should be served well done.

Veal, like beef, is divided into two categories: the loin, round or leg, and rib; and the less desirable cuts, such as breast, shoulder, neck, knuckle, shank.

The loin is roasted or braised or even sliced into cutlets.

Fig. 207 - Tournedos Beaugency (p. 334).
Fig. 208 - Tournedos Henri IV (p. 334).

VEAL BLANQUETTE BLANQUETTE DE VEAU (P.) (*For 4–5 persons*)

A real family dish, Veal Blanquette is delicious when well prepared. It may be made from neck, breast, or shoulder of veal. Take 1-1¼ lb. veal, cut it into pieces, and put it into a pot; cover with cold water and place on the fire. When it begins to boil, skim completely, then add a few small onions, 1 carrot cut in quarters, a *bouquet garni,* salt, and pepper. Cook 1¼–1½ hr., depending on the cut of meat used, the breast taking longer to cook than shoulder or neck. To determine whether the meat is cooked, pinch it between the fingers to see if it shreds. Drain the meat and save the cooking broth, which should be mixed with a roux made of 1 oz. butter and 1 heaping tbsp. flour. Cook this sauce slowly for 15 min., then bind according to the following directions.

In a separate bowl, beat the yolk of an egg with a few tbsp. cold milk, then pour in a little of the veal sauce. When it is well blended, pour this into the remainder of the sauce. Put this on a very hot fire and stir vigorously with a wire whisk until it comes to a full boil. When it has boiled a few minutes, taste it. Strain it over the meat, add 4½ oz. mushrooms cooked separately, and let everything simmer. If the sauce has not turned (and it should not, if it has been properly whipped) , there is no longer any danger of its turning, and any blanquette left over can be reheated. If 2 egg yolks are used, the sauce will be even smoother.

VEAL CHOPS CÔTES DE VEAU (E.)

Veal chops are usually sautéed or grilled. In making the sauce, leave the cooking butter and juices in the pan. Swirl around in the hot pan some liquid that will go with the desired sauce, then add it to the sauce, which is, most often, a buttered Semiglaze Sauce (p. 138) .

VEAL CHOPS BONNE FEMME CÔTES DE VEAU À LA BONNE FEMME (P.)

Using a deep skillet or Dutch oven, cook 12 small onions and 12 slices of lean bacon in butter; when they are golden brown, take them out and, in the same butter, brown the floured and seasoned veal chops on both sides; put the onions back in, with the bacon and a few mushrooms around them; pour in a little white wine and 1 cup veal gravy or bouillon. Cover and cook for about ¾ hr. Serve as is, after skimming the fat off the veal gravy, which should not be too abundant.

CREAMED VEAL CHOPS CÔTES DE VEAU À LA CRÈME (P.)

Cook the floured chops slowly in butter so as not to brown them too much; when they are cooked, pour in 4½ oz. heavy cream for 3 or 4 chops; let simmer, salt and pepper, and serve in the same pan. As there is no garnish for this dish, serve side dishes of potatoes or some other vegetable.

VEAL CHOPS WITH TARRAGON CÔTES DE VEAU À L'ESTRAGON (P.)

Salt, pepper, and flour the veal chops. Cook slowly in butter. When cooked, remove the chops and pour a little bouillon and a little tomato purée into the pan; drop a few fresh or dried tarragon leaves into this sauce and let steep. Decorate the veal chops with blanched tarragon leaves and strain the sauce over them.

VEAL CHOPS FERMIÈRE CÔTES DE VEAU À LA FERMIÈRE (P.)

Season and flour the chops and brown them in a cocotte; surround the chops with a garnish of carrots, turnips, potatoes, and onions cut in thin round slices; add 1 cup Veal Gravy (p. 134) or bouillon and 1 tbsp. tomato purée; cover and cook slowly ¾ hr.

VEAL CHOPS IN PASTRY CÔTES DE VEAU EN FEUILLETÉ (P.)

Cook the veal chops in butter until they are golden brown. Remove them and put some thinly sliced mushrooms in the same butter; cook quickly. When the mushrooms are golden, add a little chopped shallot, a little white wine, and some Veal Gravy (p. 134). To thicken this sauce, add ½ calf's brain cooked in Court Bouillon (p. 277) and mashed with a fork; mix well. Cover the chops with this dressing; next, cover them with Puff Paste (p. 544); brush with beaten egg, and bake in the oven. Serve with a separate dish of Périgueux Sauce (p. 143).

VEAL CHOPS FINES HERBES CÔTES DE VEAU FINES HERBES (P.)

Have the butcher slice the chops thick so that they stay tender. Season and flour them and cook them in butter in a pan or grill them, basting with butter. If you grill them, be sure not to have too hot a fire, since veal takes a long time to cook and must not be seared, especially if the chop is thick. Finish cooking them in a pan. Remove the chops and pour in a little white wine; cook 5 min. over a hot fire, add butter and *fines herbes*, and baste the meat with this sauce.

VEAL CHOPS FOYOT CÔTES DE VEAU À LA FOYOT (P.)

Cut the chops thick enough so that 1 will be enough for 2 persons; season them and spread the top with 1 heaping tbsp. chopped onions cooked in butter without browning; on top of this spread a thick layer of bread crumbs mixed with grated Gruyère cheese, pressing the mixture down tightly with the hand to make it stick. Place the chops side by side in a baking dish with a few browned, chopped onions in the bottom; moisten with a finger of white wine, baste with melted butter, and braise in the oven ¾ hr., basting frequently. When the white wine has evaporated, add a little water or bouillon. Serve in the baking dish.

GRILLED VEAL CHOPS CÔTES DE VEAU GRILLÉES (P.)

Salt, pepper, and flour some fine, thick chops, then baste with melted butter and place on a rather hot grill. Cook rather slowly, while turning and basting with butter frequently to keep the surface from drying. Since veal must be served well done, make sure that the heat is not too high. Depending on the thickness of the chops, it takes 12–16 min. to grill them. Serve them simply with Maître d'Hôtel Butter (p. 164), or with a gravy and a vegetable garnish.

VEAL CHOPS MARIE LOUISE CÔTES DE VEAU MARIE-LOUISE (P.)

Bread the chops. Cook them in butter and place them on a platter. Surround them with small artichoke bottoms cooked in butter and filled with a thick mushroom purée with a little Soubise Purée (p. 504) added. Serve with a thickened gravy. (Figure 211, Page 341.)

VEAL CHOPS MILANAISE CÔTES DE VEAU MILANAISE (P.)

Bread the veal chops with bread crumbs mixed with cheese; cook them slowly in butter and serve them around a mound of Macaroni Milanaise (p. 520). Some thin Tomato Sauce (p. 146) under the chops. (Figure 212, Page 341.)

VEAL CHOPS NÎMOISE CÔTES DE VEAU À LA NÎMOISE (P.)

Cook the chops in oil. Fry 1 or 2 peeled, sliced, and floured eggplants in oil, then remove the eggplant and in the same oil add 9 oz. peeled, drained, and quartered tomatoes; add salt, pepper, parsley, and a chopped clove of garlic. Arrange the chops on a platter; cover them with a mixture of eggplant and tomato and baste with gravy made by adding white wine and meat gravy to the juices in the pan used for sautéing the chops.

VEAL CHOPS POJARSKI CÔTES DE VEAU POJARSKI (E.)

Cut the meat away from the bone and trim the meat of all fat and gristle; chop it with ¼ its weight of butter and the same amount of white bread crumbs soaked in milk and pressed; season well. Reshape the minced meat into its natural state along the side of the chop bone. Cook in clarified butter, turning the chop with great care. Dress and garnish as desired.

Note: The name "Pojarski" refers only to the method of preparation without specifying any garnish. Any garnish may be used, or even use a sauce instead.

VEAL CUTLETS ESCALOPES DE VEAU (E.)

The best cutlets are cut from the tenderloin or sirloin, but, if this is not possible, they may be taken from the leg. They normally weigh 3½ oz.

Tr. Note: Veal cutlets in America are cut quite thick. The butcher will have to be persuaded to cut the cutlet French style, or somewhat less than ¼ in. thick.

VEAL CUTLETS BREADED ENGLISH STYLE ESCALOPES DE VEAU (PANÉES) À L'ANGLAISE (P.)

Season and flour rather thin cutlets, then dip them in egg white beaten with the same amount of oil and roll them in white bread crumbs; fry them in butter at low heat to avoid burning the bread crumbs before the meat is cooked. Serve them simply basted with lemon juice and butter from the cooking or garnished with vegetables. In any case, sauce or liquid should not be poured over breaded meats, since the purpose of breading is to serve them crisp.

VEAL CUTLETS CHASSEUR ESCALOPES DE VEAU CHASSEUR (P.)

Sauté the cutlets in butter without breading them; remove from the pan and place on a platter. Drop into the hot butter used for cooking the cutlets 9 oz. raw sliced mushrooms for 6 cutlets; add a little oil and brown them in the pan. Then drop in 1 chopped shallot, cook it for a moment, then moisten with ¼ glass white wine and let it reduce by ½. Add a few tbsp. brown sauce or, if this is not handy, put in 2 tbsp. tomato purée, a little bouillon, and a few drops of meat extract. Pour this over the cutlets and sprinkle with chopped parsley.

CREAMED VEAL CUTLETS ESCALOPES DE VEAU À LA CRÈME (P.)

Flour the cutlets and cook them in butter, scarcely browning them; place them on a platter. Pour into the frying pan 4½ oz. heavy cream and juice of ½ lemon for 4 cutlets and cook, while stirring up the meat glaze left in the bottom of the pan. Pour this over the cutlets and surround them with steamed potatoes.

Fig. 209 - Tournedos Marie-Louise (p. 334).
Fig. 210 - Tournedos monégasque (p. 335).

209

Fig. 210

Fig. 211

Fig. 212

VEAL CUTLETS DAUPHINE ESCALOPES DE VEAU À LA DAUPHINE (Fa.)

Sauté some large, thin cutlets in butter; next, cut out the center of each cutlet with a circular cutter about 2 in. in diameter. Then chop the pieces of meat left as trimmings, add a little chopped ham and chopped cooked mushrooms, and bind this mixture with Tomato Fondue (p. 194) or 1 tbsp. tomato purée; heighten the seasoning and spread one side of the cutlets with this mixture. Sprinkle with bread crumbs, moisten with butter, and bake 5 min. in a hot oven. Place them on a platter and pour around the gravy from the frying pan melted with a little white wine.

VEAL CUTLETS LIÉGEOISE or **VIENNOISE** ESCALOPES DE VEAU À LA LIÉGEOISE OR À LA VIENNOISE (P.)

Take cutlets cut from the leg, flatten them, dip them in flour, beaten egg, and bread crumbs, then cook quickly in clarified butter. Place them in the center of a round platter bordered with scalloped half slices of lemon; moisten them with lemon juice and brown butter; then in the center of each cutlet place a round slice of lemon and, on the lemon, a rolled anchovy in oil with a caper in the center. On either side of the cutlets tastefully arrange hard-boiled egg whites, hard-boiled egg yolks, and parsley, all chopped separately. (Figure 213, P. 344.)

Note: Cutlets can be garnished many ways, so it is useless to list them all. Since it is only a matter of vegetables, the reader can solve this problem for himself and thus augment this chapter as he wishes.

VEAL CUTLETS MILANAISE ESCALOPES DE VEAU À LA MILANAISE (P.)

Prepare the cutlets as for Veal Cutlets Breaded English Style (p. 340), then garnish with Macaroni Milanaise prepared the following way: cook some very thin macaroni, then drain it, and mix with Tomato Sauce (p. 146) ; add a little finely chopped ham and mushrooms and simmer 5–6 min.; remove from the stove and add a handful of grated cheese. Pour the macaroni into a deep platter after correcting the seasoning and arrange the cutlets around it. Allow 1 cutlet per person and 1 oz. macaroni (uncooked) per person.

VEAL CUTLETS PARISIENNE ESCALOPES DE VEAU À LA PARISIENNE (P.)

Flour the cutlets on one side only and cook them on this side, then turn them over and place on each one a pork forcemeat ball well seasoned with salt, pepper, and chopped herbs (see Forcemeats, p. 173) ; put into the oven to finish cooking the veal and the forcemeat. Surround with mashed potatoes and baste with gravy.

FRICANDEAU WITH SORREL FRICANDEAU À L'OSEILLE (P.)

Fricandeau used to be a deservedly famous dish. It is an old French recipe. Take a slice of loin of veal about 1 in. thick. Lard it with pork fat as you would a beef fillet and place it in a baking dish on a bed of carrots and onions browned in butter. Pour bouillon made from meat over it and bake in the oven. Frequently baste the top of the meat, which should project above the liquid; make this gravy brown by adding caramel coloring, season lightly several times, and cook about 1½ hr. The top should be browned as a roast. Serve with braised sorrel and pour the gravy, skimmed and reduced, over the meat.

Fig. 211 - Veal chops Marie-Louise (p. 339).
Fig. 212 - Veal chops milanaise (p. 339).

VEAL FRICASSEE FRICASSÉE DE VEAU (P.)

This recipe is prepared almost the same as Fricandeau, except that the veal is lightly browned in butter in a pot without searing, as for a ragout; then remove the veal and add 1 heaping tbsp. flour mixed with water, a *bouquet garni,* seasoning, onions and carrots, and let it all cook together. The meat is cooked in this sauce rather than in bouillon. When it is cooked, bind the sauce with egg yolk, though you risk turning the sauce. Add mushrooms and serve with fried croutons.

VEAL GRENADINS WITH SPINACH GRENADINS DE VEAU AUX ÉPINARDS (P.)

Grenadins are cutlets that are thick but not too large. Lard them with 3 intercrossing strips of pork fat; place them in a baking pan on top of some pieces of chopped pork fat, 1 sliced onion, 1 sliced carrot, and a *bouquet garni.* Cook on top of the stove until the vegetables begin to brown; pour in some bouillon without covering the meat. Salt, pepper, and put into a hot oven to braise the grenadins; baste frequently. Serve the grenadins around or in the center of a vegetable such as spinach. Skim the fat off the gravy, thicken slightly with potato starch, and strain over the meat.

VEAL LOIN or FILLET EN COCOTTE BORDELAISE LONGE ET QUASI OR ROUELLE DE VEAU EN COCOTTE À LA BORDELAISE (P.)

Veal loin, chump end, and fillet are the best cuts for cooking in a cocotte or Dutch oven. First brown the meat gently, then add sliced carrots and onions and, when these vegetables are also browned, moisten with a little water; season, cover, and cook slowly until the veal is well done, which may be determined by sticking it deeply with a knife to see if a drop of liquid clear as water forms at the opening. When the meat is cooked, place it on a platter, or serve it in the pot, and garnish with mushrooms sautéed in butter and quartered artichoke bottoms also sautéed in butter. Pour the gravy, skimmed and strained, over the meat. (Figure 214, Page 344.)

Note: Any sort of vegetable garnish may be placed around the veal: noodles, macaroni, rice, spinach, new potatoes, carrots, etc.

MEDALLIONS and NOISETTES MÉDAILLONS and NOISETTES (E.)

Medallions and noisettes are the kernel, nut, or best part of the veal fillet. The same term may be used for the choicest part of any other cut of meat. They are trimmed round and are invariably sautéed because braising dries them out and makes them tough. All the recipes and garnishes given for veal chops may be used.

VEAL MEDALLION or NOISETTE ALEXANDER MÉDAILLON OR NOISETTE DE VEAU ALEXANDRE (M.)

Stud the medallion with truffles; season with salt and paprika; sauté in butter. Place it on an artichoke bottom cooked in butter and filled with a salpicon (tiny cubes) of marrow bound with reduced Semiglaze Sauce (p. 138). Garnish with Braised Lettuce (p. 502). To make the sauce, swirl some sherry around in the pan in which the medallion was cooked, pour in some Velouté (p. 147), add fresh cream, heat until reduced, butter, and strain.

VEAL MEDALLION LAGUIPIÈRE MÉDAILLON DE VEAU LAGUIPIÈRE (M.)

Stud with truffles and pickled tongue; sauté in butter. Place on a mound of Potatoes Anna (p. 620). Garnish with an artichoke bottom cooked in butter and filled with a thick mushroom purée.

Sauce: Glaze from the cooking pan melted with Madeira and veal stock. (Figure 215, Page 345.)

VEAL JOINT WITH CARROTS MORCEAU DE VEAU AUX CAROTTES (P.)

The joint is cooked whole in a cocotte or Dutch oven. Take the loin, chump end, shoulder, round, or even the knuckle, depending upon whether you like your meat fat, lean, or gelatinous, as in the case of knuckles. Take 1½ lb. well-trimmed and tied meat, and brown it in butter on all sides, then put in around it 1 or 2 onions cut in quarters and 1 lb. peeled, sliced carrots. Cover the pot tightly and let it cook slowly at low heat for 20 min. Then pour in enough water to come just even with the top of the meat, season, and let simmer, covered, 1½ hr., or until cooked. Skim the fat off the gravy before serving.

BRAISED LOIN OF VEAL NOIX DE VEAU BRAISÉE (E.)

The loin is usually larded, but only the uncovered part touching the bone of the chump end. The best way to prepare it is to braise it. If it is to be carved at the table, it is better to roast or pan-roast it, because when it is braised it is hard to cut. On the other hand, if it is not braised completely, the meat will turn out dry and flavorless.

Various garnishes suitable for Braised Loin of Veal: Alsatian, Bouquetière, Bourgeoise, Chartreuse (Figure 216, Page 345.) Chicory, Clamart, Mushroom, Spinach, Financière, Milanaise, Sorrel, etc. (see pp. 179–185).

VEAL BIRDS PAUPIETTES (E.)

The birds are cut from the loin in slices about 4 in. long and 2 in. wide. After flattening and trimming them, spread them with filling, roll them, lard them with a strip of fat, and tie with string in several places.

VEAL BIRDS FONTANGES PAUPIETTES DE VEAU FONTANGES (E.)

Spread the birds with a buttered forcemeat (see p. 173); braise them. Arrange in a ring on small potato croquettes shaped like disks; in the center place a purée of creamed navy beans, and around the outside pour the reduced gravy from the braising.

VEAL BIRDS PORTUGUESE STYLE PAUPIETTES DE VEAU À LA PORTUGAISE (E.)

Stuff the birds with Panada-and-Cream Forcemeat (p. 173); braise them. Arrange in a ring on small stuffed tomato halves; in the center of the dish place Potatoes Château (p. 506). Around the outside encircle with a ribbon of Portugaise Sauce (p. 144). (Figure 217, Page 348.)

VEAL BIRDS RICHELIEU PAUPIETTES DE VEAU À LA RICHELIEU (P.)

Spread a thin layer of well-seasoned pork forcemeat (see p. 173) or sausage on very thin slices of veal; roll them and tie them. Then brown them in butter with a few slices of onion and carrot, moisten with a little meat gravy, and braise in the oven at least 1 hr., basting frequently. Place them on tomato halves sautéed in butter, cover with their own gravy seasoned with tomato, and garnish the center of the platter with Potatoes Château (p. 506).

VEAL BIRDS TURKISH STYLE PAUPIETTES DE VEAU À LA TURQUE (M.)

Stuff the birds with veal forcemeat mixed with chopped onions cooked in butter and finely diced pimento (see p. 173) ; braise them and glaze. On each bird place half a tomato cooked in oil. Garnish with Rice Pilaf (p. 512) . Cover the birds with the gravy from the braising.

STUFFED BREAST OF VEAL POITRINE DE VEAU FARCIE (P.)

Remove the flat bones from the breast, then split it with a knife through the center from one end to the other, to form a pocket to be filled with a stuffing made of sausage meat mixed with an equal part of leftover, chopped, cooked meat, chopped onions cooked in butter, *fines herbes*, salt, pepper, and 1 whole egg. After stuffing the breast, sew it up, then put into a braising pan on a bed of sliced onions and carrots; grease the top with a little lard and place in the oven. When it is a golden brown, pour over it 2 cups bouillon or meat gravy, if available; if not, simply use water, then salt, cover, and cook in the oven at least 2 hr. Serve the breast cut in slices, covered with its own gravy (skimmed of fat), along with some kind of garnish. If any breast is left over, it can be reheated or even served cold. (Figure 218, Page 348.)

VEAL SAUTÉ WITH MACARONI SAUTÉ DE VEAU AU MACARONI (P.)

This is simply a veal stew in which potatoes are replaced by macaroni partially cooked in advance and allowed to finish cooking in the veal sauté. Serve with a rather clear sauce highly flavored with tomato. This is a family dish.

Note: Veal Stew is made exactly like Mutton Stew (p. 357) , with this exception: Veal Stew takes 1¼ hr. to cook, while Mutton Stew takes about 2 hr.

VEAL SAUTÉ MARENGO SAUTÉ DE VEAU À LA MARENGO (P.)

Cut a shoulder of veal into pieces and brown in very hot butter and oil to sear the meat. When it is nicely browned, drop in 2 large chopped onions and a pinch of flour, which should also brown, then a crushed clove of garlic. Pour in 1 glass white wine and tomato purée to make the sauce, which can be thinned with water if it is too thick. Season, add a *bouquet garni,* and cook 1 hr., then add 4½ oz. raw mushrooms per lb. meat, and continue cooking for a few minutes. Carefully skim the fat off the sauce, sprinkle with parsley, and serve surrounded with heart-shaped croutons fried in oil.

VEAL SAUTÉ WITH FRENCH PEAS SAUTÉ DE VEAU AUX PETITS POIS (P.)

Veal Stew (see above) garnished only with small onions and small peas. When new peas are in season, they are large enough to be cooked directly in the stew; do not put in too much flour—the peas being starchy, the sauce should be thin. If canned peas are used, they should be heated first and put into the stew 5 min. before serving.

SADDLE OF VEAL CHARTREUSE SELLE DE VEAU À LA CHARTREUSE (E.)

Braise the saddle, remove the strips of fat tied about it, and glaze just before serving. Place it on a long platter with vegetables molded Chartreuse style (p. 468) at each end. These should be the same height as the saddle of veal and unmolded at the last moment. Skim, reduce, and clarify the gravy from the braising and pour several tbsp. around the meat. Serve the rest of the gravy in a sauceboat.

Fig. 213 - Veal cutlets liégeoise (p. 341).
Fig. 214 - Veal loin en cocotte bordelaise (p. 342).

Fig. 213

Fig. 214

Fig. 215

Fig. 216

SADDLE OF VEAL MATIGNON SELLE DE VEAU MATIGNON (E.)

Half braise the saddle, then cover it with a fairly thick layer of Matignon (p. 135). Cover this with strips of bacon or thin slices of ham; wrap it in a caul, or sausage casing, and cook it 2 hr. in a slow oven. Serve as is, with a separate sauceboat of the gravy from the braising, skimmed and reduced.

SADDLE OF VEAL METTERNICH SELLE DE VEAU METTERNICH (E.)

Braise the saddle. When it is ready, cut a line about 3/8 in. from the outside edges of each side and at each end, driving the point of the knife into the meat. Cut the same line the length of the bone and on each side of the bone; then gently raise the fillets of the saddle, detaching them from the bone with care. Cut these fillets into slices slightly on the bias. Spread a few tbsp. Béchamel Sauce (p. 146) mixed with paprika into the cavity of the saddle formed by removing the fillets; then, taking 1 slice at a time, place the fillets back into their original position, putting 1/2 tbsp. Béchamel Sauce and 2 slices of truffle between each slice. Finally, cover the whole surface of the saddle with Béchamel Sauce mixed with paprika and glaze quickly under a hot flame. Remove the saddle carefully with the aid of a large square spatula, and place it on a platter. Serve separately: (1) the braising stock of the meat, skimmed and reduced; (2) a dish of Rice Pilaf (p. 512).

Note: Saddle of Mutton Metternich is made the same way, as is Saddle of Venison.

SADDLE OF VEAL PRINCE ORLOV SELLE DE VEAU PRINCE ORLOFF (E.)

Braise the saddle and prepare it the same as Saddle of Veal Metternich (above). In replacing the fillets, put 1/2 tbsp. Soubise Sauce (p. 154) and 1 slice of truffle between each slice. Cover the surface of the saddle with Mornay Sauce (p. 152) mixed with 1/4 its quantity of Soubise Purée (p. 504), and glaze quickly. Serve a separate dish of the gravy from the braising, skimmed and reduced.

Note: This saddle may be accompanied by a garnish of asparagus tips or creamed cucumbers.

SADDLE OF VEAL RENAISSANCE SELLE DE VEAU RENAISSANCE (E.)

Braise the saddle and glaze it quickly just before serving. Place it on a platter and at either end arrange a large bouquet of cauliflower; place the rest of the garnish along the sides in alternate mounds. Serve separately: (1) a sauceboat of Hollandaise (p. 151) for the cauliflower; (2) the braising stock, skimmed, reduced, and strained.

VEAL TENDONS PAYSANNE TENDRONS DE VEAU À LA PAYSANNE (P.)

The tendons are pieces of the breast cut from side to side in pieces about 2 fingers wide. Cook them, as for Fricandeau (p. 341), on vegetables, in enough bouillon to cover 3/4. Bring to a boil and place in the oven without covering, season, and baste often for about 2 hr. Meanwhile, finely slice some onions, carrots, turnips, and celery and mix together in a stewpan with a little hot butter. Cover the vegetables tightly and cook them in the oven. Next, simmer them for a few minutes with the veal tendons and serve all together after skimming the gravy. Potatoes may be added, if desired. Various garnishes, cooked the same way as the above vegetables, may be added to the veal. (Figure 221, Page 349.)

Fig. 215 - Veal medallion Laguipière (p. 343).
Fig. 216 - Braised loin of veal chartreuse (p. 343).

VEAL BRAINS, LIVER, SWEETBREADS, ETC.

MARROW and BRAINS AMOURETTES and CERVELLES (E.)

We group these two items together because they are similar and may be prepared according to the same recipes. Preparation for cooking is exactly the same as for beef marrow and brains (see p. 335).

VEAL HEART BRAISED WITH CARROTS COEUR DE VEAU BRAISÉ AUX CAROTTES (P.)

Brown the heart in a cocotte with a few small onions, then, when colored, moisten with 1 cup bouillon or water, season, add 1 lb. sliced carrots, cover, and cook 1 hr. When it is cooked, there will be too much cooking juice to serve as a sauce, so, after removing the heart, skim it and reduce it a good deal. Veal heart may also be sliced lengthwise and sautéed in butter in a frying pan, like beefsteak. It is firm and crisp for those who like their meat that way.

CALVES' LIVER ENGLISH STYLE FOIE DE VEAU À L'ANGLAISE (E.)

Cut the liver into medium slices weighing about 3½ oz. Season the slices, dip them in flour, and sauté them in butter or grill them. Arrange them on a platter, alternating the liver with fine slices of sautéed or grilled bacon; moisten with the cooking butter or with brown butter if the liver has been grilled.

FRIED CALVES' LIVER FOIE DE VEAU FRIT (E.)

Cut the liver into 2-in. squares about ⅜ in. thick. Season; dip in flour, beaten egg mixed with a little oil, and bread crumbs; and fry just before serving. Arrange on a napkin with a border of fried parsley.

CALVES' LIVER LYONNAISE FOIE DE VEAU À LA LYONNAISE (E.)

Season the slices of liver, dip them in flour, and sauté them in butter and oil. Arrange them in a circle, and in the center place a garnish of onions sautéed in butter and bound with a little Meat Glaze (p. 135). Heat a finger of vinegar in the frying pan while it is still very hot, and pour over the liver just before serving.

CALVES' LIVER LOAVES VALOIS FOIE DE VEAU (PETITS PAINS DE) À LA VALOIS (P.) (*For 3 persons*)

This is a light dish good for invalids. In a mortar, pound ½ lb. very white calves' liver with salt, pepper, and a dash of spices; then add 1 teacup thick, cold Béchamel Sauce (p. 146), 2 tbsp. extra-heavy cream, 1 whole egg, and 1 egg yolk. Press through a fine sieve and fill some small, buttered baba molds with this purée. Poach them in a *bain-marie* in the oven for 12 min., then unmold and cover them with Valois Sauce, which is Béarnaise Sauce (p. 147) with a little melted Meat Glaze (p. 135) mixed in. Garnish with fried potato balls.

Note: The loaves may also be made from veal loin instead of calves' liver. (Figure 222, Page 349.)

FRIED VEAL CHITTERLINGS FRAISE DE VEAU FRITE (E.)

Wash and dry the calves' chitterlings (stomach lining or intestine); cut into pieces and season highly. Dip in flour, beaten egg mixed with a little oil, and bread crumbs; fry just before serving, and place on a napkin with fried parsley. Serve Diable Sauce (p. 140) separately.

CALVES' TONGUES LANGUES DE VEAU (M.)

Before dressing them any way, the calves' tongues should first be soaked, blanched, and braised in the usual way. Only when they are served vinaigrette, with calf's head, should they be poached like the calf's head (see Calf's Head Vinaigrette, p. 352.)

Garnishes for braised calves' tongues: Bouquetière, Bourgeoise, Breton, Fermière, Jardinière, Macédoine, Piedmontaise, purée of various vegetables.

Sauces: Chasseur, Duxelles, Fines Herbes, Italienne, Paprika, Piquante, Soubise, Tomato.

GRILLED, DEVILED CALVES' TONGUES LANGUES DE VEAU GRILLÉES À LA DIABLE (M.)

Braised tongues slit in half lengthwise. Season; coat with mustard; brush with melted butter, and cover with bread crumbs. Grill on a low fire. Serve with Diable Sauce (p. 140).

CALVES' FEET PIEDS DE VEAU (E.)

The calves' feet should first be blanched and then cooled. Next, bone them and poach them, or braise them, depending on how they are to be used.

CALVES' FEET CUSTINE PIEDS DE VEAU CUSTINE (E.)

After braising, cut the meat into small cubes; mix them with very thick Duxelles Sauce (p. 140) with sliced cooked mushrooms added; let cool. Divide this mixture into 3-oz. portions; wrap each in a pig's caul; place in a baking pan, baste with melted butter, and brown in the oven. Serve with a dish of Semiglaze Sauce (p. 138).

GRILLED CALVES' FEET PIEDS DE VEAU GRILLÉS (E.)

Braise the feet and cut each half foot in two. Coat the pieces with mustard, dip in butter and cover with bread crumbs, baste with melted butter, and grill slowly. Serve Diable Sauce (p. 140) separately.

CALVES' FEET POULETTE PIEDS DE VEAU À LA POULETTE (E.)

Cook in a Court Bouillon (p. 277); remove the large bones; divide each half foot into 3 pieces. Mix with Poulette Sauce (p. 154) and serve in a timbale with a pinch of chopped parsley.

SKEWERED SWEETBREADS RIS DE VEAU À LA BROCHE (G.)

Sweetbreads consist of two parts: the heart and the throat. The heart is the round part and the throat is the long part. Sweetbreads should always be soaked for at least 5–6 hr. in advance in plenty of cold water, which should be changed often. This will remove all of the blood and gummy substance adhering to them. They must next be blanched (placed on the fire in cold water and boiled 2 min.) to make them firm. Cool them, remove fat and cartilage, wrap them in a cloth, and place a plate and a weight on them to press them. Lard them very delicately with a larding needle, wrap them in buttered paper, and skewer them. Cook them 25 min., then remove the paper and cook for 10 or 12 min. more on the skewer to brown the pork fat, taking care to baste them with a little good veal stock. Remove from the skewer and place on a platter just before serving. Send them to the table with a separate dish of the gravy, skimmed until it is clear.

SWEETBREADS CLAMART RIS DE VEAU À LA CLAMART (P.)

Soak the sweetbreads for a long time in cold water, blanch them 3 or 4 min., then let cool completely. Trim off the cartilage and inedible parts, but be sure not to remove the top skin, as is sometimes done. Next press the sweetbreads with a weight for 1 hr. to break the fibers and keep them from shrinking while cooking. Lard them with thin strips of pork fat and braise on a bed of vegetables as for Veal Fricandeau with Sorrel (p. 341). Cook them exactly as described in that recipe, taking into consideration the size of the sweetbreads and allowing 25–40 min. in a very hot oven to brown the top. Place them on a round platter and garnish with small buttered peas. Skim the cooking gravy, reduce, thicken with potato starch, and pour over sweetbreads.

SWEETBREADS DEMIDOV RIS DE VEAU DEMIDOFF (E.)

Lard the sweetbreads with fat and stud with truffles, then braise until half done. Place them in a baking dish and surround them with carrots and turnips cut into crescents, small onions sliced in rings, and sliced celery; these vegetables should first be cooked in butter. Add 1 oz. sliced truffles per sweetbread and pour over them the strained stock from the braising; cover the baking dish and finish cooking slowly. Skim off fat and serve in the cooking dish.

SWEETBREADS EXCELSIOR RIS DE VEAU EXCELSIOR (E.)

Stud the sweetbreads with truffles and poach in white stock. Place them on a platter and garnish with 3 small mounds of mousseline forcemeat quenelles made of chicken (see p. 173), molded with a teaspoon and poached just before serving. One third of these quenelles should be made with chopped truffles added to the forcemeat; one third with very finely chopped pickled tongue added to the forcemeat; the other third plain forcemeat. Serve a separate dish of Soubise Sauce (p. 154) made with cream, with a julienne of truffles, mushrooms, and tongue added. (Figure 223, Page 352.)

GOURMETS' SWEETBREADS RIS DE VEAU DES GOURMETS (E.)

Braise the sweetbreads. As soon as ready, place them in a shallow casserole just large enough to contain them. Cover with thick slices of raw truffles; pour over this the stock from the braising; cover the casserole and seal with a band of paste made of flour mixed with a little water, so that it will be airtight. Place in a very hot oven for 10 min. and serve in the same dish. Uncover at table.

SWEETBREADS AU GRATIN RIS DE VEAU AU GRATIN (E.)

Braise the sweetbreads; slice them and put into a shallow, buttered baking dish, re-forming the sweetbreads to their original shape, pouring between each slice 1 tbsp. reduced Duxelles Sauce (p. 140). Surround with small cooked mushrooms; cover with Duxelles Sauce; sprinkle with bread crumbs; baste with melted butter, and brown quickly in a hot oven. Add a dash of lemon juice and a pinch of chopped parsley before serving.

SWEETBREADS MONTAUBAN RIS DE VEAU MONTAUBAN (E.)

Lard the sweetbreads with pork fat and stud with truffles; braise and glaze. Serve on a platter surrounded by small rice croquettes made with pickled tongue; thick slices of a forcemeat roll made of chicken, panada, cream, and truffles (see Chicken Puddings, p. 412); small fluted mushrooms. Serve a separate dish of Velouté (p. 147) made with mushroom essence.

Fig. 217 - Veal birds portuguese style (p. 343).
Fig. 218 - Stuffed breast of veal (p. 344).
Fig. 219 - Beef fillet moderne (p. 332).

Fig. 217

Fig. 218

Fig. 219

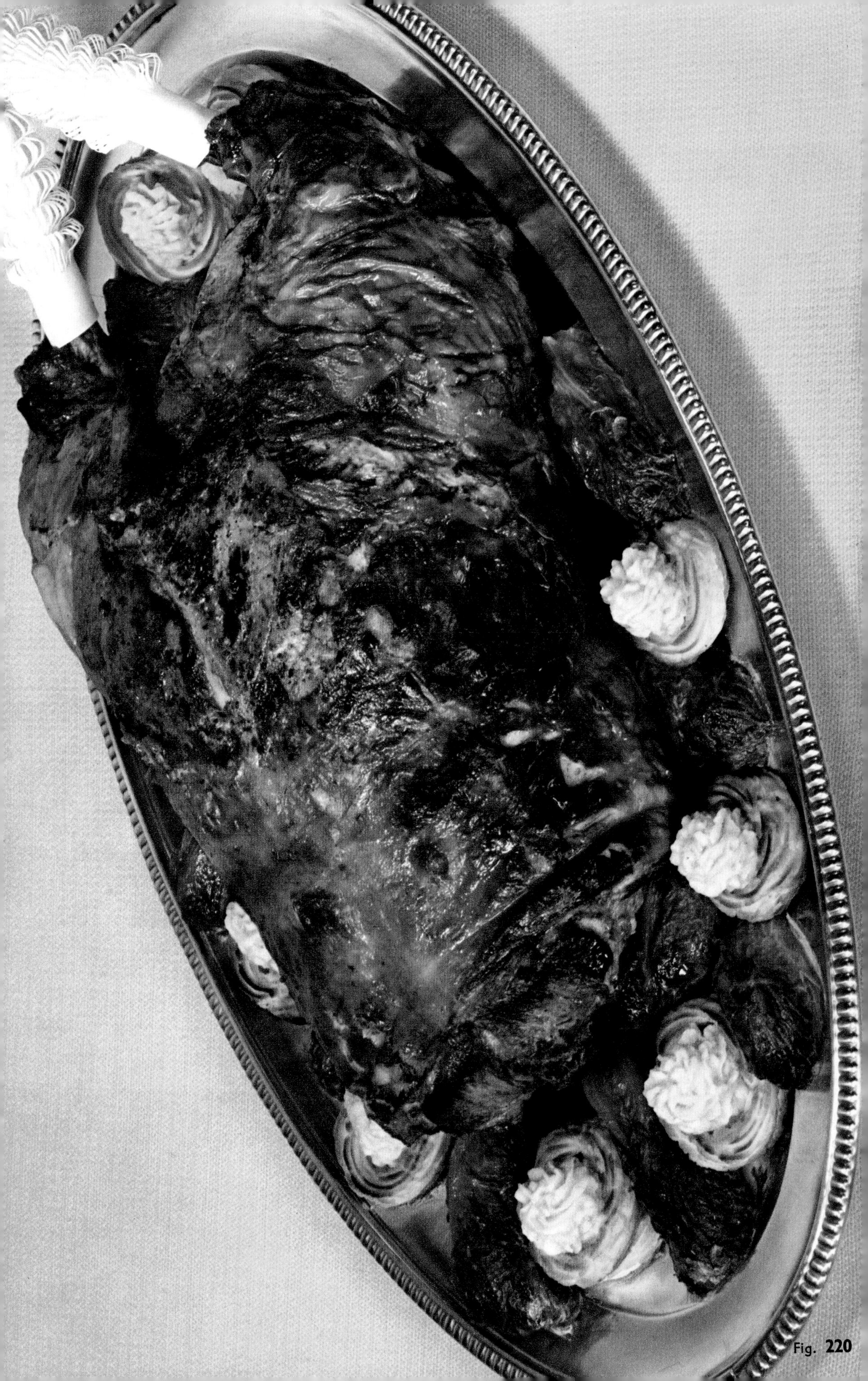

Fig. 220

Fig. 221

Fig. 222

SWEETBREADS RACHEL RIS DE VEAU RACHEL (E.)

Lard the sweetbreads, braise, and glaze just before serving. Arrange on a platter and surround with small artichoke bottoms filled with thick Bordelaise Sauce (p. 138) and a slice of poached beef marrow with chopped parsley on top. Serve the gravy from the braising separately, or pour it on the bottom of the platter. (Figure 224, Page 352.)

SWEETBREADS RÉGENCE RIS DE VEAU RÉGENCE (E.)

Stud the sweetbreads with truffles and braise or fry them. Arrange on a platter; reduce the braising stock and pour over the sweetbreads; surround the sweetbreads with a Régence Garnish. Serve a separate dish of Parisienne Sauce (p. 146) containing truffle essence.

Régence Garnish: 10 quenelles of truffled chicken forcemeat molded with a spoon, 2 large round quenelles decorated with truffles, 10 large cockscombs frizzled in a frying pan, 10 round slices of *foie gras,* 10 small fluted mushrooms, 10 truffles cut into olive shape.

SWEETBREADS TOULOUSAINE RIS DE VEAU À LA TOULOUSAINE (M.)

Stud with truffles; braise in white stock. Surround with mounds of Toulousaine Garnish. Allemande Sauce (p. 146) containing mushroom essence.

Toulousaine Garnish: Quenelles, mushrooms, olives, truffles. (Figure 225, Page 353.)

SWEETBREAD CUTLETS AND MEDALLIONS RIS DE VEAU (ESCALOPES ET MÉDAILLONS DE) (M.)

Before slicing, the sweetbreads must be made firm and easy to cut by being well blanched. The slices or cutlets of sweetbreads may be braised in white or brown stock, like whole sweetbreads, and should be fairly thick. All recipes for whole sweetbreads may be used. Most often, the raw sweetbread cutlets are sautéed in butter after being seasoned and lightly floured or dipped in flour, beaten egg, and bread crumbs. For certain recipes, the cutlets are taken from whole braised sweetbreads kept somewhat firm. The medallions are prepared the same as the cutlets, being smaller and thicker than cutlets. All recipes for veal cutlets and medallions may be applied to sweetbread cutlets and medallions.

CREAMED SWEETBREAD CUTLETS RIS DE VEAU (ESCALOPES DE) À LA CRÈME (P.)

Sauté the sweetbreads in butter without letting them brown, place them on a platter, and cover them with a few slices of mushrooms; add 5 to 7 oz. heavy cream to the juice in the frying pan. Reduce a little and season with salt, ground pepper, and lemon juice. Pour over the sweetbreads and serve.

SWEETBREAD CUTLETS FLORENTINE RIS DE VEAU (ESCALOPES DE) FLORENTINE (P.)

Cook as above. Place the cutlets on a bed of leaf spinach sautéed in butter. Cover with Mornay Sauce (p. 152), sprinkle with grated cheese and bread crumbs, baste with melted butter, and brown in a hot oven.

SWEETBREAD CUTLETS NIQUETTE RIS DE VEAU (ESCALOPES DE) NIQUETTE (M.)

Sauté in butter. Arrange in a circle with the slices overlapping, with a round

Fig. 220 - Baron of lamb byzantine (p. 360).
Fig. 221 - Veal tendons paysanne (p. 345).
Fig. 222 - Calves' liver loaves Valois (p. 346).

slice of ham turned in butter placed between each sweetbread slice. Fill the center of the dish with very small creamed carrots. Pour buttered reduced veal stock over the sweetbreads.

SWEETBREAD CUTLETS RICHELIEU RIS DE VEAU (ESCALOPES DE) RICHELIEU (P.)

Slice some carrots and turnips in thick julienne strips, add 1 or 2 sliced onions and a little celery (very little), and 4 or 5 mushrooms. Half cook all these vegetables together in butter. Sauté the sliced sweetbreads in butter and place them on top of the vegetables in a baking dish; moisten with good gravy and finish cooking in the oven, ¼ hr., basting the sweetbreads. When arranging the vegetables, mix in some green beans boiled separately so that they stay very green; arrange the sweetbreads in a circle around the vegetables or on top; skim the fat off the cooking gravy and pour it over the sweetbreads.

SWEETBREAD CUTLETS VILLEROI RIS DE VEAU (ESCALOPES DE) À LA VILLEROI (P.)

This recipe is for small sweetbreads that would not be very presentable as they are. Slice as cutlets and cook as directed, let them cool, and dry them. Make a very thick Béchamel Sauce (p. 146), or Velouté (p. 147) if you have any bouillon, and bind with 2 egg yolks; completely cover the slices of sweetbreads with this warm sauce, then dip in white bread crumbs, in beaten egg, and a second time in bread crumbs. Fry them in butter and oil, then place them on a napkin. They may be served with Tomato Sauce (p. 146) or arranged on a napkin with a garnish of French peas in the middle and without sauce.

VEAL KIDNEY BERRICHONNE ROGNON DE VEAU À LA BERRICHONNE (E.)

Brown in butter 4 oz. pork fat from the breast (diced and blanched) and 4 oz. raw sliced mushrooms. Take out the fat and mushrooms. In the same butter, quickly sauté the sliced, seasoned kidney, then take that out, too. Swirl a little red wine around in the pan, reduce, and add 4 oz. well-buttered Bordelaise Sauce (p. 138) made without marrow. Put the kidneys, pork fat, and mushrooms into this sauce; shake the pan a few times to mix well; serve in a timbale with a pinch of chopped parsley.

VEAL KIDNEY IN CASSEROLE ROGNON DE VEAU EN CASSEROLE (E.)

Trim the kidney, leaving a thin layer of fat. Season and place in an earthenware casserole with 1 oz. butter; cook slowly in the oven, about ½ hr., turning it frequently. Before removing from the oven, baste with 1 tbsp. good Veal Gravy (p. 134) and serve in the same dish.

VEAL KIDNEY WITH MUSHROOMS ROGNON DE VEAU AUX CHAMPIGNONS (E.)

Sauté the sliced kidney; remove it; make a mushroom sauce, adding the reduced cooking juice from the sautéing, and mix the sliced kidney in it. Serve in a timbale with a pinch of chopped parsley.

VEAL KIDNEY EN COCOTTE ROGNON DE VEAU EN COCOTTE (E.)

Trim the kidney, leaving a thin layer of fat, and brown in butter in a cocotte or Dutch oven. Surround it with 2 oz. diced pork fat from the breast, blanched, then browned in butter; 2 oz. raw mushrooms quartered and sautéed in butter;

2 oz. potatoes cut in the size and shape of a clove of garlic and blanched. Finish cooking in the oven; add 1 tbsp. veal stock at the last moment, and serve as is.

CURRIED VEAL KIDNEY INDIAN STYLE ROGNON DE VEAU AU CURRY À L'INDIENNE (E.)

Brown 1 chopped onion in butter, adding a pinch of curry to it. Add 3 oz. ordinary Velouté (p. 147) and strain. Sauté the kidney in butter as usual; mix it in the sauce and serve in a timbale. Serve a separate dish of Rice Indian Style (p. 512).

GRILLED VEAL KIDNEY ROGNON DE VEAU GRILLÉ (E.)

Trim the kidney, leaving a thin layer of fat. Split it in 2 lengthwise without completely separating the 2 halves; skewer it with 2 small brochettes to hold it open. Season and grill slowly, basting with melted butter. Serve a separate dish of Maître d'Hôtel Butter (p. 164), Bercy Butter (p. 163), or any other butter suitable for grilled meat.

VEAL KIDNEY LIÉGEOISE ROGNON DE VEAU À LA LIÉGEOISE (E.)

Prepare the kidney as for Veal Kidney in Casserole (p. 350); a minute before serving add: ½ jigger flaming gin, 2 crushed juniper berries, and 1 tbsp. good Veal Gravy (p. 134). Serve as is.

VEAL KIDNEY MONTPENSIER ROGNON DE VEAU MONTPENSIER (E.)

Trim the kidney, leaving a thin covering of fat around it; cut it into 5 or 6 round slices. Season, sauté in butter over a hot fire, then remove it to a plate. Add first 1 tbsp. Madeira to the sautéing pan, then 3 tbsp. melted Meat Glaze (p. 135), a finger of lemon juice, a pinch of chopped parsley, and 2 oz. butter. Arrange the slices of kidney in a circle on a platter or in a timbale and cover with the sauce; in the center of the platter place a mound of buttered asparagus tips with 12 truffle slices arranged around it.

VEAL KIDNEY PORTUGUESE STYLE ROGNON DE VEAU À LA PORTUGAISE (E.)

Slice the kidney and sauté as in the Montpensier recipe (above). Arrange the slices in a circle on a platter; place a stuffed half of a small tomato on each piece; fill the center of the platter with very thick Tomato Fondue (p. 194). Cover the kidney with the same sauce as in the Montpensier recipe.

VEAL KIDNEY WITH RICE ROGNON DE VEAU AU RIZOT (E.)

Slice the kidney, season, and sauté in butter. Place the slices inside a border of Risotto (p. 513) arranged on a serving plate. Cover with a thin layer of Risotto, top with Mornay Sauce (p. 152), and glaze quickly.

VEAL KIDNEY ROBERT ROGNON DE VEAU ROBERT (E.)

Season the kidney; brown it quickly in butter in a small cocotte over a very hot fire. Then bake it in the oven about ¼ hr. and bring to the table as is. The rest of the preparations take place at the table itself, as follows. Remove the kidney to a hot plate; place the cocotte on an alcohol stove; pour 1 glass champagne brandy into it and reduce by ½. Meanwhile, cut the kidney into very thin slices and cover with a reversed plate. Add to the reduced brandy: 1 tsp. mustard, 1 oz. butter cut into small pieces, juice of ¼ lemon, pinch of chopped parsley. Stir well with a fork; mix the kidney slices and their juice in this sauce; heat without boiling, and serve on very hot plates.

SAUTÉED VEAL KIDNEY WITH VARIOUS WINES ROGNON DE VEAU SAUTÉ AUX VINS DIVERS (E.)

Follow the recipe for Beef Kidney in Madeira (p. 336), replacing the Madeira by Chablis, Corton, Laffitte, port, Saint-Julien, Volnay, sherry, etc.

KIDNEY CRUSTS ROGNONS (CROÛTES AUX) (E.)

Cut French bread or fancy bread into 1-in.-thick slices. Hollow out the inside, leaving only a thin crust on the bottom; butter the inside and dry in the oven. Fill the crusts with veal kidneys sautéed with mushrooms, Madeira, Chablis, etc.

Note: These crusts can be made of ordinary square or rectangular white bread. In this case, they should be fried in clarified butter.

CALF'S HEAD VINAIGRETTE TÊTE DE VEAU À LA VINAIGRETTE (P.)

Have your butcher remove the bones from half a calf's head. Put it into a deep pot with plenty of cold water and boil 15 min. until a lot of froth comes to the top. Rinse it and cool it under the cold-water tap, then drain it and rub the outside with a piece of lemon to whiten it. Cut the head into square pieces and put it into a pot with cold water. A small handful of flour should first be mixed into the water with a wire whisk, then add 3 oz. vinegar, salt, peppercorns, 1 onion, 1 carrot. Cook slowly, using a cloth instead of the lid for the cover, because if it boils too strongly, the floured Court Bouillon will boil over, like milk. It takes 1½-2 hr. to cook the head, depending upon the age of the calf; while it should be well cooked, it must not be too well done. Prick it with a fork, and if the prongs penetrate easily, it should be done. When it has been cooked too long, the flesh is sticky, gelatinous, and not very appetizing to eat. It if is cooked in advance or some leftovers are returned from the table, it should be kept cold in its own cooking stock so that it stays white. Serve the calf's head hot with Vinaigrette Sauce (p. 158) to which onion, parsley, and chopped hard-boiled egg have been added. If you have a calves' tongue, it may be cooked with the head. Brains should be cooked for 15 min. in salted, acidulated water.

MUTTON AND LAMB

From the culinary standpoint, sheep are divided into 3 categories:

(1) Mutton, which has reached its full development through age.

(2) Lamb, or young weaned mutton, which is not completely grown and is considered the better the younger it is.

(3) Baby spring lamb, which has not yet been weaned and has not started to graze; the Pauillac lambs are considered the very best.

Ordinary lamb is similar to mutton, although the meat is much tenderer. The same recipes may be used for both. Only, the quality of the meat must be considered when allowing for cooking time. Baby spring lamb, with its completely different white meat, may be prepared according to a few of the recipes for mutton, but special recipes for it will be given in a separate series following those for mutton and ordinary lamb.

BARON and **DOUBLE LEGS OF LAMB** BARON and DOUBLE (E.)

The baron, which comprises the saddle and the two legs, or the whole hindquarters of the animal, is one of the finest *relevés*—a course consisting of large

Fig. 223 - Sweetbreads excelsior (p. 348).
Fig. 224 - Sweetbreads Rachel (p. 349).

Fig. **223**

Fig. **224**

Fig. 225

Fig. 226

joints of meat—to be found. The *double* is made up of the two legs unseparated. Both cuts come from ordinary lamb; they are used exclusively as *relevés* and are always roasted. For these joints, the clear gravy, or the gravy slightly thickened, is the best accompaniment. When the garnishes require a sauce, this sauce should be very thin.

Suitable Garnishes for Barons and Double Legs of Lamb: Bouquetière, Jardinière, Macédoine, Milanaise, Portugaise, Provençal, Richelieu, etc.

RACK OF MUTTON CARRÉ DE MOUTON (E.)

The rack, to be prepared whole, should be shortened as for the cutting of chops; the skin and the backbone must be removed and the meat separated from the end of each bone. The roast is then covered with strips of bacon or pork fat tied in place with string. The rack should include no more than 9 or 10 ribs, preferably fewer.

All garnishes given, above, for Baron of Lamb may be used with Rack of Lamb.

LAMB CHOPS and MUTTON CHOPS CÔTELETTES and MUTTON-CHOP (P.)

The chops include the following: the rack or rib chops, which are the finest chops to grill, the chops under the shoulder, and the chops near the neck. The last are not to be grilled, but are best used in mutton stews or in various recipes where they are braised. As for mutton chops, these are loin chops and are cut fairly thick. The ends of these chops are rolled in and skewered into place. Usually they are grilled and are served with vegetables or water cress, sometimes both. The directions for grilling will be found at the beginning of this book, in the chapter on cooking procedures. Mutton chops may be pan-broiled as well as grilled. The following garnishes are suitable: potatoes fried or souffléed, mashed or sautéed, potato croquettes, Potatoes Duchesse (p. 507), etc., or Brussels sprouts, noodles, olives, beans, peas, etc.—almost any vegetable goes well with mutton chops. The best chops are the first ribs, which contain more meat than do the second ribs. We do not think it necessary to give extensive directions, for all cooks know how to grill or sauté chops. However, the following recipe, using shoulder chops, makes a delicious entree.

CHOPS CHAMPVALLON CÔTELETTES CHAMPVALLON (P.)

Break the bones of the shoulder chops close to the meat; brown them in the frying pan on both sides; then brown a few sliced onions and mix in some sliced potatoes; place the chops in a baking pan, cover with onions and potatoes, pour bouillon over them, and braise 1½ hr. in a hot oven.

MUTTON DAUBE AVIGNONNAISE DAUBE À L'AVIGNONNAISE (Gi.)

The people of Provence insist that this stew must be made of mutton born and bred in the pastures of the Crau. This is an exaggeration, for a good grass-fed Norman lamb serves just as well. Daube is one of the finest dishes in ancient cookery, whose very name evokes the image of old hearths with iron pots sitting in the glowing embers. Today we use ovens.

Preparation of the mutton: Remove the bones from a leg or two (depending on the number of guests) and divide it into square pieces weighing about 3 oz. Bind each one of these pieces with bacon or a strip of pork fat flavored with spiced salt, and put them into a pot with enough red wine to cover them, 3 tbsp. oil, 1 finely sliced carrot and 1 finely sliced onion, a few peppercorns, 3 cloves

Fig. 225 - Sweetbreads toulousaine (p. 349).
Fig. 226 - Stuffed shoulder of lamb Mariette (p. 354).

garlic, 1 bay leaf, 1 sprig thyme, and parsley sprigs. Let marinate 1–2 hr., turning the pieces of mutton from time to time.

Preparation of the stew: A deep earthenware pot that will withstand heat is preferable to any other utensil. Line the bottom of the pot with pieces of mutton placed side by side; sprinkle onto this layer 2 tbsp. chopped onion, a pinch of crushed garlic, 12 small square pieces of blanched pork fat, and a handful of pork rind soaked 2 min. in boiling water and cut into ¾-inch squares. Sprinkle also a pinch of finely chopped thyme and bay leaf, then add another layer of mutton, onion, garlic, etc., until all the mutton has been used. Use a pot proportionate in size to the quantity of mutton so that it will be filled right to the brim. In filling the pot, be sure to put in the center a large bunch of parsley with the dried peel of ¼ orange inclosed in it. Pour into the pot the strained liquid from the marinade and ½ cup bouillon, then, as a precautionary measure, cover the last layer of mutton with thin strips of bacon or pork fat. Cover the pot and seal it hermetically with a band of flour paste.

Cooking: Cook in the oven at a low, steady heat for at least 5 hr., taking care to maintain an even temperature so that it will not suddenly boil over.

Serving: Take off the band of paste and the cover; remove the strips of pork fat and the bunch of parsley; skim the fat off the surface and clean the outside of the pot carefully before sending it to the table.

MUTTON DAUBE À LA MODE D'AVIGNON DAUBE À LA MODE D'AVIGNON (P.) (*For 8 persons*)

Cut 2 lb. boned shoulder of mutton into square pieces and marinate overnight in red wine with sliced onions and carrots, 1 or 2 shallots, 3 cloves garlic, parsley, thyme, bay leaf, spices. The next day, put it into a baking dish with 5 oz. lean salt pork cut into strips, 4 boned sheep's trotters, and 3½ oz. blanched pork rind cut into squares. Season, then pour the marinade over it, vegetables included. Add 3 chopped tomatoes; cover to seal hermetically (see recipe above), and cook slowly in the oven for 4 hr. Skim off the fat and serve in the same pot.

SHOULDER OF LAMB BOULANGÈRE ÉPAULE À LA BOULANGÈRE (P.)

Bone, season, and roll the shoulder. Tie with string, place in a roasting pan with some potatoes and onions sliced in rings around it. Salt, pepper, moisten with a little fat, and cook in a very hot oven. The shoulder should be roasted ¾ to 1¼ hr., depending upon its size, and should be rather rare. If it is a large shoulder, add the potatoes later.

STUFFED SHOULDER OF LAMB MARIETTE ÉPAULE FARCIE MARIETTE (P.)

May be made with either lamb or mutton. Bone the shoulder, open it, and spread inside a filling of forcemeat made of highly seasoned pork or sausage meat, with a little bit of bread crumbs, *fines herbes,* and chopped garlic; roll and tie the shoulder; brown it in a cocotte with pork fat; surround with quartered carrots and with onions. When everything is well browned, add a clove of garlic and moisten with a little water. Cover and cook slowly 2 or 3 hrs., depending on whether it is lamb or mutton. Skim the fat off the gravy, thicken with a little potato starch mixed in cold water, and pour the gravy over the meat. Garnish the shoulder with Risotto (p. 513), stuffed turnips, and small vegetable timbales. The turnips should be stuffed with meat or Tomato Fondue (p. 194). (Figure 226, Page 353.)

ROAST LEG OF LAMB or **MUTTON** GIGOT RÔTI (P.)

A good leg may be recognized immediately by the fine texture and bright pink color of the skin veined with fat. It should be trimmed by the butcher. It is usually studded with 3 or 4 half cloves of garlic, embedded in the knuckle end of the leg and, if one is particularly fond of garlic, stuck into the fleshy parts on both sides of the bone. Leg of lamb or mutton is roasted without water, allowing 12–15 min. per lb., depending on whether it is lamb or mutton. This roast is the main course of family gatherings and is served with any vegetable, usually beans, or a salad.

LEG OF LAMB or **MUTTON ENGLISH STYLE** GIGOT À L'ANGLAISE (P.)

Put the leg into a deep pot of boiling salted water and cook 15 min. per lb. Cook a variety of vegetables with it. When the leg has been cooked, make a White Roux with 2 oz. butter and 1 tbsp. flour (p. 136) ; moisten it with a little of the cooking liquor from the meat and a little milk to make a creamy sauce; add 2 oz. capers in vinegar to the sauce. The leg of lamb or mutton is served, already carved, surrounded by its garnish of vegetables. Serve the sauce separately.

LEG OF LAMB or **MUTTON BOULANGÈRE** GIGOT À LA BOULANGÈRE (P.)

Roast the leg in a large pan. When it is half cooked, place around it a few sliced onions and some potatoes cut in thin slices or quartered. Finish cooking together, basting frequently. You cannot get a good natural gravy cooking the lamb this way, since the potatoes absorb all the liquid, so it is a good idea to make a little gravy separately from lamb bones.

LEG OF LAMB or **MUTTON BRETONNE** GIGOT À LA BRETONNE (P.)

Having cooked some navy beans in advance, roast the leg of lamb or mutton. With the fat from the lamb, lightly brown a few chopped onions. When the onions are yellowish brown, pour in ½ glass white wine, cook 10 min., then add 2 or 3 tbsp. tomato purée. Then add the navy beans with a little of their cooking liquor so they will not be too dry, and season; simmer a little while, moisten with a little gravy from the roast, sprinkle with chopped parsley, and serve with the roast.

BRAISED LEG OF LAMB LYONNAISE GIGOT BRAISÉ LYONNAISE OF DE SEPT HEURES (P.)

Stud a good-sized leg of lamb or mutton with garlic, brown it in a cocotte with carrots and onions, and fill the pot until the lamb or mutton is half covered with a little white wine and a well-seasoned light-brown sauce flavored with tomatoes. Cover and braise in the oven 5–6 hr. Skim and strain the sauce and accompany the roast with a dish of small onions cooked in butter. Another vegetable can, obviously, be served in place of onions. This well-cooked lamb is so tender it can be served with a spoon.

ROAST LAMB or **MUTTON RICHELIEU** GIGOT RÔTI À LA RICHELIEU (P.)

Richelieu Garnish is made up of stuffed tomatoes, stuffed mushrooms (or artichoke bottoms), braised lettuce, and pan-fried new potatoes. This garnish goes with all large cuts of meat. When the roast is served rare, it is usually served sliced, surrounded by its garnish and accompanied with the gravy from the roast bound with a thin Semiglaze Sauce (p. 138) made with white wine. (Figure 227, Page 356.)

BRAISED LEG OF LAMB or **MUTTON SOUBISE** GIGOT BRAISÉ SOUBISE (P.)

Brown the lamb in a cocotte as you would a piece of veal—that is, with carrots and onions sliced in rings—then pour in 1 qt. very clear brown sauce; season, cover, and cook slowly in the oven, allowing ¾ hr. per lb. Drain off the gravy, skim, and reduce by at least ½, then bind with a little tomato purée. Turn the heat up to high in the oven for 15 min. to brown the top of the meat; serve the lamb with Soubise Purée and the gravy.

Note: Soubise Purée is made by cooking together 1 lb. thin-sliced onions, 2 oz. rice, and 1 teacup bouillon. When everything is well cooked, strain through a fine sieve, season, and butter. This purée should be very thick.

MUTTON-AND-BEAN STEW HARICOT DE MOUTON (P.)

Proceed the same way as for the ragout with turnips on p. 357, but replace the vegetables with navy beans cooked separately in water but kept firm so that they finish cooking in the ragout. A score of small onions browned in butter may also be added. Skim off the fat before serving and sprinkle with chopped parsley. Keep the sauce rather thin.

MOUSSAKA MOUSSAKA (P.)

This Oriental dish is delicious; it is an excellent way to use up leftover cooked mutton, preferably braised. Take 3 eggplants, cut them in half, salt them, chop the pulp without removing it, then flour them and fry in oil. When they are cooked, scoop out the pulp, leaving the skins whole. Grind or mince the well-cooked mutton, then heat over a fire. Add the chopped eggplant pulp, a little tomato purée, some garlic and *fines herbes*, paprika, tomato quarters sautéed in oil. Remove from the fire and bind with 2 or 3 eggs (2 eggs per lb.). Line a charlotte mold or other mold with the eggplant skins, pour in the hash, and cook 40 min. in a *bain-marie* in the oven. Let stand 10 min., then unmold onto a flat round platter containing some Tomato Sauce (p. 146) highly seasoned with pimento. Serve hot. (Figure 228, Page 356.)

Note: See other recipe, Turkish Cooking, p. 787.

LAMB NOISETTES BERGERETTE NOISETTES DE PRÉ-SALÉ BERGERETTE (P.)

Sauté the noisettes in butter. *Garnish:* Artichoke hearts garnished with a small tomato cooked in butter and sprinkled with parsley; tarragon leaves on the noisettes. Potatoes Parisienne (p. 509), Tarragon Sauce (p. 141). (Figure 229, Page 357.)

Note: Noisettes are lamb fillets that have been boned and trimmed like small *tournedos*. More often they are made from lamb chops, the bone being cut away. Noisettes are grilled or sautéed; all the recipes given for *tournedos* and cutlets may be used.

BREADED BREAST OF MUTTON or **LAMB TARTARE** POITRINE DE MOUTON OF D'AGNEAU PANÉE À LA TARTARE (P.)

Cook a breast of mutton in a Court Bouillon (p. 277) or Cabbage Soup (p. 209); remove the bones from the breast, then let cool while pressing under a weight. Next sprinkle with English mustard and cover with bread crumbs. Moisten with oil or fat and grill over a very hot fire. Cut in pieces and serve piping hot with Tartar Sauce (p. 158).

Fig. 227 - Roast lamb Richelieu (p. 355).
Fig. 228 - Moussaka (p. 356).

Fig. 227

Fig. 228

Fig. 229

Fig. 230

MUTTON or **LAMB STEW ENGLISH STYLE (IRISH STEW)** RAGOÛT DE MOUTON OF D'AGNEAU À L'ANGLAISE (P.)

This stew or ragout is made entirely differently from the ragout below. The same pieces of meat are used, but instead of browning them, put them into cold water on the stove; boil 5 min. and rinse the meat under the water tap; drain and cook again with 5 oz. thin-sliced onions and ¼ lb. sliced potatoes per 2 lb. mutton; salt, pepper, add a *bouquet garni,* and cover with water. Cook mutton 1½ hr.; lamb, 1 hr. Remove the pieces of meat, skim the fat off the gravy, and strain the gravy, onions, and potatoes through a sieve to form a sort of thin sauce. Put the meat into this sauce to finish cooking, along with small whole potatoes. Season strongly with pepper to offset the flatness of boiled meat.

RAGOUT OF MUTTON or **MUTTON STEW WITH TURNIPS** RAGOÛT DE MOUTON OF NAVARIN (P.) (*For 6 persons*)

Cut 2 lb. mutton (breast, neck, shoulder, according to taste) into pieces and brown over stove in a cocotte containing some fat. When well browned, add 2 tbsp. flour, brown some more, add 2 or 3 crushed cloves of garlic, then cover with water, season, add *bouquet garni,* 2 tbsp. tomato purée, a few drops of caramel coloring, and cover. Cook slowly 1 hr., then add some small onions, carrots, and turnips cut in quarters (all previously fried in butter) ; ¾ hr. later, add 1 lb. potatoes, whole or in pieces, depending on how they were cooked. Finish cooking, allowing a good 2 hr. for the whole preparation and even a little more for breast of mutton. Skim and serve.

MUTTON SAUTÉ WITH RICE SAUTÉ DE MOUTON AU RIZ (P.)

Make exactly as you would a ragout or stew, but do not flour the meat. Twenty min. before the meat is cooked, brown in butter 7 oz. rice per 2 lb. mutton and add to the stew; cook 16–17 min. When finished, this sauté should be almost dry, the rice having absorbed the liquid.

SADDLE OF MUTTON or **LAMB MODERNE** SELLE À LA MODERNE (P.)

This is a very pretty garnish, requiring a little work to prepare, but may be made the preceding evening. Peel some very red carrots and fine turnips and slice them about ¾ in. thick. Using a coring knife about ⅜ in. in diameter, cut these slices into small cubes. Cook these vegetables separately in salted water, drain, cool, then use them to line heavily buttered baba molds; place a row of carrots around the inside of the mold and a row of turnips on top, so that the mold is completely lined from top to bottom. This may be done the night before. Small heads of braised lettuce and tomatoes filled with Soubise Purée (p. 356) also make up the garnish.

The small baba molds are decorated *en chartreuse,* a term discussed more fully in the recipe for Chartreuse of Partridge (see p. 468) . To make the filling for the molds, cook cauliflower, drain it, press it through a sieve, season, and add 2 egg yolks. Fill the molds with this and cook in a *bain-marie* in the oven 8–10 min. Hollow out and cook the tomatoes in the same hot oven, keeping them rather firm. Unmold the *chartreuses* around the carved saddle of mutton, with a tomato filled with Soubise Purée between each mold and the braised lettuces,

Fig. 229 - Lamb noisettes bergerette (p. 356).
Fig. 230 - Kidneys en brochette vert-pré (p. 359).

sliced in half, in a fan-shaped arrangement at both ends of the platter. Serve a separate dish of gravy from the roast thickened with tomato paste. This garnish also goes well with beef fillet, but decorated forcemeat balls should be added. Apart from the few recipes mentioned here, the saddle can be garnished in a great variety of ways. Since any vegetable can be used, it is unnecessary to enumerate them. A saddle of lamb, much smaller than a saddle of mutton and served well done, may also be garnished according to taste. Served cold in aspic, it makes a very fine dish.

SADDLE OF LAMB RENAISSANCE — SELLE DE PRÉ-SALÉ À LA RENAISSANCE (P.)

The saddle called English saddle comprises the two loins, or the back of the lamb. It is the choicest cut and is served only at elegant dinners. It is roasted in the oven, 12 min. per lb. The garnish consists of fancy-cut carrots, turnips, and potatoes cooked separately in water and sautéed in butter, as well as green beans, peas, and cauliflower. Alternate the colors of the vegetables and separate them with medium-sized, hollowed-out tomatoes.

MUTTON-AND-PORK CASSOULET — CASSOULET DE MOUTON ET DE PORC (P.)

In the chapter on Provincial Cooking you will find the recipe for the real Cassoulet of Toulouse (p. 723), but if the necessary goose is not available you can make a good substitute with some mutton and a little pork. Follow the recipe on p. 723, leaving out the goose. Cook a good piece of breast of mutton with the beans. Roast a small piece of pork and cook a saveloy sausage. After preparing the beans as directed, bone the mutton and cut it into pieces; cut up the sausage; brown all of it together in the oven with the meat in the center. The roast pork should be cut into small slices and served at the same time. This dish is truly simple and good.

MUTTON AND LAMB BRAINS, TONGUES, ETC.

BRAINS (MUTTON) IN BLACK BUTTER — CERVELLES (DE MOUTON) AU BEURRE NOIR (P.)

Cook the brains in a Court Bouillon (p. 277), then drain, cut in two crosswise, place on a hot plate, and season; pour over them a good quantity of very black butter, then moisten with a finger of vinegar (previously poured into a very hot skillet). Sprinkle the brains with capers and chopped parsley.

Note: Mutton brains are prepared the same way as beef and calf brains.

BRAINS À LA MEUNIÈRE — CERVELLES À LA MEUNIÈRE (P.)

Skin the brains carefully, then cut them in two crosswise; season, flour, and pan-fry in noisette butter (butter that is just beginning to turn brown or hazelnut color). Cook slowly, arrange on a hot platter, and moisten with noisette butter and lemon juice.

BRAINS BREADED ENGLISH STYLE — CERVELLES PANÉES À L'ANGLAISE (P.)

Cut the raw brains in two crosswise, season, flour, dip in egg beaten with a little olive oil, then coat with bread crumbs. Cook slowly in clarified butter, arrange on a platter, and moisten with melted butter.

BRAINS WITH POULETTE SAUCE CERVELLES À LA POULETTE (P.)

Cook the brains in a Court Bouillon (p. 277) ; drain them; cut them in half or into 4 slices, and arrange on a round platter. Cover with Poulette Sauce (p. 154) containing cooked mushrooms; sprinkle with chopped parsley and lemon juice.

SHEEP'S TONGUES LANGUES DE MOUTON (E.)

Sheep's tongues are sometimes useful to vary the menu. Since they are prepared the same way as calves' tongues, we refer the reader to those recipes (p. 347).

SHEEP'S TROTTERS POULETTE PIEDS DE MOUTON POULETTE (P.)

Lamb or mutton feet may be bought already blanched at the market. Split them in two and remove the bone and the little tuft of hair found in the middle. Cook them 3 hr. in white stock, as outlined in the recipe for calf's head (p. 352). Then make a white sauce with some bouillon and a White Roux (p. 136). When the sauce is well cooked, neither too thin nor too thick, bind it with 2 or 3 egg yolks and some cream; add the feet and some mushrooms to the sauce; heat well together, then add juice of ½ lemon and chopped parsley.

KIDNEYS BERRICHONNE ROGNONS À LA BERRICHONNE (P.)

Blanch and brown 12 very small strips of lean salt pork; prepare a small quantity of Bordelaise Sauce with red wine (p. 138), and cook the salt pork with a few small mushrooms in the sauce ½ hr. Sauté the kidneys, add them to the salt pork, and serve at once without letting the preparation boil.

KIDNEYS EN BROCHETTE ROGNONS EN BROCHETTE (P.)

Split the kidneys in two without entirely separating the halves, remove the skin, and keep them open with small wooden or metal skewers. Butter and salt the kidneys and grill them over a hot fire; serve them rare with a nut of Maître d'Hôtel Butter (p. 164) in the center of each half kidney and with water cress around them.

KIDNEYS EN BROCHETTE VERT-PRÉ ROGNONS BROCHETTE VERT-PRÉ (P.)

Cook as in the preceding recipe. Garnish with Potato Straws (p. 509) and a bunch of water cress. (Figure 230, Page 357.)

KIDNEYS CHASSEUR ROGNONS CHASSEUR (P.)

Instead of slicing them, split them crosswise; season, flour, and cook in butter, keeping them rare. Separately, make some Chasseur Sauce (p. 139) with plenty of mushrooms; place the kidney halves on small fried bread croutons and cover with sauce. Parsley on top.

KIDNEYS IN MADEIRA ROGNONS AU MADÈRE (P.)

Prepare the same as Kidneys Sautéed in White Wine (p. 360), substituting Madeira for the white wine.

SAUTÉED KIDNEYS IN WHITE WINE ROGNONS SAUTÉS AU VIN BLANC (P.)

Trim the kidneys and cut them in very thin slices; sauté them in sizzling butter over a hot fire. As soon as they are seared, place them in timbales, and pour a little white wine into the juices in the sautéing pan and add a chopped shallot. Reduce the wine by ½ and add a few tbsp. brown sauce, a good piece of butter, a few sliced, cooked mushrooms. Boil a few moments and pour over the kidneys. Under no circumstances should the kidneys be boiled in the sauce. Sprinkle with parsley and decorate with a few heart-shaped bread croutons fried in butter.

SPRING LAMB

STUFFED ROAST SPRING LAMB AGNEAU FARCI RÔTI (P.)

Spring lamb, like suckling pig, is roasted whole, stuffed or not. It can be stuffed by chopping and mashing the liver and mixing it with a little pork forcemeat, *fines herbes*, sliced mushrooms cooked in butter and cooled, and seasoning. Sew up the opening and roast the lamb (which absolutely must be a spring lamb) 1½ hr. at least, basting frequently. Although stuffed, it may still be served with some sort of garnish, provided it is light.

BARON OF LAMB BYZANTINE BARON D'AGNEAU À LA BYZANTINE (Gi.)

The baron includes the two legs and the saddle—in other words, the whole hindquarters of the animal. It should be roasted in a rather hot oven, but the lamb should be served well done. While it is roasting, prepare some small patty shells or crusts of Potatoes Duchesse (p. 507) squeezed from a pastry bag, brushed with beaten egg, and cooked in a hot oven. Also prepare some Braised Lettuce halves (p. 502), allowing 1 for each potato shell, and a fairly thick, highly seasoned, and well-buttered cauliflower purée. Before serving, carve the saddle and put the slices back into the original shape; also carve the top of the legs; place the roast on a very large platter; moisten with a little gravy from the roast thickened with a little Semiglaze Sauce (p. 138), and surround with the Potato Duchesse shells (filled with the cauliflower purée) and the Braised Lettuce halves, alternating the two. Gravy separate. (Figure 220, Page 349.)

BARON OF LAMB MESSIDOR BARON D'AGNEAU À LA MESSIDOR (P.)

Roast and garnish like other meats. Slice the legs and the fillets of the saddle and re-form into the original shape. À la Messidor makes a very attractive garnish: after carving and reshaping the baron of lamb, place a pyramid of heads of cauliflower covered with Hollandaise Sauce (p. 151) at both ends of the roast. On both sides alternate artichoke bottoms, filled with Soubise Purée (p. 356) and topped with a croquette of Potatoes Dauphine (p. 507), and mounds of small new carrots. Decorate the ends of the legs of lamb with paper frills and serve hot, accompanying the dish with the gravy from the cooking skimmed, strained, and poured into a sauceboat.

RACK OF LAMB WITH MUSHROOMS CARRÉ D'AGNEAU AUX CÈPES (P.)

The rack consists of the unseparated chops. Roast the lamb 30–40 min.; then make rice creole and put it into a ring mold; cook the mushrooms (cepes,

Fig. 231 - Lamb chops Nelson (p. 361).
Fig. 232 - Garnished sauerkraut (p. 364).

Fig. 231

Fig. 232

Fig. 233

preferably) *à la bordelaise* (p. 502) ; do not brown the shallot before putting it in with the mushrooms. Serve the lamb roast by itself; place the mushrooms in the center of the rice ring, and serve Curry Sauce (p. 150) separately.

LAMB CHOPS CÔTELETTES D'AGNEAU (E.)

Allow 2 chops per person when serving spring lamb. Brush with melted butter and dip in bread crumbs, if they are to be grilled; if sautéed, dip in flour, egg beaten with a little olive oil, and bread crumbs.

LAMB CHOPS ARGENTEUIL CÔTELETTES D'AGNEAU ARGENTEUIL (P.)

Bread the chops and cook them in butter; arrange them in a crown with a mound of green asparagus tips in the center and a ring of Potatoes Noisette (p. 509) around the chops.

LAMB CHOPS CAPUCHIN CÔTELETTES D'AGNEAU À LA CAPUCINE (P.)

First prepare mushroom purée and, separately, some small shells of Short Paste (p. 545) , 1 for each chop. Sauté the chops in butter, then arrange them in a crown on a round platter. After skimming off the fat in the sautéing pan, pour into it ½ cup cream and juice of 1 lemon; cook 5 min., salt, pepper, and pour over the chops. Fill the small patty shells with mushroom purée and place 1 on top of each chop.

LAMB CHOPS MARIE LOUISE CÔTELETTES D'AGNEAU MARIE-LOUISE (E.)

Dip the chops in flour, egg beaten with a little olive oil, and bread crumbs; cook them in clarified butter, and place them in a circle on a platter, 1 chop overlapping the next. Surround with small artichoke bottoms cooked in butter and filled with mounds of very thick mushroom purée mixed with Soubise Purée (p. 356) , ¾ mushroom to ¼ Soubise Purée. Serve a thickened gravy separately.

LAMB CHOPS NELSON CÔTELETTES D'AGNEAU NELSON (P.)

Cook the chops in butter on 1 side only and all on the same side so that the bones point the same way. Drain them and garnish with thick Soubise Purée (p. 356) , then trim them, moisten well with butter, and bake in the oven. Arrange them in a ring on a round platter, 1 overlapping the other, with a thin Madeira Sauce (p. 142) in the center; garnish the outside of the circle with fine mushroom caps grilled and stuffed with Duxelles (see p. 176) . Decorate the chops with paper frills. (Figure 231, Page 360.)

LAMB CHOPS EN PAPILLOTES CÔTELETTES D'AGNEAU EN PAPILLOTES (P.)

Cut a heart out of white parchment paper and butter or oil it. In the center of one side of the heart put 1 tbsp. Duxelles (p. 176) . On the Duxelles lay a thin slice of cooked ham, then the sautéed lamb chop; cover with a second slice of ham, then 1 tbsp. Duxelles. Fold over paper heart, pleating the edges all the way around to enclose the chop tightly; blow into the bag before sealing it completely and place it in a very hot oven; leave in the oven until the paper turns dark brown. Serve immediately with a separate dish of Madeira Sauce (p. 142) . All dishes *en papillote* are prepared the same way. It is an old French recipe, not used much today. Mostly leftovers are prepared this way.

Fig. 233 - Ham Fitz-James (p. 367).

BREADED LAMB CHOPS CÔTELETTES D'AGNEAU PANÉES (P.)

Spring lamb is a white meat and should be breaded like veal cutlets (see p. 340).

STUFFED LAMB CHOPS À LA REINE CÔTELETTES D'AGNEAU FARCIES À LA REINE (P.)

First cook the chops on 1 side only, then mince a little leftover cooked chicken and mix it with some minced ham and 2 or 3 chopped mushrooms; blend this mixture with a little Béchamel Sauce (p. 146) bound with egg yolk; season well and, when it is thick enough, spread over the cooked side of the chops. Dip the chops into beaten egg, roll in white bread crumbs, and put them back into the pan they were first cooked in. Baste with butter and place in a hot oven to finish cooking; they should be well browned. Arrange the chops around highly seasoned creamed mushrooms. Place paper frills on the chops.

STUFFED LAMB CHOPS SOUBISE CÔTELETTES D'AGNEAU FARCIES À LA SOUBISE (P.)

Allow 2 lamb chops per person. Cook in butter on 1 side only, then cover the cooked side with Soubise Purée (p. 356); bread them and finish cooking in butter. Arrange them in a circle and fill the center with a Soubise Sauce (p. 154) made from the leftover purée thinned with cream.

LAMB CHOP SURPRISE CÔTELETTES D'AGNEAU EN SURPRISE (P.)

Salt and pepper the chops; sauté 2 min. on each side; let cool; cover both sides of the chops with a thin slice of ham and a layer of Duxelles (p. 176) containing a little garlic; wrap the chops in Paste for Croustades (p. 545). After shaping them and brushing with beaten egg, place them on a tray and bake 20 min. in a hot oven; serve a separate dish of good Veal Gravy (p. 134).

Paste for the chops: 6½ oz. flour, 3 oz. butter, 1 egg yolk, salt, pepper, and water. Stiff paste. Flaky Paste (p. 544) would be still better.

LAMB SAUTÉ PRINTANIER SAUTÉ D'AGNEAU PRINTANIER (E.) (*For 6 persons*)

Prepare the following garnish: 20 small carrots cooked in consommé and glazed, 20 turnip balls cut like elongated olives and cooked like the carrots, 15 small onions cooked in butter, 20 potato balls the size of a nut cooked in butter without browning, 3 tbsp. French peas and 3 tbsp. green beans cut diamond shape (peas and beans should be freshly boiled in salted water). Cut 2 lb. shoulder and breast of lamb into pieces weighing 1½–2 oz. each (equal parts of breast and shoulder); brown and then cook slowly in butter. Remove the pieces of meat onto a platter, then swirl around in the pan 3 tbsp. water and 5 tbsp. golden meat glaze; heat without boiling; finish with 2 oz. butter. Place the lamb and the prepared garnish in this sauce; shake the pan on the stove to mix well. Serve in a hot vegetable dish.

SADDLE OF LAMB GREEK STYLE or **ORIENTALE** SELLE D'AGNEAU À LA GRECQUE OR À L'ORIENTALE (P.)

Simply roast the saddle until it is well done, allowing 20 min. per lb. Meanwhile make a Risotto (p. 513) with tomato quarters added; stuff halves of zucchini with sautéed tomatoes mixed with a little chopped mushrooms and onions cooked in fat. Carve the saddle and place it on a platter with a mound of rice at each end and the stuffed zucchini on the sides. The sauce is the gravy from the roast flavored with tomatoes and highly seasoned.

Note: Saddle of lamb may be garnished with any vegetable. The essential point is to serve the lamb well done and not rare like saddle of mutton.

SADDLE OF LAMB STUART SELLE D'AGNEAU À LA STUART (P.)

Remove the bone from the saddle and replace it with a filling of forcemeat mixed with truffles (see p. 173). Close the opening by pressing on the middle and sewing the 2 sides together. Roast 1 hr. in a medium oven. Fry a nice slice of *foie gras* in butter (or merely heat it in butter if it is canned), allowing 1 slice per guest. Place the cooked *foie gras* on artichoke bottoms or, for economy's sake, in patty shells. Place these around the saddle (carved across like a beef fillet, since it is boned) and cover the garnish with a thin Madeira Sauce (p. 142); 1 slice of truffle on each slice of *foie gras.*

SPRING-LAMB BRAINS, SWEETBREADS, ETC.

BRAINS CERVELLES (E.)

Same recipes as for calf's brains.

TONGUES and **FEET** LANGUES and PIEDS (E.)

Same recipes as for mutton.

SWEETBREADS RIS (E.)

Same recipes as for veal sweetbreads.

PORK

Large joints of fresh pork are used more often in home cooking than for formal occasions. They are always roasted and may be served with fresh or dry vegetables, various purées, or various pastes like macaroni, noodles, polenta, gnocchi, etc.

PORK LOIN WITH APPLESAUCE CARRÉ DE PORC À LA MARMELADE DE POMMES (E.)

Roast the loin. Peel, seed, and slice 1½ lb. firm apples; cook them rapidly in a few tbsp. water containing 1½ tbsp. powdered sugar; cover tightly to keep the steam in the pot. Just before serving, beat the applesauce with a wire whisk to make it smooth. Serve the roast on a platter and pour its own gravy, with ¾ of the fat skimmed, around it. Serve the applesauce in a separate dish.

PORK LOIN COUNTRY STYLE CARRÉ DE PORC À LA PAYSANNE (E.)

Roast the loin in an earthenware dish. When half cooked, surround the pork with 2 lb. quartered potatoes and 4 sliced onions sautéed in butter. Finish cooking, basting the vegetables frequently with fat from the roast. When the roast is removed from the oven, sprinkle a handful of crushed parsley on the vegetables and serve as is.

GARNISHED SAUERKRAUT CHOUCROUTE GARNIE (E.)

If the sauerkraut is not very fresh, it should be soaked in cold water for a few hours. However, it is preferable to use fresh sauerkraut. Just before cooking, press the water out of the sauerkraut if it has been soaked, then unravel it carefully so that it will not stick together in lumps; season it with salt and pepper and place it in a braising pan lined with strips of bacon. For 10 lb. sauerkraut add: 3 carrots, 3 medium-sized onions stuck with a clove, 1 large *bouquet garni,* 3½ oz. juniper berries tied in a cloth bag, 6½ oz. goose fat or lard, 1 lb. blanched pork fat from the breast (which should be removed after 1 hr. of cooking). Pour in enough white consommé to cover the sauerkraut halfway; cover with strips of bacon; bring to a boil; then bake in a covered casserole in the oven 4 hr.

Serving: Remove vegetables, *bouquet garni,* bag of juniper berries; place the sauerkraut in a deep dish or on a platter, after draining it well; surround with thin slices of ham, rectangles of bacon, and poached Frankfort or Strasbourg sausages. (Figure 232, Page 360.)

PORK CHOPS FLAMANDE CÔTES DE PORC À LA FLAMANDE (E.)

Season the chops and brown them quickly in butter on both sides. Arrange them in a baking dish; surround with sweet apples peeled and cut in thick slices (3½ oz. apples per chop); finish cooking in the oven at low heat. Serve in the baking dish.

PORK CHOPS GRAND'MÈRE CÔTES DE PORC GRAND'MÈRE (E.)

Mince the meat of the chops and add per lb. meat: 3½ oz. butter, ½ chopped onion cooked in butter, 1 egg, a good pinch of salt, a little pepper and nutmeg. Mold the mincemeat into the shape of chops, using a bone for each one; wrap them in a pig's caul; baste with melted butter, and grill slowly. Arrange in a circle on a platter and serve with a separate dish of mashed potatoes.

PORK CHOPS MILANAISE CÔTES DE PORC À LA MILANAISE (E.)

Flatten the chops well; season them; bread them *à la milanaise* (dip in flour, then in egg beaten with a little olive oil, then in bread crumbs mixed with grated Parmesan cheese, ⅔ bread crumbs to ⅓ cheese), and cook them slowly in butter. Arrange them overlapping in a circle and, in the center, place a Milanaise Garnish (p. 183); serve Tomato Sauce (p. 146) separately.

BREADED PORK CHOPS CÔTES DE PORC PANÉES (M.)

Bread the chops, cover with melted butter, and grill; or dip in flour, in egg beaten with oil, then in bread crumbs, and sauté. Usually served with mashed potatoes and a highly seasoned sauce.

SUCKLING PIG (FORCEMEAT FOR) COCHON DE LAIT (FARCE POUR LE) (E.)

Make a Gratin Forcemeat (p. 175), using the liver of the pig; be sure only to sear the liver. To this forcemeat add the same weight of sausage meat, 6½ oz. soaked and pressed bread crumbs, 2 eggs, 3 oz. champagne brandy, a pinch of wild thyme or ordinary thyme if wild is unobtainable. Stuff the pig with this forcemeat, sew up the skin of the stomach, and place it back side up on a roasting pan or on a spit.

SUCKLING PIG (ENGLISH-STYLE FORCEMEAT FOR) COCHON DE LAIT (FARCE À L'ANGLAISE POUR) (E.)

Bake in the oven with their skins 2½ lb. very large onions; let cool. Peel them and chop very fine, then mix with 1 lb. soaked, pressed bread crumbs, 1 lb. minced beef-kidney fat, 1 oz. salt, pinch of pepper, a little nutmeg, 4 oz. blanched, finely chopped sage, 2 eggs. Mix well.

Note: This forcemeat may also be used for duck, goose, etc.

STUFFED, ROAST SUCKLING PIG ENGLISH STYLE COCHON DE LAIT FARCI ET RÔTI À L'ANGLAISE (E.)

Stuff with the forcemeat given above and sew up the belly; next place the pig on a spit, baste with oil, and roast in the usual way. Serve separately either mashed potatoes or applesauce (with very little sugar) mixed with an equal amount of dried currants that have been cleaned, washed, and soaked in warm water.

STUFFED SUCKLING PIG SERVED WHOLE COCHON DE LAIT FARCI SERVI ENTIER (Fa.)

Take a suckling pig prepared and cleaned in the usual way; season the inside and stuff in a variety of ways, either with larks, or sausages, or forcemeats, or black puddings, or olives, or apples, etc., all of which should first be cooked and cooled as it will not cook inside the pig. Sew up the belly, fold the feet under the body, and hold the head up with a wooden skewer, then roast, basting often. Roast 1½–2 hr. in a hot, but not too hot, oven.

SUCKLING PIG ST. FORTUNATUS COCHON DE LAIT SAINT-FORTUNAT (E.)

Choose a very white little suckling pig. Salt the inside a little and moisten with a few tbsp. brandy. Separately, prepare a pilaf of ½ lb. ordinary barley (see below).

Mix the barley with: the liver of the pig diced in large pieces and sautéed in butter, 2 tbsp. chopped *fines herbes,* 6½ oz. cooked chipolata sausages, 50 braised chestnuts. Stuff the pig with this dressing, sew up the belly, and truss it into position with the head resting between the two front feet. Place it in a roasting pan and baste frequently with melted butter while roasting to make the skin golden and crackling.

Serve separately: (1) Meat Glaze made from veal stock (p. 135), (2) a red-currant sauce with horseradish, (3) tart applesauce.

Barley Pilaf: Cook 3 oz. chopped onions in butter until golden brown, then add ½ lb. hulled barley, washed, drained, and well dried; heat it, stirring with a wooden spoon, and cover with 3 cups boiling white bouillon. Season with a pinch of pepper, cover, and cook in the oven slowly for about 2 hr. At the last moment moisten the barley with 2 oz. browned butter.

CHINE OF PORK ÉCHINÉE DE PORC (E.)

The chine is cut from the backbone. Generally the part containing the loin chops is selected, or the section containing the shoulder chops, but the tenderloin also makes a fine cut. It may be prepared like a carbonade (see Beef) or roasted like loin of pork, accompanied with the same garnishes as well as with braised, stuffed, or au gratin cabbage.

SHOULDER OF PORK ÉPAULE DE PORC (E.)

Boned, salted, rolled, and smoked shoulder of pork is prepared like ham. If the shoulder is only salted, it is used in the soup-stews called *potées*. Fresh shoulder should be roasted like Chine of Pork (p. 365) and served with any garnish or sauce included in recipes for loin of pork or pork chops. This cut of pork is too ordinary to be served except for family meals.

HAM (E.)

Despite Monselet's sonnet in praise of the pig and Grimod de la Reynière's dubbing it "the encyclopedic animal," pork would never hold the place it does in fine cooking if it were not for the culinary importance of the hams. Whether it is a ham from Bayonne or York, from Prague or Westphalia, it is one of the most useful items in the kitchen, and it would be hard to find a *relevé* more greatly appreciated. Which type of ham is the best is a difficult question to decide. However, we prefer the tender Bohemian ham called Prague ham for serving hot and York ham for a cold dish. The York is very good hot, but inferior to the Prague ham, whose delicate flavor is incomparable. York ham still ranks among the first in the opinion of gourmets.

COOKING THE HAM (E.)

Soak the ham in cold water for 6 hr., then scrub it, cut the bone off the chump end, and set it to boil in a deep pot of cold water without seasoning or vegetables. Once it starts to boil, reduce the heat so that the liquid simmers, which is enough to poach the ham. If the ham is to be served cold, let it cool in the cooking liquid.

Cooking time for hams depends upon the type, quality, and weight. Yorkshire, Hamburg, and Westphalia hams poach for about 20 min. per lb., while tender Bohemian and Spanish hams require only 15 min. per lb.

Note: It is easier to leave the chump-end bone on until cooked and then break it off by hand. Do not wait until the ham has completely cooled before doing this.

BRAISING THE HAM (E.)

If the ham is to be served hot, remove it from the water ½ hr. before it has finished cooking. After removing the skin, trim off the excess fat, leaving a layer about ½ in. thick. It is better to leave too heavy a layer of fat on than to cut off too much. Next place the ham in a roasting pan just large enough to hold it and pour in about 12 oz. of a heady wine like Madeira, port, sherry, or Cyprus, depending on what is to be served with the ham. Close the pan tightly and place in a low oven for 1 hr. to finish cooking the ham and to let it be impregnated with the aroma of the wine. If the ham is to be served whole at the table, glaze it just before serving. It is usually accompanied with a clear Semiglaze Sauce (p. 138) enriched with the wine used in the braising after it has been well skimmed and strained.

GLAZING THE HAM (E.)

If necessary, ham may be glazed like other braised meats, but this is not very practical and adds nothing to the quality of the dish; quite the contrary.

The most frequently employed method and the one most to be recommended is to sprinkle the ham with sugar, using a shaker. When it is evenly covered, place it in a very hot oven for a few minutes. The sugar is caramelized instantly, covering the ham with a golden, appetizing crust and adding a decided flavor to it.

Note: Since the principal directions for cooking ham have been given on p. 366, we shall not repeat these details in the following recipes, but shall indicate only the ingredients used in the braising.

HAM BAYONNAISE JAMBON À LA BAYONNAISE (E.)

Braise the ham in Madeira and glaze it. Prepare a Rice Pilaf (p. 512) with 1 lb. rice, 1 large chopped onion, and 5 cups consommé. When half cooked, add 3 medium-sized tomatoes, peeled, pressed, and crushed, 20 small, cooked mushroom caps, 20 small chipolata sausages browned in butter. Ten min. before serving, moisten the rice with 4 oz. browned butter. Arrange the ham on a platter and serve along with the Rice Pilaf in a timbale and a dish of Madeira Sauce (p. 142).

HAM BOURGUIGNONNE JAMBON À LA BOURGUIGNONNE (E.)

Braise the ham in a Mirepoix Bordelaise (p. 136) to which half its quantity in fresh mushroom peelings and Pouilly white wine have been added. Serve the ham with Madeira Sauce (p. 142) enriched with (1) thick slices of mushrooms sautéed in butter; (2) the braising stock pressed through a strainer.

HAM IN CRUST JAMBON EN CROÛTE (J.) (*For 15 persons*)

Take a small ham weighing about 9 lb., poach it, drain, and let stand until half cooled. Remove the rind and the chump-end bone, then trim off the excess fat, slice it, and enclose in a layer of Pie Paste (see p. 545) with the seam underneath. Brush with beaten egg and score or decorate with motifs cut out of paste. Make an opening in the top to let the steam out. Bake about 1¼ hr. in a moderate oven. After removing it from the oven, pour a small glass of Madeira into the steam vent on top. Place the ham on a platter, cut the crust at the base of the ham, and serve with a separate dish of Madeira Sauce (p. 142).

HAM FINANCIÈRE GODARD JAMBON FINANCIÈRE GODARD (E.)

Modern cookery almost never recommends any garnish for ham except vegetables and pastes or farinaceous dishes, while older cookery prescribed Financière and Godard Garnishes (p. 181), which may still be used. Ham served with one of these garnishes should be braised in Madeira and the garnish served separately. The wine used in the braising should be reduced and added to the garnish sauce.

HAM FITZ-JAMES JAMBON FITZ-JAMES (E.)

Braise the ham in Madeira and glaze it. In serving, surround it with timbales of tomatoed rice alternated with stuffed mushrooms. Serve Madeira Sauce (p. 142) separately, adding cockscombs, cock's kidneys, and the wine from the braising, reduced, to the sauce. (Figure 233, Page 361.)

HAM SOUFFLÉ JAMBON SOUFFLÉ (E.)

After boning all the ham except for the end bone, cook it the usual way and let it cool. Remove the skin, trim off the excess fat, then cut it horizontally about ½ in. above the bone from the round end down to the end of the bone. At this end make a vertical cut, stopping where the horizontal cut ended, so that the whole thick layer of ham may be removed, leaving only a covering of meat around the bone. Set the meat aside to use later. Trim the meat adhering to the bone neatly; envelop it in a band of buttered paper and tie it with string, to hold the soufflé mixture. Now place it on a platter and cover it with one of the two soufflé mixtures described on p. 370, reconstructing the ham in its original shape. Smooth the mixture with the blade of a knife dipped in cold water to shape it like a ham; decorate the surface with cut-out pieces of cooked ham and truffles; place the platter with the ham in a deep roasting pan containing boiling water, heated in the oven in advance. This is done to obtain as much steam as possible to poach the mixture. This soufflé may also be poached on top of the stove in a steamer. When it is well poached, remove the paper band. Serve separately one of the garnishes or sauces given in the recipes for braised ham.

HAM MOUSSES and MOUSSELINES MOUSSES and MOUSSELINES DE JAMBON (E.)

Both of these preparations are made the same way and use a ham mousseline forcemeat as the basic ingredient. A mousse is poached in a mold large enough to serve several people, while mousselines are molded with a spoon like large forcemeat balls and are more or less egg-shaped.

Preparation of the forcemeat: Mousseline forcemeat is always prepared the same way, regardless of its basic ingredient (see p. 173). However, in making ham mousseline forcemeat, care must be taken in using salt, for the ham may already be salty. If the ham meat is not very red, the forcemeat may be brightened with a few drops of red vegetable coloring to give it a distinct pale-pink shade.

HOT HAM MOUSSE (PREPARATION) MOUSSE DE JAMBON CHAUDE (E.)

Place the forcemeat in a charlotte mold or other deep mold that has been well buttered. Poach in a covered *bain-marie,* keeping the temperature of the water at 205° to 208° F. Allow 45 min. cooking time for a qt. mold. The preparation is cooked when it begins to rise and swell in the mold. Remove the mold from the *bain-marie* and let it stand 5 min. so that the mixture settles a little, then turn it upside down on a platter and wait 2 min. before unmolding. This should not be done until you have carefully wiped off all the liquid that has drained onto the platter.

HOT HAM MOUSSE (TRIMMINGS) MOUSSE DE JAMBON CHAUDE (E.)

The most suitable trimmings for ham mousse are: (1) strong but smooth brown sauces made with Madeira, port, Marsala, etc.; Suprême Sauce (p. 146); Velouté (p. 147) with curry or paprika; (2) fresh spring vegetables or a Financière Garnish (p. 181).

HAM MOUSSE AURORE MOUSSE DE JAMBON À L'AURORE (P.) (*For 3 persons*)

Follow the recipe for Ham Mousse with Spinach, p. 369. When the ham has been pressed through a sieve, mix in 3 whole eggs per lb. meat, a little red coloring and paprika, 3 tbsp. heavy cream. Put this mixture into a round, flat, buttered mold sprinkled with bread crumbs. Cook in a *bain-marie* in the oven for 35 min., then unmold onto a hot round platter and cover with Aurore Sauce (p. 147). On top of the sauce, sprinkle the yolks of 2 chopped hard-boiled eggs. Serve hot.

Fig. 234 - Ham in aspic (p. 371).

Fig. **234**

Fig. 235

Fig. 236

HAM MOUSSE WITH SPINACH MOUSSE DE JAMBON AUX ÉPINARDS (P.)

(For 3 persons)

This recipe is a way to use up leftover ham. Chop and mash ½ lb. lean cooked ham with 2½ oz. butter, ½ cup thick Béchamel Sauce (p. 146), salt, pepper, and a few drops of red coloring. Press this purée through a sieve, heat it with 2 tbsp. cream; remove from the stove and add 3 egg yolks and the white of 1 egg beaten stiff. Fill small, buttered individual porcelain cassolettes or ramekins ¾ full with this mousse. From 10–12 min. before serving, place the cassolettes in a hot oven. When cooked and souffléed, arrange the cassolettes in a circle on a platter covered with a napkin, with spinach purée in a crust of short paste in the center. Or serve with a Spinach Loaf, p. 514.

HOT HAM MOUSSELINES MOUSSELINES CHAUDES DE JAMBON (E.)

We have explained, earlier, that mousselines are molded with a spoon, but they can also be made, and this procedure is recommended, by squeezing them from a pastry bag into a buttered pan, giving them the shape of plain or fluted meringues. In either case, they should be decorated with bits of ham and truffle, then covered with lightly salted boiling water and poached 18–20 min. They may also be poached in a steamer at low heat.

HAM MOUSSELINES ALEXANDRA MOUSSELINES DE JAMBON ALEXANDRA (P.)

Decorate the mousselines with a thin diamond-shaped slice of ham and two diamond-shaped slices of truffle. Poach, drain well, and arrange them in a circle on a platter. Cover with Suprême Sauce (p. 146) made with ham essence and 3½ oz. grated Parmesan cheese per qt. sauce; glaze quickly in a hot oven. Remove from the oven and arrange around a bunch of buttered asparagus tips.

HAM MOUSSELINES FLORENTINE MOUSSELINES DE JAMBON À LA FLORENTINE (E.)

Spread out on a serving platter a layer of blanched, roughly chopped, buttered leaf spinach. Place the poached and drained mousselines on top and cover with the sauce given for Mousselines Alexandra. Glaze quickly in the oven.

HAM MOUSSELINES HUNGARIAN STYLE MOUSSELINES DE JAMBON À LA HONGROISE (E.)

Season the forcemeat with paprika; mold and poach the mousselines; drain them thoroughly and arrange in a circle on a platter; cover with Hongroise or Hungarian Sauce and glaze quickly in a hot oven. When the platter is removed from the oven, arrange a fine mound of Cauliflower au Gratin (p. 494) in the center of the mousselines.

Note: The cauliflower can be placed in the center of the mousselines, then sauced and glazed at the same time.

HOT HAM SOUFFLÉS SOUFFLÉS CHAUDS DE JAMBON (E.)

The ham soufflé mixture may be made with cooked or raw ham. The raw ham mixture, which is a kind of mousseline forcemeat, is used for quantity cooking because it may be prepared in advance and the soufflés may stand for a few minutes after cooking without being spoiled.

Fig. 235 - Ham cones russian style (p. 371).
Fig. 236 - Glazed ham medallions Monte-Carlo (p. 371).

SOUFFLÉ (MIXTURE) WITH COOKED HAM SOUFFLÉ (APPAREIL DE) AVEC JAMBON CUIT (E.) (*For 6 persons*)

Pound finely 1 lb. lean, cooked ham in a mortar, adding, bit by bit, 3 tbsp. cold Béchamel Sauce (p. 146). Press through a fine sieve into a pan and finish with 6 oz. Béchamel Sauce made with ham essence, 5 egg yolks, 7 stiffly beaten egg whites.

Note: 3½ oz. grated Parmesan cheese may be added to the mixture, for it blends well with the other flavors. Prepared this way, it is especially suitable for the Ham Soufflé given on p. 367.

SOUFFLÉ (MIXTURE) WITH RAW HAM SOUFFLÉ (APPAREIL DE) AVEC JAMBON CRU (E.)

Make ham mousseline forcemeat (p. 368), using ¼ less cream than ordinarily and replacing it by the same quantity of very cold Béchamel Sauce (p. 146). Keep the forcemeat rather firm; finish it with 4 egg whites, beaten stiff, per lb. ham.

HAM SOUFFLÉ ALEXANDRA SOUFFLÉ DE JAMBON ALEXANDRA (E.)

Prepare the mixture according to one of the two methods given above. Place it in a buttered timbale in layers alternated with layers of buttered asparagus tips. Smooth into a mound on top, decorate with fine truffle slices, and bake in a medium oven.

Note: If the soufflé is not very large, simply place a layer of asparagus tips in the center; if it is large, make 2 or 3 layers.

HAM SOUFFLÉ CARMEN SOUFFLÉ DE JAMBON CARMEN (E.)

Place the mixture in a buttered timbale in layers alternated with layers of Tomato Fondue (1 sweet pimento per qt. strained and reduced tomatoes, cooked in butter). Smooth the top up into a dome, sprinkle the surface with finely shredded red pimento, and bake in the oven at moderate heat.

Note: Instead of being used between layers of the ham mixture, the tomato purée can be mixed directly into the soufflé mixture.

GASTRONOMES' HAM SOUFFLÉ SOUFFLÉ DE JAMBON DES GASTRONOMES (E.)

Place the mixture in a buttered timbale in layers alternated with layers of sliced mushrooms sautéed in butter. Smooth the top of the mixture; sprinkle with chopped truffles; place a ball of truffles in the center of the soufflé, and bake as usual.

HAM SOUFFLÉ MILANAISE SOUFFLÉ DE JAMBON À LA MILANAISE (E.)

Place the mixture in a buttered timbale in layers alternated with layers of Milanaise Garnish (p. 183). Smooth the surface and decorate with pieces of poached macaroni dipped in melted butter, pressing the pieces lightly into the mixture. Sprinkle with grated Parmesan cheese and cook in a moderate oven.

HAM SOUFFLÉ PÉRIGOURDINE SOUFFLÉ DE JAMBON À LA PÉRIGOURDINE (E.)

Prepare the soufflé as above, alternating layers of soufflé mixture with a bed of thick truffle slices. Smooth the top, sprinkle with chopped truffles, and bake as usual.

COLD HAM

HAM IN ASPIC JAMBON À LA GELÉE (E.)

Ham served cold should, as much as possible, be allowed to cool in its cooking liquid unless it is to be boned. In this case, remove it from the liquid as soon as it is cooked and cut underneath, following the edge of the cushion, then loosen and remove the bones. Then roll the ham tightly in a cloth and set it to cool under a weight. Whether boned or not, remove the skin when the ham is cold; then trim off the excess fat. Cover it with Aspic Jelly (p. 168) until it is completely coated with a thick, even glaze. Place a paper frill over the bone and decorate the sides with chopped pieces of aspic. (Figure 234, Page 368.)

PRAGUE HAM SURPRISE JAMBON DE PRAGUE EN SURPRISE (E.)

Cook the ham in champagne and let it cool. Next trim it and carve a little bowl out of the center and fill with *pâté de foie gras*. Smooth over the surface, cover the hollow with Aspic Jelly (p. 168), and decorate with truffles. Cut the piece carved from the center into thin slices and place them around the sides of the ham. Serve each slice of ham with a spoonful of *foie gras*.

COLD HAM SOUFFLÉ JAMBON SOUFFLÉ FROID (E.)

Follow the recipe for Hot Ham Soufflé (p. 367), replacing the hot soufflé mixture with the Cold Ham Mousse mixture given on p. 372. Glaze with Aspic Jelly (p. 168) and decorate the sides with chopped pieces of aspic.

HAM CONES RUSSIAN STYLE CORNETS DE JAMBON À LA RUSSE (J.)

Use special small molds to make the cones (see directions, p. 104) ; fill them with a mousse of *pâté de foie gras* or, if preferred, *foie gras* with truffles. Cool in the refrigerator. Unmold when the *foie gras* is firm. Decorate with truffles and glaze with Aspic Jelly (p. 168). Make a mound of Russian Salad (carrots, turnips, potatoes, green beans, and peas bound with mayonnaise) on a platter. Place the ham cones on top of this mound and finish decorating with chopped aspic, using a pastry bag; spaces between the cones may be filled with whites and yolks of hard-boiled eggs chopped separately. (Figure 235, Page 369.)

HAM CONES CZARINA CORNETS DE JAMBON TSARINE (J.)

Same recipe as above, substituting chopped aspic for the Russian Salad. (Figure 272, Plate 66.)

GLAZED HAM MEDALLIONS MONTE CARLO MÉDAILLONS DE JAMBON GLACÉ À LA MONTE-CARLO (P.)

Cut some York ham into thin slices and trim into small circles. Allow 2 circles for each medallion. Prepare Cold Ham Mousse (p. 372) and place a thick slice of it between 2 circles of ham. Cover these with half-hardened Aspic Jelly (p. 168), decorate with truffles, and cover with a second coating of aspic. Fill a small timbale mold, lined with aspic, with the rest of the mousse, decorate with truffles, and chill on ice. Unmold the mousse onto the center of a round platter, surround with chopped aspic, and on this bed of aspic arrange the medallions so that they overlap one another. (Figure 236, Page 369.)

COLD HAM MOUSSE MOUSSE FROIDE DE JAMBON (E.) (*For 8 persons*)

Pound finely in a mortar 1 lb. lean cooked ham, adding 6 oz. cold Velouté (p. 147) ; press through a sieve into a bowl; correct the seasoning. Place the bowl on ice and beat the mixture for a few minutes, then blend in 4½ oz. melted Aspic Jelly (p. 168), adding it little by little. Add finally 12 oz. half-whipped cream.

COLD HAM MOUSSE ALSACIENNE MOUSSE FROIDE DE JAMBON À L'ALSACIENNE (E.)

Prepare the mousse as directed above, adding to the ham ⅓ as much cooked *foie gras*. Finish the mixture with diced *foie gras* and truffles and mold the mousse as directed. Unmold just before serving and surround with small mousselines shaped with a dessertspoon and chilled in the refrigerator.

COLD HAM MOUSSE WITH FOIE GRAS MOUSSE FROIDE DE JAMBON AU FOIE GRAS (E.)

Half fill a deep square dish with Cold Ham Mousse (above). Smooth the surface and, when the mousse has set, arrange on top some shells of *foie gras* made with a spoon dipped in hot water. Cover the shells immediately with half-set chicken Aspic Jelly (p. 168) and let it set fully. When serving, embed the dish in a block of clear ice.

HAM MOUSSE WITH BREAST OF CHICKEN MOUSSE DE JAMBON AU BLANC DE VOLAILLE (E.)

Fill a deep square dish ⅔ full of Cold Ham Mousse (above). When the mousse has set, lay on top slices of very white, poached breast of chicken coated with White Chaud-Froid Sauce (p. 149). Cover with Aspic Jelly as in the recipe above and serve the same way.

Note: If necessary, the Chaud-Froid Sauce may be dispensed with, but the slices of chicken breast must be well-covered with aspic.

COLD HAM MOUSSELINES MOUSSELINES FROIDES DE JAMBON (M.)

See Garnishes, p. 176.

VEAL-AND-HAM PIE PÂTÉ DE VEAU ET DE JAMBON

See Mixed Entrees, p. 537.

PORK LIVER, TONGUE, FEET, ETC.

PORK LIVER FOIE DE PORC (E.)

Pork liver is not highly regarded; it is chiefly used as an ingredient in forcemeats. The main, special methods of preparation are: *à la bourgeoise,* Italian style, sautéed in red wine, etc.

PORK TONGUE LANGUE DE PORC (E.)

Pork tongue is prepared like veal tongue; any of the recipes for veal tongue may be used.

PIG'S EARS OREILLES DE PORC (E.)

Singe the ears and clean them well on the inside, then cook them in salted water (½ tsp. salt per qt. water) with carrots, onions stuck with a clove, and a *bouquet garni,* if they are to be served plain or with a sauce.

If the ears are to be served with a garnish of sauerkraut, Red Cabbage Flamande (p. 510), or lentils, they should be cooked with the garnish. If they are served with the red cabbage, leave the fat out of the recipe. When the ears are served with lentils, the lentils should be mashed into a purée after the ears are cooked.

PIG'S FEET PIEDS DE PORC (E.)

Cook the pig's feet as you would the ears served plain. They can be cooked exactly like the ears, but usually they are served breaded or grilled, or studded with truffles.

BREADED PIG'S FEET PIEDS DE PORC PANÉS (E.)

Split the feet in two and bread, baste with lard or melted butter, and grill over low heat, as you would any heavily breaded food. Serve as is, or with a separate dish of mashed potatoes.

TRUFFLED PIG'S FEET PIEDS DE PORC TRUFFÉS (E.)

These pig's feet may generally be bought already prepared. Rarely are they made at home, except in large establishments, but there is nothing very complicated about preparing them.

Cook the pig's feet as described in the recipe for ears, remove all the bones, and let cool. Dice the meat in large pieces; mix it with finely minced pork meat—6½ oz. pork per foot—adding 5 oz. chopped raw truffles per lb. mixture. Separate into portions weighing 3½ oz.; shape into flat sausages pointed at one end; place 3 slices of truffle on each patty and wrap in pig's caul or sausage casing. Baste with melted butter and grill slowly so that the heat will penetrate the meat. Arrange in a circle and serve with a dish of Périgueux Sauce (p. 143). Truffled Pig's Feet may also be served with mashed potatoes.

PORK KIDNEYS ROGNONS DE PORC (E.)

Use the recipes given for veal kidneys.

PIG'S HEAD TÊTE DE PORC (E.)

The head is usually set aside to be made into cold dishes, especially head cheese. It may also be served hot, following the directions given for ears.

VARIOUS PORK PREPARATIONS

HOG'S PUDDING ANDOUILLES and ANDOUILLETTES (E.)

Andouilles (chitterlings made into sausages) usually come raw and must first be cooked in lightly salted water, the time depending upon the weight. Then they are grilled.

Andouillettes (smaller in size) are bought ready-made. All that has to be done is to pierce them and grill them slowly as they are, whether wrapped in buttered paper or greased with lard.

The most usual garnish is mashed potatoes.

BÉARN ANDOUILLE or **PUSSE** ANDOUILLE DU BÉARN or PUSSE (M.)

Preparation: Take the trimmings from the pig's neck containing the most blood, as well as the heart and the spleen. Put through a meat grinder. Season with salt, pepper, and spices. Add onion, garlic, and chopped parsley. Mix all the ingredients well and keep in a crock, in a cool place, overnight. The next day stir the mixture well and stuff into a large beef intestine; tie into pieces about a foot long. Roll in salt. Let stand in salt 8–10 days. Remove from the salt and hang up to dry for about 2 months.

To use: Boil for about 1½ hr. Serve hot or cold as hors d'oeuvres.

PUDDINGS BOUDINS (E.)

Although puddings are usually bought ready-made, we thought we should include a few recipes.

ORDINARY WHITE PUDDINGS BOUDINS BLANCS ORDINAIRES (E.) (*For 6 persons*)

Chop ½ lb. lean pork and ⅘ lb. fresh fat bacon. Pound this mincemeat in a mortar, while adding 2 oz. fresh *foie gras.* Press through a sieve, receiving the mixture in a bowl, and finish with 2 fresh eggs, 2 oz. onions cooked in butter but not browned, 3 oz. cream, ½ oz. salt, pinch of white pepper, and a little nutmeg. Mix well. Stuff this mixture into beef intestines without completely filling them; tie the pieces at the desired length; place them on a grill or wicker tray, and plunge into a pot ¾ full of boiling water. After immersing, keep the temperature of the water at an even 205° F. and poach for 12 min. Then remove and let cool. To serve, do not slit the puddings, but simply prick them with a pin; wrap each one in buttered paper and grill slowly. Serve with creamed mashed potatoes.

WHITE CHICKEN PUDDINGS BOUDINS BLANCS DE VOLAILLE (E.) (*For 8 persons*)

Pound separately 1 lb. raw chicken breasts and ⅘ lb. diced fresh fat bacon. Mix together, then pound to blend perfectly. Next add: 3½ oz. chopped onions cooked in butter without browning, a bit of thyme and bay leaf, 1 tsp. salt, pinch of pepper, dash of nutmeg, and whites of 4 eggs, the last added 1 by 1 while mashing the mixture vigorously with a pestle. Press through a fine sieve; put the forcemeat back into the mortar, then mix in, little by little, 1 pt. very cold boiled milk. Stuff the forcemeat into beef intestines, poach as directed in the preceding recipe, and let cool. Before grilling, prepare the pudding as directed above. Serve with creamed mashed potatoes.

BLACK or **BLOOD PUDDINGS** BOUDINS NOIRS (E.) (*For 6 persons*)

Put the following ingredients into a mixing bowl: 1 lb. fresh pork fat in large cubes and half fried, 12 oz. pork blood, 3 oz. cream, 6½ oz. chopped onions fried in lard without browning, 1½ tsp. salt, good pinch of pepper, pinch of spices. Mix well and stuff into beef intestines without filling them too full, for the mixture swells while poaching and might burst them. Tie the puddings at the desired length and place them on a wicker tray. Plunge the tray into a pot of boiling water; then keep the temperature of the water at 205° F. and poach 20 min., taking care to prick with a pin the puddings that rise to the surface of the water, since these puddings contain air, which, when heated, will split the intestines. When the puddings are poached, remove them from the water and let them cool on the tray. To serve, slit the puddings on both sides and grill very slowly. Serve with creamed mashed potatoes.

BLACK or **BLOOD PUDDINGS ENGLISH STYLE** BOUDINS NOIRS À L'ANGLAISE (E.)

Follow the recipe for Black or Blood Puddings (p. 374), adding ½ lb. rice cooked in consommé but kept rather firm. Poach as directed and let cool. Slit the puddings, grill them, and serve as usual with mashed potatoes.

BLACK or **BLOOD PUDDINGS FLAMANDE** BOUDINS NOIRS À LA FLAMANDE (E.)

Prepare ordinary Black or Blood Puddings (p. 374), then add: 3½ oz. brown sugar, 2 oz. dried currants and 2 oz. sultanas, picked over, washed, soaked in warm water, and well drained. Continue the recipe for Black Puddings. To serve, slit the puddings and grill slowly. Serve with applesauce. (See Pork Loin with Applesauce, p. 363.)

BLACK or **BLOOD PUDDINGS NORMANDE** BOUDINS NOIRS À LA NORMANDE (E.)

Slice cold Black Puddings (p. 374) and sauté in butter. Also sauté in butter some sliced, peeled, cored sweet apples (1 lb. apples per 2 lb. pudding). Combine the 2 ingredients, sauté together for a moment, and serve in an earthenware dish.

SAVELOY CERVELAS (M.)

Cold Dish: Chop, not too finely, 6 lb. pork (⅔ lean and ⅓ fat). Season with 3 tbsp. salt and ½ tbsp. freshly ground pepper. Mix well. Stuff this forcemeat into large pork intestines and tie in 4-in. sections. Prick the Saveloy with the point of a needle and poach gently 30 min. Drain, dry, and smoke for 40 hrs.

Note: Saveloy should be eaten cold like sausage. It is also served in salads. It can also be used as a garnish with *potées* and sauerkraut soups, in which case it should be cooked with the soups.

CRÉPINETTES CRÉPINETTES (E.)

Preparation of the forcemeat: 2 lb. fine sausage meat, 1 tbsp. chopped parsley, and a small glass of cognac. Mix well.

Forcemeat for truffled crépinettes: 2 lb. fine sausage meat, 4¼ oz. chopped truffles, 2 tbsp. cooking liquid from truffles.

For either type of *crépinette,* separate the mincemeat into 3½-oz. portions and wrap in pig's caul, giving them a rectangular shape.

CRÉPINETTES CINDERELLA I (Old Method) CRÉPINETTES CENDRILLON (MÉTHODE ANCIENNE) (E.)

Wrap each truffled *crépinette* in 2 heavy sheets of buttered paper.

Place them in the hearth and cover with a good layer of glowing cinders, renewing the cinders several times during the cooking, which should take about 20 min. Just before serving, remove the first paper and leave the *crépinettes* in the second one.

CRÉPINETTES CINDERELLA II (New Method) CRÉPINETTES CENDRILLON (MÉTHODE NOUVELLE) (E.)

Roll out Pie Paste (p. 545) into oval shapes and wrap the *crépinettes* in them. Place on a pastry tray, brush with beaten egg, score with a knife, and bake 20 min. in a moderate oven. Serve on a napkin.

GAYETTES GAYETTES (E.) (*For 8 persons*)

Cold: Cut 1 lb. pork liver and 1 lb. fresh pork fat into small strips. Add 3 crushed garlic cloves, ⅔ oz. salt, pinch of pepper, and a dash of spices. Mix together, then divide into 3½-oz. portions; wrap like ordinary *crépinettes* in pig's caul softened in warm water and well dried. Tie each *gayette* with a few bands of string, place on a buttered pastry tray, baste with lard, and bake about ½ hr. *Gayettes* are usually served cold.

PORK PÂTÉ DE FOIE PÂTÉ DE FOIE DES CHARCUTIERS (P.) (*For 6 persons*)

Cold: In winter one can make a bowl of *pâté* that will keep for several days. Take 1½ lb. pork liver, 1 lb. pork fat from the liver, and 2 lb. unsalted fresh pork fat. Cut into large cubes and grind twice. Press through a fine sieve. Season with salt, pepper, spices, nutmeg, 3½ oz. chopped onions and shallots cooked in butter. The forcemeat must be very fine. Mix with it a handful of flour and 3 whole eggs. Line a *pâté* bowl or round mold with a piece of pig's caul, with enough to fold over the top. Fill it with the forcemeat and bring the caul over the top. Cover and cook slowly in a *bain-marie* for 1¼–1½ hr. To see if it is cooked, stick a needle into the center. If the needle comes out very hot, the *pâté* is done. Let cool and then unmold. Remove the caul only as you eat the *pâté*, for it protects the outside.

PORK PÂTÉ IN A TERRINE PÂTÉ DE PORC EN TERRINE (P.)

Cold: For a medium-sized terrine (oval yellow terrine with cover) holding about 1¾ lb. meat, take ¾ lb. sausage meat, ¾ lb. lean fresh pork, a slice cut from a fresh leg or loin of pork, and 2 small slices of cooked ham. Season the sausage meat with ½ tsp. salt and pepper, season the fresh pork the same way, and line the bottom of the terrine with half the meat (sausage and pork) ; place a slice of ham on top, then the slice of leg or loin of pork, then the other slice of ham on top of this. Finally, finish filling the terrine with the remainder of the meat. Cover the terrine and make a soft paste of flour and water to seal the cover to the terrine, making it airtight. Place the terrine in an ovenware dish containing a little water, bring to a boil on top of the stove, then put into a rather hot oven for 1¼ hr. Let cool, then keep in a cool place.

SALT PORK PETIT SALÉ (E.)

Salt pork needs only prolonged cooking in unsalted water. Serve it with boiled or braised cabbage or mashed potatoes, with a separate bowl of some of the cooking liquid. It may be cooked with the cabbage, but only after being thoroughly blanched to remove the taste of brine.

SAUSAGES WITH CABBAGE SAUCISSES AUX CHOUX (E.)

Grill or poach the sausages. If the sausages are poached, the cooking fat is added to the cabbage, which is usually the green variety. They are also served with Braised Cabbage (p. 500) or with Red Cabbage Flamande (p. 510).

FRANKFORT AND STRASBOURG SAUSAGES SAUCISSES DE FRANCFORT ET DE STRASBOURG (E.)

Poach them in boiling water, with the cover on, for 10 min. Cooking them longer only spoils their flavor. They may be served plain with grated horseradish and a dish of mashed potatoes, but the usual garnish is braised sauerkraut.

POULTRY

POULTRY

This chapter includes hens, chickens, fat pullets, cocks, pigeons, ducks, geese, turkeys, guinea hens; in short, all the feathered folk raised in the poultry yard.

This provides us with a rich choice of recipes, to which we have also added those for *foie gras,* since this magnificent product of cooking is made from goose or duck. In the poultry domain, our country is far in the lead; our fine and delicate fat pullets from Bresse, our capons from Mans, our Alsatian geese, our ducks from Duclair, our chickens from Houdan, Crèvecoeur, or Nantes, are always found on gourmets' menus, and the ways of preparing them are as varied as they are delicious. We shall transcribe these recipes from the great masters of French cooking, and you will find, even in the simplest dishes, that touch of our national cooking which real gourmets always appreciate.

How to buy tender fowl: If the fowl is bought already plucked, as is usually true in the city, the texture of the skin should be smooth to the touch, white with a bluish tinge, the feet soft and not covered with rough scales, an indication that the bird is old.

If the fowl is bought with the feathers on, as it usually is in the country, feel the breastbone and if the cartilage at the tip is flexible, the bird should be tender. In old birds the cartilage becomes ossified, and their feet are covered with thick scales. They should only be used for chicken with rice or to cook in broth, for which they are excellent. There are, however, many good, simple recipes for hens, as we shall show further on (remembering Henry IV's famous hope that France might be so prosperous under him that there would be a "chicken in every pot"), and some delicious small entrees to be found in the chapter on hors d'oeuvres. Only we advise you not to roast a hen or even to cook it in a cocotte, for it would be hard and dry, without succulence or flavor.

PULLETS

Under the heading of pullets (*poulardes*) come the fine fat chickens from the great poultry centers. The Bresse is the most important and justly deserves its fame, but fine examples are found in other regions. La Flèche, for example, sends us superb specimens; Le Mans treats us to capons perfect for the spit; the Toulouse region supplies its portion for fine cooking, but it specializes above all in raising geese and ducks.

Except for roasted pullets, these chickens are served either as hot entrees, stuffed and garnished in various ways, or as fancy cold dishes to conclude a fine dinner or to decorate the buffet for a ball. In the latter case, the chicken is stuffed either before or after cooking; it is poached, pan-roasted, or braised. It is then served with a sauce usually made from its own cooking liquid and with a garnish determined by the name of the dish. If it is served cold, it is usually stuffed with a purée of *foie gras,* a ham mousse, or even a fresh vegetable salad bound with mayonnaise, and can be covered with chaud-froid sauce or chicken aspic and decorated in a variety of ways.

ROASTED PULLETS

Before roasting the pullets, they must be drawn, cleaned, and trussed. They must also be larded—that is, the breast covered with a thin strip of pork fat or bacon to protect it, since it cooks more rapidly than the legs. Also, the melting fat will baste the breast and prevent its drying out and becoming too brown if the fire is hot. When the legs and body have turned a golden brown, and the strip of fat has melted only a little, remove it so that the breast will brown, too. Pullets roasted on the spit must be frequently basted. If roasted in the oven, they need less basting, because, with the oven closed, the steam released from the cooking keeps the roast from drying out. Still, it should be basted from time to time, and salted 2 or 3 times after basting. It is a good idea to put a pinch of coarse salt inside the chicken before cooking it. To determine the cooking time for poultry, see the chapter on the different methods of cooking (p. 123).

POACHED PULLETS

Chickens served in white sauce, such as Pullet in Half Mourning (p. 384), and those served cold—in aspic, with chaud-froid sauce, or any other way—are usually poached. To poach, draw, clean, and truss the chicken and rub it with half a lemon to whiten the skin. Lard it with strips of pork fat or bacon (sometimes it may be stuffed), then place it on its back in a braising pan or deep cocotte and pour in enough white bouillon or white stock to cover it halfway (see p. 133). Add a few slices of onion, some carrots, a small *bouquet garni*, a few peppercorns, and place on the stove. When it begins to boil, cover the pan and keep at a gentle simmer, the time depending upon the weight of the chicken and whether it is stuffed.

Make the sauce from the cooking liquid, after straining it and skimming off all the fat.

PAN-ROASTED PULLETS

The chicken may be stuffed or not, according to the recipe. The breast need not be larded, as for a roasted chicken. Fry the chicken in a braising pan with clarified butter until it is golden brown on all sides. When the pullet begins to brown, place around it a few slices of onions and carrots and a few small bones or scraps of chicken (or of veal, if no extra chicken is available). Brown everything together, then pour in slowly 1 cup of whatever good wine—white or red, champagne or anything else—will go with the sauce that accompanies the dish.

Cover and simmer slowly, 40–45 min. if the pullet is not stuffed and about 1½ hr. if it is. When almost cooked, remove the cover and glaze in a very hot oven, basting often with the cooking liquid. Strain this stock through a fine sieve, skim well, and add to the sauce that is to be served with the pullet.

BRAISED PULLETS

There is less difference between braising and pan-roasting poultry than there is with meats. Braised pullet is prepared essentially the same as the pan-roasted pullet described on p. 380, except that it should be moistened after browning with some good chicken stock prepared in advance from chicken giblets, neck, feet, etc., and a few veal bones. It should be braised slowly, covered, in not too large a pan, so that the liquid will come only up to the joint of the thighs. Too much liquid would make a boiled chicken of it. When preparing braised chicken, it is a good idea to stud the breast with small strips of pork fat or pieces of truffle. When the breast is truffled, it absolutely must be protected with a strip of pork fat or bacon.

The cooking stock from the braising is generally used to make the sauce, though sometimes the pullet is braised in a sauce prepared in advance from good stock and generously flavored with wine or liquor.

Braised pullet, regardless of its finishing touches, is always served with a garnish, whether of fine vegetables, or sweetbreads, or *foie gras,* or of something else.

In old-time cookery as well as and above all in that of Carême, Dubois, and Bernard, pullet was served on a base of molded rice, or molded suet, or supports of special paste and even of wood disguised in various ways, the bird almost completely hidden under fancy and beautiful decorations. The wax and suet flowers that enhanced the appearance of food at the end of the last century produced an artistic effect, certainly, but often to the detriment if not of the quality of the dish, which was impeccable, then to the serving of it, for it could not have stayed very hot. Today, as in the last few decades, the décor has been simplified, and we are more concerned than ever with fundamentals—the quality and the service of the dishes, so they arrive at the table hot. In our day we shall no longer see the sumptuous way food was presented in olden days, when brigades of 30 and 40 cooks in a large restaurant were not uncommon. The Hôtel de Paris in Monte Carlo had 100 to 120 men in the kitchen alone.

But every era must adapt its cooking to economic necessity, and thanks to Escoffier, who created the modern techniques, France has never lost its first place in cooking.

PULLET ALBUFÉRA POULARDE ALBUFÉRA (E.)

Stuff the pullet with rice containing *foie gras* and truffles diced in large pieces. Poach it. Place it on a platter and cover with Albuféra Sauce (below). Surround it with truffles cut with a ball cutter, balls of chicken forcemeat (p. 173), small mushrooms, and cock kidneys; cover the garnish with Albuféra Sauce (below). Border the platter with pieces of pickled tongue cut into the shape of cockscombs.

Note: Albuféra Sauce is a Suprême Sauce (p. 146) to which Meat Glaze (p. 135) has been added.

PULLET AMBASSADRICE POULARDE À L'AMBASSADRICE (E.)

Stud the pullet with truffles, cover it with Matignon (p. 135), wrap it in cheesecloth, tie it at both ends, and braise. After cooking, unwrap the cloth and place the pullet on a platter. Cover it with rather thick, smooth Suprême Sauce (p. 146); surround with lamb sweetbreads studded with truffles, braised and glazed, alternated with small bunches of asparagus tips.

PULLET ANDALOUSE POULARDE À L'ANDALOUSE (E.)

Poach the pullet. Arrange on a platter and cover with Suprême Sauce (p. 146) finished with 5 oz. pimento butter (see Butters, pp. 163–166) per qt. sauce, and on either side place pimentos stuffed with rice, and eggplant sliced in rings, floured, and sautéed in butter.

PULLET ENGLISH STYLE I POULARDE À L'ANGLAISE (M.)

Poach the pullet in white stock. Garnish with carrots cut in fat bean shapes, turnip balls, hearts of celery (all these vegetables cooked with the pullet), heads of cauliflower and green beans cooked in salted water and drained. Cover the pullet with Velouté (p. 147) reduced with the cooking stock from the pullet, buttered, and strained.

Note: This pullet is sometimes served as Pullet Printanière and, in this case, can be garnished with spring vegetables.

PULLET ENGLISH STYLE II POULARDE À L'ANGLAISE (M.)

Poach the pullet in white stock. Add several tbsp. of the cooking liquid, after it has been reduced, to Béchamel Sauce (p. 146) and cook some more until further reduced; pour this over the chicken. Garnish with slices of pickled tongue, carrot and turnip balls cooked with steam, and steamed peas and celery. Serve with a separate dish of parsley sauce.

ROAST PULLET ENGLISH STYLE POULARDE (RÔTIE) À L'ANGLAISE (M.)

May be made several ways: (1) Stuff the pullet with bread crumbs lightly buttered and seasoned with salt, pepper, and powdered sage. Truss the chicken; place a few strips of bacon over the breast; roast on a spit or in the oven. (2) Stuff the chicken as directed above, but soak the bread in beef fat rather than butter. Roast the same way. (3) As above, the stuffing prepared with beef marrow. (4) Same as the first stuffing, finished with diced browned bacon. (5) Stuff the pullet with a mixture of fresh bread crumbs and diced beef suet bound with eggs. Season with salt, pepper, nutmeg, and chopped sage.

Note: If the pullet is not roasted with a covering of bacon strips, place a few slices of grilled bacon on it when serving. Usually, Roast Pullet English Style is served with Bread Sauce (p. 160) and fried bread crumbs.

GLAZED PULLET BELLE DE LAURIS POULARDE GLACÉE BELLE DE LAURIS (H.M.) (*For 10 persons*)

Cold Dish: Take 2 fat pullets weighing 3 lb. each, poach them in white chicken stock, and let cool. Use some of the cooking liquid to make chicken Aspic Jelly clarified with 2 lb. lean beef (p. 168). Use the rest of the cooking liquid to make 1 qt. Velouté (moisten the White Roux with melted Aspic Jelly) for the Chaud-Froid Sauce (p. 149). In making the Chaud-Froid Sauce, add 9 oz. fresh cream; reduce, and skim; remove from the stove and add 3 oz. cream and strain through a sieve.

Carefully remove the breasts of the chicken, cut them into medallions, cover with Chaud-Froid Sauce, decorate tastefully with floral motifs made of tarragon leaves, tomato pulp, and hard-boiled-egg yolks, then glaze with Aspic Jelly. Remove the skin from the legs of 1 of the 2 chickens, then mash the meat in a mortar and force this purée through a sieve. To this purée add an equal amount of poached *foie gras,* also mashed into a purée, and mix together in a bowl, adding 25 fine green asparagus tips pressed through a strainer. Work the mixture with a wooden spatula, adding to it 3 oz. aspic reduced by ½, 3 oz. port, and 3 oz. fresh cream lightly whipped. Place this mousse in the refrigerator and stir gently from time to time to avoid lumps. (Never chill a mousse on ice, as it will harden too rapidly and will not be smooth.) Test the seasoning of the mousse, the color of which should be emerald green. Take the chicken from which the legs were not cut but from which the breast, including bones, was removed and, using the mousse, reshape to its original form.

When the breast has been perfectly rebuilt, place a long triangle of lightly oiled sulphurized paper over it; cover the entire chicken with Chaud-Froid Sauce. When the sauce has solidified, remove the paper carefully, and the protected surface will appear a delicate green. Partially cover this triangular surface with a checkerboard motif of truffles and egg white to obtain an emerald-green, black, and white color combination. Glaze the entire bird with aspic.

Place the pullet on a low base made of molded aspic at one end of a large platter lined with aspic. Facing the chicken, spread out the medallions cut from the breast; in the center, arrange 10 small bunches of asparagus tips glazed with jelly. Around the aspic base on which the chicken rests, place small balls made of ⅔ purée of *foie gras* and ⅓ butter and balls made of the mousse used for the chicken (all molded with a vegetable spoon). Divide the balls into 3 groups: 6 green ones made of mousse, 6 cream-colored ones of *foie gras,* and 6 black ones (3 each of both, rolled in finely chopped truffles); glaze all of them with aspic. Finish the decoration with a ribbon of chopped aspic squeezed from a pastry bag. This dish (Figure 237, P. 384.) was prepared by Henri Mercier, head chef.

PULLET BOIELDIEU POULARDE BOIELDIEU (E.) (*For 6 to 8 persons*)

Stuff the pullet with ½ lb. chicken Mousseline Forcemeat (p. 173) and 5 oz. purée of *foie gras.* Stud the bird with truffles and pan-roast (p. 380). Place on a platter and in front of the pullet arrange 10 nut-sized truffle balls scooped out with a ball cutter. The garnish is completed by cutting the stuffing into large cubes when the chicken is carved. Pour 1 glass sauterne into the hot pan in which the chicken was cooked; reduce; add a little rich chicken stock; strain and bind with a little arrowroot. Serve this sauce separately.

PULLET WITH MUSHROOMS (IN WHITE SAUCE) POULARDE AUX CHAMPIGNONS (À BLANC) (M.)

Poach in white chicken stock, using as little liquid as possible. Arrange on a round platter. Surround with 18 large fluted mushrooms cooked in white stock. Cover with Velouté (p. 147) reduced with mushroom essence, buttered, and strained (the Velouté prepared with the cooking stock from the chicken).

PULLET WITH MUSHROOMS (IN BROWN SAUCE) POULARDE AUX CHAMPIGNONS (À BRUN) (M.)

Pan-roast in butter. When the pullet is almost cooked, put 18 large mushroom caps into the pan. Finish cooking together. Arrange the chicken on a platter and garnish with the mushrooms. Cover with a sauce made by adding Madeira to the butter and juices left in the pan, mushroom essence, and thickened veal stock; reduce, and strain.

PULLET CHÂTELAINE POULARDE CHÂTELAINE (M.)

Pan-roast in white stock. Arrange the pullet on a platter. Surround it with artichoke bottoms—cooked in butter (the lid of the pan tightly closed) and filled with chestnut purée with onion purée added—and Potatoes Noisette (p. 509).

Sauce: Add Madeira to the cooking juice in the pan, then thickened veal stock. (Figure 238, Page 385.)

PULLET CHEVALIÈRE or CHEVALIÈRE OF CHICKEN POULARDE CHEVALIÈRE OF CHEVALIÈRE DE VOLAILLE (M.)

This dish is a sort of chicken fricassee, but much subtler than an ordinary fricassee. Cut up the pullets as usual, taking care to keep the wings and the breasts intact. Stud the breasts with truffles and pickled tongue (cut tiny incisions and insert tiny slices of both). Cook the legs and thighs in white stock, then bind the cooking stock with egg yolks and cream. (This sauce should be very rich in chicken stock and flavored with mushroom essence.) Cook the wings and breasts in butter in a tightly closed pan, not letting them brown.

Garnish: Cockscombs and cock kidneys à la Villeroi (see p. 155); mushroom caps cooked in white stock; thick slices of truffles.

Arrangement: Place the legs and thighs on a crouton; coat with the sauce. On top of the legs place the wings and studded breasts. Surround with the garnish. Serve the remainder of the sauce separately.

PULLET CHIMAY POULARDE CHIMAY (E.) (*For 6 to 8 persons*)

Stuff the pullet with ½ lb. noodles sautéed in butter, then mixed with a few tbsp. cream and 3½ oz. *pâté de foie gras* cut in large cubes. Pan-roast slowly. Arrange on a platter and coat lightly with part of the cooking stock bound with arrowroot. Finally, cover with noodles sautéed in clarified butter. Serve the rest of the sauce separately.

PULLET CHIPOLATA POULARDE CHIPOLATA (E.)

Pan-roast the pullet and place it in an earthenware casserole with a Chipolata Garnish (below). Add the cooking stock from the roasting pan and simmer 10 min. Serve in the casserole.

Chipolata Garnish: 20 small glazed onions, 10 chipolata (tiny pork) sausages, 10 chestnuts cooked in consommé, 4½ oz. diced, browned bacon, 20 carrots cut in the shape of olives and glazed.

Sauce: Semiglaze Sauce (p. 138) with stock from the roasting pan added.

PULLET CUSSY POULARDE CUSSY (E.)

Braise the pullet. Serve on a platter surrounded by medium-sized truffles cooked in a Mirepoix containing Madeira (p. 136) alternated with large grilled mushrooms filled with artichoke purée. Between each truffle and mushroom place a cock kidney sautéed in butter. Serve Madeira Sauce (p. 142) separately, adding some braising stock to it.

PULLET IN HALF MOURNING POULARDE DEMI-DEUIL (E.) (*For 6 to 8 persons*)

Slip a few slices of very black, raw truffle between the skin and the breast of

Fig. 237 - Glazed pullet Belle de Lauris (p. 382).

Fig. 237

Fig. 238

the pullet; stuff with 6½ oz. Mousseline Forcemeat (p. 173) containing 3½ oz. grated or finely diced truffles, and poach. When the pullet is cooked, strain the cooking stock through a cloth; reduce, then add it to a Suprême Sauce (p. 146) to which slices of truffle have been added. Arrange the pullet on a platter and coat with some of this sauce. The stuffing, cut into large cubes after the chicken is carved, is the garnish. Serve the remainder of the sauce separately.

PULLET DEMIDOV POULARDE DEMIDOFF (E.) (*For 6 persons*)

Pan-roast the pullet. When it is ¾ cooked, place it in a cocotte with the following garnish, all of whose ingredients have already been cooked in butter in a tightly sealed pan: 6½ oz. carrots and 5 oz. turnips cut into fluted crescents with a cutter about 1 in. in diameter; 10 small onions sliced in very thin rings; 5 oz. diced celery. Finish cooking the pullet with the garnish and, at the last moment, add 3½ oz. truffles cut into crescents and 3 oz. reduced chicken stock. Serve in the cocotte.

PULLET DERBY POULARDE À LA DERBY (M.) (*For 6 to 8 persons*)

Stuff the pullet with buttered rice mixed with 3½ oz. *foie gras* and 3½ oz. diced truffles lightly browned in butter, moistened with 3 oz. very reduced, thickened veal stock, and seasoned well with salt and pepper. Truss the pullet so that the legs are underneath and cover the breast with strips of bacon. Place in a braising pan on a braising base made of 1 lb. lean beef cut into large cubes, 1 lb. sliced veal knuckle, 3½ oz. diced carrots, and 2½ oz. diced onions, all browned in butter. Add a *bouquet garni;* season; baste with a little melted butter. Cover and start cooking on top of the stove; roast in the oven 20 min., basting frequently. Pour in 7 oz. Madeira. Roast 1 hr. at moderate heat, basting frequently. Drain the pullet, remove the strips of bacon, untie the trussing, and glaze at the oven door.

Garnish: 6 truffles cooked in port; 6 slices of *foie gras* sautéed in butter.

Sauce: Pour some Madeira into the pan containing the cooking juices; moisten with some brown veal stock (not too thick) and consommé. Boil for a few minutes and strain. Reduce to the proper consistency and strain again.

Serving: Arrange the pullet on a long platter on top of a crouton of bread (the crust removed) fried in butter and held in place with a paste made of flour and water (first heat the dish, so the paste will harden). Arrange the garnishes around it; moisten with a little of the sauce, and serve the remainder in a sauceboat. (Figure 239, Page 392.)

PULLET DREUX POULARDE À LA DREUX (E.)

Stud the pullet with truffles and tongue, and poach. Place it on a platter and coat with Parisienne Sauce (p. 146) ; decorate the breast with a crown of truffle slices and surround the pullet with 4 medium-sized, decorated quenelles; 2 mounds of cock kidneys and 2 mounds of cockscombs.

PULLET EDWARD VII POULARDE ÉDOUARDE VII (E.) (*For 6 to 8 persons*)

Stuff the pullet with 6½ oz. rice mixed with 3½ oz. cubed *foie gras* and 3½ oz. cubed truffles; poach. Arrange on a platter and coat with Suprême Sauce (p. 146) containing curry, with 3½ oz. diced red peppers added per qt. sauce. Serve separately a garnish of creamed cucumbers.

Fig. 238 - Pullet châtelaine (p. 384).

PULLET ÉLYSÉE POULARDE À L'ÉLYSÉE (E.) (*For 6 to 8 persons*)

Stuff the pullet with 6½ oz. Mousseline Forcemeat (p. 173) with 4 oz. diced *foie gras* and 4 oz. diced truffles added to it. Make small slits in the breast and stud with small slices of truffle, and poach the pullet. Set on a platter and lay 5 whole truffles on each side of the chicken; a garnish of quenelles, mushrooms, cockscombs and cock kidneys, bound with Suprême Sauce (p. 146), at each end. Serve a separate sauceboat of Suprême Sauce. (Figure 240, Page 392.)

PULLET TARRAGON POULARDE À L'ESTRAGON (M.)

May be prepared 2 ways: poached or pan-roasted.

Poached: Stuff a bunch of tarragon sprigs inside the pullet; truss so that the legs are pulled underneath and cover the breast with strips of bacon. Poach in very rich white stock with a bunch of tarragon. Remove the tarragon from the cavity and place the pullet on a service platter. Decorate with large blanched tarragon leaves arranged in the shape of palmettes. Bind the cooking stock with a little arrowroot and serve separately.

Pan-Roasted: Put a large bunch of tarragon inside the pullet; truss it and cover the breast with bacon strips. Pan-roast in butter in the usual way. Lay on a platter. Pour some white wine into the pan juices, add tarragon, moisten with thickened veal stock; reduce, and strain. Coat the pullet with this sauce. Decorate with blanched tarragon leaves.

PULLET FLAMMARION POULARDE FLAMMARION (M.)

Stuff with buttered rice mixed with diced truffles. Truss with the legs pulled underneath and cover the breast with strips of bacon. Pan-roast in butter without letting it brown too much.

Garnish: Artichoke bottoms cooked in butter, each filled with a slice of *foie gras ;* small glazed carrots; buttered peas.

Sauce: To the butter and cooking juices in the pan, add Madeira, then fresh cream; reduce, strain, and add diced truffles. (Figure 242, Page 396.)

GASTRONOMES' PULLET POULARDE DES GASTRONOMES (E.) (*For 6 to 8 persons*)

Stuff the pullet with ½ lb. morels (mushrooms) lightly sautéed in butter and 3½ oz. raw truffles diced large; pan-roast it. Melt the solidified juices in the pan with 4 oz. champagne. Arrange the pullet on a platter and surround with medium-sized truffles alternated with mounds of chestnuts cooked in consommé and glazed. Place a cock kidney between the truffles and the chestnuts. Serve with a separate dish of Semiglaze Sauce (p.138) made with truffle essence, with the pan juices and champagne, reduced, added.

PULLET GOUFFÉ POULARDE GOUFFÉ (M.)

Poach in white chicken stock, using very little.

Garnish: Large mushrooms stuffed with a salpicon (tiny cubes) of cockscombs bound with reduced Velouté (p. 147) and gratinated in the oven; Fritters Périgourdine (stick 2 thick slices of truffles together with purée of *foie gras* in the middle; just before serving, dip lightly in Frying Paste, p. 558, and deep-fry).

Sauce: Make a Velouté, using the reduced cooking stock, truffle essence, fresh cream; reduce and, at the end, add a little sherry; butter and strain.

PULLET GRAMMONT POULARDE GRAMMONT (E.)

Poach the pullet and let it half cool. Cut off the breasts; remove the breastbones and fill the cavity in the carcass with a garnish of larks' breasts sautéed for just the right time in butter; small mushroom caps; cock kidneys and cockscombs; all bound with Béchamel Sauce (p. 146) flavored with truffle essence. Slice the breasts and place them back into position on this garnish; coat the chicken with thick Suprême Sauce (p. 146) ; sprinkle with grated Parmesan cheese; baste with melted butter; glaze quickly in the oven, and serve.

PULLET WITH COARSE SALT POULARDE AU GROS SEL (E.)

Poach the pullet in white stock; add to this same stock 10 pieces of carrots cut in the shape of elongated olives and 10 small onions. Lay on a platter and surround with mounds of carrots and onions. Serve separately: (1) a sauceboat of the cooking stock; (2) a dish of coarse salt.

PULLET WITH OYSTERS POULARDE AUX HUÎTRES (M.)

This may be made 2 ways: (1) Poach in white stock; serve on a round platter surrounded by oysters poached (but not boiled) in their own juice, trimmed, and placed on small round croutons fried in butter (2 or 3 oysters per crouton). Reduce the liquid in which the oysters were poached and add to Suprême Sauce (p. 146) ; coat the pullet with this sauce. (2) Stuff the pullet with poached, trimmed oysters bound with reduced chicken Velouté (p. 147). Poach the pullet as above; coat with Suprême Sauce with the reduced cooking liquid from the oysters added to it.

PULLET IMPÉRATRICE POULARDE À L'IMPÉRATRICE (E.)

Poach the pullet. Arrange it on a platter and at each end make a mound of lamb sweetbreads cooked in white stock. On both sides place: 2 small mounds of very white, poached calf brains cut into large cubes, with a mound of small onions cooked in a thin Velouté (p. 147) between the mounds of calf brains. Coat with Suprême Sauce (p. 146) made with cream.

PULLET ISABELLA OF FRANCE POULARDE ISABELLE DE FRANCE (E.)

Stuff the pullet with a Risotto (p. 513) with 3 oz. sliced truffles and 18 Crayfish (tails) Bordelaise (p. 315) added to it. Poach in white stock strengthened with a bottle of Chablis. Use this cooking stock to make a well-seasoned Suprême Sauce (p. 146). Place the chicken on a small crouton or other base, coat with sauce, and surround with large black truffles cooked in champagne, each on a small round bread crouton fried in butter and slightly hollowed out. Serve the remainder of the sauce separately.

PULLET WITH IVORY SAUCE POULARDE À L'IVOIRE (E.)

Poach the pullet, keeping it very white. Place it on a platter and serve as is. Serve separately: (1) a sauceboat of Ivory Sauce (p. 152) ; (2) a sauceboat of the cooking stock from the pullet; (3) some garnish such as creamed macaroni or noodles, mushrooms, cucumbers, etc.

PULLET LANGUEDOCIENNE POULARDE À LA LANGUEDOCIENNE (E.)

Pan-roast the pullet. Serve on a platter with, at each end, a mound of tomatoes sautéed in butter. Along the sides of the pullet garnish with fried slices of eggplant and sautéed mushrooms, placed in alternate mounds. Coat the pullet with a sauce made of thickened chicken gravy finished with Madeira.

PULLET LOUISE OF ORLÉANS POULARDE LOUISE D'ORLÉANS (E.)

Put a whole *foie gras*, studded with truffles and poached ¼ hr. in a little good veal stock, inside the pullet; pour in 1 glass chilled old Madeira. Brown the pullet in the oven 20 min., basting with butter. Next, completely cover it with thick slices of truffles; wrap it in strips of bacon; enclose it in rolled-out pastry crust made with lard and hot water. Completely seal the chicken in the paste; place it on a baking tray; make a small opening in the crust to let the steam escape, and bake 1¾ hr. in a moderate oven. Serve as is, hot or cold.

PULLET MAISON D'OR POULARDE MAISON D'OR (M.) (*For 8 persons*)

Take a fine, fat pullet weighing 5½ lb., 1¼ lb. fresh beautiful truffles (net weight after washing and peeling), 1 goose liver weighing about 1¼ lb., 12 large cultivated mushrooms, 10 oz. cockscombs and cock kidneys, 5 oz. raw Bayonne ham, 6½ oz. lean veal, 5 cups consommé, 6 oz. sherry (or Madeira), 1 tomato, 5 oz. butter, pepper, *bouquet garni,* salt (be careful with the salt).

Preparation: The day before serving the pullet, clean, draw, and singe it; cut off the neck, leaving the skin attached to the chicken. Wash and peel the truffles. Put inside the chicken ½ the truffle peelings, and 2 quartered truffles tossed in 3½ oz. butter, peppered and lightly salted. Sew the openings of the chicken; truss with the legs pulled back. Wrap in buttered paper and refrigerate until ready to cook. Following the classical rules, prepare a good Espagnole Sauce (p. 137) with part of the consommé added. Soak the cockscombs and cock kidneys. Cut the chicken into pieces the day you are going to cook it. Trim the goose liver and cut 8 or 10 slices from both lobes; flatten the slices a little with the palm of the hand and lightly flour, then lay them on a plate. Wash and flute the mushrooms; cook partially until they are somewhat firm. Also cook the cockscombs and cock kidneys in white stock until they are somewhat firm.

In a sautéing pan, make a Mirepoix composed of the following: cut the raw ham, veal, truffle peelings, leftover goose liver, and the liver from the pullet into ½-in. cubes. Brown these well in butter. Using a spatula, melt the hardened juices at the bottom of the pan with some sherry or Madeira and reduce to a glaze; add the rest of the truffle peelings, mushroom peelings, and the tomato previously cooked in the frying pan till it falls apart (or 2 tbsp. tomato purée); drop in a few peppercorns and the *bouquet garni;* pour over all this 2 parts Espagnole Sauce and 1 part consommé. Cook this Mirepoix slowly 1 hr., then strain the sauce through a fine sieve into another pan, pressing on the Mirepoix with a spatula or spoon, and simmer 1 hr., carefully skimming off the film that forms on the surface until it no longer forms and the sauce has been reduced to the consistency of Semiglaze Sauce. If it is too thick, thin with a little consommé or mushroom cooking liquid. But don't forget that adding the cooking stock from the pullet will thin the sauce.

At least 1½ hr. before serving, place the pullet in a buttered, covered casserole; sear it a little, uncovered, with the neck and gizzard cut in pieces, then pour in a little consommé and Madeira or sherry, previously boiled, cover with a circle of buttered paper to seal in the steam, cover, and let it cook slowly, turning and basting it from time to time. Add the truffles around the pullet, so they will cook with it, ¼ hr. before it should be done. When the pullet is cooked, remove it and let it drain over the pot; untruss; place it on a large platter, and keep warm. Also remove the truffles from the casserole and keep them hot. Reduce the cooking stock; skim off the fat and blend it into the sauce, which should be strained again; taste the seasoning; add cockscombs, cock kidneys, and truffles.

Just before serving, sauté the sliced *foie gras* quickly in hot butter; when they are nicely browned, place 4 or 5 slices on each side of the pullet, alternating them with a truffle. Place a mound of mushrooms at each end of the platter, lightly cover the chicken but not the sliced *foie gras* with sauce; serve very hot with a separate dish of the sauce and its ragout. The pullet may be decorated with 2 skewers, each holding a fine mushroom, a truffle, and a cockscomb.

PULLET MANCHINI POULARDE MANCHINI (E.) (*For 6 to 8 persons*)

Poach the pullet. Slice off the breasts; remove the breastbones without touching the wings or legs. Place the carcass on a low bed of rice or bread to hold it upright. Fill the carcass with macaroni bound with cheese and cream, with 3½ oz. cooked *foie gras,* diced, and 2 oz. julienne of truffles added. Slice the breasts; put them back into shape on the chicken over the stuffing of macaroni, alternating the breast slices with fine slices of truffles. Coat the pullet with reduced Tomato Sauce (p. 146) to which golden meat glaze, butter, and cream have been added.

PULLET HOME STYLE POULARDE MÉNAGÈRE (E.) (*For 6 persons*)

Poach the chicken in rather gelatinous white stock. Slice thin 6 carrots, 6 new potatoes, and 6 new onions; cook these vegetables slowly, uncovered, in the cooking stock from the pullet. When the vegetables are cooked and the stock is sufficiently reduced, put the pullet into an earthenware dish or casserole; cover with the vegetables and their cooking stock. Serve in the dish.

PULLET MONTE CARLO POULARDE MONTE CARLO (Fa.) (*For 6 persons*)

Prepare and truss a fine fat pullet and poach in chicken white stock; while it is cooking, prepare enough Mousseline Forcemeat (p. 173) to make 12 large quenelles, molded in little boat molds or fashioned with a soupspoon; add red coloring to half the forcemeat, to make 6 pink and 6 white quenelles. Poach them in salted water ¼ hr. before serving. Also make a Suprême Sauce (p. 146), using the cooking stock from the pullet, and color half of it pink with a few drops of carmine. It is preferable, however, to blend it with Crayfish Butter (p. 164), using the carmine only to heighten the tone. Cut the chicken in pieces and then reconstruct it in its original shape; coat one side with the white sauce and the other with the pink; place the pink quenelles on the white side and the white ones on the pink side.

Note: This pullet may also be served cold in aspic, but in that case prepare pink and white Chaud-Froid Sauce (p. 149), and use small *foie gras* mousses and small ham mousses instead of quenelles.

PULLET NANTUA POULARDE NANTUA (E.)

Poach the pullet. Place on a platter and coat with Suprême Sauce (p. 146) finished with Crayfish Butter (p. 164). Surround it with mounds of quenelles made of chicken forcemeat blended with Crayfish Butter, mounds of crayfish tails cooked in a Mirepoix, and sliced truffles.

PULLET NÉVA I POULARDE À LA NÉVA (M.) (*For 8 to 10 persons*)

Cold Dish: (1) Truss a large pullet with the legs tied back, cover the breast with strips of bacon, and poach in white stock. Cut off the breasts; remove the breastbones; stuff the inside of the chicken with a chicken-mousse mixture previously prepared the following way: (2) *Chicken Mousse:* Remove all the meat from the bones of a spring chicken poached in white stock and cooled. Cut up the meat and mash in a mortar, adding ⅓ its weight in cooked *foie gras*. Press this mixture through a fine sieve (or cloth) into a bowl; place the bowl on ice and continue mixing while adding 6 oz. reduced chicken Aspic Jelly (p. 168) that has half set and 9 oz. very stiff whipped cream. (3) Coat the underside of the stuffed pullet with White Chaud-Froid Sauce (p. 149). Place the pullet on a bed of hardened aspic in an oval crystal bowl. (4) Garnish the top of the pullet with strips of the breast cut slightly rounded at one end and pointed at the other; decorate these slices with truffles and halves of blanched pistachios glazed with aspic. (To arrange these strips of breast symmetrically and to hold them in place, use a pastry bag to squeeze a narrow band of mousse under each slice.) Glaze the whole pullet with aspic. Chill in the refrigerator. (Figure 241, P. 393.)

Notes: (1) Chicken aspic used for this sort of decoration (in crystal dish or silver bowl) should be rather stiff. (2) The quantity of cream given is understood to be before whipping. Naturally, if a crystal bowl is not available, a long silver platter may be used.

PULLET NÉVA II POULARDE À LA NÉVA (J.)

Cold Dish: Same as above, replacing the chicken mousse with a truffled *foie gras* mousse.

PULLET WITH GOLDEN EGGS POULARDE AUX OEUFS D'OR (F.)

Brown the pullet well in butter, pour 1 glass Madeira or sherry over it and ¾ cup very thin brown sauce. Season, cover, and braise slowly 50 min. Meanwhile, hard-boil 6 eggs, shell, and chop them into large pieces, then bind them with a little Béchamel Sauce (p. 146) and season highly; cool the egg mixture and reshape them into eggs on a floured board; bread them and fry in deep fat just before serving. Serve them with the pullet, a few of them at each end of the platter or in imitation egg cups made of pie crust. Serve a separate dish of the sauce from cooking the chicken.

PULLET or **CAPON WITH PÉRIGORD PEARLS** POULARDE OF CHAPON AUX PERLES DU PÉRIGORD (E.)

Stuff the chicken with fine truffles, cover it with very thin slices of veal tenderloin, and braise with brandy. Serve it with a sauceboat of the braising stock and a dish of cardoons in gravy.

PULLET PETITE MARIÉE POULARDE PETITE MARIÉE (E.) (*For 6 persons*)

Poach the pullet in very little white stock and, when beginning to cook, surround with 6 new onions, 6 small carrots, 6 small new potatoes, 4 oz. freshly shelled peas. Place pullet and garnish in an earthenware dish and coat the pullet with its own cooking stock reduced and blended with a little Suprême Sauce (p. 146).

PULLET PRINCESSE POULARDE PRINCESSE (E.)

Poach the pullet. Place on a platter and coat with Parisienne Sauce (p. 146) finished with 3½ oz. green asparagus butter (see Printanier Butter, p. 165) per qt. sauce. Surround the pullet with patties made of the Potato Duchesse mixture (p. 507) filled with buttered asparagus tips, with a slice of truffle on each patty. Alternate these with little mounds of asparagus tips. Around the garnish make a ring of round quenelles made of creamed chicken forcemeat.

PULLET À LA REINE POULARDE À LA REINE (M.)

Poach in chicken white stock, using very little liquid. Place the pullet on a service platter and coat with Suprême Sauce made with the cooking stock from the pullet (p. 146). Surround with 6 small Patties à la Reine (p. 236) and 6 truffles cooked in Madeira. Serve Suprême Sauce separately. (Figure 244, Page 397.)

PULLET QUEEN MARGOT POULARDE REINE MARGOT (E.) (*For 6 to 8 persons*)

Stuff the chicken with 10 oz. Mousseline Forcemeat (p. 173) with 2 oz. freshly blanched almond purée. Poach it; place on a platter and coat with Suprême Sauce (p. 146) finished with a little Almond Milk (p. 556). Surround with quenelles of chicken forcemeat (p. 176) finished with Pistachio Butter (p. 165) and quenelles of the same finished with Crayfish Butter (p. 164).

PULLET HOLY ALLIANCE POULARDE SAINTE-ALLIANCE (E.)

Season 10 fine truffles with salt and pepper and heat in butter; baste with 1 glass excellent Madeira; seal the pan hermetically (using paste or paper) and let them cool in their own juice. Stuff these truffles into a fine fat pullet; pan-roast the pullet just in time to be served. When it is ready, rapidly cook 1 ortolan for each guest and sauté in butter the same number of slices of *foie gras*. Send these to the table along with the pullet and the cooking stock from the pullet strained into a sauceboat.

The butler, flanked by 3 aides, and standing in front of a burning alcohol stove or chafing dish placed on the table, should be awaiting the dish. He should quickly remove the breast and slice it. He puts each slice on a slice of *foie gras*, which the first assistant has already placed on the hot plate, with 1 of the truffles from the inside of the pullet on top. The second assistant, to whom the plate is then passed, adds 1 ortolan and a little gravy. The third assistant immediately places the garnished plates before the guests. The pullet is therefore served very quickly, under circumstances that make it a dish of great gastronomical value.

SOUFFLÉED PULLET POULARDE SOUFFLÉE (E.) (*For 8 persons*)

Poach the pullet. Remove the breasts and cut them in thin slices. Remove the breastbones with poultry shears and fill the carcass with 1 lb. Mousseline Forcemeat (p. 173) mixed with 5 oz. purée of *foie gras*; lay this stuffing in layers alternated with slices of breast and slices of truffles. Smooth the surface in a mound to give the pullet its original shape; decorate with bits of truffle, pickled tongue, and hard-boiled egg white. Place the bird in an earthenware dish and set the dish in a pan containing a little boiling water (the steam from it will help poach the stuffing) and put into a low oven.

Serve a separate dish of Parisienne Sauce (p. 146) with truffle essence.

PULLET SUVAROV POULARDE SOUVAROV (M.) (*For 8 persons*)

Stuff the pullet with 10 oz. fresh *foie gras* and 5 oz. truffles cut in cubes, seasoned with salt, pepper, and spices, and moistened with cognac. Truss the pullet with the legs pulled back. Cook in butter until ¾ done. Place it in an oval terrine with 6 or 8 medium-sized peeled truffles cooked 5 min. in Madeira (in a tightly closed pan). Melt the glaze left in the pan in which the pullet was cooked with Madeira, add thickened veal stock, reduce, and strain. Pour this over the pullet. Seal the lid on the terrine with a band of paste made of flour and water. Cook in the oven 30–35 min. Serve as is.

PULLET STRASBOURGEOISE I POULARDE À LA STRASBOURGEOISE (M.)

Cold Dish: (1) Pan-roast a large pullet on a bed of Mirepoix (p. 136), then let it cool. (2) Cut away the breast meat. Fill the inside with a mousse of *foie gras* mixed with chopped truffles. Cover the underside of the pullet with Brown Chaud-Froid Sauce (p. 139) flavored with truffle essence. (3) Slice the breast meat and cut the slices into circles, using a round cutter. Coat with Brown Chaud-Froid Sauce flavored with truffle essence. Prepare an equal number of small round slices of *foie gras* decorated with truffle slices and coated with Aspic Jelly (p. 168). Arrange the circles of the breast meat and the slices of *foie gras* in an alternating pattern on the pullet. (4) Lay the pullet on a trimmed piece of bread fried in butter. Surround it with round truffles coated with aspic, each placed in a small tartlet shell. Garnish with chopped aspic.

PULLET STRASBOURGEOISE II POULARDE À LA STRASBOURGEOISE (J.)

Cold Dish: Remove the breastbones from an uncooked pullet. Stuff with *foie gras* and truffles, sew the opening, and truss. Wrap and tie the pullet in cheesecloth. Poach it the usual way, then let it cool in its own cooking liquid. After draining well, remove the cheesecloth, untruss the chicken, and cover it entirely with Chaud-Froid Sauce (p. 149). Carve the chicken, dipping the knife in hot water and drying it before each cut. Decorate with motifs made of truffles and coat with Aspic Jelly (p. 168). Serve like Pullet Néva (p. 390).

PULLET TRIANON POULARDE TRIANON (E.)

Poach the pullet. Prepare 24 quenelles of chicken forcemeat molded with a coffee spoon (p. 176). One third of these quenelles should be truffled; ⅓ mixed with chopped tongue; ⅓ mixed with *fines herbes ;* line all of the quenelles with purée of *foie gras*. In serving, surround the pullet with small mounds of quenelles, placing 1 truffle between each mound. Into the pullet stick a skewer holding 1 large fluted mushroom, 1 glazed truffle, and 1 quenelle decorated with very red tongue. Serve a separate dish of Suprême Sauce (p. 146) finished with a little *foie gras* butter (see Butters, pp. 163–166).

CHICKENS COOKED WHOLE

CHICKEN ASTURIENNE POULET À L'ASTURIENNE (M.)

Stuff the chicken with sliced chicken livers browned in butter, small slices of lean ham, sweet pimentos peeled and cut in large julienne strips, and hard-

Fig. 239 - Pullet Derby (p. 385).
Fig. 240 - Pullet Elysée (p. 386).

Fig. 239

Fig. 240

Fig. 241

boiled egg yolks, all well seasoned with paprika. Pan-roast in butter without any liquid. Place the chicken on a round platter; surround with a garnish composed of medium-sized onions or artichoke bottoms stuffed with sausage meat and braised; small tomatoes cooked in butter; cubes of zucchini sautéed in oil.

Sauce: Melt the glaze in the roasting pan with a finger of vinegar and sherry, moisten with veal stock, and reduce. (Figure 243, Page 396.)

CHICKEN BERGÈRE POULET À LA BERGÈRE (Gi.) (*For 4 persons*)

Prepare a 2½-lb. chicken for roasting, putting inside it 2 or 3 oz. butter well mixed with salt, pepper, parsley, and chopped raw mushrooms. Then truss the chicken and brown in a casserole with 20 small strips of breast of salt pork previously blanched in boiling water; add 2 onions and 2 shallots, both sliced in rings, around the chicken, and when chicken and onions are well browned, add 7 oz. chopped mushrooms. Cook 5 min. more to brown the mushrooms and moisten with 1 glass white wine; seal hermetically (with paste or paper over edges of lid) and cook in the oven 25–30 min. To serve, place the chicken, carved or whole, on a round platter. Reduce the cooking liquid by ½, remove from the stove, and add a good quantity of butter; pour this sauce over the chicken, then encircle it with a border of Potato Straws (p. 509). Sprinkle the top with chopped parsley.

CHICKEN IN WHITE SAUCE POULET AU BLANC (P.)

Can be cooked whole or in pieces; if cut in pieces, prepare like Veal Blanquette (p. 338). If it is served whole, it must be cooked with 1 pt. clear white bouillon, 1 onion, 1 carrot, a *bouquet garni,* and a few peppercorns. Poach without boiling 30 min., then make a white sauce from the strained cooking stock, and proceed as for Veal Blanquette. Bind the sauce with egg yolks and cream and garnish with mushrooms and small onions.

CHICKEN BONNE FEMME POULET À LA BONNE FEMME (M.)

Brown in butter, in an earthenware casserole, 3½ oz. cubed and blanched breast of pork and 12 small onions. Remove the onions and pork fat and brown the chicken in the same fat, after trussing and seasoning it. Cook in the oven 10 min. Replace the cooked onions and pork fat in the casserole, adding 1½ lb. potatoes cut into bean shapes. Season these vegetables and cook with the chicken in a low oven. Just before serving, baste with a few tbsp. reduced veal stock.

CHICKEN BORDELAISE POULET À LA BORDELAISE (M.)

Stuff with a mixture of Light Forcemeat (p. 173) and Gratin Forcemeat (p. 175) with chopped parsley added; pan-roast in butter. Place the chicken on a round platter. Garnish with potatoes sliced raw and sautéed in butter, small artichoke quarters cooked in butter, floured onion rings fried in oil, fried parsley, all arranged in mounds around the chicken. Melt the glaze in the roasting pan with white wine, add veal stock, reduce, butter (flavor with a clove of garlic, if desired), and pour over the chicken.

CHICKEN CHAMPEAUX POULET CHAMPEAUX (M.)

Pan-roast in butter in a casserole. Garnish with small glazed onions and Potatoes Noisette (p. 509) browned in butter. Melt cooking glaze in casserole with white wine, add veal stock, reduce, butter, and pour over chicken.

Fig. 241 - Pullet Néva (p. 390).

CHICKEN CLAMART POULET À LA CLAMART (M.)

Brown the chicken in butter in an earthenware cocotte. Half cook in the oven. Add 1 pt. half-cooked Peas French Style (p. 505). Finish cooking chicken and peas together.

CHICKEN EN COCOTTE BONNE FEMME POULET COCOTTE BONNE FEMME (E.) (*For 4 persons*)

Season the inside of the chicken with salt and pepper; stuff with 3½ oz. of sausage meat mixed with the chopped chicken liver, 1 tbsp. bread crumbs, pinch of parsley. Truss the chicken and cover the breast with strips of bacon; cook in butter in an earthenware or iron cocotte. Place the cocotte over a low fire, add 8 to 10 small onions and 12 small cubes of lean bacon. Turn the chicken from time to time to cook it evenly. When half cooked, surround the chicken with 10 oz. cubed potatoes and stir them with a fork so that they will soak up the cooking butter. Cover the cocotte and finish cooking in a low oven. Before serving, untruss the chicken and baste with a few tbsp. of rather concentrated brown Veal Gravy (p. 134); serve in the cocotte.

CHICKEN COLETTE POULET COLETTE (M.)

Stuff with Light Forcemeat (p. 173) mixed with chopped onion cooked in butter and seasoned with paprika; pan-roast in butter with large cubes of Bayonne ham. Place the chicken on pancake-shaped Potatoes Macaire (p. 508) on a round platter. Garnish with mushrooms sautéed in butter with a little chopped shallot. Melt the glaze in the pan with Chablis and butter off the stove; coat the chicken with this sauce. (Figure 245, Page 404.)

CHICKEN TARRAGON (IN WHITE SAUCE) POULET À L'ESTRAGON (À BLANC) (P.)

Prepare the same as whole Chicken in White Sauce (p. 393), but with a bunch of tarragon in the cooking stock and fresh chopped tarragon in the sauce. Skin the chicken, coat with the white sauce, and decorate the top with tarragon leaves blanched in boiling water; no other garnish. (Figure 246, Page 404.)

CHICKEN TARRAGON (IN BROWN SAUCE) POULET À L'ESTRAGON (À BRUN) (P.)

Brown the chicken in butter in a casserole, then pour over it 1 pt. good but very thin brown sauce flavored with tomatoes; add a bunch of tarragon and cook with the cover on the casserole. Skim the fat off the sauce, strain it, and add chopped tarragon. Coat the chicken with the sauce without removing the skin and decorate with blanched tarragon leaves.

CHICKEN GRAND'MÈRE POULET GRAND'MÈRE (E.) (*For 4 persons*)

Stuff the chicken with the following preparation: lightly brown in butter 1 tbsp. finely chopped onion; mix it with 2 oz. sausage meat and the chopped liver of the chicken, pinch of parsley, 2 tbsp. bread crumbs, all lightly seasoned with salt and spices. Truss the chicken and place it in an earthenware casserole with 2 oz. finely diced lean bacon, 1 tbsp. butter, and 10 small onions. Cover the casserole and place over a low fire. As soon as the chicken and onions are a golden brown, add 10 oz. cubed potatoes; continue cooking at low heat. Serve the chicken in the same casserole.

CHICKEN HENRIETTE POULET HENRIETTE (M.)

Stuff the chicken with a salpicon (tiny cubes) of *foie gras* and truffles. Pan-roast it in butter. Place it on a not-too-thick bed of Potatoes Anna (p. 506). Surround with mushrooms stuffed with chicken forcemeat (p. 176) mixed with Duxelles (p. 176), sprinkled with bread crumbs, moistened with butter, and browned in the oven, and very small heads of Braised Lettuce (p. 502).

Sauce: Melt the glaze in the pan with Madeira, moisten with equal parts of Velouté (p. 147) and brown veal stock. Reduce, butter, and strain.

SPRING CHICKEN MASCOTTE POULET (DE GRAIN) MASCOTTE (E.)

Brown the chicken in butter in a casserole and surround it with 3½ oz. potatoes cut in the shape and size of olives, 3½ oz. cubed or quartered artichoke bottoms (both previously sautéed in butter). When the chicken is almost cooked, place it in a hot terrine with its garnish, 2 tbsp. Veal Gravy (p. 134), and 10 slices of truffle. Cover the dish and keep it in an open oven 10 min. Serve as is.

CHICKEN HOME STYLE POULET À LA MÉNAGÈRE (M.) (*For 4 persons*)

Stuff with ½ lb. sausage meat mixed with the sliced chicken liver sautéed in butter and chopped parsley. Cook in butter in a casserole with 1 large onion and 1 medium-sized carrot (both quartered and previously half cooked in butter) and a *bouquet garni.* When the chicken is almost cooked, add 10 sliced mushrooms. Finish cooking everything together. Just before serving, baste with a few tbsp. reduced veal stock.

CHICKEN WITH MORELS (MUSHROOMS) POULET AUX MORILLES (M.)

Cook the chicken in butter in an earthenware casserole. When half cooked, surround with 10 oz. morels (mushrooms) previously lightly cooked in butter. Finish cooking together. At end, baste with a few tbsp. reduced veal stock.

CHICKEN NANETTE POULET NANETTE (M.)

Stuff the chicken with a very thick purée of mushrooms. Pan-roast in butter. Place it on a rather thin bed of Potatoes Anna (p. 506). Garnish with small fried Rissoles (p. 248) made with spinach, and flat croquettes (in the shape of pancakes) made with a mixture of carrots, artichoke bottoms, and asparagus tips (bound with Allemande Sauce, p. 146).

Sauce: Glaze in the cooking pan melted with Sauterne and veal stock.

CHICKEN POLONAISE POULET À LA POLONAISE (Fa.)

Stuff with Gratin Forcemeat (p. 175) mixed with ⅓ its volume in bread crumbs, soaked, and a little chopped parsley. Truss with the legs pulled back and lard the breast with strips of bacon. Roast the chicken in butter, in a flat pan, in the oven. When it is cooked, untruss and remove the bacon strips; pour a finger of lemon juice over it and, just before serving, baste with 2 oz. nut-brown butter in which 4 tbsp. freshly rolled bread crumbs have been browned.

CHICKEN WITH SPRING VEGETABLES POULET AUX PRIMEURS (M.)

Cook the chicken in butter in a casserole or an earthenware cocotte with new vegetables such as: potatoes, small carrots, artichoke bottoms or quarters, zucchini cut in large bean shapes, etc. When the chicken and vegetables are almost cooked, add 4 or 5 tbsp. Peas French Style (p. 505). At the last moment, moisten with a few tbsp. reduced veal stock.

CHICKEN RIVOLI POULET RIVOLI (M.)

Pan-roast in butter. Place the chicken on a bed of potatoes that have been cubed, sliced, fried in butter, and packed down to resemble a large pancake. Stir 2 medium-sized sliced truffles in the butter the chicken was cooked in; season; place on top of the chicken. Pour a few tbsp. rich veal stock into the cooking butter and pour over the chicken.

Note: This chicken may also be prepared *en cocotte.*

CHICKEN VAUCLUSIENNE POULET VAUCLUSIENNE (E.) (*For 4 persons*)

Clean the chicken and season the inside with salt and pepper; truss and place in a small earthenware casserole with 2 oz. chopped lean bacon and 2 tbsp. olive oil. Place the casserole on the fire and as soon as the chicken begins to brown, add 2 tbsp. finely chopped onion, 1 glass white wine, then 5 or 6 peeled, seeded, and chopped tomatoes, pinch of parsley, clove of garlic, salt, and pepper. Cover the casserole and cook at low heat. Finish with 24 black olives. Prepare, separately, 2 medium-sized eggplants: cut them in thin rings, roll in flour, and fry in oil. Place these slices around the chicken in the casserole.

CHICKEN (HEN) WITH RICE POULE AU RIZ (A.) (*For 6 persons*)

Take: ¾ lb. rice, ¼ lb. grated Gruyère cheese, 1 qt. bouillon, 1 tender young hen,[1] a *bouquet garni* (parsley, thyme, and bay leaf), some butter (the amount depends upon the amount of fat on the chicken), salt, and pepper. Place the hen in a casserole with the *bouquet garni;* season to taste, pour in bouillon until it is halfway up the side of the hen, cover the top with buttered paper and cook on a low fire 1½ hr.; remove the *bouquet.* Cook the rice 10 min. in salted water, drain, rinse with cold water; add the rice to the bouillon used in cooking the hen, which will be absorbed by the rice. Treat the rice as in the preparation of Rich Rice (p. 512). It should be fluffy, with the grains separate. Mix the rice with the grated cheese and, if necessary, a little melted butter. Place the rice on a platter with the chicken on top.

For variety, the rice may be mixed with ¼ lb. cultivated mushrooms or morels; or with 2 oz. soaked dried mushrooms cut in pieces and sautéed in butter; or with bacon, small sausages, etc. During the season for new peas, these may be substituted for the cheese and cooked with the hen. (Figure 247, P. 405.)

GRILLED CHICKEN (M.)

Ordinarily, grilled chickens, whether breaded or not, should be cooked entirely on the grill. However, in current practice this is not always done. The spring chicken is cut open and flattened and first cooked in the oven; later it is basted with butter, if necessary, and finished on the grill. This method is doubtless quicker and easier, but from the standpoint of flavor does not produce the same result as a chicken completely cooked on the grill. Spring chickens are, above all, grilled; however, large chickens can also be grilled.

Preparation: Split the trussed chicken down the back. Open it completely and lightly flatten it. Season with salt and pepper; brush with melted butter or

---

[1] An old hen needs to cook longer—3-4 hr. and even more—and certainly does not make so fine a dish.

Fig. 242 - Pullet Flammarion (p. 386).
Fig. 243 - Chicken asturienne (p. 392).

Fig. 242

Fig. 243

Fig. **244**

chicken fat (or, if called for in the recipe, oil). Cook the chicken on a grill at low heat. When the chicken is almost cooked, cover it with fresh bread crumbs, baste with butter or chicken fat, and finish cooking on the grill, browning both sides. Place the chicken on a platter bordered with fluted half slices of lemon and gherkins. Garnish with water cress and serve with the sauce indicated.

GRILLED CHICKEN AMERICAN STYLE   POULET GRILLÉ À L'AMÉRICAINE (M.)

Grill without breading. Place the chicken on slices of buttered toast. Garnish with slices of grilled or fried bacon. Baste with Maître d'Hôtel Butter (p. 164). Serve with a green salad.

GRILLED CHICKEN ENGLISH STYLE   POULET GRILLÉ À L'ANGLAISE (M.)

Dip in melted butter and roll in bread crumbs seasoned with cayenne. Garnish with slices of grilled bacon and boiled potatoes. Serve with Maître d'Hôtel Butter (p. 164) seasoned with cayenne.

GRILLED SPRING CHICKEN CRAPAUDINE   POULET (DE GRAIN) GRILLÉ À LA CRAPAUDINE (E.)

Split the chicken lengthwise from the tip of the breast to the wing joint, without separating the 2 parts. Gently flatten to break the joints and the bones; remove the bones as carefully as possible. Pin the wings back with a skewer; season with salt and pepper; baste with melted butter, and half cook in the oven. Then sprinkle with bread crumbs, baste again with melted butter, and finish cooking slowly on the grill. Serve with a dish of some highly seasoned sauce, preferably Diable Sauce (p. 140).

GRILLED DEVILED CHICKEN   POULET GRILLÉ À LA DIABLE (M.)

When the chicken is almost cooked, spread both sides with mustard seasoned with cayenne, roll in bread crumbs, and baste with butter. Finish cooking on the grill at low heat, browning both sides well. Place on a platter bordered with lemon and gherkins. Garnish with water cress. Serve with Diable Sauce (p. 140).

GRILLED CHICKEN KATOV   POULET GRILLÉ KATOFF (Gi.)

Singe the chicken, then stuff the ends of the legs into the stomach through a cut made low on each side of the breastbone. This done, split it all the way down the back, open it, remove the lungs, then flatten it gently to break the bones, which should then be removed as completely as possible. Season with salt and pepper and place in a casserole, baste with melted butter, and put in the oven 10–12 min. to brown. After removing it from the oven, cover completely with golden meat glaze and roll in fresh bread crumbs. Baste with melted butter and grill slowly 25–30 min., or a little longer, depending on the weight.

Prepare separately 1 lb. or more of mashed potatoes; dry quickly in a hot oven, bind with a few egg yolks, then add a piece of butter and a finely chopped truffle. Pour the potatoes onto a platter and shape by hand into a cake; brown in the oven 7–8 min. Place the chicken on top of the potatoes, and pour over it a few tbsp. reduced Veal Gravy (p. 134). Serve separately a sauce prepared as follows: reduce to ¾ a few tbsp. veal stock, add 1 tsp. Meat Glaze (p. 135), and butter lightly off the fire.

Fig. 244 - Pullet à la reine (p. 391).

FRIED CHICKEN (M.)

This method of cooking chicken must not be confused with *fritot,* which is especially used for preparing cooked chicken meat (see p. 414). Only small chickens such as spring chickens and squab chickens should be fried. In old-time cooking, this method was called "marinade," which is rather confusing, since chickens prepared *en fritot* are also marinated before cooking. The following recipe, taken from Plumerey, who continued Carême's work, will show how Chicken Marinade used to be made. Today's method is similar, but chickens prepared this way are called *à la viennoise,* or Vienna style.

FRIED CHICKEN or **CHICKEN MARINADE** POULET FRIT or MARINADE DE VOLAILLE (M.)

Cut up a small spring chicken (legs, wings, breast). Remove the legbones. Season with salt and pepper, and marinate ½ hr. in a few tbsp. white wine, lemon juice, thread of oil, parsley, thyme, and bay leaf. Drain the pieces and wipe them dry; roll in flour, beaten egg, and bread crumbs. Place in a frying pan containing burning hot clarified butter and cook, turning the pieces several times. Brown the pieces well, drain them, and serve on a napkin garnished with fried parsley and lemon. Serve with a rather highly seasoned sauce.

FRIED CHICKEN VIENNOISE POULET FRIT À LA VIENNOISE (M.)

Fry the pieces of marinated, breaded chicken in smoking hot deep fat. Arrange the pieces in a mound; garnish with fried parsley and lemon. Serve with Tomato Sauce (p. 146).

SAUTÉED CHICKEN

How to sauté chicken: (1) Cut the chicken in pieces. (2) Season the pieces with salt and pepper, dip in flour and shake to remove the excess flour. (The purpose of the flour is to form a light crust to hold in the juices.) (3) Cook in butter or oil, or a mixture of the two. The butter should be very hot so as to sear the meat and brown it quickly. Sautéed chicken, like anything "sautéed," should be cooked in a sautéing pan (see utensils, p. 92), a large flat pan about 2 in. deep. It must be shallow so that the steam from the cooking will evaporate rather than fall on the meat, as would be the case with a deep pan. The outside of the chicken will have a nice crust, each piece being a sort of small roast, which is a primary characteristic of a sautéed meat. The pieces will be seared on both sides and, with the help of the flour, golden brown in color.

There are two ways of sautéing chicken: after browning the pieces on both sides, put the uncovered sautéing pan into a hot oven; baste the pieces 2 or 3 times, tilting the pan to scoop the juice into a spoon. The second method is to cover the sautéing pan after the pieces have been browned and reduce the heat and cook slowly. This system, devised by Montagné, has one fault, in our humble opinion: it lets the steam condense and fall on the chicken, thereby spoiling the crusty character of the dish, which is the chief merit of a good sauté. Of course, if you are unable to put the chicken into the oven, this method must be used.

According to the directions just given, you will see that a sauté must be cooked dry, without liquid or sauce, for if it is moistened with gravy or sauce or wine, it becomes a stew.

Sauce or gravy to serve with the chicken: When the pieces of chicken are cooked, remove from the pan and place on a platter; the breast and wings, which cook faster than the legs, are removed first and kept hot. Drain off the excess fat left in the pan; melt the glaze left in the bottom of the pan with wine, cullis, sauce, etc., depending on the recipe. Place the pinions, neck, gizzard, and other pieces of carcass on the bottom of the platter to form a sort of base on which to make a pyramid of the legs, cut in two if they are large, then the breast and the 2 wings on top. After pouring the sauce over the chicken, the wing tips may be decorated with paper frills.

CHICKEN SAUTÉ ALEXANDRA POULET SAUTÉ ALEXANDRA (M.) (*For 4 persons*)

Season with salt and paprika; sauté in butter but do not brown. Remove the pieces from the sautéing pan and melt the glaze with 3 oz. chicken stock; add 6 oz. chicken Velouté (p. 147) and 12 oz. Soubise Purée (p. 504). Put the chicken pieces into this sauce. Simmer for a few moments. Remove the pieces onto a platter; take the sauce off the stove and add 2 tbsp. fresh cream and 2 oz. butter, strain through a sieve, and pour over the chicken. Garnish with bunches of buttered green asparagus tips. (Figure 248, Page 405.)

CHICKEN SAUTÉ AMBASSADEUR POULET SAUTÉ AMBASSADEUR (M.)

Sauté in butter. Place the chicken on a platter and garnish with cockscombs and cock kidneys; mushrooms (sautéed with the chicken); chicken livers sautéed in butter. On top of the chicken place 10 large, thick slices of truffle heated in chicken fat. Coat with the following sauce: melt the glaze in the bottom of the pan with 4 oz. Madeira, add 6 oz. thickened veal stock, reduce, and strain.

CHICKEN SAUTÉ ARCHIDUC POULET SAUTÉ ARCHIDUC (M.)

Season with salt and paprika; sauté in butter but do not brown. Finish as directed in the recipe for Chicken Sauté with Paprika (p. 407). Place the chicken on a thin bed of Potatoes Duchesse (p. 507) mixed with 1/3 its volume in leaf spinach cooked in butter. (This potato-spinach pancake should be browned in the oven.) Cover the chicken with Paprika Sauce (p. 151).

CHICKEN SAUTÉ ARLÉSIENNE POULET SAUTÉ À L'ARLÉSIENNE (M.)

Sauté in oil until half cooked, then add 2 cubed, peeled eggplants. Cover and cook together. Arrange the chicken on a platter and garnish with mounds of eggplant alternated with mounds of onion rings fried in oil. Cover with the following sauce. Add 2 peeled, chopped, drained tomatoes seasoned with salt and pepper and a little crushed garlic to the cooking oil. Pour in 3 oz. white wine and reduce. Add 6 oz. veal stock and 1/2 tbsp. chopped parsley.

CHICKEN SAUTÉ D'ARTOIS POULET SAUTÉ D'ARTOIS (E.)

Sauté the chicken in butter and place on a platter. Melt the glaze in the pan with 3 tbsp. Madeira and add: 1 1/2 oz. thin golden meat glaze, 4 small artichoke bottoms quartered and sautéed in butter, 10 carrot pieces cut in the shape of small olives and cooked in consommé and glazed, 8 small new onions cooked in butter. Finish the sauce with 2 oz. butter and a pinch of chopped chives, and pour over the chicken.

CHICKEN SAUTÉ BEAULIEU POULET SAUTÉ BEAULIEU (E.) (*For 4 persons*)

Sauté the chicken in butter and add: 5 oz. small new potatoes cut to about the size of hazelnuts, the same amount of small quartered artichokes (both vegetables cooked together in butter in advance). Keep hot in the oven, covered, 10 min. Next, place the chicken pieces in an earthenware casserole, along with the potatoes and artichokes, and add 12 black olives. Melt the glaze in the sautéing pan with a few tbsp. white wine and a finger of lemon juice; finish with 1 tbsp. veal stock and pour into the casserole; cover and simmer 5 min. Serve as is.

CHICKEN SAUTÉ BERCY POULET SAUTÉ À LA BERCY (P.)

Cut up the chicken and sauté in butter; when it is cooked, arrange on a platter and keep warm. Brown in the cooking pan 1 tbsp. chopped shallots, pour in ½ glass white wine, and reduce by ½, then add a good amount of meat glaze, juice of ½ lemon, 4 oz. chopped raw mushrooms. Cook 5 min., then add plenty of butter and pour over the chicken; sprinkle with chopped parlsey.

CHICKEN SAUTÉ BOIVIN POULET SAUTÉ BOIVIN (M.) (*For 4 persons*)

Brown the chicken in butter. When the pieces are well browned, add to the pan 12 small onions already colored in butter, 2 small quartered artichokes lightly blanched, and 24 small potato balls scooped out with a ball cutter. Cover and cook. Arrange the chicken on a platter and surround it with small mounds of the garnishes.

Sauce: Melt the glaze in the bottom of the pan with chicken stock, pour in some reduced veal stock, add a dash of lemon juice, and butter off the stove.

CHICKEN SAUTÉ BONNE DAME POULET SAUTÉ BONNE DAME (M.)

Heat 10 tbsp. butter in an earthenware casserole, then lay in the pieces of chicken seasoned with salt and pepper, 4 oz. strips of blanched pork fat, 12 small half-cooked onions, and 12 small carrots ⅔ cooked. Cover and cook slowly. When everything is cooked, add 24 pitted, blanched olives. Pour in 3 oz. dry white wine and simmer a few minutes. Baste with 4 or 5 tbsp. thickened veal stock; sprinkle with chopped parsley; serve in the same casserole.

CHICKEN SAUTÉ BORDELAISE POULET SAUTÉ À LA BORDELAISE (E.)

Sauté the chicken in butter and place on a platter. Surround it with small quartered artichokes cooked in butter, raw sliced potatoes sautéed in butter, fried onion rings; arrange each of these garnishes in mounds with a small tuft of fried parsley between each mound. Melt the glaze in the pan with a few tbsp. chicken gravy and pour over the chicken.

CHICKEN SAUTÉ BOURGUIGNONNE POULET SAUTÉ À LA BOURGUIGNONNE (E.)

Sauté in butter. When the pieces are well browned, place in the pan 12 small onions browned in butter, 12 small pieces of breast of pork (blanched and browned), and 12 small mushroom caps. Cover and cook together. When serving, surround the chicken with these garnishes and coat the chicken with the following sauce: melt the glaze in the bottom of the sautéing pan with 9 oz. red wine (Burgundy), season with a little crushed garlic, and reduce; pour in a few tbsp. Semiglaze Sauce (p. 138), reduce, butter, and strain.

Note: The sauce may be thickened with Flour Butter (p. 164).

CHICKEN SAUTÉ CATALANE POULET SAUTÉ À LA CATALANE (E.)

Cut up the chicken as usual, then cut the legs in 2 pieces, season with salt and pepper, roll in flour, and cook in oil with 2 heaping tbsp. chopped onion. Meanwhile, slice 5 or 6 sweet red peppers and sauté them in oil in a frying pan; when the peppers are almost cooked, add a clove of garlic. Cook at low heat 20–25 min. If desired, sliced eggplant and zucchini, floured and fried in oil, may be added. Pour the mixture of vegetables into a terrine and place the pieces of chicken on top. Melt the glaze in the bottom of the sautéing pan with 1 glass white wine, reduce, and pour over the chicken. Cover the terrine and let simmer a few moments. Serve with rice creole.

Note: Young rabbit can be prepared the same way.

CHICKEN SAUTÉ WITH CEPES (MUSHROOMS) POULET SAUTÉ AUX CÈPES (M.)

Sauté the chicken in equal parts of butter and oil. When the chicken is nicely browned, add some firm, fresh cepes (mushrooms) previously sautéed in oil. (If the mushrooms are small, use them whole; otherwise slice them.) Cover and cook together. Arrange the chicken on a platter, surround with the mushrooms, and coat it with the following sauce: drop ½ tbsp. chopped shallot into the sautéing pan, add 3 oz. white wine, and reduce; add a few tbsp. reduced veal stock.

Note: This sauté may be flavored with a little crushed garlic.

CHICKEN SAUTÉ WITH MUSHROOMS (IN BROWN SAUCE) POULET SAUTÉ AUX CHAMPIGNONS (À BRUN) (M.)

Sauté in butter. When the chicken is almost cooked, drop 12 large, fluted mushroom caps into the pan. Cover and finish cooking together. Serve the chicken surrounded by mushrooms. Coat it with the following sauce: melt the glaze in the bottom of the pan with Madeira; add well-skimmed Semiglaze Sauce (p. 138) ; boil a few moments, and strain.

CHICKEN SAUTÉ WITH MUSHROOMS (IN CREAM SAUCE) POULET SAUTÉ AUX CHAMPIGNONS (À LA CRÈME) (M.)

Sauté the chicken in butter. Add sliced raw mushrooms. Cover and finish cooking together. Arrange the chicken on a platter, surround with the mushrooms, and coat with the following sauce: melt the glaze in the bottom of the pan with sherry; add fresh cream and thicken with a little chicken Velouté (p. 147) ; strain. (Figure 249, Page 408.)

CHICKEN SAUTÉ CHASSEUR POULET SAUTÉ CHASSEUR (M.)

Sauté the chicken in equal parts of butter and oil. When almost cooked, add 4 oz. sliced raw mushrooms and, at the last moment, ½ tbsp. finely chopped shallot. Serve the chicken covered with the following sauce: melt the glaze in the pan (still containing the sliced mushrooms) with 3 oz. white wine. Add 3 oz. thickened veal stock and 1 tbsp. Tomato Sauce (p. 146) . Boil a few moments and add a good pinch of chopped chervil and chopped tarragon. Sprinkle the chicken with chopped parsley.

Note: A finger of cognac may be added to the Chasseur Sauce.

CHICKEN SAUTÉ IN CREAM SAUCE POULET SAUTÉ À LA CRÈME (M.)

Sauté in butter without browning. Cover with the following sauce before serving: stir some fresh cream into the butter left in the sautéing pan. Add 2 or 3 tbsp. chicken Velouté (p. 147), simmer, add butter, and strain.

CHICKEN SAUTÉ IN CREAM SAUCE (L'ÉCHELLE METHOD) POULET SAUTÉ À LA CRÈME (MÉTHODE DE L'ÉCHELLE) (M.)

Sauté in butter. When ⅔ cooked, add 2 large sliced mushrooms and 2 sliced artichoke bottoms (cooked in white stock). Just before removing from the stove, add 12 thick slices of truffle. Cover the chicken with the mushrooms, artichokes, and truffles, and serve coated with the following sauce.

Sauce (Crème l'Échelle): Melt the glaze in the bottom of the pan with 4 oz. sherry, add some thick fresh cream, a little chicken Velouté (p. 147), and 2 tbsp. golden chicken glaze. Boil a few moments and finish with 2 oz. butter; strain.

CHICKEN SAUTÉ CYNTHIA POULET SAUTÉ CYNTHIA (E.)

Sauté the chicken in butter and place on a platter. Pour a glass of dry champagne into the pan and reduce by ½; add 1 tbsp. thin chicken glaze, then finish with 2 oz. butter, juice of ½ lemon, 1 tbsp. dry curaçao, and pour over the chicken. Surround the chicken with 20 peeled, seeded grapes and 10 orange quarters peeled to the flesh.

CHICKEN SAUTÉ DEMIDOV POULET SAUTÉ DEMIDOFF (M.) (*For 4 persons*)

Sauté in butter. When the pieces are nicely browned, add the following vegetables, previously cooked in a closed pot, using butter but no water; 3½ oz. carrots, 2½ oz. turnips, 2 oz. small onions, and 2 stalks celery, all sliced. Cover and cook. When the chicken is cooked, add 2½ oz. sliced truffles. Arrange the chicken on a platter and cover with the garnish and the following sauce: melt the glaze in a pan with Madeira and add some well-skimmed Semiglaze Sauce.

Note: Sliced mushrooms may be added to the Demidov garnish. Vegetables used in Demidov recipes should, in principle, be cut into fluted crescents. Let us say, finally, that this chicken, after being placed on a platter, is sometimes garnished with onion rings dipped in thin Frying Paste (p. 558) and fried in clarified butter; the platter is then decorated with crescents of Flaky Paste (p. 544). (Figure 250, Page 408.)

CHICKEN SAUTÉ DURAND POULET SAUTÉ À LA DURAND (Fa.)

Cut up the raw chicken, sprinkle the pieces with salt and pepper, and flour them so that they turn a golden brown when cooked in oil and lard; add 2 or 3 onions sliced in rather thick rings and fry them until golden brown. Put the pan into the oven, without covering it, to finish cooking the chicken. Meanwhile, peel, drain, and slice 1 lb. tomatoes; salt and season the slices with red pepper and fry them in oil. To serve, pile the onions in a pyramid in the center of a round platter with the chicken pieces around it. Place a large slice of cooked ham like a funnel in the center of the onions and fill it with the tomatoes, which should then be sprinkled with parsley. Melt the glaze in the pan the chicken was sautéed in with white wine, butter well, and serve in a sauceboat with the chicken.

CHICKEN SAUTÉ ESCURIAL POULET SAUTÉ ESCURIAL (E.)

Brown in butter 3½ oz. diced raw ham and 5 oz. quartered raw mushrooms; drain. In the same butter, brown and cook the chicken pieces. Melt the glaze in the pan with 3 oz. white wine; add 3 oz. Semiglaze Sauce (p. 138) ; put the ham and mushrooms back into the sauce with 20 stuffed poached olives and 3½ oz. diced truffles and simmer 7–8 min. Make a border of rice poached in salted water, the grains separate and heated in the oven to dry for a few minutes before molding into a ring; place the chicken and garnish in the center of this rice. Surround the rice ring with very small fried eggs or fried egg yolks covered with a thin film of white.

CHICKEN SAUTÉ SPANISH STYLE POULET SAUTÉ À L'ESPAGNOLE (E.) (*For 6 persons*)

Sauté the chicken in oil. Drain off the oil and add to the chicken: 9 oz. Rice Pilaf (p. 512) mixed with 2 oz. diced pimento, 3½ oz. large fresh boiled green peas, and 2 sliced, poached sausages. Cover the pan and cook in the oven 10 min. Serve the chicken covered with the garnish and surrounded with 6 small grilled tomatoes.

CHICKEN SAUTÉ FÉDORA POULET SAUTÉ FÉDORA (E.) (*For 4 persons*)

Cook the chicken in butter without letting it brown, along with 4 oz. sliced raw truffles; arrange on a platter. To make the sauce, pour 3 oz. cream into the remaining butter and glaze in the pan, add 3 tbsp. Béchamel Sauce (p. 146) , and reduce by ½. Remove from the fire and finish with 2 oz. Crayfish Butter (p. 164) , a finger of lemon juice, and a dash of cayenne. Pour the sauce over the chicken, and surround it with bunches of buttered asparagus tips.

CHICKEN SAUTÉ FORESTIÈRE POULET SAUTÉ À LA FORESTIÈRE (P.)

Prepare the same as Chicken Sauté Chasseur (p. 401) , but first sauté the morels (mushrooms) in a pan, drain them, and put them in with the chicken to finish cooking; reduce the juice left in the pan from the mushrooms and add to the chicken sauce.

CHICKEN SAUTÉ GABRIELLE POULET SAUTÉ GABRIELLE (E.)

Cook the chicken in butter without browning, then arrange on a platter. Melt the glaze in the pan with 3 oz. mushroom cooking liquid, add 3 tbsp. Béchamel Sauce (p. 146) and 3 tbsp. cream, and reduce by ½. Remove from the fire and finish with 2 oz. butter. Pour the sauce over the chicken, sprinkle the top with very black truffles in julienne strips, and surround with palmettes of Puff Paste (p. 544) baked in the oven.

CHICKEN SAUTÉ HUNGARIAN STYLE POULET SAUTÉ HONGROISE (E.)

Cut up the chicken, season with salt and pepper, and flour the pieces. Heat 2 tbsp. butter in a sautéing pan; put in the chicken with 2 tbsp. chopped onions. When the onion begins to brown, sprinkle the chicken with ½ tsp. sweet pink paprika. Pour in 3 tbsp. white wine, add 2 or 3 peeled, seeded, and chopped tomatoes; finish cooking. Place the chicken in a terrine. Finish the sauce with a few tbsp. fresh cream, boil a few moments, and pour over the chicken. Serve with Rice Pilaf (p. 512) .

CHICKEN SAUTÉ INDIAN STYLE or CURRIED CHICKEN SAUTÉ

POULET SAUTÉ À L'INDIENNE OR AU CURRY (M.)

Cook a finely sliced onion in butter until it is transparent, then put in the chicken and cook without browning. Add a *bouquet garni.* When the chicken pieces are half cooked, sprinkle with 2 tbsp. curry. Mix well while cooking; sprinkle with 2 tbsp. flour; pour in 1 cup chicken white stock. Cover and cook slowly as you would a chicken fricassee. Remove the chicken pieces and place them on a platter. Reduce the cooking gravy and add, if needed, 2 or 3 tbsp. chicken Velouté (p. 147) ; add cream, strain, and pour over the chicken. Serve with a separate bowl of Rice Indian Style (p. 512) . (Figure 251, Page 409.)

Note: This is the recipe usually followed in Paris. Here is a recipe used by the Indian chef at the Hôtel de Paris in Monte Carlo:

CHICKEN SAUTÉ INDIAN STYLE or CHICKEN CURRY (INDIAN METHOD)

POULET SAUTÉ À L'INDIENNE OR CURRY DE POULET (M.)

Cut the chicken into 20 small pieces of the same size. Place the pieces in a deep pan in which you have previously cooked the following ingredients in lard: 2 medium-sized chopped onions, 3½ oz. chopped ham, 2 small chopped, peeled apples. Season this mixture strongly with thyme, bay leaf, cinnamon, cardamom, mace, and crushed garlic. When the chicken pieces are partially cooked, sprinkle with 5 tbsp. curry. Add 2 peeled, pressed, chopped tomatoes; mix together. Pour in 4 oz. coconut milk. Cover and simmer 35–40 min. Add a few tbsp. fresh heavy cream and juice of 2 lemons, 10 min. before serving. The sauce should be thickened, though not too much, simply by reducing it. Place the chicken in a vegetable dish or a dish with 2 compartments, 1 for the chicken and 1 for the rice, and serve with a timbale of Rice Indian Style (p. 512) . Serve the curry with Indian pancakes called "pappadums," fried in hot deep fat.

CHICKEN SAUTÉ JAPANESE STYLE

POULET SAUTÉ JAPONAISE (E.)

Brown the chicken in butter; add 1 lb. Japanese artichokes, lightly blanched, drained, and wiped dry; finish cooking the chicken and artichokes in the oven. Place the chicken on a platter with the artichokes on top. Swirl around in the pan 3 oz. lightly thickened veal stock; remove from the fire and finish the sauce with 2 oz. butter; pour over the chicken.

CHICKEN SAUTÉ JOSEPHINE

POULET SAUTÉ JOSÉPHINE (E.)

Sauté the chicken in butter and oil. When it is half cooked, drain off almost all the fat; add 1 tbsp. Mirepoix Bordelaise (p. 136) , 2 tbsp. chopped, cooked lean ham, and 2 oz. raw chopped mushrooms. Cook everything together until the chicken is done, then remove it to a platter. Melt the glaze in the sautéing pan with 3 oz. champagne brandy and 3 oz. mushroom cooking liquid; reduce by ⅔; and finish with 3 oz. thickened Veal Gravy (p. 134) . Remove from the fire and add 2 oz. butter. Pour the sauce over the chicken. Surround it with a border of medium-sized cepes (mushrooms) sautéed just before serving; the mushrooms should be well browned.

CHICKEN SAUTÉ LATHUILE

POULET SAUTÉ LATHUILE (E.)

Heat 3½ oz. butter until very hot in a pan just large enough to hold the chicken and its garnish. Place the seasoned pieces of chicken in the butter and

Fig. 245 - Chicken Colette (p. 394).
Fig. 246 - Chicken tarragon (p. 394).

Fig. 245

Fig. 246

Fig. 247

Fig. 248

add 9 oz. raw potatoes and 5 oz. raw artichoke bottoms, both cut in medium-sized cubes. When the chicken and vegetables are browned on the bottom, turn them over together and finish cooking the other side. At the end, baste the chicken with 3 tbsp. thin meat glaze and sprinkle with a pinch of chopped parsley mixed with a clove of crushed garlic. Place the chicken and vegetables on a platter in one piece, like a pancake or Potatoes Anna. Baste with browned butter and surround with mounds of onion rings fried in oil alternated with little tufts of very green fried parsley.

CHICKEN SAUTÉ LOUISETTE POULET SAUTÉ LOUISETTE (P.)

Cook in butter as above and place the chicken on a round platter. In the pan used for cooking the chicken brown 3½ oz. diced ham and 1 tbsp. diced carrots and 1 tbsp. chopped onions; cook 10 min. at low heat, then add 3 or 4 diced mushrooms. Cook 5 min. more and pour a few tbsp. rather thin Semiglaze Sauce (p. 138) flavored with tomato over the vegetables. Finish the sauce, off the fire, with a little butter. Pour over the chicken, and surround with a small ring of Rice Pilaf (p. 512).

CHICKEN SAUTÉ MALMAISON POULET SAUTÉ À LA MALMAISON (P.)

Sauté the chicken in butter and place it on a platter. Brown 3½ oz. raw ham diced fine in the same pan. Add 1 onion and 1 carrot, also diced fine. When everything is browned, drop in 1 chopped shallot, pour in ½ glass white wine, add 3 or 4 diced mushrooms, and simmer 10 min. Bind with a few tbsp. Semiglaze Sauce (p. 138) seasoned with tomato and finish, off the fire, with a piece of fresh butter. Pour this sauce over the chicken and surround it with a small border of Rice Pilaf (p. 512).

CHICKEN SAUTÉ MARSEILLAISE POULET SAUTÉ À LA MARSEILLAISE (Fa.)

Sauté the chicken pieces in olive oil with 2 cloves of garlic. Meanwhile, brown 6 sweet Spanish pimentos or green peppers in a frying pan and add 1 lb. crushed tomatoes and 2 cloves of garlic to them. Let both preparations cook, then drain the oil from the chicken, add the garnish and ½ glass white wine or bouillon, and cook for a few minutes. Serve with a sprinkling of chopped parsley mixed with a little garlic.

CHICKEN SAUTÉ MARYLAND POULET SAUTÉ MARYLAND (E.)

Cut the chicken to sauté; season with salt and pepper; roll the pieces in flour, dip in beaten egg, then roll in freshly made bread crumbs. Heat 2½ oz. clarified butter in a sautéing pan, drop the pieces into the butter, and cook at low heat, turning at the right time to brown both sides properly. Place the chicken on a very hot platter and surround with Corn Fritters (p. 747), potato croquettes, slices of grilled bacon, and bananas fried in butter. Serve an accompanying dish of creamed Béchamel Sauce (p. 146) with (depending on taste) grated horseradish added. Also serve Tomato Sauce (p. 146).

MINUTE CHICKEN SAUTÉ POULET SAUTÉ MINUTE (M.)

Sauté the chicken in butter as quickly as possible, browning all parts well. Place on a platter. Add a few tbsp. white wine and a finger of lemon juice to the cooking butter and glaze in the pan and pour over the chicken. Sprinkle with chopped parsley.

Fig. 247 - Chicken with rice (p. 396).
Fig. 248 - Chicken sauté Alexandra (p. 399).

CHICKEN SAUTÉ MIREILLE POULET SAUTÉ MIREILLE (P.)

Sauté the pieces in smoking hot oil. Place on a platter and garnish with mounds of eggplant sliced in rings, floured, and fried in oil, alternated with mounds of sautéed tomatoes. Melt the glaze in the sautéing pan with Tomato Sauce (p. 146) and white wine, add butter if needed, and pour over the chicken.

CHICKEN SAUTÉ MONSELET POULET SAUTÉ MONSELET (M.)

Sauté the chicken in butter. When ¾ cooked, drop 4 sliced artichoke bottoms (previously ½ cooked in white stock) into the pan. Cover and cook. When almost cooked, add 2 medium-sized sliced truffles. Arrange the chicken on a platter. Melt the glaze in the pan with a little white wine and add butter but no other gravy or sauce. Pour over the chicken.

CHICKEN SAUTÉ NIÇOISE POULET SAUTÉ À LA NIÇOISE (M.)

Sauté the chicken in butter (or ½ butter and ½ oil). Place on a platter and garnish with very small artichokes cooked in butter, small braised zucchini (quartered, if too large), blanched, pitted olives, and very small new potatoes browned in butter—all garnishes arranged in alternate mounds. Swirl some white wine in the sautéing pan and add thickened veal stock flavored with tomato, chopped tarragon, and, if desired, a bit of garlic; pour this over the chicken and sprinkle with chopped parsley. (Figure 252, Page 409.)

CHICKEN SAUTÉ NINON POULET SAUTÉ NINON (Gi.) (*For 4 persons*)

Cut an uncooked chicken into even-sized pieces; then heat 1 oz. butter and 1 tbsp. good olive oil very hot in a sautéing pan. Roll the pieces of chicken in flour and lay them side by side in the pan. Let the pieces brown slowly and add a finely chopped onion; sprinkle the chicken lightly with salt and turn to brown all sides. This done, remove the chicken and drain off the fat. Melt the glaze in the pan with ½ glass good white wine; add 2 chopped shallots, a pinch of garlic, and 6 oz. Semiglaze Sauce (p. 138). Let the sauce simmer, skimming off the film and fat; when it has been reduced by ⅓, replace the pieces of chicken, cover the pan, and place in a hot oven 12–15 min. to finish cooking. Remove the chicken pieces from the sauce and place in a pyramid in the middle of a round platter, surrounding the base with cucumbers cut into the shape of olives, blanched, then cooked in butter (with the lid tightly sealed); sautéed tomatoes; and fried onion rings. Alternate these garnishes in separate mounds. Then strain the sauce through a sieve and coat the chicken with it; sprinkle chopped parsley on top. Decorate the legs and wings with paper frills and serve very hot.

CHICKEN SAUTÉ NORMANDE POULET SAUTÉ À LA NORMANDE (E.)

Sauté the chicken in butter. When ½ cooked, place the chicken pieces in a terrine with ¾ lb. peeled, sliced small apples. Swirl a small glass of apple brandy around the sautéing pan to melt the glaze, and pour into the terrine; cover and put into the oven to finish cooking. Serve in the same dish.

CHICKEN SAUTÉ OPERA POULET SAUTÉ OPÉRA (M.)

Sauté the chicken in butter. Place it on a thin pancake of Potatoes Anna (p. 506). Garnish, in alternate mounds, with buttered green asparagus tips and tiny glazed carrots. Melt the glaze in the sautéing pan with Pouilly wine, add chopped shallot, bind with reduced veal stock, and, at the last moment, add a little chopped tarragon; pour this sauce over the chicken. (Figure 253, Page 412.)

CHICKEN SAUTÉ D'ORSAY POULET SAUTÉ D'ORSAY (E.)

Cut the chicken into pieces and season it; sauté in butter with raw quartered mushrooms and artichoke bottoms and slices of raw truffle. Place the chicken and garnish in a deep pie crust. Swirl 3 oz. white wine around the sautéing pan; reduce by ½; add a few tbsp. Parisienne Sauce (p. 146), a dash of paprika, and finish, off the stove, with 2 oz. butter. Pour the sauce over the chicken.

CHICKEN SAUTÉ WITH PAPRIKA POULET SAUTÉ AU PAPRIKA (M.)

Season the chicken with paprika and place it in a sautéing pan containing 1 medium-sized chopped onion (seasoned with paprika and cooked in butter until transparent). Cover and cook slowly. Melt the glaze in the pan with sour cream, add a little chicken Velouté (p. 147), strain, and pour over chicken.

CHICKEN SAUTÉ PARMENTIER POULET SAUTÉ PARMENTIER (E.)

Sauté the chicken in butter. When the pieces of chicken are nicely browned, drop into the pan ¾ lb. diced potatoes previously pan-fried in butter. Cover the pan and finish cooking. Swirl some white wine in the sautéing pan, add Veal Gravy (p. 134) bound with butter, and pour over the chicken; sprinkle with chopped parsley. Garnish with mounds of the diced potatoes.

CHICKEN SAUTÉ PIÉMONTAISE POULET SAUTÉ À LA PIÉMONTAISE (Fa.)

Cut up a chicken; remove the skin from the 2 wings (and the breast, which is left attached) and rub the meat with lemon; make small incisions in the meat and stuff with slices of Piedmont truffles. Place the chicken in a sautéing pan with butter, season, and cover with buttered white paper to cook it in the oven without browning it. The legs and the remainder of the chicken should be cooked in advance in a Court Bouillon (p. 277) for ¾ hr. Prepare Risotto Piémontaise (p. 513), adding a few slices of white Piedmont truffles to it; moisten the risotto with the bouillon used in cooking the legs and carcass. Mold the rice into a ring on a round platter and place the chicken in the center, the white meat, cooked 15 min. in the oven, on top of the dark. Decorate the risotto with truffles, and serve Suprême Sauce (p. 146) separately.

CHICKEN SAUTÉ PORTUGUESE STYLE POULET SAUTÉ À LA PORTUGAISE (P.)

Prepare the same as Chicken Sauté Parmentier (above), browning the pieces in equal parts of oil and butter. After cooking the chicken, melt the glaze in the sautéing pan with some white wine, Tomato Sauce (p. 146), and a little crushed garlic. Pour this over the chicken, sprinkle with chopped parsley, and garnish the border of the plate with small tomatoes cooked in butter (with the lid of the pan tightly sealed).

CHICKEN SAUTÉ SAINT-MANDÉ POULET SAUTÉ SAINT-MANDÉ (E.)

Sauté the chicken in butter; just before it is finished, add 4 oz. French peas and 4 oz. asparagus tips quickly boiled, thoroughly drained, but not cooled. Swirl a finger of Veal Gravy (p. 134) around in the pan, place the chicken on a pancake of Potatoes Macaire (p. 508), and cover with the garnish.

CHICKEN SAUTÉ STANLEY POULET SAUTÉ STANLEY (E.)

Partially cook the chicken in butter; cover and finish cooking with 9 oz. finely sliced onions. When cooked, place the chicken in a flat casserole with a mound of cooked mushrooms on each side. Add 6 oz. cream to the onions in the pan, simmer 10 min., and press through a strainer. Reduce this onion purée by ¼ and finish it with 1 oz. butter, a dash of cayenne, and a dash of curry. Pour this over the chicken and lay on top 10 slices of truffle.

CHICKEN SAUTÉ VERDI POULET SAUTÉ VERDI (E.)

Sauté the chicken in butter; place it in the middle of a ring of Risotto Piémontaise (p. 513). On top of the rice, make a ring of sliced *foie gras* sautéed in butter alternated with slices of truffle, both overlapping from the ring onto the chicken. Pour some Asti wine into the sautéing pan and reduce; add 3 tbsp. brown veal stock or 3 tbsp. Meat Glaze (p. 135). Pour this sauce over the pieces of chicken.

CHICKEN SAUTÉ VERONICA POULET SAUTÉ VÉRONIQUE (M.)

Sauté the chicken in oil. When it is almost cooked, add to the pan 4 tbsp. raw sliced mushrooms and 2 tbsp. sweet pimento peeled, cut in strips, and cooked in oil. Place the chicken on a bed of Risotto (p. 513) containing cheese mixed with diced ham sautéed in butter. Melt the glaze in the pan with some white wine and tomato-flavored veal stock and pour over the chicken. Sprinkle with chopped parsley.

CHICKEN SAUTÉ VICOMTESSE POULET SAUTÉ À LA VICOMTESSE (P.)

Cut up a spring chicken and sauté it in butter; when it is lightly browned, season, cover, and cook slowly 20 min. Remove the chicken pieces and pour 3 oz. white port and 1½ oz. cognac into the pan to melt the glaze; then add 4 or 5 tbsp. Béchamel Sauce (p. 146) and 6 oz. fresh heavy cream. Boil 4–5 min. over a hot fire, constantly stirring with a spatula, then add a lump of fresh butter. Reduce the heat immediately to stop boiling, and season highly. Place the chicken pieces on a platter, pour the sauce on top, and arrange mounds of asparagus tips sautéed in butter, or another vegetable, around the chicken.

CHICKEN BREASTS AND CUTLETS

The words *filet* and *suprême* are used for chicken breasts in French; the terms are synonymous and either one may be used in a recipe. They refer to the whole white meat of the breast and that tenderest part of the breast directly under the wing called the *filet mignon.*

In recipes calling for chicken *suprêmes*, the *filet mignon* is usually attached to the *filet,* being too small to be used alone. On the other hand, *filets mignons* from fattened pullets are used separately, after being skinned, studded with truffles, and cut in arc or ring shapes. Cutlets are the *suprêmes* of spring chickens with the stumps of the wing still attached. *Suprêmes,* though usually cut from spring chickens, are sometimes taken from fattened pullets. In this case, since there is so much meat, they must be cut into 3 or 4 even-sized pieces, lightly flattened, and trimmed in heart or oval shape, unless they are to be stuffed.

Fig. 249 - Chicken sauté with mushrooms in cream sauce (p. 401).
Fig. 250 - Chicken sauté Demidov (p. 402).

Fig. 249

Fig. 250

Fig. 251

Fig. 252

When the breasts are to be stuffed, they are opened from the side, like a sack, with the tip of a small knife. The opening is filled, by means of a pastry bag with a plain nozzle, with the required stuffing.

Suprêmes and cutlets are always cooked dry, or almost, because the least boiling in any liquid will toughen them. When the recipe calls for poaching, the whole chicken should be poached and the breasts cut off after cooking.

Browned Cutlets or Suprêmes: Salt, roll in flour, then place in a sautéing pan containing very hot clarified butter, and brown quickly on both sides. These pieces of chicken are so tender that they brown and cook at the same time.

Cutlets or Suprêmes Cooked White or Poached: Season and place in a sautéing pan containing fresh melted but not clarified butter. Roll the pieces in this butter; add a few drops of lemon juice; cover the pan and seal tightly and place in a very hot oven. Only a few minutes are needed to poach *suprêmes*. They are cooked when they give under the pressure of a finger.

Cutlets and *suprêmes* may be rolled in flour, dipped in beaten egg, rolled in bread crumbs, and then sautéed or fried. To grill, dip in butter after they are breaded.

Important Tip: Cutlets and *suprêmes* must never be left standing or they will toughen. They must be cooked quickly, just before serving, arranged on a platter rapidly and simply, and served tender and piping hot.

Note: For those recipes calling for a thickened gravy, we advise the following procedure. Melt the glaze in the pan used for cooking the *suprême* with white stock, without pouring off the butter, and add a few tbsp. Meat Glaze (p. 135). When melting the glaze in the pan, do not let it reduce completely, for it is needed to blend the butter and the Meat Glaze. The result will be a thickened gravy with a delicious, nutty flavor.

BREAST OF CHICKEN JEANNETTE FILETS (or SUPRÊMES) DE VOLAILLE JEANNETTE (M.)

Cold Dish: Cover poached breasts, cut into ovals, with White Chaud-Froid Sauce (p. 149); decorate with blanched tarragon leaves; glaze with Aspic Jelly (p. 168). Arrange them in a timbale or on a square silver platter, with overlapping slices of parfait of *foie gras* cut in the same shape as the breasts. Cover with half-set chicken aspic. To serve, embed the dish in a block of ice. (Figure 254, Page 412.)

BREAST OF CHICKEN ARLÉSIENNE SUPRÊME DE VOLAILLE À L'ARLÉSIENNE (E.)

Season, flour, and sauté the breasts in clarified butter. Place them on a ring of eggplant slices seasoned, floured, and fried in oil; garnish the center with crushed tomatoes sautéed in oil and surround with fried onion rings. Serve a separate dish of tomato-flavored Semiglaze Sauce (p. 138).

BREAST OF CHICKEN ELIZABETH SUPRÊME DE VOLAILLE ÉLISABETH (E.)

Remove the breasts from 2 small chickens. Cook them in brown butter and place them on a square platter. Coat with Suprême Sauce (p. 146) and on each breast place a few slices of truffle. In the center of the platter place 12 shelled oysters that have been chilled on ice at least 2 hr. in advance.

Note: This original recipe was prepared at a client's request and is given here simply as a curiosity.

Fig. 251 - Chicken sauté indian style (p. 404).
Fig. 252 - Chicken sauté niçoise (p. 406).

BREAST OF CHICKEN MARÉCHAL SUPRÊME DE VOLAILLE MARÉCHAL (E.)

Roll the breasts in flour, dip in beaten egg containing a little olive oil, and roll in fresh bread crumbs; sauté in butter. Arrange in a ring with a fine slice of truffle on each, and in the center place a garnish of buttered asparagus tips.

Note: In principle, most dishes prepared *à la maréchal* should first be breaded in finely chopped truffles; but the truffle dries out in cooking and loses its flavor. It is preferable to bread as above, only using 2 parts bread crumbs and 1 part finely chopped truffle, if you want the truffles.

BREAST OF CHICKEN MARYLAND SUPRÊME DE VOLAILLE MARYLAND (E.)

Season the breasts; roll in flour, dip in beaten egg containing a little olive oil, and roll in bread crumbs; cook in clarified butter. Place on slices of grilled bacon, surround with small fried cornmeal pancakes and fried, sliced bananas. Serve creamed Horseradish Sauce (p. 161) separately.

BREAST OF CHICKEN RÉGENCE SUPRÊME DE VOLAILLE RÉGENCE (E.)

Cut the breasts into heart shapes, flatten them gently, and poach. Place each breast on a heart-shaped slice of forcemeat made of chicken forcemeat (p. 176) containing Crayfish Butter (p. 164) ; arrange them in a circle on a round platter. Cover with Parisienne Sauce (p. 146) flavored with truffle essence; on each breast lay a truffle cut in an olive shape and a cock kidney, separating them with a cockscomb.

BREAST OF CHICKEN ROSSINI SUPRÊME DE VOLAILLE ROSSINI (E.)

Sauté the breasts in butter, place them on slices of *foie gras* sautéed in butter, and arrange in a circle on a platter. Cover with rich Madeira Sauce (p. 142) containing truffle slices.

VARIOUS POULTRY PREPARATIONS

GIBLETS BOURGUIGNONNE ABATIS À LA BOURGUIGNONNE (E.)

Fry in butter ½ lb. diced, blanched, and well-drained pork fat; in this fat fry 3 lb. giblets (except the livers, which are not added to the giblets until 10–15 min. before removing from the stove, or just enough time to poach them) with 1½ onions cut in cubes. Sprinkle with 3 tbsp. flour; cook in the oven; pour in 1 pt. red wine and 1 qt. white stock or water. Season, add a crushed clove of garlic and a *bouquet garni,* and cook slowly. About ¼ hr. before serving, drain the giblets on a cloth or fine sieve; put them into another pan and add the diced pork fat, 20 small onions cooked in butter, and the sliced livers. Simmer the sauce until reduced to the desired consistency; pour it over the giblets and garnish; finish cooking slowly. Serve in a timbale.

GIBLETS WITH TURNIPS ABATIS AUX NAVETS

Prepare the giblets as for Giblets Bourguignonne (above) , using only white stock for the liquid. When ½ cooked, put the giblets into another pan and add: the cubed pork fat, 24 small onions sautéed in butter, 1 lb. turnips cut in the shape of elongated olives, sautéed, and glazed; strain the sauce over all of this and finish cooking slowly.

WING TIPS or PINIONS AILERONS (E.)

Prepare as you would giblets, and serve as a luncheon dish. Often they are stuffed, especially those from the turkey, with fine, rather fatty sausage meat.

BROWNED WING TIPS WITH CHESTNUT PURÉE AILERONS DORÉS À LA PURÉE DE MARRONS (E.)

The wing tips of fattened pullets or young turkeys are best for this recipe.

Brown them in butter in a sautéing pan just large enough to hold them, then remove from the pan. In this same butter, lightly brown 1 carrot and 1 onion per 10 wing tips; add sprigs of parsley, thyme, and bay leaf; place the wing tips on this mixture; season with salt and pepper; cook slowly in a low oven, basting often. Add no liquid, unless perhaps a few drops of water to keep the cooking butter from clarifying if the oven is too hot; that is, cook dry.

When the wing tips are cooked, place them on a platter radiating from a center like spokes in a wheel; cover and keep hot. Add a few tbsp. clear stock to the sautéing pan, or simply water, and boil gently 10 min. When the stock is sufficiently reduced so that it will only half cover the wing tips, strain it through a cone-shaped sieve; skim lightly, if necessary, and pour over the wing tips. Serve with a timbale of fine chestnut purée.

GRILLED STUFFED WING TIPS AILERONS FARCIS GRILLÉS (E.)

Bone the wing tips, stuff them, and braise. Then cover each wing tip with 2–2½ oz. fine, truffled sausage meat; wrap each of them in a pig's caul, dip in melted butter, and grill slowly. Arrange them in a circle; pour Périgueux Sauce (p. 143) in the center or serve some sort of purée separately.

WING TIPS WITH RICE AILERONS (RIZOTTO) (E.)

Bone and stuff the wing tips with fine sausage meat mixed with 3 oz. chopped white truffle per lb. stuffing; braise in white wine. Skim the fat off the braising stock, strain, and reduce; roll the wing tips in this just before serving; place them in the center of a ring of Risotto (p. 513) on a service platter.

CHICKEN BLANQUETTE BOURGEOISE BLANQUETTE DE VOLAILLE À LA BOURGEOISE (E.)

Take a tender chicken; cut it into pieces as for a sauté; put the pieces into a pot and cover with cold water; put the pot on the fire, and when it begins to boil remove it; cool the chicken pieces in cold water and dry with a white cloth. In another pot, melt 3 tbsp. butter and blend it with 3 tbsp. flour; cook a few seconds, then add the pieces of chicken. Mix well and add enough hot water to cover the meat. Bring to a slow boil, add 1 dessertspoon salt per qt. water, a pinch of pepper, 20 small onions (1 of them stuck with a clove), a small *bouquet garni* of sprigs of parsley, bay leaf, sprigs of thyme. Cover the pot, cook slowly 50–60 min., then add some mushrooms sautéed in butter. In serving, place the chicken pieces in a deep platter and surround them with the onions and the mushrooms. Remove the *bouquet garni* from the sauce and bind it with 2 egg yolks beaten with 2 tbsp. sauce; finish the sauce by blending in a few pieces of butter. Do not let boil. Pour the sauce over the chicken.

Note: The blanquette or stew may be accompanied by Rice Pilaf (p. 512) or buttered noodles.

CHICKEN PUDDINGS and **QUENELLES** BOUDINS and QUENELLES DE VOLAILLES (E.)

Chicken Puddings belong to old-time cooking. They are shaped like small cylinders about the size of ordinary Black or Blood Puddings or are molded in small rectangular tin cases. Oval molds may also be used for quenelles, since they simplify the process of making them.

For the cylindrical puddings, the forcemeat is divided into portions weighing about 3 oz., which are rolled in the shape of a pudding and left open so that the inside may be filled with the salpicon (tiny cube mixture) called for in the recipe. The puddings are then sealed at the ends to keep in the stuffing. Molded puddings are made of a layer of forcemeat about 3 in. deep, laid in a buttered mold; this is covered with the salpicon, which in turn is covered with another layer of forcemeat smoothed into the shape of a dome.

In either case, the puddings are poached; rolled in flour, dipped in egg beaten with a little olive oil, and rolled in bread crumbs; then browned in clarified butter.

Quenelles or forcemeat balls differ from puddings in that they have no filling inside. Usually they are simply poached, but sometimes they are breaded or rolled in chopped truffles.

CHICKEN PUDDINGS CARIGNAN BOUDINS DE VOLAILLE CARIGNAN (E.)

Line small well-buttered, rectangular tin cases with fine chicken forcemeat (p. 176). Cover with a salpicon (tiny cubes) of mushrooms bound with reduced Parisienne Sauce (p. 146) ; cover with another layer of the chicken forcemeat; smooth the surface into a mound and poach in salted water. Drain and dry the puddings; roll in flour, dip in beaten egg containing a little olive oil, and roll in bread crumbs; brown in clarified butter. Arrange them, one overlapping the other, in a circle on a platter; in the center place a mound of cockscombs dipped in Frying Paste (p. 558) and fried just before serving. Serve Tomato Sauce (p. 146) separately.

Note: To poach, place the filled molds in a sautéing pan and cover with lightly salted boiling water. After a few seconds in the boiling water, the puddings will become detached from the molds and rise to the surface. Cover the pan when poaching.

CHICKEN PUDDINGS RICHELIEU BOUDINS DE VOLAILLE RICHELIEU (E.)

Chicken Forcemeat with Panada and Cream (p. 173). Mold the puddings in cases; fill the center with a salpicon (tiny cubes) of breast of chicken, truffles, and mushrooms bound with thickened Parisienne Sauce (p. 146). Poach; dry; bread (as above), and brown in clarified butter. Arrange in a circle on a napkin, one overlapping the next, with a bunch of fried parsley in the center. Serve Périgueux Sauce (p. 143) separately.

CHICKEN CAPILOTADE CAPILOTADE DE VOLAILLE (E.)

Capilotade is made with leftover roast, boiled, or braised chicken; all the bones must be removed, in any case. Cut the chicken meat into thin slices; add the meat to a pan of Italienne Sauce (p. 142) containing sliced, cooked mushrooms, and heat without boiling. Arrange in a timbale, sprinkle lightly with chopped parsley, and surround with small heart-shaped croutons fried in butter.

Fig. 253 - Chicken sauté Opéra (p. 406).
Fig. 254 - Breast of chicken Jeannette (p. 409).

Fig. 253

Fig. 254

Fig. **255**

CHICKEN CHAUD-FROID CHAUD-FROID DE VOLAILLE (E.)

Cold Dish: Poach the pullet; let it cool in its stock; then cut into even pieces and remove the skin. Dip these pieces in Chaud-Froid Sauce (p. 149) made from the chicken stock; line them up on a tray. Decorate each piece with a fine slice of truffle or bits of truffle cut in designs, glaze with Aspic Jelly (p. 168), and let set. Trim the chicken pieces before serving (Figure 256, Page 416.)

CHICKEN CHAUD-FROID MODERNE CHAUD-FROID DE VOLAILLE À LA MODERNE (M.)

Cold Dish: Either chicken or fattened pullet may be used for this dish. Cut the chicken into pieces to facilitate serving, instead of leaving the chicken whole (as in the old-style recipes), which then had to be carved after the dish was served. Cut the chicken into pieces of the same size and bone the legs. Cover the pieces with Chaud-Froid Sauce (p. 149), decorate with a slice of truffle, and glaze with Aspic Jelly (p. 168). Cockscombs and mushrooms in Chaud-Froid Sauce are always allowed with this dish. Pour a layer of Aspic Jelly into a crystal bowl or a deep round serving platter and let it set. Place the pieces of chicken, cockscombs, and mushrooms on this bed of aspic; completely cover the pieces with cold melted aspic.

CHICKEN CRÉPINETTES CRÉPINETTES DE VOLAILLE (M.)

Follow the recipe for pork Crépinettes (p. 375), using a fine forcemeat consisting of 12 oz. chicken meat (net weight after boning and skinning), 5 oz. pork, and 3½ oz. fresh pork fat, all finely chopped. Season this mixture with ½ dessertspoon salt, a good pinch white pepper, and a little grated nutmeg. Add 2 oz. diced truffles and 2 tbsp. cognac. Divide this forcemeat into portions weighing about 3 oz. Shape each portion into an oval. Place a slice of truffle on each one and wrap in a pig's caul that has been well soaked in cold water. Dip the Crépinettes in butter and grill them over a low fire.

CHICKEN CRÉPINETTES OLD STYLE CRÉPINETTES DE VOLAILLE À L'ANCIENNE (M.)

Make them with the forcemeat given in the above recipe. In the center of each Crépinette place 1 heaping tbsp. salpicon (tiny cubes) of chicken, truffles, and mushrooms bound with Allemande Sauce (p. 146). Finish in the usual way.

CHICKEN CRÉPINETTES PÉRIGOURDINE CRÉPINETTES DE VOLAILLE À LA PÉRIGOURDINE (M.)

Prepare as above, using a salpicon of *foie gras* instead of chicken.

Note: Chicken Crépinettes prepared according to any of these recipes are usually garnished with a purée, particularly of dried vegetables, potatoes, or chestnuts. Serve with Veal Gravy (p. 134) or Périgueux Sauce (p. 143).

COCKSCOMBS and COCK KIDNEYS CRÊTES ET ROGNONS DE COQ (M.)

Preparing cockscombs: Soak several hr. in cold water. Put them on the fire in fresh cold water and heat until the water becomes a little warmer than tepid. Drain the cockscombs and, while still warm, wipe them with a rough towel to remove the skin. Trim the tips of the points, skewer them on a trussing needle, and soak in cold water until they become quite white. Cook them in thin white stock. Drain, dry, and prepare according to the recipe.

Fig. 255 - Chicken galantine (p. 419).

Preparing cock kidneys: Soak in cold water until very white. Cook them in stock similar to that used in cooking cultivated mushrooms. Drain and dry, then prepare according to the recipe.

CHICKEN ÉMINCÉ BONNE FEMME ÉMINCÉ DE VOLAILLE BONNE FEMME (E.)

Place on a buttered platter, so that they overlap, round slices of potatoes that have been boiled and then lightly browned in butter. Cover the bottom of the platter with a little Velouté (p. 147) and freshly cooked, sliced mushrooms; on top place thin slices of chicken heated in advance; cover with buttered Velouté and glaze quickly in the oven.

CHICKEN ÉMINCÉ MAINTENON ÉMINCÉ DE VOLAILLE MAINTENON (E.)

Border a platter with very small chicken croquettes shaped into disks or rectangles. Place the *émincé* in the center; it should include only sliced white meat, thin slices of very white mushrooms, and slices of truffle, all bound with Parisienne Sauce (p. 146) lightly flavored with Soubise Purée (p. 504).

CHICKEN-LIVER BROCHETTES FOIES DE VOLAILLE (BROCHETTES DE) (M.)

Trim the livers, removing the gall and all adhering particles. Cut them into even-sized pieces. Season and turn in very hot butter, just enough to sear them. Place them on metal skewers, alternating them with thin squares of bacon and mushroom slices sautéed in butter. Dip these brochettes in butter and grill over a low fire. Serve with Maître d'Hôtel Butter (p. 164) or any other sauce suitable for grilled meats, such as Diable, Duxelles, Shallot, Marrow, Niçoise, etc.

CHICKEN-LIVER BROCHETTES WITH VARIOUS GARNISHES FOIES DE VOLAILLES (BROCHETTES DE) AVEC GARNITURES DIVERSES (M.)

Prepare the brochettes as above. Place them on a serving platter. Serve with one of the following garnishes (placed beside the brochettes or served separately, depending upon what it is) : various fresh vegetables, such as green beans, peas, buttered asparagus tips, buttered spinach; various vegetable purées; potatoes (creamed, Maître d'Hôtel, mashed, fried, souffléed, etc.) ; Risotto; Rice Pilaf, etc. Serve with Maître d'Hôtel Butter (p. 164) or any sauce that goes with grilled meat.

CHICKEN LIVERS IN PILAF or **PILAF OF CHICKEN LIVERS** FOIES DE VOLAILLE EN PILAF OF PILAF DE FOIES DE VOLAILLE (M.)

Season the livers with salt and pepper and sauté quickly in butter. Place them in the center of a ring of Rice Pilaf (p. 512). Baste the livers with thickened Veal Gravy (p. 134) or Tomato Sauce (p. 146).

Note: Pilaf of Chicken Livers can also be molded into a dome shape in a timbale.

SAUTÉED CHICKEN LIVERS FOIES DE VOLAILLE SAUTÉS (M.)

Prepare as you would Sautéed Mutton Kidneys (Bourguignonne, Chasseur, with mushrooms, with paprika, etc.). See p. 360.

CHICKEN FRITOT FRITOT DE VOLAILLE (E.)

Cut a boiled chicken into 5 parts: 2 legs, 2 wings, and the breast. Cut each leg into 3 pieces, the wings and the breast into 2 pieces each; place them in a deep platter, baste lightly with olive oil and lemon juice, and sprinkle with chopped parsley. Just before serving, dip the chicken pieces into thin Frying Paste (p. 558) and drop them into very hot, deep fat; drain and serve on a napkin; surround with fried parsley. Serve Tomato Sauce (p. 146) separately. May also be made with leftover chicken.

CHICKEN HASH ALSACIENNE HACHIS DE VOLAILLE À L'ALSACIENNE (P.)

Using a knife and not a grinder, chop up the leg meat and leftovers of poached chicken; blend with cream and purée of *foie gras*. Poach some noodles; mix in butter, grated cheese, and very white chopped mushrooms cooked in butter; add the proper seasoning; place the noodles around the edges of a baking dish covered with butter and grated cheese; place the hash in the center and pour a little cream over it, sprinkle with grated cheese, and brown in oven.

CHICKEN MOUSSES and MOUSSELINES MOUSSES and MOUSSELINES DE VOLAILLE (E.)

Both use Mousseline Forcemeat (p. 173) for a base, the only difference being that a mousse is usually prepared for 1 serving for all, while mousselines are made into large forcemeat balls, 1 or 2 per person.

Various recipes for mousses and mousselines are given in different parts of this book, so we shall not go any further into the subject here.

CHICKEN MOUSSELINES PATTI MOUSSELINES DE VOLAILLE PATTI (E.)

Poach the mousselines and arrange them on a platter; cover them with Suprême Sauce (p. 146) finished with Crayfish Butter (p. 164) ; in the center place a bunch of buttered asparagus tips, and, on the asparagus, a few slices of truffle covered with meat glaze.

CHICKEN NONNETTES AGNES SOREL NONNETTES DE POULET AGNÈS SOREL (E.)

Truss 12 ortolans and sear them a moment in butter. Remove the breasts from 12 spring chickens; skin the breasts, lightly flatten them, and reunite them in pairs with the edges touching, to make a larger surface. Lay 1 ortolan in the center of each one of these layers of breast of chicken; wrap the ortolan in the chicken and tie with string so they take the shape of *paupiettes,* or birds. Place these in a deep sautéing pan and, 5 min. before serving, baste with 4 oz. very hot butter. Salt lightly and bake in a hot oven. Untie the string and place each Nonnette on a square bread crouton slightly hollowed out, fried in butter, and the hollow filled with purée of *foie gras*. Coat with thin chicken glaze blended with butter; add a drop of lemon juice on each Nonnette.

CHICKEN PASCALINE PASCALINE DE POULET (E.)

Take equal parts of Choux Paste, made with milk and finished with Parmesan cheese as for Gnocchi (p. 548) , and Chicken Mousseline Forcemeat (p. 173) ; mix the 2 together. Then spread out the mixture in droplets like cookies or meringues and poach them. After poaching, place them on a buttered plate; cover them with sliced truffles and coat everything with Béchamel Sauce (p. 146) ; sprinkle grated Parmesan cheese on top, baste with melted butter, and glaze in a very hot oven or under the broiler.

CHICKEN PILAF GREEK STYLE PILAF DE VOLAILLE À LA GRECQUE (E.)

Cut the chicken into small pieces and brown in mutton fat with a large chopped onion. Sprinkle on top 1 oz. flour, pour in 2 cups white consommé; add a small diced pimento and 2 oz. dried currants and sultanas. Cook slowly. Serve in a timbale with a separate dish of Rice Pilaf (p. 512).

CHICKEN PILAF PARISIENNE PILAF DE VOLAILLE À LA PARISIENNE (E.)

Cut up the chicken as for a fricassee; season; brown in butter, and then add: 3½ oz. rice turned in butter with 1 chopped onion, 1 small bay leaf, 2 medium-sized peeled, crushed tomatoes. Pour in enough white consommé slightly more than to cover; cook 25 min. in a very hot oven. At the end of this time the chicken and rice will be cooked and the rice should be completely dry. Moisten with 3 oz. veal stock; using a fork, mix this stock carefully into the pilaf. Place in a timbale and serve with a sauceboat of Tomato Sauce (p. 146).

OLD-FASHIONED CHICKEN POULET À L'ANCIENNE MODE (P.)

Cut a chicken into pieces and cook in butter until they turn yellow but not brown. Sprinkle with flour, stir for a moment, and cover with water. Add some small onions, 1 quartered carrot, a *bouquet garni,* pepper, and salt. Cook slowly 40 min.; bind the sauce, off the fire, with 2 egg yolks mixed with a little cream. Add ½ lb. mushrooms cooked separately. Place in a deep platter with fried bread croutons around the edges and chopped parsley on top the chicken.

FONDUE OF CREAMED CHICKEN POULET À LA CRÈME (FONDUE DE) (P.)

Cut up a tender chicken as for a fricassee; place the pieces in a frying pan with a good piece of butter; add 3 sliced onions, salt, and pepper; cover the pan and simmer 20 min. at low heat; when ¾ cooked, add 1 small glass brandy, a good pinch of curry powder, and 2 cups rich cream; finish cooking the chicken. Remove the chicken, reduce the sauce until it becomes smooth, add a piece of fresh butter, and strain the sauce over the chicken, pressing the onions through the strainer. Keep hot without letting it boil, and serve very hot.

CHICKEN FRICASSEE POULET (FRICASSÉE DE) (A.) (*For 4 persons*)

Take 1¼ qt. veal and chicken stock, ½ lb. small mushrooms, 5 oz. dry white wine, 3½ oz. heavy cream, 3½ oz. butter, 1½ oz. flour, 2 fresh egg yolks, 2 onions, 1 tender, meaty chicken, 1 carrot, *bouquet garni,* lemon juice, parsley, 4 spices (see *Note,* p. 301), salt, and pepper. Cut the chicken into pieces as for a sauté; soak in water, if necessary. Peel the mushrooms and cut off the stems; set aside. Put 2 oz. butter and the chicken pieces into a pan; sear them without browning; cover the pan a few minutes to let the chicken steam; then sprinkle with flour; slowly pour in the wine and the veal and chicken stock, stirring to prevent lumps; salt, pepper, add the carrot, onions, mushroom stems, *bouquet garni,* spices to taste; cook about ½ hr. Cook the mushroom caps in the rest of the butter with some lemon juice and a little salt to keep them very white. Remove the chicken pieces; cover them and keep hot. Reduce the cooking stock and bind with the egg yolks and finish with cream. Place the chicken on a platter, surround with the mushroom caps, cover all of it with the sauce poured through a strainer, sprinkle with chopped, blanched parsley, and serve.

Garnishes most often used with chicken fricassees are: small croutons of Puff Paste (p. 544), stewed vegetables with sliced truffles, mushrooms, spring vegetables cooked in white stock, canapés spread with *foie gras,* small onions, celery, cardoons, tomatoes, artichoke bottoms, potato croquettes, noodles, Risotto, etc.

Fig. 256 - Chicken chaud-froid (p. 413).
Fig. 257 - Glazed duckling with cherries (p. 422).

Fig. 256

Fig. 257

Fig. 258

Fig. 259

CHICKEN FRICASSEE HOME STYLE POULET MÉNAGÈRE (FRICASSÉE DE) (E.) (*For 6 persons*)

Choose a tender and rather fat chicken weighing about 3 lb. Clean and cut it up as for a sauté. Put the pieces of chicken into a casserole with 1 tbsp. butter and 1 glass white wine; cover it and put it on the fire. When most of the wine has evaporated, pour in 1 qt. boiling water, add 20 small onions that have been boiled a few min.; a bunch of parsley, bay leaf, sprigs of thyme, ½ dessertspoon salt, a pinch of pepper. Boil 6–8 min., then add 2 tbsp. flour mixed with a few tbsp. cold water. Half cover the casserole and continue cooking at moderate heat 20–25 min. Finish the garnish with 15 small mushrooms sautéed in butter. Reduce the heat under the casserole until very low. Just before serving, remove the *bouquet garni,* bind the sauce with 3 egg yolks beaten in a few tbsp. sauce. Blend into the sauce 1 tbsp. butter and a pinch of chopped parsley. Buttered noodles, Rice Pilaf (p. 512), or boiled potatoes go very well with fricassee.

Note: Chicken Fricassee may also be prepared with truffles, morels (mushrooms), crayfish tails. If so, instead of water, pour in enough veal stock to cover the chicken. When the chicken is cooked, place it in a timbale; reduce the stock by ⅔, add 6 oz. Velouté (p. 147), cook a few more moments or until the sauce is thick enough to cling to a spoon. Bind the sauce with 3 egg yolks beaten with a few tbsp. fresh cream, strain through a fine sieve into a pan in which the chosen garnish has been cooking in butter, and pour over the chicken.

CHICKEN MARENGO POULET MARENGO (P.)

This well-known dish is often called Sauté Marengo, which is incorrect, since we have shown that sautéed chicken must be cooked dry and this one is cooked in a sauce. Legend has it that this recipe, conceived and first served on the battlefield of Marengo, was made from ingredients found by chance after the battle. Whether or not this is true, it is still a delicious dish.

Cut up, salt, and flour the chicken; heat the pieces in oil and when they begin to brown, add a large onion chopped in large pieces. Cook together and, when the onion has browned, add a pinch of crushed garlic, then pour in ½ glass white wine, 2 tbsp. tomato purée or ½ lb. fresh tomatoes, seeded and cut. Add 4 oz. mushrooms, salt, pepper, *bouquet garni.* Cook ¾ hr. and serve on a round platter. Garnish and decorate with fried eggs, fried croutons, and shelled crayfish. Chopped parsley on top.

CHICKEN QUENELLES WITH TONGUE QUENELLES DE VOLAILLE À L'ÉCARLATE (E.)

Chicken Mousseline Forcemeat (p. 173) mixed with 3½ oz. chopped truffles and 3½ oz. chopped, crushed raw mushrooms per 2 lb. forcemeat. Mold the quenelles in the shape of disks about 2 in. in diameter and ¼ in. thick. Poach; drain and wipe the quenelles dry; let stand until half cooled, then spread both sides with reduced Velouté (p. 147) and, on each side, stick a thin round slice of red tongue the same size as the quenelle. Roll in flour, dip in beaten egg containing a little olive oil, roll in bread crumbs; fry in clarified butter, and arrange on a napkin with a bunch of fried parsley. Serve with a sauceboat of Velouté containing very red tongue cut in julienne strips.

Fig. 258 - Nantes duckling bigarade (p. 422).
Fig. 259 - Rouen duckling sévillane (p. 428).

CHICKEN SOUFFLÉ SOUFFLÉ DE VOLAILLE (M.) (*For 5 persons*)

With uncooked chicken: This soufflé is made exactly like Chicken Mousse (p. 245), with 3 egg whites beaten stiff added per lb. mixture. It is cooked like an ordinary soufflé, except that it should cook a little longer.

Note: Chopped truffles or sliced truffles may be added to this soufflé or to the one that follows.

With cooked chicken: It is best to use braised or poached chicken white meat. Pound the meat in a mortar and press through a strainer into a sautéing pan. Per 3 cups purée, add 4 tbsp. very reduced Béchamel Sauce (p. 146); correct the seasoning and heat without boiling. Finish with 1 oz. butter, 4 egg yolks, and 5 egg whites beaten very stiff. Cook and serve the same as any other soufflé.

CHICKEN SYLPHIDES SYLPHIDES DE VOLAILLE (E.)

Mold and poach the mousselines as usual. Line the bottoms of small pastry boats with Béchamel Sauce (p. 146) mixed with shredded truffles; place a mousseline in each boat, a slice of chicken white meat on top each mousseline, and coat each lightly with Béchamel Sauce mixed with shredded truffles. Cover them with a soufflé mixture flavored with Parmesan cheese, using a pastry bag with a plain nozzle. Put the Sylphides in the oven and bake 4–5 min., just enough to cook the soufflé. Serve immediately.

TIMBALE AMBASSADRICE TIMBALE À L'AMBASSADRICE (E.)

Line the bottom of a buttered charlotte mold with rings of tongue with a circle of truffle in the center, and rings of truffle with a circle of tongue in their center; arrange the 2 kinds of rings in alternate rows. Spread this with a layer of chicken forcemeat (p. 176) and fill till ¾ full with the following garnish, alternating the noodles with the other ingredients: 7 oz. noodles with gravy, 7 oz. sliced chicken livers, 5 oz. raw, sliced mushrooms, 3½ oz. lamb sweetbreads, 3½ oz. sliced fresh truffles. The chicken livers, mushrooms, and sweetbreads should be sautéed in butter and mixed with the truffles in tomato-flavored Madeira Sauce (p. 142) containing some of the glaze from the sautéing pan. Finish filling the mold with a layer of forcemeat and poach in a *bain-marie.* Let stand several minutes after taking it out of the *bain-marie,* unmold just before serving, and pour a ribbon of Madeira Sauce around it. Serve with a separate dish of the same sauce.

POULTRY OR GAME-FOWL GALANTINE

According to Escoffier, poultry and game fowl used for a galantine can be a little tough.

After boning the poultry or game, spread it on a cloth and separate the skin from the meat. (Illustrations on pp. 108–109.)

Cut the breasts into strips; season with spiced salt and marinate in cognac with (for a medium-sized bird): 3½ oz. fresh pork fat, 2 oz. lean ham, 2 oz. red tongue, all cut into small strips, and 3½ oz. quartered truffles.

Using the meat from the legs and the remainder of the trimmings, prepare a forcemeat following the directions on p. 176. If desired, add 2 oz. chopped truffles.

Spread the skin out on a napkin and cover it with a layer of forcemeat; on top of this, place a bed of strips of white meat and truffle quarters, alternating the colors. Make another layer of forcemeat and a bed of strips of breast, and continue the operation until all the ingredients have been used. Finish with a layer of forcemeat, then draw the 2 ends of the skin together, and sew it. Next, wrap the galantine in strips of pork fat; roll it in a cloth; tie it with string, tightening it especially at both ends.

Variation: Cut the chicken breast meat, ham, tongue, pork fat, and truffle quarters into large cubes; mix them directly into the forcemeat, adding 5 oz. freshly blanched pistachios. Spread the mixture on the skin and roll into a galantine as above. This method is simpler and easier, and the galantine, when cut, is almost the same in appearance as when the strips of breast are laid out in a mosaic pattern.

Cooking the galantine: Plunge it into white stock containing blanched veal bones, chicken carcasses, ordinary flavoring agents such as onions, parsley, carrot, etc., and 1 dessertspoon salt per qt. liquid. Keep at a very slow boil; allow about 35 min. poaching time per 2 lb. galantine.

Pressing the galantine: When the galantine is cooked, drain it, unwrap it, then tie it up again tightly in the same cloth or in another clean cloth. Place it in some long utensil and cover with a board; weight the board, but not too heavily, and let cool under pressure. The purpose of pressing the galantine is simply to fuse the different ingredients, which may have become separated while cooking. If the pressure is too great, the juices run out and the galantine is dry and tasteless.

Serving: When the galantine is completely cold, unwrap it, wipe it off, and coat with cold melted Aspic Jelly (p. 168) until it is completely covered with a thick layer. Next, place it on a long, very cold platter, surround it with chopped aspic, and border the plate with squares of aspic.

CHICKEN GALANTINE GALANTINE DE VOLAILLE (A.) (*For 18 to 20 persons*)

Cold Dish: Take: 1 well-fattened chicken between 1 and 2 years old and weighing about 3 lb.; strips of pork fat or bacon.

Garnish: 10 oz. *foie gras,* ½ lb. red tongue, ½ lb. lean ham, 7 oz. pork fat, 5 oz. Madeira, port, or sherry, 3½ oz. truffles, 2 oz. cognac, 1 oz. blanched pistachios, breasts of the chicken, salt, spices.

Forcemeat: 1 lb. trimmed, lean veal, 10 oz. fresh pork, ⅘ lb. chicken meat, 1 dessertspoon salt, a pinch of pepper, 2 fresh eggs, 4 spices (see *Note*, p. 301).

Cooking Stock: 1 lb. veal knuckle, 1 lb. leg of beef, 7 oz. round of beef without any fat, 7 oz. white wine, 5 oz. carrots, 3 oz. fresh bacon rind, 2 oz. onions, 1½ oz. Madeira, port, or sherry, 1 tbsp. salt, 3 qt. water, 3 egg whites, 2 calf's feet, 2 cloves, chicken carcass and giblets, *bouquet garni.* Clean and singe the chicken without blackening it; remove the giblets and neck, leaving the skin of the neck attached to the chicken. Make a cut down the back of the chicken to the jointure of the legs and remove the bones completely. Pull the tendons out of the legs; remove the breasts from the breastbones without damaging them; set aside ⅘ lb. of meat from the thicker parts of the chicken for the forcemeat.

Preparing the cooking stock: Put into a deep pot water, veal knuckle, and calf's feet, leg of beef, chicken giblets and carcass, blanched pork rind; bring to a boil and skim; then add carrots, onions, *bouquet garni,* cloves, salt; simmer slowly 5 hr. Strain, let cool, and skim off the fat.

Preparing the garnish: Marinate the tongue, lean ham, pork fat, chicken breasts, truffles, and *foie gras* for a few hours in Madeira, port, or sherry with cognac. Remove from the marinade and cut the tongue, ham, pork fat, and breasts into fairly thick strips, the truffles and *foie gras* in cubes. Season with salt and spices.

Preparing the forcemeat: Mash in a mortar first the lean veal, then the pork, and next the chicken meat set aside for this; mix them together; mash again while mixing in salt, pepper, spices to taste, the remainder of the marinade, and the eggs; press this forcemeat through a sieve; taste.

Preparing the galantine: Spread the boned chicken on a cloth and remove all the meat uniformly from the skin; season with salt, pepper, spices; spread a layer of forcemeat on the skin and on top of this a layer of the strips and cubes of the various marinated ingredients, alternating the colors and decorating with pistachios; repeat the operation until all the ingredients have been used. Roll the stuffed chicken skin into a long even loaf completely covered by the skin, the skin of the legs completely tucked in; first wrap in thin strips of pork fat, then in a strong piece of cloth that has been soaked and wrung out; squeeze tightly and tie the 2 ends with string; also tie string around the roll in 2 or 3 places. Place the galantine, thus prepared, in the prepared cooking stock; add the white wine and simmer 2–2¼ hr. When it is cooked and cooled a bit, drain it and unwrap; wrap back in the same cloth after washing it with warm water or in another clean cloth after wetting and wringing it; press tightly and sew the cloth. Place the galantine in a long pan with the sewn side down; cover with a board not too heavily weighted; let cool under pressure. Reduce the cooking stock; let cool, and skim off the fat.

Preparing the aspic: Put the round of beef, chopped fine, and the egg whites into a stewing pan; pour the cold, skimmed stock on top; mix with a wire whisk or spatula; bring slowly to a boil, gently stirring; continue cooking at low heat ¼ hr., then add the Madeira, port, or sherry; let come to a boil a few times, then strain through a cloth; taste.

Serving: Remove the galantine from the cloth; wipe off the excess fat; coat with the melted cool aspic until the layer is about ¼ in. thick. Place on a long platter; surround with chopped aspic, and decorate the border with croutons of aspic cut in the shape of narrow triangles.

Turkey Galantine is prepared the same way. (Fig. 255, Page 413.)

TERRINES

Terrines are simply meat pies without a crust. Except for certain details in preparation, all meat pies or *pâtés* may be made into terrines. (See Mixed Entrees, p. 529.)

Preparing the Terrine: Regardless of the type of Terrine, the crock must first be lined with strips of pork fat, then it is filled with successive layers of forcemeat, slices of the principal ingredient, strips of fat, and truffles. In making Terrines of poultry and game fowl, the filling can be enclosed in the skin, as when making Duckling Pie (p. 534). Once the Terrine is filled, a strip of pork fat, a pinch of spices, and a little bay leaf are laid on top; the cover is then clamped on.

Fig. 260 - Rouen duckling Montmorency (p. 427).

Fig. 260

Fig. 261

Fig. 262

Cooking the Terrine: Place the crock in a shallow baking pan filled with a little boiling water and put into a medium-hot oven; renew the water when necessary during the cooking. Cooking time varies according to the size of the Terrine and the nature of its ingredients. For lack of any precise method of determining when it is cooked, an examination of the fat rising to the surface may give some idea. If the fat seems cloudy and uneven it is because various ingredients in the Terrine are still giving off juices, which, mixing with the fat, discolor it. But if it is clear, it may be assumed that the Terrine is thoroughly cooked. You can also stick a long needle to the bottom of the Terrine to test if it is cooked. If the needle comes out hot from one end to the other, the Terrine is cooked.

Pressing and serving: If the Terrine is to be eaten immediately, it should be finished with aspic a few minutes after it is taken from the oven, weighted with a board, and allowed to cool under not too much pressure (for the same reasons given in the recipe for Chicken Galantine). The fat is next removed, the top trimmed, and the Terrine cut into portions in the crock. If it is to be served whole, it should be pressed a little more heavily and unmolded when cold, well trimmed all around, and replaced in the crock, the bottom of which should be lined with a layer of aspic, with melted aspic poured in around the sides.

Just before serving, unmold onto a napkin and surround with croutons of aspic. If the Terrine is to be preserved, it is unmolded and trimmed as above, replaced in the mold, surrounded and covered with lard to protect it from contact with the air. Keep covered in a cool place.

TERRINES and **PÂTÉS HOME STYLE** TERRINES and PÂTÉS À LA MÉNAGÈRE (E.)

These homely recipes from olden days deserve to be included here so that they will not be forgotten. They may be made with all meats, poultry, or game fowl. The following preparation is standard. Cut the necessary quantity of veal tenderloin or fillet into large slivers; season with salt, pepper, and nutmeg; sear them quickly in butter and drop into a crock. Add strips of ham and pork fat, 4 parts of veal to 1 of them. Melt the glaze in the sautéing pan with a little cognac and Madeira, pour this over the veal, ham, and pork fat; let cool. Line a crock with strips of pork fat or make an ordinary pie crust; fill either one with alternate layers of veal and strips of bacon or pork fat; cover the terrine or pie crust and cook in a very hot oven. When the Terrine or Pâté has cooled until merely tepid, finish by filling it with ordinary Aspic Jelly (p. 168) or with aspic made from the strong stock of the principal ingredient.

VARIOUS FOWL

DUCKS AND DUCKLINGS

In French cooking, 3 types of ducks are differentiated: those from Nantes, those from Rouen, and the varieties of wild duck. The last are usually prepared as roasts or salmis.

Rouen duck is also treated as a roast rather than an entree. Since it is tra-

Fig. 261 - Duckling timbale Voisin (p. 429).
Fig. 262 - Goose alsacienne (p. 430).

ditionally served rare, it is not often braised. Unlike other fowl, which are killed by being bled, Rouen duck is choked to death.

Nantes duck, which is less fleshy than Rouen duck, is usually braised, pan-roasted, or roasted.

Note: Since it is customary to list these birds on the menu as ducklings, we shall use this term for all the recipes for Nantes and Rouen ducks.

DUCKLING ENGLISH STYLE CANETON À L'ANGLAISE (M.) (*For 6 persons*)

Bake 1 lb. large, unpeeled onions in the oven. Cool, peel, and chop fine. Add an equal amount of soaked, pressed bread and 1 oz. chopped sage leaves to the onions. Season with salt, pepper, and nutmeg. Stuff the duckling with this mixture. Roast it on a spit or in the oven. Serve with the cooking juices, unskimmed, and a dish of slightly sweetened applesauce.

GLAZED DUCKLING WITH CHERRIES or DUCKLING MONTMORENCY CANETON GLACÉ AUX CERISES OF MONTMORENCY (E.)

Cold Dish: Roast the duckling, keeping it rare. When it is cold, slice off the breasts and remove the bones to form a sort of case within the carcass. Slice each breast into 8 strips; cover with Brown Chaud-Froid Sauce (p. 139) and decorate with truffles. Fill the carcass with a mousse made from the trimmings of the meat, *foie gras,* and the duckling liver, building it up into the natural shape of the breast. Glaze with Aspic Jelly (p. 168) and place in the refrigerator to harden the mousse. When the mousse is rather firm, cover it with the slices of breast in Chaud-Froid Sauce. Place the duckling in a deep platter. Decorate the breast with a few cherries, and surround the duckling with pitted cherries poached in Bordeaux and chilled; cover these with aspic flavored with duck stock. The cherries may be placed in little tartlets. (Figure 257, Page 416.)

NANTES DUCKLING BIGARADE CANETON NANTAIS À LA BIGARADE (M.)

Truss with the legs pulled back; pan-roast in butter. Place on a platter. Cover with Bigarade Sauce (p. 138). On the edge of the platter make a border of fluted half slices of orange. Serve the remainder of the Bigarade Sauce separately. (Figure 258, Page 417.)

Note: May also be braised.

NANTES DUCKLING WITH CHERRIES CANETON NANTAIS AUX CERISES (M.)

Pan-roast in butter. Place on a service platter. Melt the glaze in the pan with Madeira, pour in a few tbsp. thickened veal stock, simmer, and strain. Poach 7 oz. pitted cherries in this sauce. Drain the cherries and arrange them around the duck. Add 1 tbsp. cherry brandy to the sauce and pour it over the duckling and cherries.

Note: Nantes Duckling with Cherries may also be served in an oval cocotte.

NANTES DUCKLING CÉVENOLE CANETON NANTAIS À LA CÉVENOLE (M.)

Braise in brown stock. When it is almost cooked, put it into a terrine or an earthenware baking dish. Surround with a garnish of lean bacon (blanched and browned), half-cooked chestnuts, and small glazed onions.

Pour the braising stock, reduced and strained, over duckling and garnish. Cover the baking dish and finish cooking in the oven at low heat.

NANTES DUCKLING LADY CATHERINE CANETON NANTAIS DAME CATHERINE (M.)

Stuff the duckling with a mixture of equal parts of Light Forcemeat (p. 173) and Gratin Forcemeat (p. 175) containing cubed lamb sweetbreads sautéed in butter and diced truffles well seasoned and moistened with a little cognac. Pan-roast in butter. Place it on a round platter on a bed of Rich Rice (p. 512). Garnish with stuffed olives, truffles, and mushrooms.

Sauce: Melt the glaze in the pan with Madeira, add thickened veal stock, reduce, and strain.

NANTES DUCKLING WITH TURNIPS CANETON NANTAIS AUX NAVETS (M.)

(*For 6 persons*)

Truss with the legs pulled back. Brown in butter in a casserole. When it is well browned on all sides, remove from the casserole. Melt the glaze in the casserole with 4 oz. dry white wine, add 4 oz. thickened brown veal stock, and reduce. Place the duckling in this sauce and add a *bouquet garni.* Cover and cook at low heat.

Brown separately in butter 1 lb. turnips cut like large beans (blanch the turnips if they are old). Sprinkle the turnips with a little sugar to assure their browning. Half cook and glaze 5 oz. small onions. When the duckling is ½ cooked, place it in another casserole. Surround it with the turnips and small onions. Pour the strained cooking sauce from the first casserole over it. Finish cooking duckling and vegetables together. Arrange the duckling on a platter and surround with the garnish.

NANTES DUCKLING WITH OLIVES CANETON NANTAIS AUX OLIVES (M.)

Braise the same as Duckling with Turnips (above). When the duckling is almost cooked, encircle it with 10 oz. pitted, blanched olives and finish cooking together.

NANTES DUCKLING WITH ORANGE CANETON NANTAIS À L'ORANGE (M.)

Prepare like Nantes Duckling Bigarade (p. 422), using sweet instead of bitter orange.

Note: This duckling may also be braised.

DUCKLING WITH RUSSET APPLES CANETON AUX POMMES DE REINETTE (R.)

Peel 2 or 3 fine russet apples. Quarter, cut out the cores, and cook them in ½ cup water. Sugar lightly, add a little cinnamon, and reduce to a purée. Stuff the duckling with the apple purée and sew the opening tightly with string so that the apples will not run out. Pour 1 wineglass vinegar into a pan, add 2 pieces of butter the size of a nut, sprinkle with 1 tbsp. powdered sugar, and bring to a boil. Roast the duckling and baste with this sauce. After it has cooked ½ hr., untruss the duck and strain the gravy from the roasting. Add 1 heaping tbsp. red-currant jelly, heat without boiling, and serve.

Wild duck and wild goose may be prepared the same way, which is not particularly unusual, since duck is cooked with oranges or cherries.

ROUEN DUCKLING IN CHAMBERTIN CANETON ROUENNAIS AU CHAMBERTIN (M.)

Stuff the duckling with Gratin Forcemeat (p. 175) mixed with *foie gras* and truffles; truss with legs pulled back. Braise it in Chambertin in the usual way. When it is almost cooked, untruss and put into an earthenware casserole or tin-lined cocotte with a garnish of strips of bacon (blanched, then browned in butter), artichoke bottoms, and sliced mushrooms. Pour the braising stock, strained and reduced (if necessary), over duckling and garnish. Cover and finish cooking in the oven at low heat. Ten min. before serving, add 3½ oz. thick-sliced truffles to the casserole. Serve in the same dish it was cooked in.

Note: Generally, Rouen ducklings are not braised. They are prepared this way only when they are to be served cold. We believe, however, in braising Rouen ducklings. We have found from experience that braised ducklings are no less flavorsome than roasted or pan-roasted ones, provided they are braised in stock very rich in meat extracts.

ROUEN DUCKLING IN CHAMBERTIN (PAN-ROASTED) CANETON ROUENNAIS AU CHAMBERTIN (POÊLÉ) (M.)

Stuff the same as the braised duckling, above; truss and pan-roast in butter.

Garnish: The same as above.

Sauce: Melt the glaze in the pan with Chambertin, add Semiglaze Sauce (p. 138) containing mushroom essence, reduce, and strain.

Note: Rouen Duckling in Chambertin may be served on a crouton of fried bread spread with Gratin Forcemeat (p. 175) and lightly browned in the oven or under the broiler.

ROUEN DUCKLING IN SKIN CANETON ROUENNAIS EN CHEMISE (M.)

Stuff the duckling as for Stuffed Duckling Rouennaise (p. 425). Truss it and put into a very hot oven 8–10 min. to brown on all sides. Place it in a pig's bladder that has been well soaked in cold water, taking care to place the tail end toward the opening of the bladder. Tie the opening tightly, to seal in the duckling completely. Wrap in a fine cloth and tie both ends. Cook in clear stock. Poach at a low, even boil 30–35 min. Drain the duckling and remove the cloth. Serve on an oval platter without removing the bladder. Carve like Stuffed Duckling Rouennaise. Serve with Rouennaise Sauce (p. 145).

JUGGED ROUEN DUCKLING CANETON ROUENNAIS (CIVET DE) (A.) (*For 8 persons*)

Take: 1 cup bouillon, ½ lb. pork fat, ½ lb. mushrooms, 3½ oz. rabbit blood, 2 oz. butter, 2 oz. brandy, 3 tbsp. flour, 2 tsp. bay salt, 1 tsp. mixture of equal parts of powdered wild thyme, oregano, savory, and hyssop, a pinch of freshly ground pepper, pinch of allspice, 1 bottle good red wine, 20 small onions, 4 shallots, 3 duck livers, 1 freshly killed Rouen duck, 1 *bouquet garni.* Cut open the duck and drain the blood, saving it. Cut the pork fat into pieces. Mash the duck liver and the 3 extra livers with the duck blood and rabbit blood. Brown the pieces of duck and pork fat in a pan with butter. When the duckling is golden brown, remove it and put the onions into the same pan. Remove the onions when they begin to brown, then stir in and brown the flour. Then replace the duck and pork fat in the pan, set aflame with the brandy; pour in the bouillon and wine; add the onions, *bouquet garni,* shallots, herbs, spices, salt, and pepper, and cook at low heat at least 2 hr. Then strain the sauce, skim off all the fat, put in the peeled mushrooms, and continue cooking ½ hr. Thicken the sauce with the mashed livers and heat for a few moments without letting it boil. Lay the duckling and onions on a platter, pour the sauce over, and serve.

This is a really remarkable dish. It is a true consolation to the sportsman in summer, when game is hard to find. Delicious the day it is made, it is even better the next day, reheated in a *bain-marie.*

The same recipe can be used for preparing Jugged Wild Goose, Pigeons, or Chicken; the last is also called Chicken in Blood.

Jugged Turkey can be made the same way, the flavor heightened with Madeira 20 min. before it is through cooking.

Potato croquettes are the best accompaniment for jugged dishes.

ROUEN DUCKLING IN DODINE or **DODINE OF DUCKLING** CANETON ROUENNAIS EN DODINE OF DODINE DE CANETON (M.)

(*Very old recipe*) (1) Truss the duckling and roast it, keeping it very rare. (2) Cut off the breasts and keep hot in a covered dish. Remove the legs (not served). Remove the tail and mash the remainder of the carcass in a mortar.

Sauce: Reduce by ⅔, as quickly as possible, 9 oz. Chambertin with 2 liqueur glasses cognac, 1 dessertspoon chopped shallot, a little ground pepper, and a dash of nutmeg. Add the mashed carcass to this reduced liquid. Pour in 9 oz. very rich, thickened brown veal stock. Boil 15 min. Press this sauce through a cone-shaped sieve. Boil again 5 min. more, remove from the fire, and add 2 oz. butter.

Serving: Slice each breast of the duckling into 3 or 4 slices. Lay these slices in a silver timbale. On top place a garnish of medium-sized mushroom caps and sliced truffles cooked in butter. Cover with the sauce above. Let simmer. Serve with fresh noodles in browned butter.

Note: Dodine is one of the oldest sauces in French cooking. As we shall show by the following recipe—taken from one of the most ancient cookbooks, *Le Grand Cuisinier de toute cuisine,* written between 1350 and 1370, and, according to Taillevent, the inspiration for Guillaume Tirel's *Le Viandier* (about 1373) —it was made quite differently in olden times from the way we make it today.

Red Dodine (recipe taken from the *Grand Cuisinier de toute cuisine*) : "Take thy black bread and roast it very brown on the grill and soak it in strong ruby-red wine; then fry onion rings in pork fat and press thy bread through a sieve; then for spices: cinnamon, nutmeg, and boil everything together with the fat from the duck. And when it is cooked, pour it on thy duck (or river bird)."

Here is another recipe for a Dodine made in those days:

White Dodine: "To make white dodine, take cow's milk, centers of hard-boiled eggs [yolks], white powder [probably flour], well-fried onion rings. Put it all through a strainer and cook it in a frying pan, not forgetting to add sugar, a little salt, and the fat of thy duck."

STUFFED DUCKLING ROUENNAISE CANETON FARCI À LA ROUENNAISE (M.)
(*For 6 persons*)

Forcemeat: May be made 2 ways. The first is simply a Gratin Forcemeat (p. 175) prepared with the liver of the duck to be cooked, with a few chicken livers added.

The second method, which we ourselves use, is as follows (proportions for a 5-lb. duckling). Cook 2 oz. finely chopped shallots until transparent in 3½ oz.

grated pork fat. Add the duck liver and 3 or 4 chicken livers, all chopped fine. Brown quickly. Season with salt, freshly ground pepper, and grated nutmeg and, at the last moment, add 3 tbsp. very reduced, thickened veal stock. Stuff the duckling with this forcemeat. Push the tail inside to close the opening. Truss the duckling. Roast on a spit or in the oven 20–25 min., depending on the size of the bird. Place on a long platter.

Serving: (1) Cut off the legs; make little slits on the undersides of the legs; season them with salt, ground pepper, a little crushed clove, and grill them. (2) Remove the forcemeat from the inside of the duckling and place it in the center of a long platter on an alcohol stove or plate warmer. (3) Slice the breasts into thin strips and place these on each side of the forcemeat. Place the grilled legs at each end of the platter; season with a little freshly ground pepper. (4) Cut the carcass into tiny pieces, pour over 2 tbsp. brandy, and press it. Add the blood that comes out to Rouennaise Sauce (p. 145). Heat this sauce without boiling it and coat the strips of breast with it. Serve rest of sauce separately.

DUCKLING ROUENNAISE I (Recipe from the Hôtel de la Couronne, in Rouen) CANETON À LA ROUENNAISE (M.)

(1) Choke a fleshy young duckling to death and immediately pluck the feathers from the breast so that the blood will rush to it.

(2) Clean it, taking care not to lose the blood; remove the breastbone, replace the liver in the stomach cavity after removing the gall. Do not season the inside of the duckling.

(3) Roast the duckling 12–14 min. in a very hot oven.

(4) Butter a long platter; sprinkle it with ½ tbsp. finely chopped shallot. Season with freshly milled salt, ground pepper, and a pinch of 4 spices (see *Note*, p. 301). Pour a finger of Meat Glaze (p. 135) around this seasoning.

(5) Cut off the legs of the duckling (which, because of the short cooking time, are almost raw), score the undersides and season them; then grill them. Slice the breasts into fine strips. Place these strips in a row on the platter. Pour a little flaming brandy over the strips and season moderately with salt, pepper, and spices.

(6) Chop the carcass and the liver. Pour ½ glass red wine over them and press well to squeeze out all the juice. Add 1 heaping tbsp. melted butter to this juice and pour over the strips of breast. Heat the platter slightly on the stove, then put for a few moments into a very hot oven to glaze the sauce. At each end of the platter place a grilled leg.

(Recipe of MM. Dorin Frères.)

Note: This dish is a sort of salmis. On the menus it is usually called Salmis of Duckling Rouennaise (*Salmis de caneton à la rouennaise*). In Rouen, a city of great gourmets, there is another famous restaurant, the Cathédrale, where this salmis is prepared slightly differently. Here is the recipe, given to us by MM. L. Convert and J. Schwartz, owners of the restaurant:

DUCKLING ROUENNAISE II (Recipe from the Restaurant de la Cathédrale) CANETON À LA ROUENNAISE (M.)

Prepare the duckling as directed in steps 1, 2, and 3 of the preceding recipe.

Reduce 1 glass wine with ½ tbsp. finely chopped shallot. Then add 1 or 2 tbsp. Semiglaze Sauce (p. 138). Season and spice moderately. Strain this sauce over the chopped raw liver of the duckling. Mix and pour into a timbale containing 3 or 4 tbsp. flaming cognac. Pour this sauce over the strips of duckling arranged on a platter as described on p. 426. Place the grilled legs at each end of the platter and simmer on an alcohol stove or plate warmer.

Here is still another way to prepare the dish, used at the Hôtel de la Poste, in Duclair. This restaurant is known to gourmets the world over, who come there to savor Denise's Duckling, the recipe for which has been kindly given to us by M. Léon Duhamel, M. Denise's son-in-law and owner of the restaurant:

FATHER DENISE'S DUCKLING ROUENNAISE (Recipe from the Hôtel de la Poste, in Duclair, Seine-Inférieure) CANETON À LA ROUENNAISE DU PÈRE DENISE (M.)

Truss the duckling (choked to death) and roast on a spit 20–22 min., depending on size, with its liver (cleaned) replaced inside and the wings entirely boned down to the joint, then resewn.

Prepare the following mixture separately: cook 1 chopped onion in butter; pour some port and Burgundy over it and reduce. After the duckling is cooked, add its crushed liver to this onion.

Serving: Cut off the legs, season, and grill them. Slice the breast into thin strips. Arrange these strips on a platter around the breastbone of the duckling; the breastbone should be covered with the puréed onions (given above) mixed with the blood obtained by pressing the chopped carcass of the duckling, all of this seasoned with freshly milled salt, pepper, and spices. Place the legs at each end of the platter.

ROUEN DUCKLING MONTMORENCY CANETON ROUENNAIS MONTMORENCY (H.M.) (*For 10 persons*)

Cold Dish: (1) *The day before serving:* Take 2 Rouen ducklings, each weighing 3 lb. or slightly more, roast them (rare), put them in a deep pan with the breasts down (so the blood stays in them).

(2) *The day of serving:* Cut up the ducks, skin the breasts, bone the legs, set aside the carcasses, necks, and wings for the aspic. Put the chopped carcasses, 2 lb. lean beef, and all the ingredients needed to make aspic into 3 qt. good clear brown veal stock; flavor it with a glass of cherry brandy (the color of the aspic should be ruby red).

(3) Remove the tendons from the legs, mash them, and press through a sieve and mix with the same quantity of poached *foie gras* also pressed through a sieve; season this purée; blend it in with 3 oz. lightly whipped fresh cream, 3 oz. very reduced aspic, and 1 glass cherry brandy, working it with a wooden spatula. Put this mousse into the refrigerator to set. Fill a pastry bag with the mousse and mold it on a round silver platter, fashioning it into the shape of an aspic with a hot metal spatula. Place the 4 duck wings on top of the mousse; decorate the sides with truffle, egg white, and tomato pulp glazed with aspic.

(4) Slice the breasts into thin strips (about 12 to each duck); place them on a wire rack, decorate them like the mousse, and glaze with aspic.

(5) Take 1 qt. pitted Montmorency cherries, cook them quickly in cherry

brandy (the lid on the pan tightly closed), let cool, and glaze them by rolling them in a tray of melted aspic. They may also be stuffed with mousse and glazed on a wire rack.

(6) *Arrangement:* Place the aspic in the center of the platter on a bed of jelly with the strips of breast fanned out around it, and a string of cherries between the edge of the platter and the slices of breast. Using a pastry bag, squeeze a ribbon of jelly around the slices of breast and in a border on the outer edges of the cherries.

Dish prepared by Henri Mercier, head chef. (Figure 260, Page 420.)

PRESSED ROUEN DUCKLING CANETON ROUENNAIS À LA PRESSE (M.)

Roast the duckling 20–25 min., depending on weight. Cut off the legs and grill them. Slice the breasts into thin strips. Place them on a silver platter on which you have previously reduced ½ glass red wine (preferably Burgundy). Keep hot on an alcohol stove or chafing dish. Chop the carcass, pour ½ glass red wine over it, and press tightly. Add to the juice obtained 2 tbsp. cognac; season, add 1 tbsp. butter, and pour over the strips of breast.

Note: Sometimes a few drops of lemon juice are added to the sauce.

ROUEN DUCKLING SÉVILLANE CANETON ROUENNAIS À LA SÉVILLANE (E.)

Cold Dish: Bone the breast of the duckling; stuff with forcemeat made of 3½ oz. Gratin Forcemeat (p. 175), 3½ oz. Mousseline Forcemeat (p. 173), 3 oz. very reduced tomato purée, and 3½ oz. raw *foie gras* cut in cubes. Truss the duckling; wrap it in cheesecloth; poach it 1 hr. in good stock. After cooking, tighten the cheesecloth and let cool in the cooking stock. Unwrap the duckling; cut off the breasts and slice into thin strips; replace these over the stuffing and coat the duckling with Chaud-Froid Sauce (p. 139) containing sherry. Glaze with Aspic Jelly (p. 168); place in an oval crystal bowl or in a deep square platter on a bed of hardened aspic; surround with large, pitted Spanish olives stuffed with purée of *foie gras* and half covered with aspic; the breasts may also be decorated with a few slices of stuffed olives. (Figure 259, Page 417.)

SOUFFLÉED ROUEN DUCKLING I CANETON ROUENNAIS SOUFFLÉ (M.)

Pan-roast a large Rouen duckling, keeping it very rare. Slice off the breasts and cut out the breastbones with scissors to make a sort of case formed by the carcass and the legs.

Forcemeat: In principle, this forcemeat, which is prepared like chicken Mousseline Forcemeat (p. 173), should be made with the meat of another duck, smaller than the first. Mash finely in a mortar the boned and trimmed raw meat of the duckling, together with the liver of the duckling being prepared, 3½ oz. raw *foie gras,* and 1 egg white. Season this forcemeat and flavor with a little brandy. Press through a fine sieve; finish like ordinary Mousseline Forcemeat. Stuff the carcass of the duckling with this composition, smoothing it into the original shape of the breast. Wrap the duckling in a double thickness of buttered paper. Cover and poach in the oven 20 min. Place the duckling on a long platter. Surround it with tartlets filled with a salpicon (tiny cubes) of *foie gras* and truffles bound with reduced Semiglaze Sauce (p. 138) flavored with truffle essence, and on each tartlet place a slice of duckling breast.

Sauce: Rouennaise (p. 145) or Périgueux Sauce (p. 143).

Fig. 263 - Squab dressed as a toad (p. 432).
Fig. 264 - Roast guinea hen (p. 433).

Fig. 263

Fig. 264

Fig. 265

Fig. 266

Note: In addition to the tartlets covered with breast of duckling, Souffléed Duckling may be accompanied by various garnishes such as: peas, asparagus tips, mushrooms, truffles, etc.

SOUFFLÉED ROUEN DUCKLING II CANETON ROUENNAIS SOUFFLÉ (M.)

Pan-roast in butter, 20–25 min., 1 large and 1 small trussed Rouen duckling. Make a circular incision around the breast of the better of the 2 ducklings, as described in the preceding recipe. Keep the breasts for garnishing the dish. Bone the second duckling completely. Trim the meat, disposing of the skins and tendons. Mash this meat in a mortar, adding ⅓ its volume in Gratin Forcemeat (p. 175) and cooked *foie gras* as well as 1 egg white. Season with salt and paprika and press through a fine sieve. Place this mixture in a bowl on ice and work into it, little by little, 9 oz. heavy cream. At the last moment add 2 beaten egg whites. Fill the first duckling with this mixture. Smooth the surface to reshape the breast. Cover with buttered paper and poach in the oven as described in the preceding recipe.

Garnish: Duckling breasts cut into tiny cubes and mixed with an equal quantity of diced truffles, bound with Semiglaze Sauce (p. 138) flavored with truffle essence. Fill small patty shells with this salpicon and arrange around the duckling.

Sauce: Melt the glaze in the roasting pan with port, add veal stock, reduce, and strain.

DUCKLING TIMBALE VOISIN TIMBALE DE CANETON VOISIN (E.)

Cold Dish: Roast a Rouen duckling, keeping it rare; let cool and remove the breasts. Use the carcass to make Salmis Sauce (p. 145) ; bind it, as for Chaud-Froid Sauce, with gelatin. Slice the breasts and cover these with the Salmis Sauce and let stand until set. Spread a layer of sauce in the bottom of a timbale crust and let stand until set; on top of this alternate the Chaud-Froid Sauced slices of breast with truffle slices and cover with a thin layer of Aspic Jelly (p. 168) ; repeat until filled. Finish with a slightly thicker layer of aspic and keep cool until serving. (Figure 261, Page 421.)

Note: This old and excellent cold entree is simply a cold salmis. The same recipe may be applied to all game birds that can be prepared as salmis. It is the simplest and certainly the best way to serve them cold.

YOUNG TURKEY

YOUNG TURKEY BOURGEOISE DINDONNEAU À LA BOURGEOISE (M.)

Truss the turkey and braise the usual way, using somewhat gelatinous white stock. After 1¼ hr. (⅔ of the cooking time), remove the turkey, strain the braising stock, and skim off the fat. Replace the turkey in the pan after rinsing it or put into a clean pan; surround it with a Bourgeoise Garnish in proportion to the size of the turkey (carrots cut in the shape of olives and blanched, small onions browned in butter, strips of browned bacon). Finish cooking. Glaze the turkey just before serving. Serve on a platter surrounded with the garnish or serve the latter separately.

Note: Generally, turkeys and young turkeys are roasted on a spit or in the oven; the few recipes given in this work should be sufficient.

Fig. 265 - Sliced foie gras Monselet (p. 436).
Fig. 266 - Small foie gras aspics (p. 438).

YOUNG TURKEY (or TURKEY) WITH CHESTNUTS DINDONNEAU (or DINDE) AUX MARRONS (M.) (*For 12 persons*)

For a turkey or young turkey weighing 6–8 lb. after cleaning and trimming, take 2 lb. fine pork forcemeat (p. 173) mixed with 2 lb. (about 60) shelled, peeled chestnuts ½ cooked in consommé and completely cooled. Remove the breastbone of the turkey and stuff with forcemeat and chestnuts. Remove the tendons from the legs, truss the turkey, and cover the breast with strips of pork fat or bacon. Roast in the oven or on a spit. Serve the roasting gravy separately.

Optional: Surround the turkey with water cress.

TRUFFLED YOUNG TURKEY DINDONNEAU TRUFFÉ (M.) (*For 12 persons*)

Proportions of stuffing for a turkey weighing 6½ lb.: 3 lb. fresh pork fat, 1½ lb. truffles (net weight after washing and peeling), 10 oz. fresh *foie gras,* if desired. If the *foie gras* is added to the stuffing, leave out that amount of pork fat.

Preparation: In a mortar mash the pork fat with the truffle peelings and, if used, the *foie gras.* Press this through a sieve with a rather large mesh. Season with salt, pepper, and spices. Sauté ¼ of this mixture and add truffles, quartered or halved, to poach with it. Add these truffles to the remainder of the pork-fat mixture. Mix well; let cool. Clean the turkey from the front end and, after removing the wishbone, stuff with this mixture. Slide large slices of truffles between the skin and flesh. Truss and cover the breast well with strips of pork fat or bacon.

Cooking: In principle, since turkey is roasted in the oven or on a spit, it should stand 1 or 2 days, once it is truffled. Cover it with buttered paper. Roast it in the oven in an uncovered roasting pan, 10 min. per lb., or 12 min. per lb. if roasted on a spit. Serve with its own roasting gravy or Périgueux Sauce (p. 143).

ROAST, TRUFFLED YOUNG TURKEY (or TURKEY) DINDONNEAU (or DINDE) TRUFFÉ RÔTI (A.) (*For 12 persons*)

Truffled turkey is often found on traditional menus. Here is an excellent way to prepare it.

Take: 1 tender, fleshy turkey, without giblets, 1 fine *foie gras*, 1 fine strip of pork fat or bacon, the desired amount of black Périgord truffles (at least 1 lb.), Madeira, salt, and pepper.

Brush the truffles carefully, peel them, and cook in Madeira; save the peelings and the Madeira used for cooking. Cut part of the truffles into thin round slices and slide them under the skin of the turkey; salt and pepper the inside of the turkey and add the rest of the truffles. Let the turkey be flavored by the truffles for 3 days. Knead the *foie gras* with the truffle peelings; let it marinate 24 hr. in the cooking Madeira you have saved. Remove the truffles from the inside of the turkey, mix them with the marinated *foie gras*, stuff the turkey with all of this, cover the breast with strips of pork fat or bacon, and roast on a spit. Serve the turkey on a platter, and the skimmed gravy in a sauceboat.

Truffled Pullet and Truffled Partridge are prepared the same way.

GOOSE

GOOSE ALSACIENNE OIE À L'ALSACIENNE (M.)

Stuff the goose with sausage meat mixed with 3½ oz. chopped onions cooked in butter per 2 lb. sausage meat—about 3 to 4 lb. of stuffing, depending upon the size of the goose. Truss and pan-roast or braise. Place the goose on a large platter and surround it with sauerkraut braised in goose fat and slices of lean pork fat cooked with the sauerkraut. Serve with the cooking stock from the goose.

Note: Goose Alsacienne is sometimes served with poached Strasbourg sausages and boiled potatoes. (Figure 262, Page 421.)

GOOSE ENGLISH STYLE OIE À L'ANGLAISE (M.)

Prepare the same as Duckling English Style (p. 422). Roast in the oven or on a spit. Serve with the gravy from the roasting and only slightly sweetened applesauce.

JUGGED GOOSE OIE (CIVET D') (M.)

Cut the goose up into even-sized pieces. Prepare the same as Jugged Hare (p. 478). Bind the sauce, at the last moment, with the blood of the goose collected while bleeding it.

GOOSE CONSERVE OIE (CONFIT D') (E.)

Since the use of this conserve is indicated in some of our recipes, we must give the directions for making it.

Choose very fat geese, each one able to supply 2½ lb. fat. Clean them carefully and cut each one into 6 parts (the legs, breast sliced in 2 parts, and the carcass in 2 parts).

Rub the pieces with bay salt mixed with a dash of spices and a little powdered thyme and bay leaf. Place them in deep platters, cover with salt, and let stand 24 hr. The following day melt in a pan all of the fat collected from the pieces and the intestines. Put the pieces in this pan after washing them in cold water and wiping them; cook them well, keeping them somewhat firm (since they must be used later), for about 2½ hr.

Place the pieces in crockery pots previously heated with boiling water, 1 pot or jar per goose. Cover the pieces with the fat from the cooking. When the pieces are well set in the fat, add enough melted lard to cover the goose fat ⅜ in. deep; let stand until solidified.

Finally, cover jars with circles of strong paper and tie well around rims.

GOOSE WITH CHESTNUTS OIE AUX MARRONS (E.)

Prepare the same way as Young Turkey with Chestnuts (p. 430).

GOOSE (VARIOUS RAGOUTS OR STEWS) OIE (RAGOÛTS DIVERS D') (M.)

Prepare the same way as Ragout of Mutton (p. 357). Ragout of Goose may also be prepared *à la bonne femme,* with celery root, with vegetables, with spring vegetables, with chestnuts, *à la paysanne,* Bourguignonne, with turnips, with tiny sausages, etc.

In Cassoulet (p. 723), goose adds an important and delectable flavor.

GOOSE LIVER OIE (FOIE D') (M.)

Goose livers that are not fattened can be cooked like chicken, pullet, and turkey livers. Prepare them on skewers, sautéed with mushrooms, Chasseur, Bourguignonne, with Rice Pilaf or Risotto, etc.

SQUAB

SQUAB ENGLISH STYLE PIGEONNEAU À L'ANGLAISE (M.)

Split the squab down the back; remove the small inside bones. Flatten it lightly and season; roll in flour, dip in beaten egg containing a little olive oil, and roll in bread crumbs. Cook in clarified butter, browning both sides well. Place it on a round platter and coat with Maître d'Hôtel Butter (p. 164).

Note: This squab may be garnished with fresh buttered vegetables or various potato dishes.

BRAISED SQUAB PIGEONNEAU BRAISÉ (M.)

Whether stuffed or not, braise like any other fowl. Braised squab is served with any of the following garnishes: Bourgeoise, mushrooms, various vegetables, olives, small onions, Risotto, etc.

SQUAB CHASSEUR PIGEONNEAU CHASSEUR (M.)

Cut up into parts and prepare the same as Chicken Chasseur (p. 401).

SQUAB IN CASSEROLE PIGEONNEAU EN COMPOTE (M.)

Truss and brown in butter, only enough to sear and color the skin. Place the squab in an earthenware casserole with 6 large cubes of blanched pork fat browned in butter, 6 small onions ½ cooked in butter, 8 pitted, blanched olives, and 6 small mushroom caps. Melt the glaze in the bottom of the pan in which the squab was browned with 1¼ oz. white wine, add 3½ oz. Semiglaze Sauce (p. 138), reduce, and add butter; pour this over the squab in the casserole. Add a small *bouquet garni.* Cook slowly 30 min. Remove the *bouquet garni.* Serve in the same casserole.

SQUAB DRESSED AS A TOAD PIGEONNEAU À LA CRAPAUDINE (M.)

Too frequently squabs prepared this way are split down the back like Grilled Deviled Chicken. This is wrong and does not justify the term *à la crapaudine.* This is how they should be prepared. Stuff the feet into an opening in the belly, then split the bird horizontally from the tip of the breast to the wing bones, dividing it into 2 parts, the carcass (or back) on one side, the breast on the other, connected by the joint of the wings. Prepared this way, the squab looks like a toad. Season with salt and pepper, baste with melted butter, and sear in the oven. Then cover with fine bread crumbs, baste with melted butter, and grill at low heat. Place on a platter bordered with gherkins and fluted ½ slices of lemon. Potato Straws (p. 509) on the sides.

It is customary to serve Diable Sauce (p. 140) at the same time, but Squab Dressed as a Toad used to be served with shallot sauce. (Figure 263, Page 428.)

MINUTE SQUAB PIGEONNEAU À LA MINUTE (M.)

Cut in 2 or 4 pieces. Lightly flatten, season, and sauté quickly in butter. When the squab is cooked, sprinkle with finely chopped onion. Cook a few minutes. Arrange on a platter. Melt the glaze in the cooking pan with 1 tbsp. cognac and a thread of lemon juice, then add 3 or 4 tbsp. reduced veal stock. Pour over the squab. Sprinkle with chopped parsley.

SQUAB WITH TURNIPS PIGEONNEAU AUX NAVETS (P.)

Follow recipe for Duckling with Turnips (p. 423).

SQUAB WITH OLIVES PIGEONNEAU AUX OLIVES (P.)

Same procedure as for Squab with Peas (below), but salted very little. Ten min. before the bird is finished cooking, add 2 oz. green pitted olives per squab.

SQUAB EN PAPILLOTE PIGEONNEAU EN PAPILLOTE (M.)

Sear the partially boned, flattened, and seasoned squab halves in butter. Lay each half on a piece of buttered paper, covering both sides with 1 tbsp. thickened Duxelles Sauce (p. 140) and a slice of lean cooked ham. Fold the paper over the squab, creasing it so that it is closed on all sides. Bake in the oven so the paper puffs up.

SQUAB WITH PEAS PIGEONNEAU AUX PETITS POIS (M.) (*For 2 persons*)

May be prepared 2 ways:

(1) Brown 2 oz. blanched, diced pork fat and 12 small onions lightly in butter. Drain these and, in the same butter, brown the squab several minutes. Remove the squab, pour off ¾ of the fat, and add 4 oz. thickened veal stock. Put the squab, pork, and onions back into this gravy, along with 4 oz. small fresh peas; add a *bouquet garni* containing a few lettuce leaves, a pinch of sugar. Finish cooking everything together.

(2) Pan-roast the squab, keeping it somewhat rare. Let it simmer a few minutes with Peas French Style (p. 505), along with pieces of lean bacon and small onions.

SQUAB VILLEROI PIGEONNEAU À LA VILLEROI (M.)

Split the squab in two. Remove the small bones; flatten the halves lightly, season, and cook in butter. When cool, dip the squab halves in Villeroi Sauce (p. 155) Roll in flour, dip in beaten egg containing a little olive oil, and roll in bread crumbs. Fry in deep fat just before serving. Arrange on a napkin and garnish with fried parsley. Serve Périgueux Sauce (p. 143) separately.

GUINEA HEN

Guinea hen (*pintade*) is not nearly so delectable as pheasant, but is sometimes served in its stead when the hunting season is over and pheasants are not available. Almost all the recipes given for pheasant may be applied to guinea hen. The recipes given for chicken in casserole or *en cocotte* may also be used for guinea hen and young guinea fowl. Grilled or roast guinea hen may be served with various garnishes: fresh vegetables, braised vegetables, chestnuts, potato chips, etc. (Figure 264, Page 428.)

FOIE GRAS

Foie gras has rightfully been called the jewel of French cooking. *Foie gras* from Périgord and Alsace, the principal centers of production, accompanied with truffles, is featured on any gourmet's menu.

These fattened livers come from either geese or ducks. Each type has its champions, and both are excellent if they have the 2 prime qualities: color and firmness. Cooking them is a very delicate matter and should be done by poaching rather than by boiling, allowing 20–25 min. per lb., depending on whether they are long or doubled into a ball.

GOOSE and DUCK FOIE GRAS FOIE GRAS D'OIE ET DE CANARD (M.)

The quality of *foie gras* is recognized by its ivory-white color bordering on pink and its being firm to the touch. If the finger can be pushed into it easily, it is safe to say that it is fatty and will melt down in cooking.

Before cooking, the parts touching the gall must be removed and also the small nerve fibers connecting the 2 lobes.

Cooking foie gras au naturel: Trim the *foie gras,* removing the gall, neighboring parts, and blood vessels. Season with salt, white pepper, and spices and moisten with a little cognac. Let it macerate in this seasoning for several hours. Wipe the *foie gras* dry and cook slowly in goose fat 45 min. to 1 hr., depending on size. Place the *foie gras* in an oval terrine. When it is almost cold, pour the cooking fat over it. When the fat has solidified, cover it with a thin layer of lard. Let cool completely. Put the cover on the terrine and seal the crack between lid and dish with a band of paper. Keep in a cool dry place.

Braised: Season the *foie gras* and let it macerate in cognac. Wrap it in very thin strips of pork fat or in a pig's caul. Place it in a small pan on a bed of braising stock containing Madeira, sherry, or any other wine that will go with the preparation. Begin cooking on the stove; cover and finish cooking in the oven at low heat, 45 min. to 1 hr., depending on size.

Pan-roasted: Season and macerate in cognac. Cook in butter in a covered pan, 45 min. to 1 hr., depending on size.

FOIE GRAS IN BRIOCHE or BRIOCHE OF FOIE GRAS FOIE GRAS EN BRIOCHE OR BRIOCHE DE FOIE GRAS (M.)

Prepare the same as the next recipe, using Brioche Paste (p. 546) instead of Short Paste.

FOIE GRAS TURNOVER FOIE GRAS EN CHAUSSON (M.)

Stud a firm *foie gras* with truffles. Season with salt, pepper, and spices and let macerate 4 hr. in this seasoning in a cool place. Sear all sides in butter. Let cool. Enclose in a layer of fine Short Paste (p. 545) folded in the shape of a *chausson* (literally, "slipper"), or turnover. Make an opening in the top to let the steam out. Decorate with motifs of the same paste and brush with beaten egg containing a drop of water or milk. Bake in the oven 45 min. Just before serving, pour a few tbsp. reduced Madeira Sauce (p. 142) flavored with truffle essence into the opening of the turnover.

TRUFFLED FOIE GRAS EN COCOTTE FOIE GRAS (TRUFFÉ) EN COCOTTE (M.)

Stud the *foie gras* with truffles and macerate 4 hr. with cognac, salt, pepper, and spices. Sear in butter. Place in an earthenware cocotte. Melt the glaze in the sautéing pan with Madeira or sherry, add reduced veal stock containing truffle essence, and reduce. Pour this over the *foie gras.* Cover the cocotte and seal the lid with a band of paste. Bake in a fairly hot oven, 45 min. to 1 hr., depending on the size of the *foie gras.* Serve in the same cocotte.

FOIE GRAS FINANCIÈRE FOIE GRAS À LA FINANCIÈRE (M.)

Stud with truffles and braise in Madeira. Drain the *foie gras* and remove the covering strips of pork fat. Place it on a crouton fixed to a round platter with a paste made of flour and water. Surround it with a Financière Garnish (p. 181). Reduce the braising stock, strain, and pour over the *foie gras.*

FOIE GRAS WITH PAPRIKA or **FOIE GRAS HUNGARIAN STYLE** FOIE GRAS AU PAPRIKA or À LA HONGROISE (M.)

Season with salt and paprika. Braise or pan-roast. Place in an oval cocotte. Cover with Hongroise Sauce (p. 151) to which some of the reduced cooking stock from the liver has been added.

Note: The liver may be studded with truffles.

FOIE GRAS PÉRIGORD FOIE GRAS À LA PÉRIGORD (M.)

Stud with truffles and season. Macerate in cognac 4 or 5 hr. Wrap in strips of pork fat or place in a pig's caul. Braise in Madeira until ½ cooked. Drain and remove the strips of fat. Place it in an oval cocotte with 6 or 7 truffles that have been peeled, seasoned, and macerated in cognac. Baste with the reduced and strained braising stock. Cover the cocotte and seal the lid with paste. Bake in the oven 20–25 min.

FOIE GRAS SUVAROV FOIE GRAS À LA SOUVAROV (M.)

This is another name for Foie Gras Périgord.

FOIE GRAS TOULOUSAINE FOIE GRAS À LA TOULOUSAINE (M.)

Stud with truffles and braise in white stock. Place it in a shallow crust of Puff Paste (p. 544) and surround with a Toulousaine Garnish (pp. 185 and 349). Suprême Sauce (p. 146).

FOIE GRAS SLICES OR MEDALLIONS

Cut the livers into slices or medallions weighing about 2½–3 oz. each. Season with salt and pepper, flour, and sauté quickly in butter. They may also be spread with melted butter, covered with bread crumbs, and grilled. *Foie gras* slices or medallions can be prepared in infinite ways. Below are a series of these preparations.

SLICED FOIE GRAS BIGOURDANE ESCALOPES DE FOIE GRAS À LA BIGOURDANE (M.)

Season with salt and pepper, flour, and sauté in goose fat. Arrange the slices in a circle, alternating them with round croutons fried in goose fat. Garnish the center of the platter with peeled grapes macerated in a little cognac. Coat the slices with Semiglaze Sauce (p. 138) finished with Madeira.

SLICED FOIE GRAS BRILLAT-SAVARIN ESCALOPES DE FOIE GRAS BRILLAT-SAVARIN (M.)

Slice the livers rather thick and make a cut in the side of each slice to form a pocket; season; fill each with a slice of truffle cooked in butter. Close the pockets of the slices and roll in flour, dip in egg beaten with a little olive oil, and cover with bread crumbs. Cook in clarified butter. Place in tartlet crusts filled with small creamed mushrooms. Serve a separate dish of Semiglaze Sauce (p. 138) flavored with truffle essence.

SLICED FOIE GRAS WITH CREAMED MUSHROOMS ESCALOPES DE FOIE GRAS AUX CHAMPIGNONS À LA CRÈME (M.)

Sauté in butter. Arrange in a circle with croutons fried in butter. Garnish the center of the platter with creamed mushrooms.

SLICED FOIE GRAS CHÂTELAINE ESCALOPES DE FOIE GRAS À LA CHÂTELAINE (M.)

Roll in flour, dip in beaten egg containing a little olive oil, and cover with bread crumbs mixed with chopped truffles. Sauté in clarified butter. Lay on artichoke bottoms cooked in butter (the lid of the pan tightly sealed) and filled with chestnut purée, sprinkled with bread crumbs, basted with butter, and browned in the oven. Semiglaze Sauce (p. 138) flavored with truffle essence.

DEVILED SLICED FOIE GRAS ESCALOPES DE FOIE GRAS À LA DIABLE (M.)

Season and dip in butter, then cover with bread crumbs. Grill. Arrange in a circle on a platter. Serve with Diable Sauce (p. 140).

SLICED FOIE GRAS FINANCIÈRE ESCALOPES DE FOIE GRAS À LA FINANCIÈRE (M.)

Sauté in butter. Arrange in a circle in a flan or pie crust (baked with fruit pits to hold its shape). Fill the center with a Financière Garnish (p. 181). Cover the liver with reduced Semiglaze Sauce (p. 138) flavored with truffle essence.

GRILLED SLICED FOIE GRAS WITH VARIOUS GARNISHES ESCALOPES DE FOIE GRAS GRILLÉES AVEC GARNITURES DIVERSES (M.)

Season, dip in butter, and cover with bread crumbs. Grill over a low fire. Arrange on a service platter. Serve with various garnishes such as: mushrooms in Madeira or cream, sliced artichoke bottoms sautéed in butter, buttered asparagus tips, Potatoes Parisienne (p. 509), truffled Risotto (p. 513), truffle ragout, etc. Serve with buttered Semiglaze Sauce (p. 138) or Périgueux Sauce (p. 143).

SLICED FOIE GRAS HUNGARIAN STYLE ESCALOPES DE FOIE GRAS À LA HONGROISE (M.)

Season highly with paprika. Sauté in butter. Arrange in a circle, alternating the sliced liver with bread croutons fried in butter. Coat the liver with Hongroise Sauce (p. 151).

SLICED FOIE GRAS ITALIAN STYLE ESCALOPES DE FOIE GRAS À L'ITALIENNE (M.)

Sauté in butter. Place on fried croutons. Cover with Italienne Sauce (p. 142).

SLICED FOIE GRAS MATIGNON ESCALOPES DE FOIE GRAS À LA MATIGNON (M.)

Season with salt and pepper; cover with a layer of fine Mirepoix (p. 136); roll in flour, dip in beaten egg containing a drop of olive oil, and cover with bread crumbs. Sauté in clarified butter. Arrange in a circle. Serve Périgueux Sauce (p. 143) separately.

SLICED FOIE GRAS MONSELET ESCALOPES DE FOIE GRAS À LA MONSELET (M.)

Sauté in butter. Place each liver slice on an artichoke bottom cooked in butter (the lid of the pan tightly sealed) and filled with a salpicon of creamed truffles. Fill the center of the platter with Potatoes Parisienne (p. 509). Garnish with a ribbon of reduced veal stock flavored with truffle essence. (Figure 265, Page 429.)

Fig. 267 - Foie gras mousse in aspic (p. 439).
Fig. 268 - Foie gras parfait (p. 439).

Fig. 267

Fig. 268

Fig. 269

Fig. 270

SLICED FOIE GRAS MONTROUGE ESCALOPES DE FOIE GRAS À LA MONTROUGE (M.)

Sauté in butter. Arrange in a circle, alternating the sliced liver with croutons fried in butter. Fill the center of the platter with a rather thick mushroom purée. Reduced veal stock with mushroom essence.

SLICED FOIE GRAS PÉRIGUEUX ESCALOPES DE FOIE GRAS À LA PÉRIGUEUX (M.)

Flour, dip in beaten egg containing a drop of olive oil, and cover with bread crumbs mixed with chopped truffles. Sauté in butter. Arrange in a circle. Cover with Madeira Sauce (p. 142) flavored with truffle essence.

SLICED FOIE GRAS WITH PORT ESCALOPES DE FOIE GRAS AU PORTO (M.)

Sauté in butter. Place on croutons fried in butter. Melt the glaze in the sautéing pan with port, add very reduced, thickened veal stock, and pour over the liver.

Note: Sliced *foie gras* may be made the same way with Madeira, sherry, Frontignan, or Marsala.

SLICED FOIE GRAS PRINCESSE ESCALOPES DE FOIE GRAS PRINCESSE (M.)

Sauté in butter and place on croutons. Garnish with buttered asparagus tips. Place truffle slices on the liver slices. Cream sauce with port.

SLICED FOIE GRAS WITH GRAPES ESCALOPES DE FOIE GRAS AU RAISIN (M.)

Sauté in butter. Place on croutons fried in butter. Garnish with peeled grapes macerated in cognac. Madeira Sauce (p. 142).

SLICED FOIE GRAS À LA REINE ESCALOPES DE FOIE GRAS À LA REINE (M.)

Flour, dip in beaten egg with a drop of olive oil, and cover with bread crumbs; sauté in butter. Place each slice in a tartlet shell filled with a purée of creamed breast of chicken. Ribbon of Suprême Sauce (p. 146). Slice of truffle on each liver slice.

SLICED FOIE GRAS TOSCANE ESCALOPES DE FOIE GRAS À LA TOSCANE (M.)

Flour, dip in beaten egg with a little olive oil, and cover with bread crumbs. Sauté in butter. Arrange in a circle, alternating with croutons fried in butter. Garnish with diced macaroni bound with Italienne Sauce (p. 142) mixed with thinly sliced white truffles. Madeira Sauce (p. 142).

SLICED FOIE GRAS WITH TRUFFLES ESCALOPES DE FOIE GRAS AUX TRUFFES (M.)

Sauté in butter. Place on croutons fried in butter. On each liver slice place 3 or 4 fine slices of truffle turned in the butter used to cook the liver. Madeira Sauce (p. 142).

SLICED FOIE GRAS WITH CREAMED TRUFFLES ESCALOPES DE FOIE GRAS AUX TRUFFES À LA CRÈME (M.)

Sauté in butter. Place on croutons. Cover with a cream sauce containing port. Garnish with truffle slices.

Fig. 269 - Foie gras Suvarov (p. 440).
Fig. 270 - Périgord eggs (p. 440).

VARIOUS FOIE GRAS PREPARATIONS

TRUFFLED FOIE GRAS ASPIC FOIE GRAS (ASPIC DE) TRUFFÉ (P.)

Cold Dish: Cut the *foie gras* (cooked as explained on p. 434) in neat slices about ⅜ in. thick; then, using a round cutter, cut the slices in circles about 2 in. in diameter; crown each circle with a large slice of truffle. Line a charlotte mold with very clear Aspic Jelly flavored with port or champagne (p. 168) and on the bottom of the mold and around the sides lay the circles of liver with the truffled side against the mold; the center may be filled with the remaining pieces of *foie gras* or with a mousse made of the leftover *foie gras ;* finish filling the mold with cold melted aspic. Place on ice; unmold onto a very cold platter, garnish with chopped aspic, and border with aspic croutons.

SMALL FOIE GRAS ASPICS FOIE GRAS (PETITS ASPICS DE) (J.)

Cold Dish: Cut cooked *foie gras* into 1-in. cubes. Line small aspic molds with port-flavored Aspic Jelly (p. 168). In the bottom of each mold place a neat round slice of truffle, then a cube of *foie gras*. Finish filling with jelly. Put into the refrigerator to set. Dip the molds in tepid water to unmold; arrange the aspics on a platter. Decorate with chopped aspic. Place a small mound of truffles in the center. (Figure 266; Page 429.)

FOIE GRAS IN CASES or **SMALL CASES OF FOIE GRAS** FOIE GRAS EN CAISSE OR PETITES CAISSES DE FOIE GRAS (M.)

Foie gras prepared this way may be served as a hot hors d'oeuvre or as a small entree. Fill small paper cases, buttered and dried in the oven, with a salpicon (tiny cubes) of *foie gras* and truffles bound with very reduced Semiglaze Sauce (p. 138) flavored with truffle essence. On each case place a slice of *foie gras* sautéed in butter and, on each slice, a slice of truffle heated in butter.

Note: Various salpicons can be served in cases: creamed mushrooms; purée of breast of chicken, asparagus tips, etc.

FOIE GRAS CUTLETS and **CROQUETTES** FOIE GRAS (CÔTELETTES ET CROQUETTES DE) (M.)

These preparations, served as hot hors d'oeuvres or small entrees, are made according to the usual recipe for croquettes (see p. 240).

FOIE GRAS CRÉPINETTES FOIE GRAS (CRÉPINETTES DE) (M.)

Follow recipe for Chicken Crépinettes (p. 413), using *foie gras* instead of chicken. In the center of the forcemeat of each Crépinette place a small slice of *foie gras*. Grill over a low fire. Serve with Périgueux Sauce (p. 143).

SLICED FOIE GRAS MARÉCHAL FOIE GRAS (ESCALOPES DE) MARÉCHAL (E.

Cold Dish: Take a crock of preserved *foie gras* and cut it into the desired number of slices, shaping each slice into an oval. With the remainder of the *foie gras* in the crock, make a Foie Gras Loaf mixture (see p. 439); cover the slices with this mixture, smoothing the tops into dome shapes. Coat the garnished slices with creamed Chaud-Froid Sauce (p. 139), decorate with truffle slices, and glaze with Aspic Jelly (p. 168). Shape some purée of *foie gras* into balls the size and shape of cherries; in the center of each ball place a small truffle ball to simulate the cherry pit; cover with reddish-brown-colored Chaud-Froid Sauce, then glaze with aspic. Arrange the sliced *foie gras* around a circular bed of aspic on a very cold platter, build the *foie gras* cherries into a pyramid on the bed of aspic, and border the platter with aspic croutons.

FOIE GRAS MOUSSE IN ASPIC FOIE GRAS (MOUSSE DE) EN ASPIC (A.)

Cold Dish: Prepare and cook a *foie gras* as described on p. 434, after seasoning it a little more highly with salt, pepper, and spice. Remove from the cocotte when cooked and press through a fine sieve. Add veal stock to the cooking liquid and clarify it; cook until concentrated, and set aside. Work the purée of *foie gras* on ice, blending into it, in small amounts, ⅕ its weight in very stiff whipped cream. Line a mold with part of the cooking liquid you have set aside, decorate it with round slices of truffle cooked in Madeira and with round slices of hard-boiled eggs. Put on ice to set, then fill the inside of the mold with the *foie gras*-cream mixture until it reaches about 1 in. below the top; finish filling the mold with the cooking liquid. Leave on ice 2 hr. Unmold onto a cake of ice placed on a platter covered with a napkin; decorate with the remainder of the congealed cooking liquid, cut or chopped, and serve. (Figure 267, Page 436.)

Chicken, winged-game, and ground-game mousses are made the same way.

Instead of a mousse, you can make mousselines, shaped in quenelle molds, egg molds, or in small pastry boats glazed with aspic or first covered with Chaud-Froid Sauce (p. 139) and then lightly glazed with aspic.

FOIE GRAS LOAF FOIE GRAS (PAIN DE) (A.)

Cold Dish: Cook some truffles in champagne, port, or Madeira; save the cooking liquid. Trim a fine *foie gras*, stud with as many truffles as you wish, and cook as directed on p. 434; let cool in the cooking liquid. When it is quite cold, cut a few nice slices off the top and press the rest through a sieve. Mix the truffle cooking liquid with that of the *foie gras* ; bind the mixture with 4 egg yolks; beat the sauce with a wire whisk, adding 6 oz. fresh butter, then blend in the purée of *foie gras* bit by bit. Line a charlotte mold with veal and chicken aspic, decorate the sides with truffles, and fill the inside with alternate layers of purée, liver slices, and truffles cut in round slices. Cover with a layer of aspic and place in the refrigerator. Just before serving, unmold onto a platter and surround with aspic cut into fancy shapes.

Note: This recipe is also called Foie Gras Parfait in Aspic. Loaves of chicken and game can be made the same way.

FOIE GRAS PARFAIT FOIE GRAS (PARFAIT DE) (E.)

Cold Dish: Foie Gras Parfait is used in many recipes. Usually it is served in a terrine or earthenware jar, coated with succulent aspic.

Simple way to prepare the parfait: Choose 2 very firm, fresh livers; carefully remove the gall, trim, remove the fibers, and stud the livers with excellent truffles carefully peeled and quartered. Place the livers in a terrine, season with salt, freshly ground pepper, and spices. Pour in 3 oz. cognac and 3 oz. Madeira. Cover the terrine; let macerate 5–6 hr. Wrap the livers in strips of pork fat, then in a napkin or cheesecloth; tie them as you would a galantine; poach 20 min. in veal stock and let cool in the cooking liquid.

As soon as cold, remove the cloth and the strips of pork fat. Place the 2 livers, pressed one against the other, in a large enough terrine and cover with fine aspic flavored with champagne or port (Figure 268, Page 436.)

STRASBOURG PÂTÉ OF FOIE GRAS FOIE GRAS (PÂTÉ DE) DE STRASBOURG

See Mixed Entrees, p. 534.

FOIE GRAS SOUFFLÉ FOIE GRAS (SOUFFLÉ DE) (M.) (*For 6 to 8 persons*)

Preparing the mixture: Press 1 lb. raw *foie gras* and 4½ oz. raw truffles through a fine sieve. To this purée add 10 oz. raw chicken meat mashed as finely as possible in a mortar with 5 egg whites, also pressed through a fine sieve. Season this mixture with salt, white pepper, and spices, and work on ice, adding 10 oz. extra-heavy cream and, when well mixed, 4 egg whites beaten stiff. Mix gently. Pour this mixture into a soufflé dish. Cook covered in a *bain-marie* 30–35 min. Serve with Périgueux Sauce (p. 143).

FOIE GRAS SUVAROV AU NATUREL FOIE GRAS SOUVAROV AU NATUREL (J.)

Cold Dish: Use a mold shaped like a *foie gras*; line with parchment lightly dampened with water. Fill the mold with 2 cooked *foie gras,* placing 2 rows of truffles in the center. Cool in the refrigerator. Unmold and take off the paper. Stick 3 fine slices of truffle on each side of the *foie gras.* Coat with Aspic Jelly (p. 168). Place on a service platter and surround with triangles of aspic.

Note: The parchment facilitates unmolding. The truffles should first be peeled before being cut. (Figure 269, Page 437.)

STRASBOURG FOIE GRAS TERRINE FOIE GRAS (TERRINE DE) DE STRASBOURG (Gi.)

Cold: Macerate a fine Strasbourg *foie gras,* weighing about 1½ lb., in Madeira and cognac for 24 hr. Then stud it with large quarters of brushed, peeled raw truffles. Prepare separately 1 lb. diced fresh pork fat and sear in a frying pan 5–6 min.; then remove the pork fat and, in the same pan with the melted fat, brown 10 oz. lean fresh pork and 4 oz. *foie gras* or, if unavailable, cubes of very pale calf's liver. Sprinkle salt, pepper, and spices on top and let cool; then chop and mash everything very fine and press it through a metal sieve. Add a little of the Madeira and cognac used in macerating the *foie gras* to this forcemeat; season to give it a rather spicy flavor.

Line a terrine or earthenware jar with strips of pork fat and spread a layer of forcemeat on the bottom and around the sides; then place the *foie gras* in the center and cover with forcemeat; the top should bulge somewhat. Cover the top with a strip of pork fat and sprinkle this with a dash of powdered thyme and bay leaf. Put the lid on the jar and seal it with a band of paste made of flour and water. Set the jar in a roasting pan containing about 1 in. water and cook in the oven about 1 hr. You can tell if it is perfectly cooked by lifting the cover: the fat should be clear and the block of forcemeat should roll easily in it without sticking to the bottom of the jar. Place a small board with a 2-lb. weight on top the forcemeat to press it, and let cool. The next day remove some of the fat from the jar and replace it with some half-set Aspic Jelly (p. 168). Place the jar on a napkin and serve with a spoon or cut in slices inside the same jar.

PÉRIGORD EGGS OEUFS DU PÉRIGORD (J.)

Cold Dish: Fill special egg-shaped molds with truffled *foie gras,* then chill. Unmold and roll the eggs in chopped truffles. Arrange in a pyramid in a small wicker basket. Finish the dish with chopped Aspic Jelly (p. 168). (Figure 270, Page 437.)

GAME

GAME

Game includes all the furred or feathered animals that live wild in the woods and fields. Large ground game (called *venaison* in French, but venison being only deer in English) are boars, roes, does, chamois or European mountain antelope, deer. The rest—hares, wild rabbits, and leverets—are merely called game. Feathered game are listed in order of merit: pheasant, partridge and young partridge, ring dove, quail, thrush, lark, figpecker, ortolan. We may also include in this list the blackbird, wood pigeon, bustard, and, among the waterfowl, the exquisite woodcock and its family, rail, moor hen, plover, curlew, lapwing, wild duckling, wild duck, teal, etc. Because other birds are less well known does not mean that they may not prove delicacies to gourmets. Enthusiasts for game, many gourmets are often hunters, besides.

GAME FOWL

LARKS

ALOUETTES

LARKS GERMAN STYLE ALOUETTES or MAUVIETTES À L'ALLEMANDE (Fa.)

A lark to be cooked in the kitchen is called a *mauviette.* According to Urbain-Dubois, William I's chef, the citizens of Leipzig were well aware of the delicacy of the fat larks native there.

Remove the heads, feet, and gizzards, and spit the larks, alternating each with a piece of pork fat or bacon; salt and roast in a hot oven 12–15 min. Then roll the whole skewer in sifted bread crumbs, baste with their own cooking fat, and put back into a hot oven 5 min. Serve basted with their fat.

LARK CHERRIES ALOUETTES EN CERISES (R.) (*For 4 persons*)

Pluck 12 or more larks without damaging the skin. Carefully bone, leaving each lark with 1 foot; push this foot through the center of the body, cutting off the end to imitate a cherry stem.

Place in a pan: mushrooms, parsley, finely chopped shallots, chicken and game giblets and livers, salt, pepper; bind with 1 egg yolk. Heat a few minutes with a piece of butter, mash into a purée, and let cool. Fill the bird with part of this forcemeat and save the rest. Sew the opening together in such a way that the lark will have a round shape. Place the larks in a pan, pressed tightly together side by side, and brown in butter.

Oil a small paper case per bird and fill the bottom with the forcemeat you have set aside. Place a lark in each, after removing the thread. Put into the oven a few minutes. Sauce with their own gravy. Serve.

COLD LARK CHERRIES ALOUETTES EN CERISES FROIDES (P.)

Same preparation as above; let cool; make a game Aspic Jelly (p. 168) and some Brown Chaud-Froid Sauce (p. 139) strongly flavored with tomato; coat the lark balls with the sauce and arrange them in a mound or as a garnish for cold game: pheasant, partridge, etc. Surround with chopped aspic.

LARKS EN COCOTTE ALOUETTES EN COCOTTE (A.) (*For 6 persons*)

Take: ½ lb. *foie gras*, ½ lb. truffles, 2½ oz. butter, 2 oz. Madeira, 1 oz. flour, 30 larks, giblets of 2 chickens, soup vegetables, salt, and pepper. Pluck, singe, and bone the larks; save the scraps and giblets. Clean the chicken giblets. Wash and brush the truffles and dry them in a cloth; cut them in slices. Cut the *foie gras* into 30 cubes; stuff them into the larks, salt, and pepper. Sew up the larks. Prepare about 1 pt. good gravy by boiling down the chicken giblets, lark scraps and giblets, and vegetables in salted, peppered water. Make a roux with 1 oz. butter and flour; add the gravy and Madeira; skim the sauce; cook until concentrated. Brown the larks in a cocotte with the rest of the butter; pour the sauce over them, add truffles, put into the oven, and cook 15 min. at low heat. Serve in the cocotte or arrange the larks on a platter after removing the thread, decorate with truffles, cover with sauce, and serve. This dish is really a salmis of larks and makes an excellent game entree.

LARKS FLORENTINE ALOUETTES À LA FLORENTINE (Fa.) (*For 8 persons*)

Pour 1 lb. corn meal slowly into 1½ qt. boiling water, stirring the while; salt, and cook 15 min. Then add 5 oz. grated Parmesan cheese and pour into a timbale mold, pressing the mixture down tightly, and let cool. Meanwhile, clean 24 larks and stuff them with Gratin Forcemeat (p. 175) containing chicken livers. Put the larks into a sautéing pan and brown them in the oven; pour a good glass of white wine over them and reduce the liquid to a glaze; add game gravy made with the lark bones and heads, and also add a few small mushrooms and some small quenelles. When the mixture in the mold has cooled and set, unmold and hollow out the center to form a sort of timbale crust. Butter the mold again, sprinkle with bread crumbs, place the timbale crust (now hollowed out) back inside, and fill with the larks and the garnish. Cover with a layer of corn-meal paste (Polenta, p. 521) and place in a hot oven for 40 min. Reverse the mold onto a hot round platter and serve with a separate dish of the stock in which the larks were cooked, strained.

LARKS IN SHROUDS ALOUETTES EN LINCEUL (A.)

Take 12 Dutch potatoes, peel and hollow them out, saving small pieces of potato pulp to make into stoppers. Pluck, singe, and bone the larks; season and stuff with a mixture of game and *foie gras* (truffled, if desired), and put each lark into a potato. Close with the potato stoppers. Place the stuffed potatoes on an ovenware service platter and cover with good game-fowl stock; cook in the oven, basting frequently. When the potatoes are no longer covered with liquid, add small bits of butter on top and finish cooking. The potatoes should be a crisp golden brown.

LARKS MILANAISE ALOUETTES À LA MILANAISE (P.)

Brown the larks quickly in a pan over a hot fire and place them in croustades filled with Macaroni Milanaise (p. 520). Serve a separate dish of Tomato Sauce (p. 146) blended with the glaze in the pan used for cooking the larks.

LARKS PARMENTIÈRE ALOUETTES À LA PARMENTIÈRE (R.)

Pluck, clean, and singe 1 or more larks. Wrap in thin strips of pork fat or bacon. Take as many fine potatoes as there are larks and of about the same size. Wash them well and, without peeling, scoop them out into nests. Butter the inside and lay them on an ovenware platter, and bake in the oven 20 min. Remove the potato nests from the oven and place a bird in each one. Salt and replace in the oven until the lark is roasted. Serve on a platter.

Note: This is a slightly different version of Ali-Bab's recipe for Larks in Shrouds.

LARKS WITH APPLES ALOUETTES AUX POMMES (P.)

Cook the larks in a pan and separately prepare some very thick, cooked-down tart applesauce. Spread the applesauce out smoothly in a deep platter and embed the larks in it. Pour 2 tbsp. heavy cream over each lark and serve immediately.

LARK PIE PÂTÉ D'ALOUETTES

See Mixed Entrees, p. 532.

WOODCOCK

BÉCASSE (M.)

"Woodcock," wrote Charles Jobey, "is one of the glories of French cooking." This is perhaps an exaggeration, but woodcock is certainly one of the most highly esteemed of our game fowl, provided it is fat and meaty. This bird has 2 seasons: the first in autumn, when it is ripe for the pot; the second in March, when it begins its northward flight. At this time, however, woodcock is not at its best, no longer having the same flavor or delicacy it has in autumn.

Before it is used, woodcock must be hung in a cool, dry, well-ventilated place sufficiently long to let its gamy flavor be absorbed into the meat (but not nearly so long as pheasant). Woodcocks are not drawn—this would amount to desecration, for the intestines are the most delicate part. Simply remove the gizzard and the eyes. Truss the woodcock by bringing the feet together and bending them back to the body; then stick the beak into the body.

WOODCOCK IN CHAMBERTIN BÉCASSE AU CHAMBERTIN (M.) (*For 2 persons*)

Note: This method of preparing woodcock, as well as pheasant, partridge, lapwing, and plover, is really a sort of salmis in red wine.

Roast the woodcock in the oven 10–12 min. Disjoint it. Place it in a buttered silver casserole. On the woodcock place 3 sliced mushrooms sautéed in butter and 6 fine truffle slices turned in butter; season with salt and pepper. Cover the casserole and keep hot without letting it boil. Melt the glaze in the pan used for roasting the woodcock with 4 oz. Chambertin. Reduce to a glaze. Pour in 6 oz. gravy made with Chambertin and game stock. Boil 3 min.; add the chopped carcass of the woodcock. Strain. Press the intestines of the woodcock through a sieve and add this to the sauce without letting it boil, then add ½ liqueur glass flaming brandy and 1 tbsp. butter. Pour this over the woodcock.

Woodcock in Chambertin may be served on a round of toast prepared at the last minute. It should be done at the table, in front of the guests, the following way. Spread Gratin Forcemeat (p. 175) on a fried crouton of white bread (or French bread) large enough to hold the bird. Just before serving, remove the insides of the woodcock. Chop the intestines, adding a little grated pork fat and ½ their volume in cooked *foie gras*. Season with salt, freshly ground pepper, and a dash of spices. Add 1 tbsp. brandy. Spread this mixture over the Gratin Forcemeat on the bread, baste with the cooking fat from the woodcock, and brown in the oven.

Some connoisseurs consider this toast the best part of the woodcock. Hunters frequently prepare it themselves. They usually make it by putting the toast into the dripping pan and spreading the top with the intestines mixed with grated pork fat and seasoned as above. It is then basted with the cooking gravy.

BRANDIED WOODCOCK BÉCASSE À LA FINE CHAMPAGNE (M.) (*For 2 persons*)

Roast the woodcock in a very hot oven 12–15 min. Cut into 6 pieces. Place these pieces in a silver casserole with the head on top, the beak in the air. Press the carcass; mix the juice obtained with the finely chopped intestines; add 3 oz. game stock. Pour 3 tbsps. flaming brandy over the pieces of woodcock (the casserole placed on an alcohol stove). Add the mixture of intestines; season with salt, pepper, spices; shake the pan to cover all the pieces with sauce, and serve immediately.

Note: Woodcock prepared this way may be served with the toast given in the recipe for Woodcock with Chambertin (p. 445). In this case, add Gratin Forcemeat (p. 175) and *foie gras* to ⅓ the intestines. This dish is often called Woodcock Flambée, which is incorrect, in our opinion, since the brandy is poured flaming over the woodcock before the intestine mixture is added, not afterward.

WOODCOCK WITH GAME STOCK BÉCASSE AU FUMET (M.) (*For 2 persons*)

Roast the woodcock in the oven 12–15 min. Cut into pieces and place in a silver casserole as directed in the preceding recipe. Melt the glaze in the roasting pan with 3 oz. sherry. Add the chopped carcass and pour in 4 oz. game stock. Boil 1 min. Strain this sauce and bind it, off the fire, with the finely chopped intestines. Season highly; add 2 tbsp. flaming brandy. Pour this over the woodcock.

Note: This dish is a variation of Brandied Woodcock.

BREAST OF WOODCOCK HUNGARIAN STYLE BÉCASSE (SUPRÊMES DE) À LA HONGROISE (M.) (*For 2 persons*)

Remove the breasts. Bone the rest of the bird, mashing the meat obtained with ⅓ its volume in *foie gras* and egg white. Season and press through a sieve. Work this forcemeat on ice, blending in 6 oz. cream. Fill small buttered cutlet-shaped molds with this composition. Poach in a *bain-marie.*

Sauce: Prepare a game stock with woodcock carcasses and trimmings, then add some Mirepoix (p. 136), truffle and mushroom peelings. Season with paprika. Add 3 oz. sherry and reduce, then pour in 6 oz. slightly thickened veal stock; boil a few moments, skimming as needed, and strain. Reduce by ½, add 3 oz. cream, strain through a cloth, and keep hot in a *bain-marie.* Season the breasts with paprika and sauté in fresh butter.

Serving: Place the breasts on the small cutlet-shaped molds. Arrange on a round platter; fill the center with a ragout of truffles cut into the shape of olives and cover the breasts with the sauce.

WOODCOCK LUCULLUS BÉCASSE À LA LUCULLUS (M.) (*For 2 persons*)

Bone the woodcock from the back and stuff it with diced *foie gras* and truffles seasoned with salt, pepper, and spices, moistened with 2 tbsp. cognac, and mixed with the intestines (pressed through a sieve). Truss the woodcock and cover with thin strips of pork fat. Cook in butter in a silver or earthenware casserole. When the woodcock is almost cooked, add 10 thick slices of truffles to the casserole. Finish cooking together at low heat. Pour over 1 tbsp. flaming brandy and 3 oz. reduced game stock. Serve in the same casserole.

WOODCOCK PÉRIGOURDINE BÉCASSE À LA PÉRIGOURDINE (M.) (*For 2 persons*)

(1) Remove the breastbone and stuff the woodcock with Gratin Forcemeat (p. 175) mixed with ¼ as much *foie gras,* the bird's intestines finely chopped, truffle, a finger of brandy, and the usual seasoning. (2) Place strips of pork fat over it and roast in a hot oven; remove while still somewhat rare. (3) Place it on a crouton; surround with small tartlet crusts filled with a salpicon (tiny cubes) of *foie gras* and truffles. Cover the bird with a sauce made by melting the glaze in the roasting pan with Madeira and woodcock stock.

ROAST WOODCOCK I BÉCASSE RÔTIE (A.) (*For 6 persons*)

Take: 2 oz. butter, 1½ oz. unsalted chicken or woodcock consommé, 1½ oz. old brandy or old Armagnac, 1 tsp. salt, ¼ tsp. freshly ground pepper, dash of nutmeg,[1] 3 young, meaty woodcocks,[2] 3 thin strips of pork fat, 3 rectangular slices of dry white bread 1 in. thick and wide enough to allow a margin of about ½ in. around the trimmed woodcocks.

Pluck and singe the woodcocks, cover with strips of pork fat without drawing them, spit them, and turn them before the fire 5 min. Remove the fat, then pour the heated consommé into the dripping pan with ⅔ tsp. salt and ½ the pepper; cook 3 min., basting; skim off the fat once more. Then put the slices of bread (which you have already grilled) into the dripping pan; from now on they will soak up all the drippings from the woodcocks. Continue cooking another 12 min., basting from time to time to avoid drying out. Remove the woodcocks from the spit, place the pieces of toast on a platter, put the woodcocks on the toast, and serve in a chafing dish.

Carefully remove the insides of the woodcocks at the table, before the guests; throw away the gizzards and hard parts; add the rest of the strips of pork fat to what is left and season with the rest of the salt, pepper, and nutmeg; baste with brandy or Armagnac; light the brandy; mix well. Butter the pieces of toast and cover with this mixture. Quickly carve the woodcocks, place the pieces on toast, and serve.

The use of the chafing dish makes it possible to do all these things at the table without anything getting cold; this is essential.

These pieces of toast (*rôties*) are different from the *tartine* I shall mention in the recipe for stuffed pheasant; they are not so thick and are grilled to keep them solid enough so they can soak as long as 10 min. in the dripping pan. However, roasted woodcocks may also be served on *tartines* (French bread sliced lengthwise).

---

[1] Minimum proportions are given for salt, pepper, and nutmeg; most chefs use more.

[2] The woodcocks should be hung for a while so that the feathers may be plucked without pulling. The time allowed depends upon the temperature and the moisture in the air. In Paris, 2 to 3 weeks are usually allowed. The woodcocks should be aged with the head down.

Some connoisseurs prefer not to light the brandy with the intestines and merely pour a little brandy or Armagnac over the spread pieces of toast. Others will not allow leftover pork fat to be used in the mixture spread on the toast; they even prefer to roast the woodcock without strips of fat, simply basting it with its own juices just enough to prevent burning. This procedure is satisfactory only if the woodcocks are very fat.

A red Burgundy, old and mellow, is absolutely essential with this game bird.

I know of nothing more flavorful than a young woodcock, properly aged and just fat enough, roasted on the spit before a wood fire, served on carefully prepared toast, and accompanied by a bottle of Romanée, Clos Bougeot, Musigny, or Chambertin.

ROAST WOODCOCK II BÉCASSE RÔTIE (P.) (*For 2 persons*)

Cover the woodcock with strips of pork fat without drawing it, except for the gizzard, and do not cut off the head or neck, for the woodcock is trussed simply by fastening down the legs with the beak. Roast in a hot oven 15–20 min. Serve on toast dipped in the roast drippings and spread with the intestines crushed in a finger of brandy or a jigger of dry champagne.

Inspired by this simple recipe, home cooks can enjoy roast woodcock without all the elaborations of Ali-Bab.

Note: May also be served in small nests of Potato Straws (p. 509). (Figure 271, Page 456.)

WOODCOCK IN SALMIS or **WOODCOCK SALMIS** BÉCASSES EN SALMIS OF SALMIS DE BÉCASSE (M.) (*For 4 persons*)

Note: In principle, Woodcock Salmis should be finished in front of the guests, like Duckling Rouennaise, which is also a salmis.

This practice has been slightly modified today to simplify serving, and salmis are usually finished in the kitchen. Roast 2 woodcocks in the oven 10–12 min. Cut off the legs, wings, breasts, and remove the skin from these pieces; put them into a buttered sautéing pan; cover with 4 oz. sliced mushrooms turned in butter and 4 oz. sliced truffles.

Sauce: Chop the carcasses and scraps, mix in 1 heaping tbsp. Mirepoix (p. 136), and brown quickly in butter. Pour in 3 oz. white wine, 2 tbsp. flaming cognac, and 9 oz. Semiglaze Sauce (p. 138) made with game stock. Boil a few moments and strain. Reduce this sauce until rather thick, add butter, and strain through a cheesecloth.

Croutons: Cut 6 bread croutons into heart shapes; slightly hollow out the center and fry in butter. Spread these croutons with the finely chopped intestines of the woodcocks mixed with an equal amount of cooked *foie gras* or Gratin Forcemeat (p. 175). Place the pieces of woodcock on a round platter. Cover them with the truffles and mushrooms; coat the woodcock with the piping-hot sauce. Garnish with the croutons browned in the oven.

Note: Woodcock Salmis may also be served on a single round crouton spread with the same mixture given above and browned in the oven. Woodcock Salmis can also be prepared according to the recipe for Pheasant Salmis (p. 461).

WOODCOCK SAUTÉED WITH TRUFFLES BÉCASSE SAUTÉE AUX TRUFFES (M.) (*For 2 persons*)

Cut the woodcock into pieces, season with salt and pepper, and quickly sear in butter. At the last moment, drop into the sautéing pan 2 oz. thickly sliced, seasoned truffles. Put the woodcock and truffles into a timbale, cover it, and keep hot without letting it boil. Brown the chopped carcass and chopped intestines in the same sautéing pan. Melt the glaze with 3 oz. Madeira; pour in 6 oz. game stock. Reduce, then press through a sieve. Reheat the sauce, add 1½ oz. butter, and pour over the woodcock.

COLD WOODCOCK MOUSSE MOUSSE DE BÉCASSES FROIDE (M.) (*For 8 persons*)

Cook 4 woodcocks. Remove bones, skin, and tendons. Chop up the meat and add ½ as much *foie gras,* season, and press through a fine strainer. Work this purée over ice, blending in 9 oz. whipped cream and 2 tbsp. Aspic Jelly (p. 168) made from very reduced game stock. Put this into a mold lined with aspic and decorated with truffles, or in a crystal bowl, as directed in other parts of this book. If the mousse has been molded, serve it on a molded bed of rice or on a solid block of ice.

WOODCOCK PIE PÂTÉ DE BÉCASSES

See Mixed Entrees, p. 534.

SNIPE

BÉCASSINE (M.)

The snipe is like a small-sized woodcock. They resemble each other in plumage and migratory periods, but are differentiated by their habits. Woodcocks live in the woods, while snipes inhabit marshy lands. The snipe belongs to a species that is subdivided into subspecies. There is the common snipe; the great snipe, whose size is halfway between that of the woodcock and the common snipe; and the half snipe or jacksnipe, which is about the size of a thrush.

As with woodcock, the best ways to prepare snipe are *en brochette* or spitted, and in a salmis, as any connoisseur knows.

It is with snipe that Grimod de la Reynière prepared his famous mustard-seasoned Bernardine Salmis, the recipe for which he gives in the sixth year of his *Almanac for Gourmands.*

Most of the recipes for woodcock and thrush can be applied to snipe.

SNIPE IN CHAUD-FROID SAUCE BÉCASSINES EN CHAUD-FROID (M.)

Cold Dish: Bone 10 snipe. Save the heads, which will be baked in the oven. Stuff them as directed in the recipe for Pheasant en Daube (p. 459). Wrap them in pieces of cheesecloth, sew them up, and poach in stock made as directed in the same recipe. After cooling in the stock, unwrap them, wipe them dry, and reshape them to their original form. Put the head back on each and coat with Brown Chaud-Froid Sauce (p. 139) made with game stock. Decorate them, glaze with Aspic Jelly (p. 168), and place in the refrigerator. Serve on a bed of molded rice.

Note: (1) The Chaud-Froid Sauce must, of course, be made from the stock the snipe were cooked in. (2) The aspic used for glazing and decorating the dish should have some game stock added to it before being clarified.

SNIPE IN CROUSTADE or OLD-FASHIONED CROUSTADE OF SNIPE

BÉCASSINES EN CROUSTADE or CROUSTADE DE BÉCASSINES À L'ANCIENNE (M.)

Bone the snipe; stuff them with *foie gras* and truffles; reshape them; cover each with a thin strip of pork fat. Lay them side by side in a sautéing pan, pressing them together to keep them in shape. Baste with butter; cook, covered, 12 min. Let cool a little; remove the strips of fat; place them in a circle in a croustade made of white bread, fried, and lined on the inside with Gratin Forcemeat (p. 175) (the croustade will have been put into the oven a few moments to poach the forcemeat). Garnish the center of the croustade with a pyramid of game quenelles or forcemeat balls. On each snipe place a large, thick slice of truffle. Coat with Semiglaze Sauce (p. 138) made with game stock (prepared with the snipe carcasses and intestines).

SNIPE AU GRATIN BÉCASSINES AU GRATIN (M.)

Stuff the boned snipe ½ full with a piece of *foie gras* studded with a large cube of truffle. Sear them quickly in butter. Place them in a buttered baking dish lined with a layer of Gratin Forcemeat (p. 175) ¼ in. deep. Embed the snipe in this forcemeat. Cover them with Duxelles Sauce (p. 140) blended with game stock, sprinkle with bread crumbs, baste with butter, and brown in the oven.

FIGPECKERS

BECFIGUES (M.)

Figpeckers belong to the flycatcher family and, according to Toussenel, may be divided into 3 kinds. The flycatcher is the most common. It is found in the South and in the departments of Ain, Isère, and Drôme. It is eaten in these regions, but its season is short. In order of excellence, Brillat-Savarin gives first place to the figpecker, among the smaller birds.

He recalls the method for eating small birds that the Canon Charcot, a natural-born gourmand and a perfect gastronome, once gave: "Take a nice fat small bird by the beak, sprinkle it with a little salt, pull out the gizzard, drop it neatly into your mouth, bite and chew quickly. A copious, succulent juice will fill your mouth, and you will savor a pleasure unknown to the common man."

We don't doubt this at all, but the author forgets to tell us whether the bird is raw or cooked.

FIGPECKERS BRYMONT BECFIGUES BRYMONT (M.)

Prepare small, oval crusts hollowed out in the center to hold 2 figpeckers. Fry the crusts in butter. Line them with *foie gras* mixed with chopped truffles. In each crust place 2 figpeckers seasoned with salt and pepper, seared in butter. Finish cooking in a hot oven.

QUAILS

CAILLES (M.)

"The quail," said Charles Jobey, "belongs to the highest aristocracy of the feathered animals." We shall add that it holds an important place in the estimation of gourmets and that it plays a considerable role in *haute cuisine*. Unfortunately, our indigenous meadow quails are becoming more and more rare, and they now have to be raised.

Certain connoisseurs will accept quail only roasted on the spit before a wood fire, repudiating all preparations that include a liquid. This attitude is excessive, since there are a number of excellent quail recipes calling for various ingredients, liquid or otherwise.

QUAILS IN CASSEROLE CAILLES À LA CASSEROLE (M.)

Cook them in butter in a special casserole. Melt the glaze with flaming cognac and game stock. Serve in the casserole in which they were cooked.

QUAILS WITH CHERRIES CAILLES AUX CERISES (M.)

Cook the quails in butter in an earthenware or silver casserole. When the quails are almost cooked, drop into the pan 12 pitted cherries per quail. Baste with 1 tbsp. cognac and a few tbsp. rich game stock. Serve in the same casserole.

QUAIL CHAUD-FROID CAILLES (CHAUD-FROID DE) (M.)

Cold Dish: Bone, stuff, and poach the quails as for Quails in the Nest (p. 543). Let cool in the cooking stock. Next, unwrap the strips of fat, dry the quails, and dip them in Brown Chaud-Froid Sauce (p. 139) made with the cooking stock; let the sauce harden, decorate with bits of truffle and poached egg white, and glaze with Aspic Jelly (p. 168).

Note: Chauds-Froids, regardless of type, are not so complicated as they used to be. On the contrary, they are prepared as simply and rapidly as possible. It is customary, in preparing *chauds-froids* of small game, to replace the heads on the birds. The heads are cooked in the oven and the eyes are simulated with hard-boiled egg white and a spot of truffle in the center. They are then heavily glazed with aspic and affixed to the bird with a small wooden pin.

QUAIL CHAUD-FROID IN CASES CAILLES (CHAUD-FROID DE) EN CAISSES (M.)

Quite frequently, and especially for large dinners or buffets for balls, quails covered with Chaud-Froid Sauce (p. 139) and decorated as above are served in oval cases. These cases are made of paper (sometimes very elegant) or of fine fluted porcelain. A quail is placed in each case, which is then encircled with a ribbon of chopped aspic.

QUAILS IN SKIN CAILLES EN CHEMISE (M.)

Stuff the quails with Gratin Forcemeat (p. 175) mixed with *foie gras* and truss them. Place them in pieces of the small intestine of a pig; tie both ends; then wrap each in a piece of cheesecloth. Poach the quails 17 min. in game stock containing Madeira.

Sauce: Reduce the game stock with some port; add finely chopped chicken livers. Strain.

Serving: Remove the cheesecloth; arrange the quails in a timbale, leaving them in their casings. Serve the reduced cooking gravy separately.

QUAILS IN PIG'S CAUL AU GASTRONOME CAILLES EN CRÉPINE AU GASTRONOME (M.)

(1) Split them down the back, remove the small breastbones, season, and spread the inside with a layer of purée of *foie gras* mixed with diced truffles. Cover each quail with 1 tbsp. vegetable Mirepoix (p. 136) cooked in butter; wrap each in a supple piece of pig's caul; cover them with bread crumbs, and cook in butter. (2) Place them in a shallow croustade containing a layer of thick mushroom purée. Melt the glaze in the cooking pan with champagne and game stock. Serve this gravy separately.

CROUSTADE OF QUAILS COURCHAMP CAILLES (CROUSTADE DE) À LA COURCHAMP (M.)

(1) Bone the quails halfway up the back; stuff them with fine chicken forcemeat (p. 176) mixed with chopped truffles. Place them tightly side by side in a buttered sautéing pan, baste with butter, and cook in the oven 10 min. Baste them with a few tbsp. game stock (prepared from quail carcasses) and finish cooking slowly, basting frequently with their own cooking stock. (2) Using white bread or Short Paste (p. 545), prepare a round croustade large enough and deep enough to contain the quails and garnish. Fry this croustade and spread the inside with a layer of fine game forcemeat; place it in an open oven to cook the forcemeat. (3) Arrange the quails in a circle in the croustade. Garnish the center of the croustade with a ragout of game quenelles, cock kidneys, truffles, and mushrooms bound with chicken Velouté (p. 147) reduced with game stock. Place a large thick slice of truffle on each quail; coat the quails with their cooking stock, reduced and strained.

QUAILS EN DAUBE WITH ASPIC CAILLES EN DAUBE À LA GELÉE (M.)

Cold Dish: Bone the quails to the joints of the legs; stuff them and poach 18 min.; finish the rest of the dish (except for poaching time) as for Pheasant en Daube in Aspic (p. 459).

QUAILS FINANCIÈRE CAILLES À LA FINANCIÈRE (M.)

Stuff the quails with truffled Gratin Forcemeat (p. 175); cook them in butter. Place them in a flan crust (baked with fruit pits to hold its shape). Fill the center of the crust with a ragout *à la financière* (see p. 181) mixed with game stock (with the glaze in the pan used for cooking the quails melted with Madeira and added to the stock). Place a slice of truffle on each quail. Coat with reduced game stock.

GRILLED QUAILS BERCHOUX CAILLES GRILLÉES À LA BERCHOUX (M.)

Split the quails down the back; open them and remove the major part of the small bones on the inside. Season with salt and pepper; brush with melted butter. Grill over a low fire. Serve the quails on mushroom purée, or serve with a separate dish of Périgueux Sauce (p. 143) made with game stock.

GRILLED QUAILS EGYPTIAN STYLE CAILLES GRILLÉES À L'ÉGYPTIENNE (M.)

Prepare and cook the quails as in the preceding recipe. Serve them on a rather thick lentil purée. Serve Duxelles Sauce (p. 140) separately.

MINUTE QUAILS CAILLES À LA MINUTE (M.)

Split them lengthwise down the back. Lightly flatten them and remove as many of the bones as possible. Cook them quickly in butter in a sautéing pan. Place them on a round platter. Melt the glaze in the pan with a finger of cognac; add the necessary amount of very reduced, rich Veal Gravy (p. 134); butter, and pour over the quails. Sprinkle with chopped parsley.

Note: They can be garnished with sliced mushrooms sautéed in butter.

QUAIL MOUSSE CAILLES (MOUSSE DE) (M.)

Prepare the same as Pheasant Mousse (p. 462), using quail meat instead of pheasant. This dish is rarely made.

QUAILS IN THE NEST I CAILLES AU NID (M.)

Bone the quails. Save the heads, which must be placed back on the bodies later on. Stuff the quails with Gratin Forcemeat (p. 175) mixed with diced *foie gras* and diced truffles; roll them into the shape of balls or small loaves and wrap each in a thin strip of pork fat; poach in very rich stock prepared with quail bones and scraps, mushroom and truffle peelings, veal stock, and Madeira. Also cook the heads in this stock. When the quails have been poached, remove the strips of fat and glaze the birds in the oven.

Sauce: Strain the quail cooking stock and reduce it by ½. Set aside ⅓ of it to coat the quails. Blend the remainder with chicken Velouté (p. 147), reduce, and finish with fresh cream and butter, and strain. This sauce should be very thick.

Garnish: Small, cooked mushroom caps, very small cock kidneys, olive-shaped truffles, all bound with the prepared cream sauce.

Serving: In advance, prepare a nest of Potato Straws (p. 509) large enough to hold the quails and their garnish. Completely line the inside of the nest with very thin pancakes (see Crêpes, p. 614). Place the quails and garnish in the nest, cover with the reduced sauce you have saved, and replace the head on each quail.

QUAILS IN THE NEST II CAILLES AU NID (P.)

Brown the quails in a casserole, then pour some thin Madeira Sauce (p. 142) over them and cook 10–12 min. Lay them on artichoke bottoms sautéed in butter or, if preferred, simply on large bread croutons fried in butter. Surround each quail with chestnut purée squeezed from a pastry bag with a tube with a small opening to imitate a nest. Baste with the well-skimmed cooking stock.

QUAILS EN PAPILLOTE MONSELET CAILLES EN PAPILLOTE MONSELET (M.)

Spread both sides of the quails with artichoke bottoms, mushrooms, and truffles, all cut in thin julienne strips and bound with chicken Velouté (p. 147) reduced with game stock; wrap each in paper and bake in the oven.

QUAILS PETIT-DUC CAILLES PETIT-DUC (M.)

Split the quails lengthwise down the back, lightly flatten them, and season with salt and paprika. Baste with melted butter, cover with fine white bread crumbs, and grill over a low fire. Lay them on small bases made of Potatoes Anna (p. 506) cooked in oval tartlet molds, and surround with grilled mushrooms filled with grated horseradish. Around the platter, pour a ribbon of game stock reduced with Madeira and lightly buttered.

QUAILS WITH PEAS CAILLES AUX PETITS POIS (M.)

Cook the quails in butter in an earthenware or silver casserole. When the quails are almost cooked, add some small French peas cooked separately with ham (6–8 tbsp. peas per quail). Cover the casserole and finish cooking together. Serve in the same casserole.

QUAILS WITH GRAPES or **QUAILS BACCHUS** CAILLES AUX RAISINS OR À LA BACCHUS (A.)

Pluck and draw some fat young quails hung until just ready, and cover with thin strips of pork fat. Prepare some game stock by cooking larks in veal stock;

strain it, pressing down on the larks; cook until concentrated. Peel and seed some golden grapes, allowing 8–10 grapes per quail. Place the quails in a sautéing pan with a little butter, salt, and cook about 20 min. in a rather hot oven. Lay the cooked quails side by side in a cocotte, add the grapes, cover, and keep hot. Pour some good white wine, Madeira, port, or sherry into the sautéing pan; reduce to 1 oz.; then pour in the prepared game stock; let boil a few moments; remove from the stove, and add some grape juice slightly acidulated with a little wine vinegar or lemon juice. Strain the sauce over the quails and serve.

Quails with Muscat can be made the same way. The glaze in the sautéing pan should be melted with game stock, with some muscat-grape juice and a little curaçao added off the fire. Garnish with large peeled, seeded muscat grapes.

Quails with Cherries can also be made the same way. Melt the glaze in the sautéing pan with game stock, then add some tart cherry juice flavored with a little cherry brandy or maraschino. Garnish with the peeled, pitted tart cherries.

Another preparation is Quails with Pineapple. Garnish with small pineapple cubes. The glaze is melted with game stock, then pineapple juice and kirsch are added.

QUAILS WITH RICE CAILLES AU RIZ (M.)

Cook the quails in butter. Arrange them in a timbale on a bed of Rice Pilaf (p. 512) to which the cooking butter used with the quails has been added. Melt the glaze in the pan with some white wine, add reduced veal gravy, and pour over the birds.

QUAILS WITH RISOTTO or **RISOTTO OF QUAILS** CAILLES AU RIZOTTO or RIZOTTO DE CAILLES (M.)

Stuff the quails with Gratin Forcemeat (p. 175) ; cook them in butter. Serve them in a timbale on a bed of Risotto (p. 513) with the cooking fat used for the quails added to it. Melt the glaze in the pan with game stock and pour over the birds.

QUAILS IN RISOTTO WITH WHITE TRUFFLES or **PIÉMONTAISE** CAILLES AU RIZOTTO AUX TRUFFES BLANCHES or À LA PIÉMONTAISE (M.)

Stuff the quails with mashed pork fat mixed with the same amount of white truffles. Cook them in butter. Place them on a bed of truffle-filled Risotto (p. 513), the white truffles cut very thin and added raw. Baste with the quail cooking glaze melted with game stock.

QUAILS ROMAINE CAILLES À LA ROMAINE (M.)

Note: Quails with Peas, the recipe for which we have already given, are frequently served under this name. But some chefs, including ourselves, prepare them the following way.

Stuff the quails with Gratin Forcemeat (p. 175) and cook in butter. Place them on croutons fried in butter. Melt the glaze in the cooking pan with a finger of vinegar, pour in a little game stock, and strain. To this sauce add some pine nuts and some dried currants and sultanas soaked in warm water, drained, and macerated in Marsala. Cover the quails with this sauce.

Note: This sauce is a variation of the one used for venison. It goes very well with the flavor of quail.

QUAILS UNDER ASH CAILLES SOUS LA CENDRE (M.)

Stuff half-boned quails with a salpicon (tiny cubes) of *foie gras* and truffles seasoned with salt, pepper, and spices and moistened with cognac. Wrap them in vine leaves and cover with thin strips of pork fat. Next wrap them in a triple thickness of buttered paper. Put them into hot ashes covered with live coals. Cook 35 min. Remove the paper in serving.

Note: Frequently, quails stuffed as above, but baked in a layer of Short Paste (p. 545) folded over like a turnover, are served under the same name.

QUAILS SUVAROV CAILLES À LA SOUVAROV (Gi.)

Quail, like woodcock, is a kitchen jewel, and the best way to cook it is on a spit. It is not without merit, however, when prepared the following way. Insert a piece of *foie gras* and a small truffle (preferably raw) into the quail. Place each bird in a small, shallow, heavily buttered earthenware cocotte along with a few pieces of truffle and ½ glass Madeira. Roll out some Flaky Paste (p. 544) until ⅛ in. thick and cut into a round shape that will fit over the cocotte, carefully sticking it to the rim so that the dish will be hermetically sealed and the aroma of quail and truffle cannot escape. Bake in the oven 15–18 min. Plan the cooking so that the quails will be removed from the oven at the precise moment they are to be served, in the same cocotte.

QUAILS TURKISH STYLE CAILLES À LA TURQUE (P.)

Quickly brown the quails in butter, then finish cooking them 12 min. in a Risotto (p. 513) rich in butter. The rice should be partially cooked in advance so that both will be finished at the same time. Place the rice in a timbale or deep platter and lay the quails on top. Baste with a thin Tomato Sauce (p. 146) blended with the glaze of the pan in which the quails were browned. (Figure 272, Page 456.)

QUAIL MOUSSE WITH FRONTIGNAN MOUSSE DE CAILLE AU FRONTIGNAN (M.) (*For 12 persons*)

Cold Dish: 16 quails, 7 oz. *foie gras*, 8 medium-sized peeled, cooked truffles, 3 qt. clarified game aspic, 9 oz. Chaud-Froid Sauce with game stock (see directly below), 9 oz. whipped cream, 12 oz. Frontignan.

Cooking the quails: Truss them and cook in a tightly sealed pot with truffle and mushroom peelings, 15 oz. game aspic, and 3 oz. Frontignan. Let cool in the cooking stock.

Chaud-Froid Sauce: Strain the quail cooking stock, add 9 oz. Brown Chaud-Froid Sauce (p. 139), and skim, adding some game aspic. Reduce this sauce to 9 oz. (as called for above).

Frontignan aspic: Clarify 3 qt. game aspic prepared the usual way, adding, before straining, the rest of the Frontignan.

Mousse: Bone the quails, keeping the wings of 12 of them intact (that is, 24 wings). Remove the skin and mash the meat, adding the *foie gras* and 3 tbsp. Chaud-Froid Sauce. Press through a sieve. Work this purée over ice, adding 2 tbsp. game aspic, then the whipped cream. Put this mixture into a dome-shaped oval mold decorated with truffles and lined with aspic. Pack the mold in ice to harden the mixture. Cover the wings that have been set aside with Chaud-Froid Sauce and glaze with aspic.

Serving: Pour a layer of melted aspic into the bottom of a shallow crystal bowl. When this layer has set, unmold the mousse on top; add a new layer of aspic to make the mousse rigid. Lay the wings covered with Chaud-Froid Sauce, alternating them with thick slices of truffle, on this last layer of aspic. Solidify this turbanlike arrangement by covering with a thin layer of aspic. Keep the bowl on ice until ready to serve. Place it on a sculptured block of ice or simply on a platter surrounded by shaved ice.

STUFFED QUAILS IN ASPIC (CANNED) CAILLES FARCIES À LA GELÉE (CONSERVE) (M.) (*Using 10 quails*)

Forcemeat: 7 oz. fine pork forcemeat and 3½ oz. Gratin Forcemeat (p. 175) made with game; mix well, season with salt and spice, and moisten with a little brandy; 7 oz. raw *foie gras* (net weight); 2½ oz. truffles (net weight after peeling), brandy, salt, pepper, spices.

Cooking stock: 5½ pt. rich meat jelly (prepared with beef, veal knuckle, chicken, calf's feet, fresh pork rind, usual vegetables and herbs); 12 oz. Madeira (or sherry).

Preparation: (1) Pluck and clean the quails the usual way; truss them and remove the backbone and breastbones. Flatten them out on the table; moisten with a little brandy and season with salt and spices. Stuff each quail with a ball of the forcemeat given above, with a piece of *foie gras* studded with a piece of truffle inserted into the middle of each forcemeat ball.

(2) Reshape the quails and wrap each in a band of buttered paper. Lay them, pressed tightly side by side, in a sautéing pan. Cover them with the carcasses turned in butter. Moisten with Madeira. Bring to a boil on the stove, then cover the pan with a buttered paper. Cook in the oven, covered, 20–25 min. (To see if they are cooked, prick them with a trussing needle, and if no blood flows they are ready.) Let the quails cool in their cooking stock.

(3) When they are quite cool, drain, unwrap, wipe them dry, and place them in tin containers with the breasts down. Cover with aspic that has been clarified after adding the quail cooking stock. Seal the containers; try them in boiling water; place them in a deep pot; cover with cold water; place weights on top so that they remain submerged. Boil the containers with 1 quail 1 hr. and 10 min., those with 2 birds 1¼ hr., and those with 4 quails 1 hr. and 25 min.

(4) Remove the containers; set them to cool on a level table, taking care to place them so that the breasts will always be down (in sealing the containers, a drop of tin should be soldered onto the sealed cover so that the top can be distinguished from the bottom). Dry the cans; clean them well by rubbing with dry sawdust. Keep them in a cool, dry place.

Note: The proportions of the forcemeat given above may be increased or diminished, depending upon the size of the quails. The same is true of the truffles. The ball of forcemeat containing the *foie gras* may be covered with an outer layer of Gratin Forcemeat and raw *foie gras* mixed together.

LITTLE BUSTARD

CANEPETIÈRE (M.)

The little bustard is, from every point of view, a smaller kind of great bustard, which has almost disappeared. It is also called the ring-necked bustard because of the 2 circles of white feathers around the neck. The small bustard used to be found in a few of our provinces, notably Berry, but it has become very rare.

Fig. 271 - Roast woodcock (p. 448).
Fig. 272 - Quails turkish style (p. 455).

Fig. 271

Fig. 272

Fig. **273**

Fig. **274**

Those found in the market usually come from Tunisia and Algeria, where they are called Carthage chickens. The plumage of a little bustard is black and white, exactly like that of the great bustard. "If a ring-necked bustard capon were fattened up in a coop in the right way," wrote Toussenel, "it would probably outdo Maine capons and even the fat pullets of Bresse."

Bustards are usually cooked on a spit, in salmis, and in cocotte.

PHEASANT

FAISAN (M.)

Only one of the many varieties of pheasants concerns us: the common pheasant with imbricated plumage, and its gray mate. The pheasant, "the pride of forests and the glory of feasts," as one writer on food put it, occupies an important place in *haute cuisine*. Brillat-Savarin has so extolled its merits that there is nothing more we can add. However, we are far from sharing his opinion that pheasants should be hung so long that they decompose. Certainly, pheasants should be hung a few days before they are used, so that the meat ages and develops its gamy taste, but we feel that it is culinary sacrilege to leave them until they are too high. Like partridge, young pheasant may be distinguished by the pointed tips of the wings, the gray color of the feet, the flexibility of the tip of the breastbone, and the tenderness of the flesh of the wings.

PHEASANT FAISAN (B.-S.)

The pheasant is an enigma understood only by experts, and only they can savor all its goodness.

Every substance has its peak of perfection; some reach this stage before they are fully developed, such as capers, asparagus, gray partridge, pigeons, etc.; others are at their best when they have fully matured, such as melons, most fruits, mutton, beef, roebuck, red partridge; still others, when they begin to decompose, such as medlars, woodcock, and especially pheasant. Pheasant eaten only 3 days after it is killed has nothing distinguished about it. It is neither so delicate as a fat pullet nor so flavorful as a quail. Aged just right, it has tender flesh and a sublime and high flavor, for it resembles both fowl and venison at the same time.

This desirable moment is reached when the pheasant begins to decompose. Then its aroma has developed and blends with an oil that needs a little fermentation to perfect it, just as the oil in coffee is produced only by roasting. This moment can be recognized by the uninitiated by a slight odor and a change in the color of the breast of the bird, but experts divine it by instinct, the kind of instinct, for example, that tells an experienced roasting chef at a glance when to take a fowl off the spit or to let it turn a few more times.

When the pheasant is ready, and no sooner, it should be plucked and carefully studded with fresh, firm pork fat. It is important not to pluck the bird too soon: experience has shown that birds aged in their feathers have a much finer flavor than those left bare any length of time. Either contact with the air neutralizes some of the aroma or some of the juices that nourish the feathers are reabsorbed into the flesh and make it too high. When the pheasant has been cleaned and drawn, it should be stuffed the following way:

Take 2 woodcocks; bone and draw them to make 2 portions: the first of the meat, the second of the entrails and livers.

Take the meat and chop it into forcemeat with steamed beef marrow, a little

Fig. 273 - Pheasant bohémienne (p. 458).
Fig. 274 - Pheasant en daube in aspic (p. 459).

grated pork fat, pepper, salt, *fines herbes*, and enough good truffles to fill the inside of the pheasant. Take care to fix the stuffing so that it will not come out, which is sometimes difficult to do, when the bird is rather high. However, there are ways—among them, cutting a crust of bread and tying it with a band of thread, to serve as a stopper.

Cut a slice of bread long enough to protrude 2 thumbs beyond the pheasant bedded on it; then take the woodcock livers and entrails and pound them in a mortar with 2 large truffles, 1 anchovy, a little grated pork fat, and a nice piece of good fresh butter. Spread this paste evenly over the bread and place it under the pheasant so that when the pheasant is roasted all the juice that flows will moisten it.

When the pheasant is cooked, serve it bedded gracefully on the bread; surround with bitter oranges; and rest easy over the outcome.

This highly flavorful dish should be basted, preferably, with wine from the vineyards of upper Burgundy. Prepared according to this recipe, pheasant, already distinguished in its own right, is enriched on the outside by the flavorful pork fat, which becomes charred; it is impregnated inside with the aromatic gasses escaping from the woodcock and the truffles. The bread, already so richly spread, is triply enriched with the juices flowing from the roasting bird. Thus, of all the delicacies gathered together, not a jot escapes the taste, and considering the excellence of this dish, I find it worthy of the tables of kings.

PHEASANT BOHÉMIENNE FAISAN À LA BOHÉMIENNE (M.)

Half bone the pheasant from the back and place inside a small *foie gras* lightly studded with truffles, seasoned with paprika, and moistened with 2 tbsp. cognac. Truss the pheasant and cover the breast with strips of pork fat or bacon. Cook in butter in a silver or earthenware casserole. Cook uncovered in the oven about 35 min. Just before serving, baste with a few tbsp. game stock reduced with Madeira. Serve in the cooking casserole. (Figure 273, Page 457.)

PHEASANT BRAZILIAN STYLE FAISAN À LA BRÉSILIENNE (R.)

Pluck, draw, and singe a young pheasant. Finely chop the meat of 1 woodcock and the same amount of pork fat; mix this with *foie gras* and truffles, season with salt and pepper, and stuff the bird with it. Cover with thin strips of pork fat. Dice some ham and cut some carrots and onions in rings; add thyme, bay leaf, parsley, and truffle peelings, and place in a casserole with a piece of butter the size of an egg; pour in 1 small glass Malaga. Cook several minutes, then let cool. Put this ragout on top and underneath the pheasant, which is wrapped in buttered white paper and tied with string, and roast. After 1 hr. remove the paper and the pork fat and brown the pheasant over an open fire. Heat the woodcock carcass and entrails (leaving out the gizzard) in butter, season with salt and pepper, and press through a strainer to make a purée; add chopped truffles and some gravy. Cut round croutons from ordinary French bread, hollow the centers slightly, and brown them in butter. Fill the croutons with the purée, cover them with the gravy from the roasting, and lay them around the pheasant on a platter.

PHEASANT IN CASSEROLE FAISAN EN CASSEROLE (M.)

Truss the pheasant and cook it in butter in the utensil in which it is to be served, either an earthenware casserole or a cocotte. Melt the glaze in the casserole with a finger of cognac and a few tbsp. game stock.

PHEASANT CHAUD-FROID FAISAN (CHAUD-FROID DE) (M.)

Cold Dish: (1) Cut up a cold roast pheasant; remove the skin and trim the pieces. (2) Dip them in Brown Chaud-Froid Sauce (p. 139) made with pheasant stock; decorate with truffle and glaze with Aspic Jelly (p. 168). (3) For serving, proceed as directed in recipes for Chicken Chaud-Froid (p. 413) and other *chauds-froids.*

PHEASANT WITH SAUERKRAUT FAISAN À LA CHOUCROUTE (M.)

Truss the pheasant and cook in butter in a casserole. Place it, whole or cut into pieces (as it is usually served), on a bed of well-braised sauerkraut. Surround with small rectangles of bacon and slices of sausage (the sausage cooked in the sauerkraut). Melt the glaze in the casserole with a few tbsp. game stock. Serve this sauce separately.

PHEASANT EN COCOTTE FAISAN EN COCOTTE (P.)

Truss the pheasant and brown it in butter in an earthenware cocotte or baking dish. When it is well browned on both sides, salt it, cover it, and let it simmer slowly 1/4 hr.; then add 15 small onions browned in butter and 15 well-washed small raw mushrooms. Pour in a little Madeira, cover, and finish cooking. Serve in the cocotte.

PHEASANT EN DAUBE IN ASPIC FAISAN EN DAUBE À LA GELÉE (M.) (*For 6 to 8 persons*)

Cold Dish: Bone the pheasant from the back, taking care to cut it only up to the middle of the back. Leave on as much skin as possible, so it can be folded over the forcemeat with which the pheasant is stuffed. Lay the pheasant on the table, breast down; stuff with 7 oz. Light Forcemeat (p. 173) and 3½ oz. Gratin Forcemeat (p. 175). Put ½ lb. seasoned, raw *foie gras* studded with 4 large peeled, seasoned truffles in the center of this forcemeat. Close the skin over and restore the bird to its original shape; wrap it in cheesecloth and tie both ends. Cook it in a braising pan containing: 2 lb. veal knuckle and 1½ lb. lean beef cut into small pieces and browned in the oven, the pheasant carcass and giblets, ½ onion and 1 carrot cut in rings. Pour in 1 pt. Madeira, bring to a boil on top of the stove, and, when the liquid has reduced by ½, add 2 qt. Chicken Aspic (p. 169). Simmer 1½ hr. Drain the pheasant, unwrap it, let it set a few moments, and then wrap again in the cheesecloth after washing it in warm water and wringing it dry. Lay the pheasant in an oval terrine. Strain the cooking stock, skim off the fat, and, when it is almost cold, pour it over the pheasant.

The following day, remove the pheasant from the terrine, unwrap it, wipe it dry, and set it in an oval crystal bowl. Clarify the Aspic Jelly in the usual way and cover the pheasant with it. (Figure 274, Page 457.)

STUFFED PHEASANT BRAISED IN PORT FAISAN FARCI BRAISÉ AU PORTO (A.) (*For 6 to 8 persons*)

Take: 1½ pt. red port, 7 oz. (at least) fine black Périgord truffles, 7 oz. duck *foie gras*, 2 oz. brandy, 1 young, fat, well-hung pheasant, 1 meaty woodcock, 1 strip of pork fat, 1 slice of bread (without crust) 1 in. thick and large enough to hold the pheasant, butter, salt, and pepper. Draw and singe the pheasant, saving the entrails. Bone the woodcock and set aside the entrails after cleaning them. Brush, wash, and peel the truffles; cook them in a little port;

save the peelings. Finely chop the meat of the woodcock, the *foie gras,* truffle peelings, the cleaned pheasant and woodcock gizzards; mix well. Prepare a smooth forcemeat with the chopped mixture, using some of the truffles cut in small pieces, salt, pepper, the port used for cooking the truffles, and 1 jigger brandy; stuff the pheasant with this forcemeat.

Cut a fine truffle in round slices and slip these slices under the skin of the pheasant; cover with strips of pork fat, and let it stand 3 days to absorb the combined flavors of the woodcock, truffles, *foie gras,* port, and brandy. Then brown the pheasant in a casserole 15 min. with more or less butter, depending upon the amount of fat on the bird; pour 1 jigger flaming brandy over it, and cook at low heat 1¼ hr., basting from time to time with the rest of the port, without any other seasoning.

Meanwhile, prepare the *tartine* or toast. Cut the slice of bread into 6 or 8 pieces and brown all sides in butter to make them firm enough. Arrange these pieces on a platter to form the original shape of the slice; keep warm.

Cook the pheasant and woodcock entrails quickly over a hot fire; pour the rest of the brandy, flaming, over them; salt and pepper. Pour the skimmed cooking gravy over the *tartine,* spread the entrails over it, place the pheasant on top, decorate with the rest of the truffles, and serve. A well-made *tartine* should be crusty outside and soft inside. Pheasant prepared this way is a fragrant, superb-tasting dish that should melt in the mouth. I do not believe there is any finer eating of its sort.

ROAST PHEASANT FAISAN RÔTI (P.)

The breast of roast game is always covered with strips of pork fat or bacon. A fine pheasant should be roasted about 40 min. and be generously basted with butter. The juices from the roast should be partially skimmed. Serve the pheasant on a canapé of white bread browned in the oven with fat from the roast. Serve with water cress and lemon quarters.

PHEASANT HOLY ALLIANCE or STUFFED PHEASANT BRILLAT-SAVARIN FAISAN À LA SAINTE-ALLIANCE or FAISAN ÉTOFFÉ BRILLAT-SAVARIN (M.)

Stuff a young pheasant with Light Forcemeat (p. 173) made from the flesh of 2 boned woodcocks, grated pork fat, poached beef marrow, and peeled, quartered truffles sautéed in butter. Season with salt and pepper. Truss the pheasant, cover the breast with thin strips of pork fat or bacon, and place on a spit. Make a forcemeat from the mashed entrails of the 2 woodcocks, including the livers, and 2 mashed truffles, adding a little grated suet, 1 soaked anchovy (pressed through a sieve), and a piece of fresh butter. Spread this mixture on a grilled bread crouton cut to the size of the pheasant. When the pheasant is ⅔ cooked, place this crouton under it so that it will soak up the juices that flow from the bird. Serve the pheasant on the crouton and surround with bitter orange slices.

Brillat-Savarin said that this masterpiece was executed in his presence by the head chef of Mme de Ville-Plaine, at the Château de la Grange. This clever preparation had a deserved success, Brillat-Savarin added (*Physiologie du goût*).

PHEASANT IN SALMIS or **PHEASANT SALMIS** FAISAN EN SALMIS or SALMIS DE FAISAN (M.)

(1) Roast the pheasant until partially cooked; cut it into 6 pieces and remove the skin. Place the pieces in a sautéing pan with 10 small cooked mushrooms, 20 slices of truffle, 1 tbsp. flamed cognac, 2 tbsp. cooking liquid from the mushrooms. Cover with buttered paper and keep hot.

(2) Add to a fine Mirepoix (p. 136) cooked in butter in advance: carcass, wings, and chopped or mashed skin, 1 tbsp. chopped shallot, and a pinch of coarse-ground pepper. Pour in 6 oz. white wine, reduce to ¾, add 7 oz. Espagnole Sauce (p. 137) and 3 oz. game stock, and cook on a low fire ¼ hr. Press through a strainer; put back on the fire and thin with a few tbsp. game stock; simmer 8 min., skimming when necessary, and strain through a cone-shaped sieve onto the pieces of pheasant and the garnish.

(3) Heat without boiling and add a little butter at the end. Serve surrounded by heart-shaped croutons fried in butter, spread with Gratin Forcemeat (p. 175), and heated in the oven a few moments.

PHEASANT SAUTÉ FAISAN SAUTÉ (M.)

Cut up a young pheasant as you would a chicken. Season with salt and pepper and sauté quickly in butter in a flat casserole. When the pheasant pieces are well seared, cover and finish cooking. Place on a round platter or in a timbale. Melt the glaze in the pan with white wine, add a few tbsp. game stock, reduce, butter, and pour over the pheasant.

PHEASANT SAUTÉ WITH MUSHROOMS FAISAN SAUTÉ AUX CHAMPIGNONS (M.)

Prepare the pheasant as above. When it is almost cooked, add 12 fluted raw mushroom caps to the sautéing pan. Finish cooking together. Place the pheasant on a platter and garnish with the mushrooms. Melt the glaze in the pan with Madeira, add some game stock, reduce, butter, and pour over the pheasant.

PHEASANT SAUTÉ WITH CHESTNUTS FAISAN SAUTÉ AUX MARRONS (M.)

Substitute braised chestnuts for the mushrooms given in the preceding recipe.

PHEASANT SAUTÉ PÉRIGOURDINE FAISAN SAUTÉ PÉRIGOURDINE (M.)

Sauté the pheasant in butter; melt the glaze in the pan with Madeira and game stock. Serve on a platter surrounded by tartlets filled with a salpicon (tiny cubes) of *foie gras* and truffles bound with rich game stock.

PHEASANT SAUTÉ WITH TRUFFLES FAISAN SAUTÉ AUX TRUFFES (M.)

Follow recipe for Pheasant Sauté with Mushrooms (above), substituting thick slices of truffle for the mushrooms.

PHEASANT SUVAROV FAISAN SOUVAROV (M.)

Stuff the pheasant with a salpicon (tiny cubes) of *foie gras* and truffles seasoned with salt and spices and moistened with cognac. Truss the pheasant, cover the breast with strips of pork fat or bacon, and cook in the oven 40 min.

Then untruss it, remove the fat, and place it in a cocotte with 8 medium-sized peeled truffles cooked in butter (the lid of the pan tightly closed). Melt the glaze in the roasting pan with Madeira and game stock. Reduce, strain, and pour over the pheasant; seal the cover of the cocotte as directed in the recipe for Pullet Suvarov (p. 392), and finish the same way.

PHEASANT VALLÉE D'AUGE FAISAN À LA VALLÉE D'AUGE (M.)

Prepare like Pheasant en Cocotte (p. 459), but without the garnish, and, when it is almost cooked, pour ½ pt. sweet cream over it. Just before serving, add the juice of 1 lemon or a finger of vinegar. Serve in the cocotte with a separate dish of unsweetened applesauce.

PHEASANT MOUSSE MOUSSE DE FAISAN (M.)

Whatever the basic ingredient, the proportions and method of preparing the mousse stay the same. In this case, pheasant meat is used, and the mousse is served with Semiglaze Sauce (p. 138) to which reduced game stock (made from the scraps and carcass of the bird) has been added. The first part of the following recipe for Pheasant Mousse Carême may be used.

PHEASANT MOUSSE CARÊME MOUSSE DE FAISAN CARÊME (M.) (*For 6 persons*)

(1) Bone a pheasant, removing the skin and all tendons; pound the flesh in a mortar, adding 3½ oz. Gratin Forcemeat (p. 175) and the same amount of cooked *foie gras*. While mashing, add 1 egg white and 3 tbsp. very reduced game stock. Season and strain through a fine sieve. Work this forcemeat over ice, gradually blending in 9 oz. fresh heavy cream; finish with 2 stiffly beaten egg whites.

(2) Pour this mixture into a plain buttered mold; poach 45 min. in a *bain-marie*.

Sauce: Brown ½ lb. cubed lean veal in butter, adding 1 medium-sized onion and 1 carrot, also cubed, and the crushed carcass and scraps of the pheasant. Melt the glaze in the pan with some sherry and add 1 pt. chicken Velouté (p. 147), 3½ oz. mushroom peelings, and 2 oz. truffle peelings. Cook very gently 1 hr., taking care to skim the sauce frequently. Strain this sauce, reduce it to a good consistency, and strain it again. Just before serving, add 6 oz. whipped cream to the sauce.

Garnish: 6 ortolans stuffed with *foie gras* and truffles, poached in sherry, and served in small oval patty shells; 6 large truffles cooked in champagne; 6 medallions of calf's sweetbreads sautéed in butter.

Serving: Unmold onto a fried bread crouton fixed to a platter with paste made of flour and water. Arrange the garnish on top, alternating the ingredients. Serve the sauce separately.

Note: The mousse composition given in this recipe may also be used for other dishes such as Pheasant Mousseline, Pheasant Soufflé, etc.

PHEASANT GALANTINE GALANTINE DE FAISAN (A.) (*For 6 persons*)

Cold Dish: Take 1 fine pheasant, 1 strip of pork fat.

For the garnish: 5 oz. *foie gras*, 2½ oz. pickled tongue, 2½ oz. York ham, 2½ oz. sherry, 2 oz. bacon, 1½ oz. truffles, 1 jigger cognac, ⅓ oz. blanched pistachios, salt, spices.

For the forcemeat: 5 oz. trimmed round of veal, 5 oz. fresh bacon without rind, 2 oz. pork fat, 1 oz. mushrooms, 1 fresh egg, 1 small shallot, 1 sprig thyme, 1 small bay leaf, chicken and pheasant livers, salt, pepper, and 4 spices (see *Note,* p. 301).

For the cooking stock: ½ lb. veal knuckle, 5 oz. leg of beef, 3½ oz. white wine, 2½ oz. lean beef or lean flesh of game fowl, 2 oz. carrots, 1 oz. lean pork rind, 1 oz. sherry, ⅔ oz. onion, 1 tsp. salt, 2 egg whites, 1 calf's foot, giblets of 1 chicken, 1 extra chicken liver, 1 clove, carcass and scraps of the pheasant, game stock, *bouquet garni.*

Pluck, clean, and singe the pheasant; bone it and gently remove the meat from the skin; slice it thin; remove the tendons. Save the scraps. Clean the chicken giblets. Put aside the 2 chicken livers and the pheasant liver.

Preparing the cooking stock: Put into a deep pot the leg of beef, veal knuckle, and calf's foot, all cut into pieces; blanched pork rind, chicken giblets, pheasant carcass and scraps. Bring to a boil; skim; add carrot, onion, clove, *bouquet garni,* salt; reduce the heat and simmer 3 hr. Strain; let cool; skim off the fat.

Preparing the garnish: Marinate the *foie gras,* tongue, bacon, York ham, and peeled truffles several hours in the sherry and cognac. Then remove them, cut into pieces, and season with salt and spices.

Preparing the forcemeat: Grate the pork fat, put it into a sautéing pan, melt it, then add chopped mushrooms, chopped shallot, thyme, bay leaf, 2 chicken livers and pheasant liver; sear them quickly without letting them cook through. Pour all of this into a mortar and mash this Gratin Forcemeat; press through a sieve. Set aside. Mash the round of veal and bacon in a mortar along with the chopped truffle peelings; season with salt, pepper, spices to taste, and mix in the remainder of the marinade and the egg; strain. Mix this forcemeat with the Gratin Forcemeat.

Preparing the galantine: Spread out the pheasant skin on a clean cloth; stop up any holes in the skin; spread out a layer of forcemeat on the skin, which you then garnish with part of the marinated ingredients, alternating the colors; sprinkle with a few pistachios; lengthwise along the galantine, place the thin slices of pheasant meat on top; make other layers in the same way until all the ingredients have been used. Roll the stuffed pheasant into an even, rather elongated loaf and sew up the skin; wrap it in the strip of pork fat, then in the cloth; squeeze it tightly and tie both ends. Cook this galantine in the prepared cooking stock, adding the white wine and a little game stock; simmer about 1 hr. Let it cool a little, then drain and unwrap it; rewrap in the same cloth after washing the cloth in hot water; squeeze it tightly and sew the cloth. Weight it down, not too heavily, and let it cool under pressure. Reduce the cooking stock; let cool and skim.

Preparing the aspic: Add the finely chopped lean beef or lean meat of game fowl and the egg whites to the cooled, skimmed cooking stock; beat; bring to a boil over moderate heat, beating gently; continue cooking at low heat ¼ hr. At the end, add the sherry; bring to a quick boil a moment or so; taste; strain through a cloth.

Serving: Take the cloth off the galantine, wipe off the fat, and pour the somewhat still liquid aspic over it until it is completely covered with a good layer. Place it on a platter, surround it with chopped aspic, and decorate the border of the platter with crescent-, star-, or triangle-shaped pieces of aspic.

Young Partridge Galantine is prepared the same way. Cook only 40 min. Galantines of small game fowl may be made with the same recipe.

GALANTINE OF PHEASANT IN PLUMAGE GALANTINE DE FAISAN EN VOLIÈRE (J.)

Cold Dish: Save the tail, wings, and head of the pheasant. Prepare the galantine as in the preceding recipe. Place the slices overlapping in an arc on the platter; surround them with chopped aspic. In the center of the platter place the head, wings, and tail of the pheasant, held into place by wooden pins stuck through each part of the bird and into a large piece of bread, which takes the place of the body of the pheasant. (Figure 275, Page 464.)

HAZEL HEN[1]

GELINOTTE (A.)

The common hazel hen is a wild fowl belonging to the order of gallinaceae, of the species Ganga, like grouse. The head is crested and the feet are tufted halfway up the leg. Its plumage is reddish, spotted with white, gray, brown, and black. In France it is found in forest-covered mountains, principally in the Vosges. The flesh of the hazel hen is delicate, with a resinous flavor owing to the pine cones on which it feeds. This flavor is lessened by marinating the bird in milk.

Hazel hen can be prepared many ways: roasted, grilled, braised, in salmis, soufflés, galantines, pies, etc. Hazel hen roasted on the spit is simply barded with pork fat or bacon like partridge, or stuffed with juniper berries. However, only young birds of fine quality should be roasted. The dryness of the meat usually makes it necessary to baste the hazel hen with melted butter or with cream (either sweet or acidulated with lemon juice) while roasting it before a very hot fire 15–20 min., depending on the size of the bird. If the hazel hen is to be grilled, it should first be boned, then rolled in melted butter, then in bread crumbs, and finally seasoned. It should be grilled 12 min. and served with Tartar Sauce (p. 158). In some regions braised hazel hen is cooked in Béchamel Sauce (p. 146). After braising, it is sprinkled with bread crumbs and placed in the oven to brown. In my opinion, the best way to prepare hazel hen is to braise it in cream. This is the way it should be done.

For 2 persons, take: 5 oz. milk, 5 oz. cream, 1 oz. butter, 1 young, fresh hazel hen (with white flesh), a strip of pork fat or bacon, juice of ½ lemon, salt, pepper. Draw the hazel hen and wash out the insides with a little milk; empty it, then pour the rest of the milk on the bird after setting it on a plate. Turn it frequently; let it soak in the milk at least 1 hr. Drain, truss, and cover the breast with a strip of pork fat or bacon. Place it in a casserole with the butter and brown on all sides 15 min. Skim off the fat, salt and pepper, add the cream, and simmer 20 min. Five minutes before it is finished, add the lemon juice, taste, and add seasoning if needed. Place the hazel hen on a platter, cover with the sauce, and serve.

---

[1] Ptarmigans imported from Russia, usually sold frozen in U. S. markets, are wrongly called hazel hens.

The best way to cook this game bird is to braise it in cream.

Fig. 275 - Galantine of pheasant in plumage (p. 464).

Fig. **275**

Fig. **276**

THRUSHES

GRIVES (M.)

French thrushes include the vine thrush, the missel thrush, the redwing, and the fieldfare. The first two are sedentary, while the others are migratory. But the most common, the one most used in cooking, is the gray-winged thrush, which feasts first in apple trees and then on the vine. The missel thrush is the largest but also the rarest.

Thrushes are not drawn; only the gizzard is removed. As for woodcock, the eyes should be taken out. The birds are trussed the same way by crossing the legs and pulling the head down and sticking the beak into the stomach.

Note: All quail recipes can be used for thrushes.

THRUSHES BACCHUS GRIVES À LA BACCHUS (A.)

Prepare the same as Quails with Grapes (p. 453). (Figure 277, Page 468.)

THRUSHES BONNE FEMME GRIVES À LA BONNE FEMME (P.)

Brown the thrushes in butter with a few tiny strips of bacon; place them in a cocotte and add some bread croutons cubed about the size of a sugar cube and fried in butter. Add a finger of white wine or cognac, season, cover, and cook in the oven 10 min. Serve as is when ready.

THRUSH CHAUD-FROID GRIVES (CHAUD-FROID DE) (M.)

Cold Dish: Bone the thrushes; stuff with Gratin Forcemeat (p. 175) lightly flavored with juniper berries; reshape them and poach as you would quails. After cooling, wipe them dry and dip them in Brown Chaud-Froid Sauce (p. 139) with some game stock made from the carcasses added. Decorate with hard-boiled egg white and truffle, glaze with Aspic Jelly (p. 168), and chill in the refrigerator. The thrushes may be dressed however the cook prefers, but the heads must always be put back on and the eyes simulated with pieces of hard-boiled egg white and a speck of truffle. Thrush Chaud-Froid is usually served in porcelain or paper cases. The birds may also be placed in crystal cups and covered with very clear aspic.

THRUSHES WITH JUNIPER BERRIES GRIVES AU GENIÈVRE (P.)

Proceeds as for Thrushes Bonne Femme (above), leaving out the bacon and the croutons and adding a pinch of crushed juniper berries to the cocotte. Also add a little cognac and a few tbsp. brown gravy. Serve in the same cocotte.

GROUSE (A.)

The red grouse of Scotland is often called heath cock. A wild bird that lives in the North, it has very delicate flesh. Grouse is common in the heather-covered mountains of Scotland and is especially good from August to October. Young birds are covered with thin strips of pork fat and roasted on the spit. *Cooking time:* 12–15 min. In England, they are served with a kind of Venison Sauce made from the grouse gravy seasoned with pepper, cloves, and cinnamon and flavored with orange peel and port, sweetened with red-currant jelly. This sauce is called Victoria Sauce. Birds not so young are braised in a good gravy containing white wine or in cream. In the first case, they are served with sauerkraut and a sauce made by concentrating the cooking gravy—the dish is called Grouse Norwegian

Fig. 276 - Chartreuse of partridge (p. 468).

Style, or *à la norvégienne.* Grouse in Cream are prepared the same as hazel hen. Finally, old birds are made into pies. In any case, only freshly killed grouse should be used, and it is a good idea to wash them several times in milk before cooking them.

ORTOLANS (A.)

The ortolan is a small bird living in middle and southern Europe. It is common in the south of France. Ortolans, like figpeckers, are captured in large groups, with a net. They are put into cages, fattened on grain, and then suffocated. They are plucked after scalding. Ortolans, like figpeckers, are usually merely roasted, without any previous preparation. This is the best way to prepare them, though they can be cooked in a cocotte.

ORTOLANS POACHED IN BRANDY ORTOLANS POCHÉS À LA FINE CHAMPAGNE (A.) (*For 4 persons*)

Take: 7 oz. chicken consommé, 1½ oz. champagne brandy, 12 fat ortolans, salt, and pepper. Put ½ the brandy inside each ortolan, salt and pepper them, group them in threes, then put them into a perfectly cleaned pork bladder and add the chicken consommé. Tie the bladder airtight and plunge into boiling water; cook 20 min. Remove the ortolans from the bladder, arrange on a platter, and keep warm. Reduce the cooking stock, skim off the fat, pour it over the ortolans, and serve.

Other small birds can be cooked the same way: figpeckers, larks, thrushes, quails, etc.

ORTOLANS IN SARCOPHAGI ORTOLANS EN SARCOPHAGES (A.) (*For 12 persons*)

Take: 13 oz. veal stock, 7 oz. purée of *foie gras,* 3½ oz. Madeira or white port, 1½ oz. Mirepoix (p. 136), 12 freshly killed ortolans in old champagne brandy, 12 large black Périgord truffles, 12 thin strips of pork fat, 3 thrushes, 4 spices (see *Note,* p. 301), salt, and pepper. Bone the ortolans and stuff them with purée of *foie gras.* Hollow out the truffles, saving a round piece to make a stopper; season to taste with salt, pepper, and spices. Roast the thrushes, press them through a strainer, add the gravy to the veal stock, also the wine and the Mirepoix. Heat this and put the ortolans into this mixture (which is an excellent game stock) for 5 min., then remove them. Concentrate the stock, skim off the fat. Insert 1 ortolan into each truffle, close the truffle with the piece you have saved for a stopper, and cover with a strip of pork fat. To cook, use one of the methods recommended for cooking truffles, especially the one called *à la maréchale* (see below). Remove the residue of the fat strips, arrange the truffles on a napkin-covered platter, and serve with a separate dish of the concentrated, skimmed cooking gravy. This dish with the picturesque but rather macabre name, Ortolans in Coffins, is one of the most delicate preparations in modern cooking. Dry champagne is an excellent accompaniment.

One of the best ways to prepare truffles *à la maréchale* is to season them with salt and pepper, cover with thin strips of pork fat, wrap them separately in paper, and cook them 1 hr. in hot wood ashes. When they are cooked, unwrap them, wipe them off, and place them on a napkin-covered platter; the napkin is then folded over the truffles. They are served as they are, with some fresh butter.

These truffles *au naturel* are simply exquisite. If wood ashes are not available, the truffles covered with pork strips and seasoned with salt and pepper can be cooked on a spit or in a pan. Truffles are also sprinkled with salt, pepper, and herbs and steam-cooked with water or a mixture of wine and brandy; or even cooked in butter, or in Madeira, port, Alicante, or champagne, enriching them with a good herb-and-vegetable-flavored stock.

RING DOVE OR WOOD PIGEON

PALOMBES

Ring doves are wild, migratory pigeons found in France in the coastal regions of the Pyrenees, especially near Biarritz, during March. They are excellent game fowl.

ROAST RING DOVES PALOMBES RÔTIES (A.) (*For 6 persons*)

Pluck and draw 3 ring doves; lay the heads and entrails aside, and stuff each dove with 8 or 10 fresh grapes; salt, cover with a thin strip of pork fat, and place on spits. Give them plenty of fire at first to sear them, then pour a little champagne brandy over them, lower the fire, and continue cooking 20 min., basting with good chicken stock. The meat should remain pink.

Meanwhile, make *tartines* by grilling 6 slices of bread. Remove the brains from the dove heads, mix them with the entrails you have saved, pour flaming brandy over them, cook a moment, mash, press through a sieve, and season to taste with salt and pepper (this purée is to be spread over the *tartines*). Place the slices of grilled bread on a platter, moisten them with the skimmed gravy from the dripping pan, and spread the purée on top; cut the doves in half, place each half on a slice of bread, and serve.

Use this recipe to prepare Hazel Hens in Armagnac and Grouse in Whisky.

PARTRIDGES

PERDREAUX (M.)

The gray partridge of the plains holds first place among the game fowl of France and is too well known to need any lengthy discussion here. We shall say only that young partridge is recognized by its gray feet and the pointed wing feathers. Birds from new broods which are only ½ or ⅔ grown are called *pouillards*. A partridge is fully grown when the plumage is speckled, and the old saying of the hunt, "On St. Rémy's Day, young partridges are old partridges," is slightly exaggerated, for in reality a young partridge does not become a partridge until the end of a year.

An old partridge has rounded tips on its large wing feathers. Though a few snips of the scissors can give it a young look, its age can still be told by the red circle around the eye, and the older it gets the more revealing does this circle become. An old partridge is hardly good for more than flavoring cabbage and is best used in forcemeat.

Note: Almost all the pheasant recipes may be used in preparing partridge.

PARTRIDGE CATALANE PERDREAU À LA CATALANE (R.)

Prepare a partridge with a thin strip of pork fat. Brown it with an egg-sized piece of butter with a *bouquet garni* (thyme, bay leaf, and parsley). Cover and cook about 20 min. Drain off the fat and put 1 tbsp. tomato purée into the pan.

Half cook 6 cloves of garlic in boiling water. Add these cloves of garlic to the partridge along with slices of lemon or bitter orange, also boiled. Let boil a few minutes together. Serve very hot.

PARTRIDGE NORMANDE PERDREAU À LA NORMANDE (M.)

Brown the trussed partridge in butter. Put it into an earthenware casserole on a bed of russet apples peeled, sliced thin, and cooked a little in butter (about 2 medium-sized apples per partridge). Place the rest of the apples around the partridge. Moisten with fresh cream and a large tbsp. Calvados (fine apple brandy). Finish cooking in the oven (18–20 min.). Serve in the same casserole.

PARTRIDGE PÉRIGOURDINE PERDREAU À LA PÉRIGOURDINE (M.)

Stuff the partridge with truffles and pan-roast it. Place it on a bread crouton spread with *foie gras*. Melt the glaze in the pan with Madeira and add to Périgueux Sauce (p. 143). Serve separately.

PARTRIDGE ST. HUBERT PERDREAU À LA SAINT-HUBERT (M.)

Open a partridge down the back; flatten it lightly after removing the small bones inside and the leg and wing bones. Season with salt and pepper and sear a few moments in burning-hot butter. Let cool and spread both sides with a Gratin Forcemeat (see p. 175) made with its liver and a little chicken liver mixed with ½ its weight in fine pork forcemeat and 1 heaping tbsp. Duxelles (p. 176). Wrap the partridge in a piece of pig's caul. Tie the skin well so that the forcemeat will not come out. Spread with melted butter and cover with freshly sifted bread crumbs. Cook on the grill over a moderate fire. Arrange the partridge on a round platter, on a bed of chestnut purée. Serve with Maître d'Hôtel Butter (p. 164) with a little chopped shallot cooked in white wine and 1 tbsp. melted Meat Glaze (p. 135) added to it.

CHARTREUSE OF PARTRIDGE PERDRIX (CHARTREUSE DE) (P.)

Blanch 1 or 2 cabbages in boiling water, drain, then braise them in fat in a cocotte, placing in the middle 1 or more partridges previously browned in butter. Also add a sausage or saveloy (see p. 375) and a piece of desalted pork fat or bacon. Flavor the cabbage with carrots, onions, *bouquet garni,* peppercorns. Cover the cocotte tightly and braise in the oven about 1½ hr. Unless the bird is tough, remove it when it is cooked and let the cabbage and pork fat continue to braise, for they cannot be too well cooked. For the dressing, the most delicate part of the work, prepare in advance carrots and turnips first sliced 1 in. thick, then cut in cylinders about the thickness of a pencil, using a special tube similar to an apple corer, only smaller. Separately, cook these vegetables in salted water. Butter a rather large timbale mold with soft but not melted butter and, when the vegetables have been drained and cooled, place them against the walls of the mold, in alternate rows, so that both sides and bottom are completely lined.

Drain the cabbage and chop it into large pieces; place it in the mold, pressing it in well and leaving a hollow in the center for the pieces of partridge. Finish filling the mold with cabbage, pressing it down tightly. Heat in the oven 5 min., reverse the mold on a round platter, and raise it carefully; arrange rectangles of the bacon and slices of sausage around it. Serve with a thin Semi-

Fig. 277 - Thrushes Bacchus (p. 465).
Fig. 278 - Venison chops with poivrade sauce (p. 472).

Fig. 277

Fig. 278

Fig. 279

Fig. 280

glaze Sauce (p. 138). This dish is very pretty and is suitable for serving at a dinner party.

Note: The carrots and turnips may be cut with a ball vegetable cutter. The partridge cooked with the cabbage may be used if it is not too tough. Partridge is also cooked with the cabbage only for the flavor and then replaced with a young roast partridge or one cooked in butter and kept slightly rare. (Figure 276, Page 465.)

PARTRIDGE WITH CABBAGE BOURGEOISE PERDRIX AUX CHOUX À LA BOURGEOISE (M.) (*For 3 persons*)

(1) Cut a Savoy cabbage (curly-leaved and mild) in quarters and remove the outer leaves and the stump. Blanch and drain it, season with salt and pepper, and put into a pot with skimmed white bouillon, 1 large carrot, 1 onion stuck with a clove, and a *bouquet garni.* Bring to a boil, then add a trussed partridge browned in the oven, 4 oz. blanched pork fat or bacon, and a small sausage. Cover with a greased paper, put the lid on the pot, and cook in the oven at low heat. (Remove the pork fat and sausage after 35 min.)

(2) Drain the partridge and cut it into pieces. Drain the cabbage in a colander, remove carrot, onion, and *bouquet,* and press the cabbage through with the back of a ladle. Place the cabbage in a timbale or on a platter; lay the pieces of partridge on top, with the pork fat or bacon cut in small rectangles, the sausage and carrot sliced.

PARTRIDGE WITH CABBAGE (As Served in Restaurants) PERDRIX AUX CHOUX (DES RESTAURANTS) (M.)

(1) Prepare partridge and cabbage as in the preceding recipe. (2) Butter a semispherical mold (a soufflé timbale) ; line it with thin round slices of sausage, slices of carrots cooked with the cabbage, small rectangles of pork fat or bacon and of green beans, alternating the colors. Line this with a thick layer of well-drained, pressed cabbage. In the center place the partridge pieces (or a young partridge cooked especially for the dish) ; finish filling the mold with cabbage and warm it 5 min. at the oven door. (3) Unmold onto a round platter; wipe up the juice spilled on the platter. Encircle with a few tbsp. clear Semiglaze Sauce (p. 138) made with game stock, and some chipolata sausages cooked in butter.

GOLDEN PLOVER

PLUVIER DORÉ (M.)

The golden plover, a wading bird, is not to be confused with the dotterel. It has been justly said that it is rather an edible bird than game fowl. The golden plover has 2 migrations: the first toward the end of October and the second in March. The golden plover's chief claim to fame lies in its having been classed Lenten game by the Council of Nicaea in the year 787. Thus, gourmands who abide by Church rules may enjoy an orthodox salmis made from this bird. Plover's eggs are very famous. In the spring, they are eaten, in the North, along with lapwing eggs.

All the recipes for woodcock and snipe can be followed for plover.

TEAL

SARCELLE (M.)

There are 2 species of teal, winter teal and summer or southern teal. The plumage of the winter teal is dark reddish brown, green, and black. It is no larger

Fig. 279 - Leg of roebuck or venison (p. 473).
Fig. 280 - Saddle of roebuck or venison Nimrod (p. 475).

than a fine pigeon, and its distinctive feature is the double border of white encircling the eye.

Summer teal is smaller than winter teal. Its plumage is sand-colored, sprinkled with black spots, and, instead of having a ring around the eye like the winter teal, it has simply a white mark over the eye in the shape of a comma.

TEAL BATELIÈRE SARCELLE À LA BATELIÈRE (R.)

Cut the teal into pieces and put it into a pan with a large piece of butter and chopped shallots and parsley. Season with salt, pepper, and grated nutmeg and brown quickly on a hot fire. Sprinkle with 1 tbsp. flour, pour in 1 glass white wine. When this ragout has come to a boil, remove it from the fire, squeeze the juice of 1 lemon into it, and serve immediately.

Note: Teal, classified by the Church as game that may be eaten on fast days, makes an excellent roast for Lent.

FRENCH GROUSE

TÉTRAS (A.)

French grouse or heath cock is a large gallinaceous bird belonging to the same family as the hazel hen and the ptarmigan. It may grow as large as a turkey. The plumage is black and dark green, marked with white on the stomach. In France it is found in high wooded mountains. The flesh of the French grouse is highly esteemed and, like hazel hen and ptarmigan, has a resinous flavor.

It is usually cooked on a spit, but may also be served in salmis, as a *chaud-froid,* etc.

All birds belonging to the grouse family that are roasted should be so cooked that the meat stays a pale pink. The breast is the most delicate part and the only one usually served. The rest is used to make game stock.

LAPWING

VANNEAU (M.)

Like the plover, the lapwing is a temporary dweller in the Dutch polders, where it nests. While its habits are the same as the plover's, its plumage is quite different, being black and white with a tuft on the head.

It has 2 migratory seasons, like the plover. During the first, at the end of October, it is fat and is called halloween lapwing. However, in March it is all skin and bones. The most interesting feature of the plover and the lapwing is the eggs, whose white will not harden in cooking like that of other eggs. These provide a delectable hors d'oeuvre. Lapwing should be prepared like woodcock.

GROUND GAME

ROEBUCK OR VENISON

CHEVREUIL

Roebuck or venison may be served as a haunch or saddle, or as chops, and is frequently marinated.

The leg: Remove the skin and all the tendons, then stud the raw flesh with bits of salt pork fat (like a piece of meat) and marinate it (the marinade penetrates the meat through the holes made by the larding). It should marinate 48 hr. Then wipe it dry and roast at high temperature to sear the meat and seal in the juices. The hoof of the roebuck should be left on, covered with its skin and wrapped in a piece of oiled paper to prevent burning. Cook 15 min. per lb. Baste frequently while cooking.

Roebuck is usually served with Poivrade Sauce (p. 143) and garnished with various vegetables, especially chestnut purée and tart applesauce.

Saddle of roebuck or *venison* makes a very rich roast. It includes the whole back from the beginning of the chops to the haunch, like saddle of mutton. Larded, marinated, and roasted, saddle of roebuck or venison is served with the same sauces and garnishes as the haunch. Chops, served 2 per person, or noisettes make a very rich small entree.

Note: We do not recommend marinating young, and therefore tender, animals.

Since red deer, fallow deer, izard, and chamois are prepared like roebuck, it is unnecessary to give special recipes for them.

JUGGED ROEBUCK or VENISON CIVET DE CHEVREUIL (E.)

The shoulders, neck, breast, and top of the loin are used. The pieces should be marinated at least 6 hr. in advance in the wine that will be used later to cook the meat, and the usual vegetables and herbs that make up a marinade. Just before putting the preparation on the fire, drain and wipe the pieces dry, then brown them over a hot fire.

The rest of the preparation is the same as for Jugged Hare (p. 478), including binding it with blood, without which the dish would be only venison stew. Since it is impossible to keep roebuck blood, the binding is done with hare blood or even, at worst, with rabbit blood.

ROEBUCK or VENISON CHOPS BÉLISAIRE CÔTELETTES DE CHEVREUIL BÉLISAIRE (P.)

Sauté the chops in burning-hot oil and arrange them in a circle with celery-root purée in the center. Serve with Poivrade Sauce (p. 143) flavored with shredded orange peel (lightly blanched in boiling water) and juice of 1 orange.

ROEBUCK or VENISON CHOPS WITH CHERRIES CÔTELETTES DE CHEVREUIL AUX CERISES (E.)

Quickly sauté the chops, keeping them rare; arrange them in a circle, sandwiching them with croutons of stale gingerbread lightly browned in butter. Fill the center with a compote of cherries. Cover with thin Venison Sauce (p. 145).

ROEBUCK or VENISON CHOPS CHÂTELAINE CÔTELETTES DE CHEVREUIL CHÂTELAINE (P.)

Sauté the chops as above, arrange them on a platter, and coat with Venison Sauce (p. 145); on each chop place a small patty shell filled with mushroom purée.

ROEBUCK or VENISON CHOPS CONTI CÔTELETTES DE CHEVREUIL CONTI (E.)

Sauté them in smoking oil; dry them and arrange them in a circle, sandwiching them in between slices of tongue cut in the shape of an elongated heart. Melt the glaze in the cooking pan with a finger of white wine, add this to a thin Poivrade Sauce (p. 143), and pour over the chops. Serve a separate dish of buttered, thin lentil purée.

ROEBUCK or VENISON CHOPS DIANE CÔTELETTES DE CHEVREUIL DIANE (E.)

Sauté the chops quickly; dry them and arrange them in a circle, sandwiching them in between triangular croutons of game forcemeat (spread in a thin layer on a buttered baking tray and poached at the oven door). Pour Diane Sauce (p. 140) over the chops; serve with a dish of chestnut purée.

ROEBUCK or VENISON CHOPS IN GIN CÔTELETTES DE CHEVREUIL AU GENIÈVRE (E.)

Sauté the chops and arrange them in a circle, sandwiching them in with heart-shaped fried croutons. Melt the glaze in the sautéing pan with 1 small glass flaming gin, add 1 pulverized juniper berry, 3 oz. extra-heavy cream, and reduce by ½. Finish with a finger of lemon juice and a few tbsp. thick Poivrade Sauce (p. 143). Coat the chops with this sauce. Serve a separate dish of slightly sweetened, hot applesauce.

MINUTE ROEBUCK or VENISON CHOPS CÔTELETTES DE CHEVREUIL À LA MINUTE (E.)

Sauté the chops quickly in very little oil, after sprinkling them with a little finely chopped onion. Arrange them in a circle. Melt the glaze in the sautéing pan with a finger of cognac, add 1½ oz. Poivrade Sauce (p. 143), and finish with 2 oz. butter and a few drops of lemon juice. Pour over the chops. Garnish the center of the platter with sliced mushrooms sautéed in butter.

ROEBUCK or VENISON CHOPS NESSELRODE CÔTELETTES DE CHEVREUIL NESSELRODE (P.)

Marinate the chops a few hours in advance, allowing 2 per person. Wipe them dry, sauté them in a little smoking oil over a hot fire, arrange them in a circle on a round platter, and fill the center with chestnut purée. Coat the chops with Poivrade Sauce (p. 143).

ROEBUCK or VENISON CHOPS WITH POIVRADE SAUCE CÔTELETTES DE CHEVREUIL À LA POIVRADE (P.)

Sauté the chops in oil or butter. Arrange them in a circle with fried croutons. Melt the glaze in the sautéing pan with 2 tbsp. vinegar; add Poivrade Sauce (p. 143); reduce; strain. Coat the chops with this sauce. Garnish the border of the platter with fluted half slices of lemon alternated with slices of beet. (Figure 278, Page 468.)

ROEBUCK or VENISON CHOPS VILLENEUVE CÔTELETTES DE CHEVREUIL VILLENEUVE (E.)

Lightly sear the chops in butter and set them to cool under a light weight. Garnish them with a cold salpicon (tiny cubes) of game; smooth the salpicon into a mound; wrap each chop in a triangle of pig's caul; lay them side by side on a baking tray; baste with melted butter, and cook in the oven 7–8 min. Arrange in a circle, with the chops overlapping each other. Serve with a separate dish of thick game gravy mixed with finely shredded truffles.

ROLLED SHOULDER OF ROEBUCK or VENISON ÉPAULE DE CHEVREUIL ROULÉE (R.)

Bone the shoulder; finely chop a little of the meat with the same amount of pork fat and white bread soaked in bouillon and dried on the fire, break in 1 egg, and mix the forcemeat. Finish with a little nutmeg, salt, pepper, chopped shallots. Pound it all together in a mortar; press through a sieve. Spread out the shoulder, salt, pepper, and cover with a layer of forcemeat, a few strips of ham and truffle. Roll the shoulder tightly, tie securely, and even sew it so that the forcemeat will not come out while cooking. Cut enough carrots and onions to cover the bottom of a casserole; lay the shoulder on top; add the bones, 1 clove, 1 clove of garlic, bouquet of parsley, thyme, and bay leaf tied with a thread, 3 glasses white wine, salt, and pepper. Cover tightly with a buttered paper and put on the lid; cook 2 hr. in the oven.

When cooked, strain the gravy. Melt an egg-sized piece of butter in a pan; blend in 2 tbsp. flour; when the roux is nice and brown, add the liquid from some mushrooms cooked several minutes in boiling water. Reduce until thickened; pour into a platter and place the shoulder on top after untying it.

LEG OF ROEBUCK or **VENISON** GIGUE OR GIGOT DE CHEVREUIL (R.)

Serve the hair-covered hoof with the leg. Cover the hoof with oiled paper to keep it from burning. Remove the skin covering the upper part of the leg, stud it with pork fat, place in a platter containing a marinade of oil, white or red wine (Burgundy makes a more highly flavored sauce, while white wine preserves the game flavor better), 4 or 5 juniper berries, peppercorns, 2 cloves, bay leaf, sprig of thyme, 2 sliced onions. Baste with the marinade several times during the day and turn the leg morning and evening. Let marinate 2–6 days, depending upon the temperature. Cook 15 min. per lb., roasting on a spit before a clear fire; baste with melted butter; salt when half cooked. Strain the cooking gravy and serve in a sauceboat with a few finely chopped shallots. Garnish with chestnut purée or braised chestnuts. (Figure 279, Page 469.)

Note: We think it better to strain the cooking gravy into Venison (p. 145) or Poivrade Sauce (p. 143).

ROEBUCK or **VENISON NOISETTES MAGENTA** NOISETTES DE CHEVREUIL MAGENTA (P.)

Prepare like chops. Sauté them in oil and place them on potato croquettes shaped like thick pancakes and breaded. Moisten them with Romaine Sauce (p. 144) and serve with a separate dish of Soubise Purée (p. 504).

ROEBUCK or **VENISON NOISETTES ROMANOV** NOISETTES DE CHEVREUIL ROMANOFF (E.)

Sauté the *noisettes* quickly; arrange them in a circle on hollowed-out thick slices of braised cucumbers filled with thick mushroom purée. In the center of the dish place a garnish of creamed large mushrooms. Serve Poivrade Sauce (p. 143) separately.

ROEBUCK or **VENISON NOISETTES VALENCIA** NOISETTES DE CHEVREUIL VALENCIA (E.)

Sauté the *noisettes;* place them in a circle, each on a round crouton of brioche fried in butter; coat lightly with Bigarade Sauce (p. 138) and surround with small orange quarters peeled to the flesh. Serve Bigarade Sauce separately.

SADDLE AND HAUNCH OF ROEBUCK or **VENISON** SELLE ET CIMIER DE CHEVREUIL (M.)

We recognize the following difference between these 2 pieces: the saddle, corresponding to the back of small animals, is the part extending from the first ribs to the rump, where it ends in a diagonal between the 2 legs. The haunch is the same piece prolonged to include the buttocks, the bones of the chops being sawed almost to the top of the loins. After the sinews are removed and the pieces are studded with pork fat, they are marinated or not, depending on their final preparation, but they should be marinated only a short time.

Method of cooking: They are roasted on a spit or in the oven. If they have been marinated, they should be roasted at intense heat at the start to sear the meat, and cooked on a bed of the vegetables used in the marinade spread on the bottom of the roasting pan. After the glaze in the roasting pan is melted, the accompanying sauce should be finished in the roasting pan.

Garnishes: Purées of green celery, celery root, lentils, chestnuts, or Jerusalem artichokes. The chestnut purée may be replaced by large chestnuts roasted in butter.

Sauces: Grand-Veneur (p. 141), Moscovite (p. 143), Poivrade (p. 143), Romaine (p. 144), Venison (p. 145).

SADDLE OF ROEBUCK or **VENISON BERNY** SELLE DE CHEVREUIL À LA BERNY (Gi.)

Remove the sinews from a fine saddle of venison and stud it with thin strips of pork fat; marinate 2 or 3 days. Thirty-five or 40 minutes before serving, remove the saddle from the marinade and wipe it off lightly. Roast in the oven or on a spit 30–35 min., basting frequently with a few tbsp. marinade.

To serve, place the saddle on a long platter with a garnish of potato croquettes shaped into round balls the size of an apricot. The croquette mixture should contain a few chopped truffles and grilled sliced almonds. Serve a separate dish of thin Poivrade Sauce (p. 143) to which grilled slivered almonds have been added, and a dish of red-currant jelly.

Notes on marinating venison: As we have said before, the purpose of marinating is to tenderize or preserve the meat or to impregnate it with the flavors of the marinade. But a saddle, leg, or rack of roebuck or venison may be marinated to preserve it and to impregnate it with the flavor of the vegetables and herbs used in the marinade, but not to tenderize it. As well perfume the violet as make the flesh of this demon of the woods tender; it would be criminal to dishonor venison by contact with corroding vinegar. We permit and advise only white wine for marinating venison, with 1/10 as much oil and just the right amount of herbs and vegetables. Economy must not raise its voice here, and vinegar should absolutely not be used, or only 1/3 vinegar and the rest wine.

SADDLE OF ROEBUCK or **VENISON WITH CHERRIES** SELLE DE CHEVREUIL AUX CERISES (E.)

Marinate the saddle 12 hr. in verjuice (the sour juice of unripe grapes). Roast it on a spit, basting with the marinade, and keep quite rare. Serve with Poivrade (p. 143) or Venison Sauce (p. 145) or a sauce containing cherries.

SADDLE OF ROEBUCK or **VENISON CREOLE** SELLE DE CHEVREUIL À LA CRÉOLE (E.)

Marinate it only a few hours, and roast on a spit, basting with the marinade. Place on a platter and surround with bananas sautéed in butter. Serve with Escoffier Sauce (p. 140) with 1/3 Poivrade (p. 143) and a little butter added.

SADDLE OF ROEBUCK or **VENISON METTERNICH** SELLE DE CHEVREUIL METTERNICH (E.)

Marinate. Proceed as for Saddle of Veal Metternich (p. 345).

SADDLE OF ROEBUCK or **VENISON NIMROD** SELLE DE CHEVREUIL NEMROD (E.)

Trim the saddle and stud with small strips of pork fat. Marinate for several hours with 2 tbsp. olive oil, 1 sliced onion and 1 sliced carrot, sprigs of parsley, bay leaf, 1 tbsp. vinegar, 1 glass dry white wine, and a few peppercorns. Baste with butter and roast, surrounded by the drained vegetables from the marinade.

Garnish: Chestnut, celery, and lentil purées arranged around the saddle. Serve Poivrade Sauce (p. 143) separately. (Figure 280. Page 469.)

ROEBUCK- or **VENISON-FILLET TIMBALE NAPOLITAINE** TIMBALE DE FILETS DE CHEVREUIL À LA NAPOLITAINE (E.)

Slice the fillets, lard them, and keep a few hours in a cooked marinade made with white wine (see p. 167). Braise them in a little veal stock and some of the marinade; glaze them, at the end of the cooking, with this stock reduced. Blanch some macaroni very lightly and finish cooking it in white consommé. Drain it well; bind it with grated Parmesan cheese, fresh butter, tomato purée, game glaze, and the braising stock used for the fillets. Place this macaroni in a shallow timbale crust and arrange the glazed slices of venison on top in a circle.

RABBIT AND YOUNG RABBIT

LAPIN AND LAPEREAU

GRILLED YOUNG RABBIT BERGÈRE LAPEREAU GRILLÉ À LA BERGÈRE (E.)

Cut off the front part of a meaty young rabbit, saving only the back and hind legs. Break the leg joints, cross the legs, and roast until ½ done. Next dredge the rabbit in flour, dip in beaten egg containing a little olive oil, and cover with bread crumbs; baste with melted butter; finish cooking slowly on the grill. Place it on a platter, surrounded with rectangles of blanched, grilled bacon; at each end of the platter make a mound of Potato Straws (p. 509). Serve a separate dish of Duxelles Sauce (p. 140) with tiny mushrooms.

RABBIT BLANQUETTE LAPIN (BLANQUETTE DE) (R.)

Skin a rabbit, cut it into pieces, and put into a pot with enough boiling water to cover it, 1 onion, 1 clove garlic, 1 clove, salt, pepper, and a bouquet of thyme, bay leaf, parsley, and wild thyme. Cook 10 min. at a rolling boil; drain and wipe off the pieces of rabbit. In another pot, blend 1 tbsp. flour in butter without letting it brown. When smooth, pour in part of the liquid used to cook the rabbit; boil 5 min.; add the rabbit and simmer on a low fire. If the sauce becomes too thick, add more of the water. Fifteen minutes before serving, drop in a handful of mushrooms. Place the pieces of rabbit on a platter; stir 1 egg yolk into the sauce without letting it boil. Pour over the rabbit and serve.

RABBIT IN CABESSOL LAPIN EN CABESSOL (P.)

[*Tr. Note:* A *cabessol* is a cushionlike roll of cloth the women of southern France wear on their heads to carry heavy loads.]

Clean the rabbit, keeping the skin of the stomach, which should be split lengthwise. Stuff it with the following mixture: 1 lb. sausage meat, 4 oz. lean cooked ham, 2 chopped onions cooked in butter, 2 crushed cloves of garlic, salt, pepper, spices, chopped parsley, powdered thyme and bay leaf (only a dash). Mix all of this well, with the ham chopped and the rabbit liver crushed; stuff the rabbit and sew it up. Place the rabbit in a cocotte large enough so the animal can roll in a circle and brown in a little lard in the oven or on top of the stove at moderate heat. Lay onions and carrots, sliced in rings, around the rabbit, then when all is well browned pour in ½ bottle white wine, season, and cover the cocotte; cook in the oven slowly 2 hr. Serve this delicious game dish with its own gravy, after skimming off the fat.

RABBIT SAUTÉ CHASSEUR LAPIN (SAUTÉ) CHASSEUR (P.)

Sauté the rabbit pieces in a cocotte containing a little burning-hot lard. Brown them well, then sprinkle with flour; add 2 or 3 chopped shallots, and when the flour has browned, pour in ⅓ white wine and ⅔ water. Add salt, pepper, *bouquet garni,* and a little tomato purée. Cook at low heat 1 hr., then add 1 oz. sliced mushrooms browned in oil in a frying pan. If preferred, raw quartered or whole mushrooms may be cooked with the rabbit. Skim off the fat and serve with chopped parsley on top.

RABBIT GIBELOTTE LAPIN (GIBELOTTE DE) (P.)

Brown the rabbit as above, sprinkle with flour, add a little chopped garlic instead of shallots, and pour in ½ red wine and ½ water. Salt and season with herbs, cook ½ hr., then add 20 small onions and 20 small strips of bacon, both browned in butter. Cook 20 min., then add a few new potatoes (if in season). If the sauce is not a real brown color, add a few drops of caramel coloring.

RABBIT INDIAN STYLE LAPIN À L'INDIENNE (P.)

Follow the recipe for Chicken Sauté Indian Style (p. 404), using rabbit for chicken and cooking a little longer.

RABBIT WITH PRUNES LAPIN AUX PRUNEAUX (E.)

Either tame or wild rabbits may be used for this recipe. Cut up the rabbit and soak the pieces 24 hr. in a strongly vinegared marinade. Drain and wipe the pieces dry; brown them in butter. Strain the marinade, reduce it by ½, and, with a little water, pour over the rabbit. Season; add 1 lb. prunes soaked in advance, and cook slowly. Just before serving, bind the sauce with a few tbsp. red-currant jelly and dress in a timbale.

CURRIED RAGOUT OF RABBIT IN A RICE RING LAPIN (RAGOÛT DE) AU CURRY, EN TURBAN DE RIZ (A.)

Skin, clean, and cut up wild rabbits, allowing 2 rabbits for 4 or 5 persons; set aside the best pieces. Place the hind pieces and scraps in a stewing pan with vegetables, salt, pepper, and enough water to make a rabbit broth; cook until concentrated, then strain. Brown the good pieces of rabbit in butter with some sliced bacon and onions; pour in the rabbit broth, add a *bouquet garni,* a little flour kneaded with butter, and curry to taste; let cook. Just before serving, remove the pieces of rabbit and bacon and keep them hot. Strain the sauce, skim off the fat, cook until concentrated, and bind with 2 egg yolks. Put the rabbit and bacon back into the sauce; heat without boiling. Meanwhile, cook Rice with

Fig. 281 - Rabbit quenelles Virgil (p. 477).
Fig. 282 - Roast saddle of hare (p. 481).

Fig. 281

Fig. 282

Fig. 283

Fig. 284

Mushrooms (p. 511) and put it into a ring mold; keep hot in a *bain-marie.* Unmold the rice ring onto a platter, pour the curried rabbit in the center, and serve.

RABBIT QUENELLES VIRGIL LAPIN (QUENELLES DE) À LA VIRGILE (Gi.) (*For 6 persons*)

Proportions for 12 quenelles: ¾ lb. rabbit meat, 7 oz. Panada (p. 171), 5 oz. butter, 6 egg yolks, and 1 good tbsp. cream, 1 tsp. salt, good pinch of white pepper, pinch of nutmeg, dash of cayenne.

Preparation: Cut the meat from the hindquarters of a rabbit killed the preceding day. Remove tendons, gristle, etc., dice it, and prepare the forcemeat as for Chicken Forcemeat (p. 176).

Cook 3 bunches asparagus tips in lightly salted boiling water; dice and drain them well, then mix with a few tbsp. reduced Béchamel Sauce (p. 146). Pour this mixture on a plate and let cool.

Forming the quenelles: Butter small boat molds. Line them with a layer of forcemeat about ¼ in. thick and fill the centers with 1 tbsp. asparagus mixture. Cover with a layer of forcemeat and smooth the surface with the blade of a knife dipped in water. Keep these quenelles cool until time to poach.

Garnish: Cut a handful of small balls from 3 carrots, using a ball vegetable cutter; cook them with bouillon, butter, and sugar as directed further on (see Glazed Carrots, p. 493). When the carrot cooking liquid has turned to a thick sirup, add 4 tbsp. small peas cooked very green and a piece of butter the size of a pigeon egg; sauté together to blend the 2 vegetables. Just before serving, finish this garnish with 1 tbsp. very heavy fresh cream. Separately, cook in butter 20 small potato balls scooped out with a ball cutter, taking care that they finish cooking exactly when they are to be served.

Poaching the quenelles and serving: Place the quenelles in a large sautéing pan containing lightly salted water at a rolling boil. Remove the pan from the fire and poach slowly ¼ hr. without letting the water come to a boil again. At first contact with the boiling water, the quenelles will come out of the molds and rise to the surface of the water. When they are poached, drain them and place them on a cloth. Arrange them in a circle, overlapping one on the other; pour the garnish of carrots and peas in the center, with the potato balls cooked in butter surrounding the quenelles. (Figure 281, Page 476.)

May be made with hare or wild rabbit as well as with tame rabbit.

GAME WARDEN'S POT-AU-FEU POT-AU-FEU DU GARDE (R.)

Skin a wild rabbit, clean it, fold the back, and put it into an earthenware marmite with a small piece of pickled pork, 2 qt. water, 7 or 8 cloves of garlic. Cook at low heat without boiling until all the scum has risen to the surface; then put in 3 stalks celery, salt and pepper, thyme, bay leaf, and parsley tied in a bouquet. When the vegetables are cooked, mash them into a purée and reheat them with a piece of butter and diced pork fat. Pour all of this into a deep platter; cut the rabbit into pieces and place on the vegetables. Cut black bread in thin slices and place in a soup tureen with a handful of chopped chives or parsley; fill the tureen with the strained broth. This is an excellent way to use an old rabbit. Cook 3–5 hr., depending on the age of the animal.

An old partridge adds flavor to an ordinary Pot-au-Feu (p. 190).

Fig. 283 - Hare fillets Sully (p. 482).
Fig. 284 - Fillet marinated wild boar (p. 484).

RABBIT TERRINE MÈRE-GRAND TERRINE DE LAPIN À LA MÈRE-GRAND (R.)

Cold Dish: Garnish a terrine or crock with bacon rind, placing the fatty side against the terrine. Take a young rabbit and cut it into pieces, 1 lb. lean veal, 1 lb. fresh lean pork, ½ lb. pork fat; cut everything into finger-thick pieces. Place a first layer of rabbit, veal, pork, and small pieces of pork fat in the crock. Cover with a layer of sausage meat about ½ in. thick; then slice carrots and onions in very thin rings and place on top the sausage meat; salt and pepper, then make other layers until the terrine is full. Do not press the layers down, for the *pâté* swells in cooking. Add 2 cloves, thyme, bay leaf, parsley, nutmeg, 4 spices (see *Note,* p. 301). Pour in white wine slowly so that it penetrates the *pâté* and almost reaches the top; cover the whole top with strips of pork fat, put the cover on, and seal it to the terrine with a paste made of flour and water. Cook 2 hr. in a low oven. Let cool until the following day.

HARE AND LEVERET

LIÈVRE AND LEVRAUT (E.)

Except for terrines, *pâtés*, or various forcemeats, old hares are not highly esteemed. Regardless of the recipe in which this game is to be used, young hare, whose weight will rarely exceed 5½ lb., should always be preferred. The fragile quality of the ear is one way to tell a young animal.

YOUNG HARE FILLETS MORNAY (Recipe of the Frères Provençaux) LEVRAUT (FILETS DE) MORNAY (E.)

Carve 2 fillets of young hare; cut them in slices about ¾ in. long and about ⅜ in. thick.

Have ready: (1) As many bread croutons as there are slices; these should be as long and as wide but not quite so thick. (2) As many thick slices of truffle, cooked, just before serving, in a little Madeira.

A few moments before serving, quickly sauté the slices of hare in clarified butter; brown the croutons in butter at the same time; then mix the slices of meat, croutons, and truffles in a casserole. Melt the glaze in the sautéing pan with the Madeira used in cooking the truffles; add a little golden meat glaze; reduce sufficiently, and strain through a cone-shaped sieve. Add a good amount of butter to this gravy; pour it over the contents of the casserole, and then dress in a very hot timbale.

Note: The Count de Mornay himself gave this recipe to the proprietors of the famous Paris restaurant. The dish was long one of the specialties of the house, which is no longer in existence.

JUGGED HARE LIÈVRE (CIVET DE) (E.) (*For 6 to 8 persons*)

When cleaning the hare, collect all the blood and save it along with the liver, immediately removing the gall and any other part contaminated by contact with it. Cut the hare into pieces and place these in a terrine with a few tbsp. cognac and olive oil, salt, pepper, and 1 onion sliced in thin rings. Let marinate 2 or 3 hr. Brown 7 oz. cubed, blanched lean bacon in butter; drain it when browned and, in the same butter, brown 2 quartered medium-sized onions. Add 2 tbsp. flour and cook until the roux is golden; place the pieces of hare in this roux after wiping them dry; sear them, turning constantly. Pour in enough good red wine to cover the meat; add a *bouquet garni* containing a clove of garlic;

cover and cook slowly at very low heat. Shortly before serving, blend this with the blood you have saved (which should have been heated slowly while adding a few tbsp. sauce and the sliced liver). Finally, put the pieces of hare into another pan, removing them 1 by 1, and add to them: the diced bacon, 20 small glazed onions, 20 small cooked mushrooms. Strain the sauce over all of it; serve, when ready, in a hot timbale and surround with heart-shaped croutons fried in butter.

JUGGED HARE WITH CHESTNUTS LIÈVRE (CIVET DE) AUX MARRONS (P.)

Follow the preceding recipe, replacing the mushrooms with 1 lb. chestnuts (already split and grilled in the oven to shell, until they are almost cooked, so that they will not fall apart when added to the hare).

HARE EN DAUBE LIÈVRE EN DAUBE (R.)

Skin a hare, bone, lard by studding with strips of pork fat, season the meat with salt and pepper, roll it into a loaf, tie securely with string, and brown in butter on all sides. Then cover the bottom of a pot with bacon rind, put the hare on top, surround it with the crushed bones (and 1 calf's foot, if you intend to serve the *daube* cold), 5 or 6 carrots and onions, 2 lumps sugar, salt, pepper, thyme, bay leaf, clove of garlic, 1 clove; pour in some white wine and add more onion, cover with buttered paper, put the lid on the pot, and cook 4 hr. on a low fire. To serve hot, ½ hr. before it has finished cooking remove a large cup of the gravy and boil this down by ½; sauce the *daube* with it, and serve with a dish of noodles boiled 10 min. and moistened with some of the *daube* gravy. To serve cold, strain the gravy into a bowl and let cool until it forms a jelly; surround the *daube* with this jelly.

SITTING HARE LIÈVRE AU GÎTE (R.)

Skin a hare, preferably a young one; scald the ears and feet, and skin them also. Soak some white bread in 1 glass cream, cook it in a pan for a few minutes with 2 or 3 onions; add this Panada to the finely chopped liver of the hare; pound together in a mortar with the same amount of butter and 4 raw egg yolks; season with salt, pepper, and 2 powdered sage leaves. Stuff the hare with this forcemeat, sew it up, break the 4 feet at the joints, fold them under the stomach, and fix them in place with a trussing needle and some string. It now looks like a sitting hare. Cover it with a strip of pork fat and buttered paper; roast in the oven or on a spit. It should take about 1½ hr. to cook, but ¼ hr. before it has finished, remove the paper and pork fat, and salt with fine salt. Thin some red-currant jelly with Madeira or port, 2 tbsp. jelly per 1 wineglass. Serve this sauce separately.

STUFFED HARE PÉRIGOURDINE LIÈVRE FARCI PÉRIGOURDINE (E.)

Clean the hare, collecting all the blood; break the leg bones to truss it more easily; remove the tendons from the fillets and legs and lard these pieces by studding with small strips of pork fat. Chop the liver, heart, lungs, and 4 chicken livers with 5 oz. fresh pork fat. Add to this mincemeat: 5 oz. soaked and pressed white bread, ½ chopped onion cooked in butter (and cold), the blood, pinch of chopped parsley, pinch of crushed garlic, 3½ oz. raw truffle peelings. Mix well together and stuff the hare with this forcemeat; sew the stomach together, truss the hare, and cover with strips of pork fat; braise it in white wine about 2½ hr., basting frequently. Glaze just before serving and place on a long platter.

To the braising stock add 12 oz. Semiglaze Sauce (p. 138) made with game stock; reduce this sauce, skim off the fat, strain, and add 3½ oz. chopped truffles. Pour a few tbsp. sauce around the hare and serve the rest separately.

HARE ROYALE LIÈVRE À LA ROYALE (A.) (*For 10 to 12 persons*)

Hare Royale is a very rich dish resembling both Hare en Daube and Jugged Hare. It is prepared with a completely boned, stuffed, and garnished hare.

Take: 1 tender hare weighing 5–6 lb., thin strips of pork fat.

For the forcemeat and stuffing: 1 lb. goose *foie gras,* ¾ lb. fresh lean pork, 3 oz. old Armagnac (flamed), 2½ oz. grated pork fat, 2 oz. mushrooms, 1 tsp. salt, chopped parsley, 1 dessertspoon powdered herbs mixed in equal parts (thyme, wild thyme, marjoram, hyssop, savory), 1 tsp. freshly ground pepper, 2 chicken livers, 2 fresh eggs, 1 shallot, as many truffles as desired, 4 spices (see *Note*, p. 301).

For the braising stock and the sauce: 2½ lb. very rich veal stock, 1 bottle very good red Burgundy, 5 oz. goose *foie gras,* 4 egg yolks, 2 medium-sized onions, 1 large *bouquet garni* containing parsley, thyme, bay leaf, a little wild thyme, and marjoram, game glaze (ground game, not fowl).

For decorating the dish: Game quenelles, large white mushrooms (stuffed or not), fine truffles.

Wash and brush the truffles; dry them in a cloth; peel them; save the peelings. Wash and peel the mushrooms; save the peelings. Skin the hare; clean it; lay aside the lungs, liver, and heart, which will go into the stuffing, and save the blood to be used in the sauce. Cut off the head of the hare; open it; remove the brains and the fleshy part of the jaws, which you will use in the stuffing. Split the feet lengthwise, then completely bone the hare without damaging the exterior. Save the bones and scraps. Chop fine: the fresh pork, chicken livers, hare lungs, liver, heart, brains, and scraps, mushrooms, mushroom and truffle peelings, shallot, parsley. Put this mincemeat into a mortar; add the grated pork fat, eggs, powdered herbs, salt, pepper, a little spices to taste; mix well, mash, and moisten with the flamed Armagnac; press this forcemeat through a sieve.

Spread out the boned hare on its back, cut off the leg meat, and distribute it over the less meaty parts of the hare; then line the whole inside with part of the forcemeat; garnish the top with the sliced *foie gras* and truffles; cover with the rest of the forcemeat. Roll the hare, shaping it well, and completely cover it with strips of pork fat; tie it and wrap it tightly in strong cheesecloth. Braise it in a mixture of the veal stock and Burgundy, with the onions, hare scraps and crushed bones (browned or not), a little game glaze, and the *bouquet garni* added to it. Cook about 4 hr. at very low heat so that it will be very soft.

Remove the hare when it is cooked; remove the cheesecloth, strings, and strips of pork fat; place it on a platter and keep hot. Strain the braising stock; skim off the fat; reduce sufficiently, constantly skimming, then bind with the blood, egg yolks, and 5 oz. *foie gras* pressed through a sieve.

Garnish the platter with assorted game quenelles, large mushrooms cooked in butter with some lemon juice (stuffed or not), and fine truffles cooked with bacon strips or in a good gravy enriched with champagne, Madeira, or port. Serve the hare with a separate dish of the sauce and a vegetable dish of potato croquettes (souffléed or not).

This royal dish leaves other preparations called Royale, which completely lack finesse, far behind—those which fall apart until they are practically a purée, containing an absolute riot of shallots, onions, and garlic.

SADDLE OF HARE NAVARRAISE LIÈVRE (RÂBLE DE) À LA NAVARRAISE (E.)

(*For 6 persons*)

Stud the saddle (which includes the hind legs) with fine strips of pork fat and keep a few hours in a red-wine marinade. Dry it off and roast it at high heat on the vegetables (drained) used in the marinade. Meanwhile, lightly brown ½ lb. sliced onions and 1½ oz. sweet garlic; sprinkle with 1 tbsp. flour, cook a moment, and pour in 6 oz. Veal Gravy (p. 134). Add a bit of thyme and bay leaf and cook slowly. Strain through a sieve, reduce this purée until very thick, and use it to fill 10 small grilled mushrooms. Place the saddle of hare on a platter and surround it with the stuffed mushrooms. Melt the glaze in the roasting pan with some of the marinade, strain this through a fine cone-shaped sieve, reduce to only a few tbsp., and heighten with butter. Serve this sauce separately.

ROAST SADDLE OF HARE LIÈVRE (RÂBLE DE) RÔTI (P.)

Stud the saddle with fine strips of pork fat and marinate 24 hr.; roast 25 min. at high heat with a piece of butter. Serve it with the gravy from the roast or cream and lemon juice, or even thin Poivrade Sauce (p. 143). Garnish with applesauce and chestnut purée. (Figure 282, Page 476.)

SADDLE OF HARE WITH SHARP SAUCE LIÈVRE (RÂBLE DE) AU SAUPIQUET (M.)

Saddle of hare is sometimes roasted when the other parts of the animal are to be used in a *civet* or a *terrine*. Remove the thin skin covering the back; stud it with fine strips of pork fat. Either marinate it very lightly or omit marinating entirely. Roast it, on a spit or in the oven, 20–25 min., depending on size. Place the saddle on a long platter, baste it with the gravy from the roast with a few tbsp. bouillon added, and serve with the Sharp Sauce, which is prepared the following way:

Sharp Sauce (*Saupiquet*): Chop the hare liver, put it into a small crock or terrine, and mix with the animal's blood. Add 1 good tbsp. cognac. While the saddle (or the whole hare) is cooking, brown in lard or oil, in a small saucepan, 2½ oz. sliced onions and 2½ oz. raw, diced ham. Add a pinch of garlic, moisten with vinegar and red wine. Season with salt, pepper, thyme, bay leaf, 1 clove. Reduce by ⅓ and strain. Bring this sauce to a boil again and, just before serving, bind it with the chopped liver and blood.

Note: In certain regions of southwestern France, *saupiquet* with onion and chopped ham is not strained. Often, too, a little chopped shallot is added to this sauce. Finally, here is another method: put 3½ oz. finely chopped onions in the roasting or dripping pan. Cook a few moments. Moisten with wine vinegar. Reduce almost completely; add a pinch of garlic. Bind with the hare blood and liver; season with salt and pepper. Heat without boiling. Add 1 good tbsp. flaming cognac or Armagnac.

Note: Sometimes "saddle of hare" includes the whole hindquarters—in other words, the saddle with the rear legs still attached. Like the back, the legs should be trimmed and studded with thin strips of pork fat.

HARE or **YOUNG HARE FILLETS SULLY** LIÈVRE OR LEVRAUT (FILETS DE) SULLY (E.)

Bone and lard the fillets; shape these and the *filets mignons* into crescents. Lay them side by side in a buttered platter; poach them, covered, just before serving, with a little melted butter and a few drops of cognac. Arrange the fillets in fours, with the points of the crescents opposing each other to form a rosette; coat with somewhat thickened Poivrade Sauce (p. 143). Fill the center of the crescents with a mound of celery purée. Between each mound of purée, place a well-glazed *filet mignon* with a slice of truffle in the center. (Fig. 283, P. 477.)

HARE or **YOUNG HARE FILLETS VENDÔME** LIÈVRE OR LEVRAUT (FILETS DE) VENDÔME (E.)

Prepare a mousse of young hare and poach it in an oval mold. Slice off the fillets, flatten them lightly, stud with truffles, and poach gently in a little hare stock. Slice the *filets mignons* ; sauté them quickly in butter with 5 oz. sliced raw mushrooms and 5 oz. sliced raw truffles. Melt the glaze in the sautéing pan with a finger of cognac and the stock the truffle-studded fillets were poached in; add a little Poivrade Sauce (p. 143), butter, and mix in: *filet mignon* slices, mushrooms, and truffles. Unmold the mousse onto an oval platter; coat it lightly with Poivrade Sauce; surround it with small pastry boats (of Puff Paste) filled with chestnut purée and topped, just before serving, with the studded fillets. Serve the ragout of sliced *filet mignon,* mushrooms, and truffles separately and a dish of fine chestnut purée.

HARE PUDDINGS LIÈVRE (BOUDINS DE) (R.)

Chop 1 fillet, the liver, and kidneys of a hare, 1 slice ham; soak white bread in bouillon and mix this Panada with the mincemeat; moisten with melted butter, add salt and pepper, and heat a few moments on the stove. Then add 2 egg yolks. Divide the forcemeat into egg-sized pieces, and roll each piece on a floured board. Poach these puddings a few minutes in boiling salted water. Drain them, dip in beaten egg, then in bread crumbs, and fry in deep fat. Melt some butter and blend it with flour; when this roux is brown, pour in some bouillon and red wine; a few minutes later, add some pitted olives, some mushrooms, or some celery root previously cooked in boiling water; simmer 15 min. Pour this ragout over the puddings.

HARE ROLLS NORMANDE LIÈVRE (PETITS PAINS DE) À LA NORMANDE (P.)

An excellent entree can be made from boned leg of hare. Pound this meat very fine in a mortar with salt, pepper, and spices; then mix in 1 cup rather thick, very cold Béchamel Sauce (p. 146), 2 tbsp. fresh heavy cream, and finally 2 whole eggs. Press this forcemeat through a sieve and poach, 10–12 min. before serving, in small buttered baba molds placed in a *bain-marie* in the oven. Unmold onto a round platter and baste these rolls or small loaves with extra-heavy cream that has been heated, salted, peppered, and flavored with a little lemon juice. Garnish the center of the platter with unsweetened applesauce.

HARE PIE LIÈVRE (PÂTÉ DE)

See Mixed Entrees, p. 535.

HARE PÂTÉ (Without Mold or Oven) LIÈVRE (PÂTÉ DE) (R.)

Cold Dish: Skin a hare, clean it, put the blood into a bowl with a finger of vinegar. Bone the hare and cut it into thin slices; cut 4 oz. veal and 4 oz. ham the same way. Finely chop the leftover scraps of hare meat, along with the liver, chives, parsley, clove of garlic, shallot. Mix this mincemeat with oil and good red wine, spices, salt, pepper. Arrange the strips of meat into a rectangular shape, alternating veal, ham, and hare, and, between each layer, placing a layer of the forcemeat. Place the *pâté* on strips of pork fat in a braising pan; surround it with the crushed hare, pork, and veal bones; add about 1 lb. lard so that when it melts it will cover the *pâté.* When it begins to boil, cover with the lid, seal hermetically, and cook at low heat about 6 hr. Then remove the *pâté* and put it into a terrine or crock; fill the terrine with the carefully strained gravy. Let cool until the following day; to serve, remove the covering layer of lard.

YOUNG WILD BOAR AND WILD BOAR

MARCASSIN AND SANGLIER (E.)

When wild boar has passed the age when it can be called young, it is rarely used in cooking, except for the haunch, and even this must be strongly marinated. Young boar, on the other hand, is highly appreciated. Noisettes, fillets, or quarters of young boar are prepared like those of venison; the same is true of the rack and the saddle roasted whole. Recipes given for roebuck or venison chops may be used in preparing the chops of young boars.

YOUNG BOAR CHOPS ROMAINE MARCASSIN (CÔTELETTES DE) À LA ROMAINE (E.)

Sauté the chops; arrange them in a circle and cover them with Romaine Sauce (p. 144). Serve a chestnut, celery, or lentil purée separately.

YOUNG BOAR CHOPS ST. HUBERT MARCASSIN (CÔTELETTES DE) SAINT-HUBERT (E.)

Sauté the chops on 1 side only and let cool under pressure. Garnish them on the browned side with a fine forcemeat made with: 1½ lb. fat young boar meat, 7 oz. small mushrooms turned in butter, 2 powdered juniper berries, and the usual seasoning for forcemeats. Wrap the forcemeat-spread chops in a pig's caul; lay them side by side in a baking pan; baste with melted butter, sprinkle with bread crumbs, and bake in the oven. Serve separately: (1) Venison Sauce (p. 145) ; (2) unsweetened applesauce.

YOUNG BOAR CHOPS ST. MARK MARCASSIN (CÔTELETTES DE) SAINT-MARC (E.)

Stud the chops with strips of pickled tongue and braise them. Arrange them in a circle; in the center make a pyramid of small chestnut croquettes molded in the shape of small balls. Serve the braising stock separately after skimming off the fat and reducing it; and a dish of cranberry sauce.

Note: Cranberry sauce is bought ready-made.

BITTERSWEET YOUNG BOAR HAM MARCASSIN (JAMBON DE) À L'AIGRE-DOUX (E.)

Braise the ham the usual way. Prepare Romaine Sauce (p. 144) from the braising stock. To this sauce add: cherries in vinegar, pitted prunes, chocolate dissolved in water (this is added to the sauce only at the last moment). This garnish-sauce is also served in southern Italy, but there they add pine nuts and candied orange rind and citron, all chopped.

MARINATED WILD BOAR SANGLIER MARINÉ (R.)

To marinate the boar, brown onion and carrot slices in butter, pour in 2 parts vinegar to 1 part water or salted red wine; add thyme, bay leaf, sage, parsley, garlic, a few juniper berries and peppercorns; put the quarter of boar into this marinade and let stand 8 days, turning it daily. Wild boar does not make a good roast, for the meat is too tough.

Cook the fillets in a braising pan with ½ lb. butter and ½ lb. fat. Brown the fillets on all sides; sprinkle with flour, pour in equal parts of hot water and marinade, using the carrots, onions, and herbs from the marinade to surround the meat. Cook at low heat, 1 hr. for the first 2 lb. and ½ hr. for each additional 2 lb.

Dissolve 2 tbsp. powdered sugar in 1 glass vinegar; heat over a hot fire until reduced by ½. Drop a few pieces of butter rolled in some flour in 2 glasses hot bouillon; when everything is very smooth, pour in the vinegar, add salt, pepper, ½ lb. seeded sultanas and dried currants; cook at low heat 15 min. Then add a few tbsp. of the boar cooking gravy and 1 tbsp. excellent cognac. Serve the fillets accompanied with this sauce. (Figure 284, Page 477.)

The chops (after being marinated and drained) should be cooked on a grill, 5 min. on each side. Serve with Robert Sauce (p. 144). To make this sauce, cut up some large onions very small and brown them in butter. Sprinkle with flour while stirring; when it is brown, pour in equal parts of marinade and bouillon, season with salt and pepper. Let simmer 20 min., then remove from the fire; throw a few drops of cold water into the sauce to raise the fat to the surface, and skim it off. Add, stirring, 1 heaping tbsp. mustard and pour this sauce over the chops.

Note: Wild boar is dressed the same as pork.

WILD BOAR'S HEAD SANGLIER (HURE DE) (R.)

Cold Dish: Bone the head of a boar after singeing the bristles and washing the ears and snout in boiling water. Season with salt, pepper, nutmeg, a little saltpeter, chopped shallots, and chopped parsley Let macerate 1 day or 2. Brush and peel 2 or 3 truffles; slice them thin. Chop ½ lb. veal with 1 lb. beef-kidney fat. Break 1 egg into this mincemeat; mix well, then add another egg; pour in some water to make the mincemeat a little runny. Season with salt, pepper, 4 spices (see *Note*, p. 301), chopped shallots and chopped truffle peelings. Lay the boar's head on a plank; fill it with successive layers of mincemeat, small, thin bacon strips, and truffles. Sew the head together with a trussing needle, restoring it to its original shape. Wrap it in a cloth. Cover the bottom of a pot with pork rind and sliced onions and carrots; put the boar's head on top; add a *bouquet garni* made of thyme, bay leaf, and parsley, clove of garlic, and the bones of the boar's head. Pour in 1 bottle white wine and enough water to cover the head. It takes about 6 hr. to cook; when you can stick a trussing needle through it easily, it is done. Let the head soak in the cooking stock until the following day, then unwrap it, wipe it dry, and serve it on a folded napkin.

Stir 2 glasses oil bit by bit into 3 egg yolks. When this is well blended, add, little by little, 3 tbsp. mustard and 1 tbsp. vinegar. Add some diced red-currant jelly. Serve this excellent sauce in a sauceboat, along with the boar's head.

VARIOUS GAME PREPARATIONS

GAME CRÉPINETTES CRÉPINETTES DE GIBIER (R.)

Cut the game flesh in slices as though for small beefsteaks; flatten these and marinate them 4 or 5 hr. in some vinegar with slices of lemon. Make a mincemeat of the trimmings and an equal quantity of pork fat, some truffles, parsley, shallots, 2 raw eggs, nutmeg, salt, and pepper. Soften a pig's caul in warm water and cut into pieces large enough to cover the fillets spread with a layer of mincemeat; close tightly to make sausages and flatten them. Sprinkle them with bread crumbs and fry them in butter.

GAME GRATIN GRATIN DE GIBIER (R.)

Put 1 chopped onion into a pan with a piece of butter, sprinkle with flour, add a little bouillon or gravy, salt and pepper, and stir while cooking 6–8 min. Dice some leftover cooked game and add it to the sauce with ½ as much in mushrooms. Heat. Cook some rice 20 min. in 1½ times its volume of boiling salted water; let dry on the fire. Add some butter, grated Gruyère cheese, and pepper. Pour ½ the rice into a deep baking dish, place the ragout of game in the center, cover it with rice, sprinkle with bread crumbs, baste with butter, and sprinkle with grated cheese. Brown in the oven. Noodles cooked only 10 min. in boiling water may be used instead of rice.

GAME MOUSSES and MOUSSELINES (HOT) MOUSSES and MOUSSELINES DE GIBIER (CHAUDES) (A.)

Hot Game Mousses and Mousselines are prepared like Chicken Mousses and Mousselines (p. 415). The accompanying sauce is made from game stock (using the game scraps and carcasses): Périgueux (p. 143), Semiglaze Sauce (p. 138), Velouté (p. 147), Suprême (p. 146), Salmis (p. 145).

In making Woodcock Mousses and Mousselines, add the liver and intestines, sautéed in butter, to the forcemeat.

GAME MOUSSES and MOUSSELINES (COLD) MOUSSES and MOUSSELINES DE GIBIER (FROIDES) (A.)

Cold Game Mousses and Mousselines are prepared like those of chicken; *foie gras* may be added, but the aspics and Veloutés should be made from game stock.

The mousses should be surrounded with the breasts or most delicate parts of the game (carved from the roasted animals), covered simply with fine Aspic Jelly (p. 168).

Mousselines may be glazed simply with aspic or covered first with thin Chaud-Froid Sauce (p. 139), either golden or brown, depending on circumstances, then glazed with aspic.

GAME LOAF WITH MORELS (MUSHROOMS) PAIN DE GIBIER AUX MORILLES (R.)

Finely chop some roasted game meat; add an equal quantity of bread soaked in bouillon and dried in the oven, salt, pepper, 2 egg yolks, and 1 egg white; mix well, press through a strainer, add chopped morels (mushrooms). Heavily butter a cylindrical mold and fill it with the purée, packing it down well. Cook in a pot filled with boiling water. Now peel 15 morels (mushrooms) and cook 5 min. in boiling water. Drain. Sauté them a few moments in a pan with a good piece of butter, salt, pepper, thyme, bay leaf; sprinkle with flour, moisten with bouillon. Let simmer. Just before pouring this ragout over the game loaf, bind the sauce with 1 egg yolk and add the juice of 1 lemon. Pour over the loaf, which you have unmolded.

GAME SOUFFLÉS SOUFFLÉS DE GIBIER (A.) (*For 6 persons*)

Game Soufflés are usually made with a Mousseline Forcemeat (p. 173) made with raw meat, but they may also be made from cooked meat.

If you use raw meat, take: 1¼ lb. raw game meat (without skin or tendons), 1½ cups fresh heavy cream, 1½ tsp. salt, ½ tsp. pepper, 7 egg whites.

Prepare a Mousseline Forcemeat: mash the game meat in a mortar, gradually blending in 3 egg whites, the cream (half whipped), salt, pepper. Press through a sieve; keep on ice 2 hr., then add the rest of the egg whites beaten very stiff and not letting them fall. Place in a buttered casserole or mold and cook in a *bain-marie,* in a low oven, 35–40 min.

If you use cooked game, take: 1¼ lb. cooked game meat (without skin or tendons), 12 oz. Béchamel Sauce (p. 146), 7 egg whites, 5 yolks, very concentrated game stock. Mash the game meat in a mortar, adding the Béchamel Sauce bit by bit; add the egg yolks and game stock; strain through a sieve; then blend in the stiffly beaten egg whites. Pour the preparation into a mold or a buttered dish and cook in a low oven. Game Soufflés are served with Semiglaze Sauce (p. 138) made from the various game stocks.

VEGETABLES
ITALIAN PASTES AND FARINACEOUS FOODS
SALADS

VEGETABLES
ITALIAN PASTES AND FARINACEOUS FOODS
SALADS

ARTICHOKES

ARTICHAUTS

Cooked simply in boiling salted water, they are eaten with Vinaigrette Sauce (p. 158) or a white sauce; but they may also be prepared various ways, the best known of which follow.

STUFFED ARTICHOKES BARIGOULE ARTICHAUTS FARCIS À LA BARIGOULE (P.)

Sometimes stuffed raw, but usually after being partially cooked in water. While the artichokes are blanching, prepare a hash of mushrooms and ham, using 2 oz. mushrooms and 1 oz. ham for a medium-sized artichoke. Chop the raw mushrooms and brown them in oil, then add 1 chopped shallot and the ham, season (very little salt, because of the ham), add 2 or 3 tbsp. rather thick tomato purée, some parsley, and a pinch of sifted bread crumbs. Pull the leaves from the center of the half-cooked artichokes, remove the choke, and fill the artichokes with this hash. Place a strip of pork fat or bacon on top, tie the artichokes with string, and braise them in a cocotte with a little white wine and a little strongly tomato-flavored brown sauce. Cook in the oven a good ½ hr. and serve as is. Remove the strings.

ARTICHOKES MIREILLE ARTICHAUTS À LA MIREILLE (P.)

Remove the outer leaves from some very small raw artichokes and cook them in a pan with 1 glass bouillon or water, 3 oz. olive oil, salt, peppercorns, and 12 small onions. Add 3 or 4 peeled, quartered tomatoes; cover the pan. Cook over a fairly hot fire ½ hr. and serve as is.

ARTICHOKE HEARTS GRAND-DUC COEURS D'ARTICHAUTS GRAND-DUC (E.)

Choose some medium-sized artichoke hearts of equal size; cook them in salted water. Drain well and arrange them in a rosette on a platter lightly coated with a fine cream sauce. Cover the artichokes with the same sauce, lightly sprinkle with grated Parmesan cheese, baste with melted butter, and glaze in the oven or under a broiler. In the center of the rosette, place a bunch of buttered asparagus tips; on each artichoke heart place a slice of truffle heated in butter mixed with melted Meat Glaze (p. 135). (Figure 286, Page 492.)

ARTICHOKE BOTTOMS COLBERT FONDS D'ARTICHAUTS À LA COLBERT (P.)

To prepare artichoke bottoms, completely peel the raw artichoke, not after cooking it, for the cooked leaves pull away part of the bottom. First break and cut the leaves clear to the base, then, using a knife, peel the bottoms as you would a potato. Flavor the bottoms with lemon juice and put them in water also flavored with lemon juice. (See Illustrations, p. 112.) To cook them, blend a little flour in a large amount of cold water, then put in the cold artichoke bottoms and add salt, pepper, and lemon juice to the water; cook until the chokes can be pulled out easily. Let cool and then scoop them out; they are then ready for every purpose—for garnishes, vegetables, soup, or purée. They may be sautéed in butter, whole or quartered, dipped in Frying Paste (p. 558) to make fritters, or filled with different vegetables.

To serve them à la Colbert, first prepare them as above, then roll in flour, dip in beaten egg, and finally roll in bread crumbs. Fry them and place on a round platter with 1 tbsp. Colbert Sauce (p. 140) in each. (Figure 285, Page 492.)

STUFFED ARTICHOKE BOTTOMS FONDS D'ARTICHAUTS FARCIS (M.)

When the bottoms have been ⅔ cooked in water, cook them in butter in a tightly covered pan. Fill them with thick Duxelles Sauce (p. 140) mixed with chopped lean ham and bread crumbs, or with any other stuffing, meat or vegetable. The stuffing should be shaped into a mound. Place the artichokes in a baking dish, sprinkle with bread crumbs or, depending on the kind of stuffing, grated cheese, baste with butter or oil, and brown in the oven.

ARTICHOKE QUARTERS ITALIAN STYLE QUARTIERS D'ARTICHAUTS À L'ITALIENNE (P.)

Prepare like Artichokes Lyonnaise, below, using Italienne Sauce (p. 142).

ARTICHOKE QUARTERS LYONNAISE QUARTIERS D'ARTICHAUTS À LA LYONNAISE (P.)

Cut the artichokes into 4 or 6 parts, depending on size; remove the choke from each piece and cut off the upper halves of the leaves; parboil the quarters in salted water. Drain them and place in a sautéing pan containing a little burning-hot oil, the bottom part touching the oil; fry them a little in the oil, then pour prepared Lyonnaise Sauce (p. 142) over them, and finish cooking in a moderate oven, letting the tops of the leaves brown a little. Serve with parsley.

ARTICHOKE-BOTTOM SOUFFLÉ SOUFFLÉ DE FONDS D'ARTICHAUTS (P.)

Cook fresh artichoke bottoms, then scoop them out and cook them in butter in a tightly closed pan. Fill them with Mousseline Forcemeat (p. 173) and cook 10 min. in the oven. Place on a round platter and top with Hollandaise Sauce (p. 151). Serve hot.

ASPARAGUS

ASPERGES (P.)

Serve with Mousseline (p.152) or Vinaigrette Sauce (p.158). These are the only 2 ways to appreciate asparagus; preparations with cheese and otherwise are not recommended. This good vegetable should be allowed to keep its own identity. (However, asparagus tips may be bound with a cream sauce.) Serve on a napkin with the sauce separate. (Figure 287, Page 492.)

ASPARAGUS TIPS WITH ORANGE SAUCE POINTES D'ASPERGES, SAUCE À L'ORANGE (P.)

Blanch the asparagus tips, cook them gently in butter for a moment, and cover with an orange sauce made as follows. Grate the peel of 1 orange and set it aside; squeeze the juice of 1 orange (preferably blood orange), then make a Hollandaise Sauce (p. 151), add the grated orange peel to the eggs; then add butter to the sauce, and finally add the orange juice and a little lemon juice; pour over the asparagus.

BEANS

HARICOTS

There are several sorts of beans: green beans, the yellow beans called butter beans, white and red haricot beans, flageolets (U.S. fresh green kidney beans).

NAVY (HARICOT) BEANS and **FLAGEOLETS** HARICOTS BLANCS and FLAGEOLETS (P.)

Fresh navy (haricot) beans should be cooked in lightly salted boiling water. Dried navy (haricot) beans should be soaked in cold water, then put on to boil in cold water, and not salted until almost cooked, for salt has a tendency to keep them hard and prevent their cooking.

NAVY (HARICOT) BEANS BRETONNE HARICOT BLANCS À LA BRETONNE (P.)

Cook 1 chopped onion in butter until golden brown, then add a few tbsp. tomato purée (fresh, if the beans are fresh). Put the beans into this sauce with a little of their cooking liquid and let simmer 20 min.; salt, pepper, and add chopped parsley.

Note: Flageolets, or small green kidney beans, are prepared the same way.

CREAMED NAVY (HARICOT) BEANS HARICOTS BLANCS À LA CRÈME (P.)

Cook the beans as above, drain, and bind with a thin Béchamel Sauce (p. 146). Since navy (haricot) beans are starchy they should not be prepared with a sauce containing too much flour.

NAVY (HARICOT) BEAN PURÉE or **PURÉE SOISSONNAISE** HARICOTS BLANCS (PURÉE DE) OR PURÉE SOISSONNAISE (E.)

Press the beans through a sieve while still very hot. Add to this purée 3½ oz. butter per lb. beans; stir briskly over a hot fire to dry; then add some milk to give it the consistency of an ordinary purée.

GREEN BEANS HARICOTS VERTS (P.)

Cook quickly in salted boiling water, without covering, to keep green. Drain, then season simply with butter or with Vinaigrette Sauce (p. 158). The beans should be rather firm.

GREEN BEANS PORTUGUESE STYLE HARICOTS VERTS PORTUGAISE (P.)

Put the raw beans into a stewpan with 3½ oz. unsalted pork fat, diced fine, per 2 lb. beans. Add ½ lb. peeled, chopped tomatoes, salt, pepper, and 1 cup bouillon. Cover and cook slowly. Serve with chopped parsley sprinkled on top. These beans do not stay green, but they are delicious. Wax beans may be prepared the same way.

BROAD BEANS

FÈVES

FRESH BROAD BEANS FÈVES FRAICHES (MODE DE CUISSON DES) (M.)

Remove the skins from the beans and cook in salted boiling water flavored with a small bouquet of savory. Prepare the same way as peas.

BROAD-BEAN PURÉE PURÉE DE FÈVES (M.)

Cook as above, then cook the beans in butter in a tightly closed pan. Press through a fine sieve. Heat the purée and finish it with fresh cream and butter.

Note: To give this purée more body, add ¼ as much mashed potatoes to the purée.

BRUSSELS SPROUTS

CHOUX DE BRUXELLES

BRUSSELS SPROUTS ENGLISH STYLE CHOUX DE BRUXELLES À L'ANGLAISE (M.)

Take small, firm, tightly closed Brussels sprouts and cook them in salted water, keeping them somewhat firm, just in time to be served. Drain well and serve in a timbale or vegetable dish.

BUTTERED BRUSSELS SPROUTS CHOUX DE BRUXELLES AU BEURRE (M.)

Boil Brussels sprouts in salted water, drain, and dry. Then sauté in a pan until lightly browned. Serve in a timbale or vegetable dish. (Fig. 295, P. 497.)

BRUSSELS SPROUTS AU GRATIN CHOUX DE BRUXELLES AU GRATIN (E.)

Cooked the Brussels sprouts, drain them, and roll in melted butter; season and mix with a little well-buttered Béchamel Sauce (p. 146). Place them on an ovenproof service platter, coat with a little Mornay Sauce (p. 152), sprinkle with grated cheese, and glaze quickly in a hot oven.

Fig. 285 - Artichoke bottoms Colbert (p. 490).
Fig. 286 - Artichoke hearts Grand-duc (p. 490).
Fig. 287 - Asparagus with mousseline sauce (p. 491).
Fig. 288 - Cauliflower Colette (p. 494).

Fig. 285

Fig. 286

Fig. 287

Fig. **288**

Fig. 289

Fig. 290

Fig. 291

CARDOONS

CARDONS

HOW TO COOK CARDOONS CARDONS (CUISSON DES) (P.)

Remove the leaves, the prickles, and the down covering them. Cut in slices, sprinkle with lemon juice, and put into water mixed with a little flour. Salt, pepper, and add the pulp of 1 or 2 lemons. Cook slowly at least 1½ hr.

CARDOONS WITH MARROW CARDONS À LA MOELLE (M.)

Stew the cardoons in reduced Veal Gravy (p. 134). Arrange them in a mound on a round platter. Place on top slices of heart alternated with slices of poached marrow. Coat with Marrow Sauce (p. 143).

Note: For variety, the cardoons coated with Marrow Sauce may be garnished with hollowed crusts or small patty shells filled with poached, diced marrow.

CARROTS

CAROTTES

CARROTS CHANTILLY CAROTTES À LA CHANTILLY (P.)

Arrange Creamed Carrots (below) and small buttered peas separately in the same dish.

CREAMED CARROTS CAROTTES À LA CRÈME (P.)

Cook the carrots in salted water—whole, if they are new carrots, or sliced, if they are large. Drain them and stir in butter, moistening with heavy cream or Béchamel Sauce (p. 146).

GLAZED CARROTS CAROTTES GLACÉES (P.)

Take new carrots, preferably round, or, if not available, cut large carrots with a small ball cutter or knife, and trim them to even-sized balls. Start them cooking in enough bouillon to cover them generously; add salt, sugar, and a little butter. Let cook slowly, uncovered, until all the liquid has been reduced, leaving the carrots covered with a glaze. These carrots are especially suitable for garnishes. Turnips can be prepared the same way.

CARROTS VICHY CAROTTES À LA VICHY (P.) (*For 3 persons*)

Cut 1 lb. very red, sugary carrots in thin round slices. Place them in a rather large sautéing pan with a large piece of fresh butter, a little salt, and 1 tbsp. sugar. Cover with cold water. Cook at a rolling boil, without covering, until all the water has evaporated and the carrots are browned in the butter. Serve with chopped parsley on top.

CAULIFLOWER

CHOUX-FLEURS

CAULIFLOWER ENGLISH STYLE CHOU-FLEUR À L'ANGLAISE (E.)

The cauliflower is served whole—even the 2 inner rows of tender leaves that enclose the flowerets are left on. After cleaning and draining, cook it in salted water, let cool slightly, and serve on a napkin or on a thick slice of toast to absorb the excess moisture.

Fig. 289 - Various kinds of potatoes (p. 508).
Fig. 290 - Celery with marrow (p. 495).
Fig. 291 - Cèpes Brimond (p. 502).

CAULIFLOWER AU GRATIN CHOU-FLEUR AU GRATIN (P.)

Place the cooked and well-drained cauliflower in a baking dish with Mornay Sauce (p. 152) beneath and on top. Sprinkle grated cheese over it, baste with melted butter, and brown in the oven.

CAULIFLOWER COLETTE CHOU-FLEUR COLETTE (E.P.)

Take a cauliflower of medium size, white and firm. After having removed the leaves, split the core in four, then blanch in boiling water for four minutes. Drain, let dry and cool.

Prepare a stuffing with 9 ounces of fresh pork, chopped very fine and pounded on a board to obtain a homogeneous mixture. Add 2 whole eggs, 9 ounces of ham, 9 ounces of cooked mushrooms, all cut rather fine. Season with salt, pepper and spices. Stuff the cauliflower from the bottom, taking care to fill all the cavities, then wrap in a dishcloth.

Place in a pan. Moisten with water. Add a good *bouquet garni* (3 or 4 sprigs of parsley, 1 sprig of thyme, ½ bayleaf, tied together) and cook for about one hour. At the end of this time, unwrap the cauliflower and put it in a shallow baking dish. Let the remaining water evaporate, and cover the cauliflower with a well-buttered tomato sauce. Serve very warm, with the same sauce. (Figure 288, Page 492.)

CAULIFLOWER POLISH STYLE CHOU-FLEUR À LA POLONAISE (P.)

Cook the cauliflower and then sauté in butter without breaking it. Place it on a platter, keeping the natural shape as much as possible. Fry a good handful of fine bread crumbs in a rather large amount of butter and pour this over the cauliflower; sprinkle the top with chopped hard-boiled egg and chopped parsley. (Figure 300, Page 501.)

CELERY

CÉLERIS (P.)

There are 2 types of celery; stalk and root (also called celeriac). Stalk celery is cut off just above the root, then split in 2, washed, and blanched 15–18 min. in salted water. Then it is well braised in rich bouillon with onions and carrots, salt, peppercorns, and a *bouquet garni*. It takes about 2 hr. to cook; test by pricking with a fork. Celery may be served, well drained, with a brown sauce made with Madeira or, like cardoons, with a sauce made with marrow.

CELERY BONNE FEMME CÉLERIS À LA BONNE FEMME (P.)

Clean and blanch the celery as above, then put it into a cocotte in which 1 or 2 onions and carrots have been lightly browned; add ½ lb. peeled, quartered tomatoes. The celery should be cut into pieces about 2 in. long before going into the cocotte. Season, moisten with a little bouillon or gravy, and cook 1½ hr.

CREAMED CELERY CÉLERIS À LA CRÈME (P.)

Braise the celery, then drain it and cover with very creamy Béchamel Sauce (p. 146).

CELERY AU GRATIN CÉLERIS AU FROMAGE GRATINÉS (P.)

Cook in bouillon (p. 494). Drain well, then place in a baking dish. Cover with Mornay Sauce (p. 152), sprinkle with grated cheese, and brown in a hot oven.

CELERY WITH MARROW CÉLERIS À LA MOELLE (M.)

Prepare like Cardoons with Marrow (p. 493). (Figure 290, Page 493.)

CELERY ROOT WITH GRAVY CÉLERI-RAVE AU JUS (P.)

Peel the celery root and cut it into even-sized pieces—small squares or quarters. Cook in salted water until ¾ done. Finish cooking in butter, with the pan covered. Serve basted with a good, tomato-flavored meat gravy.

CELERY ROOT AU GRATIN CÉLERI-RAVE AU GRATIN (P.)

Cover with Mornay Sauce (p. 152), sprinkle with grated cheese, and brown in a hot oven.

CELERY ROOT ITALIAN STYLE CÉLERI-RAVE À L'ITALIENNE (P.)

Cook quartered celery root and cover with Italienne Sauce (p. 142).

CELERY CROQUETTES CROQUETTES DE CÉLERI (P.)

Mix a small amount of potatoes with the celery, drain well, and press both through a fine sieve. Bind this purée with 2 egg yolks, divide it into small portions, and roll into balls. Roll the balls in flour, bread them, and fry in burning-hot oil or fat. The celery may also be cooked in thick round slices, the slices cut in fours, floured, breaded, and fried in very hot butter. This is another excellent kind of croquette, and is best served in a fan shape.

CHAYOTES

CHAYOTTES

The chayote, a pear-shaped vegetable belonging to the gourd family, originally came from the West Indies.

BRAISED CHAYOTES CHAYOTTES BRAISÉES (P.)

Peel the chayotes and cook 1 hr. in boiling water. Then slice the white flesh and remove the seed. Put the slices into a stewpan, cover with bouillon, and braise slowly, covered, 1 hr. Drain the chayotes and mix the liquid from their cooking with a Golden Roux (p. 136); add 3 oz. Madeira wine; reduce to a sirupy consistency, and season. Add the sliced chayotes, simmer 10 min., and serve very hot.

STUFFED CHAYOTES CHAYOTTES FARCIES (P.)

Blanch the peeled chayotes in boiling water 1½ hr. Cut in 2 lengthwise. Remove the seed and lightly hollow out each half. Fill the halves with mushroom purée, sprinkle with grated Parmesan cheese, and top with 1 or 2 pieces of butter. Place the chayote halves on a buttered tray and brown in a hot oven.

FRIED CHAYOTES CHAYOTTES FRITES (P.)

Peel the chayotes, cut in slices about 3/8 in. thick, removing the seed, and blanch 1½ hr. in boiling water. Separately prepare a bowl of Frying Paste, using 7 oz. flour, ½ tsp. salt, and 2 tbsp. olive oil (see p. 686). Thin the paste by adding warm water until it is very smooth, runny, but still thick enough to coat the finger.

This paste should be prepared at least 2 hr. in advance. Then, just before using, add 2 stiffly beaten egg whites. Before serving, dry the sliced chayotes with a clean cloth, dip them one by one into the paste until completely coated, and plunge them into burning-hot deep fat. Using a ladle, turn the slices from time to time while cooking. Cook 5 min. Drain and sprinkle with fine salt, then arrange in a circle on a napkin, with a bunch of fried parsley in the center.

CHAYOTES AU GRATIN CHAYOTTES AU GRATIN (P.)

Peel 12 chayotes and slice the white flesh very thin. Plunge the slices into a stewpan of boiling water and cook ½ hr. Drain, then place in a deep platter on a layer of Mornay Sauce (p. 152); cover the slices with Mornay Sauce and sprinkle the top with grated Gruyère cheese. Continue filling the platter, alternating layers of chayote and Mornay Sauce sprinkled with Gruyère cheese; finish with the sauce on top. Baste with melted butter and brown in a hot oven. Serve very hot.

CHESTNUTS

MARRONS (M.)

The chestnuts must be completely shelled before cooking. There are 2 ways:

First method: Make a rather deep cut in the rounded bottom of the shell. Place the chestnuts on a baking tray containing a little water. Heat a few minutes in a very hot oven. Quickly shell the chestnuts while they are still hot.

Second method: Slit the chestnuts, place them in the wire basket of a deep fryer, and plunge into smoking-hot deep fat. Cook a few moments. Drain the chestnuts and shell immediately.

BRAISED CHESTNUTS MARRONS BRAISÉS (M.)

Lay the shelled chestnuts flat in a buttered sautéing pan. Pour enough thickened rich veal stock over them to cover. In the center of the sautéing pan place a bunch of celery. Cook in the oven without turning or stirring. When the chestnuts are almost cooked, reduce the cooking stock and roll the chestnuts in it to glaze them.

Note: These chestnuts are especially used for garnishes.

POACHED or STEWED CHESTNUTS MARRONS POCHÉS OR ÉTUVÉS (M.)

Lay the shelled chestnuts in a buttered sautéing pan. Put a bunch of celery in the center of the pan. Cover the chestnuts with white consommé. Cover the pan and cook without stirring.

Note: These chestnuts are also used for garnishes. When used for stuffing fowl, they should be kept rather firm.

Fig. 292 - Stuffed mushrooms (p. 503).
Fig. 293 - Girolles with fines herbes (p. 503).

Fig. 293

Fig. 294

Fig. 295

CHESTNUT PURÉE MARRONS EN PURÉE (P.)

Chestnuts to be puréed are first shelled, then cooked in water or milk and pressed through a sieve. Butter this purée and thin it a little with fresh cream or milk; season with salt and sugar.

CHICORY

CHICORÉE

CREAMED CHICORY CHICORÉE À LA CRÈME (E.)

Blanch the chicory 10 min. in boiling water. Let cool, press out all the water, and chop it. Bind with 5 oz. Brown Roux made with butter (p. 137) per 2 lb. chicory. Add 1 qt. consommé, season with salt and a pinch of powdered sugar, and braise in the oven, covered, 1½ hr. Remove from the oven and empty the chicory into another pan; finish it with 9 oz. cream and 5 oz. butter.

CHICORY FLAMANDE CHICORÉE À LA FLAMANDE (E.)

Cut the chicory into pieces about 2 in. long. Blanch it, let it cool, and then prepare as for Creamed Chicory (above). The only difference is that the chicory is not chopped.

CHICORY LOAF PAIN DE CHICORÉE (M.)

To fill an ordinary charlotte mold, mix 6 eggs, beaten as for an omelet, with 2 lb. braised chicory. Correct the seasoning. Pour into a well-buttered mold and poach 45 min. in a *bain-marie.* After removing from the *bain,* let the mold stand a few minutes. Unmold onto a round platter. Cover the loaf with a cream or other sauce and serve with a separate dish of the same sauce.

CORN ON THE COB

MAÏS EN ÉPIS (P.)

Corn on the cob is an American import now highly esteemed in France. Cook some milky ears of corn 20 min. in salted boiling water. Shuck the leaves from the ears and serve on a napkin with melted butter. Corn on the cob may also be grilled.

CUCUMBERS

CONCOMBRES (P.)

Rarely served cooked; however, they may be stuffed and are sometimes prepared like zucchini for garnishes. (See p. 518.)

EGGPLANT

AUBERGINES

STUFFED EGGPLANTS AUBERGINES FARCIES (P.)

Split the eggplants in half lengthwise, using the point of a knife; cut around the edges to separate some of the pulp from the skin; salt the pulp and

Fig. 294 - Creamed morels (p. 503).
Fig. 295 - Buttered Brussels sprouts (p. 492).

let stand about ½ hr. so that the eggplants drain. Then flour and fry them. Remove the pulp without damaging the skins and place the skins in a baking dish. Chop the pulp and mix it with ½ as much of the chopped-mushroom mixture called Duxelles (p. 176). Season, add a pinch of garlic and *fines herbes,* and stuff the eggplant skins. Sprinkle with bread crumbs, baste with oil, and brown in a very hot oven. Serve with thin Tomato Sauce (p. 146).

The filling may also be mixed with chopped leftover meat.

STUFFED EGGPLANTS BOSTON STYLE AUBERGINES FARCIES À LA BOSTON (P.)

Prepare the eggplants as above. When the pulp is chopped, bind it with a few tbsp. very creamy Béchamel Sauce (p. 146), season, mix in 1 whole egg per 4 small eggplants and 2 oz. grated Gruyère cheese. Place on a long baking dish, sprinkle with grated cheese, and brown in a very hot oven 7–8 min. In serving, moisten the eggplants with a few tbsp. hot, salted heavy cream. Do not use any garlic.

FRIED EGGPLANTS AUBERGINES FRITES (P.)

Peel them and cut in rather thin round slices; let drain in salt; dip in flour, and fry in burning-hot oil.

EGGPLANTS ORIENTALE AUBERGINES À L'ORIENTALE (M.)

Stuff eggplant halves, cooked in oil and hollowed out, with a mixture of the chopped pulp of the eggplant, bread crumbs, very thick tomato pureé, chopped garlic and parsley, all well seasoned and flavored with a little saffron. Lay the eggplants side by side in a baking dish on a bed of Rich Rice (p. 512). Sprinkle with bread crumbs, baste with oil, and brown lightly in the oven.

EGGPLANTS PROVENÇALE AUBERGINES À LA PROVENÇALE (P.)

Peel the eggplants and cut them in slices about ¼ in. thick; salt them and let stand 15 or 20 min. to drain. Wipe them off, dip in flour, and sauté in a pan of oil. In another pan, sauté a few tomatoes drained and cut into pieces, add salt, pepper, and 1 or 2 chopped cloves of garlic. When the 2 vegetables are cooked, mix them together, add some chopped parsley, and cook for a moment so that these two products of Provence blend. Serve very hot.

EGGPLANTS SÉVILLANE AUBERGINES À LA SÉVILLANE (P.)

Cut the eggplants lengthwise into 4 or 5 rather thick slices. Dip in flour and cook in oil in a frying pan. Peel, drain, and chop 1 lb. tomatoes per large eggplant. Cook them down in oil with salt, pepper, garlic, and chopped parsley. Pour these tomatoes over the eggplant slices, sprinkle with bread crumbs, baste with oil, and brown ½ hr. in a moderate oven. Surround with clear Tomato Sauce (p. 146).

A few pitted green olives may be added to the tomato fondue (this dish resembles Eggplants Provençale).

ENDIVE

ENDIVES

ENDIVE ENDIVES (E.)

Regardless of the recipe, endive must always be cooked the following way first. After cleaning, washing, and draining, place them side by side (without blanching them) in a tin-plated casserole with, per 2 lb. endive, the juice of ½ lemon, pinch of salt, 2 oz. butter, and 6 oz. water. Place a circle of buttered paper on top, cover the casserole, bring to a quick boil, then finish cooking at low heat 30–35 min. Endive served this simple way makes a fine vegetable or garnish.

ENDIVE MEUNIÈRE ENDIVES À LA MEUNIÈRE (P.)

Wash the endives and place side by side, uncooked, in a pan containing very hot butter; do not crowd. Salt, pepper, and sprinkle with lemon juice (1 lemon per lb. endive). Cover with buttered paper and cook in the oven until the endive dries and begins to turn yellow underneath. When the pieces of endive begin to cook, they give off liquid and cook in their own juice, then, when the water evaporates, they finish cooking in butter. To serve, remove the outside burned leaves and baste simply with brown butter. Do not use the cooking butter, for it is bitter. (Figure 301, Page 501.)

FENNEL

FENOUIL (E.)

STUFFED FENNELS FENOUILS FARCIS (E.P.)

Wash the fennels. Cook them in plenty of salted water, keeping them somewhat firm. After having cooled and drained them, fill the space between leaves with the following mixture: 4½ ounces of fresh pork (fat and lean), 3½ ounces of white bread soaked in milk and pressed, a whole egg, salt and pepper. This quantity is enough for 6 fennel stalks.

Place the fennels in a pan just big enough to hold them. Add veal stock (p. 134) to fill ¾ of the pan, and braise for a good half hour. Serve in a shallow dish with the remaining liquid reduced to half. (Figure 303, Page 508.)

GREEN CABBAGE

CHOUX VERTS

CABBAGE ENGLISH STYLE CHOU À L'ANGLAISE (E.)

Quarter the cabbage, trim off the stump, remove the outer leaves, and cook in salted water. Drain and then press tightly between two flat plates to extract the water. Cut into squares, diamonds, etc. Cabbage prepared this way is served as a vegetable or a garnish.

BRAISED CABBAGE CHOU BRAISÉ (E.)

Quarter the cabbage, blanch, let cool, and drain well. Separate the leaves of the quarters; remove the outer leaves and stump. Season with salt, pepper, and nutmeg, and place in a casserole lined with strips of pork fat and containing, per 2 lb. cabbage, 1 quartered carrot, 1 onion stuck with a clove, a *bouquet garni,* and 12 oz. consommé and 3 tbsp. unclarified fat from the soup pot. Cover with strips of pork fat, bring to a boil, and braise slowly 2 hr.

STUFFED CABBAGES (FOR GARNISHES) CHOUX FARCIS (POUR GARNITURES) (M.)

Blanch the whole cabbage, cool, and drain. Remove the large outside leaves and spread them on a napkin. Separate the rest of the leaves, season them, and place a part of them on each large leaf with a quantity of mincemeat (about the size of a small egg) seasoned with *fines herbes.* Wrap the stuffed leaves in the corner of a towel or napkin and squeeze each one tightly to form a ball. Lay these balls side by side in a sautéing pan and cook as in the recipe for Dolmas of Stuffed Cabbage (below).

Note: These cabbage balls may be stuffed with various fillings. Usually they are filled with Light Forcemeat (p. 173) and pork.

DOLMAS OF STUFFED CABBAGE CHOUX FARCIS (DOLMAS DE) (P.)

Blanch 12 medium-sized cabbage leaves in boiling water 3 or 4 min. Cool and drain. Spread the leaves on the table and season with salt and paprika. Prepare in advance a hash made of braised leftover mutton, but braised or boiled beef will also do. Add to this hash a few tbsp. chopped onions cooked in a little lard, 2 oz. stale bread (soaked in cold bouillon, pressed dry, and crumbled), 3 tbsp. rice half cooked in bouillon, salt, chopped parsley, pepper, and paprika. Season and mix well, divide into balls about the size of a tangerine, and place these in the center of the cabbage leaves. Wrap the mixture in the cabbage leaf and squeeze lightly in a cloth to shape into a ball and tighten the cabbage. Lay them carefully on a bed of pork fat and sliced vegetables, pressing them tightly one against the other. Grill dry over the fire, then pour in enough tomato juice to cover. Cover with paper and cook in a moderate oven 1 full hr. Serve with the liquid from the cooking, greatly reduced, sprinkle with lemon juice, and place a slice of lemon on each one. (Figure 297, Page 500.)

CABBAGE AU GRATIN CHOUX GRATINÉS (P.)

This is an exquisite vegetable dish. Cook the cabbages in water, drain, and chop like spinach. Bind with a generous amount of Béchamel Sauce (p. 146), season, add grated cheese, then sprinkle with more grated cheese and bread crumbs and brown in the oven.

JAPANESE ARTICHOKES

CROSNES (P.)

Japanese artichokes taste rather like artichoke bottoms. Blanch, keeping them somewhat firm. Finish cooking them in butter without browning. Serve

Fig. 296 - Red cabbage Limousine (p. 511).
Fig. 297 - Dolmas of stuffed cabbage (p. 500).
Fig. 298 - Stuffed Zucchini (p. 518).

Fig. 296

Fig. 297

Fig. 298

Fig. 300

Fig. 299

Fig. 301

immediately, either sprinkled with chopped parsley and *fines herbes* or accompanied with a white sauce or as a garnish. They are also often made into fritters.

JAPANESE-ARTICHOKE FRITTERS CROSNES (BEIGNETS DE) (E.)

Clean and cook in salted water, keeping them rather firm. Drain well, then mix with a proportionate amount of very thick Parisienne Sauce (p. 146). Spread this composition on a platter and let cool. Take the composition by the spoonful, dip quickly into Frying Paste (p. 558), and fry in hot deep fat. Serve on a napkin with fried parsley.

CREAMED JAPANESE ARTICHOKES CROSNES À LA CRÈME (E.)

Blanch and cook in butter in a tightly closed pan until ¾ done. Pour boiling cream over them and finish cooking, reducing the cream. Add a little thin Béchamel Sauce (p. 146) at the end and serve in a timbale or vegetable dish.

JAPANESE-ARTICHOKE CROQUETTES CROSNES (CROQUETTES DE) (E.)

Cook the Japanese artichokes first in salted water, keeping them rather firm, then drain as thoroughly as possible and mix with very reduced Parisienne Sauce (p. 146)—10 oz. sauce per 1 lb. artichokes. Spread the mixture on a buttered platter and let cool.

Divide this composition into portions weighing about 2 oz. each. Shape them into balls, pears, disks, or otherwise. Flour, dip in beaten egg, and cover with very fine bread crumbs. Drop the croquettes into very hot deep fat 5 or 6 min. before serving. Drain them on a cloth, salt lightly, and serve on a napkin with a bunch of very green, fried parsley.

JERUSALEM ARTICHOKES

TOPINAMBOURS (P.)

Jerusalem artichokes are seldom used, even in home cooking. They may be prepared in various ways: boiled in salted water and seasoned in salads like potatoes or made into fritters, but they are best cooked in butter, browned just a little.

LEEKS

POIREAUX (M.)

This potherb is principally used for flavoring soups and as an added ingredient in shredded or mixed vegetables. However, it should be mentioned in the list of vegetable dishes, for it may also be served as such.

It is prepared like asparagus—boiled in salted water (or cooked in Pot-au-Feu, p. 190) and served, hot or cold, with one of the sauces usually accompanying boiled vegetables: melted butter, Butter Sauce (p. 148), cream sauce, Hollandaise (p. 151), etc. Cold leeks are served with mayonnaise or Vinaigrette Sauce (p. 158). Also, after blanching in salted water and cooking in butter in a tightly closed pan, leeks may be served creamed with Mornay Sauce (p. 152), sprinkled with grated Parmesan cheese, and browned in the oven.

Fig. 299 - Stuffed onions (p. 504).
Fig. 300 - Cauliflower polish style (p. 494).
Fig. 301 - Endive meunière (p. 499).

LENTILS

LENTILLES (M.)

This vegetable is used only dried. They are cooked the same as dried navy (haricot) beans. All recipes for navy (haricot) beans may be applied to lentils: buttered, *à la bretonne*, with gravy, purée. Lentil Purée is called Esau Purée.

LETTUCE

LAITUES

BRAISED LETTUCE WITH GRAVY LAITUES BRAISÉES AU JUS (P.)

Strip off the wilted leaves of rounded heads of lettuce without cutting off the root (merely scrape it). Blanch 8 to 10 min. in salted boiling water, drain, cool in a lot of water, then press the water out. Cut in half, season with salt, pepper, and grated nutmeg, and place side by side in a sautéing pan containing pork fat and slices of onions and carrots. Brown dry over the fire, then pour in enough rich bouillon to cover the heads of lettuce halfway. Cover the pan with oiled paper and braise in the oven until dry. Serve with a good gravy or thin Madeira Sauce (p. 142) poured over the heads. (Figure 304, Page 509.)

MUSHROOMS

CHAMPIGNONS

CEPES or MUSHROOMS BORDELAISE CÈPES À LA BORDELAISE (P.)

Either fresh or canned cepes may be used. Slice the cepes and drop them into a frying pan containing a little sizzling-hot butter and oil. Season with salt and pepper and sauté them until they are crisp and golden. Then add 1 heaping tsp. chopped shallots and a few chopped cepe stems. Sauté another few moments, then pour a few tbsp. brown butter over them. Sprinkle with chopped parsley.

CEPES or MUSHROOMS BRIMOND CÈPES BRIMOND (P.)

Cook in oil at moderate heat 12 fine cepes of the same size (they should be slightly hollowed out first); drain the cepes and stuff with the following mixture. Chop cepe stems and peelings, brown them in oil, add a finely chopped shallot, then chopped parsley and garlic, and 2 heaping tbsp. bread crumbs. Season with salt, pepper, and a little curry powder. Place the cepes in a baking dish on a bed of peeled, seeded, and chopped tomatoes browned in butter. Sprinkle with bread crumbs, baste with oil, and brown in the oven at low heat. (Figure 291, P. 493.)

CEPES or MUSHROOMS AU GRATIN CÈPES AU GRATIN (P.)

Wash the cepes well, chop them, and brown in butter with salt and pepper. When all the liquid has evaporated, add a small chopped onion, a pinch of garlic, chopped parsley, and Béchamel Sauce (p. 146). Place in a baking dish, sprinkle with grated cheese and bread crumbs, top with a little butter, and brown in the oven.

CEPES or MUSHROOMS PROVENÇALE CÈPES À LA PROVENÇALE (P:)

Same recipe as Cepes Bordelaise (p. 502), substituting garlic for the shallots and leaving out the butter entirely, using oil instead.

HOW TO COOK MUSHROOMS CHAMPIGNONS (CUISSON ORDINAIRE DES) (P.)

Mushrooms are usually cooked with 1 cup water, 1½ oz. butter, juice of 1 lemon, and a pinch of salt per lb. mushrooms. Cover and cook 3 or 4 min. over a hot fire. Always keep them in their cooking liquid with an oiled paper over the top.

Mushrooms with large heads may be cooked in nothing more than butter and browned a little, or they may be grilled with butter and *fines herbes* in a very hot oven.

CREAMED MUSHROOMS CHAMPIGNONS À LA CRÈME (P.)

Use small, very white mushrooms. Wash them, then cook in butter in a covered pan with salt and pepper. Add a little thin Béchamel Sauce (p. 146) and enough cream to cover the mushrooms; let them simmer. Then, just before removing from the stove, add a finger of lemon juice. If the mushrooms are too large, cut them in slices or quarters. *Giroles* or *chanterelles* are cooked the same way.

STUFFED MUSHROOMS CHAMPIGNONS FARCIS (P.)

Wash some fine, large mushroom heads without peeling them, and scoop them out slightly. Salt them and fill with the Duxelles given on p. 176. Sprinkle with bread crumbs, baste with oil, and brown in a very hot oven. (Fig. 292, P. 496)

MUSHROOM FONDUE CHAMPIGNONS (FONDUE AUX) (P.)

Wash the mushrooms well and slice very thin. Cook in burning-hot butter, salt and pepper them, and add a little Béchamel Sauce (p. 146) and some cream. Reduce well and add, at the end, a generous amount of grated cheese. Brown in the oven.

GIROLLES WITH FINES HERBES GIROLLES AUX FINES HERBES (E.P.)

Wash the girolles thoroughly. Drain, and dry them in a towel. Then cook in very hot oil in a skillet. Continue cooking until the water from the girolles is completely evaporated. Season with salt and pepper. Chop very finely a garlic clove and a small bouquet of parsley and chives, and add to the girolles just before serving. (Figure 293, Page 496.)

CREAMED MORELS MORILLES À LA CRÈME (P.)

Prepare like ordinary mushrooms (see above). They may also be used as a garnish. (Figure 294, Page 497.)

MORELS WITH FINES HERBES MORILLES AUX FINES HERBES (P.)

This delicious vegetable should be cooked in butter with a finger of lemon juice, salt and pepper, and without a cover. They should be sliced. When all the liquid has evaporated, drop them into another pan of burning-hot butter. Serve them somewhat browned, with chopped parsley.

OKRA

GOMBOS (M.)

Method of cooking: Trim, wash, and blanch 5 min. in salted water. Drain, wipe dry, and cook in butter in a tightly closed pan. May also be prepared creamed, fried, curried, with gravy, or *à l'orientale.*

ONIONS

OIGNONS

STUFFED ONIONS OIGNONS FARCIS (M.)

Slice off the top ¼ of sweet, medium-sized onions. Blanch well in salted water. Hollow them out with a curved paring knife, leaving a shell about ¼ in. thick. Chop fine the onion you have scooped out and cook it in butter in a tightly closed pan. Mix in an equal amount of thickened Duxelles (p. 176). Reduce this stuffing and season. Fill the onions with it. Lay them in a buttered baking dish. Pour some thickened Veal Gravy (p. 134) over them and braise slowly. At the last moment sprinkle the onions with bread crumbs and brown them. Place on a round platter; surround with a ring of Semiglaze Sauce (p. 138) blended with some of the strained cooking stock. (Figure 299, Page 501.)

Note: The onions may be stuffed with various compositions: pork forcemeat; chicken forcemeat; Risotto (p. 513) with tomato fondue, etc. All these fillings should be mixed with the scooped-out part of the onions chopped up and cooked in butter.

FRIED ONIONS (GARNISH) OIGNONS FRITS (GARNITURE) (M.)

Slice medium-sized onions in thin rings; separate the rings (do not use the center parts, which are too small). Flour the rings and fry in smoking hot oil; drain and salt.

GLAZED ONIONS OIGNONS GLACÉS (M.)

White: Place small onions, all of the same size, in a buttered sautéing pan. Cover with white consommé. Season with salt and a little sugar. Cover the pan and cook. When the onions are cooked, roll them in the reduced cooking stock to glaze them.

Brown: Sauté small onions in butter, sprinkling them with sugar. When they are a golden brown, season with salt, cover, and cook slowly.

ONION PURÉE or PURÉE SOUBISE I OIGNONS (PURÉE D') SOUBISE (M.)

Blanch 1 lb. thin-sliced onions and 4 oz. Carolina rice in salted water. Drain, season with salt, pepper, nutmeg, and a tiny pinch of sugar. Place in a casserole lined on the bottom and sides with strips of pork fat. Pour in some white consommé; add 2 tbsp. butter. Cook slowly in the oven with the casserole covered. Drain the onions; remove the strips of pork fat. Press the onions through a sieve, using a spatula. Heat the purée. Finish with 2 or 3 tbsp. cream and 2 oz. butter.

ONION PURÉE or PURÉE SOUBISE II OIGNONS (PURÉE D') SOUBISE (M.)

In a tightly covered pan cook in butter, without browning, 1 lb. well-blanched, thin-sliced onions. When the onions are cooked, bind them with 1 pt. thick Béchamel Sauce (p. 146). Season with salt, pepper, nutmeg, and a pinch of sugar. Cook slowly. Press through a sieve. Finish as in preceding recipe.

PEAS

POIS

SMALL BUTTERED PEAS ENGLISH STYLE PETITS POIS AU BEURRE À L'ANGLAISE (P.)

Cook the peas in plenty of boiling salted water without covering. Drain, pour into a stewpan, and let dry a moment on the stove, then add butter, salt, and a little sugar. Remove from the fire and shake well to cover all the peas with butter.

SMALL PEAS FRENCH STYLE PETITS POIS À LA FRANÇAISE (P.)

Place the peas in a stewpan with a good handful of finely chopped lettuce, a few small new onions, a piece of butter; add a little salt, a pinch of sugar, a small bunch of chervil; half cover with boiling water, and cook slowly with the pan covered. The cooking time depends upon the quality of the peas and the quantity of water.

SMALL PEAS WITH BACON PETITS POIS AU LARD (P.)

Brown 5 oz. small bacon strips in butter (after blanching 1 min.), cooking 1 chopped onion or a few small whole new onions with the bacon. When bacon and onions are browned, sprinkle with a little flour. Cook this roux for a moment, then add enough water to make a very thin sauce. Add the shelled peas, season lightly because of the bacon, and cook over a hot fire.

FRESH-PEA PURÉE or PURÉE SAINT-GERMAIN PURÉE DE POIS FRAIS OR SAINT-GERMAIN (E.)

Cook the peas with just enough boiling water to cover, adding 1 tsp. salt and a pinch of sugar per qt. Add a small lettuce and a few sprigs of parsley. When the peas are cooked, drain them; press them through a sieve, while reducing the cooking liquid. Work into this purée 4 oz. fresh butter per qt. purée; when the cooking liquid has been reduced almost to a glaze, add it to the purée.

SPLIT-PEA PURÉE PURÉE DE POIS CASSÉS (M.)

Soak the peas overnight. The following day, change the water, cover with cold water, salt, bring to a boil. Add: green of leek sliced thin, carrot, a *bouquet garni,* onions, and diced bacon. Cook slowly 1½ hr. Press through a sieve, dry the purée on the stove, and butter.

PIMENTOS OR SWEET PEPPERS

PIMENTS OR POIVRONS (M.)

Certain pimentos, such as Cayenne, are used only for seasoning. Others, such as the large sweet Spanish pimentos or the large American ones, may be cooked in various ways. However they are used, pimentos must first be skinned and the seeds removed.

To skin more easily, heat them a few moments on the grill or on the burning-hot oven grill, then plunge immediately into cold water, and skin.

Diced or shredded sweet pimento is used as an ingredient in various garnishes. It may also be used for garnishing Rice Pilaf (p. 512). Large pimentos and sweet peppers may be stuffed like tomatoes or eggplants. Finally, they may be made into a purée to serve with fish or grilled meat.

POTATOES

POMMES DE TERRE

POTATOES ENGLISH STYLE POMMES DE TERRE À L'ANGLAISE (E.)

Cut the potatoes into the shape of large cloves of garlic; cook them in salted water or steam them. They are usually served with boiled fish. The English method is to cook them without salt.

POTATOES ANNA POMMES DE TERRE ANNA (M.)

Cut the potatoes into thin round slices, wash, wipe dry, season. Place in circular rows in a pan specially made for this preparation (or, lacking one, in a flat sautéing pan with a thick bottom). The pan should be heavily buttered. Butter the first layer and continue filling the pan, buttering each layer. Cover and bake 25 min. in a fairly hot oven. Turn this potato cake over (by reversing it onto the lid of the pan) and bake in the same pan about 6 min. more. Serve on a round platter. (Figure 307, Page 512.)

BUTTERED POTATOES POMMES DE TERRE AU BEURRE (P.)

Peel new potatoes, put them into a pan of cold water on the stove, and bring to a boil. Drain them, then drop them into burning-hot butter, salt them, and put into the oven, turning them from time to time. When they are cooked, arrange them in a mound and sprinkle with parsley.

POTATOES CHÂTEAU POMMES DE TERRE CHÂTEAU (M.)

Cut the potatoes into the shape of large cloves of garlic. Cook them slowly in clarified butter, in a sautéing pan, until they are golden brown all over. Serve in a timbale or vegetable dish; sprinkle chopped parsley on top.

Note: Some cooks blanch potatoes in salted water before cooking them in butter.

POTATO CHIPS POMMES DE TERRE CHIPS (P.)

Cut the potatoes into thin round slices. Cook like Potato Straws (p. 509).

POTATO CROQUETTES (Garnish) POMMES DE TERRE EN CROQUETTES (GARNITURE) (M.)

(1) *Preparing the mixture* (*called Potato Duchesse mixture*) : Quarter some

large Dutch potatoes. Cook quickly in salted water, keeping them rather firm. Drain them; dry them a few moments in an open oven. Press through a sieve. Dry this purée a few moments on top of the stove, working it with a spatula. Remove from the stove and add, per 2 lb. purée, 3½ oz. butter and 4 egg yolks. Season. Spread this purée on a buttered platter and let cool.

(2) Divide this purée into 2-oz. portions. Roll these portions of purée in flour, shaping them as you wish (small stoppers or corks, balls, eggs, etc.). Roll the croquettes in flour, dip in beaten egg containing a drop of olive oil, and cover with bread crumbs. Fry in smoking-hot deep fat.

POTATOES DAUPHINE POMMES DE TERRE DAUPHINE (Gi.)

Take, preferably, some fine Dutch potatoes. Peel, quarter, and start cooking in lightly salted cold water. As soon as they feel soft when pressed with a finger, drain them in a colander and empty them onto a platter. Heat them in the oven a few minutes to extract all the moisture. Press the potatoes through a fine sieve. Put this purée into a sautéing pan; add salt, if needed, a pinch of white pepper, and a dash of nutmeg, and dry the purée over a hot fire. When it is sufficiently firm, remove from the fire and add 4 egg yolks and about 10 oz. (net weight) unsweetened Choux Paste (p. 548) per 2 lb. purée. Pour this mixture onto a buttered platter and let cool before using.

When the mixture is cold, separate it into portions about the size of a small egg, and roll these pieces on a floured table, shaping them into small stoppers or corks. Roll them in flour, dip in beaten egg, and cover with bread crumbs. Roll them in the hand to make them even and smooth, flattening the ends with the side of a knife. Lay them in even rows on a rack or wire basket for deep frying. Plunge into hot deep fat and drain after a few minutes—that is, when they have browned. Salt lightly.

POTATOES DUCHESSE POMMES DE TERRE DUCHESSE (P.)

Proceed as for Potato Purée (p. 509), but when the potatoes have been dried, do not add any milk; add a little more than the usual amount of butter and, off the stove, 2 egg yolks per lb. potatoes. Season with salt, pepper, and nutmeg. The purée should have the consistency of a paste. Shape as desired by hand. If you wish, make them into small round or oval pancakes, sprinkling them with flour. Cook them in a frying pan with some very hot butter or bake them on a pastry sheet in a very hot oven, after brushing the top with beaten egg. In the second case, however, the purée should be softened with a little milk or whole eggs. (Figure 305, Page 509.)

POTATOES FONDANTES I POMMES DE TERRE FONDANTES (P.)

Cut the potatoes as for Potatoes Château (p. 506), only a little larger. Blanch 5 min., then drain them. Cook them in plenty of butter, covered, in the oven. When the potatoes are cooked, baste with 2 tbsp. white bouillon, which will be absorbed by the potatoes, making them softer. Serve in a vegetable dish without parsley.

POTATOES FONDANTES II POMMES DE TERRE FONDANTES (E.)

Cut the potatoes into the shape of large, elongated olives weighing about 3 oz. each. Cook them slowly in butter or lard, in a sautéing pan, turning them frequently. When they are cooked, remove them from the pan and flatten lightly with a fork without breaking them. Pour off the cooking butter and replace the potatoes in the pan with 3½ oz. fresh butter per 2 lb. potatoes; keep them covered until they have completely absorbed the butter.

FRIED POTATOES POMMES DE TERRE FRITES (P.)

Deep frying makes it possible to serve potatoes in a variety of ways, from the simple Potatoes Pont-Neuf (p. 509) to Potato Croquettes (p. 506), including Souffléed Potatoes (p. 510), so highly appreciated but so seldom successful. (Figure 289, Page 493.)

GOURMET POTATOES POMMES DE TERRE DES GOURMETS (P.)

Boil, steam, or bake some mealy potatoes. Mash them with a fork, adding a little butter, salt, and pepper or a dash of grated nutmeg. Put them into a deep baking dish, pour a generous amount of cream over them, and bake 10 min. in a hot oven. Serve immediately.

POTATOES LORETTE POMMES DE TERRE LORETTE (E.)

Add grated cheese to the Potato Dauphine mixture (p. 507), 1 oz. cheese per lb. mixture. Divide this mixture into portions weighing 1½ oz.; mold them into crescents, flouring them lightly. Drop these crescents into very hot deep fat about 6 min. before serving.

POTATOES LYONNAISE POMMES DE TERRE À LA LYONNAISE (E.)

Cut boiled, peeled potatoes in round slices; sauté them in butter in a frying pan. Also sauté some thin-sliced onions in butter (1 part onion to 4 parts potato). When the onions are golden brown, add them to the sautéed potatoes. Season with salt and pepper, and sauté the onions and potatoes together a few minutes to mix them well. Serve in a timbale or vegetable dish with chopped parsley.

POTATOES MACAIRE POMMES DE TERRE MACAIRE (E.)

Bake medium-sized Dutch potatoes. When cooked, scoop out the pulp onto a platter; season with salt and pepper. Using a fork, work some butter into the potatoes (7 oz. butter per 2 lb. potato). Spread this mixture like a pancake in the bottom of a frying pan containing very hot clarified butter; brown both sides.

POTATOES MONT-D'OR POMMES DE TERRE MONT-D'OR (P.)

Prepare a Potato Duchesse mixture (p. 506), adding 5 oz. grated Gruyère cheese per 2 lb. mixture. Shape the potatoes into a small hill or mound on a round platter, sprinkle grated cheese on top, and bake 6–7 min. in a very hot oven. Serve immediately.

Fig. 302 - Creamed spinach (p. 514).
Fig. 303 - Stuffed fennels (p. 499).

Fig. 302

Fig. 303

Fig. 304

Fig. 305

MOUSSELINE POTATOES or **MOUSSE PARMENTIER** POMMES DE TERRE MOUSSELINE or MOUSSE PARMENTIER (E.)

Quickly make Potato Purée as directed below. To this purée, which should be kept rather firm, add (per 2 lb. purée) 3½ oz. grated Parmesan cheese, 6 tbsp. whipped cream, and 5 stiffly beaten egg whites. Place in a buttered and floured timbale, sprinkle the top with grated Parmesan cheese, and bake like a soufflé.

POTATO NESTS POMMES DE TERRE (NIDS DE) (M.)

Line the sides of a special frying basket called a "nest mold" with washed, drained, and dried potatoes cut into thin julienne strips. Trim off the pieces of potatoes extending above the rim of the mold and close it. Fry in deep fat until golden brown. Unmold after removing from the fat and serve on a napkin; fill the nests with Fried Potatoes (p. 508).

POTATOES NOISETTE POMMES DE TERRE NOISETTES (M.)

Using a ball vegetable cutter, scoop out pieces of potato about the size of a hazelnut. Cook in butter.

POTATO STRAWS POMMES DE TERRE PAILLE (P.)

Cut potatoes as fine as julienne strips, then wash them and dry well. Fry in the usual way. Dip them in very hot fat a second time just before serving.

POTATOES PARISIENNE POMMES DE TERRE À LA PARISIENNE (M.)

Very small Potatoes Noisette (above) rolled, after cooling, in melted Meat Glaze (p. 135) or in veal stock reduced to a glaze. Chopped parsley.

PARSLEY POTATOES POMMES DE TERRE PERSILLÉES (P.)

Prepare the potatoes as for Potatoes Château (p. 506). Put them into a baking dish with a little butter; half cover with white bouillon; add salt, pepper, and chopped parsley. Cover with buttered paper and cook in the oven. Serve as is with fresh parsley on top.

POTATOES PONT-NEUF POMMES DE TERRE PONT-NEUF (P.)

Cut the potatoes into long strips with square edges about the thickness of your little finger. Plunge them into very hot, but not blazing hot, deep fat or oil. Cook and drain, then just before serving plunge them again into blazing hot fat to give them a crust and make them golden brown. Drain, salt, and serve on a napkin.

POTATO PURÉE POMMES DE TERRE EN PURÉE (P.)

Quarter some mealy potatoes and cook them in salted water. Drain and press immediately through a sieve or potato masher. Work the purée in a pan with some butter and moisten it, little by little, with boiling milk. When it is rather soft, beat it briskly with a wire whisk to make it light and fluffy, still adding milk. Keep hot in a *bain-marie* if it is not to be served at once. A well-made purée is creamy and light and then deserves to be called a mousseline purée.

Fig. 304 - Braised lettuce with gravy (p. 502).
Fig. 305 - Potatoes duchesse in various shapes (p. 507).

SAUTÉED POTATOES POMMES DE TERRE SAUTÉES (M.)

May be made 2 ways: (1) Potatoes cooked in the skins, peeled, sliced in rings, sautéed in butter in a frying pan until brown and crisp. Season; sprinkle with chopped parsley. (2) Cut raw potatoes in the shape of large stoppers or corks and slice these into thin rounds. Sauté in butter in a frying pan; season. Place in a timbale or vegetable dish and sprinkle with chopped parsley.

SOUFFLÉED POTATOES POMMES DE TERRE SOUFFLÉES (M.)

Trim large Dutch potatoes along the sides to make them very regular in shape. Cut them lengthwise into slices 1/8 in. thick. (Illustration, p. 111.) Wash and wipe dry. Plunge into moderately hot deep fat. Gradually increase the heat and gently shake the pan while the potatoes are cooking. When the potatoes are cooked, drain them (using the deep-frying basket) and plunge them immediately into a second pan of burning-hot deep fat. Drain on a cloth and season. Serve on a napkin or in a nest of Potato Straws (p 509.)

Note: If Souffléed Potatoes are to be a success, use only the finest potatoes. Dutch potatoes are the best. There are 2 kinds: the long yellow ones called early English, which appear in May, and the late potatoes, which come in October.

POTATOES SUZETTE POMMES DE TERRE SUZETTE (M.)

Bake large, choice, even-sized Dutch potatoes. Make an oval cut in one side of the potatoes. Through this opening, use a small spoon to scoop out 3/4 the potato without tearing the skin. Finely mash the pulp removed or press it through a sieve. Work butter into it with a spatula; season with salt, pepper, and nutmeg. Fill the potatoes with this mixture. Sprinkle with bread crumbs, baste with butter, and brown slowly in the oven. (Figure 306, Page 512.)

POTATOES YVETTE POMMES DE TERRE YVETTE (P.)

Cut 1 lb. raw potatoes into julienne strips, wash well and wipe dry, then drop into a frying pan containing 5 oz. burning-hot butter. Season with salt and pepper. Roll them in this butter, then let them brown on one side and turn them over like a pancake. Brown the other side, and serve as a pancake.

POTATO SAVARIN SAVARIN EN POMMES DE TERRE (P.)

Cut the potatoes as for Potato Straws (p. 509). Put them into a buttered Savarin mold (ring mold), packing them in tightly. Baste with butter. Bake 20 min. in a very hot oven, then unmold. Prepare some not-too-thick Béchamel Sauce (p. 146), adding some cream, some port, a little Parmesan cheese, and paprika to it. Pour the sauce into the center of the potato ring.

RED CABBAGE

CHOUX ROUGES

RED CABBAGE FLAMANDE CHOU ROUGE À LA FLAMANDE (E.)

Cut the cabbage into quarters and remove the outside leaves and the stump; cut the quarters into fine julienne strips. Season with salt, pepper, nutmeg;

sprinkle with vinegar, and place in a well-buttered earthenware cocotte. Cover and cook at low heat. When ¾ cooked, add 4 peeled, quartered russet apples and 1 tbsp. moist or powdered sugar. Take care to cook slowly from beginning to end, and without any other liquid than the vinegar.

RED CABBAGE LIMOUSINE CHOU ROUGE À LA LIMOUSINE (E.)

Shred the cabbage, season it, and cook with a little bouillon, fat from roast pork, and peeled and broken raw chestnuts (20 chestnuts to 1 medium-sized cabbage). (Figure 296, Page 500.)

Note: Cook in an earthenware casserole.

RED-CABBAGE SALAD CHOU ROUGE EN SALADE

See Salads, p. 523.

RICE

RIZ (E.)

In preparing Rice Pilaf and Risotto the quality of the rice is the essential thing. The East Indian rice called Patna is preferred for a pilaf. If this is unavailable, Carolina rice may be used, but this is better suited to desserts and salads. Piedmont rice is the best for Risotto.

BOILED RICE RIZ AU BLANC (E.) (*For 6 persons*)

Wash ½ lb. Carolina rice and cook it 18 min. in 2 qt. salted water (1 tsp. salt per qt. water). Drain in a coarse strainer, wash in warm water, drain again completely, and spread it on a hot napkin to dry. Serve in a timbale or vegetable dish with 3 oz. melted butter.

To be served with eggs, fowl, and salads.

Note: When the rice is to be used for salad, it should be lightly seasoned with Vinaigrette Sauce (p. 158) while still warm, regardless of the subsequent preparations for the salad. When rice is completely cold, it does not absorb all of the seasoning.

RICE WITH MUSHROOMS RIZ AUX CÈPES (A.) (*For 6 persons*)

Take: ½ lb. rice, 4 oz. butter, 2 oz. dried mushrooms (cepes), salt, pepper. First rinse the rice in warm water without letting it soak, then sprinkle it gradually into a large pot ¾ full of salted boiling water (3 qt. water and 3 tsp. bay salt per ½ lb. rice). It should be cooked, uncovered, 10–25 min., depending on the rice used (Piedmont rice is one of those which cook fastest), and the water should be kept at a full boil all during cooking, to keep the grains of rice in movement and prevent their sticking together or to the sides of the pot. To determine when the rice is cooked, spoon up a few grains of rice from time to time and bite them to see if they are too hard or just right. Wash the mushrooms in cold water and let soak 1 hr.; press them to remove all excess water, and cut them into pieces. Cook them 15 min. in butter, then add the rice, salt, pepper to taste. Mix well, shaking the pan to prevent the rice from browning, then serve.

Rice with Mushrooms is an excellent garnish and goes well with Mutton Stew (p. 357), Veal Birds (p. 343), etc.

RICE CUBAN STYLE RIZ À LA CUBAINE (ARROZ A LA CUBANA) (M.) (*For 10 persons*)

Put 1 pt. washed and well-drained Carolina rice into a pot. Pour in 3 pt. cold water and season with a good pinch of salt. Bring to a boil at moderate heat. Stir the rice while it is coming to a boil. Cover the pot and cook at low heat. When the rice is cooked and fluffy, add 2 oz. lard. Mix lightly with a fork.

CURRIED RICE RIZ AU CURRY (E.) (*For 6 persons*)

Cook 1 heaping tbsp. chopped onion in 1½ oz. butter until golden brown. Add 1 tsp. curry and ½ lb. unwashed Patna rice. Shake the pan on the stove until the rice is well covered with butter and curry. Pour in 1 pt. white bouillon, cover, and cook in the oven 18 min. After cooking, fluff up the rice and mix in 1½ oz. fresh butter. Serve with eggs, fowl, fish; may also be served as is.

RICH RICE RIZ AU GRAS (E.) (*For 6 persons*)

Blanch and cool ½ lb. rice. Pour in 2¼ cups rather rich bouillon and cook slowly 25–30 min. Serve with boiled or braised meat and fowl.

RICE INDIAN STYLE RIZ À L'INDIENNE (M.) (*For 6 persons*)

Boil ½ lb. Patna rice in 3 qt. salted water. Boil until the rice is no longer crisp when bitten—usually 15 min.—and stir while boiling. Drain the rice into a large strainer and rinse it 2 or 3 times with cold water. Spread it out on a tray, cover it with a napkin, and let it dry 15 min. in a warm oven.

Note: All curried dishes must be accompanied with rice prepared this way. When perfectly served, all the grains are separate. It is important not to use any other than Indian rice and then not more than a year old. Rice that is too old chips while cooking and becomes mushy.

RICE PILAF RIZ PILAF (E.) (*For 6 persons*)

Lightly brown 2 tbsp. chopped onions in 1½ oz. butter. Add ½ lb. unwashed Patna rice and shake it over the fire until it turns a milky color. Pour in 2¼ cups white bouillon, cover, and cook 18 min. in a low oven. After cooking, pour the rice into another container and mix in 1½ oz. butter broken into small pieces. Serve with chicken, fish, shellfish, etc.

Note: The advantage of preparing rice this way is that it may be kept hot for hours without losing any of its quality, and is therefore very useful in restaurants.

RICE PILAF ASSAN RIZ PILAF ASSAN (P.)

Soak Patna rice in warm water 1 hr. Wash well in cold water, then brown it in butter. Add twice its volume in bouillon (or, for 1 bowl rice, 2 bowls bouillon) and a little tomato purée. Cook at a rolling boil until the liquid is reduced, then season, place in a baking dish, and brown in a low oven 1 hr.

Fig. 306 - Potatoes Suzette (p. 510).
Fig. 307 - Potatoes Anna (p. 506).
Fig. 308 - Risotto milanaise (p. 513).

Fig. 306

Fig. 307

Fig. 308

Fig. 309

Fig. 310

RISOTTO RIZOTTO (M.)

Brown 1 large chopped onion in butter; when the onion is golden brown, add the rice and brown together 2 min. Add the necessary amount of bouillon, seasoning, and, if desired, tomato purée. Cook 18 min. Just before serving, add grated cheese.

Note: In principle, only Parmesan cheese should be used in Risotto. However, if you have no Parmesan, Gruyère may be used.

RISOTTO MILANAISE RIZOTTO À LA MILANAISE (P.)

Same recipe as the above, with tomato purée obligatory and a pinch of saffron; mold in a buttered timbale mold only to give it shape. Unmold and surround with a border of tomatoes that have been cooked down, strained very clear, and colored with saffron. (Figure 308, Page 512.)

RISOTTO PIÉMONTAISE RIZOTTO À LA PIÉMONTAISE (E.) (*For 6 persons*)

Cook ½ chopped onion in 2 oz. butter until golden brown; add ½ lb. Piedmont rice. Shake the pan over low heat until the rice is covered with butter, then pour in twice its volume in consommé (or 1 pt.). Add ⅓ liquid at a time, or only as it is absorbed by the rice. Stir with a wooden spoon while adding the liquid. Keep covered while cooking. The result should be a creamy rice. Add 2 oz. Parmesan cheese and 1½ oz. fresh butter to the cooked rice. If desired, this risotto may be finished with fine chips of white truffles or with diced, cooked ham.

Note: Liquid may be added to the rice only once, but in this case it should not be stirred while cooking. Under no circumstances should the rice be stirred while cooking, for this will cause it to stick to the bottom of the pot.

SALSIFY OR OYSTER PLANT

SALSIFIS (P.)

Peel and cook in salted, acidulated (with vinegar), floured water. Then sauté in butter with *fines herbes*, or cook in white sauce, or dip in Frying Paste (p. 558) and fry.

CREAMED SALSIFY SALSIFIS À LA CRÈME (E.)

Cook the salsify, keeping it rather firm. Drain and cut into pieces about 1½ in. long. Thick pieces should be split in 2 or 3 parts, so that all the pieces are the same size. Finish cooking in very thin Béchamel Sauce (p. 146). The sauce should be almost completely reduced when the salsify has finished cooking. Then add a few tbsp. fresh cream, just enough to give the salsify the proper consistency.

FRIED SALSIFY SALSIFIS FRITS (E.)

Drain and cut into pieces about 2½ in. long and place in a dish. Season with salt and pepper. Add lemon juice, a few drops of oil, and chopped parsley. Let marinate 25–30 min., turning from time to time. Drain well, then dip in thin

Fig. 309 - Stuffed tomatoes egyptian style (p. 515).
Fig. 310 - Truffles in a napkin (p. 517).

Frying Paste (p. 558). Fry in very hot deep fat and drain when the paste is quite dry. Serve on a napkin with fried parsley.

Note: Marinating the salsify in advance is optional but recommended.

SAUTÉED SALSIFY SALSIFIS SAUTÉS (E.)

Cut into pieces 1½ in. long. Sauté in butter until well browned. Season and serve with chopped parsley in a timbale or vegetable dish.

SORREL

OSEILLE

SORREL CHIFFONNADE OSEILLE (CHIFFONNADE D') (M.)

Cut the raw sorrel into julienne strips. Cook it down slowly in butter until it has rendered all its vegetable juices. Season.

Note: Use as a garnish for soups or to garnish omelettes and scrambled eggs.

SPINACH

ÉPINARDS

SPINACH ENGLISH STYLE ÉPINARDS À L'ANGLAISE (P.)

Trim the stems, wash, and cook fine spinach in plenty of salted water. Drain, cool, press by hand to remove excess liquid, and sauté in butter without letting it brown. Salt and serve as soon as ready.

CREAMED SPINACH ÉPINARDS À LA CRÈME (P.)

Cook, press, and reduce to a purée; heat a little in butter and bind with Béchamel Sauce (p. 146) and cream, salt and pepper. Serve with croutons. (Figure 302, Page 508.)

SPINACH LOAF ÉPINARDS (PAIN D') (P.)

Same procedure as for Cauliflower Loaf (p. 494)—cream the spinach, bind with yolks or whole eggs, and cook in a buttered mold in a *bain-marie.* Pour a cream or Mousseline Sauce (p. 152) over the loaf. May be made in small baba molds and used as a garnish for a large cut of meat.

SWEET POTATOES

PATATES (M.)

In French slang, *patate* means a spud or an ordinary potato. However, the only thing that potatoes and sweet potatoes have in common is that they are both edible roots and both are tasty.

Botanically unrelated to the white potato, the sweet potato originated in the East Indies. A great number of varieties are cultivated in France. The favorite ones are: the yellow sweet potato, called Malaga yellow, with very fine, very sugary flesh; the pink Malaga sweet potato also has yellow flesh but very little sugar; the violet or red sweet potatoes, long and wavy, have very sweet white flesh; this last is the variety that grows best in the region around Paris.

Sweet potatoes are prepared like ordinary potatoes. They are best prepared: boiled, sautéed in butter, creamed, baked, fried, grilled, Maître d'Hôtel, and puréed.

TOMATOES

TOMATES

STUFFED TOMATOES CATALANE TOMATES FARCIES À LA CATALANE (M.)

Make a circular cut around the stem end of the tomatoes. Remove this part and squeeze the tomatoes to remove the seeds and water without spoiling their shape. Season with salt and pepper. Place on an oiled baking tray, pour a finger of oil into each tomato, and bake 5 min. in a very hot oven. Stuff the tomatoes with the following mixture. Mix well 5 oz. freshly sifted white bread crumbs, 1½ oz. raw chopped ham, and 2 chopped hard-boiled eggs. Add chopped garlic and chopped parsley; season with salt and pepper. Place the tomatoes in an oiled baking dish. Sprinkle with bread crumbs; baste with oil. Brown slowly.

STUFFED TOMATOES EGYPTIAN STYLE TOMATES FARCIES À L'ÉGYPTIENNE (M.)

Prepare the tomatoes as above, filling them with a composition of cooked mutton and cooked rice flavored with garlic and chopped parsley and seasoned with paprika. (Figure 309, Page 513.)

TOMATOES STUFFED WITH MEAT TOMATES FARCIES AU GRAS (P.)

Chop fine some leftover meat (beef, veal, or mutton). Also chop and brown in a little lard 1 or 2 onions; mix these and the chopped meat with *fines herbes,* garlic, salt, pepper. If you want a smoother mixture, add a few tbsp. thick Tomato Sauce (p. 146) and some stale bread (about the size of 2 eggs) soaked in bouillon. Cut the tomatoes in half and empty them or, if they are small, simply hollow them out. Season them, fill with the mixture, sprinkle the top with bread crumbs, baste with oil, and bake 20 min. in a very hot oven. Stuffed tomatoes to be used as a garnish for meat should be filled with a mushroom Duxelles (p. 176).

STUFFED TOMATOES PROVENÇALE I TOMATES FARCIES À LA PROVENÇALE (P.)

Crumble finely a generous amount of stale bread (cut from the crust); mix with chopped garlic and chopped parsley. Fill tomato halves with the mixture, baste with oil, and bake in a very hot oven.

STUFFED TOMATOES PROVENÇALE II TOMATES FARCIES À LA PROVENÇALE (E.)

Halve the tomatoes, remove the seeds, season, and place, open side down, in a pan containing smoking hot oil. Turn them when ½ cooked; let cook another moment. Lay them side by side in a baking dish and stuff with the following mixture. To stuff 6 tomatoes, brown 2 tbsp. chopped onion in oil; add 4 peeled, pressed, and crushed tomatoes, a pinch of chopped parsley, and a bit of crushed garlic; cook, covered, 12 min. Finish with 4 tbsp. white bread soaked in consommé and pressed through a sieve and 2 anchovies also pressed through a sieve; top off with some rather fat beef gravy. When the tomatoes are stuffed, sprinkle with bread crumbs mixed with grated cheese, baste with oil, and brown in the oven. These tomatoes may be served hot or cold.

TOMATO FONDUE TOMATES (FONDUE DE) (P.)

Cook a sliced onion in butter until transparent, then add 1 lb. quartered tomatoes; salt and pepper; add a crushed clove of garlic. Cook slowly 30 min. Serve with chopped parsley.

TOMATOES MISTRAL TOMATES À LA MISTRAL (P.)

Fry some halved eggplants, then chop the pulp with cooked onion and garlic. Stuff hollowed-out, raw tomatoes with this mixture, sprinkle with bread crumbs, and bake in a hot oven.

TOMATO SOUFFLÉ NAPOLITAINE TOMATES (SOUFFLÉ DE) À LA NAPOLITAINE (E.)

Prepare 9 oz. very reduced tomato purée. Mix in 1½ oz. grated Parmesan cheese, 2 tbsp. very thick Béchamel Sauce (p. 146), and 3 egg yolks. Add 3 stiffly beaten egg whites. Arrange in layers in a buttered soufflé dish, on each bed of the tomato mixture placing a thin layer of freshly cooked macaroni blended with butter and grated Parmesan cheese. Cook like an ordinary soufflé.

TOMATOES VAUCLUSIENNE TOMATES VAUCLUSIENNE (P.)

Peel 2 eggplants and cut them lengthwise into slices about ⅜ in. thick. Salt and let drain. Then fry slowly in oil. Peel and chop fine 2 lb. tomatoes. Cook them slowly in oil with seasoning and garlic. Add some bread crumbs to thicken the tomatoes. Place the eggplant slices in an earthenware baking dish, cover with the tomatoes, sprinkle with bread crumbs, baste with oil, and simmer ¾ hr. in a hot oven.

TRUFFLES

TRUFFES (E.)

Truffles are principally used as garnishes, but they also serve as vegetables or hors d'oeuvres. In the latter case, they should be prepared simply, for they need no delicate preparation to be perfect.

TRUFFLES IN ASHES TRUFFES SOUS LA CENDRE (E.)

Take some fine fresh truffles; clean them perfectly, but do not peel. Salt lightly and moisten with a finger of champagne. First wrap each truffle in a thin strip of bacon or pork fat, then in a double piece of buttered or greased white paper; moisten the exterior of the second with water. Place them on a bed of

Fig. 311 - Macaroni italian style (p. 519).
Fig. 312 - Cannelloni (p. 519).
Fig. 313 - Noodles alsacienne (p. 520).

Fig. 311

Fig. 312

Fig. 313

Fig. 314

blazing-hot ashes, cover with another layer of ashes, and on top of this spread some burning charcoal, replenishing it from time to time. Allow 40–45 min. to cook medium-sized truffles weighing 1½–2 oz., 50–55 min. for the larger ones weighing 2½ oz. Remove the first paper wrapper and serve on a napkin folded over them, with a separate dish of fresh butter.

TRUFFLES IN CHAMPAGNE TRUFFES AU CHAMPAGNE (E.)

Take some fine well-washed, peeled truffles; season; cover and cook with some champagne and 1 tbsp. well-cooked Mirepoix Bordelaise (p. 136) per lb. truffles. Then place them in a timbale or vegetable dish, or in small silver pans. Reduce the champagne almost completely, then add to it a little very clear but rich veal stock. Strain through cheesecloth, pour over the truffles, and heat 10 min. on the fire without letting the stock boil.

TRUFFLES IN A NAPKIN TRUFFES À LA SERVIETTE (E.)

Prepare like Truffles in Champagne (above), using Madeira instead of champagne. Serve in a napkin folded like an artichoke, placed in a timbale. However, it would be infinitely more logical to serve Truffles in Ashes under this name, simply folding them in a napkin. (Figure 310, Page 513.)

TRUFFLE BUSH WITH FOIE GRAS or TRUFFLES PÉRIGOURDINE
TRUFFES EN BUISSON AU FOIE GRAS or À LA PÉRIGOURDINE (M.)

Cold: (1) Cook 10 large round truffles in sherry. Drain and cool. Make a circular cut on the top of each and scoop out ⅔. Save the tops to use as covers after stuffing the truffles. Mash the pulp removed and mix it with an equal amount of cooked *foie gras.* Press this mixture through a fine sieve and finish as directed in the recipe for Foie Gras Mousse (p. 439). Fill the truffles with this mixture, cover them with the tops, and chill well on ice.

(2) With the truffle cooking liquid, prepare a Chaud-Froid Sauce the usual way (p. 139). Stir this sauce on ice and, when it is well chilled, cover the truffles (set on a wire rack) with it. Arrange them, on a round platter, in tiers to resemble a bush. Garnish with Aspic Jelly flavored with sherry (p. 168), and decorate the border of the platter with the same aspic cut in small diamond, triangular, or rectangular shapes.

TURNIPS
NAVETS (P.)

Turnips may be cooked in gravy or stews after browning in butter, or simply cut into slices, cooked in water, and served creamed. They may also be puréed, especially to accompany Leg of Lamb English Style (p. 355).

STUFFED TURNIPS NAVETS FARCIS (P.)

Take some round turnips, violet-colored at the top, peel them, and hollow them out with a vegetable spoon. Blanch 8–10 min., then drain and stuff with some sort of forcemeat or mincemeat, sausage, etc. Lay them side by side in a deep platter, half cover with rich bouillon, sprinkle with bread crumbs, and brown in the oven. Usually served as a garnish.

Fig. 314 - Ravioli niçoise (p. 522).
Fig. 315 - Alice salad (p. 524).

ZUCCHINI OR SMALL VEGETABLE MARROWS

COURGETTES

A very good vegetable, prepared in a variety of ways.

CREAMED ZUCCHINI COURGETTES À LA CRÈME (P.)

Peel and cut in quarters. Cook in salted water, drain, roll in butter, and cover with heavy cream. Season highly and, just before serving, add 2 egg yolks beaten in a little cream. Bind on the fire by shaking the pan, but do not let boil. Serve immediately.

STUFFED ZUCCHINI COURGETTES FARCIES (P.)

Split in 2 lengthwise and hollow out with a teaspoon. Blanch well without completely cooking. Stuff with some sort of meat hash mixed with mushrooms, or leftover meat, or pork forcemeat. Braise in a little bouillon, in the oven, 35–40 min. Serve with a tomato-flavored gravy. (Figure 298, Page 500.)

STUFFED ZUCCHINI ORIENTALE COURGETTES FARCIES À L'ORIENTALE (P.)

Peel and split in 2 lengthwise, hollow out the halves, and blanch in water 8 min. Stuff with Rice Pilaf (p. 512), with quartered tomatoes and pimentos added to it. Lay in a baking dish with a finger of rich bouillon and a few bread crumbs on top. Put in the oven and braise 25 min. Serve with Tomato Sauce (p. 146).

STUFFED ZUCCHINI SAVOYARDE COURGETTES FARCIES SAVOYARDE (P.)

Take small round zucchini, peel, and cut in half. Blanch 5 min., scoop out the insides, and season with salt and pepper. Meanwhile, make a Risotto (p. 513), adding to it, after cooking 20 min., 6 crushed tomatoes and 2 chopped shallots. Cook another 5 min., then add 4 oz. grated Gruyère cheese and 1½ oz. butter; season to taste. Stuff the zucchini halves, sprinkle with grated cheese, and dot with butter. Place in a buttered ovenware plate with a little consommé on the bottom, cook in the oven 15 min., add a little thin veal stock, and serve.

FRIED ZUCCHINI COURGETTES FRITES (P.)

Peel and cut in long, thin slices. Salt and let stand to drain off the liquid, as in preparing eggplant, then wipe dry, flour, and fry in burning-hot oil. They may also be dipped in Frying Paste (p. 558).

FRIED ZUCCHINI SURPRISE COURGETTES FRITES EN SURPRISE (P.)

Peel and cut in fairly thick slices. Salt and drain. Next, wash, dry, flour, and fry. Take some very thick Béchamel Sauce (p. 146) bound with 2 eggs and grated cheese and spread this on 2 slices, sticking them together. Roll these sandwiches in flour, dip in beaten egg, cover with bread crumbs, and fry. Serve very hot.

ZUCCHINI MEUNIÈRE COURGETTES MEUNIÈRE (P.)

Peel and slice, salt and drain, wash and dry, as above. Flour, then fry in very hot butter, browning well on both sides. Arrange on a dish, baste with very hot butter, and sprinkle chopped parsley on top.

ITALIAN PASTES AND FARINACEOUS FOODS

CANNELLONI (A.)

Cannelloni are usually made of noodle paste (see Fresh Noodles, p. 520); they can be made large or small. Begin by blanching the Cannelloni in salted water or in bouillon until 3/4 done. Drain, cool, and dry on a cloth. Next stuff them, taking care not to break them, using a paper cone or a pastry bag, or, more simply, split them lengthwise, fill with the stuffing, and roll. When thus prepared, place them side by side in a pan and finish cooking them, without boiling, in a stock that will go with the filling used. They may also be placed in a buttered dish, sprinkled with a mixture of grated Parmesan cheese and bread crumbs, basted with melted butter, and browned in the oven 1/4 hr. Cannelloni fillings can be made of fish, meat, or vegetables—shellfish, mollusks, fish, fish milt or soft roe, and fish livers; red meat, pork, brains, calf or lamb sweetbreads, chicken, chicken livers, *foie gras;* winged or ground game; vegetables, mushrooms, and truffles. All these fillings should be made of cooked ingredients bound with egg yolks. They are prepared as *salpicons* (the ingredients cut into tiny cubes and bound with a sauce) or purées. (Figure 312, Page 516.)

GNOCCHI

See Hot Hors d'Oeuvres, p. 244.

LASAGNE (E.)

A sort of paste cut in ribbons and slightly crimped. Prepare like macaroni and noodles.

MACARONI (P.)

Break into pieces and drop into boiling salted water. Boil 5 min., then reduce the heat so that the macaroni merely simmers, 25–30 min., depending on size and quality. (Spaghetti takes longer to cook than macaroni because it is not hollow.) Drain and mix with Béchamel Sauce (p. 146) and grated cheese or simply dress with butter and grated cheese.

MACARONI AU GRATIN MACARONI AU GRATIN (P.)

Blend the macaroni with Béchamel Sauce (p. 146), add cheese, and put into a baking dish. Sprinkle with bread crumbs, butter the top, and brown in a hot oven.

MACARONI ITALIAN STYLE MACARONI À L'ITALIENNE (E.) (*For 8 persons*)

Cook the macaroni in boiling water. Drain well. Put into a sautéing pan and heat over the fire to dry it. Season with salt, pepper, and nutmeg; mix with 5 oz. grated Gruyère and Parmesan cheese (equal parts of each) and 2 oz. butter (divided into small pieces) per lb. macaroni. Sauté everything together to blend well, and serve in a timbale or vegetable dish. (Figure 311, Page 516.)

MACARONI WITH GRAVY MACARONI AU JUS (E.)

Blanch the macaroni in salted water, keeping it rather firm, and drain. Then place it in a pan to simmer in gravy from braised beef until almost all the gravy has been absorbed. Serve in a timbale or vegetable dish and pour a few tbsp. of the same gravy over it.

MACARONI MILANAISE MACARONI À LA MILANAISE (P.)

Take some thin macaroni or spaghetti; partially cook it in salted water; drain while still rather firm. Pour into a sautéing pan 1 glass Madeira, 6 oz. Tomato Sauce (p. 146), and 3 oz. beef gravy; add 2 oz. pickled tongue and 2 oz. cooked mushrooms, both cut into strips. Simmer well, then pour in the macaroni and continue simmering ¼ hr. Then bind the macaroni and sauce with an egg-sized piece of butter mixed with flour, bring to a boil, remove from the fire, and add 3½ oz. grated cheese. Correct the seasoning and serve.

Note: The proportions above are for ½ lb. macaroni.

MACARONI NAPOLITAINE MACARONI À LA NAPOLITAINE (E.)

Prepare in advance an Estouffade of beef (see p. 381) with red wine and tomatoes. This should cook 10–12 hr., or until the meat falls apart and it becomes a purée. Then press through a sieve. Blanch large macaroni, keeping it rather firm. Drain, cut into small pieces, and blend with butter. Sprinkle the bottom of a timbale with grated cheese; cover with a layer of the beef purée; spread a layer of macaroni over this, and alternate the layers of cheese, purée, and macaroni until the dish is full. Serve as is.

NOODLES

NOUILLES

FRESH NOODLES NOUILLES FRAICHES (P.) (*For 4 persons*)

On a baking board, make a well or ring of 5 oz. flour and in the center put a pinch of fine salt, a nut-sized piece of butter, 1 whole egg, and 1 egg yolk. Knead by hand to make a firm but not-too-dry paste. Wrap it in a cloth and keep in a cool place for a couple of hours, then roll it out with a rolling pin into as thin a sheet as possible. Flour the paste generously, then fold and refold it on itself, and cut it into fine strips. Shake to unroll them and to let the excess flour fall off, then drop them into a large pot of salted boiling water and cook 8–10 min. at moderate heat. Drain, rinse, and then use like macaroni.

NOODLES ALSACIENNE NOUILLES À L'ALSACIENNE (P.)

Before cooking the Fresh Noodles (above), save a small portion of them uncooked and dice these as fine as if they were chopped. In one pan sauté the cooked, drained, and rinsed noodles, and, in another, the chopped noodles, which should be well browned. Mix a little grated cheese into the cooked noodles, put them into a vegetable dish, and sprinkle the top with the browned noodles. The dish has a very nice crisp appearance. (Figure 313, Page 516.)

POLENTA (E.)

(*For 5 persons*)

Drop ½ lb. corn meal into 1 qt. boiling water containing 1½ tsp. salt; stir with a spoon while pouring in the corn meal. Cook 25 min., then add 2 oz. butter and 2½ oz. grated Parmesan cheese.

If you are preparing the Polenta for a vegetable or a garnish, spread it in a thin sheet on a wet tray. When it is cold, cut it into circles or diamonds and brown in butter. Place these on a platter, sprinkle with grated cheese, and baste with brown butter.

RAVIOLI (M.)

Preparing the paste: Ravioli is made several ways. (*a*) Roll out noodle paste (see Fresh Noodles, p. 520) in a very thin square sheet. Place on this paste, in nicely spaced rows, nut-sized portions of the desired filling. Moisten the paste around the portions with cold water. Lay another sheet of paste of the same size over the top. Lightly press the paste around the small mounds of filling to join the two sheets together (it will stick together where it was moistened). Using a pastry wheel, cut the ravioli into 2-in. squares.

(*b*) Roll the paste out in thin strips about 3 in. wide. Place small portions of filling at intervals on these strips. Moisten the edges of the paste. Fold; cut the Ravioli in half-moons with a fluted pastry cutter.

(*c*) Roll out the paste and cut into circles, using a fluted round pastry cutter about 2 in. in diameter. In the center of each circle of paste place a nut-sized portion of filling. Moisten, fold like a turnover, pressing the edges together to seal.

Cooking Ravioli: Drop into a sautéing pan filled with boiling water with ¾ tsp. salt per qt. water. Lower heat and simmer 8 min. Drain on a cloth.

Fillings for Ravioli: (*a*) Mix 1 lb. well-done braised beef, chopped fine, 3½ oz. purée of brains, 5 oz. blanched spinach, pressed and chopped, 1½ oz. chopped onion cooked in butter, and 3½ oz. grated Parmesan cheese. Bind with 2 whole eggs; season with salt, pepper, and nutmeg.

(*b*) ½ lb. pork sausage, 5 oz. chopped, cooked lean veal, 5 oz. spinach, and 5 oz. blanched, pressed, chopped beet greens; pinch of garlic, ½ tbsp. chopped parsley, pinch of chopped basil, 3½ oz. Parmesan cheese, 2 eggs, salt, pepper, nutmeg.

(*c*) ¾ lb. chopped cooked chicken, 7 oz. blanched, pressed, chopped spinach, 6 oz. very reduced chicken Velouté (p. 147), 3½ oz. grated Parmesan cheese, 2 eggs, salt, pepper, nutmeg.

(*d*) ¾ lb. Gratin Forcemeat (p. 175), 7 oz. chopped, cooked lean ham, 5 oz. Dry Duxelles (p. 176), 3 tbsp. very thick tomato purée, 1 tbsp. chopped parsley and chervil, 2 eggs, salt, pepper, nutmeg.

(*e*) ½ lb. purée of *foie gras*, 5 oz. chopped, cooked calf sweetbreads, 3½ oz. Dry Duxelles, 3½ oz. chopped truffles, 2 eggs, salt, pepper, nutmeg.

Final preparation of the Ravioli: When the Ravioli has been cooked and well drained, place it in buttered and floured baking dishes, in layers sprinkled with Parmesan cheese. Baste with thickened rich beef gravy and simmer at low heat.

RAVIOLI NIÇOISE[1] RAVIOLI À LA NIÇOISE (H.)

Make a paste with flour, warm water, salt, and a little oil. No eggs. Do not make it too thick. Let stand. Roll out a first sheet of paste very thin and place to one side. Roll out a second sheet of the same size. Using a pastry bag with a plain nozzle, squeeze out portions of Ravioli filling onto the first sheet of paste. Trace parallel lines both ways between the rows of filling, separating them by about ¾ in. Moisten the paste with water along both sides of the lines, then completely cover with the other sheet of paste. Using a ruler, press the sheet down between the rows of filling, then do the same crosswise, so as to form about 1-in. squares. Cut through the lines with a pastry jagger, separating the Ravioli, and place them on a floured paper. Poach them in salted boiling water, drain them, and season each layer with salt, pepper, and grated Parmesan cheese. Pour some beef or veal gravy on top. (Figure 314, Page 517.)

Filling for Ravioli:[2] Prepare Beef Daube in advance (pp. 328 and 737). Save the stock and pound the meat in a mortar with blanched leaf spinach, calf brains, and a pinch of garlic. Press this forcemeat through a sieve into a bowl and soften it with a little of the beef stock, beaten eggs, and a handful of Parmesan cheese. Instead of beef, chicken or veal may be used. The gravy poured over the finished Ravioli should, of course, agree with the filling.

SALADS

SEASONING SALADS (E.)

(1) *With oil:* Used in all salads. 3 parts oil to 1 part vinegar; salt, pepper.

(2) *With cream:* Especially suitable for spring lettuce and romaine salads. 3 parts very fresh, not-too-thick cream to 1 part vinegar or, preferably, lemon juice; salt and pepper.

(3) *With eggs:* Use yolks of hard-boiled eggs, crumbled or pressed through a sieve, blended in the salad bowl with mustard, oil, vinegar, salt, and pepper. Whites of hard-boiled eggs, cut in thin strips, are also added to this salad. The eggs may also be seasoned with thin mayonnaise.

(4) *With bacon:* Bacon flavoring is mostly used for salads of dandelion greens, lamb's-lettuce, and red cabbage. Instead of oil, use the fat from diced bacon browned in a frying pan. Pour the hot fat along with the bits of diced bacon over the salad in a salad bowl; the salad should be hot and already seasoned with salt and pepper. Finish with a finger of vinegar heated in the same hot frying pan.

(5) *With creamed mustard:* Used chiefly with beet and celery-root salads and green salads containing beets as the main ingredient. 1 tbsp. mustard blended with 6 oz. rather thin fresh cream, juice of 1 medium-sized lemon, salt, and pepper.

(6) *With mayonnaise:* Prepared exactly according to the recipe.

---

[1] If a roller cutter is used, the first sheet of paste should be heavily covered with filling, then covered with the second sheet. Merely press heavily with the roller and separate the Ravioli.

[2] This filling is for Ravioli Niçoise. Obviously, however, the Beef Daube can be replaced by braised veal, chicken, *foie gras,* or any other filling. The spinach and garlic can be left out entirely.

Notes: (1) Mayonnaise should be used with discretion in seasoning salads. Many people find this sauce indigestible, especially at night at the end of a dinner.

(2) Raw onions should also be used sparingly in salads, since many people do not care for them. If used, they should be cut fine, washed in cold water, and squeezed tightly in a cloth to extract the bitter juice.

SIMPLE SALADS

GREEN SALADS SALADES VERTES (E.)

Lettuce, romaine, chicory, escarole, endive, celery, lamb's-lettuce, dandelion, purslane, garden or golden cress, rampion, oyster-plant leaves, wild chicory.

BEET SALAD SALADE DE BETTERAVE (E.)

Beets are mainly an extra ingredient in simple and mixed salads. It is better to cook them in the oven than to boil them. When especially prepared for salads, they are cut in thin round slices or in fine julienne strips. Flavor with onions cooked in ashes or in the oven and then chopped, and season with oil or mustard, depending on taste, adding chopped *fines herbes.*

CELERY-ROOT SALAD SALADE DE CÉLERI-RAVE (E.)

Cut the celery root in thin julienne strips and season with thin mayonnaise strongly flavored with mustard.

RED-CABBAGE SALAD SALADE DE CHOUX ROUGES (E.)

Take very tender red cabbage; separate the leaves and cut in thin julienne strips. Season with oil and vinegar at least 6 hr. before serving.

CUCUMBER SALAD SALADE DE CONCOMBRES (E.)

Peel, slice thin, and sprinkle with salt to drain the water. Wipe dry, season with oil and vinegar, and flavor strongly with chervil.

Note: Green English cucumbers do not have to be salted and drained.

POTATO SALAD SALADE DE POMMES DE TERRE (E.)

Cook the potatoes in salted water; trim the potatoes in the shape of stoppers or corks and slice thin while still warm. Season with oil and vinegar, adding chopped *fines herbes.*

TOMATO SALAD SALADE DE TOMATES (E.)

Peel and press the tomatoes; slice them extremely thin. Season with oil and vinegar, adding chopped tarragon. Surround with thin rings of fresh onion.

COMBINATION SALADS

Combination salads are served without mixing the ingredients, unless they are made in the kitchen. The various ingredients are seasoned separately in advance and placed in the salad in separate bunches. The finished salad may be bordered with beets, hard-boiled eggs, gherkins, truffles, etc. No directions are given for these decorations; they should be inspired by individual taste. We do not advise molding combination salads; they have little appeal to the eye and less to the palate. The simplest and quickest arrangement is the best. Building the salad into a mound or pyramid should not be overdone. The salad should be arranged in the center of a border of decorated Aspic Jelly (p. 168).

ALICE SALAD SALADE ALICE (P.)

Cut off the top and scoop out a fine apple. Save the top. Fill the hollowed-out apple with a salpicon (tiny cubes) of apple, celery, and banana mixed with sour cream. Place 2 leaves of heart of endive in the middle like a pair of ears, with the top of the apple cut with a cookie cutter to make a lid through which the leaves stick out. (Figure 315, Page 517.)

BAGRATION SALAD SALADE BAGRATION (E.)

Equal parts of: celery and breast of chicken cut in julienne strips; artichoke bottoms sliced thin; fine macaroni cooked rather firm and cut, still hot, into 2-in.-long pieces (twice as much macaroni as any of the other ingredients). Marinate the artichokes and celery 20 min. in oil and vinegar. Add the julienne of chicken, macaroni, and mayonnaise lightly flavored with tomato. Mix; place in a salad bowl; smooth into a mound and decorate with a star, making the points of truffle, pickled tongue, hard-boiled egg whites and yolks, chopped parsley. (Figure 316, Page 524.)

BEAUCAIRE SALAD SALADE BEAUCAIRE (E.)

Equal parts of celery, celery root, and endive cut into julienne strips and seasoned, 1 hr. in advance, with oil, vinegar, and mustard. Add a julienne of lean ham, tart apples, and mushrooms (½ the amount of the first julienne). Mix, bind with several tbsp. mayonnaise, and arrange in a salad bowl. Sprinkle the top with chopped parsley, chervil, and tarragon. Make an outer border of sliced beets and an inner border of sliced potatoes. (Figure 319, Page 524.)

BEAUTIFUL HORTENSE SALAD SALADE BELLE HORTENSE (P.)

Prepare celery with Rémoulade Sauce (p. 157) the day before. The day it is to be used, add a few chopped nuts and correct the seasoning. Smooth into a mound in a salad bowl, decorate with slices of beet and truffle and nut halves. (Figure 320, Page 525.)

CARMEN SALAD SALADE CARMEN (E.)

Equal parts of peeled and grilled sweet red peppers and breast of chicken, both cut into small cubes; Small Peas English Style, unbuttered (p. 505); rice cooked in salted water and well drained. Season with oil and vinegar, adding mustard and chopped tarragon. Decorate with tomato slices, hard-boiled eggs, and peppers or capers. (Figure 318, Page 524.)

EVE SALAD SALADE ÈVE (E.)

Hollow out some medium-sized apples as for Alice Salad (above). Dice equal parts of apples, bananas, pineapple, walnuts. *Seasoning:* cream, lemon juice, and salt. Fill and decorate like Alice Salad.

Fig. 316 - Bagration salad (p. 524).
Fig. 317 - Lily-of-the-valley salad (p. 525).
Fig. 318 - Carmen salad (p. 524).
Fig. 319 - Beaucaire salad (p. 524).

Fig. 316

Fig. 317

Fig. 318

Fig. 319

Fig. 320

Fig. 321

Fig. 322

IRMA SALAD SALADE IRMA (E.)

Equal parts of green cucumbers, asparagus tips, green beans cut diamond shape, small cauliflower flowerets. Creamed mayonnaise seasoned with chervil and chopped tarragon. Heap into a mound; cover with shredded lettuce mixed with garden or golden cress. Decorate with nasturtiums, and border with round slices of red radish. (Figure 322, Page 525.)

VEGETABLE SALAD SALADE DE LÉGUMES (P.)

The name well indicates the mixture of vegetables composing this salad, which can be made regardless of season, for vegetables out of season may be bought canned. Canned vegetables, however, should be blanched to remove the can taste. Mix together with Stiff Mayonnaise (p. 157) and decorate the top with various vegetables or chopped parsley.

LILY-OF-THE-VALLEY SALAD SALADE MUGUETTE (E.)

Equal parts of endive, sliced green apples, heart of celery cut in fine julienne strips, peeled, pressed, thin-sliced tomatoes, walnuts (⅓ of them marinated in verjuice[1]). Bind with thin mayonnaise mixed with hard-boiled egg yolk.

Decoration: Slices of pink radish, chervil leaves. Make lilies-of-the-valley with tarragon and hard-boiled egg white. (Figure 317, Page 524.)

PARISIAN SALAD SALADE PARISIENNE (M.)

Various mixed diced vegetables with diced lobster and truffles; mayonnaise. Decorate with slices of lobster and truffle.

Note: In ancient cooking this salad, usually served with cold buffets, was dressed in a mold lined with aspic. Prepared this way, it was seasoned with Stiff Mayonnaise (p. 157).

RUSSIAN SALAD SALADE RUSSE (P.)

Vegetable salads are served under this name, but actually it should contain cooked meats, either chicken or hazel hen, ham, anchovy or smoked salmon, and beets. And real Russian Salad is usually molded into an aspic and decorated with a few of its ingredients. In Russia, the custom is to make salads with the products of the country: *agourcis,*[2] *gribouis,*[3] smoked sterlet,[4] caviar, etc.

VICTORIA SALAD SALADE VICTORIA (E.)

Equal parts of lobster or rock-lobster meat trimmings, diced truffles and cucumbers, asparagus tips. *Seasoning:* mayonnaise mixed with the creamy parts of lobster and the puréed coral.

WINDSOR SALAD SALADE WINDSOR (E.)

Equal parts of celery, raw truffles, breast of chicken, pickled tongue, piccalilli, cooked mushrooms, all cut in julienne strips. Bind with mayonnaise seasoned with Derby Sauce.[5] Smooth into a mound in a salad bowl, and surround with a ring of rampion[6] half buried in the salad.

---

[1] Juice from unripe grapes or green apples.
[2] Pickles.
[3] Mushrooms.
[4] Small sturgeon.
[5] Derby Sauce is very good for seasoning many hot and cold sauces. It is bought ready prepared.
[6] A kind of campanula, the roots and leaves of which are used in salads.

Fig. 320 - Beautiful Hortense salad (p. 524).
Fig. 321 - Spinach Jacqueline (p. 221).
Fig. 322 - Irma salad (p. 525).

MIXED ENTREES

MIXED ENTREES

This short chapter is a general survey of: *vol-au-vent,* pies or *pâtés, timbales,* and tarts or *tourtes.* These preparations, as much a part of pastrymaking as of general cooking, will serve as a transition between the two parts of this book. These dishes have similarities, but each is quite different from the others.

PUFF-PASTE PATTIES BOUCHÉES FEUILLETÉES (P.)

Fold and roll out Puff Paste (p. 544) 6 times, until it is ½ in. thick. Cut it in circles with a fluted pastry cutter about 2½ in. in diameter. Place these on a baking sheet, brush with a very little beaten egg, with the tip of a knife cut a small circle to make the covers, then pierce 3 or 4 times with a knife and bake 15–18 min. in a hot oven; reduce the heat a little after 10 min.

The various fillings for patties are given in the chapter on Hot Hors -d'Oeuvres, pp. 235–237.

PATTIES À LA REINE BOUCHÉES À LA REINE (J.)

Fold and roll out the paste 6 times until ⅛ in. thick. Using a fluted pastry cutter, cut circles 2¼ in. in diameter in 2 layers of paste; with a plain pastry cutter about 1¼ in. in diameter, cut out the centers of one of these layers. Place the solid circles on a baking sheet, lightly moisten, and join the open circles to them on top. (Figure 98, p. 115.) Brush with beaten egg, taking care not to spill any of the egg on the inner or outer sides of the patty. Bake in a hot oven. When baked, remove the covers and hollow out the insides. Garnish according to the recipes given in the chapter on Hot Hors d'Oeuvres. (Figure 324, Page 532.)

VOL-AU-VENT VOL-AU-VENT (J.)

Roll out and fold Puff Paste (p. 544) 6 times until ¼ in. thick. Cut the paste lightly on the bias with the point of a knife, following the outlines of a *patron* (a sort of flattened-dome tin pattern pierced in the center to provide a hole for the finger). Repeat the same operation, removing the center from the second one with a smaller pattern than the first. (See Illustrations on p. 114.) Place the first circle of paste on a lightly moistened baking sheet. Place the second on top, joining the two pieces together, as in the preceding recipe. Score the outside of the crust with a knife. Brush the top with beaten egg. With a knife, score the center as well as the sides of the *vol-au-vent* in a diamond pattern. Bake in a hot oven. After taking out of the oven, remove the cover and hollow out the inside. (Figure 323, Page 532.)

COCK IN PASTE COQ EN PÂTE (C.)

(*Hot entree, which may also be served cold.*)

This very attractive-looking dish must be made with great care and dexterity if the fowl is to be presented whole, with the neck and head in a lifelike position.

Take a fine fowl (which need not necessarily be a cock). Bone it from the back without destroying the skin, then after removing the bones from the back, turn over and remove the breastbone. Do not remove the bones from the thighs, which should be folded under. Season the inside of the fowl and moisten the flesh with a few tbsp. port. Let macerate.

Meanwhile, prepare about 1 lb. Mousseline Forcemeat (p. 173) from chicken or, more economically, veal. Stud a *foie gras* with truffles and let it marinate 12 hr. Wipe the flesh of the chicken until dry inside and spread a very even, rather thick layer of Mousseline Forcemeat over it. Place the *foie gras* on top of this and then close the fowl around it, giving it back its natural shape. Sew up the back of the bird and then wrap it in a fine sheet of Pie Paste (p. 545), sealing the edges of the paste with a little egg where they meet down the back of the chicken.

Place the bird on a baking sheet and wrap the head and neck in a piece of the same paste. Make a support with a piece of wire or tin to hold the head upright in its natural position. Grease the support so that it can be removed easily after cooking. If you have a little paste left over, cut it in the shape of wings and fix them to the sides with egg. The wings will act as a double covering and protect the parts that cook the quickest. Brush with beaten egg, make a small opening in the middle of the top to let the steam escape, and bake in a hot oven to brown the crust a little, then cook about 1½ hr., covering with heavy paper to prevent the crust from getting too dark.

To serve, remove a rather large piece of the top of the crust, then with a sharp knife slice the breast first. This should be easy to do, since the fowl has been boned. Place the slices around the bird, if the platter is large enough, or on a separate hot platter. Serve egg-shaped pieces of *foie gras* by scooping them out with a soupspoon dipped in boiling hot water before each serving. Serve a slice of breast with a spoonful of *foie gras*. Serve a sauceboat of excellent Périgueux Sauce (p. 143) made with essence of fowl (obtained by cooking the bones).

The crust may also be served; a portion of it is placed on each plate. (Figure 325, Page 532.)

AURORA'S PILLOW OREILLER DE LA BELLE AURORE (M.) (*For 8 persons*)

Cold: I. (*a*) Take a fine, tender pheasant; cut off the drumsticks where they join the thigh, and bone the pheasant. Season with a good pinch of spiced salt; place in a platter with 5 tbsp. champagne brandy and 5 tbsp. Madeira. Take a large *foie gras;* trim it carefully and stud generously with quartered and peeled fresh truffles. Season with spiced salt and put beside the pheasant. Let marinate together 1 hr., turning both from time to time.

(*b*) Cut into large cubes: 12 oz. wild-rabbit meat; the pheasant drumsticks (skinned); 5 oz. loin of pork; 5 oz. veal fillet; 4/5 lb. fresh pork fat. Pound each of these ingredients separately in a mortar, then mix together in the mortar with 7 oz. raw *foie gras* and about 1½ oz. spiced salt (depending on the weather). Continue pounding until all the ingredients are combined, then add 2 beaten eggs little by little. Press through a sieve into a bowl, mix in 3½ oz. finely chopped fresh truffles, and keep cool. When ready to use, mix this forcemeat with the pheasant and *foie gras* marinade.

(*c*) Bone 2 properly aged woodcocks. Save the intestines. Sauté in butter 2 oz. partridge livers (or the equivalent in chicken livers) and the liver of the pheasant (these livers need only be seared); add 1 tsp. chopped shallot, pinch of spiced salt, ⅔ oz. fresh mushroom peelings. Cook all together 2 min., then melt the glaze in the pan with 2 tbsp. Madeira. Mash the livers first, then the flesh of the woodcocks. Combine these 2 ingredients; add 3½ oz. raw *foie gras,* 1½ oz. grated pork fat, the woodcock intestines, pinch of spiced salt, 1 fresh, peeled truffle (weighing about 2 oz.). Continue mashing in a mortar until all these ingredients have been combined, press through a sieve, and keep in reserve.

(*d*) Prepare some Flaky or Puff Paste (p. 544) with 1¼ lb. sifted flour, 1 tsp. salt, 9 oz. water, and 10 oz. butter; fold and roll out 5½ times.

II. *Preparing the pie:* (1) Roll out ⅔ of the paste into a 12-in. square ⅓ in. thick. Cover the center of this square (a 6-in. square) with thin strips of bacon or pork fat. This should leave about 3 in. of paste bare on each side to use in enclosing the pie filling. Spread over the bacon an even layer of ½ the first forcemeat prepared. (2) Spread the pheasant open on the table (skin down); cover the meat with ½ the woodcock forcemeat; place the *foie gras* on top, and cover with the rest of the forcemeat, then bring together the outer edges of the skin and meat of the pheasant, to enfold the liver and form a sort of flattened galantine. Place this galantine on the layer of forcemeat spread on the paste; cover it entirely with the other ½ of the forcemeat, and on top of this lay a few thin strips of bacon or pork fat. Sprinkle with a pinch of spiced salt; add a few bits of bay leaf and a little powdered thyme. (3) Roll out the rest of the paste into a square about 7 in. on each side, making it a little thinner than the first sheet of paste. Fold the edges of the first crust around the pie filling, place the second crust on top, lightly moisten the edges of the paste, and pinch the 2 crusts together with your fingers. Trim off the excess paste; crimp all around the paste where it is joined; decorate the four sides of the pie with bits of paste (cut in the shape of crescents, circles, diamonds), sticking them to the pie walls by moistening very lightly. Cover the top crust of the pie with paste leaves (fashioned with a pastry cutter or a knife), use a knife to draw the veins in the leaves, and arrange them in overlapping rows.

In the center of the pie place 3 small scalloped squares of paste, each a different size, putting the largest on the bottom and the smallest on the top; each should have a hole in the center to let the steam escape during baking. A hole should already have been carefully cut in the top crust of the pie, so that all the holes will be aligned.

Brush the top and sides of the pie with beaten egg. As a precautionary measure, wrap a strip of buttered white paper around the sides and tie with string. This should be removed after ¾ hr. in the oven.

III. *Baking:* Bake at medium, even heat, allowing 15–16 min. per lb. After removing the pie from the oven and letting it cool until it is merely warm, pour 4½ oz. very good game-fowl aspic through the opening in the top of the crust.

Note: This pie should be prepared at least 24 hr. in advance.

LARK PIE PÂTÉ D'ALOUETTES (A.) (*For 12 persons*)

For the paste: Take: 17½ oz. flour, 1 pt. warm water, 7 oz. butter, ⅔ oz. olive oil, ⅔ oz. salt, 4 egg yolks.

For the garnish: ¾ lb. fresh pork fat, 4 oz. cultivated mushrooms, 3½ oz. veal tenderloin, 3½ oz. fresh ham, 3½ oz. chicken, 3½ oz. Madeira, 3½ oz. port, ½ jigger champagne brandy, 12 larks, 12 thin strips of bacon, 12 black Perigord truffles (of the same size, if possible), 6 chicken livers, 1½ fine goose *foie gras,* shallots, powdered thyme, egg yolk, salt and pepper, allspice.

For the aspic: 2 lb. veal knuckle, 3 cups white port, 1 oz. champagne brandy, 3 qt. consommé, 1 pheasant, 1 calf's foot, soup vegetables, butter, egg whites.

Preliminary preparations: The day before the *pâté* or pie is to be served, do the following: (1) Pluck, draw, singe, and bone the larks; marinate them 24 hr. in 3½ oz. port; save the heads, the entrails, and the bones. (2) Brush, wash, and dry the truffles; marinate them in the Madeira. (3) Mix all the ingredients in the first paragraph (*for the paste*) to make a smooth paste; roll it into a ball without further kneading; wrap it in a floured cloth. (4) Cook the pheasant in the consommé, bringing it to a boil and then simmering. Put the sliced soup vegetables, veal knuckle, and calf's foot (both cut into pieces) into a stewpan with some butter; let brown over the fire; melt the glaze in the pan with the white port; pour in the pheasant consommé; let cook; skim while cooking and reduce the liquid until it makes about 1 qt. gravy. Clarify it with the egg whites; let it set until it forms a jelly.

Preparing the garnish: The following day, fry ½ lb. sliced fresh pork fat without letting the fat brown; add chopped shallots, thyme, salt and pepper to taste, the cleaned lark entrails and bones, the chicken livers (diced), and the mushrooms chopped fine; heat over a hot fire until the mushrooms produce a strong odor. Remove from the fire; pour into a mortar; mash, press through a fine sieve, then flavor this forcemeat with ½ jigger champagne brandy. You will now have a fine chicken-liver forcemeat called *gratin.* Take the strips of bacon and spread each one with a layer of the gratin forcemeat; next fill the inside of each lark with a layer of the same forcemeat. Cut the *foie gras* into 12 even slices; save the scraps. Wrap each truffle in a slice of the *foie gras* and place one in each open lark containing a layer of forcemeat. Close the larks and roll each one in a strip of the bacon covered with forcemeat.

Fig. 323 - Vol-au-vent (p. 530).
Fig. 324 - Patties à la reine (p. 529).
Fig. 325 - Cock in paste (p. 530).

Fig. 324

Fig. 323

Fig. 325

Fig. **326**

Fig. **327**

Preparing the forcemeat: Mash together the veal tenderloin, fresh ham, chicken meat, rest of the pork fat, scraps trimmed from the *foie gras;* season with salt and pepper, and moisten with all or part of the port and Madeira used in the marinades, to make a forcemeat of good consistency. Press through a sieve.

Making the pie: Roll out the paste, saving part of it for the chimney covers and plugs. Line a mold with this paste (the mold should be large and long enough to contain 2 rows of larks with 6 larks in each row). Spread a layer of forcemeat on the pie crust, place the larks on top, fill the spaces between the larks and cover with the rest of the forcemeat; smooth the surface. Prepare 2 covers of paste, 1 thinner than the other. Moisten the thinner of the covers with water and lay it over the smooth surface of the forcemeat. Make several openings to let the steam escape during the baking. Cover with the second crust, pierced 2 or 3 times to make holes for the chimneys. Pinch the covers together, decorate the top with bits of paste, brush with beaten egg, also brush the paste chimney plugs with beaten egg yolk. Let the pie stand in a cool place 3 or 4 hr.

Baking: Bake in a hot oven, 1–1½ hr. When the pie is just done, remove it from the oven, let cool, then unmold.

Final preparations: Reheat the aspic jelly, adding 1 oz. champagne brandy to it. Skim it again, let it cool partially or until it is almost ready to solidify, then pour it into the pie. Close the openings in the pie with the paste plugs, baked separately, and decorate the top of the pie with the larks' heads (which have been poached in consommé). Place the pie on a platter decorated with croutons of aspic cut into triangles. To serve, make a deep cut lengthwise down the center of the pie, then cut crosswise, so that each portion contains a lark. Heavy eaters will take a whole portion, others will be satisfied with less. This pie is an incomparable delicacy and far surpasses the famous Pithiviers Lark Pie.

This recipe may be applied to all small game birds: quails, thrushes, figpeckers, ortolans, Corsican blackbirds, etc.

PITHIVIERS LARK PIE PÂTÉ D'ALOUETTES DE PITHIVIERS (P.) (*For 12 persons*)

Cold: Although this pie is a specialty of the Gringoire restaurant, and justly famous, here is a simpler recipe, more practical for the home cook, than Ali-Bab's.

Bone 12 larks through the back; save the intestines and sauté them, then press them through a sieve and mix them with 1½ lb. mixed pork-and-veal forcemeat. Macerate the boned larks with a little Madeira. Reshape them into balls, enclosing a small cube of truffled *foie gras* in each bird. Also add a little truffle and spice to the forcemeat. Using Pie Paste (p. 545), roll out a rather thick crust, spread a layer of forcemeat in the center, lay the stuffed larks there, cover them with forcemeat, and fold the 4 sides of the paste over the top. Brush with beaten egg and make a small hole in the top, as in all pies, and bake about 1 hr. in a very hot oven if the pie is made without a mold, 1¼ hr. if baked in a mold. The Gringoire lark pies are made without molds, the crust being crimped all the way around.

After the pie is cool, game aspic made from the bones of the birds may be poured into the pie. (Figure 326, Page 533.)

WOODCOCK PIE PÂTÉ DE BÉCASSES (E.)

Cold: Bone the woodcocks; stuff them with Forcemeat for Game (p. 176) mixed with ¼ as much game Gratin Forcemeat (p. 175) and chopped intestines, alternating the layers of forcemeat with thin strips of *foie gras* and quartered truffles. Restore the stuffed woodcocks to their natural shape; place them in an oval mold lined with ordinary Pie Paste (p. 545) with thin strips of bacon on top the paste. Close the pie crust, cover it with leaves of paste or a sheet of Puff Paste (p. 544), brush with beaten egg, and bake in a medium-hot oven. After it is cool, pour some aspic made with woodcock stock into the pie.

SNIPE PIE LUCULLUS PÂTÉ DE BÉCASSINES LUCULLUS (M.) (*For 6 persons*)

(1) Bone 6 snipe. Stuff them with forcemeat containing *foie gras* and the mashed intestines of the snipe, with a large cube of *foie gras* and of truffle in the center of the forcemeat. Close and reshape the snipe.

(2) Line a heated, deep pie tin with Pie Paste (p. 545); spread the bottom and sides of the crust with a layer of forcemeat ⅜ in. thick (using the same forcemeat as above). Place the snipe in the pie, filling the spaces in between with Gratin Forcemeat (p. 175). Finish with a layer of forcemeat; cover with thin strips of bacon; close the pie with the top crust; seal, pinch the edges, and decorate with leaves or fancy pieces of Puff Paste (p. 544). Bake 45 min. (normal time for an average-sized mold) in a medium-hot oven. After removing the pie from the oven, take off the top crust and remove the bacon; pour a ragout of truffles mixed with reduced game stock finished with Madeira into the pie. Replace the top crust and serve on a platter.

DUCKLING PIE PÂTÉ DE CANETON (E.)

Cold: Prepare the forcemeat according to the recipe on p. 176, and add to it ¼ as much ordinary forcemeat. Bone the duckling; remove the breasts and slice them. Spread out the skin, garnish it as in making a galantine, alternating the layers of forcemeat, slices of breast, fat strips of *foie gras*, and quartered truffles. Reshape the duckling; place it in an oval mold lined with ordinary Pie Paste (p. 545), with strips of bacon on the paste. Cover the pie with leaves of Pie Paste or a sheet of Puff Paste (p. 544). Bake in a medium-hot oven. When the pie is cold, pour aspic made with the duckling stock inside.

FOIE GRAS PIE or STRASBOURG PIE PÂTÉ DE FOIE GRAS OR PÂTÉ DE STRASBOURG (E.) (*For 20 to 25 persons*)

Cold: Proportions for the forcemeat: 1½ lb. pork loin, 2 lb. fresh pork fat, ½ lb. raw *foie gras* trimmings, 1½ oz. spiced salt. Mash all together, press through a sieve, and finish the forcemeat with the liquid used in marinating the livers.

Garnish: 2 medium-sized *foies gras* (very firm) weighing about 1½ lb. each, studded with quarters of raw truffle, seasoned with spiced salt, marinated 3 hr. in advance with 3 oz. cognac and 3 oz. Madeira.

Preparation: Line a deep round mold grooved all around with 3 lb. very firm, well-set, Pie Paste made with lard (p. 545). Line the bottom and the sides of the pie crust with part of the forcemeat, place the *foies gras* in the center, and cover them with the rest of the forcemeat. On top place a strip of bacon, a dash of spices, and 1 bay leaf; close the pie. Finish the top crust with leaves of Pie Paste overlapping to form a dome; finish with 3 or 4 circles of Pie Paste (cut with fluted pastry cutters) of graduated size, the circles lightly moistened with water and superimposed one on the other. Make a hole through the center of these crusts to let the steam escape during the baking. Brush with beaten egg; bake at moderate heat, counting about 15 min. per lb. When the pie has cooled until slightly warm, fill it either with some excellent melted lard or with some aspic made with Madeira.

Serving the pie: Foie Gras Pie may be cut and served 2 ways:

First method: Remove the cover by cutting it all the way around with the tip of a knife and take off the fat that has congealed on the surface. Then cut the bared *foie gras* with a spoon dipped in hot water in such a way that shells of it are removed; place these shells on a platter until there are a sufficient number of servings. Then turn the top crust of the pie upside down and replace it on the pie; fill the hollow of the top crust with chopped aspic and place the *foie gras* shells on top in a pyramid.

Second method: Slide the blade of a thin knife around the inside of the pie crust to detach the desired amount of *foie gras ;* place the portion removed on a napkin and divide it into small, even-sized rectangles. Fill the empty top of the pie with chopped aspic; place the top crust back on upside down; arrange the rectangles of *foie gras* overlapping in a circle inside this top crust and fill the center with chopped aspic.

RABBIT PIE PÂTÉ DE LAPIN (P.)

Cold: Same recipe as for Hare Pie, given below. These pies or *pâtés* may also be made in terrines or crocks. Prepared this way, they may be kept much longer. (See p. 799.)

HARE PIE PÂTÉ DE LIÈVRE (E.)

Cold: Bone the saddle and thighs; save the fillets, *filets mignons,* and thigh meat. Remove the tendons from these parts and stud them with small bits of pork fat; season with spiced salt; marinate in cognac with equal amounts of lean ham and fresh pork fat, both cut in thin strips. Use the rest of the meat to prepare a forcemeat, following the proportions on p. 176. Line a buttered oval fluted mold with ordinary Pie Paste (p. 545). Line the paste with thin strips of pork fat or bacon and fill with alternate layers of forcemeat, slices of rabbit meat, and strips of pork fat and ham. Place an oval slice of pork fat on the last layer of forcemeat, sprinkle this with a pinch of powdered thyme and bay leaf, cover the pie, and bake in a medium-hot oven. After it is cool, pour some aspic made with hare stock into the pie. (Figure 328, Page 540.)

HARE PIE SAINT-ESTÈPHE PÂTÉ DE LIÈVRE SAINT-ESTÈPHE (E.)

Line a buttered charlotte mold with ordinary Pie Paste (p. 545). Spread the bottom and sides with a thick layer of hare forcemeat mixed with panada and butter (see p. 173). Slice the hare fillets, flatten them, sear quickly in butter, and roll in melted game glaze. Lay the slices on top of the forcemeat and cover them with a few tbsp. Salmis Sauce (p. 145) flavored with red wine (made from stock obtained from the carcass of the hare) ; save the rest of this sauce. Finish filling the pie with a layer of forcemeat, cover with a sheet of Pie Paste, join the cover and sides of the crust well, cut a hole in the center, and bake 1¼ hr. in a medium-hot oven. Unmold after removing from the oven; serve the rest of the Salmis Sauce separately.

CHICKEN PIE ENGLISH STYLE PÂTÉ DE POULET À L'ANGLAISE (E.) (*For 6 persons*)

Cut up a chicken as for a fricassee. Season the pieces, then sprinkle them with 3 finely chopped shallots and 1 medium-sized onion, 1½ oz. chopped raw mushrooms heated in butter, and a pinch of chopped parsley. Garnish the bottom and sides of a pie plate with thin slices of veal; lay the pieces of chicken inside, the thighs on the bottom; add 5 oz. thinly sliced, grilled bacon, 4 hard-boiled egg yolks cut in half; pour in chicken consommé until ¾ full. Cover with a crust of Flaky or Puff Paste (p. 544) ; join it onto a band of paste stuck to the rim of the plate. Brush with beaten egg, score the top with a knife, punch a small hole in the center of the crust, and bake 1½ hr. in a medium-hot oven. After removing from the oven, pour a few tbsp. rich gravy into the pie. (Figure 329, Page 540.)

SWEETBREAD (CALF) PIE PÂTÉ DE RIS DE VEAU (E.)

Line a buttered charlotte mold or a buttered round *pâté* mold with Pie Paste (p. 545). Spread a layer of Chicken Forcemeat (p. 176), ⅜ in. thick, over bottom and sides. Fill with a ragout composed of sliced calf's sweetbreads sautéed in butter and lightly browned, sliced, cooked mushrooms, and truffles, bound with Parisienne Sauce (p. 146) made with mushroom essence and reduced until rather thick. Cover the ragout with a layer of forcemeat and close with a thin crust of Pie Paste, sealing the edges. Make the lid of leaves cut from paste; brush with beaten egg; make a hole to let the steam escape; bake in a hot oven 45–50 min. Unmold after removing from the oven, and serve on a napkin. (Figure 330, Page 541.)

SALMON or **TROUT PIE** PÂTÉ DE SAUMON or DE TRUITE (E.)

Cold: Cut and skin 4 fillets from the tail end of the salmon; season. Line a buttered rectangular mold with ordinary Pie Paste (p. 545). Cover the bottom and sides with a layer of truffled Pike Forcemeat—5 oz. chopped truffles per 2 lb. forcemeat (p. 175). Place 2 of the salmon fillets on this layer of forcemeat, cover with another layer of forcemeat, and place a row of medium-sized truffles over this. Spread another layer of forcemeat and place 2 more salmon fillets on top with the pointed ends going in the opposite direction of the first 2 fillets; finish with a layer of forcemeat. Close the pie with a crust of Pie Paste and cover it with overlapping rows of paste leaves, beginning at the rim of the mold and converging toward the center. Complete with one or several layers of paste cut with a fluted pastry cutter; make an opening in the center to let the steam escape while cooking. Brush with beaten egg and bake at moderate heat, about 15 min. per lb. When the pie is cold, pour in some fish aspic.

VEAL-AND-HAM PIE PÂTÉ DE VEAU ET JAMBON (J.)

Line a fluted round mold (or a rectangular mold for larger pieces) with ordinary Pie Paste (p. 545). Cover the bottom with a thin layer of forcemeat (see directly below), lay on top a thick slice of ham, then a fine thin strip of veal tenderloin marinated in cognac. Season. Repeat the operation, alternating the layers, and finish with the rest of the forcemeat.

Close the pie with a thin crust of Pie Paste. Pinch the edges. Cover with a layer of Flaky or Puff Paste (p. 544) cut with a fluted pastry cutter. Brush with beaten egg; score the cover with a knife, making the lines radiate from the center. Bake at moderate heat about 1 hr., depending on the size of the pie.

Forcemeat: ½ lb. veal fillet and 1 lb. ham, chopped and mashed fine, 1 egg, allspice.

Note: These pies are eaten hot or cold. When serving cold, let the pie cool almost completely, then pour some aspic inside. (Figures 332-333, Page 544.)

PÂTÉ IN CRUST PÂTÉ EN CROÛTE (P.) (*Serves 6*)

Line a pâté mold with the piecrust indicated on page 545 and garnish the inside (as explained on pp. 420–421) with alternate layers of pork filling and forcemeat. One can put, for example, veal and slices of ham between two layers of pork filling, or rabbit, or fowl, game, etc.

For pâtés other than game, the filling should be seasoned only with spiced salt and flavored with cognac or Madeira. Garnish well and cover with a thin crust of pie paste (p. 545). Pinch the edges. Decorate the top with little designs of the same paste. Brush with beaten egg. Carefully make an opening on the cover and bake in a hot oven. The pâté is done when some juice comes out of the little opening in the top. Bake about one half hour per pound. (Figure 327, Page 533.)

GRILLED CALF'S SWEETBREADS CHÂTELAINE RIS DE VEAU GRILLÉ CHÂTELAINE (E.)

Bake a Brioche (leaving out the sugar) in a fluted mold with an opening a little larger than the sweetbread (see p. 546). Slice off the top of the Brioche and scoop out the inside, leaving the fluted crust, and fill this ⅔ full with a garnish composed of cubed, cooked mushrooms, truffles, and *foie gras* bound with Parisienne Sauce (p. 146). Lay the grilled sweetbreads on top of this garnish. (Figure 331, Page 541.)

SOLE-FILLET TIMBALE CARDINAL TIMBALE DE FILETS DE SOLES À LA CARDINAL (Gi.) (*For 6 persons*)

The timbale: Butter an ordinary charlotte mold and line it the following way. Roll into a ball a piece of Pie Paste (p. 545) large enough to line the mold, then roll it out into a circle ½ in. thick. Lightly dust with flour, fold it in half, then bring the 2 ends in toward the center, taking care to press out the folds. This makes a sort of dome, with which the mold is easily lined, since all that has to be done is simply to place it in the mold and then press the paste along the sides to make it take the same shape. Trim off any paste extending more than

⅜ in. beyond the rim of the mold. Prick the bottom with a fork, line bottom and sides with white paper, and fill with dried split peas. Cover the peas with a thin top crust, pinching it down all the way around the moistened rim of the timbale. Bake in a moderate oven 35–40 min., then remove the top crust by slitting it around the edges with the tip of a small knife. Pour out the peas, remove the paper, brush the inside of the timbale with beaten egg, and replace in the oven to dry 5 min. without unmolding. Take it out of the oven, turn it upside down on a rack, and keep hot. Before lining the mold, you may decorate it with a few bits of rather stiff and lightly sugared noodle paste (see Fresh Noodles, p. 520). The decorations are moistened with a little water so they will stick to the pie crust and form a part of the timbale after it is unmolded.

Garnish: Cut 12 sole fillets. Flatten them lightly, spread a thin layer of forcemeat on each, and roll them up so they form stoppers. They have now become *paupiettes,* or sole birds. Tie them with a string, lay them in a buttered sautéing pan, and cover with fish stock (or 1 glass white wine) and a little liquid from cooking mushrooms; poach slowly in the oven without boiling. Also prepare 15 small cooked mushrooms, 2 sliced truffles, and a few slices of spiny lobster or lobster. Have boiling the necessary amount of Béchamel Sauce (p. 146) to cover this garnish, and finish it, just before using, with lobster or spiny-lobster butter (made with the coral mashed with a piece of butter and pressed through a fine sieve) and 3½ oz. butter divided into small pieces. Season the sauce with a dash of cayenne pepper and color red (true red rather than pink) with a few drops of artificial coloring. Put the garnishes into the sauce (sole birds with the string removed, sliced lobster, mushrooms, and truffles) and pour into the timbale, placed on a napkin. Decorate the garnish with a large white mushroom surrounded with a few slices of truffle. This simple décor gives the timbale a more seductive appearance.

FOIE GRAS-AND-QUAIL TIMBALE CZARINA TIMBALE DE FOIE GRAS ET DE CAILLES TSARINE (E.)

Cold: Line a rather deep *pâté* mold with ordinary Pie Paste (p. 545); completely cover the inside with strips of pork fat. Place a seasoned *foie gras* upright in the center; surround it with quails (each stuffed with a piece of truffle), also upright, breast down against the strips of pork fat. Finish filling the mold with whole, raw, peeled truffles; cover with a round piece of pork fat; close the timbale with a pie crust, sealing the edges well, and cut an opening in the center to let the steam escape while cooking. Bake 1¼ hr. in a medium-hot oven. After removing the timbale from the oven, pour inside some tasty veal stock flavored with Madeira and gelatinous enough to turn to jelly. Keep in a cool place for a day or 2 before serving.

FOIE GRAS TIMBALE ALSACIENNE TIMBALE DE FOIE GRAS À L'ALSACIENNE (E.)

Bake an empty pie crust in a decorated *pâté* mold. Spread the bottom and sides of the crust with a layer of Gratin Forcemeat (p. 175) containing ¼ as much purée of *foie gras.* Keep the timbale in an open oven or warmer. Just before serving, pour into the timbale a ragout of sliced *foie gras* poached in Madeira, sliced truffles and mushrooms, bound with Madeira Sauce (p. 142). Decorate with a large fluted mushroom surrounded by truffle slices.

Variant: This dish may also be garnished the following way. Fill the timbale with alternate layers of creamed noodles, sliced *foie gras* sautéed in butter, sliced mushrooms and truffles. Finish with a layer of noodles and sprinkle the top with raw noodles sautéed in butter at the last moment. Serve with a separate dish of Suprême Sauce (p. 146) made with truffle essence.

FOIE GRAS TIMBALE CUSSY TIMBALE DE FOIE GRAS CUSSY (E.)

Bake an empty pie crust in a round, deep *pâté* mold with sides that flare out. Spread the bottom and sides of the crust with a layer of Chicken Forcemeat (p. 176) ; poach this forcemeat in an open oven. Along the walls of the crust, place a ring of *foie gras* slices trimmed round and sautéed in butter; alternate the rounds of *foie gras* with rounds of pickled tongue; arrange them so that they overlap. Fill the center with a garnish of mushrooms, cock kidneys, and truffles cut in the shape of olives, bound with Madeira Sauce (p. 142). Finish with a garland of cockscombs placed between the garnish and the ring of *foie gras.* Serve Madeira Sauce separately.

TIMBALE NAPOLITAINE TIMBALE À LA NAPOLITAINE (Gi.) (*For 6 to 8 persons*)

Crust: Line a buttered charlotte mold exactly as directed in the recipe for Sole-Fillet Timbale Cardinal (p. 537), with this difference: when the timbale is filled with dried peas, covered, and pinched all the way around, lay a few rows of paste leaves on the top crust to make a lid. Bake as directed in the recipe.

Garnish: Boil 3/4 lb. elbow macaroni in salted water. Drain the macaroni as soon as cooked, then heat in a sautéing pan to remove all the moisture. Season with salt, pepper, nutmeg, and dash of cayenne pepper; add 4 oz. Gruyère or 5 oz. grated Parmesan cheese, and sauté over the fire to melt the cheese and bind the macaroni. Then add 1 tbsp. reduced tomato purée and 3½ oz. butter divided into small bits; mix well, still sautéing the macaroni, being careful not to break the macaroni. Meanwhile, reduce 1 glass Madeira, add 1 tbsp. Semiglaze Sauce (p. 138) and ½ tbsp. tomato purée, and bring to a boil. Pour into this sauce the following garnish, prepared in advance: slices of truffled Chicken Pudding (p. 412), small mushrooms fluted and cooked, cockscombs and cock kidneys, and sliced truffles. Let this garnish simmer 8–10 min., and season with a dash of cayenne. Fill the bottom of the timbale with a layer of the prepared macaroni, pour part of the garnish over it, cover this with another layer of macaroni, then the garnish, and so on. Place the timbale on a napkin, put the cover on top, and, if possible, serve immediately.

TARTS TOURTES (A.)

The precursors of *vol-au-vent,* tarts are shallow crusts usually filled with garnished forcemeats, ragouts, Godiveau (veal-and-beef-kidney forcemeat), fish, *foie gras,* mushrooms, etc.

Originally, tarts were made with bread dough. Today they are made of Short Paste like timbales (and almost as deep), with or without cover, or of Flaky or Puff Paste with a cover.

Tart is also the name given to preserved fruits, or fruit jellies with cream, served in tart shells and glazed with sirup.

QUAIL TART CARÊME TOURTE DE CAILLES À LA CARÊME (M.)

(1) Stuff the boned quails with *foie gras* and truffles. Place them tightly side by side in a buttered sautéing pan so they will not lose their shape. Cook them in the oven 10 min. Let cool.

(2) Place the quails on a round crust of Short Paste (p. 545) filled ¾ in. from the top with a layer of Light Forcemeat (p. 173), mixed with an equal amount of Gratin Forcemeat (p. 175). The tart crust should be placed on a tin baking sheet. On top of the quails lay thick slices of truffle seasoned with salt and pepper and heated in butter. Cover with a round top crust of Short Paste. Seal the edges.

(3) Decorate the top of the tart with flower-shaped ornaments made of Puff Paste (p. 544); brush with beaten egg; make an opening in the center to let the steam escape. Bake 45 min. in a medium-hot oven. At the end, pour a few tbsp. game stock (prepared with the quail bones and trimmings) into the crust.

Note: The tart crust may also be made of Flaky or Puff Paste. In this case, it is a good idea to place a collar of Flaky Paste around the top of the bottom crust to seal on the top crust. The tart can be filled and baked directly on the serving dish.

OLD-FASHIONED FOIE GRAS TART TOURTE DE FOIE GRAS À L'ANCIENNE (E.)

Cut a raw *foie gras* in even slices; season and marinate them in cognac with the same number of slices of raw truffle. Add the *foie gras* trimmings (pressed through a sieve) and 3½ oz. chopped truffles to 1¼ lb. very fine sausage meat. Using half of this forcemeat, fill a round crust, made of ordinary Pie Paste (p. 545), to within 1¼ in. of the top; lay the sliced *foie gras* and truffles on this; spread the rest of the forcemeat on top; cover with a top crust. Seal the 2 crusts together, moisten the edges, and encircle with a band of Puff Paste (p. 544). Score the band of Puff Paste all around (see Figure 103, p. 115), brush with beaten egg, and bake 45 min. in a medium-hot oven. After removing the tart from the oven, detach the top crust with the tip of a knife and pour some thick Madeira Sauce (p. 142) over the filling.

Fig. 328 - Hare pie (p. 535).
Fig. 329 - Chicken pie english style (p. 536).

Fig. 328

Fig. 329.

Fig. 330

Fig. 331

PASTRY

Fig. 330 - Sweetbread (calf) pie (p. 536).
Fig. 331 - Grilled calf's sweetbreads châtelaine (p. 537).

PASTRY

This chapter on pastrymaking is just as interesting as the one on cooking—if not more so. For you must admit that French pastry has as great a reputation as its older sister, French cooking. In the same rank we also place what used to be called "sweet dishes," designated under the term *entremets* (literally, "between dishes"). Formerly, the same term included vegetables, and we even find Antonin Carême's menus listing, under *entremets*, a galantine of chicken and a glazed ham, peas, cucumbers, asparagus, etc. Today, the term is used exclusively for the desserts that usually wind up a meal.

We have therefore reserved a chapter or, more exactly, a large part of this book for pastries and other desserts. Just as in the first part of this book you found fancy recipes, from the chefs who were the glory and honor of French cooking, as well as simpler recipes easily prepared in the average household, so in the second part you will find recipes for the experts alongside those better suited to the housewife. Her recipes have been taken from cookbooks especially written for the home cook—the Cordon Bleu school books, the *Traité de cuisine familial,* Mlle Rose's, Andrée Beaujard's, and others. Thus we shall have fulfilled our aim: to present a work intended for fine chefs as well as for the most modest homemaker.

PASTRY BAKING (J.)

At the end of each recipe you will find conventional terms to designate the necessary temperature at which the pastry should be baked. Obviously, indications are only a guide and cannot be rigidly applied; the exact temperature of an oven cannot always be given. In this part of the book, as in others, theory does not take the place of practice.

	American	*English Electricity*	*English Gas Regulo*
Very hot oven:	460° to 500° F.	475° to 500° F.	8 to 9
Hot oven:	410° to 445° F.	425° to 450° F.	6 to 7
Medium oven:	320° to 355° F.	375° F.	4
Slow oven:	250° to 265° F.	275° to 300° F.	1 to 2
Very slow oven:	210° F.	250° to 275° F.	½ to 1

Closed: an oven from which steam does not escape.

Note: Small pieces are baked in a hotter oven than large. It is sometimes necessary to double and even triple the pastry trays.

BASIC PASTES

All pastrymaking begins with a paste; the two words belong together. There are almost as many pastes or mixtures as there are cakes. We say "almost" because so many cakes look different but have the same basic paste. These pastes and mixtures are classified and enumerated only once in this chapter so that they do not have to be repeated for each recipe.

Even though listed in the chapter on pastrymaking, some of these pastes are, of course, associated strictly with cooking: patty shells, *vol-au-vent, pâtés,* hot entrees, etc. These recipes have been given in their respective chapters. Only the pastes used in making them are detailed here.

FLAKY PASTES

PÂTES FEUILLETÉES

PUFF PASTE FEUILLETAGE (P.)

Proportions: ½ lb. sifted flour, 7–8 oz. butter, about 6 oz. cold water, ¾ tsp. salt.

Shape the flour into a ring resembling a well and put the salt and water in the middle. Quickly mix with the tips of the fingers without kneading the paste, so it has no elasticity. The mixture should be done quickly and produce a paste having exactly the same consistency as the butter used, which should always be firm rather than soft and have some body.

This first step in making Puff Paste—called the *détrempe*—can mean success or failure, so do it carefully. It is a good idea not to put in all the water in the beginning, lest the paste turn out too soft, for all flours do not absorb liquid at the same rate. This is why it is impossible to give in advance the exact weight of the butter to be used. To know the necessary quantity, you must weigh the flour-and-water mixture. The proportion of the butter should be exactly ½ this weight. For example, for 1 lb. flour-water-salt mixture, use ½ lb. butter. Working this way, you will obtain a Puff Paste that is always right, regardless of the nature of the flour used.

Mixing the butter into the paste: Let the flour-and-water paste stand ¼ hr. in a cool place; pound it out flat with the fist; then place the firm butter in the center and fold the edges of the paste over it until completely enclosed.

Using a rolling pin, roll the paste out into a long, even strip until it is thin enough so that you can see the butter. Press very lightly with the rolling pin and flour as little as possible so as not to change the proportions given. When the paste has been rolled out into a long straight strip, fold it in 3 by bringing 1 end over to the center and laying the other end on top of the first. This is called the first "turn." Next turn the piece of paste in the other direction (not upside down) and again roll out with a rolling pin, then fold again in 3; this second "turn" has thus been rolled in the opposite direction to the first. After making these first 2 turns, let the paste stand 20 min. in a cool place before giving it another 2 turns, each one always in the opposite direction. Then let stand 20–30 min. in a cool place. Finally, give it another 2 turns, bringing the total to 6,

Fig. 332 - Veal-and-ham pie (p. 537).
Fig. 333 - The same, open (p. 537).

Fig. 332

Fig. 333

Fig. 334

Fig. 335

which is the necessary number to make Puff Paste. Paste turned 6 times should be used immediately, without standing, and may be made into a variety of cakes, large and small, patties, and *vol-au-vent.* The proportions given here will make a *vol-au-vent* for 6 persons or 10 fine patty shells.

TWELFTH CAKE PASTE (Home Style) PÂTE À GALETTE DES ROIS (DE MÉNAGE) (P.) (*For 8 persons*)

Proportions: ½ lb. flour, 6 oz. butter, ½ tsp. salt, 4½ oz. water.

Place the sifted flour on a marble slab and form into a well; in the center put salt, water, and well-kneaded butter; then knead all together delicately and rapidly without trying to obtain a perfect mixture. As soon as the ingredients have been more or less blended, roll into a ball, wrap in a cloth, and let stand a good ½ hr. in a cool place. Then give it 4 turns, as for Puff Paste (p. 544), letting it stand ¼ hr. after the second turn. This paste is used after 4 turns instead of 6. With this recipe the *galette* or flat cake can be made almost instantly. A flakier *galette* can be made by using leftover paste from patty shells or *vol-au-vent.* These paste scraps or trimmings should be gathered gently together into a ball, rolled and turned once, and then used in making the *galette.*

PASTES FOR LINING

PÂTES À FONCER

SHORT PASTE PÂTE BRISÉE or PÂTE À FONCER (Ga.)

Proportions: 1 lb. flour, 10 oz. butter, 1 egg, 1 tsp. salt, 2 tsp. sugar, water.

(Made without sugar, this paste is used for timbales and croustades in cooking.) Shape the sifted flour into a well on the marble slab; put the salt, sugar, and egg into the center. Knead the butter, place it in the center of the flour well, and begin kneading with ½ glass water. When all the flour has been mixed in, press it out twice with the palm of the hand. (See Figure 104, p. 116.) Roll it into a ball and wrap in a damp cloth. This paste, like certain others, is better when prepared the day before using.

Use: Tarts, tartlets, *petits fours,* croustades.

Note: For economy, you can use 2 oz. less butter for this paste.

PIE, CROUSTADE, and **TIMBALE PASTE** PÂTE À PÂTÉS, CROUSTADES ET TIMBALES (P.)

Proportions: ½ lb. flour, 3 oz. butter, 1½ oz. lard or 2 tbsp. olive oil, 1 tsp. fine salt, 2 egg yolks, 6 oz. cold water.

Make the flour into a well and put the rest of the ingredients into the center; then knead all together, and when the mixture is almost completed, perfect it by patting it out with the palm of the hand—flatten it on the table with the palm of the right hand, pushing it toward you. Repeat this operation twice to make a well-mixed paste with enough body for a crust that can hold a heavy filling, such as meat or other garnish, whose liquid content would soften too delicate a paste or make it soggy. Let stand several hours in a cool place before using. This paste should be rather firm.

Note: The proportions given above are for a small pie serving about 6 persons. Increase the proportions according to need.

Fig. 334 - Alcazar (p. 562).
Fig. 335 - Anniversary or Birthday cake (p. 563).

SWEET PASTE or DRY PASTE PÂTE SUCRÉE OR PÂTE SÈCHE (P.)

Proportions: ¼ lb. flour, 2 oz. butter, 2 oz. sugar, pinch of salt, 1 whole egg (small).

Shape the flour into a well on the baking board; put the sugar into the center, also making it into a well; then, in the center of the sugar, put the salt, butter, and egg. Knead all together, beginning with the sugar, butter, and egg, then incorporate the flour, to make a very smooth paste. Make this paste 2 or 3 hr. in advance and let it stand in a cool place. It is used for making the shell of a great number of cakes and tarts, large and small, the inside filled with various mixtures. In summer, when butter is soft, substitute 2 egg yolks for the whole egg, to make a firmer paste. This paste can also be used for making small tea cakes.

RAISED OR LEAVENED PASTES

PÂTES À LEVAIN

BABA PASTE PÂTE À BABA (P.)

Babas are made with Savarin Paste (p. 547), but, at the end, add (for the same proportions given) 3 oz. raisins—dried currants and sultanas mixed (or 2 oz. dried currants and 1 oz. sultanas).

BRIOCHE PASTE PÂTE À BRIOCHE (P.) (*For 8–10 persons*)

Proportions: ½ lb. flour, 7 oz. butter, 1½ tsp. sugar, pinch of salt, ¼ oz. yeast, 3 small whole eggs.

Take ¼ of the flour, or 2 oz., and shape it into a well on the baking board; put the yeast into the center and pour 3 oz. warm water over it. Knead the yeast with the tips of the fingers to dissolve it, then incorporate the flour, adding, if needed, enough warm water to make a moderately soft paste. Roll it into a ball, indent it to make a deep cross, and plunge it into a pot of warm water.

At this stage the paste is called leaven; leave it in the water while finishing the preparation as follows. Take the rest of the flour and shape it into a well, too; break 2 eggs into the center. Work the flour by hand into a paste, gradually adding the last egg; knead until it becomes very elastic and has plenty of body. To do that, lift the paste high and let it fall hard on the baking board or marble; it should not stick to the fingers. Now add salt and sugar and knead a few more minutes; add the butter, which should first be worked to soften it somewhat. Mix the butter and paste well together without letting the paste lose its elasticity. Meanwhile, the leaven in the warm water should have swelled to twice its original size and should now float on the surface. Lift it gently out of the water and place it on a cloth to dry it a little; then spread it on the paste, and mix it carefully with it.

When the paste is finished, put it into a floured bowl, cover with a plate, and place it in some part of the kitchen where it will be warm, but not too warm. Let it stand about 3 hr. to rise. At the end of this time, sprinkle it with flour, put it back on the marble slab or baking board, and pat it with the hands to restore it to its normal size; this is called breaking it down. Replace in the bowl, cover, and let stand at least 6 hr. in some cool place, even the cellar; this hardens it and makes it easier to shape just before baking. Even though kept in a cool place, the paste will rise a second time and must be broken down again. To make good, attractive Brioches, the paste must rise once in a warm and once in a cool place before being used. It is a good idea, therefore, to make the paste at about 6 o'clock in the evening the day before using; let it stand in a warm place until 9, then put in a cool place for the rest of the night. The next morning, break it down at once to stop the fermentation. If you don't want to bake it immediately, put it back in a cool spot, but be sure to break it down every time it starts to swell. This way, the paste may be kept 24 hr. before baking it. (See p. 565 for the different ways of shaping Brioche Paste.)

KRAPFEN or PLAIN BRIOCHE PASTE PÂTE À KRAPFEN OR À BRIOCHE COMMUNE (P.) (*For 8–10 persons*)

Proportions: ½ lb. flour, 3½ oz. butter, 1 tsp. sugar, ½ tsp. salt, ¼ oz. yeast, 2 whole eggs, 3 oz. warm milk.

This paste is made exactly like the preceding Brioche Paste, except that the proportions are different, the milk being used to dissolve the yeast. It is therefore useless to go over the details; follow the explanations given above. With the sugar left out, this same paste can be used for certain entrees.

KUGELHOFF or CUGLOFF PASTE PÂTE À KUGELHOFF OR CUGLOFF (P.) (*For 8–10 persons*)

Proportions: ½ lb. flour, 3 oz. butter, 1 oz. powdered sugar, ½ oz. yeast, 4 oz. Malaga raisins, ⅔ tsp. salt, 2 whole eggs, 6 oz. milk.

This paste is very similar to Savarin Paste and is made almost the same way. Put ¼ of the sifted flour into a warm bowl and in the center place the yeast; pour in ⅓ cup tepid milk to dissolve the yeast; mix the flour until you have a very soft, almost liquid paste in the bottom of the bowl; sift the rest of the flour on top without mixing it. Place the bowl in a warm place and let stand until the leaven in the bottom of the bowl rises and comes through the flour on top. Then mix all together, little by little, while adding the eggs 1 by 1. If necessary, add the rest of the warm milk until you have a moderately soft paste similar to Savarin Paste. Next, mix in the softened, kneaded butter, then the salt, and, last of all, the sugar. This paste should be beaten by hand until very elastic. Complete with seeded Malaga raisins. The paste can be used the same day or even as soon as finished.

SAVARIN PASTE PÂTE À SAVARIN (P.) (*For 8 persons*)

Proportions: 4 oz. flour, 1½ oz. butter, ¼ oz. yeast, ¼ oz. sugar, pinch of salt, 2 whole eggs, 3 oz. warm milk.

First slightly warm a bowl in an open oven; then sift the flour into it, making a hole in the center for the yeast. Pour the tepid milk on top of the yeast to dissolve it, then, when it has completely melted, break in the 2 eggs and mix them immediately with the flour. The paste should be very soft, almost liquid. Beat 2 or 3 min. by hand, then cover the bowl and place in a warm spot for about ¾ hr., or until the paste has doubled in volume. Knead the butter until it is creamy, then mix it into the paste along with the salt and sugar. Beat in the bowl by hand, lifting the paste with the tips of the fingers and letting it drop back into the bowl, but with less force than when making Brioche Paste; do this 4 or 5 min. only. The paste is now finished and can be used immediately.

Note: This way of making the paste enables you to serve Savarins and Babas about 2 hr. after the order is placed and gives perfect results.

COOKED PASTES

PÂTES SUR LE FEU

CHOUX PASTE PÂTE À CHOUX (P.)

Proportions: ¼ lb. flour, 3½ oz. butter, ½ oz. sugar, dash of salt, 1 cup water, 4 whole eggs.

Put the hot or cold water, salt, sugar, and butter into a medium-sized saucepan. Place the pan on the fire and, when it boils and the butter is melted, remove from the stove and pour in the sifted flour, stirring with a spatula to mix it well and make a very thick and compact paste. Put the pan back on the fire and stir the paste with a spatula, reaching well to the bottom. The purpose of this operation is to cook the flour; continue cooking until the paste no longer sticks to the spatula or pan. Remove from the fire and, while the paste is still warm, blend in the whole eggs 1 by 1, beating well after adding each egg and before adding the next. The finished paste should be soft, but not liquid, and should form a lump. The number of eggs given may not be sufficient, depending on the flour and the size of the eggs. If needed, beat a fifth egg in a saucer and then incorporate as much of it as will give the right consistency. If, on the other hand, the paste is soft enough when the first 3 eggs are incorporated, add only a little of the fourth. This is a matter of practice, which alone will give you the necessary experience to judge and regulate these details. Choux Paste is used as the base of many pastries, such as: Saint-Honoré, Paris-Brest, Cream Puffs, Éclairs, Salambos, Praline Puffs, Profiteroles, etc. It is the first paste usually taught beginners.

ORDINARY CHOUX PASTE PÂTE À CHOUX D'OFFICE (J.)

Put 2 cups water, 3½ oz. butter, and ½ tsp. salt into a saucepan. Bring to a boil. Remove from the fire and add 10 oz. flour. Heat on the stove to dry. Remove again from the fire and incorporate 6–7 eggs, 1 by 1, into the paste.

GNOCCHI PASTE I PÂTE À GNOCCHI (J.)

Follow the recipe directly above, incorporating at the end 1½ oz. grated Parmesan or Gruyère cheese and a little grated nutmeg. Put this mixture into a pastry bag with plain metal opening, and cut off the gnocchi with the point of a wet knife over a sautéing pan or a saucepan filled ¾ full with boiling salted water. When cooked, the gnocchi will rise to the surface of the water and will be springy to the touch. Drain.

GNOCCHI PASTE II PÂTE À GNOCCHI (D. and D.)

2 cups milk, 3½ oz. butter, ½ tsp. salt, pepper, grated nutmeg, ½ lb. flour, 6 or 7 eggs, 3½ oz. grated Parmesan cheese. Same procedure as the proceding recipe.

CAKE BATTERS

PÂTE À BISCUITS

FINE SPONGE CAKE WITH BUTTER BISCUIT FIN AU BEURRE (P.) (*For 8–10 persons*)

Proportions: ¼ lb. sugar, 3½ oz. flour, 2 oz. butter, 4 eggs.

Put the sugar into a bowl with the 4 egg yolks, mix with a spatula until the batter becomes pale and creamy, then add the sifted flour, mixing it in gently

Fig. 336 - Chocolate cake (p. 567).
Fig. 337 - Harlequin (p. 563).
Fig. 338 - Baba au rhum (p. 563).
Fig. 339 - Savarin Chantilly (p. 581).

Fig. 337

Fig. 336

Fig. 338

Fig. 339

Fig. 341

Fig. 340

Fig. 342

along with the 4 stiffly beaten egg whites. As soon as these ingredients are blended, add the melted butter. In mixing, observe the precautions given in the recipe for Génoise (below), for which this batter may be substituted in many cases.

SPONGE-CAKE ROLL BISCUIT ROULÉ (P.) (*For 10 persons*)

Proportions: 2½ oz. powdered sugar, 2½ oz. flour, 1 oz. butter, 3 whole eggs, 1 egg yolk.

Put the sugar and 4 egg yolks into a bowl and mix together with a spatula until pale, then gradually mix in the flour along with the 3 stiffly beaten egg whites. Finish by mixing in the melted butter. (The butter can be left out entirely.) Spread this paste out on a sheet of buttered paper placed on a baking sheet. The paste should be spread out smoothly and of equal thickness so that there are no thin parts to dry out during baking. It should be about ½ in. thick, sometimes less, depending on what it is to be used for. Bake 7–8 min. in a hot oven, then turn the cake over on a marble table, cover with a cloth, and let the underside cool, to make it softer and easier to roll.

This sponge cake is used in making several kinds of cakes and desserts and may also be served cut in even slices after being filled with different creams or jams and rolled.

SAVOY SPONGE CAKE BISCUIT DE SAVOIE (P.) (*For 12 persons*)

This cake is too often confused with Génoise Cake, ordinary sponge, and other similar cakes. The composition is, however, not the same, and even though the true Savoy Sponge Cake is not often made any more, we shall nevertheless give the recipe.

Proportions: ½ lb. sugar, 3½ oz. flour, 3½ oz. potato flour or cornstarch, 7 egg yolks, 7 whites, vanilla.

Directions: Beat the sugar and egg yolks for a fairly long time as in making any sponge cake. Then, using a spatula, mix in very lightly, at the same time, flour and potato flour. Next mix in the beaten egg whites stiffened with 1 tbsp. powdered sugar. Mixing is the most important detail; do it gently, taking a long time. Butter and sprinkle the molds or tins with potato flour and bake 45 min. in a moderate, even oven.

FINE GÉNOISE CAKE GÉNOISE FINE (P.) (*For 8–10 persons*)

Proportions: 3½ oz. flour, ¼ lb. sugar, 3½ oz. butter, 4 whole eggs, flavoring as desired.

Put the sugar and whole eggs into a copper bowl. Place this bowl over a very low fire, such as a bed of warm cinders; then beat this paste until it has at least doubled in volume and is slightly warm. Remove from the fire and continue beating until it is almost cold. Then mix in the flour with a spatula, then the melted butter. The butter must not be too warm or it will not mix well and will not have the same taste. Mixing must be done gently to keep the Génoise light. As soon as the ingredients are mixed, the batter should no longer be stirred, to avoid making it heavy, the most deplorable effect of which is to make it greenish —the despair of inexperienced cooks, and owing simply to incorrect or too much mixing. Pour quickly into buttered, floured molds. Medium oven.

Fig. 340 - Tub of mushrooms (p. 564).
Fig. 341 - Tub of macaroni (p. 564).
Fig. 342 - Brioches (p. 565).

ORDINARY GÉNOISE CAKE GÉNOISE COMMUNE (P.)

The procedure is the same as in the preceding recipe, except that you use ½ the amount of butter. Also use only 3 eggs and ¼ lb. flour. To lighten this batter, you can add 1 tsp. baking powder. This batter is used principally for small Génoise Cakes cut in sections or for glazed Petits Fours.

VARIOUS MIXTURES USED IN MAKING DESSERTS, PASTRIES, PETITS FOURS, ETC.

REDUCED APRICOT ABRICOT RÉDUIT (Ga.)

Greatly reduce apricot jam. Apply with a small brush. Can be colored pink (using carmine coloring) for Neapolitans, Ambrosia, Mirrors, etc. This Reduced Apricot is used for coating pastries before glazing them with Fondant.

ALMOND CREAM FOR PITHIVIERS CRÈME D'AMANDES POUR PITHIVIERS (E.) (*For 8 persons*)

Proportions: 3½ oz. almonds, 3½ oz. sugar, 1½ oz. butter, 2 egg yolks, 1 liqueur glass rum.

Mash the almonds fine with the sugar; then add the egg yolks, next the butter, and, last, the rum. Work well together with a spatula. Use this cream to fill various pastries, of which the best known is a Puff-Paste cake called Pithiviers (p. 578).

ENGLISH CREAM CRÈME ANGLAISE (P.) (*For 6 persons*)

Beat 4 oz. powdered sugar and 4 egg yolks together with a spatula, then pour in 1 cup boiling milk flavored with vanilla. Spoon it, put back on the fire, and stir gently with a spatula (not a beater) until it is almost to a boil but not boiling, then strain through a fine sieve. Use hot or cold as needed. If you want this cream to be rather thick, add ½ tsp. arrowroot with the sugar. Flavor according to taste.

COFFEE ENGLISH CREAM CRÈME ANGLAISE AU CAFÉ (M.)

Prepare as in the preceding recipe. Add to the mixture of egg yolks and sugar 6 oz. milk containing 1½ oz. coffee essence.

CHOCOLATE ENGLISH CREAM CRÈME ANGLAISE AU CHOCOLAT (M).

Prepare the cream the usual way, adding 2 oz. chocolate melted in the oven and dissolved in a few tbsp. milk.

ENGLISH CREAM WITH GELATIN CRÈME ANGLAISE COLLÉE À LA GÉLATINE (P.)

Use the same proportions as in making liquid English Cream, but leave out the arrowroot and add to the cream, when it has been taken off the fire and allowed to set, ⅙ oz. gelatin previously soaked in cold water. Strain the cream when the gelatin has melted and let it cool. This cream is used in making Bavarian Creams, Charlotte Russes, etc. We rarely advise the use of gelatin.

BUTTER CREAM CRÈME AU BEURRE (P.)

This Butter Cream, made in several flavors for Petits Fours or cakes, is prepared the following way. Make a liquid English Cream (p. 550) and, when it is cold, mix it with the right amount of butter, depending on how it is to be used. This butter should be very smooth and rather soft. The butter should be blended in the cream gradually, while the desired flavoring is also added. Instead of this recipe, we prefer using Mousseline Butter Cream. See directly below.

MOUSSELINE BUTTER CREAM (VANILLA) CRÈME AU BEURRE MOUSSELINE (VANILLE) (P.)

Proportions: 4 oz. lump sugar, 3 oz. water, 5 egg yolks, vanilla, ½ lb. butter.

Cook the sugar with the water, adding vanilla if you want vanilla cream. Cook this sirup until it is sticky enough to form a thread between 2 fingers; this is called the "thread stage." Break the egg yolks into a bowl, then pour the sirup slowly over them, stirring with a small wire whisk. When the sirup is mixed, beat the mixture until completely cold; it should then be foamy and light. Soften the butter in a bowl, work it with a whisk to smooth it, then blend in the cream little by little. If the cream starts to turn, it means that there is too much sirup. In this case, add a little melted or softened butter. (This cream is far superior in smoothness to the one above.)

Note: If you want to make creamed Petits Fours with assorted flavors, make the sirup without flavoring, then add flavoring to each portion of the butter cream needed for the number of Petits Fours. Liquid flavorings such as kirsch, anisette, coffee, etc., are blended at the same time the beaten sirup is added to the butter.

CHOCOLATE BUTTER CREAM CRÈME AU BEURRE CHOCOLAT (P.)

Proceed as for Vanilla Mousseline Butter Cream (above), adding, when the cream is finished and completely cool, 3 chocolate tablets melted in a little water or 1 oz. cocoa melted the same way and cold.

CHOCOLATE PRALINE or **COFFEE PRALINE BUTTER CREAM** CRÈME AU BEURRE AU CHOCOLAT or CAFÉ PRALINÉ (P.)

Coffee or Chocolate Praline Creams are made by adding 1½ oz. powdered Praline (p. 559) to the basic recipes.

BUTTER CREAM WITH KIRSCH OR ANY OTHER LIQUID FLAVORING CRÈME AU BEURRE AU KIRSCH or TOUT AUTRE PARFUM LIQUIDE (P.)

Mix the liqueur into the Butter Cream (above) at the same time as the sugar mixture.

CHESTNUT BUTTER CREAM CRÈME AU BEURRE AUX MARRONS (D. and D.)

Mix 2 lb. broken pieces or scraps of candied chestnuts with 5 oz. butter; mix well and beat with 1 cup sirup at 30° on the saccharometer (see p. 560). Flavor with rum, kirsch, or vanilla.

MOCHA BUTTER CREAM CRÈME AU BEURRE AU MOKA (P.)

Make a simple Butter Cream (above), mixing it with coffee essence instead of vanilla. If the cream is meant for a mocha cake, it is better to cook the sugar with very strong coffee instead of water. The coffee essence should be added just the same, to heighten the color.

PISTACHIO BUTTER CREAM CRÈME AU BEURRE AUX PISTACHES (P.)

Same procedure as for vanilla Butter Cream (p. 551). Add 2 oz. blanched pistachios mashed fine with a little kirsch. Darken the color with a tiny bit of green vegetable dye. Prepare Hazelnut Butter Cream the same way.

PRALINE BUTTER CREAM CRÈME AU BEURRE PRALINÉ (P.)

Prepare like vanilla Butter Cream (p. 551), adding 1½ oz. powdered Praline (p. 559).

CHANTILLY CREAM CRÈME CHANTILLY (P.)

Chantilly Cream is Whipped Cream (see below) with 2–2½ oz. powdered sugar and some vanilla flavoring added. This cream is used to fill meringues, on Vacherins (p. 655), and on many other cakes and desserts.

WHIPPED CREAM CRÈME FOUETTÉE (P.)

Chill on ice, 1 or 2 hr., ½ pt. sweet cream mixed with ½ as much extra-heavy cream. Whip it until it becomes frothy and firm, then drain it on a silk or hair sieve. Do not whip too long, or it will turn to butter.

FRANGIPANE CREAM CRÈME FRANGIPANE (E.)

Proportions: ½ lb. sugar, ½ lb. flour, 4 whole eggs and 8 yolks, 3 pt. milk, 1 vanilla bean, tiny pinch of salt, 2 oz. crumbled macaroons, 3½ oz. butter.

Procedure: Bring the milk to a boil and drop in the vanilla bean to steep. Mix together in a pan: sugar, flour, eggs and yolks, salt; mix and work with a spoon; blend in the vanilla-flavored milk little by little. Heat, stirring constantly; let boil 2 min., then pour into a bowl. Add the butter and macaroons; spread the surface with a piece of butter.

CHOCOLATE CREAM CRÈME GANACHE (D. and D.)

Melt 6 chocolate tablets (½ lb.) on the stove or in the oven; pour into a bowl and add 2 oz. butter, then ½ pt. sweet cream; let cool a little before using. (If cream is unavailable, use boiled milk.)

PASTRY CREAM CRÈME PATISSIÈRE (P.)

Proportions: 7 oz. sugar, 2½ oz. sifted flour, 6 egg yolks, 1 pt. vanilla-flavored milk.

Beat the egg yolks and sugar in a pan with a small wire whisk. When the mixture has lightened, add the flour; pour in the boiling milk flavored with vanilla. Stir the cream with a wire whisk until it comes to a boil. Because this cream is thickened with flour, it should boil so that the flour can do its work; there is no danger of its turning.

CREAM (COOKED) FOR SAINT-HONORÉ CRÈME (CUITE) POUR SAINT-HONORÉ (D. and D.)

1 lb. powdered sugar beaten with 16 egg yolks and 3½ oz. flour; pour in 1 qt. boiling milk, beat well with a wire whisk, then bring to a boil while stirring with the whisk. Pour into a bowl, flavor with vanilla, or coffee, or melted cocoa, then add, as desired, 24–30 stiffly beaten egg whites. Work with a spatula to make a perfect mixture. Some chefs add gelatin to preserve the cakes for sale in pastryshops. In this case, add to the cream, before mixing in the egg whites,

Fig. 343 - Yule Log (p. 566).
Fig. 344 - Carrack (p. 566).
Fig. 345 - Breton (p. 564).

Fig. 343

Fig. 344

Fig. **345**

Fig. 346

Fig. 347

Fig. 349

Fig. 348

6–8 leaves of gelatin soaked in advance in cold water and then pressed in the hands to squeeze out all the water.

Note: It is a good practice to blend the sugar and egg yolks alone, before adding the flour, to avoid lumps or strings in the cream; this is advice we have given frequently.

SAMBAYON or SABAYON CREAM CRÈME SAMBAYON (P.) (*For 8 persons*)

Sambayon or Sabayon is more a sweet sauce than a cream. It is served hot with all sorts of puddings, but it can also be served cold. Using a wire whisk, beat 4 egg yolks and 5 oz. sugar together in a deep saucepan. When the mixture has whitened, stir in 1 wineglass good white wine. Place the saucepan in a *bain-marie* or double boiler and heat the cream, beating briskly with a wire whisk by rolling it between the hands; continue beating until it is very frothy and the water in the *bain-marie* or double boiler begins to boil. At this moment add some rum, kirsch, or other flavoring and serve immediately while the cream is foamy, for it will fall very quickly. If Sambayon must be made in advance, it is a good idea to add a pinch of arrowroot to the sugar—the cream will stand up better—but this procedure is not recommended. Sambayon may also be made with port, Madeira, Frontignan, champagne, etc.—in which case, substitute one of these wines for the white wine.

ICED SAMBAYON or SABAYON CREAM CRÈME SAMBAYON GLACÉE (P.)

Prepare the same mixture as above, adding 2 more egg yolks. When it is set, pour it into a bowl placed on ice and whip until it is completely chilled. Flavor at the end with maraschino, kirsch, or other flavoring. These cold Sambayons are served with certain ice creams or iced desserts and are usually made with champagne brandy or other liqueur.

FONDANT FONDANT (Ga.)

Melt 2 lb. cubed sugar at moderate heat in a pan containing a little water. When the sugar is melted, bring it to a boil and, as in all sugar-cooking operations, wash down the sides of the pan with the hand after dipping it in cold water; skim carefully. When the sugar reaches the "ball" stage—when it forms a soft ball when tried in cold water—add a quantity of glucose about the size of an egg (see pp. 561–562). Remove from the fire and pour onto a clean marble slab moistened with a little water. Let cool a little and turn the sugar with a spatula until it becomes white and solid. Then put it into a bowl and keep cool with a damp cloth on top. Fondant prepared this way keeps a long time.

Usage: To obtain a white glaze, put some Fondant into a saucepan and heat it slightly with a little kirsch, rum, or sirup, depending upon its use. For colored Fondants, follow the same procedure, adding very little green, red, or yellow coloring. For Coffee Fondant, add a little commercially prepared coffee flavoring or essence. For Chocolate Fondant, prepare the Fondant with sirup as for a white glaze. Melt 2 chocolate tablets on the stove (without any addition) and then add it to the Fondant. If the mixture is too thick, dilute it with a little sirup.

Note: Never heat Fondants until more than tepid, for if they get any hotter the glaze loses its shine.

Fig. 346 - Croquembouche (p. 567).
Fig. 347 - Dacquoise (p. 568).
Fig. 348 - Danicheff (p. 568).
Fig. 349 - Checkerboard (p. 568).

LAYERS FOR BRAZILIAN CAKE FONDS DE BRÉSILIEN (Ga.) (*For 12 persons*)

7 oz. almonds, 5 oz. fine sugar, 3 grated chocolate tablets.

Sift these 3 ingredients into a bowl with a few drops of vanilla and 2 oz. flour. Add enough stiffly beaten egg whites to make a rather soft paste, then add 1 oz. melted butter. Spread in very thin layers in buttered, floured baking tins. Slow oven. Let dry. (See Brazilian Cake, p. 564.)

LAYERS FOR DACQUOISE FONDS DE DACQUOISE (Ga.) (*For 12 persons*)

½ lb. powdered almonds, ½ lb. powdered sugar, 1 oz. cornstarch, 8 beaten egg whites.

Beat the egg whites very stiff, add the other ingredients listed above, mix gently with a spatula. Pour into 2 buttered, floured round cake tins of the same size, smooth the top, and bake in a slow oven. May be prepared in advance and kept several days. (See Dacquoise, p. 568.)

LAYERS FOR FRIANDS FONDS DE FRIANDS (Ga.) (*For 12 persons*)

½ lb. powdered almonds and ½ lb. fine sugar.

Put the ingredients into a bowl and add 8 egg yolks (1 by 1), 3½ oz. chopped, preserved fruits, kirsch and vanilla, 1⅔ oz. flour. Beat 8 egg whites stiff, mix all together, and bake in buttered round cake tins with paper in the bottom. Slow oven. May be kept 5–6 days, covered. Use for various Petits Fours. May also be used as is. (See Friand, p. 570.)

LAYERS FOR PROGRESS CAKE FONDS DE PROGRÈS (Ga.) (*For 12 persons*)

4 oz. almonds, 4 oz. hazelnuts (grilled), ½ lb. sugar.

Reduce these ingredients to a powder in a mill or mortar. Beat 8 egg whites very stiff, remove the beater, and gently mix in the powdered ingredients with a spatula. Bake in buttered, floured cake tins at low heat. May be kept 6–15 days if carefully dried and sealed in tins. (See Progress Cake, p. 579.)

LAYERS FOR SUCCESS CAKE FONDS DE SUCCÈS (Ga.) (*For 12 persons*)

½ lb. almonds, ½ lb. sugar, both pulverized as in the preceding recipe, 8 beaten egg whites.

Mix powdered ingredients and egg whites. Fill a pastry bag with the mixture and squeeze into the desired shape on buttered, floured cake tins for large layers and on paper (on baking sheets) for small cakes. Slow oven. (See Success Cake, p. 582.)

JELLIES GELÉES (E.)

Gelatin with the required amount of water is the base for jellies. The best gelatin is made by cooking calf's feet, but since its preparation is rather complicated, commercially made gelatin is frequently used instead.

CALF'S-FOOT JELLY GELÉE DES PIEDS DE VEAU (E.)

Take some fine, soaked calf's feet; place them in a stewpan; cover with cold water; place on the stove and when it begins to boil remove at once. Cool the feet, then set them to cook with 2 qt. water per foot. Skim carefully, cover the pan, and cook very slowly about 7 hr. At the end of this time, strain the cooking liquid and skim off all the fat. Test the strength of the gelatin by chilling a few tbsp. on ice; correct it if necessary by adding a small quantity of filtered water and trying it again on ice. Per qt. jelly, add 8 oz. sugar, ½ orange peel, and juice of 1 orange and 1 lemon. To clarify, use commercial gelatin and proceed as directed below.

JELLY MADE FROM PREPARED GELATIN GELÉE À BASE DE GÉLATINE (E.)

Dissolve 1 oz. gelatin in 1 qt. water; add ½ lb. sugar, peel and juice of ½ lemon and 1 orange. Bring to a boil, then let stand 10 min. off the fire.

To clarify: Beat together in a very clean saucepan 2 egg whites and 1 wineglass white wine. Pour the sticky sirup over the egg whites little by little, whisking briskly all the while. Place the saucepan on the fire; continue beating until it comes to a boil. At this moment, lower the heat, cover, and keep at low heat (without boiling) ¼ hr. At the end of this time, the clarification is completed; strain the jelly through a bag or clean napkin placed over a porcelain bowl. If the jelly is not completely clear at the first straining, strain it a second time until it comes out quite clear. Let it almost cool before adding any flavoring. Liqueurs, fine wines, or fruits are used for flavoring jellies. When flavoring with liqueurs, allow 1 part liqueur—kirsch, maraschino, rum, curaçao, anisette—per 9 parts jelly.

Fine wine jellies made with champagne, Madeira, Marsala, etc., should contain 3 parts wine per 7 parts jelly. Fruit jellies made with strawberries, raspberries, gooseberries, cherries, bananas, peaches, etc., may be flavored with some liqueur. The fruits are placed by rows in a mold surrounded with crushed ice, with a layer of jelly poured over each row of fruit; as soon as the first layer has set, another is added, and so on until the mold is full. Keep the mold surrounded with ice until ready to serve the jelly. Jellies are also made with fruit juices, such as strawberry, raspberry, and cherry. These delicate jellies should be served in attractive champagne glasses.

Preparation: Proportions: 10 oz. strawberries, 7 oz. raspberries, both fresh and carefully picked over; place them in a white bowl and cover with 21 oz. vanilla-flavored simple sirup at 215° F., half cool (see p. 560). Cover the bowl; let macerate 2 hr. in the refrigerator. Pour into a sieve over a bowl and let the juices filter through without pressing. Add to the sirup 6 oz. any desired liqueur and ⅓ oz. agar-agar dissolved in 3 oz. water. Pour immediately into sherbet glasses. Keep in the refrigerator. This way of serving jelly is almost a standby at social functions and makes a delightful dessert for afternoon tea. If desired, the sherbet glasses may be garnished with fresh fruits such as quartered peaches, strawberries, raspberries, cooked cherries, bananas, etc.

Note: This jelly sets very quickly and should be poured slightly warm into the glasses. We should add that jellies are served much more simply today. Molded jellies have almost completely disappeared. Today jellies are served in deep silver dishes or in crystal bowls. The fruits or mixture of chopped, chilled fruits are put in first, then the jelly is poured on top, and the dish is put into the refrigerator. Prepared this way, jelly doesn't have to be unmolded, need not be stiffened, and therefore turns out even finer.

ORANGE JELLY GELÉE D'ORANGES (P.)

Here is the best of several ways of making this jelly. Cut 12 ripe oranges in half; use a silver spoon to scoop out the insides. Be sure to remove all the white skin and seeds, for they are bitter. Crush the orange pulp in an unplated copper pan and bring to a boil, then drain through a cloth and press to extract all the juice. Put this juice back into the pan with the same weight of lump sugar and 5 or 6 more pieces rubbed over the oranges to take in their flavor; let simmer, skimming carefully with a silver spoon. When it no longer needs skimming, remove from the fire and, before completely cooled, add ¼ oz. gelatin melted in a *bain-marie* or double boiler and 6 oz. curaçao. Place on ice; when the jelly begins to set, pour it either into the half shells of scooped-out oranges,[1] or into small, individual porcelain or silver ramekins, or into little Puff-Paste shells, etc. The jelly may be colored with a little carmine if used judiciously.

SUGAR GLAZE or PLAIN ICING or FROSTING GLACE À L'EAU (Ga.)

Confectioners' sugar moistened with a little water, flavored according to choice, and slightly warmed. Use with a brush to glaze Lady Disks (p. 596), Mirrors (p. 595), Babas (p. 584).

ROYAL GLAZE, ICING, or FROSTING GLACE ROYALE (Ga.)

Sifted confectioners' sugar beaten with egg white to the desired consistency, flavored with a little lemon juice. Keep in a bowl with a damp cloth on top. Use for Conversations (p. 587), Petits Fours, Matches (p. 584).

DUTCH GRANITÉ GRANITÉ HOLLANDAIS (Ga.)

For frosting Dutch Galettes (p. 591) and other cakes: 3½ oz. almonds, 3½ oz. fine sugar, 1 egg. Make a paste of these ingredients and spread a thin layer on the pastry selected. Watch carefully when baking, for this glaze browns very quickly in the oven.

ALMOND MILK LAIT D'AMANDES (P.)

Mash 5 oz. freshly shelled almonds, pouring in, little by little, 3 oz. cold water. The almonds should be mashed to a very fine paste and the water added drop by drop to prevent the almonds' turning into oil. Then squeeze in a cloth to extract the water, which has now become just like milk. This composition is used for such desserts as Blancmange (p. 636), etc.

MERINGUE MERINGUE (D. and D.)

Meringue is made of beaten sugar and egg whites. There are 4 different ways of preparing it, each with its own name.

Ordinary Meringue is made cold by blending powdered sugar with stiffly beaten egg whites. The proportion of egg whites may vary from 6–12 per lb. sugar.

Italian Meringue is made by pouring cooked sugar (at the ball stage) over stiffly beaten egg whites, continuously beating. The proportion of whites varies from 6–8 per lb. sugar. This meringue is used for decoration and Petits Fours.

Cooked Meringue is made by beating confectioners' sugar with egg whites over a low fire. This meringue is used for making Petits Fours decorated with bits of fruit and nonpareilles.

Swiss Meringue is made by first beating the sugar with a little egg white and a few drops of lemon juice, as for Royal Glaze, and then adding the rest of the beaten whites.

---

[1]In this case, fill only at the last minute, since the white skin of the orange is very bitter.

Fig. 350 - Gift from Nice (p. 569).
Fig. 351 - Milk flan (p. 570).

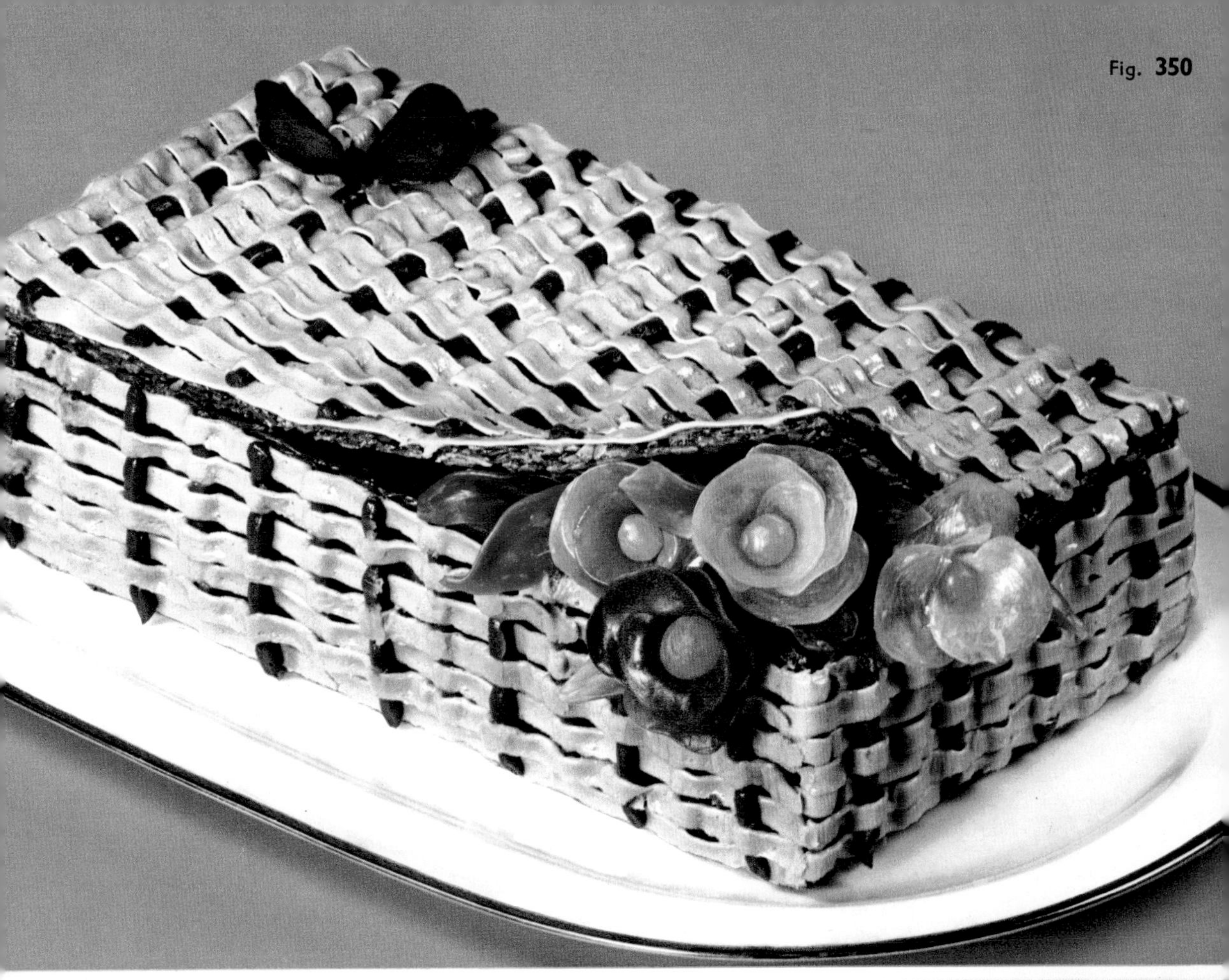

Fig. 350

Fig. 351

Fig. 353

Fig. 354

ORDINARY MERINGUE MERINGUE ORDINAIRE (P.)

Proportions: 4 egg whites, ½ lb. powdered sugar, vanilla.

Put the egg whites into a copper basin made for this purpose and beat with a wire whisk until very stiff; then, using a spatula, quickly mix in the powdered sugar and a little vanilla; if this takes too long, the mixture will be too soft. The essential thing for success is to keep the egg whites stiff. This meringue is used for meringue shells to be filled with Chantilly Cream and for other cakes.

COOKED MERINGUE MERINGUE CUITE or SUR LE FEU (P.)

Proportions: 4 egg whites, ½ lb. confectioners' sugar, vanilla.

Put everything together into the copper basin and beat over a very low fire, as in making Génoise Cake (p. 549), until the mixture becomes too stiff to spread. It should be fairly hot, but not enough to cook the egg whites. Use this meringue for making very light Petits Fours such as Lady Fingers, fake mushrooms (for Tub of Mushrooms), Rocks, etc. Bake it in a hot oven and it will remain creamy inside.

ITALIAN MERINGUE MERINGUE ITALIENNE (P.)

Proportions: 3 egg whites, ½ lb. lump sugar, 3 oz. water, 1 vanilla bean.

Put the sugar into a very clean pan, add the vanilla bean and water, and cook over a hot fire until the sirup reaches the "ball" stage. To test if it is thick enough, take a little of it on your wet finger and dip it in cold water. If the cooled sugar can be rolled between the fingers like a ball and offers slight resistance to pressure, somewhat like a wad of gum, it has reached the proper stage. Now put the pan in a *bain-marie* or over a double boiler to keep it hot without cooking it. Then beat the egg whites until very stiff. Pour the sugar over the whites, continuously beating with a whisk. Better have someone help you with this, for the hot sugar can cause serious burns. When cool, this meringue is used for filling various cakes or pastries and can take the place of whipped cream in regions where it is not available.

Though this meringue is not baked in the oven, it may be put there a few moments to give it a crust, if necessary.

SWISS MERINGUE MERINGUE SUISSE (D. and D.)

Beat ½ lb. confectioners' sugar with 1 egg white, add a few drops of lemon juice; when beaten stiff, flavor with vanilla and mix in 2 stiffly beaten egg whites.

NOUGAT (for desserts, Petits Fours, and frostings) NOUGAT (Ga.)

Put 5 oz. powdered sugar and some glucose the size of a hazelnut into a heavy, round-bottomed pan. Weigh 7 oz. chopped or shredded almonds. Melt the sugar over a hot fire, stirring constantly. When the sugar has completely melted, drop in the almonds, mix well, and pour onto an oiled, marble slab; keep warm on the marble slab in an open oven. The knife and roller should also be lightly oiled.

ALMOND PASTE or **FROLLE PASTE** PÂTE D'AMANDES or PÂTE FROLLE (P.)

Proportions: ½ lb. flour, 5 oz. shelled almonds, 5 oz. butter, 5 oz. powdered sugar, 2 small whole eggs, pinch of salt, 1 piece of lemon peel (grated).

Mash the almonds very fine, adding the sugar little by little to keep the almonds from turning to oil; when the almonds are finely mashed, add 1 whole egg. Shape the flour into a well and put the paste in the center; add the butter,

Fig. 352 - Meringue flan (p. 570).
Fig. 353 - Roquefort-cheese cake (p. 570).
Fig. 354 - Brie-cheese surprise (p. 570).

second egg, salt, and lemon peel (or orange peel). Knead this paste quickly until it has the consistency of Pie Paste and can be rolled out with a rolling pin. Let the paste stand 1 hr. before using. It is used for Neapolitans and small dry or cream pastries.

ALMOND-PASTE FONDANT I PÂTE D'AMANDES FONDANTE (Ga.)

Mash fine 1 lb. freshly shelled, washed, and dried almonds with ½ lb. confectioners' sugar. Pour in 1 glass kirsch, keeping the mixture very firm, and put into a round-bottomed, heavy pan. Cook 1½ lb. sugar with a vanilla bean until it reaches the ball stage, then pour it in a thin ribbon into the almond paste, stirring until completely cold. Add any artificial coloring you wish. If kept in a cool place, in a bowl covered with a cloth, it can be preserved a long time.

Use for various Petits Fours, green leaves for decorating large cakes, and imitation fruits.

ALMOND-PASTE FONDANT II PÂTE D'AMANDES FONDANTE (P.)

Reduce ½ lb. shelled, well-dried almonds to a fine powder, then mix this powder on a table with 7 oz. Fondant (p. 553) and a little vanilla powder. This will make a paste similar to the one in the preceding recipe, but it will not be quite so white and fine. However, it is more easily made and serves the same purpose.

PASTE FOR DÉLICIEUSES or **DAINTY CAKES** PÂTE À DÉLICIEUSES (D. and D.)

Beat 11 oz. pulverized almonds with 18 oz. sugar and 6 egg whites. Then blend in 10 stiffly beaten egg whites and ½ lb. flour. Spread the paste out until it is about ⅔ in. thick, shape into small balls, and bake on paper in a slow oven. Sprinkle with powdered sugar. Serve as Petits Fours.

DUTCH PASTE PÂTE À HOLLANDAIS (D. and D.)

Mash ¼ lb. almonds with 3 egg whites. Place in a bowl with ½ lb. sugar, add 2 whole eggs and 12 yolks, 1 by 1, while working the paste. Add ¼ lb. flour, ¼ lb. melted butter. Place in a cake pan with buttered paper on the bottom. Moderate oven.

PARISETTE PASTE PÂTE À PARISETTE (D. and D.)

Mash ¼ lb. fresh almonds, ¼ lb. sugar, 3 eggs; mix well together in a mortar.

PARISIAN PASTE PÂTE À PARISIENNE (D. and D.)

Mash ½ lb. almonds with ½ lb. sugar, vanilla, 2 egg whites. Mix into this paste 6 stiffly beaten egg whites and 1 oz. flour. Spread this paste out on a sheet of paper, making a layer about ⅛ in. thick. Bake in a slow oven. This paste is cut into various fancy shapes and combined with other pastes to form Petits Fours or other small pastries.

FRYING PASTE PÂTE À FRIRE (D. and D.)

In a bowl mix ½ lb. flour, ½ tsp. salt, 2 tbsp. olive oil, 6 oz. warm water. Make a smooth paste; let stand 1 hr., then, just before using, add 2 beaten egg whites. If the Frying Paste is to be used for sweet desserts, add ⅔ oz. sugar and 2 tbsp. cognac.

FRYING PASTE FOR FRUIT AND FLOWER FRITTERS PÂTE À FRIRE POUR BEIGNETS DE FRUITS ET DE FLEURS (E.)

Proportions: ½ lb. sifted flour, ½ tsp. salt, 2 tbsp. melted butter, 4 oz. beer, 6 oz. warm water, 1 tbsp. cognac, 2 stiffly beaten egg whites.

Procedure: Mix flour, salt, butter together in a bowl; slowly mix in the beer and water without working the paste, then add the cognac. Finish the paste, just before using, with the beaten egg whites.

FRYING PASTE FOR FRUIT FRITTERS GLAZED IN THE OVEN PÂTE À FRIRE POUR BEIGNETS DE FRUITS GLACÉS AU FOUR (E.)

Proportions: 1 lb. flour, 2 tbsp. melted butter, pinch of fine salt, pinch of sugar, 1 egg, 4 oz. beer, and a little warm water.

Blend the paste with a spoon, shortly before using, without working it too much. Keep it in a rather warm place to let it ferment, then break it down just before using—that is, pat it by hand until it is back to its former size.

PRALINE I PRALIN (P.)

Place in a copper frying pan an equal weight of powdered sugar and raw almonds (not blanched). Using a spatula, stir over the fire until the sugar has melted into dark-brown caramel and the almonds are well grilled. Pour the mixture onto an oiled marble slab and let cool. Reduce this Praline to powder by pounding in a mortar or by grating.

PRALINE II PRALIN (Ga.)

Take ½ lb. grilled, blanched hazelnuts. Cook 7 oz. sugar to the ball stage, drop the nuts into the sugar, and mix. Continue stirring on the fire until the sugar starts to brown; continue until the sugar has caramelized around the nuts. Pour onto a marble slab, let cool, and pound in a mortar. Three different Pralines can be made from this.

(1) Granulated Praline is made by lightly pounding in a mortar and straining through a coarse sieve. This is sprinkled on Petits Fours, cakes, or frosting.

(2) Powdered Praline. Pound for a long time, until reduced to a powder. Use for Praline creams and frosting.

(3) Praline paste. Continue pounding until the Praline turns into a paste of its own accord. This Praline is used for creams, frostings, and for cake and Petits Fours fillings. It can be kept 2 weeks in a closed tin container. If desired, use half almonds and half hazelnuts.

RICE CONDÉ RIZ CONDÉ (D. and D.)

Blanch some Carolina rice in very little water, drain well, and finish cooking with a little vanilla-flavored, thin sirup. Bring to a boil on the stove and finish in the oven, stirring from time to time with a fork. Keep the rice in separate grains. Bind it with the right number of egg yolks (10 per lb.), remove the vanilla bean, and mold in a savarin or ring mold. Unmold after packing it and filling it according to the recipe.

Note: This rice is served with all preparations called *à la Condé.*

DESSERT RICE or **RICE WITH MILK** RIZ POUR ENTREMETS or RIZ AU LAIT (E.) (*For 15 persons*)

Proportions: 1 lb. Carolina rice, 10 oz. sugar, pinch of salt, 2 qt. milk, 12 egg yolks, 1 vanilla bean, lemon or orange peel, 3½ oz. butter.

Procedure: Wash, blanch, and drain the rice, then rewash it in warm water. Drain again and set it to cook with the boiled milk (already flavored by the vanilla bean and mixed with the sugar), salt, and butter. When it comes to a full boil, cover the pan and cook slowly in the oven 25–30 min. Do not touch the rice during this time, or the liquid will be displaced and cause the rice to stick to the bottom of the pan. After removing from the oven, add the yolks; blend them in carefully with a fork—do not break the rice; it must stay in whole grains.

APRICOT SAUCE SAUCE ABRICOT

See Fruit Sauces, below.

ENGLISH SAUCE SAUCE ANGLAISE

See English Cream, p. 550.

CHOCOLATE SAUCE SAUCE AU CHOCOLAT (M.)

This is prepared 2 ways: (1) Mix 7 oz. dissolved chocolate in 1 pt. Vanilla Sauce (below). Strain through cheesecloth. (2) Dissolve ½ lb. chocolate in 9 oz. water. Add 6 oz. cream and 1 heaping tbsp. vanilla-flavored sugar. Strain through cheesecloth.

FRUIT SAUCES SAUCES AUX FRUITS (D. and D.)

Peach and apricot sauces are prepared by poaching very ripe fruit in sirup at 215° F. When the fruit is well cooked, strain it through a sieve and mix with the sirup. For strawberry and raspberry sauces, strain the fruit through a sieve, then add the sugar without heating it, in the following proportions: out of season, use the pulp of preserved peaches, apricots, strawberries, and raspberries, strained and sugared (½ lb. sugar per lb. pulp). Depending on the case, the sauce is flavored with Madeira, kirsch, rum, etc. Color according to need.

VANILLA SAUCE SAUCE À LA VANILLE (M.)

Creamed: Simply English Cream (p. 550) strongly flavored with vanilla.

With sirup: Steep a vanilla bean in sirup heated to 210° F. Bind with arrowroot. Strain.

SIRUP AND SACCHAROMETER SIROP ET PÈSE-SIROP (P.)

Sirup is made of sugar and water, sometimes sugar and fruit juice. The density of the sirup is determined by the amount of sugar in a specific amount of water. To know the specific weight of the sirup, you can figure out the amount of sugar needed in 1 qt. water—to take an example—to make a sirup at 20°. But this method isn't always exact, and better results are obtained with a saccharometer, which is a sort of small thermometer. It is inexpensive, easy to use, and accurate. When the sirup is boiling, pour some of it into the tube that serves as a case for the saccharometer, provided it is made of metal and not cardboard, then plunge the graduated saccharometer into the case. You will be able to read the degree of the sirup just as easily as reading a bath thermometer. For example, if pure water weighs zero, the more sugar you put in, the higher the saccharometer will go. You can weigh boiling sirups for preserves, for example, without any risk of breaking the instrument.

The saccharometer is indispensable in the kitchen, for it is needed for all sirups for pastrymaking and candymaking. To conclude this short study of sirups, we give below the proportions of sugar and water needed to produce the degree you wish.

Fig. 355 - Twelfth cake (p. 571).
Fig. 356 - Norman cake (p. 575).
Fig. 357 - Kugelhoff (p. 571).

Fig. 355

Fig. 356

Fig. 357

Fig. 358

Fig. 359

Water	Sugar	Degrees
1 pt.	2 lb.	32
1½ pt.	2 lb.	30
1 qt.	2 lb.	25
2½ pt.	2 lb.	22
3 pt.	2 lb.	20
2 qt.	2 lb.	17

This little table should be enough to guide you. It should be noted, however, that a sirup registering 28° on the scale will actually be 31° or 32° when cooled, because of the evaporation of water in cooling and because the saccharometer goes down slower in cold sirup, which is thicker.

COOKING SUGAR CUISSON DU SUCRE (J.)

Stage	Saccharometer	Degrees F.	Stage	Saccharometer	Degrees F.
Melted	20°	212	Soft Ball	39°	239
Sticky	25°	215	Ball	40°	244
Very Sticky	30°	217	Hard Ball	41°	250
Pearl	33°	221	Soft Crack	—	257
Thread	35°	223	Crack	—	286
Soufflé	37°	226	Hard Crack	—	293
Thick Soufflé	38°	233	Caramel	—	298–302

In cooking the sugar, use 1 oz. glucose per lb. sugar, except for meringues, sirups, and certain macaroons. Moisten with 4½ oz. water per lb. sugar. When the sugar reaches the soft-ball stage, it is tested by finger or thermometer. At this stage of the cooking, the sugar has too much density to be measured by a saccharometer.

Note: To test the stage of the cooking by finger, dip the thumb and index finger into cold water, then into the sugar, bringing the 2 fingers together and dipping them again into water. This should be done quickly to avoid burning. While cooking the sugar, clean the sides of the pan, using the same method. Use the thumb alone, one finger or several fingers, holding the handle of the pan in the other hand to avoid tilting it. This can also be done with a small clean cloth dipped in cold water. The purpose of this is to dissolve the bits of sugar spattered on the sides of the pan from boiling, and to prevent them from caramelizing and then falling back into the sugar, causing it to become thick and brown.

If no saccharometer is available, here is how to tell the various stages by hand:

Melted: Dip a skimming ladle into the sugar and let it drain; the sugar, or rather the sirup, should cling to the spoon.

Sticky: Use the finger, as directed above. When the thumb and index finger are drawn apart, a small thread that does not hold should form.

Fig. 358 - Manon (p. 572).
Fig. 359 - Marcelin (p. 572).

Very Sticky: The thread of sugar stretches a little more and is a little solider.

Pearl: The thread stretches still further and falls as a "pearl" or drop on the finger.

Thread: The thread lengthens without breaking. Use for butter creams.

Soufflé: Dip a skimming ladle into the sugar, lift it, and blow hard through the holes; the sugar comes out in small bubbles that burst immediately.

Thick Soufflé: The bubbles should be larger and will last a moment.

Soft Ball: The sugar forms a small ball that can be rolled with the tip of the fingers. Use for Fondant.

Hard Ball: The ball is larger and harder. Use for Italian Meringue, soft caramels, etc.

Soft Crack: The sugar no longer sticks enough to roll, and breaks. If crunched, it sticks to the teeth.

Hard Crack: The sugar breaks and no longer sticks to the teeth when crunched. Use for making sugar flowers, for glazing cherries, sliced oranges, and various Petits Fours.

Caramel: The water has completely evaporated, and the sugar has begun to brown. If left on the fire, it becomes black, porous, and no longer usable.

SPUN SUGAR SUCRE FILÉ (P.)

Spun Sugar is used for decorating certain cakes and built-up pieces such as Croquembouche, Nougat, Christmas Stocking, etc. It is very easy to make. Cook the sugar to the hard-crack stage (see above), then let it cool a bit until it becomes very thick. Now dip a very clean fork or spoon into it and raise it, holding it in your right arm, as high as you can reach. Work it quickly backward and forward over an oiled spatula so that the sugar, thrown to each side of the spatula, will stick there in long, thin threads. Dip the fork again into the sugar and continue the operation until you have enough Spun Sugar for your needs. This sugar is very pliable and can be shaped by hand into any desired form. Do not confuse Spun Sugar with sugar cooked to the "thread" stage, as explained above. Only a silver fork or spoon should be dipped into cooked sugar, for it is delicate and turns easily—that is, crystallizes. Should this happen, add water, a finger of vinegar, and cook again to the hard-crack stage.

DESSERT PASTRIES

ALCAZAR ALCAZAR (D. and D.)

Line the bottom of a plain round mold or cake pan with Sweet Paste (p. 546); place a thin layer of Reduced Apricot (p. 550) on top, then fill the mold with Financier Paste (p. 569); bake in a hot oven. Unmold or remove from pan and make a diamond pattern on top of the cake with Almond Paste (p. 557) softened with egg white and squeezed from a pastry bag with a fluted opening; then make a border, using the same paste, and put back into the oven to brown lightly. Pour Reduced Apricot into each diamond pattern, with a half a pistachio or a pinch of chopped apricot in the center of each diamond. After removing from the oven, brush the Almond Paste with apricot sirup. (Figure 334, Page 545.)

ALEXANDRA ALEXANDRA (P.) (*For 8 persons*)

¼ lb. sugar, 2½ oz. cornstarch, ⅔ oz. flour, 2½ oz. almonds, 2½ oz. butter, 3½ oz. chocolate, 4 whole eggs.

Put the sugar, pulverized almonds, 1 whole egg, and 3 egg yolks into a mixing bowl and work briskly with a spatula. Melt the chocolate in very little water until it becomes a cream, then add to above mixture. Blend in the flour and cornstarch, along with 3 stiffly beaten egg whites. Finish by mixing in the melted butter. Pour this mixture into a buttered and floured square cake pan; bake about 50 min. in a very slow oven. When the cake has cooled, cover it with Reduced Apricot (p. 550) and frost it with Chocolate Fondant (p. 553). This cake has neither decoration nor garnish, but is nonetheless exquisite.

AMANDINE AMANDINE (D. and D.) (*For 20 persons*)

1 lb. sugar well beaten with 4 yolks and 4 whole eggs. Add ½ lb. finely pounded almonds (including ½ oz. bitter almonds), 1 tsp. salt, grated peel and juice of 2 lemons; at the end, add ½ lb. flour, 1½ oz. cornstarch, 11 oz. melted butter, 4 stiffly beaten egg whites. Bake in round cake tins in a slow oven. Using a brush, spread the sides and top with apricot jam and cover with chopped, grilled almonds; sprinkle with powdered sugar.

ANNIVERSARY or **BIRTHDAY CAKE** ANNIVERSAIRE (GÂTEAU D') (J.)

Fill and cover a Génoise Cake (p. 549) with Chocolate Butter Cream (p. 551). Glaze the top with Chocolate Fondant (p. 553). Cover the sides with chopped, grilled almonds. Decorate with Royal Glaze (p. 556), writing either the first name of the person for whom the birthday party is given or simply "Happy Birthday" or "Happy Anniversary."

Prepare separately, using sugar in the hard-crack stage (p. 562): small flowers, leaves, and a ribbon of green sugar to give the effect of a stem (the 2 ends will be joined to make a circle). Arrange flowers, leaves, and stems. Stick a candle in each flower, holding it in place with a little Royal Glaze, and set the arrangement on the cake. (Figure 335, Page 545.)

Note: This cake can be filled and frosted with any flavor. It usually has white frosting when made for a young girl.

HARLEQUIN ARLEQUIN (P.)

The only difficult thing about this cake is the decoration. Make a Fine Génoise Cake (p. 549) filled with Pastry Cream (p. 552) mixed with chopped, preserved fruits and flavored with kirsch. Brush the cake with apricot jam, frost with green pistachio, and decorate it artistically with Royal Glaze (p. 556), using a paper cone or a pastry bag. In the center make a rectangle crisscrossed in a diamond pattern, the openings filled with 2 colors of Fondant (p. 553), either white and pistachio or coffee and chocolate, the main idea being the contrast of colors. Finish with a pretty and delicate decoration around the outside. (Figure 337, Page 548.)

Without attempting this difficult decoration, any fairly skillful cook can make this cake rather simply.

BABA AU RHUM BABA AU RHUM (D. and D.)

Half fill a special baba mold with Baba Paste (p. 546). Let rise, then bake in a medium oven. Sirup and flavor with rum.

Note: Unmold the baba after taking it from the oven, and let cool before dipping it in the hot sirup. Use cold sirup if you intend to soak the cake as soon as baked. (Figure 338, Page 548.)

SAVORY BABA BABA SAVOUREUX (D. and D.)

Pour Baba Paste (p. 546) into a fluted brioche mold, let rise, and bake. Then cut off the top, hollow out slightly, soak in Almond Milk (p. 556), fill with vanilla-flavored Chantilly Cream (p. 552), replace the top, and frost white. Sprinkle grilled, chopped almonds on top.

TUB OF MUSHROOMS BAQUET DE CHAMPIGNONS (J.)

Fill and frost a round Génoise Cake (p. 549) with somewhat flaring sides with coffee-flavored Butter Cream (p. 551). Stick Cat Tongues (p. 601) all around the outside. Use only halves of Cat Tongues, except for 2 longer ones, on opposite sides, pierced at the top with a small round cutter to resemble the handles of the tub. Fill the top with small mushrooms made of Cooked Meringue (p. 557). (Figure 340, Page 549.)

TUB OF MACARONI BAQUET DE MACARONI (J.)

Same procedure as above, using Vanilla Butter Cream (p. 551) instead of coffee Butter Cream. Cover the top with imitation macaroni, using a pastry bag with a small round opening. Do not overload it. Sprinkle with a few finely chopped, grilled almonds. (Figure 341, Page 549.)

BIBESCO BIBESCO (D. and D.)

Take 15 stiffly beaten egg whites; add ½ lb. powdered sugar and ½ lb. pulverized filberts to the egg whites. Using a pastry bag, lay out even-sized rings of this mixture. Bake in a medium oven. When baked, superimpose the layers one on top of the other, with a layer of chestnut purée between each. With a pastry bag with a fluted tube, cover all around with chestnut purée. Fill the hole in the center with whipped cream and top with a dome of red sugar poured from a spoon. The dome is made of sugar cooked to the crack stage (see p. 562), colored red, and poured from a spoon in a thin trickle on the outside of an oiled copper hemisphere or the back of a ladle.

HAZELNUT SPONGE CAKE BISCUIT NOISETTE (D. and D.)

10 oz. sugar, 7 oz. hazelnuts, 2 oz. almonds crushed with 2 whole eggs; beat with 8 egg yolks and mix in 3½ oz. flour, a little kirsch, 8 beaten egg whites. Bake in a slow oven in shallow round cake pans. Frost to taste, sprinkling a few chopped, grilled hazelnuts on top.

BRAZILIAN CAKE BRÉSILIEN (Ga.)

Brazilian Layers (p. 554) filled with Chocolate Butter Cream (p. 551) and glazed with chocolate.

BRETON BRETON (D. and D.) (*For 25 persons*)

Take 1 lb. sugar beaten with 16 egg yolks, then mix in ½ lb. almonds pounded in a mortar with 4 eggs, ½ lb. flour, and 16 egg whites beaten stiff. Fill some molds with 6 rounded sides, called Breton molds, to the top and bake 35–40 min. in a medium oven. Remove from the oven and unmold. When cold, trim each part. Brush with apricot jam and frost the layers with Fondant (p. 553), half of one color and the other half of a different color. Alternate the colors in

Fig. 360 - Marignan (p. 572).
Fig. 361 & 362 - Chestnut cake (p. 573).

Fig. 360

Fig. 362

Fig. 361

Fig. 363

Fig. 364

assembling the layers. Using a pastry bag with a fluted opening, decorate with 2 different colors of Butter Cream (p. 551).

When this cake has been made several layers high, for a wedding or a banquet, it should be adorned with flowers made of Royal Glaze (p. 556) and crowned, depending on the circumstances, with a bride, a small imitation vase, or a sugar flower. Especially in summer, well-beaten, frothy Royal Glaze can be used instead of Butter Cream; or decorate the cake with fruits, if it is filled with jam. (Figure 345, Page 552.)

BRIOCHE RING BRIOCHE COURONNE (D. and D.)

Brioche Paste (p. 546) for rings should be rather softish. To shape it, form the paste into a floured ball, then make a hole in the center with the finger; progressively enlarge this hole until the ring has the desired dimensions. Place on a buttered baking sheet. Let rise, brush with beaten egg, cut notches around the top, and bake in a hot oven. A very attractive effect can be made by fashioning small raised peaks around the top of the ring. To do this, take scissors in the right hand and make small cuts with the points of the scissors, from the inside of the ring; each time you make a cut, push the paste outward into a peak with the thumb of the left hand; take exactly the same amount of paste at each cut, being careful not to cut too deeply into the brioche, or it will not rise as it should. On the other hand, if enough paste is not cut, the peaks will not stand upright. Dip the tip of the scissors in water to prevent sticking. Brioche Ring requires a hotter oven than Brioche with a Cap. (Figure 342, Page 549.)

MOUSSELINE BRIOCHE BRIOCHE MOUSSELINE (D. and D.)

This brioche is made in smooth-sided, deep, buttered molds. Let it rise in a cool place so as not to hasten fermentation and spoil the quality. In winter it is sometimes necessary to force the fermentation. Sometimes it is made with a puffed top, but too often this falls inside or outside, and it is therefore better not to make one but to cut the surface (after brushing it with beaten egg) crosswise with scissors. Fasten a band of paper around the top of the mold with beaten egg. Bake in a medium oven. (Average time: 45 min.)

You can dispense with the paper band if you use a rather deep mold without a bottom; this way, the brioche is unmolded more easily and the bottom is neater. (Figure 342, Page 549.)

BRIOCHE WITH A CAP BRIOCHE À TÊTE (D. and D.)

The Brioche Paste (p. 546) should be rather firm. Take about ¼ of it to form the cap or puff; make a ball of the rest and place in the buttered mold. Roll the cap into a pear shape; use your finger to make a hole in the center of the ball, then stick the point of the pear-shaped piece into this hole; let it stand to rise. Next, brush with beaten egg, being careful not to spill any between the brioche and its cap, causing them to stick together. Before placing in the oven, use scissors to make a few cuts around the outside of the brioche. Bake in a medium oven.

It is better not to use much sugar in the paste for Brioche with a Cap, or it will brown too much in the oven. If there is danger of this happening, brush with water instead of egg. If the brioche turns brown enough before it is through baking, you can cover the top with a wet or buttered paper. (Figure 342, Page 549.)

Fig. 363 - Marquis (p. 573).
Fig. 364 - Millefeuille (p. 574).

MILANESE BRIOCHE BRIOCHE MILANAISE (D. and D.) (*For 10 persons*)

Roll out 1 lb. firm Brioche Paste (p. 546) into a strip 4 in. wide; spread 3½ oz. creamed butter on the paste, then sprinkle the top with dried currants and sultanas. Cut into 2-in. strips, roll them, and place them side by side in a buttered cake tin; let rise, then bake in a medium oven.

After baking, brush with apricot jam and sprinkle with dried currants, chopped pistachios, and granulated sugar.

PARISIAN BRIOCHE BRIOCHE PARISIENNE (D. and D.)

Cut off the top of a Mousseline Brioche (p. 565) ; cut out the soft inside, leaving a shell about ¾ in. thick; be careful not to stick the point of the knife all the way to the bottom—try to cut the inside out in a solid block. Fill the timbale thus formed with a mixture of preserved fruits bound with Apricot Sauce (p. 560) flavored with kirsch or maraschino; put the top back on, and, if you wish, use a shaker to sprinkle sugar on it.

Sometimes Parisian Brioche is finished by brushing the outside with apricot jam and then sprinkling it with chopped pistachios and granulated sugar. Instead of scattering the pistachios and sugar, you can place strips of paper on the bias across the brioche, sprinkle the granulated sugar in the spaces between the paper, and then remove the paper to set the pistachios in place. Serve hot.

YULE LOG BÛCHE DE NOËL (D. and D.)

The log can be made by joining layers of cake together with cream, but the best way is to use a rainpipe-shaped mold about 20 in. long to cook the paste in one piece. It can then be cut to make 3 cakes without any waste. Place the logs on a wide and rather thick base of Sweet Paste (p. 546), cover with a layer of coffee, chocolate, or chestnut Butter Cream (p. 551), and imitate the bark of the log with the same cream, using a pastry bag with a specially made small, flat, fluted tube. Spread the ends with white or coffee Butter Cream, making 2 or 3 lines with a knife to imitate the grain of the wood; use some finely chopped pistachios to simulate moss.

Note: The moss can also be imitated by pressing Almond Paste (p. 557) through a sieve. Gather it with the point of a knife. Make a trimming of ivy with green Almond Paste or sugar. (Figure 343, Page 552.)

CARRACK CARAQUE (P.) (*For 12 persons*)

¼ lb. sugar, 2 ⅔ oz. flour, 2 oz. cocoa powder, 2 oz. butter, 1 oz. grilled, grated almonds, 4 egg yolks and 4 stiffly beaten whites, baking powder. Beat the yolks with the sugar, then add cocoa and almonds; beat the whites, then add them with the melted butter and flour, mixing gently. Place in a Génoise mold with paper on the bottom to prevent sticking and bake 25 min.

Then make the cream. Beat over the fire, as in making a Génoise, 3 egg whites with 6 oz. confectioners' sugar to make a Cooked Meringue (p. 557). Then melt a little cocoa with a little water in a pan, add an egg-sized piece of butter, beat it when it is hot only, then add the meringue and 5 oz. creamed butter.

Split the cake in 2 and fill it, cover the sides with chocolate chips, and decorate the top with chocolate shavings in long rows. To make the shavings, melt some chocolate in a pan on the stove and let it cool, then reheat it to make it thicker. Pour it onto a marble slab, spread it out, and cut into shavings with a pastry wheel. Place these on the cake. They can also be shaved with a knife. Place 2 narrow strips of paper over the cake and sprinkle with confectioners' sugar. (Figure 344, Page 552.)

CHAMBORD CHAMBORD (P.) *(For 16 persons)*

Proportions: ½ lb. grilled hazelnuts, ½ lb. almonds, 1 lb. sugar, 16 stiffly beaten egg whites. For the butter cream: ¼ lb. sugar, ¼ lb. butter, ¼ lb. Praline (p. 559).

Grate the almonds and hazelnuts into a powder; mix with 1 lb. powdered sugar. Beat 16 egg whites until stiff and blend these carefully with the sugar-and-nut mixture; shape into circles on a buttered, floured baking sheet. Bake in a slow oven until crisp on the outside. Then make a praline butter cream by beating ¼ lb. sugar with 2 egg whites over a low fire as for meringue, and afterward blending in ¼ lb. butter and the Praline. Spread a layer of this cream between each cake circle; when the cake has thus been formed, frost the top and sides with an even layer of this same cream.

In the center of the cake set a fleur-de-lis made of sugar or Almond Paste (p. 557), and cover the sides and the rest of the surface with finely chopped, grilled almonds.

APPLE TURNOVER CHAUSSON AUX POMMES (D. and D.)

Prepare a round crust of Puff Paste (p. 544) or, better, of the paste trimmings; roll it out with a rolling pin to give it an elliptical shape and fill the center with applesauce or finely sliced apples sprinkled with vanilla-flavored sugar. Lift one part of the crust over the other after moistening the edges, then seal by forming a ridge with the fingers. Brush with beaten egg; make indented lines on the top without cutting the paste; bake in a medium oven. Glaze in the oven with powdered sugar or sirup. (Figure 375, Page 580.)

CHOCOLATE CAKE CHOCOLAT (GÂTEAU) (P.)

Fill a Génoise Cake (p. 549) with Chocolate Butter Cream (p. 551), then frost with chocolate. Rapidly stick grilled, powdered almonds to the frosting around the sides (¾ of the way up) before it has hardened and decorate with Royal Glaze (p. 556), using a pastry bag or a paper cone. (Figure 336, Page 548.)

CORNEVILLE CORNEVILLE (D. and D.)

Fill a round Génoise Cake (p. 549) with Vanilla Butter Cream (p. 551), brush with apricot jam, and cover with white frosting. Next, make some very small cones of Almond Paste (p. 557), or of Cat Tongue paste (p. 601). Fill 1 group of cones with pink Butter Cream, the rest with pistachio Butter Cream; set a rosette on the mouth of each cone, squeezing the rosettes from a pastry bag with a fluted tube. Plant 1 cone upright in the center, lay 6 flat around it, and make a border of green and pink cones, alternating the colors and pointing the tips toward the center.

CROQUEMBOUCHE CROQUEMBOUCHE (J.)

Prepare in advance the following of Nougat (p. 557): (1) A bottom layer molded in a round cake tin or mold. (2) Some small triangles cut with a knife and placed while still hot on a cylindrical form (rolling pin, bottle, etc.). (3) Crescents and other shapes cut with a pastry cutter, to be combined later to form the finial of the piece. Use cooked sugar to stick the triangles to the bottom layer.

Separately, prepare some small puffs, using Choux Paste (p. 548). Fill them with rum-flavored Butter Cream (p. 551) and glaze them with caramel. Stick these little puffs together with sugar cooked to the crack stage (see p. 562), using a special *croquembouche* mold. When they are held together well, place them on the bottom layer. Put the finial on top. Depending upon the occasion, this topmost ornament can be replaced by a flower, a bride, or a communicant. (Figure 346, Page 553.)

Note: Some or all of the puffs can be replaced with fruits glazed with caramel: prunes, dates, oranges, etc.

CUPID CUPIDON (P.)

Using a pattern, cut 5 thin heart-shaped layers of Puff Paste (p. 544); prick them with a fork and bake in a medium oven. Let cool completely. Spread the tops of 4 hearts with a layer of meringue cream with strawberries; then place the layers one on top of the other, with the fifth uncovered layer on top. Trim the sides of the cake, keeping its heart shape. This done, brush the top and sides of the cake with a layer of Reduced Apricot (p. 550), and stick chopped almonds over it. Frost the top with white Fondant (p. 553) flavored with kirsch. Using a pastry bag or a paper cone, decorate the top with a bouquet of leaves and stems made of melted green Fondant. Using another pastry bag or paper cone filled with pink Fondant, make flower petals, and place small rosettes at intervals all around the edge of the cake.

DACQUOISE DACQUOISE (Ga.)

Take 2 Dacquoise cake layers of the same size (see p. 554) and put them together with a thick layer (¾ in.) of Butter Cream (p. 551) in the middle: vanilla, coffee, pistachio, or chocolate praline. Carefully smooth the sides and keep in the refrigerator until serving time. (Figure 347. Page 553.)

Note: This cake is more attractive when frosted with powdered sugar.

CHECKERBOARD DAMIER (P.)

The decoration gives this cake its name. Bake a Génoise Cake (p. 549) in a buttered, floured square mold or cake tin, in a medium oven. When cooled, fill it with Chocolate Butter Cream (p. 551) or other flavor to taste. Spread a little of the cream around the sides, sticking grilled, chopped almonds over it; glaze the top neatly with Reduced Apricot (p. 550) and trace small squares with a paper cone filled with Royal Glaze (p. 556). These squares must be perfectly even, so it is a good idea to mark the divisions with the back of a knife over the Reduced Apricot. Merely follow these lines when squeezing out the Royal Glaze. Next, fill these squares, always using a paper cone, with chocolate Fondant (p. 553) for one group and white Fondant for the other—alternate the 2 colors as on a checkerboard. Use a paper cone to border the top of the cake with a chocolate-cream garland. (Figure 349, Page 553.)

DANICHEFF DANICHEFF (P.)

Fine Sponge Cake with Butter (p. 548) baked in a plain square mold or cake tin. Let cool; slice in half crosswise to make 2 layers and put together again with raspberry jam between the layers. Then prepare Italian Meringue (p. 557), using 4 egg whites. Cover the cake with a layer of this meringue about 1¼ in. thick; spread it smoothly on top and around. Heat a thin, rather long iron rod in the fire until red hot and draw a crisscross pattern over the meringue with it;

reheat it in the fire whenever necessary. This iron rod need only be pressed very lightly over the meringue to make the lines. Lay small diamonds of candied angelica between the spaces. Then re-cover everything, top and sides, with well-cooked (but cold) apricot jam. Remove the excess jam and stick chopped, grilled almonds all around the base of the cake. (Figure 348, Page 553.)

GIFT FROM NICE ENVOI DE NICE (J.)

Stuff and coat a rectangular Génoise Cake (p. 549) with a fine Mocha Butter Cream (p. 551). Prepare a layer of Nougat (p. 557) the same shape as the Génoise, but raised slightly along one side. Decorate the top and sides, imitating the braiding of a basket, with 2 Butter Creams: Coffee and Chocolate (p. 551). The directions are given below.

Place a bouquet of roses and mimosa with green leaves, all made of pulled sugar, on the cover. (Figure 350, Page 556.)

Braiding with Butter Creams: For this decoration, use a pastry bag with a tube with a small, plain, round opening filled with Chocolate Butter Cream, and a pastry bag with a tube with a wider, flat opening filled with Coffee Butter Cream.

(1) Make a perpendicular band with the chocolate cream (round opening). (2) Using the coffee cream (flat opening), lay 3 small, equally spaced horizontal bands on top. (3) Make another perpendicular band of chocolate. (4) Using the coffee cream, lay 3 more strips over this second chocolate band, interweaving them between the other 3 bands and reaching the first chocolate one. (5) Lay another perpendicular band of chocolate, and continue until finished. (Figure 116, p. 118.)

FINANCIER I (Recipe for many-layered cakes) FINANCIER (D. and D.) (*For 16 persons*)

Beat 1 lb. sugar over the fire with 16 egg whites; when the meringue is very stiff, add ½ lb. flour, 6 oz. finely powdered almonds, 4 oz. melted butter, kirsch, and vanilla. Mix well together before pouring into savarin molds of graduated size, buttered and sprinkled with chopped almonds. Bake in a rather hot oven, then arrange the layers one on the other, the smallest on top, brush with apricot jam, and frost with vanilla Fondant (p. 553). Decorate with Pistachio Butter Cream (p. 552).

FINANCIER II FINANCIER (D. and D.)

Use the proportions in the recipe for Genoa Loaf (p. 577); flavor generously with rum and vanilla. Bake, in rosette molds buttered and sprinkled with chopped almonds, in a medium oven. When the cake layers are cooked and cool, brush with red or natural-colored apricot jam, sprinkle with chopped pistachios and chopped almonds grilled in the oven.

FINANCIER III FINANCIER (P.) (*For 8 persons*)

5 oz. powdered sugar, 2½ oz. butter, 2½ oz. flour and cornstarch, 2 oz. powdered almonds, 2 oz. preserved fruits, 4 whole eggs and 2 yolks, 1 liqueur glass curaçao.

Work the paste over a slow fire, as in making Génoise Cake; then add the mixed flour, cornstarch, and almonds, the melted butter, and the curaçao. Next, butter a round cake mold or tin and sprinkle with very dry, finely shredded almonds and confectioners' sugar; half fill the mold with the paste; sprinkle the preserved fruits, finely diced, on top; finish filling with paste, and bake 45–50 min. in a medium oven. After removing from the oven, sprinkle with powdered sugar and serve very cold.

FLAMMARION FLAMMARION (D. and D.) (*For 8–12 persons*)

Make several round layers on a buttered, floured baking sheet, using the following mixture: ½ lb. almonds, ½ lb. granulated sugar, pinch of flour, 1½ oz. melted butter, and 5 stiffly beaten egg whites; make a layer in the shape of a crescent the same size as the round layers, and bake in a slow oven.

Cover the round layers with Chocolate Praline Butter Cream (p. 551) and put together, 2 or 3 layers high; place the crescent on top at one side. Frost the entire top of the cake with chocolate and cover the top and sides of the crescent with chopped, grilled almonds. On the chocolate frosting place 3 or 4 small stars made of Almond Paste (p. 557) and sprinkle with granulated sugar. Finish by decorating the edges of the crescent with Pistachio Butter Cream (p. 552), using a paper cone.

MILK FLAN FLAN AU LAIT (P.) (*For 8 persons*)

Line a round flan tin about 6 in. in diameter with Short Paste (p. 545), and prick the bottom with a fork. Make a cream by using a fork to beat 3 whole eggs with ¼ lb. vanilla-flavored sugar; then add 2 oz. flour and 12 oz. cold milk. When well mixed, strain it through a fine sieve into the tart shell; bake in a hot oven, especially hot on the bottom, since the paste takes longer to cook than the cream. It takes about 25 min. It can also be made without flour. (Figure 351, P. 556.)

MERINGUE FLAN FLAN MERINGUÉ (P.)

Make a Milk Flan, as described above, then, when cool, cover with a layer of Italian Meringue (p. 557) about 1¼ in. thick. Smooth the top and sides of the meringue until it has a very flat surface; then, using a pastry bag with a tiny opening, decorate the top with some of the same meringue, sprinkle with sugar, and heat a few minutes in a very slow oven to cook the meringue. Then fill the hollows in the decoration with a little red-currant jelly and clear apricot jam. (Figure 352, Page 557.)

FRIAND FRIAND (Ga.)

Friand layers (see p. 554), filled with strawberry jam, the top frosted pink. Crushed Praline (p. 559) around the sides.

BRIE-CHEESE SURPRISE FROMAGE DE BRIE EN SURPRISE (P.)

Make a Génoise Cake (p. 549) in a fairly large flan tin, and bake in a rather hot oven. When the Génoise is cold, cut it into 2 layers, placing between them a filling of Butter Cream (p. 551) flavored with kirsch or vanilla. Cover the outside with the same cream and sprinkle generously with granulated sugar tinted light green. Next, cover the top with powdered sugar. Imitate the cheese by making streaks with the back of a knife. (Figure 354, Page 557.)

ROQUEFORT-CHEESE CAKE FROMAGE DE ROQUEFORT (P.)

Make an Ordinary Génoise Cake (p. 550); after baking, cut the cake to imitate a wedge of Roquefort cheese. Fill with Butter Cream (p. 551) flavored with kirsch and mixed with finely chopped pistachios; cover the outside of the slice with the same cream, imitating the natural marbling of Roquefort. (Figure 353, Page 557.)

TWELFTH CAKE[1] I GALETTE DES ROIS (P.)

Make Twelfth Cake Paste (p. 545). Gather the paste into a round ball and flatten it with a rolling pin, keeping it very round and ½ in. thick; make a notch in the bottom to insert the bean; brush the top with beaten egg, make a crisscross pattern with the back of a knife, prick it 6 or 8 times with the tip of a knife, and bake about 20 min. in a very hot oven. (Figure 355, Page 560.)

TWELFTH CAKE II GALETTE DES ROIS (P.) (*For 8 persons*)

Gently knead, using the tips of the fingers, 12 oz. flour with ½ lb. butter, some fine salt, and 3 oz. cold water; make a softish, imperfectly mixed paste and finish this flour-and-butter mixture by rolling it out, folding, and rolling again 2 or 3 times—that is, if the butter has not been well blended into the mixture after the second time, fold and roll again. Let stand 15 min., then spread out the paste to make the cake as described above.

FROSTED GÉNOISE CAKE GÉNOISE GLACÉE (P.)

Bake a Génoise Cake (p. 549) in a buttered, floured mold or tin. When the cake is cool, split it into 2 layers and fill with any jam or Butter Cream (p. 551) flavored to taste; frost it with a Fondant (p. 553) flavored and colored to go with the filling. Finish by decorating with preserved fruits, almonds, cream, or Royal Glaze (p. 556).

GRAND CROSS GRAND-CROIX (J.)

Fill and frost a Fine Génoise Cake (p. 549) with Mousseline Butter Cream (p. 551) flavored with maraschino. Cover with Chocolate Fondant (p. 553). Cover the sides with chopped, grilled almonds. Place a beautiful red ribbon of pulled sugar on top and a cross of the Legion of Honor made of Almond Paste (p. 557) and decorated with a brush. Finish with a delicate decoration of Royal Glaze (p. 556).

HEDGEHOG HÉRISSON (D. and D.)

Bake Génoise Cake (p. 549) in oval flan tins in different sizes, to be able to form the humped back of the hedgehog without using too many paste trimmings. Stick these layers on an oval base; fill with 3 or 4 layers of Praline Butter Cream (p. 552); round off the back and cover completely with the same cream; sprinkle with granulated Praline (p. 559) and stick the back with slivered, grilled almonds; imitate the ears with 2 almond halves and the eyes with Royal Glaze (p. 556).

KUGELHOFF KUGELHOFF (P.)

Fill special glazed pottery molds for Kugelhoff half full of Kugelhoff Paste (p. 547). Let rise; bake in a medium oven. Sprinkle with powdered sugar before serving. (Figure 357, Page 560.)

MAGENTA MAGENTA (P.) (*For 8 persons*)

Mash ¼ lb. almonds with ¼ lb. sugar, first moistening with 1 egg; then, when the paste is quite fine, add 2 more whole eggs, 1 by 1, and 1 yolk. Beat the paste thoroughly, then finish it by mixing in ¼ lb. creamed butter and finally 1½ oz. rice flour (cream of rice). Pour this paste into a round mold lined with Sweet Paste (p. 546) and pricked on the bottom; moisten the Sweet Paste with

---

[1] A cake that used to be served at a feast on Twelfth Night, the person receiving the slice with the bean in it being acclaimed king of the feast.

a little water so that the paste with the almonds will stick to it. Sprinkle slivered almonds on top and bake 40–45 min. in a medium oven. When it is cold, cover the top with Reduced Apricot (p. 550) containing a little red coloring and stick a small ring of chopped pistachios around the sides of the cake.

MANON MANON (P.)

Half fill a buttered charlotte mold with Savarin Paste (p. 547) ; let rise to ¾ the height of the mold, then bake about 40 min. in a hot oven. Prick with a long needle to test if properly cooked, then unmold. When it is cold, split it crosswise into 5 layers, moistening each one with kirsch. Rebuild the cake, spreading the first layer with vanilla Pastry Cream (p. 552), the second with Chocolate Cream (p. 552), vanilla cream on the third, and chocolate on the fourth; cover with the fifth layer. When the cake has been rebuilt, spread kirsch-flavored Reduced Apricot (p. 550) over it and cover top and sides with slivered, grilled almonds; sprinkle with confectioners' sugar. (Figure 358, Page 561.)

MARBLE CAKE MARBRÉ (D. and D.)

Fill a round Génoise Cake (p. 549) with Chocolate Butter Cream (p. 551). Cover entirely with apricot jam. Frost the top of the cake with almost cold Chocolate Fondant (p. 553) ; then, using a paper cone, make a few spots of white Fondant; with the tip of a knife, draw fine lines outward from these white spots, then make other white lines in between, tracing them back toward the center. Cover the sides with chopped, grilled almonds.

Various flavors and colors can be used for the frosting. The lines may also be made with paper cones filled with red-currant or apricot jam.

MARCELIN or **ROYAL** MARCELIN OF RÉAL (D. and D.) (*For 30 persons*)

Line flat, round cake tins with a thin layer of paste for lining Marcelins (see directly below) or, if that is impossible, a thin layer of Sweet Paste (p. 546), and fill them to the brim with the following paste. Mash 1½ oz. freshly shelled almonds with kirsch and anisette; beat separately 1 lb. powdered sugar with 10 egg yolks, mix in the mashed almonds, ½ oz. flour, and 10 beaten egg whites. Sprinkle rather heavily with powdered sugar so that in baking it will form a crust; bake in a very slow oven. (Figure 359, Page 561.)

Paste for lining Marcelins: 2 lb. flour, 1 lb. confectioners' sugar, 4–5 whole eggs, depending on size, rum and vanilla, 1 lb. butter (for 5 or 6 cakes). This paste should, preferably, be made in advance, and the flan tins also lined in advance—say, the night before. This sweet paste, intended simply to support the almond paste, should be as thin as possible. This is a very old French cake, highly appreciated for its lightness.

MARIGNAN MARIGNAN (D. and D.)

Make Savarin Paste (p. 547), let rise, and bake in a cake tin. Soak in Savarin sirup, drain well, cut a thin slice off the top for a lid, and garnish with a rather heavy layer of Italian Meringue (p. 557). Cover the lid and sides with apricot jam and decorate with meringue. This cake may also be finished by cutting off the top for a lid, filling with meringue in such a way that it looks like the two raised sides of a hamper, and replacing the lid cut in half. Simulate the handle with a narrow band of candied angelica or a thin ribbon of pulled sugar; decorate with meringue. (Figure 360, Page 564.)

Fig. 365 - Orange mousse (p. 575).
Fig. 366 - Neapolitan (p. 575).

Fig. 365

Fig. 366

Fig. 368

Fig. 367

Fig. 369

CHESTNUT CAKE I MARRONNIER (D. and D.)

Fill a round Génoise Cake (p. 549) with Chestnut Butter Cream (p. 551), brush with apricot jam, and frost with chocolate. Write the word "Marron" (Chestnut) and decorate with Royal Glaze (p. 556), using a paper cone. (Figure 362, Page 564.)

CHESTNUT CAKE II MARRONNIER (D. and D.)

Make an oval Génoise Cake (p. 549); lay it on a base of Sweet Paste (p. 546); fill it with kirsch-flavored Chestnut Butter Cream (p. 551); cover with pale-green or chestnut-colored frosting. In the center place some chestnuts with half-open burrs made of Almond Paste (p. 557), green for the burrs and dark brown for the inside. (Figure 361, Page 564.)

CHESTNUT CAKE CORRÉZIENNE MARRONS (GÂTEAU DE) À LA CORRÉZIENNE (Gi.) (*For 8 persons*)

This is real home pastry, doubly recommended because it is easy to make and keeps for several days.

The paste: Sift onto the baking table 7 oz. flour and shape it into a ring. Place in the middle 2½ oz. powdered sugar, 2½ oz. creamed butter, pinch of salt, 2 egg yolks, and 3 oz. milk. Mix well together, and flatten out the paste twice with the palm of the hand, then roll it into a ball and keep in a cool place; this should be done at least 2 hr. in advance.

The chestnuts and cake filling: Slit the shells of 1 qt. chestnuts, plunge them into a pot of boiling water, and leave 5 min. Then drain them and peel off shell and skin. Place them in a stewpan with 12 oz. boiling milk, ½ vanilla bean, a pinch of salt, and cook slowly. As soon as cooked, mash them in the pan with a pestle, or press them through a sieve. It is preferable simply to mash them, so the cake keeps its original character. Remove the vanilla bean and add: 2 tbsp. powdered sugar, 4 tbsp. heavy fresh cream, 3 stiffly beaten egg whites. (Note that the sugar is added to the chestnuts after cooking because they cook better and faster without sugar.)

Baking the pastry: Heavily butter a flan or round cake tin 7 in. in diameter. Roll out the paste about ⅛ in. thick. Line the tin by letting the paste fall and pressing it against the tin with the tip of the fingers. Cut off the excess paste around the edges, using a pastry roll cutter. Then make a ridge along the rim by thickening the paste with the fingers. Using special pincers (see Figure 105, p. 116), pinch the edges of the crust. Set the flan on a baking sheet and prick the bottom of the paste with a small knife to avoid producing blisters while baking. Pour in the chestnut mixture and bake 35–40 min. in a slow oven. Before serving, powder the surface with vanilla-flavored sugar, and serve warm or, preferably, cold.

MARQUIS MARQUIS (P.) (*For 8 persons*)

Make a Génoise Cake with 3 eggs (p. 549); bake it in a round cake mold in a medium oven. When it is cold, slice it in 3 layers and fill with Chocolate Praline Butter Cream (p. 551); brush with apricot jam and stick on chopped, grilled almonds. On top make a dome of strongly vanilla-flavored Chantilly Cream (p. 552); around the cream place diamonds of Nougat (p. 557). Using a pastry bag with a very fine tube, squeeze the remaining Chocolate Butter Cream like small vermicelli over the Chantilly Cream. (Figure 363, Page 565.)

Fig. 367 - Walnut cake (p. 576).
Fig. 368 - Hazelnut cake (p. 575).
Fig. 369 - Cake in shape of whole-meal bread (p. 576).

MARYSE MARYSE (P.)

Line a pie tin with Puff Paste (p. 544), prick the bottom with a fork, and fill with Almond Cream for Pithiviers (p. 550); bake in a medium oven. Cover with Swiss Meringue (p. 557); using a pastry bag, decorate as artistically as possible; powder with sugar, and replace in a slow oven 6–8 min. to dry the meringue and give it a crust without browning it too much.

MASCOT MASCOTTE (P.)

Bake Génoise paste (p. 549) in a buttered, floured cake pan, 35–40 min. in a medium oven; unmold and let cool. Meanwhile, prepare Hazelnut Butter Cream (p. 552) with which to fill the cake when it is cold. Cover with Reduced Apricot (p. 550), then frost with Coffee Fondant (p. 553). While still moist, quickly stick chopped, grilled almonds to the sides; decorate the top with halved, grilled hazelnuts.

MEXICAN CAKE MEXICAIN (P.) (*For 8 persons*)

¼ lb. powdered sugar, 3 oz. flour, 2½ oz. butter, 1 oz. cocoa powder, 4 whole eggs and 1 yolk.

Mix the batter as in making a sponge cake, with egg yolk and sugar beaten in a bowl; then add cocoa, flour, and stiffly beaten egg whites at the same time; add the melted butter last. Bake about 40 min. in a buttered, floured cake pan in a medium oven. When the sponge cake is cold, cut it into 2 layers and fill with Chocolate Butter Cream (p. 551). Put the layers together and cover with Reduced Apricot (p. 550); frost with Chocolate Fondant (p. 553). While the Fondant is still warm, trace fine parallel lines of Royal Glaze (p. 556) across the top, using a heavy paper cone. As soon as this is done, cross these lines with the tip of a knife at regular intervals, first in one direction and then in the other. This makes a simple, but pretty, decoration.

MIKADO MIKADO (P.) (*For 10 persons*)

Make a Swiss Meringue paste (p. 557) with 2 egg whites and ¼ lb. vanilla-flavored sugar. Shape this paste into 3 round, equal-sized pancakes on a buttered, floured baking sheet. Powder with sugar and bake in a slow oven; loosen the paste from the baking sheet, return to the oven, and let finish drying at low heat.

Meanwhile, make some Ordinary Génoise paste (p. 550) with ¼ lb. sugar, 3 eggs, ¼ lb. flour, 1½ oz. butter, vanilla. Prepare a cream with 5 oz. butter well blended with 3½ oz. sugar, then mix in 4 or 5 tbsp. very cold rum-flavored Pastry Cream (p. 552).

Build the cake by placing a layer of Génoise Cake, about ⅜ in. thick, on the bottom; cover it with the cream, place one of the meringue pancakes on top, and then another layer of cream; all in all, 3 layers of each paste. Spread the cream over top and sides and sprinkle with chopped, grilled almonds. If a little cream is left over, use it in a paper cone to decorate the top of the cake.

MILLEFEUILLE MILLEFEUILLE (P.)

Cut some round crusts of Puff Paste (p. 544). Place them on moistened baking sheets and cut out the center part; make 2 other circles larger than the first, without the centers cut out, to be used as top and bottom; sugar, prick with a fork, and bake in a hot oven. The number and size of the crusts depend upon the number of guests. Place the crusts, one on top of the other, alternating the layers with apricot jam and red-currant jelly; cover the sides with meringue and lightly frost the top white. On top place 20–25 hollow, baked Puff-Paste rings, arranging them in circles with the rings overlapping; powder lightly with confectioners' sugar. All around the sides, cover with dried currants and chopped, grilled almonds. (Figure 364, Page 565.)

Note: May also be made in a square shape.

MOCHA MOKA (D. and D.)

Make a round Génoise or sponge cake (p. 549) ; fill the layers with Coffee Butter Cream (p. 551). Spread this same cream over top and sides of the cake; sprinkle granulated sugar (not the finely granulated kind, but the kind called "mocha" sugar) all around the sides, and, using a pastry bag with a fluted tube, decorate the top. The rule says the sugar is stuck all around the sides of the cake, but chopped, grilled almonds are better.

ORANGE MOUSSE MOUSSE À L'ORANGE (P.) (*For 8 persons*)

¼ lb. powdered sugar, 1½ oz. flour, 1½ oz. potato flour, 4 egg yolks, 3 beaten whites, peel from 1 orange.

Place the sugar in a bowl with the grated orange peel; add the egg yolks and beat with a spatula until you have a creamy, whitish paste; pour in a few drops of carmine to give it a pink tint; then carefully blend in the sifted flours along with the stiffly beaten egg whites. Mixing must be done carefully so that this mousseline cake will not lose its characteristic lightness. Bake 40 min. in a slow oven, in a buttered, floured cake pan. When cold, frost with white or pink Fondant (p. 553) and decorate with candied orange peel. (Figure 365, Page 572.)

NEAPOLITAN (Many-layered cake) NAPOLITAIN (D. and D.) (*For 12 persons*)

¾ lb. powdered almonds, ¾ lb. sugar beaten with 4 eggs, ¾ lb. butter, 1 lb. flour, vanilla.

Press out the paste with the palm of the hand, then roll out a sheet ⅜ in. thick; cut out 6 or 8 circles, cutting out their centers, so they become rings; make 2 larger, solid circles for top and bottom, and bake in a medium oven. Stack the open circles on one of the solid layers, covering each one with hot Reduced Apricot (p. 550) ; trim, then cover with the second solid layer and glaze with Reduced Apricot or rather thin rum-flavored Fondant (p. 553.) Decorate with fruits or Royal Glaze (p. 556). (Figure 366, Page 572.)

HAZELNUT CAKE NOISETTINE (J.)

Fill and frost a Génoise Cake (p. 549) with Coffee Butter Cream (p. 551) containing grilled, crushed hazelnuts. Cover with Coffee Fondant (p. 553). Stick chopped, grilled almonds or hazelnuts all around the sides. Write the word *Noisettine* on top, using Chocolate or Coffee Fondant.

Prepare a little green Almond Paste (p. 557) ; cover 3 hazelnuts with the Almond Paste, making little balls; cut notches with a knife to simulate hazelnuts in buds. Roll out the rest of the Almond Paste and cut 3 leaves with a fluted, oval cookie cutter; imitate the veins in the leaves with the tip of a knife. Place the leaves and then the nuts under the name on the cake. (Figure 368, Page 573.)

NORMAN CAKE NORMAND (J.)

Make 2 square crusts of Puff-Paste (p. 544) trimmings. Prick with a fork. Using a flat-bladed knife, spread a thin layer of Royal Glaze (p. 556) on one of these crusts. Bake about 25–30 min. in a slow oven. Let cool, then fill with Norman-style apples—quartered apples reduced in butter. Place the glazed crust on top. Sprinkle chopped, grilled almonds on the four corners and center of the cake. (Figure 356, Page 560.)

WALNUT CAKE NOYER (D. and D.)

Slice a square Génoise Cake (p. 549) into layers and fill with Praline Butter Cream (p. 552) containing chopped walnuts; frost the top with Coffee Butter Cream (p. 551) ; cover the sides with grilled, slivered almonds. Decorate with halves of walnut shells made of Almond Paste (p. 557), with green Almond-Paste leaves in the spaces between. (Figure 367, Page 573.)

CAKE IN SHAPE OF WHOLE-MEAL BREAD I PAIN COMPLET (Du.) (*For 24 persons*)

Beat ½ lb. powdered sugar with 16 egg yolks in a bowl; add 5 oz. flour, 5 oz. potato flour, a little vanilla-flavored sugar; then, separately, beat 16 egg whites until very stiff and blend in ½ lb. sugar; combine the 2 mixtures. Then, using a pastry bag, shape the mixture into large balls on buttered, floured baking sheets. Have ready a mixture of 3½ oz. cornstarch and 3½ oz. powdered sugar, put into a shaker; sprinkle the paste generously with this powder. Cross-hatch the surface by bearing down on it with a piece of string; bake in a slow oven. When baked, place the cake on a rack with a pad under the cake to keep it from sinking and to preserve its dome shape; fill the inside, without leaving any trace of where it was cut, with a Butter Cream (p. 551) lightly flavored with Praline, kirsch, and vanilla. When the cake is filled, follow the cross-hatch lines on top with lines of apricot jam (with the aid of a paper cone with a fine opening), using it sparingly; lay thin bands of paper about ⅜ in. wide crosswise over these lines, repeating the cross-hatch pattern; finish by powdering generously with confectioners' sugar, and then remove the bands of paper. (Figure 369, Page 573.)

Note: To conceal the cut made for the filling, you can cut the cake through the bottom, removing a cone of paste from the inside and then filling it. This cake can be made of ordinary sponge-cake paste (p. 548), but the above is preferred.

CAKE IN SHAPE OF WHOLE-MEAL BREAD II PAIN COMPLET (P.)

Roll out 2 crusts of Puff Paste (p. 544) ⅛ in. thick; in the center of one crust place Frangipane Cream (p. 552) with rum or other flavoring; weld the 2 crusts together with a little water and evenly spread the following composition on top: 1½ oz. sugar, 1½ oz. powdered almonds, ½ egg white; powder with confectioners' sugar and make a few shallow furrows on the surface; bake 20 min. in a medium oven.

SPICE LOAF PAIN D'ÉPICE (A.)

Spice Loaf has been known since ancient times; it was probably invented right after bread. From the Orient, where it was greatly appreciated, it spread to Europe. The Greeks served it for dessert, and the Romans made offerings of it to their gods. In the Middle Ages in France, it was served at court dinners, especially at Rheims. During the reign of Louis XIV, rye flour, honey, molasses, anise, clove, and cinnamon were added to its composition.

Fig. 370 - Genoa loaf (p. 577).
Fig. 371 - Motley or National cake (p. 577).

Fig. 370

Fig. 371

Fig. 372

Fig. 373

Today there are many recipes for Spice Loaf. Here is one with which I have had good results. Take 1 lb. flour, 10 oz. water, ½ lb. honey, ½ lb. sugar, 1½ oz. rum, 1 tsp. bicarbonate of soda, ½ tsp. powdered green anise, pinch of powdered cinnamon, dash of salt. Dissolve the sugar, honey, bicarbonate of soda, and salt in boiling water; add the rum, anise, and cinnamon. Blend in the flour to make a smooth, unlumpy paste. Heavily butter a mold, pour in the mixture, begin baking in a very hot oven, then continue in a medium oven—1 hr. baking is enough.

Serve Spice Loaf with fresh butter.

If you do not like Spice Loaf too firm, use less flour and add more water.

For variety, any of the following ingredients may be added to the recipe: almonds or pistachios plain or grilled, coriander seed, star anise, clove, ginger, preserved fruits, candied orange or lemon peel, candied angelica, raisins, pitted prunes, fresh angelica, citron soaked in rum, kirsch or maraschino, jams, fruit jellies, liqueurs, etc.

GENOA LOAF PAIN DE GÊNES (P.) (*For 8 persons*)

5 oz. powdered sugar, ¼ lb. butter, 3½ oz. almonds, 1¼ oz. flour or potato flour, 3 whole eggs, pinch of salt, 1 liqueur glass of kirsch.

Pound the almonds very fine, gradually adding ½ the sugar to keep them from turning to oil; put the butter, softened a little with heat, into a rather large bowl; add the rest of the sugar and beat thoroughly with a whisk. When the mixture begins to whiten, add the mashed almonds and continue beating; then mix in the 3 eggs, 1 by 1, at 2- or 3-minute intervals; do not be disturbed when you see the mixture turn when the last egg is added. Continue beating this cream for a moment and finish by adding the salt (very little), flour, and, finally, the kirsch (which can be replaced by any other flavoring). Pour this batter into a buttered Genoa mold (square cake pan) with buttered paper on the bottom; bake 40 min. in a medium oven at even temperature. This cake can be made in advance and served as is, without any sort of frosting or decoration.
(Figure 370, Page 576.)

Note: When pounded or mashed almonds are needed for a cake, they can be grated into powder with a small grater that can be bought in stores. These are easier to find than a mortar, and it is less tiring to grate than to pound, especially if the almonds are dry.

MOTLEY or **NATIONAL CAKE** PANACHÉ OR NATIONAL (P.)

Fill and decorate a Fine Génoise Cake (p. 549) in quarters with 4 different Butter Creams (p. 551): coffee, chocolate, pistachio, and vanilla. The top decoration is made by squeezing the Butter Cream into small points, using a pastry bag with a small fluted tube. Cover the sides with chopped, grilled almonds. (Figure 371, Page 576.)

BASKET OF FRUIT PANIER DE FRUITS (J.)

Fill and frost an oval-shaped Génoise Cake (p. 549) with Chocolate Butter Cream (p. 551). Take a sheet of white paper and, with a pencil, trace the shape of a basket handle, taking the size of the Génoise Cake into consideration; the handle should be stuck to opposite sides of the cake.

Using a paper cone, fill the pattern of the handle with thick chocolate enriched with cocoa butter, and containing a little sugar; do not try to smooth it

Fig. 372 - Paris-Brest (p. 578).
Fig. 373 - Easter cake (p. 578).

out—let it give the impression of wood and bark. Let cool. Meanwhile, using the same paper cone and filling, make imitation interwoven twigs around the sides of the cake. Turn over the piece of paper filled with chocolate to make the handle; if the chocolate is cold, it should be detached easily in 1 piece. Repeat the same operation on the flat side of the handle and let cool again.

The fruits are made of Sponge Cake (p. 548) cut in various shapes and filled with Pastry Cream (p. 552) or simply stuck together with Reduced Apricot (p. 550). Cover them with melted Almond Paste (p. 557), shaping and coloring to resemble some fruit: banana, apple, pear, peach, fig, etc. Make a few leaves of green Almond Paste. When all this has been done, put the handle on the cake, holding it in place with a little of the chocolate mixture. Decorate the top with the Almond-Paste leaves, then arrange the imitation fruit. If desired, the cake may be decorated with a ribbon of pulled sugar.

PARIS-BREST or **PARIS-NICE** PARIS-BREST OR PARIS-NICE (D. and D.)

Lay a ring of Choux Paste (p. 548) on a buttered baking sheet (see Figure 107, p. 117); brush with beaten egg, and bake. Then slice the ring through and fill with Saint-Honoré Cream (p. 552) containing Praline (p. 559). Powder the top with vanilla-flavored confectioners' sugar. (Figure 372, Page 577.)

EASTER CAKE I PASCAL (GÂTEAU) (J.)

Fill and cover a square Génoise Cake (p. 549) with Praline Butter Cream (p. 552). Frost the top with chocolate Fondant (p. 553). Cover the sides with chopped, grilled almonds. Prepare Nougat (p. 557) in the shape of half an egg (using a special egg mold); place the half egg on the cake and decorate with Royal Glaze (p. 556). Finish with a border of Chocolate Butter Cream (p. 551) squeezed from a pastry bag with a small fluted tube. (Figure 373, Page 577.)

EASTER CAKE II (Children's) PASCAL (GÂTEAU FANTAISIE) (J.)

Fill a Génoise Cake (p. 549) with any desired cream. Frost with green Fondant (p. 553). Cover the sides with chocolate shot. Decorate the top, using thick chocolate enriched with cocoa butter and containing a little sugar, and white and yellow Fondant. This is a cake for children.

PEACE CAKE PAX (GÂTEAU DE) (P.) (*For 8 persons*)

Beat together 1/4 lb. sugar and 2 1/2 oz. powdered almonds with 4 egg yolks and 1 whole egg; then mix in 7 oz. chocolate cooked with very little water or milk to make a paste; when perfectly cool, mix in 2 1/2 oz. flour with 4 stiffly beaten egg whites; finish with 3 1/2 oz. butter melted to a cream. Bake this paste, in 1 or 2 well-buttered, floured savarin molds, 25–30 min., in a fairly hot oven. Unmold and frost with chocolate Fondant (p. 553), then fill the center of the cake with a cream made by mixing together 3 egg yolks, 3 1/2 oz. sugar, 3 1/2 oz. chocolate, 1 1/4 oz. cocoa powder, 1 1/2 oz. cream of rice, and 1 cup milk. Bring to a full boil, then remove from the fire and add 3 1/2 oz. butter. Let cool before filling the center of the cake. This is also called Bridge Cake.

PITHIVIERS PITHIVIERS (D. and D.)

Prepare a round crust using Puff-Paste (p. 544) trimmings; fill the center with rum-flavored Almond Cream (p. 550), moisten the edges with water, then cover with another whole crust of Puff Paste cut with a pastry cutter with a very keen blade; brush with beaten egg; then, using the tip of a knife, streak the top crust like a rosette or a pinwheel; gently press the sides in a scallop pattern; powder with a sugar shaker, and bake in a medium oven. It is a good idea to let it stand a few minutes before putting it into the oven, to avoid shrinking.

A cake 8 in. in diameter takes 7–7½ oz. Puff Paste and about 5¼ oz. Almond Cream. (Figure 374, Page 580.)

Note: Sometimes, if the oven is not quite hot enough, the sugar will not melt. If this happens, simply brush the surface with sirup, return to the oven to dry, and the cake will have the same shiny glaze.

HOMEMADE PLUM CAKE PLUMCAKE DE MÉNAGE (P.) (*For 8 persons*)

Using a whisk, beat in a bowl ¼ lb. soft butter with ¼ lb. powdered sugar; when this is very frothy, add 1 whole egg, beat briskly 3 min., then add another egg; beat another 3 min. and add the third and last egg; when the last has been well beaten, use a spoon to blend into this paste 5¼ oz. flour, ½ tsp. salt, ½ tsp. baking powder, and, finally, 5 oz. diced, candied fruits macerated in rum. Bake in buttered cake pans lined bottom and sides with white paper. Bake 5 min. in a very hot oven, then reduce to medium heat and bake 35–40 min. Can be kept fresh several days. (Figure 376, Page 580.)

Professional bakers advise mixing the fruits into the paste before the flour, to prevent their sinking to the bottom while baking.

STRAWBERRY SPRING CAKE PRINTANIER AUX FRAISES (GÂTEAU) (D. and D.)

Bake 2 Génoise Cakes (p. 549) in 2 circles of the same size. Crush 7 oz. tiny strawberries and mix with 3½ oz. sugar and 1 liqueur glass of kirsch; spread this purée on one of the cake layers and cover with the other. Spread a layer of meringue over top and sides and sprinkle with finely chopped pistachios. Then, using a pastry bag with fluted tube, make a border of meringue. At intervals on the meringue border lay candied cherries alternated with pistachio halves. Lightly brown in the oven, then finish by placing fresh strawberries, covered with red-currant jelly flavored with kirsch, in the center. (Fig. 377, P. 581)

PROGRESS CAKE I PROGRÈS (D. and D.) (*For 15 persons*)

Crush dry ¼ lb. hazelnuts, ¼ lb. almonds, ½ lb. sugar, then mix in 10 stiffly beaten egg whites and 2 oz. melted butter. Prepare like Layers for Success Cake (p. 554), put several layers together with Praline Butter Cream (p. 552) between, spread a layer of this cream over top and sides, stick chopped, grilled almonds around the sides, and write the word "Progress" in the Butter Cream on top.

This cake is also made with Coffee or Chocolate Butter Cream, the top frosted only with Fondant (p. 553). In this case the name is written with a paper cone filled with Fondant.

PROGRESS CAKE II PROGRÈS (P.)

Prepare a Progress Cake mix (p. 554). Spread this paste into 3 or 4 round pancakes no thicker than a half dollar on 1 or more floured, buttered baking sheets. Bake 10 min. in a medium oven, then, as soon as cooked, loosen the cakes and trim the edges so they are all perfectly round, since they may have lost their shape while baking. Cool them on a flat surface. Place one layer on top of another with a thick layer of Chocolate Praline Butter Cream (p. 551) between. Spread this cream over the top and sides of the cake, then stick chopped, grilled almonds to the sides; powder the top with confectioners' sugar, then, with a paper cone filled with Chocolate Butter Cream (without Praline), write the word "Progress" in the center.

For variety's sake, a thin round layer of melted Almond Paste (p. 557) can be placed in the center of the cake and the name written over it. (Figure 378, Page 581.)

ROYAL RÉAL (D. and D.)

Also called Marcelin. (See p. 572.)

REGENT CAKE RÉGENT (P.)

Make 3 round layers of Génoise Cake (p. 549) with a filling of Butter Cream (p. 551), thick jam, or chestnut purée between each layer, but none on top. When the layers have been assembled, cover the cake with very reduced apricot jam, then decorate the center with a round slice of candied fruit surrounded with almond halves to imitate a daisy. Frost the whole cake with a rum-flavored Fondant (p. 553) thin enough so that the almond decoration shows through. To make the Fondant translucent, heat it a little more than usual, and frost the cake quickly and generously. The surplus Fondant that drips off can be gathered up afterward for other uses. A very old French cake. (Figure 379, Page 588.)

NUN RELIGIEUSE (D. and D.)

Line a round cake mold with Short or Sweet Paste (p. 546); fill with dried fruit pits or beans, and bake. Then make some Éclairs (p. 589) larger at one end than at the other, and 2 or 3 Cream-Puff shells (p. 587), 1 large, the others smaller. Fill them with Saint-Honoré Cream (p. 552) flavored with vanilla, coffee, or chocolate, and frost them with Fondant (p. 553) of the same flavor. Fill the empty cake crust with Saint-Honoré Cream, building it into a dome shape; stand the Éclairs upright around the cream dome, sticking them into place with cooked sugar; put the Cream Puffs on top and decorate the spaces between with Butter Cream (p. 551). (Figure 380, Page 588.)

ROSEMARY ROSE-MARIE (P.) (*For 8 persons*)

Prepare in advance an almond sponge cake by beating in a bowl ¼ lb. sugar with 4 egg yolks. Then mix in 2 oz. powdered almonds and 1 whole egg. Whip 4 egg whites until stiff and blend them into the mixture, along with 2½ oz. flour. Finally, add 3½ oz. melted butter. Bake in a buttered, floured round cake pan. Let the cake cool, cut it into 3 layers, and fill with a cream made by pounding in a mortar 3½ oz. almonds with 3½ oz. sugar and mixing with 2½ oz. melted butter and 2½ oz. melted chocolate. Brush the entire cake with Reduced Apricot (p. 550), then frost with chocolate Fondant (p. 553). Decorate with a bouquet of roses made of pulled sugar and a delicate motif of Royal Glaze (p. 556). (Figure 381, Page 589.)

ST. CHRISTOPHER SAINT-CHRISTOPHE (P.)

Make a round layer of Sweet Paste (p. 546) like a large pancake; prick

Fig. 374 - Pithiviers (p. 578).
Fig. 375 - Apple turnover (p. 567).
Fig. 376 - Plum cake (p. 579).

Fig. 374

Fig. 375

Fig. 376

Fig. 377

Fig. 378

with a fork and bake in a hot oven. Meanwhile, using an ordinary éclair pastry bag, lay out some rings of Choux Paste (p. 548) on a clean baking sheet; make 5 rings of graduated size, the largest being slightly smaller than the Sweet-Paste crust and the others diminishing in size, with the smallest still quite open in the center; brush them with beaten egg and bake in a hot oven, keeping them rather dry. Next frost them with coffee Fondant (p. 553) flavored with kirsch and place them on the cold layer of Sweet Paste, 1 on top the other; when 3 have been put in place, fill the center with Chantilly Cream (p. 552) mixed with strawberries or candied chestnuts, depending on the season. Place the last 2 rings into position and finish filling with cream until the cream stands higher than the top ring.

SAINT-HONORÉ SAINT-HONORÉ (P.)

Make a flat cake of Short Paste (p. 545) about 1/8 in. thick and cut it to the size of a small plate. Prick it well with a fork and, using a pastry bag with a tube as thick as a finger, lay a ring of Choux Paste (p. 548) around the edges. Brush the top with beaten egg and cook in a fairly hot oven. Make about 15 balls of Choux Paste half as large as walnuts and bake them in a hot oven. When everything has been baked and has cooled, cook 5 oz. lump sugar with a little water until melted, and cook until it reaches the "crack" stage (see p. 562); dip the small Choux-Paste balls into this sugar and stick them around the border of the Saint-Honoré, filling the center with Saint-Honoré Cream (p. 552). (Figure 382, Page 589.)

CASUAL CAKE SANS-GÊNE (D. and D.) (*For 6 persons*)

Beat in a bowl 7 oz. powdered sugar and 4 egg yolks, then blend in gradually 2½ oz. flour, ¾ oz. starch, 1½ oz. powdered almonds, and ½ tsp. vanilla-flavored sugar; add to this paste 2½ oz. melted butter and 1 liqueur glass of maraschino. Pour into a buttered, floured mold and bake in a slow oven. Once baked, let cool. Then moisten with maraschino and spread apricot jam over the cake. Frost with vanilla Fondant (p. 553) and sprinkle a few chopped pistachios on top.

SAVARIN CHANTILLY SAVARIN CHANTILLY (D. and D.)

Bake a Savarin (see p. 547), then soak it in kirsch; spread a light coating of apricot jam on top. Place the Savarin on a layer of Sweet Paste (p. 546) spread with apricot jam; fill the hollow center with Chantilly Cream (p. 552) until it bulges up into a dome beyond the cake; decorate the inside (at the top) of the Savarin with cream, also decorate across the top of the cake. Saint-Honoré Cream (p. 552) can also be used this way with a Savarin. (Figure 339, Page 548.)

SINGAPORE SINGAPOUR (J.)

Fill the inside of a Génoise Cake (p. 549) with Reduced Apricot (p. 550) and candied pineapple macerated in kirsch. Spread the top and sides with apricot jam and stick chopped, grilled almonds or sugar crystals at the base of the cake. On top the cake, in the center, place a square of candied pineapple, and around the border small pineapple triangles alternated with candied cherry halves. Glaze with very golden apricot jam. (Figure 383, Page 592.)

Fig. 377 - Strawberry spring cake (p. 579).
Fig. 378 - Progress cake (p. 579).

SUCCESS CAKE I SUCCÈS (Ga.)

Fill Success Cake layers (p. 554) with Coffee Butter Cream (p. 551). Frost with coffee Fondant (p. 553) and sprinkle chopped pistachios on top and sides.

SUCCESS CAKE II SUCCÈS (D. and D.)

Take 3 or 4 layers of Success Cake (p. 554), fill them with Hazelnut Butter Cream (p. 552), trim the sides, brush a thin coat of Reduced Apricot (p. 550) all over, and frost with white vanilla Fondant (p. 553), or Fondant tinted pale pink, if you prefer; sprinkle the top with chopped, grilled hazelnuts. If you wish, write the word "Success" on top with chocolate Fondant. (Figure 384, Page 592.)

THREE BROTHERS I TROIS FRÈRES (D. and D.) (*For 16 persons*)

Beat over the fire, in a heavy metal mixing bowl, 13 oz. sugar with 12 eggs; continue beating off the fire until cold; then, using a spatula, blend in 12 oz. rice flour, 10 oz. melted butter, vanilla. Pour into special fluted ring molds for this cake and bake in a slow oven. After baking, spread with Reduced Apricot (p. 550) and decorate the top at intervals with squares of candied angelica and Pralined Almonds (below).

Note: To make Pralined Almonds, dice the almonds, heat them, then pour them over sugar (cooked to the "ball" stage) in a heavy mixing bowl (5 oz. sugar to ½ lb. almonds); stir with a spatula to keep the almonds from sticking together.

THREE BROTHERS II TROIS FRÈRES (D. and D.) (*For 8 persons*)

7 oz. sugar beaten with 4 whole eggs and 4 yolks, 7 oz. powdered almonds, 1 cup whipped cream, and 4 stiffly beaten egg whites; flavor with orange. Bake in fluted ring molds in a slow oven. Frost, then decorate with preserved fruits.

TARTS

TARTES

APRICOT TART TARTE AUX ABRICOTS (P.)

Roll out an ⅛ in.-thick layer of Short Paste (p. 545) that has been standing for a while, butter a tart circle, and lay the paste inside, pressing it gently with the fingers; let about ⅜ in. overlap at the top, but trim off the surplus. Pinch the paste all around the edges with a special tart or pie pincers, then place on a clean, unbuttered baking sheet; prick the bottom of the crust a few times with the tip of a knife; sugar the edges of the crust, and fill with apricot halves (see p. 806). Bake about ½ hr. and finish by coating the top with hot Reduced Apricot (p. 550) or apricot jam. (Figure 385, Page 593.)

CHERRY TART TARTE AUX CERISES (P.)

Line a tart circle as described above, prick the bottom with a knife, and sprinkle the bottom with a handful of powdered sugar (this is done for all tarts with fresh fruits that yield juice when baked); pit fresh cherries (when in season) and fill the whole tart with the cherries packed tightly together; bake 25–30 min. in a very hot oven. Let cool and coat the top with red-currant jelly. In winter, use preserved cherries, but make sure they are carefully pitted.

STRAWBERRY TART TARTE AUX FRAISES (P.)

This is altogether different—the strawberries are not baked; therefore, the crust must be baked alone. Prepare the tart crust as explained on p. 582, prick the bottom in the same way, and cover the bottom with a piece of tissue paper; fill it with some dry vegetable—rice, for example—then bake in a very hot oven. This is done to keep the shape of the tart, the rice providing the necessary weight inside. Otherwise the crust would blister and have no shape, once baked. When the tart shell is almost done, remove the dry vegetable and tissue paper, since there is no longer any danger of its losing shape, and bake another 6 or 7 min. to cook it through and even dry it a little. Let the crust cool, then fill it with carefully stemmed strawberries, wild or cultivated, but in any case so clean that, if at all possible, they do not have to be washed. Then coat the strawberries with red-currant jelly.

LINZER TART or **TORTE** TARTE LINTZER or LINTZER-TART (D. and D.) (*For 20 persons*)

Line a flan circle with Linzer Paste (see below), making the bottom a little thick; fill ⅔ full with raspberry jam cooked with the seeds. Crisscross the surface with strips of the same paste about ⅘ in. wide, cut with a pastry wheel cutter, and join the strips to the crust by moistening with a little water (the raspberry should show through in a diamond-shaped pattern) ; be careful not to leave any trace of flour on the tart; prick with the tip of a knife, and bake, without brushing with egg, ½ hr. in a medium oven. Small Linzer Tortes are made the same way. (Figure 386, Page 593.)

Linzer Paste: 1 lb. flour, ¼ lb. powdered almonds, ¼ lb. sugar, ¼ lb. brown sugar, ¼ tsp. powdered cinnamon, pinch of salt, pinch of baking powder, 5 oz. butter, 2 eggs. Make a rather firm paste.

PEAR TART BOURDALOUE TARTE AUX POIRES À LA BOURDALOUE (Ga.)

Line a flan circle with Short Paste (p. 545), spread a layer of Frangipane Cream (p. 552) on the bottom, and bake. After baking, spread another thin layer of Frangipane Cream on top and lay quartered pears, cooked in sirup, on this. Spread Reduced Apricot (p. 550) over top and sides, and over the places where there is no fruit, put crushed but not ground Praline (p. 559) or even dry, crushed macaroons.

APPLE TART or **ENGLISH FLAN** TARTE AUX POMMES or FLAN ANGLAIS (D. and D.)

Line a flan circle with Short or Pie Paste (p. 545) and form a ridge around the edges with pincers; fill ¼ full of applesauce and lay thin slices of apple on top, making a rosette pattern. (Cut the apple in half, remove seeds and core, then cut in thin slices.) Lay the slices so that they half overlap each other, beginning at the outer edge of the circle. Brush the sides with beaten egg, bake, remove from oven, then spread rather thin apricot jam over the top. Baking time: 35–40 min.

Note: This can be made in a square shape. (Figure 387, Page 596.)

PLUM TART TARTE AUX PRUNES (P.)

All tarts can be made the same way, whether they are filled with cherries or Mirabelle plums (small yellow plums) ; the large plums should be cut in half like apricots. Spread red-currant or apricot jam on top, depending on whether or not the fruit is red.

TARTS WITHOUT MOLDS TARTES SANS MOULE (P.)

Anyone can make tarts this way. Instead of rolling out the Short Paste (p. 545) into a round shape, use a rolling pin to roll it into a square, keeping it a little thicker than usual, then fold the 4 sides to form a rim, sticking the corners together by moistening with a little water. Pinch all the way around with the thumb and index finger or with pincers. Place on a baking sheet, prick the bottom with a fork, and lay either thick slices of apple or cold applesauce on the bottom; arrange the thin slices of apple as shown in Figure 453, Plate 151. Halved apricots or plums can also be used, and even pitted cherries, but these tarts are not very practical for fruits that render juice while baking; the shallowness of the crust causes the juice to spill over and the crust bakes poorly.

SMALL PASTRIES

GLAZED MATCHES ALLUMETTES GLACÉES (P.)

Roll out a strip of Puff Paste (p. 544) 5 in. wide and about 1/8 in. thick. Spread the top with Royal Glaze (p. 556) made by beating 1/2 egg white with enough powdered sugar, added bit by bit, to make a thick cream that can be spread in a very thin layer over the paste, using a knife. Then cut with a floured knife into small strips about 1 in. wide; place them on a baking sheet, and bake 12–15 min. in an oven that is fairly hot on the bottom but less hot at the top.

BABAS BABAS (P.)

Generously butter some baba molds and fill 1/3 full with Baba Paste (p. 546); let rise in a warm place and, when the mold is full, bake 8–10 min. in a very hot oven. Cool, then soak in hot rum- or kirsch-flavored sirup. (Figure 388, Page 596.)

FLEMISH STICKS BAGUETTES FLAMANDES (P.) (*18 sticks*)

1/4 lb. sugar, 1/4 lb. flour, 2 oz. chopped almonds, 1 whole egg, 1 yolk, vanilla or orange-flower water.

Put the sugar into a bowl with the whole egg and yolk and beat briskly. When it has whitened a little, add the vanilla and flour, then press it from a pastry bag, or mold it with a spoon, onto a buttered, floured baking sheet, shaping the paste into sticks or rods about as thick as your little finger and twice as long. Cover these sticks with chopped almonds and bake 8 min. in a medium oven. Very good with tea.

CHERRY BOATS BARQUETTES AUX CERISES (J.)

Line little pastry-boat molds with Short or Pie Paste (p. 545). Finish according to the recipe given for Cherry Tartlets (p. 600). (Figure 394, Page 605.)

FLEMISH BOATS BARQUETTES FLAMANDES (Du.)

Line little boat molds with Short Paste (p. 545). Then make a pastry cream with 2 egg yolks, 2 1/2 oz. sugar, 1 oz. flour, 1 1/4 oz. powdered almonds, 1 cup milk, and a little kirsch. Bring to a boil, then mix in 2 tbsp. chopped, candied cherries. Fill the molds with this, place a half almond on top, and powder with sugar; bake 12 min. in a hot oven.

MACAROON BOATS BARQUETTES MACARONNÉES (Du.)

Line boat molds with Short or Sweet Paste (pp. 545, 546), prick the bottoms, and fill with the following cream: 3½ oz. almonds mashed with 7 oz. vanilla-flavored sugar and whites of 2 small eggs; pour this paste into a pan and heat until too hot to touch; finish, off the stove, with 1 stiffly beaten egg white and 1 tsp. apricot jam. When the boats have been filled, sprinkle the tops with slivered almonds. Powder with sugar and bake 12–15 min. in a fairly hot oven.

HAZELNUT BOATS BARQUETTES NOISETTINES (Du.)

Same pastry as above, with hazelnuts instead of almonds. Lightly grill the hazelnuts in the oven to remove the skin by rubbing them in a towel. Wait until they are cold before mashing.

STRAWBERRY BOATS BATEAUX DE FRAISES (Du.)

Make small ovals of Sweet Paste (p. 546) and place them in buttered boat molds; the paste should extend a little beyond the rim. Prick the bottoms and bake in a very hot oven. After they are cold, fill them with wild strawberries and coat with red-currant jelly.

CURRANT BOATS BATEAUX AUX GROSEILLES (Du.)

Prepare the same as above and fill with small red or white currants; red-currant jelly on the red and apricot on the white.

CHESTNUT BOATS BATEAUX AUX MARRONS (J.)

Line boat molds with Short Paste (p. 545) and fill to the brim with Pastry Cream (p. 552). Bake 10 min. in a hot oven. Unmold and let cool. Garnish with Chestnut Butter Cream (p. 551). Frost one side with coffee Fondant (p. 553), the other with chocolate Fondant. (Figure 393, Page 605.)

BABIES BÉBÉS (P.)

This excellent little pastry has several names: Brazilians, Duchesses, Dora, etc., depending on the restaurant or bakeshop.

The paste is made by mixing 4 stiffly beaten egg whites, 1¼ oz. powdered, grilled almonds and hazelnuts, 2½ oz. sugar, 1 oz. flour, and 1 oz. melted butter. Using a pastry bag, lay out in small flat ovals on a buttered, floured baking sheet. Bake in a hot oven, remove from the baking sheet, and let cool on a flat surface, then put them together in twos, with a thin layer of Praline (p. 559) mashed into a paste in between. These can also be shaped like small Petits Fours. (Figure 392, Page 604.)

BERNARDINS BERNARDINS (D. and D.) (*28 pieces*)

13 oz. sugar, 7 oz. powdered almonds, 1 lb. flour, 3 egg whites; mix all together, roll out the paste, and cut into pieces the same size as Glazed Matches (p. 584). Bake in a medium oven. After removing from the oven, glaze with sirup.

BIARRITZ BIARRITZ (P.)

Soften 3½ oz. butter, add 3½ oz. powdered almonds, 3½ oz. powdered sugar; beat well; when the paste begins to turn whitish, blend in, bit by bit, 2 egg whites; last of all, add 1½ oz. flour. Put this paste into a pastry bag with a plain tube; butter and flour a baking sheet, and squeeze onto it balls of paste about the size of a hazelnut; flatten these balls by tapping the baking sheet;

bake 7–8 min. in a hot oven. When cold, cover the flat sides with thick chocolate enriched with cocoa butter and not too sweet. (Heat the chocolate mixture in a double boiler and, when it becomes creamy, spread a thin layer of it on the pastries, using a knife.) (Figure 389, Page 597.)

SPONGE FINGERS BISCUITS À LA CUILLER (P.) *(22 to 24)*

2½ oz. sugar, 2½ oz. flour, flavoring, and 3 eggs.

The batter is made like the Sponge-Cake Roll mixture on p. 549; mix it gently without trying to blend it too thoroughly, so that it will not be too soft and crack while baking. Taking a pastry bag with a wide, plain tube, lay the sponge biscuits out very straight, about the size of the index finger, on a buttered, floured baking sheet; sprinkle generously with fine sugar, shake the excess sugar off onto a paper, and bake 15–18 min. in a medium oven. Do not be afraid to let them dry a little. (Figure 391, Page 604.)

DRY BISCUITS (for champagne) BISCUITS SECS (P.) *(40 pieces)*

Though usually manufactured commercially, these biscuits can be made easily at home.

Beat over a slow fire, like a Génoise mixture (p. 549), ½ lb. sugar and 5 whole eggs. When the paste is very foamy, remove from the fire and blend in with a spoon ½ lb. flour, ½ tsp. cream of tartar or baking powder, and a little vanilla.

Using a pastry bag, squeeze this paste into special molds containing 10 biscuit shapes; they should first be buttered and floured. Generously sprinkle the top with fine sugar, shake off the excess sugar, and bake, like all biscuits, in a very slow oven.

BLIDAHS BLIDAHS (P.)

Beat 3 egg whites until stiff; using a spatula, blend in 3½ oz. sugar, 3½ oz. powdered almonds, ½ oz. flour, the grated peel of 2 oranges, and a few drops of carmine to give an orange color. Make thick, oval cakes on a buttered, floured baking sheet, spreading the top of the paste very smooth with a flat-bladed knife. Sprinkle generously with confectioners' sugar and bake 12–15 min. in a medium oven. (Figure 389, Page 597.)

CHOCOLATE PATTIES BOUCHÉES AU CHOCOLAT (P.)

Make the same paste as for Sponge Fingers (p. 586). Using a pastry bag, squeeze out, on a buttered, floured baking sheet, drops of paste about the size of large macaroons. Bake 12–15 min. in a medium oven, then hollow them out a little from the bottom and fill these hollows with Pastry Cream (p. 552) or Frangipane Cream (p. 552); put 2 cookies together and frost with warm chocolate Fondant (p. 553). Do not frost the bottom.

BRAZILIANS BRÉSILIENS (D. and D.)

Lightly grill ½ lb. raw almonds and ½ lb. hazelnuts; rub them on a wire sieve to remove the skins, then add 1 lb. powdered sugar and beat with 2 egg whites. Put into a bowl and add ¼ lb. melted butter, ½ cup milk, then 8 unbeaten egg whites. Using a pastry bag, squeeze out oval shapes onto lightly buttered baking sheets. Bake in a slow oven.

These small cakes are then treated like Babies (p. 585)—in other words, 2 put together with a layer of soft Praline (p. 559) in between.

PRETZELS BRETZELS (P.) (*10 to 12 pieces*)

Don't confuse these pastry pretzels with the pretzels seen on café tables. Mix a paste by hand, using 7 oz. flour, 3½ oz. butter, 1¼ oz. sugar, a pinch of salt, and some flavoring—cinnamon, lemon, or crushed anise—with 1 whole egg and 1 yolk. Make into a firm paste and let stand 1 hr. Then divide into pieces weighing a little over 1 oz.; roll them, on a floured baking table, into the shape of rather elongated spindles, the center part thick and the ends thin. Lightly moisten the middle and bring the 2 ends together, crossing them to form a knot. Turn them over, brush lightly with beaten egg, sprinkle with granulated sugar, and bake on a baking sheet, 8–10 min., in a medium oven. (Figure 392, Page 604.)

BRIOCHES BRIOCHES (P.)

Mold the same as large Brioches (p. 565), using small, individual molds, and filling them only half full; let rise, then bake 7–8 min. in a hot oven.

SICILIAN CUP CAKES CAISSETTES SICILIENNES (P.)

Mash 3½ oz. almonds with 3½ oz. vanilla-flavored sugar; color this paste green with a dash of green vegetable coloring and moisten with a few tbsp. orange-flower water. Make into a softish paste by blending with 3 stiffly beaten egg whites. Put this mixture into special small, oval paper cups; place a half almond on top and powder generously with confectioners' sugar; bake about 10 min. on a baking sheet in a moderate oven.

CARRACKS CARAQUES (J.)

Same recipe as for the large Carrack (p. 566), baking the mixture in a square cake pan. Fill the usual way, then cut into small squares. After frosting them, cover the sides with chocolate paillettes. Decorate the tops with chocolate shavings or cigarettes. Powder with confectioners' sugar.(Figure 393, Page 605.)

APPLE TURNOVERS CHAUSSONS AUX POMMES (P.)

Make fairly large rounds of Puff Paste (p. 544) and fill the centers with rather reduced cold applesauce. Moisten the edges and fold the paste over to form a sort of half circle; pinch the edges together tightly. Brush with egg and prick the turnovers 3 times with a paring knife. Bake 12–15 min. in a hot oven; powder with sugar and let it melt.

CHEVREUSE CHEVREUSE (P.) (*12 pieces*)

Cook 1½ oz. semolina in a cup of boiling milk; beat 1 whole egg with 1½ oz. vanilla-flavored sugar; pour in the cooked semolina and mix together, then add a few dried currants. Fill 12 tartlet molds lined with Short Paste (p. 545) with this cream and bake 10–12 min. in a hot oven.

CREAM PUFFS CHOUX À LA CRÈME (P.)

Squeeze small balls of Choux Paste (p. 548) from a pastry bag onto a clean baking sheet; brush with egg; bake 15 min. in a hot oven. Open them and fill with Saint-Honoré Cream (p. 552) or Chantilly Cream (p. 552). Powder with confectioners' sugar. The top may be replaced after filling. (Figure 393, Page 605.)

CONVERSATIONS CONVERSATIONS (P.)

Line tartlet molds with Short Paste (p. 545) or Puff-Paste (p. 544) trimmings; prick the bottoms and fill to the brim with Pastry Cream (p. 552) or Frangipane Cream (p. 552); cover with a very thin round of paste, and spread the top with a thin coat of Royal Glaze (p. 556). Finish by laying 4 tiny strips of paste in crisscross on top (making a diamond-shaped center). Bake 15 min. in an oven hot on bottom and slow on top. (Figure 390, Page 597.)

CREAM CONES CORNETS À LA CRÈME (P.)

For this recipe you need some of those inexpensive tin molds in the shape of small cones; roll out some scraps of Puff Paste (p. 545) into a fairly thin strip, then cut it lengthwise into ribbons 1 in. wide; slightly moisten the outside of the tin cones and cover them with the paste ribbons, spiraling them from the tip to the top. Place the cones on a baking sheet, brush the top with egg, and bake 10 min. in a hot oven. Remove the molds and fill the baked cones with a cream or some other mixture.

CRESCENTS CROISSANTS (P.) (*18 pieces*)

No more difficult to make than Brioche. The paste is made the day before, with the following ingredients (to make 18 crescents) : 7 oz. flour, 2½ oz. butter, ⅓ oz. yeast, pinch of salt, ¼ cup milk, and a little water. Prepare like Brioche Paste (p. 546)—the leaven made with ¼ of the flour, the yeast, and warm water. While the leaven is rising in a warm place, knead the flour with the salt, milk, and only ½ the butter. Beat this paste just as you do Brioche Paste (p. 546), then mix in the leaven and keep in a bowl until the following day. Put the paste back onto the baking table, enclose the rest of the butter, and fold and roll for 2 "turns," as in making Puff Paste (see p. 544). Let stand 20 min., then give it 2 more turns. Roll out the paste; cut into triangles and roll by hand into crescents; place them on the baking sheet with plenty of room in between. Let them rise ½ hr., brush with egg, and bake 8–10 min. in a hot oven.

ALMOND CRESCENTS CROISSANTS AUX AMANDES (P.) (*16 to 18*)

5 oz. almonds, 5 oz. powdered sugar, 2 egg whites, 1 tbsp. thick apricot jam, vanilla.

Pound the almonds fine, adding the sugar little by little; mix in the apricot jam and, bit by bit, the egg whites. Make a paste firm enough to be rolled by hand. Divide the paste into pieces the size of a walnut shell, and roll them in a little flour until they are shaped into cylinders as large as a finger. Next, moisten them with a little egg, roll them in slivered or chopped almonds, and place them on a sheet of paper on a baking tray, fashioning them into crescents. Brush the top with egg and bake 10 min. in a medium oven. As soon as baked, loosen them from the baking sheet. (Figure 394, Page 605.)

ALMOND CROQUETS CROQUETS AUX AMANDES (P.)

Blend 5 oz. flour, 2½ oz. sugar, 2 oz. butter, 2½ oz. whole, unpeeled almonds, a little salt, grated peel of 1 orange or lemon, and 1 whole large egg or 1½ eggs. Make a firm paste and chop it a little with a knife to break up the almonds. Roll the paste by hand into a large sausage shape, place it in the center of a baking sheet, and flatten it a little so that the bottom is flat but the top rounded. Brush with egg, crisscross with a fork, and bake 18–20 min. in a medium oven. When cold, cut into finger-thick slices. (Figure 389, Page 597.)

BORDEAUX CROQUETS CROQUETS DE BORDEAUX (D. and D.)

Blend with 1 glass water and a little orange-flower water: 20 oz. flour, 13 oz. sugar or brown sugar; add 10 oz. chopped raw almonds, 1 tsp. baking powder. Roll out this paste into thin strips and cut into rectangles 4 in. long; brush with egg, and bake on buttered baking sheets. (Figure 389, Page 597.)

Fig. 379 - Regent cake (p. 580).
Fig. 380 - Nun (p. 580).

Fig. 379

Fig. 380

Fig. 381

Fig. 382

SLICED CROQUETS CROQUETS COUPÉS (D. and D.)

½ lb. sugar, ½ lb. coarsely chopped raw almonds, 1 lb. flour, 4 eggs, 1 tsp. baking powder. Make a firm paste, using only 3 eggs if necessary. Roll out in a strip as long as the buttered baking sheet, brush with caramel, crisscross with a fork, and bake in a hot oven; slice as soon as baked.

LADIES' CROQUETS CROQUETS DE DAMES (D. and D.)

Make a well of ½ lb. flour; in the center put ¼ lb. powdered sugar, ¼ lb. blanched, chopped almonds, ¼ lb. butter, 2 eggs, a little rum. Blend into a paste and let stand a little; cut into tiny loaves, brush with egg, and roll in granulated sugar. Place on a buttered baking sheet. Bake in a very slow oven.

DARIOLES DARIOLES (D. and D.) (*12 pieces*)

Nowadays these little pastries are forgotten and neglected, which is a shame. They used to be made by the dozens. Line 12 small round or oval baba molds with very thin Pie Paste (p. 545). Separately prepare a bowl of the following mixture: 2 oz. powdered sugar and 1 oz. sifted flour beaten with 2 eggs and orange-flower water. Thin the mixture with 4 oz. milk. Fill the molds with this mixture and place a small piece of butter on each. Bake in a slow oven. Powder with sugar after baking. (Figure 394, Page 605.)

DARTOIS DARTOIS (P.)

Roll out a strip of Puff Paste (p. 544) as long as the baking sheet and as thick as a half dollar; moisten with water and fill the center from end to end with Almond Cream (p. 550) or some jam. Cover with a second, thicker strip of paste, pressing it firmly down onto the first strip. Trim the edges even with a knife, brush with egg, and lightly mark into sections the width of 2 fingers. Streak each section with the tip of a knife, prick with a fork, and bake in a hot oven. Cut the sections while still warm.

DUCHESSES DUCHESSES (P.)

3½ oz. vanilla-flavored sugar, 1 oz. powdered almonds, 1 oz. powdered, grilled hazelnuts, 1 oz. flour, 1 oz. butter, 3 egg whites. Beat the egg whites very stiff, then, using a spoon, blend in the sugar, powdered almonds and hazelnuts, and flour; mix all this together at the same time. Finally, add the melted butter. Place this paste on a buttered, floured baking sheet, forming small, thin, flat oval cakes with a cookie cutter. Bake in a hot oven, letting it dry out a little. Place the ovals together in twos with creamed Praline (p. 559) in the middle.

ÉCLAIRS ÉCLAIRS (D. and D.) (*12 pieces*)

Using a pastry bag with a plain tube, lay out, on a baking sheet, rods of Choux Paste (p. 548) about 3 in. long. Bake in a slow oven and, when cold, fill with a cooked coffee or chocolate cream; lightly brush the surface with Reduced Apricot (p. 550) and then frost with coffee or chocolate Fondant (p. 553). For 12 Éclairs, use 8–11 oz. Choux Paste or more, depending on size, and the same amount of cream. (Figure 390, Page 597.)

FANCHONNETTES FANCHONNETTES (D. and D.) (*12 pieces*)

Line round tartlet molds with leftover pieces of Puff Paste (p. 544), then fill with the following cream: 3½ oz. sugar beaten with 2 yolks and 1 whole

Fig. 381 - Rosemary (p. 580).
Fig. 382 - Saint-Honoré (p. 581).

egg, 1½ oz. powdered almonds, 2 oz. flour, 1 oz. butter, a pinch of salt. Fill ⅔ full. Remove from the oven before completely baked, and top with meringue; sprinkle with a little granulated sugar and finish baking. After removing from the oven, let cool, then fill the hollows in the meringue with red-currant jelly. (Figure 394, Page 605.)

FLORETTES FLORETTES (P.)

Beat 2 egg whites very stiff, then blend in 3½ oz. vanilla-flavored sugar and 2½ oz. powdered almonds. Make tartlet crusts of Short Paste (p. 545), prick the bottoms with a fork, and put in ½ tsp. apricot jam; fill with the above almond paste, sprinkle the top with a little coarsely chopped almond, sugar, and bake about 12 min. in an oven that is hot on the bottom.

FRIANDS FRIANDS (P.)

Mix ¼ lb. finely ground, dried, skinned almonds with ¼ lb. powdered sugar. Beat a good ¼ hr. with 4 egg whites, adding them a bit at a time; then blend into this paste 1¼ oz. flour, a little vanilla, ¼ lb. butter cooked until almost black and cooled; fill small buttered, floured molds with this mixture and bake 8–10 min., depending on the size of the molds, in a hot oven.

AMIENS GALETTES GALETTES D'AMIENS (D. and D.)

Mix ½ lb. flour with 2 whole eggs, then ¼ lb. sugar, ¼ lb. butter. Roll out the paste with a rolling pin, cut with a fluted cookie cutter, brush with egg. Bake in a hot oven and glaze with gum arabic after removing from the oven.

BASEL GALETTES GALETTES À LA BÂLOISE (P.)

Proportions: ¼ lb. almonds, 5 oz. flour, ¼ lb. sugar, 1¼ oz. butter, 3 yolks or 1 whole egg, vanilla, salt.

First finely pound the almonds and sugar, adding the 3 egg yolks, then put this paste in the center of the flour; add the salt and vanilla, and knead by hand to make a firm paste; let stand 1 hr. in a cool place; roll it out and cut into oval pancakes; brush the top with egg and place a half almond in the center.

BRETON GALETTES GALETTES BRETONNES (P.)

Proportions: 5 oz. flour, 2 oz. butter, 2 oz. dried currants, 2 oz. sugar, 1 whole egg, pinch of salt, pinch of powdered cinnamon.

Knead the paste and roll it into a ball; let stand; roll it out and divide it into pieces the size of an egg; flatten these pieces by pressing a floured box or mold on top; brush with egg and streak each piece with a knife; place a pinch of dried currants on the center (these are in addition to the 2 oz. mixed into the paste). Bake in a hot oven. Very good with tea. Since cinnamon does not appeal to everyone, another flavor can be substituted.

FLAKY GALETTES GALETTES FEUILLETÉES (Ga.)

Make a round ball of Puff Paste (p. 544), flatten it by hand, and finish shaping it round with a rolling pin. Brush with egg, streak with a knife, bake, turn over when half baked, and finish baking until quite dry.

FONDANT GALETTES GALETTES FONDANTES (D. and D.)

Put into a mixing bowl: 8 oz. sweet cream, 11 oz. powdered sugar, vanilla, and ½ lb. flour; mix well, then add 7 stiffly beaten egg whites. Using a pastry bag (with a special tube for making Cat Tongues), squeeze out this mixture, onto a lightly buttered baking sheet, into pieces the size of a hazelnut. Bake in a hot oven.

DUTCH GALETTES GALETTES HOLLANDAISES (Ga.)

Prepare the same as Flaky Galettes (below), but spread the top with the mixture called Dutch Granité (p. 556). Streak with a knife and bake in a slow oven until quite dry.

RAISIN GALETTES GALETTES AUX RAISINS (P.) (*18 pieces*)

5 oz. flour, 2 oz. butter, 2 oz. sugar, 2 oz. dried currants (raisins), salt, a good pinch of powdered cinnamon, and 1 whole egg. Knead, divide into 18 pieces, and roll these into balls in the palms of the hands; place these on a buttered baking sheet, spaced well apart, and flatten them by pressing on top with some floured, flat utensil; brush with egg, place 6 or 8 raisins in the center. Bake in a hot oven.

SALTED GALETTES GALETTES SALÉES (P.) (*24 pieces*)

¼ lb. flour, 2½ oz. butter, ½ tsp. salt, 3 or 4 tbsp. cold milk or 1 egg yolk and some milk.

Knead without working the paste too much, or it becomes too elastic, because of the absence of sugar. Let stand 1 hr. Roll it out very thin, prick the surface thoroughly with a fork. Cut into circles about 2 in. in diameter and place on a buttered baking sheet. Moisten the tops with a brush dipped in salted milk. Bake 4 or 5 min. in a very hot oven. As soon as baked, brush again with salted milk.

ANISE CAKES GÂTEAUX À L'ANIS (P.)

Beat well 2 whole eggs with ½ lb. powdered sugar, 1 tbsp. crushed anise, ½ lb. flour; make a very smooth paste, then add 1 tsp. baking powder. Cut into rounds, place on a buttered, floured baking sheet, and bake in a slow oven. Put a nut of butter into the paste; if you want the cakes higher and not so wide, leave out the baking powder; to make them less dry, put in a little more butter.

FLAKY CAKES GÂTEAUX FEUILLETÉS (P.)

Roll out the Puff Paste (p. 544) into a sheet between ⅛ and 1⁄16 in. thick, and cut into diamonds, squares, or small rounds; place them on slightly moistened baking sheets, brush with egg, streak with a knife, and bake 6–8 min. in a hot oven. When almost finished, powder with confectioners' sugar so that it will melt and caramelize a little on the cakes, making them shine.

MILAN CAKES GÂTEAUX DE MILAN (P.)

Proportions: 5 oz. butter, ½ lb. flour, ¼ lb. sugar, 4 or 5 egg yolks, a few grains of salt, 1 grated lemon peel, 1 tsp. cognac or rum. Shape the flour into a well on the baking table, put all the ingredients in the center, mix; then roll the paste into a ball; roll it out with a rolling pin until ⅛ in. thick; cut with a cookie cutter; place on a buttered baking sheet, brush with egg, and bake 10–15 min. in a hot oven.

YEAST WAFFLES GAUFRES À LA LEVURE (D. and D.)

10 oz. powdered sugar, 13 oz. flour, 2 oz. yeast, 1 lb. butter, 18 egg yolks, 15 stiffly beaten egg whites, ½ tsp. salt, 1 qt. whipped cream.

Cream the butter and beat it with the egg yolks; add the sugar, then the flour; make a leaven with the yeast and mix it into the paste; let the paste rise and, just before using, add the 15 egg whites, then the whipped cream. Cook in a flat waffle iron.

FLEMISH WAFFLES I GAUFRES FLAMANDES (D. and D.)

20 lb. flour, 2 lb. melted butter, 8 qt. milk, 2¼ oz. salt, 10 oz. yeast, 150 egg yolks, 120 beaten egg whites, 2 qt. whipped cream; mix, strain through a sieve, let stand 2 hr. in a warm place; cook in rectangular waffle irons. Powder the cooked waffles with confectioners' sugar.

FLEMISH WAFFLES II GAUFRES À LA FLAMANDE (D. and D.)

Sift 1 lb. flour into a mixing bowl, place in the center ½ oz. yeast dissolved in a little warm milk, add 4 eggs, 1 tsp. salt, and enough milk to make a smooth and rather liquid batter. Finish with 1½ oz. powdered sugar, ¼ lb. melted butter, vanilla. Let stand in a warm place to double the volume. Finish the usual way.

ORDINARY WAFFLES GAUFRES ORDINAIRES (D. and D.)

Put into a mixing bowl 7 oz. flour, 7 oz. sugar, 5 egg yolks, powdered vanilla. Mix, then blend in, bit by bit, 12 oz. milk and 3½ oz. melted butter. The batter should be liquid enough to be poured with a spoon; if necessary, add a little more milk. Heat the waffle iron and lightly grease it with a brush dipped in butter; pour 1 tbsp. batter on the bottom of the waffle iron, close it, and cook. Remove from the waffle iron and powder with sugar before serving.

TUILERIES WAFFLES GAUFRES DES TUILERIES (D. and D.)

Beat 9 oz. confectioners' sugar and 6 oz. sifted flour in a bowl with 3 eggs and 1½ oz. melted butter; blend in about 12 oz. milk to make a rather thin batter; flavor with orange-flower water, and cook in a rectangular waffle iron.

SHUTTERS JALOUSIES (P.)

Same procedure as Dartois (p. 589), but filled only with red-currant jelly; and the top crust is cut across in narrow slits to give the impression of shutters. Let cool before cutting into pieces about 1½ in. wide.

JAVANESE JAVANAIS (P.)

Ordinary Génoise paste (p. 550) with chocolate or cocoa powder added (1 tbsp. to 4 oz. sugar). Make the paste about 1 in. thick and bake on a square baking sheet. After cooling, cut into 1½-in. squares; split them and fill with Chocolate Butter Cream (p. 551); cover them with the same cream and roll them in granulated chocolate, then decorate the top as follows. Spread out 5 oz. chocolate enriched with cocoa butter (but not too sweet) very thin on a marble slab. When it is almost cold, scrape it with a wide knife to make shavings that roll up like wood shavings. Scatter these shavings unsymmetrically on the cakes and lightly powder the tops with confectioners' sugar.

FLAKY TONGUES WITH CARAMEL LANGUES FEUILLETÉES AU CARAMEL (P.)

Cut small rounds of Puff Paste (p. 544) with a fluted cookie cutter; place them on a baking board powdered with sugar and roll them once with the rolling pin to shape like a tongue; bake 10–12 min. in a medium oven, or until the sugar on top melts into a golden caramel.

MACAROONS MACARONS (P.)

4 oz. almonds, ½ lb. sugar, 3 egg whites, vanilla. Mash the almonds, gradually adding the sugar, and, after the almonds are well crushed, add the egg whites 1 by 1. The paste should be softish but not liquid. Using a pastry

Fig. 383 - Singapore (p. 581).
Fig. 384 - Success cake (p. 582).

Fig. 383

Fig. 384

Fig. 385

Fig. 386

bag, squeeze out the Macaroons in small drops on sheets of paper (Figure 110, p. 117). Lightly moisten the tops with a brush dipped in water, powder with confectioners' sugar, and bake 12–15 min. in a moderately slow oven. Place the paper on a damp surface to loosen the Macaroons. Stick them together in pairs. (Figure 391, Page 604.)

MACAROONS (SOFT) MACARONS (MOUS) (P.)

Same proportions as above, using confectioners' sugar. Make the paste a little firmer, stirring it while heating it gently; shape the Macaroons from the warm paste. Let them stand a good hour before baking; put neither water nor sugar on top; bake 10 min. in a medium oven.

CHOCOLATE MACAROONS MACARONS CHOCOLAT (P.)

4 oz. almonds, 7 oz. sugar, 2½ oz. grated chocolate or chocolate melted in very little water, 2 egg whites, ½ tsp. arrowroot. Prepare like ordinary Macaroons; bake 12 min. in a slow oven.

NANCY MACAROONS MACARONS DE NANCY (D. and D.)

1 lb. almonds peeled the preceding day, then crushed with ½ lb. fine granulated sugar. Put into a mortar and beat with 7 egg whites added 1 by 1; while continuing to beat, gradually add 1½ lb. sugar, then, at the end, ½ lb. sugar cooked at 226° F. Let the paste stand 1–2 hr., then blend in 4 or 5 stiffly beaten egg whites, and drop onto a paper like ordinary Macaroons. Moisten them with a brush or by spreading a damp cloth over them, and bake in a medium oven. This kind of Macaroon is easily prepared and turns out light and spongy. Keep the Macaroons in closed cookie tins.

COCONUT MACAROONS MACARONS À LA NOIX DE COCO (A.)

Take: ½ lb. powdered sugar, 7 oz. finely grated fresh coconut, 2 oz. heavy cream, pinch of white salt, 4 fresh egg whites. Beat the egg whites until stiff. Mash the coconut in a mortar with the sugar and salt, add the cream, then fold in all the beaten egg whites at once. Put the mixture into a pastry bag and squeeze out the Macaroons either on a lightly buttered baking sheet or on a piece of white paper powdered with sugar and placed on a baking sheet. Bake in a rather hot oven without browning; keep careful watch while baking.

Coconut Macaroons are outstanding among Petits Fours. They have a special flavor and are unique.

MADELEINES MADELEINES (D. and D.) (*40 pieces*)

1 lb. sugar beaten with 9 eggs, then 13 oz. flour; add 13 oz. creamed butter, ½ tsp. baking powder, lemon flavoring. Butter the molds; bake in a hot oven. (Figure 390, Page 597.)

COMMERCY MADELEINES MADELEINES DE COMMERCY (P.)

In a mixing bowl, soften 2½ oz. fine butter without melting it; beat 10 min. with a whisk, while mixing in 3½ oz. sugar; then add 1 whole egg and beat another 3 min.; add a second egg, beat 3 min. more; add a third and last egg and beat a little more; then, using a spoon, mix in 3½ oz. flour containing ½ tsp. baking powder, and flavor with orange-flower water or other flavoring. Bake in buttered, floured molds, 8–10 min. (depending on the size of the molds), in a hot oven.

Fig. 385 - Apricot tart (p. 582).
Fig. 386 - Linzer tart or Torte (p. 583).

MANONS MANONS (Du.)

Use the same paste as for Sponge Fingers (p. 586), but shape into Macaroons. Bake in a slow oven; hollow them a little and fill with chopped, preserved cherries or strawberries flavored with kirsch. Cover with white frosting and a sprinkling of pink granulated sugar on top.

MARCELINS MARCELINS (D. and D.)

Same recipe as the Marcelin on p. 572. Line small tartlet molds with Sweet Paste (p. 546) and fill ⅔ full with the mixture given. (Figure 390, Page 597.)

MARCELLES MARCELLES (Du.)

Bake Parisian Paste (p. 558) and put 2 strips together with Mocha Butter Cream (p. 551) in between; let harden in the refrigerator, then cut into triangles; frost with Coffee Fondant (p. 553) and place a crystallized coffee bean on each.

MARIGNANS MARIGNANS (D. and D.)

Fill small boat-shaped molds ½ full of Savarin Paste (p. 547), let them rise, then bake. Soak them with baba sirup (p. 584); cut an opening in the side and, using a pastry bag, fill with Cooked Meringue (p. 557); spread the top with Reduced Apricot (p. 550). (Figure 388, Page 596.)

MARQUISE MARQUISE (Du.)

Bake Parisian Paste (p. 558) and put 2 strips together with a layer of vanilla-flavored chestnut purée in between. Cut into small diamonds and frost with chocolate, placing a few slivers of pistachio on top of the frosting.

MARS MARS (P.)

Turn up the edges of a long strip of Puff Paste (p. 544) and fill the center with Pastry Cream (p. 552); bake 15 min. in a hot oven; let cool a little, then cover with 1 in. of Swiss Meringue (p. 557). Cover heavily with powdered sugar, mark into 1-in. squares with the back of a knife, and decorate each section with 2 almond halves and 3 raisins. Put back into a slow oven 10 min.; let cool; cut into squares, following the marked lines and without breaking the crust.

MASCOTS MASCOTTES (J.)

Bake a Génoise Cake (p. 549) in a square mold; let cool. Fill with Praline Butter Cream (p. 552). Cut into small, even squares. Cover the top and sides with the same cream and then stick on shredded, grilled almonds. (Figure 393, Page 605.)

MERINGUES MERINGUES (P.)

Following the recipe for Ordinary Meringue (p. 557), use a pastry bag or a spoon to lay out Meringues on a buttered, floured baking sheet. Cover them with sugar and bake 10 min. in a slow oven. Detach them from the baking sheet and return to the oven to let dry completely. (Figure 391, Page 604.)

MERINGUES CHANTILLY MERINGUES CHANTILLY (P.)

Fill 2 meringue shells with Chantilly Cream (p. 552), using either a pastry bag or a spoon.

SMALL CHOCOLATE MERINGUES MERINGUETTES AU CHOCOLAT (P.)

Cook a meringue over a slow fire (see Cooked Meringue, p. 557), then mix in 1½ oz. unsweetened cocoa powder. Using a pastry bag with a very small tube, squeeze out some small Meringues or little sticks called Lady Fingers onto a buttered, floured baking sheet. Bake in an oven just hot enough to dry them and crust the tops. Add a little coffee essence to make coffee-flavored ones.

MILLEFEUILLES or NAPOLEONS MILLEFEUILLES (P.)

Make some very thin strips of scraps of Puff Paste (p. 544). These should be cut evenly and about the width of a hand. Place them on a baking sheet, prick them all over with a fork, and bake in a rather hot oven, letting them dry thoroughly. Place these strips of paste in 3 layers, with a layer of cream—Pastry Cream (p. 552), Frangipane Cream (p. 552), or Chantilly Cream (p. 552) with strawberries—between each layer of paste. Powder the tops with sugar and cut into pieces with a special saw-edged knife.

ROUEN MIRLITONS MIRLITONS ROUENNAIS (P.) (*12 pieces*)

Line tartlet molds with Short (p. 545) or Puff Paste (p. 544). Beat together with a fork 3½ oz. sugar and 2 whole eggs until rather foamy, then add 2 or 3 coarsely crushed dry macaroons. Prick the tartlet crusts with a fork and place a slice of apricot in the bottom of each; fill with the mixture given above; place 3 almond halves on top in the form of a trefoil; powder heavily with sugar, and bake in a rather hot oven, especially hot on the bottom. (Figure 392, Page 604.)

MIRRORS MIROIRS (P.)

Stiffly beat 3 egg whites; mix in 4 oz. dry, powdered almonds and 4 oz. sugar. Squeeze this paste from a pastry bag (with the special tube used for Cat Tongues) into small ovals with open centers. Sprinkle with powdered almonds, turning over the baking sheet to shake off the surplus, then fill the centers with the following paste: ¼ lb. almonds mashed with ¼ lb. sugar, 1 whole egg and 1 yolk, 1½ oz. melted butter, and a finger of rum. Bake in a rather hot oven; let cool; glaze only the centers with a brush dipped in Reduced Apricot (p. 550) and on top of this a very thin rum Fondant (p. 553), to keep a bright glaze. (Figure 389, Page 597.)

MOCHATINES and CHOCOLATINES MOKATINES and CHOCOLATINES (P.)

These are made in the shape of small cakes or Petits Fours. They are small squares of Ordinary Génoise Cake (p. 550), split, filled with Coffee or Chocolate Butter Cream (p. 551), covered on the outside with the same cream, then rolled, those with coffee in granulated sugar, those with chocolate in chopped, grilled almonds. Using a pastry bag with a fluted tube, dot each one once or several times with the same cream. They are made the same way for Petits Fours, but in a very small size, about 30 to the lb. (Figure 393, Page 605.)

NARCISSUS NARCISSES (P.)

Made of Choux Paste (p. 548) and shaped like large commas. Brush with egg and sprinkle the tops with a pinch of shredded almond; bake in a hot oven. Split on the side and fill with Pastry Cream (p. 552) or Saint-Honoré Cream (p. 552).

ENGLISH ROLLS PAINS ANGLAIS (D. and D.)

Mash 7 oz. almonds and ½ lb. sugar with 6 egg yolks; add 7 oz. butter, ½ lb. flour, 1 level tsp. baking powder. Mix into a paste, press the ball of paste on the marble slab with the palm of the hand, shape into small loaves or rolls, brush with egg yolk, and split in the middle with the back of a moistened knife.

ENGLISH TEA ROLLS PAINS ANGLAIS POUR LE THÉ (P.) (*15–18*)

¼ lb. flour, ¼ lb. sugar, 3½ oz. butter, 3 oz. almonds, salt, grated lemon peel, 1 whole egg. First mash the almonds with the sugar, moistening with a little egg, to make a very fine paste. Place this mixture in the center of the flour with the rest of the egg, butter, salt, lemon peel. Knead the paste and divide it into even-sized pieces. Roll the pieces by hand into small loaves or rolls and place them on a buttered baking sheet. Dent them in the middle, brush with egg, and bake in a hot oven.

MILK ROLLS PAINS AU LAIT (P.)

Taking a paste similar to that used for Crescents (p. 588), but without butter, make Milk Rolls for sandwiches. Shape like small rolls rather than crescents. Let rise well, brush with egg, and bake in a hot oven.

MECCA ROLLS PAINS DE LA MECQUE (P.)

Make oblongs of Choux Paste (p. 548); sprinkle sugar on top; lightly dent in the middle as for other rolls; bake in a hot oven. May be filled with cream or jam, or eaten as they are.

RAISIN ROLLS PAINS AUX RAISINS (D. and D.)

Make from sugared Brioche Paste (p. 546) a little hardened with flour; add ¼ lb. dried currants (raisins) per lb. paste. Shape into rounds on buttered baking sheets, brush with egg, and cut a cross on top with scissors.

PUFFED ROLLS PAINS SOUFFLÉS (P.)

Proportions: ¼ lb. flour, 2 oz. butter, 2½ oz. sugar, 1 whole egg, grated lemon peel, pinch of bicarbonate of soda.

Mix and knead all together, then let stand. Divide into pieces about the size of a walnut, then roll them out like long cigars. Place on a baking sheet and brush with egg. These little cakes puff up in baking.

LADY DISKS PALETS DE DAMES (P.)

Proportions: 2 oz. butter, 2 oz. sugar, 2½ oz. flour, 1¼ oz. dried currants, a finger of rum, 1 whole egg.

Soften the butter in a mixing bowl, then mix in the sugar and beat 3–4 min. with a whisk. Next add the whole egg and continue beating; finish by mixing in the flour, then the cleaned raisins (which have been soaked in rum). Lay out like macaroons on a buttered, floured baking sheet; bake 5 min. in a very hot oven.

PALM LEAVES PALMIERS (P.)

These are usually made of scraps of Puff Paste (p. 544) left over from making a cake or *vol-au-vent.* Fold and roll out these scraps twice more, sprinkle liberally with powdered sugar. Make a large thin square of the paste and fold 1 side twice, bringing it to the center of the square; make the same double fold on the other side, joining it to the first. These 2 double folds should be folded again, 1 on the other, so that you have 4 thicknesses of paste. Cut into slices ⅜ in. thick or a little more if you want them larger, for the Palm Leaf can be either a Petit Four or a small cake. Place them flat on a baking sheet, allowing plenty of space between each one, for they spread out rather than rise. Bake 10 min. in a rather hot oven, but not too hot on the bottom.

Fig. 387 - Apple tart (p 583).
Fig. 388 - 1. Baba (p. 584). 2. Marignans (p. 594).
3. Pomponnettes (p. 597). 4. Savarin with cream (p. 599).

Fig. 387

Fig. 388

Fig. 389

Fig. 390

PARISETTES PARISETTES (P.)

Make the paste for Lady Disks (p. 596), leaving out the dried currants. Then shape into large wafers on a buttered, floured baking sheet and sprinkle with chopped or shredded almonds. Bake 5–6 min. in a very hot oven.

PATRICIANS PATRICIENS (D. and D.)

Cook 1 lb. sugar to the "soft-ball" stage (p. 562); pour it over 5 stiffly beaten egg whites. Mix into this meringue ½ lb. almonds crushed into a soft paste with ½ lb. sugar and a little egg white; add vanilla. Squeeze the mixture from a pastry bag, in round or oval shapes, onto buttered, floured baking sheets. Dry them in the warmer 3 hr., then bake in a slow oven. Put these cookies together in pairs with a layer in between of vanilla Butter Cream (p. 551) mixed with Cooked Meringue (p. 557) that has been crushed and pressed through a coarse sieve; powder the top with vanilla-flavored confectioners' sugar. (Figure 391, Page 604.)

POLKAS POLKAS (P.)

Cut thin rounds of Short Paste (p. 545) with a cookie cutter or water glass; prick them with a knife. Then, using a pastry bag with a rather small round tube, lay a ring of Choux Paste (p. 548) around the edges (see Figure 106, p. 117). Brush with egg and bake in a hot oven. Fill the hollow with thick Pastry Cream (p. 552), powder heavily with sugar, and caramelize the sugar rapidly and lightly by holding a red-hot iron over it. (Figure 390, Page 597.)

POTATOES I POMMES DE TERRE (D. and D.)

Place 2 small patties (see Chocolate Patties, p. 586) together with a filling of white Almond Paste (p. 557) between and a covering of the same paste. Cover with sirup and roll in chocolate powder. Indent the eyes of the potatoes with a small piece of wood. These are also made of chestnut paste enriched with a little Almond Paste.

POTATOES II POMMES DE TERRE (D. and D.)

Mash 1 lb. Sponge-Cake scraps (p. 548) with 5 tbsp. apricot jam and ¾ oz. melted cocoa to make a fairly soft paste; let it stand several hours. Prepare 13 or 14 pieces of Sponge Fingers about ⅜ in. wide and 1¼ in. long (p. 586). Soak them in a thin sirup flavored with curaçao. Roll out the cocoa paste with a rolling pin, brush the surface with apricot jam, and wrap each Sponge Finger in a layer of this paste. Shape by hand into potatoes and roll in chocolate powder; prick here and there, as directed above.

POMPONNETTES POMPONNETTES (D. and D.)

Half fill small, deep, round molds with Baba Paste (p. 546) containing dried currants and sultanas; let rise, then bake in a hot oven. Soak in punch, decorate with half a candied cherry, and frost white or pink with rum-flavored icing. (Figure 388, Page 596.)

PONTS-NEUFS PONTS-NEUFS (P.)

Line tartlet shells with Short Paste (p. 545), prick the crust, and fill heaping full with a mixture of equal parts of cold Choux Paste (p. 548) and Pastry Cream (p. 552). Brush the top with egg and lay 2 strips of Short Paste over it in the shape of a cross. Bake 12–15 min. in a moderate oven. (Figure 393, Page 605.)

Fig. 389 - 1. Biarritz (p. 585). 2. Blidahs (p. 586). 3. Almond croquets (p. 588). 4. Bordeaux croquets (p. 588). 5. Mirrors (p. 595).

Fig. 390 - 1. Conversations (p. 587). 2. Eclairs (p. 589). 3. Madeleines (p. 593). 4. Marcelins (p. 594). 5. Polkas (p. 597). 6. Cherry tartlets (p. 600). 7. Visitants (p. 600).

CHOCOLATE PROGRESS CAKES PROGRÈS CHOCOLAT (J.)

Prepare small layers of Progress Cake (see p. 554) about 2 in. in diameter. Lay a filling of Chocolate Praline Butter Cream (p. 551) between 2 layers (a pastry bag makes this step faster and cleaner). Be sure the smooth side of the top layer is up. Cover with cocoa powder. (Figure 393, Page 605.)

PRALINE PROGRESS CAKES PROGRÈS PRALINÉ (J.)

Same procedure as in the preceding recipe. Fill with Praline Butter Cream (p. 552) and powder with vanilla-flavored sugar. (Figure 393, Page 605.)

WELLS OF LOVE or JAM PATTIES PUITS D'AMOUR OR BOUCHÉES AUX CONFITURES (P.)

Cut a thin round of Puff Paste (p. 544) about 2 in. in diameter for the bottom crust and place it on a baking sheet; moisten it slightly with water and place on top a second and slightly smaller circle of Puff Paste with the center cut out. This makes a ring around the bottom crust. Brush with egg and bake 12 min. in a rather hot oven. Then fill the well in the center with red-currant jelly. (Figure 392, Page 604.)

NUNS RELIGIEUSES (D. and D.)

Line small tartlet molds with Pie Paste (p. 545); fill with Frangipane Cream (p. 552); bake, cool, place on each a Cream-Puff shell (p. 587) filled with cooked cream and frosted with Coffee or Chocolate Fondant (p. 553); a stippled border of Butter Cream (p. 551) around the puff and a rosette in the center.

ALMOND ROCKS ROCHERS D'AMANDES (P.)

Beat 3 egg whites and 5 oz. vanilla-flavored powdered sugar over a very low fire until the mass becomes rather compact and no longer spreads. Then mix in 3½ oz. very dry shredded almonds and place on a baking sheet or on paper in irregular droplets; bake in a very slow oven without browning.

COCONUT ROCKS ROCHERS À LA NOIX DE COCO (P.)

Mix together 2½ oz. grated coconut, 2 oz. powdered almonds, 4½ oz. sugar, and 2 egg whites; beat thoroughly, then add 2 egg whites beaten stiff and mixed with 1½ oz. vanilla-flavored sugar. Drop spoonfuls of this paste onto a buttered, floured baking sheet, leaving plenty of space between. Bake 8–10 min. in a very slow oven. (Figure 394, Page 605.)

ALMOND SHORTBREAD COOKIES SABLÉS AUX AMANDES (P.) (*18 pieces*)

¼ lb. flour, 3½ oz. butter, 2 oz. powdered almonds, 2¼ oz. sugar, 2 egg yolks, salt, and grated lemon peel.

Make the paste as directed in the recipe for Shortbread Cookies with Hard-Boiled Eggs (p. 599), using raw egg yolks and more almonds (proportions above). Roll out the paste, cut it into rounds with a cookie cutter. Cut each round into 4 equal parts to obtain triangles with one rounded side—in other words, like wedges of a pie. Brush these cookies with beaten egg, streak them with a knife, bake 7–8 min. in a hot oven.

NANTES SHORTBREAD COOKIES SABLÉS NANTAIS (P.) (*18 pieces*)

¼ lb. flour, 2 oz. butter, 2 oz. sugar, 1¼ oz. powdered almonds, 2 egg yolks, ⅓ tsp. salt.

Make a very smooth paste, roll it into a ball, and let it stand 1 hr. in a cool place. Roll it out ⅛ in. thick and cut it with a fluted cookie cutter into circles 2 in. in diameter. Place them on a lightly buttered baking sheet and brush with beaten egg. Streak them both ways with a fork, making a checkerboard pattern. Place a pinch of powdered almonds in the center, with a dash of powdered sugar on top. Bake 7–8 min. in a hot oven.

SHORTBREAD COOKIES WITH HARD-BOILED EGGS SABLÉS AUX OEUFS DURS (P.) (*18 pieces*)

¼ lb. flour, 3 oz. butter, 2 oz. sugar, yolks of 2 hard-boiled eggs, ⅓ tsp. salt, 1 grated lemon peel.

Shape the flour into a well and in the center put the other ingredients and the hard-boiled eggs pressed through a sieve. After kneading, let stand 2 hr. in a cool place. Roll it out with a rolling pin until 3/16 in. thick. Cut it into triangles with a cookie cutter. Place them on a buttered baking sheet and make a rather deep crisscross design with the prongs of a fork. Let stand 1 full hr. Bake in a very hot oven without brushing with egg.

SACRISTANS SACRISTAINS (P.)

These can be made with scraps of leftover Puff Paste (p. 544). Roll out in a long, very thin strip, as for Glazed Matches (p. 584). Brush with beaten egg, cover with powdered almonds, powder with sugar, and cut into strips the width of a finger. Take the 2 ends of each strip and twist them twice like a corkscrew. Place them on a baking sheet and pinch the ends tightly to stick them together so that they will bake without unwinding. Bake 5–6 min. in a very hot oven.

SALAMBOS SALAMBOS (D. and D.)

Oblong Cream Puffs (p. 587) made of Choux Paste (p. 548) and filled with vanilla Pastry Cream (p. 552), then frosted with sugar cooked to the "crack" stage (p. 562); chopped pistachios sprinkled on top before cooling.

SAVARINS SAVARINS (P.)

Make them like the large Savarins (p. 547), using small savarin molds. When they are baked and soaked, they are sometimes filled with Chantilly Cream (p. 552) or some cooked cream. (Figure 388, Page 596.)

FRUIT SAVARINS SAVARINS AUX FRUITS (P.)

Make small Savarins, soak them, and brush with apricot jam; fill the center with fruit compote or jam.

SELIKAS SELIKAS (Du.)

Small puffs like Salambos (above). Fill with vanilla Butter Cream (p. 551); frost with Chocolate Fondant (p. 553), a grilled almond half on top.

SIGHS SOUPIRS (Du.)

Line tartlet molds with Pie Paste (p. 545); fill with Frangipane Cream (p. 552); bake. Then, using a pastry bag held vertically, top with a point of Italian Meringue (p. 557). Let dry, and frost with Fondant (p. 553) of different flavors and colors.

SUZANNE SUZANNE (Du.)

Savarin Paste (p. 547) in small, deep, round molds; let rise, bake, and soak in kirsch-flavored sirup. Split on side and fill with Chantilly Cream (p. 552).

TARTLETS TARTELETTES (P.)

Have some small tartlet molds; roll out Short Paste (p. 545) very thin and cut it with a fluted cookie cutter the same size as the molds; prick with a fork and fill as directed in making tarts (p. 582).

CHERRY TARTLETS TARTELETTES AUX CERISES (D. and D.)

After lining the molds, follow the method given above; sugar the bottom, place the pitted cherries in tightly against each other; bake, and sugar after removing from the oven or coat with red-currant jelly. Baking time: 15 min.

Fresh cherries will keep their natural color if you roll them in powdered sugar before placing them in the tartlet shells. (Figure 390, Page 597.)

MAZURKA TARTLETS TARTELETTES MAZURKA (Du.)

Line molds with leftover scraps of Puff Paste (p. 544) and put a little cooked cream (without beaten egg whites) in the bottom; bake. After baking, add a little of the same cream; cover the surface with powdered sugar, and burn in a design with a red-hot iron.

MERINGUE TARTLETS TARTELETTES MERINGUÉES (P.)

Make small round or rectangular tartlets of Short (p. 545) or Puff Paste (p. 544); fill them with Pastry Cream (p. 552), Frangipane Cream (p. 552), or applesauce; and bake them in a hot oven. Then cover the top with a layer of meringue; sprinkle with powdered sugar and replace a few minutes in a very slow oven to bake and lightly brown the meringue. (Figure 392, Page 604.)

TOMMIES TOMMIES (D. and D.)

½ lb. sugar, 11 oz. grilled, crushed, sifted hazelnuts.

Shape 20 oz. flour into a well and place the ingredients above in the center, then add 1 lb. butter and 3 tbsp. light cream. Mix well into a paste and let stand. Roll out with a rolling pin and cut with a fluted cookie cutter about 1¼ in. in diameter; place on unbuttered baking sheets. Bake in a hot oven. Put together by twos with Reduced Apricot (p. 550) in the middle. Spread a little Reduced Apricot over the center of the top and, when cold, frost with powdered sugar.

VISITANTS VISITANDINES (P.)

This little cake, one of the simplest and best, may be found in all pastry shops. Put into a mixing bowl 5 oz. very dry mashed almonds and 7 oz. vanilla-flavored sugar; then, using a spatula, mix in, little by little, 4 egg whites (not beaten). When the paste has been beaten about 10 min., mix in 2½ oz. flour and 7 oz. butter. (The butter should be cooked slowly until it begins to brown, turning into what we call nut butter.) Mix it almost cold and bake, in round or oval buttered, floured molds, in a hot oven. (Figure 390, Page 597.)

PETITS FOURS or FANCY LITTLE CAKES

A chapter on Petits Fours could be extremely long, but we shall include only the easiest to make at home. Unless you have an excellent chef, you had better buy these pretty little cakes ready-made for dinner parties, for you won't be able to get away with only mediocre Petits Fours.

Note: Many small cakes—Mirrors, Biarritz, Brazilians, Palm Leaves, Sacristans, etc.—are also made as Petits Fours. Since these recipes have already been given, we shall not repeat them in this chapter.

Petits Fours are divided into 3 kinds: dry, frosted, and meringue.

DRY PETITS FOURS

DRY-PASTE FOURS FOURS EN PÂTE SÈCHE (P.)

Make a Sweet Paste (p. 546) well flavored with lemon or orange; roll it out with a rolling pin until not quite 1/8 in. thick, then cut the paste with different-shaped cookie cutters, or with a knife, into diamonds, rectangles, or small squares. Place them on a baking sheet, brush with beaten egg, and decorate each in a different way, with a half almond, Malaga raisin, candied fruit, etc. Bake 5–6 min. in a hot oven.

DRY FOURS WITH ALMONDS FOURS SECS AUX AMANDES (P.)

Add to the Sweet Paste mentioned above, 1½ oz. powdered almonds, an extra egg yolk, and ½ tsp. baking powder. Shape small bits of this paste by hand into different forms: rolled like thick pencils; shaped like rolls dented in the center; braided; in very tiny pancakes. Brush with beaten egg and bake in a hot oven.

ALMOND-PASTE FOURS FOURS EN PÂTE D'AMANDES (P.)

Finely pound 7 oz. almonds in a mortar with 7 oz. powdered sugar. Then moisten, bit by bit, with 1 egg white until the paste becomes soft enough to be squeezed from a pastry bag. Flavor with vanilla and squeeze from a bag with a fluted tube onto a sheet of paper. These Petits Fours are of the macaroon type, but made in different shapes—rings, droplets, S-shaped—then decorated with almonds, cherries, raisins, etc. Bake 8–10 min. in a rather hot oven. Place the paper on a damp board to make it easier to remove the cakes. (Figure395P.608.)

CAT TONGUES LANGUES DE CHAT (P.)

Proportions: 3½ oz. butter, 3½ oz. sugar, 4¼ oz. flour, vanilla, 3 egg whites, 6 tbsp. heavy cream.

Preparation: Put the butter into a mixing bowl and knead it gently until creamed but still rather firm; beat it with a wire whisk while mixing in the vanilla-flavored sugar. Beat the mixture well 5 min., then add the egg whites in 4 parts, always beating 2 min. after adding each part. Do not worry if the paste seems to turn. When all the egg whites have been blended, remove the wire whisk and mix in all the flour at one time with a spatula, and finish with the cream. Put the paste into a pastry bag with a special tube for Cat Tongues (plain round tube no. 11) and squeeze, onto lightly buttered, floured baking sheets, small strips as wide as a pencil and as long as a finger; leave enough space between, for the tongues spread out in baking. Bake in a very hot oven. Baking time: 4–5 min. These Cat Tongues are exquisite. If you want to keep them a day or two, they must be tightly covered in a tin box, like all dry cakes, for the air softens them.

SMALL SOUFFLÉS WITH ALMONDS PETITS SOUFFLÉS AUX AMANDES (P.)

Pound 2 oz. almonds in a mortar with 4 oz. confectioners' sugar, vanilla, and 1 egg white; the paste should not be hard, but able to be rolled by hand into balls the size of Mirabelle plums. Moisten very lightly with egg white and roll in confectioners' sugar until entirely covered. Place them in small paper baking cups especially for Petits Fours, which they should fill 3/4 full, and bake 10–12 min. in a slow oven. They will puff up in these cups, and should be served in them.

SMALL SOUFFLÉS WITH HAZELNUTS PETITS SOUFFLÉS AUX NOISETTES (P.)

Same as above, with lightly grilled, peeled hazelnuts instead of almonds.

ALMOND TILES TUILES AUX AMANDES (P.) (*30 pieces*)

Proportions: 3 oz. vanilla-flavored powdered sugar, 1½ oz. flour, 1½ oz. butter, 2 egg whites, 1¼ oz. shredded almonds.

Preparation: Beat the sugar and 2 egg whites together 3 or 4 min., then mix in the flour, melted butter, and shredded almonds. The paste should be made quickly. Butter and flour a baking sheet or 2, then use about 1 tsp. paste at a time to lay small drops on the baking sheet, and spread them out a little into round wafers. Sprinkle them with a shaker of powdered sugar and bake 4–5 min. in a very hot oven. As soon as they are baked, pick the wafers up with a knife and place them on a rolling pin or any other round object, so they will take the shape of roof tiles while cooling. They are rather fragile.

FROSTED PETITS FOURS

FROSTED FOURS OF GÉNOISE CAKE FOURS EN GÉNOISE GLACÉS (P.)

Cut a Génoise Cake (p. 549) baked the previous day into small squares, triangles, diamonds, rounds, crescents, etc. Split them crosswise and fill with a little jam. Then prepare Fondant (p. 553), flavor and color it, and dip the different pieces of cake into various colors and flavors of Fondant. Decorate lightly with candied fruits.

FROSTED CREAM FOURS FOURS À LA CRÈME GLACÉS (J.)

These are the most difficult to make because of their delicacy, brittleness, and the impeccable appearance they must have. They can be made with a base of Génoise Cake (p. 549) or macaroon-type Almond Paste (p. 557). Use a pastry bag filled with Mousseline Butter Creams (p. 551) of various flavors and colors to garnish the tops (see Illustrations, p. 119). Put them into the refrigerator 1–2 hr., then frost them with variously colored Fondants (p. 553).

(Figure 396, Page 608.)

No. 1. Rectangles of Génoise Cake filled with raspberry jam. Frost with raspberry-flavored pink Fondant. *Décor:* 2 small strips of chocolate Fondant, made with a paper cone.

No. 2. Rounds of Sponge Cake (p. 548) filled with Coffee Butter Cream (p. 551). Frost with coffee Fondant.

No. 3. Diamonds of Génoise Cake filled with jam. Frost with green Fondant flavored with kümmel. Dot of chocolate Fondant on top.

No. 4. Rounds of Sponge Cake filled with cherry-flavored Butter Cream. Frost with cherry-flavored pink Fondant. Dot of coffee Fondant on top.

No. 5. Long pieces of Sponge Cake filled with Chocolate Butter Cream. Frost with chocolate Fondant. Sprinkle a pinch of chopped, grilled almonds on top.

No. 6. Rounds of Sponge Cake filled with Chestnut Butter Cream (p. 551). White Fondant frosting. Spirals of chocolate Fondant made with a paper cone.

No. 7. Long pieces of Sponge Cake filled with Coffee Butter Cream. Coffee Fondant frosting. Place half a walnut on each. (Figure 397, Page 609.)

No. 1. Rounds of Sponge Cake filled with kirsch-flavored Butter Cream. Place half a candied cherry on top. Frost with kirsch-flavored Fondant.

No. 2. Rounds of Sponge Cake filled with Coffee Butter Cream and chopped hazelnuts. Coffee Fondant frosting. Grilled hazelnut on top.

No. 3. Long pieces of Sponge Cake filled with curaçao-flavored Butter Cream. Curaçao-flavored, pink Fondant frosting. Dot of chocolate on top.

No. 4. Rounds of Sponge Cake filled with Butter Cream flavored with crème de cassis. Mauve Fondant frosting with same flavoring.

No. 5. Long pieces of Sponge Cake filled with anisette-flavored Butter Cream. Green Fondant frosting with same flavoring. *Décor:* 2 small bands of chocolate Fondant.

No. 6. Rounds of Sponge Cake filled with Chocolate Butter Cream, shaped into a pointed cone. Chocolate Fondant frosting. Stick 3 small triangles of hard chocolate into the top.

DISGUISED CHERRIES CERISES DÉGUISÉES (P.)

Drain and dry some brandied cherries; taking them by the stems, dip them into white or pink kirsch-flavored Fondant (p. 553), which should be rather thick and a little hotter than usual. Space them evenly on a surface well covered with powdered sugar, then place them in small paper cups. (Figure 397-7, Page 609.)

May be decorated with a small leaf of green sugar. (Figure 398, Page 609.)

MOCHATINES and CHOCOLATINES MOKATINES and CHOCOLATINES (R.)

Cut Génoise Cake (p. 549) into very small squares; split them crosswise and fill them lightly with Coffee or Chocolate Butter Cream (p. 551), depending on the case. Spread the top and sides of these little squares with the same cream. Roll the Mochatines in granulated sugar and the Chocolatines in finely chopped, grilled almonds or in granulated chocolate.

FROSTED PETITS FOURS

with a Choux-Paste base

COFFEE AND CHOCOLATE CAROLINES CAROLINES CAFÉ ET CHOCOLAT (P.)

Small Éclairs (p. 589) hardly as large as a little finger, filled and frosted like the large ones.

PRALINE PUFFS CHOUX PRALINÉS (P.)

Small Cream Puffs (p. 587) brushed with beaten egg and powdered with chopped almonds, sugared, and baked in a medium oven. Fill them with Praline Butter Cream (p. 552) and powder with confectioners' sugar.

SALAMBOS SALAMBOS (P.)

Small puffs of Choux Paste (p. 548) like those used for a Saint-Honoré (p. 581), filled with vanilla Butter Cream (p. 551) and the top dipped in sugar cooked to the "crack" stage (p. 562).

MERINGUE PETITS FOURS (P.)

Take Cooked Meringue (p. 557), flavored coffee, vanilla, or chocolate, and squeeze it from a pastry bag, onto buttered, floured baking sheets, into different shapes, imitating mushrooms or other forms. Bake in a very slow, open oven.

COFFEE BISCUITS BISCUITS CAFÉ (D. and D.)

Prepare the same as the Chocolate Biscuits, below, but cook the sugar to the "crack" stage (p. 562) and reduce it to the "ball" stage with strong coffee or coffee essence; add a little confectioners' sugar to form a crust and finish as described in the chocolate recipe.

CHOCOLATE BISCUITS BISCUITS CHOCOLAT (D. and D.)

Beat 5 egg whites very stiff; pour in 1 lb. sugar cooked to the "soft-ball" stage (p. 562), continuing to beat; add ¾ oz. confectioners' sugar and 6 oz. melted cocoa diluted with a little sirup to facilitate blending. Squeeze from a pastry bag into long strips onto waxed baking sheets, and bake in a very slow, open oven.

RASPBERRY or STRAWBERRY BISCUITS BISCUITS FRAMBOISE OF FRAISE (D. and D.)

Same proportion of sugar and egg whites as for Chocolate Biscuits, above. Cook the sugar to "crack" stage (p. 562) and bring back to the "soft-ball" stage with raspberry or strawberry juice; color pink.

VANILLA BISCUITS BISCUITS VANILLE (D. and D.)

Same preparation as above; flavor with 2 vanilla beans cooked in the sugar (cooked only to the "soft-ball" stage) or use vanilla-flavored sirup to bring sugar cooked to the "soft-crack" stage back to the "soft-ball" stage (see p. 562).

COFFEE LADY FINGERS DOIGTS DE DAMES AU CAFÉ (D. and D.)

Pour 1 lb. sugar cooked to the "hard-ball" stage (p. 562) onto 5 very stiffly beaten egg whites; immediately add ½ lb. confectioners' sugar previously moistened in a mixing bowl with coffee essence. Using a pastry bag with the appropriate tube, squeeze the mixture onto lightly buttered, floured baking sheets. Slow oven.

CHOCOLATE LADY FINGERS DOIGTS DE DAMES AU CHOCOLAT (D. and D.)

Proceed as above with 1 lb. sugar cooked to the "hard-ball" stage poured over 8 stiffly beaten egg whites; add ½ lb. grated chocolate, 10 oz. confectioners' sugar, caramel, and a little carmine. Bake the same way as Chocolate Biscuits (above).

REAL AND IMITATION FRUIT GLAZED WITH CARAMEL

ALMONDS ABOUKIR AMANDES ABOUKIR (P.)

Shape green Almond Paste (p. 557) into large green almonds by rolling it between the hands; slit them on the side and insert a dry, peeled almond, allowing about half of it to show. Dip in sugar cooked to the "crack" stage (p. 562) by sticking the tip of a small knife into the Almond Paste. Let them drain for a moment over some sugar, then place on an oiled marble slab to cool. All of these Fours should be served in tiny paper cups. (Figure 399, Page 612.)

Fig. 391 - 1. Sponge fingers (p. 586). 2. Macaroons (p. 592). 3. Meringues (p. 594). 4. Patricians (p. 597).
Fig. 392 - 1. Babies (p. 585). 2. Pretzels (p. 587). 3. Mirlitons (p. 595). 4. Wells of love (p. 598). 5. Meringue tartlets (p. 600).

Fig. 391

Fig. 392

Fig. 393

Fig. 394

CARAMEL CHERRIES CERISES AU CARAMEL (P.)

Drain and dry brandied cherries at very low heat. Taking them by the stem, dip them in sugar cooked to the "crack" stage (p. 562). Let them drain, then place in tiny paper cups. These cherries may also be decorated with a little leaf made of green sugar. (Figure 398, Page 609.)

Other recipe: Roll kirsch-flavored Almond-Paste Fondant (p. 558) into balls. Embed half a candied cherry on top of each ball. Glaze with caramel. (Figure 399, Page 612.)

STUFFED DATES DATTES FARCIES (P.)

Split the dates on the side to remove the pit, replacing it with a pit made of Almond Paste (p. 557); make the Almond-Paste pit larger than the original stone so that it sticks out of the date and can be seen. Dip in sugar cooked to the "crack" stage (p. 562). Finish as for Almonds Aboukir (p. 604). (Figure 399, Page 612.)

STUFFED WALNUTS NOIX FARCIES (P.)

Neatly shell some large walnuts to remove 2 perfect halves; press the 2 halves together again, embedding them in a small ball of Almond-Paste Fondant (p. 558) to imitate the shell. Dip in sugar cooked to the "crack" stage (p. 562) and finish as in the recipe for Almonds Aboukir (p. 604). (Figure 399, Page 612.)

GLAZED ORANGE SLICES ORANGES (TRANCHES D') GLACÉES (P.)

Peel the oranges, remove the white skin, then separate into sections and place them upright on a wire rack or grill. Dry them in the kitchen 3 or 4 hr. at moderate temperature; do not use a drier or oven. Cook sugar to the "crack" stage (p. 562) and dip each orange slice in it, holding the slices at one tip, which of course will not be glazed. After draining them, place on an oiled marble slab, then take them 1 by 1 and dip the unglazed part. If the sugar cools, it will thicken, and must be brought to a boil again to keep it liquid. It takes about 10 oz. sugar for 6 oranges.

STUFFED PRUNES PRUNEAUX FARCIS (P.)

Soft, raw prunes. Follow the directions given for Stuffed Dates (above). (Figure 399, Page 612.)

GLAZED PEARS POIRES GLACÉES (J.)

Roll by hand some small pieces of yellow-colored Almond-Paste Fondant (p. 558) into the shape of pears. Place a small dried currant in the wide part to imitate the core. Lightly color the middle part of the pear with carmine. Glaze with sugar cooked to the "crack" stage, following the method already given. (Figure 399, Page 612.)

LADY APPLES POMMES D'API (J.)

Mold by hand small balls of Almond-Paste Fondant (p. 558) colored pink or pale green. Color a slightly darker shade around the side and stick a dried currant in the top. Glaze with sugar cooked to the "crack" stage, following the method already described. (Figure 399, Page 612.)

Fig. 393 - 1. Chesnut boats (p. 585). 2. Carracks (p. 587). 3. Cream puffs (p. 587). 4. Mascots (p. 594). 5. Mochatines (p. 595). 6. Ponts-Neufs (p. 597). 7. Progress (p. 598).

Fig. 394 - 1. Cherry boats (p. 584). 2. Almond crescents (p. 588). 3. Darioles (p. 589). 4. Fanchonnettes (p. 589). 5. Coconut rocks (p. 598).

CONFECTIONERY

CHOCOLATE CARAMELS CARAMELS AU CHOCOLAT (Ga.)

1½ pt. milk, 13 oz. powdered sugar, egg-sized piece of glucose, 3¼ oz. chocolate in tablets, 1½ oz. butter, ½ vanilla bean. Put milk, sugar, vanilla bean, and glucose into a stewpan. Put the chocolate into a round-bottomed copper pan and melt it slowly on the stove. Meanwhile, heat the mixture in the stewpan, not letting it boil, since you merely want to melt the sugar and glucose. When completely melted, pour this mixture, bit by bit, into the chocolate, while stirring. When thoroughly mixed, cook at moderate heat, constantly stirring. Cook to the "ball" stage (p. 562). Remove from the fire, add the butter, mix well, and pour onto an oiled marble slab in an oiled, iron framework. Let cool and cut.

SOFT CHOCOLATE CARAMELS CARAMELS MOUS AU CHOCOLAT (Ga.)

½ lb. sugar, 9 oz. fresh heavy cream, 2 oz. cocoa powder, 1¼ oz. honey. Cook together in a copper pan (or a pan not lined with tin) until the mixture reaches the "ball" stage (p. 562). Pour this cooked sugar onto an oiled marble slab, keeping it at an even thickness of ⅔ in., using 4 oiled rulers to make a framework. Let cool and cut.

SOFT COFFEE CARAMELS CARAMELS MOUS AU CAFÉ (D. and D.)

Weigh 1 lb. lump sugar and place on top, in the scales, 5 oz. glucose; pour into a pan large enough to let it boil; dilute with ½ pt. milk and begin cooking over a very hot fire, stirring constantly. Add 1 pt. milk, bit by bit, making a total of 1½ pt. milk, then 1 oz. butter, and cook to the "ball" stage (p. 562). Flavor with coffee essence and pour onto a buttered marble slab in a framework or between iron rulers.

Let stand a few hours, then turn it over and roll out with a rolling pin (keeping it between the rulers) to the desired thickness. Rub the surface with the palm of the hand, lightly buttered, to give it a gloss. Roll with a ridged candy roller or mark with a caramel cutter and saw into squares with a large knife.

To better the quality, use 1 qt. milk, adding it in very small amounts, for if too much is poured in at one time, it may turn. If you increase the amount of milk, it's not a bad idea to leave out the butter; in fact, if you do leave it out, the caramel will keep longer. We don't advise using cream—it has a tendency to turn. It is wise to lower the heat toward the end of the cooking.

ALMOND MOCHETTES MOKETTES AUX AMANDES (Be.)

For these sweets, you need: 5 oz. chocolate, 1 tbsp. coffee concentrate, ¼ lb. confectioners' sugar, 2½ oz. sweet almonds, 2 tbsp. milk.

Preparation: Shell the almonds, lightly grill them, then pulverize them in a mortar with some rum (about 1 tbsp.). Grate the chocolate into fine powder; work it with the milk into a paste, then add the coffee, sugar, and almonds. Mix well together. Make into balls and roll in grated or granulated chocolate. Let stand 5–6 hr. to harden before serving.

MONTÉLIMAR NOUGAT NOUGAT DE MONTÉLIMAR (Be.)

Take 1 lb. white honey, 3 egg whites, ¾ lb. sugar, 9 oz. almonds, ½ lb. pistachios.

Bring the honey to a slow boil in a pan and fold in the stiffly beaten egg whites. When the mixture becomes brittle, remove from the fire. Cook the sugar to the "crack" stage (p. 562) and add it to the honey mixture. Stir the paste until cold. Shell and dry the almonds and, while still hot, blend them into the paste. Then add the pistachios, also shelled.

Line the sides of one or several tins with unleavened or wafer bread (this can be bought ready-made). Fill the tins with the nougat, cover with a sheet of unleavened bread, and put a heavy weight on top. Do not unmold until the next day.

CHOCOLATE TRUFFLES I TRUFFES AU CHOCOLAT (Be.)

Take 3 oz. chocolate, 1½ oz. butter, 2 oz. powdered sugar, 2 tbsp. fresh cream.

Preparation: Put cream, butter, and grated chocolate into a pan. The chocolate need not be grated fine. The cream can be replaced by skimming the top off raw milk poured into a wide basin and allowed to settle. Melt butter, chocolate, and cream in a double boiler, stirring to mix well. When melted, remove the double boiler from the fire, leaving the hot water in the bottom to keep it warm. Sift the powdered sugar in slowly, so that it will not form lumps, stirring constantly.

Let stand 24 hr. in a cool place. (In winter, 12 hr. in a cold room will do.) At the end of this time, cut a piece of this chocolate about the size of a small nut, using a knife or spoon. Roll it into a ball in the palm of the hand until the outside of the bonbon begins to melt a little. Then roll it in grated or granulated chocolate, which will stick to it perfectly. Let stand 2 hr. before serving, but in a place that is not too cold, because these truffles are better when they are a little soft. Instead of rolling them into balls, you can also shape them to look more like truffles.

CHOCOLATE TRUFFLES II TRUFFES EN CHOCOLAT (Ga.)

½ lb. good chocolate, a little water (about ½ glass), 3 egg yolks, 3 oz. butter.

Slowly melt the chocolate in the water, bring to a gentle boil, remove from the fire, and add the yolks, beating with a spatula, then replace on a low fire to poach the eggs in the chocolate. Do not stop beating. Remove from the fire and add the butter. Let cool, beating from time to time (this cooling takes a rather long time). When the mixture begins to solidify, take some with a spoon, place it in some grated chocolate (prepared in advance), and shape to resemble real truffles. These truffles keep a week. To keep a longer time, substitute vegetable shortening for the butter.

PRALINE TRUFFLES TRUFFES PRALINÉES (Ga.)

Proceed as above, adding 1½ oz. Praline paste (p. 559) after mixing and before cooling. Praline paste is made simply by pounding the Praline in a mortar until it becomes a paste that can be rolled by hand. Crushing extracts the oil from the almonds, giving the Praline a pastelike consistency. Stop pounding when the Praline can be rolled in the hands—the paste must be neither too soft nor too gritty.

SUGAR ARTWORK

This chapter is intended only for professionals and those rare first-rate cooks who may be inspired by it. From the several works on artistic sugar creations, we have selected Émile Duval's *Traité de confiserie moderne* (*Modern Confectionery*), since it is the clearest for the cook unfamiliar with working cooked sugar. We have borrowed—and boiled down—the material on sugar flowers from Duval's book.

There are 2 ways to make these flowers: one by turning the sugar in the hands while working it, and the other by using satiny sugar, which makes brilliant but not such natural-looking flowers. Moreover, the turned flowers can be kept in the open air without using any preservative.

TURNED-SUGAR FLOWERS FLEURS EN SUCRE TOURNÉ

Put 8–10 oz. sugar into a copper pan with 6 oz. water and only a few drops of acetic acid (or lemon juice). Do not use glucose with the sugar, or you will not be able to turn it. Cook the sugar to the "soft-crack" stage (see p. 562), but not beyond—this is the most important point in working with turned sugar. Grease a marble slab with vaseline or oil and, when the sugar has cooled until it is merely warm, pour it on top. Mark into squares with a caramel cutter. Keep the sugar in a covered tin can to keep out the air—it should not be used at once.

To make flowers, heat each sugar square in the flame of an alcohol lamp and pull it out, thinning it until it is as thick as a petal; cut off the surplus with scissors (these won't be needed, once you have acquired a little experience). The petals should be of diminishing size and are fashioned by wrapping them around the tip of the thumb: when the sugar is worked between the fingers, it turns. Of course, to make pink or red roses, you must color the sugar while it cooks. To make tea roses, add a drop of carmine to yellow coloring.

When enough petals have been made, they must be put together. First, shape a small sugar base, around which the petals are stuck, beginning with the smallest; make them look as much as possible like a flower by turning back the outer edges or cupping them to give a delicate effect. The best way to imitate a rose is to have a real one before you as a model.

When the rose has been finished, the same process must be followed with green sugar; pull it between the fingers and stick it to the base of the rose; the leaves are made by pulling a little green sugar between the thumb and index finger and pressing it on a metal mold to imprint the veins of the leaf. The stems are made by pulling this green sugar to the desired length. The flowers can be arranged on top of a cake or in a bouquet in a vase made of Nougat (p. 557) or sugar.

Important Note: Your fingers must be very dry when working with sugar.

PULLED-SUGAR FLOWERS FLEURS EN SUCRE TIRÉ

These flowers must be kept under a glass bell with some sort of preservative. For professional use, flowers should always be kept on hand in tightly sealed containers to keep them dry. When they are needed to fill an order, all you have to do to finish them is to make the stems and leaves.

Put into a pan 10 oz. sugar moistened with just enough water to melt it; add 3 pinches of cream of tartar. Cook to the "hard crack" stage (p. 562), then remove from the fire and put the bottom of the pan into cold water to

Fig. 395 - Almond-paste fours (p. 601).
Fig. 396 - Frosted cream fours (p. 602).

Fig. 395

Fig. 396

Fig. 397

Fig. 398

stop the cooking. Pour the sugar on a marble slab greased with oil or vaseline. Fold the edges toward the center with a spatula until cool enough to hold in the hands without discomfort. When the sugar is very shiny, gather it into a ball, lay it on a wire rack or tray, and place in the opening of the oven. To have a very satiny sugar, pull the sugar only when it is almost cold. To make a flower, begin by shaping petals as thin as possible between the fingers. To do this, take a little sugar between the thumb and index finger of the right hand and, with the left hand, pull off a pinch. Thin it quickly, shaping it like a petal, and place it on a sieve or rack. To make a rose, first stick a central bud to the end of a sugar stem, then stick the petals around it, heating the base with an alcohol lamp. Begin with the smallest petals and finish with the larger ones. Do not use too many petals. Rosebuds are made by wrapping 2 or 3 petals around a small cone-shaped center base; finish by sticking on long, narrow leaves of green sugar. The sugar can be worked more easily if it is cooked with a little glucose, but it does not keep so well.

The directions given in Duval's book, clear as they are, are not worth a practical demonstration; they simply help the practitioner perfect the technical knowledge he already possesses.

PULLED-SUGAR RIBBONS RUBANS EN SUCRE TIRÉ

Sugar ribbons should have a more satiny sheen than flowers and call for even more dexterity and experience. They are made in all colors and sometimes in several colors with contrasting borders. They are a magnificent specimen of the French art of confectionery. Sugar for ribbons is worked the same way as for satin flowers, but much more delicately when made into a wide ribbon with several colors. Sugars of various colors are pulled separately, then stuck together and pulled over the stove to maintain pliability. Use the fingers as little as possible on the surface, so as not to spoil the brilliancy. When the ribbon has reached the right length, cut it and soften it slightly so that it may be curved and whorled gracefully. Bows are made by folding the loops of sugar and welding the 2 ends together.

BOUQUET OF FLOWERS BOUQUET DE FLEURS

This piece is entirely made by hand. Vase of Nougat (p. 557) decorated with Royal Glaze (p. 556). Flowers and ribbon of pulled sugar.

HOT SWEETS or DESSERTS

APRICOTS COLBERT ABRICOTS À LA COLBERT (P.)

Poach some fine apricot halves, keeping them rather firm, then wipe them dry and put the 2 halves together with 1 tbsp. Rice Condé (p. 559) containing chopped candied cherries in the middle. Shape like a whole, large apricot, roll in flour, then in beaten egg, and finally in white bread crumbs. Stick a small piece of candied angelica into the apricot to imitate the stem, and fry, just before serving, in very hot deep fat. Arrange a mound of these apricots on a napkin, powder with sugar, and serve with a separate dish of kirsch-flavored Apricot Sauce (p. 560) or Sabayon (p. 553).

Fig. 397 - Frosted cream fours (p. 603).
Fig. 398 - 1. Disguised cherries (p. 603).
2. Caramel cherries (p. 605).

APRICOTS CONDÉ ABRICOTS À LA CONDÉ (P.)

Cut the apricots in 2 and poach them in vanilla-flavored sirup. Do not let them cook too long. Drain them and place them on a ring of Rice with Milk (p. 559) made with sugar and vanilla and bound, on the stove, with 2 egg yolks per 5 oz. rice and a good piece of butter. While this rice should be fluffy, it must also be firm enough to support the weight of the fruit. Place the apricot halves open side down on the rice, decorate them with candied cherries and angelica, and pour a thin apricot sirup flavored to taste over them.

Note: Any fruit can be prepared *à la Condé.* (Figure 400, Page 612.)

APRICOTS CUSSY ABRICOTS CUSSY (E.)

Cover the flat sides of some large Soft Macaroons (p. 593) with a layer of finely chopped fruits bound with apricot purée; place a fine, poached apricot half on each macaroon; cover with Italian Meringue (p. 557). Arrange in a circle on a platter and place in a slow oven a few minutes to dry the meringue without coloring it. Serve a separate dish of kirsch-flavored Apricot Sauce (p. 560).

APRICOTS RÉGENCE ABRICOTS À LA RÉGENCE (P.) (*For 8 persons*)

Soak 4 oz. Sponge Fingers (p. 586) in vanilla-flavored boiling milk; when they are thoroughly saturated, press through a sieve; bind this purée with 2½ oz. sugar and 4 whole eggs. Poach this pudding in a flat mold in a *bain-marie,* first buttering and sugaring the mold. Cook about 20 min., then unmold the pudding onto a round platter large enough to accommodate a border of fine apricot halves poached in sirup. Place the apricots open side up and lay a candied cherry in the hollow of each half. Cover everything with reduced apricot sirup thickened with a little apricot jam.

APRICOTS SULTANE ABRICOTS À LA SULTANE (E.)

Bake a Génoise Cake (p. 549) in a ring mold with a rather high rim. After unmolding, use some apricot sirup cooked to the "thread" stage (p. 562) to stick it to a base of Dry Paste (p. 546) of the same size. Cover the sides with Ordinary Meringue (p. 557); decorate with a paper cone and color a golden brown in a slow oven. Then fill the center of the ring with a composition of vanilla-flavored rice mixed with a little Frangipane Cream (p. 552) and shredded pistachios, keeping the mixture firm enough to build into a dome. On top the rice place fine apricot halves poached in vanilla sirup and sprinkle the apricots with chopped pistachios. Serve a separate dish of sirup made with Almond Milk (p. 556) and finished with a hazelnut-sized piece of butter. (Figure 401, P. 613.)

PINEAPPLE BOURDALOUE ANANAS À LA BOURDALOUE (P.)

Bake Ordinary Génoise paste (p. 549) in a buttered, floured savarin mold. Unmold onto a round platter and lay on top some thin slices of fresh or canned pineapple simmered 10 min. in vanilla sirup. The pineapple slices should be curved so that they cling tightly to the rounded top of the cake. Fill the center with Bourdaloue cream or Frangipane Cream (p. 552) piled into a dome; sprinkle the top with crushed macaroons or chopped almonds; baste with butter, and brown the top of this cream in a hot oven. Then moisten the pineapple slices with a thin apricot sirup flavored with kirsch and decorate them with candied cherries and angelica.

Note: Any fruit may be prepared *à la bourdaloue.*

PINEAPPLE CREOLE ANANAS À LA CRÉOLE (P.)

Prepare some well-bound but fluffy Dessert Rice (p. 559). Poach some thin pineapple slices, cut in 2 like half moons, in sirup. Drain these slices and place them overlapping in a dome-shaped mold until it is completely lined. Spread a thick layer of the Dessert Rice over the pineapple, leaving a hollow in the center of the mold. In this hollow place the rest of the pineapple, diced and mixed with apricot sirup; finish filling the mold with the rest of the rice, and bake 6–7 min. in a hot oven. Unmold onto a round platter, and lay banana halves poached in pineapple sirup around it. Put a few cherries between or on the bananas, and cover the whole with rum-flavored apricot sirup. (Fig. 402, P. 613.)

DEVILED PINEAPPLE ANANAS À LA DIABLE (M.)

Poach pineapple slices in sirup, drain them, and place each slice on a slice of stale Brioche (p. 565) toasted in butter. Cover with Praline (p. 559) thinned with a little cream. Sprinkle with shredded almonds and sugar. Glaze quickly in a hot oven. Moisten with kirsch and set aflame when serving. Serve with kirsch-flavored Apricot Sauce (p. 560).

BANANAS FLAMBÉ BANANES FLAMBÉES (E.)

Split peeled bananas in 2 lengthwise and powder with sugar. Roll them in flour, in beaten egg, and again in flour. Fry them in clarified butter. Place the banana halves side by side on a long platter; powder with sugar, cover generously with heated kirsch, and light when serving.

SOUFFLÉED BANANAS BANANES SOUFFLÉES (E.)

Cut off the top ¼ of the bananas and remove the pulp without breaking the skins. Press the pulp through a sieve; add it to a cream soufflé mixture (see p. 629); finish it with the necessary amount of stiffly beaten egg whites. Fill the skins with this mixture. Arrange the bananas like the spokes of a wheel on a platter, and bake 6 min.

FAVORITE FRITTERS BEIGNETS FAVORIS (E.)

Take 2 Soft Macaroons (p. 593) per fritter. Lightly hollow out the centers. Fill them with apricot jam; stick the 2 macaroons together and soak them, just before using, in kirsch-and-maraschino-flavored sirup or rum-flavored sirup; dip them in Frying Paste (p. 558) and plunge them into hot deep fat. Drain, sprinkle with sugar, and serve on a napkin.

Note: Following this same procedure, you can replace the apricot jam with any other jam and liqueur, such as curaçao with orange marmalade or strawberry jam. Instead of dipping the macaroons in Frying Paste, simply dip them in flour, beaten egg, and bread crumbs and brown on both sides in butter. The jam may also be replaced with Frangipane Cream (p. 552) mixed with finely chopped candied fruits macerated in kirsch. These simple fritters can be varied a great number of ways and served with a fruit sauce flavored with rum, kirsch, maraschino, or curaçao.

ACACIA-FLOWER FRITTERS BEIGNETS DE FLEURS D'ACACIA (E.)

Pluck clusters in full bloom, place them in a deep dish, sprinkle with sugar, pour champagne brandy over them, and let them macerate ½ hr. When ready to serve, dip them in Frying Paste (p. 558) and fry in very hot deep fat; drain, sprinkle with sugar, and serve on a napkin.

Note: Fitters may be made the same way with elderberry, squash, or bindweed flowers. All fruit fritters—in fact, all fritters—are best fried in pure olive oil.

FRITTERS GRAND'MÈRE BEIGNETS GRAND'MÈRE (E.)

Spread fruit jam on slices of stale Brioche (p. 565) moistened with kirsch or rum. Dip in Frying Paste (p. 558) and fry in very hot deep fat. Drain, powder with confectioners' sugar, and glaze in a hot oven.

DAINTY FRITTERS BEIGNETS MIGNONS (E.)

Take 2 Soft Macaroons (p. 593) per fritter. Lightly hollow out the centers; fill with apricot jam; stick the macaroons together in pairs and soak them in kirsch-flavored sirup. Dip them in flour, beaten egg, and very fine bread crumbs, and fry in hot deep fat. Drain, arrange on a napkin, and powder with fine sugar.

APPLE FRITTERS BEIGNETS DE POMMES (P.)

Peel and core some fine russet apples, then slice in rounds. Sprinkle them with sugar and moisten with rum or kirsch. Let the slices macerate 1 hr., then wipe them dry, dip in Frying Paste (p. 558), and plunge into burning-hot deep fat. Turn them several times while cooking, and drain them on a cloth. Heap them on a plate and sprinkle with vanilla-flavored sugar.

FRITTERS REGINA BEIGNETS RÉGINA (E.)

Drop some Sponge Finger paste (p. 586) onto a baking sheet in the shape of thick-bulging macaroons; bake in a slow oven, and let cool. Hollow out the inside and fill with apricot jam; stick them together in pairs, and soak them in fresh cream flavored with maraschino. Dip them in flour, beaten egg, and bread crumbs and proceed as for Dainty Fritters, above.

SEMOLINA FRITTERS SUZETTE BEIGNETS DE SEMOULE SUZETTE (P.) (*For 8 persons*)

1 qt. milk, 3¼ oz. medium semolina, 2½ oz. sugar, 1 oz. butter, 2 egg yolks.

Cook the semolina in vanilla-flavored boiling milk until it becomes a thick paste; add the sugar and butter, then the egg yolks, and bring again to a boil for a moment or two. Spread this paste in an even layer about ⅔ in. thick on a marble slab and, when cold, cut in rounds with a cookie cutter about 2 in. in diameter. Cut out the centers with a smaller cutter to form rings and bread these in white crumbs and fry in butter. Arrange them in a circle on a round platter and place a candied cherry in the center of each fritter. Powder with sugar and serve with a separate dish of kirsch-flavored Apricot Sauce (p. 560).

SOUFFLÉED FRITTERS or **NUNS' PUFFS** BEIGNETS SOUFFLÉS OR PETS DE NONNES (P.)

Make some Choux Paste (p. 548), using very little butter, and drop small round balls of it into moderately hot deep fat, which should get hotter as the fritters fry and finally be burning hot when they are cooked. They are cooked when they no longer turn by themselves and are uniform in color. Drain them and serve in a heap on a napkin. Sprinkle with vanilla-flavored sugar. Serve with a separate dish of vanilla English Cream (p. 550), or stuff the inside with jam (but these are exceptions to the classic recipe, which calls for no trimmings). (Figure 404, Page 620.)

Fig. 399 - 1. Almonds Aboukir (p. 604). 2. Caramel cherries (p. 605). 3. Stuffed dates (p. 605). 4. Stuffed walnuts (p. 505). 5. Glazed pears (p. 605). 6. Lady apples (p. 605). 7. Stuffed prunes (p. 605).

Fig. 400 - Apricots Condé (p. 610).

Fig. 399

Fig. 400

Fig. 401

Fig. 402

VIENNESE FRITTERS or **KRAPFEN** BEIGNETS VIENNOIS OR KRAPFEN (P.)

Roll out some Krapfen Paste (p. 547) to the thickness of a half dollar, then cut in rounds 2 in. in diameter; moisten the edges of half these rounds with a little water, garnish the centers with a little apricot jam, and cover with the other rounds, sealing the edges together. Place them on a floured cloth, let them rise ½ hr. in a warm place, and fry in burning hot, but not too much, fat; cover them 2 min. Remove the cover and turn the fritters over with the tip of a knife. Let finish cooking 4–5 min., turning them once more. Drain and sprinkle with sugar. (Figure 403, Page 620.)

APPLE DUMPLING BOURDIN (P.)

Peel and core a fine ripe apple and fill the center with a nut-sized piece of butter and a pinch of sugar. Wrap the apple in fine Short Paste (p. 545) as thick as a half dollar and place it on a baking sheet. Moisten the top and cover it with a small, round, fluted piece of the same paste. Brush with beaten egg and bake 20 min. in a hot oven. Serve with a pitcher of very fresh sweet cream or a dish of Apricot Sauce (p. 560). (Figure 405, Page 620.)

CHERRIES JUBILEE CERISES JUBILÉES (E.)

Pit some fine cherries, poach them in sirup, and place them in small silver timbales. Reduce the sirup; bind it with arrowroot mixed with a little cold water (½ tbsp. arrowroot per 9 oz. sirup) or with red-currant jelly. Cover the cherries with this thickened sirup; pour 1 dessertspoon heated kirsch into each timbale, and light it when serving.

APPLE CHARLOTTE CHARLOTTE AUX POMMES (P.)

Cut 12 small triangles of white bread; dip them in melted butter and lay them in the bottom of a charlotte mold, dovetailing, so that they cover the entire bottom. Cut other slices of bread into rectangles the width of 2 fingers and the height of the mold. Dip these also in butter and place them upright around the sides of the mold, overlapping them so that there are no spaces in between. Fill the mold with applesauce made with 5 oz. sugar per 2 lb. apples and reduced as much as possible over a hot fire. (Flavor this applesauce with vanilla, pour rum over it, and set aflame, before filling the mold.) Set the mold in a hot oven, but not too hot on the bottom, or, if it is, place it on something so that the bottom of the mold, which will be the top when served, will not darken. It takes a good ¾ hr. to bake Apple Charlotte so that the bread lining will be golden brown and dry enough to support the weight of the unmolded charlotte. Pour hot Apricot Sauce (p. 560) flavored with rum over the dessert. (Figure 406, Page 621.)

Note: Charlottes with other fruit purées can be made the same way. Since the purée must be very thick, it is sometimes a good idea to mix in a few crushed Sponge Fingers (p. 586) to absorb the liquid from the fruit.

APPLE CLAFOUTI CLAFOUTI AUX POMMES (J.) (*For 6 persons*)

½ lb. apples, 2 oz. flour, 1 egg, 1 pt. milk, 1 oz. sugar, 1 oz. butter, cognac.

Line a flat tart pan with Pie Paste (p. 545); fill it with the apples, quartered. Beat the flour, egg, and sugar in a mixing bowl, then add the milk, a little cognac, and the melted butter. Cover the tart with this mixture. Bake 35–40 min. in a medium oven. Sprinkle with sugar before serving.

Note: For Cherry Clafouti, see Provincial Cooking, p. 725.

Fig. 401 - Apricots sultane (p. 610).
Fig. 402 - Pineapple creole (p. 611).

FRIED CREAMS CRÈMES FRITES (P.) (*For 8 persons*)

¼ lb. sugar, 2½ oz. rice flour, 3 whole eggs, 9 oz. milk, vanilla or other flavoring.

Blend the eggs with the sugar in a saucepan; add the sifted flour, then the milk and flavoring. Bring to a boil for a moment so that it becomes very thick, almost pasty. Pour this cream onto a buttered, floured baking sheet, spreading it out till about as thick as a finger, then let it cool. Cut it into 12 small diamonds and bread these first in flour, then in beaten egg, and finally in white bread crumbs. Just before serving, plunge into burning-hot deep fat; powder with sugar and serve heaped on a napkin.

CRÊPES and PANCAKES (Various Mixtures) CRÊPES and PANNEQUETS (M.) (*60–80 pieces*)

MIXTURE A. *Proportions:* 1 lb. sifted flour, 7 oz. powdered sugar, 12 eggs, 4 tbsp. melted butter, 3 pt. boiled, chilled milk, dash of salt, 1½ oz. cognac, rum, or other liqueur. Any flavor you wish—vanilla; orange, tangerine, or lemon peel; orange-flower water, etc.

Preparation: Blend flour, sugar, and salt in a mixing bowl; add the eggs, mix well to avoid lumps; add the flavoring, liqueur, and butter. Thin with the milk. Let stand a few hours before making into crêpes.

Note: In certain regions of France, especially the southwest, oil is used instead of butter.

MIXTURE B: *Proportions:* 1 lb. sifted flour, 5 oz. sugar, 6 whole eggs, 4 yolks, 4 tbsp. brown butter, 2 qt. milk, dash of salt, 6 stiffly beaten egg whites. Any flavor you wish.

Preparation: Proceed as above. At the end, fold in the beaten egg whites.

MIXTURE C: *Proportions:* 1 lb. sifted flour, 5 oz. sugar, 10 eggs, 9 oz. fresh cream, 2½ oz. melted butter, 1 qt. milk, pinch of salt, 1½ oz. cognac, rum, or other liqueur, 1½ oz. orgeat (sirup made from almonds), 3½ oz. crushed macaroons. Any flavor you wish.

Preparation: Mix the flour and sugar with the eggs; add the salt. Thin this mixture with the cream; add the melted butter and liqueur. Dilute with the milk. Strain through a cone-shaped sieve and, finally, add the orgeat and crushed macaroons.

MIXTURE D: *Proportions:* 1 lb. sifted flour, 5 oz. sugar, 10 eggs, 9 oz. fresh cream, 1 qt. milk, pinch of salt, 1½ oz. cognac or other liqueur, 7½ oz. whipped cream. Any flavor you wish.

Preparation: Proceed as above. Add the whipped cream at the end.

Cooking: Using a brush dipped in melted butter, lightly butter a well-heated, small, heavy frying pan made especially for crêpes. Pour enough mixture to cover the bottom, remembering that the crêpe must be extremely thin; cook over a hot fire. As soon as bubbles begin to appear in spots, flip the crêpe over. As the crêpes are done, place them one on top the other, sprinkling them lightly with sugar, and keep hot.

Serving: Serve them as they are, one on the other, or fold them in quarters after spreading them with the mixture given in the recipe.

Serving a pancake: After spreading with the given mixture, roll up the crêpes or pancakes and cut them into diamonds. Place the pancakes on a baking sheet, powder with confectioners' sugar, and glaze them quickly in the oven. Serve them on a napkin or paper doily.

Note: The proportions given by Montagné are for restaurants and should make about 60–80 crêpes.

CRÊPES ALSACIENNE CRÊPES À L'ALSACIENNE (M.)

Flavor Mixture A with raspberry brandy. Spread the crêpes with Frangipane Cream (p. 552) mixed with raspberries. Fold them in quarters. Arrange on a silver platter, pour some raspberry brandy on them, and light when serving.

CRÊPES BONNE FEMME CRÊPES À LA BONNE FEMME (M.)

Mixture A flavored with grated orange peel and rum. Spread the crêpes with some rather thick applesauce. Fold them in quarters. Sprinkle with lightly grilled, chopped almonds. Pour rum over; light when serving.

CHARTREUSE CRÊPES CRÊPES DES CHARTREUX (M.)

Mixture A flavored with Chartreuse. Spread the crêpes with the following mixture. Work 3½ oz. butter into a paste with 1½ oz. powdered sugar and 1½ oz. pulverized macaroons. Add 1½ oz. green Chartreuse. Mix well. Fold the crêpes in quarters. Powder with confectioners' sugar.

THIN CRÊPES CRÊPES FINES (P.)

Lightly butter some very hot, small frying pans and cover the bottoms with a thin layer of crêpe batter. When they are done on one side, turn them over, and when they are cooked, powder them with vanilla-flavored sugar; fold in half and serve on a hot platter.

CRÊPES GEORGETTE CRÊPES GEORGETTE (P.)

Pour the batter into the frying pan as directed above, then place a thin slice of pineapple on top and cover with a little of the batter. Cook these crêpes the usual way, but, naturally, do not fold them in half.

CRÊPES LONGUEVILLE CRÊPES LONGUEVILLE (M.)

Mixture A mixed with finely chopped almonds, flavored with orange peel. Spread the crêpes with very thick applesauce mixed with ⅓ as much Pastry Cream (p. 552) ; season with a dash of cinnamon. Fold the crêpes in quarters, powder with sugar; glaze quickly in the oven.

CRÊPES SIMONE CRÊPES SIMONE (M.)

Mixture D flavored with cherry brandy. Spread the crêpes with Frangipane Cream (p. 552) mixed with chopped candied cherries. Fold them in quarters. Set them aflame with champagne brandy.

CRÊPES SUZETTE CRÊPES SUZETTE (M.)

Mixture C flavored with curaçao and tangerine juice. Spread the crêpes with the following butter. Cream 3½ oz. butter with 3½ oz. powdered sugar. Add 1½ oz. curaçao and the grated rind of a tangerine. Fold the crêpes in quarters; powder with sugar. They are sometimes set aflame with champagne brandy.

CRÊPES YVONNE CRÊPES YVONNE (M.)

Mixture B flavored with crème de cacao. Make the crêpes very small. Spread them with Frangipane Cream (p. 552) mixed with melted chocolate. Stick them together in pairs, with the cream between. Place them on a silver platter; powder with confectioners' sugar. Glaze quickly in the oven.

MERINGUE CRÊPES or PANCAKES CRÊPES OR PANNEQUETS MERINGUÉS (D. and D.) (*For 10–12 persons*)

Mix in a bowl: ½ lb. flour, 3½ oz. powdered sugar, 3½ oz. melted butter, then thin with 1 pt. milk, 3 whole eggs and 3 yolks, or 5 whole eggs, salt, vanilla. Make small crêpes, lightly buttering the pan each time; turn them over to color both sides. If you use fresh cream instead of milk, the pancakes are much superior. Roll the pancakes after spreading them with jam. Arrange them in a dome shape, cover with meringue, and put into the oven for a moment. (Figure 407, Page 621.)

CHESTNUT CROQUETTES I CROQUETTES DE MARRONS (P.)

Peel the chestnuts as directed on p. 496, cook them in thin sirup flavored with vanilla, and lay aside 1 small, whole chestnut for each croquette. Press the rest through a sieve; dry the purée over a hot fire; bind it with 5 egg yolks and 1½ oz. butter per lb. purée. Let cool. Next, divide the composition into portions the size of a pigeon egg; roll into balls, enclosing a chestnut in the center of each. Dip in flour, beaten egg, then very fine bread crumbs; fry in very hot deep fat, and arrange on a napkin. Serve a separate dish of vanilla-flavored Apricot Sauce (p. 560).

CHESTNUT CROQUETTES II CROQUETTES DE MARRONS (E.)

Take some leftover candied chestnuts (*marrons glacés*), mash them fine with a fork, mix them well with ⅓ as much macaroons soaked in kirsch or rum and finely crushed. Divide this mixture into portions the size of a small egg; roll them into balls and flatten them into the shape of small disks. Dip them in flour, beaten egg, and very fine bread crumbs and, just before serving, brown them on both sides in clarified butter. Serve with a dish of Apricot Sauce (p. 560) flavored with kirsch and a dish of Chantilly Cream (p. 552).

RICE CROQUETTES CROQUETTES DE RIZ (P.) (*For 6 persons*)

Proportions: 3¼ oz. Carolina rice, 2½ oz. sugar, 3 egg yolks, 9 oz. milk, vanilla.

Blanch the rice in water, then finish cooking it in milk (flavored with vanilla) until well done; add the sugar and egg yolks and continue stirring on the fire until it separates from the pan. Spread this mixture on a platter and, when cold, divide it into small egg-sized pieces and roll them into loaves or large stopper shapes on a floured marble slab; dip them in beaten egg and bread crumbs and fry them. Serve on a napkin; serve, at the same time, English Cream (p. 550) or Apricot Sauce (p. 560).

RICE CROQUETTES WITH FRUIT CROQUETTES DE RIZ AUX FRUITS (P.) (*For 8 persons*)

Make ordinary Rice Croquettes, above, but add to the mixture 4 oz. diced, candied fruits macerated in kirsch. Make the croquettes a little larger than those above, and shape them like pears. Bread them by rolling them first in beaten egg, then in shredded or chopped almonds. Use a small piece of candied angelica to imitate the stem. Same treatment and same sauce as above.

CRUSTS BONNE FEMME CROÛTES À LA BONNE FEMME (J.)

Cut thick, rectangular slices from leftover white bread or stale Brioche (p. 565). Fry them in butter on both sides without drying them. Cover each slice with thick applesauce. Glaze heavily with confectioners' sugar and criss-cross the top with a red-hot iron. Serve immediately, with kirsch-flavored Apricot Sauce (p. 560). (Figure 412, Page 625.)

GOLDEN CRUSTS CROÛTES DORÉES OR PAIN PERDU (P.)

Cut some slices of stale Brioche (p. 565) or white bread about ⅜ in. thick and soak them in very liquid, vanilla-flavored English Cream (p. 550), to sop up the flavor. Drain them and dip in well-beaten egg. Brown on both sides in burning-hot butter. Place on a napkin and powder with sugar.

FRUIT CRUSTS CROÛTES AUX FRUITS (E.)

Cut a stale Savarin Cake (p. 547) that has not been soaked in sirup into slices ¼ in. thick, allowing 2 per person. Lay these slices on a baking sheet; powder them with sugar; place them in the oven to dry and glaze at the same time. Arrange the slices in a heavy ring, overlapping the slices and alternating them with thin slices of pineapple cut exactly the same size. On top of the ring, place quarters of stewed apples and pears. The dish may be made more attractive by cooking the pears in pink sirup. Decorate with candied cherries, diamonds of candied angelica, quarters of green and yellow kumquats. Coat with kirsch-flavored Apricot Sauce (p. 560).

CRUSTS LYONNAISE CROÛTES À LA LYONNAISE (E.)

Prepare the crusts as explained above; cover them with a fine vanilla-flavored chestnut purée; then coat them with apricot jam cooked to the "thread" stage (p. 562). Sprinkle with finely shredded almonds and arrange in a ring, the slices overlapping, on a service platter. Fill the center of the ring with chestnuts cooked in sirup; seeded Malaga raisins, dried currants, and sultanas, all soaked until swollen in warm water; everything bound together with apricot purée thinned with a few tbsp. Malaga.

MADEIRA CRUSTS CROÛTES AU MADÈRE (E.)

Arrange the glazed crusts in a ring as described above. Fill the center with a garnish of equal parts of candied fruit cut in cubes; seeded Malaga raisins, dried currants, and sultanas, soaked in warm water, all blended together with Madeira-flavored apricot sirup.

CRUSTS NORMANDE CROÛTES À LA NORMANDE (E.)

Prepare the crusts the usual way; spread them on one side with very thick applesauce and place them in a ring, with the slices overlapping, on a service platter. Fill the center with applesauce prepared as for Apple Charlotte (p. 613); on top of the sauce make a pyramid of pink and white apple quarters cooked in sirup. Cover with reduced apple sirup thickened with a little applesauce and flavored with kirsch.

CRUSTS VICTORIA CROÛTES VICTORIA (E.)

Prepare a ring of crusts as for Madeira Crusts, above; fill the center with cherries half cooked in sirup, and whole candied chestnuts. Serve a separate dish of rum-flavored Apricot Sauce (p. 560).

Note: (1) Any number of fruit crusts can be prepared, each taking its name from the principal garnish, such as Cherry Crusts or Crusts Montmorency, Peach Crusts or Crusts Montreuil, etc. (2) The slices of stale Savarin Cake can be replaced by Savoy Sponge Cake (p. 549) or Génoise Cake. (p. 549)

CARAMEL RICE CAKE GÂTEAU DE RIZ AU CARAMEL (P.) (*For 4 persons*)

Proportions: ¼ lb. Carolina rice, 3¼ oz. sugar, 1½ oz. butter, 2 egg yolks, 1 pt. milk, vanilla.

After blanching the rice 3 min. in water, add it to the milk and vanilla. Cover the rice and cook in the oven without stirring; it takes about ½ hr. and should then be almost dry. Mix the egg yolks, butter, and sugar in a bowl and pour in the rice. When well mixed, put the mixture into a timbale mold lined with caramel and poach it, in a *bain-marie,* in the oven. Do not let the water in the *bain-marie* boil. This should take about 20 min. Unmold the dessert onto a round platter and pour a little caramel sirup around it. This dessert is fluffier and superior to Rice Pudding made with egg whites (p. 627).

SEMOLINA CAKE WITH DATES GÂTEAU DE SEMOULE AUX DATTES (A.) (*For 6 persons*)

Take: 13 oz. very ripe dates, 10 oz. butter, 3½ oz. semolina, 2 oz. sugar, pinch of salt, dash of powdered cinnamon, 1 qt. milk, 1 fresh egg, vanilla bean, honey.

Put the milk, sugar, salt, and vanilla into a stewpan; bring to a boil; sprinkle in the semolina a little at a time and let cook 20 min. Remove the pan from the fire and take out the vanilla bean. Bind the semolina with the beaten egg. Let the semolina paste cool, then shape it into 2 round pancakes about 8 in. in diameter. Cover a baking sheet with a buttered paper and lay 1 of the pancakes on it. Pit the dates and press the pulp through a sieve. Mix the date purée well with the butter; spread this mixture on the semolina pancake on the baking sheet; sprinkle with cinnamon, and cover with the second pancake; brush the top with honey and bake in a medium oven. Serve this cake warm, preferably, and with a separate dish of vanilla cream. This delightful dessert is of Arabian origin.

Following the same idea, you can make a semolina cake with vanilla-flavored chestnut purée.

OMELET CÉVENOLE OMELETTE À LA CÉVENOLE (M.) (*For 6 persons*)

Make a 3-egg flat omelet (see p. 270) with sugar. Place it on a round platter. Cover it with a thick layer of creamed chestnut purée flavored with kirsch. Place a second sweet omelet on top. Sprinkle with chopped almonds and sugar, pour kirsch over it, and light when serving.

JAM OMELET OMELETTE AUX CONFITURES (P.)

Beat the eggs as for an ordinary omelet (p. 270), adding a little sugar and a dash of salt; cook the omelet as usual, but before rolling it, place 2 or 3 tbsp. of some sort of jam in the center. Lay it on a long platter and cover generously with powdered sugar; then, with a red-hot iron, burn a pattern on top. Rum or kirsch can also be poured over it and lit at the table. (Figure 408, Page 624.)

OMELET MONTMORENCY OMELETTE MONTMORENCY (M.)

Make an Omelet Cévenole (p. 618), substituting cherries cooked in sirup and bound with red-currant jelly for the chestnut purée. Pour kirsch on and light when serving.

OMELET NORWEGIAN STYLE OMELETTE NORVÉGIENNE (E.)

See p. 667.

VANILLA SOUFFLÉED OMELET OMELETTE SOUFFLÉE À LA VANILLE (P.) (*For 8 persons*)

Proportions: 5 oz. vanilla-flavored powdered sugar, 3 egg yolks, 5 stiffly beaten egg whites.

Beat the yolks and sugar in a mixing bowl until the mixture whitens, then add the beaten whites, folding them in very carefully, but not bothering to see that everything is completely blended. Place this mixture on a long, buttered, sugared platter, shaping it into an oval mound with a hollow in the center. Smooth the sides with a knife and bake about 20 min. in a very slow oven. This omelet will fall faster than a regular soufflé and must be served as soon as ready.

OLD-FASHIONED SURPRISE OMELET OMELETTE EN SURPRISE À L'ANCIENNE (P.) (*For 8 persons*)

Fill a 2-egg omelet with red-currant jelly (or other red jelly). Make another omelet with 6 beaten eggs, 2 tbsp. crushed macaroons, and 2 tbsp. finely chopped green citron. When folding this omelet, wrap it around the smaller one. Place it on a long buttered platter. Cover entirely with a thin layer of Vanilla Souffléed Omelet mixture (above). Using this same mixture in a pastry bag, decorate the top. Powder with confectioners' sugar. Brown quickly in the oven. Surround with a band of kirsch-flavored Apricot Sauce (p. 560).

DEVILED PEACHES PÊCHES À LA DIABLE (M.)

This is a variant of Peaches Flambé in kirsch (or other liqueur). Place the peaches, poached in sirup and well drained, on small, round slices of Brioche (p. 565) fried golden brown in butter. Coat with Praline (p. 559) thinned with a little cream; sprinkle with shredded almonds; powder with sugar; lightly brown in the oven. Pour the liqueur over them and light when serving.

Note: Restaurants usually serve a dish like this with fruit sauce flavored with the same liqueur the dish was flambéed with—a custom we recommend.

PEACHES FLAMBÉ PÊCHES FLAMBÉES (E.)

These can be prepared 2 ways:

(1) Poach the peaches, whole, in kirsch-flavored sirup; place each one in a small timbale. Thicken the sirup with arrowroot and pour it over the peaches. Add heated kirsch and set it aflame when serving.

(2) Poach the peaches as above; place them on a purée of fresh strawberries. Pour the heated kirsch on top and light just before serving.

PEACHES IMPÉRATRICE PÊCHES IMPÉRATRICE (E.)

Line the bottom of a shallow timbale with a layer of Dessert Rice (p. 559) flavored with kirsch and maraschino. Place halved peaches cooked in vanilla-flavored sirup on the rice and cover with a light layer of the same rice. Spread a layer of Apricot Sauce (p. 560) over the top, sprinkle with crushed macaroons, and set the timbale in an open oven 10–12 min. Do not let the surface brown.

PEACHES ORIENTALE PÊCHES À L'ORIENTALE (M.)

Poach peach halves in vanilla sirup; drain; place them on a ring of Dessert Rice (p. 559) mixed with chopped pineapple macerated in kirsch. Sprinkle the peaches with chopped almonds and sugar. Glaze lightly in the oven. Fill the center of the ring with a mound of very small Fried Creams (p. 614) flavored with orange peel. Serve with red-currant sauce flavored with kirsch.

PEARS BOURDALOUE POIRES À LA BOURDALOUE (H.)

Made various ways. Here are the most usual:

(1) Place them in a timbale and coat completely with Pastry Cream (p. 552) flavored with maraschino and kirsch and containing crushed macaroons; sprinkle the top with sugar and chopped macaroons; glaze in the oven.

(2) Place the pears on a border of semolina, coat them with the same Pastry Cream, fill the center with apricot jam, and glaze in the oven.

(3) Place the pears in a large tart shell on a layer of Pastry Cream, decorate with candied angelica and cherries, and lightly cover with Apricot Sauce (p. (Figure 409, Page 624.)

STUFFED PEARS CARMELITE POIRES (FARCIES) À LA CARMÉLITE (P.)

Take some medium-sized pears (1 per person), peel, sprinkle with lemon juice, and don't cook them too much. When they have cooled a little, cut off ⅓ each pear nearest the stem. Hollow out the center of the pears with an apple corer and fill with a mixture of hot, diced preserved fruits bound with a little apricot purée. Replace the part cut off the pears and arrange them on a bed of Dessert Rice (p. 559) made with sugar and vanilla-flavored milk but no egg yolks. Coat the pears only with hot red-currant jelly thickened with arrowroot. This dessert can also be served cold, but it is better hot.

PEARS DUCHESSE POIRES DUCHESSE (P.)

Cook a Cabinet Pudding (p. 625) in a savarin mold; unmold and fill the center with a compote of pears. Coat with English Cream (p. 550).

PEARS FLAMBÉ POIRES FLAMBÉES (P.)

Poach the pears in rather sweet, vanilla-flavored sirup; place them in a silver timbale or soufflé dish; reduce the sirup and add a little apricot jam, then thicken with a very little arrowroot, and pour over the pears; baste them with a little heated kirsch or rum and light when serving.

The pears can also be arranged on a bed of reduced applesauce and finished the same way. Cherries, peaches, and almost any other fruit can be treated the same way.

PEARS MÂCONNAISE POIRES À LA MÂCONNAISE (M.)

Poach whole or halved pears, depending on size, in sweetened Mâcon wine. Drain the pears; place them on round slices of Brioche (p. 565) glazed with sugar. Just before serving, coat them with the reduced cooking sirup flavored with a little red-currant jelly and champagne brandy and strained. Sprinkle with grilled, shredded almonds.

Fig. 403 - Viennese fritters or Krapfen (p. 613).
Fig. 404 - Souffleed fritters or Nuns' puffs (p. 612).
Fig. 405 - Apple dumpling (p. 613).

Fig. 404
Fig. 403

Fig. 405

Fig. 406

Fig. 407

SOUFFLÉED PEARS POIRES SOUFFLÉES (M.)

Cut 6 large pears in half. Scoop them out without breaking the skin. Press the pulp through a sieve. Dry a few moments on the stove. Add to 12 oz. Soufflé Mixture (p. 629) prepared the usual way. Flavor with kirsch. Fill the pear halves with this mixture. Smooth the surface; powder with sugar. Bake 8–10 min. in the oven. Serve on a napkin.

PEARS SULTANE POIRES SULTANE (E.)

Cook peeled pears, halved or quartered, in vanilla sirup. Follow the rest of the recipe for Apricots Sultane (p. 610).

APPLES BONNE FEMME POMMES À LA BONNE FEMME (P.)

Cut the tops off some russet apples, core them without cutting them up or peeling them, and place in a baking dish; put a small piece of butter and some sugar in the centers, baste with a little white wine or simply water, and bake in the oven. Thicken the cooking juice left in the baking dish with a little apricot jam and pour it over the apples when serving.

APPLES BOURGEOISE POMMES À LA BOURGEOISE (P.)

Peel and core medium-sized apples, cut them in 2 crosswise, and poach them in vanilla sirup. Place them in a baking dish and fill the center of each apple with a mixture of chopped preserved fruits. Cover with a good layer of very thin vanilla Pastry Cream (p. 552)—that is, made with less flour than the recipe calls for. Sprinkle the top with finely chopped almonds, powder with sugar, baste with melted butter, and put into a very hot oven to brown the tops.

APPLES CHANOINESSE POMMES À LA CHANOINESSE (J.)

Cut a thin round crust of Pie Paste (p. 545), using a plate or pattern as a guide. Place on a moistened baking sheet. Prick the surface all over with a fork. Using a pastry bag with a large plain tube, lay a ring of Choux Paste (p. 548) around the inside edge of the crust. Fill the center with a thin layer of Pastry Cream (p. 552). Brush the Choux-Paste border with beaten egg and place in the oven. Baking time: 35–40 min. After removing from the oven, place apples poached in sirup on top. Decorate with candied angelica and cherries. Coat with kirsch-flavored Apricot Sauce (p. 560). (Figure 410, Page 625.)

APPLES CHÂTELAINE POMMES CHÂTELAINE (E.)

Take medium-sized apples; peel and prepare them as for Apples Bonne Femme (above). Place them in a buttered baking dish; fill the centers with diced cherries half cooked in sirup and bound with apricot purée; cover with clear Frangipane Cream (p. 552); sprinkle with macaroon and sponge-cake crumbs; baste with melted butter, and brown in a very hot oven.

APPLES CHEVREUSE POMMES CHEVREUSE (E.)

Fill the bottom of a baking dish with a semolina croquette mixture. Line the sides with overlapping apple quarters cooked in vanilla sirup; fill the center with a mixture of diced preserved fruits and raisins bound with apricot purée; cover with a thin layer of semolina. Completely cover with Ordinary Meringue (p. 557) shaped into a dome; sprinkle with chopped pistachios, powder with confectioners' sugar, and color in a slow oven. After removing from the oven,

Fig. 406 - Apple charlotte (p. 613).
Fig. 407 - Meringue crêpes (p. 616).

decorate the top of the dome with a rosette of candied angelica cut in long diamonds; place a small apple cooked in pink sirup in the center of the rosette; surround the base with a circle of overlapping apple quarters, alternating white and pink apples.

APPLES GRIMALDI POMMES À LA GRIMALDI (M.)

Quarter russet apples and poach in vanilla sirup. Drain. Place them in a flan crust (baked with beans to hold its shape) and fill ⅔ full with Dessert Rice (p. 559) mixed with chopped preserved fruits flavored with curaçao. Sprinkle with crushed macaroons and sugar and baste with melted butter. Glaze in the oven. Serve with English Cream (p. 550) flavored with curaçao.

HOME-STYLE APPLES POMMES À LA MÉNAGÈRE (J.)

Cover the bottom of a platter with apple quarters cooked in butter. Prepare separately some ½ slices of grilled Brioche (p. 565) about ⅜ in. thick. Arrange these slices in a circle, overlapping them. Coat with warm Apricot Sauce (p. 560) flavored as you wish. (Figure 411, Page 625.)

APPLES WITH RICE CREOLE POMMES AU RIZ CRÉOLE (J.)

Fill the bottom of a platter with Dessert Rice (p. 559) cooked in milk; place on top apple quarters poached in vanilla sirup. Decorate with candied angelica and cherries. Coat with thin Apricot Sauce (p. 560). (Figure 413, Page 628.)

APPLE MERINGUE WITH RICE POMMES AU RIZ MERINGUÉES (P.)

Prepare Apples Condé, following the recipe for Apricots Condé (p. 610). Then, when the dessert is ready, instead of covering with apricot, spread a smooth layer of Swiss Meringue (p. 557) over it, completely covering all the apples; use this same meringue in a pastry bag with fluted tube to decorate the top. Powder with sugar and bake the meringue in a slow oven without coloring it too much. Before serving, the hollows in the meringue decoration may be filled with red-currant or apricot jelly, using a paper cone. Instead of placing the apples on a bed of rice, they can be placed on very reduced applesauce, as for Apple Charlotte (p. 613), or even covered with meringue without any rice or applesauce base. (Figure 414, Page 628.)

SOUFFLÉED APPLES POMMES SOUFFLÉES (M.)

Hollow out 12 large apples without breaking the skins. Moisten the insides with a few drops of champagne brandy and let them macerate. Prepare 18 oz. very thick applesauce with vanilla and very little sugar. Fold in 8 stiffly beaten egg whites. Fill the apple shells with this mixture. Smooth the surface; powder with confectioners' sugar; bake in a very hot oven. Serve the apples on a napkin.

APPLE FLAN BATELIÈRE POMMES (FLAN DE) À LA BATELIÈRE (E.)

Line a flan circle or tart pan with Short Paste (p. 545); fill it with applesauce prepared as for Apple Charlotte (p. 613). Cover this with a dome of very fluffy Dessert Rice (p. 559) mixed with 4 stiffly beaten egg whites per lb. cooked rice.

Bake the flan the usual way. After removing from the oven, powder generously with confectioners' sugar and glaze with a red-hot iron held over the top.

APPLE FLAN NINON POMMES (FLAN DE) NINON (E.)

Prepare a flan crust and bake it. Fill it with applesauce prepared as for Apple Charlotte (p. 613), shaping it into a dome. On this, alternate pink and white apple quarters; lightly brush these quarters with reduced white sirup.

PLUM PUDDING PLUM-PUDDING (M.) (*For 20 persons*)

Proportions: 1 lb. very dry beef-kidney suet, 19 oz. bread crumbs, 5 oz. flour, 7 oz. seeded Malaga raisins, 7 oz. dried currants, and 7 oz. sultanas washed and soaked in warm water (all 3 varieties of raisins macerated in rum), 3¼ oz. candied orange peel, 3¼ oz. candied citron peel, 3¼ oz. candied lemon peel (all of these candied peels diced very fine), 5 oz. (net weight) peeled, chopped russet apples, 2 oz. chopped candied ginger, 3¼ oz. dry figs soaked (to swell) in warm water and chopped fine, 3¼ oz. chopped, shelled almonds, ½ lb. brown or white sugar, peel and juice of 1 orange, peel and juice of ½ lemon, ½ oz. spices, 12 oz. rum or cognac, 6 eggs.

Mixture: Put all the ingredients listed above, except the eggs and rum (or cognac), into a large bowl. Mix well. Moisten with the rum and mix again. Cover with a cloth and let the mixture macerate 6–8 days in a cool place. Every day, stir the mixture and add a few tbsp. rum (or cognac). The day it is to be used, add the eggs and mix well.

Molding Plum Puddings: Butter and fill special Plum-Pudding molds with the mixture given above. Fill the molds well and pack the mixture down. Cover the mold with a napkin after buttering and flouring the part that touches the mixture. Tie the ends of the napkin under the mold and bind tightly with a string. If you do not have a special mold, you can put the mixture into a buttered, floured cloth, tying it tightly with string, shaping the pudding like a large ball.

Cooking: Plunge the pudding into a large pot of boiling water and, keeping a steady boil, cook 5 hr. (for a Plum Pudding weighing 3 lb.).

Sauces and Serving: Plum Pudding is usually served flaming. Pour a generous amount of heated rum or cognac over the pudding and set it aflame when serving. It may also be served with a separate dish of one of the following sauces: Sabayon (p. 553) with rum or Madeira; hot English Cream (p. 550) flavored with any liqueur; cognac sauce thickened with arrowroot; Brandy Butter prepared the following way: cream 5 oz. butter with 5 oz. powdered sugar; add 3 oz. cognac.

Note: We have tried the above recipe countless times and it has always given excellent results. But we hasten to add that there are many other ways to make this typically Anglo-Saxon dessert. As is true of any popular dish—each cook has his own method and believes it to be the only right one. To tell the truth, the differences in preparation are slight. They consist chiefly in increasing or decreasing the proportions of certain ingredients or in leaving them out altogether and substituting others—for example, milk and stout.

Once boiled, Plum Puddings can be kept a long time—simply keep them in a dry, cold place. In serving Plum Pudding for Christmas dinner, it is customary to stick a branch of green holly with its red berries in the top.

ENGLISH PLUM PUDDING PLUM-PUDDING ANGLAIS (P.) (*For 20 persons*)

This dessert is to the English at Christmas what our Twelfth Cake is to us on the day of Epiphany, and needs long, careful preparation.

Proportions: 1 lb. beef-kidney suet, 1 lb. mixed dried currants, sultanas, and Malaga raisins, 12 oz. brown sugar, 5 oz. candied lemon, orange, and citron, 1 tsp. salt, ½ lb. flour, ½ lb. bread crumbs, 1 boiled lemon, pinch of spices, grated nutmeg and ginger, ½ bottle rum, 6 whole eggs.

Peel and chop the suet; put it into a large pot or mixing bowl; add the cleaned raisins (the Malagas seeded), brown sugar, chopped candied fruits, spices and seasoning, the lemon (boiled whole 2 hr.), and the rum. Mix well and pack down tightly so that everything is soaked in the rum; keep covered in a cool place at least 15 days.

When the time comes to cook the Plum Pudding, mix in the flour, eggs, and bread crumbs (pulverized and then sifted). Since this paste should be dark brown, add caramel coloring if necessary. Wrap the mixture in buttered, floured cloths. Roll the cloth in the shape of a galantine or loaf as thick as a fist and cook it 2 hr. or longer in boiling water. Slice it, powder with sugar, and pour hot rum over it; bring it flaming into the dining room. It should, of course, be served in a fireproof dish.

With the proportions given above, the pudding should serve 20 persons. The mixture can be macerated several months, and the flour, bread crumbs, and eggs added only when it is to be used.

ALMOND PUDDING PUDDING AUX AMANDES (M.)

Use Souffléed Saxon Pudding mixture (p. 628), adding 1⅓ oz. finely chopped almonds to it just before blending in the beaten egg whites. Put this mixture into a plain mold buttered and sprinkled with lightly grilled, shredded almonds. Bake in a *bain-marie* in the oven. Serve with Sabayon (p. 553) or English Cream (p. 550) flavored with vanilla or a liqueur.

Note: If you wish, use Almond Milk (p. 556) for milk in the mixture.

SPONGE-CAKE PUDDING PUDDING DE BISCUITS (M.)

Put ½ lb. crumbled Sponge Fingers (p. 586) into a pan. Pour in 18 oz. boiling milk containing 5 oz. sugar. Cook this mixture on the fire a few moments, stirring well with a spatula. Remove from the fire and add 5 oz. diced, candied fruits and washed dried currants macerated in rum or kirsch. Bind with 3 egg yolks; add ¼ lb. melted butter and fold in, at the last moment, 3 beaten egg whites. Pour into a buttered mold lined with bread crumbs. Bake in a *bain-marie* in the oven. Serve with Apricot Sauce (p. 560) flavored with kirsch or rum.

PUDDING CHEVREUSE PUDDING À LA CHEVREUSE (P.)

This is a Tapioca Pudding (p. 628) made of semolina instead of tapioca, with candied fruits macerated in kirsch added, and served with Sabayon Cream (p. 553) flavored with the same liqueur.

Note: These paste puddings can be varied a number of ways—adding fresh or candied fruits, molding them, flavoring and coloring them different ways.

DATE PUDDING WITH ALMOND CREAM PUDDING AUX DATTES, À LA CRÈME D'AMANDES (A.) (*For 8 persons*)

(1) *For the pudding:* 19 oz. fresh dates, ½ lb. dried currants and sultanas, Sponge Fingers (p. 586), powdered sugar, butter. (2) *For the cream:* ½ lb. shelled almonds, ½ lb. sugar, ½ lb. butter, 3 oz. heavy cream, 6 eggs, kirsch or vanilla.

Fig. 408 - Jam omelet (p. 618).
Fig. 409 - Pears Bourdaloue (p. 620).

Fig. 408

Fig. 409

Fig. 410

Fig. 411

Fig. 412

Pit the dates, press the pulp through a sieve, seed the raisins. Butter a mold, sprinkle the inside with a little sugar, line the bottom and sides with Sponge Fingers, sprinkle again with sugar, place a layer of date purée over this, a layer of raisins on top, sugar again, then more Sponge Fingers; continue alternating the layers until all the ingredients have been used.

Prepare the Almond Cream. Pound the almonds in a mortar with a little egg white, add the sugar, pound again; then blend in the melted butter, eggs, kirsch or vanilla and stir well, bringing the paste to the center of the mortar. The mixture should be light and fluffy. Finally, add the cream. Pour part of this mixture into the mold, almost filling it; let it set in a *bain-marie;* cook the rest of the mixture on a low fire until it has a rather good consistency. Watch the cooking carefully. Unmold the pudding carefully onto a platter, cover with the rest of the Almond Cream, and serve hot.

As a variant, this pudding can be served with Hazelnut Cream.

To make Hazelnut Cream, take: 12 oz. milk, ½ lb. grilled hazelnuts, 5 oz. sugar, 2 oz. butter, ¼ tsp. salt, 4 fresh eggs.

Pound the hazelnuts in a mortar and press them through a sieve. Break the eggs into a saucepan and, using a wire whisk, beat them with the sugar over a slow fire. As soon as the eggs are well beaten, add the nuts, butter (softened on the fire), and milk (which has been boiled); mix well, then heat gently until the cream has the right consistency.

DIPLOMAT or **CABINET PUDDING** PUDDING DIPLOMATE or DE CABINET (P.) (*For 8 persons*)

Proportions: ¼ lb. Sponge Fingers (p. 586), 3 oz. powdered sugar, 3 whole eggs, 3¼ oz. raisins and candied fruits, 1 pt. milk.

Boil the milk with vanilla, then pour it into a mixing bowl in which the eggs have been beaten with the sugar. Stir with a fork while pouring in the milk, then let this cream stand and skim the foam off the top. Meanwhile, butter and sugar a pudding mold; fill it with broken Sponge Fingers (or Génoise Cake or any leftover Sponge Cake). Alternate the layers of Sponge Fingers with raisins and diced, preserved fruits macerated in rum. When the mold is quite full, pour in the cream bit by bit, allowing time for the Sponge Cake to soak it up and swell. If the cream is poured in too quickly, it will collect in the bottom of the mold, and the Sponge Cake, not having time to soak it up, and being lighter, will come to the top. Moisten the Sponge Cake very slowly until the mold is full, then poach 25 min. in a *bain-marie* in the oven, without letting the water boil. To see if it is done, stick a small knife into the pudding. If the blade comes out with no trace of cream on it, it is cooked. Unmold 5 min. after removing from the oven; cover the pudding with rum-flavored Sabayon (p. 553) or with English Cream (p. 550). (Figure 415, Page 629.)

PUDDING FLEUR DE MARIE PUDDING FLEUR DE MARIE (P.) (*For 8 persons*)

3 oz. semolina flour, 3 oz. butter, 3 oz. sugar, 4 egg yolks and 3 whites, ½ pt. milk, vanilla, salt.

Cook the semolina in vanilla-flavored boiling milk; when it becomes a thick paste, add the sugar and butter; remove from the fire and add the egg yolks and beaten whites. Pour this mixture into a plain pudding mold with a hole in

Fig. 410 - Apples chanoinesse (p. 621).
Fig. 411 - Home-style apples (p. 622).
Fig. 412 - Crusts bonne femme (p. 617).

the center, lined with sugar that has been caramelized to a golden color. Cook in a *bain-marie* and serve covered with English Cream (p. 550) to which the rest of the caramel has been added.

FRANKFORT PUDDING PUDDING DE FRANCFORT (M.) (*For 12 persons*)

Mixture: Put ½ lb. butter and 6 oz. powdered sugar into a mixing bowl. Cream this mixture, then add 8 egg yolks, 1 at a time, and ¼ lb. black bread soaked in red wine and pressed through a sieve. Add 6 oz. mashed almonds and 2 tbsp. chopped, preserved fruit. Season with a pinch of powdered cinnamon and a little salt. Mix well with a spatula and blend in, finally, 8 stiffly beaten egg whites. Put this mixture into plain molds buttered and lined with bread crumbs; bake in a *bain-marie* in the oven. Serve with Fruit Sauce (p. 560) flavored with kirsch.

CHESTNUT PUDDING PUDDING AUX MARRONS (M.) (*For 8 persons*)

Mixture: Dry on the fire 1 lb. chestnut purée (prepared with peeled chestnuts cooked in thin vanilla sirup) mixed with 2½ oz. sugar and 1½ oz. butter. Remove from the fire and bind with 4 egg yolks. Fold in 3 stiffly beaten egg whites. Cook in a plain buttered mold, in a *bain-marie*, in the oven. Serve with English Cream (p. 550) or Sabayon (p. 553) flavored with kirsch or rum.

MOUSSELINE PUDDING PUDDING MOUSSELINE (M.) (*For 10 persons*)

Mixture: Cream ¼ lb. butter and ¼ lb. powdered sugar in a mixing bowl. Add 10 egg yolks, 1 at a time. Flavor with vanilla or other flavoring. Heat this mixture on the fire until it thickens enough to cling to a spoon. Then remove from the fire and fold in 7 stiffly beaten egg whites. Pour into a large, high, well-buttered ring mold. Fill the mold only halfway. Bake 30 min. in the oven, in a *bain-marie*. Let the pudding stand for a few minutes before unmolding. Serve with Sabayon (p. 553) or Fruit Sauce (p. 560).

BREAD PUDDING ENGLISH STYLE PUDDING AU PAIN À L'ANGLAISE (P.) (*For 6 persons*)

Proportions: 1 pt. milk, 3¼ oz. vanilla-flavored sugar, 2 oz. bread, 2 oz. dried currants, 4 yolks or 2 whole eggs.

Cut enriched white bread into thin slices, spread with a little melted butter, and dry in the oven without browning; place it in a deep ceramic dish (an English pie dish) used for puddings. Scatter raisins with the bread. Beat the egg yolks and sugar together, and pour in the boiling milk. Strain this cream through a cone-shaped sieve and pour it bit by bit over the bread, allowing time to soak. Poach about 25 min., in a *bain-marie*, in the oven. Powder the top with vanilla-flavored sugar and serve in the cooking dish.

BREAD PUDDING FRENCH STYLE PUDDING AU PAIN À LA FRANÇAISE (M.)

Soak 10 oz. white bread in milk boiled with ½ lb. sugar and flavored with vanilla or other flavoring. Press the bread through a sieve into a mixing bowl; bind it with 4 whole eggs and 6 egg yolks. Just before cooking, fold in 4 stiffly beaten egg whites. Pour into a mold with a center hole, buttered and lined with bread crumbs. Poach in a *bain-marie* in the oven at low heat. Serve with English Cream (p. 550), Sabayon (p. 553), or Fruit Sauce (p. 560).

RICE PUDDING PUDDING DE RIZ (D. and D.) (*For 8 persons*)

¼ lb. sugar and ¼ lb. rice flour mixed with 1½ oz. milk; beat well with 4 eggs, then add 3 beaten whites and 3¼ oz. melted butter; flavor with chopped orange peel. Pour into a heavily buttered charlotte mold and cook ½ hr. in a slow oven. Serve hot.

CREAMED RICE PUDDING PUDDING DE RIZ À LA CRÈME (E.)

This pudding is an excellent accompaniment for hot fruit compotes. Cook the rice the usual way, with a suitable flavoring, and, after cooking, bind with 4 egg yolks and 3 oz. fresh cream per qt. cooked rice. Place on a service platter and glaze quickly in the oven.

PUDDING ROYALE PUDDING À LA ROYALE (M.) (*For 8–10 persons*)

(1) Prepare a Sponge Finger mixture (p. 586). Spread this mixture in thin layers on sheets of paper. Bake these layers in a medium oven. After taking out of the oven, remove the paper and spread the layers with red-currant jelly. Roll up the layers into long loaves. Slice into rounds about ⅜ in. thick and use them to line the sides and bottom of a large, round buttered mold.

(2) *Mixture:* Bring to a boil 1 pt. milk with ¼ lb. sugar, ¼ lb. butter, and a pinch of salt; sift ¼ lb. flour into the milk. Work the mixture over the fire, as when making Choux Paste (p. 548). Remove from the fire and add 10 yolks and 2 whole eggs. Flavor with rum and blend in, finally, 3 stiffly beaten egg whites.

(3) Fill the mold with this mixture. Cook in the oven the usual way. Serve with orange-flavored English Cream (p. 550).

SOUFFLÉED PUDDING DENISE PUDDING SOUFFLÉ DENISE (E.) (*For 8 persons*)

Pound ¼ lb. freshly shelled and washed almonds in a mortar, adding a few drops of water from time to time. When the almonds become a fine paste, add enough water to make 1 pt. almond milk. Strain through a cheesecloth, twisting it to extract the milk. Mix this milk with 3¼ oz. flour and 3¼ oz. cream of rice, taking care to avoid lumps; strain through a cone-shaped sieve and add 5 oz. sugar, 3¼ oz. melted butter, and a little salt.

Place over the fire and bring to a boil, stirring vigorously with a spatula; cook until the mixture becomes as dry as Choux Paste (p. 548) and comes off the spatula cleanly. Pour this paste into a mixing bowl; first add, bit by bit, 1½ oz. butter, then 8 egg yolks, 1½ oz. almonds mashed fine with 1 tbsp. kirsch, 1 tbsp. maraschino, and 5 very stiffly beaten egg whites. Cook in a *bain-marie* in 1 of the following ways:

(1) In a buttered pudding dish. In this case, when the pudding is removed from the *bain-marie,* sprinkle the surface with confectioners' sugar and mark into squares with a red-hot iron.

(2) In a buttered, floured deep charlotte mold.

(3) In a dome-shaped mold, not too deep, buttered and lined with circles of Génoise (p. 549) or Sponge Finger (p. 586) paste, cut with a round cookie cutter, about ⅜ in. thick and ¾ in. in diameter.

In the last 2 cases, coat the pudding with Apricot Sauce (p. 560) made with Almond Milk (p. 556), and serve a separate dish of the same sauce.

SOUFFLÉED CHESTNUT PUDDING PUDDING SOUFFLÉ AUX MARRONS (P.) (*For 8 persons*)

1 lb. chestnuts, 2 oz. butter, 2½ oz. sugar, 4 egg yolks and 3 whites, vanilla, salt.

Peel the chestnuts and cook them in vanilla-flavored milk. When cooked, drain them and press them through a fine sieve; put this purée into a saucepan with the butter and sugar, and dry it 6–7 min. over a very low fire. Remove from the fire and mix in the egg yolks, then the stiffly beaten whites. Cook, as on p. 627, in a buttered, sugared mold. Serve with English Cream (p. 550) or hot Apricot Sauce (p. 560) flavored with rum.

SOUFFLÉED PUDDING À LA REINE PUDDING SOUFFLÉ À LA REINE (E.)

Souffléed Saxon Pudding mixture (see below), flavored with vanilla. Take a mold with a hole in the center and butter the inside, then sprinkle with chopped pistachios and crushed macaroons. Fill the mold with layers of the Saxon mixture, alternating them with layers of chopped pistachios and crushed macaroons. Poach in a *bain-marie* in the oven. Serve with English Cream (p. 550) containing Praline (p. 559).

SOUFFLÉED RICE PUDDING PUDDING SOUFFLÉ AU RIZ (P.)

Follow the recipe for Pudding Fleur de Marie (p. 625), using 12 oz. milk to cook the rice. Instead of caramelizing the mold, simply butter and sugar it or line it with white bread crumbs. Blend 3 stiffly beaten egg whites into the mixture.

SOUFFLÉED SAXON PUDDING PUDDING SOUFFLÉ SAXON (P.) (*For 8 persons*)

2½ oz. butter, 2½ oz. sugar, 2½ oz. flour, 6 oz. milk, 3 egg yolks and 3 whites, vanilla, salt.

Cream the butter in a mixing bowl, then mix in the sifted flour; pour the milk (boiled with vanilla) over this mixture. When well mixed, pour into the pan in which the milk was boiled and dry this paste on the fire until it no longer sticks to the spatula and is a little greasy to the touch. Remove from the fire and add the sugar, then the egg yolks, a dash of salt, and, finally, when the paste has become a very thick cream, blend in the stiffly beaten egg whites. The whites should be well mixed in and stirred for quite a while, so that the paste is not too thin. Pour this paste into a deep mold with a center hole; the mold should first be buttered and sugared, then filled only ¾ full. Bake 35–40 min., in a boiling *bain-marie*, in the oven. When the top has turned a light golden brown, protect it with a paper covering. It should puff up while cooking and rise about 1½ in. above the rim of the mold. When cooked, let it settle a few minutes before unmolding onto a deep round platter. Cover with English Cream (p. 550) flavored with vanilla or lemon or, if you prefer, sauce with a Sabayon (p. 553) made with white wine.

TAPIOCA PUDDING ENGLISH STYLE PUDDING AU TAPIOCA À L'ANGLAISE (P.) (*For 6 persons*)

Proportions: 1 pt. milk, 3¼ oz. sugar, 3¼ oz. tapioca, 2 oz. raisins, 3 egg yolks, vanilla.

Fig. 413 - Apples with rice creole (p. 622).
Fig. 414 - Apple meringue with rice (p. 622).

Fig. 413

Fig. 414

Fig. **415**

Fig. **416**

Cook the tapioca in the milk 10 min., then pour it over the egg yolks beaten with the sugar. Next add the raisins and pour into an English pudding dish; poach in the oven, in a *bain-marie*, about 15 min.

Note: In England, puddings are made from all sorts of pastes: semolina, vermicelli, macaroni, etc., using the proportions given at bottom of p. 628.

RHUBARB PIE RHUBARBE-PIE (P.)

Stick a band of Puff Paste (p. 544) with a little water to the rim of a ceramic English pie dish; fill the dish with small pieces of peeled rhubarb, heaping it into a dome; add a few good handfuls of brown sugar (or powdered sugar). It takes a good deal of sugar to counteract the acidity of the rhubarb. Cover with a thin crust of Puff Paste, brush with beaten egg, and bake 25–30 min. in a hot oven. Serve cold or warm.

This same dessert can be made with other fruit: sliced apples, gooseberries, plums, etc., using a little less sugar than with rhubarb.

Note: This dessert may also be classified as pastry.

FRUIT RISSOLES RISSOLES DE FRUITS (P.)

Roll out some scraps of Puff Paste (p. 544) into a sheet about as thick as a dime; cut into large rounds with a fluted cookie cutter, moisten the edges with water, and fill the centers with fruit purée or jam; fold the bottom crust over as in making turnovers and pinch the edges together. Fry in burning-hot deep fat. They can also be baked in the oven, but then they become regular turnovers. Rissoles can also be made with Krapfen Paste (p. 547), usually filled with strawberry jam. These are called Rissoles à la Dauphine.

SOUFFLÉS (MIXTURES FOR) SOUFFLÉS (APPAREILS POUR) (M.) (*For 4 persons*)

CREAM MIXTURE NO. 1: 4½ oz. milk, 1½ oz. sugar, 1 oz. cornstarch or arrowroot, ½ oz. butter, small pinch of salt, 3 egg yolks, 4 stiffly beaten whites. Any flavor you wish.

Preparation: Bring the milk to a boil with the sugar and salt; add the starch mixed into a paste with a little cold water. Cook 2 min. Remove from the fire and add the butter, egg yolks, and, at the very last, the beaten whites.

CREAM MIXTURE NO. 2: 4½ oz. milk, 1½ oz. sugar, 1 oz. flour, ½ oz. butter, small pinch of salt, 3 egg yolks, 4 stiffly beaten whites. Any flavor you wish.

Preparation: Mix the flour and milk in a saucepan; add the sugar and salt. Cook until the mixture thickens. Remove from the fire and add the butter, egg yolks, and, finally, the beaten whites.

FRANGIPANE MIXTURE: Prepare Frangipane Cream (p. 552), adding, on the fire, only ½ the usual number of egg yolks. Remove from the fire, add the rest of the yolks, and fold in the whites just before using.

Note: This is the most practical mixture for restaurants and quantity cooking.

MIXTURES FOR FRUIT SOUFFLÉS (for 8 persons): Cook 1 lb. sugar to the "crack" stage (p. 562), then add 13 oz. fruit pulp called for in the recipe. Bring the mixture to the "ball" stage. Pour it over 10 very stiffly beaten egg whites. Mix rapidly.

Fig. 415 - Diplomat or Cabinet pudding (p. 625).
Fig. 416 - Vanilla soufflé (p. 631).

Cooking Soufflés: Soufflé mixtures are cooked in special timbales, buttered and sprinkled with sugar, or in the false bottoms of these utensils, also buttered and sugared. Smooth off the surface of the mixture. Bake in a medium oven. When the soufflé is almost cooked, powder the surface with confectioners' sugar and glaze quickly in a hot oven.

APRICOT SOUFFLÉ SOUFFLÉ AUX ABRICOTS (M.)

Prepare the soufflé mixture with apricot pulp, as directed in the recipe on p. 629. Lightly flavor with kirsch.

Note: Chopped, preserved apricots can be added to the mixture.

ALMOND SOUFFLÉ SOUFFLÉ AUX AMANDES (M.)

Add 4 oz. finely crushed almonds to one or another of the cream mixtures given on p. 629. Flavor with kirsch. Decorate the top with shredded almonds.

FILBERT SOUFFLÉ SOUFFLÉ AUX AVELINES (M.)

Like Praline Soufflé (p. 631), using filbert Praline (p. 559).

SOUFFLÉ BAR-LE-DUC SOUFFLÉ BAR-LE-DUC (M.)

Prepare a vanilla-flavored soufflé mixture. Add to the mixture, when pouring it into the baking dish, small clusters of red currants and diced macaroons soaked in plum brandy.

SOUFFLÉ BRILLAT-SAVARIN SOUFFLÉ BRILLAT-SAVARIN (M.)

Make a cream soufflé mixture flavored with vanilla, and, when pouring it into the baking dish, add crushed Sponge Fingers (p. 586) soaked in rum and lumps of very thick applesauce. Decorate the top of the soufflé with a border of cherries half cooked in sirup.

SOUFFLÉ ELIZABETH SOUFFLÉ ÉLISABETH (E.)

Alternate layers of vanilla-flavored cream soufflé mixture with layers of macaroon pieces soaked in kirsch and pralined violets. After removing from the oven, cover with a veil of Spun Sugar (p. 562) and serve immediately.

SOUFFLÉ PALMYRE SOUFFLÉ PALMYRE (M.)

Vanilla-flavored soufflé mixture. Garnish the soufflé, when filling the timbale, with pieces of Sponge Fingers (p. 586) soaked in anisette and with diced, candied cherries and angelica.

HALF-AND-HALF SOUFFLÉ SOUFFLÉ PANACHÉ (H.)

Fill one half of the soufflé timbale with a vanilla soufflé mixture and the other half with a chocolate soufflé mixture, carefully separating the colors. Since the chocolate makes the mixture heavy, add a little more of the beaten egg whites to it. If successful, this dish is most attractive, with the soufflé all puffed up and the 2 colors distinctly separated. The English call it "half and half," and the French, *moitié, moitié.*

PEACH SOUFFLÉ or **SOUFFLÉ MONTREUIL** SOUFFLÉ AUX PÊCHES OR À LA MONTREUIL (M.)

Prepare a fruit-soufflé mixture, using peach pulp. When pouring into the baking dish, garnish with small quartered peaches cooked in sirup and well drained and pieces of Sponge Fingers (p. 586) soaked in kirsch.

PRALINE SOUFFLÉ SOUFFLÉ PRALINÉ (M.)

Add finely crushed Praline (p. 559) to a vanilla soufflé mixture. Decorate the top of this soufflé with lightly grilled, chopped almonds.

SOUFFLÉ ROTHSCHILD SOUFFLÉ ROTHSCHILD (M.)

Vanilla soufflé mixture. Garnish the soufflé mixture with preserved fruits macerated in kirsch. When the soufflé is almost cooked, lay a ring of large strawberries around the top or, if out of season, semisweetened cherries.

Note: Another way to vary this recipe is to macerate the preserved fruits in Goldwasser.

SOUFFLÉ SAINT-SYLVESTRE SOUFFLÉ SAINT-SYLVESTRE (M.)

Vanilla soufflé mixture with finely chopped walnuts. When pouring the soufflé into the baking dish, garnish with a mixture of diced russet apples cooked in butter and sugar and small cubes of Baba (p. 584) soaked in rum.

SOUFFLÉ SARAH BERNHARDT SOUFFLÉ SARAH BERNHARDT (E.)

Fill the soufflé timbale with alternate layers of a vanilla cream soufflé mixture and pieces of macaroon soaked in dry curaçao. Cook as usual. Serve with large sugared strawberries macerated in curaçao, covered with puréed strawberries, and a separate dish of Chantilly Cream (p. 552).

TEA SOUFFLÉ SOUFFLÉ AU THÉ (M.)

Make a cream soufflé mixture, using tea instead of milk.

SOUFFLÉ TSARINE SOUFFLÉ TSARINE (M.)

Cream soufflé mixture flavored with kümmel. When filling the soufflé timbale, garnish it with candied violets and Sponge Finger (p. 586) pieces soaked in kümmel.

VANILLA SOUFFLÉ SOUFFLÉ À LA VANILLE (M.)

Prepare with one of the cream mixtures previously given; strongly flavor with vanilla. (Figure 416, Page 629.)

SOUFFLÉ VÉNITIENNE SOUFFLÉ À LA VÉNITIENNE (M.)

Vanilla soufflé mixture. Garnish with macaroon pieces soaked in maraschino and with 1½ oz. peeled, chopped pistachios per 3 oz. milk.

PINEAPPLE TIMBALE CREOLE TIMBALE D'ANANAS À LA CRÉOLE (M.)

Line a charlotte mold with leftover scraps of Puff Paste (p. 544). Fill by alternating layers of Dessert Rice (p. 559) with layers of thinly sliced pineapple and red-currant jelly. Cover the timbale with a crust of the same paste, and bake in a hot oven—35 min. for a 3-pt. mold. Unmold the timbale and coat with Apricot Sauce (p. 560) flavored with kirsch or other liqueur.

CHERRY TIMBALE MONTMORENCY TIMBALE DE CERISES MONTMORENCY (E.)

Bake a Brioche (p. 565) in a mold large enough to make the timbale. When it is cold, scoop out the inside, leaving a crust about ½ in. thick. Brush the outside with apricot sirup cooked to the "thread" stage (p. 562); decorate with bits of Puff Paste (p. 544) cut into crescents, diamonds, small circles, etc., and bake in a slow oven, with nothing inside the Brioche. Just before serving, fill the Brioche shell with pitted cherries cooked in a thin sirup mixed with raspberry-and-red-currant jelly.

FRUIT TIMBALE BOURDALOUE TIMBALE DE FRUITS BOURDALOUE (E.)

Make a dry Sweet Paste (p. 546), adding to it ¼ lb. finely chopped almonds per lb. flour. Line a buttered timbale mold with this paste; fill with various stewed fruits alternated with layers of Frangipane Cream (p. 552). Cover with a crust of the same paste and bake in a medium oven. After unmolding, coat with vanilla-flavored apricot sirup.

FRUIT TIMBALE PARISIENNE TIMBALE DE FRUITS À LA PARISIENNE (H.)

Bake Brioche Paste (p. 546) in a charlotte mold; slice off the top, scoop out the inside, spread a layer of apricot jam around the inside of the shell, and fill it with a hot mixed-fruit compote flavored with kirsch and maraschino. Replace the top that was sliced off and decorate with preserved fruits.

PEACH TIMBALE MONTREUIL TIMBALE DE PÊCHES À LA MONTREUIL (M.)

Line a charlotte mold with Puff Paste (p. 544). Fill it, in alternate layers, with quartered peaches poached in sirup and with rather thick applesauce. Cover with a crust of the same paste and bake 30–35 min. in a medium oven. Coat with Apricot Sauce (p. 560) flavored with kirsch or other liqueur.

PEAR TIMBALE D'ARENBERG TIMBALE DE POIRES À LA D'ARENBERG (M.)

Line a charlotte mold with ordinary Brioche Paste (p. 546). Fill it, in alternate layers, with quartered pears lightly poached in vanilla sirup and with rather thick apricot jam. Cover with a top crust of paste, sealing the edges tightly. Bake 35–40 min. Unmold and coat with kirsch-flavored Apricot Sauce (p. 560).

Note: A variant of this recipe is to replace the apricot jam with applesauce.

PEAR TIMBALE SWEDISH STYLE TIMBALE DE POIRES À LA SUÉDOISE (M.)

Line a charlotte mold with ordinary Brioche Paste (p. 546). Fill it, in alternate layers, with pear quarters poached in vanilla sirup and with Pastry Cream (p. 552). Cover with a top crust of the same paste; seal the edges. Bake 35–40 min. Serve with Sabayon (p. 553) made with white wine.

SMALL FRUIT TIMBALES PETITES TIMBALES AUX FRUITS (M.)

Usually made with ordinary Brioche Paste (p. 546). Line small, plain, shallow molds with this paste. Fill with various fruits: cherries, quartered pears or apples, apricots, peaches, plums, etc., lightly poached in vanilla sirup and bound with apricot jam. Cover the timbales with a crust of the same paste; seal the edges. Bake in a medium oven. Serve with Fruit Sauce (p. 560) flavored with a liqueur.

HASTY PUDDING TÔT-FAIT (D. and D.) (*For 6 persons*)

Mix 3½ oz. powdered sugar and 3½ oz. flour or cream of rice in a bowl with 1½ oz. milk; beat in 3 whole eggs, then add 2½ oz. melted butter, 2 beaten egg whites, tiny pinch of salt, and flavor with chopped orange peel or vanilla. Pour the mixture into a buttered charlotte mold or baking dish and bake about ½ hr. in a slow oven; serve hot.

Fig. 417 - Apricots Banville (p. 633).
Fig. 418 - Pineapple Alexandra (p. 633).
Fig. 419 - Pineapple Belle de Meaux (p. 633).
Fig. 420 - Bavarian cream Fontanges (p. 635).

Fig. 417

Fig. 418

Fig. 419

Fig. 420

Fig. 421

Fig. 422

Fig. 423

Fig. 424

ZAMORA ZAMORA (D. and D.)

Soak a Savarin Cake (p. 547) ring in kirsch-flavored sirup, frost with white Fondant (p. 553), and place on a base of Sweet Paste (p. 546); fill the center with Saint-Honoré Cream (p. 552) smoothed into a dome, powder the top heavily with confectioners' sugar, and caramelize it with a red-hot iron; decorate the Savarin with a ring of cherries half cooked in sirup. Serve with a dish of Apricot Sauce (p. 560) flavored with kirsch, with chopped cherries in it. Serve hot or cold.

COLD SWEETS or DESSERTS

APRICOTS BANVILLE ABRICOTS À LA BANVILLE (J.)

Poach pitted apricots in thin sirup; arrange them in a ring on a platter, placing each on a small macaroon. Fill the center of the ring with Chantilly Cream (p. 552) shaped into a mound with a pastry bag with a fluted tube. Decorate with candied cherries and angelica. Serve very cold. (Figure 417, Page 632.)

APRICOTS MIREILLE ABRICOTS MIREILLE (E.)

Peel and halve some fine ripe apricots. Arrange them in a timbale with their shelled almondlike stones, powder with sugar, and keep on ice 1 hr. Just before serving, moisten with kirsch; cover with sugared, vanilla-flavored whipped cream; sprinkle the surface with crystallized jasmine flowers and violets.

APRICOTS ROYALE ABRICOTS À LA ROYALE (E.)

Place apricot halves, poached in vanilla sirup and chilled, in rather deep tartlet molds. Finish filling the molds with very clear, kirsch-flavored jelly. Prepare a low ring of Génoise Cake (p. 549), glazed with red-currant jelly cooked to the "thread" stage (p. 562) and sprinkled with chopped pistachios. Unmold the apricot tartlets and place them around the top of the cake ring; fill the center of the ring with chopped pink jelly flavored with anisette.

PINEAPPLE ALEXANDRA ANANAS ALEXANDRA (J.)

Peel a very ripe pineapple. Neatly cut half slices and macerate them in kirsch and sugar. Dice the scraps and macerate them with tiny wild strawberries. Just before serving, make a mound of the diced mixture in the center of a platter, cover with very stiff Chantilly Cream (p. 552), and surround with a border of pineapple slices. Sprinkle the top with wild strawberries. Cover the border with thin Apricot Sauce (p. 560) flavored with kirsch. (Figure 418, Page 632.)

PINEAPPLE BELLE DE MEAUX ANANAS À LA BELLE DE MEAUX (Fr.)

Pineapple served this way makes it easier for the guests to help themselves. It is rather awkward to help oneself from a pineapple shell standing on end. In this recipe, the pineapple is split in half lengthwise, including the leaves, then hollowed out, leaving a little thickness of pulp. Dice the pulp removed and macerate it in sugar and kirsch with an equal amount of tiny wild strawberries, the bowl set on ice.

Serving: Prepare and cook in advance a layer of Ordinary Génoise Cake (p. 550) long enough to hold both halves of the pineapple placed end to end.

Fig. 421 - April breeze (p. 636).
Fig. 422 - Charlotte russe (p. 639).
Fig. 423 - Strawberries Chantilly (p. 641).
Fig. 424 - Strawberries diva (p. 641).

Fill the pineapple halves with the macerated strawberries and diced pineapple and cover generously with very stiff Chantilly Cream (p. 552). Decorate the top of the dessert with large chilled strawberries. Serve very cold.

Note: When strawberries are out of season, the pineapple can be filled with pineapple ice (made from the pulp scooped out), but then the recipe no longer deserves the name Belle de Meaux, a beautiful variety of strawberry.

Dish carried out by M. Fressinet, head chef. (Figure 419, Page 632.)

PINEAPPLE GEORGETTE ANANAS GEORGETTE (E.)

Cut off the top of a fine pineapple and hollow it out, leaving about ⅜ in. pulp on the bottom and around the sides of the shell. Save the top slice with the leaves. Fill the pineapple shell with a mixture of frozen pineapple mousse and thin slices of the pineapple removed from the inside. Chill in the refrigerator. Put the top of the pineapple back on to restore its appearance and serve on a napkin.

PINEAPPLE WITH MIXED FRUITS AND LIQUEURS ANANAS À LA MACÉDOINE AUX LIQUEURS (M.)

Cut the top off a fresh pineapple and hollow it out without breaking the shell. Moisten the inside with kirsch, maraschino, and sugar. Fill with diced fruits in season mixed with the diced pulp removed from the pineapple. Moisten with kirsch and maraschino (or any other liqueur). Chill 2 hr. in crushed ice. Replace the top with leaves and serve on a napkin.

Note: Melon is served the same way.

PINEAPPLE NINON ANANAS NINON (E.)

Line a soufflé dish with vanilla ice cream, packing it in on the bias—in other words, slanting it from the rim to the center of the bottom so that it forms a hollow like an inverted cone. On this bed of ice cream lay 2 or 3 rows of thinly sliced fresh pineapple so that the last row of slices sticks out past the rim of the dish.

PINEAPPLE ROYALE ANANAS À LA ROYALE (E.)

Cut the top off a fresh pineapple and hollow it out, leaving a layer of pulp about ⅜ in. thick. Save the top slice with the leaves. Fill with diced mixed fruits macerated in kirsch; place in the center of a crystal bowl; surround the base with a ring of fine peaches poached in vanilla sirup; between each peach place a large strawberry macerated in kirsch. Put the top back on the pineapple.

BANANAS PRINCESSE BANANES PRINCESSE (D. and D.)

Dice apricots and bananas (split the banana skins in half lengthwise and save them); mix the diced fruit and macerate in kirsch; fill the half peels with this mixture; using a pastry bag with a fluted tube, cover the top with Chantilly Cream (p. 552).

VANILLA BAVARIAN CREAM BAVAROIS À LA VANILLE (P.) (*For 8 persons*)

Prepare 6 oz. vanilla English Cream (p. 550), remove it from the fire, and add ¼ oz. gelatin dissolved in cold water. Strain this cream and let it cool, then, when it has almost set, add 9 oz. whipped cream. Pour this mixture into a mold with a center hole, moistened on the inside with cold water, and chill it in a bed of crushed ice. To unmold, run a small knife around the edges, separate the cream from the side of the mold slightly, and blow into the empty space. Then turn it upside down on a plate and let it loosen by itself, without shaking. In midsummer, or when ice is unobtainable, add a little more gelatin, taking care not to add too much, or the flavor will be disagreeable.

Note: The name Bavarois has been changed to Muscovite. However, we prefer to leave the original name given by the author. (See p. 645.)

BAVARIAN CREAM BEAU-RIVAGE BAVAROIS BEAU-RIVAGE (D. and D.)

Vanilla-flavored Chantilly Cream (p. 552) in the center of a ring mold of Caramel Cream (p. 640) and sprinkled with very finely chopped pistachios.

COFFEE BAVARIAN CREAM BAVAROIS AU CAFÉ (P.)

Same as Vanilla Bavarian Cream (p. 634), except that the English Cream is made with ½ milk and ½ very strong coffee, with a few drops of coffee essence for coloring.

CHOCOLATE BAVARIAN CREAM BAVAROIS AU CHOCOLAT (P.)

Same procedure as for Vanilla Bavarian Cream (p. 634), adding 4 chocolate tablets, or 2 tbsp. cocoa dissolved in milk, to the English Cream. If cocoa is used, add a little more sugar to the cream.

BAVARIAN CREAM FONTANGES BAVAROIS FONTANGES (P.)

To make this dessert, prepare two Bavarian cream mixtures with different but harmonizing flavors, so that they do not offend the palate. Chocolate and strawberry, for example, are not good together. With this word of advice, proceed as follows. To mold the cream, take 2 molds, one a little smaller than the other, so that when it is placed inside the larger mold there will be an empty space of about ¾ in. Embed the larger mold in crushed ice and pour in some of 1 mixture--vanilla, for example. Then fill the smaller mold with crushed ice and place it inside the larger one so that its weight will make the vanilla cream rise to the rim of the mold, on which the handles of the inner mold are resting.

After a few minutes, when the cream has set, empty the ice from the small mold with a spoon, and fill it with hot water. Half a minute later, the small mold can be easily removed, and you will have a well-lined mold in which to pour the second Bavarian cream—strawberry, raspberry, etc. Serve on a napkin. It makes a pleasant-looking dessert. (Figure 420, Page 632.)

STRAWBERRY BAVARIAN CREAM BAVAROIS AUX FRAISES (P.) (*For 8 persons*)

This recipe can be considered standard for all Bavarian creams with fruit, no matter what the fruit. Press ½ lb. delicately flavored, tiny wild strawberries through a silk or wire sieve. Put this purée into a bowl with 5 oz. powdered sugar, juice of ½ lemon, and a little carmine coloring; add ⅓ oz. gelatin (a little more than for plain Bavarian cream) dissolved with a little water in a double boiler, and let cool until the mixture begins to congeal. Then fold in ½ pt. whipped cream and mold as directed above.

Note: Using this recipe, you can make Bavarian creams with any fruit.

PISTACHIO BAVARIAN CREAM BAVAROIS AUX PISTACHES (P.)

Same procedure as for Praline Bavarian Cream, below, adding 2 oz. shelled pistachios mashed very fine with a little kirsch to the vanilla cream. Heighten the color with a drop of green vegetable coloring.

PRALINE BAVARIAN CREAM BAVAROIS PRALINÉ (P.)

Same procedure as for Vanilla Bavarian Cream (p. 634), adding, at the same time as the whipped cream, 2½ oz. finely powdered Praline (p. 559) to the English Cream.

WHIPPED-CREAM CAKE MONTE CARLO BISCUIT MONTE-CARLO (E.)

Place 5 large flan circles on a dampened baking board covered with heavy paper. Half fill the circles with meringue; bake the meringue and keep in the warmer 24 hr. so that it becomes very dry. Stack the meringue layers 1 on the other like a cake, with a filling of Chantilly Cream (p. 552) sprinkled with grated chocolate between each layer. Frost the top layer with chocolate, then border the top with Chantilly Cream squeezed from a paper cone.

Border the sides of the cake with small rosettes of Chantilly Cream and place a pralined violet in each rosette.

BLANCMANGE ENGLISH STYLE BLANC-MANGER À L'ANGLAISE (E.) (*For 8 persons*)

Bring 1 qt. milk to a boil with ¼ lb. sugar. Pour it, stirring briskly, onto ¼ lb. cornstarch mixed into a paste with 7 oz. cold milk. Beat with a whisk until smooth, then cook a few minutes over a hot fire, constantly stirring. After removing from the stove, flavor as desired; pour it while very hot into molds previously brushed with thin sirup to make the dessert smoother and shinier. Let set and serve very cold, either plain or with a fruit compote.

BLANCMANGE FRENCH STYLE BLANC-MANGER À LA FRANÇAISE (E.) (*For 8 persons*)

Mixture: Shell 1 lb. sweet almonds and 4 or 5 bitter almonds; soak them in cold water to make them very white. Pound them in a mortar as fine as possible, while adding, spoonful by spoonful, 24 oz. filtered water; press very tightly by squeezing in a cloth. Dissolve 7 oz. lump sugar in the almond milk thus obtained (about 21 oz.) and add 1 oz. gelatin dissolved in warm sirup; strain through cheesecloth and flavor as you wish.

Molding: Use an oiled mold with a center hole, the same kind used for making Bavarian creams. Put on ice to set and unmold as usual.

Note: The method of making almond milk given above is the old-fashioned way. In modern cooking, the almonds are pounded with only a few spoonfuls of water and some very light cream.

APRIL BREEZE BRISE D'AVRIL (J.)

Using a pastry bag, fill small individual cups with strawberry-flavored Chantilly Cream (p. 552) tinted a delicate pink. Decorate with a few crystallized violets. (Figure 421, Page 633.)

SPRING BREEZE BRISE DE PRINTEMPS (E.)

Violet-flavored Chantilly Cream (p. 552), lightly chilled, served in elegant, small crystal cups. Place a few pralined violets on top.

Fig. 425 - Chilled fruits (p. 643).
Fig. 426 - Floating island (p. 644).

Fig. 425

Fig. 426

Fig. **427**

CHERRIES DUBARRY CERISES DUBARRY (E.)

Line a large flan circle with Short Paste (p. 545), lay it on a tart pan, and prick the bottom with a fork to avoid bubbles while baking; powder with confectioners' sugar and fill with pitted cherries, packing them in tightly one beside the other. Bake the flan the usual way and let cool. When it is cold, cover the cherries with Chantilly Cream (p. 552) mixed with either ordinary Praline (p. 559) or crushed macaroons. Smooth the surface of the cream, also smoothing it over the crust of the flan; cover with powdered macaroons; decorate with pink and white Chantilly Cream, using a paper cone.

CHERRIES MIREILLE CERISES MIREILLE (E.) (*For 8 persons*)

Take 1 lb. very fine Montmorency cherries; pit them and put into a frying pan with 7 oz. very fresh raspberries pressed through a sieve, 7 oz. sugar, 1/3 vanilla bean. Cover the pan, bring to a boil a few times, and keep hot, 10–12 min., at the back of the stove. Then put the cherries into a bowl and let them cool in their sirup.

Prepare 1½ pt. Chantilly Cream (p. 552) and add about 10 very small meringues. Pour the cream into an ice-cream mold lined on the bottom and sides with white paper. Close the mold and chill on ice the usual way. When ready to serve, unmold the mousse onto a platter, surround with a few cherries, and cover lightly with the sirup. Serve the rest of the cherries in a separate bowl.

Note: As a variant, small macaroons soaked in kirsch, maraschino, curaçao, or rum can be used instead of the small meringues. This kind of mousse can be garnished or accompanied with peaches, strawberries, or apricots, poached or not in vanilla sirup, and named according to the fruit selected—for example, Peach Mousse Mireille, if peaches are used. Strawberries should never be cooked; simply macerate them in sugar and some liqueur.

CHERRIES VICTORIA CERISES VICTORIA (P.)

Prepare a Bavarian cream with currants: squeeze the juice from ½ lb. currants and melt ¼ lb. powdered sugar in it; add 4 leaves of gelatin dissolved in a few tbsp. cold water. When the mixture begins to congeal, blend in 5 oz. whipped cream, then fill small porcelain dessert cups, which have been chilled on ice, ¾ full. Next, poach 1 lb. pitted cherries in a light, sweet red wine; drain them and chill on ice. Cover the cream with these cherries, top with Chantilly Cream (p. 552), and serve ice-cold.

CHERRIES WITH BORDEAUX or **CHERRY SOUP FRENCH STYLE**

CERISES AU VIN DE BORDEAUX or SOUPE AUX CERISES À LA FRANÇAISE (E.)

Pit 1 lb. Montmorency cherries and put them into a silver bowl; add ½ lb. powdered sugar, a very small stick of cinnamon, ½ orange peel, and 5 or 6 tbsp. red-currant jelly. Pour in 1½ bottles good Bordeaux. Cover the bowl, bring to a boil, and keep hot, 10–12 min., at the back of the stove, to poach the cherries. Let cool. Serve these cherries in crystal cups, along with Dry Biscuits (p. 586) or macaroons. This delicious dessert is especially good at teatime.

CHARLOTTE CHARLOTTE (M.)

Line a charlotte mold with Sponge Fingers (p. 586). (Charlotte molds should always be lined, first, on bottom and sides, with paper.) The mold is

Fig. 427 - Melon surprise (p. 645).
Fig. 428 - Chesnut Mont Blanc (p. 645).

lined the following way. Cover the bottom of the mold with Sponge Fingers cut into long triangles (leaving one side with its usual rounded shape) and laid in a rosette radiating from the center. Place the fingers vertically around the sides, tightly against each other, which will be done more easily if the edges are slightly trimmed. Fill the mold with the Bavarian-cream mixture called for in the recipe. Let set in the refrigerator or on ice. Unmold the Charlotte onto a napkin or doily.

Note: In addition to the method given above, charlotte molds can be lined with flat or rolled waffles, with ordinary Sponge Cake (p. 548), punch biscuits, frosted or plain rectangles or rounds of Génoise Cake (p. 549), or very tiny Meringues (p. 594) stuck together with sugar cooked to the "crack" stage (p. 562).

CHARLOTTE CHANTILLY CHARLOTTE CHANTILLY (M.)

This can be made 2 ways:

Method A: Make a small tub or bucket, using Dry Paste (p. 546) for the round bottom and waffles for the sides; fill with sugared, vanilla-flavored whipped cream, heaping it into a dome. Decorate the top with whipped cream squeezed from a paper cone and with preserved fruit.

Method B: Line a charlotte mold with Sponge Fingers (p. 586) stuck together with sugar cooked to the "crack" stage (p. 562). Place on a doily. Fill with sugared, vanilla-flavored whipped cream. Cover the top of the charlotte with Sponge Fingers cut in points toward 1 end and fitted together to make a rosette.

CHARLOTTE MALAKOFF CHARLOTTE MALAKOFF (P.) (*For 8 persons*)

¼ lb. almonds, ¼ lb. powdered sugar, ¼ lb. butter, ¼ lb. whipped cream, vanilla, and kirsch.

Take 15 Sponge Fingers (p. 586), trim the sides to make them straight and trim off 1 end to stand them up around the sides of a charlotte mold, pressing them tightly together as explained above. Line the bottom of the mold simply with a round piece of white paper. When the mold is properly prepared, pound the almonds in a mortar until very fine, adding the sugar and vanilla bit by bit. When this is well mashed, mix in the slightly softened butter and work in the mortar with a pestle to make the paste white and smooth. Add 1 liqueur glass of good kirsch, put into a mixing bowl, and mix with the whipped cream.

Pour this cream into the biscuit-lined mold and embed it in unsalted crushed ice. When it is very firm, slice off the biscuits sticking above the mold, to make them even with the cream, and turn over onto a platter covered with a napkin or doily; remove the paper circle and decorate the top with sugared, vanilla-flavored whipped cream, using a pastry bag with a fluted tube. This exquisite dessert has a delicacy of flavor far superior to Charlotte Russe.

CHARLOTTE MONTREUIL CHARLOTTE MONTREUIL (E.)

Line the bottom and sides of a charlotte mold with Sponge Fingers (p. 586). Fill it with a Bavarian-cream mixture containing 12 oz. peach purée per qt. English Cream and the usual proportion of whipped cream (see p. 635). Add some very soft, thin-sliced, sugared peaches when pouring the mixture into the mold.

CHARLOTTE NESSELRODE CHARLOTTE NESSELRODE (M.)

Line the mold with rectangles of Génoise Cake (p. 549). Fill with Vanilla Bavarian Cream (p. 634) mixed with some tiny bits of candied chestnuts and some seeded Malaga raisins and dried currants that have been washed, soaked in sirup to swell, and macerated in maraschino.

CHARLOTTE OPÉRA CHARLOTTE OPÉRA (E.)

Line the mold with Palmer's Sugar Wafers (brand name); fill with Vanilla Bavarian Cream (p. 634) mixed with ¼ as much very fine purée of candied chestnuts and a mixture of diced candied fruits macerated in maraschino.

CHARLOTTE PARISIENNE CHARLOTTE À LA PARISIENNE (M.)

Line the mold with waffles. Fill with Bavarian Cream (p. 634) mixed with diced candied fruits macerated in kirsch.

CHARLOTTE RUSSE CHARLOTTE RUSSE (P.)

Make some very dry Sponge Fingers (p. 586) to line a charlotte mold. First cut the fingers in slender triangles (leaving 1 end rounded) and then place them in the bottom of the mold with the points together in the center, pressing them tightly against each other. Trim the sides of the other fingers so that they will fit closely together around the sides; trim off 1 end of the fingers so that they will stand up straight with the rounded side out; do not bother about the fingers being all of the same height or sticking out past the mold. Fill the mold with Vanilla Bavarian Cream (p. 634), or of any other flavor, but containing less gelatin than usual. Let set in a cold place, then trim off the tops of the fingers to make them even with the cream and, when ready to serve, unmold onto a doily. (Figure 422, Page 633.)

CHARLOTTE SAVOISIENNE CHARLOTTE SAVOISIENNE (H.)

Bake a Génoise Cake (p. 549) in a charlotte mold, hollow it out, and fill with a heaping mound of Chantilly Cream (p. 552). Decorate with candied fruit.

CHOCOLATE HEART COEUR DE NÈGRE (A.) (*For 4 persons*)

Take: 1 qt. Chantilly Cream (p. 552) molded in a heart shape, ¼ lb. fine chocolate with or without vanilla flavoring, 1¾ oz. sweet butter, 12 thin sponge biscuits, 2 egg yolks. Melt the chocolate with a few tbsp. water, then add the butter and egg yolks; stir over a low fire, then let cool. Place the cream heart on a platter, coat it with the chocolate, and put the biscuits all around the base. This is a very light and tasty dessert that takes only a little time to prepare.

CREAM CAPRICE CRÈME CAPRICE (E.)

Add ½ cup coarsely broken meringues to 1 pt. Chantilly Cream (p. 552). Place the mixture in a madeleine mold (a mold with a small base and flaring, fluted sides) lined with white paper; cover the top and tie on tightly and keep on ice 2 hr. Unmold when ready to serve; remove the paper, and, using a pastry bag with a fluted tube, decorate with Chantilly Cream colored pink with a little strawberry or raspberry juice.

FAVORITE CREAM CRÈME FAVORITE (P.) (*For 8 persons*)

3½ oz. vanilla-flavored powdered sugar, ½ lb. raspberries, 3 oz. sugar icing, 1 pt. whipped cream, 8 meringue shells, 1 liqueur glass maraschino.

Mix the vanilla-flavored powdered sugar into the whipped cream, along with the maraschino and the meringue shells, which should be very dry and broken in large pieces. Pour into a plain bombe mold, cover tightly, and bury 2 hr. in lightly salted crushed ice. Unmold onto a well-chilled plate, then cover with a sauce made by dissolving the sugar icing in the raspberries, which have been pressed through a sieve.

FRENCH CREAM CRÈME FRANÇAISE (P.)

Make a simple molded vanilla cream or custard (see directly below), without caramel, and poach it in a charlotte mold. After chilling and unmolding, decorate, using a pastry bag with a fluted tube, with very stiff Chantilly Cream (p. 552).

MOLDED CARAMEL CREAM or **CUSTARD** CRÈME RENVERSÉE AU CARAMEL (P.) (*For 8 persons*)

¼ lb. powdered sugar, 1 pt. milk, 2 whole eggs and 4 yolks, vanilla.

Beat the eggs, yolks, and sugar in a bowl; when the mixture is smooth, pour in the boiling milk flavored with vanilla. Let stand a few minutes; skim the foam off the top, which would immediately burn in the oven; pour this cream through a strainer into a mold of any shape lined with caramelized sugar. Poach in a *bain-marie*, without boiling, in the oven, until the cream feels a little firm to the touch. These creams or custards can also be tested, like cakes, by sticking a knife in to see if it comes out dry. Let the cream cool before unmolding.

Note: This recipe is standard for all molded creams or custards, regardless of the flavor used. It is therefore unnecessary to repeat the recipe for each flavor, except to say, however, that ½ milk and ½ very strong coffee are needed to make Molded Coffee Cream.

VIENNA CREAM CRÈME VIENNOISE (A.) (*For 8 persons*)

Take 3½ oz. sugar, 3½ oz. Italian Meringue (p. 685), 1⅓ oz. flour, 1 oz. sweet butter, pinch of salt, 1 pt. milk, 6 egg yolks, vanilla bean.

Bring the milk to a boil with the vanilla bean to flavor it well. Remove the bean. Put the flour into a saucepan; mix it well with the milk, avoiding lumps; cook it. Remove from the fire and add the butter, egg yolks, sugar, salt; mix well; heat gently without boiling, constantly stirring until the cream takes on a good consistency. Strain the cream, let cool, then mix it with the meringue.

JOINVILLE RING CROÛTE JOINVILLE (E.)

Moisten fresh slices of Savarin Cake (p. 547) with kirsch-flavored sirup; make a ring of overlapping cake slices, alternating them with thin slices of pineapple macerated in kirsch; fill the center of the ring with vanilla-flavored Chantilly Cream (p. 552) heaped into a pyramid and sprinkle it with grated chocolate. Pour kirsch-flavored apricot sirup over the cake ring.

SEMOLINA PUDDING I FLAMRI DE SEMOULE (P.) (*For 8 persons*)

6 oz. white wine, 6 oz. water, ¼ lb. semolina flour, ¼ lb. sugar, 5 egg whites, vanilla.

Bring the white wine and water to a boil together, then sift in the semolina, and cook well; add the sugar and vanilla, then remove from the fire and mix in, first, 2 egg whites (unbeaten)—so quickly that they have no time to cook; then add 3 more egg whites, this time stiffly beaten. Pour the mixture into a buttered, sugared mold with a center hole; and poach slowly in a *bain-marie*, in the oven, 35 min. Let cool, then unmold onto a cold plate, and serve surrounded by kirsch-flavored red-currant sauce (see Fruit Sauces, p. 560) and with a separate dish of the same sauce.

SEMOLINA PUDDING II FLAMRI DE SEMOULE (P.) (*For 8 persons*)

This recipe is quite different from the one above. Bring 1 cup vanilla-flavored milk to a boil and cook 2½ oz. semolina; add ¼ lb. sugar, then remove from the fire and add ⅕ oz. gelatin soaked in cold water and dissolved with very little water in a double boiler. While the semolina mixture is still boiling hot, mix in 4 stiffly beaten egg whites and pour into a mold moistened with a little water. Embed in ice to set, unmold, and serve, as the above, with red-currant sauce and a decoration of candied fruits, if desired.

STRAWBERRIES CARDINAL FRAISES À LA CARDINAL (P.) (*For 6 persons*)

Chill 1 lb. large, firm strawberries on ice. Press ½ lb. raspberries through a sieve and add 5 oz. powdered sugar and 1 tsp. lemon juice to this purée, and let the sugar melt while chilling the purée on ice. Arrange the strawberries in a well-chilled bowl or timbale, cover them with the raspberry sauce, and sprinkle with fresh shredded almonds.

STRAWBERRIES CHANTILLY FRAISES À LA CHANTILLY (P.)

Whip cream until very stiff with plenty of sugar and vanilla. Then, using a pastry bag with a fairly large tube, make a ring of this cream on a chilled platter or in a bowl and fill the center with fine strawberries that have been chilled on ice; powder with vanilla-flavored sugar. There are a variety of ways of serving whipped cream and strawberries. (Figure 423, Page 633.)

STRAWBERRIES CREOLE FRAISES À LA CRÉOLE (M.)

Equal parts of diced strawberries and pineapple macerated on ice with kirsch and sugar. Serve heaped in a mound in a compote or crystal bowl in the center of a ring of half slices of pineapple also macerated in kirsch and sugar and arranged so that they overlap.

Note: Raspberries can be prepared the same way.

STRAWBERRIES DIVA FRAISES DIVA (M.)

Macerate large strawberries in sugar and kümmel. Chill well. Heap the strawberries into a pyramid in the center of a Molded Vanilla Cream ring (see p. 640). Decorate the strawberries with Chantilly Cream (p. 552) squeezed from a paper cone. Sprinkle with shredded pistachios and decorate the ring mold with a border of pralined violets. (Figure 424, Page 633.)

STRAWBERRIES FÉMINA FRAISES À LA FÉMINA (P.)

Prepare a Peach Bavarian Cream (p. 635) with a little more gelatin than usual and mold it in a ring mold. When it has set, and just before serving, unmold onto a well-chilled platter; fill the center with large fine strawberries macerated on ice with a little sugar and kirsch. Cover the strawberries with a purée of wild strawberries sugared with its own weight in powdered sugar and thickened with a few tbsp. red-currant jelly to form a sauce. This sauce should be prepared in advance and kept on ice.

STRAWBERRIES GISMONDA FRAISES GISMONDA (M.)

Macerate large strawberries on ice with champagne and sugar. Cut off the tops of some oranges and hollow them out without breaking the skin. Place the strawberries in these shells, with orange quarters peeled to the quick arranged on top. Chill well in the refrigerator.

STRAWBERRIES IMPÉRATRICE FRAISES À L'IMPÉRATRICE (J.)

Cover the bottom of a bowl with Rice Impératrice (p. 654), leaving out the gelatin. Cover with a mound of Chantilly Cream (p. 552) decorated with a pastry bag with a fluted tube. Lay a ring of large strawberries around it, coating them with red-currant jelly. Serve very cold.

STRAWBERRIES JEANNE GRANIER FRAISES JEANNE GRANIER (E.)

Take 1 lb. very fine strawberries, clean them carefully, place them in an earthenware bowl, sprinkle with sugar, moisten with Grand Marnier curaçao. Cover the bowl and place on ice. Just before serving, spread the bottom of a crystal bowl or timbale with a layer of orange ice. Place the strawberries with their juice on the orange ice and cover with a Curaçao Mousse mixture (p. 646) or a sirup flavored with curaçao and not iced.

STRAWBERRIES LÉRINA FRAISES LÉRINA (E.)

Take a ripe, medium-sized cantaloupe; cut off a plug about 2 in. in diameter (with the stem mark in the center) and save it. Remove the seeds and threads in the melon, then cut out the pulp with a dessertspoon; place the pulp in a bowl and mix it with 1 lb. tiny wild strawberries. Sprinkle with sugar and moisten with 3 oz. Lérina liqueur, also called Liqueur des Moines des Îles de Lérin. Cover the bowl and let macerate 1 hr. Place the melon on a service plate covered with a doily, and fill with the strawberries and melon pulp, mixing the fruit with a few tbsp. orange ice.

STRAWBERRIES MAGALI FRAISES MAGALI (P.)

Crush 3½ oz. fresh almonds in a mortar; put them into a saucepan containing ½ bottle sparkling Asti (or, if unavailable, any other sparkling wine), and bring to a boil over a low fire. Meanwhile, beat 4 egg yolks with 5 oz. powdered sugar in a mixing bowl; pour in the boiling wine and almonds. Mix well together; pour this mixture into a flat round mold that has been buttered and sugared; poach in a *bain-marie* like a molded cream (p. 640), without letting the water boil. When the cream feels a little firm to the touch, let cool. To serve, unmold onto a cold platter, and in the center place a mound of large red strawberries that have been rolled in granulated sugar; surround the strawberries with a ring of Chantilly Cream (p. 552) tinted pink with some carmine. Chill in the refrigerator. When ready to serve, pour some red-currant jelly mixed with Asti around the bottom of the mold; coarsely chopped pistachios can be sprinkled on top.

STRAWBERRIES MARGOT FRAISES MARGOT (P.)

Make a Strawberry Bavarian Cream (p. 635) with very little gelatin; pour it into a rather large timbale or crystal bowl embedded in crushed ice. When the Bavarian cream has set, place some large strawberries on top and, between each strawberry, a peak of Chantilly Cream (p. 552) squeezed from a pastry bag with fluted tube. Sprinkle a few shredded pistachios over the whole top.

STRAWBERRIES MELBA FRAISES MELBA (E.)

Fill the bottom of a timbale with vanilla ice cream. Put a layer of strawberries over the ice cream; cover with a thick, lightly sweetened purée of raspberries.

STRAWBERRIES MONTE CARLO FRAISES MONTE-CARLO (E.)

Pick and clean some fine strawberries. Put them into a bowl, sprinkle with sugar, moisten with curaçao, and keep on ice. Using more ordinary strawberries and a few raspberries, make a fine purée; sugar it lightly; keep cold on crushed ice. Just before serving, mix into the purée ½ as much Chantilly Cream (p. 552). You will already have prepared Curaçao Mousse (p. 646) in an ice-cream mold called Countess Marie and chilled it on ice; also, as many meringue shells as there are guests. Surround the meringue shells with Spun Sugar (p. 562), just before serving, to simulate pretty little birds' nests.

Serving: Unmold the mousse onto an oval platter; place the nests at both ends of the platter. Fill the bottom of each nest with 1 tbsp. strawberry purée with Chantilly Cream; lay 2 or 4 strawberries macerated in curaçao on this. Cover the mousse with the strawberry purée with Chantilly Cream and then cover again with a thin veil of Spun Sugar sprinkled with crystallized Monte Carlo violets.

STRAWBERRIES RITZ FRAISES RITZ (E.) (*For 8 persons*)

Put 1 lb. fine strawberries into a silver timbale or crystal bowl, sprinkle with sugar, and keep on ice. Press 5 oz. small strawberries and 5 oz. very fresh raspberries through a fine sieve; add to the purée almost the same amount of very stiff Chantilly Cream (p. 552), and completely cover the strawberries with this mixture.

STRAWBERRIES ROMANOV FRAISES À LA ROMANOFF (H.)

Place strawberries in a crystal bowl, sprinkle with powdered sugar, flavor with kirsch and maraschino, chill, and decorate with Chantilly Cream (p. 552).

STRAWBERRIES SINGAPORE FRAISES À LA SINGAPORE (P.)

Macerate 1 lb. wild strawberries and ½ lb. fresh pineapple, diced fine, in sugar and kirsch. Chill on ice and, meanwhile, prepare Rice Impératrice (p. 654) in a ring mold. Unmold onto a well-chilled round platter and place the strawberries and pineapple in the center. Thicken the sirup from the macerated fruit with fresh apricot purée and pour it over fruit and rice.

STRAWBERRIES TOSCA FRAISES TOSCA (E.)

Macerate some very beautiful strawberries in a silver timbale with sugar, orange juice, and kirsch. Cover with a purée of raspberries mixed with as much Chantilly Cream (p. 552). Sprinkle the top with powdered macaroons.

CHILLED FRUITS WITH VARIOUS LIQUEURS FRUITS RAFRAÎCHIS AUX LIQUEURS DIVERSES (M.)

You can prepare any fruit in season this way. If they have to be, the fruits are peeled, pitted, sliced thin or left whole. Mix them together in a silver timbale or crystal bowl. Cover them with sirup cooked at 217° F. and flavor them with some liqueur. Usually fruits are flavored with a mixture of kirsch and maraschino. Decorate the top of this *macédoine* with strawberries, raspberries, pitted cherries, currant clusters, grapes, and fresh almond halves, depending on the season. Chill 2 hr. (Figure 425, Page 636.)

CHILLED FRUITS TORTONI FRUITS RAFRAÎCHIS À LA TORTONI (M.)

Place a *macédoine* of fresh fruit, prepared as on p. 643, in a crystal bowl. Drain the fruit well. Cover with a layer of strawberry ice cream. Decorate with Chantilly Cream (p. 552) and large strawberries.

FLOATING ISLAND ÎLE FLOTTANTE (P.) (*For 8 persons*)

2 oz. grilled, crushed almonds or 3½ oz. coarsely crushed pink Praline (p. 559), 4 oz. sugar, 4 egg whites, vanilla.

Beat the egg whites very stiff; mix in the sugar, vanilla, and Praline or almonds. Pour this mixture into a buttered, sugared timbale mold—or, better, a mold lined with caramelized sugar—and poach 20 min. in a *bain-marie* in a very low oven. Let cool a little, then unmold in a compote or deep dish containing a layer of excellent, very cold English Cream (p. 550).

The Floating Island may be sprinkled with dried currants or coarsely chopped pistachios or almonds. (Figure 426, Page 636.)

JELLIED MACÉDOINE OF FRUIT MACÉDOINE DE FRUITS À LA GELÉE (P.)

This dessert, usually made in the summer, when the supply of fruit is abundant, is one of the most delightful and perhaps the simplest of all to make. As the name indicates, it is composed of all sorts of fruits, such as strawberries, raspberries, red and white currants, a few black currants, cherries, peaches, apricots, fresh peeled almonds, etc. All these fruits should be ripe enough not to need cooking. After cleaning them well, mix them together in a beautiful salad bowl or silver timbale. Naturally, the larger fruits such as peaches or apricots should be peeled and quartered.

Pour over the fruit a cold jelly made with kirsch, maraschino, or champagne, as directed on p. 555, but stiffened with ½ as much gelatin. Keep on ice until ready to use and then serve the bowl on a doily.

MARQUISE ALICE MARQUISE ALICE (P.)

Prepare Chocolate or Strawberry (depending on the season) Bavarian Cream (p. 635), using ½ as much gelatin as usual. Pour ½ this Bavarian cream into a round, flat mold moistened with a little water, then on top of this put a layer of Sponge Fingers (p. 586) soaked in kirsch, cover with the rest of the Bavarian cream, and let harden on ice.

Unmold onto a cold, round platter and cover completely with cream whipped very stiff with sugar and vanilla. Smooth the cream carefully on top and sides and decorate with a paper cone filled with thin red-currant jelly. Around the base, pour a ribbon of red-currant jelly thinned with kirsch.

CHILLED MELON MELON FRAPPÉ (E.)

Take 2 ripe, medium-sized melons; remove the pulp from 1, discarding skin, seeds, and threads, then press it through a sieve and prepare a Granité (p. 669).

Cut a round plug in the stem end of the second melon and open it. Remove all the seeds and threads and cut out pieces of the pulp with a silver spoon; macerate these pieces on ice with a little sugar and wine or some liqueur such as port, curaçao, rum, or maraschino. Keep the hollowed-out melon rind in the refrigerator about 1 hr. When ready to serve, place the empty melon in a small block of carved ice; fill with alternate layers of Granité and macerated pulp. When the melon is filled, close it with the plug.

Fig. 429 - Orange surprise (p. 647).
Fig. 430 - Peaches Chevreuse (p. 648).

Fig. 429

Fig. 430

Fig. 431

Fig. 432

Note: This melon frequently replaces sherbet or ice cream at the end of a dinner. Serve it by spoon on chilled plates.

MELON ORIENTALE MELON À L'ORIENTALE (E.)

Take a ripe melon; cut a round plug from the stem end. Remove the seeds and threads; scoop out the pulp with a silver spoon and cut it into large cubes. Powder the inside heavily with confectioners' sugar; fill it with wild strawberries and the diced pulp, in alternate layers, powdered with sugar. Finish with 3 oz. kirsch. Close the melon with the plug that was removed; solder the jointure with a band of butter; keep in the refrigerator 2 hr., and serve on a napkin. Serve along with some wafer biscuits.

MELON SURPRISE MELON EN SURPRISE (E.)

Hollow out a melon as above and fill it with a *macédoine* of fresh fruit, with the scooped-out pulp, diced, added, bound with wild-strawberry purée sweetened with sugar and flavored with kirsch. Put the plug back on the melon and keep in the refrigerator 2 hr. (Figure 427, Page 637.)

MERINGUES GERMAINE MERINGUES GERMAINE (E.)

Take 3 small, very fresh packages of cream cheese; crush them with a wooden spoon in a salad bowl, adding an equal amount of fresh heavy cream, 3 tbsp. powdered sugar, and 3 tbsp. wild-strawberry purée. If the color of the composition isn't pink enough, add a few drops of red vegetable coloring. It may be flavored with vanilla, kirsch, or grated orange peel, but this is optional. Arrange it in attractive, very dry meringue shells.

STRAWBERRY MONT BLANC MONT-BLANC AUX FRAISES (E.)

Add small wild strawberries, macerated in cold vanilla-flavored sirup and well drained, to some very stiff Chantilly Cream (p. 552). The proportions are ¼ lb. strawberries per qt. cream. Arrange in a dome shape; encircle the base with large strawberries rolled in sugar; decorate the dome with large, very red, halved strawberries.

CHESTNUT MONT BLANC MONT-BLANC AUX MARRONS (E.)

Cook some chestnuts in sugared, vanilla-flavored milk; press them through a sieve over a plain ring mold in such a way that the chestnut purée drops like pieces of vermicelli from the sieve, filling the mold naturally. Finish filling the mold with the purée dropped on the sides. Unmold on a serving platter. Fill up the center of the ring with Chantilly Cream (p. 552), piling the peak up irregularly like a mountaintop. (Figure 428, Page 637.)

Note: In filling the center of the ring with chestnut purée, a pastry bag with a tube pierced with small holes may also be used. This method is neater and quicker.

MUSCOVITE MOSCOVITE (E.)

Molding and Serving: Muscovites are usually made in molds with a hollow center. The mold should be lightly greased with sweet almond oil. When the molds are filled, the mixture is covered with a circle of white paper and they are embedded in crushed ice.

When ready to serve, dip the mold quickly into warm water and wipe it dry; turn it over onto a service plate (covered with a folded napkin, if you wish).

Fig. 431 - Peaches Melba (p. 649).
Fig. 432 - Peaches sultane (p. 649).

Instead of oiling the molds, they may be covered with a thin layer of sugar cooked to a light caramel. This gives the dessert an attractive appearance and an excellent flavor.

Another highly recommended procedure is to mold the Muscovite in a silver timbale or deep silver dish, surrounded with ice. In this case, since the dessert does not have to be unmolded, the mixture does not have to be so stiff (so less gelatin may be used) and the flavor is more delicate.

When molded this last way, the Muscovite is sometimes served with a *macédoine* of fresh fruit. However, these side dishes of fruit go better with cold puddings, which are, of course, similar to Muscovites. Finally, whether molded or not, they may be decorated, just before serving, with a pastry bag or paper cone filled with pink or white Chantilly Cream (p. 552).

CREAM MUSCOVITE MOSCOVITE À LA CRÈME (E.) (*For 18 persons*)

Beat 1 lb. powdered sugar with 16 egg yolks in a pan; pour in 1 qt. vanilla-flavored boiled milk. Add 1 oz. gelatin soaked in cold water. Thicken the mixture over a low fire, without boiling, until it clings to a spoon. Strain through a cone-shaped sieve into a glazed bowl; let cool, stirring from time to time, and, when the mixture begins to set, blend in 1 qt. whipped cream, 3½ oz. powdered sugar, and 1 oz. vanilla-flavored sugar.

Note: A Muscovite is nothing more than Bavarian cream rechristened. (See p. 635.)

FRUIT MUSCOVITE MOSCOVITE AUX FRUITS (E.) (*For 10 persons*)

15 oz. purée of fruits thinned with 15 oz. sirup cooked at 217° F. Add the juice of 3 lemons, 1 oz. dissolved, strained gelatin, 1 pt. whipped cream.

Raw fruits such as strawberries, raspberries, currants, etc., or pulpy fruits such as pears, peaches, apricots, etc., poached in sirup, may be added to the Muscovite mixture.

CURAÇAO MOUSSE MOUSSE AU CURAÇAO (E.) (*For 8 persons*)

Beat 8 egg yolks with 1 cup sirup cooked at 215° F. and still slightly warm, then strain the mixture through a fine sieve into a saucepan. Beat over a low fire or in a double boiler, as in making a Génoise Cake (p. 549). When the mixture has thickened enough to make a ribbon, remove from the fire; continue beating over ice until completely cold. Add 1½ oz. curaçao and, when ready to serve, 1½ oz. whipped cream.

STRAWBERRY MOUSSE MOUSSE AUX FRAISES (P.) (*For 8 persons*)

Press 1 lb. strawberries through a wire sieve; mix this purée with a sirup made of 7 oz. sugar and 2 tbsp. water (the cold sirup should register 30° on the saccharometer). Pour this mixture into the top of a double boiler and add 6 egg yolks; beat, as for a Génoise Cake (p. 549), over a low fire. When it becomes frothy, pour it into a bowl and let it cool. Then mix in 1 pt. whipped cream, a little kirsch, and juice of ½ lemon; heighten the color with a little red vegetable coloring. Pour into a square mold, seal tightly, and embed in salted, crushed ice; leave in the ice 3 or 4 hr. To serve, unmold onto a cold plate, cover the mousse with thick vanilla English Cream (p. 550), and sprinkle the top with a few wild strawberries.

EGGS IN THE SNOW OEUFS À LA NEIGE (P.) (*For 6 persons*)

Beat 3 egg whites until very stiff and add 3½ oz. vanilla-flavored powdered sugar. Bring 1 pt. milk to a boil in a frying pan with a spray of vanilla, and drop the egg white in a spoonful at a time; let poach without boiling, and, with a fork, turn the eggs over after 2 min. When they have become a little firm to the touch, drain them on a cloth, and use the milk they cooked in to make an English Cream (p. 550). Let the cream cool and pour it into a shallow dish; set the eggs on top. Serve very cold.

EGGS À LA REINE OEUFS À LA REINE (P.)

Prepare very small eggs of beaten whites, as directed above; make the English Cream (p. 550) and, after removing it from the fire, add ⅓ oz. gelatin. When the cream is cold, pour a layer of it into the bottom of a mold with hollow center embedded in ice. Next, arrange a row of eggs in the mold, letting them set in the cream before pouring more cream into the mold; otherwise, the eggs, being very light, will float to the top. When everything has set, unmold onto a doily and serve with a separate dish of very cold red-currant or raspberry sauce (see Fruit Sauces, p. 560).

NUN'S EGGS OEUFS À LA RELIGIEUSE (P.)

Prepare the eggs as in the recipe for Eggs in the Snow (above), but mix in 2 oz. ground Praline (p. 559) at the same time as the sugar. Cook the same way, and make the English Cream (p. 550), but flavor it with chocolate.

When serving, first place the eggs in a shallow bowl, coat them generously with the cold cream, and sprinkle with grilled, shredded almonds. The eggs should be rather small.

ORANGE SURPRISE ORANGES EN SURPRISE (P.)

Slice off the top ¼ of the oranges and hollow them out. Fill the rinds with orange ice; cover the ice with Italian Meringue (p. 557); place them in a baking pan of crushed ice, and put into a rather hot oven to brown the meringue quickly.

After removing from the oven, replace the slice of orange cut off the top and stick a leaf and stem made of pulled sugar into the top. Serve on a doily. (Figure 429, Page 644.)

ORANGES TSARINE ORANGES À LA TSARINE (P.)

Cut the top ¼ off 6 or 8 fine oranges; hollow them out with a silver spoon without breaking the rinds. Fill the rinds a little more than ½ full with semi-congealed orange jelly; embed them in shaved ice. When the jelly has set, mix the rest of the jelly (about 4 oz.) with 1 cup whipped cream, add a little carmine coloring, and, using a pastry bag with a fluted tube, finish filling the oranges, heaping the cream on top. Serve on a doily when it has completely set.

PEACHES ADRIENNE PÊCHES ADRIENNE (E.)

Take 1 tender, ripe peach for each guest. Plunge them quickly into boiling water, remove them immediately with a skimming ladle, and plunge them into water containing chopped ice; remove the skins; arrange them on a platter, sprinkle with sugar, and keep cold. Have ready some strawberry ice cream, some vanilla-flavored fresh cream, and as many meringue shells as there are peaches.

Make a layer of the ice cream in the bottom of a shallow crystal bowl and embed the meringue shells in it. Place a peach in each shell and cover it with a light coating of unchilled Curaçao Mousse (p. 646). Cover with a thin veil of Spun Sugar (p. 562), sprinkled with crystallized rose petals. Embed the bowl in a block of ice, or simply surround it with shaved ice.

PEACHES AIGLON PÊCHES AIGLON (E.)

Prepare the peaches as in the preceding recipe and, after removing the skins, place them in a mixing bowl, cover with boiling sirup cooked at 215° F., and let cool in the sirup.

Just before serving, drain the peaches and place them on a bed of vanilla ice cream in a silver timbale. Sprinkle pralined Parma violets on the peaches, embed the timbale in the base of a block of ice carved to imitate a rock surmounted by an eagle, and cover the timbale with Spun Sugar (p. 562).

PEACHES ALEXANDRA PÊCHES ALEXANDRA (E.)

Poach the peaches in vanilla sirup and let cool in the sirup. Arrange them in a timbale on a bed of vanilla ice cream covered with strawberry purée. Sprinkle the peaches with pink and white rose petals and cover with a veil of Spun Sugar (p. 562).

PEACHES AURORA PÊCHES À L'AURORE (E.)

Peel the peaches, poach them in kirsch-flavored sirup, and let them cool in the sirup. Drain them, place them in a silver timbale on a bed of frozen Strawberry Mousse (p. 646), and cover with a cold Sabayon (p. 553) flavored with curaçao.

PEACHES CARDINAL PÊCHES À LA CARDINAL (E.)

Poach the peaches in vanilla sirup. When they are completely cold, arrange them in a timbale on a bed of vanilla ice cream. Cover them with a purée of very red sugared raspberries flavored with kirsch; sprinkle the surface with fresh, very white, shredded almonds.

PEACHES CHEVREUSE PÊCHES À LA CHEVREUSE (J.)

Prepare a base of Semolina Pudding (p. 640). Place a ring of fine peaches poached in vanilla sirup, with candied fruits in the spaces between, on top this base. Chill.

When ready to serve, fill the center with Chantilly Cream (p. 552), using a pastry bag with a fluted tube. Sprinkle with chopped pistachios. Coat the peaches with thin Apricot Sauce (p. 560) tinted pink and flavored with curaçao. (Figure 430, Page 644.)

PEACHES EUGÉNIE PÊCHES EUGÉNIE (P.)

Carefully remove the stones from some well-ripened peaches. Peel them and place them in a timbale with tiny wild strawberries in between. Moisten with a few tbsp. kirsch and maraschino, powder with fine sugar, and keep on ice. When ready to serve, cover the peaches with very cold Sabayon (p. 553) made with champagne.

PEACHES GRAND-DUC PÊCHES GRAND-DUC (P.)

Bake a Génoise Cake mixture (p. 549) in some rather deep tartlet molds. Take some fine, not-too-ripe peaches, slice them in half, and poach them in

Fig. 433 - Pears impériale (P. 650).
Fig. 434 - Rice impératrice (p. 654).

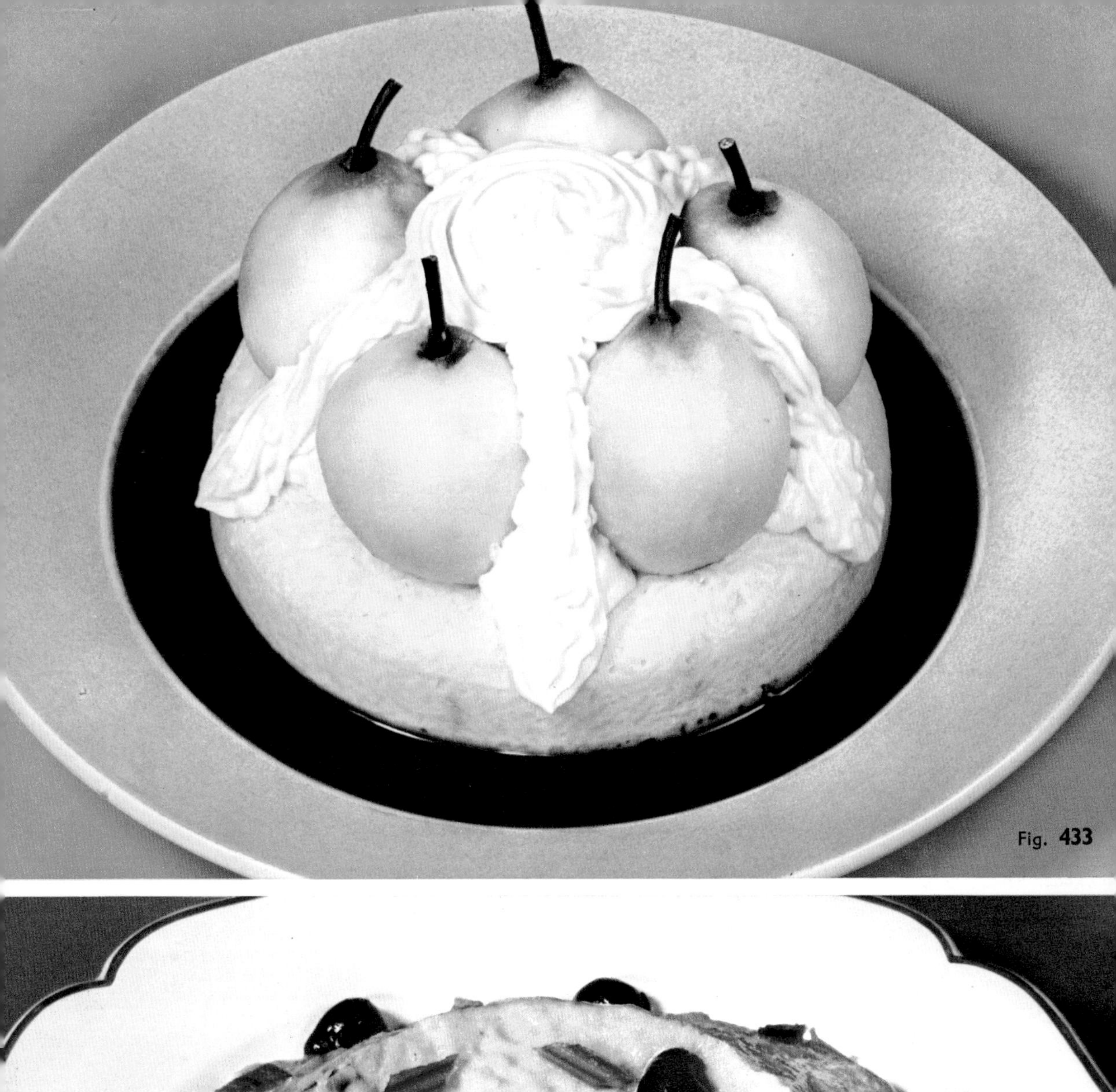
Fig. 433

Fig. 434

Fig. 435

Fig. 436

vanilla sirup. Chill them over ice, then place a half peach, hollow side up, in each cold tartlet shell; fill the peach hollows with 1 tsp. red-currant jelly; using a pastry bag, decorate the edges of each peach with a ribbon of Chantilly Cream (p. 552), and fill the center of the dish with the same cream.

PEACHES MELBA PÊCHES MELBA (E.)

Poach the peaches in vanilla sirup. Arrange them in a timbale on a layer of vanilla ice cream and cover with raspberry purée. (Figure 431, Page 645.)

Note: When green almonds are in season, shred them finely and sprinkle them on top, if you wish, but never use dry almonds.

PEACHES NINON PÊCHES À LA NINON (P.)

Make Rice Impératrice (p. 654) and mold it in a small bombe mold. Also make a stiff English Cream (p. 550) with gelatin, mixed with a good amount of diced, candied fruits macerated in kirsch. Pour this cream into a ring mold large enough to hold the rice in the center. When both mixtures have set, unmold the ring of English Cream onto a platter and, in the center, unmold the rice. Place some fine poached, well-chilled peach halves around the ring, leaning them against the rice, and cover with a sirup made from the sirup the peaches were cooked in, thickened with apricot jam and flavored with kirsch.

PEACHES RÉJANE PÊCHES À LA RÉJANE (P.)

Prepare in advance, in tartlet molds, some small crusts of Sweet Paste (p. 546). When cold, cover the bottom with 1 tbsp. kirsch jelly (see p. 555); put into the refrigerator to set. In each tartlet place an upturned peach half poached in sirup and chilled, then lay a ring of tiny wild strawberries between the peach and the rim of the tartlet crust. Fill each peach hollow with Chantilly Cream (p. 552) squeezed from a pastry bag. Serve on a doily.

PEACHES ROSE-CHÉRI PÊCHES ROSE-CHÉRI (E.)

Carefully remove the stones from some fully ripened peaches. Peel them and place in a bowl, cover with boiling sirup, and let cool in the sirup.

Prepare separately, for 6 peaches, 1 lb. Montmorency cherries; pit them and put them into a copper frying pan with 5 oz. powdered sugar; cook 6–8 min., then add 5 oz. red-currant jelly. When the jelly has melted, pour the cherries into a bowl and let cool. When ready to serve, place the peaches in a crystal bowl on a bed of vanilla ice cream, with the cherries in their sirup in the spaces in between. Mix some of the cherry sirup with twice as much Chantilly Cream (p. 552) and cover the peaches with this.

PEACHES SULTANE PÊCHES À LA SULTANE (E.)

Place poached peaches in a timbale on a bed of pistachio ice cream. Cover with a thick sirup flavored with attar of roses. Sprinkle with chopped pistachios.

Note: Usually, the peaches are placed over a block of ice and covered with a veil of Spun Sugar (p. 562). (Figure 432, Page 645.)

PEARS ALMINA POIRES ALMINA (P.)

Poach very ripe pear halves in vanilla sirup; let cool. Meanwhile prepare a cream with 3 egg yolks, 3½ oz. sugar, and ½ tsp. cornstarch or arrowroot; add 6 oz. milk and some grated orange peel and thicken over a low fire without boiling. After the cream has cooled, add 2 tbsp. fresh extra-heavy cream and the peel of 1 orange cut in thin julienne strips. Arrange the pears side by side in a

Fig. 435 - Chocolate head (p. 654).
Fig. 436 - Turin loaf (p. 655).

deep dish, coat them with the cream, and place 1 tbsp. Chantilly Cream (p. 552) between each.

PEARS BORDELAISE POIRES À LA BORDELAISE (M.)

Poach very ripe pears in a sirup made with red Bordeaux and flavored with a little cinnamon. Chill the pears on ice; drain them and wipe them off. Arrange them in a pyramid in the center of a ring of Molded Caramel Cream (p. 640). When ready to serve, cover the pears with the sirup they were cooked in, thickened with a little apple jelly, reduced, strained through cheesecloth, and chilled on ice. Garnish the outside of the ring with peeled grapes.

PEARS BRISTOL POIRES À LA BRISTOL (P.)

Bake some Cream Puff shells (p. 587) and slice off the tops. Fill the shells with maraschino-flavored Pastry Cream (p. 552), place the pears on top, and cover with red-currant jelly. Decorate all around with preserved fruits and Chantilly Cream (p. 552).

PEARS CARMEN POIRES À LA CARMEN (P.)

Poach pear halves or quarters, depending on size, then let cool. Prepare Strawberry Bavarian Cream (p. 635), using very little gelatin; pour it into a beautiful crystal bowl, and let it set on ice. Place the pears on top and coat them with an excellent vanilla English Cream (p. 550). Sprinkle the top with chopped pistachios.

PEARS CECILIA POIRES À LA CÉCILIA (D. and D.)

Prepare Vanilla Molded Cream (p. 640) in a savarin or plain ring mold; unmold onto a silver platter. Then, in the center, arrange a heaping mound of pear quarters cooked in vanilla sirup; lay some cooked pears tinted pink on top of the ring; cover with the pear cooking sirup reduced, tinted pink, and thickened with a little red-currant jelly.

PEARS FLORETTA POIRES À LA FLORETTA (P.) (*For 8 persons*)

Cook 2 oz. semolina in 1 cup milk, add 2½ oz. vanilla-flavored sugar and ¼ oz. gelatin melted in a double boiler, and let cool. When the mixture begins to congeal, mix in 1 cup whipped cream. Then pour into a ring mold moistened with water and let jell on ice.

Unmold onto a round platter. Fill the center of the ring with a compote of quartered pears cooked in a sirup made with red Bordeaux and sugar and flavored with a little cinnamon or vanilla. The pears must be well chilled when ready to serve; cover them with their reduced cooking sirup thickened with a little red-currant jelly; neatly pour a ribbon of sirup around the ring and decorate it with pistachio halves.

PEARS HÉLÈNE POIRES HÉLÈNE (E.)

Poach the pears in vanilla sirup and let cool. When ready to serve, place them in a timbale or crystal bowl on a bed of vanilla ice cream sprinkled with pralined violets. Serve hot Chocolate Sauce (p. 652) separately.

PEARS IMPÉRIALE POIRES À L'IMPÉRIALE (J.)

Prepare Rice Impératrice (p. 654) in a savarin mold. Cook the usual way, let cool, and unmold onto a service plate. Fill the center with very stiff Chantilly

Cream (p. 552) shaped into a dome. Around the dome, stand some fine pears poached in thin sirup. Decorate with Chantilly Cream, using a pastry bag with a fluted tube. Surround with a ribbon of red-currant jelly. (Figure 433, Page 648.)

PEARS JOINVILLE POIRES À LA JOINVILLE (P.)

Make Molded Caramel Cream (p. 640) in a plain ring mold; when it is cold, unmold onto a round platter and, in the center, place a compote of pears cooked in sirup flavored with vanilla and lemon juice. Cover the pears with a mound of very stiff Chantilly Cream (p. 552), then decorate the cream with more Chantilly Cream, using a pastry bag with a very small fluted tube (but tint this cream pale pink with a few drops of carmine). Surround the ring with kirsch-flavored Apricot Sauce (p. 560) thinned with a little of the pear sirup.

PEARS MARIE-ANNE POIRES À LA MARIE-ANNE (J.)

Prepare Rice Impératrice (p. 654); unmold onto a service plate. Arrange very ripe pears, poached in vanilla sirup, around it. Decorate with preserved fruits and Chantilly Cream (p. 552) squeezed from a pastry bag with a fluted tube. Cover the fruit with chilled, kirsch-flavored Apricot Sauce (p. 560).

PEARS RICHELIEU POIRES RICHELIEU (E.)

Make a Semolina Pudding mixture (p. 640) in a plain ring mold decorated with preserved fruits. Poach, let cool, and unmold onto a round platter.

In the center of the ring, arrange a pyramid of quartered pears cooked in vanilla sirup; coat the pears with Frangipane Cream (p. 552) mixed with 1/4 as much dry, crumbled macaroons and twice as much very stiff Chantilly Cream (p. 552). Decorate the top with a paper cone filled with Chantilly Cream and serve kirsch-flavored Apricot Sauce (p. 560) separately.

APPLES CHARCOT POMMES À LA CHARCOT (P.)

Peel and hollow out some firm apples to form shells that can be filled after cooking. Poach these apples lightly in vanilla- and lemon-flavored sirup, drain them, and chill on ice. Meanwhile, mold Vanilla Bavarian Cream (p. 634) in a round, flat mold. When the cream has set, unmold onto a cold platter, place the apples on top, and fill them with quince jelly mixed with orange peel cut in thin julienne strips and blanched 5 min. Coat the apples with raspberry jelly.

Note: In most cases, apples can be prepared the same way as pears. It is therefore unnecessary to repeat all the recipes.

CREAM POTS POTS DE CRÈME (D. and D.)

Fill small porcelain ramekins or pots with a molded cream mixture (see p. 640), place them in a *bain-marie,* and poach in the oven. Serve cold. For 12 3-oz. pots: 27 oz. milk, 9 oz. sugar, 2 whole eggs and 8 yolks, vanilla, caramel, or rum. Cook 1/2 hr.

CHOCOLATE PROFITEROLES PROFITEROLES AU CHOCOLAT (P.)

This dessert may be served hot or cold. Make very small Cream-Puff shells as for a Saint-Honoré (p. 581). Fill them with Chantilly Cream (p. 552) or Saint-Honoré Cream (p. 552). Then arrange them in a pyramid on a round platter and cover them with Hot Chocolate Sauce.

Hot Chocolate Sauce: Melt 5 oz. fine chocolate in 1 cup water. Cook until it becomes a smooth cream, then, since it is rather liquid, thicken it with a little arrowroot or cornstarch mixed with water; stir in a piece of butter the size of a walnut; and pour over the profiteroles to coat them completely. Two other recipes for Chocolate Sauce are given on p. 560.

STRAWBERRY AND OTHER PROFITEROLES PROFITEROLES AUX FRAISES ET AUTRES (D. and D.)

Make some very small Cream-Puff shells (p. 587) ; when cold, fill them with Chantilly Cream (p. 552) mixed with strawberry purée. Prepare some Sabayon (p. 553) separately, adding a little strawberry sirup to it, and pour into a silver timbale. Place the filled Cream Puffs on top. (The filling and Sabayon can be flavored vanilla, chocolate, etc., for variation.)

AMERICAN PUDDING PUDDING À L'AMÉRICAINE (M.) (*For 10 persons*)

Bring 1 qt. milk and 1 pt. cream to a boil with 7 oz. sugar and 1 oz. vanilla-flavored sugar. Add ¼ lb. cornstarch mixed with 1 cup cold water. Mix well. Cook over the fire a few moments, stirring with a wire whisk. Pour this mixture into buttered baba molds. Chill on ice. Dip in hot water; unmold onto a service plate. Pour a ribbon of uncooked strawberry purée or raspberry jam around the pudding, or surround with a ring of brandied peaches.

Note: American Pudding can also be made with coffee (substitute 6 oz. very strong coffee for 6 oz. milk) and with chocolate (add 6 oz. dissolved chocolate to the milk) .

BOHEMIAN PUDDING PUDDING BOHÉMIENNE (E.)

Prepare some very small crêpes (p. 614) ; spread them with a mixture of diced, preserved fruits and raisins soaked in warm water and bound with thick pear jelly and applesauce. Fold the crêpes into rectangles or roll into balls; lay them side by side in a buttered ring mold; finish filling the mold with a molded cream mixture (p. 640) enriched with whole eggs. Poach in a *bain-marie.* Let cool in the mold; unmold when ready to serve; cover the pudding with Sabayon (p. 553) flavored as you wish.

CHERRY PUDDING ALSACIENNE PUDDING AUX CERISES À L'ALSACIENNE (P.)

Soak a Brioche (p. 565) in milk and drain. Cream some butter in a bowl; add powdered sugar and vanilla; mix in the Brioche; add 4 whole beaten eggs and 1 lb. pitted cherries. Put the mixture into a buttered mold sprinkled with chopped almonds. Poach ½ hr., unmold, and serve cold with kirsch-flavored red-currant sauce (see Fruit Sauces, p. 560) .

CLERMONT PUDDING PUDDING À LA CLERMONT (M.)

Prepare a Vanilla Bavarian Cream mixture (p. 634) with ½ its weight in chestnut purée added, and garnished with bits of candied chestnuts. Pour into an oiled Bavarian-cream mold. Let set on ice.

DIPLOMAT PUDDING PUDDING À LA DIPLOMATE (P.)

Make a Bavarian-cream mixture (p. 634) strongly flavored with vanilla, pour it into the bottom of a mold with hollow center, and place on ice to set.

Cover with a layer of broken Sponge Fingers (p. 586) soaked in kirsch, and sprinkle with diced, preserved fruits macerated in kirsch; cover with another layer of vanilla cream, then a layer of Sponge Fingers and fruits, and so on, finishing with the cream. Let set on ice, then unmold onto a napkin or doily. Serve with very cold kirsch-flavored Apricot Sauce (p. 560) or red-currant jelly flavored with Cointreau.

MALAKOFF PUDDING PUDDING MALAKOFF (E.)

Prepare: (1) An English Cream (p. 550) made with gelatin and 15 oz. fresh extra-heavy cream per qt. English Cream. (2) Pear jam and applesauce as for Apple Charlotte (p. 613), dried currants and sultanas soaked in warm sirup, shredded fresh almonds, diced candied orange peel, slices of stale Sponge Cake (p. 548) or Sponge Fingers (p. 586) soaked in liqueur.

Oil a charlotte mold; pour in a layer of cream about ⅜ in. thick; on the cream make a layer of the sliced Sponge Cake spread with the jam and applesauce. Sprinkle this with the raisins, almonds, and orange peel. Cover with another layer of cream, then a layer of Sponge Cake, and so on. Let set in the refrigerator. When ready to serve, unmold onto a service plate and cover with kirsch-flavored Sabayon (p. 553).

NESSELRODE PUDDING PUDDING NESSELRODE (P.)

Blend ½ lb. chestnut purée (cooked in vanilla-flavored milk) in a very sweet Vanilla Bavarian Cream (p. 634). (While mixing in the whipped cream for the Bavarian, sprinkle in 5 oz. crumbled candied chestnuts.) Let set on ice, then unmold onto a very cold platter and surround with a ring of very stiff and strongly vanilla-flavored Chantilly Cream (p. 552).

The Chantilly Cream may be replaced by very cold, Madeira-flavored Apricot Sauce (p. 560).

QUEEN OF THE FAIRIES CREAM or PUDDING PUDDING OR CRÈME REINE DES FÉES (E.)

Prepare Italian Meringue (p. 557) with 4 egg whites and sugar, adding, while cooking, an equal amount of quince jelly and, just before removing from the stove, 2 oz. diced, preserved fruits macerated in kirsch and carefully drained. Drop balls of this meringue onto a sheet of paper. In a utensil large enough to hold the sheet of paper, bring 4 qt. water to a boil with 2 lb. sugar and 4½ oz. kirsch. Slide the paper into the boiling sirup; pull it out as soon as the meringues are detached from it; let them poach, then drain on a cloth and let cool.

Prepare 2 Bavarian cream (p. 634) or Muscovite (p. 645) mixtures separately: 1 white with vanilla, the other with curaçao. Beat into these mixtures double the usual amount of whipped cream and reduce the gelatin by ½. Lay these mixtures in alternate layers of equal thickness in a chilled and lightly oiled madeleine mold, distributing the meringues between each layer. Cover the mold with a paper and its own cover, seal tightly, and chill 2 hr. When ready to serve, unmold onto a doily.

CREAMED RICE PUDDING PUDDING DE RIZ À LA CRÈME (E.)

This pudding can be served alone or accompany cold fruit compotes. It is prepared the same as hot Creamed Rice Pudding (p. 627), but instead of glazing it in the oven, mix in a little whipped cream, 4 dissolved leaves of gelatin per lb. rice, and 4 oz. coarsely crushed Soft Macaroons (p. 593) soaked in kirsch, and chill it on ice. Place on a service plate, chill again, powder with confectioners' sugar, and burn a decoration in it with a red-hot iron.

RICE PUDDING JOSEPHINE PUDDING DE RIZ JOSÉPHINE (E.) (*For 6 persons*)

Wash 10 oz. fine Josephine rice, put it into a pan, cover with plenty of cold water, and place on a hot fire. When it first begins to boil, drain the rice, put it back into the pan, and pour in 20 oz. boiling milk, dash of salt, 2 tsp. butter, and a little vanilla. Cover the pan, bring to a full boil, remove from the stove, and place in an open low oven. After cooking 12 min., add 5 oz. sugar and cook another 10–12 min. By this time, the milk should be absorbed and the rice sufficiently cooked. Remove the pan from the heat and bind the rice with 3 egg yolks beaten with 9 oz. cream. Flavor the rice with kirsch and maraschino and pour immediately into a fine crystal bowl. Let cool.

Have 1 lb. carefully picked strawberries ready. Macerate 11 oz. of the prettiest ones in sugar, kirsch, and maraschino and press 5 oz. of them through a sieve, adding this purée to the macerating strawberries.

When ready to serve, make an attractive ring of strawberries inside the bowl and in the center heap a mound of Chantilly Cream (p. 552). Serve the rest of the strawberries in a silver timbale.

RICE IMPÉRATRICE RIZ À L'IMPÉRATRICE (P.) (*For 8 persons*)

3½ oz. Carolina rice, 3½ oz. sugar, ¼ lb. preserved fruits, ⅕ oz. gelatin, 4 egg yolks, 1 pt. milk, 1 cup whipped cream, vanilla.

First blanch the rice 2 min. in water, then drain and finish cooking with 9 oz. milk and ½ vanilla bean. Meanwhile, prepare an English Cream (p. 550), adding to it, while cooking without boiling, the 4 egg yolks beaten with sugar, vanilla, and the remaining 7 oz. milk. When the cream is thick, remove from the fire and add the dissolved gelatin, then strain through a cone-shaped sieve. Add the rice when well cooked and let cool until the mixture begins to set. Now mix in the whipped cream and the preserved fruits (diced fine and macerated in kirsch). Pour this mixture into a fancy mold with hollow center and let set on ice. If you have no ice, better add ½ leaf of gelatin. Unmold onto a very cold platter and surround with very smooth red-currant jelly thinned with kirsch. If you wish, decorate with preserved fruits. (Figure 434, Page 648.)

CHESTNUT SULTANA WITH CHANTILLY CREAM SULTANE DE MARRONS À LA CHANTILLY (P.)

Prepare 1 cup English Cream (p. 550) with plenty of vanilla and stiffened with gelatin and, when it is cold, add chestnut purée (as in recipe for Nesselrode Pudding, p. 653). When well mixed, pour into a ring mold and embed in crushed ice. When set, unmold and fill the center with a mound of sugared, vanilla-flavored whipped cream. Cover the top with a veil of Spun Sugar (p. 562) or a sugar decoration. Stick candied chestnuts in the cream ring.

CHOCOLATE HEAD TÊTE DE NÈGRE (P.) (*For 8 persons*)

Prepare a rice-pudding mixture with 5 oz. rice, 1 pt. milk, 4 oz. vanilla-flavored sugar, 3 egg yolks, and 3 stiffly beaten whites. Cook in a semispherical mold; after unmolding and cooling, cover completely with rather thick Chocolate English Cream (p. 550). Stick a finger into the cream to make the eyes and the mouth. Surround with a collar of Chantilly Cream (p. 552). (Figure 435, Page 649.)

AGEN RING TURBAN D'AGEN (P.) (*For 8 persons*)

Cook ¼ lb. rice in vanilla-flavored milk (1 pt.); sweeten, when cooked, with 5 oz. sugar; add ⅓ oz. dissolved gelatin, and, when the mixture begins to cool, mix in 1 cup whipped cream; pour this mixture into a ring mold and let set on ice. Unmold onto a round platter and fill the center with a compote of prunes cooked in red wine, bound with a few tbsp. apricot jam.

If rice is not available, 3½ oz. semolina may be used.

TURIN LOAF TURINOIS (P.) (*For 8 persons*)

Proportions: 1 lb. chestnuts, 3½ oz. butter, 3½ oz. grated chocolate, 3½ oz. vanilla-flavored sugar.

Preparation: Split the chestnuts and bring them to a boil, then peel them and finish cooking by dropping them a few at a time into boiling water. When cooked, drain and press through a fine sieve, then, while still hot, mix this purée with the sugar, butter, and grated chocolate. When the mixture is very smooth, pour it into a buttered mold with a paper lining on the bottom. Pack the paste down and keep in the refrigerator until the following day; without cooking, unmold and cut in slices. (Figure 436, Page 649.)

VACHERIN VACHERIN (D. and D.)

Mark buttered, floured baking sheets with round flan circles of the size desired for the layers. Beat 8 egg whites very stiff, then blend in 1 lb. powdered sugar; use a pastry bag with a large plain tube to lay this meringue in the marked circles on the baking sheets; bake in a very slow oven. Stack 2 or more of these meringue layers on a base of Sweet Paste (p. 546), decorate top and sides with meringue, and dry in the oven. Garnish with Chantilly Cream (p. 552) in various flavors. (Figure 437, Page 656.)

FROZEN DESSERTS

These are among the most delightful desserts and include plain ice creams, such as vanilla ice cream; fruit ices, such as strawberry ice, which need no milk or eggs; frozen mousses, which are light and fluffy, as the name indicates; parfaits, very light, too; bombes, made with a frozen outside and an inside of variously colored and flavored bombe pastes.

Besides these, we have ice-cream fancies, frozen cups, frozen soufflés, marquises, granités, spooms, punches, and sherbets. While they contain different mixtures, they all stem, nevertheless, from the other recipes.

NOTES ON MAKING FROZEN DESSERTS NOTES SUR LES GLACES (Ga.)

Ice-cream molds are always filled to the brim and carefully covered with white paper; they must be sealed airtight. Remember that while salted ice is indispensable to freezing, it is always a danger. If you have an ice-cream freezer with a small screw opening in the bottom and are making ice cream with only one flavor, you need not empty it into another mold and set it in salted ice 1–2 hr. before serving. Simply leave it in the freezer, and then, when ready to serve, all you have to do is run a knife around it, let in a little air through the opening in the bottom, and unmold onto a serving plate.

Take, for example, a 1-qt. mold: plain ice cream freezes in ¾ hr.; ice cream lined with another flavor of ice cream takes 1–1¼ hr.; bombes, parfaits, and ice-cream cakes take 1¼–1½ hr.; a frozen soufflé, 2½–3 hr.

Bear in mind when making any frozen dessert that the more sugar the mixture contains, the less solid it will be. That is why you must not exceed the proportions of sugar given in this chapter—weigh and measure everything. If a mixture will not freeze, no doubt it contains too much sugar. Also take care with liqueurs: add them in moderation and only after the mixture has frozen. Use liqueurs sparingly in making mousses and parfaits, too. You will have less trouble with a frozen dessert containing too little liqueur than one highly flavored, which falls apart before it is served. Don't wait till the last moment to unmold a frozen dessert—a well-made frozen dessert will keep 10–15 min. and be only smoother and less icy for having been unmolded ahead of time. Even an Omelet Surprise (p. 667) baked in the oven, if well made and properly frozen, may be kept 5–10 min. before being brought into the dining room.

ICE and **ICE-CREAM FANCIES** FANTAISIES EN GLACE (Ga.)

Special tin molds for molding ices and ice creams in a variety of shapes may be bought in stores. These molds come both large and small, made in the shape of swans, beehives, melons, pineapples, bunches of asparagus, etc. The small ones, usually in the shape of fruit, are for individual servings. Use these molds to make lovely baskets of fruit: peaches, pears, apricots, and flowers. Imitate real fruit by filling each mold with 2 different ice creams—for example, vanilla and strawberry for peaches, vanilla and pistachio for pears.

PLAIN ICE CREAMS

VANILLA ICE CREAM GLACE VANILLE (Ga.) (*For 10 persons*)

1 qt. milk, 10 oz. powdered sugar, 8 or 10 egg yolks, 1 vanilla bean. Bring the milk to a boil with the split vanilla bean. Beat the egg yolks in a bowl with a wire whisk, adding the sugar bit by bit; beat 10 min. When the milk comes to a boil, remove from the fire and pour the beaten egg yolks in little by little; put the mixture back over a medium flame, stirring gently with a spatula. You can tell if it is cooked: (1) when the foam disappears; (2) when the mixture clings to the spatula. As soon as cooked, remove from the fire, strain through a fine sieve, and set aside in a bowl. Preferably, prepare this mixture in the morning to use that evening. When ready to freeze, pour 1 cup sweet cream into the mixture, then pour into the freezer, cover, pack with salted ice, and turn the crank until the ice cream becomes so stiff that you can no longer turn it. The ice cream is now ready to be used, and only now add a liqueur, if you wish, but a moderate amount. (It takes 15–20 min. to freeze 1 qt. ice cream.)

Fig. 437 - Vacherin (p. 655).
Fig. 438 - Ice cream bombe (p. 658).

Fig. 438

Fig. 439

Fig. 440

HAZELNUT ICE CREAM GLACE AVELINE (Ga.)

Make some Hazelnut Praline as directed in the recipe for Praline (p. 559), grind it coarse while hot, and drop it into the hot ice-cream mixture. Let macerate 7–8 hr., strain through a sieve, pressing to extract all the oil from the hazelnuts, and freeze as usual. Allow 7 oz. Praline per qt. ice-cream mixture, and use 1½ oz. less sugar.

COFFEE ICE CREAM GLACE CAFÉ (Ga.)

Same procedure as for Vanilla Ice Cream, substituting ½ cup very strong coffee for the vanilla and using ½ cup less milk.

CARAMEL ICE CREAM GLACE CARAMEL (Ga.)

Make 1 qt. mixture with ½ lb. sugar. Cook 1⅔ oz. sugar to a golden caramel. Mix when cold and freeze as usual.

CHOCOLATE ICE CREAM GLACE CHOCOLAT (Ga.)

Substitute 4 oz. chocolate for the vanilla in the Vanilla Ice Cream recipe and leave out 2 oz. sugar (use sweet chocolate).

ICE CREAM WITH LIQUEURS GLACE AUX LIQUEURS (Ga.)

The basic mixture may be flavored with any liqueur: rum, kirsch, champagne brandy, anisette, curaçao, etc. Use these liqueurs moderately, for their alcoholic content will soften the ice cream. Add them only after freezing.

CHESTNUT ICE CREAM GLACE AUX MARRONS (Ga.)

Make 1 qt. Vanilla Ice Cream mixture, adding, before freezing, 7 oz. chestnut purée flavored with vanilla and a little sugar. Instead of the purée, you can use the same amount of candied chestnuts mashed and pressed through a sieve. Finish with a small glass of kirsch or cognac.

FRUIT ICES

GLACES AUX FRUITS (E.)

These are prepared the following 2 ways.

(1) Press the fruit through a fine sieve—after mashing, if needed. Dilute the purée with an equal amount of simple sirup measuring 32° on the saccharometer when cold (see p. 688); add some lemon juice, the amount depending on the acidity of the fruit. Always mix the ingredients cold and use a saccharometer. If the scale shows too much sugar, thin it with a little water. On the other hand, if it does not register high enough, add the right amount of sirup.

(2) Mash the fruits with sugar, allowing about 10 oz. sugar per lb. fruit. This is only an approximate amount and depends upon the amount of sugar in the fruit. Press through a sieve; add the necessary amount of filtered water to get the proper degree on the saccharometer.

Fruit ices should register 18–22° on the saccharometer.

Fig. 439 - Snowball bombe (p. 659).
Fig. 440 - Ice cream countess Marie (p. 664.)

APRICOT ICE GLACE À L'ABRICOT (E.) (*For 10 persons*)

15 oz. purée of fresh apricots, 15 oz. sirup, and juice of 2 lemons. The mixture should register 18–19° on the saccharometer.

BANANA ICE GLACE AUX BANANES (E.) (*For 10 persons*)

Macerate 1 pt. mashed banana pulp 2 hr. in 1 pt. sirup flavored with kirsch. Add the juice of 3 lemons and strain through a sieve. The mixture should register 20–21°.

CHERRY ICE GLACE AUX CERISES (E.) (*For 10 persons*)

Crush 1 pt. pitted cherries and pound the stones in a mortar. Macerate everything 1 hr. in 1 pt. sirup flavored with kirsch. Add the juice of 3 lemons and press through a sieve. The mixture should register 21°.

LEMON ICE GLACE AU CITRON (E.) (*For 10 persons*)

Macerate the grated peel of 3 lemons 2 hr. in 1 pt. cold sirup. Add the juice of 4 lemons and 2 oranges; press through a cone-shaped sieve. The mixture should register 22°.

STRAWBERRY ICE GLACE AUX FRAISES (E.) (*For 10 persons*)

Mix 1 pt. strawberry purée with 1 pt. sirup; add the juice of 2 oranges and 2 lemons. Or instead: mash 2 lb. strawberries with 1 lb. powdered sugar, add the same amount of orange and lemon juice, press through a sieve, and add the necessary amount of filtered water to obtain a mixture registering 16–18°.

RASPBERRY ICE GLACE AUX FRAMBOISES (E.)

Prepare the mixture the same as for Strawberry Ice, using the same proportions.

MELON ICE GLACE AU MELON (E.) (*For 10 persons*)

Mix 1 pt. very ripe melon pulp with 1 pt. sirup, juice of 2 oranges and 1 lemon, 1 tbsp. orange-flower water. Press through a sieve. The mixture should register 22°.

PEAR ICE GLACE AUX POIRES (E.) (*For 10 persons*)

Peel, seed, and mash very soft pears with 1 lb. powdered sugar per lb. fruit; add the juice of 1 lemon per lb. pears. Press through a sieve and add filtered water until the saccharometer registers 22°.

VIOLET ICE GLACE AUX VIOLETTES (E.) (*For 10 persons*)

Put ½ lb. washed violet petals into 3 cups boiling sirup. Let steep 10 min.; press through a sieve; let cool, and finish with the juice of 3 lemons. The mixture should register 20–21°.

ICE-CREAM BOMBES

BOMBES GLACÉES (A.)

(*For 36–40 persons*)

Bombes are made of plain ice creams or ices as a covering around a more or less soft bombe mixture. Formerly, bombes were molded in spherical molds, which accounts for their name. Today, they are made in molds in the shape of truncated cones with rounded top. Bombe mixtures are made with 32 egg yolks per qt. sirup registering 28° on the saccharometer. Blend the mixture with a wire whisk over a slow fire; when it is very smooth, remove from the fire, strain, put on ice, and continue beating until completely cold. Flavor it then, and add 2 cups very stiff whipped cream.

In molding the bombe, begin by lining the bottom and sides of the mold with a rather thin layer of the desired ice or ice cream frozen in a freezer. Then fill the inside with the bombe mixture, flavored to taste, or with a mousse. Cover with a round of white paper, seal tightly, and embed the mold in salted ice, leaving it there at least 2 hr. When ready to serve, unmold the bombe onto a plate covered with a folded napkin. Bombes may be made in all flavors, with creams and frozen sirups; they are garnished with diced or minced preserved fruits, and, finally, decorated. (Figure 438, Page 656.)

BOMBE AÏDA BOMBE AÏDA (E.)

Line the mold with strawberry ice; fill the inside with a bombe mixture flavored with kirsch.

BOMBE ALHAMBRA BOMBE ALHAMBRA (E.)

Line the mold with vanilla ice cream; fill with a strawberry bombe mixture. After unmolding, surround the bombe with a ring of fine, fresh strawberries macerated in kirsch.

AMERICAN BOMBE BOMBE AMÉRICAINE (E.)

Line the mold with strawberry ice; fill with a tangerine bombe mixture. After unmolding, decorate the bombe with pistachio ice cream.

SNOWBALL BOMBE BOMBE BOULE DE NEIGE (P.)

Vanilla ice cream mixed with a generous amount of preserved fruits macerated in kirsch. After unmolding, cover completely with vanilla-flavored Chantilly Cream (p. 552) and decorate with a pastry bag with a fluted tube. Stick on several crystallized violets. (Figure 439, Page 657.)

BOMBE BOURDALOUE BOMBE BOURDALOUE (E.)

Line the mold with vanilla ice cream; fill with a bombe mixture flavored with anisette. After unmolding, decorate the bombe with pralined violets.

BOMBE CAMARGO BOMBE CAMARGO (E.)

Line the mold with coffee ice cream; fill with a vanilla bombe mixture.

BOMBE CARMEN BOMBE CARMEN (D. and D.)

Line a bombe mold with chocolate ice cream and fill the center with a creamy mixture tinted pink with maraschino.

BOMBE CHANTILLY BOMBE CHANTILLY (D. and D.)

Line a bombe mold with chocolate ice cream lightened with whipped cream and fill the inside with sweetened, vanilla-flavored Chantilly Cream (p. 552).

BOMBE COLOMBIA BOMBE COLOMBIA (E.)

Line the mold with kirsch-flavored ice; fill with a bombe mixture made with pears. After unmolding, decorate with cherries half cooked in sirup.

BOMBE COPPELIA BOMBE COPPELIA (E.)

Line the mold with coffee ice cream; fill with a Praline (p. 559) bombe mixture.

WHITE LADY BOMBE BOMBE DAME BLANCHE (E.)

Line the mold with vanilla ice cream; fill with an Almond-Milk (p. 556) bombe mixture.

PINK DEVIL BOMBE BOMBE DIABLE ROSE (E.)

Line the mold with strawberry ice; fill with a bombe mixture flavored with kirsch and containing cherries half cooked in sirup.

DIPLOMAT BOMBE BOMBE DIPLOMATE (E.)

Line the mold with vanilla ice cream; fill with a maraschino bombe mixture containing preserved fruits.

BOMBE FALSTAFF BOMBE FALSTAFF (E.)

Line the mold with praline ice cream, then fill with Strawberry Mousse (p. 646). After unmolding, sprinkle with powdered Praline (p. 559).

BOMBE FAUVETTE BOMBE FAUVETTE (E.)

Line the mold with pistachio ice cream; fill with a banana-mousse mixture flavored with kirsch.

FROU-FROU BOMBE BOMBE FROU-FROU (E.)

Line the mold with vanilla ice cream; fill with a rum-flavored bombe mixture containing preserved fruits.

BOMBE GISMONDA BOMBE GISMONDA (E.)

Line a mold with praline ice cream; fill with a bombe mixture flavored with anisette and containing white currants.

HAVANA BOMBE BOMBE HAVANAISE (E.)

Line the mold with coffee ice cream; fill with a vanilla- and rum-flavored bombe mixture.

BOMBE JAFFA BOMBE JAFFA (E.)

Line the mold with praline ice cream; fill with an orange bombe mixture.

JAVANESE BOMBE BOMBE JAVANAISE (P.)

Line the mold with coffee ice cream mixed with 4 or 5 tbsp. fresh extra-heavy cream, then fill the center with rum-flavored banana mousse. Mix 2 oz. coffee beans soaked in liqueur (a kind of bonbon easily bought) in the mousse.

Fig. 441 - Ice cream cheese (p. 664).
Fig. 442 - Armenonville cups (p. 665).

Fig. 441

Fig. 442

Fig. 443

Fig. 444

BOMBE JEANNETTE BOMBE JEANNETTE (P.)

Line the mold with strawberry ice and fill with vanilla Chantilly Cream (p. 552) mixed with crystallized violets. After unmolding, sprinkle the top with crystallized violets.

BOMBE MADELEINE BOMBE MADELEINE (E.)

Line the mold with almond ice cream; fill with a vanilla- and kirsch-flavored bombe mixture containing preserved fruits.

MALTESE BOMBE BOMBE MALTAISE (P.)

Line the mold with orange ice containing candied orange peel cut in small strips, then fill the center with curaçao-flavored vanilla mousse. Serve this bombe surrounded with glazed orange slices.

BOMBE MARIE-LOUISE BOMBE MARIE-LOUISE (E.)

Line the mold with raspberry ice; fill with a vanilla bombe mixture.

BOMBE MASCOTTE BOMBE MASCOTTE (E.)

Line the mold with peach ice; fill with a kirsch-flavored bombe mixture.

BOMBE MONTMORENCY BOMBE MONTMORENCY (E.)

Line the mold with kirsch ice; fill with a cherry bombe mixture. After unmolding, encircle it with preserved cherry halves.

BOMBE NELUSKO BOMBE NELUSKO (E.)

Line the mold with praline ice cream; fill with a chocolate bombe mixture.

BOMBE PAUL BOMBE PAUL (P.)

Line the mold with praline ice cream and fill with Chantilly Cream (p. 552), then pour 2 oz. granulated chocolate into the center of the cream. The chocolate should stay in a lump and not mix with the cream, so that, when served, it will be in grains.

BOMBE SELIKA BOMBE SELIKA (P.)

Make a purée of equal amounts of strawberries and bananas and mix it with twice as much cold sirup registering 20° on the saccharometer, a little lemon juice, and carmine coloring. Freeze in an ice-cream freezer and, when hard, mix in 1 cup whipped cream. Let stand 1–2 hr. embedded in salted ice, then unmold and decorate with a ring of fine strawberries or, if not in season, with preserved cherries.

WITCH'S BOMBE BOMBE SORCIÈRE (P.)

This frozen dessert is both original and exquisite. Prepare a very thin layer of Génoise Cake (p. 549) baked in a flan circle, cut it into triangular slices, and use it to line a dome mold or a semispherical bombe mold. Fill with chocolate ice cream mixed, after freezing, with 1 cup whipped cream to make it soft and

Fig. 443 - 1. Midinette cups (p. 666). 2. Denise cups (p. 665).
Fig. 444 - Omelet norwegian style (p. 667).

mousselike. Close the mold very tightly, sealing it with butter, and embed in salted ice; then unmold onto a cold plate or a well-chilled tray and cover it quickly with warm chocolate Fondant (p. 553). Sprinkle with shredded grilled almonds, wipe away the chocolate running around the edges, and slide the bombe onto a service plate covered with a napkin. This bombe must be decorated and served very quickly to avoid melting.

SUCCESS BOMBE BOMBE SUCCÈS (E.)

Line the mold with apricot ice; fill with Chantilly Cream (p. 552) flavored with kirsch and mixed with diced, preserved apricots.

SULTANA BOMBE BOMBE SULTANE (E.)

Line the mold with chocolate ice cream; fill with a pistachio bombe mixture.

BOMBE ZAMORA BOMBE ZAMORA (E.)

Line the mold with coffee ice cream; fill with a curaçao-flavored bombe mixture.

ICE-CREAM CAKES AND DECORATED ICES

BISCUITS GLACÉS ET GLACÉS DÉCORÉES (Ga.)

Ices and ice creams can be served more attractively by molding them or decorating them with a pastry bag. The color of the ice cream and its decoration should contrast pleasantly—for example, a strawberry decoration with vanilla ice cream; raspberry decoration for pistachio ice cream; pistachio or chocolate decoration for coffee ice cream; chocolate or vanilla decoration for praline ice cream; vanilla decoration for chocolate ice cream. A used pastry bag still in good condition is best for this work. It is better than a new one because the weave in the cloth is tighter and there is less chance of leakage. Fit the pastry bag with a wide, fluted tube having 6 well-opened sides. Shortly before serving, soften the ice cream to be used in the decoration by working it with a spatula in a bowl. If executed quickly and tastefully, this pastry-bag decoration produces a very pretty effect. Ices and ice creams can be decorated much more easily with whipped cream.

Ice-cream cakes are molded with any bombe mixture. They should be molded in plain squares or rectangles. Because of their simplicity, these cakes are especially suitable to be decorated with a pastry bag, as described above.

OLD-FASHIONED ICE-CREAM CAKE BISCUIT GLACÉ À L'ANCIENNE (Ga.)

Line a bombe mold with Sponge Fingers (p. 586) moistened with kirsch and stuck together in pairs with a little apricot jam; fill with a vanilla bombe mixture (see p. 658). After unmolding, decorate with a pastry bag filled with whipped cream.

ICE-CREAM CAKE GRAND CARÊME BISCUIT GLACÉ GRAND CARÊME (Ga.)

Make a square layer of Génoise Cake (p. 549) of proportionate size for the number of guests; make it 1¼ in. thick and split it in 2 lengthwise. Stick 1 slice to a service plate with a little jam and moisten this slice with champagne brandy. Sauce the other slice lightly, too. Prepare vanilla ice cream, a little raspberry or strawberry ice, and some whipped cream. When ready to serve, spread a thick layer of vanilla ice cream on the first slice of Génoise Cake, smooth it with a flat knife, and cover it with the second slice. Spread this with a ⅜-in. layer of strawberry or raspberry ice; carefully smooth the top and sides and finish by decorating lightly with Chantilly Cream (p. 552), using a pastry bag.

ICE-CREAM CAKE MARIE-ROSE BISCUIT GLACÉ MARIE-ROSE (E.)

Add to 1 pt. Chantilly Cream (p. 552) ½ cup coarsely crumbled meringues. Pour the mixture into a Countess Marie sponge-cake mold lined with white paper; seal tightly, embed in salted ice, and chill 1½–2 hr. Unmold onto a service platter, remove the paper, and decorate with a cone filled with Chantilly Cream. Serve with a separate bowl of strawberries macerated in curaçao and sugar, with some sugared strawberry purée added at the last moment.

MEXICAN ICE-CREAM CAKE BISCUIT GLACÉ MEXICAIN (Ga.)

Mold a praline bombe mixture (see p. 658) and decorate with chocolate ice cream.

ICE-CREAM CAKE POMPADOUR BISCUIT GLACÉ POMPADOUR (Ga.)

Fill an iced sponge-cake mold with a vanilla bombe mixture (see p. 658); prepare strawberry or raspberry ice. When ready to serve, beat the strawberry or raspberry ice until very smooth and use it for decorating the cake.

VENETIAN ICE-CREAM CAKE BISCUIT GLACÉ VÉNITIEN (Ga.)

Same procedure as Ice-Cream Cake Grand Carême, (p. 662), but filled with pistachio ice cream and decorated with raspberry ice.

VARIOUS ICES AND ICE CREAMS

ALHAMBRA ICE GLACE ALHAMBRA (E.)

Line the bottom and sides of a madeleine mold with vanilla ice cream. Macerate some fresh strawberries 2 hr. in noyau (a liqueur flavored with fruit stones), mix the strawberries with Chantilly Cream (p. 552), flavor with some of the noyau, then fill the mold with the mixture.

Note: When strawberries are out of season, use Strawberry Mousse (p. 646) instead of the fresh berries.

CHAMPAGNE ICE GLACE CHAMPENOISE (D. and D.)

Line a shallow mold with raspberry ice and fill with an ice made with champagne and diced pineapple; decorate with a pastry bag filled with vanilla ice cream.

ICE CREAM CHATEAUBRIAND GLACE CHATEAUBRIAND (D. and D.)

Prepare a vanilla ice-cream mixture, using milk in which peeled fresh almonds and a few mashed bitter almonds have soaked 1–2 hr. After straining the milk through a napkin, prepare the vanilla ice cream the usual way; let the mold stand in salted ice until the cream is very hard, then add kirsch and maraschino and a little whipped cream. Use a fancy mold.

ICE CREAM COUNTESS MARIE GLACE COMTESSE MARIE (E.)

Use a special square mold, either plain or with a design stamped on top: line it with strawberry ice; fill with vanilla ice cream. After unmolding, use a pastry bag with a fluted tube, filled with vanilla ice cream, to decorate it. The procedure can be reversed and strawberry ice be used for the filling and decoration. (Figure 440, Page 657.)

SUNSET ICE GLACE COUCHER DE SOLEIL (E.)

Take 1 lb. very ripe strawberries; put them in a silver timbale; sprinkle with 10 oz. powdered sugar; moisten with 6 small liqueur glasses Grand Marnier. Cover the dish and keep on ice ½ hr. Then press the strawberries through a sieve and use the purée to prepare a mixture as described in the section on Fruit Ices (p. 657). Freeze in an ice-cream freezer and, when frozen, mix in 1 pt. Chantilly Cream (p. 552). Cover the freezer and put it back into the ice 35–40 min. Carefully serve the ice in pyramids in crystal cups.

EVENING STAR ICE GLACE ÉTOILE DU BERGER (E.)

Use a star-shaped mold or a madeleine mold with a star on the bottom: line it with raspberry ice and fill with a mousse flavored with benedictine. Unmold onto a platter covered with an uneven but thick disk of Spun Sugar (p. 562). This Spun Sugar will set off the ice and give the impression of light shed between the points of the star.

ICE FLEURETTE GLACE FLEURETTE (E.)

Fill a square mold with even layers of strawberry and pineapple ice superimposed on each other. After unmolding, decorate with lemon ice.

ICE-CREAM CHEESES FROMAGES GLACÉS (D. and D.)

Ice-cream cheeses are made of very hard ice cream molded in a fluted bombe mold, using 1, 2, or 3 flavors. To fill them, place a tin divider upright in the mold and fill each side with a different flavor, usually an ice cream and a fruit ice; then remove the divider and tap the mold to eliminate any air bubbles. Close the mold and pack in salted ice. The ice cream can be unmolded after ½ hr. (Figure 441, Page 660.)

VARIOUS FROZEN PREPARATIONS

CUPS COUPES (J.)

Cups used for this purpose should be silver or crystal. They are filled with different flavors of ice cream, and sometimes Chantilly Cream (p. 552) or fruits are added.

D'ANTIGNY CUPS COUPES D'ANTIGNY (E.)

Fill the cups ¾ full with strawberry ice with light sweet cream added to the ice. On the ice in each cup place a half peach poached in vanilla sirup and cover with a light veil of Spun Sugar (p. 562).

ARMENONVILLE CUPS COUPES ARMENONVILLE (J.)

Fill the cups with vanilla ice cream. Encircle with a band of warm Chocolate English Cream (p. 550). (Figure 442, Page 660.)

BOHEMIAN CUPS COUPES BOHÉMIENNE (E.)

Fill the cups with a cone of vanilla ice cream mixed with broken bits of candied chestnuts macerated in rum. Cover lightly with rum-flavored Apricot Sauce (p. 560).

CREOLE CUPS COUPES À LA CRÉOLE (H.)

Dice pineapples and bananas; cover them with kirsch or Liqueur des Îles, place in cups, garnish with lemon ice diluted with rum. Decorate the top with preserved fruits.

WHITE LADY CUPS COUPES DAME BLANCHE (E.)

Fill the cups ¾ full of almond-milk ice cream. On the ice cream place a half peach poached in vanilla sirup, and fill the peach with white currants. Surround the peaches with a band of lemon ice squeezed from a pastry bag.

DENISE CUPS COUPES DENISE (E.)

Fill the cups with mocha ice cream; sprinkle the ice cream with bonbons filled with liqueur (preferably rum) or with tiny wild strawberries. Top with 1 tbsp. Chantilly Cream (p. 552) or squeeze it from a pastry bag with a fluted tube. (Figure 443, Page 661.)

EUGÉNIE CUPS COUPES EUGÉNIE (E.)

Fill the cups with vanilla ice cream mixed with broken, candied chestnuts. Cover with Chantilly Cream (p. 552) and sprinkle pralined violets on top.

FAVORITE CUPS COUPES À LA FAVORITE (E.)

Fill the cups with vanilla ice cream flavored with kirsch and maraschino. Encircle the top with a band of pineapple ice; in the center place some Chantilly Cream (p. 552) blended with puréed strawberries.

JACQUES CUPS COUPES JACQUES (H.)

Diced pineapple, bananas, cherries, and strawberries mixed and macerated in kirsch and maraschino. Half fill the cup with the fruit and garnish with fruit ice. Decorate the top with candied angelica and finish with a strawberry and a cherry.

MALMAISON CUPS COUPES MALMAISON (E.)

Fill the cups with vanilla ice cream mixed with peeled Muscat grapes. Cover with a veil of Spun Sugar (p. 562).

MANON CUPS COUPES MANON (H.)

Chill crystal cups in the freezer and fill the bottom with a layer of vanilla ice cream; sprinkle the ice cream with cherries half cooked in sirup and macerated in kirsch. Cover the top of the cherries with chestnut purée squeezed out in the shape of vermicelli from a pastry bag. Also use a pastry bag to encircle the top of each cup with a ring of Chantilly Cream (p. 552).

MIDINETTE CUPS COUPES MIDINETTE (E.)

Half fill with vanilla ice cream. Place on top a small meringue turned upside down, with a small, poached half peach inside the meringue. Surround with a border of Chantilly Cream (p. 552).

Variant: Cover the meringue with Chantilly Cream tinted pink with puréed fresh raspberries and squeezed from a pastry bag with a fluted tube. (Figure 443, Page 661.)

MIREILLE CUPS COUPES MIREILLE (H.)

Peaches sliced thin, moistened with maraschino, and placed in the bottom of the cup. Cover the top with vanilla ice cream softened with maraschino. Decorate with shredded almonds and a cherry.

BABY'S DREAM CUPS COUPES RÊVE DE BÉBÉ (E.)

Fill the cups ½ full with pineapple ice and the other ½ with raspberry ice. Place a row of small strawberries macerated in orange sugar between the 2 ices. Encircle the top with a border of Chantilly Cream (p. 552) and sprinkle the cream with pralined violets.

THAÏS CUPS COUPES THAÏS (H.)

Half fill the cups with vanilla ice cream. On top place a half peach; surround with Chantilly Cream (p. 552). Chocolate shavings on the cream.

VENUS CUPS COUPES VÉNUS (H.)

Half fill the cups with vanilla ice cream. In the center of each cup place a small peach poached in vanilla sirup, with a small, very red strawberry on top. Surround the peaches with a border of Chantilly Cream (p. 552).

VICTORIA CUPS COUPES VICTORIA (E.)

Cover the bottom of the cups with broken bits of candied chestnuts macerated in kirsch. Finish filling with vanilla ice cream and strawberry ice. Place a whole candied chestnut in the center of the cup.

FROSTED TANGERINE SURPRISE MANDARINES GIVRÉES EN SURPRISE (P.)

Prepare tangerine ice with the pulp from 12 tangerines. Do not damage the rind—cut a circular opening, the size of a quarter, in the stem side of the fruit and remove the pulp. When the ice is made, fill the hollow rinds and close with the circular piece you have removed. Place them in a freezing compartment or in a large charlotte mold embedded in salted ice. Let chill ½ hr., then use a brush to sprinkle a few drops of water on them and let frost form until ready to serve. Then place them quickly on a napkin. If possible, use tangerines that have stems and a few leaves, for these have more eye appeal.

CHOCOLATE MOUSSE MOUSSE AU CHOCOLAT (Ga.) (*For 10 persons*)

Make ½ pt. vanilla bombe mixture (see p. 658) with a sirup registering no more than 20° on the saccharometer; melt 1 lb. chocolate in 3 cups water. Let cool. When ready to use, mix the chocolate, which should be very thick, with the bombe mixture and add 3 cups whipped cream. Mold. This mousse is also used as a filling for bombes.

STRAWBERRY MOUSSE MOUSSE AUX FRAISES (Ga.) (*For 10 persons*)

Purée 1 lb. strawberries without adding water or sirup, sweeten with 10 oz. powdered sugar, add 1 pt. whipped cream and a pinch of powdered vanilla. Mix and mold. This is also used as a filling.

APRICOT, PEACH, or **PEAR MOUSSE** MOUSSE À L'ABRICOT, AUX PÊCHES, or AUX POIRES (Ga.) (*For 10 persons*)

Press 13 oz. fruit poached in sirup through a fine sieve. Make a vanilla bombe mixture with 8 egg yolks and sirup registering 30° on the saccharometer (see p. 560) ; mix with the puréed fruit and add 3 cups whipped cream. If fresh fruits are not available, fruit compote may be used. These mousses usually serve as fillings for bombes.

Note on the whipped cream: The quantities of whipped cream given for each recipe should be measured before the cream is whipped.

SURPRISE OMELET or **OMELET NORWEGIAN STYLE** OMELETTE EN SURPRISE or À LA NORVÉGIENNE (E.)

On a long platter, place an oval layer of Génoise Cake (p. 549) about ½ in. thick and large enough for the omelet you want to make. Spread ice cream or fruit ice on the cake. Cover this with a layer of Ordinary Meringue (p. 557) or very stiff Italian Meringue (p. 557) ; smooth it with the blade of a knife, making it about ½ in. thick; decorate with a cone or pastry bag filled with the same meringue, and place in a very hot oven to cook and color the meringue rapidly without melting the ice cream. (Figure 444, Page 661.)

PARFAITS PARFAITS (E.)

The name "parfait" used to mean only coffee parfait, but now it is given to frozen desserts made with bombe mixtures with only 1 flavor, which is logical enough, since the bombe mixture, except for a few insignificant details, is exactly the same as a parfait mixture. Therefore, parfaits can be made in all flavors, such as vanilla, chocolate, praline, etc., as well as coffee.

COFFEE PARFAIT PARFAIT AU CAFÉ (Ga.) (*For 16 persons*)

Add coffee to ½ pt. sirup registering 40° on the saccharometer when hot. The mixture should register 26 or 28°. Blend with 16 egg yolks as in making a bombe mixture and finish the same way. Flavor with ½ vanilla bean. (Figure 445, Page 668.)

BALMORAL PARFAIT PARFAIT BALMORAL (Ga.) (*For 10 persons*)

Make a sirup with 10 oz. sugar, 1½ pt. water, and 1 vanilla bean. Bring the sirup to a boil. Grill 10 oz. hazelnuts and drop them hot into the sirup. Cover and remove from the fire for ¼ hr. Strain through a cone-shaped sieve into a frying pan; pour 1 glass water over the hazelnuts and put them back on the fire to wash off the sirup and extract all the hazelnut flavor; strain this juice and add it to the first sirup. Cook this sirup until very thick. Let cool and mix in 1 pt. whipped cream. Freeze like any ice cream and serve with Chocolate Sauce (p. 560).

PARISIAN PLOMBIÈRE PLOMBIÈRE À LA PARISIENNE (D. and D.) (*For 12 persons*)

Pound 7 oz. fresh, shelled almonds in a mortar with a little water to keep the oil from separating. Put into a mixing bowl. Bring 1 pt. milk to a boil and pour it over the mashed almonds; cover and let steep awhile. Then strain through a cone-shaped sieve and blend smoothly with 12 egg yolks and 1 pt. cold sirup registering 35° on the saccharometer. Flavor with vanilla and thicken on the fire, like an English Cream (p. 550), without boiling. Strain again into a mixing bowl, beat the mixture until it is cold, add ⅓ as much whipped cream, and pour the mixture into a bombe mold, alternating it with thin layers of diced, preserved fruit macerated in kirsch or maraschino. Freeze at least 2 hr.

JAVANESE FROZEN PUDDING PUDDING GLACÉ JAVANAIS (Gi.)

Line a dome-shaped ice-cream mold with a layer of vanilla ice cream. Fill the inside with 2 ice-cream mixtures, tangerine and curaçao, in alternate layers (see directly below). Finish filling the mold with a layer of vanilla ice cream. Seal it tightly, then embed it at least 2 hr. in crushed, salted ice. When ready to serve, unmold the pudding and sprinkle the top with crushed red Praline (p. 559).

Tangerine Ice Cream: Peel 3 very ripe and well-washed tangerines and steep the peel 15 min. in 1 qt. boiling milk. Beat 12 oz. powdered sugar with 12 egg yolks. When the mixture is very frothy, dilute it with the tangerine-flavored milk; then bind this cream by stirring it over the fire with a spatula. Color it a deep orange and strain it through a sieve. Let this cream cool, then freeze it like ordinary ice cream.

Curaçao Ice Cream: Beat 5 oz. sugar with 6 egg yolks. When the mixture is frothy, dilute it with 1 pt. boiling milk, then bind it on the fire, and strain. When the cream has cooled, flavor it with 1½ oz. curaçao. Pour it into an ice-cream freezer. When it is ¾ frozen, mix in another 1½ oz. curaçao and finish freezing.

FROZEN SOUFFLÉS SOUFFLÉS GLACÉS (Ga.)

Frozen Soufflés are made with all bombe mixtures. They are served in the same dishes as hot soufflés or in specially made cups of pleated paper. In either case, extend the height of the mold by attaching to it a band of paper projecting about 1 in. above the rim. Fill the soufflé containers with the chosen bombe mixture, piling it up about ⅔ in. higher than the soufflé dish or cup. Place in the freezing compartment, or in a special ice-cream container, sealing the edges with butter, and embed it in a tub of salted ice, taking care not to let the water rise above the rim of the container. It takes 5 hr. to freeze a soufflé. When ready to serve, remove the paper band and the frozen bombe will look like a hot soufflé. Frozen Soufflés are usually made with a vanilla, hazelnut, praline, Balmoral, or chocolate bombe mixture and are named accordingly.

NEAPOLITAN SLICES TRANCHES NAPOLITAINES (J.)

Use special rectangular molds opening on both top and bottom. Place one of the covers in the bottom of the mold and spread with a layer of coffee ice cream.

Fig. 445 - Coffee parfait (p. 667).
Fig. 446 - Neapolitan slices (p. 668).

Fig. 445

Fig. 446

Fig. 447

Fig. 448

Freeze 15–20 min. at 14° F. Put in a second, rather thick layer of Plombière ice cream (see p. 668). Replace in the freezer. Finish filling the mold with a fruit ice: strawberry, raspberry, etc. Put on the top cover and leave in the freezer at least 2 hr. To unmold, put the mold under cold running water and then remove the 2 covers, gently pressing on the ice cream to slide it out. When ready to serve, cut in slices about 3/8 in. thick.

Note: The mold should be put into the freezer after each layer of ice cream is added, so the various mixtures do not run together. (Figure 446, Page 668.)

VARIOUS SHERBETS

For all sherbet and punch recipes, allow 1 qt. mixture for 15 persons.

SHERBETS SORBETS (Ga.)

Sherbets are flavored sirups registering 16° on the saccharometer, which are frozen by machine and used 2 ways: (1) served in cups before the roast at large dinners; (2) as a filling for ice cream hollowed out with a spoon just before serving.

PLAIN SHERBET SORBET SIMPLE (Ga.)

Flavor with any desired liqueur. Bring to a boil 2 qt. sirup registering 10° on the saccharometer and drop in the peel of 2 lemons and 2 vanilla beans. Simmer till the sirup reaches 14°, remove from the fire, let cool. Just before freezing, add the juice of 2 lemons. After freezing, flavor with the desired liqueur or wine.

Liqueurs and Wines Used for Flavoring: Wines—champagne, sherry, port, Samos, Cyprus, Lacryma Christi. Wine sherbets are especially suitable for the middle of a dinner. Those made with liqueurs—rum, kirsch, champagne brandy, anisette, curaçao, chartreuse, benedictine, cherry brandy, cassis—are best used as ice-cream fillings. These liqueurs must be first quality. If desired, a 2-egg-white Italian Meringue (p. 557) may be added to the sherbet, but this should be done only after freezing the sherbet and before adding the liqueur or wine.

GRANITÉS GRANITÉS (E.)

Granités serve the same purpose on the menu as sherbets. They may also be used in some culinary preparations. The base is a thin fruit sirup not exceeding 14° on the saccharometer. Granités are quite simply frozen sirups without the addition of Italian Meringue or anything else. Even more important than when making sherbets, the sirup must not be stirred or beaten while freezing or it will break down. When frozen, it should form a lightly granulated mass.

MARQUISES MARQUISES (E.)

Marquises are usually made with strawberries or pineapple and kirsch. Make a kirsch sherbet mixture registering 17° on the saccharometer. Freeze like a Granité, but a little firmer. When ready to serve, mix in, per qt. frozen mixture, 12 oz. very stiff Chantilly Cream (p. 552) blended with puréed strawberries or pineapple.

Fig. 447 - Cheeses Tray. 1. Brie. 2. Camembert. 3. Goat Cheese. 4. Maroilles. 5. Pont-l'évêque. 6. Port-salut.
Fig. 448 - Cheeses Tray. 1. Cantal. 2. Gruyère. 3. Livarot. 4. Roquefort.

ROMAN PUNCH PUNCH À LA ROMAINE (E.)

Mix the necessary amount of dry white wine or dry champagne with 1 pt. sirup registering 22° on the saccharometer to bring it down to 17°. Add the juice of 2 oranges and 3 lemons and a piece of orange peel and lemon peel; cover and let steep 1 hr. Strain the sirup and bring it to 18°. Freeze until somewhat firm, then mix in ¼ as much Italian Meringue, made in the proportions of 2 egg whites and 3½ oz. sugar (see p. 557). Just before serving, finish with 3 oz. rum added bit by bit. Serve in glasses like sherbets.

SPOOMS SPOOMS (E.)

Spooms are sherbets prepared with sirup registering 20° on the saccharometer. Add twice as much Italian Meringue (p. 557) as in ordinary sherbets, for they must be very light and frothy. Spooms may be made with fruit juices, but are usually made with such wines as champagne, Samos, muscatel, Zucco, etc. Serve in glasses like sherbets.

CHEESE AND FRUITS

CHEESE (A.)

Cheese is a highly digestible[1] albuminoid food containing peptone, which aids digestion.[2] For this reason it is served at the end of a meal. I believe I should say a few words about it.

The art of cheesemaking dates back more than 2000 years. Originally a matter of trial and error, it is now manufactured more and more along scientific lines, and many distinguished scholars have written important treatises on the subject.

Today a good cheesemaker must know how to choose[3] and mix the types of milk to be used, depending on the case; to determine in each case the proportion of rennet, the physical and chemical condition of the atmosphere (temperature, acidity) to ensure proper coagulation; to drain the curds, which contain almost all the casein in milk and the greater part of butter, in order to obtain a firm, compact, homogeneous, elastic product, containing only the amount of serum needed to cause proper fermentation; to encourage the development of certain species of microbes in the drying room or cellar and to prevent the development of certain others that might "sicken" the cheese, for, according to present scientific knowledge, cheese diseases are incurable.

All cheeses have a base of curdled milk, and may be grouped in 4 classes:

(1) Cheeses made from fresh curds; (2) cheeses made from fermented curds at low temperature and without outside pressure, having a soft texture;

---

[1] Along with bread, cheese is almost a complete food.

[2] Peptones especially help the digestion of fats and carbohydrates.

[3] The quality of cheese depends upon the quality of the milk used in the preparation, and, all things being equal, the best cheese is made with the milk of animals raised in good pastures. For a long time, no other kind of milk was used in France, and the ancient reputation of French cheeses stemmed from this fact; but for some time, at the risk of killing the goose that laid the golden egg, the producers have tried to increase the yield of dairy animals and have succeeded, to the detriment of quality, by feeding their beasts oil cakes and beets.

(3) cheeses made from curds fermented at a rather high temperature, having a hard, compressed texture; (4) moldy cheeses.

(*A*) In the class of cheeses made from fresh curds, we have white cheese, plain, drained curds of cow's milk; cream cheese, *petit-suisse,* curds of cow's milk beaten with cream, especially good from May to September; Gournay and Neufchâtel-en-Bray cream cheese, molded curds of cow's and ewe's milk, or simply ewe's milk alone, mixed with cream and sown with a mold that is usually *Penicillium candidum,* good from May to October; half-salted cheese, lightly salted cream cheese, and the Alpine *vacherin,* curds combined with cream and kept several days to give it a sourish flavor.

(*B*) In the class of curd cheeses fermented to a soft texture, we should cite: Brie, one of the most famous French cheeses, Camembert, Coulommiers, Port-Salut, Livarot, Maroilles, Gérome, Munster, Tome, Mont-dore, Saint-Marcellin, Banon, and Chabichou.

Brie, good for 5 months of the year, from December to April, should be soft, but not runny, and pale yellow in color; the cheese from Olivet, near Orléans, has a great local reputation and belongs to the Brie family. Camembert, made like Brie, is different only in that it contains a lactic ferment (*Oïdium camemberti*) that probably gives it its special flavor; Monsieur Fromage's cheese, made by that firm, is a variety of Camembert with a fine flavor. Coulommiers[1] is a spring and summer cheese with a very smooth, fat texture oily to the touch; the rind is grayish white. Port-Salut is a salty summer cheese with a smooth yellow texture. Livarot and Maroilles, autumn and winter cheeses, are appreciated only by a few connoisseurs because of the rather ammoniacal odor of the cheeses. Gérome is a salty cheese mixed with cumin seeds, good from October to March. Munster is a highly flavored winter cheese, usually eaten sprinkled with cumin seeds; Tome, from the Hérens Valley, is aromatic and fatty. Finally, Mont-dore, Saint-Marcellin, Banon, and Chabichou are excellent goat cheeses; the first of these is soaked in white wine before being put into the cellar.

(*C*) In the class of curd cheeses fermented to a hard texture, we include: Gruyère, a cheese cooked at a temperature of 50–60° C., of which Emmenthal is the best, Cantal, Dutch or Edam, Parmesan, Cheshire, and Stilton. All of these cheeses keep.

A good Gruyère or a good Emmenthal should have an even texture, light yellow color, and regular but not too many large holes; old Emmenthal, moistened with white wine and kept in the cellar several years, is an incomparable product. Cantal is made from salted cow's milk. Dutch or Edam cheese is made by treating unskimmed cow's milk at 36° C.; it should be reddish yellow in color, delicate, smooth, and buttery; it is excellent chilled in summer. Parmesan, also made from cow's milk, is primarily a seasoning cheese. When it is of good quality and mature, it is slightly moist and a golden yellow. The saffron-colored Cheshire is prepared somewhat like Dutch cheese and is highly appreciated in England, but the king of English cheeses is Stilton. When aged, and eaten while sipping old Madeira, it is really marvelous.

(*D*) A typical moldy cheese is Roquefort, prepared with ewe's milk. The moldy spots are made by cultivating a mold (*Penicillium glaucum*) on white

[1] The double-cream Coulommiers, a de luxe fresh cheese, is prepared at low temperature with freshly drawn milk, the curds being mixed with the cream.

bread, which produces the green marbling. Roquefort matures in a cavelike cellar, maintained at a constant temperature of 6–8° C.

Among the other moldy cheeses, we should mention the Auvergne blue and Gorgonzola, a yellowish-blue cheese highly regarded in Italy.

People who despise cheese are fairly rare; however, there are those who, because of some incomprehensible idiosyncrasy, cannot stand any food flavored with even the blandest cheese and who flee from even simple macaroni au gratin.

Connoisseurs of cheese, however, are legion; there are even fanatics who would prefer dry bread and cheese to the finest dinner served without it; and we must admit that cheese is an admirable conclusion to any meal; it completes the meal if it has been insufficient and it crowns it if it has been good.

People who don't want to add to their diet may enjoy cheese by taking only a tiny piece and pressing it with the tongue against the palate until it has melted. This way, they may enjoy all the flavor and aroma and the healthful effect of the cheese without overeating or any ill effects.

Cheeses should be served with wines from the same region, but remember that a good cheese calls for a good wine, more often red than white, but both of equal quality.

Camembert, Livarot, Pont-l'Évêque: Grands Bordeaux or Burgundy, Pommard, Côtes du Rhône, Beaujolais.

Maroilles: Saint-Émilion, Côtes de Nuits.

Various Brie cheeses: Médoc, Beaune, Beaujolais, Saint-Julien, red Bouzy, Algerian.

Port-Salut: Fleury or Moulin-à-vent.

Roquefort: Rhône wines.

Gruyère: sweet wines of Lorraine.

Sweet cheeses (*petits-suisses, demi-sel,* Gournay, *coeur à la crème*) : sweet wines: Monbazillac, Barsac, sauternes, Vins de Paille, *demi-sec* champagne.

Gérome, Munster: Alsatian wines, Moselle or Meursault, Montrachet.

Dutch: Alsatian wines or white burgundy.

Cheshire: red Bordeaux.

For cheese illustrations, see Figures 447-448, Page 669.

Fig. 449 - Basket of summer fruits.

Fig. 449

Fig. **450**

FRUITS

The variety of fruits grown in France, along with the exotic imports, makes it possible to supply the table with all sorts of fruits all year round. Fruit is one of the most important foods and should be included in any well-planned menu. We feel, therefore, that it would be useful to write about some of the principal varieties:

APRICOT (*abricot*) : from May to August. Come principally from the South of France, Algeria, and Spain. The most famous are those from Murcia, the clingstone (a white-fleshed variety), and the peach-apricot, very flavorful, juicy, and sweet.

GREEN ALMOND (*amande verte*) : from June to September. Found principally in the South of France and in the Mediterranean region. There are 2 varieties: the sweet almond and the bitter almond. Sweet almonds are both soft and semihard. The favored almond is the Princess, which can be broken with the fingers.

PINEAPPLE (*ananas*) : an exotic fruit imported from the Azores, Hawaii, Martinique, Guinea; sold in Paris in all seasons, especially winter. Juicy and flavorful pulp.

Preparation: Slice off the top and half the bottom, and run a knife all around the inside, removing the pulp in 1 piece and leaving the pineapple shell whole by pressing the pulp up through the hole in the bottom. Slice the pulp, removing the hard core. Replace in the shell, sugar, flavor with kirsch or maraschino, and serve cold.

FILBERT (*aveline*) : a variety of large hazelnut from Spain and Sicily.

AVOCADO (*avocat*) : an exotic fruit resembling a large pear and containing a large seed. Its soft pulp looks like butter; it has a bland flavor and is therefore seasoned: as an hors d'oeuvre, with oil and vinegar; or as a dessert fruit, with sugar and port.

BANANA (*banane*) : throughout the year. Exotic fruit, imported chiefly from the Antilles, Canaries, South America. Its pulp is flavorful, soft, and sweet.

Fig. 450 - Basket of winter fruits.

The most famous bananas are the curved ones from the Canaries, smaller than the American variety. Should be eaten very ripe.

CITRON (*cédrat*) : a sort of lemon with a very thick rind; grown on the Mediterranean coasts. This fruit is usually candied and used in pastrymaking.

CHERRY (*cerise*) : from April to August. A highly esteemed and very refreshing fruit. There are a great many varieties in France, the heart cherries with soft pulp and red juice, the bigarreau with firm pulp and clear juice, the Burgundy variety with firm pulp, red juice, and a delicious flavor; the rather tart English cherries, and the Montmorency cherries, usually brandied.

KUMQUAT (*chinois*) : a sort of small orange, either green or yellow, that comes from China. Like citron, this fruit is used in pastrymaking after being candied.

LEMON (*citron*) : throughout the year and especially from November to May. A very acid fruit containing many vitamins. The best grow around Naples and Murcia, but may be found almost anywhere in the Mediterranean region.

DATE (*datte*) : from November to March. A very nourishing and sweet North African fruit. There are many varieties, but the best is the Deglet-Nour with its soft pulp and shiny brown color.

FIG (*figue*) : from July to October. Grows in Europe and North Africa. Among the many varieties the principal are: the world-famous Loukums from Smyrna, with fine white skin; the Marseilles fig, with yellowish-white skin and white pulp (August-September) ; the Bellona fig, with violet skin and red pulp (July-October) ; the Banissotte, with violet skin and red pulp (ripe from October until the first frost).

STRAWBERRY (*fraise*) : June to October. Found all over Europe. Classified in 2 groups: the small strawberries, of which the wild or wood strawberry is the best known, with firm pulp and full flavor; and the large strawberries, which include many varieties, the most esteemed being: Héricart de Thury, la France, Belle de Meaux, etc.

RASPBERRY (*framboise*) : July to October. Flavorful and juicy fruit, must be eaten very ripe. Principal varieties are Belle de Fontenay, Hornet, etc.

POMEGRANATE (*grenade*) : October-November. A globular fruit with a very tough skin. The pulp is composed of numerous transparent seeds. A very juicy and decorative fruit.

CURRANT (*groseille*) : July to September. May be divided into three principal species: currants in clusters, with red or white berries; the gooseberry, a larger berry with a greenish veined skin; the black currant, also called *cassis.*

JUJUBE (*jujube*) : September to November. A fruit grown in North Africa and the South of France. It looks like a large red-skinned olive and contains a hard stone. It has a bland flavor and is only eaten when overripe.

PERSIMMON (*kaki*) : October-November. Originally from Japan, now cultivated in Provence. Has the shape and color of a large orange. It is picked green, but eaten only when very ripe and soft. The pulp is refreshing, but stringy and somewhat tasteless.

TANGERINE (*mandarine*) : November to January. A species of small orange brought from China and now grown in southeastern France. The best known varieties come from Nice and Algeria. There is another variety called Clementine, which ripens earlier than the ordinary tangerine and is sweeter.

CHESTNUT (*marron*) : from October to the end of February. A farinaceous and nourishing fruit. A little larger than the horse-chestnut. Chiefly grown in Ardèche, Auvergne, Périgord, and Italy. May be used in various ways, especially grilled and in pastry.

MELON (*melon*) : May to September. Asiatic in origin. May be eaten at the beginning of a meal as an hors d'oeuvre or at the end as a fruit. There are 2 principal species: the melon with a mottled skin and the cantaloupe. Melons cultivated in the region around Paris are generally excellent and are grouped under the name *maraîchers ;* Kroumir melons, originally from Cyprus, have a yellow pulp, grow in the Paris region, and ripen later than the others. They have an excellent quality. The Charente melon, grown in the South of France, is one of the best known melons. It has an exquisite flavor. There are still other species of melons, such as the golden or Spanish melon with yellow skin.

It is not easy to choose a good melon. It should be weighed in the hand to determine whether it is full or hollow, and there should be a marked crown around the stem if the fruit is sweet and properly ripened.

MIRABELLE (*mirabelle*) : August to September. A small, golden-yellow plum, very sweet. The best known are those from Lorraine.

MEDLAR (*nèfle*) : November to February. Grown in Europe. The fruit is bitter when picked, but becomes sweet and flavorful after ripening.

LOQUAT (*nèfle du Japon*) : October to November. Grown in Provence and Algeria; tart, refreshing.

HAZELNUT (*noisette*) : August to November (dry: all year). Grows wild all over Europe; widely used in pastry- and candymaking.

WALNUT (*noix*) : August-September (dry: all year). Grown in Europe, provides a very good oil.

COCONUT (*noix de coco*) : all year. Colonial fruit. The shell is as hard as wood and the inside contains a milky liquid. The flesh is firm and white. Grated coconut is used in pastry.

ORANGE (*orange*) : November to March principally (all year, depending on where they come from). This is one of the best known fruits; it is juicy, refreshing, and rich in vitamins. Raised principally in Algeria, Morocco, Spain, and America. Majorca and California oranges are the finest.

GRAPEFRUIT (*pamplemousse*) : November to March. This pale yellow fruit is like a very large orange with a more acid taste. Cut horizontally, make an incision between the pulp and the rind with a special knife, and remove the core. Separate each section with a knife; powder with fine sugar. Grapefruit is eaten with a spoon.

WATERMELON (*pastèque*) : August to November. Cultivated principally in the South of France and Italy. The pulp is very juicy, red, and rather bland. It contains many black seeds.

PEACH (*pêche*) : July to September. The peach is one of the best fruits of France; there are 2 principal types: the fuzzy peach with a rather soft pulp and the nectarine with a smooth skin and rather firm pulp. The favorite varieties come from Montreuil and Fréjus. Much of the fruit is raised in the eastern Pyrenees and the Rhone Valley.

WINTER CHERRY (*physalis*) : November to January. A very tart fruit especially used as a garnish. Grown in the region of Rennes.

PISTACHIO (*pistache*) : October-November. Imported from Turkey and Sicily. It is about the size of an olive and has a shell; its green meat has a very fine flavor. It is eaten like almonds and hazelnuts, and is especially used in pastrymaking.

PEAR (*poire*) : June to March. There are so many varieties of pears that it is impossible to list all of them here. The principal and best known are: the Williams or Bartlett (July-August), very fine and soft, the best of the summer pears; Louise-Bonne (end of September-October), very soft, usually small; Hardy butter (end of September-October), very fine; Doyenné de Comice (October-December), the best and most appreciated, known the whole world over; Passe-crassane (January-March), a very large, soft, tart fruit that keeps a long time. Let us also mention the Saint-Jean pear, of mediocre flavor; the July Doyenné, very flavorful; the Giffard butter; the Dr. Jules Gruyot, with a fine, juicy pulp; the English butter, very good, but not long-lasting.

APPLE (*pomme*) : September to April. There are 2 categories: eating apples and cider apples. The principal eating apples are: the large Alexander (September-October), a large, red, sweet, flavorful fruit grown on espaliers in the region around Paris; the Canadian russet (December-March), with a flavorful and crisp pulp; the white Calville, ivory-white, very fine and sweet, keeps well, grown on espaliers; the red Calville, with light-pink flesh and a delicate raspberrylike flavor; the russet, rather large, with crisp, flavorful flesh, keeps well; the queen of russets, large, round, etc.

PLUM (*prune*) : July to September. Cultivated in Europe. There are many varieties of plums, the best of which are the greengage (end of July), with a very sweet, flavorful pulp; the golden greengage (end of August) ; the violet greengage (mid-September) ; the mirabelle (see p. 679) ; the quetsche, used principally for compotes, jellies, and pastry; the Agen plum, violet pink in color (September), etc.

GRAPE (*raisin*) : July to October (hothouse: all year). Among the many varieties, here are the best for the table: the very popular fine-skinned *chasselas ;* the Thomery, of the same quality, which keeps until March; the Malaga, very large and sweet, from Spain; the white Muscat (October), with a very distinct flavor, good for both table and brandied preserves; the Colman: this black grape is very large, has a fine skin, and keeps very well; these are grown throughout the year in hothouses; the white date grape with a thick skin (July-August) ; the black hothouse Alicante (end of October-November) ; the black-skinned hothouse Frankenthal (October) ; the Saint-Janer from the Côte d'Azur (October-December), etc.

PROVINCIAL COOKING

PROVINCIAL COOKING

French cooking should be considered in its entirety, for not only the large cities have created its fame; every province has contributed specialities and local dishes to help establish its world-wide reputation. Countryside tours have provided the best propaganda for this culinary folklore. Thanks to touring and the car, one may lunch at a fine lodge in the Chevreuse Valley and dine at Saulieu or at Bourg-en-Bresse.

You will therefore find good provincial recipes in this book on the art of cooking—recipes mothers have religiously passed on to their daughters, just as they received them from their mothers and jealously guarded them.

We have grouped the local dishes by province, or at least the principal, best known, and most characteristic dishes of the territory.

The *potées:* each region of France has its own soup, called *potée,* and all include pretty much the same ingredients. We have highlighted a few of these to serve as a base: Auvergne, Burgundy, and Champagne *potées.*

Note: The recipes for each province are listed according to the order they are served in: soups, hors d'oeuvres, fish, meat, poultry, vegetables, pastry.

ALSACE

(Lower Rhine—Upper Rhine)

SOUP ALSACIENNE SOUPE À L'ALSACIENNE (M.)

Cook 1¼ lb. new sauerkraut in butter (in a tightly closed pot) after washing, pressing, blanching, and coarsely chopping it. Pour 2 qt. white consommé over it. Cook 45 min. Serve with long, slender French bread.

TROUT MOLLAU TRUITES À LA MOLLAU (S. F.)

Brown some small, sliced onions in good butter; add equal parts of white wine and water, salt, pepper, parsley, bay leaf, 1 clove, a little bouillon if possible. Let this court bouillon cook a few minutes before dropping in the brook trout, which cook very quickly. Place the trout on a platter, and baste them with very hot butter in which some bread crumbs have been toasted golden. Pour a little of the court bouillon over them and serve very hot.

BEEKENOHFE BEEKENOHFE (M.)

Cut equal parts of boned shoulder of pork and shoulder of mutton as for a stew. Put the cubed meat on a thick bed of thin-sliced potatoes in an earthenware casserole. Cover the meat with thin-sliced onions. Season with salt and pepper. Cover with another layer of sliced potatoes. Dot with bits of butter. Moisten with white Alsatian wine. Bring to a boil on the stove, cover, and finish cooking in the oven (preferably a baker's oven) 2 hr. Serve as is, in the same casserole.

GOOSE ALSACIENNE OIE À L'ALSACIENNE

See Goose, p. 430.

PULLET STRASBOURGEOISE POULARDE À LA STRASBOURGEOISE

See Pullets, p. 392.

PHEASANT ALSACIENNE FAISAN À L'ALSACIENNE (S. F.)

Take: 1 pheasant or 1 pheasant hen, 2 lb. raw sauerkraut, 1 lb. sausage without garlic, ¼ lb. lean bacon, 1 truffle. Wash the sauerkraut in tepid water, drain and press it. Brown 1 large sliced onion in a cocotte with 3 tbsp. goose fat; add the sauerkraut, salt, pepper, and cook slowly 3 hr.

Meanwhile, truss the pheasant, lard the breast with strips of pork fat, and brown it lightly. In the bottom of the cocotte put a layer of sauerkraut, the bacon cut in thin slices, the truffle cut in round slices and previously cooked in Madeira, and the pheasant. Cover with the rest of the sauerkraut; cook another 2 hr.

Before serving, heat the sliced sausage on top of the sauerkraut.

Serve this dish like Partridge with Cabbage (p. 469).

Note: The truffle may be omitted, but then the dish loses much of its finesse.

SAUERKRAUT ALSACIENNE CHOUCROUTE À L'ALSACIENNE (S. F.) *(For 6 persons)*

Take 3 lb. Alsatian sauerkraut and wash it in plenty of water. Press it well and sprinkle it with a pinch of cumin.

Put into an earthenware casserole 1 pt. water, ½ pt. white Alsatian or Burgundy wine, 1 fresh calf's foot, 1 large carrot. Add the sauerkraut and cook together 1 hr. Next, put on top ½ lb. smoked pork fat and a Montbéliard sausage; cook another hour at low heat. A few minutes before serving, add a few small Vienna sausages or frankfurters and reheat.

Separately: (1) Cook smoked shoulder of pork, changing the water twice. (2) Boil potatoes in the jackets. Serve all together (except for the calf's foot and carrot, which should be removed from the sauerkraut), and drink a white Alsatian or Burgundy wine with it.

Note: Before preparing it, taste the raw sauerkraut, which should tell you how much to wash it and the right amount of white wine to add.

STRASBOURG PÂTÉ DE FOIE GRAS PÂTÉ DE FOIE GRAS DE STRASBOURG

See Mixed Entrees, p. 534.

LIVER KNEPFEN KNEPFEN AU FOIE (S. F.) (*For 4 persons*)

7 oz. calf's liver. Chop the liver after removing the membrane and veins. When it has been chopped to a pulp, add bread soaked in milk and squeezed dry, chopped parsley and shallots, salt, pepper, and 2 whole eggs. Mix well, adding a little flour. Drop this mixture by the spoonful into boiling water to poach it. When the knepfen are cooked (about 20 min.), drain and let them cool. Then fry them in very hot deep oil. Sprinkle with chopped parsley and serve. (Very old Alsatian recipe.)

POTATO KNEPFEN KNEPFEN AUX POMMES DE TERRE (S. F.)

Cook 5 or 6 large potatoes, mash them well, mix that purée with an equal weight of flour; blend in 4 or 5 eggs, a little salt, and make into a fairly thick paste by adding a little milk from time to time. Bring some water to a boil, then drop in spoonfuls of the paste about the size of a walnut, keeping the water at a boil. The balls are properly cooked when they rise to the surface of the water. Drain them and brown in butter in a pan. Knepfen are very popular and may be served alone or with a roast, a daube, or a blanquette.

PFLÜTTEN PFLÜTTEN (S. F.) (*For 6 persons*)

Mash 1½ lb. potatoes. Thin with 1 pt. milk until almost liquid, and salt to taste. Bring to a boil, taking care to stir the composition to keep it from sticking. Sprinkle in ¼ lb. fine semolina and continue stirring until the semolina is cooked. The mixture should have the consistency of gruel. Remove from the fire and mix in 2 whole eggs. Pour onto a platter large enough so that the paste will not be much more than 1 in. thick. Let stand until the next day.

When ready to use, put ⅛ lb. butter into a frying pan and, when it is hot, lay in squares of the paste. (These should be about ¾ in. square.) Cook both sides until golden brown. These delicious pflütten may be served with prune compote or salad. They also make a fine garnish around a platter of sliced roast beef.

ONION TART ALSACIENNE TARTE AUX OIGNONS À L'ALSACIENNE (S. F.)

Line a square tart pan with ordinary Pie Paste (p. 545). Peel and chop 2 lb. onions and cook them with just enough water (almost 1 glass) to keep them from burning.

When they are cooked, add a good piece of butter and leave on the fire a few more minutes. Remove from the stove and add enough flour to bind them, then salt, pepper, 2 beaten eggs, and 1 tbsp. cream, to make a rather thick mush. Spread this onion mixture in the pie crust, pour a few tbsp. cream over it, and bake in the oven until brown.

BIREWEKA (PEAR LOAF) PAIN DE POIRES (S. F.)

Take 1 lb. dried pears. After removing the stems and seeds, soak them in water overnight. The next day cook them in plenty of water.

Also take: ½ lb. pitted prunes, also soaked overnight and heated; 10 oz. figs cut in half, ¼ lb. pitted dates cut in half, ¼ lb. hazelnuts cut in half, 10 oz. walnuts, ¼ lb. Malaga grapes (seeded, macerated in red wine or pear juice, and cooked a few minutes), 1 oz. candied citron, 1 oz. each of candied lemon and orange peel, and 1 oz. candied angelica, all diced.

Mix with 6 oz. powdered sugar, ⅓ oz. green anise, washed and crushed fine, ½ tsp. powdered cinnamon, ¼ tsp. powdered clove, 1 small glass kirsch, and 1 small glass rum, and several scraps of candied fruits melted over the fire. Mix well. The day before preparing the recipe, make a paste of ½ lb. flour, pear juice, and ⅙ oz. yeast, and let it rise overnight.

The next day, mix all together (with the fruits mixed in advance), except the nuts, which should be added last. Put this paste on a floured baking board, flour your hands, and shape it into 2 or 3 long, narrow loaves. Sprinkle with chopped almonds, place on buttered, floured baking sheets, and bake 1¼–1½ hr.

PRETZELS BRETZELS

See Pastry, p. 587.

KUGELHOFF KUGELHOFF

See Pastry, p. 571.

SCHAUKELE SCHAUKELE (S. F.)

Proportions: 3 eggs, 1 lb. sugar, ½ lb. crushed almonds, and 2 lb. flour.

Beat the sugar and eggs together well, then add the almonds, flour, and a little grated lemon peel. The paste should be very smooth. Mold it in the shape of cigars and fry in deep fat.

SCKENKELEES SCKENKELEES (S. F.)

Proportions: 2 oz. butter, 3 eggs, 2½ oz. crushed almonds, cinnamon, grated lemon peel, ½ lb. powdered sugar, 2 tbsp. kirsch, and 1 lb. flour.

Mix the eggs, flour, and sugar into a very smooth paste. Add the melted butter, then the lemon peel, cinnamon, kirsch, and crushed almonds. Mix well together. Roll out the paste and cut it into pieces the size of a finger and not too thick; fry them in very hot oil. Drain carefully on a rack and powder with confectioners' sugar. This kind of Alsatian pastry may be kept a long time in tins.

ANGOUMOIS

(CHARENTE)

CALF'S HEAD GROSSE NOUNOU TÊTE DE VEAU GROSSE NOUNOU (S. F.)

Bone a calf's head, spread it out, and fill it with a forcemeat made with ¾ lb. neck of pork, ½ lb. veal, 1 egg, mushrooms, truffles, salt, pepper, spices (do not be afraid to season highly). Roll the head and sew it carefully to keep in the stuffing. Cook it 5 hr. in water containing the bones removed from the head, vegetables for a pot-au-feu, a bay leaf, and 1 onion.

When it is cooked, remove it from the cooking broth. Make a roux (p. 136), moisten it with the cooking liquid and a finger of cognac; add a little tomato purée, truffles, small pieces of ham, and olives, and cook very slowly. A few minutes before serving, add the calf's brains (cooked in advance and cut into pieces) and the calf's head cut into quarters. This calf's head tastes even better when reheated.

ANJOU

(MAINE-ET-LOIRE)

PIKE WITH WHITE BUTTER SAUCE BROCHET AU BEURRE BLANC (M.)

The towns of Nantes and Angers both pretend to hold the secret of preparing white butter. Connoisseurs have long argued the respective merits of these recipes. Some insist that the white butter prepared in Anjou is the best, while others refuse to recognize any but that of Nantes. This white butter is served not only with pike. In Anjou and Brittany it is also served with various other fish, notably with shad from the Loire, whose delicate flavor harmonizes admirably with this sauce.

Cooking the fish: Prepare a court bouillon made with white wine from the Loire Valley, water, a little wine vinegar, thin-sliced carrots and onions, parsley, thyme, bay leaf, and 1 or 2 cloves of garlic (see p. 277). Season with salt and ground pepper. Boil the court bouillon 25 min. Strain it; let cool until tepid. Place the cleaned, washed pike on a rack in a fish kettle and pour the court bouillon over it. Bring to a boil over a hot fire. As soon as it comes to a boil, lower the flame, cover, and poach slowly 25–30 min., depending on the size of the fish.

White Butter Sauce: Put 2 tbsp. finely chopped shallots, 4½ oz. vinegar, salt, and freshly ground pepper into a small saucepan. Reduce by ¾. Thicken by adding, bit by bit, while mixing well with a wire whisk or spoon, some very fine butter, about 2½ oz. per person. If the mixture is prepared properly, it should be very white and a little foamy.

Serving the fish: Drain the pike. Place it on a large, long platter. Split it lengthwise with a fish knife, remove the fillets, and take out the spine in 1 piece. Put the fillets back into place and cover the fish with the White Butter Sauce, to which a good pinch of chopped parsley should be added just before using.

ROAST BURBOT WITH CURRY LOTTE RÔTIE AU KARI (S. F.)

Scale a fine burbot and put it into the oven with a little water, a little white wine, and a piece of butter. Cook 2 qt. mussels to open them, and keep them hot. Put a good piece of butter into a saucepan and add ½ lb. rice; stir on the fire and season with 2 heaping tsp. curry and a dash of cayenne. Cover with some good gravy, put the lid on the pan, and cook slowly ½ hr. Place the burbot on a platter, surround it with the rice and mussels, and decorate with slices of lemon.

For the sauce: Melt a piece of butter, mix in 1 tbsp. flour, and add the burbot cooking liquid and a little of the mussel cooking liquid. Bind the sauce with 2 egg yolks and finish with a good piece of butter and some lemon juice. Cover the fish with the sauce or serve it in a sauceboat.

POILLETTES POILLETTES (S. F.)

Take a 10-lb. side of pork, preferably fresh, containing the bacon, with as much fat as meat on the ribs. Remove the rind, bone the meat, and cut the meat and fat into 1-in cubes. Put meat and fat into a caldron or cocotte or earthenware pot. Add 3 glasses water, 7 oz. coarse salt, ½ tsp. ground pepper, and, according to taste, a pinch of spices (not indispensable). Bring to a boil and let simmer 6 hr. uncovered, stirring from time to time to prevent the meat from sticking to the pot.

At the end of this time, remove the bones and rind. Mash the remainder with a pestle and place in small jars; after cooling, cover with a good layer of fat. Made this way, it will keep 5–6 months.

MOTHER GOOSE OF LOWER MAINE'S RILLETTES RILLETTES DE LA MÈRE L'OIE DU BAS-MAINE (S. F.)

Better make these rillettes from December on. Cut ½ goose or 1 whole goose into pieces, removing the giblets and liver. Weigh these pieces and take an equal weight of pork, lean and fat, also cut into small pieces. Put 1 glass water into a large pot, then the goose, the pork, a *bouquet garni,* salt and pepper, 1 carrot and 1 small onion, both chopped fine. Cook 8 hr. at low heat and stir from time to time. After this long period of cooking, the bones are loosened from the meat and are easily removed (make sure there are no bone splinters in the meat).

Heat some small stoneware pots glazed on the inside in the oven, then pour the cooked mixture into them. In cooling, the fat will rise to the surface, but the next day, nevertheless, you must cover it with some good lard. Cover with sulphurized paper and keep in a cool, dry place.

ARTOIS

(PAS-DE-CALAIS)

STUFFED BEEFSTEAKS BOULONNAISE BIFTECKS FARCIS À LA BOULONNAISE (S. F.) (*For 6 persons*)

6 slices of sirloin of beef, ¼ lb. sausage meat, 1 glass bouillon, ½ glass red wine, 1⅓ oz. butter, 1 tbsp. tomato purée, chopped parsley and shallot, salt and pepper.

Cut the beef into very thin slices. Mix the chopped parsley and shallot with the sausage meat. Spread a layer of this forcemeat on each slice of beef, roll it, and tie with a string. Heat the butter in a pan and brown the steaks 20 min. on a low fire. When they are browned, pour in the bouillon, wine, and tomato purée. Cover the pan and cook slowly 1½ hr.

WILD DUCK CABIN STYLE CANARD SAUVAGE DE HUTTE (S. F.)

Roast a wild duck, preferably a small black pintail, with the insides and coagulated blood removed. Mix the insides with parsley, shallots, garlic, all chopped very fine, and 1 small glass Madeira; make a sort of salmis of this and add the juice of 1 orange to it. When the duck is roasted, prick it with a fork and pour the orange salmis over it.

MINING-COUNTRY CRÊPES or **PANCAKES** CRÊPES DES PAYS MINIERS (S. F.)

Mix 1 lb. flour with 10 egg yolks and 1 qt. warm milk, 2 tbsp. powdered sugar, 2 tbsp. cognac or rum, and a little salt. Brown an egg-sized piece of butter and add it to the paste with 1 oz. yeast dissolved in a little beer. Beat the egg whites until stiff, fold them into the batter, and let rise a few hours in a warm place.

Melt a little butter in a frying pan, then pour in some batter, spreading it out so that the crêpe will be as thin as possible. As each crêpe is made, sprinkle it with confectioners' or brown sugar. (Grease the pan with lard after each pancake.)

AUNIS AND SAINTONGE

(CHARENTE-MARITIME)

EELS CHARENTAISE ANGUILLES CHARENTAISES (S. F.)

Put garlic, shallots, and a little onion, all cut in tiny pieces, into a pan. Brown them in butter, then add flour and let it brown slightly. Add water and white wine (1 part wine to 3 parts water), salt, pepper, and cook the sauce 20 min. Add skinned, cleaned slices of eel, 1 tsp. sugar, and boil gently 20 min.

FISH STEW CHARENTAISE CHAUDRÉE CHARENTAISE (S. F.) (*For 6 persons*)

The main stipulation for success: use very fresh fish.

Clean and gut 2 fine soles, 1 salt-water eel, 2 small skates, 4 or 5 small squid or cuttlefish. Remove the black skin from the soles, the skin of the skates, the "bone" and pocket containing the black liquid from the squid. Cut each sole crosswise into 2 or 3 pieces, the eel in sections, and the small skates in 2 lengthwise.

Begin by cleaning the squid, so that you can start them cooking in enough salted water to cover, while preparing the other fish, for they take longer to cook. When the fish are ready and cut into pieces, put 15 peeled garlic cloves and a *bouquet garni* (parsley, thyme, bay leaf) into the bottom of a large pot. Place the fish in layers and season each layer well with salt and pepper. When this is done, pour in enough white wine until the top layer is almost covered. Cover the pot and set it on the stove. When it begins to boil, add the almost cooked and drained squid. Cook about ½ hr. This should make a good deal of broth. When the fish have cooked, pour the stew into a deep dish and add, when serving, ¼ lb. good fresh butter.

MUSSELS IN SAUCE AUNIS STYLE MOUCLADE DE L'AUNIS (S. F.)

Scrape and wash some fine mussels and open them raw, leaving all the meat in 1 shell. Lightly brown some chopped onions in butter, add some cream, and bind with egg yolks, using suitable proportions for the number of mussels. Season with a little saffron or curry. Drop the mussels left in their shells into this sauce and cook 5 min. Serve very hot.

TRIPE SAINTONGEAISE TRIPES À LA SAINTONGEAISE (S. F.)

Proportions: For 4 lb. tripe and calf's feet: 2 fine leeks, 1 lb. carrots, 7 oz.

turnips, a few stalks of celery, mushrooms, 20 small onions, clove of garlic, salt, pepper, spices, nutmeg, clove, a *bouquet garni.*

Split and cut up the calf's feet, cut the tripe, and chop the vegetables. Put a layer of tripe and calf's feet into a pot, then a layer of vegetables, seasoning, then another layer of tripe, a layer of vegetables, seasoning, etc., until all the ingredients have been used. Pour in ⅔ bouillon to ⅓ white wine until covered. Bring to a boil and simmer 16–18 hr. Skim off the fat and serve on hot plates.

SAINTONGE CORN-MEAL CAKES WITH JAM CRUCHADE DE SAINTONGE AUX CONFITURES (S. F.)

Heat 1 qt. water in a large pan with 1½ oz. powdered sugar and a little salt. When the water begins to boil, sprinkle in 1 lb. very fine corn meal, stirring constantly with a wooden spoon. When the mush is thick and cooked, flavor it with rum. Spread it out very thin on a floured baking board, let cool, then cut into triangles and fry in very hot deep fat. When the triangles are browned on both sides, drain them and spread with orange marmalade, apricot jam, or currant jelly.

AUVERGNE

(CANTAL—PUY-DE-DÔME)

AUVERGNE POTÉE POTÉE À L'AUVERGNATE (M.) (*For 8–10 persons*)

Meats: 1 pickled pig's head cut into 4 pieces, 2 lb. bacon, 1 lb. ham knuckle, a 1-lb. cervelat. *Vegetables:* 10 oz. carrots, 7 oz. turnips, 3½ oz. onions, 3½ oz. leeks, 2½ oz. celery, all quartered, 1 green cabbage (quartered and blanched), 1 pt. half-cooked navy beans, 8 large quartered potatoes, 2 crushed cloves of garlic, *bouquet garni. Liquid:* 4 qt. water (or white consommé). *Seasoning:* supplied by the pickled pork and bacon.

Preparation: Put the pig's head, bacon, and ham into a large pot or marmite. Cover with the water, bring to a boil, and skim. Add the carrots, turnips, leeks, celery, crushed garlic, and *bouquet garni.* Cook 1 hr. Add the cabbage (blanched, cooled, and pressed) and the half-cooked beans. Cover and cook 1½ hr. Then add the potatoes and cervelat and simmer 40 min. to finish cooking. If needed, add a little hot water while cooking.

To serve: Drain the pork and other meats. Place them on a large platter and surround with ⅔ the vegetables arranged in alternating heaps. Serve the rest of the *potée* in a tureen with thin slices of bread dried in the oven in the soup or separate.

Note: To make the dish even more savory, add a piece of beef blade to the other meats. Fresh pork rind cut in small squares can also be added.

STOFINADO STOFINADO (S. F.)

Stofinado is a favorite dish in the canton of Maurs (Cantal). It is made from stockfish—salt cod with a strong, penetrating odor. Soak the cod at least 24 hr.

before using. If you can, leave it under running water during this time. When the fish has been well soaked, cut it into very thin slices and put them into a pan containing boiling walnut oil. Keep stirring, always in the same direction, until the oil becomes a sort of white purée, then break some eggs into the pan and add a bowl of fresh cream. Season highly with garlic and parsley and serve very hot.

TURKEY BALLOTTINE STUFFED WITH FOIE GRAS BALLOTTINE DE DINDE FOURRÉE AU FOIE GRAS (S. F.)

Bone a turkey hen the usual way, taking care to leave no meat on the carcass; remove all the tendons from the meat. Open the fowl out, skin side down; spread with a layer of fine pork forcemeat, prepared as for *pâtés*, and on this lay a whole *foie gras* studded with brushed, peeled truffles, then a new layer of forcemeat.

Close the turkey by bringing the outer edges of the skin together and sewing securely. Wrap it in a white linen cloth and sew it tightly. Cook slowly in chicken bouillon, figuring on a minimum of 20 min. per lb. After cooking, remove from the bouillon and let cool. Do not remove the cloth until completely cold.

Prepare a jelly with chicken feet, giblets, calf's foot, onions, carrots, and *bouquet garni.* Cook for a long time at low heat. Clarify it and, when it is cold and set, use it to garnish the turkey. When carefully prepared, this dish is exquisite.

COCK IN WINE COQ AU VIN (A. C.)

Cut up a young cock and save the blood, setting it aside with a finger of vinegar. Brown the pieces in a casserole with butter and a few strips of bacon; add 12 small onions and 12 mushrooms. Add 1 whole clove of garlic or 2 crushed, pour over 1 glass brandy and set it aflame, then add 1 pt. good red wine, salt, pepper, and *bouquet garni.* Cook covered, then bind the sauce with the blood. Just bring to a boil once to thicken, then pour into a deep dish and garnish with grilled, buttered bread croutons.

POUNTI or POUNTARI POUNTI OR POUNTARI (S. F.)

This is one of the favorite dishes of the Auvergne countryside. First make a mincemeat of pork fat, onions, parsley, and chard, chopping very fine until it has a pastelike consistency. Salt and pepper. Mix in enough milk, flour, and eggs for the amount of Pounti desired and, when smoothly blended, add the mincemeat. Pour this paste into a cocotte and place in the oven; cook about 1 hr. The Pounti is cooked when covered with a crisp, golden crust. It is eaten hot or cold. Leftovers cut in slices and pan-fried in butter make a delicious entree.

ALIGOT ALIGOT (S. F.)

Cook some potatoes in salted water, press them through a sieve, leave the purée on the stove, and blend in a piece of fresh butter, a bowl of cream, and a large amount of *tome grasse.* (*Tome grasse* is made in winter. It is a special skimmed-milk cheese from Planèze. Since it dries poorly in winter, it stays fatty and becomes runny. It should not be confused with *tome* used in making *truffade.*)

Stir until very smooth and serve very hot. In the canton of Chaudesaigues (Cantal), the land of Aligot, it is sometimes served powdered with sugar, basted with rum, and flaming.

BOURRIOLS BOURRIOLS (S. F.)

Buy 1 lb. paste at the baker's. Thin it with a bowl of warm milk to make a thin paste. Add a little buckwheat flour and let stand about 1½ hr. to rise. Lightly brush a small frying pan with oil, pour a ladleful of paste into the cold pan, set it over a hot fire, and brown 1 side only. Before cooking a second Bourriol, cool the pan by dipping the bottom in cold water. Bourriols should be very thin and are delicious eaten hot, spread with fresh butter or jam. In Auvergne, Bourriols are eaten instead of bread.

CADET MATTHEW OF AUVERGNE CADET MATHIEU AUVERGNAT (S. F.)

This is a thick mush of flour and milk flavored with vanilla or orange-flower water and bound with a few egg yolks. When cold, it is spread in a pie crust. A thick layer of thinly sliced raw apples is laid on top. These are sugared and covered with a pie crust top, with a large hole pierced in the center and a few small holes here and there to keep bubbles from forming. It is brushed with beaten egg and baked. This Cadet Matthew is still eaten in Auvergne.

BÉARN

(BASSES-PYRÉNÉES)

GARBURE GARBURE (S. F.)

Garbure is the common name for any vegetable soup cooked with pork or goose fat or chopped bacon and thin slices of bread. But the classic Garbure should consist of the vegetables cooked with a potted meat in fat (pork, duck, goose, turkey, or chicken) or at least with a salted meat: ham, ribs, sausage, or neck of pork. Here are a few recipes for Garbure.

(1) Start the water boiling in an enamel pot (metal gives an unpleasant taste). When the water boils, drop in some peeled potatoes cut into large pieces and other fresh vegetables in season such as peas, green beans, broad beans. Salt and pepper, using red pimento if you have no pepper; season further with garlic, branch of thyme, parsley, or marjoram, all fresh. Let cook, keeping the water at a boil.

Have ready some tender green cabbages shredded fine after the outer leaves are removed. When the other vegetables are cooked, add the cabbages and cover the pot to keep the cabbages green; when the cabbages have begun to cook (about ½ hr. before serving), plunge a piece of potted meat with the fat adhering to it into the pot.

If pork is used, a little goose fat added will lend more finesse to the Garbure. Lay some thin slices of brown bread in the tureen and pour the boiling soup over them. The piece of meat should be on top.

(2) A good Garbure can be made without potted meat, but the meat flavor is still needed. In this case, put a knuckle of ham, or a slice of fat ham, or some garlic sausage into a pot of cold water. Add twice as much chopped bacon. White or white-heart cabbage may be used instead of green. If green is preferred, it is only because white cabbage has only recently come into use.

(3) For an everyday Garbure (since it isn't practical to cook a piece of potted meat every day), the soup vegetables may be enriched with salt pork, cured bacon, ham fat, or pork fat crushed with garlic. In winter, slices of pink turnip or grilled chestnuts may be added to the cabbage; dry beans should be precooked and the water thrown away, for if it is added to the soup, it will spoil the flavor.

The meat cooked in the soup should be served separately, as for pot-au-feu, either with some vegetables or alone.

GALLIMAUFRY or HODGEPODGE BAYONNAISE GALIMAFRÉE À LA BAYONNAISE (S. F.)

Cut a very thick slice of raw Bayonne ham and brown it in a cocotte with a little lard. Add 4 artichokes, a few new onions and carrots, broad beans, green beans, and 2 sweet peppers. After cooking ½ hr., add 1 glass white wine; cook at low heat 1 hr. Then add the separated leaves of 3 small heads of lettuce and ½ lb. tomatoes; salt lightly, for the ham is already salty. Cook another hour and serve.

SANGUÈTE SANGUÈTE (M.)

This dish is a specialty of Montanerez and Vic-Bilh.

Take the blood of some cooked veal, lean of calf's jowl, tripe, and spleen, all boiled in advance in water seasoned with salt and pepper. Dice and brown in a cocotte. Add 1 finely chopped onion and stir. Do not let the onion burn. When the onion is cooked, add chopped garlic and parsley. Stir and cook a moment more. Sprinkle with 2 tbsp. flour, stir, and mix well. Pour in gradually, continuing to stir, 1 cup water or bouillon; let simmer ½ hr. Add gherkins or capers 15 min. before serving. (Simin Palay, *La Cuisine en Béarn.*)

CABBAGE GRATIN GRATIN DE CHOUX (S. F.)

Boil the leaves of a winter white-heart cabbage in a pot of water with salt and pepper. Grind some leftover meat—boiled beef or other meat, or roast chicken. Brown some onion in butter and add the ground meat. Cook a few moments at low heat, then add 2 or 3 tbsp. tomato purée. Salt and pepper to taste.

When the cabbage is sufficiently cooked, drain it well and chop coarsely; mix it with the ground meat, then, after testing the seasoning, put the mixture into a baking dish. Sprinkle with bread crumbs and brown in the oven. A delicious and economical dish.

BASQUE PEPPER OMELET PIPERADE BASQUAISE (Fa.)

Brown 2 or 3 seeded, quartered tomatoes; add 2 grilled yellow or green sweet peppers (seeded and sliced thin). When tomatoes and peppers are cooked, add them to the eggs and make an omelet the usual way, but in oil (see p. 270). The omelet may be filled with the peppers and tomatoes instead of being mixed with them.

CORN-MEAL CAKES BÉARNAIS ESCOTONS BÉARNAIS (Fa.)

Make a very thick corn-meal mush with water and a little salt; cook 20 min., constantly stirring to avoid lumps. Pour onto a buttered platter, spreading it out until ⅔ in. thick, and let cool. Then cut into pieces, dredge with flour, and fry in fat or butter. Sprinkle with sugar and serve very hot.

BERRY

(CHER—INDRE)

CHICKEN IN BLOOD BERRICHONNE POULET AU SANG À LA BERRICHONNE (S. F.)

Kill a young chicken. Keep the blood and add a small glass of wine vinegar to it. Cut the chicken into pieces and sauté them in butter; add 3 medium-sized, quartered onions and brown with the chicken. Sprinkle in 1 tbsp. flour; let brown; add a crushed clove of garlic; pour in some water and 1 glass good white wine; add a *bouquet garni* (parsley, ½ bay leaf, sprig of thyme, and stalk of celery). Cook slowly. When cooked, lower the flame as much as possible and gradually add the blood, stirring constantly. Test the seasoning and do not let the dish boil again, or the sauce will turn.

BERRY PIE or **EASTER PIE** PÂTÉ DE BERRY OR PÂTÉ DE PÂQUES (S. F.)

Prepare a Short Paste (p. 545), using 1 lb. flour, 10 oz. butter, ¾ cup water, 1 tsp. salt, 2 tbsp. sugar. Hard-boil 6 eggs, cut them in 2 lengthwise, salt and pepper lightly. Have ready 1¼ lb. fine sausage meat. Roll out your paste until it is as thick as your little finger, giving it a rectangular shape and cutting off the angles. Place ½ the sausage meat in the center of the crust, letting it cover ⅓ of the crust. Lay the egg halves on top, side by side, with the cut side down. Cover them with the rest of the sausage meat and close the paste by folding over the sides and sealing them together lengthwise on top. With scissors, cut openings in the top of the crust about ⅜ in. apart. Take the small pieces of paste cut from the openings and stick them on the sides of the crust. Do the same at both ends to seal the paste. Brush with beaten egg and bake 1½ hr. in a hot oven. This pie should be served cold as an entree.

MUSHROOM PIE SOLOGNOTTE PÂTÉ DE CÈPES À LA SOLOGNOTTE (S. F.)

Line a tart or pie pan with Short Paste (p. 545). Lightly grill some large mushroom caps (cepes) to remove the water, then wipe them dry.

Separately, take the mushroom stems, chop them, and add a little Bayonne ham. Heat some butter in a frying pan, add some finely chopped onion and garlic and the mushroom mincemeat; brown, sprinkle with flour, pour in a little bouillon, and add 1 tbsp. butter. This forcemeat should have a thick consistency.

Lay a slice of uncooked Bayonne ham as wide as the pan on the bottom crust of the pie, spread a layer of forcemeat on top, place the mushroom caps on the forcemeat, spread another layer of forcemeat, then another slice of ham, mushrooms, and so on, until the pie is filled. Cover with the top crust and make a little cardboard chimney in the center through which to pour in some good gravy after cooking. Bake about 3/4 hr. and serve hot.

MATAFAN MATAFAN (M.)

Put 3½ oz. flour, 3½ oz. sugar, and a pinch of salt into a mixing bowl. Mix with 4 beaten eggs, added bit by bit, and 6 oz. milk, making a paste. Heat 2 oz. butter in a pan large enough so that the paste, when spread out, is 2/3 in. thick in the bottom. Pour the paste into the pan and keep over a very low fire to harden it and color it underneath, then put it into the oven to harden the top and make it easy to turn over. Brown the bottom and slide it onto a plate. Spread with rum butter, currant jelly, or marmalade.

Note: Matafan should not be compared to an omelet; it is simply a thick pancake.

APPLES BERRICHONNE POMMES À LA BERRICHONNE (S. F.)

Make a very thick sugar sirup. Drop in some quartered apples. (The apples must be firm enough not to turn into purée.) Simmer very gently 3–4 hr. The apples should become lightly candied, without crushing. After cooking 4 hr., pour the apples into a plain buttered mold. When they are almost cold, add 1 large wineglass good rum. Prick the apples with a fork so that they will soak up the rum.

The next day, unmold the apples onto a fruit dish. Stick preserved fruits on the top and cover with a very thick vanilla English Cream (p. 550).

BOURBONNAIS

(Allier)

MEURETTE OF YOUNG RABBIT BOURBONNAISE MEURETTE DE LAPEREAU BOURBONNAISE (S. F.)

Skin and clean a young rabbit; cut it into pieces as for a stew.

Heat 3½ oz. butter in a sautéing pan, add 12 small white onions, and brown them. Put the rabbit pieces into the pan, salt, pepper, cover, and cook slowly until the meat is lightly browned. Sprinkle with 1 tbsp. flour; cook without browning too much, then pour in 2 glasses dry white wine and 1 wineglass water; add a *bouquet garni,* bring to a boil, and cook covered. Mix in a bowl 2 egg yolks, 1 wineglass fresh cream, 5 or 6 small pieces of fresh butter, juice of ½ lemon. When the rabbit is cooked, take the pan off the fire, and add the contents of the mixing bowl. Serve in a deep dish, sprinkled with chopped parsley, and surrounded with croutons fried in butter.

Since this dish must be made carefully, it is better to have 2 rabbits and use only the saddles and legs in the fricassee. The smaller pieces can be used in a stew.

CHICKEN SAUTÉ BOURBONNAIS POULET SAUTÉ BOURBONNAIS (S. F.)

Take a tender young chicken raised in Bourbonnais. Drain the blood and add a drop of vinegar to it. (This may be done the preceding day.) Cut up the chicken for sautéing, brown it in butter, salt and pepper to taste, sprinkle with flour, let cook a few moments, then pour in equal parts of red wine and veal stock; add a *bouquet garni.* Bring to a boil, cover, and cook slowly.

Glaze some small onions and sauté some small strips of bacon in butter. When the chicken is cooked, add the onions and bacon; bind the sauce with the blood, and add a little butter. Test the seasoning. Serve the chicken surrounded with fried heart-shaped croutons.

POTATO PANCAKE MORVANDELLE TOURTIÈRE MORVANDELLE (S. F.)

Grate 6 large raw potatoes into a bowl, add ¼ lb. grated Gruyère cheese and 3 eggs, pour in 1 small glass rum, season with a little salt, and mix together well, sprinkling with a pinch of flour. Put some oil, fat, or even small pieces of pork fat into a frying pan the size of a plate. When the oil or fat is very hot, pour in a ladleful of the potato paste or enough to make a rather thick pancake. Cover and, after 2 or 3 min., turn to brown the other side.

To keep the pancake from sticking to the bottom of the pan, raise the edges with a fork while tilting the pan; repeat this operation as long as there is any liquid paste.

BURGUNDY

(AIN—CÔTE-D'OR—SAÔNE-ET-LOIRE—YONNE)

BURGUNDY POTÉE POTÉE À LA BOURGUIGNONNE (M.) (*For 8–10 persons*)

Meats: 2 lb. salt pork back, 1 lb. fresh pork knuckle, 1 lb. garlic cervelat. *Vegetables:* 10 oz. carrots, 8 oz. turnips, 4 oz. leeks, 4 oz. onions, all quartered, 1 medium-sized green cabbage (blanched), 8 quartered potatoes. *Liquid:* 4 qt. water (or white consommé).

Preparation: Put all the meat ingredients into an earthenware pot or marmite, except the sausage, which should be added 30 min. before serving. Cover with water, bring to a boil, and skim. Add all the vegetables, except the potatoes. Simmer 3½ hr. Add the sausage and potatoes ½ hr. before serving.

Serving: Pour the broth into a soup tureen containing household bread cut into thin slices. Add part of the vegetables from the soup pot. Serve the meats separately, with the rest of the vegetables heaped in alternate piles.

GOUGÈRE GOUGÈRE (S. F.)

Gougère is the traditional cake of Lower Burgundy. It is also made in the Aube district.

Ingredients: 10 oz. water, ½ lb. Gruyère cheese, ½ lb. sifted flour, ¼ lb. butter, 5 eggs.

Put the water, a pinch of salt, and the butter into a pan and bring to a boil.

When it starts to boil, remove from the fire and add the flour. Mix well with a wooden spoon. Replace on the fire, continuing to stir to keep the paste from sticking. Cook until almost dry, then remove from the fire. Break 1 egg into the pan and stir. When it is well blended in, add another, and so on.

Dice the Gruyère cheese fine and mix it into the paste, taking care to save about 2 tbsp. cheese. Place 1 tbsp. paste at a time in a buttered baking pan to form a ring (like a Brioche ring, p. 565). Brush the top with beaten egg, sprinkle with the rest of the Gruyère cheese, and bake in a medium-hot oven.

This cake should be eaten cold and is excellent with Burgundy wines.

BURGUNDY TART TOURTE BOURGUIGNONNE (S. F.)

At least 2 hr. in advance, prepare a paste with 1½ lb. flour, ¾ lb. butter, ½ oz. salt, and about 12 oz. water. Let stand in a cool place.

Dice 1 lb. fresh pork fat and 1 lb. lean veal. Chop them and add salt, pepper, spices, 2 crushed cloves of garlic, 1 chopped onion, 1 tbsp. chopped parsley, and 1 small glass cognac. This mincemeat does not have to be very fine. Choose a baking pan large enough to hold the tart. Divide the paste into 2 equal parts. Roll 1 part out into a crust, place it in the pan, and fill it with the mincemeat rolled into balls the size of a small egg, leaving a little space between each. Lightly moisten the edges of the crust. Roll out the other part of the paste, place it over the meat balls, seal the 2 crusts together, and pinch the edges all around. Brush with beaten egg, streak with a fork, cut a hole in the center to let the steam escape, and bake about ¾ hr. in a medium oven.

This is one of the traditional dishes of Burgundy. In Lower Burgundy especially, it always used to be included on the menu for marriage and patron-saint's day feasts. It may be eaten hot or cold.

MATELOTE OF EEL BOURGUIGNONNE MATELOTE D'ANGUILLE À LA BOURGUIGNONNE

See Fish, p. 306.

SUPRÊME OF PIKE DIJONNAISE SUPRÊME DE BROCHET DIJONNAISE (C. and R.)

Remove the fillets, without bones, from a fine pike, and then remove the skin. Stud them with pork fat as you would a beef fillet and let the fillets marinate 1–2 days at most with finely chopped shallots, 2 or 3 small *bouquets garnis* (parsley, thyme, bay leaf), salt, pepper, cognac, Madeira, and white wine.

Heavily butter a baking dish, lay in the fillets, surround them with sliced mushrooms, pour in the marinade and seasoning, and cook about 20 min. in a rather hot oven, basting frequently. The fillets should be golden brown. Add 2 tbsp. fresh cream and 2 or 3 pieces of butter. Serve hot.

MORVAN CARP or TENCH AU GRATIN CARPES OU TANCHES GRATINÉES DU MORVAN (S. F.)

Stuff the fish with Choux Paste (p. 548) mixed with diced Gruyère cheese, and place in a baking dish. Make some Gnocchi (p. 548) with this same paste and place them along with mushrooms as a garnish around the fish. Season with salt and pepper, and pour in some white wine and a little Madeira. Cover the fish with a light layer of bread crumbs dotted with bits of butter.

Bake in a medium oven ½ hr. or more, depending on the size of the fish. It is better to cook the fish slowly at moderate heat than too fast in a hot oven.

BURGUNDY MEURETTE MEURETTE DE BOURGOGNE (S. F.)

Meurette is the national dish of Burgundy. To prepare it, take 1 small eel, 1 small pike or pickerel, 1 small carp, and 2 trout. All these fish should be alive until ready to use, and then cleaned and cut into slices.

Bring 1 qt. wine to a boil in an earthenware casserole; put in the slices of fish, along with 1 onion and a bouquet of parsley enclosing ½ bay leaf, a few cloves, and 4 crushed cloves of garlic. The fish should be barely covered by the wine. Bring to a quick boil over a hot fire, add 2 small glasses of cognac, and set aflame. Cook the fish ¼ hr., then lower the flame under the casserole, bind the sauce with a piece of butter kneaded with flour, and let simmer another 10 min. Finish by adding small bits of butter. Meanwhile, grill 2 large slices of household bread, rub them with garlic, moisten with oil, and place them in a deep platter. Place the pieces of fish on the bread, and pour the sauce over the top, after removing the *bouquet garni.*

PAUCHOUSE FROM THE BANKS OF THE SAÔNE PAUCHOUSE DES BORDS DE LA SAÔNE (SAINT-JEAN-DE-LOSNE) (S. F.)

In making Pauchouse, 4 kinds of freshly caught fish are generally used: eel, pike, tench, and large perch. Clean and scale the fish and cut in slices. Line the bottom of the casserole with diced pork fat and crushed garlic, bouquet of thyme (no bay leaf) and, in summer, a little tarragon. Place the pieces of fish on top, season with salt and pepper, and cover with white wine. Bring to a quick boil, bind with a good piece of butter kneaded with flour, swirling the casserole to mix well (do not stir with a spoon). Cook 20–25 min., then reduce the heat and let simmer.

Cut 2 small loaves of French bread lengthwise, rub with garlic on all sides, and fry in butter. Place them in a deep platter, cover with the pieces of fish, and pour the sauce over the top. Serve very hot.

For 2 lb. fish use: a handful of garlic cloves, ½ lb. butter kneaded with flour, ¼ lb. pork fat.

SOLE FILLETS BOURGUIGNONNE FILETS DE SOLE À LA BOURGUIGNONNE

See Fish, p. 293.

SNAILS BOURGUIGNONNE ESCARGOTS À LA BOURGUIGNONNE (S. F.)

Wash the snails several times in fresh water and brush them to remove the dirt. Soak them 1–2 hr. in vinegar and salt and wash them again. When they are completely clean, cook them at a rolling boil in a large pan of water with a handful of salt about 5–6 min. Remove the pan from the fire and take the snails from the water 1 at a time, to remove them from the shells with the point of a knife. Cut off the black end, wash well in fresh water several times to remove whatever slime remains, and drain in a sieve. Cook the snails 2 hr. or more with white wine, a little water, salt, pepper, 1 onion, 2 or 3 cloves of garlic, 1 carrot, *bouquet garni,* and a piece of pork fat. Be sure that the snails are well cooked, or they won't be good. Drain them in a sieve, then on a cloth.

To make a stuffing for 100 snails, take: 13 oz. butter, finely chopped parsley with a little chervil, 4 or 5 cloves of garlic (depending on size and taste), 2 shallots, a small slice of chopped raw pork fat, salt, pepper, juice of 1 lemon. Chop and mix well together. The snail shells should be perfectly clean both inside and out, drained and dried. Take a little of the stuffing and place it in the bottom of the shell, put in the snail, and then some more of the stuffing to fill the shell. Place them in special baking dishes, slide them into the oven for a few minutes, and serve.

The snails are even better prepared the day before. This recipe has been followed by several generations and always with success.

BEEF BOURGUIGNON BOEUF BOURGUIGNON (S. F.) (*For 7 or 8 persons*)

Use 2 lb. well-hung round of beef (no other cut will do) sliced into cubes about as thick as a beefsteak. Lard a small iron cocotte and line it with sliced carrots and onions, thyme, bay leaf, and fresh parsley. Lay a row of beef cubes on top, sprinkle a little chopped garlic, onion, and shallot and sliced mushrooms on the meat. Continue adding layers until all the meat has been used. Don't forget to salt and pepper each layer.

Finally, pour in good champagne brandy and excellent Madeira, the liquid reaching to about ⅓ the height of the cocotte. Place a fine strip of pork fat on top, cover, and seal the cocotte with a band of paste made of flour and water to keep in the steam. Bring to a boil and then cook very slowly 6 hr. Be sure not to uncover the cocotte before serving. Serve in the cocotte on a tray with a folded napkin and allow 1 of your guests the pleasure of breaking the crust and opening the pot. I leave to your imagination the wonderful aroma that will be released.

SMOKED BEEF TONGUE LANGUE DE BOEUF FUMÉE (S. F.)

Take a fresh beef tongue; put it into a dish with enough salt to cover it completely, spices, garlic, shallots, chopped onions, celery, carrots, parsley, a few juniper berries, and set in a cool place.

Let macerate at least 15 days, turning from time to time so that it becomes thoroughly impregnated. Make sure that it is always covered with salt. At the end of this time, remove it from the dish and hang it on a hook inside the chimney. Procure some green juniper or other aromatic wood, light it, and let it smoke. If the wood starts to flame, put it out with a little water so that it merely smokes. Do this at least 8 times, ½ hr. at a time.

At last you may take the tongue off the hook, clean off the salt and other condiments, and cook it. To do this, put it into plain water (in a pan long enough so that the tongue lies flat) and cook 5–6 hr. It should stay firm. While still hot, remove the outer skin, which should come off very easily, then place it on a long platter to cool.

To serve, cut in thin slices and decorate with parsley. This tongue keeps for quite a while and should be eaten cold.

BREAST OF VEAL EN MEURETTE POITRINE DE VEAU EN MEURETTE (C. and R.)

En meurette is a way of preparing fish or meat. The following is an example.

Brown some pieces of breast of veal in butter with salt, pepper, and diced pork fat. Add a little flour for thickening, then pour in some red wine and a little hot water or bouillon. Stir well and cook over a low fire, adding a *bouquet garni,* some small onions, 1 or 2 cloves of garlic; test the seasoning. When cooked, serve on a platter with the small onions around the meat.

HAM WITH PARSLEY BOURGUIGNONNE (Indispensable Dish for Easter) JAMBON PERSILLÉ À LA BOURGUIGNONNE (C. and R.)

Soak a piece of or a whole country ham. Blanch it 1 hr. and wash it under running water. Start it cooking in a good stock made with a piece of veal knuckle including the bone, 2 calf's feet, the usual soup vegetables, chervil and tarragon in the *bouquet garni,* 5 or 6 shallots, and 2 bottles of white wine. When the ham is well cooked, remove it from the cooking broth and crush it with a fork, mixing the fat and lean, then press it in a salad bowl. Clarify the cooking stock and correct the seasoning to make fine-colored jelly. When it begins to jell, add a large amount of chopped parsley, 1 tsp. good vinegar, and 1 wineglass white wine, then pour it over the ham and place the bowl in the refrigerator. The ham is usually served in the salad bowl.

CREAMED MORVAN HAM JAMBON DU MORVAN À LA CRÈME (C. and R.)

Soak a country ham 24 hr. in cold water, changing the water frequently, depending on the age of the ham. Cook it with plenty of seasoning, but without salt, 15–20 min. per lb. Keep it rather firm; otherwise, if too well cooked, it will be difficult to cut after braising. Braise the ham, basting it with some sherry. After braising, melt the glaze in the pan with veal gravy and finish the sauce with extra-heavy cream; taste, correct the seasoning. Slice the ham and cover generously with the sauce. Serve very hot.

GIBLETS BOURGUIGNONNE ABATIS À LA BOURGUIGNONNE

See Fowl, p. 410.

BURGUNDY COCK IN WINE COQ AU VIN DE BOURGOGNE (S. F.)

Cut a young cock into pieces and brown them in an earthenware casserole with a few pieces of blanched pork fat and some small onions. Pour in 1 glass champagne brandy, set aflame, and add 1 bottle old Burgundy and a little white stock; season with salt and pepper and add 2 cloves of garlic and a *bouquet garni.* When it comes to a boil, cover tightly and cook slowly, the time depending on the tenderness of the cock. After cooking, remove the garlic and *bouquet garni;* add small cooked mushrooms. Thicken with butter kneaded with flour, simmer a few moments, and serve.

CHICKEN WITH CHAMBERTIN POULET AU CHAMBERTIN (S. F.)

Brown the pieces of chicken in butter with a pinch of crushed garlic; sprinkle with flour, cook a few minutes in the oven, moisten with Chambertin, set aflame, and add a little chicken stock, *bouquet garni,* and seasoning. Cover and cook 20 min. Prepare a garnish of small onions, bacon strips, and quartered mushrooms, all sautéed in butter. Remove the chicken pieces from the pan, reduce the stock, correct the seasoning, and thicken slightly with a little blood. Pour this sauce over the chicken with its garnish. Simmer everything together ¼ hr., and serve with diced croutons and chopped parsley.

CHICKEN SAUTÉ DUKES OF BURGUNDY POULET SAUTÉ AUX DUCS DE BOURGOGNE (C. and R.)

Take a fine Bresse chicken, cut it into pieces, season with salt and pepper, and brown in a sautéing pan. Cook slowly in the oven about 1 hr., then remove the chicken pieces from the pan and put them into another, keeping them warm.

Pour into the first pan used in cooking the chicken 1 good glass port and another of champagne brandy, 1 glass whisky, and some kirsch; reduce, then add 1 pt. cream and 2 egg yolks; mix together and strain. Place the chicken pieces in a timbale and pour the sauce over the top. Serve.

Note: The egg yolks should be added only at the last moment.

SADDLE OF HARE PIRON RABLE DE LIÈVRE À LA PIRON (C. and R.)

Marinate a fine saddle of hare with shallots, garlic, celery, thyme, bay leaf, and marc brandy for 2 or 3 days.

Roast the saddle, surround with purple and white peeled and seeded grapes, set aflame with marc brandy, and, just before sending to the table, baste with the gravy from the roast mixed with 1 tbsp. Poivrade Sauce (p. 143) and 1 tbsp. heavy cream.

HOT PÂTÉ or PIE ROUSSOTTE PÂTÉ CHAUD ROUSSOTTE (C. and R.) (*For 6 persons*)

18 larks, 11 oz. fresh pork tenderloin, 4 oz. fresh pork fat, 3½ oz. cooked ham.

Bone the larks, leaving only the thigh bones (save the intestines) ; marinate them at least 2 days in cognac, Madeira, salt, pepper, and spices.

Lightly brown the pork tenderloin and diced pork fat over a hot fire. Let cool completely, then pound in a mortar, mixing in the cooked ham, 5 or 6 fine truffles, and the lark intestines sautéed in butter; taste, and correct the seasoning.

Reshape the larks with a little forcemeat with a piece of truffle and a piece of *foie gras* in the middle.

Line a mold or straight-sided casserole with a crust of Short Paste (p. 545) . Line the inside with very thin slices of bacon, put a little forcemeat in the bottom, and lay in the larks, separating each row of larks with a thin layer of forcemeat; cover the top with a crust of Short Paste (without making the usual chimney as for ordinary meat pies) .

Put 2 or 3 pieces of fresh butter on top of the pie and bake about 1¼ hr. in a slow oven. Unmold and serve as is.

Note: This *pâté* or pie can be made to be served cold, but then place fine pieces of *foie gras* studded with truffles in the center of the larks and pour some good game jelly into the cold pie. Thrush, quail, etc., many be substituted for the larks, but M. Roussotte, who created this recipe, made the pie only with larks.

CORN CAKE GÂTEAU DE MAÏS (S. F.)

Ingredients: 2¼ oz. corn meal, 4 oz. wheat flour, 4 oz. powdered sugar, 3½ oz. fresh butter.

Mix the 2 flours and the sugar well. Melt the butter slowly and pour it over the mixture. Mix well again and then, using the back of a spoon, spread the paste in a shallow spring cake pan. Bake 15–20 min. in a medium oven; watch carefully while baking, for sometimes the cake is done very quickly and it should not brown. Turn the cake upside down onto a cake platter, remove the pan, and slice while still hot, for the cake will crumble when cold. Very good with tea.

BURGUNDY RAISINÉ RAISINÉ DE BOURGOGNE (S. F.)

Pick some good, ripe grapes and press out the juice. Boil the juice until reduced by ½, carefully skimming off the foam and stirring. Add some pears of any sort, cut in quarters and peeled; reduce again by ⅓, stirring constantly. The fruit should now be cooked.

Pour the grape-pear mixture into jars and let set overnight in an oven that has been on all day. If pears are not available, tender young carrots cut slantwise to about the same size as pear quarters may be used; drop them into the grape juice when it is first put on the stove, because it takes them longer to cook.

If the grapes are not ripe enough, the Raisiné will not be fit to eat. In this case, add 3 lb. sugar per 10 lb. reduced grape juice (including the pears). Also, do not reduce the grape juice quite so much.

BRITTANY

(CÔTES-DU-NORD—FINISTÈRE—ILLE-ET-VILAINE—LOIRE-ATLANTIQUE—MORBIHAN)

WHITE BUTTER NANTAIS BEURRE BLANC NANTAIS (S. F.)

Chop fine some shallots and parsley. Put them into a pan with 2 fingers of vinegar, salt, and pepper, and reduce completely but without drying out. Lower the flame as much as possible and add walnut-sized pieces of butter, stirring constantly, until you have enough sauce. Strain through a sieve to remove the shallots. Be very careful not to let the sauce cook at too high a heat, or the butter will turn to an oil instead of staying a cream. Allow about ½ lb. butter for 1 lb. fish.

This butter sauce is usually served with fresh-water fish previously cooked in a court bouillon. It is especially good with pike, small barbel, perch, etc., and is not out of place with salt-water fish.

EELS WITH PRUNES ANGUILLES AUX PRUNEAUX (S. F.)

This dish takes a long time to prepare and cook, but it can be reheated.

Ingredients: 8 or 10 eels, 6 small onions, 2½ oz. lean sliced bacon, 12 prunes, 3 wineglasses white wine.

Clean and skin the eels, wipe them off, cut them in slices, and drop them into very hot deep fat; remove them when they are golden brown. Meanwhile, brown the bacon and onions in lard, sprinkle with flour, moisten with white wine, and add thyme, bay leaf, salt, spices.

Place the eels in this sauce, let simmer 2 hr. at low heat; add the prunes, and continue to cook 1 hr. over a very low fire.

NANTES DUCKLINGS CANETONS NANTAIS

See Fowl, pp. 422-423.

BRETON RAISIN CAKE FAR BRETON (S. F.)

Ingredients: 1 qt. milk, ½ lb. flour, ½ lb. powdered sugar, 6 fresh eggs, 4 oz. Malaga raisins, 5 tbsp. rum. Mix sugar and flour in a bowl; make a hole in the center and break in the 6 whole eggs. Blend in the eggs bit by bit, working this paste a good ¼ hr., then begin to thin it with about ¼ the milk, poured in very hot and little by little. Next add the rest of the milk, a little at a time, and, finally, the raisins and the rum.

Pour the mixture into a buttered cake tin and bake about 1½ hr. in a slow oven. Unmold when cold.

BRETON COFFEE CAKE GALETTE BRETONNE (S. F.)

Ingredients: 2 lb. flour, 1 lb. salt butter, 6 eggs, 1 lb. sugar, desired flavoring (the usual Breton flavoring is orange-flower water), a few pieces of candied angelica.

Blend the sugar in the well-beaten eggs, then mix in ⅔ of the flour. Put the rest of the flour on a cloth, lay the well-mixed paste on top, and put the butter in the center of the paste. Using your hands, work the butter and the rest of the flour into the paste. Shape into a flat cake, brush the top with egg yolk, and bake about ½ hour in a medium oven.

REAL BRETON CAKE VÉRITABLE GÂTEAU BRETON (S. F.)

Ingredients: ½ lb. wheat flour, ½ lb. very fresh butter, 4 oz. sugar, 3 oz. crushed almonds, 3 eggs, 3 or 4 drops of cherry-laurel, a few drops of vanilla.

Work the butter in a warm bowl with a wire whisk to cream it; continuing to beat, add 2 egg yolks, 1 whole egg, and the drops of cherry-laurel. Put the flour with the sugar and almonds on the baking board. Make a hole in the center and place the butter in this well; work it in gradually, add the vanilla, and knead the paste well. Place in a mold and bake 20–30 min.

CHAMPAGNE

(Ardennes—Aube—Haute-Marne—Marne)

CHAMPAGNE POTÉE POTÉE CHAMPENOISE (S. F.)

Pour 2½–3 qt. water into a large enamel boiler, then add ½ lb. streaked salt pork fat and 1 lb. salt pork. When it comes to a full boil, skim, and add 3 carrots, 2 turnips, 3 kohlrabi, 1 cabbage cut in quarters. The vegetables should be cooked about 2½ hr., the pork 3 hr. Add some potatoes cut in large pieces ½ hr. before serving. Sausages and smoked ham may be added, if desired. Place strips of household bread in the bottom of a soup tureen and pour the broth on top. The vegetables and meat should be served together: the vegetables on the bottom of a large platter and the meat and pork fat on top.

This simple but excellent dish used to be the daily fare in the Champagne countryside, until a few years ago.

CHEESE FONDU FONDUS AU FROMAGE (S. F.)

Make a very thick Béchamel Sauce (p. 146) ; blend in some egg yolks, the number depending on the amount of Fondu desired, and equal parts of grated Parmesan and Gruyère cheese. Stir briskly a few moments on the fire, and pour this paste into small plain tartlet molds. Smooth the top of the molds with a knife (it is useless to grease them) . Let cool 1–2 hr.

Unmold, dip in flour, then in beaten egg containing salt and pepper, and next in golden bread crumbs. Fry in boiling oil and serve very hot.

STUFFED SHEEP'S TROTTERS RÉMOISE PIEDS DE MOUTON FARCIS RÉMOISE (S. F.)

After carefully washing the feet, cook them 3 hr. in water mixed with 1 or 2 tbsp. flour, with carrots, onions, *bouquet garni,* salt, and pepper added.

When they are cooked, drain them and remove the bones. Stuff the feet with sausage meat mixed with chopped parsley. Next wrap each foot in a pig's caul, baste with butter, and roll in bread crumbs. Grill slowly in the oven and serve very hot.

HAM CRÊPES or **PANCAKES** CRÊPES AU JAMBON (S. F.)

Beat 2 eggs as for an omelet and make 6 small crêpes. Prepare in advance a filling made with ham, cooked mushrooms, and 1 small shallot cooked in butter. Spread the crêpes with this filling and then roll them, place them in a baking dish, sprinkle with grated Gruyère cheese, and brown in the oven.

PRUNE SURPRISE PRUNEAUX SURPRISES (S. F.)

Cook the prunes, remove the pits, and stuff with almonds. Dip the prunes in Frying Paste (p. 558) and fry like fritters. Immediately after removing the prunes from the deep fat, roll them in grated chocolate.

COMTAT VENAISSIN

(VAUCLUSE)

COD BENJAMIN (Lenten Dish) MORUE À LA BENJAMIN (S. F.)

Choose some first-quality cod with thick fillets. After soaking to remove the salt, poach it and remove the skin and bones.

Place nice slices of the cod in a buttered baking dish sprinkled with sliced mushrooms sautéed in butter and mixed with fresh truffles cut in julienne strips. Cover the cod with the same amount of mushrooms and truffles, and coat everything with Hollandaise Sauce (p. 151) mixed with ⅓ as much extra-heavy cream.

Place in a very hot oven to glaze rapidly without letting the sauce turn.

MUTTON DAUBE À LA MODE D'AVIGNON DAUBE DE MOUTON À LA MODE D'AVIGNON

See Meats, p. 354.

CHICKEN VAUCLUSIENNE POULET À LA VAUCLUSIENNE

See Fowl, p. 396.

COMTÉ DE FOIX

(ARIÈGE)

CORN-MEAL CAKES MAS D'AZIL MILLAS DU MAS D'AZIL (M.)

These corn-meal cakes are prepared in the Ariège country usually at hog-slaughtering time and when preserved goose is made—in other words, during the winter. The fat of these animals is used in making the cakes.

Pour water (or, preferably, milk) into a caldron containing a few tbsp. fat. Season with salt. Bring to a boil. Sprinkle corn meal into the boiling liquid. Stir the gruel constantly with a wooden handle having 4 to 6 small prongs at the end (in Ariège this implement is called a *toudeillo*).

Cook 25 min., stirring constantly. When the corn meal is cooked, pour it out onto a cloth sprinkled with corn meal, making a layer about ⅔ in. thick. Let cool.

Millas may be eaten grilled, dipped in milk, or fried in fat and sprinkled with sugar. It may also be used in cabbage soup instead of bread. When soup is garnished this way, it is called *soupe aux tailluts.*

SAUPIQUET OF BEANS or **BRAISED BEANS** SAUPIQUET DE HARICOTS or ÉTUVÉE DE HARICOTS (M.)

Put 1 lb. already soaked navy beans into an earthenware pot. Pour in some cold water. Add 5 oz. fresh pork rind cut in small pieces, 2 oz. raw ham, and 1 carrot. Bring to a boil, skim, and let simmer.

When ½ cooked, add 1 soup sausage (an *andouille*—a large pork sausage made of tripe or pork) or, if unavailable, 1 ordinary sausage, ¼ jar of preserved goose, 1½ oz. pork fat chopped fine with a large clove of garlic.

Note: This bean dish should cook very slowly, about 3 hr. The stock should be white and sufficiently reduced to cover the beans.

COMTÉ DE NICE

(ALPES-MARITIMES)

NONAT OMELET OMELETTE AUX NONATS (M.)

(Nonats are very small Mediterranean fish eaten only where caught.)

Sauté the nonats in butter and mix them with the eggs while beating. Make the omelet the usual way.

Note: These omelets are usually made flat.

MOISTENED BREAD PAN BAGNA or PAIN MOUILLÉ (M.)

Rub a slice of bread with a little garlic and moisten with olive oil. Garnish the bread with sliced tomatoes, peppers, anchovy fillets, and capers.

COD NIÇOISE MORUE À LA NIÇOISE (S. F.)

Take 2 fine fillets of soaked cod. Make some Frying Paste (p. 558), dip the pieces of cod in the paste, and fry them in hot deep oil. Drain them and let cool. Put a little of the oil used in frying the cod into a pan and brown 1 chopped onion, 2 cloves of garlic, and 1 large, peeled, seeded tomato in it. Make into a sauce with a little flour and water. Peel some firm potatoes and cut into pieces. Put the potatoes into the sauce so that they are completely covered; add a *bouquet garni* with green and black olives. Cook at low heat. Add the pieces of cod to the sauce, without breaking them, ¼ hr. before serving.

Serve on a hot platter with the potatoes underneath and the cod on top.

RED MULLET NIÇOISE ROUGETS À LA NIÇOISE

See Fish, p. 293.

ZUCCHINI or **SQUASH NICE STYLE** COURGETTES OF COURGERONS À LA MODE DE NICE (M.)

Slice the zucchini in 2 lengthwise; loosen the pulp from the skin with a circular cut of the knife. Blanch a few minutes in salted water. Drain, wipe the zucchini dry, and remove the pulp. Chop this pulp and put it into a sautéing pan containing 1 chopped onion cooked in hot oil. Add bread crumbs, chopped garlic, and chopped parsley; bind with egg yolks; season.

Fill the squash skins with this stuffing, dip them in flour, beaten egg, and bread crumbs, and fry just before serving.

Note: This dish is also prepared the following way. Split the zucchini in 2; slip a knife in a circular cut under them; season with salt, and let drain 1 hr. on a cloth. Remove the pulp without breaking the skin. Chop the pulp. Brown it with a chopped onion cooked in oil; flavor with chopped garlic and parsley, and add ⅓ as much Rich Rice (p. 512) to this mixture. Season well. Stuff the zucchini skins with this filling. Place them on an oiled baking dish. Sprinkle with golden bread crumbs, baste with oil, and brown slowly.

RATATOUILLE or **STEW** or **RAGOUT NIÇOISE** RATATOUILLE OF SAUTÉ À LA NIÇOISE (M.)

Brown 1 sliced onion and 3 sliced sweet peppers in oil in a frying pan. Add 2 crushed tomatoes and 4 zucchini and 4 small eggplants cut in round slices; season with salt and pepper. Brown well. Just before removing from the stove, add chopped parsley and garlic.

Note: Somtimes small new potatoes are added to this dish. The potatoes should be fried with the onion and peppers.

RAVIOLI NIÇOISE RAVIOLI À LA NIÇOISE (S. F.)

Make Beef Daube (p. 328) and save the gravy to season your ravioli. Chop the meat and add to it chopped spinach (in Nice they use the cooked, chopped green leaves of spinach-beet), 1 whole egg, onion, salt, pepper, and grated Gruyère cheese.

Prepare some noodle paste (see p. 520) and roll it out very thin; place small dabs of your mincemeat at regular intervals on top. Cover with a second sheet of noodle paste, and cut into cushionlike squares with a pastry wheel. Let stand 10 hr. Cook the ravioli about ½ hr. in boiling water, drain carefully without breaking the paste, and serve hot, flavored with beef gravy and grated Parmesan or Gruyère cheese.

CORSICA

SMALL TRIPE TRIPETTES (M.)

Cut the small intestine of a sheep into pieces the width of a hand and sauté them in lard with some tomatoes; season well with salt, pepper, and spices. Just before removing from the stove, sprinkle with chopped parsley.

WOODCOCK CACCIATORE BÉCASSE À LA CACCIATORE (M.)

Pluck the woodcock but do not draw it (only remove the gizzard). Season it and skewer it on a toasting fork or a branch of myrtle. Roast it the following way. Set some spitted pieces of pork fat aflame before a hot myrtle or vine-branch fire. Let the fat drip gently over the bird, turning it to cook on all sides.

MICISCA MICISCA (M.)

Cut a pork tenderloin into long tonguelike slices, leaving them joined together at 1 end. Macerate a long time in a heavily spiced marinade. Drain, wipe dry, and smoke. Dry well.

To serve, grill the tongues of pork.

FRESH CHEESE BROCCIO (M.)

Warm the milk to curdle it, but do not add the rennet until the milk is from 140° to 148° F. Through this process, the boiling of the milk will separate the casein from the serum. Boiling causes the casein to combine with the butter and the lactic acid to make the cheese very smooth. Drain the cheese in a basket made of thin, supple, plaited rush.

CHEESECAKE FIJADONE (M.)

Make a rather thick cream with some Broccio (see above), egg yolks, sugar, and flavoring (vanilla, lemon, or orange). Line a pie tin with Short Paste (p. 545) and fill with this cream. Bake in a slow oven. This cake is usually made at Eastertime.

DAUPHINÉ

(ISÈRE—DRÔME—HAUTES-ALPES)

PORK CAILLETTES CAILLETTES DE COCHON (S. F.)

Take 1 lb. pork liver, ¼ lb. pork fat, 1 lb. spinach, 1 glass rum, salt, and pepper. Cut the liver and fat into small pieces, and cut up, but do not chop, the spinach.

Take some pig's caul and cut it into 3-in. squares. Put an egg-sized ball of the above forcemeat in each square and wrap it to form a ball. Place these on a baking dish, put a small piece of fat on each one, and bake in a very hot oven.

Run hot water over the raw fat to make it softer.

POTATOES AU GRATIN DAUPHINOIS GRATIN DAUPHINOIS (S. F.)

In the bottom of a buttered baking dish place a layer of potatoes sliced in thin rounds, season with salt and pepper, and sprinkle with grated Gruyère cheese. Make a second layer of potatoes and season these the same way. Beat 1 egg yolk in 1 pt. fresh milk and pour this mixture over the potatoes.

On top of the potatoes add small pieces of butter about 2 in. apart, and place in a very hot oven until the top turns a golden brown. A baker's oven is preferred to an ordinary kitchen oven.

POTATO PIE DAUPHINOIS MICHON DAUPHINOIS (S. F.) (*For 4 persons*)

Slice 1 lb. potatoes, but not too thin. Mix ½ lb. flour with 1 pt. milk and stir it into the potatoes. Butter a pie pan, pour in the mixture, and bake about ¾ hr. in a country oven.

COFFEE RING ROMANS-SUR-ISÈRE POGNE DE ROMANS (M.)

Ingredients: 1 lb. wheat flour, ½ lb. bread yeast, ½ lb. butter, 6 eggs, 7 oz. powdered sugar, 1 tsp. salt, 2 tsp. orange-flower water.

(1) Shape the flour into a well; put the salt and orange-flower water in the center, make it dissolve, then add the butter, the leaven, and 4 eggs. Mix together, knead the paste to give it body, and then blend in the other 2 eggs and the sugar, adding the sugar 1 tsp. at a time, continuing to knead the paste to keep it elastic.

(2) Put this paste into a bowl, cover it, and let rise 10 hr. in a fairly warm place. At the end of this time, break down the paste (that is, pat it with the hand a few times on the baking board), divide it into 3 parts, and shape into a ring (like an ordinary Brioche Ring, p. 565). Let the paste rise ½ hr., brush with beaten egg, and bake in a hot oven.

CHOCOLATE TRUFFLES DAUPHINOISE TRUFFETTES DAUPHINOISES (S. F.)

The proportions given are for 4 oz. chocolate. They may be doubled or tripled, depending on the number of chocolate truffles desired. Melt 4 oz. chocolate in 3 tbsp. milk, stirring it well over a very low fire; add 2 oz. fresh butter, continuing to stir; let cool a little, then add 1 egg yolk. Mix well, and let stand a few hours in a cool place. Next, form into small balls and roll in grated chocolate. Repeat this last operation several times. Finely chopped, grilled hazelnuts or almonds may be added to the melted chocolate, but this is not usually done in Dauphiné.

FLANDERS

(NORD)

FLEMISH TART FLAMICHE FLAMANDE (S. F.)

Ingredients (*for 2 tarts*): 3 eggs, a little yeast, ½ pt. milk, 13 oz. sifted flour, at least 2 oz. salt butter.

Put ⅔ of the flour into a mixing bowl. Break the eggs in and mix gently by hand, keeping the hand limp. Warm the milk until tepid and pour it in; dissolve the yeast in a little milk or water and add it to the paste; mix in the butter in small pieces without melting it. Continue to beat by hand, gradually adding the rest of the flour. Cover the bowl and place it in a warm spot near a low fire to let the paste rise 3 or 4 hr. When it has risen, butter 2 large tart or pie tins, dip a spoon in cold water, and spread out the paste, without adding flour, simply by moistening the spoon. When it has been evenly spread, prick it with a knife. (This paste is excellent for making tarts. If fruits are used, the paste should be sprinkled with fine dry cake crumbs.) Lay slices of Maroilles cheese, about as thick as a half dollar (half-crown), on the bottom crust, then dot with small pieces of fresh butter.

For a fine tart, beat 3 whole eggs with a little milk or cream and pour this mixture on the tart just before putting it into the oven. Bake in a hot oven. Serve immediately after taking out of the oven (at the beginning of the meal, before the soup). Each guest should spread his slice with fresh butter. Eat very hot with a glass of dry white wine.

CHEESE TART VALENCIENNOISE GOYÈRE VALENCIENNOISE (S. F.)

Ingredients: ¼ lb. white cheese, ¼ of a Maroilles cheese, 2 eggs.

Cut the Maroilles cheese into small pieces and put it into a deep dish. Add the white cheese, mixing it well by crushing it with a fork, then the 2 beaten eggs.

Make a Short Paste (p. 545) without sugar and line a tart pan with it; dry it slightly in the oven before pouring in the preparation given above. Bake about 20 min. at moderate heat. The top should be a light golden brown and the paste well cooked. It can also be cooked on top of the stove without too much trouble.

If Maroilles cheese is not available, grated Gruyère cheese may be used, but then the dish loses its particular flavor. Serve hot after placing a few pieces of butter on the cheese.

KIDNEY RAMEKINS (Douais recipe) RAMEQUINS AUX ROGNONS (S. F.)

Cook a whole veal kidney in a stewpan and chop it. Have ready some small dinner rolls; split them in 2 and remove the soft bread inside. Soak this bread in milk; mix it with the chopped kidney, 1 beaten egg, *fines herbes* chopped very fine, salt, and pepper. Fill the hollow half rolls with this mixture, heaping it into a small dome. Place a piece of butter on each ramekin, brown in the oven, and serve very hot.

BLACK PUDDING FLAMANDE BOUDIN NOIR À LA FLAMANDE

See p. 375.

RABBIT FLAMANDE LAPIN À LA FLAMANDE (S. F.)

1 rabbit (weighing about 3 lb.), ¼ lb. breast of pork, ¼ lb. prunes or more, if desired, ¼ lb. raisins, 24 small onions.

Cut up the rabbit. Slice the breast of pork into small, thin strips. Melt 1½ oz. butter in an iron cocotte. When it is very hot, lightly brown the strips of pork and put them on a plate. Then brown the pieces of rabbit in the same butter, remove them also to the plate, and then brown the onions. Put all of this back into the pot, sprinkle lightly with flour, mix, and add a little water or skimmed bouillon. Add salt, pepper, a sprig of thyme, and simmer gently on a low fire. After cooking 1 hr., add the prunes and raisins, both well washed; cook another hour.

In a small saucepan, make some caramel by heating 3 tbsp. sugar; dissolve it with 1 tbsp. vinegar, and add this just before serving. This gives the sauce an attractive color and taste.

HUCQUELIERS CAKE or TARTINES GÂTEAU HUCQUELOIS OR TARTINES (S. F.)

Ingredients: 1½ lb. flour, 7–9 eggs, ¼ lb. butter, about 1 pt. cream, 1 oz. bakers' yeast, ¼ lb. dried currants, sugar to taste.

Break the eggs the night before, if possible. Separate the whites from the yolks, and put the yolks into a mixing bowl with a little fine salt. This reddens the yolks and makes the cake yellower.

The following day, dissolve the yeast in a little warm cream. Mix the butter, the cream (which should be warmed a little in winter), and the sugar.

Shape the flour into a well, put the egg yolks in the middle, and blend gently with the butter, cream, and sugar mixture. Add the dissolved yeast, then the washed, dried raisins and 4 or 5 stiffly beaten egg whites. Do not knead the paste too much, and let it stand ¼ hr. before turning it. Shape the cake into a large round loaf and brush it with egg yolk diluted with a little water. If the paste does not have enough body, add a little flour. If, on the other hand, it is too thick, add cream or milk.

This excellent cake will keep 3 weeks. It is usually eaten with a cup of fine chocolate.

FRANCHE-COMTÉ

(Doubs—Haute-Saône—Jura)

CANCOILLOTTE CANCOILLOTTE (S. F.)

Take some sour milk, let it cook in its whey until the curds are dry enough to crumble in the fingers. Then press and drain it, until all the liquid has disappeared; you will now have what people in Franche-Comté call the *mettou.*

After draining this *mettou,* put it into an earthenware jar with cover on top and let it ferment, stirring it several times each day. The jar should be kept in a fairly warm place at a constant temperature, so that the fermentation takes place evenly. Fermentation should be stopped when the *mettou* has turned yellow. Take a good piece of butter (about 3 oz. per qt. *mettou*) and melt it in a pan over a low flame, then add the *mettou;* stir constantly while gradually adding warm water until it has completely melted. When poured into bowls, this delicious Cancoillotte may be eaten hot or cold, as you wish.

CHICKEN STUFFED WITH BRAINS POULET FARCI À LA CERVELLE (S. F.)

Pluck, draw, and singe a fine chicken; lightly salt and pepper the inside, after making a fairly large opening. Meanwhile, soak a calf's brain in water (in running water, or in a bowl, changing the water from time to time) and remove the outer membrane.

After seasoning and sprinkling it with tiny pieces of truffles, place it carefully inside the chicken, sew up the opening, and roast in the oven. After the chicken has been well cooked, cut it up and place the pieces in a circle on a hot platter, with the whole calf's brain in the center. Serve the gravy separately in a sauceboat. The guests should eat the chicken and brains at the same time.

HEN IN THE POT GRAY STYLE POULE AU POT À LA MODE DE GRAY (S. F.)

Clean and singe a plump hen; remove the liver, gizzard, lungs, eggs (if there are any), and chop fine together. Add a small jar of good creamed *foie gras,* bind with egg, and season. Stuff the hen with this paste; sew tightly to keep in the stuffing. Lightly brown the hen, then put it into a soup pot with leeks, carrots, small white turnips, parsnips, salt, pepper. As soon as it starts to boil, reduce the heat and cook slowly 2–2½ hr.

Serve a dish of rice, cooked in a little of the hen broth, along with the hen. The skimmed broth is delicious with pearl or ordinary tapioca.

HASTY PUDDING FRANC-COMTOISE GAUDES FRANC-COMTOISES (S. F.)
(*For 4 persons*)

Gaudes, or corn-meal pudding, is the usual winter's evening meal of the old Franche-Comté peasants. This 1-dish supper may be a frugal repast, but it makes the peasant live to be a hundred and sleep soundly during the long winter night.

Mix 8 heaping tbsp. corn meal with 4 heaping tbsp. wheat flour and a little salt. Add cold water gradually (to avoid making lumps) until it has the consistency of gruel. Pour into an earthenware casserole and cook over a very hot fire, stirring constantly. As the gruel thickens, gradually add hot water until it has the consistency of rather thin gruel; stir until it reaches the boiling point. Lower the heat and let it simmer very slowly, without a cover and without stirring, 1½–2 hr.

Serve it in the Franche-Comté style: in hot, deep dishes, at least 2 servings per person. Put butter and fresh cream in the bottom of the dish, then a few ladlefuls of the golden-yellow pudding on top. Keep the plates hot 5 min. to let a thick skin form on the top.

Watch the children for a prank—they will poke a small hole in the middle of the skin and blow strongly through it, until the top of the pudding rises in a cone. The pudding is tastier when each guest spoons his pudding to blend it with the cream and butter.

GUYENNE ET GASCOGNE

(AVEYRON—DORDOGNE—GERS—GIRONDE—HAUTES-PYRÉNÉES—
LANDES—LOT—LOT-ET-GARONNE—TARN-ET-GARONNE)

CRAYFISH SOUP SOUPE AUX ÉCREVISSES (L. M.)

The peasants almost never make this excellent soup, but it is a favorite of some of the old families of Périgord. Begin by browning the white of 1 leek, 2 onions, and 1 carrot, cut in slices, in some good fat; add salt, pepper, and a *bouquet garni.* When the vegetables are well browned, sprinkle with 1 tbsp. flour, add a little hot water, and start to cook in an earthenware pot containing 2 qt. water.

Take 12 crayfish—more, if you can. Remove a part of the tail, pulling away the bitter intestine with it. Heat and flame 2 glasses of good Monbazillac or other white wine, cook the crayfish in the wine until they are red, drain them on a cloth, and peel them. Put the cooking wine into the pot with the vegetables. Next, mash the crayfish shells and tails with a pestle and add them to the soup.

Let cook ¾ hr. over a rather hot fire. When ready to serve, strain the soup and reheat it to bind it with 1 egg yolk, and pour it over the crayfish on slices of grilled bread lightly rubbed with garlic.

HARE SOUP SOUPE AU LIÈVRE (L. M.)

Quite frequently during the hunting season in Périgord, the kitchen is stocked with 2 or 3 hares. One of them can be made into an excellent stew, another roasted on a spit, and the forequarters of 1 or 2 hares can be made into soup if the liver and blood have been saved. This spicy soup is always welcomed by hunters who come home worn out from chasing all over the countryside.

If you have some leftover rich beef or veal bouillon, you will find it very useful for enriching the soup. If not, use a little good meat extract. Marinate part of a hare about 2 hr. in 1 glass good white wine with a few tbsp. brandy. Put it into an earthenware marmite and cover it with hot water and the beef bouillon; salt, pepper, and drop in a pinch of powdered spices (clove, nutmeg, white pepper, ginger). Add a good *bouquet garni* (thyme, bay leaf, wild thyme) and the wine and brandy used in the marinade. Brown some carrot slices in good fat and add them, along with 4 or 5 more carrots, to the hare soup. The carrots, a stalk of celery, and 3 or 4 small white onions are the only vegetables you should allow in the soup, to keep the particular flavor of the hare.

Cook 3 or 4 hr., strain the broth, then add the mashed hare liver and the blood mixed with 1 tbsp. broth. After heating 5–10 min. without boiling, pour over fried or grilled bread croutons lightly rubbed with garlic.

In his book *Code de la bonne chère*, Ed. de Pomiane tells how this soup is made in Périgord, and he recommends port for the marinade rather than white wine mixed with a little of the local brandy.

PÉRIGORD SOUP TOURAIN PÉRIGOURDIN (L. M.)

This soup, so famous in southern and southwestern France, is a favorite in Périgord. At present, it is well known all over, for it appeals to everyone. It stimulates the appetites of those with even the most delicate stomachs, and, moreover, it is one of the least expensive and easiest soups to make. However, it must be made according to instructions.

Bring 1 or 2 qt. water to a boil in a marmite; meanwhile, melt 1 heaping tbsp. fat in a frying pan. Peel 1 or 2 large onions and slice them thin. If you want to avoid red eyes from the acid fumes of the onions, peel them near an open window and have a small piece of bread stuck on the tip of the knife. The onions sliced, fry them in the pan without letting them turn brown, which would give the soup a bitter taste. Add a crushed clove of garlic to the onions; sprinkle them with 1 tbsp. flour and let it brown a little.

Thin this fricassee with 1 tbsp. boiling water. Pour it into the marmite with the boiling water and add salt, pepper, and 1 lb. drained tomatoes. Crush the tomatoes with a pestle when they are cooked. If the onions are to be digestible, the soup must cook ½–¾ hr. The usual 10-min. onion soup is difficult to digest and hasn't had time to develop any real flavor. When ready to serve, break 1 or 2 egg yolks into the soup and keep hot without boiling.

Pour the strained soup over large, thin slices of bread. Those huge loaves of country bread which sometimes weigh 15 lb. are especially suitable. However, well-baked, stale city bread is good for soaking up the soup. To make the soup even better, put a thick layer of grated Gruyère cheese between the slices of dry bread. Pour the soup over the top and heat a few moments in the oven. In those country regions where the inhabitants have no kitchen oven, they merely place a metal cover heaped with burning embers on top of the soup tureen for a few minutes.

LAMPREYS IN WINE SOUTHWESTERN STYLE LAMPROIES AU VIN DU SUD-OUEST (L. M.)

Take some fine, live lampreys. After stunning them, tie them at the head and hang them. Hold the body with one hand wrapped in a rough towel and with the other hand, using the point of a knife, make an incision in the head to bleed the lamprey. Place a bowl underneath to receive the blood. Let the lampreys drain several hours. Next, remove the skins by soaking a few moments in hot water. Wipe with a cloth, gut, clean, and cut the lampreys in thick slices. Meanwhile, peel and wash about 1 lb. leeks, depending on the number of lampreys, and cut them in small round slices. Make a roux by browning a sliced onion in 1 tbsp. fat. Add 2 tbsp. flour and let it brown.

Now heat 1 bottle good red wine in a pan and set it aflame. When the flame dies down, extinguish it with a cover. Pour the flamed wine into the roux. Brown the sliced leeks in a little olive or walnut oil. Mix all together with salt, pepper, 2 cloves of garlic, and a large *bouquet garni.* Let simmer 2 hr. at very moderate heat.

The time has now come to put the lampreys into the sauce. This is where opinion differs. Some believe in searing the lamprey slices a few minutes in hot oil, and others want to put them into the sauce raw. I believe in the latter method because it makes it easier for the wine to penetrate the flesh of the fish and keeps it whiter. It takes about ¾ hr. to cook the lampreys. Taste the sauce; if it is a little strong, add a pinch of sugar. When ready to serve, add the blood mixed in a little of the sauce. Heat for a moment without boiling and finish with a good piece of butter.

Serve the lampreys surrounded with croutons fried in oil, and coat them with the sauce.

LOTE or **BURBOT BORDELAISE** LOTTE BORDELAISE (S. F.)

Take a lote weighing about 2 lb. Skin it and cut into slices about ¾ in. thick. Put 4 or 5 tbsp. oil into a sautéing pan and, when very hot, fry the lote slices on both sides. Remove them and put into the same oil ¾ lb. peeled, pressed tomatoes cut into pieces, 2 shallots, sprig of thyme, ½ glass Madeira, and ½ glass white wine; salt, pepper, and cook over a hot fire until the tomatoes are puréed. Lay the slices of lote in this sauce and cook 15 min. at very low heat. Serve with fried croutons.

CRAYFISH BORDELAISE ÉCREVISSES À LA BORDELAISE (S. F.)

Take some live crayfish, wash in running water, detach the phalanx from the middle of the tail, and remove the black intestine. Cook in butter at low heat without browning: diced carrots, onions, and shallots, parsley, thyme, bay leaf; salt and pepper. Pour in some good white wine and, when it begins to boil, add the crayfish. Pour 3 tbsp. cognac over them and light it; sauté the crayfish until completely cooked. Drain them, place them in a deep platter, and keep hot.

Reduce the cooking sauce to ⅔. Blend in a good piece of butter, add a dash of cayenne, pour over the crayfish, and serve.

DAUBE SAINT-ANDRÉ DAUBE DE LA SAINT-ANDRÉ (L. M.)

Who in the entire southwest doesn't know Daube Saint-André made with red wine? The secret of this highly flavorful dish lies entirely in very slow, even cooking.

In the back country, it is cooked all night on the hearth in the last glowing embers. In the city, since it takes 7 hr. slow cooking, the Daube should be put into the cocotte early in the morning to be ready by dinnertime.

Cut a 3-lb. piece of sirloin with no gristle into even slices as for very small beefsteaks. Line an iron pot with strips of pork rind and lay in the salted, peppered slices of beef. Cover with a layer of chopped pork fat, parsley, garlic, and shallots. Place more slices of beef on top, then the chopped items, and continue till all the meat has been used. Pour in ½ bottle old red wine. Add 1 onion stuck with a clove, a *bouquet garni*, salt, pepper, and a pinch of powdered spices (clove, white pepper, nutmeg, ginger). Bring to a boil, then close with the lid, reduce the heat as low as possible, and leave it to its own devices.[2]

Toward evening, you will be surprised to discover that, without bothering about it, you have prepared one of the most appetizing dishes in your repertoire. Before serving, be sure to skim some of the fat off the gravy.

RIB STEAK BORDELAISE ENTRECÔTE À LA BORDELAISE

See Meats. p. 330.

LAMB CROWS BORDELAISE FRAISES D'AGNEAU BORDELAISE (S. F.) (*For 6 persons*)

Prepare 2 lamb crows according to the usual method for tripe. Cook them in salted water with a little vinegar, 2 medium-sized onions cut in quarters, and a carrot split lengthwise in quarters. Cook 1 good hr. When the crows are completely cooked, remove them from the cooking water, drain well, and dry carefully with a cloth. While they are cooking, prepare the sauce in which they are to be served, as follows.

Chop 3 tbsp. shallots. Put this into a fireproof porcelain dish with 6 tbsp. good white vinegar; boil until the vinegar is reduced by ½, and set to the back of the stove. Melt 2 oz. butter in a small saucepan and blend in 1 heaping tbsp. flour with a wooden spoon; do not let this mixture get any darker than a golden color. Then pour it bit by bit, stirring with the wooden spoon, into the first preparation in the porcelain dish, which you put back on the fire. When it comes to a boil, let it boil ¼ min., no more. Remove again from the fire and, while the sauce is still very hot, pour in 1½ oz. first-rate olive oil, a bit at a time, continuing to stir. Put 3 tbsp. of this sauce into a bowl and mix in 1 tbsp. mustard. When perfectly blended, pour it into the sauce. If the sauce is finished before the lamb crows are cooked, keep it hot in a *bain-marie* or double boiler.

When about to serve, have ready a deep round platter heated very hot, and,

---

[1] This is a good dish for winter, when you have a cook for the whole day.
[2] Be sure not to let the fire go out.

separately, a pinch of tarragon and burnet leaves; add these herbs to the sauce at the last minute, pour it over the crows, and serve without delay in very hot plates.

POTTED PORK-LIVER PÂTÉ PÂTÉ DE FOIE DE PORC (EN TERRINE) (L. M.)

Remove the skin and membranes from a fine pork liver. Chop it very fine until it forms a paste. Add 1 lb. lean fresh pork and 1 lb. pork fat, both chopped. Salt, pepper, and mix well together. Put in a crushed clove of garlic and a few finely chopped shallots. Add a good pinch of powdered spices (clove, white pepper, nutmeg, ginger). Spread a piece of pig's caul on the table. Put the mincemeat in the center. Fold the pig's caul around it and tie with a string, making a sort of pudding or large ball.

Line a cocotte or caldron with strips of pork rind. Put in the ball of *pâté* and pour 1 glass white wine and 1 small glass brandy over it. Surround the *pâté* with a few marrow bones, sliced carrots and onions, and a large *bouquet garni.* Cook 2½ hr. over a very low, even fire, taking care to put live coals on the lid of the pot.[1] Baste the *pâté* frequently with the cooking liquid. When it is completely covered with a bronze crust, drain the *pâté* and place it while still hot into a round terrine. When it is cold, cover it with about 1 in. melted fat. Tie a round of paper over the top, or even two thicknesses of paper, and cover the terrine. Pork-Liver Pâté, prepared this way, has a remarkable flavor resembling potted game and keeps well 2 or 3 months.

PULLET or **CAPON WITH PÉRIGORD PEARLS** POULARDE or CHAPON AUX PERLES DU PÉRIGORD

See Fowl, p. 390.

CHICKEN WITH MUSHROOMS SAINT-ASTIER POULET AUX CÈPES DE SAINT-ASTIER (L. M.)

Clean and singe a fine chicken, cut it into pieces, and sear it in a well-greased iron pot. When the pieces have begun to brown, add a few small onions and 12 cèpe caps (or other large mushroom caps) washed in several waters, drained on a cloth, and browned 10 min. in very hot oil. Pour 1 glass white wine into the pot and add a little pork fat, parsley, and 2 cloves of garlic, all chopped. Salt and pepper and simmer ¾ hr. in a covered pot without removing the lid.

Chicken with Mushrooms may also be prepared by braising the whole chicken in fine fat. When it has browned on all sides, add the large mushroom caps and a few drained whole tomatoes. Salt and pepper and, on the mushrooms, add a little pork fat, garlic, parsley, and mushroom stems, all chopped. Pour in ½ glass white wine, cover, and let simmer ¾–1 hr. Serve it surrounded with the mushrooms and tomatoes; reduce the cooking gravy and pour it on top. The mushrooms may be served on croutons fried in oil.

HEN IN THE POT WITH SORGES SAUCE POULE AU POT À LA SAUCE DE SORGES (M.)

Clean and singe a good fat young hen, preferably a common local hen called "plucked necks" by the peasants. The meat has a fine flavor.

[1] You can cook the *pâté* in the oven, too.

Make a forcemeat with the mashed chicken liver, 1 slice crumbled stale bread, the blood (if you have been able to save it), a little pork fat, pinch of garlic, parsley, chervil, and scallion, all chopped. Bind with 1 or 2 egg yolks, salt and pepper, and, when the mixture is smooth, stuff the hen with it and sew up the opening. Brown it on all sides in a little goose or pork fat, put it into a marmite, cover with boiling water, salt, pepper, add 1 onion stuck with a clove, carrots, turnips, leeks, celery—all sorts of soup vegetables.

When it comes to a full boil, skim carefully, and cook, with the cover tightly sealed, 2½ hr. over a very moderate fire.

The chicken is cooked when it can be easily pierced with a knitting needle. Drain it a little and keep hot with the vegetables placed around it.

After the broth has been strained, pour it over toasted slices of bread, or cook some vermicelli in it 10 min.

The Sorges Sauce to go with the boiled hen is simply a Vinaigrette Sauce (p. 158) made with oil, salt, pepper, scallions, *fines herbes*, and finely chopped shallots, mixed with one or two 3-min. soft-boiled eggs. The success of the sauce depends on the cooked eggs; recook the whites a bit in the broth and chop into tiny pieces before adding to the sauce.

PRESERVED GOOSE CONFIT D'OIE (L. M.)

Preparation: When forced feeding has been finished, the time has come for geese and ducks to die. They are killed, and the blood is carefully collected to make those good little dishes of Sanguète[1] so dearly loved in the southwest. Then the geese and ducks are plucked and the feathers used in down quilts.

At last we come to the actual cooking of the conserve.

When the goose has been plucked and cleaned, cut it into 4 parts, taking care to cut off the excess fat without spoiling the appearance of any of the pieces.

Salt the meat, using 2 tbsp. salt per lb. goose. Place the pieces in layers in a large terrine with thyme and bay leaf, and let them stay 1 day and 2 nights. Next, skin the neck and bone it.[2]

Separate the head from the neck, clean and singe it, and cut the beak on the underside to remove the digestive and respiratory tubes. Cut the wings very close to the shoulder joints. Cut off the feet, which, like the wing tips, are easily cleaned by boiling them in water or holding them over a live flame; also clean the gizzard. When these have been well cleaned, put them in salt in the terrine already containing the other parts. Also put in the neck bone.

If the liver is a large fine one, soak it a few hours in fresh water, then drain it on a cloth before making it into a *pâté*. Dark livers are used with sausage meat to stuff the necks.

When you clean the geese, be sure to remove all the fat from the entrails.

Cooking: Cut the fat into very thin pieces, put them into a large pot with 2 or 3 glasses water, melt over a moderate fire, taking care not to burn them (which is what happens if the fire is too hot). When the fat is almost melted, put in the goose quarters 1 at a time after shaking off the salt. Also put in the wing tips, neck bone, and gizzard. Keep the fire even around the pot. When it has come to a moderate boil, cook 2½ hr., but remove the neck and gizzard earlier, since they cook faster.

[1] Recipes given on pp. 693 and 724.

[2] Save the skin to make delicious Stuffed Goose Neck, p. 717.

To see if they are done, prick the pieces of goose with a straw. It should pierce the flesh completely without difficulty. Remove the pot from the fire, pour off part of the fat into a terrine, then remove the pieces of goose and place them 1 by 1 in a stoneware jar. Allow about 8 pieces for a medium-sized jar of preserved goose. Use a cleaver to chop the bones, which have become separated from the meat during cooking.

Put the scraps (neck, wing tips, etc.) into a separate jar and cover with the impure fat from the bottom of the pot—the fat with the meat gravy.

The gizzard must be covered with good clear fat. Usually the gizzards of the geese are put together in the same jar. You have not yet covered the goose quarters with goose fat, for the fat has not finished cooking. Let it boil a little longer in the pot until the surface is covered with a veil of foam, the fat underneath being clear. Remove the pot from the fire and, when it has stopped boiling, skim carefully. After letting the fat stand a few minutes, pour it over the goose meat. When the fat has solidified, cover with white paper and the lid of the jar.

Further preservation: In May the conserve should be boiled again a few minutes after it has reached the boiling point. This is called renewing it, and is necessary because it might spoil during the summer heat.

STUFFED GOOSE NECK COU D'OIE FARCI (L. M.)

It is assumed that you have removed the skin from the neck of the goose and put it aside. To stuff 1 neck, take 1 lb. sausage meat and a little *foie gras* (about 3½ oz. should do). Use the dark livers to stuff the necks—they are very good, though not attractive enough to use for *pâtés*.

Knead all together with salt, pepper, and a pinch of powdered spices (cloves, white pepper, nutmeg, ginger); let stand at least 1 night. The next day, sew up the small end of the neck—that is, the head end. Stuff the neck and sew up the other end. After you have removed the goose quarters from the boiling fat (see above recipe), cook the stuffed necks in it until they float to the surface. Remove them with a skimming ladle, and place them in a stoneware jar. When they are cold, cover with the clear fat. In May, "renew" them with the rest of the goose (see above).

Stuffed Goose Neck is served as an hors d'oeuvre, merely heated in a frying pan, or over mashed potatoes, or even with fresh peas. It may also be served with Périgueux Sauce (p. 143).

PÉRIGUEUX TRUFFLED FOIE GRAS FOIE GRAS CLOUTÉ DE PÉRIGUEUX (L. M.)

Here is a dish enjoyed everywhere, but one that can be made only under certain conditions, for it needs a fine liver with no imperfections. Soak the liver overnight in cold water; drain, salt, and pepper. Next, peel ½ lb. perfectly round truffles and cut from each some pieces pointed at one end and flat at the other; save the scraps for the sauce. Stud the liver with these dark aromatic pegs. Then wrap a strip of bacon fat around it, enfold it in a greased paper, and tie with string. Place it in a baking dish, baste with 1 tbsp. goose fat, and cook over a very low fire 30–40 min. basting frequently with the fat in the dish. While cooking the *foie gras*, prepare a little sauce with lightly browned shallots and good white wine. Salt, pepper, and add a roux made with a browned onion and flour mixed with bouillon. To finish, add the scraps of truffles left from the studs. When the liver is cooked, remove it carefully from the paper, place it on a hot platter, and pour the truffle sauce around it.

SNIPE CINDERELLA BÉCASSINE CENDRILLON (S. F.)

Pluck, singe, and clean 6 snipe, saving the insides.

Put all the snipe insides, except the gizzards, into a mortar; add a piece of goose or duck liver, a fine truffle, salt, pepper, spices, a few drops of champagne brandy, and pound well. Butter the snipe with this preparation, wrap and sew each in a thin strip of fresh pork fat. Place them in a dish just large enough to hold them. Pour 1 glass or more Madeira over them, add a sprig of thyme, a few slices of lemon, 1 sliced truffle, a few strips of lean bacon, and some mushrooms cut fine. Let marinate 3 days, turning every day. Place the snipe on a spit and roast them before a hot fire. Meanwhile, reduce the marinade, and prepare a piece of toast for each bird by burning champagne brandy on the bread and then rubbing it with lemon juice, a little garlic, and nutmeg. Baste the pieces of toast with the reduced marinade, place the snipe on the toast, and serve on a platter. Don't forget to put a bottle of fine old wine, brought to room temperature, on the table.

This recipe seems complicated, but it really isn't; the main thing is to have the snipe.

STUFFED HARE PÉRIGOURDINE LIÈVRE FARCI À LA PÉRIGOURDINE

See Game, p. 479.

HARE ROYALE LIÈVRE À LA ROYALE (L. M.)

We don't have to praise this ultra-famous dish. But you should know that there are several sorts of Hare Royale: Mâcon style, with a stuffing consisting basically of 10 cloves of garlic and 20 shallots; Saint-Hubert style; Orléans style; one stuffed with truffles, etc.

This Périgord recipe for Hare Royale is so delicately stuffed that it is a marvel of culinary art. To be successful, you need only time and patience, since it takes at least 7 hr. to cook and first-rate ingredients. If these conditions are met, any cook can make a successful Hare Royale.

Take a fine hare between 3 and 6 months old and skin and clean it. Save the heart, liver, kidneys, and blood (mixed with a little vinegar to keep it from clotting), and crush the liver and heart with a few cloves of garlic. Cut off the head and neck and remove the tender bones along the sides.[1] Marinate it a whole day in good red wine with 1 glass oil and such spices as salt, pepper, sliced onion, thyme, clove, bay leaf, etc.

The following day, grease a large *tourtier,* which is a special iron pot still used in the country for cooking this dish. If you haven't one, use an ordinary cocotte or large sautéing pan. Brown in it a slice of pork fat cut in small pieces and about 10 small onions. Meanwhile, stuff the hare with long, thin slices of veal. Alternate these slices with strips of fresh pork fat and a forcemeat made with bread crumbs, 1 lb. chopped pork meat, a few shallots, parsley, salt, and pepper, and bound with 1 egg.[2] Next sew up the hare with a strong thread and,

[1] The bones separate from the meat and are easily removed after the long period of cooking.

[2] Some people improve on this recipe by alternating the slices of veal with slices of truffled *foie gras.*

after tying strips of pork fat around the body, sear it in the pot. Baste it with 1 or 2 small glasses brandy and ½ bottle excellent wine, white or red. Salt, pepper, and add a roux made with flour and a well-browned onion. Cover the pot and place coals on top as well as underneath; cook 7–8 hr. at moderate but even heat. The hare is cooked when the meat falls away from the bones by itself. Cook the liver crushed with garlic in a separate pan, at low heat, 1 hr., with a little vinegar. Remove the pot of hare from the fire, skim the gravy, remove the bones, and add the crushed-liver mixture and the blood mixed with the sauce. Cook another ¼ hr. without boiling. Now add a few peeled, sliced truffles, and your hare is ready to be served. Remove it carefully, place it on a heated platter, and pour the sauce, with its royal flavor and aroma from the truffles, around it. Serve very hot and, naturally, eat the exquisitely stewed meat with a spoon.

For another recipe, see Game, p. 480.

QUERCY DUMPLING FARCIDURE DU QUERCY (S. F.)

Ingredients: 2 lb. salt pork cut from the back or side, 1½ lb. flour, 3½ oz. butter, 2 or 3 eggs, 1 tsp. salt, ⅔ oz. yeast.

Dissolve the yeast with some warm water and the salt, mix the flour with the melted butter and the eggs, and knead well. Roll the paste into a ball on a floured baking board, then wrap it in a floured napkin. Put it into a bowl and let stand 3 hr. to rise; it has risen enough when it begins to split.

Meanwhile, start the salt pork cooking in a large pot with 5–6 qt. water; the pot should not be full. Put the paste into the boiling water with the salt pork 1 hr. before the meal. Cover and let simmer. After ½ hr., turn the dumpling over with a skimming ladle. At this point it should resemble a large brioche. Let it cook another ½ hr. and remove it from the water just in time to go on the table. This dumpling is eaten hot with the salt pork, instead of bread, and can be used only with salt pork. It may seem a little heavy, but it is very nourishing and highly digestible.

CORN-MEAL MIQUES MIQUES DE MAÏS (L. M.)

This is one of the oldest dishes known in Périgord. In this region, where a great deal of corn is raised to feed the pigs, geese, chickens, etc., the peasant is also used to eating it ground and doesn't turn up his nose at it. Brought up on *fougasse,* a badly risen, heavy corn-meal bread, he considered *miques* a good dish, especially when wheat bread was thought a luxury. The younger generation looks down on Corn-Meal Miques. With what disdain do they call misers "*mique* eaters"! However, there are still those who like it, and to them it is very good, even though a little too heavy for most people. It has a fine, pleasant taste, like all corn-meal dishes. Slices of *miques* fried with eggs and sprinkled with sugar, for which I shall give you the recipe, were a real treat in my childhood. *Miques* are extremely simple to prepare. For 3 *miques*, take about ½ lb. corn meal and ½ lb. wheat flour. With these equal proportions you will make finer *miques*. Mix the 2 flours well and knead them with 1 tbsp. fine fat, a little salt, and 1 cup warm water. This will make a very thick paste. Take about ⅓ of it and, with the palm of the hand, make it into a smooth, round ball about the size of an orange. When the *miques* are ready, bring some salted water to a boil, and drop them in, turning them once or twice to cook on all sides. After about ½ hr., they should be cooked; drain them on a cloth and keep hot. Corn-Meal Miques are eaten instead of bread with salt pork and cabbage or with civet of hare or rabbit. They may also be served as a dessert, fried in beaten eggs and covered with currant jelly or honey. They are best this way.

BRANDY CORN-MEAL FRITTERS MICHES (S. F.)

Mix a good handful of corn meal and the same amount of wheat flour in a small bowl; make a hole in the center and break 2 eggs into it; add a pinch of salt, a good wineglass old Armagnac, and ½ glass cold water. Mix thoroughly, then fry in very hot oil, dropping the paste in 1 tbsp. at a time. Drain well and powder with vanilla-flavored sugar.

BORDEAUX CROQUETS CROQUETS DE BORDEAUX

See Pastry, p. 588.

GREEN WALNUT PRESERVES CONFITURE DE NOIX VERTES (S. F.)

This little known but excellent preserve should be made in mid-June, since only green walnuts tender enough to stick a pin all the way through should be used. Shell the nuts, leaving the very fine underskin. Wash them carefully in cold water, then cook them in a kettle of water a fairly long time so they can be crushed with a spoon.

Drain them; put them in a plain coarse linen cloth because they stain a good deal; weigh them, and put them back into the water they were cooked in.

Take the same weight of sugar as you have walnuts; put the sugar into a bowl, cover with cold water, and cook this sirup at least 2 hr. At the end of this time, add the nuts; bring to a boil and simmer 1 hr.; pour the preserves into jelly jars.

Eight days later, recook the sirup only, without the nuts, until it becomes sufficiently thick, which will take a rather long time. It will never have exactly the consistency of jelly. Do not add the nuts, or they will harden. When the recooked sirup is cold, pour it over the nuts and place in small jelly jars.

This preserve should not be prepared in a copper bowl because of the verdigris that might form during the various operations. Better use an enameled utensil.

ILE-DE-FRANCE

(AISNE—OISE—SEINE—SEINE-ET-MARNE—SEINE-ET-OISE)

EGG RING COURONNE D'OEUFS (S. F.)

Allow 1 egg per person. Butter a ring mold, break the eggs in a circle, cook in a *bain-marie*, and let cool. Meanwhile, take an ordinary collop of veal, cook it and let cool. Chop it very fine with 2½ oz. cooked York ham. Unmold the egg ring, surround it with the chopped ham and veal and a few small bunches of water cress. Pour mayonnaise in the center of the ring.

GLAZED SEA BASS AMÉRICAINE BAR GLACÉ À L'AMÉRICAINE (S. F.)

Cook a fine large bass in a well-seasoned Court Bouillon (p. 277). Drain it, remove the head, tail, skin, and bones. Cut it into servings and arrange it on a service platter so that the fish seems whole.

Sauce: Brown some finely chopped onions in some good butter with a tiny bit of oil. Pour in some good dry white wine, some rum, and some tomato sauce. Season with pepper and a dash of cayenne, and let simmer. Test the seasoning, pour this sauce over the fish, glaze in the oven, and serve surrounded with lemon quarters.

COD ÎLE-DE-FRANCE MORUE ÎLE-DE-FRANCE (S. F.)

Soak some fine cod fillets to remove the salt, cook them, and put them on a cloth to cool. Prepare a marinade with 2 tbsp. water to 2 tbsp. vinegar, adding peppercorns, parsley, finely chopped scallion, 1 small clove of garlic cut in 4 pieces, 1 onion sliced in thin rings, and 2 cloves.

Flake the codfish, carefully removing bones and skin, and put it into a deep platter. Pour the marinade over it.

Carefully remove the cod flakes 2 hr. later, place them on a dry linen towel, and wipe them dry. Then prepare a fairly thick Frying Paste (p. 588) with flour, milk, 3 or 4 egg yolks, and grated Gruyère cheese. Dip the flakes in this batter until they are completely covered, then dip them in beaten egg white, and drop them into very hot deep fat. When they are a golden brown, drain them from the fat. Place them in a hot platter and serve with a sauce prepared the following way. Add 1 tbsp. flour to 2 oz. fresh butter; thin with a little milk, enough to make a rather thick sauce, and season with salt, pepper, and a little grated nutmeg. Let the sauce simmer a moment, then add 2 diced hard-boiled eggs and serve in a sauceboat.

THIÉRACHE PORK-LIVER PÂTÉ PÂTÉ DE FOIE DE PORC DE LA THIÉRACHE (S. F.)

Ingredients: ½ lb. pork liver, ¼ lb. pork fat, ¼ lb. pork blood, 7 oz. onions.

Melt the fat, chop the onions, and cook them in the fat without browning; then add the chopped liver and blood and cook a few moments, stirring; season with salt and pepper and let cool.

Prepare a paste made with: flour (enough to make a soft paste), 1 cup milk, 2 whole eggs, 2 oz. butter, salt, and ⅓ oz. yeast. Shape the flour into a ring, break the 2 eggs into the center, add salt and butter, dissolve the yeast in the warm milk and add that. Mix and knead the paste until it becomes elastic and no longer sticks to the fingers; let it rise in a warm place. When the paste has risen, butter a plain mold and lay in ⅔ of the paste, spreading it out with the fingers to line the bottom and sides of the mold. Fill the mold with the prepared force-meat and cover it with the rest of the paste, sealing the edges tightly. Make a small opening in the center and bake in a hot oven, about ¾ hr. This *pâté* or pie is eaten cold or may be slightly reheated.

PHEASANT PARISIENNE FAISAN À LA PARISIENNE (S. F.)

After cleaning the pheasant, slide round slices of truffles between the flesh and skin. Quarter a few peeled truffles, moisten them with cognac and Madeira, season with a pinch of salt and ½ pinch of pepper, and let them marinate about 1 hr.

Peel ¼ lb. mushrooms, chop them fine with the truffle peels, 1 onion, and 1 shallot, and mix with the quartered truffles and their marinade, a few grilled chestnuts, and ¼ lb. pork fat melted and cooled.

Heat this mixture slightly and stuff the pheasant with it. Sew it, and let it soak up the flavors about 48 hr. in a cool place.

Roast the pheasant on a spit, if possible, or, if not, in an oven, taking care to wrap it in a thin strip of pork fat, which should be removed when the pheasant is almost cooked, so that it will turn a beautiful golden brown.

Serve on a hot platter, surrounded by fried croutons, and baste with the cooking gravy.

CHARLOTTE MARCELLE CHARLOTTE MARCELLE (S. F.) (*For 8 persons*)

Ingredients: 6 oz. fresh butter, ¼ lb. almonds, 5 oz. powdered sugar, ½ glass kirsch, ½ lb. Sponge Fingers (p. 586).

Grill the almonds in a low oven without peeling the skin, then rub them in a towel to remove the grilled skins. Pound them in a mortar or, better still, grind them, using the finest blade.

Put them into a bowl with the butter, sugar, and kirsch and beat this mixture about 20 min.

Line the bottom and sides of a charlotte mold with the Sponge Fingers, fill the center with the butter-almond mixture, and cover with Sponge Fingers. Keep in a cool place a few hours. To serve, unmold and cover with cold caramel English Cream (p. 550). It is wise to make this dessert the day before serving.

In addition to these few simple recipes, many specialties were created in Île-de-France, mainly in Paris, despite the opinion of certain epicures. These recipes have become a part of French cooking and are in their rightful place, in the first part of this book.

LANGUEDOC

(ARDÈCHE—AUDE—GARD—HAUTE-GARONNE—HAUTE-LOIRE—HÉRAULT—LOZÈRE—TARN)

POT-AU-FEU ALBIGEOISE POT-AU-FEU À L'ALBIGEOISE (M.)

Meats: 2 lb. leg of beef, 2 lb. knuckle of veal cut in round pieces, 1 lb. raw ham, ¼ preserved goose, 1 small dry sausage (previously blanched).

Vegetables: The usual Petite Marmite vegetables (p. 190) sliced up, 1 heart of cabbage cut in thick julienne strips, 1 qt. dry navy beans (half cooked), 2 crushed cloves of garlic, a *bouquet garni.*

Liquid: 3 qt. white consommé (containing very little salt, since the ham and sausage are already very salty).

Preparation: Put the beef, veal, ham, and blanched sausage into an earthenware marmite. Cover with the cold consommé. Bring to a boil. Skim. Add the vegetables given above, crushed garlic, and *bouquet garni.* Cook at a slow boil, the pot only ¾ covered, 2½ hr. Put the preserved goose into the pot and finish cooking together 1 hr. more. During this last hour, prick the meats, removing those already cooked and keeping them hot.

Serving: Serve the soup in the cooking pot. Along with it, serve the meats, surrounded with part of the vegetables, on a large deep platter. Serve with toasted sliced bread.

Note: This dish is also served as *potée à l'albigeoise.* In this case, increase the amount of cabbage and navy beans.

CASTELNAUDARY CASSOULET or RAGOUT CASSOULET DE CASTELNAUDARY (S. F.)

Ingredients: 1 lb. shoulder of mutton, ½ lb. fresh pork, ¼ lb. pork fat, 7 oz. Toulouse sausage, 1 garlic sausage weighing about 10 oz., 1 qt. navy beans, 10 chopped cloves of garlic, 1 lb. tomatoes or 4 tbsp. tomato purée.

Soak the beans several hours, then start them cooking in salted cold water and continue till half cooked. Meanwhile, bone the shoulder of mutton and cut it into pieces along with the pork and the fat. Brown all of it in butter or good fat, drop in the garlic, turn it a couple of times, and add the drained beans. Cover with water, pepper heavily, salt; cook 3½ hr., watching it closely, adding hot water to make up for that boiled away. After cooking 2 hr., put in the garlic sausage; brown the Toulouse sausage separately in a pan and make a purée of the tomatoes.

Put the meat, beans, Toulouse sausage (cut in thick slices), and garlic sausage (cut in rather thick slices) into a baking dish. Pour the tomato purée over it, sprinkle with bread crumbs, and bake in the oven about ¾ hr. Serve in the baking dish.

TOULOUSE CASSOULET or RAGOUT CASSOULET DE TOULOUSE (S. F.)

After soaking navy beans 12 hr., cook them 1 hr. in salted water with pieces of blanched pork rind tied in a bundle, sliced carrots, and a few cloves of garlic. Add a small garlic sausage and cook together another ½ hr.

Brown ¼ jar of preserved goose in some lard with crushed garlic. Pour in some of the liquid the beans were cooked in, add tomato purée and a *bouquet garni,* and cook 2 hr.

Put the cooked pork rind, goose, and sausage (all sliced) in the bottom of a deep platter. Pour the beans on top, cover with brown bread crumbs, and bake 1 hr. in a slow oven, basting from time to time with the liquid the beans were cooked in.

SWEETBREADS TOULOUSAINE RIS DE VEAU À LA TOULOUSAINE

See Meats, p. 349.

PULLET LANGUEDOCIENNE POULARDE À LA LANGUEDOCIENNE

See Fowl, p. 387.

PULLET TOULOUSAINE POULARDE À LA TOULOUSAINE (S. F.)

Ingredients: 1 young, fat pullet, 13 oz. Toulouse sausage, 1 lb. pitted olives, 1 or 2 whole cloves of garlic, 2 raw tomatoes, and the pullet liver.

Clean, draw, and singe the pullet and remove the neck, leaving the skin attached to the pullet. Make an incision on the inside with the tip of a knife and remove the breastbone without injuring the wings. Cut up the sausage and brown it in a frying pan along with the liver and garlic. Let cool and add the olives; stuff the pullet with this mixture and sew up the opening.

Cook the pullet in butter until a golden brown all over, add 2 small onions, a *bouquet garni,* salt, pepper, 1 good glass white wine, and bring to a boil. Cover tightly and cook about 1½ hr., basting frequently. When only a little gravy remains, strain the 2 tomatoes through a fine sieve and add the purée to the reduced gravy. Let cook another 5 or 6 min.

Place the pullet on a round platter, remove the trussing string, the onions, and the *bouquet garni,* and pour the gravy over it.

WARBLERS SAINT-GERVAIS BECS-FINS À LA SAINT-GERVAIS (S. F.)

Melt about 3½ oz. salted raw ham fat in an earthenware casserole and add 3½ oz. pork fat. Clean the warblers, ortolans, larks, etc., and stuff them with both lean and fat ham. When the ham and pork fat in the casserole is melted and hot, put the birds in it 2 or 3 min. only (time enough to brown them). Remove immediately.

Meanwhile, soften 2 whole garlic heads in boiling water, then separate the cloves and mash them with about 5 oz. tomato paste to make a very smooth new paste. Pour this paste into the casserole left on the stove and stir briskly, adding ½ glass water a little at a time. This last operation contains the secret of the recipe, for the water is indispensable to the smooth blending of the paste and melted fat. Heat this sauce until it comes to a boil, then put in the warblers, stirring gently. Salt, pepper, and cook 10 min. While the warblers are cooking, pound 2–3 oz. juniper berries to powder in a mortar and, when the birds are just cooked, add this powder to the sauce and remove from the fire. The juniper berries must not be allowed to cook.

Serve the warblers in a ring on a very hot platter, and pour the sauce in the center.

COOKED BLOOD SANGUÈTE (M.)

This dish used to be very popular when people killed their own chickens, a custom that now survives only in the country. The chicken should first be bled into a dish containing chopped garlic and parsley and sometimes thin strips of fried bacon. Fry the blood quickly in goose fat or lard. When it is cooked—it cooks very quickly—serve it in a round platter, basted with 1 tbsp. vinegar heated in the same pan.

PRESERVED GOOSE AND FOIE GRAS CONFITS D'OIE ET FOIE GRAS (J.)

The department of Haute-Garonne in Languedoc is a great raiser of geese. For the preparation of geese and *foie gras,* see the recipes on pp. 431 and 433.

BOUGNETTAS or OREILLETTES BOUGNETTAS OR OREILLETTES (M.)

Ingredients: 1 lb. flour, 1½ oz. melted butter, 1 oz. sugar, 1 oz. yeast dissolved in warm water, 4 eggs, 4 tbsp. milk, 4 tbsp. water, 4 tbsp. rum, 1 tbsp. grated lemon peel, ½ tsp. salt.

Mix all these ingredients in a bowl with a wooden spoon, and beat the paste for a few minutes to make a smooth mixture.

Cover the bowl and let rise 6 hr. in a warm place. Drop small parts of the paste into very hot deep oil. Fry until golden brown, drain on a cloth, and sprinkle with sugar.

KALOUGA KALOUGA (S. F.)

Ingredients: 4 eggs; flour, sugar, butter, and chocolate, all weighing the same; 5 oz. Praline (p. 559).

Cut the chocolate into small pieces and melt it in a double boiler with the butter. Keep stirring while you add the whole eggs (1 at a time), powdered sugar, Praline, and flour, which should be sprinkled in so that lumps won't form. Stir the paste until it becomes very smooth. Pour into a buttered mold and bake, keeping the interior of the cake soft. Let cool, unmold, and serve with a coffee-flavored cream.

LIMOUSIN

(CORRÈZE—HAUTE-VIENNE)

PRESERVED GOOSE CONFIT D'OIE (S. F.)

Pluck a fine fat goose, cut it into pieces, and bone. Remove all the fat from the intestines and skin, cut the fat and skin into tiny pieces, and melt them slowly in a copper pot. Then drop the pieces of goose into the fat and cook slowly until any remaining bones have separated from the meat. Place the goose in a glazed stoneware jar with 2 small brackets sterilized in boiling water in the bottom; cover the goose with the fat strained through a fine sieve, and let cool. Next, cover the jars and keep them in a dry place.

HARE AU CABESSAL LIÈVRE AU CABESSAL

Limousin name for Hare Royale; see p. 480.

CHERRY or RAISIN CLAFOUTI CLAFOUTI LIMOUSIN (S. F.)

Beat 3 eggs as for an omelet, add 1 tbsp. powdered sugar, a pinch of salt, ½ cup milk, and blend in 3 heaping tbsp. flour. Mix into this paste 1 lb. black cherries or, if unavailable, 1 lb. large Muscat raisins. Pour into a buttered tin and bake ½–¾ hr. After removing from the oven, sprinkle with vanilla-flavored sugar.

CHESTNUT CAKE LIMOUSINE GÂTEAU DE CHÂTAIGNES À LA LIMOUSINE (S. F.)

Take 3 lb. good chestnuts, split the shells all the way around, and start them cooking in water. When they are ½ cooked, remove the shells and the skin underneath. Put them in another pan to finish cooking, and strain them through a fine sieve. Add to this purée, while it is still hot, 7 oz. fresh butter, 7 oz. powdered sugar, 3 eggs, and a generous amount of vanilla; mix well.

Butter a mold, pour the mixture into it, cook covered in a *bain-marie,* and let cool. Serve the next day with whipped cream, or a chocolate cream made the following way. Take 4 eggs, 4 grated chocolate tablets, 4 lumps of sugar melted and almost caramelized, 4 tbsp. powdered sugar. Beat the egg yolks well, add the chocolate, caramel, and powdered sugar, beating constantly, and fold in 3 stiffly beaten egg whites.

LORRAINE

(MEURTHE-ET-MOSELLE—MEUSE—MOSELLE—VOSGES)

QUICHE LORRAINE QUICHE LORRAINE (S. F.) (*For 6 persons*)

Make a Short Paste (p. 545) with 7 oz. sifted flour, 2 oz. fresh butter, 1½ oz. lard, a good pinch of salt, 2 tbsp. water. Do not work this paste too much; kneading it 2 or 3 times should suffice.

Let it stand 1 hr., then roll it out in a circle the size of your tart pan, which should be about 8 in. in diameter. Lift the paste and carefully place it in the pan without tearing, lining the pan to the rim. While the paste is standing, fry 20 thin strips of lean, smoked bacon in a little butter. Cover the tart crust with this bacon.

Meanwhile, beat about 1 cup very fresh cream in a bowl with 2 eggs and a pinch of salt. When the mixture is smooth, pour it over the bacon and place the *quiche* in the oven. Bake about ½ hr. in a very hot oven, making sure that it cooks equally well on top and bottom. The top should be a golden brown. Serve the *quiche* hot, as an entree, but not piping hot—that is, about ½ hr. after taking it out of the oven.

POPPY-SEED TART TARTE AU PAVOT or QUICHE AU SEMZAN (S. F.)

Make a Short Paste (p. 545) and line the tart pan with it.

Take 1 pt. poppy seeds, moisten them with a little hot milk, and crush them; add a little semolina cooked in lightly salted milk, 2 eggs, ½ cup fresh cream, and some salt. Mix well; pour it into the bottom crust, cover with the top crust, brush with beaten egg, and place in the oven. It should bake a rather long time—¾–1 hr., depending on the oven.

This tart is eaten as a cold entree and is greatly appreciated by gourmets. It is a Lorraine dish, a specialty of Toul.

TROUT LORRAINE TRUITES À LA LORRAINE (S. F.)

Take some fresh, medium-sized trout (7 oz. trout per person). Choose French trout rather than American rainbow trout, which are less delicate and flavorful. Scale and clean them carefully, then wipe them dry in a towel. Roll each trout lightly in flour.

Melt a large piece of fine butter in a frying pan—don't let it brown—and fry the trout in it till golden brown, a few minutes on each side; salt, cover the pan, and cook 7–8 min. on a very low flame.

Place the trout on a hot platter; drop about 2 oz. butter into the frying pan and pour in about ½ pt. very fresh extra-heavy cream; let the mixture get hot, then pour it very hot over the trout. Serve on very hot plates.

HOME-STYLE CHITTERLING SAUSAGES LORRAINE ANDOUILLES DE MÉNAGE À LA LORRAINE (S. F.)

Take a blanched calf's crow, the same weight of pork meat, and ½ this weight of fresh pork fat. Cut all of it into tiny pieces. Chop garlic, shallots, onions, and parsley and mix with the meat. Add 1 tsp. salt per lb. mixture and a generous amount of pepper. Mix well in a pan, and add 1 onion stuck with 2 cloves, and 2 bay leaves, which should be removed when the sausage is stuffed. Let macerate 2 days, stirring it from time to time, without mashing it. Stuff it into lengths of intestines, tie the ends like sausages, and leave overnight in brine. Remove and store in a dry place. This keeps 5 or 6 months and can be eaten after 5 or 6 days.

LYONNAIS

(LOIRE—RHÔNE)

PIKE QUENELLES LYONNAISE QUENELLES DE BROCHET LYONNAISE

See Fish, p. 307.

TRIPE LYONNAISE GRAS DOUBLE À LA LYONNAISE (M.)

Sauté 3 lb. tripe cut in strips in smoking-hot oil (or lard); season with salt and pepper. Add 10 oz. thin-sliced onions cooked in lard (or butter). Sauté together until well browned. Place in a dish; heat a finger of vinegar in the sauté-ing pan and pour it over the tripe and onions; sprinkle chopped parsley on top.

PULLET IN HALF MOURNING POULARDE DEMI-DEUIL

See Fowl, p. 384.

GRILLED CHICKEN LYONNAISE POULET GRILLÉ À LA LYONNAISE (M.)

Cover the chicken, when it is almost cooked, with chopped onion cooked in butter. Bread it. Finish cooking it on the grill. Garnish with slices of grilled ham and sautéed Potatoes Lyonnaise (p. 508). Serve with Lyonnaise Sauce (p. 142).

LYON FRITTERS BUGNES DE LYON (S. F.)

Make a fritter batter (see p. 558) with ½ pt. milk, flour, 1 whole unbeaten egg, dash of salt, powdered sugar, chopped lemon peel or orange-flower water; mix as for ordinary fritters.

Special long-handled molds are needed to make *bugnes;* dip them in the hot fat to heat them, then into the batter, which should be fairly thin. They should be dipped in ¾ of the way, to take in the necessary amount of batter, and then dipped quickly into the very hot fat, where the fritters will separate from the mold and finish cooking; remove them when they are golden brown, and drain them on a cloth. Repeat the process quickly until all the batter has been used. Sprinkle the fritters with powdered sugar. They may be eaten cold as well as hot, and keep very well.

CRUSTS LYONNAISE CROÛTES À LA LYONNAISE

See Pastry, p. 617.

MAINE

(MAYENNE—SARTHE)

APPLE DUMPLINGS BOURDAINES (S. F.)

First prepare a rather thick paste with 1 egg, a piece of butter, flour, water, and a little salt. Pare and core some fine large apples, without splitting them, and fill with preserves, preferably plum; wrap each apple in a piece of paste about 3/16 in. thick. Seal the paste carefully around the apples so that it will not open while baking. Brush the surface with a little milk or cream and bake in the oven. May be eaten hot or cold.

Note: This province has almost the same specialties as its neighbor, Orléanais. (See pp. 731-732.)

MARCHE

(CREUSE)

CRAYFISH VILLEDARY ÉCREVISSES À LA VILLEDARY (S. F.)

To prepare 50 crayfish, brown in 3 tbsp. oil in a copper pan, over a very hot fire, 1 large, thin-sliced onion and 3 thin-sliced shallots, 1 bay leaf, 5 or 6 sprigs of parsley, 2 sprigs of chervil, 1 sprig of tarragon, 2 cloves of garlic, 2 small pimentos, 2 small diced carrots.

Sauté 5–6 min., then add 1½ pt. old white wine, salt to taste, ½ tsp. peppercorns, 2 pinches of powdered pepper, 1 pinch of spices (powdered clove, white pepper, ginger, nutmeg), 2 cloves. When it comes to a boil, put in the crayfish, and add 1 wineglass brandy. Cover and cook at a rapid boil 6–8 min. at most. Remove the crayfish; place them in a deep platter or in a vegetable dish and keep very hot. Strain the cooking stock, reduce it by ⅓, and thicken it with 3 or 4 tbsp. tomato sauce and 2 tbsp. meat extract. Bring to a quick boil a couple of times and remove from the stove. Blend 3½ oz. butter into the sauce bit by bit; finish with a light dash of cayenne pepper, a little chopped parsley, and lemon juice. Pour the sauce over the crayfish and serve very hot.

POTATO PIE CREUSOIS PÂTÉ CREUSOIS AUX POMMES DE TERRE (S. F.)

Take 1½ lb. flour, make a well in the center, and place 13 oz. butter, a pinch of salt, and 1 glass milk in it. Make a smooth, softish paste and work it a good while. Put ⅓ of it aside.

Roll out the other ⅔. Line a buttered baking tin with the paste, making the sides extend above the rim of the pan. Put a layer of very thinly sliced potatoes into this bottom crust; salt, pepper, and sprinkle with chopped parsley. Pour a good layer of fresh cream on top of the potatoes. Repeat this operation until the pie has been filled. Finish with a layer of cream. Roll out the rest of the paste, and cover the pie with it. Roll edges of the bottom crust over the top, pinching all around to seal the pie tightly.

Bake 1½–2 hr. in a hot oven.

NIVERNAIS

(NIÈVRE)

NIVERNAIS OMELET OMELETTE NIVERNAISE (M.)

Lightly brown some thin slices of ham and cook down some finely shredded sorrel and chopped chives in a frying pan with butter. Pour in the beaten and seasoned eggs. Make the omelet in the shape of a pancake.

BRAISED VEAL IN RED WINE ÉTUVÉE DE VEAU AU VIN ROUGE (M.)

Use boned knuckle of veal. Cut the meat in even-sized pieces and season; brown in butter with thin-sliced onions. Sprinkle with flour, then pour in some red wine. Season with garlic and a *bouquet garni.* Cover and cook slowly.

CRACKLING GALETTES GALETTE AUX GRIAUDES (M.)

Griaudes is a Nivernais term for those small pieces of browned pork fat, or cracklings, which remain in the sieve after the fat has been rendered and strained. Prepare these galettes by mixing cracklings into ordinary Brioche Paste (p. 546). Shape the galette into a ring. Bake in a medium-hot oven.

PEAR LOAF PÂTÉ AUX POIRES (M.)

Shape bread dough into a long rectangular loaf. Fill it with peeled, thin-sliced pears bound with a mixture of fresh cream and egg yolks. Bake in a low oven.

When the dough has cooked, pour a few tbsp. fresh cream bound with egg yolks through an opening made in the top.

NORMANDY

(CALVADOS—EURE—MANCHE—ORNE—SEINE-MARITIME)

MACKEREL FILLETS FÉCAMP STYLE FILETS DE MAQUEREAUX À LA MODE DE FÉCAMP (S. F.)

Slice the fillets from 6 mackerel and cook them in butter with very little white wine. Cook 2 qt. fine mussels with white wine, chopped shallots, pepper, and parsley.

Save the mussel cooking liquid to make a creamy white sauce, adding to it, at the last moment, some chopped parsley and butter. Reduce the mackerel cooking liquid a good deal and add this to the sauce. Remove the mussels from the shells. Place the mackerel fillets on a platter, arrange the mussels around them, and pour sauce over all.

SOLE FILLETS NORMANDE FILETS DE SOLE À LA NORMANDE

See Fish, p. 301.

TRIPE À LA MODE DE CAEN TRIPES À LA MODE DE CAEN

See Meat, p. 337.

TRIPE CHAPLAIN STYLE TRIPES À LA MODE CHAPLAIN (S. F.)

This recipe has been handed down faithfully for generations in my Norman family. It is different from all other tripe recipes in cookbooks because it doesn't call for a drop of water or lard. This will give you an incomparable dish, which, though cooked the usual way, is smooth, exquisite in flavor, and golden in color. To succeed, you must first have a good earthenware marmite or soup pot with a cover. Here are the ingredients:

3 lb. beef tripe (including various parts of the stomach), 1 quartered calf's foot, 1 lb. fresh butter, 3 large carrots, 3 onions, 3 cabbage leaves, 2 bay leaves, 3 cloves, 1 sprig of thyme, salt, pepper, and spices.

Cover the bottom of the marmite with sliced carrots and onions, thyme, bay leaf, cloves, spices, salt, and pepper; sprinkle with small bits of butter (about ⅓ lb.). On top of this make a layer of tripe cut in good-sized pieces and ½ the calf's foot. Now make another layer of carrots, onions, clove, pepper, etc., then a second layer of tripe and calf's foot, and so on, until the pot is full. Finish with a layer of carrots sprinkled with butter, cover with the cabbage leaves, and seal tightly with a sheet of buttered paper between the edge of the pot and the cover.

The best way to cook it is to place it in a very hot oven at 5 o'clock in the evening, keep the fire up until 10 o'clock, and leave the pot in the hot oven for the rest of the night (with no fire); relight the fire at 8 o'clock in the morning to have the tripe ready for the noon meal. Serve from the cooking pot onto very hot plates.

The Normans claim that only cider is fit to accompany this dish.

BLACK PUDDING NORMANDE BOUDIN NOIR À LA NORMANDE

See Meat, p. 375.

CHICKEN ROUENNAIS POULET ROUENNAIS (S. F.)

Cut up a very tender chicken. Put a good piece of butter into a sautéing pan on a very hot fire; when the butter is clarified, lay in the pieces of chicken seasoned with salt and pepper. When the pieces begin to brown, turn them, then cover and place in the oven. When ¾ cooked, add raw mushrooms cut in thick julienne strips.

After the chicken is fully cooked, reduce the gravy, pour 1 glass brandy over it, and set it aflame; add 3 oz. extra-heavy cream and let simmer a few moments.

Arrange the pieces of chicken in a ring on a round platter. Butter your sauce, then in the center of the ring place a fine slice of smoked ham rolled into a cone. Fill the cone with very green asparagus and serve.

ROUEN DUCKLING CANETON ROUENNAIS

See Fowl, pp. 423-429.

PHEASANT VALLÉE D'AUGE FAISAN À LA VALLÉE D'AUGE

See Game, p. 462.

CRUSTS NORMANDE CROÛTES À LA NORMANDE

See Pastry, p. 617.

NORMAN POTFUL or RICE PUDDING TERRINÉE NORMANDE (S. F.)

Ingredients: ¼ lb. Carolina rice, 2½ oz. sugar, 2 qt. boiled milk, ½ tbsp. cinnamon, a pinch of salt.

Put the rice, sugar, salt, and cinnamon into a baking dish and mix well; pour in the milk and, finally, add a good piece of fresh butter. Cook 3 hr. in a medium oven. If the top begins to brown too much, cover it with buttered paper.

This rice is served hot or cold in the same baking dish.

ORLÉANAIS

(EURE-ET-LOIR—LOIR-ET-CHER—LOIRET)

ORLÉANS SOUP SOUPE ALÉNOISE OR ORLÉANAISE (M.)

Cook 1 lb. sliced potatoes in white consommé (or, simply, salted water).

When the potatoes are cooked, break them a little by beating with a wire whisk. Add 7 oz. picked, washed, coarsely shredded garden cress. Cook 6 min. at a rapid boil. When finished, add 3½ oz. butter and chervil leaves (with no stems).

HEN BEAUCERONNE POULE À LA BEAUCERONNE (S. F.)

Be a good housekeeper and don't let hens grow old in the chickenyard after they have stopped laying. To begin preparing a luncheon for some gourmet friends, put an end to one of those plump birds which are fattening themselves at your expense.

Pluck and clean the hen and let it become tender. Over a low fire, melt the fat taken from the inside of the bird and save it.

When the day arrives, put your chicken on the chopping board and cut it into neat pieces; place these in a sautéing pan in which you have heated the fat mentioned above and a large piece of butter. Turn the chicken until it is evenly browned on all sides, then take out the pieces, put on a platter, and keep warm at the back of the stove. Pour 1 cup veal or chicken stock into the pan, season with salt and pepper, add 4 heaping tbsp. shredded onions and a bouquet made of parsley and very little thyme, and let simmer 1 good hr. Allow enough time for the hen to cook and drop the pieces into the sauce, which the onions should have thickened. When it is time to serve, the pieces of onion should have disappeared completely. Place the chicken on a hot platter and pour the strained sauce over it.

Do not add any cornstarch unless the sauce is too liquid.

PITHIVIERS LARK PIE PÂTÉ D'ALOUETTES DE PITHIVIERS

See Game, p. 533.

ORLÉANS QUINCE JAM COTIGNAC D'ORLÉANS (S. F.)

Take some beautiful ripe quinces; slice them, remove the core, but leave the peel. Place them in a pan with enough water to cover, bring to a boil, then simmer till soft and stewed down. Pour them with their juice into a sieve placed over a bowl to catch the juice.

Soften the same amount of quinces as in the first preparation, but instead of water use the strained juice of the first quinces. Strain them as before, weigh this second juice, and add to it an equal weight of sugar, and cook it again.

The *cotignac* is cooked when the sirup boils with a heavy swelling movement. It now has only to be put into jars like jam.

PITHIVIERS (ALMOND CAKE) GÂTEAU AUX AMANDES DE PITHIVIERS

See Pastry, p. 578.

PICARDY

(SOMME)

PICARDY BLOOD PUDDING BOUDIN PICARD (S. F.)

Ingredients: 1 lb. hog fat, 4 lb. onions, 1 pt. fresh pig's blood.

Peel and slice the onions. Cut the hog fat into small pieces and melt in an iron pot. When the fat has melted, drop in the onions and cook them on a low fire, stirring from time to time. Season with salt, pepper, and a pinch of powdered clove.

When the onions are well cooked, remove them from the fire and let them cool until merely warm, then add the blood, mixing it with a wooden spoon. Stuff this into well-cleaned links of pork intestine, and tie at both ends. Prick them lightly with a pin. Plunge the puddings into a potful of boiling water and then poach them ¼ hr. on a low fire. Don't let the water come to a boil again.

Remove the puddings, drain, and let them cool on racks. To serve, grill them with mustard.

LEEK TART FLAMICHE AUX POIREAUX (S. F.) (*For 6 persons*)

(In Picardy dialect: *el flamique à porgeons.*)

The leek filling: Wash 12 very white leeks and remove the first skin; leave on only ¼ of the green. Quarter the leeks lengthwise and then slice them in ¼-in. pieces.

Boil them 5 min. (This will take away their strong taste.) After draining them, drop them into a second pot of boiling water salted to taste; after 1 hr. at a rapid boil, the leeks should be properly tender. Drain them carefully; if necessary, press with a skimming ladle.

Make a white sauce in a stewpan with 2 oz. butter and 1 tbsp. flour; add the leeks, salt, a dash of pepper, and mix well, over a very low fire, with 2 or 3 tbsp. cream or, if lacking, milk and 1 egg yolk. Keep warm off the fire.

The paste: Prepare the paste the night before or at least far enough in advance to let it stand 3 hr. Take 7 oz. flour, 3½ oz. butter, 1 egg yolk, 1 tsp. salt, ½ glass water. Make the flour into a well in a mixing bowl and in the center put the water, egg yolk, and salt; mix well, then blend in the butter in small bits; knead by hand without working it too much.

Wrap your ball of paste in a linen cloth and let it stand overnight in a cool place. Set aside ¼ of your paste to use in making the top crust; roll out the rest until it is just a little thicker than a tart crust. Use this to line a heavily buttered tart pan. Fill this bottom crust with the leek filling.

Roll out a round top crust from the paste you have saved, cover the tart with it, and bring the edges of the bottom crust over the top, rolling it over lightly and sealing it to look like a twist. Brush with beaten egg and bake 40 min. in a hot oven.

POITOU

(DEUX-SÈVRES—VENDÉE—VIENNE)

FISH STEW FOURASINE CHAUDRÉE FOURASINE (S. F.) (*For 8 persons*)

Take 10 oz. medium-sized soles, 1 lb. small rays (skate), 10 oz. plaice, 1 lb. eels.

Carefully clean the sole and plaice; skin the rays (skate), saving only the wings; skin and clean the eels and cut each into 3 or 4 pieces. Wash all the fish in several waters and drain a few moments. Put into a stewpan 10 or 12 cloves of garlic, salt, a copious amount of pepper, 1 bay leaf, a little thyme, a bunch of parsley, white wine and water if the wine is strong; if it isn't, 2⁄3 wine and 1⁄3 water—enough to cover the fish. Boil 10–15 min. Now add 1½–2 oz. good butter and simmer about 20 min. Before serving, add another 2 oz. butter and serve very hot. Only the freshest fish should be used.

BEEFSTEAKS POITEVINE BIFTECKS À LA POITEVINE (S. F.)

Cut the fat and sinews from about 1 lb. lean beef and chop it very fine. Mash fine the marrow of 2 marrowbones and mix it with the chopped meat. Put this into a terrine with salt, pepper, nutmeg; mix well together, adding, bit by bit, 1 tbsp. fine semolina and 3 or 4 whole eggs. Meanwhile, have soaking in a bowl 7 oz. soft white bread with enough milk to saturate it. Mash the bread, drain it, and put it into a terrine. Next heat 1 finely chopped onion in butter without letting it brown; add it to the bread soaked in milk, and mix together with the ground meat. Let stand 1 hr.

Take 2 spoons and shape the ground-meat mixture, which should be a rather solid paste, into small beefsteaks about 1 in. thick.

Place them in a pan containing very hot butter. Cover and cook ¼ hr. over a moderate fire, turning the beefsteaks when they are ½ done. Place them on a hot platter. Pour ½ glass white wine and a few tbsp. bouillon into the pan, boil a few minutes, and finish with chopped parsley and lemon juice. Pour this gravy over the beefsteaks before serving them. They should be very soft on the inside and slightly crusty on the outside. The addition of truffles will further improve this tasty, though simply prepared, regional dish. It may be served with a dish of sorrel, spinach, or the 2 mixed, chicory, or tomato purée.

POITOU CAKE GÂTEAU POITEVIN (S. F.)

Ingredients: 6 eggs, 1 lb. butter, 1 lb. flour, and 1¼ lb. sugar, angelica flavoring or orange-flower water.

Preparation: Knead the butter until soft; add the sugar bit by bit, working it with a wooden spoon, then the egg yolks, 1 by 1, a few grains of salt, and finally the flour. Beat the mixture well, for this will make the cake lighter. Fold the stiffly beaten egg whites into the paste; flavor with orange-flower water or, more common in this region, Niort angelica cut into small pieces.

Spread the paste with a fork on oiled brown wrapping paper and spread the surface with a light layer of stiffly beaten egg whites. Fold the edges of the paper together and sew them to prevent the cake from spilling over while baking. Bake 15–20 min. in a rather hot oven. When removed from the oven, the cake should be golden brown on both sides. The paper can be easily removed.

This delicious pastry is made for all family feasts and reunions, and many of the local citizens prefer this country dessert to city-made brioches.

PROVENCE

(Basses-Alpes—Bouches-du-Rhône—Var)

AÏGO-BOUIDO or BOILED-WATER SOUP soupe aïgo-bouido (soupe à l'eau bouillie) (M.)

Put 10 crushed cloves of garlic, a sprig of sage, some coarse salt, and a pinch of pepper into a soup pot. Add 3 oz. olive oil. Pour in 2 qt. water and boil 8–10 min.

Pour into the soup tureen onto slices of household bread sprinkled with chopped parsley.

Note: Aïgo-Bouido can also be garnished with eggs poached in the broth.

AÏGO-SAOU or FISH SOUP soupe aïgo-saou (M.)

Put 1 medium-sized, sliced onion, 2 chopped tomatoes, 2 crushed cloves of garlic, and a *bouquet garni* (parsley, bay leaf, and fennel) into a soup pot. On top of this put 2 lb. sliced white fish and 3 quartered potatoes. Season with salt and pepper. Pour in 3 pt. water. Cook 20 min. at a rapid boil.

Pour the broth into a tureen containing slices of bread moistened with olive oil and seasoned with freshly ground pepper.

HOME-STYLE AÏGO-SAOU SOUP soupe aïgo-saou à la ménagère (M.)

Lightly brown in oil 1 sliced onion and the sliced white of 3 leeks. Add 2 drained, chopped tomatoes, 4 crushed cloves of garlic, a *bouquet garni,* a little dried orange peel, and a sprig of fennel. Add 3 sliced potatoes; season with salt and pepper. Pour in 3½ pt. water. Bring to a boil. Let cook 15–18 min. at a rapid boil. Poach 1 egg per person in this broth. Soak some thick slices of bread in a deep dish with a few tbsp. of this broth.

Serve the potatoes on a separate plate, put the poached eggs on top, and sprinkle with chopped parsley. Serve the rest of the soup separately.

Note: Aïgo-Saou Soup is also made in Provence with fresh sardines.

GARLIC SOUP soupe à l'ail (M.)

Put 20 cloves of garlic, 1 or 2 cloves, 4 sage leaves, salt, and pepper into a soup pot. Pour in 2 qt. water. Cook 15–18 min. Sprinkle some thin slices of bread with cheese, brown them in the oven, line the tureen with them, and pour 2 tbsp. oil over them. Then strain the soup over the tureen, pressing down with the ladle.

SARDINE SOUP SOUPE BOURRIDE DE SARDINES (M.)

Proceed as for ordinary Bouillabaisse (below), using fresh sardines as a base and leaving out the tomato and saffron.

When the Sardine Soup is cooked, finish it the following way. Put 1 egg yolk and 1 tbsp. *aïoli* (garlic crushed with olive oil) per person into a soup pot. Mix these ingredients well, off the stove, gradually adding some of the Sardine Soup, beating with a wire whisk. Cook this mixture on the stove, stirring constantly as when making an English Cream (p. 550). It may also be cooked in a double boiler.

Pour this thickened soup into a deep dish garnished with slices of bread. Place the sardines on top. Serve the rest of the soup separately in a tureen.

BOUILLABAISSE BOUILLABAISSE (M.)

This dish is a symbol of Provence: the poets have duly celebrated it, and epicures rave about it. It is difficult, if not impossible, to make this dish, as it should be made, outside the sun-drenched regions bordering the Mediterranean. Only there can one find all the fish needed for this saffron soup whose origin is lost in the mist of the ages.

Hogfish is the base of this dish. This bizarre-looking fish flavors the Bouillabaisse with the iodine that characterizes all rock fishes and provides the gelatin to give the soup the proper thickness.

The number of different fish used in Bouillabaisse is very large:[1] the multicolored *rouquier;* purple-and-blue-striped *girelle;* John Dory, bristling with spikes; the *baudroie*, or angler fish, with its deformed body; the black-and-silver conger eel; the moray, speckled with golden rings; and, finally, all shellfish: spiny lobsters, prawns, squillfish, edible crabs, etc.

All these ingredients, dominated by a note of garlic, combine and blend their flavors. The action of the live heat extracts the essential juices from their cells and fixes them in a bath of oil, tomato pulp, saffron, and fragrant herbs. Bouillabaisse must be cooked quickly, for prolonged cooking will make it lose its flavor.

Bouillabaisse is truly a poem, and it is not surprising that Provençal legends trace its invention to the goddess Venus.

(*For 10 persons*)

Skin and trim the fins and tails from 8–10 small, salt-water fish described above. Cut them into even-sized chunks, and add 13 oz. sliced conger eel. Split 2 small spiny lobsters in 2. Add a few crabs, squillfish, and prawns. Season the fish and put them into a deep pot with the firmest fish on the bottom. The following ingredients should be put into the pot before laying in the fish: 2 chopped onions, 3 crushed tomatoes, a crushed clove of garlic, thyme, bay leaf, fennel,

---

[1] These fish are peculiar to the Mediterranean coast, but almost any of our small, salt-water fish may be substituted.

parsley. Sprinkle with 1 tbsp. powdered saffron; pour in 6 oz. oil and 3 qt. fish stock; cover the pot and bring to a quick boil. Cook 15 min. at a rolling boil.

This amount of cooking should suffice if the fish have been cut into the proper sizes (fish that take longer to cook should be sliced smaller). Remove the fish and crustaceans and place them in a large deep dish. Reduce the bouillon a few minutes over a good fire and strain through a cone-shaped sieve. Pour it boiling hot into a soup tureen containing 20 thick slices of bread.

Note: There are several ways of preparing this Provençal soup. Some chefs add sliced leek, others first lightly brown the onion in oil. These methods seem to be a departure from the typical recipe given above.

In some of the river regions near the Mediterranean a completely different fish soup is served as Bouillabaisse. In Perpignan, Bouillabaisse includes potatoes and is often made without saffron. In Béziers, Agde, and Sète, a fish soup is made with oil heavily seasoned with garlic and fortified with a large amount of chopped parsley. This dish resembles Waterzoi rather than Bouillabaisse, except that the Waterzoi is made with fresh-water fish, while the Béziers soup uses salt-water fish as a base.

To conclude these remarks on Bouillabaisse, we should like to add that it is not necessary to add even a small amount of cognac to the soup; it only spoils the fresh taste that comes from combining the flavors of various fish with oil, tomato, saffron, and aromatics.

MARSEILLES BOUILLABAISSE BOUILLABAISSE DE MARSEILLE (S. F.) (*For 10 persons*)

Take 3 lb. various fish such as: hogfish, angler fish, weever, John Dory, *galinette,* whiting, and 2 spiny lobsters.[1] All these fish must be alive.

Scale, clean, wash the salt-water fish and cut them in chunks. Put into a large pot with a thick bottom: 2 onions, 4 tomatoes, 4 cloves of garlic, all coarsely chopped, and 3 oz. excellent olive oil. Flavor with 2 fennel tops, bay leaf, and a good pinch of powdered saffron. Season with ½ oz. coarse salt and a good pinch of pepper. Mix well together; add the fish with firm flesh and set aside the tender ones to be added after 5 min. cooking. Pour in enough boiling water (not white wine, which would take away the fresh flavor of the fish) to cover those fish yet to be added. Place on a very hot fire and cook 12–15 min. at a rolling boil. Success depends upon this boiling.

Meanwhile, cut a long loaf of French bread into rather thin slices, allowing about 4 per person; dry them a few moments in the oven without toasting.

When the Bouillabaisse is ready, gently place the pieces of fish in a platter; pour the bouillon through a strainer into a bowl containing the slices of bread sprinkled with chopped parsley.

If the Bouillabaisse is well made, you should be able to distinguish the flavor of each variety of fish. The pepper should be noticeable and the bouillon naturally thickened by the violent boiling.

FRIED ANCHOVIES ANCHOÏADE (A. C.)

Cut some fine anchovies into fillets, dip them in milk, then in flour, then in

[1] Since most of these fish are not found in American waters, almost any variety of small, salt-water fish and 2 lobsters or rock-lobster tails will do.

vinegar, and a second time in flour. Fry them in burning-hot oil. Brown a few cloves of garlic, add a little flour and vinegar to form a thin sauce, reduce it, and pour over the anchovies. Serve hot with some onion.

ANCHOVY CRUSTS ANCHOÏADE (C.)

Soak the salt from some anchovies, slice off the fillets, and crush them with a fork. Make a little sauce with a crushed clove of garlic, a little pepper, a finger of vinegar, and a few tbsp. olive oil. Mix this with the anchovy purée and spread it on small canapés of stale bread, pressing it well into the bread; brown these crusts in the oven and serve hot.

ANCHOVY TART PISSALADIERA (C.)

Make a tart crust with bread dough or even some unsweetened Flaky Paste (p. 544) and prick the bottom with a fork. Cook a generous amount of sliced sweet onions in oil with salt, pepper, clove, and 2 crushed cloves of garlic. Put this into the tart and cover with anchovy fillets, sprinkle a few black olives on top, baste with olive oil, and bake ½ hr. in a medium oven.

BEEF DAUBE (Old Provençal Recipe) BOEUF À LA DAUBE (S. F.)

Chop fine an egg-sized piece of pork fat; put it with 1 good tbsp. pure lard into the bottom of an earthenware pot; lay in a fine piece of beef (preferably fillet or sirloin), 1 whole onion stuck with 1 or 2 cloves, ½ bay leaf, a few cloves of garlic. Brown over a low fire.

When the lard is completely melted and the beef browned on all sides, completely cover the meat with good red wine. Cook at a rapid boil 8–10 min., then add ½ glass boiling water; salt, pepper heavily, seal the pot tightly with the cover and a piece of butcher's paper placed between the cover and the pot. Let cook, covered, 5 hr. at very low heat. When ready to serve, remove what is left of the onion, garlic, and other garnishes that have not completely disappeared. Keep very hot and be careful to take the sauce from the bottom of the dish, to avoid the fat on top (this fat may be used in making a delicious macaroni dish, adding the cheese just before serving).

To have the finest quality, Beef Daube should be cooked in a tightly sealed earthenware pot so that none of the juice is lost.

PROVENÇAL SAUSAGES GAYETTES À LA PROVENÇAL (Gi.)

These are the equivalent of Parisian Crépinettes (p. 375) and Burgundy *griblettes*. They are served either hot or cold.

Ingredients (for 15 *gayettes,* each weighing about 2½ oz.) : 1 lb. pork liver and 1 lb. fat cut from the intestines (as our colleague Reboul, the eminent author of *Cuisinière du Midi,* advises), ½ lb. pork mincemeat, 3 crushed cloves of garlic, 1 tbsp. parsley. 1 oz. spiced salt, and about 12 oz. very fine pig's caul.

Preparation: Dice the liver and fat fine, place in a dish, and sprinkle with spiced salt. Let stand about 20 min. to let the seasoning penetrate. Mix it well in a bowl with the mincemeat, garlic, and parsley.

This done, cut the pig's caul (which should first be soaked in cold water to soften it) into rectangles 4 in. long and 2½ in. wide; lay them side by side on a cloth. Place about 2½ oz. mixture on each piece of pig's caul and wrap them carefully.

Cooking: Place the sausages in a shallow baking or roasting dish, baste heavily with lard or fat from the stew pot, and bake 35 min. in a medium oven.

Serving: If they are to be served hot, accompany them with mashed potatoes or purée of split peas. When served cold, accompany them with aspic and gherkins, but, in this case, instead of making 15, only make 5, cutting the pig's caul into larger pieces. Since the sausages will be larger, they will take longer to cook —50 min. instead of 35. These large ones should be cut into slices like a galantine and arranged in a ring on a platter.

MARSEILLES FEET AND BUNDLES PIEDS ET PAQUETS MARSEILLAIS (S. F.)

Chop some lean bacon, garlic, and parsley. Cut mutton tripe into sections, fill the center of each with the chopped mixture, and shape into small bundles.

Brown sliced onions, leeks, and carrots and cloves of garlic in oil in an earthenware pot. First put in the mutton feet and then the bundles, pour in some white wine, add a few chopped tomatoes, and season with salt and pepper. Cover tightly and bake in the oven. To serve, skim the fat off the sauce, place the bundles and feet on a platter, and pour the sauce on top.

STUFFED CANNELLONI CANNEBIÈRE CANNELLONI FARCIS CANNEBIÈRE (S. F.)

Take a box of cannelloni containing 12 squares. Poach them 4–5 min. in lightly salted boiling water. Remove them carefully and place them on a cloth to sponge them dry.

Prepare the following stuffing. Take some leftover lean stewed or braised beef (or, if you have none, veal or chicken). Add some lean ham, a little bread soaked in milk, 1 tbsp. tomato purée, salt, and pepper, and heat in butter a few minutes. Spread this filling on the squares of paste and make into large tight rolls. Place the rolls in a baking dish, tightly press together side by side, and cover with the following gravy. (Allow 2 or 3 cannelloni per person.)

Gravy for cannelloni and other Italian pastes: Put a good piece of butter, 1 tbsp. tomato purée, some meat gravy, salt, pepper, *bouquet garni,* and 1 glass good dry white wine into a saucepan, and cook 20 min. Pour this gravy over the cannelloni, but not too heavily. Sprinkle lightly with grated Parmesan or Gruyère cheese or ⅔ Gruyère and ⅓ Parmesan. Cover with a buttered paper. Brown 15–20 min. in a slow oven.

Variation: The cannelloni may be filled with a mixture of spinach, veal, and brains, and covered with creamed Béchamel Sauce (p. 146) and cheese as described above.

ROUSSILLON

(PYRÉNÉES-ORIENTALES)

FISHERMEN'S STEW BOUILLINADE DES PÊCHEURS (M.)

Put 3 oz. olive oil and 2 or 3 tbsp. slightly rancid lard (this is one of the characteristics of the dish), chopped onion, garlic, and parsley, and 1 Spanish pimento into an earthenware pot.

On these ingredients place 1 lb. potatoes cut in pieces and, on the potatoes, ½ lb. red gurnet, ½ lb. angler fish, ½ lb. John Dory, ½ lb. sea bass, all cut in even slices, a few small crabs and some mussels (scraped and washed). Sprinkle with flour; pour in enough water to cover the fish. Season. Cook 20 min. at a fast boil.

When the *bouillinade* is cooked, thicken the broth the following way. Mash the liver of the angler fish in a mortar with 5 cloves of garlic. Bind this mixture with 1 egg yolk and 2 or 3 tbsp. oil. Pour a few tbsp. fish broth into this composition, mix well, and pour all of it into the *bouillinade.*

GRILLED SNAILS GARGOLADA (M.)

Cleaning the snails: This consists principally of removing the whitish membrane from the opening of the shell, using the tip of a knife. As each snail is cleaned, place it on a grill with the bars close together to keep the snails from falling through.

Meanwhile, prepare the salt, called *sel de cardona* in Roussillon. Put a good handful of grains of salt and some dry red peppers into a large marble mortar. Using plenty of elbow grease, crush it until it becomes a powder. The pepper used is called *bit-xou* in Catalan and belongs to a class of condiments termed *enragés,* or fiery hot.

When the snails are lined up on the grills, stomach up, they are salted. The grills are placed over a fire of dry vine shoots. The snails sizzle, while exuding a red foam colored by the salt. When the snails are cooked, they should be "baptized." This operation consists of the following. A piece of pork fat stuck on the end of a skewer is wrapped in white paper and the paper is set aflame; the melting lard is allowed to fall on each mollusk.

This highly spiced dish should be washed down with a Spanish wine such as Rancio, Cosperons, Rivesaltes, or Maury.

BRAISED BEEF CATALAN ESTOUFFAT CATALAN (M.)

Stud a 4-lb. rump roast with large pieces of pork fat and cloves of garlic. Moisten the beef with vinegar and roll in flour.

Put it into a large earthenware pot lined with fresh pork rind, 2 sliced onions, 2 sliced carrots, and 2 sliced turnips. Add 3 peeled, seeded, crushed tomatoes, a large *bouquet garni,* a whole head of garlic with the outer skin removed, and 2 cloves.

Pour in 1 qt. full-bodied red wine, season with salt and pepper, and cover with a sheet of buttered paper. Bring to a boil on top of the stove; cover the pot. Cook 3½ hr. in a medium oven. When the beef is cooked, take it out of the pot. Put cooked navy (haricot) beans or macaroni (⅔ cooked) into the pot containing the cooking stock. Put the beef back into the pot and let simmer together.

Note: Sometimes, dried mushrooms (previously soaked in water) are added to this dish.

SAVOY

(HAUTE-SAVOIE—SAVOIE)

SAVOY OMELET OMELETTE SAVOYARDE (S. F.)

Dice and boil fresh bacon. After draining and wiping it dry, brown it in a frying pan in lard. Remove the bacon and brown finely diced potatoes in the fat. Cook the sliced white of 1 leek separately in a little butter.

Break the eggs into a bowl, season, beat, drop in the bacon pieces, potatoes, and leek, a few tiny cubes of Gruyère cheese, and a good pinch of chopped parsley. Brown some butter in a pan and cook the omelet flat, without rolling it; stir the eggs slowly while cooking. Place the omelet in the pan in an open oven and watch it carefully so it doesn't cook too much; it should be soft and moist. Slide it onto a hot platter, and serve.

This omelet is a real treat and rivals that of Mother Poulard.

SAVOY PUDDING FARCEMENT SAVOYARD (S. F.)

This is a traditional dish of the high Arve Valley in Savoy and is served on feast days and for almost every family Sunday dinner in winter. It may be served as the principal course, side dish, or dessert.

To make the pudding, grate 6 or 8 raw potatoes (a grated pear may be added) ; add 1 lb. raisins and 2 lb. prunes (with or without pits) . In the country, dried cherries are sometimes used; they give the dish a delightful flavor.

Flavor with 1 tbsp. brandy; add 1 tbsp. flour and very little sugar. Brown 2 lb. diced pork fat in butter and pour it into the mixture and stir well. Pour all this into a buttered cake mold with an opening in the center and a cover. Seal the mold tightly with a cloth between the mold and cover, and place it in a vessel containing enough water to cover the mold halfway up the sides. Poach 3½–4 hr.

SAVOY PEARS POIRES SAVOIE (S. F.)

Peel and quarter some not-too-ripe pears. Put them into a baking dish, sprinkle heavily with powdered sugar, and dot with bits of butter. Place the dish in a hot oven, baste the pears with their own juice, and stir them carefully in order not to break them. When they are brown and the sugar burnt, baste with ½ cup fresh cream, let it cook down a little, and serve the pears very hot in the baking dish.

TOURAINE

(Indre-et-Loire)

MATELOTE OF LAMPREY WITH PRUNES MATELOTE DE LAMPROIE AUX PRUNEAUX (S. F.)

Take a fine lamprey; clean it as you would tench; cut into pieces and brown in hot butter. Sprinkle with 1 tbsp. flour, blend it with a little hot water, and cover the pieces of lamprey with good red wine having a fine color; add salt, pepper, spices (powdered clove, white pepper, ginger, and nutmeg) , bunch of parsley, 1 onion. Cook until the fork easily pierces the lamprey. When half cooked, add 20 large prunes, and place them around the edge of the platter when serving.

TOURS RILLETTES (HOME STYLE) RILLETTES DE TOURS (DE MÉNAGE) (S. F.)

Take 2 fine rabbits; bone them and cut the meat into small pieces; cut up 4 lb. pork tenderloin and 3 lb. pork fat the same way.

Pour 1 qt. water into a pot with ½ tsp. salt per lb. meat; dissolve the salt, add the pork fat first, then the pork meat and the rabbit. Let cook 2½ hr. at moderate heat, taking care to prevent the mincemeat from sticking to the bottom of the pot. Stir from time to time with a wooden paddle, scraping the bottom well; when it is almost cooked, stir constantly. When the pieces of meat may be crushed easily with a fork, mash them a little and, when they begin to brown, remove from the fire and immediately pour in 1 glass white wine. Cover the pot with a cloth, let stand a few minutes, and put into jars. These Tours Rillettes keep several months.

For another recipe, see Preserving, p. 797.

TOURS GREAVES RILLONS DE TOURS (S. F.)

Take 2 lb. pork neck and the same amount of fresh bacon; dice the meat and bacon and cook it slowly, 4 hr., in a pot with a little water, salt, pepper, and cayenne. Stir frequently. When finished cooking, the bits of bacon and pork should be golden brown. Strain, and put the bits of meat and bacon into a stoneware jar and cover with hot fat; seal the jar and keep in the kitchen cabinet. May be served as an hors d'oeuvre and with salad.

TOURAINE PEACHES ROYALE PÊCHES DE TOURAINE À LA ROYALE (S. F.)

Peel some fine peaches, cook them a few minutes in sirup, and let them cool in the sirup. Press ½ lb. tiny wild strawberries through a sieve or strainer. Mix this strawberry purée with Chantilly Cream (p. 552) and ½ glass champagne brandy. Place the peaches in a compote dish and cover them with the strawberry whipped cream. Serve very cold.

FOREIGN COOKING

FOREIGN COOKING

Even though this work is done in homage to French cooking, we feel that a glimpse at a few foreign dishes might be a pleasant reminder to our gourmets and, at the same time, give them information for future travel.

Most of these recipes have been taken from books written by French chefs who worked on the scene. Thus, we have Alfred Suzanne, famous chef of the good old days, to document English cooking for us; Urbain-Dubois on German cooking; Victor Petit on Russian cooking, etc.

We have chosen from these writers only the most typical and representative recipes of the various countries.

AMERICA

CORN SOUP POTAGE DE MAÏS (T.)

1 can kernel corn, 1 qt. milk, 1 pt. boiling water, 2 tbsp. flour, 2 tbsp. butter, 2 tsp. salt, a little pepper, a little paprika.

Bring the milk to a boil and pour in the corn. Add the butter mixed into a smooth paste with the flour, the salt, pepper, and paprika. Cook the mixture 20 min., strain, and pour into a tureen.

CHICKEN GUMBO SOUP POTAGE À L'OKRA (T.)

1 sliced onion, 4 tbsp. butter, 1 qt. veal or chicken broth, ½ can okra (or gumbo), 2 tsp. salt, ¼ tsp. pepper, ½ sliced green pepper.

Cook the onion 5 min. in the butter, stirring it. Add the chicken broth mixed with the other ingredients. Bring to a boil, then let simmer 40 min.

PHILADELPHIA PEPPER POT POTAGE AU POIVRE DE PHILADELPHIE (T.)

¼ cup thin-sliced celery, ¼ cup thin-sliced green peppers, ¼ cup sliced onions, 4 tbsp. butter, 3 tbsp. flour, 5 cups veal broth, ½ lb. tripe cut into cubes, 1½ cups cubed potatoes, ¾ tbsp. salt, ½ cup cream, ½ tsp. ground pepper.

Cook the vegetables 15 min. in 3 tbsp. butter; add the flour, stirring it till well mixed, then the broth, the tripe, potatoes, ground pepper, and salt. Cook 1 hr. in a closed pot. When ready to serve, add the rest of the butter and ½ cup heavy cream.

MOCK TURTLE SOUP POTAGE (FAUSSE) TORTUE (T.)

1 calf's head, 1 knuckle of veal, 1 lb. marrowbone, 4 qt. cold water, 2 sliced onions, 3 sprigs of thyme, 2 sprigs of marjoram, 1½ tbsp. butter, ½ tsp. cloves, ¼ tsp. celery seed, 1½ tbsp. flour, 1 tbsp. lemon juice, ½ cup Madeira.

Clean and wash the calf's head and put it into a pot with the veal knuckle and marrowbone; add the 4 qt. water, cover, and let simmer until the meat falls off the bones. Set aside the brains and jowls and dice them. Chop the rest of the meat from the calf's head, the tongue, and the veal knuckle, and put into the broth. Add the vegetables and seasoning and let simmer 2 hr. Strain through a sieve, cool, skim off the fat, reheat, and add the butter and flour browned together. Put in the diced brains and jowl, lemon juice, Madeira, and, to taste, salt and pepper. Add Egg Balls (see below).

OYSTER STEW SOUPE AUX HUÎTRES (T.)

1 qt. oysters, 4 cups milk brought almost to a boil, ¼ cup butter, ½ tbsp. salt, ⅛ tsp. pepper.

Put the oysters into a strainer and pour ½ cup cold water over them; save the resulting liquid and bring it to a boil. Strain through a sieve, add the oysters, and cook them until the edges begin to curl. Remove the oysters with a skimming ladle and put them into a tureen with the butter, salt, and pepper. Add the liquid from the oysters and the hot milk.

EGG BALLS FOR SOUPS BOULETTES DE JAUNES D'OEUFS (T.)

Crush the yolks of 3 hard-boiled eggs, mix them with an equal amount of calf's brain, season well with salt and pepper, and add enough beaten egg to make a paste that can be worked. Shape the paste into small balls the size of a marble, roll them in flour, and sauté them in butter.

VEAL LOAF PAIN DE VEAU FROID (T.)

1 lb. lean veal, 1 oz. salt pork, 4 eggs, 1 cup bread crumbs, 6 soda biscuits, 1½ tsp. thyme, 1½ tsp. sage, 1½ tsp. sweet marjoram, 1 tsp. mustard, 3 tbsp. melted butter, salt, pepper.

Chop the veal and salt pork, add the other ingredients, and mix well. Shape into a loaf by hand, dot the top with pieces of salt pork and butter, and bake in the oven. This loaf is sliced and eaten cold.

CORNED BEEF BOEUF SALÉ (T.)

3 pt. coarse salt, 1 qt. ordinary salt, 1 qt. brown sugar or molasses, 4 oz. saltpeter, 7 qt. water.

Boil the beef well in this mixture, and let it cool before serving. If the brisket of beef is used, the bones must be removed after cooking, and the meat pressed between 2 planks.

CORN FRITTERS BEIGNETS DE MAÏS (T.)

1 can of kernel corn, 1¼ cups flour, 1 tsp. baking powder, 2 tsp. salt, 2 eggs, ¼ tsp. paprika.

Chop the corn and dry it; add the flour and salt, the paprika and baking powder, all sifted together; the well-beaten egg yolks and the stiffly beaten whites. Fry in very hot deep lard.

BOILED SWEET POTATOES PATATES BOUILLIES (T.)

Clean the sweet potatoes well. Boil 20 min., without peeling, in enough salted water to cover. Eat them hot with butter.

CANDIED SWEET POTATOES PATATES CONFITES (T.)

For 6 sweet potatoes, peeled and boiled in salted water, take ¾ cup brown sugar, ½ cup melted butter, and a little salt. Cut the sweet potatoes in 2 lengthwise, put them into a buttered baking dish, cover with the brown sugar and melted butter, add the salt, and bake them 2 hr. in a slow oven.

SWEET POTATOES GEORGIA STYLE PATATES À LA GÉORGIENNE (T.)

Mash the sweet potatoes, add butter, salt, pepper, and a little sherry. Pour in some cream and beat well 5 min. Boil 2 tbsp. molasses and 1 tsp. butter together 5 min. Put the sweet potatoes into a buttered baking dish, cover with the sirup, and bake in the oven until brown.

PRESERVED PINEAPPLE SALAD SALADE D'ANANAS DE CONSERVE (T.)

Place the slices of pineapple on lettuce leaves. On each slice place 1 dessertspoon mayonnaise and, in the center, a small ball of cream cheese sprinkled with paprika.

MUFFINS MUFFINS (T.)

¼ cup butter, ¼ cup sugar, ½ tsp. salt, 1 egg, 2 cups flour, 3 tsp. baking powder.

Blend the butter and sugar and add, bit by bit, the beaten egg, the flour and baking powder sifted together, then the milk. Put into small, deep, round molds and bake 25 min. in the oven.

GRIDDLE CAKES CRÊPES AMÉRICAINES (M.)

They are cooked not in a pan, as for ordinary crêpes, but on a heavy griddle placed on the stove and greased with fresh lard.

The batter should be a little thicker than that used for ordinary crêpes and is poured on the griddle with a small ladle. The griddle cakes, which should be 2 or 3 in. in diameter, are turned over with a metal spatula called a cake turner.

American griddle cakes are served with maple sirup and fresh butter.

WHEAT GRIDDLE CAKES CRÊPES DE FROMENT (M.)

Sift 1 lb. flour into a bowl and add 1½ oz. sugar, ½ tsp. salt, ½ tsp. baking powder.

Add 4 whole eggs; mix well to remove lumps. Thin with ⅔ milk and ⅓ fresh cream to make a slightly thicker batter than that used for ordinary crêpes. Mix well. Let stand a short while before using.

CORN-MEAL GRIDDLE CAKES CRÊPES DE MAÏS (M.)

Sprinkle ¼ lb. fine yellow corn meal into 1 pt. boiling water seasoned with a pinch of salt. Add 2 oz. butter; mix well; boil a few moments. Remove from the fire, cover, and let cool. Add this mixture to the wheat-cake batter described above, using only ½ the proportions given in the recipe. Add enough milk to make a paste as thick as Frying Paste (p. 558).

HOMINY GRIDDLE CAKES CRÊPES (À LA SEMOULE) DE MAÏS (M.)

Made like yellow Corn-Meal Griddle Cakes, above, with white corn meal cooked in milk.

RICE GRIDDLE CAKES CRÊPES AU RIZ (M.)

Mix into wheat-cake batter, prepared as above, rice cooked in milk and well beaten, allowing ⅔ batter to ⅓ rice.

BUCKWHEAT CAKES CRÊPES DE SARRASIN (M.)

Put 1 lb. buckwheat flour into a bowl; add ½ tsp. baking powder and a pinch of salt. Mix well; pour in 6 oz. light molasses and milk, enough of the latter to make a paste as thick as Frying Paste (p. 558). Let stand before using.

FLANNEL CAKES FLANNEL-CAKES (Gi.) (*For 12 cakes*)

This dessert, a sort of pancake of American origin, is not well known and is made only in certain Paris restaurants. The cakes are made on a griddle—2 cast-iron disks joined by hinges. One of them has 4 hollows to hold the paste, while the other is flat. The Flannel Cakes are turned over and finish cooking on the flat side. If you haven't a griddle, very small frying pans will do, but the Flannel Cakes will not be quite so elegant.

Batter: Put into a small bowl ¼ lb. sifted flour, 2 oz. powdered sugar, ½ tsp. fine salt, 1 tsp. baking powder, 1 whole egg and 3 yolks. Mix with a wooden spoon, then thin the mixture, bit by bit, with 6 oz. cold, boiled milk, and then, after it is well mixed, add 3 stiffly beaten egg whites.

Cooking: Heat the griddle on the stove, then grease it with lard. Wipe it off immediately and grease it with a brush dipped in melted butter. Pour 3 tbsp. batter into each hollow, carefully smoothing the surface, for this batter is rather thick. The batter will swell instantly, and, after a minute—that is, when the surface in contact with the heat is brown—turn the Flannel Cakes over onto the other side of the griddle, which is easy to do, thanks to the handle. Let the other side brown, then remove the Flannel Cakes and keep them hot. As soon as the first ones have been turned to the flat side, butter the hollows again and fill with more batter, and so on, in a continuous operation. Follow the same procedure if you use frying pans.

According to the American method, this kind of pancake is served with maple sirup. In France they are generally served with very thin rounds of butter, with currant jelly, quince jam, or very fine applesauce.

CHOCOLATE CAKE GÂTEAU AU CHOCOLAT (T.)

1 egg, 1 cup sugar, ½ tsp. baking soda, 1 cup milk, 1½ cups sifted flour, 2½ oz. unsweetened chocolate, an egg-sized piece of butter.

Beat the white and yolk of the egg separately; add the sugar, the milk with the baking soda dissolved in it, and the flour. Melt the chocolate in the butter and add it to the mixture. Put it into a cake pan and bake about 30 min. in a slow oven. Frost with chocolate.

Very economical cake. Must be eaten immediately.

LEMON-JELLY CAKE GÂTEAU À LA GELÉE DE CITRON (T.)

¾ cup butter, 2 cups sugar, 1 cup milk, 1 tsp. baking powder, 4 cups flour, 4 eggs, 1 tsp. vanilla extract.

Beat the butter and sugar together well, add the beaten egg yolks, the milk, the flour mixed with the baking powder, the vanilla, and finally the well-beaten egg whites. Bake in 4 small tart molds about 10 in. in diameter. When the cakes are cooked, place them one on top of the other, filling the spaces between layers with the following mixture. Take 1 cup sugar, 1 egg, juice and grated peel of 1 lemon, an egg-sized piece of butter. Cook this mixture and, while it is still hot, add 1 tsp. arrowroot dissolved in hot water, then make it into a paste with some boiling water. Let cool before using in the cake.

MOLASSES COOKIES PETITES GALETTES À LA MÉLASSE (T.)

1 cup molasses, ½ cup butter and lard mixed, 2½ cups flour, 1 tbsp. hot milk, 1 tsp. salt.

Bring the molasses to a boil, add the butter and lard, 1 tsp. baking soda dissolved in warm water, the salt, and flour. Mix well, roll on a floured baking board, cut into thin rounds, place on a buttered baking sheet, and bake 8–10 min. in a slow oven. While working the mixture, the paste must be kept cool, or you will have to add flour and the cookies will turn out hard instead of crisp.

GOOSEBERRY FOOL MOUSSE AUX GROSEILLES À MAQUEREAU (T.)

1 qt. gooseberries, 1 pt. water, 1 tbsp. butter, 1 cup sugar, 4 eggs, 2 heaping tsp. powdered sugar.

Cook the gooseberries in the water until they are soft. Press through a strainer to remove the skins. Add the butter, sugar, beaten egg yolks, and let cool. Beat the egg whites until stiff and add the 2 heaping tbsp. powdered sugar bit by bit. Beat this mixture until very firm, add it to the gooseberries, and serve very cold in sherbet glasses.

BAKED HOMINY HOMINY AU FOUR (T.)

¾ cup fine hominy, 1 tbsp. sugar, ¼ cup butter, 1 egg, 2 cups milk, 1 tsp. salt, 1 cup boiling water.

Add the hominy little by little to the boiling water and salt. Boil 2 min., then cook in a double boiler until all the water has been absorbed. Now add 1 cup milk, mix well, and cook 1 hr. Remove from the fire, add the butter, sugar, slightly beaten egg, and the rest of the milk. Put into a buttered mold and bake 1 hr. in a slow oven.

AUSTRIA

STEAMED DUMPLINGS or DAMPFNUDELN (Sch.)

Sift into a heated bowl: 1 lb. flour and 1 tsp. fine salt; put in the center 4 tbsp. yeast dissolved in warm milk; add 1 whole egg and 4 yolks, 3½ oz. melted butter, 2 oz. powdered sugar. Work the paste with the warm milk until it is smooth, cover, and let rise at moderate temperature.

When the paste has risen, pour it onto a floured board, shape into walnut-sized balls, place these on a floured cloth, cover with another cloth, and let rise again.

Meanwhile, put 1 pt. sweet cream into a large pan with a large piece of butter, vanilla, and powdered sugar; bring to a boil, then remove the pan from the fire, remove the vanilla bean, put the paste balls inside, cover the pan, and heat 15 min. over a moderate flame without removing the cover. Let a crust form on the underside; unstick the balls with a small skimming ladle, place them on a round platter, cover with English Cream (p. 550), and serve very hot.

APPEL STRUDEL or APFELSTRUDEL STROUDEL AUX POMMES (Sch.)

Sift ½ lb. flour onto the baking board, shape into a well, and, in the center, put a pinch of salt, ⅓ oz. butter, 1 whole egg, and some warm water. Mix this paste with a fork until smooth and work it until it forms bubbles; cover with a cloth and let stand ½ hr.

Meanwhile, peel 12 apples, cut them in thin slices, and place in a bowl; sprinkle with sugar and a little cinnamon, add ¼ lb. sultanas. Put a cloth over a square table, powder it well with flour, and roll your paste out on it until ⅛ in. thick. Put your hands under the paste and stretch it with the back of the hands. When the paste becomes transparent, place it on the cloth and pull it on all sides with your fingers. Take care not to tear it, for by now it should be as thin as paper. Spread your apples evenly on top and sprinkle them with bread crumbs fried in butter and with powdered sugar. Raise both ends of the cloth quite high to make the paste roll into a long rope. Place the pastry on a square, long, or round shallow buttered dish, brush it with beaten egg, and bake ¾ hr. in a medium oven, basting it with melted butter. When cooked, slice it, place on a platter, and powder with sugar. Serve hot.

Very good eating. This dessert is also made with pitted cherries, pears, and other fruits.

TYROLEAN STRUDEL STROUDEL À LA TYROLIENNE (Sch.)

Make a Wuchteln paste (p. 751), roll it out very thin, cover it with a layer of the following mixture. Mix 2 oz. blanched, crushed almonds with the finely chopped peel of ½ lemon, 2 oz. powdered sugar, a handful of dried currants and sultanas, and candied citron cut in fine strips. When this mixture has been spread on the paste, roll it into the shape of a long sausage. Place this roll on a buttered baking sheet and let rise, then brush with beaten egg and bake in a medium oven. Let cool and slice.

WUCHTELN or BUCHTELN (Sch.)

Beat with a spatula 5 oz. butter, 2 whole eggs and 4 yolks, a pinch of salt, 1 tbsp. powdered sugar, finely chopped peel of ½ lemon, ⅔ oz. yeast dissolved in warm milk. Blend in about 1½ lb. flour, mix until the paste is very smooth, and let it rise. When it has risen well, turn it onto a floured baking board, roll it out until ⅛ in. thick, and cut into 1¼-in. squares. Put some plum jam on the center of each piece, roll up the pieces, and lay them side by side on a buttered baking sheet, sticking them together with melted butter so they will separate easily after baking. Let rise, then bake in a medium oven. Turn over the baking sheet onto the baking board and separate the pieces. Powder with sugar and serve with a separate dish of plum jam.

BELGIUM

EELS IN GREEN SAUCE ANGUILLES AU VERT (M.)

Skin 2 eels weighing 10–12 oz. and slice each into 8 pieces about 1½ in. long.

Brown them in a sautéing pan in which the following ingredients have first been cooked in 2 oz. butter: 2 handfuls stripped, washed, finely shredded sorrel leaves, 1 handful spinach leaves (prepared the same way), a pinch of tarragon leaves, 2 tbsp. crushed parsley, a pinch of burnet, and a few leaves of green sage.

Season the pieces of eel with salt, freshly ground pepper, and a slight dash of powdered thyme and bay leaf. Pour 15 oz. white wine over them. Bring to a boil over a hot fire. Cover the pan, lower the flame, and cook slowly 10 min. Bind the cooking stock with 3 egg yolks and add a finger of lemon juice. Turn into a bowl. Keep in a very cool place.

To serve, place the pieces of eel in long relish dishes and cover with the cooking sauce. If they have been turned into a utensil that may be sent to the table, serve them as is.

BEEF CARBONNADES FLAMANDE CARBONNADES À LA FLAMANDE (M.)

Slices of beef braised with sliced onions and beer. (See Beef Carbonnades, p. 329.)

SWEETBREADS CHOESELS (M.)

Belgian connoisseurs of good food are fond of this Brussels specialty. Some restaurants serve it on set days.

(1) Put 1 oxtail cut into pieces and 2 trimmed beef sweetbreads into 4 tbsp. smoking-hot fat from a beef roast. Let brown 45 min. Add 2 lb. breast of veal cut into pieces; continue cooking ½ hr. At the end of this time, add a trimmed beef kidney cut into thick slices and 2 large sliced onions sautéed in butter. When the kidney has been seared, pour in 1½ glasses lambic (a strong Belgian beer), season with salt and cayenne pepper, and add a *bouquet garni.*

(2) Let cook another ½ hr., then add the *choesels* (see *Note,* below) and a sliced calf's sweetbread. Add 1 bottle lambic and 1 cup mushroom cooking stock. Now thicken the sauce with flour or starch and cook another 1½ hr.

(3) ¼ hr. before serving, add 6 cooked mutton feet split in 2 and 10 small *fricandelles* (small, thin fried cakes of chopped beef or veal, like hamburger patties). When ready to serve, skim the sauce and finish it with 1 lb. cooked mushrooms and 1 glass Madeira.

Note: The word *choesel* is not used by French butchers. It means the stomach sweetbread.

CHICKEN WATERZOIE WATERZOIE DE POULET (S. F.)

Take a fine, tender chicken; clean, singe, and truss it. Cut celery, white of leek, and mushrooms into thin julienne strips.

Put a piece of butter into a braising pan with the chicken and vegetables; salt and pepper; start cooking over a hot fire, then cover and let cook slowly 1 hr., taking care not to let the vegetables brown.

When cooked, remove the chicken and vegetables. Melt the glaze in the pan with cream, bind it with 3 or 4 egg yolks, strain this sauce, and mix it with the vegetables. Disjoint the chicken and place it on a platter and cover it with the creamed vegetables. Serve very hot.

Once the sauce has been bound with the eggs, do not let it boil. Instead of cream, the sauce may be made with veal stock enriched with truffle essence and slightly thickened with starch. In this case, add a few shredded truffles to the vegetables when ready to serve.

CHINA

BIRD'S-NEST SOUP CONSOMMÉ AUX NIDS D'HIRONDELLES (M.)

Note: The high price of sea swallows' nests almost prohibits this soup being made often in Europe.

Most of the soup's succulence comes not from the nest, but from several nutritive ingredients such as beef and chicken, from which the consommé is made, the gelatinous fibers of the nest being added at the end. According to Payen and other chemists who have analyzed these nests, their matter is rich in alkaline salts and nitrogen.

Method: Soak the nests a long time in cold water. When the filaments have swollen and become somewhat translucent, clean them as carefully as possible, to remove all impurities.

Blanch the nests 6–8 min., drain them, and put them into the boiling chicken consommé, to poach about 1 hr. at a simmer.

Below is a recipe for preparing sea swallows' nests, taken from a Chinese cookbook by Yuan Nei, of the Tsing dynasty, who was considered the Brillat-Savarin of the Celestial Empire.

SEA SWALLOWS' NESTS NIDS D'HIRONDELLES

"Swallows' nests are a precious dish. When you wish to eat them, you should allow 2 oz. [Chinese] per bowl. First cook them in rain water, using a silver pin to remove the down clinging to the nests.

"Next, use chicken bouillon, some good ham, and some fresh mushrooms to season them, and continue to cook until the swallows' nests become flesh-colored. This dish must stay pure, without being mixed with fat. It is very tender and should not be served with anything hard. Some people flavor the swallows' nests with meat or chicken cut in fine strips. Thus, they eat the strips of meat or chicken rather than the swallows' nests."

The author of *My Garden Cookbook* (the title of this interesting work) adds that when a host offers his guests swallows' nests in a stingy manner, "just enough to garnish the top of the bowl," it is just as though he had spread out a few white hairs. He concedes, however, that, "if absolutely necessary [to flavor the swallows' nests], you may use mushrooms, young bamboo shoots cut in strips, the stomach of the 'tchi' fish, and young pheasant cut in tiny pieces.

"But," he adds, "the important secondary ingredients for swallows' nests are chicken and mushroom sauces," which we Occidentals translate as chicken consommé and mushroom essence.

SOY SAUCE SAUCE SOYA (M.)

Shell some soybeans and cook them in salted water until they become a purée. Meanwhile, roast the pods and cook them separately with a seasoning of ginger, mace, and a purée of salted anchovies. Blend the 2 mixtures, strain, and heat in a pan, stirring with a spatula until it is reduced. The reduced sauce is then put into bottles.

SOY CHEESE FROMAGE DE SOYA (M.)

Cook the shelled soybeans in unsalted water. When they are almost cooked, pour off the excess water, leaving just enough to cover the beans. Let them continue to cook until they can be crushed between the fingers. Then pour them into a bowl or enameled pan and let cool completely. The following day, reheat the soybeans. Then strain them through a sieve and add a little yeast to this jellylike purée to produce fermentation. Salt the preparation, wrap it in cheesecloth, and put it on a sieve to drain the water from the soy jelly. This is now the cheese, which must be placed in wicker molds. Moisten the cheeses with brine and dry them on racks. They may be eaten as soon as they have dried.

ENGLAND

Most of the material in this section is taken from M. Alfred Suzanne's highly opinionated book, "La Cuisine Anglaise" (1904).

TURTLE SOUP POTAGE TORTUE (Su.)

This soup is a specialty of English cooking and is obligatory for diplomatic and ceremonial banquets. It is made from the meat of ocean turtles from different regions: South America, Australia, Africa, or the West Indies.

The animal is bled and its meat taken from the carapace, cut into pieces, and cooked 3 or 4 hr. in plenty of salted water.

Next, a sort of pot-au-feu is made with beef, knuckle of veal, old hens, calf's feet, and part of the flesh from the inside of the turtle. The liquid for this pot-au-feu comes from the liquid the turtle is cooked in, garnished with the usual soup vegetables, and is cooked until all the meat is done. After the broth has been strained through a cloth, the already cooked pieces of turtle meat are added, it is cooked another 20–30 min., and the soup is finished by adding an infusion of aromatic herbs made by dropping a pinch of basil, sage, sweet marjoram, and savory into 1 small glass boiling Madeira. Add pepper and serve the soup as is—that is, clear—or slightly thickened with a dash of starch dissolved in a little turtle broth.

This soup is served with pieces of turtle in it; it is not unusual to find pieces of meat in English soups. Oxtail Soup, for example, is served with meat from the tail of a steer.

OXTAIL SOUP POTAGE QUEUE DE BOEUF (Gi.)

Cut 3 oxtails into pieces at the joints and let them soak 3 hr. in cold water. Then put them into a pot with 3 qt. cold water, salt moderately, and bring to a boil. Skim carefully, then drop into the pot 2 quartered carrots, 1 onion stuck with 2 cloves, and a *bouquet garni* composed of 2 leeks, a celery stem, a few sprigs of parsley, 1 clove of garlic, a little thyme, and bay leaf. Lower the heat and simmer 3 hr. Remove the oxtails and keep them hot in another pan with a little of the bouillon.

Meanwhile, cube 1 carrot and the white of 2 leeks. Finely chop 2 lb. lean beef, put it into a pan with the vegetables and whites of 2 eggs, and add the skimmed, strained oxtail bouillon. Bring to a boil and let cook 30–35 min. The purpose of this operation is to clarify the bouillon and to strengthen it with the chopped meat.

While the oxtails are cooking, prepare a garnish with 2 carrots, 2 turnips, 1 onion, 1 celery stem, and the white of 2 leeks, all diced fine. Brown these vegetables in butter and finish cooking them with a little white bouillon.

When the bouillon has been clarified, strain it through a cloth, correct the seasoning, add the browned vegetables and the pieces of oxtail, and serve. If you prefer, serve the oxtails separately.

Historical Note: One of our eminent colleagues, M. Suzanne, in a very interesting study of English cooking, has explained the origin of this soup:

"At the time of the revocation of the Edict of Nantes, there were a great number of Huguenot refugees in London, where they formed a sort of French colony in a quarter of the city occupied by the tanners' guild.

"The buyers of oxhides, having no use for the tails, gave them to the poor of the neighborhood, who made them into a sort of pot-au-feu.

"One day, a rich and philanthropic gourmet, visiting these poor exiles, was initiated into the mysteries of this excellent soup. He introduced it into high society, where it immediately became rather fashionable under the name 'tanners' soup.' "

HODGEPODGE POTAGE AU MOUTON (Su.)

Make a sort of pot-au-feu (see p. 190) using boned mutton cut into small pieces and some diced bacon. After skimming the bouillon, garnish it with carrots, onions, turnips, leeks, lettuce, cabbage, celery, green beans, thyme, and pearl barley. Cook 1 hr., then add green peas and chopped parsley, cook another hour, and serve as is.

A simple mutton broth may be made the same way, using only mutton, a few soup vegetables, and pearl barley, of which our neighbors are especially fond in soups.

GIBLET SOUP POTAGE AUX ABATIS (Su.)

Chicken, turkey, or even goose giblets may be used for this soup. The giblets are understood to include the wing tips, neck, liver, gizzard, head, and feet; all these should be cleaned and singed, cooked in bouillon, preferably veal, with a few vegetables, basil, sweet marjoram, and parsley. Remove the giblets as they are cooked, since some cook more quickly than others, then thicken the bouillon with a little arrowroot mixed with water, and finish the soup with a dash of cayenne, a little chopped parsley, and a finger of Madeira.

The giblets are served in the soup. In some restaurants, fluffy dry rice is added as a garnish.

FISH POISSONS (Su.)

Eel: The Thames eel is famous and plentiful. It can be served in a pie, fried, in a loaf, in stews, or on small spits, but since wine is not widely used in England, they do not prepare eel *matelotes* with red wine as we do (see p. 342).

Haddock: This smoked fish is very common in England. The English bake or boil it and fill it with a forcemeat called "veal stuffing," though, oddly enough, not a speck of veal is used. This stuffing is a mixture of beef-kidney suet and bread crumbs, highly seasoned, and bound with 1 or 2 eggs. Bake the haddock in a hot oven or cook it in salted water and serve with melted butter.

Salmon and Turbot: These fish are greatly appreciated in England, but have no special preparation.

Whitebait: This very small fish is caught at the mouth of the Thames. It must be strictly fresh and is only served fried. Like turtle soup, it is an indispensable dish for all diplomatic dinners in London.

Crustaceans and Oysters: Our neighbors prefer these to ordinary fish, but there is nothing distinctive about the way they prepare them.

BEEF BOEUF (Su.)

England is the land of roast beef. It used to be the custom in aristocratic English families to roast a whole steer for a wedding or the coming of age of the eldest son. We can well understand why this custom is now only a memory, even in a country so bound by tradition.

BEEFSTEAK PIE PÂTÉ DE BEEFSTEACK (Su.)

For this a special earthenware dish is needed, with a flat rim about ½ in. wide, which can be bought in any china shop.

A strip of Pie Paste (p. 545) is fastened to this rim with a brush dipped in water. When this is done, cut a beef fillet into rather thin slices, season with salt, pepper, and *fines herbes,* roll up each slice, and lay them side by side in the dish with several small potato balls browned in butter; it will be even better if you add 3 or 4 sliced mushrooms and 1 or 2 sliced, hard-boiled eggs. Pepper a little, then moisten the meat with a little bouillon or even water; cover the dish with a top crust of ordinary Pie Paste and seal it onto the strip of paste fastened around the rim with a little water. Trim off the edges, brush with beaten egg, and decorate the top of the crust with scraps of Pie Paste cut into small leaves. Bake 1 hr. in a medium oven and serve as is.

SALT BEEF BOEUF SALÉ (Su.)

The English are masters in the preparation of Salt Beef and Pressed Beef.

The composition of the brine is rather special. Dissolve 13 lb. bay salt in 50 qt. water; let steep in it a bunch of thyme, 6 or 8 bay leaves, 24 cloves, 2 tbsp. mace (which is the outer covering of nutmeg), a handful of black peppercorns, 4 oz. saltpeter, and 7 oz. brown sugar (or ordinary sugar, if you have no brown).

The beef should first be rubbed strenuously with bay salt and left in the salting tub ½ day or overnight. Then it is put into the brine, where it should stay 15–20 days, depending on size.

PRESSED BEEF BOEUF PRESSÉ (Su.)

Soak a brisket of beef 15 days in brine, then drain, wash, and cook 6 hr. in a good deal of water. Then bone it completely. Put it into a square earthenware or ceramic dish just large enough to fit; keep it under heavy pressure (30 or 40 lb.) 24 hr. Trim the beef, glaze it with aspic, and serve sliced.

IRISH STEW RAGOÛT IRLANDAIS (Su.)

This way of preparing ragout of mutton is quite different from our ragout, but it makes a fine entree, which we French will like as a change.

Take a neck of mutton and cut it into pieces as for stew; put the meat into a pot with 3 or 4 onions and 10 potatoes, all sliced thin. Season with salt and a generous amount of pepper, cover with cold water, and cook 2 hr. When cooked, the liquid will be thickened by the crumbled potatoes. Serve as is. To make a richer dish, add some small potatoes ½ hr. before serving; these will stay whole, while the other potatoes thicken the sauce. Sprinkle with chopped parsley and pepper the sauce heavily.

BOILED LEG OF MUTTON GIGOT DE MOUTON BOUILLI (Su.)

Chop off the extending bone from a leg of mutton, trim it, and plunge it into a pot of salted boiling water (1 tsp. salt per qt. water). For a medium-sized leg add: 3 carrots, 2 onions, each pricked with a clove, a *bouquet garni,* and 2 cloves of garlic.

Cook 15 min. per lb. meat, keeping the liquid at a slow boil. Place the joint on a platter and surround it with the carrots and onions. Serve English Butter Sauce (p. 159) separately, with 3½ oz. capers added per qt. sauce. Boiled Leg of Mutton may be served with mashed turnips or celery, cooked with the meat. It may also be served with mashed potatoes or bean purée, or with any boiled vegetable placed around it.

MUTTON PUDDING PUDDING DE MOUTON (Su.)

The English eat a number of meat puddings, a dish that would hardly please French taste. Make a suet paste by kneading together 13 oz. flour and 7 oz. finely chopped beef suet (weighed after being skinned and trimmed).

Salt, and moisten this paste with a little cold water to make it firm enough to be rolled out. Roll it out into a large pancake and lay it in a large, special pudding bowl; in the center place thin-sliced mutton sautéed in butter with onions and shallots; add a little bouillon and ketchup. Fold the paste, which extends past the rim of the dish, over the meat.

To seal the opening, cover the top with a buttered cloth; turn the pudding over, and tie the cloth under the bowl, then plunge it into boiling water and cook 3 hr. Unmold the pudding and serve very hot.

In England, this same paste is used with kidneys, lamb, liver, and beef, and even sweet desserts.

PORK PORC (Su.)

Pork is first rate in England, and French gourmets have only praise for bacon, which is an unbeatable English specialty. In France, bacon is grilled in thin slices to accompany eggs or sautéed meats. In England, it is cooked the following way. Cut it into thin slices and roll up the slices like veal birds, then spit them on small skewers and grill them over a hot fire or in a very hot oven. Serve on toast.

BOILED CHICKEN AND OYSTERS POULET AUX HUÎTRES (Su.)

Of the few fowl recipes peculiar to the islanders on the other side of the Channel, we have chicken or turkey with oysters.

Cook the chicken in a Court Bouillon (p. 277) with a bunch of parsley, then cook the oysters in their own liquor. Using the chicken cooking stock and the oyster cooking liquor, make a rather thick white sauce seasoned with cayenne and grated nutmeg. Skin the chicken and cover it with the sauce, with the oysters added to it.

Nothing extraordinary about the flavor. The English are keen on boiled meats. They also serve rabbit and game this way.

GROUSE GROUSES (Su.)

Among our Channel neighbors, grouse has a reputation equal to that of partridge and quail, which are considered the finest game fowl in France. Grouse, which belongs to the Lagopus family, is essentially a British game bird, found principally in the heathland of Scotland, Ireland, and Norway. Grouse is eaten roasted, in pies, and as cutlets.

ROAST GROUSE ENGLISH STYLE GROUSE RÔTIE À L'ANGLAISE (Su.)

The characteristic of this game is that it is roasted and eaten very fresh, just the opposite of other game. Truss the grouse and band the breast with strips of pork fat as you would pheasant; roast it about 40 min. over a hot fire. Since the meat should be kept a little underdone, cooking time should be based on the size of the bird.

Roast grouse is not served on the usual bread canapé, but is accompanied by Bread Sauce or red-currant jelly. Bread Sauce is made by mixing a piece of fresh white bread, 1 cup milk, ⅓ tsp. salt, a small onion stuck with a clove, and a walnut-sized piece of butter in a casserole. Let it simmer ¼ hr., then remove the onion and beat the sauce until it is smooth; if it is too thick, thin it with a little milk or, better yet, sweet cream.

VEGETABLES LÉGUMES (Su.)

Their vegetables have nothing in particular that needs mentioning. Nor does the pastry, except for a few special things we shall close this chapter with.

SWEET DISHES PLATS SUCRÉS (Su.)

All fruits are made into pies, as are beefsteaks, kidneys, chickens, and pigeons.

A special dish called a pie dish, covered with a Flaky Paste (p. 544), is used for apples, rhubarb, gooseberries, and all fruits in general.

Everyone knows that Christmas is the greatest English holiday, and that it is traditional to serve flaming Plum Pudding. It is less known that another Christmas specialty is Mince Pie.

We shall not speak about the plum cakes, which are as French as possible and English in name only. But we must include Plum Pudding, for England and America are the only 2 countries where pudding is king. They make it out of anything, fruits, vegetables, meat, pumpkin, and whatnot.

CUSTARD PUDDING CUSTARD PUDDING (E.)

This is made with a molded-cream mixture (see p. 640), using these proportions: 6 eggs and 6 oz. sugar per qt. milk. Cook it in a pie dish in a *bain-marie,* an oven, or a steamer. Often, too, it is made on top of the stove like an English Cream (p. 550) and served in special glasses.

The number of eggs may be increased or diminished, depending on whether you like a heavy or light custard. The amount of sugar depends on individual taste; if need be, it can be left out and saccharine or glycerine substituted—this is done for diabetics.

Custard is usually flavored with vanilla, but any dessert flavoring may be used.

PLUM PUDDING PLUM PUDDING (A.)

Plum Pudding is the English national dessert. It is made with a variety of fruits and flavored in various ways: with rum, cognac, Madeira, etc. Here is the recipe for a Plum Pudding serving 18–24 persons.

1 lb. skinned, finely chopped beef-kidney suet, ½ lb. flour, ½ lb. sifted bread crumbs, 7 oz. seeded Malaga raisins, 7 oz. dried currants, 7 oz. light brown sugar, 3 oz. rum, 6 oz. milk, 2½ oz. finely diced, candied orange, 2½ oz. finely diced, candied citron, 2½ oz. chopped almonds (optional), 2½ oz. pitted, dried cherries (optional), 1 tsp. salt, pinch of powdered cinnamon, pinch of powdered nutmeg, pinch of powdered ginger, pinch of cloves, 4 fresh eggs, 1 peeled and finely diced russet apple, finely chopped peel of 1 lemon, and 1 whole lemon boiled 2 hr. and then crushed.

Put into a mixing bowl: suet, flour, bread crumbs, brown sugar, orange peel, citron, apple, almonds, raisins, dried currants, dried cherries, lemon peel, milk, rum, eggs, salt, cinnamon, nutmeg, ginger, cloves; mix well.

Butter a pudding mold, fill it with the mixture, and tie on the cover. If you have no mold, put the mixture into a buttered, floured napkin and tie it with a string. Put a plate into the bottom of a deep pot and fill the pot ⅔ full of water; bring to a boil, place the Plum Pudding on the plate in the pot, and continue boiling 5 hr., replacing the water that evaporates with boiling water. Unmold the pudding onto a hot platter and serve with a Sabayon (p. 553) or simply sprinkled with sugar and moistened with 7 oz. old rum set aflame when ready to serve.

Note: It is a good idea to put everything together, except for the flour, bread crumbs, milk, and eggs, and let it macerate in rum 3 weeks, stirring from time to time. When the Plum Pudding is to be cooked, mix in the other ingredients and cook as directed.

MINCE PIE MINCE PIE (Su.)

While Plum Pudding is known the world over as the English Christmas dessert, another dessert is also highly esteemed and very popular at this time of year, though it is hardly known in our country. An English Christmas without Mince Pie would be as unthinkable as our Mardi Gras without crêpes. Preparations are made a month in advance so that the fruits will have time to macerate and be impregnated with the liquors.

The recipe is not very different from the above; while there are no flour and bread crumbs, there is meat. Here is a copy of the recipe:

1 lb. finely chopped beef-kidney suet, 1 lb. seeded, chopped Malaga raisins, 1 lb. washed, picked sultanas and dried currants, 1 lb. light brown sugar, 1 lb. peeled, chopped apples, ½ lb. chopped, candied citron and candied orange peel, ½ oz. salt, 1 oz. same spices used in the pudding, ½ bottle cognac, 1 cup rum, 1 cup Madeira, 1 lb. chopped roast beef (this last is not obligatory).

All these ingredients, chopped separately, are put together in a large stoneware crock, which is tightly sealed and stored in the cellar for a month. The mixture is stirred every 8 days with a wooden spoon.

Line tartlet molds with Pie Paste (p. 545), prick the bottoms with a fork, and fill with the mincemeat mixture. Cover the tartlets with a top crust of the same paste with a hole cut out in the center about the size of a quarter. Tightly seal the top crust to the bottom crust, brush with beaten egg, and bake in a very hot oven.

Serve immediately with a sauceboat of flaming cognac or pour 1 tsp. hot cognac into each tartlet and set aflame.

CHRISTMAS OMELET OMELETTE DE NOËL (Su.)

The same mincemeat as above is also served a different way. Make an omelet with 6 eggs, 1 tbsp. rum, 1 tbsp. cream, a little grated lemon peel, and fill this omelet with the mincemeat. After turning it onto the platter, powder it with sugar, and baste with hot rum. Set the rum aflame when sending the omelet to the table.

GERMANY

GERMAN CHERRY SOUP SOUPE AUX CERISES À L'ALLEMANDE (U. D.)

Although this soup is not very distinguished, it is quite popular in Germany. Pit and stem 1½ pt. freshly picked sour cherries. Put ⅔ of them into an earthenware pot or a pan without a tin lining (tin spoils the color of the fruit), pour in 1 qt. hot water, add a stick of cinnamon and a lemon peel, put the pan on a very hot fire, and cook the cherries 10 min. Thicken the liquid with 2 tbsp. cornstarch mixed with a little cold water; 10 min. later, strain the cherries and liquid through a sieve. Put the soup back into the same pan, add 1/3 of the cherries you have saved and a pinch of sugar; bring to a boil, then lower the flame. Meanwhile, pound 2 handfuls of cherry pits in a mortar and put them into a small saucepan with 2 or 3 glasses Bordeaux. Let boil a few moments, remove from the fire, and strain over a napkin into the soup; mix, and then pour the soup into a tureen. Serve with a plate of sponge cake cut into small cubes.

BERLIN BEER SOUP SOUPE À LA BIÈRE À LA BERLINOISE (U. D.)

Melt 5 oz. butter in a pan and mix in 5 oz. flour to form a thin paste; cook a few seconds, stirring, without letting it brown. Pour in 2 qt. beer, light or dark, but not too strong. Stir the liquid on the fire until it comes to a boil, then lower the flame and let it simmer 25 min., skimming when necessary.

Pour 1/2 glass rum and 1/2 glass white Rhine wine into a saucepan; add a piece of ginger, a stick of cinnamon, 3 1/2 oz. sugar, and lemon peel; cover the pan and keep it hot in a *bain-marie* or double boiler. When the soup has been well skimmed, bind it with 15 beaten egg yolks. Cook without boiling or even heating too much; strain the soup into another pan; blend in 7 oz. butter in small bits and, immediately after, mix in the strained infusion of rum; pour into a soup tureen. Serve with thin slices of toast.

LOBSTER HAMBURG STYLE HOMARD À LA MODE DE HAMBOURG (U. D.)

Cook 4 small, live lobsters in salted water with a little vinegar. As soon as cooked, cut off the claws and remove the meat, then split the body lengthwise. Remove the meat from the half tails, trimming it quickly, and arrange it in a circle on a hot platter; place the claws in the center of this ring. Mix 6 oz. melted Meat Glaze (p. 135) in a small saucepan with 3 oz. Madeira; boil the liquid 2 min. and set to the back of the stove.

Knead in a bowl 3 tbsp. crumbled fresh white bread with 4 oz. butter, dash of cayenne, pinch of chopped parsley. Divide this paste into small particles and blend it bit by bit into the liquid, constantly stirring, to make a thick sauce; do not let it boil. Finish the sauce by mixing it with the mashed, strained lobster intestines, along with 2 tbsp. good vinegar or lemon juice. The sauce should be rather thick. Pour it over the lobster.

BEEF BERLIN STYLE (SCHMORBRATEN) BOEUF À LA BERLINOISE (U. D.)

Cut a 4–6 lb. flank steak (without bone) ; lard the meat along the grain with thin strips of pork fat and raw ham. Sprinkle it with salt and place it in a bowl. Add parsley and celery roots, sliced carrots and onions, thyme, bay leaf, basil, spices. Pour enough light beer over it barely to cover it. Macerate the beef 3 days (in winter) ; keep it in a cool place and turn it from time to time.

Line a pot with a few scraps of pork fat and some vegetables. Place the meat on this bed, pour the marinade over it, and add enough beer to cover; also add a few strips of pork rind. Bring to a boil and skim. Cover with strong paper, put the lid on, and reduce the heat until very low, or put the pot on warm cinders, with coals on top of the cover, to keep the liquid simmering. Turn the meat over 3 hr. later and continue simmering another 3 or 4 hr. When it is ready, remove the pot from the fire, strain the cooking stock through a sieve, skim it carefully, and pour the fat over the meat. Cover the pot and keep the meat warm. Let the skimmed gravy stand ½ hr. Pour it carefully into another pan, leaving the sediment in the bottom of the first pan, and boil it with 3½ oz. gingerbread softened in a little water and mashed; reduce the heat and let simmer.

20 min. later, add a piece of orange peel, pulp of 1 lemon without rind or seeds, and a *bouquet garni* (parsley, thyme, and bay leaf). 10 min. later, skim the fat off the sauce again, strain it into another pan, mix in 2 tbsp. red-currant jelly, and, after boiling a few minutes, pour it over the beef arranged on a platter. Place a few thin slices of lemon on top of the beef and send it to the table with a plate of salted cucumber cut into pieces and replaced in its original form.

MUTTON AND POTATOES GERMAN STYLE HAMMELKARTOFFELN À L'ALLEMANDE (U. D.)

Although this is not a luxury dish, it is one that even masters of the hunt order on hunt days. A dish for a hunter doesn't have to be fancy, but it must be good and tasty.

Take 2 lb. raw mutton without skin or fat, 3 lb. raw, peeled potatoes, 7 oz. chopped onions, 7 oz. butter, salt, a generous amount of pepper, dash of cayenne, a little bouillon, and a little good gravy.

Cut the meat from a raw leg of mutton, remove the tendons and fat, and cut it into large cubes. Cook the onion in butter until golden, add the meat, sear it a few minutes, season, cover, and cook 3–4 hr. at low heat. In the beginning, the natural meat juices will provide enough liquid, but as it continues to cook, you will have to baste the meat from time to time with a little bouillon and, toward the end, some good gravy, so that the meat is always kept moist. Cook the potatoes in salted water 20 min. before serving; drain, dry them a few minutes in an open oven, then mash them with a large fork into a purée without ricing them or pressing them through a sieve. Mix ¾ of this purée into the meat ragout and keep the rest to be used as needed if the ragout seems too liquid. It should have the consistency of a good hash. Keep covered 2 or 3 min., and place it in a dish to be served as soon as possible.

At hunting parties, this ragout is usually served as is, but I have sometimes surrounded it with small cooked sausages or with poached eggs, and neither of them seemed to detract from the dish.

ROAST HAMBURG CHICKENS GERMAN STYLE POULETS DE HAMBOURG RÔTIS À L'ALLEMANDE (U. D.)

In winter the city of Hamburg supplies a large part of Germany with small chickens, sometimes fat but always tender. They are about the size of a large partridge; the meat is white and delicate; they are really worthwhile in those regions where only mediocre chickens are to be found after November.

Take 5 oz. butter for each chicken; knead this butter with fresh bread to form a firm paste; add salt and chopped parsley. Stuff the chickens with the paste; truss, tie them across a small spit, and roast them 14–15 min., basting with butter. Salt them, remove them from the spit, place them on a platter, and baste them with the butter from the dripping pan.

ROAST GOOSE GERMAN STYLE OIE RÔTIE À L'ALLEMANDE (U. D.)

Clean a goose, saving the fat and giblets; wipe out the inside and stuff with small whole potatoes (the eyes cut out, but not peeled) and a small bunch of mugwort. Sew up the opening and truss the goose; place it in a roasting pan lined with the fat cut off; add 1 glass hot water. Sprinkle the goose with a little salt, cover it with buttered paper, and roast it in the oven 3 hr., basting frequently. It must be well done. Salt, untruss, and place the goose on a platter. Skim the fat from the cooking stock and mix in a little good gravy; bring to a boil, strain, and pour into a sauceboat.

HAUNCH OF VENISON GERMAN STYLE CIMIER DE CERF À L'ALLEMANDE (U. D.)

Neatly trim a haunch or saddle of young deer. Shorten the ribs, remove the skin from the fillets, and macerate the meat 24 hr. in a cooked marinade. Then drain it, stud the fillets with strips of pork fat, braise it with part of the marinade and some red wine. When it is cooked, remove it and let cool somewhat. Cut off the 2 fillets, slice them, and put them back into place. Brush the surface of the fillets with beaten egg and cover them with a 3/8-in. layer of pumpernickel crumbs (or plain brown bread) seasoned with a little cinnamon-flavored sugar and moistened with red wine. This covering must remain solid; sprinkle it with a few dry bread crumbs and baste with melted butter. Place the saddle or haunch on a flat pan with a little of the fat skimmed off the braising liquid and heat 1/2 hr. in a low oven, basting from time to time with melted butter. Serve the haunch or saddle on a platter with a separate dish of Cherry Sauce.

Cherry Sauce: Soften 2 handfuls of the dried black cherries commonly sold in Germany—in other words, with their pits. After softening them in water, pound them, and mix them with 1 glass red wine. Pour the mixture into a skillet (not tin-lined) ; add a stick of cinnamon, 2 cloves, a slight pinch of salt, a piece of lemon peel; boil the liquid 2 min.; thicken it with a little starch mixed with water. Lower the flame, cover the pan, and cook slowly 1/4 hr. Strain the sauce through a sieve.

POUND CAKE NAPFKUCHEN (U. D.)

Napfkuchen is a national cake prepared all over Germany.

Sift 1 lb. flour into a bowl and heat it a little in the warmer. Dissolve 1 dessertspoon yeast in 3/4 glass hot milk. With this liquid and 1/4 of the flour make a leaven in a hot bowl; let it rise in the warmer until it has doubled in volume.

Meanwhile, with your hands shape the flour in the bowl into a well. Pour 1/4 glass warm milk into this well. Beat 5 eggs and heat them in a double boiler until they are tepid, then mix in 6 oz. melted butter, and pour 1/2 this mixture into the flour well; add it bit by bit, to form a consistent paste. Work it 7–8 min. to give it body, while blending in the rest of the butter and eggs little by little.

When the paste is thin and elastic, mix in the leaven. Work it another 7–8 min. Add 3 1/2 oz. crushed sweet and bitter almonds, 7 oz. dried currants and sultanas, a pinch of chopped orange peel, and finally a pinch of mace. Cover the bowl and let the paste rise. Butter a cylindrical mold made of copper or earthenware, sprinkle it with chopped almonds. When the paste has risen, break it with your hand; taking small pieces of it at a time, fill the mold 3/4 full.

Let the paste rise again until it reaches the rim of the mold. Lay the mold on a baking sheet and bake ¾ hr. in a medium oven. Unmold and let cool. The amount of flour given in this recipe will make 2 large cakes.

HOLLAND

DUTCH SALTED HERRINGS HARENGS SALÉS DE HOLLANDE (U. D.)

The first salted herrings to arrive on the market in Holland are very expensive, for the Dutch are rather ostentatious about eating the first to arrive. The price goes up because of the scarcity of the fish, and some Dutch gourmets pay exorbitant prices in proportion to the real value of the herring. Salted herrings are not eaten very much in France, which is a pity, for they are wholesome and whet the appetite. They have the further advantage of being simple to prepare and inexpensive.

Wash, dry, and skin the herrings, then cut them into pieces and place them back in their original shape on a plate. Cover them with a Vinaigrette Sauce (p. 158) flavored with mustard; garnish with new onions, gherkins, capers, and pickles.

If the herrings are not newly salted, they should be soaked a few hours in cold milk before being seasoned.

DUTCH PUDDING PUDDING HOLLANDAIS (U. D.)

Soak 7–9 oz. bread in milk; press out the liquid. Put it into a pan and crumble it; mix in 6 oz. beef marrow and 6 oz. chopped beef-kidney suet; add 8 egg yolks, 3 whole eggs, a little chopped lemon peel, 7 oz. sugar, 7 oz. seedless raisins, 6 tbsp. diced, candied fruit peel.

Pour the mixture into a buttered mold and place it in a pan containing enough boiling water to cover ½ the mold. Cover the pan and cook 1 hr. at moderate heat; the water must be kept boiling and replenished as it evaporates.

When ready to serve, unmold the pudding onto a platter and cover it with apricot jam thinned with sirup and rum.

DUTCH COOKIES COUQUES HOLLANDAISES (U. D.)

A simple and good pastry, which I recommend serving with desserts, ices, or ice creams, or with tea.

Prepare a Flaky Paste (p. 544) with ¾ lb. butter and 1 lb. flour; roll it and fold it 6 times. After letting it stand, roll the paste out ¼ in. thick; cut it with a fluted cookie cutter into circles 2 in. in diameter.

Spread a layer of powdered sugar on the baking table. Take the rounds of paste, 1 by 1, and press 1 side in flour and the other side in the powdered sugar. With the cookies lying sugar side down, roll them out until they are about 3½ in. long. Place them, flour side down, on a baking sheet, powder with grilled, crushed almonds, and bake in a medium oven.

HUNGARY

RIB STEAK ESTERHAZY ENTRECÔTE À LA ESTERHAZY (Sch.)

Cut 12 slices from the middle of the sirloin, flatten them, and season with salt and pepper. Quickly sauté them over a hot fire, turning them over. Lay them in a long casserole or pan and cover them with 1 pt. coarsely shredded carrots, turnips, onions, celery, and leeks. Pour in enough Espagnole Sauce (p. 137), 1 glass white wine, and 1 glass sour cream to cover completely; add 1 tsp. paprika. Cover the casserole and cook in the oven. When the meat is properly cooked, place it on a long platter, skim the fat from the cooking sauce, pour the sauce over the steaks with the vegetables, and sprinkle the top with thin strips of lemon peel.

HUNGARIAN GOULASH GOULASH À LA HONGROISE (Sch.)

Goulash is a sort of beef stew that holds a position of honor in Central Europe; it is, moreover, an excellent entree. Cube 1½ lb. rump of beef. Lightly brown 7 oz. chopped onions in lard and add the beef without letting it brown; mix well and cover the pot so that the meat can render its juice. At the end of ¼ hr., add a good amount of tomato purée, 1 glass water, and, if in season, 1 lb. peeled, chopped fresh tomatoes. Season with salt and paprika (indispensable), add a *bouquet garni,* and let cook slowly 2–3 hr. with the pot covered.

Skim the fat from the sauce and serve in a ring of small potatoes cooked in butter or water.

VEAL GOULASH (KALBS GULYAS) GOULASH DE VEAU (Sch.)

Cut breast or neck of veal in large cubes. Brown a good number of finely chopped onions in lard with 1 tsp. paprika, add the meat, sear it over a hot fire, stirring with a spatula, season with salt, add 1 tbsp. flour, and cover with bouillon, 1 glass sour cream, and 1 tbsp. vinegar. Let simmer until well done. Serve surrounded by Gnocchi (p. 548) or noodles or with a separate dish of either one.

NUT ROLLS NUSSBEUGELN (Sch.)

This pastry is well known in Austria and Hungary, especially in Pressburg. It has the same shape as a crescent or a stuffed crescent.

Here is the recipe: 1 lb. flour, ⅓ oz. yeast dissolved in hot milk, 5 oz. butter, 3½ oz. lard, 1 tsp. salt. Knead all together until you have a firm paste. Then take 2 oz. good walnuts and mash them with 2 oz. sugar, 1 tbsp. cinnamon or nutmeg, 1 tsp. mace; mix with 2 egg whites and set to one side.

Cut the paste into 2-oz. pieces and flatten them with a rolling pin as when making Crescents (see p. 588). Put 1 tbsp. nut mixture in the center of each piece, wrap them, and roll them into crescents. Place on baking sheets and brush with beaten egg. Let rise at least 1 hr. When the brushed egg has dried and begun to crack, they are ready to be put into the oven. Brush them again with beaten egg and bake in a slow oven. Exquisite.

ITALY

Italian cooking comes after French cooking, in the opinion of gourmets. It is stimulating, highly seasoned, and has many similarities to Provençal cooking. We must remember, too, that the Italian chefs who came to France with Catherine de' Medici at the time of her marriage to Henry II were in on the beginning of the ascendancy of French cooking, contributing new ingredients and seasonings, which they brought with them, and so inspiring our chefs of the time that they lost no time in outclassing the Italians.

FRITTO MISTO FRITURES MÊLÉES (Gr.)

Clean and prepare the following ingredients: artichokes, zucchini, squash flowers, cauliflower (broken into small flowerets and blanched in salted water), lambs' brains, lamb sweetbreads, beef marrow (*stienali*), calf's liver, borage leaves. Cut all into slices, including the brains, which have been blanched in advance. Dip all of these pieces into Frying Paste (p. 558) and drop them into very hot deep fat. Arrange them on a napkin-covered platter garnished with fried parsley and lemon halves, along with small croquettes made of meat or rice, as you prefer. Celery cooked in advance and cut into quarters may be added, also crescent rolls cut into pieces, soaked in milk, dried in a cloth, dredged with flour, dipped in beaten egg, and fried separately.

Note: When this fried mixture is carefully prepared, it is always favorably received by foreigners. When I was in Vienna with Prince Demidov, who was the guest of Prince Gortschakov, he often asked me to make this Fritto Misto, and each time sent me his compliments.

POLENTA POLENTA (Gr.)

Sift corn meal (10 oz. per qt. liquid) and sprinkle it gradually into boiling consommé mixed with 1/3 water, stirring constantly. Let thicken and cook, continuing to stir, until the paste separates from the side of the pan and a skin forms on top. Reverse it onto a floured cloth and wrap it. Cut it first into slices and then into other shapes. Sprinkle the pieces with cheese and butter and brown in the oven.

FRIED CANNELLONI (LARGE MACARONI) FRITURE DE CANNELLONI (Gr.)

Cook 1/2 lb. cannelloni in salted water. Drain well, let cool, and drain again. Spread them out on a clean cloth to dry. Use a paper cone to fill them with the following stuffing. Take 1/2 lb. cooked meat (any type will do, but chicken is preferred). Chop it fine and mash it in a mortar. Add salt, pepper, a little grated nutmeg, and 3 egg yolks. Strain through a sieve into a bowl. Mix well with a wooden spoon and add a little grated Parmesan cheese. Dip each cannelloni into Frying Paste (p. 558) and drop it into very hot deep fat. Fry until a golden brown and serve on a napkin. The cannelloni may be breaded and prepared like Fritto Misto, described above.

Note: Cannelloni may be served, like macaroni, with Tomato Sauce (p. 146) or any other sauce. However, instead of frying it after filling it with the meat mixture, poach it 10 min. in salted water or, better still, in bouillon. Drain well and serve in a deep dish, covered with the sauce of your choice. Serve grated Parmesan cheese separately. This dish may be considered an entree.

SMOTHERED COD (INZIMINO) MORUE À L'ÉTOUFFADE (Gr.)

Put into a baking dish 1/2 glass olive oil, 3 or 4 cloves of garlic cut fine, a number of chard leaves cooked in advance in salted water, well drained, and slightly chopped; add salt, pepper, and spices; fry 3 or 4 min., turning with a spoon to keep anything from sticking. Pour in 1 pt. liquid Tomato Sauce (p. 146), cover the baking dish, and let simmer. When the chard leaves are tender, place 12 pieces of cod on top. Boil rapidly 2 min. Turn the cod over, cook another 2 min., and serve hot.

Note: The chard leaves should be tasted to see if the flavor is right before putting in the cod.

RAGOUT FLORENTINE (STUFATINO) RAGOUT À LA FLORENTINE (Gr.)

Cut ¼ lb. raw ham and 2 lb. leg of beef into small pieces and put them into a pan. Add 1 clove of garlic. Heat over the fire until the meat turns light brown, then add salt, pepper, spices, and a *bouquet garni.* Pour in 3 glasses very liquid Tomato Sauce (p. 146), bring to a boil, and simmer 2–2½ hr. When the ragout is cooked and the sauce reduced, test the seasoning and serve.

The same recipe may be used for knuckle of veal or pork, but shorten the cooking time.

SLICED BEEF NAPOLITAINE (BRACIOLINE) TRANCHES DE BOEUF À LA NAPOLITAINE (Gr.)

Cut 12 very thin slices from a round of beef; flatten them very thin with a mallet; sprinkle with salt, pepper, and spices. Mash in a mortar 1 lb. of the same meat, very lean, with a piece of bread soaked in tomato juice and pressed by hand to squeeze out all the liquid. Mix in some *fines herbes,* which have been finely chopped without mashing, 1 tbsp. dried currants, 1 tbsp. sultanas, and 1 tbsp. sliced almonds. Test the seasoning. Remove from the mortar, divide into 12 equal portions, and place each portion on a slice of meat, flattening it out. Roll them into the shape of an egg. Line the bottom of a deep pot with slices of raw ham, 1 finely sliced onion and 1 finely sliced carrot, a *bouquet garni.* Place your stuffed meat on top. Brown a few minutes, turning the meat on both sides; add 1 good glass white wine or ½ glass Madeira. Cover with a sheet of buttered paper, put the lid on the pot, and let simmer 1½ hr. Put the meat on a platter, strain and skim the cooking gravy, add ½ glass Tomato Sauce (p. 146), boil 2 min., pour over the meat, and serve. It must be served very hot. Each portion may be served on a toasted crouton.

FEGATELLI FLORENTINE FEGATELLI À LA FLORENTINE (Gr.)

Put salt, pepper, spices, and 1 tbsp. fennel seeds into a dish and mix well. Cut fresh pork liver into 12 egg-sized pieces, put them into the dish with the seasoning, and roll them around until completely covered. Wrap each piece of liver in a little pork casing; spit them on skewers, alternating a piece of liver, a small chipolata sausage, and a bread crouton. Grill on the spit or in the oven, basting with good olive oil. Serve on a very hot platter.

NORTH AFRICA

The culinary repertoire of North Africa is much more extensive than one would believe in France. According to the French chef Léon Isnard, hospitality in a Moslem country is so widespread and obligatory for all that no expression is more insulting to a family than to say of it, "They showed poor hospitality."

Young Arab women belonging to the leisure classes always have an extensive knowledge of cooking. They know recipes for countless dishes calculated to please their husbands' guests.

COUSCOUS or COUSCOUSSOU couscous (M.)

Couscous is the national dish of North Africa: neither poor nor rich ever tire of it.

This dish is easily prepared and nutritious; it is appropriate to the climate of the country and is especially useful for those who live in the desert, where there is often no bread.

In some regions, the inhabitants make Couscous of roasted corn meal and in others they use roasted ground acorns. In the oases, the natives don't always have the necessary semolina to make their Couscous and so grind barley or hard grain between 2 stones.

Today, many ready-made cereal preparations can be used to make first-rate Couscous, steamed with water or bouillon vapor.

COUSCOUS-TAM couscous-tam (M.)

Put 1 lb. semolina into a wide bowl or wooden dish *(djefna)* ; moisten with lightly salted water and work between the hands to remove all lumps. Continue working the semolina while adding 15 oz. salted water until it has soaked up all the water and resembles buckshot. When the semolina has reached this stage, strain it through a sieve and put it into a special colander *(keskès)* that fits over a straight-sided pot containing 1 qt. water (the water must not touch the semolina while boiling) . Cook 30 min., then add 2 oz. butter to the semolina, stirring with a fork until melted. This should make about 2½ lb. Couscous. Add milk, honey, hard-boiled eggs, raisins, powdered sugar, and melted butter, if it is to be served as a dessert.

COUSCOUS À LA MARGA couscous à la marga (M.) *(For 5 persons)*

This is the outstanding Couscous served at African feasts.

Preparation: 1 hen, 3 lb. breast and shoulder of mutton, 3 tomatoes, 3 artichoke bottoms, 3 small squash or zucchini, 5 oz. turnips, 5 oz. cardoons, 3½ oz. onion, 3 sweet peppers, 5 oz. fresh broad beans, 3½ oz. chickpeas, 1 tbsp. salt, 1 tbsp. Spanish paprika, a pinch of cumin and spices, 2 cloves, 3½ qt. water.

Cut the mutton into even-sized pieces and the hen into joints and put them into a narrow-necked but deep earthenware pot. Pour in the water. Bring to a boil and skim.

Add the tomatoes, zucchini, peppers, turnips, cardoons, artichoke bottoms, onions cut into even pieces, chickpeas (already half cooked) , fresh broad beans.

Season with the salt, paprika, cumin, and cloves. Put the Couscous basket or colander containing the Couscous over the pot. Cook over a low fire about 2 hr.

To serve: Place the Couscous in a large dish. Arrange the mutton, chicken, and vegetables symmetrically on top. Pour the bouillon into a tureen, reserving a little of it to mix with cayenne pepper (this sauce for connoisseurs of spicy dishes) .

How to eat Couscous: The large wooden dish containing the Couscous is placed on a small round table about 20 in. high. The guests sit cross-legged, on a large mat, around this table. Using a large wooden spoon in the right hand, they eat from the same dish without offending their neighbors.

While eating, the Arabs drink cow, ewe, camel, or goat milk or even, simply, fresh water. Needless to say, no bread is eaten with Couscous.

MÉCHOUI or ROAST MÉCHOUI OR RÔTI (M.)

Méchoui is the *pièce de résistance* at feasts given by Arab chieftains. This holiday roast is cut from a sheep or lamb. According to Léon Isnard, author of *Afrique gourmande,* this is the way to prepare it.

The sheep or lambs for a Méchoui must be fat and fleshy. To give the meat its peculiar flavor, a large bouquet of aromatic plants—juniper, thyme, fennel, wild mint, and parsley—should be placed inside.

Cooking the roast requires great attention: Méchoui is not perfect unless constantly basted with melted butter and salted water and cooked slowly over a glowing fire kept at a constant temperature.

Preparation: Spit the sheep from head to tail on a pointed rod. The spit should extend beyond both ends.

Tie the shoulders to the neck with a few twists of string. Tie the legs to the rod with string. Season with salt and pepper. Place the 2 ends of the spit on 2 large rocks or on 2 Y-shaped supports stuck in the earth (this roast should be prepared in the open air), on which the spit can turn.

Dig a pit 1 yd. long and 1 ft. deep beside the spitted sheep. Light a wood fire in the pit and wait until the embers are hot and glowing. Place these embers about 2 ft. under the sheep. Turn the spit slowly to roast the animal on all sides.

Using a large brush, baste with melted butter and salted water while cooking. The Méchoui is cooked when a long skewer stuck through it no longer lets out red juices; it should be evenly browned all over.

As soon as it is cooked, the Méchoui should be served and carved. The guests themselves do this, pulling off strips of hot meat with their fingers.

In various regions of Morocco and Tunisia, Méchoui is cooked in a clay oven. Méchoui is also made of young camel, moufflon (wild sheep), and gazelle.

HONEY CAKE MESELMEN (M.)

Take 1 lb. stone-ground wheat flour. Place it on the table in a ring; put a pinch of salt, 5 oz. sugar, 3 oz. olive oil, and a little water in the center.

Knead this paste without pounding it. Then roll it out and cut with a cooky cutter into circles 2 in. in diameter. Plunge these rounds of paste into burning-hot deep fat. As soon as you take them out of the fat, cover them with honey and sprinkle with shredded pine-cone almonds.

SEBAS-EL-AAROUSSA SEBAS-EL-AAROUSSA (M.)

Shape 1 lb. sifted flour into a ring on the table. In the center put 3 whole eggs, 3½ oz. sugar, a pinch of salt, and a little water.

Work together to make a very smooth, firm paste. Roll out the paste and cut into narrow strips 2 in. long. Roll these strips into long, slender fingers on the floured table.

Plunge them into burning-hot oil, drain the sticks, and roll them immediately in honey. Serve hot or cold.

Note: The words *sebas-el-aaroussa* mean "fiancée's finger."

RAHAT-LOUKOUM RAHAT-LOUKOUM (U. D.)

Dissolve 2 lb. sugar in 2 glasses water, add 1½ pt. water, and pour into a copper bowl with a walnut-sized piece of butter and ¼ lb. well-sifted wheat flour; mix well to avoid lumps. Add the juice of 1 lemon. Stir constantly over a hot fire, blend in ¼ lb. gum arabic dissolved in water, and skim. Lower heat and cook 1 hr., stirring constantly. It is through cooking when a drop of the liquid, falling on confectioners' sugar, stays a globule and is coated with the sugar. Finish by adding 5 oz. almonds, hazelnuts, and pistachios, all slivered fine. Then add a little pink coloring (cochineal or amaranth sirup), and flavor with attar of roses. Pour into a metal frame on an oiled marble slab, and powder with sifted sugar to avoid sticking. Cut into squares or strips and roll in the sugar. Keep in a cool place.

POLAND

BARSZCZ[1] BARSZCZ (A.)

Barszcz is the Polish kind of sour soup found in most Slavic cooking. It may be prepared many ways, but its tart flavor always comes from sour beet juice.

(*For 4 persons*)

Here is one of the simplest recipes. Take: 2½ cups excellent chicken and beef consommé, 3½ oz. carrots, 3½ oz. raw beets, 3½ oz. oven-cooked beets, ⅓ oz. onion, ⅓ oz. dried mushrooms, 1 heaping tsp. parsley, 1 heaping tsp. chopped fennel leaves, 1 heaping tsp. powdered sugar, salt, pepper, sour beet juice.[2]

Peel and slice the carrots and raw beets thin, sprinkle them with sugar, and let them stand. Bring the consommé to a boil and put in the drained carrots and beets, parsley, onion, mushrooms, salt, and pepper. Bring to a boil again. Cut the cooked beets into slices and pickle them in the sour beet juice, which you have heated without boiling, and add beets and juice to the first preparation. Boil for a moment, taste, and finish the seasoning if needed, correct the acidity,[3] and color the soup.[4] Strain; add the chopped fennel and some poached eggs or slices of cooked, peeled sausage or even ravioli. Serve very hot.

As a variant, any of several vegetables cut into julienne strips can be added to the soup: carrots, leeks, celery, turnips, cabbage, beets, tomatoes, and beans. In this case, do not strain the soup.

---

[1] This word is pronounced *brachtch.*

[2] Sour beet juice is made with raw or cooked beets. Connoisseurs prefer the first. The raw or cooked beets are peeled, sliced thin, and put into a stoneware jar with hot water. Keep the jar in a warm place 8–15 days, depending on the temperature, and you will have the proper sour juice.

If you add crumbled rye bread to the jar, you will speed up the operation. Using hot cooked beets, you should have the desired sour juice in 48 hr.

If you are in a hurry, instead of sour beet juice, you may use a sour juice made by pickling slices of cooked beets a few hours in wine vinegar.

[3] If the soup is too acid, it is sweetened with a little cream. If it is not acid enough, the juice of cooked beets mixed with red wine vinegar should be added.

[4] The soup should be a beautiful red. If it is too pale, darken it by adding the natural juice of cooked beets.

Another variant is to add to the soup, strained or not, thin-sliced meats such as pork, bacon, fowl, or game. The meat should be cooked in the broth.

Finally, vegetable bouillon may be used instead of meat bouillon, but, in this case, better add some cream to thicken the soup and give it body.

In Russia they make tart soups called borscht, some with meat, more or less like the variants given above, the meats being served separately with a dish of sour cream. The meatless ones have a base of fish bouillon flavored with fennel, sweet marjoram, and clove; these are served with ravioli stuffed with chopped fish.

There is still another sour soup made with the juice of cucumbers pickled in brine instead of the sour beet juice. In Moldavia, there is a soup called Borge, belonging to the tart soups, but different from Barszcz in that a sour concoction of bread dough and bran, or lemon juice, is substituted for the sour beet juice.

Here are a few directions for Borge made with lemon juice. Cut cabbages, sweet pimentos, red and green tomatoes, squash, beets, onions, and potatoes into small pieces. Cook these vegetables a long time in bouillon and flavor to taste with lemon juice. 10 min. before serving, put a few raw egg yolks into a soup tureen with 1 tbsp. extra-heavy cream per person, mix with a little bouillon, then slowly pour in the rest of the soup, stirring the tureen.

POLISH BORSCHT (BORTSCH POLSKI) BORTSCH POLONAIS (Pe.)

Cut beets, leeks, celery root, parsley root, and 1 onion into julienne strips; add a small head of kale cut the same way. Heat all this in butter in a medium-sized pan. When it all turns golden, pour some good bouillon over it and 1 ladleful sour beet juice. Add a good duckling already ¾ roasted, then about 2 lb. brisket of beef already blanched, and a *bouquet garni* of marjoram, 2 or 3 dried mushrooms, 1 bay leaf, and 1 clove. Let simmer until the duckling and beef have cooked thoroughly. Remove them both from the soup, cut up the duckling the usual way, and cube the beef. Remove the *bouquet,* skim the fat off the soup, correct the seasoning, add a binding composed of ½ ladleful sour cream diluted with the juice of 2 grated, very red beets and a good pinch of chopped, blanched parsley and fennel. When ready to send the soup to the table, add the pieces of beef and duckling along with some small chipolata sausages (grilled and skinned).

CZERNINA CZERNINA (A.)

Czernina, or black broth, is a blood soup of Polish origin.

Use duck, chicken, game, or pork blood as you wish.

To make Czernina, take some good chicken consommé, cook semolina, rice, or one of the Italian pastes in it, then take the pot off the fire, add fresh blood, quantity depending on taste, heat over a low fire without boiling, thicken with a purée of fowl or game livers, and serve.

Fried bread croutons may be added to the soup just before serving in place of the semolina, rice, or paste.

KRÜPNIK KRÜPNIK (A.) (*For 8 persons*)

Krüpnik is a Polish soup made with pearl barley.

Take: (1) *For the soup:* 1 lb. knuckle of veal, 1 oz. bay salt, dash of pepper, 2 qt. water, giblets of 3 chickens, 3 medium-sized carrots, white of 2 medium-sized leeks, 1 medium-sized turnip, 1 small piece of parsnip, 1 small piece of celery, ½ bay leaf, ½ parsley root, ½ onion.

(2) *For the garnish:* ½ lb. pearl barley, 2 oz. carrots diced into ⅛-in. cubes, 2 oz. butter, 1 roast chicken wing sliced thin.

Prepare a white bouillon by simmering the ingredients mentioned in the first paragraph; strain it. Put the barley and butter into a pan, cover with bouillon, and let simmer 2½ hr., stirring from time to time with a wooden spoon and replacing the liquid as it evaporates, to keep the barley from burning. Cook the carrots separately in the same bouillon. Keep the sliced chicken hot.

When ready to serve, combine the bouillon, barley, carrots, and chicken.

As a variant, use a vegetable bouillon instead of the white bouillon, but then bind the soup with egg yolks or with cream with or without a little lemon juice.

POLISH KOLODNIK (POLSKI KOLODNIK) KOLODNIK POLONAIS (Pe.)

Wash and blanch 3 or 4 good handfuls of very tender beet leaves. Chop fine and mix with a good pinch of tarragon, chervil, chives, fennel, and shallots, all chopped fine and blanched. Put into a soup pot on ice and cover with 1 pt. salted cucumber juice and 1 pt. kvass.[1]

Dice fine 10 fresh cucumbers, 50 crayfish tails, and ½ lb. braised sturgeon, and keep on ice until ready to serve. Strain 3 cups good sour cream and blend it into the soup. Then add the cucumbers, crayfish, and sturgeon, and a few pieces of clean ice; season with salt and a pinch of powdered sugar. Serve a separate plate of 12 quartered, hard-boiled eggs sprinkled with finely chopped chervil and fennel.

CARP FOR CHRISTMAS EVE POLISH STYLE (KARPE PO POLSKI DLA ROJEDE STWENNSKAGO SOTSCHELNIKA) CARPE À LA POLONAISE POUR LA VEILLE DE NOËL (Pe.)

Scale, clean, and wash a fine carp. Place it on the heavily buttered grid of a fish poaching pan; put in a *bouquet garni* and a few trimmings of various vegetables; season with salt, pepper, and nutmeg and cover with 2 bottles sauterne and 1 bottle Bordeaux. Place in the oven 2 hr. before serving, and cook slowly. When the fish is ¾ cooked, strain and skim the cooking stock, replace the carp in the poaching pan, and finish cooking in an open oven. Meanwhile, reduce the stock, adding to it 6 tbsp. good honey and 6 tbsp. spice bread soaked in milk, heated over a fire till dry, and pressed through a sieve. When ready to serve, drop a handful of slivered almonds into the sauce and pour it over the carp. Serve the rest of the sauce in a sauceboat.

CHICKEN CRACOVIENNE POULET À LA CRACOVIENNE (Fa.)

Cook 1⅓ oz. semolina in 1 pt. bouillon, stirring constantly; season generously with pepper, fennel, and chopped parsley. Cook 20 min. and add a piece of fresh butter. Let cool, and use this dressing to stuff a chicken prepared for roasting. Roast the chicken on a spit and then, when done, about 50 min., roll it in

[1] An intoxicating beverage, a sort of liquor made by fermenting barley with hot water. A great favorite of the muzhiks of old.

golden bread crumbs, place it on a platter, and baste heavily with brown butter. Serve the gravy separately.

(Recipe given to J. Favre by the Polish chef, Stanislas Tarkowski.)

CREAM-CHEESE BALLS (KLUSKI) BOULETTES AU FROMAGE BLANC (A.)

(For 4 persons)

Take: 1 lb. well-drained cream cheese, 5 oz. butter, 3½ oz. golden bread crumbs, 1½ oz. wheat flour, ½ oz. salt, 3 egg yolks, 2 whites.

Put the cheese, flour, salt, egg whites and yolks into a bowl and mix well. Add 1½ oz. butter melted in a double boiler. Work well to form a smooth, rather liquid paste without lumps.

Boil salted water (½ oz. salt per qt. water) and drop the paste by the tbsp. or dessertspoon into the boiling water; each spoonful will form into a ball. Remove the balls as soon as they rise to the surface of the water, drain them in a strainer, and keep them separated; then roll them in the bread crumbs. Heat the rest of the butter in a fireproof dish, lay in the cheese balls, brown them on both sides, and serve in the same dish.

When well prepared, these balls should be firm outside and soft inside. They can take the place of a side dish of vegetables on the menu.

As a variant, first roll the boiled cheese balls in a mixture of egg white and grated Gruyère or Parmesan cheese, and then in the sifted bread crumbs. Fry them in very hot deep fat. Serve with Tomato Sauce (p. 146).

RUMANIA

Rumanian cooking resembles Russian cooking in some respects, Italian in others. Don't lose sight of the fact that Rumania is a Latin country and that, while its nearness to the Slavic nations has made it take on certain tastes and customs, in its cooking there are resemblances to both zones. Rumanians, like the Russians, love hors d'oeuvres; at the same time, they serve most of their dishes with *mamaliga,* which is nothing but Italian polenta.

BORCHE BORCHE

The best Rumanian soups are the sour soups, which have an exquisite flavor and are both appetizing and digestible. They are usually prepared with canned cabbage juice, Borche, sour grapes, small raw plums that are very acid, lemon juice, or sour beet juice.

Bran Borche, which is slightly alcoholic, is preferred above all other liquids in preparing these soups. It is fermented in a large, earthenware crock. Take 3 lb. bran, 1 lb. corn meal, 1 slice dry brown bread, rind of ½ lemon, a few cherry leaves, 3 qt. water, a piece of charcoal.

Separately, prepare a leaven (you will have to do this only the first time you prepare the Borche) with ½ lb. bran, 5 oz. corn meal, 1 qt. water, 1 lb. dry brown bread. Mix the bran with the corn meal and bread; heat in the oven with 1 qt. cold water. Let stand overnight, or at least 6 hr., in a warm place. This leaven may be used any time you want to induce the fermentation of the Borche. Keep it in the crock and use it whenever you want to make fresh Borche.

Mix the bran with corn meal and very little cold water, just enough to dissolve the albuminous part of the bran. Pour boiling water over it, mix well, and let cool. When the mixture is tepid, add the leaven prepared the night before (or a handful of old leaven taken from the bottom of the crock), add a few cherry leaves, lemon rind, bread, and charcoal. If necessary, add more water. Let stand a few days in a warm place. Taste the Borche each day to see if it has become acid and skim off the foam. Each time you use some of it, replace the liquid removed with warm water.

If, after some time, the Borche begins to lose its sour quality, repeat the process by adding 1 or 2 good handfuls of leaven from your storage crock.

Borche is used instead of vinegar in recipes for tart dishes and sour soups. Its flavor and aroma add a special note to these dishes. Every humble kitchen in Rumania uses it because it is easy to make, inexpensive, and can be bought in even the smallest grocery.

TCHORBA TCHORBA

All sour soups made with Borche (above) or canned cabbage or pickle juice are called Tchorba.

Drop ½ lb. veal or pork, or both together, cut into pieces, into 1 qt. boiling Borche. Add salt and pepper, 1 sliced onion, 1 small carrot cut into julienne strips, celery leaves, coarsely chopped parsley and fennel, 2 or 3 peeled tomatoes cut into pieces, 1 green pepper cut into pieces, 1 tbsp. rice, and, when almost cooked, a handful of chopped lovage.[1]

LAMB TCHORBA TCHORBA D'AGNEAU

This spring soup is very good. Cook some small pieces of lamb along with the head and the vegetables cut in julienne strips as above. Add some boiling Borche (p. 772), parsley, fennel, and lovage. Remove the head, press it between 2 platters (the bones come out very easily), and put the brains, tongue, and pieces of meat detached from the bones into a soup tureen. Add the lamb pieces from the soup, then pour in the Tchorba with the vegetables. Sprinkle with chopped lovage.

POLENTA MAMALIGA

This national dish is the Rumanian peasant's daily bread. It is easy to prepare, nourishing, highly digestible, and may be served a number of ways.

Heat 1 qt. salted water over a hot fire and, when it first starts to boil, drop in a heaping handful of corn meal. Mix rapidly with a wooden spatula. Increase the heat and continue stirring until firm. If necessary, add a little more corn meal.

This gruel should be very smooth and without lumps. Leave on the stove about ¼ hr. When it is thick enough, press it with a wet wooden spoon and reverse it onto a wooden platter. It should keep the shape of the pot it was cooked in and have the consistency of a pudding.

POLENTA BALLS BOULETTES DE MAMALIGA

Mix the Polenta (above) with butter and cheese. Shape into egg-sized balls

[1] An aromatic plant, similar to angelica, widely used in Rumania.

and fry in butter. The balls may be filled with mushrooms, leftover stew meat, diced bacon, or ham. Serve them as a garnish around green vegetables sautéed in butter or cover them with fresh cream.

PIKE CAVIAR CAVIAR DE BROCHET

After black caviar (sturgeon eggs), which is expensive and served only on special occasions, Pike Caviar occupies an important place among Rumanian hors d'oeuvres.

We must caution you never to boil or fry Pike Caviar. Be sure to save it when you prepare pike, for it is so delicious that it is worth more than the fish itself.

Gently lift out the caviar, remove the skin and small blood vessels, salt it, and let stand ½ day without washing. Beat it lightly with a fork, adding, 1 drop at a time, 1 glass good olive oil, juice of 1 lemon, and, from time to time, a few drops of cold water. Do not stop beating until the caviar has become firm and light like a beaten egg white. It should be pale pink, and each fish egg should be separate in the white foam formed by the oil and lemon juice. Season to taste with a little finely chopped onion. Serve garnished with black olives or as small open-faced sandwiches.

BLACK OLIVE PÂTÉ PÂTÉ D'OLIVES NOIRES

Pit some fine black olives and press them through a sieve. Mix this purée with an equal amount of fresh butter; add pepper and a little chopped onion to taste. Serve very cold as is or make into sandwiches.

CARP STUFFED WITH OLIVES CARPE FARCIE D'OLIVES

Clean a carp and stuff it with 3½ oz. pitted black olives mixed with some Béchamel Sauce (p. 146), fennel, parsley, 1 clove of garlic, pepper, lemon juice, and oil. Sew up the carp and lay it on a bed of sliced onions, peppercorns, and lemon slices. Pour burning-hot oil over the top, make a few slits in the fish, and bake in the oven.

STURGEON WITH ONION ESTURGEON À L'OIGNON

Cut the sturgeon into slices and dredge them in flour mixed with paprika; brown them in oil. Using the oil left in the pan, brown a good number of sliced onions, add salt and pepper, ⅔ oz. flour, Tomato Sauce (p. 146), and water. Pour this sauce over the fried fish, bring to a boil over a low fire, and finish cooking in the oven. Salmon and cod may be prepared the same way.

PAPRIKA FISH PAPRIKA DE POISSON

Cut the fish (any kind of fat fish) into pieces. Lightly brown sliced onions in oil, add 1 tsp. paprika, salt, and pepper, and enough water to cover the fish. Boil the fish in this sauce about ¼ hr., without stirring. Add either fresh cream or 1 small glass red wine. Serve with Polenta (p. 773).

BEEF RAGOUT RAGOÛT DE BOEUF

Cut a piece of brisket of beef into small cubes and brown in fat; lightly brown a few sliced onions along with the meat. Cover and let simmer, adding a few drops of water from time to time. Stir the pan to keep from burning. Add peeled tomatoes cut into pieces and continue cooking 2 hr., stirring occasionally and adding a little water, 1 tsp. paprika, salt, and pepper. Just before serving, add some fresh cream. Surround with slices of Polenta (p. 773) or serve with potato balls made of mashed potatoes mixed with 2 eggs and a little flour.

MITITEIS (HOME-MADE SAUSAGES) PETITES SAUCISSES DE MAISON

Chop 1 lb. beef cut from the tender part of the neck. Add salt and pepper, a few chopped cloves of garlic, 1 tsp. baking soda (to make the sausages swell), powdered spices, 1 clove, 1 English pepper, a little beef suet chopped with the meat. Wet the hands and shape the mincemeat into little sausages about 3 in. long. Cook them on a grill, using special flat pincers to turn them until done all over.

ZUCCHINI STUFFED WITH CHEESE COURGETTES FARCIES AU FROMAGE

Peel 6 zucchini, scald them, hollow them out, and fill with the following stuffing: 5 oz. fresh cheese mixed with 3½ oz. grated Gruyère, ⅓ oz. semolina, ½ cup cream, a few tbsp. Béchamel Sauce (p. 146), and 3 eggs (the whites beaten separately). Put them into a baking dish, baste with butter, and bake in the oven.

GUIVETCHE GUIVETCHE

Take equal amounts of: diced potatoes, sliced carrots, handful of peas, green beans cut lengthwise, diced eggplant, cabbage cut into small pieces, cauliflower, large green bell pepper, onions cut into ½-in. cubes, chopped parsley, sliced turnip, sliced leek, diced zucchini, a chopped *bouquet garni,* a bunch of green grapes, a handful of okra, a few thick-sliced tomatoes, 2 apples or 1 orange. Put everything into an earthenware pot. Pour boiling oil on top, salt, and pepper; add 3–4 tbsp. water, and cook in the oven. Serve hot or cold.

EGGPLANT SALAD SALADE D'AUBERGINES

Take some fine eggplants and fry them until they are cooked and tender inside. The skin will turn black. Let them cool somewhat, then wet your hand in cold water and carefully remove the skin and any other black spots. Put the eggplants on a chopping board and pour a little oil on top while still warm; chop them fine with a special wooden chopper (metal blackens them). Put the chopped eggplant into a porcelain bowl, add salt, and mix the purée with a wooden spoon while adding, drop by drop, as when making mayonnaise, ½ cup olive oil and a little lemon juice. Serve this paste with a little sliced onion, if you wish. Garnish with slices of tomato.

SOUR CABBAGE SALAD SALADE DE CHOUX AIGRES

Shred the cabbage very fine, rub with salt, add a little cumin, press well into a crock, add very little water. Keep at a warm temperature near the stove in winter or in the sun in summer. Each day skim off the foam that forms on top. Depending on the degree of heat, the cabbage should sour in 3–7 days. Serve with oil, chopped onion, olives, and hard-boiled eggs.

Another way to sour cabbage is to slice it thin, salt it without rubbing, add caraway or not, put it into a glass jar with a small green or red pepper, add a generous amount of pepper, cover with warm water, and let stand a few days in a warm place.

RUSSIA

One of the specialties of Russian cooking, at least as Petit practiced it, is *zakouskis*—hors d'oeuvres. The Russians don't serve them at the table as we do, but, in a separate room next to the dining room, lay out a wide variety of hors d'oeuvres, both hot and cold, with numerous decanters of liqueurs and whiskies and plates of black and white bread. The guests pass before this sort of buffet and serve themselves hors d'oeuvres and 1 or 2 small glasses of spirits before being seated at the table.

The list of hors d'oeuvres includes all those we know: radishes, cucumbers, onions, various salads, eggs, etc., and such native dishes as smoked or salted herrings, apple mixtures, small canapés of fish, caviar, crayfish, shrimp, etc.

Among the soups peculiar to the Slavs, we shall give the recipes for Borscht (made with slight variations in Russia, Poland, and Lithuania), Stschi, and Batwinia, which is served cold.

Note: The proportions given are for about 10 persons and may be increased or diminished, depending on the number of guests.

CONSOMMÉ WITH BUCKWHEAT KLOSKIS (CONSOMMÉ C'KLETSKAMI GRETSCHNEVOI) CONSOMMÉ AUX KLOSKIS DE SARRASIN (Pe.)

Make the Kloskis the following way. Heat ½ cup cream with ¼ lb. butter, salt, and a pinch of powdered sugar. When the butter has melted, make a panada by adding about 6 oz. buckwheat flour. Let dry over a low fire, then add 5 or 6 eggs, 1 by 1, to give it the consistency of Choux Paste. Using a pastry bag or paper cone, squeeze this paste into small balls onto a buttered sautéing pan. Poach, drain, and serve in boiling consommé.

FISH BORSCHT (BORSCHT IS RIBA) BORSCHT AU POISSON (Pe.)

Cut up vegetables, beets, and cabbage as for ordinary borscht. Cook slightly in butter, and cover with equal parts of sour beet juice and fish bouillon. Season and add a *bouquet garni* (parsley with a little sweet marjoram); simmer and skim. Season with salt and pepper, and bind with sour cream.

10 min. before serving, cook a few fillets of breaded fish (perch or dace) until golden brown and put them into the soup. When serving, add chopped fennel and parsley.

You can add some small fish ravioli to this soup. Cook 1 shallot in butter, add a few pieces of whitefish or salmon, and cook together. When the fish is cooked, put it on the chopping board and cut into pieces. Mix the fish with some very thick Allemande Sauce (p. 146) made with fish essence. Season with salt, pepper, nutmeg, and chopped parsley. Let cool, then use to fill small ravioli. Blanch the ravioli and put into the soup when ready to serve.

RUSSIAN CABBAGE SOUP WITH BUCKWHEAT (STSCHI-GRESCHENE-VAI-KACHE) POTAGE AUX CHOUX À LA RUSSE AVEC GRUAU DE SARRASIN (Pe.)

Dice 2 medium-sized onions very fine and cook them in butter. Add about 1½ lb. or more, depending on the number of guests, coarsely chopped sauerkraut; heat it with the onion. Then add 1 tbsp. buckwheat flour and 3 tbsp. sour cream. Mix well, then fill the pot with good bouillon. Add a whole duckling (half-roasted), a few pieces of blanched brisket of beef, and a few sausages. Lower the fire and let the pot simmer. Remove the duckling, beef, and sausages when they are thoroughly cooked. Cut them up the usual way, and put them back into the soup, just before serving, after skimming it and thickening with 4 or 5 tbsp. sour cream. Season to taste and add a good pinch of chopped, blanched parsley.

ROSSOLNICK SOUP WITH CUCUMBERS (SOUPE ROSSOLNICK Ç'AGOURTZAMI) POTAGE ROSSOLNICK AUX CONCOMBRES (Pe.)

Make a garnish of celery root and parsley root cut in the shape of small carrots; cut the top of each root to form a cross and blanch in cold water. After boiling 10 min., let cool and put into a soup pot. Cut 10 salted cucumbers (*agoursis*) into diamond-shaped slices and blanch them quickly so they stay very green. After boiling 2 min., drain them on a cloth, let cool, and put into the pot with the blanched roots. Prepare a thin Velouté (p. 147), using rich chicken consommé. Skim and strain the sauce and pour it into the soup pot containing the vegetables. Add ½ cup cucumber juice, and bind the soup as usual with egg yolks and extra-heavy cream. Just before serving, add 2 young, disjointed chickens (cooked to make the Velouté for the soup or braised separately) to the soup. Instead of chicken, you can use Chicken Quenelles or Godiveau (p. 174).

STSCHI LAZY STYLE (STSCHI LIENIWOUI) STSCHI À LA PARESSEUSE (Pe.)

Clean a fine fresh cabbage and cut it into 8 sections. Cut up carrots, turnips, parsley, and leeks as for pot-au-feu. Blanch all together and let cool. Cut 2 or 3 lb. brisket of beef into cubes, blanch, cool, and put into the soup pot with the vegetables. Fill the pot with clear bouillon and boil slowly until the beef is thoroughly cooked; 15 min. before serving, mix ¼ lb. butter with flour to make a White Roux and stir it into the soup. Season with salt and pepper, skim off the fat, bind with 2 or 3 tbsp. sour cream, and add a good pinch of chopped parsley.

ROASTED BUCKWHEAT CAKES TO SERVE WITH STSCHI STSCHI (GRUAU DE SARRASIN RÔTI POUR SERVI AVEC LE) (Pe.)

Soak 1 lb. ground buckwheat seeds with enough warm water to make a thick paste; salt, and put into an earthenware pot glazed inside, or, if unavailable, a large charlotte mold. Put it into a hot oven and let cook almost 2 hr. Remove the thick crust that has formed on top and turn the soft, center part into a bowl with an egg-sized piece of butter. Mix well with a spatula; press the mush between 2 pot covers until it is only about ⅜ in. thick. After it has cooled, cut it with a plain cooky cutter and brown on both sides in clarified butter. Serve these buckwheat cakes very hot on a napkin and send to the table with the Stschi.

BATWINIA BATWINIA (Pe.)

Cook down 2 lb. sorrel, drain, and press through a sieve; put it into a soup pot and chill on ice. Do the same thing with 3 lb. spinach and a good handful of new beet leaves, and add to the sorrel. Dice fine 12 fresh *agoursis*[1] and mix them with the sorrel and spinach. Pour in enough *kislischy*[2] to fill the soup pot. Season with salt and a good pinch of powdered sugar, a little tarragon, chervil, fennel, and shallots, all chopped. A few minutes before serving the soup, drop in a few cubes of ice.

Serve, on a separate, napkin-covered platter, a cold salmon steak surrounded by green parsley and small mounds of grated horse-radish.

Sometimes, instead of salmon, braised sturgeon chilled under pressure is served. The sturgeon should be cut crosswise into very thin slices and served with grated horse-radish on a platter without a napkin.

SMOLENSK KASHA (SMOLENSKI KACHE) KACHE DE SMOLENSK (Pe.)

Mix 1 lb. Smolensk semolina (called *Smolenski kroupa*) with 2 beaten eggs until the semolina is thoroughly moistened. Put it into the warming oven to dry and then press it through a fine sieve. Boil 2 bottles of milk with ½ lb. butter, salt lightly, pour in the semolina, and mix well to keep from sticking to the bottom of the pan. When well cooked, place it in a silver baking dish. Serve with a sauceboat of melted butter.

BEEF FILLET WITH RAISINS (FILET PO NEAPOLITANSKI S' IZIOUME) FILET DE BOEUF AUX RAISINS (Pe.)

Trim a beef fillet and lard it the usual way; braise with equal parts of Madeira and Malaga and 1 lb. fresh, crushed grapes. While the beef is braising, pick and wash ½ lb. dried currants, ½ lb. sultanas, and ½ lb. Malaga raisins; put these 3 types of raisins into a saucepan. 15 min. before serving, strain ½ the stock from the braising beef, skim off the fat, and pour the stock over the raisins; boil a few minutes. Just before serving, mix ½ lb. red-currant jelly with 2 tbsp. grated horse-radish and add this to your boiling raisins; shake as when buttering peas. Cut up the beef fillet and place it on a platter with the raisins surrounding the meat; glaze it in the oven, and serve. Accompany the platter with a sauceboat of good Espagnole Sauce (p. 137) reduced with Madeira.

PASTE FOR KULIBIAK AND PIROJKY (TIESTA DIA COULIBIAC I ROUSSK PIRAJKIS) PÂTÉ À COULIBIAC ET PETIT PÂTÉ RUSSE (Pe.)

Put 1 glass warm milk and a little yeast into a stewpan; add ½ lb. flour, then beat with a spatula to form a smooth leaven. Let rise in a warm place. When it is ready, pour into the same pan ½ lb. flour, ½ lb. soft butter, 6 whole eggs, and a little salt and beat with a spatula to make a very smooth paste. Next sprinkle the baking table with flour, turn the paste onto it, and knead it a little. If the paste has the proper consistency, it will not stick to the fingers. Put the paste into a bowl and let it rise again in a warm place ¾ hr. The paste is now ready to be made into Kulibiaks or small Russian *pâtés* called Pirojky.

---

[1] Salted cucumbers.

[2] A Russian beverage. However, if it is not available, you can substitute a young and rather sharp white wine, which I have done quite successfully.

For Kulibiak, roll out your paste until it is ½ as thick as your finger. Put the filling for your Kulibiak—fish, meat, cabbage, etc.—on the paste, fold the edges over, and seal together after brushing with beaten egg. Shape the Kulibiak into a long rectangle on a napkin. Place a buttered baking sheet on top of the Kulibiak, then, taking the edges of the napkin that extend beyond the baking sheet, turn the Kulibiak over quickly. This way, the sealed edges will be on the bottom of the tray and the smooth side up. Brush off the excess flour on top and let stand ½ hr. in a warm place. Brush with beaten egg, sprinkle the top with bread crumbs, and bake in the oven. When it is cooked, baste the top with a brush dipped in melted butter, cut crosswise and lengthwise into 12 pieces, and slide the whole Kulibiak onto an oval platter covered with a napkin. (Figure 190, Page 308.)

Prepare Pirojky the same way as small fish *pâtés* or pies or Salmon Rastegaïs, the recipe for which is given below.

SALMON AND LAVARET[1] KULIBIAK (COULIBIAC IS LOSSOSSE I SIGUI) COULIBIAC DE SAUMON ET LAVARET (Pe.)

Prepare Kulibiak paste as directed above. Sauté a few fillets of salmon and lavaret in butter and lemon juice and let cool. Chop some cooked *vesiga*,[2] heat a small shallot in butter, add the chopped vesiga, a little parsley and fennel, and mix well on the fire. When the mixture is well heated, put it into a bowl to cool and lightly mix in 4 or 5 thinly sliced hard-boiled eggs. Have ready some cooked semolina kasha pressed through a bread-crumb sieve (cooked rice may be used instead, provided the grains are separate). Fill your Kulibiak with these ingredients as described in the article above and finish the same way.

SALMON RASTEGAÏS (RASTEGAÏS S' LOSSOSSE) RASTEGAÏS AU SAUMON (Pe.)

Fill small *pâtés* or pies with chopped *vesiga* (see n. 2, below) mixed with chopped, hard-boiled eggs, and lay on top small pieces of raw salmon seasoned with salt and pepper and chopped parsley. When ready to serve, pour 1 tsp. clarified fish bouillon into the small hole in the top crust.

LITHUANIAN VARENIKIS (LITOFFSKI WARENIKIS) VARÉNIKIS LITHUANIENS (Pe.)

Chop ¼ lb. raw beef (preferably fillet) ; chop separately ¼ lb. beef-kidney suet. Heat a finely sliced onion in butter. When the onion begins to brown, add the beef and suet. Season with salt, pepper, nutmeg, and chopped parsley. When cooked, add 1 heaping tbsp. reduced Béchamel Sauce (p. 146) and let cool.

Roll out a very thin sheet of noodle paste (see p. 520) made with 5 eggs. At intervals lay portions of filling ½ the size of an egg, and cut the paste into large ravioli with a fluted pastry wheel. Poach the ravioli in boiling water 5 min. before serving, drain, and place in a very hot silver serving dish. Pour a little melted butter on top and serve.

---

[1] Variety of grayish-blue salmon found in the Atlantic and Baltic; very abundant in Russia.
[2] Spinal marrow from the sturgeon, highly esteemed by the Russians.

BEARS' PAWS (LAPPE MEDWEDE) PATTES D'OURS (Pe.)

Skin and wash the bear paws and marinate them at least 48 hr. Blanch them, let cool, and cook in a good stock with various vegetables and herbs. When they are cooked, drain them onto a platter and cut lengthwise into 5 parts. Dip them in flour, beaten egg, and bread crumbs, and grill them. Serve with a sweet-and-sour sauce or Piquante Sauce (p. 143).

BUCKWHEAT BLINIS (BLINIS GRETSCHNEVOI) BLINIS DE SARRASIN (Pe.)

Make a leaven with 2 lb. buckwheat flour and warm water;[1] cover the pan and keep in a moderately warm place; let stand 4 hr. Then add 1 lb. fine wheat flour, 6 egg yolks, 1 cup warm cream, and a little salt. Mix well together, beating lightly, to make a smooth, thin batter. Next fold in 6 very stiffly beaten egg whites; spoon the batter while mixing, as when making sponge cake. Let stand another 20 min. before cooking.

COOKING BLINIS CUISSON DES BLINIS (Pe.)

The day before cooking your Blinis, put a small, square firebox of logs in the opening of your oven so that you will have dry wood, for the Blinis must be cooked under a flame. The fire is not to be lighted until the beaten egg whites have been added to the mixture—that is, 30 min. before serving. Meanwhile, prepare your small *scowarodes* (small, round frying pans without handles, about 2½ in. in diameter and ⅜ in. deep). Heat the pans over the flame to dry them. Have ready at hand, at the right of the oven opening, a saucepan full of good, clarified butter and a brush; at the left, 2 silver serving dishes in which to put the Blinis as they are cooked; on the ground, a small pile of dry wood to be added to the fire from time to time as needed, to keep an even flame; on the right beside you, a stool on which to place your batter.

Now, after all these little details are seen to, is the time to start cooking your Blinis. To do this, brush 6 small pans with butter and put 1 tbsp. batter into each. (Be sure to dip your spoon just under the surface of the batter; it is unnecessary to stir up the whole mass.) Using a wooden paddle about 1 yd. long, place the small pans under the flame. As the Blinis brown, brush them with melted butter and turn them over with the tip of a knife. When the other side browns, remove them and put them into the silver dishes on your left. When 30 have been cooked, send them to the table, for Blinis must be eaten hot, and should be light, crisp, and transparent. While these are being eaten, you will have time to make another 30 to put into the second silver dish, and so on until all the batter has been used. Blinis are served at luncheon as the first course, and at dinner after the soup. Serve them with a sauceboat of very fine melted butter, a dish of sour cream, and a small dish of fresh caviar.

SMALL BLINI PATTIES WITH TRUFFLES (PIRAJKI IS BLINOWS' TROUFELEME) PETITS PÂTÉS DE BLINIS AUX TRUFFES (Pe.)

Make 20 very thin Blinis (above) and cover 10 of them with sliced truffles rolled in thick Béchamel Sauce (p. 146); cover with the other 10 Blinis, press

[1] 3 tbsp. liquid leaven, or 3 oz. solid leaven, will do.

well together, and let cool. Cut each pair into 2 ovals or circles with a cookie cutter, dip twice in egg, and fry. Serve piled into a pyramid on a napkin.

COLORED EGGS (YAITSA KRASCHENIE) OEUFS COLORÉS (Pe.)

The Russians serve not only red eggs, but various other shades such as pink, yellow, blue, and marbled. For a simple color, steep sandalwood in boiling water with a pinch of alum; let cool. Meanwhile, clean the eggs by rubbing them with a little salt and place them in cold water. Then put them carefully into the sandalwood brew and cook them 10 min. Remove the pot from the fire and let the eggs stand ¼ hr. in the cooking liquid. Remove the eggs and dry them twice; first with a slightly oiled cloth and then with a dry cloth. They are also wrapped in onion skins before being cooked or in small bits of variously colored silk; this way, the eggs are marbled. Arrange them in a pile on a napkin.

BUTTER LAMB (BARAECHKE IS MASSIA) AGNEAU DE BEURRE (Pe.)

Take a block of butter weighing about 2 lb. Wash it in a bowl of ice water, place it on a small board, and shape it into a sleeping lamb. Make the fleece with butter squeezed through a towel, mark the eyes with 2 small dots of truffle, place a bit of palm leaf in the mouth, and slide it onto a small base of lard prepared in advance. This is an Easter specialty.

EASTER SALT (TSCHETWERGOWAI SOLE) SEL DE PÂQUES (Pe.)

On Holy Thursday mix about 2 lb. fine salt with egg white to form a thick paste. Wrap this mixture very tightly in a cloth and put it into the glowing coals of the oven hearth. Let it burn until the following day. You will then find a small block of oxidized salt—naturally, without the cloth that covered it. Crush the salt and sift it to use in filling the salt cellars.

On the night of Holy Saturday, the Russians carry such dishes as paskas, kulitsches, eggs, butter lambs, salt, etc., to the church to have them blessed before putting them on the table.

MUSHROOMS RUSSIAN STYLE (GRIBOUIS PA ROUSSKI) GRIBOUIS À LA RUSSE (Pe.)

Gribouis (a kind of mushroom that usually grows around birch trees) are very plentiful in Russia, where they are greatly appreciated and widely eaten. They keep very well canned, in vinegar, or dried.

Remove the dirt and wash the white *gribouis.* Dry them with a cloth and cut them in halves or quarters. Put them into a sautéing pan with plenty of butter and a *bouquet garni* of parsley, green onion, and fennel. Season with salt, pepper, and nutmeg, and simmer; 5 min. before serving, remove the *bouquet* and add 2 tbsp. very thick Béchamel Sauce (p. 146) and 1 tbsp. sour cream. Bring to a boil again, add a pinch of chopped fennel, and serve.

VATRUSHKIS WITH CREAM CHEESE (VATROUSCHKIS S'TWAROGUE) VATROUSCHKIS AU FROMAGE BLANC (Pe.)

Press ½ lb. *twarogue*[1] through a sieve into a bowl and mix with ½ lb. soft-

[1] Cream cheese.

ened butter and a little salt, add 2 eggs, and beat well. This should make a smooth, thick cream like Pastry Cream (p. 552). Use it to fill the centers of round crusts made of Brioche (p. 546) or Short Paste (p. 545). Smooth off the tops with a knife, moisten the rim of the crust, and build it higher with another ring of paste as when preparing *tourte* crusts. Brush the rim and top with beaten egg and bake 15 min. in the oven.

Serve in a pyramid on a napkin.

CRANBERRY KISSEL (KISSEL IS KLOUKWA) KISSEL DE CANNEBERGE (Pe.)

Crush 2 lb. cranberries in a mortar, add about 1 qt. water, and squeeze through a cloth into a bowl. Put 6 tsp. arrowroot into a saucepan, mix with the cranberry juice, add some lump sugar, and stir while heating over a fire. When the mixture comes to a boil, you should have a thick, transparent composition. If you wish to serve it hot, pour it into a silver casserole and serve with a sauce-boat of extra-heavy cream. If you wish to serve it cold, however, fill a jelly mold with ice water to chill it, then pour out the water and fill the bowl with the hot cranberry mixture; let harden on ice and unmold onto a napkin. Since the mold has already been moistened with cold water, it should not be necessary to dip it into hot water to loosen the mixture from the mold.

Kissels are made with all sorts of fruit sirups as well as with almond, walnut, and hazelnut milk and are always served with a separate dish of extra-heavy cream or jam.

PRESERVED APPLES (YABLOKE MATSCHONE) POMMES CONFITES (Pe.)

Boil enough water to fill the keg or jar you are going to use to preserve your apples. Remove the water from the fire and add a pinch of white pepper, a few bay leaves, some mace, cloves, cardamom, salt, honey, and vinegar to make a pleasant-tasting, bittersweet liquid. Bring this mixture to another boil and let cool.

Meanwhile, place freshly picked apples, without peeling them, on a bed of fresh rye straw laid in the bottom of a keg; continue filling the keg with alternate layers of apples and straw. When the keg is full, pour in the very cold liquid and seal tightly. Leave in cold storage. Serve the apples in the wintertime in a salad bowl with a little of the juice. Pears, apricots, grapes, gooseberries, peaches, cherries, plums, wild cherries, black and white currants, cranberries, huckleberries, and white raspberries can all be preserved this way, except that cherry and vine leaves should be used instead of rye straw, and the small fruits should be preserved in large jars.

These preserved fruits are served in winter as salads.

SCANDINAVIA

HOT TURBOT PIE DANISH STYLE PÂTÉ CHAUD DE TURBOT À LA DANOISE (U. D.)

Bone a small fresh turbot or ½ turbot. Cut the meat crosswise into long strips about 1 in. thick. Put these fillets into a bowl and season with salt and spices. Cook 5 or 6 hard-boiled eggs. Cut them in quarters, season, sprinkle with chopped parsley, and keep covered.

Sift 1 lb. semolina; mix in 2 egg yolks, 1 after the other, while kneading by hand. Next spread it on a board and dry in the warmer. Crumble it again in your hands, breaking the lumps, and cook it in salted water, keeping it thick and dry. Chop onions, mushrooms, and parsley.

Brown the onions and mushrooms in butter; sprinkle with 1 tbsp. flour, moisten with ½ glass white wine, and add a bay leaf. Cook a few minutes, stirring, then add the chopped parsley and turbot fillets. Cover the pan, let the sauce come to a boil twice, then lower the flame and keep hot 5 min. Then let the sauce and fish cool together.

Make a Flaky Paste (p. 544) with 1¼ lb. good flour, 1¼ lb. butter, and the necessary amount of water. Roll out and fold the paste 6 times and let stand; set aside ¼ of the paste and roll out the rest into a long rectangle about 1 ft. wide and a little over 2 ft. long. Roll the paste around the rolling pin and then unroll it onto a baking sheet. Moisten with water all around. In the center make a thickish layer of the cooked but cool semolina, spreading it out in a long rectangle narrower than the crust. Lay the fish fillets on this layer, interspersing them with *fines herbes,* hard-boiled eggs, and 2 dozen blanched oysters. Cover the top and sides of this mixture with the rest of the semolina; shape the filling into a smooth, even loaf. Fold the sides of the crust over the top to cover the filling completely, fold the 2 ends over, press the edges together and seal them; moisten the top of the pie with water.

Roll out the Flaky Paste held in reserve into a long rectangle; stick it to the top of the pie, brush the surface with beaten egg, and make a small hole through the center. Then, with the tip of a knife, trace a small design in the crust. Bake the pie in a medium oven. When the crust is dry, cover it with paper, tying it on the sides. Bake the pie 1¼ hr.

Meanwhile, blanch 2 dozen oysters with 1 glass white wine. With the head and bones of the fish, some water, some white wine, and vegetables, prepare 1 qt. bouillon. Make a light golden sauce with this bouillon and the oyster cooking juice. Bind it with 3 egg yolks and finish with butter, chopped parsley, and lemon juice. Add the oysters, and serve at the same time as the pie.

SALTED RED SALMON NORWEGIAN STYLE SAUMON ROUGE SALÉ À LA NORVÉGIENNE (U. D.)

In northern Europe, as much salmon is salted as beef or pork. Before cooking the salted salmon, soak it 48 hr. in water. Drain, then put it into a pot with plenty of cold water. Bring the liquid to a boil, remove it from the stove, and keep covered; 10 min. later, drain it and place it on boiled, unchopped spinach. Cover generously with melted butter.

PERCH SWEDISH STYLE PERCHES À LA SUÉDOISE (U. D.)

Place a few clean, medium-sized perch side by side in a buttered flat pan. Season them and barely cover with water. Add some chopped parsley. Cover and cook over a hot fire so that by the time the fish is cooked the liquid is reduced by

½; thicken it with a piece of butter kneaded with flour. Place the perch on a platter and cover with the sauce.

RICE WITH MILK SWEDISH STYLE riz au lait à la suédoise (U. D.)

This is one of the national dishes of Sweden. Prepare Rice with Milk (p. 559). When it is cooked, finish it with a piece of fine butter. Spread a layer of it in a platter, sprinkle it with sugar, and glaze the surface with a red-hot iron spade. Sprinkle the sugar with a pinch of powdered cinnamon and make another layer of rice on top of the first. Glaze it again, and continue until all of the rice has been used. Glaze the top, too.

ROD-GROD rod-grod (E.)

Put 1 lb. red currants, ½ lb. raspberries, and 24 oz. water into a copper skillet. Bring to a boil and strain through a fine sieve. This should make 1½ qt. liquid. Add to the liquid 1¼ lb. sugar, 1 oz. arrowroot and 1 oz. potato flour, both mixed with a little cold water, 6 oz. red wine, and ¼ vanilla bean. Boil the mixture 2 min., stirring with a spatula.

Pour this preparation into special ceramic molds that have been moistened and sprinkled with powdered sugar or simply lined with sirup. Let stand 24 hr. in a cool place before serving. Unmold at the last moment onto a service platter and serve with a pitcher of fresh cream or milk. (A Danish dessert.)

SPAIN

COCIDO or SPANISH POT-AU-FEU pot-au-feu espagnol (U. D.)

Put into an earthenware pot 2 lb. beef, a piece of raw ham, the knuckle of roast leg of mutton, 1 hen, 2 or 3 handfuls soaked chickpeas, 5 or 6 qt. cold water. Put the pot on the fire, and skim the liquid. When it first comes to a boil, lower the flame and cook slowly. 2 hr. later, add 1 small blanched kale tied with a string, 2 leeks, 1 cut tomato, 1 carrot, a few cloves; 1 hr. later, plunge 2 smoked sausages into the liquid. When the meats have cooked, strain the broth into a pan and keep it hot.

Chop 1 onion and brown it in a little lard. Mix it with 1 lb. good rice, then pour in the strained broth until it is 3 times as high as the rice. Cover and let cook very slowly. When it is dry and well cooked, mix in 1 tbsp. Spanish paprika and 1 tbsp. Tomato Sauce (p. 146). Skim the rest of the strained broth and use it to prepare tapioca or semolina soup. When it is ready, pour it into a tureen. Remove the meats from the soup pot: beef, hen, ham, and sausages; place them together on a long platter and surround them with the chickpeas and the kale divided into portions. Serve the rice separately.

BISCAY COD SPANISH STYLE morue de biscaye, à l'espagnole (U. D.)

Cut 2 lb. raw salt cod into medium-sized squares and soak to remove the salt. Cook in salted water without boiling. Drain and remove the bones.

Grill or heat 3 or 4 large red Spanish peppers in the oven to be able to remove the skins. Cut them in strips lengthwise; season with salt and pepper.

Brown 2 chopped white onions in oil; add 4 tomatoes cut in pieces, 1 clove of garlic, a bunch of parsley, salt, and pepper (if fresh tomatoes are unavailable, add 6 oz. canned tomato purée) ; add a little bouillon or simply some of the liquid the cod was cooked in. Cook 10 min. Slightly thicken the sauce with a little starch or flour mixed with water, cook a few more minutes, then remove the parsley.

Boil 12 potatoes in their jackets, peel and slice them. Spread a layer of the potatoes in a baking dish; on top of the potatoes make a layer of cod; pour part of the sauce over it. On top of the cod, make a layer of peppers, then begin again with the potatoes, cod, and peppers. Cover with the rest of the sauce, sprinkle with bread crumbs, and bake 35 min. in the oven. If fresh red peppers are unavailable, use canned pimentos instead; they are excellent for this dish.

PAËLLA SPANISH STYLE PAËLLA À L'ESPAGNOLE (U. D.)

Paëlla is the indispensable dish for Spanish feast days, for it is too costly to be served every day. In certain cases, it may be the whole dinner or at least the only cooked dish. I advise cooks to serve this dish only to Spaniards.

The meats used are: beef fillet, pork fillet, *chorizos* (smoked pork sausages seasoned with pimento) , and ham. Fowl and game: chickens, pigeons, partridges, and rabbits. Fish: eels, sea bream, and snails. Vegetables: tender artichokes, sweet pimentos fried in oil and peeled, peas, broad beans, carrots, tomatoes. Proportions depend on the number of guests or, rather, the number of plates to be filled, for each kind of fish or meat must have its own plate.

To prepare, brown all the meats, fowl, game, and fish separately, the meat with lard, and the fish with oil.

When the meats have been browned, place them in a large braising pan and braise them with very little liquid. When half cooked, add the sausages and then part of the chosen vegetables. The meats and garnishes must finish cooking at the same time. ¼ hr. before removing them from the stove, add liquid to the braising stock, enough to cover the meats and vegetables, and then strain off. For each qt. cooking stock, add 1¼ cups unwashed rice, a little saffron, a little red pepper; cook the rice, keeping it a little firm. Prepare the chicken, game, and fish, separately, the same way. The fish stock should be diluted with hot water.

When ready to serve, place the meats in one dish or several dishes with part of the vegetables and some rice. Arrange the chicken, game, and fish the same way in different dishes.

ALMONDIGILLAS or **SPANISH MEAT BALLS** ALMONDIGILLAS ESPAGNOLE (U. D.)

Carefully trim 10 oz. from the thick end of a raw beef fillet; chop it very fine. Also chop 5 oz. fresh pork fat and then chop both fat and meat together. Season with salt, red pepper, and a pinch of garlic; add 2 or 3 whole eggs to bind the mincemeat. Divide it into egg-sized pieces; roll them on the table and flatten them lightly; dip them in beaten egg, bread them, and plunge them into hot lard just long enough to sear them. Remove them immediately and place them side by side in a shallow pan; cover them with a thin Tomato Sauce (p. 146) containing gravy. Let simmer ½ hr. Place them on a platter and pour the sauce over the top. This is a very tasty dish for people who like to eat tender meat.

BOILED CHICKPEAS GARBANZOS BOUILLIS (U. D.)

The vegetable called *garbanzos* in Spanish and *cecci* in Italian are very common in Provence, but the best and most famous chickpeas come from Castile, in Spain. They are larger and have the incomparable advantage of cooking well in a short time.

Plunge the peas into warm water in a deep pot with a handful of crushed salt. Keep the water 15 hr. at the same low temperature, stirring the peas from time to time.

When they are very soft and swollen, drain, wash, and plunge them into boiling salted water. Cook them slowly until very tender, about 3–4 hr.

If after cooking you discover that you have tough peas, add a bit of ammoniac (about the size of a pea) to the water; this harmless acid will soften the peas; however, do not use too much. Potash may be used instead of ammoniac.

MANTECADOS or **SPANISH COOKIES** MANTECADOS À L'ESPAGNOLE (U. D.)

Mix with 1 lb. good, firm, white, odorless lard 12 oz. powdered sugar, 2 tbsp. roasted, crushed sesame, pinch of powdered cinnamon, and enough good wheat flour to make a firm paste.

Divide this paste into walnut-sized particles, roll them in the hands until round, and space them out on a baking sheet covered with paper. Bake them in a medium oven until they are golden. Remove and serve the cookies either hot or cold.

SWITZERLAND

CHEESE FONDUE CHAUDEFONNIÈRE FONDUE AU FROMAGE À LA CHAUDEFONNIÈRE (Ma.)

Mix ½ tsp. flour in a cup with 1 liqueur glass kirsch. Rub the inside of a glazed earthenware casserole with a clove of garlic and melt a walnut-sized piece of butter in it; add 1 lb. grated or thinly sliced fatty cheese and 6 oz. white wine. Place the casserole over the fire and stir the cheese until it is almost completely melted; at this point, pour in the kirsch and flour and finish with a pinch of pepper and nutmeg. Send to the table immediately in a chafing dish.

FONDUE GENEVOISE FONDUE À LA GENEVOISE (Ma.)

Mix 8 egg yolks in a pan with 7 oz. grated cheese, pepper, nutmeg, a pinch of sugar, and 5 oz. butter divided into bits. Put the pan on the fire and let the mixture thicken, stirring with a spoon. As soon as it begins to thicken, add ½ glass cream and finish thickening, stirring constantly. Pour into a deep dish and surround with bread croutons fried in butter or a garnish of noodles blanched in salted water.

LAKE TROUT WITH GENEVOISE SAUCE FÉRA À LA SAUCE GENEVOISE (Ma.)

Clean 2 lake trout[1] and put them into a pan with 1 sliced carrot and 1

[1] Lake trout belong to a different species than other trout and resemble salmon and lavaret.

sliced onion, a *bouquet garni,* a few peppercorns, and 1 pt. white wine. Bring the liquid to a boil, lower the flame, cover, and barely simmer 10 min. Serve the trout on a platter covered with a napkin and accompany it with a sauceboat of the following sauce:

Genevoise Sauce: Melt 2 oz. fresh butter in a pan and mix in 1 oz. flour; add 2 egg yolks; beat with a wire whisk, while gradually pouring in the almost cool fish cooking stock. Cook the sauce at moderate heat, stirring. When it first comes to a boil, remove it from the fire and beat briskly while adding 2 oz. butter and the juice of 1 lemon.

Note: It is interesting to note the difference between this Genevoise Sauce and the one given by Escoffier on p. 141.

TROUT GENEVOISE TRUITE À LA GENEVOISE (U. D.)

Clean 4 or 5 small, fresh trout. Heavily butter a flat pan, lay the trout in side by side, pour 1 glass white wine over them, salt lightly, cover, and cook 10–12 min. over a hot fire. Arrange the fish on a platter, brush them with melted butter, and keep hot in an open oven. Add a little melted fish glaze to the cooking pan, bring the liquid to a boil, and remove from fire. Add a piece of Maître d'Hôtel Butter (p. 164) and finish the sauce with the juice of 1 lemon. Pour the sauce alongside the trout. At each end of the platter make a mound of small potato balls boiled in water or fried in butter. Garnish the sides of the platter with lemon slices.

BASEL COOKIES LÉCRELETS DE BÂLE (Ma.)

Proportions: 10 oz. honey, 10 oz. sugar, ¼ lb. shredded almonds, ½ oz. powdered cinnamon, ⅓ oz. powdered clove, 1 tsp. grated nutmeg, ¼ oz. potash, grated peel of 1 lemon, 2 oz. candied orange peel, 2 oz. candied citron, 4 small glasses cherry brandy, 1 lb. flour.

Put the honey and sugar into a pan or basin, bring to a boil, and pour into a bowl. Add the almonds, candied orange and citron peel, cinnamon, lemon, clove, and cherry brandy. Mix well with a wooden spoon. Dissolve the potash in ½ cup warm water; pour it into the bowl. Add the flour, and mix well. Let stand 2 or 3 days. Roll the paste out ⅜ in. thick. Sprinkle a square baking sheet with flour, lay the paste on it, and bake in a hot oven. Turn the sheet of pastry over onto the baking table, brush off the flour, replace it on the baking sheet to warm it, and divide into pieces 1½ in. long by 1 in. wide, without cutting all the way through. Cook ¼ lb. sugar with ½ glass water; bring it to the "soufflé" stage (see p. 562). Glaze the top of the pastry with a brush dipped in the sugar; this should be done with a single stroke, for the same place must not be brushed twice. When the glazed surface is dry, break into rectangles along the lines you have marked, pack the cookies in a tin, and keep dry.

TURKEY

MOUSSAKA TURKISH STYLE MOUSSAKA À LA TURQUE (E.)

(1) Split 6 fine eggplants lengthwise, slit all around the skin so that the pulp will be easily removed later, and fry.

(2) Peel 2 other eggplants; cut them in slices about ¼ in. thick; season, dip in flour, and fry in oil.

(3) Chop the pulp removed from the fried eggplant halves; put it into a bowl with 1½ lb. very lean, cooked mutton (chopped or diced fine), ½ finely chopped onion browned in butter, ¼ lb. crushed raw mushrooms sautéed in butter, 1 crushed clove of garlic, 2 eggs, 3 oz. thick, tomato-flavored Espagnole Sauce (p. 137), a pinch of chopped parsley, salt, and pepper. Mix well.

(4) Butter a shallow charlotte mold and line the bottom with the eggplant skins. Fill the skins with alternate layers of the chopped mixture and the fried eggplant slices; cover with the rest of the skins, and cook 1 hr. in a *bain-marie.*

Take the mold out of the water bath and let it stand a few minutes to let the filling settle. Just before serving, unmold the Moussaka onto a round platter and sprinkle the surface with chopped parsley.

For another recipe, see p. 356.

BEURRECKS TURKISH STYLE   BEURRECKS À LA TURQUE

See Hot Hors d'Oeuvres, p. 234.

JEWISH COOKING

ALSACE

CARP JEWISH STYLE   CARPE À LA JUÏVE (Rou.)

Buy a live carp, if possible. Kill, scale, wash, and gut it, saving the roe, and cut it into pieces. Sprinkle the pieces lightly with salt and pepper and keep in a cool place until the following day.

Finely chop a good handful of parsley, 2 large onions, 2 cloves of garlic (per 2 lb. fish).

Heat a little oil in a cocotte until it smokes, mix in 2 or 3 tbsp. flour and the chopped herbs; let the flour and herbs brown. Then pour in some hot water; season well with salt, pepper, and ginger, and lay in the pieces of fish. Cook 20 min. over a hot fire without covering. When ½ cooked, add the roe or milt and, if you wish, some chopped mushrooms. (Some cooks do not brown the herbs.)

Arrange the pieces of fish on a service platter as nearly as possible in the original shape of the fish. Reduce the sauce until it is very thick. Pour it over the fish; it will turn to jelly when cold.

CHICKEN JEWISH STYLE   POULET À LA JUÏVE (A.) (*For 4 persons*)

Take: 2 oz. raw chicken fat or fat from a roast chicken or, if unavailable, veal-kidney fat, 1½ oz. butter, 1 oz. chopped shallots, ½ oz. flour, good pinch of garlic, 1 tsp. chopped parsley, 1 chicken, soup vegetables, salt, and pepper.

Cut the chicken up as for fricassee; save the giblets. Prepare 13 oz. stock by simmering the giblets and vegetables in salted water. Melt the fat in a deep skillet, put in the pieces of chicken, and brown them lightly. First add the shallots and garlic, turn for a few minutes, then add the flour and stir without letting it brown. Cover with the chicken stock, salt and pepper, cover, and cook on a medium fire about 1–1½ hr., depending on the size of the chicken.

Skim the sauce and add butter to it; test the seasoning, which should be rather peppery, sprinkle with chopped parsley, and serve.

CHALEUTH CHALEUTH (Rou.)

Soak 5 oz. fancy bread in water, press out the water, and put it into a bowl. Add 2 lb. potatoes cut fine, 3 pinches of salt, 3 liqueur glasses rum, 2 pinches of cinnamon, 1/4 lb. Malaga raisins, 3 or 4 egg yolks and the lightly beaten whites, 1/2 lb. powdered sugar. Mix all the ingredients well by hand.

Heat a little oil in a cocotte. When it begins to smoke, pour in the mixture and let it simmer 5 min. over the fire. Then send it to a hot oven and bake, uncovered, 1/4 hr. Be sure to push the raisins on the surface into the cake to prevent their burning. Let cool a little before unmolding and serve warm.

CRIMSELICH CRIMSELICH (Rou.)

Soak 5 oz. fancy bread in water. Squeeze it out well and put it into a bowl. Add 1/4 lb. dried currants, 1/4 lb. crushed sweet almonds and 5 or 6 bitter almonds, 3 tsp. rum, 1 tsp. salt, 1/4 lb. powdered sugar. Mix well and fry by the spoonful in very hot oil.

Let them turn golden brown. Put them on tissue paper to dry them and sprinkle with powdered sugar. Serve warm.

PURIM COOKIES PURIM-KUCHLICH (Rou.)

Put 1/2 lb. flour into a bowl, making a well in the center. Dissolve a walnut-sized piece of yeast in a little warm milk and put it into the well with 2 pinches of cinnamon, 1 pinch of salt, 1/2 cup powdered sugar, 1/4 lb. melted butter. Mix well and beat with a wooden spoon. Roll out the paste until about as thick as a half dollar, cover with a cloth, and let rise 2 hr. Then cut into small triangles and fry in very hot oil.

GERMANY

OATMEAL KUGEL KUGEL D'AVOINE (Rou.)

Mix 1 tbsp. fat with 7 egg yolks, 3 *Semmel* (sweet rolls) soaked in water and pressed, 1/4 lb. sweet almonds, 4 or 5 bitter almonds, a pinch of salt, 1/2 lb. oatmeal. Add 7 stiffly beaten egg whites. Pour into a baking dish and bake in a slow oven.

When half cooked, place quetsche plums on top, and cover.

LEMON TART TARTE AU CITRON (Rou.)

Beat the juice of 10 lemons with 1/4 lb. powdered sugar. Let stand. Add 3 1/2 oz. almonds, grated peel of 3 lemons and 3 oranges, a good pinch of powdered cinnamon, and 2 oz. dry sponge-cake crumbs. Line a tart tin with Pie Paste (p. 545), fill it with the above mixture, and cover it with crossed strips of the paste. Bake 1 hr. in a medium oven.

CHOLLA HALÉ (Rou.)

Cholla is the bread served on holidays and Saturdays. Plaited, golden, covered with poppy seeds, it is almost a pastry compared to the daily barley bread. But let us not run down the latter; give a Jew who has left his native Russian town a long time ago a crust of dry black bread and he will chew it with his eyes closed in delight. He will recall the days when, just a lad, he went to the distant school along a road hemmed in by walls of snow, a hot potato in each pocket of his caftan. Perhaps he imagines he still breathes in the aroma of the days of his youth, good or bad, but as sweet in remembrance as the perfume of the acacias in bloom in Odessa.

If you rub the crust with garlic or spread it with a little goose fat, the illusion will be even more perfect.

But let us return to our Cholla. On Thursday night, make a small ball of paste by mixing 2 cups flour, 1 tbsp. oil, 1 whole egg, and 1 oz. yeast dissolved in a little warm water. The next day, add 2½ lb. flour, 4 tbsp. oil, salt, and water to make a rather soft paste similar to bread dough. Knead it thoroughly by hand and let stand a few hours. Divide the paste, pull it into coils, and twist them into braids; 2½ lb. flour should make 5 or 6 Chollas, depending on size. Let the loaves stand 1–2 hr., then brush with beaten egg and sprinkle with poppy seeds. Bake ½ hr. in a hot oven. When putting the loaves into the oven, throw a small piece of paste into the fire, repeating the holy prayer, "Ribene che l'oïlom . . . mitzveh cholle," a touching reminder of the tithe given the temple servants in the ancient days of the glory of Israel.

Cholla has always been a great treat for the Jews, as witness that old, naïve plaint: "America is the land of opportunity, a real paradise for everyone—truly marvelous! There they eat Cholla all week long, my son."

TCHOLENT TCHOLENT (Rou.)

Tcholent is a typical Sabbath dish. It is prepared the day before and placed in the oven, where it is left until the noon meal of the next day. When the cover is lifted from the tightly sealed pot, a delicious aroma escapes from the tender, browned meat soaking in its smooth, rich sauce.

Here is the recipe:

Put into a glazed earthenware casserole some brisket of beef cut into pieces, chopped onions, 1 clove, 1 clove of garlic, salt, pepper, potatoes, and kasha (or grains of buckwheat). Cover with water, put the lid on tightly, and place in the oven.

The potatoes and buckwheat may be replaced by pearl barley or rice. The latter should be cooked in a small cheesecloth sack.

CALVES FEET IN JELLY PETCHIA (Rou.)

Here is another typical dish from Russian Jewish cooking.

Cut 2 calves feet into pieces, wash and blanch them, and cook in salted, peppered water; add 2 cloves of garlic. Cook 3–4 hr.

When cooked, carefully pare the meat from the bones, avoiding small bone splinters. Chop the meat, put it into a dish, and cover with the cooking liquid, adding 3 or 4 sliced hard-boiled eggs and 1 grated clove of garlic. Let stand until the following day to jell.

GOOSE GRIEBENES AND SCHMALTZ GRIBENÈS D'OIE ET SCHMALTZ (Rou.)

Take a very fat goose. Trim off the skin with its layer of fat from the meat. Cut the skin and fat into pieces, put into a cocotte, and cook over a low fire. When all the fat has melted and the pieces of skin are nicely browned, drop in 6 finely cut onions. Brown the onions to a good chestnut color, then strain the fat through a sieve into jars. Salt lightly.

The pieces of skin and fried onions are greatly appreciated and should be eaten very hot. If you leave a little meat on the skin, they are even better. Griebenes are a great treat for Chanukkah. They are usually served with buckwheat fritters or Gretchene-latkas (see below).

GRETCHENE-LATKAS or BLINIS GRETCHENÈ-LATKESS (Rou.)

The day before using, prepare a paste by mixing ½ lb. buckwheat flour with 3 eggs, 1 oz. yeast dissolved in a little warm water, some water, and a pinch of salt. Cover the bottom of small pans with this paste and place them in the oven so the pancakes brown on both sides. Serve with a mixture of cream and melted butter.

JERUSALEM ALMOND COOKIES GÂTEAUX D'ÉCUME DE JÉRUSALEM (Rou.)

Mix ½ cup powdered sugar with 1 cup finely chopped almonds and 1 stiffly beaten egg white. Roll the paste out on a board and cut into rounds with a liqueur glass. Place the cookies on a buttered baking sheet with enough space between each and bake 10 min. in a medium oven. These cookies should not brown in baking, to keep the inside soft when cooled.

KUGEL KUGEL (Rou.)

Put some soaked, pressed bread into a mixing bowl. Add 2 eggs, 4 tbsp. powdered sugar, 1 apple chopped fine, a handful of crushed almonds, ½ cup sultanas or Malaga raisins (seeded and cut), grated peel of ½ lemon, 3 tbsp. goose fat or oil, and 2 pinches of cinnamon. Mix well until the paste looks like a sponge.

Grease the mold and flour it lightly. (Turn it upside down to shake out the excess flour.) Pour in the paste and bake 2 hr. in a medium oven. While baking, baste frequently with goose fat or oil to keep the cake soft. Serve hot, covered with the following sauce.

Kugel Sauce: Put 1 whole egg into a saucepan with ½ glass white wine and 1 tbsp. powdered sugar. Place on a low fire and beat constantly, always in the same direction, until foamy. Pour over the Kugel.

HOME CANNING AND PRESERVING

HOME CANNING AND PRESERVING

GENERAL PRINCIPLES

Cans with the tops soldered on can be completely submerged and stacked one on top the other. However, when glass jars are used, the water should come only to the neck of the jar and the pot should be covered to let the steam heat the top.

PRESERVING VARIOUS FOODS

BUTTER BEURRE (P.)

Whenever butter is low-priced, it is a good idea to stock up on it. There are 2 recommended ways to preserve it: by salting and by cooking.

SALTED BUTTER BEURRE SALÉ (P.)

First knead the butter in a bowl under running water to extract any whey left in it. Then, when the water is perfectly clear, place the butter on a moistened board and crush it with 1 oz. fine salt per lb. butter. Mash and knead until butter and salt are perfectly combined. Put it into a glazed crock and pour a finger of salted water on top.

COOKED BUTTER BEURRE CUIT (P.)

Put the butter into a pot or deep saucepan that seems larger than necessary, for if, by chance, it heats too rapidly it will foam and rise. Therefore, it might boil over if the utensil is too small. Cook the butter slowly until it is very clear, limpid, and a brownish sediment forms in the bottom of the pan. Let the butter cool a little and put it into jars, decanting it to separate the sediment. Do not throw the sediment away, but use it with dried vegetables, cabbage, sautéed potatoes, etc.

Note: These butter recipes are especially practical for the country. Naturally, in Paris or any other large city they are not quite so useful.

FOIE GRAS FOIE GRAS (P.)

If you happen to raise a few geese or ducks to make a *confit* (see below), which is a sort of preserved food, you will probably want to keep the livers for important dinners during the social season.

With the tip of a knife, carefully remove the greenish part that has touched the gall; also remove the bloody veins that streak the surface. Then lay the livers in a sautéing pan or deep baking tray with a tight-fitting cover; salt, pepper, and arrange the livers upside down and pressed close together without destroying their shape. Pour some very good, hot, melted lard, goose fat, or a mixture of both over them. Cover the pan and place it in a *bain-marie ;* poach the livers until they are too hot to hold in the fingers. Let them cool in their cooking liquor until the following day.

Pack in tins with a bay leaf; the liver should almost fill the tin. Pour in a little of the cooking fat without adding any of the bottom residue containing blood and liver gravy. After wiping the tins clean, cover and solder them immediately, then boil them. A 1-lb. tin takes about 40 min. cooking.

To get very white livers, salt them lightly and let them soak overnight in cold milk; dry them before poaching in lard or goose fat.

EGGS OEUFS (P.)

Thanks to today's science, we have an extremely simple way to store eggs. Barral and Ovidal tablets, Ovigarde and Alban powders, for example, make it possible to preserve the eggs without doing more than dipping them in the composition as fast as they are laid.

In addition to the above, there are other processes, though not so famous. The important thing is to use only the freshest eggs. All methods considered, preserving eggs in limewater is still about the best.

LIMEWATER FOR PRESERVING EGGS LAIT DE CHAUX POUR CONSERVER DES OEUFS (P.)

Place very fresh, uncracked eggs in an open-end keg. Use 1 qt. quicklime for 5 qt. cold water. If the quicklime is fresh, it will combine immediately with the cold water. Mix with a wooden paddle, then let stand until the water becomes very clear; pour it over the eggs without disturbing any of the quicklime in the bottom. Since the eggs must be well covered, proportion the amount of limewater to the number of eggs. Before using, wash the eggs in running cold water.

PRESERVED GOOSE OIE (CONFIT D') (P.)

The glory of Toulouse Cassoulet (see p. 723), this goose preparation, being a preserve, belongs in this chapter.

Furthermore, it is very simple to make, and all home cooks in the South make it.

Quarter the goose and salt the pieces 24 hr.; wipe them off and poach slowly in melted goose fat. Do not let the fat get too hot—it should merely simmer—or the goose will be fried instead of poached. The goose is cooked when you can stick a needle through it and no blood flows out. Put the quarters of goose into earthenware or stoneware jars and cover completely with goose fat from the cooking (decanted to separate the meat gravy).

If there is not enough fat to cover the meat, let what you have poured harden, then finish covering with melted, but not too hot, lard. This Preserved Goose keeps a long time. Better keep it in several small jars that can be used up completely, once uncovered, rather than in one big jar that might spoil in time after being partially used.

Note: Use young, fat geese and kill them by bleeding; pluck them immediately and let hang in a cool place 2 or 3 days to settle the meat.

Do not put the pieces into jars until they are cold, and pour in the fat almost cold, too, and just fluid enough to fill up all the spaces between the pieces.

For another recipe, see Fowl, p. 431.

GOOSE or PORK RILLETTES RILLETTES D'OIE OR DE PORC (P.)

Rillettes can also be classed among the preserves, for they will keep a long time. They are made with goose and pork mixed in equal parts, with pork alone, or with a mixture of pork and some other meat such as rabbit, for example, following the recipe given below for Tours Rillettes.

MOTHER GOOSE RILLETTES RILLETTES DE LA MÈRE L'OIE

See Provincial Cooking, p. 688.

TOURS RILLETTES RILLETTES DE TOURS (P.)

Cut 1 lb. half-lean, half-fat fresh pork and 1 lb. breast of goose into cubes. Put this meat into a pot with enough water to cover ¾; add salt, pepper, a *bouquet garni* of savory and 2 sage leaves. Cover and cook slowly 3 hr. to let the meat cook down and the water almost completely evaporate. Pour everything into a large, deep dish, carefully remove the bones and *bouquet,* and mash with a fork. Let cool and, when the mixture begins to solidify, stir well again and put into stone jars. This will keep a long time in a cool place.

For another recipe, see Provincial Cooking, p. 740.

TERRINES (P.)

Terrines should keep several months, whether filled with fowl, game, or *foie gras.* We shall first give a few outstanding recipes, then the proper steps to take for perfect preserving. The Terrine of Truffled Foie Gras is, without doubt, the most highly regarded of all.

TERRINE OF TRUFFLED FOIE GRAS TERRINE DE FOIE GRAS TRUFFÉ (P.)

Macerate a fine 1¼–1½ lb. *foie gras* with salt, pepper, spices, Madeira, and a finger of cognac; put 3 or 4 well-peeled and brushed truffles around it. Cover to keep in the aroma and then, on the same day, prepare the paste given below.

The next day, prepare the following forcemeat. Dice ¾ lb. unsalted pork fat and sear it in a frying pan. Turn it into a dish and drop into the fat it has rendered 10 oz. fresh pork, 5 oz. calf's liver, and 5 oz. leg of veal, all diced. Sear quickly without browning, then let cool together with the fat while blending in the following seasoning: ⅓ oz. salt, pepper, spices, thyme, and bay leaf. When cold, put through the meat grinder, then mash the mixture and press it through a sieve. Add the Madeira used in macerating the *foie gras*.

Stud the *foie gras* with quarters of peeled truffles. Chop the peelings and mix them into the forcemeat (optional). Line the bottom and sides of the terrine with strips of pork fat, then fill with the forcemeat, leaving room in the center for the *foie gras*. Cover the *foie gras* with forcemeat and finish filling the terrine. Fold the ends of the pork-fat strips over the top or lay 1 new strip on top and sprinkle with a pinch of spices (powdered cinnamon, clove, white pepper, and nutmeg). Cover and seal the terrine with paste made of flour and water; cut an opening in this top crust to let the steam escape. Cook in the oven, in a *bain-marie,* allowing 50 min. for a terrine containing 2 lb. of ingredients. Let cool under light pressure and preserve as directed further on.

SNIPE TERRINE TERRINE DE BÉCASSINES (P.)

After boning the plucked, cleaned, and singed snipe, cut them into 4 parts, season, and stud with pork fat and ham. Brown the livers and intestines of the birds with a little grated pork fat; add 4 oz. calf's liver for each snipe used, and let cool.

For each snipe, chop ¼ lb. lean, fresh pork with ¼ lb. pork fat. Add the cold snipe intestines and livers and calf's liver. Season properly and press through a sieve to make a fine forcemeat. Cover the bottom of an ovenware terrine with a thin strip of pork fat; fill with ½ of the forcemeat and lay the snipe quarters on top; cover with the rest of the forcemeat, fold the strip of pork fat over the top, cover with a paste made of flour and water, and cook.

Terrines of hare or rabbit are prepared the same way.

PITHIVIERS LARK TERRINE TERRINE DE MAUVIETTES DE PITHIVIERS (P.)

Pithiviers is famous for its lark pies, which are sent all over France. But while a pie can't be kept, larks can be prepared the same way and preserved in cans or earthenware terrines.

Bone 8 larks through the back (this should be done in advance). Use the bones to flavor an aspic. Season the birds and macerate them overnight in Madeira. Make a Gratin Forcemeat (p. 175), adding the lark livers and intestines sautéed in a pan and then crushed. Put a little of this forcemeat into each lark, with a small cube of truffled *foie gras* in the center, and close the birds. After stuffing the larks, mix ¼ lb. forcemeat left over with 1 lb. fine pork forcemeat. Line the terrine with strips of pork fat and spread a layer of forcemeat on top. Lay the larks on this, cover with the rest of the forcemeat, fold the strips of pork fat over the top, cover, and cook. Let cool, then proceed as directed on p. 799.

HOW TO COOK TERRINES CUISSON DES TERRINES (P.)

To cook the terrine, place it in a deep tray or roasting pan containing about 1 in. water. Bring to a boil and place in an oven hot enough to continue boiling the water. The contents of the terrine are cooked when, after 40 or 50 min., you remove the cover and see that the fat rendered in the terrine is very clear. Place a plank of wood with a 2-lb. weight directly on the meat to pack it down while cooling. All terrines are treated the same way.

HOW TO STORE TERRINES FOR SEVERAL MONTHS COMMENT CONSERVER DES TERRINES PLUSIEURS MOIS (P.)

If the terrines are to be served 8–10 days after they are made, merely put them in a cool place and, when cold, cover them with lard. If they are to be kept all winter, however, unmold them after they cool, then remove all fat, strips of fat, and gravy on them. Even wipe them off, leaving only the edible part. Clean and dry the terrines (crocks), put the meat back in, and cover completely and generously with warm, melted lard. The meat must be completely covered to keep out all air. When the lard has solidified, place a sheet of tinfoil on top. Put the cover on and seal the rim with paper to make it airtight. Keep in a cool, dry place.

PRESERVING WITH SALT (P.)

In the country, pork is preserved by salting, but it is not always done as carefully as it should be, and one sometimes eats rancid bacon, which is very disagreeable. Here is how to avoid this situation.

SALTED TONGUE LANGUE SALÉE (P.)

Beef tongue sold in France as "scarlet tongue" is only salted or pickled tongue. It is salted the same way as pork, but it should first be pricked all over with a sharp-pointed fork and then beaten with a board or held by the tip and struck on the table. This is to force the air out of the meat and to help the brine penetrate better. Keep 12–14 days in the salt preparation described later on for pork, with a weighted board on top.

The following liquid brine may also be used. After pricking, beating, and rubbing the tongue, soak it in brine about 8 days. Soak it in fresh water 24 hr. and boil 2 hr. in unsalted water. Let it cool with a weight on top, place it in goldbeater's skin (a skin made with the large intestine of beef or mutton), tie the 2 ends, plunge into boiling water 5 min., take it out, prick with a fork to let out the air, and color with carmine or caramel. Hang it in a cool place. This keeps a long time.

BRINE SALAISON LIQUIDE OR SAUMURE (P.)

Boil 4 qt. water with 3 lb. bay salt, 2½ oz. saltpeter, ¼ lb. sugar, ⅓ oz. pepper, ⅓ oz. juniper, a sprig of thyme, and 2 bay leaves. Let cool after cooking 10 min. and test the brine by dropping in a raw, fresh egg, which should float. If it sinks, add salt.

SALTING or CURING PORK salaison de porc (P.)

Cut the pork into equal-sized pieces, except the hams, which should stay whole. Mix some very dry, fine salt with saltpeter—⅔ oz. saltpeter per lb. salt.

Vigorously rub the salt into the pieces of pork with the palm of the hand. Put a layer of coarse salt mixed with saltpeter (only ¼ oz. per lb. salt) into the bottom of a large wooden tub or glazed earthenware jar. Place a layer of meat between each layer of salt. Let stand about 3 weeks. Turn the meat once a week with a wooden pike; never use your hands. Afterward, hang the meat in a cool, ventilated place. Once dry, it will keep as long as you like. Soak well before cooking.

CURING AND SMOKING HAMS salaison et fumage des jambons (P.)

Hams should not be salted until 24 hr. after slaughtering the pigs. Treat them the same as beef tongues, adding 10 per cent more sugar to the salt and saltpeter. Then plunge them into brine and let stay 15 days for small ones and 20 for the large ones. Wipe them off, hang them in the open air to dry, and smoke them over a fire (not too close) of aromatic wood: beech, oak, laurel, etc.

PRESERVING VEGETABLES

ARTICHOKE BOTTOMS artichauts (fonds d') (P.)

Sprinkle the bottoms generously with lemon juice and cook them until they become a little soft. Then cool and remove the chokes, which should come off easily. Put the bottoms into jars or cans, 1 on top of the other, without leaving too much space between. Pour in lightly salted water boiled with a good deal of lemon juice to fill the jars or cans, cover them, and boil 45–50 min. for the narrow jars or cans containing 10–12 bottoms. To use these artichoke bottoms, put them into a pan of cold water with lemon juice and bring to a boil. Then drain them and dry them in butter before cooking them according to need.

ASPARAGUS asperges (P.)

Though asparagus is rarely canned at home, we shall include it for the benefit of those who grow their own asparagus and would like to preserve it for winter.

This is a rather delicate canning operation, since the asparagus should stay whole and be cooked just right, without mushing the tips.

June is the best month to can asparagus. Take purple-tinged, medium-sized asparagus, too large rather than too small. Peel them, instead of scraping them, with a vegetable knife; this will lessen the danger of breaking the stalks. Wash them and tie them into bunches after cutting them to fit the cans or jars.

Stand the bunches upright in a pot. Pour in boiling salted water until ⅔ the height of the asparagus, cook 3 min., then add more boiling water until the asparagus is ¾ covered—in other words, until the water comes just below the tips. Boil another 3 min., then add more water without quite covering the tips. Cover the pot and cook 2 min. at a rapid boil to steam the tips.

This makes 8 min. blanching. Put the pot under the cold-water tap and let the water run 2 or 3 hr., then drain the asparagus and put it into cans or jars. Canned asparagus, which must be opened with a can opener, should be placed in head down, so the asparagus is not injured by opening, while those in jars should stand upright. Fill with water boiled with 1 oz. salt per qt., seal, and boil 40 min. for medium-sized cans containing 16–18 asparagus.

WHITE MUSHROOMS CHAMPIGNONS BLANCS (P.)

Cultivated mushrooms should be prepared immediately after picking. Mushrooms are difficult to preserve because they are apt to ferment and become poisonous. They are prepared commercially under a blue light to keep them white and protected from daylight. Peel and wash them quickly in water with lemon juice, then boil rapidly 2 min. in salted water containing a good amount of lemon juice. Put them into cans with their cooking liquid and boil 1½ hr. if pt.-sized, 2 hr. if qt. cans.

SAUERKRAUT CHOUCROUTE (P.)

Take large, solid cabbages with white hearts. Strip off the green leaves and shred all the white except the hard parts. There is a special shredder, but a large knife will do as well. Take a keg that formerly contained white wine or vinegar, drill a hole near the bottom for a spigot, then place a layer of coarse salt in the bottom and, on this, a 4-in. layer of cabbage; season it with peppercorns, juniper berries, and coriander seeds. Make another layer of salt and tamp it down with a plank to press the water out of the cabbage. Continue filling the keg with alternate layers of salt and cabbage and cover with a round, wooden lid. Place a 40-lb. weight on the lid to press the cabbage down. It is a good idea to place a cloth between the last layer of cabbage and the wooden lid. After a few days the cabbage starts fermenting. You can speed up the process by drawing the liquid from the bottom and pouring it over the top. Complete maceration takes about 1 month. After this time, the keg should be sealed to protect the sauerkraut from the air, which darkens it. When finished, it should be drained until almost dry.

GHERKINS CORNICHONS (P.)

There are 2 procedures: hot and cold. Cold: put them into cold pickle jars with small onions, tarragon, and a bay leaf and cover with vinegar. They can be eaten 6 weeks later. Prepared this way, they stay soft because the water drains out of them, which weakens the strength of the vinegar.

Here is the hot method, for crisp and very green gherkins. Wrap them well in a cloth with a good handful of fine salt and rub and shake them vigorously until they are wet with the water that drains from them. Hang the cloth over the sink until the next day. Then dry them in another cloth and put them into a pan. Heat a copper frying pan (not tin-lined) and pour in enough vinegar to cover the gherkins. When the vinegar boils, pour it over the gherkins and let stand 24 hr. The next day, boil the same vinegar again and repeat the operation. The following day, repeat this operation, using fresh vinegar, small onions, pimentos, peppercorns, and tarragon. The gherkins can be eaten 3 weeks later.

SPINACH ÉPINARDS (P.)

Spinach is expensive enough in winter, when it can be found, to justify canning it when in season. This is extremely simple. Wash the spinach carefully in water after trimming off the thick stems, and cook as usual in salted water. Drain and cool in running water, then press well between the hands to extract all the water. Next, chop or press through a sieve, and boil again, stirring to avoid burning. When the spinach comes to a good boil, salt lightly, add 1 tbsp. sugar per lb. spinach, to remove the tartness, then put into cans or jars, seal, and boil 1-qt. jars or cans 2 hr.

Since this vegetable spoils quickly, we advise boiling the purée before canning it and using only cans with plated linings. Better yet, use wide-necked jars or bottles.

GREEN BEANS HARICOTS VERTS (P.)

Green beans should be picked, stringed, and separated into small, medium, and large. In general, large beans are not preserved; if they are, they must be split in 2 or 3 lengthwise, which is more work than the beans justify.

The beans must be picked fresh, shortly after dawn, during dry weather, and then trimmed carefully. Separate the very small from those a little larger. Wash these beans well and plunge them into lightly salted, boiling water. To make them nice and green, cook the smallest 2 min. at a rapid boil, and the medium-sized 4 min. Drain, cool in running water, drain again, and lay them tightly in the cans or jars.

I say lay them in tightly and not pack them in bulk because the can will seem full until you have to open it, and then it will be only ¾ full when the beans have settled.

Put them in a small bundle at a time, and even crowd them a little, leaving only about ⅜ in. empty space. Then pour boiled water containing a little Vichy salt into each can or jar and seal the containers. Do not cover completely with water, because the beans will render their own water while cooking in the jars.

Boil qt. jars 1½ hr., and pt. jars 1 hr.

SALTED GREEN BEANS HARICOTS VERTS AU SEL (P.)

2 methods: After stringing and blanching the beans as when preserving in jars, make alternate layers of beans and coarse salt in a small keg. Better still, I think, prepare a brine by boiling enough salted water to cover the beans amply. The brine should register 10° on the salt scale (an inexpensive instrument), but if you haven't one, here is what to do. Put some salt into cold water and, when it has dissolved, drop an egg into the brine. If the egg floats, it contains enough salt. Then bring the brine to a boil, let it cool, and pour it cold over the green beans. After 4 or 5 days, test the density of the brine the same way, for the beans will have diluted it with their own water. Boil this brine again until it has a density of 10° and, when cold, pour it again over the beans. Using this system, you can salt the beans as they are picked. Since they should always be com-

pletely covered with water, you must put a wooden lid weighted with a brick over them to keep them from floating to the surface. When ready to use, soak the beans 24 hr. in frequently changed cold water, and cook as you would fresh beans.

SORREL PURÉE OSEILLE EN PURÉE (P.)

Clean the sorrel like spinach, but cook it down with very little salted boiling water. Spinach must be cooked in a good deal of water to keep it green, which is not necessary for sorrel, for it will never be green. When cooked, drain it thoroughly, but not by squeezing it in the hands. Press through a sieve and prepare like spinach but without adding any sugar. Same cooking time.

SORREL WITH BUTTER OSEILLE AU BEURRE (P.)

The preceding recipe for preserving sorrel is useful when preparing sorrel with gravy, cream, or hard-boiled eggs for a vegetable or a garnish.

When you want to preserve it for soup in winter, it is just as easily done, but differently. After trimming and washing the sorrel, cut it into strips by taking a handful at a time in the left hand and shredding it into a julienne. Heat 2 oz. butter in a pan per 4 lb. sorrel and drop the sorrel in. Cook it down completely as for soup and, when it is completely mushy, salt it and put it into small, conveniently used jars or cans. A large qt. can would be wasted before it could be fully utilized.

Boil these small containers 1 hr. at most, and you can make soups just as delicious as when using freshly picked sorrel.

PICKLES PICKLES (P.)

Put gherkins, cauliflower flowerets, carrot slices, onions, celery, fennel, and all sorts of raw vegetables into wide-mouthed pickle jars. Add some vinegar and crushed peppercorns. Macerate 1 month.

SMALL PLAIN PEAS or **PEAS AU NATUREL** POIS (PETITS) AU NATUREL (P.)

This is one of the most useful and appreciated of all preserved vegetables. Although green beans, tomatoes, and mushrooms may be found in any season in the big city markets, the same is not true of peas. They are easy to preserve if you follow these directions. You'll be able to delight your guests with French peas all through the winter season.

As when preparing green beans, you must sort the peas into very small, small, and medium.

Pick the peas when they are mature and the pods are a brilliant, transparent green, or at least give this illusion. Shell them quickly and, if you have a good quantity, spread them out, for when piled up, they warm up quickly. After sorting them, put aside the tiny ones to prepare *au naturel,* the small ones for French peas (p. 804), and the larger ones for Peas in Lard Bonne Femme (p. 804).

Boil a large pot of salted water and add 1 gram powdered copper sulphate per qt. water if you want to keep the peas very green. However, this is not obligatory. Cook the tiniest peas 5 min. at a good boil, 6–7 min. for the others, depending on size. Then pour cold water over them to wash them, skim off the foam, and cool thoroughly. Drain and put immediately into cans, jars, or bottles, packing them well. To do this, knock the bottoms of the containers on a towel. Pour in water boiled with ⅓ oz. salt and ¼ oz. sugar per qt. water. Cool this boiled liquid before pouring it into the containers. Boil qt. containers 1¼ hr., and pt. containers 1 hr. Don't let cool completely in the water bath. If you use soldered cans, remove them immediately. Since it is dangerous to transfer glass quickly from boiling water to cold air, jars should be left in the water bath ½ hr.

FRENCH PEAS POIS (PETITS) À LA FRANÇAISE (P.)

Canned French peas bought in stores, including brands with well-deserved reputations, are not canned according to the following recipe, which is designed for home use.

Wash small peas immediately after shelling and drain them. Put them into a thick-bottomed pot and blend them with 1 oz. butter and 1 tbsp. flour per qt. peas. When the peas are evenly coated, add a few tiny new onions and a few well-cleaned, halved or quartered lettuce hearts (drop the lettuce hearts into boiling water for a few moments to soften them; rinse, drain, and put them over the peas). Pour in only enough water to cover the peas ⅓, salt, and add 2 lumps sugar per qt. peas. Cook the peas until they feel tender to the touch and put them immediately into cans or jars, removing the lettuce and onions.

If you use glass jars, be sure to preheat them gradually in water to prevent the sudden change in temperature from breaking them. Seal, and boil qt. containers 1¾ hr. and pt. containers 1¼ hr. Remove from the water as directed in the preceding recipe.

PEAS IN LARD BONNE FEMME POIS (PETITS) AU LARD À LA BONNE FEMME (P.)

You may use the medium-sized peas for this recipe. Prepare them as for French peas, above, but blanch them first. In a frying pan, heat 2 oz. salt pork fat per qt. peas. The pork fat should first be cut into pieces the size of the first joint of the little finger and boiled awhile to remove the excess salt. Brown them a little in the pan and cook your peas as directed above. Though this recipe does not include lettuce, a few green leaves chopped fine and mixed with the peas can only improve them. Since peas, like all vegetables, settle down while cooking, fill the containers well and rap the bottoms on a folded cloth to pack the peas down as much as possible. Otherwise, after the bottles are boiled, they will be only ½ full.

TOMATO PURÉE TOMATE EN PURÉE (P.)

Here we have one of the most useful preserves for the kitchen and also one of the easiest to make.

August, or September at the latest, is the time to preserve tomatoes. August is best, for the tomatoes have ripened quickly under a hot sun. This is not always the case in September.

Take good red, ripe tomatoes; they should be firm, and by ripe we don't mean squashed and soft. Cut them in 2 crosswise and remove the stem end; squeeze out the juice and seeds. Many people cook them as they are, just crushing them; this is a mistake and spoils the quality of the purée, for the tomato juice is very acid and must be eliminated or it will make the purée acid while cooking.

Very often, tomatoes are cooked with nothing more than a little salt. This makes them rather tasteless, and it is better to heighten the flavor of their sun-reddened flesh with seasonings you would use in a sauce you were going to serve immediately. These seasonings are onions, garlic, parsley, thyme, bay leaf, peppercorns, and salt. For 10 lb. tomatoes, take: 5 oz. thin-sliced new onions, 1 whole clove of garlic (which should be removed before making the purée), 1 large *bouquet garni* (parsley containing 1 bay leaf and 1 sprig of thyme or, better still, savory).

Take a large pot, wide rather than deep. I prefer the rounded copper pot used in cooking sugar and jams, not only for its shape, but because the copper preserves the natural color of fruit and the tomato is, after all, a fruit (copper is by no means harmful if the tomatoes aren't left to cool in it). Press half your tomatoes, crushing them a little, then sprinkle the seasoning over them; cover with the rest of the tomatoes and cook first over moderate heat to extract the juice from the tomatoes (you need not add water). When they come to a boil, stir from time to time with a spatula. Cook at high heat a good ½ hr., then drain well in a strainer. The juice may be saved, since it is good tomato juice, the acid water having been extracted before cooking; make soup with it or add it to vegetable soup.

When thoroughly drained, remove the *bouquet* and garlic; remove the onion or not, as you wish; press through a fine sieve. Boil this purée, stirring constantly with a spatula, for as long as you wish—that is, depending on how thick you want the purée. For economy's sake, it is a good idea to cook the purée until concentrated and thick, since it will need fewer containers.

Put it into small jars or cans that can be used up at one time and not left to spoil after being opened. However, I have noticed that tomato purée, when sufficiently thick, will keep 3 or 4 days without spoiling after being opened.

Seal the containers and boil ½ hr. if they contain no more than ½ pt. purée. Larger ones take 50 min. Having put your tomatoes boiling hot into the containers and sealed them immediately, the preserving is already half done. Some cooks can them while still boiling hot, seal them immediately, and feel that no further boiling is needed. Don't let bottles cool in the water, and seal them with wax the following day if you have merely cooked them.

Preserving may be done without sterilization if you add 1 gram salicylic acid to every 2 lb. preserves. Those with weak kidneys should abstain.

TRUFFLES TRUFFES (P.)

Soak the truffles ½ hr. in warm water, then brush them carefully. Remove particles of dirt embedded in holes with the tip of a knife and rinse well. Put them all into a pot with salt and pepper. Half cover the truffles with Madeira or white wine (or equal parts of each). Put the lid tightly on the pot and cook 30–40 min. in a *bain-marie.* Put them into ½-pt. or ¼-pt. cans (which need not be completely filled), solder them, and boil 40 min. Truffles can also be put raw into the cans and then boiled, but since they settle down, the cans, when opened, will be only ½ full.

FRUIT PRESERVES

PLAIN APRICOTS FOR TARTS ABRICOTS AU NATUREL POUR TARTES (P.)

Although called plain or *au naturel,* the apricots must nevertheless be sugared, though not so much as when preserved in sirup. The sugar will keep them fresher and preserve the flavor. July is the best time to preserve apricots. Pick them when barely ripe and save the finest and largest to preserve in sirup and set aside the smaller ones for tarts. Carefully clean the apricots and cut them in half. Lay them in jars 1 by 1, packing them tightly together with the cut side toward the opening. They must be laid in by hand. Fill the jars to within ½ in. of the top. Cover them completely with a thin cold sirup made with 3½ oz. sugar per qt. water and a piece of vanilla bean. If you wish, crack a few of the apricot stones, peel the almonds inside and split them in half, and add about 10 to each jar. These almonds, placed on top of the finished tart, will add to its flavor and appearance.

Seal the jars the usual way and boil qt. jars 15 min., pt. jars 6–8 min. Remove them from the water 20 min. later, but don't let them cool completely in the water or the apricots will overcook, and for tarts they should stay whole and firm.

Because the apricots are picked before completely ripe, they are not well flavored, and vanilla must be added to the juice.

APRICOTS IN SIRUP FOR COMPOTES ABRICOTS AU SIROP POUR COMPOTES (P.)

Use somewhat riper apricots than those called for in the recipe above, but not so ripe that they are soft to the touch. Halve them, put them carefully into jars, and cover with a sugar sirup registering 24° or 25° on the saccharometer, or 1 lb. vanilla-flavored sugar to 1 qt. water, boiled and cooled. When you use cans to preserve apricots, carefully wipe the rims, or the sugar will make the soldering difficult.

Apricots preserved in sirup are good for compotes and desserts, but should not be used for tarts, for they will turn into jam when baked with a crust.

Boil the jars as directed above, but let them cool in the water because the sugary sirup needs time to penetrate the fruit. Also, there is less danger of overcooking, since these apricots don't have to be cooked a second time.

PLAIN CHERRIES FOR TARTS CERISES AU NATUREL POUR TARTES (P.)

Don't try to preserve the large plump cherries, delicious for eating when they're not wormy, as these are better eaten fresh. The preserving season is the end of June and the beginning of July for English cherries to be used in tarts, cherries in brandy, and Montmorency cherries in sirup for compotes. The Montmorency cherries are also very good in brandy. Choose cherries that are perfect and just ripe but no more, like all fruit for preserving. Grade them and reject any that have the least spot or imperfection. Do the work quickly in the morning, before the heat of the day, to prevent this delicate fruit from spoiling.

Stem them with one of those little pitters bought in the stores, and neatly remove the pit through the hole. You can make your own pitter with a bit of wire bent like a hairpin with a small hook on one end and a cork stopper stuck on the other to hold it; you will find that it speeds up the work without spoiling the fruit. Hold the cherry gently with the tips of the fingers of your left hand and avoid pressure, or the juice will run out. As the cherries are pitted, put them into large-necked bottles and rap the bottoms on a folded cloth to pack the fruit down as much as possible. Otherwise, after the bottles are boiled, they will be only ½ full.

Pour sugared water over the cherries, as directed in the recipe for Plain Apricots for Tarts, but fill the bottle only ¾ full, to allow for the juice rendered by the cherries. Stopper the bottles with good corks, which must be forced in, and tie them on with string or, better still, with fine brass wire sold especially for home preserving.

Place the containers in a deep pot—or even a washtub—with straw between them to keep the bottles from hitting each other and smashing. Boil qt. bottles 5 min., pt. bottles 3 min., and let cool completely in the water.

The cherries will provide you with excellent tarts in winter, and adding a small glass of kirsch to the juice, sweetened a little, will make a delicious drink.

CHERRIES IN SIRUP FOR COMPOTES AND DESSERTS CERISES AU SIROP POUR COMPOTES ET ENTREMETS (P.)

Sort out fine, ripe cherries, cut the stems midway, and pack them down gently in jars in order not to leave too much space. But since these cherries are not pitted, they will cook down less than those which are.

Pour a cold sirup registering 28–30° on the saccharometer over them. Because cherries render more water than apricots, the sirup must contain more sugar—about 1½ lb. per qt. water and, of course, a little vanilla. Boil qt. containers 15 min. and pt. jars 10 min. Remove the jars before the water cools, taking care not to place them on a cold surface, which would crack any defective glass.

STRAWBERRY JUICE JUS DE FRAISES (P.)

There is a strawberry preserve I am very fond of and recommend to you—preserved strawberry or raspberry juice. In winter you can make ices or mousses with it and it will also be useful for other things.

Choose well-flavored strawberries. They can be rather ripe, but sort them carefully so that only perfect berries are used. To improve the flavor, mix in a small amount of tiny wild strawberries with the large ones. Wash the picked berries and press them through a hair sieve—never use wire, even plated, for straining fruits. Pour this juice into ½-pt. bottles without any other ingredients, stopper them well, and boil 25–30 min. Let cool in the water, then seal the bottles with wax. By adding simple sirup, lemon juice, and carmine to heighten the color, this juice will make ices, mousses, or other desserts with all the flavor of fresh fruit.

STRAWBERRIES or RASPBERRIES IN SIRUP FRAISES OR FRAMBOISES AU SIROP (P.)

Because the fruit is so fragile, this is the most delicate of all preserves to prepare. It is not often made by home cooks, who would rather make jam. Raspberries are even more fragile than strawberries. You must have fine red strawberries; carefully pick the stems without spoiling the berries by holding the berry just beneath the stem and giving it a twist. It is better not to wash the berries unless absolutely necessary. But if they must be, wash them quickly in a large bowl of ice water—above all, don't let them soak in the water. Lift them out by hand and spread them out on clean cloths to dry and drain.

The berries can then be preserved the same way as Cherries in Sirup (p. 807), but just a little too much cooking and you will have strawberry purée. Moreover, after boiling, the strawberries will all float to the top of the jar while the bottom will be nothing but sirup.

Here is another and recommended method. Make your vanilla sirup with 1½ lb. sugar per qt. water; test it with a saccharometer to bring it to 28° or 30°. After carefully packing the berries in the jars, cover with boiling sirup and seal each jar as it is filled. After sealing the jar, no cooking is necessary. Keep in a cool place, and the next day test the cap to make sure that it is tightly sealed.

Raspberries can be prepared the same way, but this preserving is rarely done in the ordinary home, only on large estates where raspberries are grown on a big scale.

PEACHES IN SIRUP PÊCHES AU SIROP (P.)

Take medium-sized, ripe but not overripe, flavorful, juicy peaches, and you will find these same qualities when you taste the peaches in the middle of winter. August is the month peaches are ripe enough to pick and preserve. The early ones in June and July do not can so well and, furthermore, are so delicious to eat as they are that it would be a sacrilege to cook them. They must be wiped clean if you want to preserve them with the skins on. Not only does the skin retain the flavor, but the color of the fresh peach will be found when you peel it before eating.

This recipe is for preserving whole peaches. However, whole peaches take up more room than quartered ones and need more jars. Whole peaches cannot be preserved like other fruits; they must be pricked clear to the stone 6–8 times with a large silver needle and then blanched. Put the peaches into a large pot used for making jam, cover them with plenty of cold water, and cook at moderate heat. When they rise to the surface, lift them out with a skimming ladle and put them into a large container of cold water. Do not let the water come to a full boil while blanching the peaches.

After cooling and draining, place the peaches in qt. jars, which should be able to hold 8 or 9, and cover with sirup registering 28° on the saccharometer. Boil qt. jars 45 min., and pt. jars 30 min.; let cool in the water.

Nectarines are prepared exactly the same way.

MIXED FRUITS TOUS FRUITS (P.)

This is a sort of macédoine of fruits, best made in August or September, for it requires pears, plums, apples—in short, fruits that aren't ripe in early summer. Except for strawberries, which contribute nothing because of their fragility, you may put in all sorts of fruits: cherries, peaches, apricots, pears, apples, quetsche and mirabelle plums, greengages, etc. Quartered pears and apples should first be cooked a little in sirup.

Place a mixture of these fruits in each jar, cherries and mirabelle plums pitted; apricots, peaches, greengages, and quetsche plums cut into quarters. Cover ¾ full with sirup registering 28° on the saccharometer; use the vanilla-flavored sirup the pears and apples were first cooked in, with more sugar added and then reduced. Seal the jars; boil qt. jars 50 min., and pt. jars ½ hr. Cherries are very good in this macédoine, but, unfortunately, they color the sirup and tint the other fruit. This doesn't change the flavor; the pink sirup simply spoils the appearance.

In winter, you can serve these Mixed Fruits chilled. Keep the jar on ice, then pour the contents into a bowl and, if you wish, add sliced pineapple and a little kirsch or champagne, maraschino, etc.

DRIED FRUITS

Drying is a good way to preserve fruit, and dried fruits take up less space than cans or jars. However, they don't make so fine a compote.

When drying fruits, never let the pieces touch.

Malaga raisins are much too complicated to prepare at home. Good raisins are best bought.

DRIED APRICOTS ABRICOTS DESSÉCHÉS (P.)

Take apricots that are not too ripe, split them in half, and place them on wicker racks, then put them into a baker's oven a few hours after bread has been taken out. This way, the heat will be only as high as in a drying oven. Leave them in the oven several hours, 3 days in a row.

Take them 1 by 1 and flatten them, rubbing them a little since the heat will have shriveled them. Lay them side by side and leave them in the air 2 or 3 days, preferably in sunshine. Take them in at night to prevent the dampness from softening them, and put them into boxes when they are well dried.

Peaches are prepared like apricots.

DRIED APPLES POMMES SÉCHÉES (P.)

Peel the apples, remove the seeds with an apple corer, cut crosswise into slices ⅜ in. thick, and dry in a very slow oven to avoid cooking them. Let them dry overnight in the oven or drier and then in the sun, turning them several times.

The same procedure is used for dried pears.

PRUNES PRUNEAUX SÉCHÉS (P.)

These can be prepared several ways. Boil them as soon as picked and dry them on racks in the sun without letting them touch each other. Let dry until they are covered with a light coat of white powder.

Another method is to lay them on racks and put them into a drier heated to 105° F., as for drying apricots. When they are shriveled, dry them several days in the sun. There is nothing complicated about this method; it only takes watching. All plums can be dried this way.

JAMS AND JELLIES

This chapter is of particular interest to the homemaker and will show how to lay in a winter supply of wholesome, tasty desserts and delicious jam spreads for children home from school. The general principle of jam making is to cook fruit with an equal weight of sugar. However, each sort of fruit has its special rules relating to degree of ripeness, amount of water or sugar, etc.—rules that must be known if the jam is not to turn out too liquid or crystallized. These are the 2 pitfalls in jam making, which takes a good deal of trouble and uses up precious time in the kitchen.

APRICOT JAM CONFITURE D'ABRICOTS (P.)

Halve very ripe apricots, then weigh them and measure ¾ their weight in sugar. Cook the sugar with enough water to melt it. When the sirup has boiled 7–8 min., add the apricots. Cook over a hot fire, constantly stirring to the bottom of the pan, so that nothing sticks to it. When the sirup clings to the skimming ladle and drops through slowly in lumps, add a few shelled almonds and put into jars. When the jam is cold, cover the top with rounds of wax paper or paper smeared with white vaseline; this is better than the customary alcohol, which evaporates. Seal the jars with 2 rounds of paper.

APRICOT or **PLUM JAM** CONFITURE D'ABRICOTS ET PRUNES (P.)

Halve the apricots the preceding day, put them into a bowl, and mix them with granulated sugar—6 lb. sugar for 8 lb. apricots. Shake them well together and cover the top of the bowl. Then let macerate overnight. The following day you will find that the fruit has rendered its water and is covered with a sort of sirup. Cook everything together without adding water and stir while cooking.

Prepared this way, the jam is perhaps less attractive to the eye, but in my opinion it tastes better. Plum jam is made the same way.

BLACK-CURRANT JELLY CONFITURE DE CASSIS (P.)

Pick and seed very ripe black currants, carefully removing the stems, which is the longest part of the task. They may then be treated like raspberries (p. 811) or prepared the following way.

Melt in water 1½ lb. sugar per lb. black currants and cook it to the "soufflé" stage as for Strawberry Preserves (p. 811). Drop in the black currants and cook ¼ hr. at a very slow boil. Then drain, reduce the juice, and press the currants through a hair sieve; put the purée back into the sirup and cook until it clings to the spoon. This will form a jelly instead of a jam, but has the advantage of containing no seeds.

CHERRY JAM CONFITURE DE CERISES (P.)

Same procedure as for strawberries, but use 1 lb. sugar per lb. cherries if they are tart and only ¾ lb. sugar if they are sweet. Naturally, the cherries should be pitted.

QUINCE PRESERVES CONFITURE DE COINGS EN MORCEAUX (P.)

Quinces are especially used to make jelly, but the fruit can later be utilized to make a good preserve. To do this, save a little of the cooking liquid, add ¾ lb. sugar per lb. fruit, and cook the quinces for a long time until they are well done. This crushes them, naturally, and they cannot be kept very long, but the answer to that is to eat them up first.

They can also be used to make Jellied Quince Candy (p. 814).

STRAWBERRY PRESERVES CONFITURE DE FRAISES (P.)

Strawberry and cherry preserves very often crystallize at the end of a few weeks; this is caused by using too much sugar—½ lb. sugar per lb. picked strawberries is sufficient. Cook the sugar with enough water to melt it, but not so much that time is wasted in bringing it to the desired consistency. Cook the sirup over a hot fire until it comes to the "soufflé" stage; in other words, until the rather thick sirup forms small balls like soap bubbles when you blow on it through a skimming ladle. When the sugar is ready, drop the strawberries in and let them poach, without boiling, 10 min. Drain them on a hair sieve and cook the sirup again, for it will have been diluted by the strawberry juice. Bring the sirup again to the "soufflé" stage, drop in the strawberries, let them simmer again, and this time drain them thoroughly, at least 1 hr. Cook the sirup a third time until it reaches a thick "soufflé" stage and then let the strawberries simmer in it 20 min.

This preserve should not be allowed to come to a real boil, or the strawberries will lose their juice and turn into tasteless, rubbery bits of sponge.

Pour the preserves into a bowl and let cool. When almost cold, stir with a spoon, for all the strawberries will be on top, and put into jars; this way, the strawberries will be evenly divided.

PRESERVED WHOLE RASPBERRIES CONFITURE DE FRAMBOISES ENTIÈRES (P.)

Put raspberries with ¾ their weight in granulated sugar into a round-bottomed jam pot and cook, stirring slowly to keep from burning on the bottom. When you can see the bottom of the pot, remove from the fire and pour into jars immediately. This preserve is delicious.

CHESTNUT JAM CONFITURE DE MARRONS (P.)

Peel and cook 4 lb. chestnuts in water. Drain, then press them through a fine sieve. Cook 3 lb. granulated sugar with 1 qt. water and vanilla in a jam pot until it is very thick and forms small bubbles on top that do not break easily. Put the chestnut purée into this sirup and continue cooking, stirring with a spatula, at least 30 min. This jam should look like a thick paste and, when dropped into water, should settle on the bottom like a little pellet. Store in jars.

MELON JAM CONFITURE DE MELON (P.)

Take a melon that is just ripe, peel it, and cut the pulp into cubes. Macerate 24 hr. with 1 lb. sugar per 2 lb. melon. Strain the resulting juice and cook it to the "thread" stage (see p. 562). Put the diced melon into this sirup and continue cooking with a piece of tangerine or orange peel until you have a thick jam; flavor with vanilla.

MIRABELLE PLUM JAM CONFITURE DE MIRABELLES (P.)

Pit very ripe, tiny yellow plums called mirabelles and macerate them, as directed in the recipe for apricots, with ¾ lb. sugar per lb. fruit. If the plums are very sweet, reduce the amount of sugar. The following day, cook them like apricots until the sirup clings to a spoon, and put into small jars.

BLACKBERRY JAM CONFITURE DE MÛRES (P.)

Blackberries also make a nice jam. Take care in picking them to remove any worms, which are found quite frequently, wash them, and cook like elderberries (p. 813). Children love this jam.

ORANGE MARMALADE CONFITURE D'ORANGES (P.)

Take 12 good-quality oranges, prick the skin all over with a fork, and soak 3 days in cold water, changing the water twice a day and keeping them well covered. The third day, put them on to cook whole in a large amount of cold water. They take a long time to cook and are done when they can be easily pierced with a straw. Next, soak in cold water until the following day to remove most of the bitterness. Cut the oranges into quarters or 6 sections, depending on size, remove the seeds, and weigh the fruit; add the same weight in granulated sugar. Moisten with the juice of 6 fresh oranges. Cook the sugar and oranges until the sirup is thick enough to cling to the spoon. Skim carefully while cooking.

PEAR PRESERVES CONFITURE DE POIRES (P.)

Peel the pears, sprinkle with lemon juice, cut into quarters, remove the seeds, and blanch in water flavored with lemon juice until half cooked. Then make a sirup with the same weight in sugar as the pears. Cook this sirup 5–6 min. with enough water to cover the pears amply; drop in the well-drained pears. Cook slowly until the fruit is completely cooked. Increase the heat to thicken the sirup and, when it is thick enough, put pears and sirup into jars.

The small English pear is very good for preserving but does not make good jelly. If you want the fruit to jell, mix 1 part apple juice to the pear cooking water and the sugar.

GREENGAGE-PLUM JAM CONFITURE DE PRUNES REINES-CLAUDE (P.)

Same procedure as for Apricot Jam (p. 810); cook quickly to keep the green color.

FOUR-FRUIT JAM CONFITURE DE QUATRE-FRUITS (P.)

Take equal amounts of peaches, apricots, greengages, and mirabelle plums; stone them, macerate 12 hr. with 1½ lb. granulated sugar per 2 lb. fruit, and cook as for Apricot or Plum Jam (p. 810).

FOUR-FRUIT JAM or **CONVENT JAM** CONFITURE DE QUATRE-FRUITS or CONFITURE DU COUVENT (P.)

Use red fruit such as red currants, raspberries, strawberries, and cherries.

Prepare the Cherry Jam as directed on p. 810 and, when it is ½ cooked, add the 3 other fruits (the red currants separated from the clusters, but whole). Finish cooking everything together. Use equal weights of sugar and fruit.

RHUBARB JAM CONFITURE DE RHUBARBE (P.)

Peel the rhubarb, cut it into small pieces, and macerate it 2 hr. in a bowl with an equal weight of granulated sugar. Then cook sugar and rhubarb until it forms a thick jam and put into jars. Rhubarb takes a long time to cook because it renders so much water.

ELDERBERRY JAM CONFITURE DE SUREAU (P.)

Elderberry Jam, like Tomato Jelly (below), would not sell very well in stores, but has its place among homemade sweets. The cost of the sugar is about the only expense involved, for the country is full of elderberries for anyone who wants to pick them, as it also is of barberries, which have a rather agreeably tart flavor.

Pick very ripe, black elderberries; separate them from the clusters and wash them, for they are always dusty. Put them into a jam pot with ¾ lb. sugar per lb. berries and start cooking at moderate heat, stirring with a spatula. Increase the heat when the berries have split and rendered their juice.

Cook a fairly long time so that the jam becomes quite thick.

TOMATO JELLY CONFITURE DE TOMATES (P.)

Seed and slice the tomatoes thin, then boil 5–6 min. Drain, press the tomatoes through a fine sieve, and weigh the purée. Cook the same weight of sugar with a little vanilla until it reaches the "ball" stage (p. 562), then add the tomato purée and stir constantly to prevent burning. Cook a long time, for the mixture will not jell by itself; if you add a little red-currant or apple juice, the quality is improved and the preparation will jell better.

BLACK-CURRANT JELLY GELÉE DE CASSIS (P.)

Take equal parts of black-currant juice and red-currant juice and cook with ⅘ lb. sugar per 2 lb. juice.

QUINCE JELLY GELÉE DE COINGS (P.)

Peel, core, and quarter the quinces. Sprinkle them with lemon juice. Save the cores with the seeds and wrap them in a square of cheesecloth. Cook the quinces in a large amount of cold water along with the bag of cores, which are extremely gelatinous. When the quinces are well cooked, which does not take so long as you think, drain them, weigh the cooking juice, and cook it with an equal weight of sugar, and orange or lemon peel, until jelly forms on the skimming ladle as described in the recipe for Red-Currant Jelly (below).

RASPBERRY JELLY GELÉE DE FRAMBOISES (P.)

Same procedure as for Red-Currant Jelly (below); add 1 part red currants to 3 parts raspberries.

RED-CURRANT JELLY GELÉE DE GROSEILLES (P.)

Crush the red currants by hand, then bring them to a boil. Drain them and, when they have cooled a little, squeeze them in a cloth. Weigh the juice obtained and cook over a moderate fire with an equal weight of sugar. Skim carefully until the sirup is thick enough to cling to the spoon. The jelly forms very quickly and must be watched closely, for if it passes the right degree of cooking, it will be like pitch instead of jelly. Add a little raspberry juice to the currants to give a finer flavor.

RED-CURRANT JELLY PREPARED COLD GELÉE DE GROSEILLES À FROID (P.)

Red-Currant and Raspberry Jelly with an even finer flavor nearer the taste of the fruit itself can be made without any cooking. Press the juice from cold red currants and add 1½ lb. sugar per lb. juice. Let the sugar melt in a bowl, then put into jars and expose them to the sun 5 or 6 hr. at a time for 2 days. Seal the usual way. This jelly doesn't keep as long as cooked jelly.

APPLE MARMALADE MARMELADE DE POMMES (P.)

Quarter the apples and cook them (without paring them) in enough water to cover, then drain and press through a sieve. Cook this purée again with an equal weight of sugar or only ½ the weight, according to taste. Cook a good ¼ hr. and pack in jars.

JELLIED QUINCE CANDY PÂTE DE COINGS (P.)

When preserving quinces, this is a good supplementary recipe and can be made 2 ways.

Real Jellied Quince Candy should be made with grated raw fruit cooked with an equal weight of sugar until the purée is so thick that you can see the bottom of the pan when you stir with a spatula. It must be stirred constantly. Pour it onto a marble surface or on sheets of white paper sprinkled with sugar. Spread it out about 1 in. thick and let cool. Cut into lozenge-shaped pieces, roll them in granulated sugar, and let them dry further on a grill or sieve before packing them in cans with a layer of parchment between each layer of quince candy.

This candy can also be made with cooked quinces used to make jelly. In this case, use ⅓ more sugar than the weight of the purée because the gelatinous part of the quince has already gone into the jelly. This candied jelly is reddish in color, and, if cooked a long time, will keep very well.

Jellied Apple Candy can be made the same way, but it is rather tasteless.

HOMEMADE RAISINÉ RAISINÉ DE MÉNAGE (P.)

Cut the spoiled parts from soft or wormy pears, slice them thin, and cook in water. Press very ripe grapes in a cloth to squeeze out the juice and use 1 lb. sugar per 2 lb. juice; cook into a thick sirup. Then put in the drained pears and continue cooking over a hot fire, constantly stirring, until it becomes a thick mass.

For another recipe, see p. 702.

BRANDIED FRUITS (P.)

It is always a good idea for a wide-awake housewife to have a reserve of brandied fruits on hand. If she has made them herself, they will seem all the more attractive to possible visitors and more out of the ordinary than bought liqueurs.

You will also find in this chapter a few recipes for homemade liqueurs that are easily prepared. Here are the directions for preparing brandied fruits properly. The fruit must be just ripe, so that it will have all its aroma and flavor, and of the best quality. The fruit must be without blemish and firm to the touch. If you use fruit from your own orchard, pick it on a dry morning after dawn and before the sun has heated the pulp. The best results are obtained by preserving the fruit in glazed crocks or glass jars.

The larger fruits should first be blanched; others may be put directly into the alcohol. Let us not be concerned with recipes used in industry for fruits that have to appeal to buyers, which are much too complicated for you to prepare. Let's stick to simplicity.

BRANDIED CHERRIES I CERISES À L'EAU-DE-VIE (P.)

Montmorency cherries are the best because of their firm flesh, but the English cherry is also very good. Take fine, perfect cherries that are not sticky, as sometimes happens; cut the stems midway and arrange them in rows in your jars. Cover them completely with white brandy 50° strong or stronger if you wish, and add a piece of vanilla or a stick of cinnamon to each jar. Stopper carefully and let stand 1 month or 5 weeks, and not in the sun, as some do; stir from time to time by gently rocking the jars. Next, prepare the following sirup. Heat 1 lb. sugar in 1½ pt. water until melted, then let cool. Drain the brandy from the cherries and mix with this sirup, ⅓ sirup to ⅔ brandy. Pour the mixture over the cherries, stopper, and seal the cork with a piece of pig's bladder tightly tied on to keep the alcohol from evaporating, which it would do even through the cork. Ready to eat after 15 days.

BRANDIED CHERRIES II CERISES À L'EAU-DE-VIE (P.)

Though not so traditional, this second recipe is simpler to prepare. Put the cherries into jars and add 5 oz. sugar per lb. cherries; powdered sugar is best because granulated sugar will not melt in alcohol and will injure the fruit. Cover with fruit alcohol, seal airtight, and let macerate 5–6 weeks. Vanilla and cinnamon should also be included.

With this method, there will be no water in your preserves, which is the case when you use sirup as directed above, so 45° alcohol is sufficient, since it is not cut by the sirup. This procedure is simpler and more practical for the home.

BRANDIED MIRABELLE AND QUETSCHE PLUMS MIRABELLES ET QUETSCHES À L'EAU-DE-VIE (P.)

These 2 varieties of plums are brandied like ordinary plums (below), but the mirabelles should be blanched only once.

BRANDIED PLUMS I PRUNES À L'EAU-DE-VIE (P.)

Greengages are recommended for this preparation. Here are 2 different methods.

Plums are slightly more difficult to prepare than cherries. Take fine, not-quite-ripe plums picked before the sun rises. Wipe them off and prick them to the stone 7 or 8 times with a silver or copper pin. After each is pricked, drop it into cold water; blanch in lightly salted water at moderate heat. As the plums rise to the surface, lift them out with a skimming ladle and cool them in salted water.

To keep the plums very green, put them back into the tepid salted water (the same water will do), set over a moderate fire, and heat them, without boiling, 10 min. Drain and rinse again, then place in jars and macerate in white brandy (50° strong) 1 month to 6 weeks. Drain off the brandy and mix it with ⅓ its volume of sirup cooked to 20° on the saccharometer. Arrange the plums in several jars and cover them with their sugared alcohol.

BRANDIED PLUMS II PRUNES À L'EAU-DE-VIE (P.)

Take greengages that are not too ripe; wipe them off and prick them all over with a needle, then put them into a copper basin filled with water; drop in 1 gram copper sulphate per qt. water to preserve the color of the fruit. Heat until the water just begins to simmer—in other words, when tiny bubbles no larger than pinheads rise to the surface. Cool immediately, then drain. Put into jars and cover with a mixture of sirup and white brandy (45° strong), ⅓ simple sirup to ⅔ brandy; be sure that the plums are amply covered. Let macerate 6 weeks.

BRANDIED MUSCAT GRAPES RAISIN MUSCAT À L'EAU-DE-VIE (P.)

Put fine, firm grapes into jars without filling them too full. Cover them with white brandy and let macerate 3 weeks. Then finish filling the jars with cold sirup made with 1 lb. sugar per 9 oz. water. Shake the jar to mix well. Other grapes than muscat can be used, provided they are whole and perfect.

All fruits—red currants, raspberries, strawberries, and black currants—can be preserved this way. They can also be prepared like cherries (see above, second recipe).

PICKLED FRUITS (P.)

When you have so much fruit in the garden that the trees are weighted down, pick the smallest before they are completely ripe. This thinning will benefit the rest of the fruit by giving it more sap. The unripe fruit, then, may be used as follows.

PICKLED CHERRIES CERISES AU VINAIGRE (P.)

Take firm cherries that are not quite ripe. Pluck the stems or cut them short; leave the pits. Place the cherries in glazed crocks. Prepare the vinegar as directed in the recipe below and pour it over the cherries when cold.

The difference between such large fruit as plums, apricots, and peaches and such small fruit as cherries, grapes, etc., is that the latter group need not be cooked to be pickled clear to the center. These pickled fruits are served with certain meats, game, pork, fowl, and even cold beef.

PICKLED PLUMS PRUNES AU VINAIGRE (P.)

Wash the plums and prick them 6–8 times with a pin. Bring 1 lb. sugar to a boil in 2 qt. good wine vinegar. When the sirup is boiling, drop in the plums, lower the fire, and cook 5 min. without boiling. Remove them gently with a skimming ladle and put them into glazed crocks. Pour in the vinegar, let cool, cork, and keep in a cool place.

LIQUEURS

CURAÇAO FOR FLAVORING CREAMS AND CAKES CURAÇAO POUR PARFUMER CRÈMES ET GÂTEAUX (P.)

Dry orange rinds on top of the stove until they split. Put the rinds into a bottle with enough rum to cover. Let macerate 1 month to 6 weeks. Filter the rum and add it to a sirup prepared in the proportions given in the recipe for Quince Liqueur (below).

BLACK-CURRANT LIQUEUR LIQUEUR DE CASSIS (P.)

Put 4 lb. stemmed black currants in 1 qt. 90° alcohol. Let stand 2 months. Make a sirup by boiling 2 lb. sugar and 1 pt. water; add the macerated black currants and alcohol and press through a fine sieve or cloth. Pour into bottles.

QUINCE LIQUEUR LIQUEUR DE COINGS (P.)

This liqueur is easily obtained. We're not dealing with a well-known brand of liqueur, but a delicious drink you can make at home. Peel well-washed quinces and put the peelings into a jar with good 60° white brandy; let macerate 6 weeks. Then cook together 11 oz. sugar and ½ pt. water per bottle brandy. When this sirup has boiled 5 min., let it cool, then blend it with the quince brandy strained through a cloth. This liqueur is invaluable for stomach-aches.

MOCHA LIQUEUR LIQUEUR DE MOKA (P.)

Mix ½ lb. well-roasted, finely ground good coffee with 1 qt. alcohol. After 15 days, add 1 qt. sirup made with 1½ pt. water and 1¼ lb. sugar; let the sirup cool before mixing. Let stand 8 days, then strain through a filter.

BLACKBERRY LIQUEUR LIQUEUR DE MÛRES (P.)

2 lb. blackberries, 1 bowl raspberries, and 1 bowl red currants. To 1 qt. this juice, add 1½ lb. granulated sugar; let melt a little and add 3 pt. to 2 qt. 50° white brandy. Let stand 3 weeks, stirring from time to time, to finish melting the sugar; filter and pour into bottles.

The same liqueur may be made with raspberries mixed with ⅓ red currants.

WILD-PLUM LIQUEUR LIQUEUR DE PRUNELLES (P.)

Crush 1–1¼ lb. very ripe wild plums; leave the pits. Put into a jar with 1 qt. fruit brandy, a little vanilla, and ½ lb. sugar. Cork, and let macerate 6 weeks before filtering.

SIRUPS

BLACK-CURRANT SIRUP SIROP DE CASSIS (P.)

4 lb. sugar and 1 qt. water. Boil 10 min., add 3 lb. stemmed black currants, boil another 10 min., strain by pressing the fruit in a cloth. Boil again and bottle.

CHERRY SIRUP SIROP DE CERISES (P.)

Pound 6 lb. cherries in a mortar, also crushing the pits. Let macerate 24 hr. Extract the juice by squeezing in a cloth and add 5 lb. sugar per 4 lb. juice. Proceed as for Red-Currant Sirup (p. 818).

LEMON SIRUP SIROP DE CITRONS (P.)

1½ lb. sugar and 1 qt. lemon juice. Heat without boiling, adding the grated rind of 3 lemons. Strain this sirup through cheesecloth, let cool, and bottle.

STRAWBERRY SIRUP SIROP DE FRAISES (P.)

Macerate an equal weight of strawberries and sugar 24 hr. Mash and strain through a sieve; cook the juice ¼ hr. at low heat. Let cool and bottle.

RASPBERRY SIRUP SIROP DE FRAMBOISES (P.)

Same procedure as above, using raspberries.

GRENADINE SIRUP SIROP DE GRENADINE (P.)

Seed 12 pomegranates, removing all the white skin; crush the seeds and squeeze the juice through a cloth. Cook with 1½ lb. granulated sugar per qt. juice. Let boil 10 min., skim, and pour into bottles.

RED-CURRANT SIRUP SIROP DE GROSEILLES (P.)

Extract the juice from 4 lb. red currants and let stand 24 hr. Then weigh it and put on the fire in a copper basin with twice its weight in sugar; boil a few moments, skim, and let cool. Bottle and seal airtight. Don't cook this sirup too much or it will turn to jelly.

ORANGE SIRUP SIROP D'ORANGES (P.)

Prepare like Lemon Sirup (p. 817), flavoring well with orange rind; mix the juice of 2 lemons with that of 15 oranges.

BIBLIOGRAPHY

AND ABBREVIATIONS OF AUTHORS' NAMES

ABBRE-VIATION *	AUTHOR	TITLE	PUBLISHER
(A.)	ALI-BAB	*La Gastronomie pratique*	Flammarion
(Be.)	BEAUJARD, ANDRÉE	*Faites votre confiserie vous-même*	Flammarion
(B.-S.)	BRILLAT-SAVARIN	*Physiologie du goût*	Flammarion
(A.C.)	DE CROZE, AUSTIN	*Les Plats régionaux de France*	Montaigne
(C. & R.)	CURNONSKY and ROUFF, MARCEL	*La France gastronomique*	Rouff
(Da.)	DAGOURET	*Le Barman universel*	Flammarion
(D. & D.)	DARENNE, E. and DUVAL, E.	*Pâtisserie moderne*	
(Du.)	DUVAL	*Traité de confiserie moderne*	
(E.)	ESCOFFIER, A.	*Le Guide culinaire*	Flammarion
(E.)	ESCOFFIER, A.	*Ma Cuisine*	Flammarion
(Fa.)	FAVRE, J.	*Dictionnaire de cuisine*	
(Ga.)	GAUDEFROY, O.	*Guide pratique de la pâtisserie et des glaces*	Flammarion
(Gi.)	GILBERT, PHILÉAS	*Cuisine de tous les mois*	Ollendorff
(H.)	HEYRAUD, H.	*Manuel du restaurateur*	Flammarion
(L.M.)	LA MAZILLE	*La Bonne Cuisine du Périgord*	Flammarion
(Ma.)	MAILLARD	*La Cuisine pratique*	Payot & Cie.
(M.O.)	MAYOR, OLIVIER	*Le Barman*	
(M.)	MONTAGNÉ, PR. and SALLES, PR.	*Le Grand Livre de la cuisine*	Flammarion
(P.)	PELLAPRAT, H.-P.	*Comment faire ses conserves*	Flammarion
(P.)	PELLAPRAT, H.-P.	*La Cuisine de tous les jours*	Le Cordon Bleu
(P.)	PELLAPRAT, H.-P.	*Le Guide des hors-d'oeuvre*	Le Cordon Bleu
(P.)	PELLAPRAT, H.-P.	*La Pâtisserie pratique*	Le Cordon Bleu
(P.)	PELLAPRAT, H.-P.	*Traité de la cuisine familiale*	Flammarion
(Pe.)	PETIT, A.	*Traité de la cuisine russe*	Flammarion
(Ro.)	ROSE, MADEMOISELLE	*Cent Façons de préparer le gibier*	Flammarion
(Ro.)	ROSE, MADEMOISELLE	*Cent Façons de préparer les potages*	Flammarion
(Rou.)	ROUKHOMOVSKY	*Gastronomie juive*	Flammarion
(S.-F.)	LES SANS-FILISTES GASTRONOMES	*Les Belles Recettes des provinces françaises*	Flammarion
(Sch.)	SCHEIBENBOGEN, A.	*Cuisine et pâtisserie austro-hongroise, balkanique, orientale*	Flammarion
(Su.)	SUZANNE, A.	*La Cuisine et la pâtisserie anglaise et américaine*	L'Art Culinaire
(T.)	TOUZALIN, LIDA-M	*L'Amérique à table*	Flammarion
(U.-D.)	URBAIN-DUBOIS and BERNARD	*La Cuisine illustrée*	Joinville
(W.)	WERNER, F.	*Traité général des hors-d'oeuvre et savorys*	Flammarion

(C.) Caillat, A. (Fr.) Fressinet (Gr.) Grandi, F. (J.) Jourlet (H.M.) Mercier, Henri

* These abbreviations are used after the title of each recipe to indicate the original author of the recipe.

GLOSSARY OF CULINARY TERMS

Abatis. Giblets, winglets, and neck of fowl.
Acidulate. Add vinegar or lemon juice.
Agar-agar. A vegetable gelatin.
Aiguillette. Long strip of cooked meat, fowl, etc.
À la. In the style of.
Alexandra. With asparagus.
Algérienne, à l'. Algerian style. With green or red peppers.
Allemande, à l'. German style. A basic white sauce. Applied to meat, it often means garnished with sauerkraut, sausage, or noodles.
Allumettes. "Matches"—applied to pastry, potatoes, and canapés cut in matchstick shapes.
Almond. Bitter or sweet fruit of almond tree. Green almond is the pistachio nut.
Almond Oil. For cooking, prepared from sweet almonds.
Alsacienne, à l'. Alsatian style. Sometimes, garnished with sauerkraut or cabbage and sausage; sometimes, with *foie gras.*
Américaine, à l'. American style. Lobster or tomatoes form part of garnish or sauce. Or dishes popular in the United States.
Amiral, à l'. Admiral style. With mussels and oysters or shrimp.
Anchovy Essence. Anchovies pounded and simmered, sold ready-prepared.
Ancienne, à l'. Old-fashioned style. Applied to soups, garnishes, fowl, etc.
Andalouse, à l'. Andalusian style. A mayonnaise with puréed tomatoes and pimento. With fish, fowl, and meat dishes, usually denotes eggplant and tomato or pimento.
Andouille. Large hog pudding.
Angelica. Plant used to flavor various liqueurs. Tender stems candied and sold for decorating pastries.
Anglaise, à l'. English style. Usually means in a plain style.
Archiduc. Archduke. Usually, with a cream sauce containing paprika and truffles.
Argenteuil. With asparagus.
Arlésienne, à l'. Arles style. Contains tomato, onion, sometimes eggplant, and garlic.
Arménienne, à l'. With rice, lemon, and tomatoes.
Arrowroot. An easily digested starch.
Aspic. A clear, savory jelly used to coat eggs, meat, fish, etc.
Au Beurre. With or cooked in butter.
Au Bleu. Fish simmered in wine.
Au Naturel. Foods cooked or served in plain fashion.
Aurore, à l'. Aurora style. Color of food or sauce is rosy-dawnlike.
Bacchus. With grapes.
Bain-marie. A large pan containing water, holding smaller pans. Substitute either double-boiler or (for oven) water-filled pan.
Ballotines. Small meat, fish, or poultry balls. Also applied to stuffed game birds.
Bard. To cover with strips of pork fat or bacon to keep meats from drying out during roasting.
Barigoule, à la. Containing artichokes, mushrooms, and a brown sauce.
Barquettes. Boat-shaped pastry shells filled with various mixtures.
Baste. To pour liquids from cooking food over it to prevent its toughening.
Bavaroise. (*a*) Cold cream pudding. (*b*) A beverage called a posset. (*c*) Bavarian style.
Béchamel. White sauce with added cream.
Beef Marrow. Fatty substance in beef bones.
Bercy. With an herb-and-butter sauce.
Bergère, à la. Shepherdess style. With mushrooms and parsley.
Bigarade. Made with a bitter-orange sauce.
Bind. To add egg, butter, or liquid to hold mixture together.
Biscuit. Literally, "twice-cooked." Brittle cakes or cookies.
Bisque. A shellfish purée and cream soup.
Black or **Brown Butter.** Butter cooked until it darkens.
Black Pudding. Sausage containing pig's blood.
Blanch. To boil foods a short time to remove bitter or strong taste. Also, to put fruits or nuts into boiling water to remove skins.
Blanquette. A stew with a white sauce.
Bombe. A molded ice cream or pudding.
Bonne Femme, à la. Goodwife style. Usually, with potatoes.
Bordelaise, à la. Bordeaux style. Rich brown sauce flavored with Bordeaux.
Bouillon. A clear stock made of beef bones, veal, and vegetables.
Bouquet Garnis. A bunch of herbs—parsley, tarragon, thyme, bay leaf, etc.—tied together (often in cheesecloth), cooked with the food, and removed before serving.
Bouquetière. With fresh, young vegetables arranged in separate mounds.
Bourgeoise. Simple family style. With carrots and onions; sometimes, potatoes and bacon.
Bourguignonne. Burgundy style. With onions, mushrooms, and red wine.
Bread. To cover with bread crumbs.
Bretonne, à la. With string beans.
Brochette, en. Cooked on a skewer.
Broil. To cook food on a grill under heat.
Brown Butter. See **Black Butter.**
Brunoise. Cut-up or cubed fresh vegetables.
Case or **Caisse.** Round porcelain dish, formerly made of paper.
Cancalaise. Cancale style. With oysters.
Carbonnade. Braised or stewed meat.

Cardinal. With red color, usually with shellfish.
Carmine. A red pigment used for coloring confectionery.
Catalane. Catalonian style. With tomato and pimento.
Caul. Pig's membrane used for wrapping chopped meats and sausages.
Cendrillon. Cinderella style. Cooked in embers or hot ashes.
Cepes. Large brown mushrooms.
Cervelas, Cervelat. A highly seasoned, smoked pork sausage. Also called saveloy.
Chanterelles. Yellow mushrooms.
Chantilly. With cream (town of Chantilly is noted for its rich cream).
Charlotte. A fruit or cream mixture molded in a biscuit or bread lining.
Chartreuse. Besides the liqueur, the name applies to molded jellied vegetables, fruits, fowl, or game.
Chasseur. Hunter style. With mushrooms and tomatoes.
Chateaubriand. A double filet mignon.
Châtelaine. With chestnuts and artichoke bottoms.
Chaud-froid. Literally, "hot-cold." Food prepared hot but served cold, coated with sauce and glazed with aspic.
Chiffonade. Vegetables shredded in long strips.
Chipolata. Small sausages seasoned with chives.
Choux Paste. Named because of cauliflower-like shape when baked for cream puffs and such.
Clamart. With peas.
Clarified Butter. Butter melted and poured off, leaving the residue on bottom of pan.
Clarify. To clear. Clouded liquids—soups, liquid jellies, etc.—are cleared by using meat or egg white, etc.
Cockscombs and Cock Kidneys. "Kidneys" is a euphemism; they are the cock's testicles, often prepared with, sometimes without, the combs.
Cocotte. A small earthenware pot or pan.
Cognac. Brandy distilled from wine in the Cognac district.
Colbert. With a tarragon-flavored butter sauce.
Compote. A fruit stew in which fruits have kept their natural shape.
Condé. With rice.
Consommé. Broth.
Coquilles. Shells.
Coral. Red part of stomach in lobster, rock lobster, and scallop.
Court Bouillon. Liquid containing wine and vegetables in which fish are simmered.
Crapaudine. Birds split down the back and cooked spreadeagle style.
Crécy. With carrots.
Crème, à la. Served with or cooked in cream or a cream sauce.
Creole. With rice.
Crêpes. Thin pancakes.
Crépinette. Kind of pork or chicken sausage.
Croquettes. Crisp-fried mixture breaded on outside.
Croustade. Pastry or bread case containing a cooked meat mixture.
Croutons. Sliced bread toasted or fried; cubed for soups; spread with mixtures for hors d'oeuvres.
Currant. Fresh fruit—red, white, and black. Also, a small seedless raisin. "Currants and sultanas" always means the two types of raisins.
Curry. Mixture of powdered spices.
Dariole. Small cup-shaped mold.
Daube. Meat or fowl braised or stewed in earthenware dish.
Decant. To separate the good from the bad part of a liquid.
Demi-deuil. Half mourning. White sauce with black truffles.
Demidov. With truffles and Madeira.
Derby. With rice and *foie gras.*
Deviled. With hot seasoning or sauce.
Dice. To cut into small cubes.
Dieppoise, à la. Seafood style—with mussels, etc.
Dubarry. With cauliflower.
Duchesse. With creamed potatoes.
Dugléré. With tomato-flavored sauce.
Duxelles. Chopped mushroom garnish.
Egyptienne, à l'. Egyptian style. Sometimes, with lentils; sometimes, with rice and curry.
Émincé. Meat (usually, leftover) sliced and sauced.
Escalope. A collop or small slice, usually of veal.
Escalloped or **Scalloped.** Baked with sauce and bread crumbs.
Espagnole, à l'. Spanish style. With tomatoes, pimentos, and oil. Or the basic rich brown sauce.
Essences. Boiled-down stocks with pronounced flavor: mushroom essence, truffle essence, fish essence, etc.
Fermière, à la. Farmhouse style. Simply prepared, usually with young vegetables, sometimes with ham.
Filet Mignon. Small beef fillet.
Fillet. Fish: flat slice boned. Fowl: cut from breast. Meat: cut from loin or tenderloin.
Financière, à la. Financier style. With Madeira sauce and truffles, etc.
Fines Herbes. Finely chopped herbs—mainly chives, chervil, parsley, tarragon.
Flamande, à la. Flemish style. Usually, with chicory.
Flambé. Flamed. The liquor is heated, then set afire and poured over food.
Flan. Open tart or pie.
Florentine. With spinach.
Foie Gras. Fattened goose liver.
Fondant. Melting. Also, an icing.

Forcemeat. Any kind of stuffing.
Forestière, à la. Forest style. With mushrooms.
Four Spices. Mixture of white pepper, ground cloves, grated nutmeg, and ginger.
Française, à la. French style. With young fresh vegetables, or with a rich tomato-flavored sauce, or particularly native dishes.
Frappé. Frozen or iced.
Freneuse. With turnips.
Fricassée. Braised or stewed food.
Galantine. Roll of meat, fowl, or game elaborately stuffed, glazed with aspic.
Garbure. Mixture between a soup and a stew.
Garnish. To decorate around a dish or add on food.
Gelatin. An odorless animal protein used in making jellies.
Genevoise, à la. Geneva style. Usually, with anchovies.
Génoise. Genoese style. In pastry, a rich cake forming the base of fancy cakes. Otherwise, usually means with anchovies.
Glaze. (*a*) In meat recipes, a thick, concentrated gravy. (*b*) Icing a cake with fondant, sugar, etc. (*c*) Using a thick gravy or sirup to give a glossy finish to any meat or sweet dish.
Godard. With rich brown sauce and mushrooms.
Grand-duc. Grand Duke. With cheese sauce and asparagus.
Grand'mère. Grandmother style. Usually, with croutons and parsley.
Gratin, au. Covered with bread crumbs and/or grated cheese and browned in oven.
Gratinate. To garnish with bread crumbs and brown in oven or under broiler.
Grecque, à la. Greek style. Usually, fried in oil.
Grenadins. Small trimmed pieces of veal.
Grill. To cook food on a grill over a fire. Today, grilled food is usually cooked under a broiler. All recipes calling for "grilling" can be broiled.
Gum Arabic. Gum of the acacia.
Hash. Sliced or chopped (leftover) meats heated in a sauce.
Haricot. Mutton stew with vegetables; originally, bean stew.
Hongroise, à la. Hungarian style. With paprika.
Indienne, à l'. Indian style. With curry.
Irlandaise, à l. Irish style. With potatoes.
Italian Paste. Macaroni, spaghetti, etc.
Italienne, à l'. Italian style. With macaroni, or with an espagnole sauce with mushrooms, tomatoes, and garlic.
Ivoire. With smooth white sauce.
Japonaise, à la. Japanese style. With Japanese artichokes.
Jardinière, à la. Gardener style. With mixed cooked vegetables.
Jelly. Meat and fruit liquids stiffened with gelatin.
Joinville, à la. With shrimp or with crayfish.
Jugged. Meat, fowl, but especially game stewed in a covered earthenware pot.
Julienne. Vegetables cut into thin, matchlike strips.
Jus, au. With gravy or own juice.
Kromeski. Deep-fried croquette.
Lait, au. Served with or in milk.
Langouste. Rock lobster.
Larding. Pork-fat or fat-bacon strips pulled through meats with a special needle to keep the meats from drying out during cooking.
Livournaise, à la. Leghorn style. With tomatoes.
Lucullus. Lavishly prepared dishes.
Lyonnaise, à la. Lyon style. With onions.
Macédoine. Mixture of fruits or vegetables.
Macerate. To steep in wine or liqueur to impart flavor.
Madrilène, à la. Madrid style. With tomatoes.
Maître d'Hôtel, à la. With butter sauce and parsley.
Marchand de Vin. Wine-merchant style. Flavored with claret.
Maréchale, à la. Marshal style. With bread crumbs and truffles.
Marie-Louise. With artichoke bottoms.
Marinate. To place fish and meats in marinade (wine-and-spice liquid) to enrich flavor.
Marmite. An earthenware stock and soup pot.
Marseillaise, à la. Marseille style. With garlic and tomatoes.
Masséna. With artichoke bottoms.
Matelote. Sailor style. With fish, or a fish stew.
Medallion. Small round meat fillet.
Meunière, à la. Miller's-wife style. Floured and cooked in butter.
Milanaise, à la. Milan style. With macaroni and cheese.
Minute, à la. Cooked quickly.
Mirabeau. With anchovies.
Mirabelle. Small yellow plum.
Mireille. Usually, with tomato, mushroom, and onion.
Monselet. With artichoke bottoms and truffles.
Montmorency. With cherries.
Montreuil. With peaches.
Morels. Delicate mushrooms.
Mornay. With cheese sauce.
Moscovite, à la. Moscow style. With caviar. Also, a Bavarian cream.
Mousse. Literally, "foam," "froth." Molded, poached dishes. Souffléed cream dishes.
Nantua. With crayfish.
Napolitaine, à la. Naples style. With macaroni and cheese sauce.

Navarin. Stew with turnips.
Nesselrode. With whipped cream, candied chestnuts, and raisins.
Newburg. With lobster, cognac, and fortified wine.
Niçoise, à la. Nice style. With olives, tomatoes, and anchovies.
Nivernaise. With carrots.
Noisette. Best part, or eye, of lamb or mutton.
Normande, à la. Norman style. With fish or fish sauce. Or with apples.
Noyau. Liqueur flavored with almond kernels.
Orgeat. Almond-flavored sirup.
Orientale, à l'. Oriental style. With rice, curry, spices, or tomato.
Panada. Bread and milk or stock mixture used to bind forcemeats.
Papillote, en. Cooked in paper bag or buttered paper to preserve flavor.
Parmentier. With potatoes.
Pâté. Pie.
Paupiettes. Thin slices of meat rolled with a filling to form "birds."
Paysanne, à la. Peasant or country style. Foods prepared simply, with fresh root vegetables.
Périgord or **Périgueux, à la.** With truffles.
Piémontaise, à la. Piedmont style. With tomato or truffled risotto.
Pilaf. Rice dish containing other ingredients.
Poaching. Simmering just below the boiling point.
Polonaise, à la. Polish style. With beets, bread crumbs, sour cream, or horseradish.
Portugaise, à la. Portuguese style. With tomato, onion, or garlic.
Pot-au-feu. Literally, "pot on the fire." Broth, meat, and vegetables boiled together.
Potée. Soup with boiled meats and vegetables.
Potted. Game, fowl, or meat pounded to a paste (or sliced) and preserved in jars.
Poulette. White sauce with mushrooms and parsley.
Princesse. With asparagus.
Printanière, à la. Spring style. With fresh spring vegetables.
Provençale, à la. Provence style. With tomatoes, garlic, and olive oil.
Purée. Cooked food pressed through a sieve or reduced to a pulp.
Quenelles. Small forcemeat balls.
Ragout. A stew.
Raisiné. Fruit cooked in grape juice.
Ramekins. Small porcelain or earthenware molds.
Reduce. To boil down.
Régence. With crayfish and truffles.
Reine, à la. Queen's style. With suprême sauce and truffles.
Rissoles. Meat or fish mixtures wrapped in pastry, breaded, and fried.
Rossini. With *foie gras* and truffles.
Roux. Flour-butter mixture for saucemaking.
Rouennaise, à la. Rouen style. With duck.
Royale. With mushrooms and truffles.
Russe, à la. Russian style. With beet juice, sour cream, or horseradish.
Saint-Germain. With peas.
Saint-Hubert. With game.
Salmis. Game or poultry hash with a rich sauce.
Salpicon. Cubed mixture bound with sauce.
Sauté. To brown food in butter to sear it.
Score. To cut grooves or gashes.
Skim. To remove the impurities floating on surface of soups, sauces, etc.
Smitane. With sour cream and onions.
Soissonnais. With navy beans.
Soubise. With onions.
Spoon. To stir a sauce or cream with a spatula to prevent its separating, or, while cooling, so that a skin doesn't form on top.
Stock. Beef, veal, chicken, or fish broth kept "in stock" for use in sauces, etc.
Strasbourgeoise, à la. Strasbourg style. With *foie gras* or sauerkraut.
Sultanas. Small seedless yellow raisins.
Suprême. Best part of fowl or fish.
Surprise. Something unexpected, like orange ice in an orange shell or ice cream inside a soufflé.
Suvarov. With *foie gras,* truffles, and Madeira.
Tartare. With tartar sauce.
Tartine. Toast on which game birds are served.
Terrine. Earthenware pot or jar. Or meat pies without a crust.
Timbale. A drum-shaped mold or dish.
Tournedos. Small steaks cut from tenderloin for quick cooking.
Turque, à la. Turkish style. With rice and saffron, eggplant or zucchini.
Velouté. White sauce with a velvet finish.
Venison. Flesh of all kinds of deer.
Vénitienne, à la. Venetian style. With a green sauce.
Verjuice. Unripe grape or apple juice.
Vert-pré. With green-colored garnish.
Vichy. With new carrots.
Villeroi. Breaded and fried.
Vin Blanc, au. With or cooked in white wine.
Vin Rouge, au. With or cooked in red wine.
Vol-au-vent. Round or oval puff-paste shells containing creamed mixtures.
Work. To stir or beat a mixture by hand, spatula, or whisk.
Zest. Outer part of orange or lemon rind.
Zingara. With paprika and truffles.

INDEX

Imprimé par DÉCHAUX - Paris